ISBN 978-0-265-65155-1
PIBN 10876159

# HISTORY OF THE
# ARCHDIOCESE OF ST. LOUIS

Benedictio Domini super vos

Pius PP. XI

# HISTORY OF THE ARCHDIOCESE OF ST. LOUIS

*In its Various Stages of Development
from A. D. 1673 to A. D. 1928*

by

## REV. JOHN ROTHENSTEINER

*Archivist of the Catholic Historical Society
of St. Louis*

---

## VOLUME II

---

Containing Part Three

ST. LOUIS, MO.

1928

———

*Copyright 1928*

*Rev. John Rothensteiner*

———

PRESS OF

BLACKWELL WIELANDY CO.

ST. LOUIS, MO., U. S. A.

# PREFACE

St. Louis has now been an archdiocese for eighty years during which it has had three Archbishops. As to length of service, however, Archbishop Kenrick outranks the years of both his successors combined. During this comparatively long period of time, material, political, and social conditions have changed so very much that a faintly adequate description cannot be given within the limited space of an introduction. It is as if two distinct worlds here came in contact, the one emerging into the light of day, the other passing away into night. Only a few of the leading characteristics of the earlier and the latter portions of this period of cultural and scientific transition can here be set down to form the background for the grand panorama of the Church's steady growth and expansion.

When Peter Richard Kenrick became Archbishop of St. Louis his immediate charge was confined to the State and the Territory of Missouri. Chicago had become an episcopal see with all Illinois under its jurisdiction. The State of Arkansas also was severed from St. Louis and formed into the diocese of Little Rock. The general Government of the Church as well as the marvelous growth, from decade to decade, of its young offshoot in the United States will clearly appear from the subjoined table:

| Year | Pope | Cardinal Prefect of Propaganda | Dioceses in United States | Priests in United States | Catholic Population |
|------|------|-------------------------------|--------------------------|-------------------------|---------------------|
| 1852 | Pius IX | Philip Fransoni | 32 | 1,421 | 1,600,000 |
| 1862 | Pius IX | Alexander Barnabo | 43 | 2,284 | 2,000,000 |
| 1872 | Pius IX | Alexander Barnabo | 56 | 4,184 | 4,829,900 |
| 1882 | Leo XIII | John Simeoni | 63 | 6,438 | 6,370,858 |
| 1892 | Leo XIII | Miecislaus Ledochowski | 80 | 9,067 | 8,647,221 |
| 1902 | Leo XIII | Jerome M. Gotti | 87 | 11,986 | 10,759,330 |
| 1912 | Pius X | Jerome M. Gotti | 98 | 17,608 | 15,019,074 |
| 1922 | Pius XI | William Van Rossum | 103 | 21,164 | 17,616,676 |

The State of Missouri had a lion's share in this progress.

As in the ancient days the power of the Roman Empire built the great military roads and highways into every part of its vast possessions to hold them in subjection, and to bring all nations into closer communion, yet under the Providence of God, served the cause of the Gospel by opening the way for Christ's ambassadors to these very nations and to bring them into subjection to the Kingdom of Christ: so the busy and restless world of later days built the network of the railways that covers the entire State of Missouri and connects it with all parts of the country, to serve commerce and agriculture and the mining industries, but really serving the messengers of peace and truth in their laborious endeavors to raise the hearts of the people for God. After the first railway train west of the Mississippi had connected St. Louis with the little suburb of·Cheltenham, five lines were started with State aid.

1. The Pacific Railroad of Missouri, due West from St. Louis to Kansas City.

2. The North Missouri R. R. northwest from St. Louis to Omaha.

3. The Southwestern Branch of the Pacific R. R. southwest from St. Louis.

4. St. Louis and Iron Mountain, due south from St. Louis.

5. The Hannibal and St. Joseph R. R.

Only the latter two were completed by 1859, the others were delayed for six years. These railroads opened vast stretches of rich and beautiful country to immigration, which was then in full swing, and at the same time kept them from isolation. They also made it possible for one minister of God to serve several farflung Congregations on the same Sunday, and to visit the sick and dying far more readily. Of all the contributary causes of the unprecedented progress of the Church in Missouri during the last eighty years, the enjoyment of perfect liberty by the Church, the mighty and constant flow of immigration, and the services of the Railroad are the most notable. It has been well said by a writer in Blackwood, that ''for the fullest measure of civilization, freedom and enjoyment of which earth is capable, the one thing needful is the fullest intercourse of nation with nation, of man with man. . . . It cannot, therefore, be doubted that the whole system of railways, must be acknowledged as having given the mightiest propulsion to the general improvement of mankind.'' It may be that the more modern inventions of the automobile and aeroplane will in a measure supersede the railways: but the honor of having been the first really rapid transportation system in the world in general and in Missouri in particular must remain with the railways.

As to immigration it is well known that Ireland and Germany have formed the main streams. The hightide of Irish immigration was reached in the decade 1850-1860, the hightide of German immigration is the decade 1880-1890. In the latter decade German immigration outnumbered the Irish by over 800,000, and established the Germans as the most considerable foreign element in our population. Of the sixteen million immigrants and immigrants' children of Irish and German descent there was a vastly larger proportion of Catholics among the Irish than among the Germans: yet a very large proportion of the Germans came from predominantly Catholic points of Germany, as Westphalia, the Rhine Province, Bavaria, Alsace, Baden, Württemberg, Tyrol and the other German crownlands of Austria. How much of this Catholic emigration came to Missouri is impossible to tell at present. It is plain, however, that the ethnic composition of the Church in Missouri cannot be explained without assuming an almost overwhelming influx of these two Catholic elements.

The Civil War of 1861-1865 retarded the progress of the Church in a measure, but the forward march was resumed immediately after the return of peace. The reconstruction measures of the Government, though careless of religious liberty, offered no serious hindrance, but on the contrary gave a fresh impulse to religious fervor. Slavery was abolished in Missouri on January 11th, 1865. The Order of Knights of Father Matthew was organized in St. Louis in November 1872 and made a state organization in 1881. The first Missouri Branch of the Catholic Knights of America was established in St. Louis in May 1879. On April 30th, 1904 the Louisiana Purchase Exposition in St. Louis was opened; and in August, Centennial Celebrations of Missouri's Statehood were held in many cities and towns of the State.

In the first quarter of the Twentieth Century there was a remarkable advance over former years in the magnitude of building operations entered upon by the Archdiocese as such, as well as by individual institutions and parishes. Money was becoming more plentiful, and the credit of Catholic institutions was maintained at a high and honorable level. The Des Moines Register lately quoted the following words with hearty approval: "Roman Catholic institutions throughout the world have an enviable record of never defaulting in their obligations."

The great inventions of these later days, as the automobile, the Zeppelin and the aeroplane have brought people much closer together, road improvement has proceeded at a truly wonderful celerity, and the telephone and the radio have established a human intercourse that was not dreamt of in the days of our fathers. They too were made tributary by friend and foe for or against the Church's progress. What the outcome shall be we cannot say. Only this we know: Divine Providence that has guided and guarded us so far, will guide and guard us to the end.

# TABLE OF CONTENTS

PART III

## THE ARCHDIOCESE OF ST. LOUIS

BOOK I

*Peter Richard Kenrick, Archbishop*

(ix)

## BOOK II

### *Archbishop John Joseph Kain*

## Book III

### *Archbishop John Joseph Glennon*

# LIST OF ILLUSTRATIONS

PART THREE

THE ARCHDIOCESE OF ST. LOUIS

BOOK I

*Archbishop Peter Richard Kenrick*

+ Peter R. et Kenrik
Arp.

## CHAPTER 1

## PETER RICHARD KENRICK, ARCHBISHOP

Up to the year 1847, Baltimore was the one and only archdiocese in the United States, and the other sees of the country, St. Louis included, were suffragans of the Archbishop of Baltimore. But late in that year there were two: Baltimore and St. Louis. Peter Richard Kenrick attended the Seventh Provincial Council of Baltimore in 1849, as Archbishop of St. Louis, whilst his brother Francis Patrick still bore the title of Bishop of Philadelphia. Peter Richard, therefore, held a more exalted position at that Council than his brother Francis Patrick, who was ten years his senior and had, until then, acted as counsellor and guide to the seemingly less able and certainly much less experienced Bishop of St. Louis. What had happened in the interim, and what was the meaning and true inport of the change?

It is well known, at least among Catholics the world over, that the Bishop of Rome, as successor of St. Peter, and heir to the glorious promises made to him by Christ, the Son of the Living God, is and must ever be, the Head of the Church, the chief Shepherd of the flock, the Vice-Gerent of the Lord. He alone enjoys full authority over all the Church, and over all its members, be they bishops, or priests or laymen. The bishops too, are called to rule the Church of God, but only in the part assigned to them by the Supreme Ruler. In his own diocese every bishop is independent of every other, only not of the Bishop of Rome. Yet it is necessary that all should work in harmony, not only with the center of unity, the Pope, but also with one another. The authority of the Supreme Ruler is the mighty principle by which this unity of effort is effected but, as the bearer of this supreme authority cannot be personally present among all nations, and as "nations always will differ, in inherited characteristics and predilections and traditions and modes of thought and feeling," it was certainly most expedient that the Pope should, wherever feasible, band together a number of bishops into a province and endow the bishop of the chief city in each province with a limited particiation in the supreme pastoral office of which he himself is primarily the custodian and dispenser. The

(1)

leading bishop in a Province is, therefore, called the Metropolitan, or the Archbishop. An archdiocese remains a diocese and holds the same relation to its ordinary as it did before it attained metropolitan rank. Yet the Archbishop's power extends beyond his own diocese, it includes in its jurisdiction his suffragan bishops also and their diocese, though only in a limited way. This extraneous power is his, not by divine right, but only through concession from the Supreme authority, which resides in the Pope.

The Archbishop's dignity is not one of mere honor, although deserving of highest honor. It is the arch that spans the pillars and holds them together by giving them a closer union with the center of unity, Rome. Thus the greatest diffusion of spiritual power is attained, whilst the union of purpose and action is maintained *in Urbe et Orbe.*

By a Brief of His Holiness, Pope Pius IX under date of January 30, 1847, the diocese of St. Louis was raised to the dignity of an Archdiocese, and Peter Richard Kenrick was appointed its first Archbishop.[1] This matter was not touched upon in the petition for the erection of new dioceses sent to Rome by the Sixth Council of Baltimore, held in May 1846. The majority of the bishops then, no doubt, desired the previous erection of some eastern or southern diocese into a metropolitan See. Bishop Francis Patrick Kenrick was suspected by some as having designed and accomplished the western project in favor of his brother. He himself denied this, saying: "I made no request for the erection of a metropolitan see at St. Louis. Though, when Cardinal Fransoni asked me what city in the West I thought ought to be raised to that dignity, I told him that it was St. Louis, as I judged the various claims. After the Council I opened my mind to the Fathers, and I submitted to the Holy See a plan for the initial division of provinces, suggesting the new sees of Albany and Buffalo to (be subject to the future metropolitan see of) New York. It would be more just, perhaps, if they charged me with favoring the promotion of the Bishop of Buffalo whom I very strongly commended."[2]

Philadelphia's plan must have found favor with the Holy See, though not in the case of the Bishop of Buffalo: for St. Louis received the palm of victory over the older Sees, New York, Boston, Bardstown, and the claims of New Orleans.

His Holiness Pius IX. on June 13, 1847 wrote to the Archbishop of Baltimore that he had referred the petition of the Council to the Congregation of the Propaganda.[3] On July 7, of the same year, Bishop Francis Patrick reports a rumor that Peter Richard had become an

---

[1]  Original in Chancery of St. Louis Archdiocese.
[2]  Kenrick-Frenaye Correspondence, p. 278.
[3]  Concilia Baltimorensia, p. 249.

Archbishop, and on the 20th, the rumor has grown in prominence. Peter Richard then promised his brother he would be with him in Philadelphia about November 1, 1847. On October 6, Francis Patrick sends his congratulations to Peter Richard, ''and to the entire church of America upon the newly erected Metropolitan See. May you govern it many years with a tranquil mind.''[4] The source of this information is the Archbishop of Baltimore. ''But he wonders,'' writes the Bishop of Philadelphia, ''that you, Peter Richard, have not written to him after receiving the Apostolic Letters. Acknowledgement is due to him for his kindness.''[5] Six days later, Francis Patrick counsels his brother of St. Louis, that it seems ''proper to request our Very Rev. Friend, Paul Cullen, to do the kind office of asking for the Pallium. He then should send the Pallium when a fair opportunity offers, so that it may reach you here in Philadelphia.''[6] But time went on and the Pallium did not arrive, and no word had come as to the bishops who were to be his suffragans. This caused Peter Richard no slight worry. For an Archbishop without the Pallium, the symbol of Metropolitan authority, really seemed to have less power and dignity than the simple Bishop of St. Louis. By law he was debarred from the exercise of of pontifical functions, as ordinations and consecrations, although Francis Patrick surmised, that the law did not apply to the Bishop of St. Louis, now raised to metropolitan rank.[7] In any case, Peter Richard thought it prudent to abstain from ordinations until he should receive the Pallium: in the meantime he had Bishops Barron and Loras to perform these functions for him.[8]

At last, early in June, 1848, came the welcome news-item from Philadelphia. ''On the ninth day of April, the priest, James O'Connor brother of the Bishop of Pittsburg, left Rome to bring the Pallium to you. He will go to Malta, London and finally to America. He is said to be broken in health, and almost without hope, so that there is another point of peril to your honor: for, if anything should happen, to him, I dare not conjecture when the Pallium will come to you.''[9] On the 13th, Francis Patrick wrote that the priest, James O'Connor, planned to remain three weeks in London. July had passed and August was in full swing and still there was no sign of the Pallium. The Archbishop-Elect of St. Louis proposed to write to the Pope about the matter: but his brother counselled him to address the Prefect of

---

[4] Kenrick-Frenaye Correspondence, p. 260.

[5] Kenrick-Frenaye Correspondence, p. 260. Archbishop Eccleston.

[6] Kenrick-Frenaye Correspondence, p. 263. Paul Cullen, the future Primate of all Ireland.

[7] Kenrick-Frenaye Correspondence, pp. 270 and 271, 272.

[8] Chancery Records, St. Louis.

[9] Kenrick-Frenaye Correspondence, p. 279.

the Propaganda, whose business it was to obtain and expedite the Pallium to the Metropolitans under his authority.[10] "In the meantime you will have patience, and wait," wrote the Bishop of Philadelphia. This time he was not deceived: for on August 24, 1848, Francis Patrick could note in his diary—: "The Rev. James O'Connor brought here the Pallium." "This I conferred on him (Peter Richard Kenrick) in accordance with the solemn rite in St. John's Church (Philadelphia), September 3, (1848).'"[11] Peter Richard Kenrick was now in full possession of his metropolitan rights, but had no suffragans upon whom to exercise his authority. The long delay was probably occasioned by Francis Patrick of Philadelphia, who in the Sixth Council of Baltimore had advised that it would be an act of consideration due to the Bishops to leave the designation of the suffragans to them. In the Bishop's opinion the Congregation of the Propaganda was awaiting the judgment of the next Council of Baltimore.[12] The Seventh Provinical Council of Baltimore, which assembled in May 1849, under Archbishop Eccleston was meant, which, in its first private session, sent a petition to the Holy Father requesting that New Orleans, Cincinnati, New York be made Metropolitan Sees; and that the Metropolitan See of St. Louis receive as suffragans the Bishops of Dubuque, Nashville, Chicago and Milwaukee; and that the Metropolitan See of Baltimore be made the Primatial See of the United States, with all the other Archbishops and Bishops as subjects.[13] All these requests were granted except the last. Baltimore had to content itself with the primacy of honor, not of jurisdiction.

But the official declaration of these points was again delayed, and that more than a year, by the revolutionary outbreak in Rome. On August 9, 1850, Cardinal Fransoni, Prefect of the Propaganda, notified the Archbishop of Baltimore that the Holy Father had approved the Decrees of the Seventh Provincial Council of Baltimore, the erection of the new Metropolitan Sees, and the assignment of the four Bishops already mentioned as well as of the bishop of the newly erected see of St. Paul, as suffragans to the Metropolitan of St. Louis. He added to this, that the Apostolical Letters had been forwarded to the individual Metropolitans.[14] Archbishop Kenrick's Apostolical Letters was dated July 19, 1850. Thus the diocese of St. Louis took its rightful place as the first Archdiocese erected in the Mississippi Valley, and third in the entire country from the Atlantic to the Pacific, from the St. Lawrence River and the Great Lakes to Gulf of Mexico. On the eve of Christmas 1849, Bishop Francis Patrick offered the most beauti-

---

10   Kenrick-Frenaye Correspondence, p. 277.
11   Kenrick-Frenaye Correspondence, p. 263, note.
12   Kenrick-Frenaye Correspondence, p. 263.
13   Concilia Baltimorensia, pp. 269 and 270-281.
14   Concilia Baltimorensia, pp. 287 and 288.

ful and tender tribute to his brother, Peter Richard, the Archbishop of St. Louis. Alluding to a number of prominent converts to the faith, he wrote: "It is the prayer of the Mother of God, whose sinless conception we venerate, that these conversions, are, beyond doubt, to be attributed. The faithful invoke her as the Patron of the United States and by prayer attain for themselves and for their fellow-citizens gifts of divine grace and the light of faith . . . She has been close to you for your devotion to her in the Month of May, for your vindication of the translation of her house to Loretto, she stood by you placing on your head the insignia of Metropolitan, the promise of a more precious crown of your work in heaven."[15]

On the death of Archbishop Eccleston, in 1851, the Right. Reverend Francis Patrick Kenrick was promoted to the See of Baltimore, and as such presided over the First Plenary Council of all North America. From that time on the two Kenricks stood before the world as the most honored and most influential members of the American hierarchy of their time.

---

[15] Kenrick-Frenaye Correspondence, pp. 303 and 304.

## CHAPTER 2

# FATHER JOSEPH MELCHER, VICAR-GENERAL

Early in March 1843, Bishop Rosati departed from Rome on his way to Marseilles and Paris. He intended to return to Hayti to complete the arrangements with President Boyer for the Concordat. The companion of his journey was a young priest whom he had lately won for the diocese: Father Joseph Melcher, a man who was destined to become a power for good under Bishop Kenrick, and to attain the mitre in the far North. Bishop Rosati introduced his latest acquisition to his coadjutor in a letter from Marseilles: "I have found an excellent travelling companion in the person of an excellent German priest, whom I met in Rome. He is so attentive to me and so full of activity and intelligence, that I have unloaded all the cares of the journey upon him;" and again, from Paris: "Mr. Melcher has already set sail for St. Louis. I was very much pleased with him."[1]

. Father Melcher, the last acquisition Bishop Rosati made for St. Louis, was born on March 8th, 1807, in the imperial city of Vienna, Austria. In his seventh year the Melcher family removed to Modena, one of the little Italian principalities subject to an Austrian ruler. The father of the family had obtained a position at the ducal court. To the son, Italian became as familiar as German. In his early student days an aged half-blind priest engaged the young man to read the Breviary to him day by day, a circumstance that must have exerted a great influence on the choice of a vocation. He was raised to the holy priesthood in Modena by the Bishop of the place, March 27th, 1830. On April 2nd, he attained the degree of Doctor of Divinity and on April 7th, said his first holy Mass. His first appointment was that of chaplain to the Court of Modena; with the incidental duty of holding services for the German Catholics of the city. Thus quietly the first twelve years of Father Melcher's life were spent: but then the desire for a wider field of activity, a more strenuous life of priestly charity and selfsacrifice, broke forth and urged him on to seek a change. Obtaining a leave of absence, he went to Rome and offered himself to Propaganda for the Foreign Mission. But he was told, that the Foreign Missions were in the hands of the Religious orders, and a secular priest could not be accepted. Into this dark night of sorrow, at seeing his generous offer unavailing, there suddenly fell a ray of light. Bishop Rosati of St. Louis in the far West, was pointed out to him as one that was seeking priests. The good Bishop was de-

---

[1] Original in Archives of St. Louis Archdiocese.

BISHOP JOSEPH MELCHER

lighted to find a new co-laborer, and when he learnt that the young priest, spoke German, in fact was a German, he at once adopted him into his diocese.[2]  Arriving in St. Louis Father Melcher was cordially received by Bishop Kenrick, who at once gave the courtly gentleman from Modena a touch of American missionary life by sending him to the Poste of Arkansas.  If the young missionary, under his fine appearance and polished manners, had not possessed a heart  as true as gold, he might have lost in this mission all his fervor and interest. But the time of trial was shortened by the erection of the diocese of Little Rock.  Father Melcher was recalled by his bishop, and sent to what was designated, Meramec, comprising Mattese Creek in St. Louis County, Merrimack, now Maxville in Jefferson County, Gravois, now Kirkwood and St. Martin's Church in Central Township of St. Louis County on the Bonhomme Road.  His residence was at Mattese Creek where there was a church, but no house for the priest. Yet, the people, though poor, were of good will.  Soon a log house was raised to place a roof over the head of the shepherd of souls.  As for the rest, the hard floor had to serve for a bed, a box for a writing table: and a few blocks of wood for chairs.  No meals were served in the house, but the priest had a standing invitation to the homes of his parishioners, who seasoned the rough and plentiful fare with a hearty welcome.  Such extreme poverty was bound to tell on the gently-reared body of Father Melcher: the usual fever infesting all newly cultivated lands, attacked and threatened to undermine his strong constitution.[3]  Bishop Kenrick, remembering that the young missionary was a Doctor of Divinity, invited him to accompany him to the Sixth Provincial Council of Baltimore as his theologian (1846).

On returning to St. Louis from the Council, Bishop Kenrick appointed Father Melcher one of his Vicars-General and sent him to Europe for the purpose, of securing some German priests for the rapidly increasing German settlements of his diocese.[4]

Vicar-General Melcher on his journey passed through Lorraine, Alsace and Switzerland.  Four priests and twelve theological students

---

2  Holweck, F. G., Bishop Joseph Melcher ''Pastoral-Blatt,'' vol. 51, 5.

3  Idem, ibidem.

4.  Littel's ''Living Age,'' 1847, p. 147, has an article entitled Italy and the Carnival, in which this notice of Vicar-General Melcher's activities occurs:  ''I have not the least idea that the 'Successor of St. Peter' will ever leave the halls of the Vatican for the Valley of the Mississippi, but the Propaganda are sending over a large recruiting force.  A Mr. Melcher, Vicar-General of Missouri, is collecting German priests for the diocese of Bishop Kenrick, of St. Louis, and I understand that a detachment is soon to start from the South of France for the new diocese of Walla-Walla in Oregon, 'established,' says a Roman paper, 'under the protection of President Polk who has pledged himself to permit none but the true Faith in the conquered provinces of Mexico.' ''

joined him on his return trip to St. Louis: The priests were: Joseph Meister of the diocese of Bale, George Ortlieb, of the diocese of Nancy, Cajetan Zapotti of the diocese of Linz in Austria, and Francis Rutkowski of the archdiocese of Breslau. Father Ursus Meister[5] became pastor of Apple Creek; March 1847, he was promoted to Jefferson City; in 1853, he was sent to Maniteau County, and 1859, he left the diocese for Vincennes. He was killed by a falling tree, February 25th, 1864.

Father George Ortlieb[6] received as his first appointment the pastorship of Our Lady of Mount Carmel, Carondelet, but, after a few years, returned to his native city Nancy. Father Cajetan Zapotti was entrusted with the church at Benton, Scott County, but left the diocese in 1848, for Cincinnati and Chicago. Father Francis Rutkowski became pastor of Weston, Platte County; from 1852 to 1856, he was stationed at Dardenne, St. Charles County.

Of the twelve students brought over by Father Melcher only seven attained the dignity of their vocation: Francis Weiss, Simon Siegrist, both of the diocese of Strassbourg, John Anselm, of the diocese of Nancy; Francis Blaarer, of the diocese of St. Gall in Switzerland, Louis Rossi of the diocese of Modena, Francis Trojan, of the diocese of Leitomischl in Bohemia, Jacob Stehle, of the diocese of Nancy.

All these students entered the Seminary of St. Mary's of the Barrens, and were there ordained to the holy priesthood:

The other students mentioned on the list of the Annals of the Propagation of the Faith (19. 520): Bernard Siedert of Muenster in Westphalia; Peter Curlot of Nancy; Mathias Cobbin of Freibourg, in Baden; and Joseph Girard of Nancy seem to have come to St. Louis, but left no trace behind. Sebastian Brutscher promised to come along with Father Melcher, but failed to keep his word.

Simon Sigrist,[7] became pastor of Meramec in 1847, and in 1849, was commissioned to found the parish of S.S. Peter and Paul, but leaving the diocese for Vincennes in 1858, died October 28th, 1873. He enjoyed the reputation of being a forceful preacher.

John Anselm was ordained in the Cathedral of St. Louis by Archbishop Kenrick on September 29th, 1848, and was immediately after sent to French Village. During the year 1849, he served as assistant to Father Gandolfo in Ste. Genevieve; and in the following year he founded the German church of the Holy Trinity in North St. Louis. Here he labored earnestly for the upbuilding of the parish, until 1856, when he was transferred to his first place of service, Little Canada or French Village. In 1865, his name no longer appears on the list of priests.

---

5   Holweck, F. G., "Pastoral-Blatt," vol. 51, 11.
6   Chancery Records.
7   Holweck, F. G., Vater Sigrist, "Pastoral-Blatt," vol. 58, 1.

Joseph Aloysius Blaarer was raised to the holy priesthood on April 29th, 1848, at the Seminary. He received the appointment to the Parish of Herman. After short stays at Mattese Creek, Maxville and the German Settlement in Ste. Genevieve County (Zell) Father Blaarer was sent to Deepwater in the western part of the State where he labored faithfully until his transfer to Jefferson City in 1853. In 1855, he returned to the German Settlement and ultimately became Chaplain to the Ursuline Nuns.

Father Aloysius Rosi, or Rossi from Modena, is sometimes credited to Tyrol. After his ordination at the Barrens, April 29th, 1848, he was appointed pastor of the ancient parish of New Madrid: and from 1849 to 1853, had charge of St. Stephen's Church at Richwoods. In 1853, Father Rosi became pastor of Little Canada (French Village) where he lost his life by being drowned in a swollen branch of the Establishment Creek, whilst on an urgent sick call, August 29, 1853.

Father Francis Trojan, born in Jaromere in Moravia, was ordained on January 12th, 1851, and at once received charge of the Parish of Apple Creek in Perry County. In 1856, he became pastor of the Bohemian Church of St. John Nepomuc in St. Louis in succession to its founder Father Henry Lipowski. He left the diocese in 1846, for Chester, Illinois.

Jacob Stehle, probably a nephew of the Lazarist Nicholas Stehle, who entered the Seminary at the Barrens in 1844, labored since 1844, among the immigrants in Scott County. In 1869, he is mentioned as pastor of Hazel Green, Grant County Wisconsin. Probably the best and ablest, certainly the most persevering member of this little caravan of Father Melcher's first gathering was Francis Xavier Weiss, who is justly styled the patriarch of Ste. Genevieve County. German Settlement, Reviere aux Vases, and the ancient city of Ste. Genevieve were the successive scenes of his priestly labors; but in all the churches that cluster around Ste. Genevieve, like the beautiful daughters around a more beautiful mother, the name of good Father Weiss is still a household word. He died March 3rd, 1901.

The acquisition of an entire community of religious, daughters of St. Ursula, was another fruit of Father Melcher's first journey to Europe. In Oedenburg, Hungary, not far from Vienna, he found them and prevailed upon them to establish a convent of their Order in St. Louis. The interesting story of this foundation must however be reserved for another chapter.

On his return from Europe Father Melcher received the appointment as pastor of St. Mary's Church in place of the ailing and rather discouraged Father Fischer, who however remained with Father Melcher as his assistant. In 1845, the diocese had three Vicars-General, John Timon, C.M., Francis Cellini, and Joseph Anthony Lutz. But when Father Timon was made Bishop of Buffalo, in 1847, and Father Lutz resigned his position, Father Cellini remained Vicar-General for the English speaking part of the diocese, and Father Melcher received the appointment for the Germans.

Archbishop Kenrick was wont to appoint a man for a position or place for which he seemed to be fitted by nature and grace, expecting him to work out the problem without let or hindrance on his part. The case of Father Melcher as Vicar-General for the Germans is a case in point. The Archbishop, who had learnt to place confidence in his Vicar-General, allowed him a free hand to act. Thus it came that the German priests of the archdiocese, all through Peter Richard Kenrick's regime, looked to their Vicar-General, Melcher, and, following him, Muehlsiepen, for direction, counsel, comfort and promotion. It was a real godsend that Father Fischer was willing to remain at St. Mary's in a subordinate position: for the Vicar-General's duties drew him away more and more from his pastoral cares.

The Congregation had a church worthy of the name; although it was far from being completed: but there was as yet no proper rectory for the priests. An old log house, which had been used by a negro family, now served Father Fischer and Father Melcher as their home. Father Melcher laid plans for the erection of a commodious dwelling: but some of the hard-headed parishioners reported him to the Archbishop as if he were about to waste the goods of the parish. The Archbishop quietly ordered the completion of the building.

In the cholera year 1849, when so many of the children of the Catholic immigrants suddenly became orphans, and the two existing diocesan Orphan Asylums could only with great difficulty take care of the children of the English speaking parishes, it was Vicar-General Melcher that set in motion the desire of the German Catholics of St. Louis to provide a German Orphan Home for the children of their nationality.

On the 9th of May, Father Melcher started on his second journey to Europe in quest for new subjects for the ministry. The places he visited were in the northern parts of Germany, particularly the diocese of Paderborn. As many of the German Catholics in the diocese of St. Louis were natives of Westphalia and Hanover, priests, or candidates for the priesthood, of North-German stock were most acceptable. When the stately and most affable representative of the Archbishop of St. Louis arrived at the Jesuit College in Paderborn, he raised high enthusiasm in the hearts of a number of young men whose names are now imperishably interwoven with the history of the Church in St. Louis. One of them, Stephen Schweihoff, was already in priestly orders. There were three subdeacons: Francis Goller,[8] Caspar Doebben-

---

8 Holweck, F. G., Franz Goller, Priester, in ''Pastoral-Blatt,'' vol. 51, 7.

er, and Christopher Wapelhorst.[9] Then came the two students of Theology: John Boetzkes, and Conrad Tintrup. Henry Müchlsiepen who had just completed his classical studies, a native of the Rhineland, hurried to Paderborn from his home in Mintard, to offer himself for the American mission, and was gladly accepted. Two others, August Reinecke, and Francis Schreiber[10] came to Paderborn after Father Melcher's departure for Modena, but followed the call in 1856.

The student Francis Ruesse, also a native of Paderborn diocese, preceded this ecclesiastical exodus by more than a year: he was ordained on June 29th, 1855, in the Cathedral of St. Louis and became successively, assistant at St. Joseph, Mo., Pastor of Deepwater, Pastor of Herman and since 1866 first assistant priest at S. S. Peter and Paul's Church in St. Louis. Father Ruesse was, therefore, the first priest of low German stock in Missouri. Father Schweihoff is the well known and revered founder and life long pastor of St. Liborius Church in St. Louis.

Francis S. Goller, ordained priest at St. Louis Cathedral on November 1st, 1855, became Father Anselm's assistant at Holy Trinity, then assistant priest to Father Siegrist, and in 1858 Pastor of the Church of S. S. Peter and Paul. Father Goller was one of the mainstays of the Catholic Parochial School System in the United States, in favor of which he ever spoke and labored in season and out of season, as some thought, with a singleness of purpose that was truly admirable. As Theologian to Archbishop Kenrick at the Third Plenary Council of Baltimore, Father Goller wielded a wide and incisive influence in favor of the Council's legislation in regard to the Catholic Parochial School policy, now showing such wonderful strength and salutary fruit.

Caspar Doebbener was raised to the priesthood by Archbishop Kenrick on the same day and in the same place as his friend Francis Goller. After serving a short time as Assistant in S. S. Peter and Pàul's, he became Pastor of the Holy Trinity church in what was then called Bremen, a suburb of St. Louis, where he remained until 1865. A brief stay at St. Michael's Church closed his career in St. Louis.

Christopher Wapelhorst, as priest, professor, rector of a Seminary, diocesan Chancellor, distinguished member of the Franciscan Order, and author of the best text book on Sacred Liturgy ever published in America, looms up large in the history, not only of St. Louis Archdiocese, but of the United States at large. He certainly was one of the most learned, most zealous and efficient priests St. Louis ever had. On his arrival in St. Louis, October 4, 1855, he was sent to the Seminary in Carondelet to learn English and to teach Philosophy and Theology. After his ordination by Archbishop Kenrick on June 28th, 1856, he

---

9  Holweck, F. G., Vater Innozent, Wapelhorst, ''Pastoral-Blatt,'' vol. 51, 4.
10  Author of Amanda and other poems, German and English.

was sent to the Germans at Dutzow. Here he paid the usual tribute to the climate of Missouri. But the attack by the fever prepared the way for his advancement to the chair of Philosophy in the Seminary at Carondelet. In 1857, Father Wapelhorst was appointed to the Church of St. Peter, the Parish church of the German Catholics of St. Charles on the Missouri River. In 1865 the founder of the Salesianum near Milwaukee, Dr. Joseph Salzman, who had long since made the acquaintance of the bright and energetic priest, obtained from the Archbishop the permission to take Father Wapelhorst with him as Professor in the Seminary. Father Wapelhorst, in 1879 returned to St. Louis to join the humble Sons of St. Francis. He was a man without guile, *anima candida,* yet an ever watchful defender of Holy Church, a man with the courage of his convictions.

Father John Matthew Boetzkes, a native of the Rhineland, did effective, though humbler duty in Dardenne, St. Charles County and in Benton, Scott County. The war of the rebellion which reduced the promising church of South East Missouri to ruins drove Father Boetzkes to St. Louis, where he was employed until 1865 as assistant priest to Father Goller of S. S. Peter and Paul. Leaving the diocese Father Boetzkes founded the church at Helena, in Arkanas 1875, and died in Lancaster, Pa., February 28th, 1891.

Father Conrad Tintrup, ordained priest on January 5th, 1857, was sent to Weston as Pastor, then to Elm Prairie, St. Charles County, then to Wellsburg, then to Dog Prairie, afterwards called St. Paul's, where he continued until 1902. About ten years before his death he was afflicted with total blindness, spending the remainder of his life at Arcadia College.

Of Fathers Reinecke and Schreiber there is no need to write, as they spent almost all of their priestly life in the State of Illinois after its severence from the Archdiocese of St. Louis. Both were faithful and true servants of Holy Church in the sphere assigned to them. Father Schreiber served as Pastor of Weston, Missouri for three years until 1861 when he left the diocese for that of Alton.

Of Henry Muehlsiepen,[11] Vicar-General of St. Louis under three Archbishops, the untiring shepherd of souls, the helpful friend of all his priests, the co-founder of a magnificent series of churches for the Catholic Germans entrusted to his loving care, we will have to treat at length in another chapter of this History. A man not highly talented as preacher or organizer, Father Muehlsiepen would not seem to have been called to leadership in the high sense of the term. It was his burning zeal for the spread of religion, his honesty of purpose, and his childlike winning ways, that carried him to success in almost all his undertakings. He was at times pushed into untenable positions,

---

11  Holweck, F. G., Vater Muehlsiepen, ''Pastoral-Blatt,'' vol. 51, 1.

either by force of circumstances, or by designing persons: but no one ever doubted his absolute honesty of purpose.

After completing his studies in the Seminary at Carondelet under such Professors as the future Archbishops Feehan and Hennessey, Henry Muehlsiepen was ordained by Archbishop Kenrick on the Feast of the Immaculate Conception 1857, and received the appointment as Assistant to Vicar-General Melcher at Our Lady of the Victories. In 1862 he took a post-graduate course in theology at the Seminary of Treves in the Palatinate.

But we must return to Vicar-General Melcher. It was in 1864 that Father Melcher made his third and last voyage across the sea for the purpose of gaining new recruits for the needs of the diocese. Once more did he visit the homes of his former followers, Muenster and Paderborn. In Muenster he found only one enthusiastic student, willing to sacrifice home and friends and a rich inheritance to serve God and Holy Church amid the privations and dangers of American missionary life, Henry Groll, the late dean of all the clergy of Missouri. We need do no more than apply to him the words of Fitz Green Halleck:

> None knew him but to love him,
> Nor named him but to praise.

Wending his way to the ancient city at the fountain head of the Pader the genial Vicar-General from the American wilderness, secured the free and spirited consent of one deacon, the Rhinelander William Faerber, four subdeacons: William Klevinghaus, George Hartmann, Edward Vattman and William Sonnenschein. The other recruits were the theological students, John Gruender and Julius Heerde and the student Boden.

William Faerber,[12] the Pastor of St. Mary's, editor of the *Pastoral-Blatt,* and general writer on theological subjects, was for many years one of the leading spirits among the German priests of the United States. From 1865 to 1868, he was rector of the church at Dutzow, and after that, Pastor of St. Mary's until his death in 1905 (April 17th).

William Klevinghaus, the son of a very wealthy family, was ordained in St. Mary's Church, April 5th, 1865 and held the rectorship of the Church of Herman from 1866 to 1868, and at Koeltztown from 1868 to 1872. The last forty years of Father Klevinghaus were spent as assistant priest at S. S. Peter and Paul. Father George Hartman was ordained on the same day and at the same place as his friend Father Klevinghaus. After a year of apprenticeship at S. S. Peter and Paul, he was appointed pastor of the German Catholics in St. Joseph, Missouri, and after the erection of the diocese of St. Joseph remained there until his death.

---

12 Holweck, F. G., Vater Faerber, "Pastoral-Blatt," 51, 2.

Edward Vattmann, after three years of priestly labor in St. John's, Franklin County, left the diocese in 1867 and, after several new departures, entered the United States army as Catholic Chaplain, attaining in the course of service the distinguished title of dean of the U. S. Army Chaplains.

William Sonnenschein was raised to the holy priesthood by Archbishop Kenrick on August 29th, 1865. In the fifteen years of his stay in the diocese Father Sonnenschein held the pastorship of the churches of St. Peter in the town of St. Charles, then in St. John's, Franklin County, from 1871 to 1875 of St. Charles church at O'Fallon, then of the Church of the Annunciation at Cape Girardeau, then of Mattis Creek and once more of Cape Girardeau. In November 1880, he was sent to Holstein, Warren Co., and soon after received leave of absence for a trip to Europe, from which he never returned. His ultimate destiny remains unknown, for which he seems to deserve neither blame nor praise.

John Gruender, after his ordination in St. Vincent's Church by Bishop Feehan, then Bishop of Nashville, officiated as Pastor of Deepwater until 1870, when he was transferred to Vienna, Maries Co. In 1872 he was promoted to the parish of Koeltztown, and in 1875 to Taos in Cole County. After a visit to Europe in 1885, Father Gruender, received the flourishing parish of Loose Creek which he held up to a few weeks of his death.

Julius Heerde was raised to the holy priesthood by Archbishop Kenrick in the Seminary chapel at Cape Girardeau on May 30th, 1867. After serving as assistant at the church of the Holy Trinity in St. Louis until 1868, he labored in the holy ministry at the church of the Annunciation in Cape Girardeau until 1870. After that period his name no longer appears in the Directories. Of the student Boden we have found no traces. It is probable that he was ordained for St. Louis, but drifted southward, probably to Baton Rouge. All of these clerics were from the diocese of Paderborn, except Henry Groll, whose diocese was Muenster.

Owing to the uncertainties of war times, Father Melcher's hopeful band made the journey from New York, over the soil of Canada, to Chicago by way of Detroit. On January 7th, they were placed safely in the Seminary of St. Francis, near Milwaukee. Here they resumed their studies; only the deacon William Färber was adjudged sufficiently prepared for ordination. Accordingly, he followed Father Melcher to St. Louis within three weeks and was raised to the priesthood by Archbishop Kenrick on February 4th, 1865, in the pro-cathedral of St. Louis, the Church of St. John the Apostle.

Through these valuable accessions to the clergy of St. Louis, Vicar-General Melcher's prestige and influence had grown to such a degree that the attention of those, to whom the selection of candidates for episcopal honors was confided, was turned upon the Vicar-General of St. Louis. When in 1854, the diocese of Quincy was erected out of the southwestern territory of Chicago diocese, and Chicago itself had become vacant through the resignation of Bishop Van de Velde the Archbishop of Baltimore wrote to Archbishop Kenrick: "I am at a loss to know why you did not prevail upon Joseph Melcher to accept the burden, or at least, to undertake the administration of (Chicago) until the Holy See gives further orders. My mind is that he ought to be made to accept the see of Quincy."[13]

Vicar-General Melcher would probably have accepted the see of Quincy, but in Chicago conditions were such, that no one cared to go there. Father Melcher, after due consideration declined to make the sacrifice. The administration of Chicago was then confided to Bishop Henni of Milwaukee, and that of Quincy to Archbishop Kenrick. In the following year Father O'Regan was appointed, much against his will, as Bishop of Chicago and administrator of Quincy.

But Father Melcher could not escape the mitre. By a Brief of Pope Pius IX dated March 3rd, 1868, the diocese of Green Bay in northern Wisconsin was erected with Joseph Melcher as its first Bishop. The Bishop-elect could not decline the honor for a second time: reluctantly he accepted what he knew would be a purgatory for him. He was consecrated in St. Mary's Church on Sunday, July 12th, 1868, by Archbishop Kenrick, assisted by the Bishop of Milwaukee and Quincy. The German Catholics of the state of Missouri owe Bishop Melcher undying gratitude and love. The memory of his noble priestly life, and his great achievements is a priceless legacy for all time!

---

[13]  Kenrick-Frenaye Correspondence, p. 357.

## CHAPTER 3

# DURING THE CHOLERA EPIDEMIC OF 1849

The transition of St. Louis from a big rambling village to a well-ordered modern city was attended by several distressing visitations, that partly depressed, partly spurred on, the latent energies of the people. The Catholic portion of the population, which in 1848 was about one-half of the total, naturally shared in these afflictions and in the efforts to ameliorate them: but it was among the clergy and the Catholic Sisterhoods that the spirit of charity shone forth most beautifully during these trying days of sorrow and bereavement.

Of the cholera of 1833 and 1834 we have already spoken: the memorable flood of 1844 worked severe hardships on many, and spread the germs of disease far and wide; the great conflagration of 1849 in which five hundred houses were destroyed, and the Cathedral and Orphan Asylum stood in greatest danger, was a dreadful calamity: yet, the severest of all the visitations that had so far come upon the city, was the cholera of 1849.

In a way, St. Louis had brought the tragedy upon itself. Through the negligence of its officers the city was in a most unsanitary condition. "Most of the alleys were unpaved, and were used as repositories for all kinds of filth thrown from the dwellings."[1] Whenever they were cleaned, only the surface was scraped, and the underlying clay, deeply saturated with the poisonous effluvia, was left to exhale its infections. In many parts of the city the cellars, were filled with water, which became stagnant, and sent its deadly odors through the houses, and into the streets.

"Imagine," wrote Father De Smet, "a city, of 70,000 inhabitants crowded and packed together in new brick houses, in the dampest and worst drained prairie in existence, undulating, imperfectly drained and interspersed with sink-holes and stagnant waters. The city has hardly a sewer, and in the new streets, mostly unpaved, all the offal of the horses runs out or is thrown out in the omnipresent mud. Add to this that outside the center of the corporate limits is a dirty pond, a mile or more in circumference. Around this natural 'slop-bowl,' at short intervals, you find breweries, distilleries, oil and white lead factories, flour mills and many private residences of Irish and Germans,

---

[1] Edward's "Great West," p. 406.

(16)

into this pond goes everything foul—this settles the opinion as to the real cause of all the dreadful mortality here.''[2]

Warnings had come at various times, but they were not heeded: at last in April 1849 the messengers of death, where followed by the mysterious lord himself. According to the Report made by Robert Moore, civil engineer, ''the disease had been brought to New Orleans on emigrant ships, early in December 1848, and in a few weeks was carried to all the principal cities on the Ohio and Mississippi Rivers. During the last week in December several boats with cholera on board arrived in St. Louis, one of them being the steamer which arrived on the 28th, with no less than thirty cases of cholera amongst passengers and crew.''[3] Other steamers followed with even larger number of cholera patients. The immigrants were landed at the wharf and, with all their baggage, scattered throughout the city in boarding houses, and private homes, without the slightest care on the part of the city authorities.

On January 9th, the morning paper announced, that ''several cases of cholera were reported in the city yesterday, one or two fatal.'' The disease, did not, however, become epidemic at once. In January the deaths from cholera were thirty-six, in February twenty-one. But in March the number rose to seventy-eight, and in April to one hundred and twenty-six. Now the public became alarmed. After the night of the great fire, May 17th, the dread visitant seemed to have received a check: the daily mortality from cholera which for a week before had been twenty-six, fell below twenty; but on June 9th, it began to rise again, and continued to rise to fifty-seven, then to eighty-six per day. The city seemed helpless in the grasp of the cholera. The city council was strongly denounced for its inaction. In fact almost all the members of the city government had fled the doomed city, the Mayor, James G. Barry, alone remaining at his post of duty. A Committee of safety was now appointed. Among a number of salutary measures adopted by the Committee, was the appointment of ''Monday, June 2nd, as a day of fasting and prayer.'' It was not until late in the month of July that the number of victims began to decrease. About the middle of August the disease had nearly disappeared.. The season of greatest virulence was from the end of April to the first week in August.[4]

---

2 De Smet, August 20, 1849, cited by Garraghan, ''Early Chapters in the History of St. Louis University,'' ''St. Louis Catholic Review,'' vol. V, p. 114.

3 Hyde and Conard, ''Encyclopedia of the History of St. Louis,'' vol. II, p. 681.

4 Cr. Edward's ''Great West,'' pp. 406-409, passim.

More than one-tenth of the entire population of 70,000 had been swept away within five months. What the exact number of victims from among the Catholic people was cannot be stated: yet the daily report of interments as published in the Missouri Republican gives us a clew. There were three Catholic Cemeteries in use at the time of the cholera. The Old Catholic Cemetery, the New Catholic Cemetery, and St. Vincent's Cemetery. Of the interments made in these three Catholic burying grounds from June 12th to July 30th, when the epidemic was at its high tide we have found the records in an old scrapbook, which obviously were inserted day by day. The sum total of burials for these two months alone was 1,556, of which there were 1,182 victims of the cholera, that is about four-fifths of the total of 1,556 St. Louisans that died of the epidemic within the brief period.

No doubt many Catholics were hurriedly laid away in the City Cemetery. Those that died before June 12th, or after July 31st, are not given here. Their number would, no doubt, swell the total of Catholic victims of the cholera to 2,600 or 2,700, that is three-eighths of 7,000.[5]

At the end of its Mortality Reports, Monday July 30th, the morning paper from which these items were taken, writes: "We are glad to be able to announce that the cholera no longer remains with us as an epidemic. Our people are going into business again with their usual activity, and in a short time we expect to see but little of the dullness induced by the raging of the pestilence with which we have been so long and so terribly afflicted.

"We know there are many sad hearts and desolated homes in our city, but trust that all will bow submissively to the terrible decree that has been so heavily laid upon us, and with renewed energy go forward in the performance of the duties of the mission, directing us to develop the resources of the Great West, and never failing to do good for others who may be thrown, as yet, to some extent upon our claims for assistance and protection. We have suffered greatly—let us bear all with becoming bravery."[6]

Like every visitation of God the cholera certainly worked for good: not only in rousing the citizens to a higher sense of their civic responsibility, but also of producing the most beautiful manifestations of divine charity in the hearts of God's ministers and of the people. The thirty or more priests with the Archbishop at their head, were

---

5 The burials of cholera victims for April and May, were 1,224 out of a total of 2,179. Of these burials we have no record as to the religious affiliation of the victims of this epidemic. The buirals after August 1, will no doubt make up the grand total of 7,000 deaths in 1849. Our Scrapbook Records were originally the property of T. J. Delamere.

6 Delamere's Scrapbook.

untiring in their service to the afflicted, waiting on them day and night for their spiritual comfort and help, and piously burying the dead: "Seven of our Fathers were night and day, for months together, among the dead and dying." wrote Father De Smet. The Archbishop himself daily visited the Hospitals. The old missionary, Peter Richard Donnelly, now chaplain of the Hospital, was faithfully assisted by his brother priests of the city. Not one left his post of duty, and it is owing to a special Providence of God that not one of them was claimed by the plague.

The St. Louis Hospital of the Sisters of Charity, on the corner of Spruce and Fourth Streets, had during the cholera year received to its care two thousand seven hundred and five patients. Almost one half of this number, namely 1,330 were attacked by cholera. Five hundred and ten died of that disease, and eight hundred and twenty were cured. Five hundred and twenty-seven were charity-patients.

But these numberless acts of charity to the poor and afflicted were not the fullness of the sacrifice offered by the Sisters of Charity. Two of their members, Sister Columba Long and Sister Patricia Butler willingly and cheerfully gave their lives for their friends, the suffering and disconsolate. That others might live, not only in body but also in soul, these angels of the sick-wards were ready, one and all, to immolate themselves, to see death stare them in the face, day and night, and to feel his mysterious presence and his ghastly touch whereever they turned to go. That was true heroism, far greater and nobler than the soldiers death on the battlefield. All honor to their names. The Sisters of Charity also had charge of one of the diocesan Orphan Asylums. In the year of the cholera, there were one hundred and twenty orphan girls in their care, about fifty of them having lost their parents by the cholera. There were two schools attached to St. Mary's Orphan Home, one German, the other English, attended regularly by four sisters from the Asylum. The number of pupils in both was two hundred and fifty. This institution was situated on Biddle and Tenth Streets. There was also St. Philomenas Free School, on Walnut and Fifth Streets with five Sisters of Charity and two hundred and twenty pupils. During the prevalence of the cholera, however, these schools were closed, and all the Sisters attended the public cholera hospitals established by the Committee of Safety, the quarantine and also poor families who called for their assistance.

"What a world of good these Sisters wrought, during the awful year of Asiatic cholera!" exclaims Father Kenny. "Such was their success that both the general and the city government made choice of this hospital for all patients, and when, in 1845, the city had its own hospital, the Sisters were put in charge and remained until the fire of 1856, when prejudice, the Knownothing craze, took it from them.''[7]

The Sisters of Charity were not the only heroic souls in these trying days.

The Sisters of St. Joseph had at their Mother House in Carondelet a Novitiate of their Order, an Academy with 130 pupils, an Asylum for the Deaf and Dumb and an Orphan Asylum containing twenty-eight orphans. Sister Celestine was in charge as Superior with seven professed Nuns. In St. Louis they conducted a day-school near St. Vincent's Church with three Sisters and two novices, and one hundred and twenty pupils.

Another House of the Community in St. Louis had under its direction the diocesan Orphan Home for boys of whom there were one hundred and twenty. Sister Felicite with five professed Sisters formed the community:

In 1849 the Sisters stationed at St. Vincent's Convent, having closed their school, "fearlessly gave themselves to the relief of the sick and dying neighbors." Two of their number, Sisters Frances Nally and Justine Mulhall, were seized with the dread symptoms of cholera. Sister Justine was but eighteen years of age "a young woman of rare innocence, and extraordinary personal beauty," in the agony of dying had but one wish, that of renewing her vows on the morning of the Visitation. Archbishop Kenrick remained at her bedside until after midnight that her dying wish might be fulfilled. On July 28th, 1849, the Archbishop wrote to his friend Mark Anthony Frenaye in Philadelphia: "The epidemic which has made frightful ravages among our people is now abating in its violence day by day, and there is hope that this afflicted city may have a little time to breathe. The malady has not, up to the present time, claimed as a victim any of our priests, though they have devoted themselves to the service of the sick with great zeal, and the fatigue of this alone would be enough to bring them to the grave. Eleven religious women are among the victims, two of the Sisters of Charity, two of the Sisters of St. Joseph, one of the Visitation and six of the Sacred Heart.''[8]

Of the first four, the honored names have already been given. The name of the Visitandine Sister was Veronica Corcoran, the names of the Ladies of the Sacred Heart were: M. Rose Proudhon, M. Rachel-Gardiner, Madam Rohe, a novice, and Madam Griffin, also a novice. The name of the other two are hidden with God. There is another

---

[7] Kenny, Rev. Lawrence, "The Mullanphys of St. Louis," "Historical Records and Studies," vol. XV, p. 96.

[8] "Records of the American Catholic Historical Society," vol. XXX, p. 343.

Sister of St. Joseph mentioned in the Catholic Directory of 1850, as having died of the cholera at St. Joseph's Orphanage, Sister M. Antoinette-Kinkaid.[9]

The plague left many children homeless. When St. Joseph's Orphanage was transferred, in the late summer of 1849, to the new building on Clark Avenue and Thirteenth Street, the number of boys had increased from eighty in the previous year to one hundred and fifty. The diocesan orphanages were crowded. As about half of the Catholic population of the city consisted of German immigrants, the number of Catholic orphans of German parentage was very large. "Why cannot our German Catholics provide for the needs of the orphans of our race and creed?" The idea struck root. The German Catholic Clergy under the leadership of Vicar-General Joseph Melcher showed a deep interest in the plan.

There were at the time only two German Parishes in the city. St. Mary's and St. Joseph's. Father Melcher was pastor of the former, with Father Simon Sigrist as assistant; St. Joseph's was attended by the Jesuit Fathers Hofbauer and Seisl. St. Vincent's served as a Parish church for both the German and the Irish; SS. Peter and Paul's and Holy Trinity were in their initial stages.

The German Catholics of St. Louis of that time were mostly young beginners. Not one could be called wealthy. But they possessed the two virtues, so characteristic of the pioneer age, generosity and strong faith; and these were sufficient to clear away all the obstacles they met in their pathway.

On the 12th day of June 1850 the following appeal to the German Catholics of the city was issued by a Committee of priests and laymen: "For a long time the Catholics of St. Louis have felt the need of a German Roman Catholic Orphan-Home, and the wish to found such an institution has often been expressed by the charitably disposed. Such an institution would have certainly been established long since, if the necessary means could have been raised by individuals. Now, as the means of the few are not sufficient to carry out the difficult project of satisfying this pressing demand, it seems advisable to organize a society. The undersigned German Catholics avow it as their intention to build a German Catholic Orphanage, so that support and education may be provided for the helpless orphans of both sexes, and they entertain the hope, that their compatriots, both far and near, will join the society, or at least, give their support to the undertaking."[10]

---

9   Records of the American Catholic Historical Society, vol. XXX, p. 343 note.

10   Diamond Jubilee of the German St. Vincent Orphan Society, p. 11.

This appeal was signed by Very Rev. Joseph Melcher, Vicar-General of St. Louis, and by three other members of the clergy. Fathers Hofbauer, S. J., Simon Siegrist, Michael Seisl, and the following laymen: Val. Reis, G. Eberle, Anton Schroeder, F. A. Stuever, Christ Pieper, Anton Holle, Franz Saler, John Mauntel, Peter Ludecke, Edward Buse and Charles Blattau.

The appeal found an immediate response. On June 14th, a meeting of German Catholic men was held at the Rectory of St. Mary's Parish under the presidency of Vicar-General Melcher, at which it was unanimously resolved to organize under the name of the German St. Vincent Orphan Society. The following officers were elected: Frank A. Stuever, President; J. F. Mauntel, Vice President; Francis Saler, Treasurer; Charles Blattau, 1st Secretary; Edward Buse, 2nd Secretary.

A committee was appointed to formulate a Constitution and By-laws, and to report to the next meeting. After being submitted to Archbishop Kenrick and approved by His Grace, both were adopted. The Society numbered 82 members. Within a month the President of the Society, Frank A. Stuever, died, and Valentine Reis was chosen to fill the vacancy.

The Society at once began operations. A plot of ground on Hogan Street between Cass Avenue and O'Fallon Street was bought for the Society by Father Elet, S. J., at a cost of $950.00.

Construction work was begun immediately, the contract price was $5,980.00. The corner-stone was laid in September 1850. In May 1851 Archbishop Kenrick performed the ceremony of dedication.[11]

In his pastoral letter of 1850 Archbishop Kenrick showed his deep appreciation of this excellent work:

"Besides the two asylums already in existence, we have deemed it advisable to approve the erection of a German Male and Female Asylum, as well to comply with the wishes of that portion of our flock who use the German language, as to diminish the burdens on the existing Asylums, and to obviate the necessity of making additions to them, which otherwise would soon be necessary. A large and suitable lot has been secured for this purpose, on very favorable terms, and at a price far below its actual value; and we earnestly recommend the undertaking to your charitable consideration."[12]

On March 1st, 1851 the German St. Vincent Orphan Society was incorporated by the State Legislature, with F. J. Heitkamp, B. Heidacker, J. Degenhard. F. Heitkamp, J. F. Mauntel and F. Beehler as incorporators.

---

11   Diamond Jubilee of the German St. Vincent Orphan Society, p. 11.
12   Pastoral Letter of 1850.

Five sisters of St. Joseph, from Carondelet, Angela, Febronia, Adelheid, Stanislaus and Ignatia took charge of the new Orphan Home on July 3rd, 1851. Mother Angela served as Superior of the community.

Archbishop Kenrick ordered that two collections be taken up annually for the German orphans in all the German Churches of the city. The first collection realized the sum of $369.05; from St. Joseph's Church $116.25; St. Mary's $87.50; Holy Trinity $74.00; S. S. Peter and Paul's, $64.80 and St. Vincent's $26.50.

On July 25th, 1851, the first orphan girl, Anna Schwerdt, was received into the home; in the following week two boys, Andrew Schwartz and John Gehrig, were entered. Two months later the Home harbored 30 children.

The first Festival conducted for the benefit of the Orphan Home realized $1900.

The annual report submitted by Mr. Droege, the Secretary, gave the number of members in the Society as 200, and the total receipts as $1827.00. By the end of the year the membership had increased to 350. Nine Trustees had control of the funds.

The Jesuit Fathers of St. Joseph's Church were chaplains during that time: Father Joseph Patshowski being the first to say Mass in the institution. In its long career of seventy-five years the German St. Vincent Orphan Home experienced many sad vicissitudes, from fire, pestilence and other evils. The saddest was the recurrence in 1854 of the dreadful epidemic that in 1849, had led to the foundation of the Home, the cholera. Within the brief period of two weeks, one sister, Ignatia, and fourteen children fell victims to the awful scourge. On one sad day six little corpses lay in the house; and for fear of contagion, the sisters had to lay them away in the old disused cemetery within the enclosure, until proper burial could be held.

In the year previous to the outbreak of the cholera there were 40 boys and 30 girls in the Home. But through the havoc wrought by the plague within the city, the number of orphans increased to such an extent, that they could no longer be properly accommodated. To provide for the newcomers, an addition was made to the building, to serve as chapel, the temporary chapel being vacated for other purposes.

The new chapel was dedicated by Father Patshowski, on March 17th, 1855. From this time on the Orphan Society held the anniversary celebration of its foundation in the Orphan Home.

Within a few years the constant increase of the number of orphan children, and of the Sisters that were required for their proper care and instruction, urgently called for another addition to the building. In 1859 the south wing was erected, and dedicated by Father Niederkorn, S.J., on Easter Monday, 1860. This new structure was set apart for the girls, the boys remaining in the old place.  The number of pupils was 110.

Up to this time Mother Angela had been Superior of the institution; now she was succeeded by Mother Theresa, and after an interval of two years, by Mother Martha.  But, owing to declining health, she too was forced to retire, and Mother Angela returned, to the great joy of the Sisters.

The January assembly of the Society in 1869 adopted the new Constitution, by which the organization of branch-societies in the various parishes was authorized.  The following were erected during the year 1869; St. Mary's in April, Holy Trinity in May, St. Joseph's in June, St. Liborius in July, St. Vincent's and St. Nicholas in December.  The branch-societies of S. S. Peter and Paul's was organized on January 1st, 1870, and of St. Francis de Sales in 1871.  The Orphan Society as a centralized society, had become unwieldy, by reason of numbers: From now on business was transacted by delegates from the branches who form what is called the Main society.

On the 29th day of December 1888 the "Daughters of the Blessed Virgin of the Immaculate Conception," or as they are now better known the "Sisters of Christian Charity" succeeded the Sisters of St. Joseph in the administration of the German St. Vincent Orphan Home. The Sisters of Christian Charity have their mother house in Paderborn. Their foundress, the venerable Mother Pauline Mallinckrodt will, it is justly hoped, right soon receive the honor of beatification.  Driven out of Germany by the so-called Kulturkampf the Sisters came to America in 1873 and took up their abode, first in New Orleans, and then at Wilkesbarre, Pa., until several years ago, when the mother house was removed to Wilmette, Ill.

Four sisters came, under Mother Theresa, as Superior to assume the duties of the German orphanage at St. Louis.  Ere long two others were added to the little community.  They found 141 children placed under their care; and still the number continued to increase and to call for better housing faculties, a call that was to meet its proper response in the fine new Home in Normandy.  With real Christian charity have these gentle sisters given their consecrated lives to the noble purposes of the Orphan Society.  Truly wonderful results have been attained.  Many of the pupils hold or held distinguished positions in the world and in the church.  Monseignor Hoog's success in life is know to all.  But it may not be so well known that the German St. Vincent Orphan Home has given eleven priests to Holy Church, four of them members of the Society of Jesus, three Benedictines, one Franciscan, one Capuchin, and two of the diocesan clergy.

Then there are ten boys of the German Orphan Home that have chosen the service of God in some religious Order or Congregation; and forty-three girl pupils who entered some Sisterhood, as the Order of St. Joseph, of St. Francis, of the Precious Blood, of St. Mary, and of Christian Charity.[13]

Such results as these spiritual vocations sufficiently characterize the excellent spirit of the Home, and the high ideals cultivated in it.

It is worthy of note that the Catholic Orphan Association of St. Louis, founded February 13th, 1841, but incorporated in 1849 under the new name *The Roman Catholic Male and Female Orphan Asylum of St. Louis* were assigned the control and support of the two diocesan Orphan Asylums of St. Joseph and St. Mary in the city of St. Louis, and also of the Catholic Protectorate at Glencoe, an institution where it was proposed to send Catholic orphan boys to be taught farming or the trades. The latter Asylum has ceased to function. The proper designation at present is the Catholic Orphan Board of St. Louis.

The diocesan orphan Asylums are supported by annual collections taken up in all the English speaking parishes of the diocese and liberal allowances from the Calvary Cemetery Board.

---

13  Diamond Jubilee, passim.

## CHAPTER 4

## THE SISTERS OF THE GOOD SHEPHERD

The cholera epidemic of 1849 not only furnished the religious Orders, already established in the city, with rare opportunities for practicing the virtue of charity in the sublimest manner, but also brought to St. Louis another institute of religious women, equally devoted to the work of christian charity, the Sisterhood of Our Lady of Charity, better known as the Sisters of the Good Shepherd. Their main purpose was the work of reclaiming fallen members of their own sex and of preserving young girls in danger. The work of building up a strong pure and high-minded womanhood by means of a higher Christian education was already in good hands among the existing Orders and Congregations: to labor for the salvation of the outcasts of society was to be the work of the Sisters of the Good Shepherd.

The Order of the Good Shepherd was founded early in the seventeenth century by the Blessed John Eudes, a native of Normandy, in France. While engaged in missionary work, there came under his direction some souls who, like Mary Magdalen of old, had fallen; and now, like Mary Magdalen, desired to change their ways. At his request some pious women took them into their care, but soon tired of the work. Then the idea of a Religious Order devoted to the work of preservation and reformation of these unfortunate outcasts of society was aroused in his mind. He organized such a community at Caen, and, in addition to three usual vows of chastity, obedience and poverty, added as a fourth: the vow namely, to labor for the salvation of the souls of the penitent women, who would enter their houses. For a time they lived under the direction of the Nuns of the Visitation; but Pope Alexander VI constituted them an independent religious congregation. Father Eudes died on August 19th, 1680: his last words: "My God and my All." He was beatified by Pope Pius X April 25th, 1909. The Congregation spread all over France, but its career was arrested for a time by the French Revolution. In 1818, after Napoleon had partly restored liberty of worship, the Convent of Tours was reopened. One of the members of the convent, Sister Euphrasia, was chiefly instrumental in bringing the foundation of Father Eudes to a higher degree of usefulness. She became Superior of the Convent of Angers in 1831, and as such took steps to unite the different houses of the Order under one head. Pope Gregory XVI warmly approved of the union under the title "Our Lady of Charity, of the Good Shepherd of Angers." Bishop Flaget, on his travels in France in 1835, came to Angers, and asked for a colony of Sisters for his diocese. Five

Sisters, each of a different nationality, were chosen for the mission. They established themselves near Louisville, Kentucky. God blessed their efforts, and in 1849 they were sufficiently well-established to send a colony to St. Louis.

The Sisters appointed to make the foundation were: Mother Mary of the Infant Jesus, Gress, Superior; Sister Mary of St. Reparata, Deleuse, and Sister Mary of St. Peter, Bongar. Mother Mary of the Infant Jesus, who was of German extraction, had made her Novitiate at Angers, and in 1845 had been a member of the second colony of Sisters sent to Louisville. Sister Mary of St. Reparata, an Italian Sister, was one of the pioneers of Louisville. Sister Mary of St. Peter was not long visibly to aid the new foundation, for she was called to her reward in 1853, but the fragrance of her virtues still lingers in the Community of St. Louis.

"The trip was made by steamer and the travelers left Louisville on the 21st of January 1849. The winter was unusually severe and the Sisters, while on board, suffered much from the cold as it was impossible to prevent its penetrating their cabins from which, because of the uncongenial company on the boat, they hardly dared venture. At one point the river became so blocked with ice that the Captain questioned whether it was safe to continue the journey. Alarmed at the mere idea of turning back, the Sisters started fervent prayers, and in the later years when speaking of their first journey on the river, they attributed to their humble persevering prayers the fact that it was accomplished without any serious accident."[1]

On the 24th the steamer reached St. Louis, and what was the Sisters' surprise to see at the landing the commanding figure of their Reverend Archbishop Kenrick, who was waiting to greet them.

The next morning the good Archbishop wrote to his friend Mark Anthony: "We have here a house of our dear Mother of Charity, that is, the Sisters of the Good Shepherd, who arrived last Thursday evening, and took possession of a fine house already furnished, with a chapel nicely decorated and fitted up. A good priest dying left this by will, together with other properties, in order to make of it, one or other of them, an establishment for the care of old priests, or those who are no longer able to labor on the missions by reason of poor health. Happily, we have no one now of these classes of priests, and I see nothing better to do than to lay the foundation of the house mentioned above. The good Sisters are very well satisfied with their new home: and, it is needless to say, that I am pleased that the number of our establishments has been increased with so little expense, and in particular, this work of noblest Christian charity."[2]

---

[1] From a circular published August 23, 1925, and sent us by the Sisters.

[2] Kenrick, P. R., to Frenaye in "Records of the American Catholic Historical Society," vol. XXX, pp. 340 and 341.

The house here mentioned as the first home of the Sisters of the Good Shepherd was built by Madam Mary Sentee Smith, who had formerly lived on her large plantation at Grand Couteau, La., but later moved to St. Michael's at Fredericktown and eventually to St. Louis. She was permitted to have a private chapel in her house and also a private chaplain, Father Francis Cellini, one of the earliest Lazarist Fathers in the Louisiana Mission and finally Vicar-General of the archdiocese of St. Louis. Mrs. Mary Smith had bequeathed all her property to Father Cellini and he, in turn bequeathed all to Archbishop Kenrick. This house and garden the Archbishop now set apart for the little Community of the Good Shepherd until a suitable Convent should be built for them. He had also provided for the spiritual needs of the Sisters by calling upon the Lazarist Fathers of St. Vincent's Church to minister to them. In his Pastoral of February 2nd, 1849, the Archbishop writes of his new acquisition:

"We have great satisfaction in being able to state to you, that we have added to the number of the religious houses already established in this diocese, a small community of Our Lady of Charity, or Sisters of the Good Shepherd, who have lately arrived in this city from Louisville, Kentucky. The object of this institute is to afford an asylum, and means of restoration to those, who after having followed in the steps, may feel inclined to imitate the repentance of Magdalene. In this Asylum, in a house separate and apart from the residence of these admirable and devoted ladies, who consecrate their lives, under the solemnity of the religious engagement, to this most Divine work of imitating the Good Shepherd and bringing back to the fold the strayed sheep, such persons will be trained to habits of virtue and industry, until they can return to the world, with greater security among its dangers. We earnestly recommend this truly good work to your encouragement and support. The inmates of the establishment will, under the direction of the religious ladies already mentioned, occupy themselves with every species of work suitable to their sex and situation; and thus will be enabled to contribute to the support of a house to which they will owe so much."[3]

Archbishop Kenrick was, of course, well aware that Father Cellini's old mansion was but a temporary expedient in as far as the work of the Good Shepherd was concerned. On February 6th, 1849, he wrote to Frenaye: "You have been told before that we have here the Sisters of the Good Shepherd. A kind Providence has given me the means of doing or rather, of beginning this good work without actual outlay of money, a work moreover which was much needed. According to the Constitutions of these good Sisters, they should have a house apart from their own for the penitents, and as there was a house which ad-

---

3  Pastoral of February 2, 1849.

joined our grounds, I bought if for $1400, in order to have the Sisters begin their work for poor sinners. They have already received one."[4]

In the meantime Madam Anne Lucas Hunt, so well known for her magnificent charities, had become interested in the work, and donated to the Archbishop a piece of ground on which to build the future Convent. This property, located in what was then the suburbs, is now the block bounded by 16th, 17th, Chestnut and Pine Streets.[5]

The Sisters had come to St. Louis with absolutely no funds, and had no means with which to build a Convent, but the Most Reverend Archbishop, ever their friend, came to their aid, and both by his own liberal contributions and exerting his influence, with the citizens of St. Louis, succeeded in accomplishing the apparently hopeless task. Under his personal supervision a Convent suitable for their needs, was erected and paid for. As years went on the work extended, other buildings were added, until the St. Louis Convent became a model of its kind.[6]

The Reformatories, of which there were two, one for juvenile offenders, and the other for older women, usually sheltered about three hundred. The Preservation Class, in which were received children or young women, exposed to the dangers of vice, either through their own depravity or the evil surroundings of their childhood, averaged about one hundred and fifty inmates. The Community of Magdalens, which is a religious Order established for the benefit of those among the inmates of the Reformatories who desired to spend their remaining years in prayer and penance, had a membership of sixty.[7] These Magdalens, however, can never become members of the Order of the Sisters of the Good Shepherd, among whom none are admitted except ladies who have always led pure, irreproachable lives. An untarnished reputation is an absolutely necessary qualification for membership, not only in the individual herself, but freedom from any moral stain on the immediate relatives. "Our Lord, the Good Shepherd," said Archbishop Ireland in one of his most eloquent sermons, "thinks not of others safe within the fold, but rushes in loving pursuit that He may rescue the lost one from all peril, and, finding it, clasps it in His arms and brings it back to the haven of love and mercy. So the Sisters of the Good Shepherd. There are those children of misfortune whom the world views as the lowliest, from whom it shrinks as from contagion to whom doors are closed, save the doors of sin and dereliction. To such the house of the Good Shepherd is ever open.

---

4 Records, vol. XXX, pp. 341 and 342.

5 The Community moved to the new Convent in 1852.

6 Adolphus Busch who donated the site of the present Convent, was not a Catholic, yet a public-spirited man.

7 Brief notices communicated by the Sisters.

There the light of love is ever burning, beckoning to hope and to salvation: there the welcoming hand is ever at the threshold: there safety is insured.　There, to keep and guard, to heal and comfort the woe-stricken victims of cruel storms, to form them into new and happier life, to instruct and strengthen mind and heart against future trial and temptation, there do dwell the Sisters of the Good Shepherd, women so strong in their own purity that no peril of nearness to the woe-stricken breeds alarm, so mighty in self-sacrifice that no call upon their courage suggests a surcease of zeal.　Little is known by the outside world of the Sisters of the Good Shepherd and of the work they are doing.　Little should be known.　Through very respect to their wards they are bidden to do their work in isolation and silence.　But what is it that holds those Sisters in their isolation, in their silence? in their life-long self-sacrifice?　This and this alone—the love springing from the heart of the Good Shepherd of the Gospel: the knowledge that doing good to the poor and lowliest, is doing good to the Shepherd Himself.''[8]

In 1859, the St. Louis Convent was made a Provincial or Novitiate House and in subsequent years branch houses were established in St. Paul, Chicago, New Orleans, Havana, Memphis, Denver, Kansas City, Omaha, Milwaukee, Detroit, Peoria, Sioux City, Los Angeles, Normandy, an Industrial School in Chicago, and the Government Reform School for Girls in Havana.　The Novitiate supplied Religious for all these foundations.

The City of St. Louis extended rapidly, and the location at 17th and Pine Streets became the center of a business district.　The quiet and retirement necessary for carrying on the work of the Good Shepherd were wanting.　The old Convent had also become too small for the ever increasing number seeking its shelter, and when the need of more room became imperative, the Sisters, with the advice of their benefactors, decided that it was advisable to seek a more suitable location on which to build.　Mr. Adolphus Busch donated eleven acres of ground out on the Gravois Road, and the proceeds of the sale of the old property, augmented by a legacy of seventy-five thousand dollars from Mrs. Winifred Patterson, and contributions from other generous friends, enabled the Sisters to erect the present large, but incompleted building, which they entered November 25, 1895.

---

[8]　Archbishop Ireland, Sermon.

CHAPTER 5

## THE SISTERS OF MERCY

It is to the foresight and energy of the Jesuit Father Arnold Damen that the Congregation of the Sisters of Mercy owes its establishment in the city of St. Louis. Father Damen was the pastor of St. Xavier Church, or as it was usually called, the College Church, from 1847 to 1857. On all sides he met poverty, sickness and ignorance among the motley population of his parish.

The hard struggle for life during the years when immigration from Ireland and Germany, was at its high tide, brought about in many a dangerous relaxation of moral principles. Extreme poverty and helpless misery usually tend to evil, unless extraordinary efforts are made by the shepherds to surround the flock with every influence of christian charity. The religious Orders of women had a special calling to this work. But they were few and all were over-burdened with work; yet in their various fields, the Madams of the Sacred Heart, the Sisters of Loretto, the Sisters of Charity, the Visitandines, and lately, the Ursulines and the Sisters of the Good Shepherd were doing excellent work, but not of the special kind that Father Damen's people seemed to require. The work of going forth from the cloister, at the bidding of God, on errands of charity to the poor and the sick in their homes, to feed the hungry, to bring healing balm to the afflicted, to instruct the ignorant and to recall the wayward, was the special demand of the hour.

Where shall he get such ministering angels? There was a Congregation of Sisters, founded in Ireland in its darkest days of misery and want, 1827, by a fervent soul, Catherine McAuley, who had chosen for the Sisters of Mercy the undying love for our Lord in the person of the poor, the sick and the ignorant. The most assiduous application to the education of poor girls, the visitation of the sick and the protection of poor women of good character, was to be the cherished object of her foundation, whereever established. That was the Sisterhood Father Damen's parish required: to get this Sisterhood established in the parish of St. Francis Xavier his every effort was now bent.

Archbishop Kenrick heartily approved Father Damen's plan, and on May 19th, 1856 wrote to the Mother Superior of St. Catherine's Convent at New York:

"I esteem it as a great blessing for the Catholics of the Diocese that a house of the Sisters of Mercy should be established here; and that I shall always esteem it a duty and a consolation to bestow whatever aid

(31)

and encouragement I may be able to command in facilitating the success of the Order in this city.''[1]

As to the business arrangements made by Father Damen with the Superior of the Sisters, Archbishop Kenrick writes in the same letter:

''1· The house is not, I presume, such a house as would be deemed suitable for a convent; it being a private residence which may be used for such purpose. I have not myself seen it, but rely on Father Damen's assurance as to its suitableness in the above sense.

''2· The moderate support which the Sisters will receive will be $800 a year at the least. I have no doubt that small as is this sum, the Sisters will have no reason to complain of insufficient support. Unless I am greatly mistaken they will find the Catholics of St. Louis well disposed to assist them, not only in the matter of support, but also in the provision for a permanent establishment of the Community.

''3· The Chaplain and Director, ordinary, and extraordinary, will be furnished by the Jesuits, at my request, and by my appointment.

''Father Damen authorized me to say that all the expenses of the Sisters, either for preparations for the journey or for traveling expenses will be defrayed by him. He has promised to write to Mr. Dunigan, the publisher, to advance to the Sisters whatever sum they may call for.''[2]

On the receipt of the Archbishop's letter, Rev. Mother Agnes O'Connor selected six of her Sisters for the new mission, appointing as Mother Superior, Sister M. de Pazzi Bentley, who had been, up to that time, Mother Assistant in the New York House.

They made the overland journey mostly by rail, in care of Father Patrick J. Ryan, and arrived on Friday morning June 27th, in St. Louis. Without delay they drove to St. Xavier's Church, where Father Damen gave them welcome and brought them to their new home, at the corner of Morgan and Tenth Street.

The convent was placed under the protection of St. Joseph. Adverting to the poverty of their surroundings, the Archbishop, on his first visit, remarked:

''Nothing great has great beginnings.''

''On the feast of the Visitation of the Blessed Virgin, July 2nd, within one week of their arrival from New York, the Sisters commenced their visits of mercy. Seeking out the sick and the poor in their homes, and attending to both temporal and spiritual needs, a vast field of neglected humanity spread out before them on every hand. Most rapidly, stories of their ministering kindness passed among the suffering people,

---

1  Smith, M. C., ''A Sheaf of Golden Years,'' p. 13.
2  Ibidem, pp. 13 and 14.

and even where charity was never sought before, the Sisters were wanted now."[3]

As the community grew in numbers the visitation of the sick and the poor was extended over the entire city. On these rounds the Sisters, always going two and two, took especial interest in keeping Catholics up to the practice of their religion. Among them they found many who had not made their first Communion: these they instructed and then introduced them to a priest. During the terrible years of the war, the number of wounded soldiers and of prisoners was very great, and the accommodations for them were not of the best. The Sisters of Mercy visited them day by day and did much to alleviate their sufferings and distress. McDowell's College was turned into a prison for Confederate soldiers. Its forlorn inmates regarded the visits of the Sisters as so many messengers of hope and comfort.

The Sisters of Mercy made their first visit to the St. Louis Jail on July 16th, 1856. In this work they have continued up to the present time, and though arduous it is performed cheerfully for the love of God. Many a conversion of hardened sinners was effected through their meekness and humility of heart."[4]

In August 1856, they opened St. Francis Parish Free School with a large attendance. A Sunday School for Negro women and girls was also opened. A House of Mercy, a free shelter for young girls out of employment was established on December 12th, 1856. The establishment of an Industrial School for little girls whose parents were unable or unwilling to care for them, was their next venture.

Thus there was work in abundance for the Sisters: but whence should the means be derived to carry on all these charities? In addition to the Convent, Father Damen had given them two houses, the rent of which was intended for the upkeep of the Institution; but the good Sisters were often disappointed in their expectations of rent due them from their tenants, who thought it cheaper to move than to pay up. To make full their measure of tribulations, Father Arnold Damen, who had been their chief adviser and support from the beginning, was transferred to Chicago. The good Sisters were reduced to the necessity of taking in sewing and laundry work in addition to their manifold other duties. Nightwork soon told on the health of the Sisters; which moved the New York Superior to write: "Do not undertake more work than you are reasonably able to perform. If you do not succeed return to us."[5]

---

[3] "A Sheaf of Golden Years," p. 19.
[4] Ibidem, p. 29 ss.
[5] Ibidem, p. 49.

In this crisis Archbishop Kenrick was appealed to, and not in vain. "God is only trying you," answered the generous Prelate, "You must not think of leaving St. Louis where there is so much good to be done. When I go home I will send you one hundred dollars, and if your creditors are dunning you, give them an order on me. During the coming year I will see what can be done."[6]

In spite of the dire poverty of the Sisters their Community increased and flourished. In 1860 the lack of larger accomodations was pressing heavily upon them: the house on Morgan and Tenth Streets had but poorly served its purpose until 1860. But now a change had to be made. There was no available building in St. Xavier's Parish. In this predicament the Archbishop once more proved himself as the Guardian Angel of the Sisters. He offered to give them a large building lot on Morgan and Twenty-Second Street and to purchase from them a part of their property holdings at the old place. The offer was gratefully accepted. The Sisters now proceeded with building the fine commodious structure long known to the people of St. Louis as "St. Joseph's Convent of Mercy."[7] The Jesuits furnished a chaplain to the Sisters free of charge: a number of wealthy people of the city enlisted as patrons of the institution, prominent among them were the Kerens, Chouteau, Maffit and Peugnet families.

In the basement of their new Convent the Sisters opened a school for little girls. A small monthly fee was asked but rarely paid: and the Sisters had no complaint but, in many cases, added food and clothing to the educational benefits bestowed by them on their pupils. Five years later, when the attendance reached six hundred children, it was found necessary to erect a parish school.

The former school rooms were converted into an infirmary. This was the beginning of the Sisters Hospital in St. Louis under the title of St. John of God. It was at first intended for women and children only, but finally it was enlarged to a general Hospital, to receive men and women without distinction of creed or nationality. The Hospital was opened March 1, 1871.

The kind and attentive care accorded by the Sisters to all patients who came to them for help and relief in suffering soon made larger accommodations imperative. The city, too, was growing rapidly, and the urgent need of larger hospital facilities was strongly impressed upon the Sisters. So, without special pecuniary assistance from friends or benefactors, stimulated by zeal for Christ's suffering, strong in their

---

6 "A Sheaf of Golden Years," p. 50.

7 The Archbishop contributed $600 in 1840. The Sisters took possession of this Convent in 1860.

confidence in God, they purchased the property at Twenty-third and Locust streets. This they converted into a hospital which was opened in 1890, August 5, and was known as The "New St. John's Hospital."

Originally a private mansion of magnificent proportions, it was enlarged with two wings, until it attained a frontage of one hundred and five and a depth of one hundred and fifty feet. The growth of the hospital necessitated the establishment of a clinical dispensary for outside patients. This consists of a number of departments: Medical, Surgical, Eye, Ear, Nose, Throat, and many others.

The establishment of the Hospital brought on a trying ordeal for the community. Two rival medical colleges of the city, the Marion-Simms and the Missouri Medical College, were anxious, the one to obtain, the other to retain the privilege of having their physicians attend the patients at St. John's. The Missouri Medical College was in possession and had given the best possible service: but the Marion-Simms College having been incorporated in the St. Louis University, claimed a superior right as being a Catholic institution. The matter was settled through the intervention of Archbishop Kain, the main points of whose letter are here subjoined:

"All of us desire to see flourishing schools of higher learning under Catholic management. The lack of these has been a reproach to us in the past. If such schools are necessary in other lines, especially are they necessary in medicine."

"The St. Louis University is spending many thousands of dollars, and expects no pecuniary advantage from this enterprise. Now that it is an assured fact, we should all lend it our support, as it is for the common good of the Church in this section. . .

"We all know that a medical school can not be successful without ample hospital or clinical facilities. It would seem, therefore, altogether natural that the Catholic hospitals should grant their clinical facilities to a Catholic medical college, rather than to any other."[8]

In the year 1890 the Sisters of Mercy received a call from Springfield, Mo. Not only Rev. Father Porta, pastor of the Immaculate Conception church, but the leading doctors and citizens of that city joined in the earnest solicitation. When Bishop Hogan, of Kansas City, added his word of invitation, they consented to go to Springfield.

A house with a large piece of ground was purchased at the corner of Washington Avenue and Chestnut street, and a hospital started on a small scale. After securing a somewhat firm foothold a frame addition was added to the original building.

---

8  "A Sheaf of Golden Years," p. 65.

St. John's at Springfield, like every institution of its kind conducted by the Sisters of Mercy, is strictly non-sectarian, no distinction of creed or nationality ever being made.

Here the Sisters also visit the sick and the poor, and have charge of the parochial school attached to St. John's church.

A terrible smallpox epidemic descended upon Springfield, in 1899, and then, more than ever before, the citizens realized the true heroism that actuates a daughter of Mother McAuley.

In November 1901, responding to an invitation from Bishop Fitz-Gerald, of Little Rock, the Sisters of Mercy opened a hospital and a school in Eureka Springs, Ark.

As the crowning glory of their charity to the sick and convalescent the Sisters of Mercy on November 24th, 1912, opened their magnificent and admirably appointed new St. John's Hospital on Euclid Avenue and Parkview Place. Subsequently they removed their Mother House and Novitiate to Webster Groves one of the beautiful suburbs of St. Louis.

From their loved home in Ireland the Daughters of sainted Catherine McAuley had come across the sea to our land, "to gladden the expectant eyes of far-off nations in a world remote." But they formed a happier home in the great cities of our country, where sin and poverty and misery hide in the dark, waiting with expectant eyes the coming of the angels of mercy in human form. Divine Providence did indeed try them severely, but they were not found wanting in humility, meekness and patience. To these virtues, and to the underlying virtue of charity is due the grand success of the Sisters of Mercy.

## Chapter 6

## THE URSULINE NUNS

"They that are learned shall shine as the brightness of the firmament: and they that instruct many unto justice as stars for all eternity," is a saying of the Holy Spirit, that may well be applied to the Ursuline Nuns, who have now been engaged, for upwards of seventy-five years, in educational work in the archdiocese of St. Louis.

The Order of St. Ursula was founded early in the Sixteenth Century by St. Angela Merici, a native of Desenzano on Lake Garda in northern Italy. Owing to the Founder's long connection with the neighboring city of Brescia, she is often called St. Angela of Brescia. It was at this city that the pious maiden gathered around her twelve companions who, on November 25th, 1535, pronounced the vows that united them to Christ, the divine Lover of childhood.

The institute of the Ursulines was approved in 1545: their special work was to be: to instruct little children, to save the lambs of Christ's flock and, through them, their parents.

The St. Louis Convent of the Ursulines is indebted to the ancient Catholic Empire of Austria for its foundation. In the year 1846 Very Reverend Joseph Melcher, then Vicar-General of St. Louis, was sent to Europe to procure priests and students for the diocese. He was also on the lookout for German Sisters that might undertake the work of educating the swarms of German children growing up in the city.

"Divine Providence," says the Convent Chronicle, "placed in his path a Redemptorist Brother whose sister, an Ursuline, was most desirous of raising the standard of Saint Ursula in the vast "Wilds of America." This religious, Mother Magdalen Stehlin, was Superior of a convent at Oedenburg, a town about thirty-seven miles from Vienna. Thither the good priest bent his steps, and great was his joy to find in Mother Magdalen the spirit of a true apostle of education.[1]

On his return to St. Louis, in 1847, Father Melcher told Archbishop Kenrick of the possibility of securing Ursulines. His Grace heartily approved of the project, and Father Melcher wrote immediately to Mother Magdalen to come on.

Accordingly, May 9th, 1848, our brave Mother Magdalen with Mother Marian von Pann and Mother Augustine Schragl started on the long and tedious journey. They partook of the hospitality of the

---

[1] Daniel, XII, 3, "Souvenir of the Golden Jubilee," May 31, 1899, p. 5.

Ursulines of Landshut, Bavaria, en route, and there awakened such lively interest in their enterprise that a postulant, Miss Rosine Bruiding, joined them, and some of the Sisters promised to follow as soon as they could secure permission from their Bishop.[2]

The little missionary band embarked on the *Andalusia,* June 22nd, and arrived in Baltimore, August 21st. Here they were met by the sainted Bishop Neumann, then rector of the Redemptorist convent in Baltimore, and conducted to the Sisters of Notre Dame by whom the weary, travel-stained daughters of St. Angela were received with true religious charity. Archbishop Kenrick was in Philadelphia at the time, but no sooner was he apprised of the arrival of the Sisters in Baltimore than he hastened thither to welcome them, and then charged Reverend W. R. Wheeler to escort them to St. Louis.

September 5th, 1848, brought them to the Mound City where they were met by Vicar-General Melcher and conducted to the Sisters of the Visitation with whom they found a hospitable home until October 4th. On that day they were installed in a small domicile on Fifth Street, and here they opened school November 2nd.

The Landshut nuns were as good as their word: the 25th day of May, 1849, brought to the miniature community, Mothers Aloysia Winkler, Isabella Weinzierl, Seraphine Pauer, Angela Oberdofer, Sisters Frances Mangold and Ottilia Osterried.

Mother Augustine Weinzierl, superior of the Landshut Convent, continued to be one of the best benefactors of the St. Louis house. The chaplain, too, Reverend Donat Eder, manifested much interest in the American foundation; while Reverend Joseph Mueller, chaplain at the Royal Court of Bavaria and almoner to the king, espoused the cause so enthusiastically as to secure from King Louis the sum of four thousand dollars towards purchasing land for a new convent; and from 1849 till 1866 the Sisters received sums averaging six hundred dollars a year from the "Ludwig Missions-Verein" at Munich of which Father Mueller was an influential member."

King Louis I of Bavaria must be regarded as one of the greatest benefactors of the American Church. The Arch-Abbey of St. Vincent's in Pennsylvania owes its existence to him: the Franciscans in Cincinnati, the Friars Minor in Texas and in Pennsylvania, the Premonstratensians in Sauk City, Wisconsin, and the Redemptorists in their numerous residences throughout the country acknowledge him as "the illustrious Protector of the German Missions in the United States of America." Among the religious communities of women, the Dominicans in Williamsburg, New York, in Green Bay and Racine, Wisconsin, the School-

---

[2]  Souvenir, p. 7.

Sisters de Notre Dame in Milwaukee, and the Ursulines in St. Louis, Morrisania, New York, and Alton, Illinois, have received for a number of years very generous allowances from the King personally, and from the Ludwig Missions Verein, founded and patronized by him.

The Ludwig Missions-Verein grew out of the work done by Bavarian Catholics in union with the Society for the Propagation of the Faith established at Lyons in 1822. In fact, all the German states with the exception of the Austrian Empire, were at one time associated with the French Society; and sent their contributions to Lyons or Paris. In the years 1836 and·1837 a priest of Munich, the Rev. Karl Stumpf, began to promote this work with special zeal. He soon enrolled seven hundred members, the proceeds of whose weekly contributions were sent to Lyons. But, as there was a law in Bavaria against gathering money without government sanction; these activities had to cease.

Meantime Vicar-General Rezé submitted a plan to the King by which the various organizations of Bavaria, dedicated to the extension of the Catholic Faith in foreign countries, could be brought under one management, and their connection with the French Association might be dissolved. The King accepted the plan, and established the new missionary society under the Presidency of the Archbishop of Muenchen-Freising. Its official name was to be "The Ludwig Missions-Verein." This was in 1848. From that time on the Society published its own Annals with numerous letters from those who had received favors. The income was distributed annually, the greater part of it fell to dioceses and religious institutions in the United States. The King himself contributed 1,204,000 Marks, or about $350.000. During the first fifty years of its existence the "Ludwig Missions-Verein" of Bavaria assisted the Church in America with the sum of 3,339,343 Marks. Two Plenary Councils of the American Episcopate, a number of individual bishops, missionaries and parishes bore witness to the great and glorious things that were accomplished through this generous Catholic King.[3]

The Sisters from Landshut had brought along $960. On December 8th, 1849, the first allotment made by the Ludwig Verein added $800. to their sum, and in April 1850 the King himself sent $4,000.00.

A large plot of ground, southwest from the Cathedral, was bought by Archbishop Kenrick, and there among the oak trees, the new convent was built. The Architect and builder was Francis Saler. The industry of the Sisters, the annual allowances from Munich, and, last but not least, the generosity of friends succeeded in paying for all.

---

[3] On the activities of the Ludwig Missions Verein, cf. Schabert, Joseph A., "The Ludwig Missions Verein," in vol. II, pp. 23-41 of Catholic Historical Review.

The Sisters entered their new home the 13th of the following November, and four days later the convent was solemnly blessed.[4]

As early as 1855, the community had grown sufficiently strong to enable them to found another convent. In May of that year, eleven Sisters with Mother Magdalen as superior left for East Morrisania, New York.

Mother Aloysia now became Superior of the St. Louis Convent. During her incumbency of the office, in 1858, Bishop Juncker of Belleville applied for Ursulines for his diocese. In response to his call seven Sisters proceeded to Alton, Ill., and on the 8th of December, 1862, Father Melcher and Mother Aloysia had the happiness of assisting at the blessing of the new convent in Alton.

In 1866 an addition was built to the Convent, the present north-wing, for the purpose of housing the pupils of the Academy, whilst the day-school was carried on in older part of the building.[5]

Vicar-General Melcher, the Ursulines' best friend and patron, was promoted in 1868 to the See of Green Bay, Wisconsin, but found a worthy successor in the Archdiocese as well as at the Convent of the Ursulines, in the person of Father Henry Muehlsiepen, V. G. Father Muehlsiepen was the strong and uncompromising advocate of the Parochial School. "The School first and then the Church," was the principle that governed his official life in the diocese. As Archbishop Kenrick placed full confidence in the young, and energetic and no less prudent young man, he gave him the full powers of Vicar-General for all the German priests and parishes in the Archdiocese. Father Muehlsiepen was bishop, for all practical purposes, of the German part of Archbishop Kenrick's diocese. It was Vicar -General Muelsiepen that made the appointments and ordered the promotions and demotions. The Archbishop was content to exercise a general supervision.

Now, as Father Muehlsiepen was firmly convinced of the necessity and feasability of the Parochial School, he was anxious to obtain as many Sisters as possible to undertake this educational work. In the Convent of the Ursulines Father Muehlsiepen soon discovered a magnificent opportunity, one that was to be of incalculable benefit to the Archdiocese in the matter of Parochial Schools. There was one difficulty: the Ursulines were cloistered Nuns, and therefore, every foundation must be regarded as an independent convent.

According to the rule, it seemed impossible for the Sisters to live in small scattered communities, such as their taking up parochial school work would imply. Archbishop Kenrick, however, thought it proper

---

4   Souvenir, 10.
5   Souvenir, p. 14.

and right to change the rule in so far as to permit such members of the Order, as were specially designated for the purpose by the Spiritual Director, to appear in public for the purpose of attending Church and school, and for this only. At the end of the scholastic term, however, all must return to the Convent in St. Louis. This change in the rule paved the way for the Ursulines to take under their care a number of parochial schools in the poorer country districts, where schools were otherwise unattainable.[6] The first Parochial School thus taken charge of by the Ursuline Nuns was that of St. Paul, Missouri, whither Mother Angela took a small band of Sisters. Mother Aloysia's successor, Mother Johanna Blum, carried on the good work, eight other schools being taken by the Sisters in her lifetime, Mother Seraphine Tintrup raised the efficiency of these schools to a high degree of perfection.

The blessing of God was visibly present with the self-sacrificing efforts of these Sisters. Thousands and thousands of Catholic children have been instructed and prepared by them for a nobler, brighter life, who otherwise might have perished in the shadows of the valley of death.

As an asylum for the sick Sisters of the Order and at the same time, as an Academy for young ladies, the Arcadia College was established in 1877. The Methodist Brethren had chosen the spot for a College of their own, but were obliged, by lack of patronage, to sell out to the Ursuline Sisters. The price was moderate, $20,000; but the cost of necessary repairs was $10,000. more. About thirty Sisters find employment in the institution. The small congregations of Arcadia and Ironton are privileged to use the Sisters beautiful chapel for divine service. The parish priest, is also chaplain of the Convent. The first Chaplain was Father John Hennessy, his successor and present incumbent of the office is the Very Reverend Dean, Father Lawrence Wernert.[7]

---

6 Souvenir, pp. 20 and 21.

7 Souvenir, pp. 22 and 23.

## CHAPTER 7

## KANSAS CITY AND ITS DEPENDENCIES

The northwestern corner of the State of Missouri remained for the decade 1835-1845 the almost exclusive spiritual hunting ground of the Jesuits, who visited its widely scattered settlements from their missionary centers among their Indian neophites. The time had now come when the more advanced frontier towns should receive resident pastors of the diocesan clergy. There was Independence in Jackson County which had risen into prominence as the western terminus of the Santa Fe trade. The town of Westport, however, near the confluence of the Kansas and Missouri Rivers, soon drew this rich trade to itself, and began to develop into the great emporium now known as Kansas City. The course of proceeding was that a stock company bought from the Proudhomme heirs a large tract of land in the vicinity of the town of Westport and at once subdivided it into lots, which readily sold at about $55. each. The town developed rapidly, attaining within the first year a population of about five hundred. It was officially organized on May 3rd, 1845, and, having absorbed the trade of Westport, eventually absorbed the town also, and in 1889 exchanged the name of the town of Kansas for that of Kansas City.[1]

Having thus briefly given the genesis of Independence and Kansas City, it seems proper to review the facts connected with the planting of religion on its soil.[2] Father Felix Van Quickenborne, the first Superior of the Jesuits in Missouri, visited Independence in 1837 on one of his missionary journeys from the Kickapoo Mission; Father Verhaegen passed through the town in 1838 on his way to the Potawatomi Mission on Sugar Creek; Father Aelen in 1839 administered the sacrament of Baptism in this place to two converts. Father Point, during his residence at Westport from November 1840 to April 1841, attended to the spiritual needs of the Catholics of Independence. After his departure Father Verreydt, Superior of the Sugar Creek Mission, made quarterly visits to Independence, until in 1845, the care of the small Catholic Congregation in that town passed into the hands of the diocesan clergy.[3]

The beginnings of the Church in Westport date back beyond the earliest Jesuit Fathers to the days of the secular priest Joseph Anthony

---

1 Cf. Miller, W. H., ''The History of Kansas City,'' 1881, p. 28 ss. passim.

2 ''Catholic Beginnings in Kansas City,'' by Father Garraghan, S.J. is the only Church History of Kansas City.

3 Garraghan, Beginnings, passim.

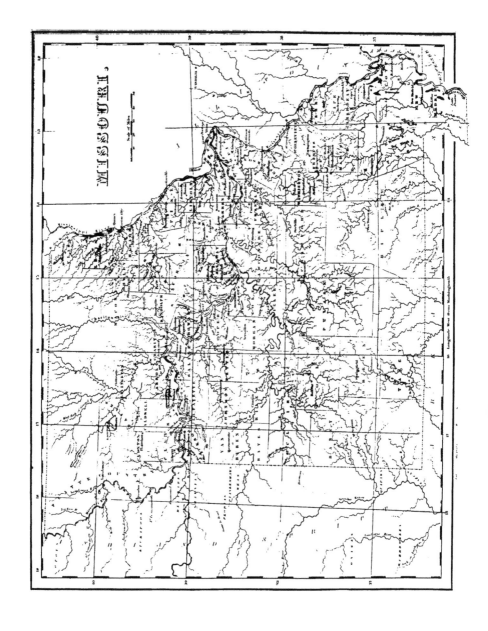

MISSOURI,

Lutz, who in 1828 resided for a few months among the wild Kansas Indians, about sixty-five miles above the mouth of the Kaw, and on his way to and fro, sojourned for a while at what he called Kawsmouth. Father Lutz was succeeded by Father Benedict Roux who arrived at Kawsmouth, November 14th, 1833, and in the following summer took up his abode in a house two miles from the temporary chapel at Wesport. After Father Roux's departure, a log chapel and a presbytery were built by the Chouteau brothers on land purchased by Father Roux. It was for a long time simply designated as Chouteau's Church, until, on November 17th, 1839, it received the official title of "St. Francis Regis near the town of Westport."

On July 3rd, 1835 Father Van Quickenborne appeared at the French settlement at Kawsmouth, the first Jesuit on the site of Kansas City. He held service and administered the sacraments in "Chouteau's Church" then, and once more in July 1836, when he baptized fourteen Indian children, Flatheads, Koutenaes and Iroquois, all belonging to the group of Rocky Mountain Indians, who had descended the Missouri River in 1831 and made a settlement on the Kansas River near its mouth. Father Van Quickenborne's last visit at Kawsmouth was on May 28th, 1837. His successor as Superior of the Kickapoo Mission, Father Christian Hoecken, and his assistant, Father Verreydt, then took up the labor of visiting the Catholics around Chouteau's Church until the Indian Mission was closed in the Autumn of 1840.

But the Jesuits did not forsake the scattered flock along the border of the state . . . . Since 1839 they came from the Potawatomi Mission on Sugar Creek in Kansas. A number of Baptisms are recorded in the "*Sugar Creek Register*" as having been administered by Jesuit Fathers " in the church near the town called Westport." It was Father Herman Aelen, S.J., who, with Bishop Rosati's concurrence, changed the name of Chouteau's Church to that of "St. Francis Regis."

In October 1840 the French Jesuit, Nicholas Point, the founder of the Jesuit College at Grand Couteau in Louisiana, was sent to take charge of the Church of "St. Francis Regis near Westport." He remained there until May 10th, 1841 when he joined Father De Smet on his way to establish the historic Oregon Mission.

The Congregation at Westport, as Father Point informs us, consisted of an assemblage of twenty-three families, each family-group comprising a Frenchman with his Indian wife and half-breed children. In regard to the female portion of his flock Father Point bears this beautiful testimony: "It is a fact that in all the twenty-three families living here, there was not a young girl whose moral conduct was not above reproach."[4]

---

4 Garraghan, op. cit., p. 106.

Once more did the Missionaries of the Sugar Creek Mission take up their labor of holy love and zeal in behalf of the Creole Catholics by the Kansas River. Father Felix Verreydt, Superior of the Sugar Creek Mission, from 1841-1848, was the last of the Jesuit Missionaries in Westport as he had been in Independence. The man selected by Archbishop Kenrick from among his recently ordained priests was Father Bernard Donnelly, an accession from the diocese of Kilmore, in Ireland. Father Donnelly took charge of Independence in 1845, although the town had neither church nor parochial residence. His field of labor, however, was not confined to the little congregation of Catholics of that town, but extended in a wide semicircle south of the Missouri River. The most promising town in his district, both from a commercial and religious point of view, was the town of Westport at the mouth of the Kaw.[5]

Father Donnelly at once turned his face to the rising sun, figuratively speaking, for geographically Westport lay westwards of Independence. In 1845 he styled himself Pastor of Independence, but in the two following years, Pastor of Kansas City, to revert in 1848 to the old style of Pastor in Independence. The Chancery Records of the latter year give the name of Rev. August Saunier as Pastor of Kansas City in 1848, and the fact of his removal to Little Canada in 1849.[6] In October 1849 having built a church at Independence Father Donnelly again took charge of Kansas City, without, however, changing his residence for the present. Bishop Barron, at the request of Archbishop Kenrick, went to Independence, where Father Donnelly was Pastor, for the purpose of administering Confirmation, and in company with Father Donnelly rode from Independence to the town of Kansas, and there also administered Confirmation.

With the exception of one year, therefore, Father Donnelly was in charge of Kansas City, as well as of Independence from 1845 to 1857, when he transferred his residence to Kansas City and resigned Independence in favor of his friend D. Kennedy. The church at Independence bore the name of The Most Holy Redeemer. One of the leading merchants of Independence, by the name of Davy, a fervent Catholic and generous benefactor of the Church, was mainly instrumental in building it, as Canon O'Hanlon informs us.[7] Whilst residing here the pastor like an old time missionary was constantly moving about in his wide district, in search for lost sheep, or for the purpose of feeding with the bread of life the Catholics in Sibley and Lexington

---

5  Chancery Records.

6  August Saunier is no mythical personage. His name is given in the Church Directory as well as in the Chancery Records. After serving two years in St. Louis diocese, he returned to the East.

7  "Life and Scenery in Missouri," p. 132 and 133.

in Lafayette County, and in Liberty, Clay County beyond the great river. But his main attention was even then directed to the growing town of Westport. "Two Sundays of the month were devoted to Kansas," the young O'Hanlon wrote in 1847. In a long, sympathetic communication, published in the *St. Louis News Letter,* the same writer gives a picturesque account of Father Donnelly's little kingdom near the mouth of the Kaw. There were in his care about two hundred souls almost exclusively of French and Indian extraction. The old log church of Father Roux's day occupied an elevated site on a finely wooded ridge between the Kansas and Missouri rivers. The residence of the pastor adjoined the Church. The church measured thirty feet in length, by twenty in width, and was surmounted by a cupola and cross of rather humble proportions. A clear-toned bell summoned the faithful to prayer and mass. The great benefactress of the congregation was Madame Chouteau, the widow of Francis Gesseau Chouteau. Highmass at 10 o'clock with an instruction in French, Vespers at 3 o'clock in the afternoon with lecture constituted the religious services on Sundays.[8] At this time civilization had not made much headway in all these places. Westport itself, as Parkman tells us, was still a typical frontier town, "full of Indians whose little shaggy ponies were tied by dozens along the houses and fences. Sacs and Foxes with shaved heads and painted faces, Shawnees and Delawares, in calico frocks and turbans, Wyandots dressed like white men, and a few wretched Kansas wrapped in old blankets, were strolling along the streets, or lounging in and out of the shops and houses."[9]

In 1847 the newly appointed Bishop of Walla-Walla, A.M.A. Blanchet and a party of Canadian missionaries journeyed over the Oregon trail to the Pacific seaboard and on his way kept notes of the towns and rivers and deserts and people he met. Among the many places mentioned the town of Kansas comes in for a brief notice:

"May 1. After a four days' trip during which we had covered about 381 miles, we came to Kansas. This town, just coming into existence, numbers eight houses, some of which are not yet finished. At Kansas and in the neighborhood there are one hundred and eighty Catholics, almost all Canadians. They have a frame chapel a mile from town. Rev. Mr. Donnelly is their resident pastor and visits several neighboring missions. Mrs. Chouteau, a widow, and a good fervent Catholic, seems to be the soul of this colony. We lodged at a hotel kept by a fanatical Methodist; however, his conduct toward us was entirely satisfactory.

"May 2. Sunday. Having made up the sleep lost on the trip we had services in the chapel. Father Ricard sang the Mass and gave

---

8 St. Louis News Letter, May 1847.
9 Parkman, "The Oregon Trail," c. i., p. 7.

an instruction. The vespers were chanted as never before in this part of the country. How happy these poor people were to have us with them. Their missionary is full of zeal, but he doesn't speak French very well, which keeps many of them away from Confession. I had Father Ricard give them a mission, which almost all attended. "May 7, we went over to Westport, about four miles from Kansas. There we had to make our last travelling preparations while waiting for Mr. Wiggins, to whom I was introduced at St. Louis as a man capable of being of service to us."[10]

In the summer of 1848 a party of Jesuits consisting of Fathers Verreydt, Gailland and Van Mierlo and Brother Thomas O'Donnell passed through Westport on their journey to Sugar Creek. Father Donnelly received them with joy and invited them to his humble home. "He gave us the best entertainment that his house and his old housekeeper could afford," wrote Brother O'Donnell to his Superior in St. Louis, adding this word of noble praise: "Indeed, the Father's place would call to your mind the situation of the early missionaries."[11] But the spirit of progress was in the air. The conclusion of the Platte Purchase which opened about three thousand square miles of excellent land to settlement, brought a goodly number of hardy immigrants into the country, thus increasing the trade of Kansas City, which was, even at that early date, the great emporium of the Far West. The enterprising Pastor of the place was the man who knew how to take opportunity by the forelock, but like Bishop Kenrick, he combined the man of business with the man of religion.

Father Bernard Donnelly was, indeed, a remarkable man, worthy to be named with "the early missionaries," for whom he had such a high regard, and Providence favored him accordingly. The ten acres of land deeded to the Bishop of St. Louis for the Parish of St. Francis Regis by Father Roux in 1839, proved to be a veritable gold mine. The sale of the two acres set apart for a cemetery, furnished the means to Father Donnelly, by which he not only purchased the new St. Mary's Cemetery, but also donated ten acres of land to the Sisters of St. Joseph in 1879. The amount realized from the sale of a half-block on Washington Street erected the Orphan Asylum. Another block in the heart of the city, also a part of Father Roux's purchase, was deeded to the Sisters of St. Joseph at the request of Father Donnelly. The enterprising pastor also realized large sums for the church by operating a brickyard and lime-kiln on his land and selling stone from a quarry he had opened. The proceeds of these business ventures were used to establish St. Joseph's Hospital. The second parish established in Kansas City received substantial aid from Father Donnelly's brickyard,

10  Hamilton, R. N., in "Illinois Catholic Historical Review," vol. IX, p. 212.
11  Archives of St. Louis University.

as also did the Parish of St. Patrick. The Redemptorist Fathers, whom Father Donnelly brought to Kansas City, always found in him a munificent patron.[12]

The old church of St. Francis Regis, the parish church of Father Donnelly, had to make room in 1857 for a new brick structure, and also a parish house. During the three years from 1854-1857 Father Donnelly styles himself Rector of Independence; in 1858 he assumes the exclusive title Pastor or Rector of Kansas City. On completing the church at Kansas City he requested Archbishop Kenrick to appoint a pastor for the place. The Rev. D. Kennedy was then commissioned to take the place, but on learning that there was a debt of $3,000 on church and residence, he forthwith declined. Father Donnelly then proposed to take Kansas City himself and to leave open Independence for Father Kennedy. Father Donnelly now became Pastor of the church of the Immaculate Conception of Kansas City, the title of St. Francis Regis was extinguished with the demolition of the old log church.[13] At the erection of the diocese of Kansas City the parish church of the Immaculate Conception became the Cathedral of the new Episcopal See.

Soon after his arrival at Independence and before his settling down in Westport Father Donnelly was relieved of the care of his farthest outmission, Liberty, by the arrival there of Father Patrick Ward. This pioneer in Western Missouri came to America from the diocese of Limerick, entered the Seminary at the Barrens, and was raised to the priesthood of May 29th, 1847. The first years of his priestly life was spent in the wild and lonely frontier town of Liberty, in Clay County, about three miles from the Missouri River. From 1852 on he held successively the pastorates of St. Michael's and St. Patrick's Churches in St. Louis. In 1848 Father Ward had the deed for eight lots which he had secured for the Congregation, recorded. Among the outmissions attended from Liberty were the town of Far West, in Caldwell County, Fredericksburg in Ray County, and Carrolton. Father Ward's successor in Liberty was Father James Murphy. After 1855 Father Patrick Ward resided with his mother in St. Louis, not being attached to any church. He died on November 1st, 1863.[14]

Father Donnelly's mission of Weston in Platte County, was in 1847 taken over by Father Francis Rutkowski, one of Vicar-General Melcher's acquisitions.[15] Weston was the center of a Catholic Congregation numbering 350 souls, and had a church that was dedicated

---

12 Dalton, W. J., "Catholic Church in Kansas City" in Conard's "Encyclopedia of the History of Missouri," vol. I, pp. 538-546.

13 Idem, ibidem, p. 541, and Chancery Records.

14 Church Records.

15 F. Rutkowski was pastor of Weston, Platte Co., 1847-1852; 1852-56 he was stationed at Dardenne, St. Charles Co.; then he disappears from the directory.

to the Holy Trinity. Its dependencies were the church of the Holy Savior at Kessler's Settlement and the Immaculate Conception church at Deuster's Settlement, both predominantly German, and Fort Leavenworth in the Indian Territory.

Prior to 1851, Father Donnelly had but three stations to attend from Independence, Westport, Sibley and Lexington, work enough, indeed for any missionary. After that date he attended only Kansas City.

The first division of Immaculate Conception Parish took place in 1866, when the German Catholics erected the church of S. S. Peter and Paul. "German Catholics" as Father Dalton tells us in his article on the Church in Kansas City, " were among the principal supporters of Father Donnelly from his coming to Kansas City to reside. They rapidly grew in numbers, until Archbishop Kenrick felt justified in giving them a pastor of their own. Father Francis Rüsse used to aid Father Donnelly in hearing German Confessions, and in giving missions to the Germans of Kansas City. He came here frequently for years for that purpose from his Parish in Henry County."[16] It was Father Henry Grosse, however, who received the appointment for S. S. Peter and Paul's in Kansas City. As early as August 7th, 1855, Father Francis Rüsse, who had been ordained but recently, was sent to St. Joseph, the rising city on the Upper Missouri River, to organize the German Catholics of that place into a separate parish. But in the following year he was ordered to Deepwater in Henry County, long since occupied by a Catholic colony from Northern Germany. The church was not dedicated as yet. Father Rüsse soon undertook the erection of new church, at Deepwater, the old log structure being dilapidated and too small for the Congregation.

One of the leading parishioners, Theodore Schmedding, had willed his farm of 160 acres to the Church. A good part of it was still in timber; but the cleared part, about sixty acres, was selected by the Congregation as a more centrally located spot for their new church. This place was about one mile southeast of the old church. To put the parish on a sound financial basis, a brother of this benefactor, Edward Schmedding, willed 3,000 dollars as an endowment for the support of the priest. The size of the new church was forty by eighty feet, and had a bell tower fifty feet in height, all built of native blue rock. The corner-stone was blessed by Vicar-General Muehlsiepen in 1858. The following year Vicar-General Patrick Ryan dedicated the new structure to divine service. St. Ludgerus was given it for its titular saint. After the dedication the pastor started on a collection tour in Ohio. During his absence Father Nicholas Staudinger supplied his place.

---

16 Dalton, l. cit., p. 543. The name of the priest is not Reusse but Ruesse. From the Catholic Register of Kansas City, December 4, 1924.

In May Father Rüsse was sent to St. Joseph as substitute to Father Scanlon, and pastor of the German Catholics of the place. With youthful energy he organized building operations, but dissensions arising among his people discouraged him, so much so, that he left the new church half-completed and returned to Deepwater in September 1861.

In 1862 the Civil War caused sad havoc in the settlement. The so-called bushwhackers stole the horses, cattle, sheep, from the farmers and destroyed much of their property. Father Rüsse's life was threatened, his horse was stolen, and his own people were dispersed. At last he gave up the unequal contest and retired to Herman among the vine-clad hills of Gasconade County. The church he had built with such glowing anticipations was occupied as a barracks by a company of soldiers whom the government had stationed there, as ward and watch for the surrounding country.[17]

---

[17] Germantown Parish a Pioneer Missouri Settlement,'' by Bishop Thomas Lillis in ''The Catholic Register'' of Kansas City, December 4, 1924.

## CHAPTER 8

## FATHER JOHN HOGAN AND NORTH CENTRAL MISSOURI

Between the partly christianized Counties along the Upper Mississippi and those on the northern reaches of the Missouri there lay a mighty ridge-shaped extent of land, the last unclaimed great prairie of the state. At its rather blunted point in the south it rested on Chariton and Carroll Counties. Its chief river was the Chariton. The main causes of its settlement being delayed so long were the wide extension of its prairies and the lack of timber. Beck in his *Gazetteer of Missouri, 1823*, ventures the opinion, that the interior of these prairies could not be inhabited on account of the northern and western blizzards by which the snow is drifted like hills and mountains, so as to render it impossible to cross from one side to the other. "In summer ,on the contrary, the sun acting on such an extensive surface, and the southerly winds which uniformly prevail during the season, produce a degree of heat almost insupportable."[1]

The building of the Hannibal and St. Joseph Railroad through the very heart of this treeless praireland soon disproved the fallacy of this prediction.[2] The Irish laborers on the road were the advance guard of civilization in this hitherto silent wilderness. And the Irish Soggarth Aroon, followed his people whithersoever they led. The Apostle of North-Central Missouri was the earnest enthusiastic missionary John Hogan.[3]

Father Hogan as a man of studious habits and fine attainments did not seem destined to the hard rugged life of a missionary. Ordained on April 10th, 1852. Father Hogan passed his first year of the priesthood as assistant to Father Fox at Old Mines, and the next two years as pastor of Potosi. After a brief stay at the Cathedral and then at St. John's in St. Louis, he became pastor of St. Michael's Church, where he remained two most laborious years.[4] During his stay at St. John's Church Father Hogan had observed that there were three hundred or more Catholic servant girls attending the early mass and receiving holy Communion on Sundays. On enquiry he found

---

1  Beck Gazetteer, 1823.

2  The last spike of this first railway across the State was driven February 13, 1859, near Chillicothe; the first complete run was made February 14, 1859. The trip of 206 miles was made in 12 hours forty-five minutes.

3  Bishop John J. Hogan is the author of a very interesting book, "On The Missions in Missouri" from which we have derived most of the facts here related.

4  Chancery Records.

that at some of the other city-churches their numbers were even greater. Why did so few of them marry? And where were the young men? The Catholic young Irishmen, not finding ready employment in the city, were obliged to seek employment on the railroads, then under construction, and to live in camps, and to move from place to place, as the work progressed. This seemed to him an anomalous condition, a kind of servitude, from which the ownership or cultivation of land alone could save them. Thus the plan of forming colonies to which he might draw his countrymen, and enable them to attain a higher standard of living, and a better opportunity of leading a life worthy of the principles they had inherited, became his constant study. North Missouri appeared to him as the proper place for such an undertaking. To go on into the wilderness and to seek a place or two where this work could be mostly readily accomplished appeared to him as his particular vocation. He communicated his desire to Archbishop Kenrick, and, after repeated requests to be freed from the pastorship of St. Michael's he received permission to make a scouting-trip through the churchless and priestless Counties of North Missouri.[5]

The North Missouri Railroad carried him to Warrenton, the terminus of the line at that time. One of the contractors extending the road farther west offered the priest the loan of a horse. With a hearty God bless you, Father Hogan mounted his steed, a common cart-horse by the way, and rode away through Montgomery, Audrian and Randolph Counties and thence through Macon County westwards to the Chariton River. There was no farm, no human habitation in sight: the rolling prairie around him and the heavens above.[6] As he crossed the Chariton Swamp on the confines of Macon and Linn Counties, a young man mounted on a spirited horse, rode up to him, and made the usual inquiries of men that meet on a desolate road. Father Hogan mentioned his name and his profession of a Catholic priest, and his intention to locate a church somewhere in those parts. "There are no Catholics here, what then is the use of a Church? was the quick answer. "True, sir," answered Father Hogan, "there are no Catholics here now, but they will be here before long, and you and I may see the day, when there will be a Catholic Church on every hill around him."[7] Riding on, the weary pilgrim came to a house on the stagecoach road leading to Linneus, where he was hospitably entertained. Next morning he rode to a place near by on the Hannibal and St. Joseph Railroad to quell one of those, half-playful, half-earnest disturbances that so frequently occurred among the Irish workmen in the camps along the line of the railroad. To the right and left of the camps were the

5   Hogan, op. cit., p. 37.

6   Idem, ibidem., p. 2.

7   Idem ibidem, p. 3.

shanties of the warriors. Father Hogan passed from Camp to camp to bring both parties to terms. His efforts were crowned with success. Resuming his journey the good shepherd and friend of peace rode through the counties of Linn and Livingston and, on August 11th, rested himself at the little Hotel at Utica in Livingston County. Thence he rode on westward into the high open prairie land of Caldwell County, which he made the turning point of his journey. Returning eastward he stopped for the night in a place called Garryowen. a railroad camp of good sober Irishmen working on the Hannibal and St. Joseph Railroad. Early in the morning he set out for Utica ten miles distant and then rode forty-five miles without rest or refreshment, traveling fifty-five miles in one sultry August day, to Brunswick on the Missouri River. Here he boarded the steamer *Spread Eagle* for Boonville, eighty miles down stream, where there was a Catholic Church.[8]

Unfortunately, the pastor of Boonville, Father Hillner, was away on some distant mission, and had with him the only chalice the church possessed. It was the Feast of the Assumption. "Having heard mass in spirit before the lonely little altar," as Father Hogan himself relates, he was called away to a place called Otterville, thirty miles distant to quell a riot. He obeyed the call of duty, and found peace restored. On Monday night Father Hogan embarked with his horse, on a passing steamer, and floated down on the rushing waters of the muddy Missouri heading for St. Louis. Next day the boat touched at Jefferson City, and towards evening the good Father and his faithful horse were landed at the head of Loutre Island, a place that is now designated Starkenburg. From this place to Warrenton was sixteen miles. At Warrenton the missionary returned the horse to its owner, took the train and arrived in time that day to report to His Grace the Archbishop. Again the zealous man of God requested his Superior's Sanction to start work in the beautiful land as yet unknown to the Church. Two days later His Grace called on Father Hogan at St. Michael's Rectory and said: "I would not think of sending you out to North Missouri on that mission. But since you are willing to undertake it, you may do so in God's name. I give you these light missionary vestments, with chalice and portable altar stone: They are from my own private chapel. I hope you will succeed in your undertaking. But if you ever wish to return to the city, I will give you your parish back, or one as good in place of it."[9]

On September 8th, Father Hogan started by rail for Jefferson City and thence travelled by boat to Brunswick, and then by stagecoach to Center Point, a new town in Linn County on the Hannibal and St. Joseph Railroad. The town of Center Point had but one house on

---

8 Hogan, pp. 5 and 11.
9 Hogan, p. 12.

the ground, the rest of it was on paper and lived on hope. Father Hogan rented the house and converted one of its rooms into a chapel and the other into a study. The congregation consisted of a few railroad laborers living in shanties nearby. But a crowd from the backwoods came to that strange thing, a Catholic priest. Center Point was not to be Father Hogan's Mission Center. So one morning he rode away on a borrowed horse, and arrived towards evening in a delightful little town, charmingly situated in an open prairie surrounded by woods. It was Chillicothe in Livingston Co., a place of about one thousand inhabitants. The people were mostly Kentuckians, the Baptists, Methodists, Presbyterians and Campbellites, each had a separate church: there was but one Catholic person in town, the cultured wife of a prominent lawyer. The visiting missionary was invited to say mass at her house. The children of the family were baptized soon after. The presence of a priest in town caused quite a stir: People were on the lookout for him: He was at last found to be ''a tall thin man, wearing black travel-stained clothes.'' Being denied the use of the Protestant churches, Father Hogan preached in the courthouse. John Graves, the first settler in the town donated a lot to him, on which to build a church. There were no Catholic settlers in the vicinity, only a few Irish laborers along the railroad. In the far northwest part of Linn County Father Hogan found a Catholic farmer, known all over the country as Irish Brown. He and his wife were good Catholics. Father Hogan said mass at their house and baptized their children. Grundy and Davies Counties were searched for stray Catholics, but without success. The same results, or rather non-results, were met with in Clinton and Caldwell. Only the hamlet of Mirabile on the confine of Caldwell and Clinton Counties had about seven Catholic families, for whom he said mass. Throughout all North Missouri there was not one Catholic church, or hope of one. All that the church possessed was the lot in Chillicothe. In Chillicothe Father Hogan decided to take up his residence. But before he entered upon his difficult task of building a church there, he made a visit to Wayne and Ripley Counties near the southern borders of the state for the purpose of examining the government lands around the headwaters of Current River. Here there was a mill owned by a man named Appolinaris Tucker, a near relative of good old Father Tucker of Fredericktown. His wife was in the last stages of mortal illness. She longed for the last sacraments and she received them from the hands of the first priest known to have come into that forlorn region, since the days of Father James Maxwell of Ste. Genevieve.

During the period from November 1858 to December 1859 Father Hogan was kept moving to and fro between his missions in North Missouri and his colony near the Arkansas border. The first visit to the southern parts of the state was made in company with Father Fox of Old Mines who was deeply interested in the question of landowner-ship and Catholic Settlements.  In December of that year Father Hogan was back once more in Chillicothe, seeking Catholic settlers and rail-road camps saying mass and administering the sacraments whenever he found any children of the Church.  In his Book of Reminiscences he recorded a number of touching incidents of those days of pioneering.

His companion of the second journey to South Missouri was the devoted pastor of St. Peter's church, Jefferson City, William Walsh. After looking at many localities recommended to them, they came to the conclusion that Ripley, Oregon and Howell counties were best adapted to their purpose.  The land was fairly productive and very cheap.  Improved property might be bought for ten dollars an acre, with house and barn and fences.  The winters were not so long and severe as on the prairies of North Missouri.  Timber was plentiful. The proposed settlement becoming known, a large number of applica-tions for Government land came in to the land-office at Jackson, in Cape Girardeau County.[10]  But the busy Father's attention was again drawn to his mission at Chillicothe, where the erection of a church was in contemplation.  The building was to be frame, 70x20 feet, with bell tower, sacristy, pews, and stained glass windows.  A dishonest con-tractor got away with full payment for the foundation that had to be replaced by new work ere the construction of the frame work could go on.  The stained glass "windows, which were really beautiful, were not suffered to shower their rainbow tints very long over the secluded little sanctuary."[11]  They were destroyed by a crowd of olden time Kukluxers at the solemn midnight hour, when all good people are wrapped in sleep.

When the church at Chillicothe was completed, the happy pastor was called away once more to his people in the South.  Appreciating the impossibility of doing justice to his two fields of labors, separated as they were by almost the full length of the State and connected only partially and in a round about way with one another, Father Hogan re-quested the appointment of another priest for North Missouri, whilst he would attend to the colony that was forming in South Missouri. His Grace the Archbishop could not spare any one of his priests, as they were all busily occupied.  Father Hogan resolved not to abandon either place.  For the present the southern mission seemed to be most in need of his presence, as well as most in accordance with his original plan.  Going by rail to Pilot Knob he travelled by wagon into Southern Misouri.  On the confines of Ripley and Oregon Counties, along the tributaries of Curren and Eleven Point Rivers, about twenty miles north of the state of Arkansas.  Father Hogan's colony was es-

---

10    Hogan, p. 47.
11    Hogan, p. 56.

tablished. It seems proper to give a description of the place and its surroundings as well as of its old settlers in the very words of the Founder of this Catholic Colony: ''On a wide and fair tract of ground bought and donated by Reverend James Fox of Old Mines, Missouri, a one story log house forty feet square was erected and partitioned into two apartments, one for a chapel and the other for the priest's residence.    Soon improvements went on apace; cutting down trees, splitting rails, burning brushwood, making fences, grubbing roots and stumps, building houses, digging wells, opening roads, breaking and ploughing land, and sowing crops.    Already in the spring of 1859, there were about forty families on the newly-acquired government lands, or on improved farms purchased east and west of Current River in the counties of Ripley and Oregon; and many more were coming, so that the settlement was fairly striding towards final success.    The little chapel amid the forest trees in the wilderness was well attended.    Mass, sermon, catechism, confessions, devotions went on as in old congregations.    The quiet solitariness of the place seemed to inspire devotion.''[12]

Of the scattered people of Protestant faith, among whom the Catholic Father's newcomers were to live and seek the peace and happiness of their homes, Hogan writes: ''In keeping with these scenes were the simple, quiet ways of the early settlers of southern Missouri, who were mostly from North Carolina and Tennessee, and of whom much may be said in praise.    They were kind-hearted honest, sincere and sociable. No stranger ever travelled amongst them without feeling his heart warmed with the fullest conviction, that if worthy, his presence gave them pleasure, that he was treated to the best they had or could afford, and that his person, money and property were safe and sacred in their keeping.    Vice was little known amongst them.    Intemperance was nowhere observable, although they usually took, as a matter of course, their morning dram, or a drop with a friend, from a keg of the best, distilled by themselves or by some neighbor willing to share or barter on accomodating terms.    Every one smoked, men and women.    The weed grew abundantly, and was usually the best tended patch of crop on the place.''[13]

As to their social customs and manner the writer says: ''The maidens and swains married young, usually before twenty, often at sixteen, and their married life was remarkably virtuous and happy. The Marriage dowry was usually a one-room log house.    The young man was fortuned by his father with a yoke of oxen and a plow.    The bride was dowered by her mother with wealth of homespun dresses and household fabrics of like manufacture.    Timber from a neighboring saw mill was easily framed into a variety of articles of house-

---

12  Hogan, pp. 59 and 60.
13  Hogan, pp. 60 and 61.

hold furniture, and the eyes of the young couple were none the less delighted with it, for being pure of veneer or varnish, of which their rural surroundings gave them no knowledge whatsoever. Uncle Sam had given them a homestead of three hundred and twenty acres, at twelve and a half cents an acre. There was no reason in the world why they should not be happy. Moreover the young wife had been taught by her mother, to knit, spin, weave and sew. The young husband had been taught by his father to tend sheep and cattle, and to cultivate cotton and corn. The education of husband and wife could be depended upon to procure them a living. The plow cultivated plots and furrows in the field. The wheel and loom wrought fabrics at home. There was no need of the merchant's ship, bringing goods from afar. No need of town fashions, or of store clothes. Willing hands and humble hearts made the one room log cabin a sacred place and a happy home.''[14]

The manner of these people showed curiosity more than prejudice. Some of them told Father Hogan that their forefathers in North Carolina and Tennessee had been Irish Catholics who had been brought there in early days, and left without the means of practicing their religion, and so had fallen in with the prevailing churches of their surroundings. A number of these Catholics in spirit were won over to the Mother Church by the zealous missionary. This aroused the displeasure of the Protestant preachers. One of their fanatical adherents made an attack on the life of Father Hogan, but he was saved from direct harm by the interposition of Judge Hutchinson.[15]

The Catholic colony was hardly under way, when the cry of distress from the North reached Father Hogan's ear: ''We have not heard mass nor received the sacraments since you left us, many have died without the last sacraments, there are many children unbaptized, and many sick people need to be prepared for death. The good Father told them to call on Father Scanlon at St. Joseph or Father Murphy at Hannibal to attend them in their spiritual needs. To Archbishop Kenrick he appealed once more for a priest in Chillicothe, but in vain. Indeed two Lazarists were sent a little later from Cape Girardeau or the Barrens, but they could not stay long at any place they visited. Complaints came in again, and a new difficulty at Chillicothe called for immediate solution. The church was in debt, the people of the parish declined to pay it, since they saw that they were abandoned. The creditors entered suit. To save the church, and to reanimate the people of Chillicothe, Father Hogan rode home, and was received with joy. This happened during the last day of October 1859. The church-collection

---

14 Hogan, pp. 61 and 62.
15 Hogan, pp. 62-68.

turned out well, the debt was paid and all seemed happy and prosperous once more.[16]

During Father Hogan's absence in the South a number of new Catholic settlers had come into the country round about Chillicothe. After a brief stay with his good people in the North, the claims of the South again obtruded themselves upon his mind. Both places were equally clamorous, and yet only one could be gratified at a time. The church in North Missouri seemed ripe for a great harvest. So northward once more went the journey. The last day of December 1859 found the restless bird of passage in Chillicothe, meditating much work to do the next few years.

By 1860 the railroads had opened the country to an evergrowing flood of immigration. Cities and towns sprang up by the hundreds, farmstead joined farmstead for miles in all direction. The number of Catholics increased in due proportion: Father Hogan selected four principal places, at each of which he promised to hold services once a month, and about a dozen of less important places where he would say mass once in three months. Father Hogan placed a missionary time-table in every family he could reach, showing where the priest could be found on any particular day, if a sick-call should require his presence. For several years, during which this order was in force, the missionary's travels amounted to about 10,000 miles a year. The cost of this would have been about $400, if the Railroad Companies had not granted free transportation to the missionary.

On May 17th, 1860, the Feast of the Ascension of Our Lord, the Catholics of Chillicothe were gladdened by the coming of Bishop James Michael O'Gorman, Vicar-Apostolic of Nebraska, who dedicated the church. Father Thomas Scanlon of St. Joseph's, and Father James Murphy of Hannibal honored the occasion by their presence. The church was named St. Joseph's. The missions that had sprung up recently were Bancroft in Davies County Bethany, sixteen miles northwest from Bancroft, where a few Catholic families lived that had almost lost the Faith, then Eagleville, still farther north, where indifference held sway among the few Catholics it contained. In a southeastern direction there was Hickory Branch, or the watershed of the Grand and Chariton Rivers, where a truly Catholic family of Germans rejoiced to see a priest once more. Brookfield was visited by Father Hogan for the first time on December 20th, 1859. Mass was said there once a month at the home of James Tooey, or at that of Michael McGowan. Macon City was also one of the principal missions at this time. Brookfield built a church in 1860, Macon City soon afterwards. During the war the Macon City church was often occupied by soldiers and in 1864 almost demolished. The other principal stations of

---

16 Hogan, pp. 69 and 70.

Father Hogan's were Mexico in Audrian Co. and Cameron on the confines of De Kalb and Clinton. The war's devastation in North Missouri was very great, indeed, but not comparable with those to the South. Ripley County suffered more than any other part of the State. Murder and rapine were the order of the day. All that could get away fled. Father Hogan's colony was destroyed, the settlers dispersed, the whole country was a howling wilderness once more.

In the northern part of Missouri railroad wrecks were extremely common, sometimes as a direct result of battle, sometime owing to negligence, or malice. Father Hogan passed through twenty-one such wrecks of more or less destructiveness. Death seemed very near to him in those days that so severely tried the courage of men.[17]

Amid these battles and alarms of battle Father Hogan, as a man of peace, started a school in the town of Chillicothe, the more advanced pupils teaching the little ones, and they themselves receiving instructions in the higher studies by the Principal, Father Hogan. Of course such a man of principle and eminent courage refused to take the so-called test-oath, that had been imposed by the Drake Constitution, and also refused to abstain from the performance of his duty as a Catholic priest. Father Hogan, like many another priest, was arrested, arraigned and finally discharged, when Archbishop Kenrick won his case against the test-oath in the Supreme Court of the United States. It was a matter of special satisfaction to Father Hogan that his people at Brookfield at a public meeting, condemned "the arrest of Rev. John Hogan as an act of unmitigated tyranny, alike revolting to our feelings and provoking to our passions."

The last church built in 1865 by Father Hogan as the missionary of North Missouri was that of St. Bridget, at a place called Peabody, on the line of the Hannibal and St. Joseph Railroad. The congregation was composed of pious, honest and virtuous people, mostly Irish. Through the carelessness of some travellers incamped near by, the church was burnt: The fire they had kept burning all night was, after their departure, scattered and blown against the side of the building. It was soon ablaze, and burned to the ground. On December 8th, Archbishop Kanrick administered confirmation at Brookfield, and on the following day at Chillicothe.

Bishop Kenrick's visit to North Missouri was a farewell call: for soon after March 3rd, 1868 the Holy Father erected the diocese of St. Joseph and appointed Father John Hogan its first Bishop. His new diocese included all the Counties of the State between the Missouri and the Chariton Rivers, with two parishes in the episcopal city of St. Joseph and one each in Chillicothe, Liberty, Weston and Conception.

---

17  Hogan, pp. 94-96.

## CHAPTER 9

## ST. JOSEPH AND THE PLATTE PURCHASE

About seventy-six miles northwest of Kansas City, on the left bank of the Missouri River, stands on a beautiful eminence the City of St. Joseph, now an episcopal see, and a fine commercial center, but a hundred years ago a line of thickly wooded bluffs with a trader's hut and a landing place for voyagers and Indians. The lonely trader is Joseph Robidoux, the third of that name in a direct line. In 1830, six years before Congress authorized the purchases of the triangle of land that is now comprised in the six counties Platte, Buchanan, Andrew, Holt, Nodaway and Atchison, Joseph Robidoux acquired all the land on which the City of St. Joseph was to rise. Joseph Robidoux had his land platted for a town; lots were sold to all comers; the town grew into a city and in 1864 had a population of 20,000 souls. The Jesuit Fathers from the Kickapoo mission were the first priests to administer the sacraments to the widely scattered Catholics of this part of the Indian frontier, and to evangelize the roving bands of Iowa, Sauk and Fox Indians, that then claimed its ownership.[1] The Potawatomi Indians, for a time, encamped here on a spot opposite to Fort Leavenworth. Father Quickenborne found a number of Catholics among them. Later on they took possession of their reservation near Council Bluffs. It was mainly through the efforts of Senator Benton that the Platte Purchase became an accomplished fact in 1836. As the soil was excellent, game abundant, and timber plentiful, immigration at once poured in. Two years after the conclusion of the Treaty with the interested Indian, Platte County alone contained 4,500 white settlers.

As for the town of St. Joseph, religious ministrations can be said to have begun with the visit in May 1838 of Father Peter De Smet, who was then on his way under Father Verreydt to open the Mission of Council Bluffs. "We stopped for two hours at the Black-Snake Hills," wrote the renowned missionary. "There I had a long talk with Joseph Robidoux, who keeps a store and runs his Father's fine farm. He showed me a great deal of affection and kindness, and expressed a wish to build a little chapel there, if his father can manage to get some French families to come and settle near them. The place is one of the finest on the Missouri for the erection of a city."[2]

---

[1] History of Buchanan County and St. Joseph, 1898.
[2] Chittenden and Richardson, Father De Smet, vol. I, p. 151.

It is Father Anthony Eysvogels' name, sometimes abbreviated to Vogel, that occurs most frequently in the early Church records concerning Buchanan County.

But Fathers Christian Hoecken and Felix Verreydt, his companions at the Kickapoo Mission, were also active in the ''Platte Purchase.'' In March 1841, Father Eysvogels was at Weston, Platte County. In a missionary trip which lasted from July 8th, 1842, to November 20th, he administered twenty-two Baptisms in Clay County, at English Grove in Holt County, at the Black Snake Hills (Robidoux's Landing) at the Third Ford of the Platte, at Kickapoo Village in Platte County, and on Fishwing River in Ray. Father Hoecken's Baptisms were all recorded as having been performed in the *Platte Purchase*. It would seem, according to Catholic Almanac for 1845, that Father Eysvogels was in charge of a mission at St. Joseph, with Westport, Weston and Independence as stations visited by him: but it is not probable that he resided there at any time, or built a church at the place. The first resident priest and builder of the first church at St. Joseph was the Rev. Thomas Scanlon,[3] a member of the diocesan clergy, who entered the Seminary at St. Louis in 1843 and was ordained on September 21st, 1845, to be sent at once to the mission of St. Joseph, October 25th, 1845. An authentic account of the origin of the church at St. Joseph was left on record by Canon O'Hanlon, who was living there at the time of its erection.

''Among the most enterprising and intelligent traders in that town, Mr. John Corby, an Irish Catholic and a native of Limerick, had started a successful business house, well-stocked with general merchandise and having large stores for country produce provided for export and import goods. He was then unmarried, and he proposed to maintain a resident priest in his house, until a Catholic Church was built, and a parochial dwelling could be provided.[4] Mr. Robidoux was willing to grant an eligible site, and accordingly, application having been made to the Bishop of St. Louis, the Reverend Thomas Scanlon, a native of Tipperary, was elected to open a mission and there to reside. A small but handsome church was soon commenced and the work of building was proceeding very rapidly, while a temporary place of worship was provided in the town.''[5]

---

[3] On December 28, 1850, Father Christian Hoeken writes from the Territory of the Platte, ''that he reached St. Joseph at the foot of the Black-Snake Hills, and borrowed an Indian pony from Father Scanlon, and left his own in care of the kind priest.'' History of North-West Missouri, vol. I.

[4] The so-called Corby Chapel, dedicated to St. John the Baptist, contains the tomb of John Corby. It is a beautiful structure of stone. It is not used for public service. The Fathers and Brothers of the Holy Crown have charge of it.

[5] O'Hanlon's ''Life and Scenery in Missouri,'' p. 106.

The location of the church, which was dedicated by Bishop Kenrick, June 17th, 1847, was at the corner of Fifth and Felix Street.[6]

Father De Smet was a visitor in St. Joseph, while Father Scanlon's church was in process of erection. "Eastward and at the foot of the Black Snake Hills stands the town of St. Joseph. We reached there on the 23rd of November 1846, and paid a visit to the respectable curate, Rev. Mr. Scanlon. In 1842 St. Joseph did not exist; there was only a single family there. Today there are 350 houses, 2 churches, a city hall and a jail; it is in the most prosperous condition. Its population is composed of Americans, French Creoles, Irish and Germans.'"[7]

The city of St. Joseph was, at the time of Father Scanlon's coming the fartherest western outpost of civilization, still savoring of savage life, yet striving after the ideals of security, justice and power. Business was brisk. The farmers came in from the newly claimed homesteads to exchange the product of their lands for the various necessaries and comforts of life, to which they had been long accustomed. The red children of prairie crossed the river in their canoes to exchange skins and game for blankets, powder and shot. As money was scarce, trade was largely carried on by accommodation in kind. Toward evening came a lull in business, when suddenly the spirit of myrth and jollity would flare up in the young clerks and shopmen, and lead to boisterous, though more or less innocent scenes. Among the Indian visitors were the noted Iowa war-chiefs Massourent and White Cloud, great warriors in the day, but now only a shadow of their former selves.[8] The city was proud of its *St. Joseph Gazette.* Father Scanlon's congregation was small, but the individuals composing it, were of good social standing, very respectable and moral, and also highly esteemed by the non-catholic portion of the inhabitants. The services were frequently attended by Protestants, who came to hear a plain but instructive sermon. Father Scanlon was respected and loved by all. A goodly number of converts to the Faith stand to his credit.[9]

The town of Weston in Platte County and the English Grove Settlement, where the Jesuits had built a little chapel, were at first under the care of the pastor of St. Joseph. In both places the Catholics were of English, Irish and German origin.

Many blood-curdling stories were told by the firesides of these pioneers, about the dangers and hardships encountered by them in

---

6 Chancery Records.

7 Chittenden and Richardson, Father De Smet, II, p. 612. Canon O'Hanlon alludes to this visit of the great missionary, p. 126.

8 Life and Scenery, pp. 109 and 110.

9 Life and Scenery, p. 124.

subduing the wilderness, and its still wilder claimants. Lawlessness and rapine were not all on the side of the Indians; horse thieves made a business of crime. Lynch law was often resorted to by the infuriated settlers. But with the rapid increase of population stern justice was taken in hand by the regularly constituted authorities. When in the later forties the Hannibal and St. Joseph railroad penetrated the wilderness that separated, like a blunted wedge, the east from the west, St. Joseph and the surrounding territory began to bloom like an earthly paradise.

It has already been recorded that the German Catholics in St. Joseph had received the promise of a church of their own, but that two attempts of Father Francis Ruesse from his parish of Deepwater, the first in 1856, the second in 1860, to carry out the plan, failed through the stubbornness of the people and the lack of prudence and patience in their spiritual leader.

As Archbishop Kenrick wrote to Father Henry Van der Sanden in his letter appointing him to the vacancy "Rev. Ruesse built the Church, till the roof was put on, and then left." The future Chancellor's appointment to the German Church in St. Joseph was, "as he himself naively observes, superseded, as Rev. Van der Sanden was too necessary in Jefferson City."[10]

Father E. A. Schindel was sent in his place to organize the German parish started by Father Francis Ruesse, and was succeeded after an interval of about five years by Father George Hartmann, the former assistant priest at SS. Peter and Paul's Church in St. Louis. The church begun by Father Ruesse was now completed and dedicated under the invocation of the Immaculate Conception.[11]

Father Hartmann was succeeded in April 1865 by Father Christopher Linnenkamp.[12]

This excellent priest received ordination on March 19th, 1864, and his first appointment was that of assistant to Father Francis Goller of SS. Peter and Paul's Church in St. Louis. The Parish of Weston at that time numbered fifty German families who were reported to Archbishop Kenrick as trouble-makers of the worst kind. One of their former priests had introduced himself to them by saying: "Everywhere there is order. In heaven God rules, in hell the devil, and in Weston I, your pastor," which announcement seems to have cowed the "Kickers;" for Father Linnenkamp succeeded in establishing a parochial school, which, within two years, was attended by one hundred children. On the erection of the diocese of St. Joseph Bishop Hogan appointed

10   Chancery Records of St. Louis.
11   Chancery Records.
12   Holweck, F. G., "Pastoral-Blatt," vol. 57, No. 3.

Father Linnenkamp his Vicar-General, and pastor of the German Parish in the episcopal city.

From Weston, the original parish of Platte County, Father Linnenkamp visited the mission at Platte City, East Leavenworth and Easton. At Plattsburg he built the first church.

The Congregation at Liberty, Clay County, for a time an outmission of Father Donnelly's, built a brick-church in 1847 at a cost of $2700. It was consecrated by Archbishop Kenrick in 1848 under the title of St. James; the succession of priests at Liberty was: Bernard Donnelly, Patrick Ward, 1847-1849 and James Murphy.

Father Ward and Murphy also attended the Congregation of Carrolton until the year 1869, when it received its first pastor in the person of Father Richard Nagel.

Father James Power, the founder of the Church in Nodaway County, was born in 1815 in County Waterford, Ireland and, coming to Philadelphia in 1845, was in the same year ordained to the priesthood. In 1856 he organized a Catholic Colonization Society under the name "Felix, O'Reilly and Company." Father Power was the moving spirit of the undertaking. In the Fall of 1856 he came with three companions to Nodaway County and selected 20,000 acres of land.

When they came to Plattsbury to enter their land they found the land-office closed. Felix and O'Reilly entered suit in the General land office in Washington for the possession of the land which had in the meantime been assigned to other claimants. After two years litigation they won their case.

The colonists, about sixty in number, thereupon started from Philadelphia and arrived at St. Joseph in the middle of April. Only fourteen proceeded to their destination, the others remained in the city of St. Joseph. The names of these Catholic pioneers proclaim their Irish nativity. In five wagons drawn by oxen they conveyed all their belongings. On the fourth day of their journey through brush and mireland, they arrived at what was to be their home. The town of Maryville was about fifteen miles distant. An American farmer offered them the use of a house which he was then building. After finding their land, they built a small community house: and three smaller houses. Then began the work of clearing their land.[13]

In June of the same year Father Power paid a visit to the struggling colony. He found his people thoroughly discouraged.

The colony became known as Irish Settlement. But Father Power suggested the name of Conception. The improvised names, Irish Settlement, Bradyville, McCloskeyville, gradually fell out of use.

---

13 Die Benedictiner in Conception, Mo. 1885, pp. 24 ss.

On St. Columba's day, June 9th, 1860, Father Power dedicated the chapel in the Community house under the invocation of St. Columba. From that day on he came frequently from St. Joseph's to say mass for the colonists; and then made his home with them as their resident pastor. Father Power was anxious to get some religious Order to take charge of the colony and parishes.

In 1860 he prevailed upon the Archbishop of St. Louis to offer the place to the Trappists of Ireland. The offer was declined. Then the Civil War rendered all efforts in this line hopeless. During the year 1861 to 1866 Father Powers labored in Illinois and other adjoining states, but visited his colony at least twice in the year. On returning to his parish of St. Columba in 1865 he opened a parochial school. In the same year Father Power made another effort to place his colony in care of a religious Order, this time the Benedictines. The Abbot of St. Vincent's accepted the offer; but Archbishop Kenrick refused his consent. A third Order was tried, the Fathers of the Precious Blood in Ohio: but nothing came of the move.

Father Power seemed fated to stay at the place he had founded. He now built a small church and blessed it on the Feast of the Immaculate Conception, but under the invocation of St. Columba.[14]

At the Second Plenary Council of Baltimore all the Missouri territory between the Missouri and the Chariton Rivers was erected into a separate diocese with the city of St. Joseph as the episcopal See, and John Joseph Hogan as its first Bishop. Father Power's desire was now fulfilled: the colony and parish of St. Columba in Conception was offered to the Benedictines and they accepted the charge. The first Fathers, destined to found the great Abbey of Conception were P. P. Adelhelm, Fintan and Frowin. Father Power retired from active service in the ministry leaving his missionary stations also in charge of the Benedictines. The diocese of St. Joseph, in the year of its erection, numbered only seven parishes with resident pastors. The city of *St. Joseph* had two parishes:

The Cathedral of St. Joseph with Fathers James Doherty and Eugene Kenny, and The parish of the Immaculate Conception, for the German Catholics under Father George Hartmann.

*Easton*, Buchannan County was largely composed of Germans. The church was not dedicated; Father A. J. Abel was its pastor.

The town of *Conception* had the Church of St. Columba under Father James Power.

---

14 ''Die Benediktiner in Conception, Mo.,'' p. 29.

*Liberty* in Clay County, with Father James Ledwith.

*Cameron* in Clinton County, with Father Richard Nagel.

*Weston*, in Platte County, with Father Linnenkamp had churches that were as yet nameless.

But *Chillicothe* in Livingston County had a resident pastor, Father Robert S. Tucker and a church dedicated to St. Columba.

Plattsburg having a German congregation was attended from Easton.

Brunswick in Chariton County and Richmond in Ray were attended from Carrolton, whilst Brookfield and Buckley in Linn, were attended from Chillicothe.

## CHAPTER 10

# THE VINCENTIANS AND THEIR SUCCESSORS IN PERRY AND STE. GENEVIEVE COUNTIES

Whilst this consolidation of the Church in the Northern portion of Missouri was carried on by secular priests, the parishes of the southeastern portion also were gradually passing from the care of the Vincentian Fathers into the hands of the diocesan clergy. The enforcement of the rule of the Congregation of the Mission, that the Fathers must not be withdrawn from community life, brought about this change. There was no longer any great necessity of leaving single members all alone in an exposed out of the way place, where many of the rules could not be observed. The fact that it had been done for a long time, could be justified only on the plea of urgent necessity: But as a new auxiliary force of secular priests had grown up, the necessity was no longer pressing. Bishop Rosati was at first greatly troubled: "Father Nozo," he wrote to Bishop Anthony Blanc of New Orleans, "has taken away Doutreluigne from Cahokia and Dahmen from Ste. Genevieve, and he wants no less than three priests of the Congregation to live together. Therefore, he has three priests in Old Mines, whilst other parishes are without priests. All this kills me."[1]

The Superior of the Lazarists was, of·course, more interested in the good of his Congregation, whilst the Bishop had in view, above all things, the necessities of the Congregations in his diocese.

There were four missionary centers under Vincentian rule; St. Vincent's Parish in St. Louis, St. Mary's of the Barrens, Cape Girardeau, Ste. Genevieve, and Old Mines. The St. Louis center had no outmissions: but for a time the diocesan Seminary was conducted near St. Vincent's Church, to be discontinued in favor of the Seminary of Carondelet in charge of secular priests.

St. Mary's of the Barrens was the mother house of the Congregation in America. Here stood the Seminary, the College, and the parish-church of St. Mary's.

The highest office in a Province of the Congregation of the Mission is that of Visitor. The American Lazarist Province was erected in 1835 with Father John Timon as Visitor. When he, in 1848, became Bishop of Buffalo, he was succeeded in the office of Visitor by Reverend Mariano Maller, first Lazarist Superior of St. Charles Seminary in

---

[1] Bishop Rosati's Letter-Book, Archives of St. Louis Archdiocese.

Philadelphia. To Father Maller succeeded Very Reverend Anthony Penco, who had come with Father Maller to Philadelphia. When Father Penco was called to Europe in 1855, Father Masnou was appointed Pro-Visitor. He was also called to Europe and made Visitor of the Lazarist Province in Spain, his native country. Reverend Stephen Ryan, afterwards Bishop of Buffalo, became in 1857 the next Visitor. He had succeeded Father Masnou as President of St. Vincent's College at the Cape. After Father Ryan came Reverend John Hayden. Father Hayden died in November 1872 and had as his successors Reverend James Rolando and Reverend Thomas J. Smith. Father Rolando died in November 1833.

In the spring of 1867 the mother house was removed from St. Louis to Germantown to the extensive and beautiful grounds secured by the Rev. Denis Leyden, then pastor of St. Vincent's church, and successor as such of Bishop Domenec, with the good will and kind encouragement of Archbishop Wood.

When the province was divided in 1888 the eastern portion was placed in charge of Father James McGill, a veteran missionary of varied experience in many fields. Father McGill had been superior at Cape Girardeau, Mo., Los Angeles, Cal., St. Louis and Germantown, Pa. and had everywhere endeared himself to all by his unfailing charity.[2]

The Diocesan Seminary and the College having been removed, the one to St. Louis and the other to Cape Girardeau, and the mother house itself having been transferred to far away Pennsylvania, there remained but little more of the ancient glories of the Barrens than the church of St. Mary's and the parishes established by the Vincentian Fathers in Perry County, Bois Brule Bottom and Brazeau Settlement. These churches were attended in 1840 from the Barrens, by Fathers Timon, Paquin, Domenec, and Burke. In 1842 the number of outmissions had increased by two: Baily's Landing and New Tennessee. Rev. Hector Figari and his assistants at the College attended these places. In 1843 Apple Creek also fell to the care of the Lazarists of the Barrens. In 1845 Father Thaddeus Amat, the President of St. Mary's Preparatory Seminary, was now at the head of the missionary band for Perry County.[3]

The Mission of Apple Creek was the first one to be severed from the Vincention circuit in Perry County, and established into a parish under secular priests. A brief account of the antecedents of the place is here given according to the researches of Msgr. Holweck:

---

[2] Tercentenary of Vincentian Foundation, January 25, 1917, in "Church Progress," April 1925.

[3] Chancery Records.

"At Apple Creek Joseph Schnorbush, a colonist from Baden, Germany, under the supervision of Father Odin, C. M., had built a small log chapel in 1828.[4]

The original settlers on Apple Creek, like those of the Barrens, were English speaking Americans from Kentucky, but after 1820, under the leadership of Schnorbush, some families arrived from Baden who drew others after them; consequently, the German element in the parish became quite strong. As most of these immigrants were unfamiliar with English, Father Loisel, the French-Canadian Creole, to help these poor abandoned Catholics, undertook the study of German, and he learned enough of it to preach a simple sermon in their native language.

In February 1833, Father Loisel began to erect a stone church at Apple Creek and Bishop Rosati, March 7th, gave him permission to lay the cornerstone; the church was 30 by 40 feet and had a large sacristy which was to serve as residence to the priest on his weekly visits.[5]

The church was blessed by the Bishop November 30, 1834; Father Timon, C. M., preached in English, Father Loisel in German. But Father Loisel, at the death of Father Condamine on August 8th, 1836, was promoted to the old and venerable parish of Cahokia. Apple Creek continued to be attended from the Seminary as it had been by Father Loisel. Neither of the Reverend gentlemen, however, were Lazarists.

On August 1st, 1847 the Church of St. Joseph, Apple Creek, received its first resident pastor in the person of the Reverend Ursus Joseph Meister. Father Meister was native of Canton Solothurn, Switzerland. He came to America at the invitation of Vicar-General Melcher in 1847. He was fifty-three years of age, and had served in the sacred ministry for a number of years, in his native land. On his arrival in St. Louis he was sent to Apple Creek. Msgr. Holweck has given a good character sketch of this picturesque figure of our early days. Father Meister must have been doing some building at Apple Creek, for his account-books are full of notices in quaint curious English, concerning the clap-boards his parishioners did or did not bring him. The venerable missionary did not stay very long in Apple Creek. He departed for St. Louis in October 1848, and in the Spring of the following year he was appointed to succeed Father James Murphy at St. Peter's Church, Jefferson City.[6]

---

4   Statistics written by Father Wiseman, 1839, Archives.

5   Cf. Holweck, F. G., "St. Louis Catholic Historical Review," vol. I, pp. 103-108.

6   Cf. Holweck, F. G., "Pastoral-Blatt," vol. 51, No. 11.

During the vacancy between Father Meister's departure and the coming of Father Francis Trojan in 1850 Apple Creek was attended from the Barrens. Father Trojan in 1856 became pastor of the Bohemian church of St. John Nepomuc in St. Louis. He was succeeded at Apple Creek by Rev. Joseph Becker.

In the Report of 1851 the outmissions of the Lazarists in Perry County are given as follows: Mattingly's, Reiney's, Mannings, and Vysfel's Settlements, St. Mary's Landing and Bois Brule Bottom.

Since the early days of the Spanish regime the parish of St. Genevieve exerted its missionary efforts within a wide semicircle, north and west and south.

Fathers Meurin and Gibault visited the congregations at St. Louis and on the Missouri River. Father Maxwell did the same service to New Bourbon, St. Michael and his proposed colony in Reynold's County. Father Henry Pratte built the first churches at Old Mines and St. Michael. During Father Dahmen's incumbency Ste. Genevieve supplied three outlying missions: 1) Little Canada with its chapel of St. Anne's; 2) the Establishment, and 3) Reviere aux Vases, the two latter congregations were as yet without churches, but had services once a month in some private residence. The church at the Establishment received the title of St. Philomena; the Church of Reviere aux Vases that of SS. Philip and James.

In 1837 the log-chapel built by Father Pratte at St. Michael's was removed by Father Cellini to a four acre lot adjoining the village of Fredericktown. It was, as we have already shown, in this quiet parish of about three hundred souls, French Creoles and Germans for the most part, that Father Francis Cellini, after leaving the Congregation of the Mission, held spiritual sway as a member of the diocesan Clergy of St. Louis.

In 1840 Father F. X. Dahmen and H. Gandolfo, both of the Congregation of the Mission preached to the French, English and German Catholics of Ste. Genevieve in their respective languages. They also attended the German settlements of Reviere aux Vases, and the Establishment, now Zell. In 1842 Father Dahmen was withdrawn to the Barrens and Father Brands, C. M. sent to Ste. Genevieve as Assistant to Father Gandolfo. The Fathers have now Little Canada on their list of outmissions. In 1845 Father Nicholas Stehle, C. M. succeeds Father Brands. In 1846 there are four Vincentians at Ste. Genevieve, in 1848 only two, Fathers Gandolfo and Francis Barbier, reside there, whilst the secular priests, John Anselm, is stationed at Little Canada, with the Establishment and Valle's Mines as outmissions, and Father F. X. Weiss has charge of German Settlement now known as Zell. In 1850, Rev. August Saunier succeeds Father Anselm at Little Canada, and

Father John Mary Ireneus Saint Cyr, the founder of the church in Chicago, succeeds the Vincentian Gandolfo in the parish of Ste. Genevieve. He has for his assistant the Reverend S. Grugan.[7]

Father Francis X. Weiss, the first pastor of St. Joseph's church, at Zell, was born at Schlettstadt, Alsace, on July 27th, 1821. Having joined Vicar General Melcher's first band of missionaries in 1847, he came to St. Louis and was raised to the sacerdotal dignity by the missionary Bishop John Barron, on April 29th, 1848. In that very year Father Angelo Hyppolite Gandolfo, then pastor of Ste. Genevieve, had built a little stone church in honor of St. Joseph at the German Settlement, as the place was then called. Father Weiss was appointed pastor of the new parish. He immediately started to build a parish residence, also of stone. When the civil war began, Father Weiss returned to his native land. He was succeeded at the Establishment by Father Theodore Stein, January 1st, 1862.

On his return from Europe Father Weiss received the appointment to Reviere aux Vases, where Father Gandolfo, as early as June 1842, had blessed a chapel dedicated to St. Anthony. This chapel stood on the bank of the river, at the foot of the hill on which the Church now stands. In December 1849 a tract of land was bought for the Parish. After this no mention is made of the place until 1863 when Father Weiss enters upon the care of the Congregation. He built the stone church in 1863.[8]

The pastorship of Father Saint Cyr in Ste. Genevieve lasted from October 17th, 1849 until April 1st, 1862. It was a rather uneventful period in the history of the ancient church. "Father Saint Cyr," as Father William Walsh tells us in his sketch on the Life of Archbishop Kenrick "seemed fitted rather for the cloister of religion than for the field of the missionary priest. He was almost totally blind for several years before his death. This must have been a great affliction to him, as we never knew a greater reader. He never did very much in the way of building churches and schools, but he labored very zealously in the ministry. His life was a constant example and a constant sermon."[9]

But one great thing he certainly did for the parish: he brought the Sisters of St. Joseph to Ste. Genevieve. In the very year that saw the consecration of the church of Father Dahmen by Bishop Rosati, witnessed the advent of the Sisters of Loretto. These spiritual daughters of Father Nerinckx founded a Convent and School for young ladies, which continued its course of usefulness under varying fortunes. Mother

7    Chancery Records.

8    Ste. Genevieve, Historical Sketch of the Town and Parish in "Church Progress," November, 1910.

9    L. Cit., p.

Odile, Sister Catherine, Sister Teresa Augusta were the Superiors. This Academy was still in operation, though already on the decline, when Father Saint Cyr assumed charge of the parish; In 1858 they sold Convent and academy to the Sisters of St. Joseph of Carondelet. The Catholic Directory of 1859 brings the announcement of ''The Convent and Academy of the Sisters of St. Joseph, Ste. Genevieve, which formerly belonged to the Sisters of Loretto, but which has been recently bought by the Sisters of Carondelet.'' Mother Gonzaga is given as Superior over nine Sisters.

In regard to the advent of this new teaching body in the quaint old town, we quote the beautiful description from Sister Mary Lucida Savage Account:

''In response to this request (of Father Saint Cyr) Sisters Gonzaga Grand, Bridget Burke, Theodore McCormack, Clemence Motschman, Dorothea Rufine and Dosithea Grand left Carondelet, August 28th, and reached Ste. Genevieve by boat the same day. From the landing at the foot of the village Main street, they looked upon an attractive rural scene. Grouped about the old stone church as a center, the low white houses with gabled roofs, broad verandas, and outside chimneys built from the ground. The gardens were bright with late summer flowers, and elm and pecan trees shaded the graveled roads. Opposite the church, in a cultivated plot of several acres, was the convent, a large frame building; and nearby stood the quaint dwelling of Felix Valle, son of Don Francois Valle, last Spanish commandant of Sainte Genevieve. Felix Valle and his estimable wife were generous benefactors of the new academy, which, under the patronage of St. Francis de Sales, drew boarders from the surrounding towns and day pupils from the oldest families in the state.

The Superior, Sister Gonzaga, one of the four Sisters who had come from France in 1854, was an accomplished woman of striking personality and dignified bearing. An habitual reserve gave her the appearance of sternness; but in reality covered a great sweetness and gentleness of character, as well as a delightful sense of humor that relieved of awkwardness many an otherwise embarrassing situation. She quickly endeared herself to the kindly villagers, and pupils and parents were her devoted friends. Her regime was short, however; she returned to Carondelet in 1860, though not before the academy was well launched on its long and prosperous career.''[10]

---

[10]  Savage, Sister M. Lucida, ''The Congregation of St. Joseph,'' pp. 115 and 116, Archives of Ste. Genevieve Parish. Father Saint Cyr's death occurred shortly before the fiftieth anniversary of his ordination. This was what he had wished, to die before the exercises of a golden jubilee celebration could bring him undesired notice. ''I want to go to heaven,'' were his last words. Sr. Mary Lucida Savage, op. cit., p. 170.

The Catholic Directory of 1881 mentions among the "Religious Institutions" the Convent and Academy of St. Francis de Sales, by the Sisters of St. Joseph at St. Genevieve, and among the Parochial Schools: "St. Genevieve, one secular teacher, Pupils 40; four Sisters of St. Joseph, Pupils 218." This arrangement was in force since June 1874, as the following document would show:

"A Writ by which the Sisterhood of St. Joseph of Carondelet is engaged to keep in perpetuity a free parochial school for girls and boys in the Catholic Congregation of Ste. Genevieve, City and County of Ste. Genevieve, State of Missouri.

The first of June in the year of our Lord one thousand eight hundred and seventy-four, the Sisters of St. Joseph of Carondelet in the county of St. Louis, State of Missouri, in consideration of the sum of seven thousand and five hundred dollars, paid to that purpose by Felix Valle, Esq., for the benefit of St. Francis de Sales Academy of Ste. Genevieve, promise to furnish annually for all coming years three able teachers for the Catholic Congregation worshipping in the church dedicated to Ste. Genevieve in the city and county of Ste. Genevieve, State of Missouri, to wit.: Two Sisters for the girls' parochial school and one sister for the boys under twelve years of age. The Sisters of the aforesaid Academy taking charge of the little repairs of the school-house of the girls and furnishing the fuel and other necessaries for the same in consideration of the sum of twenty-five cents to be paid monthly by each pupil except those who may be exempted by the Pastor of the church and the church furnishing everything necessary for the boys' school.

"In faith whereof we have set our signature to this document."[11]

But now we must return from our digression to the fortunes of St. Genevieve parish in 1862. Father Saint-Cyr, who was then in his sixtieth year, requested of his Bishop the favor to be relieved of the burden of his parish, and the Bishop granted the request, and appointed the Rev. Philip Lawrence Hendrickx as his successor. Father Hendrickx had served for six months as Father Saint-Cyr's assistant. The saintly old man left Ste. Genevieve for Carondelet, to enter upon his duties as Chaplain to the Sisters of St. Joseph, at whose Convent of Nazareth he died February 21st, 1883. Father Hendrickx remained pastor of Ste. Genevieve until 1865. It is said of him that he had no care for the appearance of the church property, in fact, that he left church and rectory in a rather dilapidated condition. Though the fact of dilapidation seems undeniable, the imputation of neglect does not seem altogether justified. At the very outset of his career as pastor of Ste.

---

11   Original in Archives of Ste. Genevieve Parish.

Genevieve, on Sunday, June 1st, 1862, Father Hendrickx called a parish-meeting in the rectory of the church at which the Pastor explained the present condition and the future requirements of the church, and immediately withdrew from the deliberations. The Secretary then made the following statement substantially derived from the books of the church, viz., that the total income for the year ending on the 31st of December last, was but $349.75 derived from the following sources, viz.

| | |
|---|---|
| From rent of pews.............................. | $305.25 |
| From the annual tax of $1.00 per family........ | 30.50 |
| From the annual tax of .50 per family for paying the sexton...................... | 14.00 |
| Making together.......................... | $349.75 |

And that the expenses of the church for the same period were as follows :

| | |
|---|---|
| Salary of the organist.......................... | $100.00 |
| Salary of the Sexton........................... | 25.00 |
| Salary of the Organ-blower.................... | 7.50 |
| | $132.50 |

Leaving only the sum of $217.25 for the support of the priest, and for supplying the other wants of the church, such as candles, wine for the altar, altar-linens, the probable expenditure for which would amount to 75 to 100 dollars per annum—leaving the totally inadequate sum of $107.00 to $132.00 for the support of the priest and the expenses of his housekeeping.

| | |
|---|---|
| The rent of the pews at the present rates of rent would, if all collected, amount to..................... | $409.50 |
| But the amount actually collected was but.............. | 305.25 |
| Showing a defict of................................. | 104.25 |

The vestry is in want of many articles among others,

| | |
|---|---|
| A stole for preaching to cost about.............. | $15.00 |
| A chasuble for every day masses................ | 25.00 |
| A chasuable for Holy Days.................... | 45.00 |
| A Black chasuble for Funerals................. | 20.00 |
| | $105.00 |

Then must also be had a horse for the use of the priest.''

The meeting then adopted seven rules for the government of the temporal affairs of the parish, some pertinent, other impertinent. We can give only the substance of the lengthy document, but always in the wording of the original.

"Rule 1. The rent of the pews in the church from and after the first day of July next will be at the following rate, viz. The front pews on each side of the middle aisle of the church, will pay the annual rent of Ten Dollars each. The second pew twenty-five cents less than the front one, and so on towards the door of the church, each pew paying twenty-five cents less than the one immediately preceding it. The annual rents of the front pews on each of the side aisle will be eight and a half dollars with a like diminution of twenty-five cents on each pew going towards the church door.

"Rule 2. Concerns itself with the manner and time of payments and the penalties of default.

"Rule 3. In view of the annual tax of one dollar per family, and of the Sexton's tax of fifty cents per family, both of which have been abolished, there should be levied on each member, white or colored, of every family, over the age of seven years, the sum of fifteen cents, every month, payable at the same time as the pew rents."

Now comes a matter, which was not in the power of the assembly to decide, but which was taken in for good measure:

"Rule 4. The parish priest will be entitled to receive the following fees,

1. For a funeral high mass or service, Five dollars and one dollar additional for the organist; the candles for the altar being furnished by the church.

2. For the burial of a grown person two dollars and of a child under seven years of age one dollar."

3. For baptizing an infant or other person, no fixed fee will be required, but the ancient custom of attesting the record of the baptism and receiving voluntary contributions from the persons present, will be restored.

4. For marrying a couple, the contributions will continue as heretofore to be voluntary, but it is expected that the groom will at least pay for the recording the marriage certificate."[12]

It would seem that the appeal of Father Henrickx for better financial support met with but little more than the fine words of the parish assembly, and that the upkeep of the parish buildings suffered by neglect as well as from the ravages of time. In any case, it remained to Father Francis X. Weiss, whose appointment to Ste. Genevieve is dated March 5th, 1865, to restore the old and build the new.

---

[12] Book of Minutes of Ste. Genevieve Parish.

In 1863 we find Father Weiss at Riviere aux Vases, building the new stone church, and in 1865, on March 1st, when Father Weiss reached Ste. Genevieve he found the old stone church and an old rickety house for the priest. In 1871 the Sisters of St. Joseph erected the beautiful convent used partly for a residence and partly as an academy and music parlor. In 1873 the fine stone mansion, until quite recently the parochial residence, was erected, and up to the completion of the new school house, the lower story was used as a school for the boys, and the upper story as a pastoral residence.

Under the rectorship of the Rev. F. X. Weiss, the parish increased rapidly in numbers, the country around Ste. Genevieve being steadily settled by German farmers, until it became evident, that the old church was far too small to accomodate the ever increasing number. Either the parish had to be divided, or a new church had to be built. It was unanimously decided to build a new church. Ground was broken in 1875 and the corner stone laid on April 30, 1876, by Rev. Charles Ziegler, pastor of St. Malachy's, St. Louis, and a native of Ste. Genevieve, assisted by Reverend Clergy of the County, and a great number of the faithful. In 1880 the new church was completed and solemnly blessed by the Right Rev. P. J. Ryan, the coadjutor to St. Louis. After the dedication the Rev. Chas. Ziegler sang the solemn High Mass Coram Episcopo. There were seventeen priests present and vast crowds from the surrounding parishes. The parish at this time had over 400 Catholic families, 150 of which are German. There were also about 30 colored Catholic families.[13]

In this connection we feel it our duty to insert a tribute of praise to a few of the distinguished parishioners of Ste. Genevieve in Father Weiss time; and first of Felix and Odile Valle, neé Pratte, a noble pair, worthy of the heroic days of the Church.

Felix Vallé, the great benefactor of the Catholic schools was the youngest of the four sons of Jean Baptiste Valle, Sr., the last commandant of the Post of Ste. Genevieve—and was born at Ste. Genevieve on February 12th, 1800. He was educated at Bardstown, Ky., became a member of the firm of Menard & Valle who controlled a large Indian trade throughout Missouri and Arkansas and was largely interested in the mining enterprises of Missouri.

On January 7th, 1823, he married Odile Pratte, born December 24th, 1804, as the daughter of Joseph Pratte, Jr., commandant of the Post. God blessed this union with one son, Louis Felix Valie, who grew

---

[13] Ste. Genevieve Historical Sketch of the Town and Parish, ''Church Progress,'' 1910.- Cf. Mrs. Ida Schaaf's ''Quaint Ste. Genevieve a Colonial Town of Missouri,'' in ''Church Progress,'' March 13, 1919.

up to manhood and died without issue. After the death of their only heir, Mr. and Mrs. Valle gave their special attention to the establishment of a good school for boys and applied certain funds to perpetuate their work. Mr. Felix died October 1st, 1877. After the death of her husband "Mamma" Valle who had led a most exemplary Christian life and possessed "un coeur," gave her whole attention to works of charity, education and religion. The beautiful new church and interior decorations are greatly due to her munificence and the new Valle Spring cemetery with surrounding farms is another monument of her royal generosity. Mrs. Valle died August 16, 1894, and was by a special privilege laid to rest at the old Catholic cemetery in the center of the city, and amidst the inhabitants she loved so well."[14]

The names of other distinguished parishioners of the oldest parish in Missouri, are Louis and F. J. Ziegler, Eloi Lecompte, Edmund D. Janis, S. A. Guignon, F. C. Rozier, L. C. Menard and John L. Detchmendy.

Four of the brightest jewels in the crown of the venerable though ever-youthful Mother are the four priests that were born to her: Father Henri Charles Pratte, the first native priest of Missouri, Father Charles Frederick Ziegler, the one time pastor of St. Malachy's Church, St. Louis: Father Leon Dufour and Father Martin Bahr. The Rev. Leon Dufour is the only survivor of these priestly sons of a noble mother.

In the county of Ste. Genevieve there were in the days of Father Weiss, seven parishes, branched off from the old mother parish: St. Mary's, 200 families; Riviere Aux Vases, 175 families; Zell, 80 families; Weingarten, 70 families; Bloomsdale, 100 families; Lawrenceton, 40 families and French Village, 45 families.[15]

The Parish of St. Philomena at Bloomsdale formerly called La Fourche a Duclos on the Establishment Creek, is another one of the missions of the Lazarists in Ste. Genevieve County, that passed into the hands of the secular clergy about this time. The first resident pastor of Bloomsdale was Father Louis Rosi, whose heroic death Father Saint Cyr immortalized by the following entry in the Book of Burials:

"On the first of September 1853 I, the undersigned parish priest of Ste. Genevieve, buried on the epistle side of the sanctuary of the church of St. Philomena, Rivière a l'establishment, the remains of Louis Rosi, who was drowned on the night of the 30th of August last, near Bantz's mill on his way to the German Settlement to assist a sick man. His funeral was attended by both the congregations of Little Canada

---

14   "The Fair Play," Ste. Genevieve, April 30, 1898.
15   Ibidem in Chancery Records of St. Louis.

and Fourche a Duclos and was deeply regretted by all. May he rest in peace, for he laid down his life for his sheep.

J. M. I. St. Cyr. P. P.[16]

St. Mary's, though situated in Ste. Genevieve County, was for all practical purposes, a dependency of St. Mary's of the Barrens, being in reality the landing for the Seminary. The boats land there no more, but the parish is still a thriving one. Weingarten, Ozora and Coffman are much later foundations. Weingarten was formed out of Zell, and both Ozora and its neighbor Lithium out of St. Mary's, whilst Coffman covers about what was formerly known as New Tennessee. There remains only French Village, that is, the ancient Little Canada, situated in St. Francois County. Here Bishop Joseph Rosati on October 8th, 1836, blessed the chapel of St. Anne, and Father Gandolfo, C.M., on the fifth Sunday after Pentecost (1833) blessed the Cemetery of the Chapel of St. Anne. This chapel, however, was not the first house of prayer erected at Little Canada. In 1828 Father Dutreluingne had blessed an oratory that stood on the land of Pierre Lerrard. The new oratory however, was situated near the house of Antoine Aubuchon. It was enlarged to double its size in 1845.

On November 29th, 1847 a chapel built at the point called Byrne Chardon Place was blessed by Father Gandolfo assisted by Father Nicholas Stehle, under the title of St. Peter. Prince of the Apostles. This place was at a later date renamed Ozora: the Church received the title of Sacred Heart.[17]

---

[16] Cf. "The Story of Father Rossi," in "The Fair Play" of Ste. Genevieve.

[17] Chancery Records and Archives of Ste. Genevieve Parish.

## CHAPTER 11

# THE VINCENTIANS AND THEIR SUCCESSORS IN
# WASHINGTON COUNTY

The country around Old Mines was explored as early as 1723, by French officers and mining experts in search of fabled gold and silver mines. They found lead in abundance, and on the strength of their report to Paris, a large company of miners and negro slaves under Renault was settled on the headwaters of the Big River, a tributary of the Meramec. The Jesuit Fathers of Kaskaskia, and after 1793, the Jesuits of Ste. Genevieve, had charge of the spiritual interests of these pioneers. A short time before 1820, Father Henry Pratte built a log church at Old Mines and made regular visits to the Congregation. This connection with Ste. Genevieve was continued by Father Dahmen from 1822 to 1828, as the Records of the parish show. The oldest Book of the Parish begins with the 20th day of April, 1820, and for many pages contains the signature of Henri Pratte, Curé of Ste. Genevieve.

Old Mines became a separate parish in 1826, when the Lazarist John Bouillier took up his residence at the Church of St. Joachim. As the old log structure seemed unworthy of a progressive community, Father Bouillier built a new church of brick, the cornerstone of which was laid in 1828, and the consecration of which was held by Bishop Rosati under the invocation of St. Joachim. The church had a frontage of thirty, and a length of one hundred and ten feet. Its steeple rose fifty feet in air.

From 1828 to 1841, the parish of Old Mines was a Lazarist Center, usually holding a community of three or four. Among them we find Fathers John Brands, P. J. Doutreluingne, B. Rolando, J. M. Mignard, J. B. Tornatore, Joseph Demarche and others. From this center the following stations in Washington County were regularly attended: St. Stephen's at Richwoods, and St. James at Potosi: Besides these missions, the Fathers occasionally visited Valle's Mines and Grande Riviere (Big River).

The first secular priest to hold the pastorship of Old Mines was the rough and ready John Cotter. For ten years, from 1841, to his tragic death, he was pastor of this ancient church. According to Msgr. William Walsh, "He was neither a scholar nor a preacher, but he was a most sincere and self-sacrificing man. Whilst a student at the Barrens, he was infirmarian and thus acquired quite a practical knowledge of medicine. This served him to good use, when he became a priest, and many and many a time by night and by day, did he hasten over the roads of Washington County bringing corporal as well as spiritual health to the poor of his flock. On the 5th of June 1851, whilst accompanying the Rev. Francis Barbier, a French Lazarist, from the Old Mines to the Barrens, the horse on which he rode shied and threw him violently against a tree. He was mortally injured. He survived, however, for about two days, and save the words, Ora pro nobis, and our Saviour's sacred name, which he was heard occasionally to utter, he spoke, as far as we know, not a word. His remains lie buried beneath the sanctuary of the Old Mines Church. From what you may hear, even to this day from the people of the Old Mines and surrounding country, you would infer that he must have been almost worshiped by Protestants as well as Catholics."[1]

His successor, the saintly Father James Fox, was born in County Wicklow, Ireland, and studied for the priesthood at Carlow. He came to St. Louis early in 1849, and was ordained on June 9th, of the same year, by Archbishop Kenrick. After doing duty for a while in Carondelet Seminary and at St. John's church, St. Louis, he was appointed pastor of St. James' Church, Potosi. After the death of Father Cotter, James Fox was transferred to Old Mines. He remained in the country mission for 18 years, building churches at Irondale, and De Soto, and enlarging the Church of Old Mines, which was then reconsecrated by Bishop Duggan, November 15th, 1857. Father Fox also built a school at Old Mines. He was assisted in these years by Father Hogan, afterwards Bishop of Kansas City, and Father Robert Hayes.

Bishop Hogan tells in his reminiscences, "of consulting with his dear friend and worthy brother priest, Rev. James Fox, rector of St. Joachim's Church, Old Mines, Missouri, who was deeply concerned in the matter of landownership and occupancy by Catholic emigrants." He also made a visitation of the district with the Pastor, both, of course, on horseback. And later he tells of founding a new settlement in the winter of 1858-59, "on a wide and fair tract of ground bought and donated by Rev. James Fox of Old Mines."[2]

It is but just to add that in his many works of zeal and charity Father Fox was greatly assisted by Madame LaMarque, a long time resident of Old Mines and a most worthy Christian matron.[3]

The town of Potosi was long known as *Mine a Burton*, a corruption of the French *Mine a Breton*. In the early days when Father Timon came to visit the few scattered Catholics of the neighborhood, he found a wooden church-building. In 1829, Father Bouillier, C.M. ac-

---

1 Walsh, William, "Life of Peter Richard Kenrick," pp. 51 and 52.

2 Hogan, Bishop John, "On the Mission in Missouri," pp. 40, 59 and 60.

3 Mrs. La Marque of Potosi, made a bequest of $20,000 to Archbishop Kenrick, for charitable purposes, which the Archbishop forfeited by not taking the so-called Test-Oath.

quired a half acre lot for the use of the Church. In 1831, Father Philip Borgna, C. M., built on it a brick church, which was consecrated by Bishop Rosati, April 27th, 1834. The place was regularly visited by Fathers Borgna and Bouillier from Old Mines, until 1835, when Father Lewis Tucker, a secular priest, became its pastor. Father Tucker was a native of Perry County, and after completing his studies at St. Mary's of the Barrens, was ordained by Bishop Rosati in the Cathedral of St. Louis, September 21, 1835. One year after his coming, the young priest, who had endeared himself to all the people of Potosi "by his indefatigable labors" in their behalf and in his zeal for gaining converts, was unexpectedly sent to the mission of New Madrid. The people of *Mine a Breton,* however, sent an earnest petition to Bishop Rosati that he "in order to show them his kindness and to confirm their attachment toward him, let their dearly beloved pastor continue to reside with them." This document signed by Firmin Desloge and thirty-nine substantial church-members, almost exclusively of Irish descent, had its proper effect, and Father Lewis Tucker remained in Potosi until 1844.[4] Under his gentle rule the Congregation grew from year to year until in 1844 numbered two hundred souls. Father Lewis Tucker now entered upon his long pastorate at St. Michael's, Fredericktown. Concerning his labors and successes in Potosi Father Tucker wrote to Bishop Rosati on May 6th, 1835: "I have been here since the first day of February. I spoke to the congregation in consequence of the subscription list, that had been presented to them previous to my arrival, by the Reverend Mr. Bouillier: The Irish have all subscribed according to their means, and some of the French also, but the others have as yet done nothing towards it. They all attend Mass when they can, and have nearly all made their Easters, and in general appear desirous of practicing their religion. Some also among the non-professors are curious enough to take a peep at popery, so that five of them are pleased with its charms, and I am preparing them for the reception of Baptism. I trust, with the grace of God, others will follow their example."[5] At the end of 1835 Father Tucker could report seventy-seven baptisms, thirty-one of which were conferred on former Protestants." On October 8th, 1838, Father Tucker informs his Bishop of a proposed visit to Stoddard County; "A young man residing in Bloomfield, the county-seat of Stoddard County, told me that he would give ten acres of land for a church, if there was any possibility of having a priest. A priest cannot, as yet, be supported there, but I will obligate myself to give them Mass there on four times in the year, until they are able to provide for one."[6] On December 7th, 1838 Father Tucker

---

4  Original in Archives of St. Louis Archdiocese.
5  Lewis Tucker to Rosati, in Archives.
6  Lewis Tucker to Rosati, in Archives.

describes Stoddard County as a proper place for Catholic immigrants; the land being very good and well-timbered. The climate also is reported to be as healthy as in any place in the state, so much so that the only Doctor of Bloomfield had to turn farmer for lack of patients. Father Tucker then proposes to buy a lot for church purposes on the outskirts of the town of Bloomfield.

Father Tucker left Potosi in 1843 and was succeeded by the Rev. Joseph V. Wiseman. Father Wiseman was a near relative of the celebrated Cardinal of the same name. He was above the average as a scholar and, though, he read his sermons, he was considered a very eloquent preacher. As the congregation of Potosi was small and hardly able to support a pastor, Father Wiseman, in order to meet his expenses, taught school for some time. During his time as pastor the people built a small frame house of two rooms as a priest's residence. It was located in a corner of the church yard, without as much as a rail fence between it and the graves of the dead.

Father Wiseman remained pastor of Potosi for about three years. He died in the Hospital of the Sisters of Charity, St. Louis, in the summer of 1848.[7] He was succeeded by Father John Higginbotham in 1846 who came to St. Mary's Seminary from the archdiocese of Dublin and was raised to the priesthood by Archbishop Kenrick on September 21st, 1845.

Father Higginbotham remained in Potosi until May or June 1848, when he removed to St. Louis. He founded St. Michael's parish and was for a time pastor of St. Patrick's. All the older English-speaking people of St. Louis remember him as a most zealous advocate of temperance. He spent the declining years of his life in Ireland where he died in the fall of 1882.

Father Saint Cyr filled the position for a brief space in 1848, and was relieved by Father James Fox in 1849-1852. After a two-years' administration by Father John Hogan, the future Bishop of St. Joseph and Kansas City, and another two years' pastorship by Father Simon Grugan, followed the short periods of Father James O'Brien's and Eugene O'Hea's pastorates in 1856 and 1857.

After Father O'Hea's time Potosi was for a longer period without a resident pastor, being attended from Old Mines. It was during this time in 1859-60, that Father James Fox, pastor of Old Mines, built the present Potosi church. It was dedicated by Archbishop Kenrick in September 1860. About 1867 Rev. Michael O'Reilly became pastor and remained until the close of 1871. Michael O'Reilly, a native of County Leitrim, Ireland, while persuing his ecclesiastical studies in the Irish College at Paris, was adopted by the diocese of St. Louis, and trans-

---

7  ''The Old Town of Potosi,'' in ''Church Progress,'' 1894.

ferred to St. Vincent's College at Cape Girardeau. Here he was ordained by Archbishop Kenrick on May 27th, 1866.[8]

His first appointment was as assistant to Father Fox at Old Mines. But on hearing of this appointment, a delegation from Potosi came to remind Archbishop Kenrick of his promise to send them a resident priest. Mr. Connolly the spokesman, had already fitted up a part of his house in which to entertain the promised pastor. In the fall, young Father O'Reilly was transferred to Potosi, where he found a royal welcome. He lived at Mr. Connolly's for about a year, in the meantime erecting a pastoral residence. He taught the boys of his parish Latin, devoting much time to this. Among these boys were the future Monsignor Connolly, Father Francis Jones, late pastor of St. Thomas of Acquin, St. Louis, and Judge Teasdale, of Kansas City.[9]

The church of St. Stephen at Richwoods, in the northern part of Washington County, dates back to the year 1831. On the 12th day of October of that year Bishop Rosati wrote in his Diary: "I came to Richwoods, and looked at the place where Mr. Roussin and other inhabitants propose to build another church of cedar-posts."[10] The church was dedicated to St. Stephen. The place was originally called Mine a la Baume. The church was attended for a time by Lazarist Fathers from Old Mines; mainly by Rolando and Mignard. In 1842 Richwoods became an independent parish with Father Joseph Wiseman, a secular priest, as its first pastor. Father Wiseman divided his attention among his two charges, Potosi and Richwoods. On his departure for the Hospital in St. Louis, Fathers O'Brien and L. Galtier filled the vacancy until October 17th, 1847, when the Reverend James Duggan came and remained for about a year. Then the place was visited by Father S. A. Bernier and by Father Saint-Cyr: but in 1849 the parish received its own exclusive pastor in the person of Louis Rosi. After five years service at Richwoods Father Rosi was transferred to Ste. Genevieve County. His successor, the Rev. John McCaffrey, like his predecessor, Father Rosi, met a tragic death being drowned in crossing the Meramec River on February 7th, 1856.[11]

Rev. John J. McCaffrey," says Father William Walsh, "was pastor of the Richwoods at the time of his death, and was comparatively a young man, being only thirty-six or thirty-seven years of age. He had excellent qualities of head and heart. We never knew a man more familiar with the text of the Holy Scripture. Give him the least idea of the passage of the Holy Scripture which you wanted to find, he would find it immediately. One cold afternoon, in the beginning

---

8  Chancery Records.
9  Cf. "Our Pastors in Calvary," by Mary Constance Smith. pp. 36 and 37.
10  Rosati's Diary in Archives of Archdiocese of St. Louis.
11  Chancery Records, St. Louis.

of February, 1856, he left his humble home, the home which he was destined never to re-enter, to go on a distant sick call. In fording the Meramec River, which lay in his way, the horse he rode took fright at some object and threw him. And that was the last seen alive of poor Father McCaffrey. It was supposed that in falling he was injured by his horse, and, being thus rendered insensible he became incapable of saving himself. His dead body was found some days after and was conveyed to the Old Mines, where a Mass of Requiem was sung for the repose of his soul. And then friendly hands tenderly and respectfully carried the dead priest to his last resting place. A few of the priests of the diocese united and placed a modest tombstone over the grave of the priest that had died in the discharge of his duties.''[12]

---

[12]  Walsh, 1. c., p. 53.

## CHAPTER 12

# LAZARIST ACTIVITIES IN CAPE GIRARDEAU

Of the four counties of Southeast Missouri having residences of the Vincentian Fathers, Washington, Ste. Genevieve, Perry and Cape Girardeau, it was the latest foundation, St. Vincent's of Cape Girardeau, that vied in importance with the earliest one St. Mary's of the Barrens in the County of Perry. Both possessed the Seminary, and the College for a time, and both have formed strong parishes and still hold them: they differ in this, that St. Mary's of the Barrens still attends most of its former outmissions in Perry County, whilst St. Vincent's of Cape Girardeau has long ago turned over its stations and missions in New Madrid, Scott, and Cape Girardeau Counties to the secular clergy. This chapter treats of the Lazarist activities in Cape Girardeau County during the earlier years of Archbishop Kenrick's administration.

The parish of St. Vincent's, Cape Girardeau, was founded from the Barrens. In 1816 the entire town held only eight Catholic families. Many converts to the Faith from among the native Americans, and at a later period, numerous Catholic immigrants from the Eastern States and from Ireland and Germany, so strengthened the Congregation, that in 1836 the Rev. John Bouillier, C. M., was appointed as its first resident pastor. Then came Father J. Brands, and in July 21st, 1839, Bishop Rosati consecrated the new stone church, that was to supplant the wooden structure of earlier days.[1]

In October 1838 Father Brands founded St. Vincent's Academy, a school for boys and placed it in charge of a Mr. M. Flynn. On the 23rd of October of the same year, a community of seven Sisters of Loretto with six boarders, came to Cape Girardeau for the purpose of founding a house of their order. They came from Bethlehem, their house near the Barrens Seminary. For their immediate use, Father Brands vacated his house, taking up his own abode in a little dwelling on the other side of the street. The sisters availed themselves of that kind accomodation until the following July, when they entered a house of their own. Since that day, so long past, the Sisters of Loretto have continued in Cape Girardeau, and have done much to advance the cause of religion and education.[2]

During Father Brands' ministry in Cape Girardeau district, besides their own parish, the priest of St. Vincent's had to attend the out-

---

[1] Cf. Cape Girardeau, a series of articles in the "Church Progress" of 1894.
[2] L. Cit., February, 1894.

missions of Jackson, Tywappity Bottom, and Cairo beyond the Mississippi. The Congregation at Jackson had no church as yet, but services were held in the house of one or the other parishioner. At Cairo a church was being built, and at Tywappity Bottom stood the Church of St. Francis de Sales, a poor lonely log house amid its cluster of century-old trees.[3]

The novitiate of the Congregation and the Preparatory Seminary were established at Cape Girardeau in the former residence of the Spanish Governor on the banks of the river. Reverend Michael Domenec, afterwards Bishop of Pittsburg, was Superior of the Seminary, and Reverend James Rolando was master of novices. In 1843, when the College building on the river bank was finished, the professors and students of St. Mary's College were transferred to its spacious halls and rooms, whilst the Preparatory Seminary and the Novitiate left the old Governor's Mansion for the hallowed retreat of St. Mary's of the Barrens.[4]

The first President of the College was Father Hector Figari and its first Prefect of Discipline the Rev. John Francis Gerry. It was expected that a large number of students would be drawn from the Southern States to the new College, but these expectations were not fully realized. The great flood of 1844, when the lowlands around Cape Girardeau were suddenly transformed into a billowy sea, did great damage to the farms that belonged to the College. When the waters at last subsided, the effluvia from the recently submerged district hung like a pall of death over the city and countryside, spreading sickness to an alarming degree. In the College no less than forty of its inmates were at one time suffering from one or the other of the prevailing diseases. Father McGerry and one student were the only persons that were not attacked. Students and professors were disheartened at the prospect. In October Father Figari resigned as President and Father Thaddeus Amat took his place.[5]

But the number of students remained small, and two of the Professors died. Father Ricini, a young Italian priest, who had just made his novitiate, was seized with the sickness that carried him off in a few days. He was buried on Good Friday, Fathers Cercos and McGerry officiating. Father Cercos was taken sick at the altar on Easter Sunday and died on the following Wednesday. Father Amat filled the office of President for a year or more, when he was transferred, to the Barrens and made Superior of that institution.[6]

---

3  "Church Progress," February 1894.
4  Ibidem, January 4.
5  Cape Girardeau, 1. c., February 3.
6  Ibidem.

In the fall of 1845, Rev. Anthony Penco became President of the College. He was a man of great personal popularity, a native of Genoa, descended from one of the wealthiest families of that city. "M. Penco," as Bishop Stephen Ryan of Buffalo writes, "was one of nature's noblemen; his appearance and manner indicated his gentle character; his presence at the altar evidenced the saintly priest . . . . But by extravagant speculation his brother wrecked his princely fortune and, at his death, left his family destitute. Father Penco was able to save his own patrimony, and he educated his brother's children. To this he devoted himself during the remainder of his life, acting, at the same time as chief Director of the Missionary College Brignole-Sale in his native city, Genoa. This explains the somewhat mysterious words on his tombstone in the Campo Santo at Genoa:

"A zealous missionary in America. In his native country a worthy priest, as he was a true father to his family."[7]

During Father Anthony Penco's presidency the number of students began to increase, and the prospects of the college took on a brighter hue. In the night of January 4th, 1848, a singular accident befell the College. The steamer Seabird, with an immense cargo of powder, 1500 kegs, on board was tied up to the river bank near the college. During the night the steamer caught fire, and exploded, shattering the doors and windows of the building and destroying the plastering. There was, however, no loss of life, as the inmates of the college had received timely warning from the captain of the boat. But the severest trial was still to come, the almost total destruction of St. Vincent's College and Church.[8]

On the 27th of November 1850 at 3 P. M. a most violent and destructive hurricane passed over the City of Cape Girardeau, the course of the wind was from the Southwest to Northeast. This storm was threatening for some hours, the day was very sultry, and heavy dark clouds flying in great confusion portended something dreadful. The heavens seemed in great confusion and all were expecting torrents of rain. For more than an hour the winds presaged destruction. When it came, all was confusion and terror. It carried every thing before it; trees, fences, houses, everything was swept from the face of the earth. The roof of St. Vincent's College was carried away, and not a particle of it was ever found again. The walls of the S. W. corner were thrown down to the second story, the gable ends carried away and all the chimneys thrown down. The brick bake house in ruins, the large new, two story frame house, used as tailor shop, shoemaker shop, trunk and

---

7  "Catholic Historical Review," vol. II, 182-184.
8  Cape Girardeau, 1. c., February 3.

clothes room, was razed to the ground. Two men who were in the garret of this house were blown more than 50 yards, one was not hurt, the other had his leg broken. Four of the brothers were caught under the floor of the second story, but happily the trunks and some large boxes, saved them from being crushed to death. It was with difficulty they were removed from the ruins without any serious injury. They were sorely pressed and bruised. Old Henry, a servant of the college, was found dead in the garden, being struck by a beam in the fall of the brick quarters for the negroes. His wife and daughter were in the same room but not hurt. Two only of the collegians who were outside the college at the time, were hurt. There were seventy persons bruised and covered with wounds from being carried and rolled by the wind along with the ruins of fences and houses. They were found buried in the ruins of the Methodist meeting house which was on the opposite side of the street from the college.

The fine stone church of St. Vincent's had the roof and steeple carried away, and not a vestige of it could be found; the walls were down almost to the ground. The two large frame houses near the church lay in ruins. The fine painting of *Our Saviour in the Garden of Olives* was never found. The collegians and priests passed the night in the college yard, the weather was cold and rainy.

It was resolved to send the students to their families, consequently the boys from St. Louis departed at 10 A. M., by steamboat in company with Rev. Richard Hennessy; those from the South started at 4 P. M., the same day on steamboat *Alton*, 52 in number, accompanied by Fathers McGerry and Verina.

The convent near the college was entirely destroyed, and a great portion of the houses in town, more or less injured. The students all arrived safe at their respective homes.[9]

As soon as the students were disposed of, Father Penco, the President, had the ruins examined by a mason and soon decided to repair the college. The weather being fine, the work commenced immediately, and by the 1st of January 1851, the walls of the college were repaired and under roof. On the 28th of March Father McGerry returned from Louisiana with 30 boys. Rev. Richard Hennessy having returned the day previous with some boys from St. Louis.

On March 31st, 1851 studies and classes recommenced with 33 students and prospects for a large number very soon.

Rev. Anthony Penco was still President. The college appeared more solid and substantial than before the storm. The bake house, wash house and quarters for the servants were all rebuilt in brick. Rev.

---

9  ''American Catholic Historical Researches,'' vol. XIII, pp. 78 ss.

P. Chandy was very active, and soon after the return of the students, he had all the fences around the play-garden replaced. Everything began to look cheering, the year went on well and closed with Exhibition and Distribution of Premiums as usual.[10]

About six months after this diaster there was another inundation of the College farms, entailing serious losses. Nothwithstanding all these frowns of fortune it was resolved in council to rebuild the church. The workmen who had been hired for the year to cultivate the farm, were employed to clear away the ruins of the old stone church and, on the spot, to erect the new church. The work went on rapidly, and all was soon cleared, and a large and deep foundation dug out.

When the Rev. Anthony Penco was promoted to the office of Visitor or Pro-Visitor, Father Richard Hennessy became President. It was during his Presidency that the present parish church of St. Vincent de Paul was built and dedicated.[11] The chief and almost only support Father Penco had under the distressing circumstances that accompanied his course as President of the College of Cape Girardeau, was the bright and buoyant spirit of his Prefect of Discipline, Father John Francis McGerry. He was a native of Maryland and, like the Rev. John O'Reilly, was a secular priest before he joined the Lazarists. Old Father Time dealt kindly with him, whitening indeed his locks, but not dimming in the least the light of his spirit. He was graphically described in his three score years and ten, by one, who knew him well, as ''a beautiful old man.''

When he was far beyond seventy, he was of a more hopeful and cheerful disposition, than many a man of forty. He was not a learned man; but he knew a little of almost everything and loved to back his comments and answers with an innocent appropriate story. Father McGerry died at Cape Girardeau on January 25th, 1872.[12]

Father James Rolando was an Italian by birth, served by preference as Master of Novices, was considered by some as a fine church-singer, though according to others, his voice had more volume in it than sweetness. He died at Germantown, Pa., in November 1884. After the death of Father Richard Hennessy the presidency of the College devolved upon the Spaniard, Father John Masnou. After three years service he returned to his native country, where he was appointed Visitor of the Lazarists.[13]

---

10  ''American Historical Researches,'' vol. XIII, pp. 78 ss.
11  Cape Girardeau, 1. c., February 10, 1894.
12  Cape Girardeau, 1. c., February 10, 1894
13  Ibidem, February 17.

Father Masnou was succeeded as president of St. Vincent's College by Rev. Stephen V. Ryan, the future Bishop of Buffalo. Father Ryan filled the office until 1858, when he removed to the Barrens. He had been appointed Visitor of the Lazarists the preceding year.[14]

In 1857 St. Vincent's College under the presidency of Father Thomas J. Smith was converted into a seminary for the training and educating of candidates for the priesthood.[15]

---

[14] Cape Girardeau, l. c.
[15] Ibidem.

## CHAPTER 13

## ST. MICHAEL'S, FREDERICKTOWN UNDER FATHER TUCKER

After Father Cellini's departure from St. Michael's, Fredericktown, the Rev. Nicholas Savelli became pastor; yet remaining there only about three years, (1842-1845), he did not make himself felt so much in the history of the parish as Father Cellini before him and Father Tucker after him. Who he was, and whence he came, we could not discover. In 1845 he left the diocese of St. Louis and died in Louisana 1857, by an assassin's hand. From the *Catholic Cabinet* of St. Louis, we learn, that during his pastorship, on September 10, 1843, the Coadjutor Bishop Peter Richard Kenrick administered the sacrament of Confirmation in the church of St. Michael, Fredericktown Mo., to fifty-six persons, among whom were several converts. During the Mass the Coadjutor Bishop preached on the devotion of Catholics to the Blessed Virgin. In the afternoon of the same day, and on the two following days he delivered lectures in the church, "On the Principles of Roman Catholics."[1] A few days later, September 25, 1845, Bishop Rosati died in Rome at the age of fifty-four years, and Peter Richard Kenrick was Bishop of St. Louis.

From 1845-1880 the Parish of St. Michael was in charge of Father Lewis Tucker, the former pastor of Potosi. "Good old Father Tucker," as he is affectionately called by the people of Fredericktown and all the country round about, was born February 11th, 1806, in Perry County, Mo. Lewis and Hilary, both destined to become priests, were the sons of Nicholas Tucker of Perryville, and grandsons of Joseph Tucker who settled on the Saline in 1797, and at whose house Father Dunand the Trappist stayed on his first visit to Perry County. Both entered the seminary of St. Mary's of the Barrens. Hilary, however, in company with George Hamilton, had the distinction of being the first student from St. Louis Diocese sent to Rome, whilst Lewis completed his studies at the Barrens where subdeaconship was conferred on him by Bishop Rosati, on Ascension day 1832.[2]

On this occasion the Bishop congratulated the Congregation of the Barrens at seeing the children of their own country admitted to the Sanctuary.[3]

---

1 "Catholic Cabinet," vol. I, October.

2 Hilary Tucker, George Hamilton, and Joseph Marie Dunand, have been treated in previous chapters.

3 "Shepherd of the Valley," II, 1.

In the following year, September 21, 1835, having received deacon-ship, Lewis Tucker was ordained priest in the Cathedral of St. Louis by Bishop Rosati. Father Tucker's first appointment was at St. Michael's for one year, then at Potosi for nearly ten years, and at New Madrid for one year to 1845. In New Madrid the young priest's health began to fail, and brought on his removal to St. Michael's, where he was already well known as the former assistant to Father Cellini. The trip from New Madrid to Fredericktown had to be made in a rough wagon, as the good Father was too ill to ride. For the subsequent years of his life, St. Michael's and Father Tucker were almost synonymous terms.

Towards the end of Father Cellini's pastorate the congregation of St. Michael's had increased to such an extent in numbers and im-portance, that everyone realized the necessity of a larger and more becoming church than the old log structure, and a subscription of two thousand and eight hundred dollars in money and labor was ob-tained for that purpose. Deeming the amount rather uncertain in part and altogether insufficient in toto to erect such a church as seemed desirable, Father Cellini declined to commence building operations, and soon afterward removed to St. Louis. His successor, Father N. Savelli did nothing to further the project; but Father Tucker on his accession in 1845 devised plans, and began the building of what is even now the main-part of St. Michael's church.[4]

The records of St. Michael's contain the following entry made by Father Tucker in 1846. ''Church Building: Fredericktown, Madison County, Mo. Dimensions: 35 ft. by 55. 20 ft. high. After holding three meetings on the subject above-mentioned the members of this Congregation have come to the conclusion of erecting a new church near the old one, on a lot of ground donated for the use of the church by Rev. F. Cellini. A committee of three have been appointed to super-intend the work, viz.; Henry Janis, A Guignon, and L. Tucker.

Father Tucker, himself, besides contributing $30.00, actually per-formed a part of the manual labor, and was always present during the progress of building. The architecture of the new building was rather primitive: Straight walls, with square windows, the ceiling rounded, with elevated galleries along the side walls of the sanctuary. One of these lofts was for the choir, and the other for the colored members of the Congregation, of whom there were quite a number. The church was completed towards the end of 1846. On the 16th day of June the pews were sold to the highest bidders.

---

[4] Father Tucker's church was razed in 1927, to make room for the present fine edifice erected by Father Francis Mispagel.

Father Tucker was no less solicitous for the education of the children. From 1851-1860, St. Michael's had a parochial school, conducted by the Misses Margaret and Mary Anne Barron. The war, that blasted so many flourishing hopes, ruined this second educational institution of St. Michael's Parish. But in obedience to the decrees of the Council of Baltimore in regard to parochial schools, Father Tucker made the third venture with a layman James F. Fox as teacher.

A beautiful "Ecce Homo," dated 1867, reminds us of the fact, that the well-known artist, Emile Herzinger, was a native of Fredericktown, and a great admirer of Father Tucker.

Up to 1840 the congregation of St. Michael's was composed of the descendants of the old French settlers, speaking a language that was in derivation and substance French, though intermingled with many words of English and perhaps Indian origin, a people possessing in the main the natural characteristics of their ancestors, courage, love of adventure, respect for truth, sobriety and honesty, but at the same time their easy-going, pleasure-loving and somewhat unprogressive ways especially as compared with the American restlessness and hurry. But after 1840 there came a steady stream of immigration of German Catholics spreading over Madison County and especially Mine La Motte. It was about 1864 that these German Catholic miners and mechanics built of their own slender means on a lot donated by Eberhard Priggel, the little chapel that was afterward dedicated to the "Dear St. Elizabeth of Thuringia." As the German Catholics, however, gradually withdrew from the work at the diggings, and crushers and smelters of Mine La Motte for the more congenial occupation of farming, the little church of St. Elizabeth fell into neglect and disuse and final destruction, and the land on which it had been built reverted to the owners of Mine La Motte.

For many years, Father Tucker made regular pastoral visits to Pilot Knob, Iron Mountain, Valle Forge, New Tennessee-Settlement, as well as Mine La Motte and Marquand, and during the construction of the Iron Mountain Railroad to Iron Mountain and Pilot Knob. From 1855 to 1859, and again from 1866 to 1869 he visited the various camps up and down the line for priestly ministrations. All these excursions were made on horse-back and with every possible inconvenience. In the early days, when priests were few and far between, Father Tucker would now and then journey to St. Louis on horseback, about a hundred miles, for the purpose of making his confession. On one of these journeys it happened that the horse he was riding, showed signs of lameness. At Carondelet, about ninety miles from home, the kind-hearted rider took the horse by the bridle and led it along, trudging on and on the many weary miles, stopping over night at Herculaneum, Ste. Genevieve and Reviere aux Vases, until he reached his home in Fredericktown.

In a financial way these missionary trips to the construction camps or works as Father Tucker called them, were not unprofitable. It is a notable tribute to the generosity of the workmen along this new Railroad, as well as to the popularity of Father Tucker with the men, that in fourteen years, from 1855-1869, they gave him of their savings at least $5,000.00 by actual count.

Among the Works visited by Father Tucker during this period of railroad building it may be of interest to note the name of Coffey, the father of Rev. James Coffey of St. Leo's church, mentioned six times in the record; the names of Johnson, Griffin, Scott and Murray, occur a number of times, all between October 1868 and August 1869.

The parochial residence with its commodious front porch, almost hidden behind an immense old apple-tree, was built in 1861, and in 1873 an addition, including a little spire was made to the front of the church, which enlarged it to almost double its former size. Of these two building operations we have no further record.

Father Lewis Tucker was, no doubt, the most popular, the most endeared pastor St. Michael's ever had. If the life of Father Cellini can be compared to an impetuous mountain stream, somewhat turbid and strong and always tending forward to the accomplishment of some great design, the life of his successor, good old Father Tucker, may find its corresponding image in some remote woodland lake, reflecting from its placid surface the happy surroundings during the day, and at night the peaceful stars of heaven. Father Tucker was a plain, unassuming man and strictly attentive to his duties. He was of a retiring disposition, a great reader, proficient in English and French controversial literature, and not averse to entering a friendly discussion on the grounds of his Faith and the merits of his Church. Judge Robert A. Anthony remembers a religious controversy, conducted in the columns of the *Fredericktown Bee* by Father Tucker and the Rev. Dr. Farmer a Methodist minister of some note. The two controversialists were personal friends and remained friends until death. As the files of almost all the old papers of Fredericktown have fallen a prey to the tooth of time, we could not verify this fact by some quotations from Father Tucker's literary effort. It would have, no doubt, added a touch of quaintness to our narrative.

Father Tucker had a fine voice for singing, and a good delivery in preaching, though his sermons were liable to be rather long. He loved the common people, and always had a kind word for every one. With strangers he was reserved. Yet, if you got into a conversation with him, you would find him excellent company. Archbishop Kenrick once said: "Father Tucker must be a very good man; I have heard or seen nothing of him for the last ten years." His motto seems to have been: early to bed and early to rise; for he rose at four, and after his meditation said Mass at five o'clock every day winter and summer, and he invariably retired for the night at eight. Father Tucker's life was truly spiritual. He cared little for creature comforts, and for personal appearance. Like Chaucer's model priest, Father Tucker was the flower of charity and kindness.

Father Tucker had ordered a marble slab to be placed above the church door, bearing the inscription of Matthew 21, 13: "My house shall be called a house of prayer." The sculptor, on opening the Bible at the place indicated, read the entire verse: "My house shall be called a house of prayer, but you have made it a den of theives," and so he chiseled it all in the patient stone. Father Tucker was surprised, perhaps a little indignant; but realizing that the man meant no harm, his kind old heart would not permit him to send back the marble with the obnoxious inscription, as he was urged to do. Quietly covering up the "Den of thieves" with putty, he placed the corrected slab in its proper place above the portal. But alas, in the course of months, the marble grew darker and the putty whiter, and, after some time, the somewhat blurred legend "My house shall be called a house of prayer" was read with even greater attention, because it was followed by the refrain in snow-white letters: "but you have made it a den of thieves."

This anecdote in some manner found its way into Harper's Weekly, and many a good soul had a hearty laugh at the simplicity of Father Tucker, without knowing what kindly motive inspired the singular performance. The celebrated inscription was removed from its place of honor by Father B. V. Tannrath, and can now be seen beneath the old spreading hickory tree near the church.

In our Father's early days the march of progress had not yet made obsolete the pleasant glow of the fireplace and the cheerful light of the candle, and clocks were still regarded as a luxury. Times had changed in his declining years but the good Father did not change with them. He remained faithful to the old-fashioned fireplace and to candle-light in thought and word and deed. Archbishop Ryan of Philadelphia, then Coadjutor to the Archbishop of St. Louis, who frequently lectured to the people of Fredericktown, was wont to say that he never could tell the precise time when he was to begin his lecture, as Father Tucker would always announce it for "early candle-light." But there is a word of Archbishop Ryan's in regard to Father Tucker, that is of far greater importance. Many years ago His Grace of Philadelphia wrote me a letter about good old Father Tucker, his dear friend, in which he bore eloquent testimony to the holiness of his life and stated, that if Father Tucker's beautiful character could be made known, he might be adjudged worthy of beatification.

Msgr. William Walsh, in his interesting life of Archbishop Kenrick writes: "Speaking of Father Tucker old Father St. Cyr said in our presence somewhat to the effect: "He is a very holy man. When I had to leave Ste. Genevieve owing to the loss of sight, I suggested to him that he should take my place. At first he seemed favorable to the suggestion. But after a little thinking he said: ''No, he would remain where he was. Ste. Genevieve would surely get a pastor, but his poor little place might not.''[4]

In his later years Father Tucker bore a striking resemblance to the sainted Curé of Ars, not only in the simplicity and holy austerity of of his life and character, but even in the form and expression of his countenance.

Father Tucker was indeed the spiritual Father of his people. Often, I have been told, when people brought him a load of hay or corn for his horse, the kind Father would thank them for their good will, but ask them to take the gift to some poor neighbor who, he said, needed it more than himself. Father Tucker's highest rent for a pew in church was two dollars, ($2.00). Not being in need of more liberal contributions, he never thought of asking more; but somehow, the parishioners did not always appreciate his generous motives, and, it is to be feared that some of them

''The less he sought their offerings, pinched the more,
And praised a priest contented to be poor.''[5]

But Father Tucker, though poor in spirit, was never destitute. Whatever he needed for his simple household, the people might easily furnish; and when the good priest died, he could leave not a little to charity; to the infirm Priest's fund, five hundred dollars, and to the Little Sisters of the Poor, four hundred dollars. Except two small bequests to near relatives, Father Tucker's estate was given to the Archbishop to be used for good purposes, as His Grace might see fit. A little more than eight thousand dollars was found stowed away in odd corners and hiding places of the old house. Probably the good Father himself had forgotten as to where most of it lay hidden. Certainly he was not a believer in the modern doctrine of high interest, or he might have doubled or trebled his wealth; but as it came to him almost unsought, he laid it away without any solicitous care. It was a talent entrusted to him for safe keeping which would, in due time, bring fruit for the church; yet it was Father Tucker's personal property. The main source of income, besides the small salary, and the monthly contributions or donations from the very numerous Irish and German workmen in the construction camps, along the railroad from 1855-1869, were the very liberal offerings at the marriages of the old French families of St. Michael's. For it was the custom, that every more or less prominent wedding guest should come up and sign his name in the Record and make an offering of at least one dollar. Father Tucker seems to have had the practice of bundling up all the money he received,

---

4    Walsh, l. c., p. 53.

5    Dryden, Translations from the *Canterbury Tales*.

gold, silver, and paper, and putting it away in some box or tin-can. And thus his wealth grew from year to year, and the good Father was none the wiser or richer for it. This lack of business sense adds a new grace to Father Tucker's character of unworldliness; for the money was derived, not from any investment or enterprise but from the free gifts of a devoted people. And the people were to profit in return for their liberality; for among other benefactions, the St. Michael's Library Hall and School, afterwards built by his successor, the Rev. B. V. Tannrath with a portion of Father Tucker's bequest to Archbishop Kenrick, remains as a monument to the priest who provided the funds, as well as to the priest who erected the building.

The first great reverse the Parish of St. Michael sustained was occasioned by "the War of the Rebellion." "Poor Old Missouri" was debatable ground during the entire period, being traversed again and again by northern and southern armies. The sympathies of most of the people were with the South; and many of the young men of St. Michael's left their homes to join the boys in gray. Yet, St. Michael's furnished not a few of the "boys in blue," especially from the ranks of the German settlers. In consequence of the ravages caused by the war, or the resulting distrust and ill-feeling, a number of St. Michael's oldest and best families moved to the more secure and peaceful haunts of Ste. Genevieve, whence they never returned. A memorial to those trying days can be found in the old cemetery near the church, the monument marking the last resting place of Col. Adine Lowe who fell in the battle of Fredericktown, October 21, 1861.

The coming of the railroad seemed destined to repair the injury done by the war, especially as a roundhouse was built and operated in the town. But this advantage was not permanent. The roundhouse was removed, and then the Parish lost a number of substantial families, mostly of Irish descent. The loss of these families proved only a temporary setback to St. Michael's congregation. For during all the years of Father Tucker's administration a constant change was going on in the population of the County; the old French families were losing ground before the steady though slow advance of the German and American immigration. One by one the farms in the bottom lands and mining claims in the hills passed into the hands of enterprising newcomers. The wild lands were gradually reclaimed by new settlers, and the remaining descendants of the pioneers adopted the language and some of the customs of the Americans, many of whom were Catholics from Maryland and Kentucky, and others converts to the Catholic Religion. St. Michael's is, to a great extent, a congregation of converts thoroughly assimilated with the older elements and, although the complexion of the parish is now greatly modified by these changes, yet the old traditions have left their impress on the character of its people. Those that had loved and revered Father Tucker in life keenly felt his loss as a personal bereavement, and many a soul that was admitted into the Church in after years, received its first inspiration of Catholic truth from the saintly life of Father Lewis Tucker.

Some few years before his death Father Tucker thought it best to retire and rest from active duties. At the invitation of Archbishop Kenrick, his personal friend, he went to St. Louis, where he made all necessary arrangements to reside and prepare himself for the eternal years. When he returned to Fredericktown for his last leave-taking, the people, having heard of his determination, gathered around him like children and besought him to remain with them. With tears in his eyes he gave way to them, and said: "My children, I will not leave you until God calls me."

God called him on the eve of November 30th, 1880. Around his deathbed knelt Father O. J. McDonald of Potosi, Father Coony of Iron Mountain, and Father L. C. Wernert of Arcadia. His earthly remains were laid to rest in the old churchyard of St. Michael's by the Most Rev. Archbishop P. J. Ryan. After some time they were conveyed to their final resting place within the sanctuary of St. Michael's Church. And his memory is still in benediction.

## CHAPTER 14

## ST. JOHN'S AND ST. MICHAEL'S IN ST. LOUIS

The rapid growth of St. Louis since 1845 when St. Vincent's Parish was founded, from 45,000 to 62,000 souls in 1848, led to the organization of four additional parishes before the end of 1849: St. John the Apostle and Evangelist and St. Michael for the English-speaking Catholics, Holy Trinity and S. S. Peter and Paul of the Germans. The state of progress in the city may be indicated by the two significant facts, that in 1847 city-lighting with gas began, and in 1848 the telegraph was installed. Only a little more than a quarter century previous to these events, the first steamboat had arrived in St. Louis. From now on the forward march of civilization was assured. The Church was not slow to fall in line.

In November 1847 Father Patrick O'Brien was charged by the Archbishop with the organization of a new Congregation, in what was then the West End of St. Louis. Rev. Patrick O'Brien was born on St. Patrick's day, 1815, in the County of Cork, Ireland. His father, Daniel O'Brien, emigrated with his family in 1839, and settled in the town of Potosi, a short distance from St. Louis. As the young Patrick had received an excellent education, under the immediate care of some learned priests in Cork, and as he had always felt an inclination to the religious life, he entered the Seminary of the Lazarists at the Barrens and, after a course of five years, was ordained priest by Bishop Kenrick in 1846. After ordination the young priest was attached to the Cathedral of St. Louis, and from there was sent on a missionary tour through the entire state. He was accompanied by Father Thomas Burke, C. M.

Father O'Brien was eminently qualified to explore the wild and sparsely settled portions of the country. His father was one of the best civil engineers and surveyors of the day, and had naturally imparted some of his practical knowledge to the youthful Patrick. On his return from the tour, he was again attached to the Cathedral. Father O'Brien's first church was a little frame chapel. He then built the small St. John's Church, the people bringing him bricks for the purpose. The corner stone of this was laid in 1847, Father Timon officiating. This second church became "St. John's Library" and still stands next to St. John's Basilica, which was built a few years later by Father John Bannon. The neighborhood was as yet forest and farmland. Washington Avenue ended in an orchard on Seventh Street, and the devout worshipers had to plod their way along the wood-

ST. JOHN'S CHURCH
Pro-Cathedral during Archbishop Kenrick's Later Years

land paths and unpaved streets to attend mass at St. John's.[1] But
with happy smile and ever ready joke Father O'Brien was there to
greet them. From 1854 to 1858 a number of distinguished priests
served as assistants at St. John's: John O'Hanlon, John Hogan, Eugene
O'Hea.[2]

In 1857 Father O'Brien took a leave of absence and started on
a holiday trip to Ireland from which he returned in May 1858, to become pastor of St. Michael's. On November 4th, 1858, John Bannon
assumed the charge of St. John's Church, Myles Tobyn being assigned
as his assistant. Father Bannon, who until then had been pastor of
the Immaculate Conception Church[3] was transferred to St. John's for
the purpose of erecting a church, suitable to the position of the Coadjutor Bishop Duggan, who was to take up his residence at the new
St. John's. A presbytery, also of large proportions was to be built
in connection with the church. St. John's was planned and built
for the exercise of pontifical functions.

Father O'Brien's departure was keenly· felt by the people as a
bereavement, and the coming of Father Bannon, met no kindly reception; but courage did not forsake the youthful pastor and finally he
triumphed over all opposition. "On Sunday afternoon, the fourteenth of November," he states in his Diary, "at a called
meeting held in the church of St. John, the pastor explained the object of his mission in this parish, his relation to
the Rt. Rev. Coadjutor, and the most Rev. Archbishop's desire to
have a new church in the parish. In response to this address the gentlemen present subscribed their names to the amount affixed thereto in
the list to be found at the other side of this record book, amounting to $4,070.00, which sum, at a subsequent meeting two weeks after-
wards was increased to $5,287.00. The balance of the subscription list
was filled by the solicitations of the· pastor."[4]

The plan for the new edifice was presented by Patrick Walsh and
approved by the Archbishop. Work was begun on February 2nd, 1859.
Contracts for masonry, brick-work and iron casting, were assigned.
On May 1st, the Archbishop laid the corner-stone. The celebrated Jesuit
F. Smarius preached on the occasion. Fathers Feehan, Henry and
O'Reilly, C. M., attended His Grace, and Fathers Ziegler and Tobyn
acted as chanters. Outside the wall the Roman Catholic Total Abstinence
and Benevolent Society were drawn up in double file, surrounding the

---

1 Cf. Rev. Patrick O'Brien, in "Our Pastors in Calvary," pp. 20-22.

2 Chancery Records, St. Louis.

3 This was the first church of the Immaculate Conception in St. Louis. It
stood on Eighth and Chestnut Streets.

4 "Diary of Rev. John Bannon" in "The Church Progress," May 19, 1921.

wall. "Owing to a sudden shower of rain which fell about 4:30 o'clock, the people were thrown into such confusion that the contemplated arrangements for collecting the subscriptions were frustrated, and in consequence only a trifle was received. The rain likewise detracted much from the solemnity of the ceremony as it prevented our using the rich vestments on hand for the occasion."[5]

In October 1859, the roof was constructed on the finished side walls, but, owing to some faulty construction, the lateral pressure caused them to bulge. After a few experiments to rectify matters, the architect sent in his resignation. Father Bannon suggested to his successor, a Mr. Mitchel, the idea of resting the foot of the circular roof on pillars, secured to the walls. This was done and the construction of the building was completed according to the original plan.[6]  It was dedicated on November 4th, 1860, by Archbishop Kenrick. But neither Bishop Duggan nor Father Bannon long enjoyed the use of the stately basilica, Bishop Duggan being appointed to the see of Chicago 1859, and Father John Bannon resigning his rectorship of St. John's after the Fall of Camp Jackson in 1861, to join the Confederate Army as chaplain. Archbishop Patrick J. Ryan, on the occasion of his own leave-taking from his beloved Church of St. John, graciously and tenderly expressed his affection for him, who built the Church, and was his personal friend, Rev. John O'Bannon:

"He built this church, and, having completed it, and being so deeply attached to it, as a priest will be to a church for which he has begged and for which he has fought, loving it tenderly, and loving with that great heart of his, he sacrificed all, and without hesitation left everything; because he heard that there were Catholic young men of this city in the Confederate Army without a chaplain to minister to them who might fall in battle at any moment. He risked his life crossing the lines, was for a time pursued, but with the same high motive and sense of duty and self-sacrificing charity for the young men whom he knew and loved, he made this sacrifice and left an imperishable record of his personal courage and devotedness to the great cause. Twice did the Commanding General order him off the field, and threaten him with arrest because he did not keep within the proper lines when someone had fallen among the rushing balls in the midst of the greatest danger. His heart I am sure is with us tonight."[7]

Father John Bannon after the war went to Ireland and became a member of the Society of Jesus. In 1878 he was residing at Gardiner Street, Dublin.[8] He died in 1905 in his eighty-fifth year.

5   "Diary of Rev. John Bannon," 1. c.

6   Diary, 1. c.

7   Archbishop Ryan, Sermon, in St. John's Church, St. Louis.

8   From a letter of Rev. John Bannon, S.J., to Father Tobyn, July 24, 1883.

Father Bannon's successor at St. John's was the Reverend Patrick Ring.

"Father Ring was born on the 14th of May 1828, in Castlecomer, Kilkenny, Ireland. He came to America in boyhood and made his earlier studies here, but returned to Ireland and entered Carlow College, where he was ordained to the priesthood on the 2nd of June 1860.

He officiated for a brief period in his native land and then came back to St. Louis, crossing the Atlantic on a ship that was burned on the voyage. All were rescued, but the awful experience wrecked the nerves of Father Ring, and Archbishop Kenrick was very considerate of him in consequence."[9]

"In his responsible position, at the head of one of the most prosperous congregations in St. Louis, he won the affections of all, and his unusal learning was appreciated by priests and people. In his pastoral duties he was ably assisted by Father Constantine Smith, but poor health finally compelled him to ask for a transfer to Potosi. The country air and easy duties of this charge failed to restore him, and after a few years he was compelled to take up his residence at Mullanphy hospital. His condition permitted him to be of great use there in the exercise of his priestly offices. Father Ring died at the hospital on February 7th, 1887."[10]

The same causes that led to the foundation of St. John's in 1847, two years later brought on the organization of another Irish-American Church in North St. Louis, St. Michael's on Eleventh and Clinton Streets. This eldest daughter of St. Patrick's was entrusted to the care and priestly zeal of the Rev. John Higginbotham, the one time pastor of Potosi. Father Higginbotham was born on February 2nd, 1830, and came to St. Louis from the diocese of Dublin, in Ireland. He was ordained priest on September 21st, 1845. He was in the prime of manhood when appointed to St. Michael's. He found about one hundred Catholic families within the territory assigned to him. The first church, a frame one, with several rooms attached, stood on the site of the present parochial residence. School there was none, save the public school across the street.[11]

Father Higginbotham remained at St. Michael's until May 1854 when he started on a trip to his native land. After a brief interval filled by Father Patrick Ward, the Reverend Michael Prendergast became pastor of the parish in December 1852. During his pastorate the public school children from the school across the street had a sort of

---

9   Smith, Miss Mary Constance, "Our Pastors in Calvary," p. 35.

10 - Ibidem.

11   Chancery Records.

affiliation with the little church. One of these early pupils, now a Sister of Mercy in St. Louis, remembers that Father Prendergast was often invited to be present at the regular public examinations and afterwards asked to make a little speech. ''And on one occasion his remarks included such an apt comparison between examination day and the last great day of final judgment that reference to it was made again and again by the teachers and children during the rest of the year.'' Father Prendergast prepared me for First Communion,'' says this Religious, ''and I remember we were all under the usual age. He believed, like the late Holy Father, in admiting very little children to the Holy Table. And, as a consequence, we had wonderful confidence in our pastor.''[12]

After the death of Father Prendergast in February 1854 the Rev. William Wheeler succeeded to the rectorship of St. Michael's. ''Father Wheeler was born on January 31st, 1815, a short distance from Dublin, Ireland. His father was an Englishman, a convert to Catholicism, and his mother of Irish parentage. He came to this country about the year 1845 with a band of students and, landing in New York, repaired to St. Louis, where he was ordained on April 25th, 1845. In the following year he was made pastor of St. Patrick's and in September 1852 accompanied Father Higginbotham on his European tour. After his return, Father Wheeler served two years as curate at the Cathedral, and in 1854 he was appointed to the Church of St. Michael as its pastor, to remain there until the Fall of 1855. ''The first ministerial charge of Father Wheeler, was in connection with St. Patrick's Church, and with the exception of a few brief interruptions, he was identified with this parish for twenty-two years . . . . These however, were but episodes in his career, which was usually associated with St. Patrick's Parish.

''In November 1870, Father Wheeler again left for Europe to attend the Council of the Vatican. His position in that body was that of theologian for Bishop Feehan of Nashville, whom he accompanied to Rome. He left St. Louis about the first of February, and in a letter to Father Ryan stated that he proposed making a short tour through Germany and other portions of Continental Europe, and expected to return to St. Louis about the first of May. Father Wheeler was a hard-working and devoted divine, and during the cholera epidemic of 1849 he labored ceaselessly in his ministrations among the sick and dying.''[13] His work at the prisons during the period of the Civil War also forms a glorious chapter in his life. Father Wheeler died in Munich, Bavaria on February 28th, 1870.

---

12  Cf. St. Michael's Church, ''Our Pastors in Calvary,'' p. 169.
13  Scharf, C. T., ''History of St. Louis,'' p. 1659.

On August 1st, 1855, Rev. John Hogan became pastor of St. Michael's, but owing to his missionary zeal left the pleasant parish for the rough and lonesome life in the wilds of North and South Missouri.

In June 1857, Father Patrick A. Feehan came to take his place. During Father Feehan's brief administration, the parish seemed to experience a new springtide. On December 20th, 1857, Bishop Duggan, Coadjutor to Archbishop Kenrick blessed the new Church of St. Michael, the Archangel. Father Feehan never was a good money-gatherer. He never could ask for money. He was both glad and grateful when some ladies of the parish organized a Church Fair to help him meet his building obligations. Father Feehan, also, like his predecessors, was not destined to remain long in the parish of St. Michael. On the occasion of Father Bannon's appointment to St. John's, Father Feehan was transferred to the Church of the Immaculate Conception, at the corner of Eighth and Chestnut Streets.

Father Patrick O'Brien of St. John's in 1857 sojourned in Europe. On his return to St. Louis, he received the appointment to St. Michael's Church. With his old vigor and enterprise he entered upon the discharge of his new and laborious duties; paying off in a very short time the debt of $8000.00 that had for a while burdened the church. Then came an undertaking of still greater importance, the building of the parochial school on Eleventh and Benton Streets, and the Sisters' convent. This was done at a cost of $50,000.00, all of the large sum was paid within a few years.

But the constant strain of building and procuring the means to build proved too much for body and mind. Again a trip across the sea was considered the best, if not the only, remedy. Early in July 1873, Father O'Brien started from New York by the steamer *France* of the National Line. In a few days the good Father found himself growing weaker, and on Sunday, July 13th, he passed peacefully away. His body was committed to the sea.

During his long rectorship of St. Michael's, from 1859-1872, Father O'Brien was assisted in his work by Fathers Ledwith, James O'Brien, Patrick O'Neil, James McCabe and Martin J. Brennan. His immediate successor was the Rev. Andrew Eustace, a cousin of Archbishop Kenrick.

## CHAPTER 15

## THE PARISH OF S. S. PETER AND PAUL

The year of Our Lord 1849 is memorable in the history of St. Louis for the foundation of two of its most prosperous and influential churches, S. S. Peter and Paul's and Holy Trinity, both under German control.

The Records of the former parish begin with June 17th, 1849. For some time previous the spiritual needs of the German Catholics living south of Carroll St. were supplied by the priests of St. Vincent's and of St. Mary's. But the number of Catholics in South St. Louis increased so rapidly, that the Bishop gave way to their wishes and appointed the Rev. Simon Sigrist as their pastor. Simon Sigrist was born February 13th, 1822, at Stotzheim in Alsace.[1] He pursued his theological studies at Strassburg, and was there engaged for the diocese of St. Louis by Vicar-General Melcher in 1847. The company in which he came to America consisted of four priests and five clerical students: among them was Francis X. Weiss and John Anselm. Bishop Kenrick received them with a German address of welcome, July 5th, 1847. After a brief stay at the Seminary on Soulard Street, Simon Sigrist received holy Orders at the hands of Bishop Kenrick. Immediately after his ordination the energetic man was sent as pastor to what was called Meramec. This congregation comprised the Catholic settlers on both sides of the River Meramec, south of the city, and had two churches: the one south of the river dedicated to the Immaculate Conception, and situated at what is now called Maxville, and the other north of the river dedicated to the Assumption, at Mattese Creek. It is probable that the youthful pastor took up his abode at Mattese, and from there paid a monthly visit to Maxville.

Father Sigrist remained at Meramec about one and a half years. Early in 1849 he was appointed to organize the Parish of S. S. Peter and Paul. A building lot on Eighth and Allen Avenue was bought from Thomas Allen, and a small frame church erected upon it. Ere long an addition to the church and a residence for the priest became necessary. The Congregation now decided to buy the entire block, but was prevented from so doing by a lawsuit instituted by Mr. Soulard against Thomas Allen, as to the ownership of the land. After two years' litigation the case was decided in favor of Allen, who then sold the block to Father Sigrist. In the meantime the foundation for a commodious brick church

---

1 Cf. Holweck, F. G., in "Pastoral-Blatt," vol. 58, No. 1.

had been laid. Now, after the title to the land was clear, the building operations that had been suspended were resumed, and on October 23rd, 1853, the second church of S. S. Peter and Paul was dedicated by Archbishop Kenrick with all possible solemnity, Patrick J. Ryan, the future Archbishop, but then only in deacon's order, preaching the sermon. The little frame church was then torn down. School had to be held from the beginning in a private dwelling on Geyer Avenue.

The new structure was built of brick: it had three aisles, a balcony for parishoners on both sides of the organ loft, two rows of windows, and an abbreviated tower. Architecturally it was in nowise remarkable:' yet it seated a large congregation. The cost of building was $18,000.00[2]

From 1854 to 1856 Father Sigrist had as assistants Fathers Bernard Watermans and Casper Doebbener. The Congregation grew still more rapidly than before, but the debt resting on the property had grown to $20,000, by the time that Father Francis S. Goller was transferred from Holy Trinity to S. S. Peter and Paul's, as assistant. Father Sigrist was a man of imposing presence and oratorical ability, but no such financier as the times seemed to require. Dissatisfaction arose among the parishioners. A small but active party began a campaign of abuse, for one reason or another, against Father Sigrist, whilst the better part of the Congregation upheld him. Father Sigrist grew nervous under the strain, and when the malcontents turned their favor to the young assistant, without however finding any encouragement from him, the pastor and his household made it rather unpleasant for Father Goller. At last the assistant priest approached the Archbishop with the request for his removal from S. S. Peter and Paul's or his exeat from the diocese. Thereupon the Archbishop, realizing that Father Sigrist's stay in the rebellious parish could not be productive of any good, appointed Father Goller in his place. Father Sigrist felt chagrined and a large part of the Congregation, which had always admired him as an able and good priest, raised a sullen protest against his sudden and seemingly groundless demotion. As Father Goller was small of stature, especially when compared with the magnificent physique of Sigrist, the people mocked him as being but a child. But Francis Goller soon showed them that, when measured from the chin upwards, and not downwards, he was of a higher stature than their temporary hero, Father Sigrist. No doubt, Father Goller sympathized with the good, though imprudent man: yet the call of the Archbishop and the critical condition of the parish demanded that he remain at his post of duty, however unpleasant or even dangerous it might become. For a short while there seemed to be signs of a schism. Father Sigrist,

---

2  S. S. Peter and Paul's Parish, ''Souvenir of the Diamond Jubilee.''

who regarded the whole proceeding as an act of truculent injustice, seems to have entertained the idea of placing himself at the head of the discontented elements and of forming them into an independent Parish. The fact is that Father Sigrist remained in St. Louis until the end of 1857, without interfering, however, in the affairs of Father Goller's parish. About Christmastide 1857 Father Sigrist received an urgent call from Bishop Maurice de Saint-Palais of Vincennes to take charge of the German Catholics of Indianapolis. Here, at St. Mary's Church, Father Sigrist labored with exemplary zeal and great success until his death, October 28th, 1873.[3]

Father Francis Salesius Goller, the new rector of S. S. Peter and Paul's was born October 27th, 1831, at Freiheit Hagen, Westphalia, of an ancient family of Saxon farmers on the mother's side, and of a Rhineland family of artisans, on the father's part. Westphalian depth of thought and feeling was mingled in their son Francis with Rhineland quickness of wit and genial spirit. Full of the joy of life and fired by youthful ambition, "Arens Franz," as he was called from his mother's ancient farmstead, sought admission in the Collegium Germanicum at Rome, but the outbreak of the cholera in Italy upset the plan. Having a deep admiration for Professor Doellinger, then at the height of his fame, the young student decided to pursue his studies in Munich. But this plan also falling through for reasons unknown, it was determined that Francis Goller should go to the University of Tuebingen, where men of the quality of a Hefele, Kuhn, Albert and Welte were then the bright luminaries of ecclesiastical science. Here in the genial atmosphere of Suabia, amid the monuments of German greatness and solidity, Francis Goller imbibed that love for the deeper parts of theology, and for the great and renowned thinkers of antiquity, an Augustine, a Thomas Aquinas, a Bonaventure, and others, that distinguished him all through life. After his graduation at Tuebingen, the young theologian entered the Seminary of his native diocese of Paderborn. It was here, in the winter 1854-1855 that Vicar-General Melcher met Francis Goller and enkindled in him the liveliest enthusiasm for the missions of America. Having received sub-deaconship in the Cathedral of Paderborn, on Pentecost Sunday 1855, he joined the company of St. Louis missionaries under the guidance of Vicar-General Melcher and started with them for New York and St. Louis, where they arrived in October 1855.

Goller and his friend Casper Doebbener were raised to the priesthood on the Feast of All Saints of the same year, by Archbishop Kenrick in the Cathedral. It was the day of the terrible railway accident caused by the collapse of the new bridge over the Gasconade

---

3 Holweck, 1. c.

River, at which a large number of St. Louis Catholics lost their life. Father Goller filled the position of assistant to Father Anselm at Holy Trinity Church for a brief space of time; then after another short stay at St. Mary's, was appointed assistant, and soon after, successor to Father Sigrist at S. S. Peter and Paul's.[4]

From January 1st, 1858 until his death August 18th, 1910, Father Goller's life was so intimately and inseparably connected with the parish of S. S. Peter and Paul that one cannot think of one without thinking of the other. The congregation soon learnt to understand and appreciate the great qualities of their pastor. Few priests have found deeper love and reverence among their parishioners than Father Francis S. Goller of S. S. Peter and Paul's. His grand monument is the imposing Gothic Church building of stone he began to erect in the Spring of 1873, and which was completed and dedicated to divine service on December 12th, 1875. Bishop Ryan officiated at the dedication services; Bishop Fitzgerald of Little Rock preached the English sermon, Bishop Michael Heiss of Milwaukee was celebrant of the Pontifical Highmass, and Bishop Krantbauer preached in German. Two other Bishops, Seidenbusch of Duluth, and Louis Fink of Leavenworth, Kansas, were in attendance. The Congregation overflowed with joy and gladness in spite of the debt of $92,000.[5]

It was a heavy burden; but the Pastor's far-sighted prudence and the unselfish cooperation of his assistants, Fathers Francis Ruesse, Henry Groll and William Klevinghaus, who were like the early Christians of Jerusalem, "but one heart and one soul," enabled him to liquidate the entire debt by January 10th, 1887. It was now determined to complete the tower, and to erect a parish residence of suitable proportion and architectural beauty. The priests took possession of their new home on January 2nd, 1889. The tower was completed in 1890 at a total cost of $33,000. Five new bells were installed in March the next year. The Parish Church of S. S. Peter and Paul is counted even today, as one of the finest churches in the United States. At the time it was built, St. Louis did not have many beautiful churches. Father Goller's example, no doubt, had a notable influence on the development of church architecture in the West. Father Goller's main motive in devoting all his energy and income to the erection of a worthy temple of God, was besides this highest of all motives, his pious solicitude for the poor: "I wanted," he said, "this church to be as beautiful as possible, that the poor, of whom there are many among us, might also

---

4 Abbelen, Father. Zum Goldenen Jubilaeum des Hochw Franz S. Goller. Holweck, Father F. G., "Franz Goller, Priester," in "Pastoral-Blatt," vol. 51, No. 7.

5 Holweck, 1. c.

have a beautiful house which they could call their own.''[6]     Many an
assembly of the highest dignitaries of the Church, Cardinals, Archbishops and Bishops, has this sublime house of God and of God's poor,
witnessed within its walls.    Its fame went out to all corners of our
country.    Many a priest received his inspiration there for an equally
noble effort.

But great as a church-builder, Father Goller was greater still as
a builder of schools.    As early as 1859 he introduced the Poor School-
Sisters de Notre Dame into the schools of S. S. Peter and Paul.    This
was the second colony of these excellent teachers and religious in the
diocese.    S. S. Peter and Paul's Parish was a fruitful field for the
growth of the Order: at least one hundred and sixty members were
added to it in the course of time from the ranks of S. S. Peter and
Paul's Congregation.    The Schools of the Parish had an average attendance of 1,300 pupils.

The boys were at first under the care of lay-teachers, then under
the members of a religious community founded by Father Goller himself in 1867, and approved by Archbishop Kenrick, and when they disbanded in 1872, by secular teachers and Sisters de Notre Dame.    On St.
Bernard's Day, however, on August 20th, 1897, the Brothers of Mary
arrived from Dayton.    Brother Albert the Superior was already on the
spot to receive them.    The boys of the Parish were placed in their care.
In 1898 the High School Building was erected, and Brother Louis joined the community.    The High School was continued until the establishment of the diocesan High Schools claimed most the pupils, and so
brought on the closing of the parochial institution.    The higher grades
of the boy-school, however, are still in charge of the Brothers of Mary.[7]

Father Goller's efforts in behalf of the parochial school, were of
decisive influence at the Third Plenary Council of Baltimore, which he
attended in an official capacity.    Fathers Bonacum and Goller were
Archbishop Kenrick's theologians at the Council.    It was well-known
that the question of the necessity of parochial schools would come up
for discussion.    Former Councils had praised and advocated, and highly recommended the establishment of such schools: Father Goller and
his friends saw that, if there was no legislation on the matter, all
recommendations would be in vain.    They, therefore, set their heart upon
getting a few clear-cut statutes requiring the establishment of parochial
schools wherever it was possible.    There were many who agreed with
this view and purpose: but it was to be feared that, among the multiplicity of important matters, this most important matter might be
placed in a position where only doomsday should awaken it:    Father

---

6  Holweck, l. c.
7  Diamond Jubilee, Souvenir, pp. 17 and 18.

Goller used his thorough knowledge of the question, and his wide acquaintance with members of the Council, to secure the legislation which the Council actually adopted: "that within two years after the promulgation of the Council a parochial school be established and perpetually sustained at every church, where such a school does not already exist," and "that a priest, who prevents by his negligence or after repeated episcopal admonitions takes no steps to erect and sustain a school, deserves to be removed from his church," and "that all parishes are bound to support such schools, and all parents to send their children to them, unless they be legitimately dispensed." These decrees contained in Titulo VI, of the Council, and form the Magna Charta of our present magnificent Catholic School-System.

Of course, Father Goller was not the only member of the Council that fought for this legislation: but he certainly was one of its foremost advocates. In season and out of season, he spoke of the parochial school, the Catholic School, heartening his friends, enlightening his opponents, and jolting the careless with some searching question, giving a tired feeling to some, exasperating others, but never tiring, never exasperated himself, but ever cheerful, though earnest, and pushing on to victory. Father Goller was not alone in the fight, but he was in the very midst of it, and his cause was right, as the issue has amply proved. That is high merit for any man.[8]

And so, when for the last time, danger threatened the parochial school system from distinguished churchmen, of best intentions, but of misguided judgments, Father Goller was among its foremost defenders, by clear exposition in writing, and caustic speech, repelling attacks and clearing up ramifications of the matter. His zeal was not a gentle rivulet ending in a stagnant pool, but a restless fire that burnt away the rust from the iron. He knew no hatred or ill will: the welfare of God's people was ever his highest law. When, on the 9th day of April, Cardinal Satolli, in company with Archbishop Kain, visited S. S. Peter and Paul's, finding an assembly of 1,200 children of the School to greet him in the Sacred Place, Father Goller addressed the Pope's Representative in classic Latin, emphasizing the absolute necessity of the Parochial School in a country that had no traditions and no liberty of teaching religion in the public school:

"Your Eminence: Entering our church of S. S. Peter and Paul you meet more than twelve hundred children who are acquiring the rudiments of Christian Doctrine in our parochial school and receive from the care and zeal of our good Sisters instructions in good morals

---

[8] Of course, Father Goller met severe condemnation at the hands of the "Western Watchman" and others, but as it was not a personal matter with him, he never paid any attention to rude personalities.

as well as in the sciences and arts, so that they may become good citizens of the State and worthy members of the kingdom of God. For this, our country, where the Catholics are living dispersed among the many unbelievers and heretics, it is almost impossible, certainly, very difficult, that Catholic truth should remain the rule of life, unless it be instilled into the minds of the young from their earliest years. Therefore, I do not hesitate to affirm, that, in the shadow of every church that is really flourishing and ·bringing forth fruit for everlasting life, you will find a parochial school; where, however, you find no parochial school, the church will appear neglected, and I fear, will soon fall into ruin.

"And if you should find at times such a parish showing some life and progress, it is because it is drawing its vigor and vital spirit from other parishes, that are blest with parochial schools, whilst its own offspring is gradually dying out. This temple has been built by the parents of these children, and it is filled three times on every Sunday and feast day, from the altar to the portals, by the multitude of the faithful. But I am fully convinced, that, if the parochial school should be suspended, after thirty years only a few pious women and their infants would be present at the solemnities of the church."[9]

In response His Eminence congratulated the priests and the people on the magnificence and solidity of their Church edifice and for their zeal in caring for the lambs of the flock by laying even deeper and building more solidly, the foundation and superstructure of the spiritual edifice ·in their souls by·thorough Catholic education.

That the distinguished pastor of S. S. Peter and Paul was fully alive to the dangerous tendencies of the times is further evinced by the loyal interest he extended to the *Daily Amerika*, a newspaper in the German language, conducted in the spirit of Catholic principles and ever ready to meet the rude and aften impudent attacks of infidel and heretic on the Church. Through his influence the noble convert, Dr. Edward Preuss, was appointed editor of the paper at a time when infidel snobbery needed a gentlemanly dressing.

And Dr. Preuss was the man to bring down many a proud Goliath from his cocksure position. Every Sunday found Dr. Preuss as a most welcome guest at the hospitable board of his staunchest friend, Father Francis Goller.

The parish of S. S. Peter and Paul has given to the Church at least twenty-two priests:[10] the number of Sisters has already been mentioned.

---

9  The address in Latin and German may be found in the "Daily Amerika" of April 10, 1896; and in English in the "Church Progress" of April 10, 1896.

10  A list of these priests is given in "Souvenir of Diamond Jubilee," pp. 15 and 16.

The terrible cyclone of May 27th, 1896 struck the church of S. S. Peter and Paul with indescribable fury; the roof was torn to pieces and scattered to the winds, but the heavy walls stood firm under the shock and counter-shock, as firm as the confidence of the Pastor, that all would soon be repaired and restored. This hope was not disappointed.[11]

The daily life of the pastor and his assistants at S. S. Peter and Paul's was an ideal one. The supreme direction was with the pastor, who on his part, wished to be no more than "primus inter pares." Each had his particular duties and offices, each had his own circle of penitents and parishioners, each had his Cathechism classes to attend, and each made the pastor, or rather the church of S. S. Peter and Paul's, his main beneficiary. One by one they took their departure: Father Francis Ruesse, on April 13, 1898; Father Goller himself, August 18, 1910; and Father William Klevinghaus, on February 2nd, 1915: leaving us only the dearest one of all, the present senior of the archdiocese, Father Henry Groll.[12] Five years before his death, on the occasion of his Golden Jubilee of the priesthood, the pastor of S. S. Peter and Paul was honored by the Pope with the title of Domestic Prelate of His Holiness. His successor as pastor of S. S. Peter and Paul was another Domestic Prelate, the Very Reverend O. J. S. Hoog, Vicar-General of the Archdiocese.

---

[11] At sunrise the next day Father Goller engaged a Building Firm to restore what the cyclone had just destroyed.

[12] Since these words were written, the good Father Groll died, rich in years, and rich in merits, November 20, 1926.

## CHAPTER 16

## HOLY TRINITY PARISH, AND ITS ELDEST DAUGHTER

North of the city-limits of St. Louis a small settlement had sprung up during the forties of last century, which was incorporated in 1845 and bore the name of Bremen. Among the first citizens of the town we find the names of Angelrodt and Mallinckrodt. But within ten years Bremen lost its separate entity being incorporated in the city of St. Louis. The name Bremen, however, like that of Carondelet, the southern surburb, still retains its former place in the memory and use of the people.

The nearest church for the German Catholics of Bremen was St. Joseph's: but even this place of worship was sufficiently remote from their habitations to excite in their hearts a desire for a Church of their own. In the Spring of 1848 a representative Committee of six was sent to Vicar-General Melcher, to represent to him their forlorn condition in spiritual matters, and to ask him for permission to build a church in Bremen. The number of Catholics in the district, however, seemed too small as yet, to warrant the erection of a church among them, and the cautious Vicar-General counselled to wait a year or so. But nothing daunted by the polite refusal, they marched to Archbishop Kenrick, and explained conditions. The Archbishop cordially acceded to their request. The people of Bremen, Catholics and non-catholics, were over-joyed at the prospect of having a church in their town. Mr. Mallinckrodt donated a lot on Mallinckrodt and Eleventh Streets, and Bernard Farrar gave a large plot of land on Mallinckrodt and Fourteenth Streets, on which the erection of a church building and a schoolhouse was begun in July 1848. The schoolhouse was a two story building, the upper story was intended for the pastor's apartments. There was, as yet no priest assigned to the place. At the cornerstone laying the Jesuit Father Patschowski of St. Joseph's preached the sermon. When the Church was completed Archbishop Kenrick dedicated it under the in-vocation of the Most Holy Trinity, having appointed the Rev. Theodore Laurensen as its first pastor in January 1849. On the day of dedication, Trinity Sunday 1849, Mr. Mallinckrodt gave a bell to the new congrega-tion. All things seemed to be going as merry as the proverbial marriage bell: but there were some surprising changes in store.[1]

---

1 "Das Katholische Deutschtum von St. Louis in Seinen 20 Gemeinden" 1896, pp. 42-53. "Das Katholische Deutschtum," p. 43.

Before the close of the year 1849 Father Laurensen left the parish; and the Rev. Joseph Blaarer took his place; but only until September 1850, when Father John Anselm succeeded him. The number of Baptisms during Father Anselm's administration of five years rose from seventy-one to one hundred and fifty-five annually, and the number of marriages from twenty-seven to fifty-eight.

Archbishop Kenrick came year by year for Confirmations. In the summer of 1851 the Congregation bought a tract of land on Florissant Road west of O'Fallon Park for the purpose of establishing a cemetery. At the blessing of this "God's Acre" as the Germans called it, the Fathers Siegrist, Patschowski, S. J., Weber, S. J., Wheeler, Alleman and Anselm, the pastor of Holy Trinity were present. The large sum of money which was borrowed from the Archbishop's Bank for the church became due in 1854, but as the Congregation could not raise the amount, the cemetery property was offered and accepted in part-payment.[2] But other pressing needs demanded new loans: the church was entirely too small for the rapidly growing parish, and on May 18th, 1856, the cornerstone of the new brick church was laid with appropriate solemnities. Father Simon Sigrist preaching the sermon, and the two German Catholic organizations, the Orphan Society and the Benevolent Society, taking part in the festivities.[3]

In November Father Francis Goller was appointed by Vicar-General Melcher as assistant to Father Anselm at Holy Trinity Parish. Father Anselm, a native of Nancy in Lorraine, was a truly pious priest, a member of the Third Order of St. Francis, and very exact in the observance of its rules, but rather exacting in his demand that his assistant conform to the same rigid practices.

Father Goller demurred. His view of life did not coincide with that of his pastor, and perhaps in consequence of this, Father Goller was transferred to St. Mary's Church, and soon after to S. S. Peter and Paul's. A good deal of dissatisfaction ensued. Father Anselm was blamed for the removal of his able assistant, and the clamor against the pastor grew so loud and wide-spread, that the Archbishop felt obliged, for the peace of the Congregation, to replace Father Anselm with the newly arrived and very capable Father Casper Doebbener, a special friend of Francis Goller.[4] On June 22nd, 1856, Father Doebbener organized a Building Society of ninety members, with the

---

2 Cf. "Calvary Cemetery" in Part III, Book I, ch. 24 of this History. The old Trinity Cemetery having been long disused was given to the city by Archbishop Glennon.

3 "Das Katholische Deutschtum," pp. 43 and 44.

4 "Das Katholische Deutschtum," p. 44. Also Holweck, "Pastoral-Blatt," 51, 7.

purpose of providing funds for the Church, but with the result of piling up debts. The latent rigor of the Congregation, however, is shown in the fact ·that a large part of its territory could be safely de-tached from it, and erected into the new flourishing parish of St. Lib-ory's. The new Holy Trinity Church was consecrated by Archbishop Kenrick, on November 1859. On the very day of the dedication three Redemptorist Fathers started an eight-day mission which had a salutary quieting effect upon the Congregation.

The old church was remodelled for a school, which was now placed in charge of the Franciscan Sisters, from the Motherhouse at Olden-burg, Indiana. Three Sisters of this Congregation arrived in St. Louis December 28, 1859, and opened school with one hundred and thirty-five pupils on January 1860. The boys, however, were taught by a lay-teacher.

The founder of this Sisterhood, Father Francis Joseph Rudolf, came in the autumn of that year to visit the little Community. On paying his respects to Archbishop Kenrick, he was invited to transfer the motherhouse of the Congregation to St. Louis; but after due con-sultation with the Bishop of Vincennes and Mother Superior Antonia, he firmly declined the invitation. Father Doebbener had freely given the lot on which the school building stood to the Sisters: the Sisters later on bought the adjoining property, and also a small farm of forty acres in the county. In 1884 the new commodious school building and convent of the Sisters was completed under the pastorship of Father Brinkhoff, and in January 1894 the Sisters, at the request of Father John N. Hoffman took charge at St. Henry's Church having an attend-ance of one hundred and ninety-three pupils.

In order to have room for a proper parochial residence the parish bought the adjoining lots at a cost of $4300. Building operations were begun, but owing to hard times had to be suspended indefinitely, referring the pastor and his assistant, the Franciscan Father, Servatius Altmicks, to the shelter of the old narrow quarters, until 1864, when the new commodious residence was completed at an expense of $7500.

In spite of his many cares and sacrifices, Father Doebbener's en-ergies did not relax, but even sought new fields to conquer for God. Towards the north lay the little German settlement called Baden. Its few but earnest Catholics attended services at Holy Trinity Church, at a distance of at least three miles. But there was a convent of the Carme-lite Nuns in the Old Clay Mansion on what is now Calvary Cemetery where Father Edmund Saulnier was chaplain. The Chaplain had the residence at some distance from the Convent, in a four room house, one room serving as the priest's private chapel, where the people of the neighborhood were privileged to attend mass and receive holy Communion. For Confessions they rode or walked to Holy Trinity Church. Thus it came about that the pastor of Holy Trinity became interested in the Catholics of Baden, the majority of whom were German immigrants, the others of French and Irish extraction. Father Doebbener expressed himself as ready to help them in every way to get a Church of their own. Two plots of ground were offered; Archbishop Kenrick decided to buy the two acres of woodland in the town of Baden, the site of the present parish building.[5]

Father Doebbener, the old Prussian cavalry soldier, brought new energy into the proceedings. The parishioners hauled the rock and ,sand for the foundation. In 1864 the foundation was completed; the corner stone for the brick superstructure was laid September 27th, by the pastor who also made an eloquent address. Two train loads of Catholics, among them the members of the German and Irish Catholic Societies of St. Louis, graced the occasion. Father Phelan also made an address to the assembled multitude in his crisp and clear English. The winter 1863-1864 was very mild. The bricks were made and burnt on the place. Sand was brought from the Mississippi, and thus the walls of the new Temple of God began to rise higher and higher until the roof covered all and the church was ready for dedication on May 3rd, 1864. It was the Feast of the Finding of the Cross. Accordingly the church was named for the Holy Cross of Christ, but the exaltation of the Holy Cross was chosen as Titular Feast. Of course, many things were still lacking in the new church: there was no ceiling, no plastering, no communion rail, no proper altar, and no pastor. All the money the parish had raised was spent.[6]

At first the Sunday services were performed by the founder and builder of the church, Father Doebbener: later on they were performed alternately by Father Doebbener and his assistant, Father Frederick Brinkhoff. One of them would binate at the Holy Trinity Church, whilst the other rode to Baden to say mass and preach and then to gallop back to Bremen to sing the Highmass there. The parish of the Holy Cross grew and prospered and in 1864 built a small brick house for the pastor's residence. Father Brinckhoff took possession of the parish in November 1864, as the first Pastor of Holy Cross Parish; but, his regime was cut short by his transfer to Holy Trinity Parish as successor to Father Doebbener. Father Casper Doebbener in 1865 seems to have felt a certain exhaustion after the herculean effort of the last few years and accordingly asked Vicar-General Melcher for a leave of absence. A visit to his old home would surely restore his health and equanimity,

---

[5] Wigger, Peter, ''Goldenes Jubilaeum der Hl. Kreuz-Gemeinde zu Baden,'' St. Louis, 1914.

[6] Wigger, op. cit., pp. 15 and 16.

but the Vicar-General thought the priest's ability and resourcefulness could not be spared under present circumstances. Father Doebbener was determined to leave, transferred the entire financial care and responsibility to the Board of Trustees of the Parish that were elected by the Building Society, and departed for Europe without express permission. It was a mistake, as Father Doebbener found on his return from Europe: he was no longer persona grata in the diocese, and he wended his way regretfully to Terre Haute, Indiana, where he labored with pious zeal and success among the German Catholics; until in the seventies he returned to St. Louis.[7]

Father Frederick Brinckhoff on his accession to the pastorate of the Holy Trinity Church, found a church-debt of $20,000, and general discontent in the Congregation. One of the new pastor's first official acts was the dissolution of the Building Society, after this the spirit of peace once more hovered over the disturbed elements, and grateful calm returned with all its blessings. Within the next twelve months Holy Trinity Church three newly ordained priests celebrated their first holy Mass in the Church: Father Herman Wigger, on June 25th, 1865; Theodor Kussmann and Joseph Helwig on June 5th, 1866.

Financial matters were not so favorable. Archbishop Kenrick had advanced $22,000.00 to the Congregation, and in 1868 demanded repayment, as he intended to close his banking business. In order to meet this call, the parishoners decided to organize a bank of their own. With the proceeds of the sale of the stock, they paid the Archbishop's claim. The Bank continued operations until the year 1876.[8]

From now on the course of Holy Trinity Parish ran smoothly in the grooves assigned it. Societies were formed, missions given, a fine church choir was organized and a large school building erected; and lastly the Parish itself was incorporated under the state-laws.[9] In 1886 Father Brinckhoff made a journey to his old home, and on his return in the Fall of the year received an enthusiastic reception from his parishioners. But the good Father's health was undermined by the labors of years spent in building up the parish. He died on March 31st, 1887, in the fifty-first year of his age.

For a short period Father John L. Gadell administered the affairs of the Church but on May 12, Father Joseph Schroeder became pastor. At a parish meeting held on June 12th, the trustees made the announcement that a debt of $33,000.00, was resting upon the church. Father

---

7   Chancery Records.

8   Archbishop Kenrick's Account Book in 1870, charges the Holy Trinity Parish with $5,576.68 and marked it ''remitted.''

9   ''Das Katholische Deutschtum in St. Louis,'' p. 42.

Schroeder set to work resolutely to cancel the debt, and to raise a fund for a new church. All this was accomplished in due time and before his death the grand Gothic structure, one of the finest in the city, was completed in the Fall of 1899 and was dedicated by Archbishop Kain on October 22nd, 1899. Father Joseph Schroeder was a good faithful priest, of a quiet, retiring nature, but of a firm character. He was born in St. Louis on November 19th, 1849, made his studies with the Franciscan Fathers of Teutopolis and at the Salesianum in Milwaukee. Before his appointment to Holy Trinity Church, Father Schroeder had served with patient zeal the churches at Portage des Sioux, Bridgeton, and Linn. He died on June 17th, 1907, and was succeeded by Father Joseph Schaefers, October 1st, 1907, who died before the end of the year, to be succeeded in turn by the Rev. Joseph Lubeley.

The parish numbers nine hundred families, and has nine hundred children in its school. In 1909 a fine rectory was built on the site of the old one, and the church was tastefully frescoed. The beautiful church was severely damaged by the cyclone of 1927, but has been restored and, in a manner, improved, since the cataclysm.

## Chapter 17

## THE REDEMPTORISTS AT THE CATHEDRAL

During the pastorship of Father Simon Augustin Paris from 1844 to 1856, the affairs of the Cathedral parish ran in smooth, perhaps even sluggish courses. The establishment of the new and vigorous parishes all around the old mother drew away from her many of her best supporters.[1] The usual ministrations of the church were, no doubt, zealously offered to the remnants of the old Creole families. Father Patrick J. Ryan, from 1857 to 1861, brings back to the venerable monument of Bishop Rosati's Cathedral an after-glow of its former glories. His commanding and graceful presence, his lambent play of wit and kindly humor, and his truly remarkable flow of language gave Father Ryan a widespread fame and popularity. From all parts of the city the people would flock to the Cathedral whenever Father Ryan was announced as the preacher. But this enthusiastic audience was directed from the Cathedral to the new Church of the Annunciation, which had been built for Father Ryan during his absence in Europe with the Archbishop.[2] Father Ryan's successors at the Cathedral were Rev. Raphael Cappezuto (1861-1862) and Father F. M. Kielty 1863-1866. In 1866, the care of the Cathedral parish was entrusted to a band of Redemptorist Fathers, under the Rev. Louis Dold as Superior. As early as 1861, the Redemptorist Fathers had received a hearty invitation from the Archbishop to found a house of their Order in the archdiocese. The invitation was repeated in 1865, and the offer of the Cathedral parish as a temporary field of labor was made to them; the Bishop retaining for his own use the office and adjoining parlor in the Residence at a rental of $1,000 per year. The new Pastor, Rev. Louis Dold, arrived on August 27th, 1866 and was joined within two days by his assistants Egidius Smulders and Ferreol Girardey, and the Brothers Jacques and Peter. The three men chosen to rule over

---

1 Every year of this period showed a deficit of a thousand dollars more or less which the Archbishop invariably made good. Towards the end of Father Paris' administration, the Archbishop built the present Cathedral dwelling, (in 1852), and in the following year made some changes and improvements in the Cathedral, erected the present society and school house. The cost of these improvements was $15,923.19; the Parish subscription amounted to $4,416.26, which left a deficit of $11,506.92, to be paid by His Grace.

2 Under Bishop Ryan's pastorship at the Cathedral this annual deficit ran merrily on, reaching within twenty-five years the sum of $57,082.98. Archbishop Kenrick, however, balanced this account from year to year by contributing the required amount.

the destines of the Cathedral, and to lay the foundations of their Order in St. Louis, were remarkable men, each in his own way.

Father Louis Dold the Superior was born at Mons, Belgium October 28th, 1821. He made his religious profession November 6th, 1843, and was ordained priest December 21st, 1850. He possessed an extraordinary talent for languages. He was Lector of Dogmatic Theology in the Redemptorist Seminary at Cumberland, Md. In the fifties, he was sent on a most difficult mission to the Island of St. Thomas, the account of which, in his graphic descriptions, reads like a romance. He was a missionary in Chili, South America, in 1861, after which, returning to the United States, he worked with zeal in many capacities, especially as a missionary preacher of great power. He made a voyage to Palestine, an account of which he has left in his writings.[3]

Father Giles Smulders was born November 1st, 1815, he is a Hollander by birth, and was educated in Belgium. He was one of the Redemptorist Pioneers in the United States. He founded the Redemptorist house in Detroit, Mich., and also founded a Religious Order of Women, "The Sisters of the Immaculate Heart of Mary," who labor principally in teaching parochial schools in the Diocese of Detroit. When the Paulist Fathers, under Father Hecker, seceded from the Redemptorist Order, in the year 1858, Father Smulders, with great courage, energy and faith in God, took charge of the English missions. At the outbreak of the war between the States, Father Smulders, being an intense sympathizer with the Southern cause, became a Chaplain in the Confederate army. He loved to preach the word of God in its native simplicity and strength.[4]

Father Ferreol Girardey was born in France April 21st, 1839, came to United States very early in life, he received his education in New Orleans, at St. Charles College, Maryland, and at the Seminary of the Redemptorists at Cumberland, Maryland. He was raised to the priesthood on June 11th, 1862. A Compendium of the History of Philosophy was the literary fruit of his years of teaching in College. He was one of the contributors to the *New Orleans Catholic Morning Star*. He had ever shown himself devoted to the Catholic press, and generally contributed to the Catholic papers in his vicinity. *The Western Cross*, Kansas City, and *The Michigan Catholic*, have both been favored by the strength of his support.[5]

When the Fathers arrived in St. Louis the city numbered a population of about 204,000. The cholera, in its most virulent form, was epidemic. The death rate for a while was more than one hundred daily. Though the Fathers were frequently called upon day and night

---

3 Leaves from The History of St. Alphonsus Church, St. Louis, pp. 3 and 4.
4 Ibidem, pp. 4 and 5.
5 Ibidem, pp. 6 and 7.

to minister at the bedsides of cholera patients, God protected them and they escaped unscathed.

The Cathedral parish, comprising the business and manufacturing district of the city, was large in extent, though small as to the actual number of its families. It entailed, however, much labor on the priest. Within the parish limits were situated the St. Louis Hospital, founded nearly sixty-five years ago, and under the direction of the Sisters of Charity; a boys' school, under the care of the Christian Brothers, with an attendance of about sixty boys; a girls' school, located on the corner of Fifth and Walnut Streets, with an attendance of one hundred pupils, in charge of the Sisters of Charity; also several large hotels, which gave employment to many Catholic men and women. Owing, doubtless to the troubled condition of the times, the parish and church were in a most neglected state. Smoke and dirt gave to the church a forbidding aspect. High Mass was no longer sung on Sundays and Holydays. As only a few people came to church, they were regaled with a very short sermon. Many persons belonging to the parish stayed away or went elsewhere. Few pews were rented. The yearly expense exceeded the income by thousands of dollars. Temporal and spiritual ruin threatened.[6]

The Fathers, long accustomed to such labors, took in the situation at a glance, and immediately threw themselves with great zeal into the work of reorganization. High Mass on Sundays and Festivals was resumed. The church was soon cleaned and repainted. Restored to its pristine beauty, it once more became attractive in the eyes of the people.

In October 1866, a mission was given at the Cathedral, with gratifying results. A special effort was made to bring back to the church the French Catholics scattered throughout the parish. A special Sunday service at 9 o'clock with Mass and French sermon was inaugurated.[7]

On May 8th, 1867, the Community received a most valuable acquisition in the person of Rev. Joseph Henning.

Father Henning was born in New York City, November 17th, 1838. He was educated principally in New York and Cumberland, Maryland. Having pronounced his vows as a Redemptorist, December 10th, 1855, he pursued his studies and was elevated to the sacred priesthood June 11th, 1862.[8]

In the meantime the Fathers were laying the plans for their church and residence on Grand Avenue. It was the first day of Our Lady's month, 1867, that ground was broken for the St. Alphonsus Church. Father Dold, who had made special studies in architecture, drew the

---

6  Leaves from the History of St. Alphonsius Church, p. 10.

7  Ibidem, pp. 10 and 11.

8  Ibidem, p. 12.

plans for the edifice, a strictly Gothic structure, entirely of stone. A big-hearted Irishman, John Doyle, promised a donation of $7,000 and paid $1,000 at once, and the remaining $6,000 by bequest. As the work was progressing but slowly, the Fathers determined to remove to the new location before the completion of the church. December 1st, 1868, was the memorable day on which they bade farewell to the Cathedral residence and turned westward, while Father Myles W. Tobyn took possession, and continued the good work until February 1886.

Of the sixteen bishops consecrated by Archbishop. Kenrick the three first and the six last, received the episcopal dignity, not in the St. Louis Cathedral, but some in the churches of their Order, some in their own parish churches, and some in other Cathedrals.

Bishop James Van de. Velde of Chicago and Bishop John B. Miége, Vicar Apostolic of Indian Territory, both being Jesuits, chose for the place of their consecration the Church of St. Francis Xavier in St. Louis; the one on February, 11th, 1849; and the other on March 25, 1851.

Bishop John McGill of Richmond was consecrated in the Cathedral of Bardstown, November 10th, 1850. The following seven Bishops were consecrated by Archbishop Kenrick in the St. Louis Cathedral: Anthony O'Regan of Chicago, on July 25th, 1854; James Duggan, Coadjutor Bishop of St. Louis, and third Bishop of Chicago, on May 3rd, 1857, Clement Smith, a Trappist, Bishop of Dubuque, on the same day; James Whelan, a Dominican, Bishop of Nashville, and James O'Gorman, Trappist, Bishop of Raphanea and Vicar Apostolic of Nebraska on May 8th, 1859; Thomas Grace, Bishop of St. Paul, on July 24th, 1895; Patrick Feehan, Bishop of Nashville, was the last of the Bishops consecrated in the old St. Louis Cathedral, the Archbishop officiating as consecrating Prelate. He was consecrated on the 1st of November 1865, the thirteenth Anniversary of his ordination as a priest. Bishop Feehan governed the Diocese of Nashville for fifteen years, until the 10th of September, 1880, when he was created the first Archbishop of Chicago. Of the remaining six Bishops John Hennessey of Dubuque was consecrated in St. Raphael's Cathedral of his own episcopal See, on September 30th, 1866, and Bishop Joseph Melcher of Green Bay, in St. Mary's Church, St. Louis on July 12th, 1868. Bishop John Hogan of St. Joseph, Bishop Patrick J. Ryan, Coadjutor of St. Louis and Archbishop of Philadelphia, Bishop Thomas Bonacum of Lincoln, Nebraska, and Bishop John J. Hennessey of Wichita were all consecrated in the pro-cathedral, the Church of St. John the Apostle.

## ECCLESIASTICAL POLITICS

The Seventh Provincial Council of Baltimore held under Archbishop Eccleston in May 1849, was attended by Archbishop Peter Richard Kenrick. His Theologians were Fathers Simon A. Pavis and Thomas Foley.[1] The opening sermon preached by the new Archbishop of the West made a deep impression on the assembled prelates: The main business of the assembly was the extension and regulation of the ecclesiastical organization. The outstanding matter for discussion was the mode of selecting candidates for the episcopal office: It has appeared good to the Fathers of the Council that the commendation of priests to be elevated to the episcopal dignity should be made according to the usage already sanctioned by the Holy See: the Archbishop however, of the Province, to which the diocese, that is to be provided with a new pastor, belongs, shall send the commendation of the priests that are proposed, to the other archbishops, who shall then make known their judgment on the priests to recommend, to the Holy See''[2] The Sacred Congregation of the Propaganda approved of this mode of selecting candidates for the episcopacy, on August 10, 1850.[3] This new Decree refers to a former Decree, June 14, 1834, in which it is stated that the bishops can only speak of recommending, never of electing, nominating or demanding the appointment of any priest they propose.[4]

Archbishop Samuel Eccleston of Baltimore died on April 22nd, 1851. Four days later the Bishop of Philadelphia wrote to his brother: "On occasion of the burial of the Archbishop of Baltimore we held a conference to consult upon the choice of his successor, as we knew of no disposition made by (The Archbishop) himself on this point. The choice of all who were present, that is, Pittsburg and Richmond and myself, agreed upon the Bishop of Buffalo (John Timon) whom we hope to see transferred (to Baltimore) by the Holy See. We wish to have you send your choice to the S. Congregation as soon as possible. I wrote this hastily April xxvi day, MDCCCLI.''[5] But the writer himself Francis Patrick Kenrick was promoted to the See of

---

1 Concilia Baltimorensia, 1851, p. 266.
2 Concilia Baltimorensia, pp. 290 and 291.
3 Concilia Baltimorensia, p. 117.
4 Concilia Baltimorensia, p. 120.
5 Kenrick-Frenaye Correspondence.

(122.)

Baltimore August 3rd, 1851, and appointed Apostolic Delegate to preside at a Plenary Council to be held in May of 1852.

Archbishop Kenrick's suffragan see of Chicago was deprived of its first Bishop, William Quarter, by a sudden and unexpected death on April 10th, 1848. According to the rule then in force, the American Bishops were called upon to submit a so-called "terna," three names of those, whom they considered worthy and competent. Bishop Francis Patrick wrote to Archbishop Peter Richard: "I consider James Van de Velde as worthy of the first choice on account of the natural gifts and qualities of the man, and I think that his promotion is to be urged, even by the Pope's instruction, at this time particularly, in order to give this testimonial of the American Bishops in favor of the Society of Jesus so much vexed and harassed."

On June 1, the Bishop of Philadelphia returns to the subject:

"In the meantime I am praying for the appointment of Father Van de Velde as Bishop of Chicago; for aside from his good moral life he has piety, and he knows languages, German also (as I think), in which case he will be acceptable to the people of his own tongue."[6]

Towards the end of 1848, the news arrived that Father Van de Velde, S.J., had been nominated Bishop of Chicago. In the beginning of December the Brief "freeing him from allegiance to the Society of Jesus and appointing him to the vacant see of Chicago" was placed in his hands. The humble Jesuit was reluctant to accept; but on being assured by Archbishop Kenrick that the Pope's words implied a command, Bishop Van de Velde submitted himself to the will of the Holy Father. He was consecrated by Archbishop Kenrick in the College Church at St. Louis, on February 11, 1849.

Bishop Van de Velde entered upon his new and grave duties, but he soon found them too onerous and disagreeable for a man of his shattered health and peace-loving disposition. He resigned. The Prefect of the Congregation of the Propaganda, Cardinal Fransoni, wrote him a letter of encouragement and high appreciation. The Bishop then dispatched a second letter to Rome, tendering his unqualified resignation. The Sacred Congregation referred the matter to the First Plenary Council of Baltimore, which assembled at Baltimore in May, 1852. But instead of accepting the Bishop's resignation, the Fathers of the Council agreed to divide Illinois into two dioceses and make Quincy the see of the southern portion. Bishop Van de Velde now offered to accept Quincy, but was refused. It was then that the Bishop decided to go to Rome in person. Concerning this matter Archbishop Francis Patrick Kenrick, now archbishop of Baltimore, wrote on the Vigil of Christmas, 1851: "The Bishop of Chicago

---

6  Kenrick-Frenaye Correspondence.

thinks there should be a new see established in the lower part of the State of Illinois.''[7]

From this it would appear the Bishop Van de Velde had no objection to the dismemberment of his diocese; yet he may have consented to it mainly in the hope of getting rid of Chicago.

In the meantime the Archbishop of St. Louis was beginning to feel the weight of his laborious years and looking around for an available coadjutor. The thought of selecting the Bishop of Chicago for this office may have been in his mind at that time, 1852. That it was in the mind of Bishop Van de Velde seems quite probable from what he states about his first interview with Pius IX: ''The Holy Father seems inclined to either accept his (Van de Velde's) resignation, or at least to make him coadjutor, or Auxiliary Bishop to some other Prelate.''

No name of any prelate seeking a coadjutor is mentioned here: yet the probabilities point to Archbishop Kenrick.

On November 24, 1851, Francis Patrick Kenrick had tried to dissuade his brother from taking a coadjutor, and more particularly, one that offered his services: ''There are many inconveniences connected with the assistance offered by a coadjutor, so that a Bishop may hardly be said to govern his diocese, once a coadjutor has been appointed—I believe moreover, that one who has offered himself of his own accord should never be appointed.''[8]

So far it has become clear that Archbishop Kenrick of St. Louis had asked for a coadjutor, and the Bishop Van de Velde had asked the Pope among other things to appoint him coadjutor to some American Prelate. That the two lines of action had a bearing on the same coadjutorship, becomes clearer from what the Archbishop of Baltimore wrote to his brother on the Feast of the Holy Name, 1852:

''As to the question of a coadjutor, I cannot approve the plan of choosing one who is bound already to another see, just because he wishes to get away from the burden of its care. I think therefore that there should be absolutely no yielding to the aims of such a Bishop. But if you wish to make the request to have him named as your successor, in the event of any misfortune to you, I shall not oppose such a measure. The Holy See, I think, would permit him, while retaining the government of his own see, to hold the title of Coadjutor (to St. Louis) with the right of succession.''[9]

But the Archbishop of Baltimore was plainly not in favor of such a move. As open resistance, however, was out of question, he sought to gain time and the support of others. For in the same letter

---

7  Kenrick-Frenaye Correspondence, p. 321,
8  Kenrick-Frenaye Correspondence, p. 328.
9  Kenrick-Frenaye Correspondence, p. 325.

he said: "I think you ought not to make known your plans to the Bishop Chicago, until the whole affair can be made the subject of deliberation here (in the Council).[10]

On October 20, 1852, the Archbishop of Baltimore sent a lengthy exposition of the new turn of affairs to his brother of St. Louis: "You have learned that our plan did not succeed, as I think: and the Bishop of Chicago is now on his way to return to his see. The Bishop of Pittsburgh thinks that he is confident of your requesting him as coadjutor: but the Bishop of Chicago declared to the S. Congregation and to me that he would be willing to undertake the government of the District of Columbia together with the southern counties (of Maryland) under the title of Vicar-Apostolic, if it were so determined. This indeed does not seem to me to be quite the right arrangement. It remains for you to decide whether it would be a better plan to ask for his appointment as your coadjutor. To find a successor (for Chicago) will be another big problem. At the suggestion of the Bishop of Pittsburgh the Bishop of Chicago recommended Edward Purcell, to whom he knew that the S. Congregation was unfavorable. My letter also written on the complaint of the Bishop of Charleston was a bar (to the recommendation), more especially because the Bishop of Pittsburgh (in his letter) spoke as representing me. Now he (the Bishop of Pittsburgh) asks me to tell the S. Congregation that I am not opposed (to Purcell), also to have you write (to Rome) *in favor of* Edward (Purcell). He thinks that this (appointment) would put an end to discord, which, in the event of another (appointment) will, he believes, end in schism. I wish you to use your own judgment in this case.

"As to the Diocese of Quincy, the priest Obermeyer is hardly the man for the place, as I see it. Though his moral life is without blame, and he is quite a stranger to the vice of money greed, he is yet a little severe, and too much attached to his own opinion. Your own Vicar-General (Joseph Melcher) would, in my opinion, be preferable, though I am not unmindful that, in your judgment, he has no administrative ability.

"The Bishop of Chicago was opposed to the choice of George Carrell as Bishop of Covington. David Deparcq, who was the second choice, worn with labors and years, hardly has the qualities to be desired in a bishop. Louis Senez is mentioned by the Bishop of Chicago for the see of Natchez. If this should be done, there is hardly one left for the Vicariate Apostolic of Florida; for the Superiors of both candidates who have been recommended, request that neither one of them be appointed. Perhaps it would be well to give this post (Florida) to Edward Barron. It would be a tribute of honor to his good life, and

---

[10]   Kenrick-Frenaye Correspondence, p. 326.

provide means of support, for he is working in Columbus as a parish priest, and it is probable that he will suffer financial loss.''[11]

This letter proves beyond a doubt that the Archbishop of St. Louis had serious thoughts of asking for Bishop Van de Velde as his coadjutor, and that Bishop Van de Velde had some sort of an understanding on the matter with the Archbishop of St. Louis. It follows, therefore that the Bishop, whom the Archbishop of Baltimore represents as offering his services to Archbishop Kenrick of St. Louis as his coadjutor, was no one else but Bishop Van de Velde of Chicago. On November 8, 1852, Francis Patrick of Baltimore wrote to Peter Richard of St. Louis: ''I think the (present) Bishop of Chicago should be transferred to the see of Natchez or Natchitoches. But by no means to be made coadjutor. He lacks good judgment.''[12]

In the meantime the resignation of Bishop Van de Velde was accepted in Rome, and the Metropolitan of St. Louis was requested to send in three names for the diocese of Chicago. For on December 14, 1852, the Archbishop of Baltimore writes: ''In reference to the choice of candidates for the see of Chicago I have nothing in writing; but the Bishop of Pittsburgh, and the Bishop of Chicago, both have told me that this is the wish of the S. Congregation. If the Bishop of Chicago is transferred to Natchez, which appears to me to be much desired, then William Elder, John Loughlin, Patrick Reilly, of Wilmington, might be proposed.''[13]

As the Metropolitan of St. Louis hesitates to send his terna, his brother urges him on, saying: ''The Bishop of Pittsburgh thinks you ought to present the names; as the Bishop of Chicago, by the very fact of resigning the see, is hardly the one to make provision for its future government. As William Elder and Josue Young are already recommended for other sees, it would not be the proper thing to name them. Anthony O'Regan is one worthy of recommendation.''[14]

Anthony O'Regan was at that time President of the Diocesan Seminary of St. Louis. He was placed on the list as first choice. But Bishop Van de Velde seems to have resented the action of the two Kenricks. In his letter of January 18, 1853, the Archbishop of Baltimore rather angrily animadverts upon the course pursued by Bishop Van de Velde: ''The man from Chicago has unsettled everything, stating that the Archbishops arrange things just as they choose: that they determined upon the erection of this new diocese (Quincy) without consulting him, and recommended priests (to head the new see) without his knowledge. He moreover proposes Alton as better deserving

11   Kenrick-Frenaye Correspondence, pp. 335 and 336.
12   Kenrick-Frenaye Correspondence, p. 340.
13   Kenrick-Frenaye Correspondence, p. 342.
14   Kenrick-Frenaye Correspondence, p. 347.

(the honor of an episcopal city): and he also expresses the wish to have a Vicar-Apostolic (for the district) with no city determined (as the seat of episcopal government), leaving it to the Vicar's judgment and experience to choose his own cathedral city."[15]

No doubt, Bishop Van de Velde's suggestions were wise. In fact, Alton did become the episcopal city, only to lose the honor, after three administrations, to the capital of the State, Springfield. Yet, as we have seen, Bishop Van de Velde had favored Quincy at the time of the Baltimore Council, and the Archbishop of St. Louis, as Metropolitan was fully within his competence in recommending candidates for Quincy as well as Chicago.

It seems the case of Bishop Van de Velde was still undecided at Rome. "We ought, I think, not too readily depart from what has been done in the Council and approved. It is my judgment, that the Bishop of Chicago should be transferred to another see, preferably to Natchez. But. if the Holy See does not approve this, then Joseph Melcher appears to me the most worthy of those recommended (for Natchez)."[16]

Joseph Melcher was then the Vicar-General of St. Louis for the German portion of the Archdiocese.

As Bishop Van de Velde was transferred to Natchez on July 29, 1853, the question of filling the sees of Chicago and Quincy took on new interest. "I am sending you documents from Rome," wrote Francis Patrick on September 10, "from which you will understand that the case of the Bishop of Chicago will be up for another consideration. They whom you recommended, had, it appears, no weight."[17]

And again on October 17, he writes: "I believe that Anthony O'Regan is the best choice. There is nothing against him but a weak voice. I fear however, that the S. Congregation will go slow (in the appointment of O'Regan), by reason of the complaints made against the Irish."[18]

It would follow from these indications that the favorite candidate for the diocese of Chicago was Anthony O'Regan, and for that of Quincy, Joseph Melcher. Both of them were unwilling to accept the burden. Yet both were favored by Rome. Some opposition to them must, however, have been at work, as the appointment was delayed so long. An administrator, at least, was needed at Chicago to keep matters from going from bad to worse. On July 23, 1853, Joseph Melcher was appointed Bishop of Quincy and Administrator of Chicago, but he declined to accept the double burden: Hence Francis Patrick complains on October 17, 1853: "I am at a loss to know why

15 Kenrick-Frenaye Correspondence, pp. 347, s. s.
16 Kenrick-Frenaye Correspondence, p. 348.
17 Kenrick-Frenaye Correspondence, p. 355.
18 Kenrick-Frenaye Correspondence, p. 356.

you did not prevail upon Joseph Melcher to accept the burden, or at least to undertake the administration of Chicago, until the Holy See gives further orders. My mind is, that he ought to be made to accept the see of Quincy. I wish, however, to know what you think of it.''[19]

Still, Father Melcher remained obdurate. He might have accepted Quincy, but Chicago, never. Our Baltimore Prelate wrote October 20, 1853: ''As you believe it not advisable to urge Joseph Melcher too much, my mind turns to Leonard Ambrose Obermeyer, as a name to be recommended, against whom there is no objection, but his unbending rigor in habits of thought and unyielding firmness in holding to his own judgment. But I fear that he would reject an honor, that had been first offered to another. You may now ask for a coadjutor, if you know one fitted for the office.''[20]

It was now that Archbishop Peter Richard made a change in the terna he had submitted to Rome for Chicago, upon which his brother animadverts as follows, on December 30, 1853: ''I am sorry to see that you have changed your choice of candidates. Anthony O'Regan has qualities for a Bishop. He should have retained the place of first choice.''[21]

Still, Anthony O'Regan received the appointment for Chicago; yet like Joseph Melcher, declined the honor. ''I am sorry,'' wrote Francis Patrick on March 14, 1854, ''that Anthony O'Regan refuses to bear the burden. I think that you ought to send James Duggan to the city of Chicago without delay, giving him the title and the authority of Administrator in accordance with the Pope's brief, of which I hope you have received a copy.''[22]

The Archbishop of St. Louis accordingly sent James Duggan, his Vicar-General, to Chicago as Administrator of the diocese.

''I confidently expect,'' wrote Francis Patrick, ''that the Holy See will soon name a Bishop for Chicago, and prevent further evils by longer delay.''[23]

Bishop Elect Anthony O'Regan yielded at last to the persuasions and remonstrances of his friends, and allowed himself to be cousecrated on July 25, 1854, in the Cathedral of St. Louis. At Chicago, he also assumed the administration of what was set apart for the new diocese of Quincy. This arrangement continued until January 9, 1857, when the city of Alton became the see, instead of Quincy, and received its first Bishop in the person of Henry Damian Juneker.

---

19 Kenrick-Frenaye Correspondence, p. 357.
20 Kenrick-Frenaye Correspondence, p. 358.
21 Kenrick-Frenaye Correspondence, p. 362.
22 Kenrick-Frenaye Correspondence, p. 364.
23 Kenrick-Frenaye Correspondence, p. 365.

Now the question of a coadjutor for St. Louis demanded a solution. Here is what Francis Patrick wrote on Palm Sunday, 1854:

"The Bishop of Buffalo (Timon) thinks as I do, that you ought not to ask for a coadjutor: for usually he (a coadjutor) is more in the way of a bar, than a help, and readily offends in the reverence due to a Bishop. However, if you will not give up your design, then choose one whom you know well, and who is in disposition not out of harmony with yourself. Do not, in a choice of such moment, trust to the recommendations of others. It will have a bearing on the peace and tranquility of all that remains to you of the years of life."[24]

Archbishop Kenrick, on January 9, 1857, received what he had so persistently sought: Father James Duggan was appointed as coadjutor, and consecrated by him under the title of Bishop of Antigone, May 3, 1857. "Bishop Duggan was born at Maynooth, Ireland, May 22nd, 1825, and educated at the Seminary of Ballaghadereen. He was one of several ecclesiastics who responded to a call of Archbishop Kenrick in 1842, and completing his course at St. Vincent's, Cape Girardeau, he was ordained May 29th, 1847. Having been assigned to the Cathedral parish, he attracted attention by his zeal and devotedness, by his instructions to children, by his scholarly, eloquent discourses."[25] Archbishop Kenrick felt delighted as well as relieved. But his satisfaction was not to be of long duration. The Bishop of Chicago, Anthony O'Regan, left no stone unturned to effect his release from what had proved to be an unbearable burden. Both the Kenricks begged him to be patient and to await better times, yet all in vain. It was, therefore, the part of prudence to prepare for the emergency. "I advise you therefore," wrote Francis Patrick to his brother, on May 9, 1858, "if you get news of the resignation of the Bishop of Chicago, to call a Provincial Synod at once, to present names of priests for the see, and to consider other problems, things needful and fitting. . . . If you recommend priests of known good qualities and put together a few simple and clear decrees, the Holy See will approve with very little delay. This matter is urgent, so as not to let the diocese of Chicago go headlong to ruin."[26]

The Provincial Council, the second and last one ever held in St. Louis, was convened in the month of December, 1858, about two months after Bishop O'Regan's resignation had been accepted. The Coadjutor-Bishop of St. Louis, James Duggan, attended it in his quality of Administrator of Chicago. Archbishop Francis Patrick wrote on July 4, 1858:

---

24 Kenrick-Frenaye Correspondence, p. 368.

25 Shea, J. G., "History of the Catholic Church in U. S.," vol. IV, p. 620.

26 - Kenrick-Frenaye Correspondence, p. 412.

"I hope that your Coadjutor may get things in order soon in Chicago. All good men are deploring the wounds of that church. While the see is vacant, these wounds are readily made to bleed again."[27]

His name was placed before Rome in the usual terna, and in due time he was nominated Bishop of See of Chicago, January 21st, 1859. Thus invested with full power he showed ability and masterful hand. "Priests and people gave every evidence of renewed confidence, and the spirit of the new Bishop electrified all hearts, so that the visible fruits of Bishop Duggan's immediate action in the government of the diocese was noticed everywhere."[28] During his absence in Europe charges were made against his administration, on learning of which he removed some of the remonstrants, among them the future Bishop of Davenport, John McMullen, and his friend James J. McGovern. It soon became evident that the Bishop's mind had given away. In 1869, he was removed to an Asylum in St. Louis. He never recovered.

As for the See of Quincy, the name of the saintly Bishop of Philadelphia, John B. Neuman, who in 1856, had expressed a wish to be relieved of his burden, was proposed for the new diocese, as being predominantly German. But nothing came of the suggestion. On January 9th, 1857, the see was transferred to Alton, and the Lorrainer Damian Juncker, was appointed its first Bishop. In our review of Archbishop Kenrick's strenuous years from 1845 to 1852, we repeatedly met with Edward Barron, Bishop of Eucarpia, as performing episcopal functions in the Archdiocese of St. Louis. Though never a member of the diocese he did right noble service to God under the direction of his friend Peter Richard Kenrick. His career was a strange one, marked with many a failure, his character was as innocent of the world's way, and as helpless, and yet full of merriment as that of a child. He was born at Ballyneal, County Waterford, Ireland in 1801. He won the degree of Doctor of Divinity in the College of the Propaganda at Rome. After his ordination he was stationed for eleven years in his native diocese. During the summer of 1837, Bishop Kenrick invited him to Philadelphia. Here he was placed in charge of the Seminary as a priest whom, "piety, learning and other qualities mark out as a man of distinction and character." He was conversant with the French and German languages in addition to his own. When in 1840, the Holy See made an appeal for missionaries to go to Liberia, on April 1st, Father Barron and Father John Kelly of New York immediately offered their services. Dr. Barron had a deep sympathy for the colored race. On December 20th, 1841, Dr. Barron set out

---

27  Kenrick-Frenaye Correspondence, p. 469.
28  Shea, op. cit., 1. c.

from Baltimore for his distant mission. Father Kelly was with him and about thirty colored persons, ten of whom were Catholics. The United States Government, at that time, was intent upon shipping back to Africa the freed negroes that would consent to go. On his visit to Rome he was consecrated by Cardinal Fransoni under the title of Bishop of Constantia and Vicar-Apostolic of two Guineas.

Passing through Paris the new Bishop made a pilgrimage to the Shrine of Our Lady of Victories. Here he met the celebrated convert from Judaism, Father Libermann, who had recently founded the Congregation of the Missionaries of the Immaculate Heart of Mary for the conversion of the colored race. Delighted with piety and enthusiasm of Bishop Barron, he agreed to furnish him seven priests and three brothers for his missions. The Bishop and his band sailed from Bordeaux for Cape Palmas, September 13th, 1843. The future looked bright and cheering. But the deluge of sorrow was about to start. On Saturday December 30th, 1843, one of the priests died of fever, and all his companions were taken ill. One after another they died, priests and brothers, until there was but one left. Bishop Barron in sadness of heart and anguish of soul tendered his resignation to the Holy See, January 1845. After a short stay in Ireland, he returned to America. The two brothers Kenrick lovingly provided for his temporal wants, and cheered him with the golden glow of their cordial yet discerning friendship. They knew him as a dreamer, a man full of the spirit of romance, instead of practical judgment and prudence: but they also knew the holiness of his life, his simple faith, sincere convictions and greatness of soul. Among the most poignant sorrows of his later life was the remembrance of the colored people he had taken to Africa. Again and again he tried to bring them home. "I would willingly make any sacrifice to bring those poor Catholics back." he wrote to his friend Dr. Cullen.

In St. Louis Archdiocese, the great missionary field of his friend Peter Richard Kenrick, Bishop Barron spent about eight years of his life in visiting the remote congregations, administering holy Confirmation and even Holy Orders. In the Indian Territory he "confirmed seventy Potawatomi near Sugar Creek, not far from the Osage River.

In 1854, Bishop Barron went South. In early Summer the scourge of the Yellow fever fell upon Savannah, the home of his friend Bishop Gartland. At the first call Bishop Barron hurried to the assistance of Bishop Gartland, and Fathers Barry, Kirby and O'Neil.[29] Archbishop Kenrick wrote his obituary in a letter to his brother:

---

[29] Clarke, Richard H., "The Lives of our Deceased Bishops," vol. II, pp. 595-600.

·  ''Our very dear friend Edward Barron departed this life in the Lord a few days ago, September 12th, in the city of Savannah.  He died of the fever.  He was helping the Bishop of the diocese in the urgent work of visiting the sick; but soon after his arrival was forced himself to go to bed.  I need not tell you of the confidence in which I feel secure that he is now one of the number of those priests who serve Christ in heaven.  You know the quality of his spiritual life, his piety, charity, humility and the other virtues which gave nobility to his character.   God grant that we too may be found as well prepared and free from all blame when the Judge shall come.''[30]

---

[30]  Cf. Ella M. E. Flick, The Rt. Rev. Edward W. Barron, D. D., 1801-1854, in R. A. C. H. S., vol. XXXIV, pp. 99-112.

## CHAPTER 19

## PETER RICHARD KENRICK'S CONCILIAR ACTIVITIES

The conciliar activities of Peter Richard Kenrick extended from 1843 to 1870, thirty-seven years. As Bishop of Drasa and Coadjutor to the Bishop of St. Louis he attended the V Provincial Council of Baltimore that was held under the presidency of Archbishop Eccleston, in May 1843. As Bishop of St. Louis he was one of the leading prelates of the VI and VII Provincial Councils, convened by Archbishop Eccleston, the one in May 1846, and the other in 1849. In 1847, the Archdiocese of St. Louis was erected by Papal decree, but as yet received no suffragans. In 1848, Archbishop Kenrick was invested with the Pallium, and still later in 1850, five suffragan sees were assigned to the archdiocese, Chicago, Milwaukee, Dubuque, Nashville and St. Paul. Meanwhile Francis Patrick Kenrick had become Archbishop of Baltimore, and was nominated Apostolic Delegate, to preside over the first Plenary Council of Baltimore. The country was now divided into six ecclesiastical Provinces: Baltimore, Oregon, St. Louis, New Orleans, New York and Cincinnati.[1]

Archbishop Peter Richard of St. Louis selected as his theologians for the Council the President of his Seminary Dr. Anthony O'Regan and the parish priest George Ortlieb. The main points the Council decided on were: the solemn renewal of the Decree of the Council of Florence that "the Roman Pontiff is the successor of Blessed Peter, the Prince of the Apostles, and the true Vicar of Christ, and Head of the Universal Church and the Father and Teacher of all Christians, and that to him as in the Blessed Peter the full power, to feed and rule and govern the universal Church was given by our Lord Jesus Christ. They, therefore, acknowledge that the Most Blessed Pontiff Pius IX is constituted by divine right as the head of the entire episcopate, and that it is His office to confirm his brethren in the Faith, as He alone is the Shepherd of all."[2]

The Council exhorts the bishops that they endeavor to establish schools in connection with every church in their diocese.

The Council also suggests that in each diocese a Chancery be established, and Consultors as well as a Censor Librorum be appointed.[3]

In order to enforce the Decrees of the Plenary Council a Provincial Council of his suffragans was called by Archbishop Kenrick

---

1 This Council was held in May, 1852, Collectio Lacensis, vol. III, pp. 129-154.
2 Collectio Lacensis, vol. III, p. 145, No. 1.
3 Ibidem, No. XII, et XIII.

for the month of October 1855. ᐟ The Bishops of Dubuqe, Nashville, Milwaukee, St. Paul and Chicago assembled on October 19th, at the Cathedral of St. Louis, the Archbishop presiding. 'The decrees of the Plenary Council as well as those of the seven Provincial Councils of Baltimore were declared the ecclesiastical law of the Province.[4] It was resolved that candidates for vacant sees within the Province should be proposed by the Archbishop and the Bishops of the Province: that every Bishop should establish and support a Preparatory Seminary, and that one Theological Seminary should be kept in the Province. As an aftermath of the Council the following facts may be stated here. The proposition that Prairie du Chien be recommended to the Holy See as a diocese, was voted down by Propaganda. The transfer of the See of Quincy was made to Alton, and the appointment of Henry Damian Juncker as its first Bishop was approved by the Pope. Archbishop Kenrick's petition to have Father James Duggan appointed as his Coadjutor was also granted: The letter of Cardinal Barnabo transmitting these items of information is dated, Rome, February 17th, 1857.[5]

On September 5th, the Fifteenth Sunday after Pentecost 1858, the Second Provincial Council of St. Louis was convened at the Cathedral. The Bishops of Nashville, Milwaukee, (Henni), Santa Fe, (Lamy), Alton, (Juncker) Dubuque, (Smith), the administrator of St. Paul, (Ravoux), the Coadjutor of St. Louis, (Duggan) and the Bishop of Mesanna, Vicar Apostolic of the Indian Territory, (Miege). Vicar-General Melcher was chosen as Promoter, Father Saulnier, Notary, and John Bannon, one of the Secretaries. The Archbishop's theologians, were Patrick Feehan, Patrick O'Brien, Thomas Burke, C.M., and Joseph Patschowski, S.J. As the Tridentine Decree Tametsi "in regard to clandestine marriages, was published in various parts, and not in others, thus causing confusion in the minds of many, a proposition was submitted to the Fathers of the Council that Rome be petitioned to extend the Decree to the entire Province. All but one, Bishop Duggan, voted in the negative. The proposition was then made and passed unanimously that the Decree be abrogated in the Province. As the Decrees of this Council were approved by the Sacred Congregation of the Propaganda, and by Pope Pious IX on January 31st, 1859, it would seem that the Decree, *Tametsi* ceased to have binding force in the Province of St. Louis.[6] Yet, when the Fathers of the Second Plenary Council petitioned Rome that the Tridentine Decree be abolished in all the dioceses of the United States with the sole exception of New Orleans, the answer came that the Holy did not consider it well that

---

4   Collectio Lacensis, p. 307, No. II.
5   Collectio Lacensis, vol. III, p. 311. Conc. Prov. St. Ludovici, 306.
6   Collectio Lacensis, vol. III, pp. 313-322.

this be done.[7] The new Codex Juris has now removed all doubt and difficulties in this regard. In regard to Matrimony, the faithful are to be admonished to shun mixed marriages to prepare themselves for the worthy reception of the sacrament by Confession, and to receive it at holy mass, and to sanctify it still more by the reception of Holy Communion.

The Second Plenary Council of Baltimore was in session from the 17th to the 26th day of October, 1866.[8] Archbishop Martin John Spalding of Baltimore presiding as Delegate Apostolic. It was the great legislative assembly of the Church in the United States. Parliamentary rules were in force for the first time. The Acta et Decreta form a large volume, treating under fourteen distinct titles of Faith and the errors opposed to Faith, of Church-government of the Sacraments, of Divine worship, of monks and Nuns, of Catholic Youth, of the Zeal for souls, of Books and Perodicals, of Secret Societies, of New Sees and of a more efficacious observance of the Decrees of the Council. At the suggestion of the Holy See the Fathers of the Council proposed these Decrees as the Norm which the teachers in the schools of Theology and Canon Law were to follow and explain, and which their pupils were to study accurately and diligently.[9]

As these Decrees have been substantially embodied in the Decrees of the Third and last Plenary Council of Baltimore, and are consequently still in force in all parts of the United States, we need not here advert to them. The Acts of the Council however contain some very interesting historical information for the Archdiocese of St. Louis.

There were seven Archbishops and thirty-seven Bishops, one Administrator and one Abbot in attendance. Archbishop Kenrick, second in dignity to the Apostolic Delegate, stood alone and foremost in reputation for learning, wisdom and strength of character. As theologians he brought with him his Vicar-General Joseph Melcher, and Fathers Patrick J. Ryan and Charles Ziegler.

At the opening of the Council the Apostolic Delegate handed to the Archbishops and Bishops a printed schema containing the matter to be treated under fifteen Titles. Three of the Titles were devoted to matters pre-eminently dogmatic in character. Archbishop Kenrick held that the minute discussion of these doctrinal matters, which were partly of Faith, and partly of more or less theological certainty, would consume too much of the appointed time of fifteen days, so as to render

---

7 Collectio Lacensis, vol. III, 315, et. Decr. II, p. 317. Cf. p. 384 No. 2.

8 Decree No. II was simply a petition, "Visum est Patribus a S. Sede implorare."

9 Collectio Lacensis, vol. III, pp. 323-574. A reprint of the Baltimore edition of 1868.

the full and thorough treatment of the real business of the Council, that is, the matters of Christian practice, impossible. He, therefore, moved that the dogmatic matters be referred to a special committee, and that the Council proceed with the discussion of practical matters. The Report of the Special Committee should then be submitted and, if necessary, amended, and finally included, not among Decrees, but among the Acts of the Council.[10]   The Titulus Secundus "De Hierarshia at Regimine Ecclesiae," was the subject of a fiery debate, the leaders in which were the Archbishop of St. Louis and the Archbishop of Cincinnati. It was, of course, no question about matters of faith, but there were some controverted theological opinions in the Title to which the Archbishop of St. Louis objected.   As there was not sufficient time to discuss these matters as fully as they deserved, he thought it best to refer them to Rome in the manner proposed. This view was adopted.[11]

The accepted doctrine of the Church was then freed from the incumbrance of mere theological opinion, and the rest of Titulus Secundus was unanimously adopted.   Another clash came when the proposition to publish Archbishop Francis Patrick Kenrick's English version of the Sacred Scripture, revised, however, and augmented with the notes of Bishop Challoner, was brought before the Council. The chief oponent of this measure was Archbishop Kenrick of St. Louis.[12]

In the seventh private Congregation of the Fathers on the 5th day of October it became plain, that the matter submitted, could not be completed within the time remaining. The Delegate proposed that a Committee of Bishops select from the proponenda such questions as seemed to be of greater importance, for the discussions, but that the Fathers should, if these were approved, subscribe to them in the sense they had in connection with the other dogmatic and pastoral matters that could not be treated by the Council and in this way to transmit them to the Supreme Pontiff for correction or approbation.   All the Fathers, with the exception of the Archbishop of St. Louis, voted in the affirmative.[13]   One more proposition was made by Archbishop Kenrick, and adopted by the Council, namely that Rome be petitioned to allow priests to be ordained "titulo missionis," without them taking an oath to serve in the missions forever. This petition was not granted by the Holy Father. At the last public session of the Council on Sunday October 21st, the Archbishop of St. Louis preached the sermon. Then all the members of the Council signed the Decrees and departed for home.

---

10   Collectio Lacensis, vol. III, p. 353, ad calcem.
11   Collectio Lacensis, vol. III, p. 356.
12   Collectio Lacensis, vol. III, p. 357.
13   Collectio Lacensis, vol. III, p. 358.

Among the Dogmatic Decrees of the Titulus II. those that had
reference to the mutual relations between the Bishops of the Church
and the Pope seem to have been most earnestly discussed. In this
regard the Ecumenical Council of the Vatican, which was to be called
only three years later, seems to have cast its shadows before. The
doctrine of the Baltimore Council on all matters was, of course, perfectly orthodox. Yet, it showed that a movement was on its way, not
to introduce anything new, but rather to bring out more clearly what
had always been accepted, the infallibility of the Pope as the Supreme
teacher of the Church. That the Church is infallible in its teaching on
matters of Faith and of Morals, was always held as a fundamental
part of divine revelation. That the body of the bishops, either in
Council assembled, or dispersed throughout the world, but united with
the Pope as their Head and chief teacher, spoke with divine authority
and consequently without danger of teaching anything that was not
true. But whilst all were in agreement thus far, some went still farther
and claimed that the Pope, as Head and Supreme Teacher of the Church,
must be infallible when deciding questions of Faith and Morals, even
before and without the concurrence of the body of the Bishops.

The official report on these theological discussions at the Council,
being very brief, it does not appear what stand on the question Archbishop Kenrick took, and whether the word papal infallibility was
used by him or by the opponents: it is certain that it was not used in
the Acta et Decreta which were submitted to the judgment of the Holy
Father. The question was not as yet "spruch-reif," as the Germans
say, "ripe for a decision." The council in its Decrees laid the stress
on the inerrancy of the Church represented by the body of the bishops
in union with the Pope, and left the question as to the inerrancy of
the Pope, as such, and even without the concurrence of the body of the
bishops, to future consideration and final decision. Practically it
had always been accepted by the Church. No official decisions in
matters of Faith and Morals, issued to the Christian world, have ever
failed of acceptance. On the Archbishop's return to St. Louis a noteworthy demonstration was arranged in his honor. For the 30th of
November, 1866, marked an epoch in the Archbishop's life. It was
the day of his Silver Jubilee as Bishop. Owing to the fact that the
Archbishop was averse to any public display, there was only a partial
celebration of the anniversary. The clergy presented him with a fine
set of canonicals both costly and beautiful,[14] and the German Catholics

---

[14] The Archbishop mentions this gift from the clergy in his Account Book
p. 70. "The Archbishop received from the Clergy, on the 25th year of his
episcopacy, a crozier, gold chain and ring, red cope and soutane, together with
somewhat above $1,600. The money and somewhat more were expended by the
Archbishop on himself and his two theologians, when he attended the Council of
Baltimore, that year."

honored him with a torchlight procession. The English-speaking Catholic laity did nothing in the way of celebrating the anniversary.

In 1867, the Archbishop paid his first visit to Rome since his consecration as Bishop. He visited the Eternal City for the purpose of uniting with the Catholic Episcopacy of the world, in the celebration of the Eighteen Hundredth Anniversary of the Martydom of St. Peter and to join them in their formal protest against the despoiling of the Pope of the greater part of his temporal dominions, and in a declaration that, in order to preserve the freedom of the Church, the temporal power was a necessity. He remained away for more than a year, visiting several parts of Europe. He did not, of course, neglect to visit his own dear native Ireland. Whilst in Dublin, he was the recipient of many marks of affectionate respect from the friends of his youth and first years of his priesthood. Father O'Dwyer, his former pastor, was so overjoyed to see him that he embraced him with the forgetful familiarity of the days of his curacy. Whilst in Dublin, he preached in one of the churches of the city. In his sermon he used the remarkable words, "whilst other nations have given many martyrs to the Church, Ireland is the Martyr Nation in the world." The saying was so remarkable that it was cabled to this country next day. On his return to St. Louis, he was the recipient of an ovation, the greatest that the Catholics of St. Louis had ever given to any man, if we except those given to our present Holy Father and to Pius IX. Members from all the parishes and all the Catholic societies of the city joined in the welcoming procession. Archbishop Kenrick arrived in East St. Louis on the morning of June 24th, 1868 accompanied by Father Patrick J. Ryan. He was met there by Rev. Thomas O'Neill President of St. Louis University, Rev. W. Wheeler of St. Patrick's and Rev. R. P. Tschieder of St. Joseph's; and the Messrs. O'Neill, Amend, and Donovan, who escorted him to his residence in this city, where he was received by Vicar-General Joseph Melcher and several of the Reverend Clergy. A public demonstration was announced to take place on the Sunday following.

Of the several new bishops appointed in consequence of the late Council of Baltimore Archbishop Kenrick, on his return from Europe, consecrated Joseph Melcher, Bishop of Green Bay, Wisconsin, at St. Mary's Church, on July 12th, and John Hogan, Bishop of St. Joseph, in St. John's Church on September 13th, 1868. Bishop Melcher had been considered worthy of episcopal honors for the previous twenty years. In his old home in Modena he no doubt would have received the appointment, if he had not chosen the hard and rough course of a western missionary. After the brief Episcopate of a little more than five years and five months, he died on the 20th of December 1873.

Bishop John Hogan resigned the pastorate of St. Michael's Church to enter the mission in the wildest parts of Missouri, where he founded a few parishes and also a Catholic colony. He ·was little known, even among the clergy. When at the Second Plenary Council of Baltimore, the Archbishop spoke of him as a fit and proper person to fill the new See of St. Joseph, some one asked,—"But who is Father Hogan?" "O, I know who he is," answered the Archbishop. He remained Bishop of St. Joseph twelve years, when, on September 10th, 1880, he was promoted to the new and more important See of Kansas City. He died February 21, 1913.

## CHAPTER 20

## PETER RICHARD KENRICK'S PASTORALS

Peter Richard Kenrick being a truly zealous bishop, and at the same time a capable writer naturally took up the ancient custom of communicating with the members of his diocese by means of pastoral letters. These documents, nine in number and dating from 1842 to 1865, form a beautiful monument of the great churchman's deep interest in all matters conducive to the advancement of holy Church, and of his singular affection for the priests and people under his charge. The tone of these letters is so unaffectedly earnest, and accordingly convineing, that a few extracts will, even at this late day, prove interesting and helpful. The first pastoral letter of Peter Richard, Bishop of Drasis and coadjutor of the Bishop of St. Louis, is dated February 16, 1842. It is countersigned by Joseph Lutz, Secretary. Its subject matter was Christian Temperance:

"Being charged with the administration of this vast diocese, during the absence of the venerable prelate, who has long and so successfully presided over it, we felt it our duty, thus publicly to address you, on occasion of the proposed formation of a society, the chief object of which is, to promote the virtue of temperance. Our motives in so doing are, a sincere wish to aid, as far as in our power lies, in attaining the important end which is the object of the proposed association; to proclaim clearly and distinctly the principles of morals which the Catholic Church has ever professed, and which, in the present instance, we seek but to apply; and to state the conditions on which we have given our approbation to the formation of a society, the establishment of which has been called for by the zeal of several among the clergy and laity of this diocese."[1]

"How afflicting the spectacle, to behold a creature, endowed by God with honor and glory, and placed over the works of His Hand;—a soul which has not been purchased with corruptible gold and silver, but by the precious blood of the immaculate Lamb;—a soul, which by baptism, has been made the temple of the Holy Ghost, and been, perhaps, subsequently enriched with the choicest gifts of God's house;— a soul which has been thus prepared to enjoy the eternal possession of God, for which alone she was drawn forth from nothing: how afflicting to behold such a soul, unmindful of her origin, and of the glorious destinies which await her, sacrifices all the hopes of happiness, in order to indulge in the brutish pleasures of intemperance, it is

---

[1] Bishop of Drasis, Coadjutor of St. Louis, February 16, 1842, p. 1.

not necessary to dwell on the temporal evils that result from this degrading vice; the loss of character and of self-respect; the enfeeblement, no less of the physical powers of the body than of the mental faculties of the soul; the distress and ruin in which the drunkard involves his unhappy family, whom, but too often, having been taken off by the diseases engendered by excess, he leaves behind him, to depend for support on the charity of strangers, or to be victims of every evil to which unprotected destitution may be exposed. Great as are these evils, and loudly as they plead for our sympathy and lamentations, they are, but temporal, and therefore, not to be compared with that eternal anathema pronounced by the unspired apostle on the intemperate, when he says:—"Drunkards shall not obtain the kingdom of heaven."[2]

"But while, beloved brethren, we thus raise our voice against an evil, which has ever been a subject of affliction to the Christian pastor, and against which he has at all times, contended, with a zeal inspired by the greatness of the prize that was to reward his efforts, we must not permit ourselves to be hurried away by the spirit of excitement from the maintenance of correct principles, and from observing the form of sound words, so necessary for the preservation of Christian faith. We should be loud and vehement in the condemnation of the vice of intemperance; but we must not involve in indiscriminate condemnation the lawful use of those creatures of God, which the intemperate man abuses to his own perdition. We must remember that such a principle is impious and irrational; that it is opposed to the direct declaration of the inspired apostle, that, "Every creature of God, is good, and is to be received with thanksgiving," that it implies an error formally condemned by the Church, and that therefore no favorable result can be expected from any system in which it incorporated, or from any zeal to which it may give an impulse."[3]

Here we have the safe and sound doctrine on Temperance in a nutshell, clearly and purely expressed.

The second pastoral letter is dated June 1, 1842, in answer to a cry of anguish from the Catholics of Spain suffering at that time, all the evils of religious oppression and persecution. The Bishop orders that the collect *"Contra persecutores Ecclesiae"* be added in the celebration of the mass.

"The voice of the common father of the faithful has reached our ears, imploring on behalf of our fellow Catholics in Spain, our co-operation with him and the rest of our brethren, in seeking to avert the evils that appear to impend over that once flourishing portion of the Church. From the apostolical letter of His Holiness, a translation of which accompanies this our pastoral letter, you will learn the na-

---

2   Pastoral of February 16, 1842, p. 2.
3   Pastoral of February 16, 1842, p. 2.

ture of the causes which have moved the Vicar of Jesus Christ to call on all the members of the Church to unite with him in offering, by prayer and penitential supplication, a holy violence to Heaven, on behalf of this afflicted portion of the flock committed to his care. These motives are of the gravest character, and are well calculated to excite the sympathies of every Christian breast. Not only have the Spanish clergy, and the religious communities of that country, been made the victims of outrage, insult, and, in many cases, of sanguinary persecution; not only have the rights of ecclesiastical property been flagrantly violated, the monuments of religion and of art, in many instances, demolished, or become the prey of sacrilegious rapine and cupidity, and the sacred asylums of learning and sanctity-consecrated by the most glorious recollections of the Church—been invaded and profaned, but an effort has been made to perpetuate these evils by the introduction of an irreligious and anti-Christian system, which, if permitted by a chastening Providence to be successfully adopted, would rob our Holy Mother the Church of the brightest gem that sparkles in the mystic crown of piety and faith, wherewith her Divine Spouse crowned her in the day of her exaltation. To perpetuate the more easily these enormous evils, the sacred name of Liberty has been made use of by those whose acts show that they know not what true liberty is, since they respect not the liberty of the Church—the surest bulwark of the people's rights— but seek by a thousand unworthy acts, to bind her in the degrading trammels of subserviency and absolute subjection to the civil power.

"In giving this public expression to our feelings of just indignation at the occurrences to which we refer, we most explicitly disclaim any intention of passing any judgment on the changes which have of late taken place in Spain. With such matters, in our public character, we have no concern; it is only the evils of the Church that we deplore, in common with the Father of the Faithful, in common with our brethren, the bishops of the Catholic Church, and in common with moderate and just men of every party. It is only for the liberties of the Church that we are willing to contend, with the only arms that become us as ministers of Christ, prayer and supplication.''[4]

History repeats itself, now here, now there. Liberty is made the cloak of evil, but always finds a defender in the Church.

The pastoral letter of September 14, 1846 concerns itself exclusively with the Christian duty of supporting the Church and its clergy. The provisions heretofore made for the support of the ministers of religion, were plainly inadequate. The laity were not to blame for this; the clergy were partly at fault, because, through a feeling of delicacy, they often failed to make known their wants. Then many of the laity were poor and had not much to give: others coming from countries

---

4  Pastoral of June 1, 1842.

having state provision or endowment of the clergy, did not feel the necessity of contributing to the support of the church. After summing up the probable causes of delinquency and presenting the cure, Bishop Kenrick concludes:

"The provision which we seek to obtain for the support of the clergy, is not to be regarded as a salary, given by the employer to the employed, but as an offering made by Christians to God, in the persons of His Ministers. We need not say that no human reward could adequately compensate for the services of a zealous and devoted priest. No, Brethren, we look not here for our reward:—"We are the ministers of Christ and the dispensers of the mysteries of God." He is our Master: to Him are we answerable for the service we render the souls He has redeemed with His precious blood; and from Him are we to receive, if found faithful among the dispensers, the imperishable crown of eternal recompense. The offerings you make to us,—whether towards our support, or to enable us to give the example of that charity which the poor so naturally expect to receive at our hands, and which we are so constantly called upon to exercise,—are offerings to God, Whom you thus honor with your substance, in recognition of the source whence you have derived whatever you possess, and as the expression of your gratitude to the Giver of all good gifts. Let us remind you that God loves the cheerful giver."[5]

Peter Richard Kenrick had now become Archbishop of St. Louis. His pastoral letter of February 2, 1849 treats of the proper observance of the season of Lent:

"The contrast between the austerity that characterized the observance of Lent in the first days of Christianity, and for many centuries afterwards, and our modern practice, is humiliating in the extreme, and should convince us that if "we are the children of the saints, and look for that life which God will give to those that never change their Faith from Him," we have much degenerated from the fervor and earnestness, which distinguished our forefathers in the faith. And yet, brethren, we serve the same God whom they served; we have the same enemies, from within and from without, as they had to contend with, the apprehension of the endless and unspeakable torments of which rendered the severest practices of penance easy to those who, perhaps were less criminal than we are, and peopled the desert with thousands who sought either to preserve their innocence or retrieve their fall; and we have the same heaven to gain, we hope for the same future glory, in comparison with which they esteemed the severest trials of this life as light and momentary. Whence, then, arises our apathy and indifference for those salutary observances of penance, which formed so prominent

5 - Pastoral of September 14, 1846, p. 7.

a character of the Christian life,\ as exhibited in primitive times? Whatever be its source, we must be convinced that there is nothing in the Gospel of Jesus Christ to warrant or excuse it; and that, if circumstances exempt us from the obligation of observing the Lenten fast, with all the strictness and severity of ancient discipline, they cannot diminish for us the obligation of doing penance, which is an essential part of the Christian duty. The spirit of penance must always be the same, although the manifestation of that spirit by outward acts, may be, and in the nature of things, must be different in different times and different places. No relaxation of the ancient discipline of the Church can dispense us with the obligation of offering to God the sacrifice of a contrite and humble heart, which at all times He requires, and which He never will reject. The exact and conscientious observance of the fast of Lent, even as at present prescribed, is well calculated to produce within us, and develop, this feeling of contrition and humility; for it is not, and never can be, the intention of the Church, in the relaxations of exterior discipline which she grants to the weakness of her children, or to the calamity of the times, to exempt them from the obligation of sanctifying a fast, in order the more easily and the more securely to appease the anger of God.''[6]

In the same letter the Archbishop adverts to the sufferings of holy Church in the persecution sustained by the Holy Father, Pope Pius IX.

''You have, doubtless, brethren, heard with feelings of deep affliction of the trials to which it has pleased God to subject our Most Holy Father, Pius IX, and you have, we are confident, sympathized with him in all the indignities which he has suffered, and in the voluntary exile which he has preferred to a departure from the character of his office as Vice-Regent of the Prince of Peace, and Minister of the Gospel of universal concord. You are too well instructed in the nature of the obedience we owe to him, to be told that it rests on the ''foundation other than which no man can lay, which is Jesus Christ,'' and that it is entirely independent of his temporal character as Sovereign of that portion of Italy, known as the States of the Church. His predecessors were the Chief Pastors of the flock of Jesus Christ before they acquired the rank and power of secular princes; and should it be the providence of God to deprive the Bishop of Rome of his temporal authority, we should not the less regard him as the Vicar of Jesus Christ, the center of Catholic unity, the rock on which Christ built and continues to sustain His Church, the shepherd to whom He has committed His lambs and sheep, that is His whole flock, Pastors no less than people. His authority will be for us, who are not his temporal subjects, the same,

---

6   Pastoral of February 2, 1849, p. 1.

whether he is enthroned in the Vatican, or wanders in exile, or languishes in captivity.—''[7]

In the same letter the Archbishop speaks of the support the archdiocese has received from the pious association of Europe, and declares the use he has made of their contributions:

"The fact that for several years past, large sums of money have been placed at our disposal by charitable societies in Europe, especially by the Society for the Propagation of the Faith in Lyons, France, may have, and in some instances, undoubtedly has, produced the impression, that the clergy were not entirely dependent on the contributions of the people towards their support. A few words of explanation will remove this erroneous notion. The funds received by us from the associations referred to, have been applied principally to the support and education of candidates for the ministry, in the two seminaries in this diocese; and, the expenses of which, in any one year during the last six years, have exceeded the total amount of the subscriptions received in the diocese for that object, during the same space of time. Next, we have had to aid the establishment of new missions, either by the purchase of lots for churches, or by contributions towards their erection, or by supplying what was indispensably necessary for Divine Service, or by giving the priest sent to such places the means of defraying the first and most necessary expenses attending on his own personal wants;— and sometimes, have we been obliged to comprise all these various objects in our efforts to establish religion, where there were but few Catholics, and these not of the most opulent class. Again, we have had to defray the expenses incurred by ourselves in the administration of the diocese; expenses, at all times, considerable, but which were still more so, when we had to visit the various congregations beyond the city in which we reside. The canons of the Church, indeed, authorize us to demand from the clergy an annual contribution towards our own support, and for the purpose of defraying the expenses to which we have referred, and this contribution is cheerfully and liberally made by the clergy of several of the dioceses of the United States, towards their respective Bishops. But how could we look to the clergy for this aid, when we were aware of the privations to which many of them were exposed? and when we were obliged, in several instances, to afford them assistance, in order to enable them to provide what was necessary for their own support?"[8]

The Pastoral Letter of October 2, 1854, in announcing the Jubilee has this beautiful passage in regard to the power of charity:

"It is by the exercise of mercy towards the poor, as well as by the discharge of all the other duties of a Christian life, that we can best

---

[7]  Pastoral of February 2, 1849, p. 5.

[8]  Pastoral of February 2, 1849, p. 8.

vindicate our Religion from the charges which are so unjustly brought against it, and disarm those prejudices which are arrayed, at the present time, against the church of Christ. We must not forget, brethren, that not from the suggestions of passion, but. from the sacred oracles of Religion, we are to learn the best means of vindicating both ourselves and the Church of which we are members. It is not by returning railing for railing, evil for evil, but by blessing those that curse, and by praying for those that calumniate us, that we are to show our zeal for truth and approve ourselves disciples of Our Heavenly Master.''[9]

As a fitting conclusion to this chapter of extracts from the Pastorals of Archbishop Kenrick we would subjoin the following strong passage from the Letter of the Second Provincial Council of St. Louis held under the presidency of Archbishop Kenrick in 1858 :

''How often must it be repeated that mere secular knowledge is not education, and that, of itself, it contributes little, if anything, to the real happiness of the individual. Education, is surely as the term itself imports, something more than mere science, or the acquisition of knowledge. It implies an unfolding, and a direction of the powers of the mind, and a training of the affections of the heart, so as to mould the character, and form the Christian and the man—a result never attained by the mere acquisition of science. Should not the experience of all times convince us that mere human knowledge is not always virtue and happiness to man, and that the possession of the highest talents and of the most extensive acquirements are often found to be associated in the same individual with the greatest. misery and the most deplorable degradation? This has been the sad lesson taught us by the past, and it is, what we may too easily discern, at the present time. It is the natural consequence of the unnatural divorce of religious from secular knowledge, of separating the knowledge that passes away,—a mere transitory acquisition,— from the only knowledge that is eminently worthy of an immortal being, which will. continue through all eternity ''the Science of the Saints''—''The Knowledge of Salvation.''[10]

---

9  Pastoral of October 2, 1854.
10  Pastoral of the Second Provincial Council of St. Louis, 1858.

## Chapter 21

## ARCHBISHOP KENRICK AS A BANKER

There are few lawful avocations that would seem to be more incompatible in their practice than those of a Bishop and a Banker. The one is concerned with the salvation of souls, the other with the accumulation and investment of money. It may, therefore, strike many minds as a contradiction in terms to speak of Archbishop Kenrick as a Financier, and to dwell with approval on the so-called Bishop's Bank. Yet Archbishop Kenrick exercised for a number of years, and with marked success, the functions of a Bishop of souls and a money-changer. Not that he loved money or the business of banking. Far from it. His trend of thought, and the aspirations of his soul ran in a far different direction. It was dire necessity alone, that held him captive for a number of years at the counting house. The diocese was indebted for Fifty-eight thousand dollars, the notes bearing 6%, 8% & 10% per annum. On the death of Bishop Rosati, these debts were assumed by Bishop Kenrick; the landed property left by Bishop Rosati to his successor was partly unproductive, partly bringing rent, the net amount of which, however, did not suffice to pay one-half of the interest due to the creditors.[1] After 1842 the contributions from the Society for the Propagation of the Faith ceased until 1849, and the contributions from the Leopoldine Society were applied to the erection of the earliest German churches of the city. The Cathedral income always fell two or three hundred dollars below the expense.[2] And yet the Seminary required a heavy annual outlay, and the new missions also put the Bishop's purse under contribution. Bishop Kenrick was poor and running deeper into debt, from year to year. But, to be poor, meant to Bishop Kenrick, to be deprived of the means of advancing the Kingdom of God; to be in debt meant to be forced to retrace his steps. To get pecuniary help from any honorable source, was the Bishop's prime necessity, and to ask for it he felt no shame nor reluctance.

He tried repeatedly to raise a loan in Philadelphia, but without success. On December 4th, 1843 his brother of Philadelphia wrote to him: "As to (your) getting a loan here, I think it hardly expedient to look for it, unless the need is very urgent. It is not at our command but would have to be borrowed from a creditor of Mr. Lopez and

---

[1] Archbishop Kenrick Book of Accounts and Financial Statements, marked on back, "Thornton Estate," quoted in this chapter: Kenrick's Account Book.

[2] Kenrick's Account Book, p. 47.

from the bank: the interest, as you know, is deducted beforehand, and the note must be renewed every three months. It is better, therefore, to await a time more opportune, unless there is danger threatening of a suit (in law). But, if I see any chance of helping you, I will do so without delay. I will follow your advice, and write to France (for aid). In this case, I will change my former determination; for I had resolved fully to ask for no more help from abroad."[3]

If the worst should come to the worst, that is, if a law suit should be threatened, Mr. Frenaye, the Bishop of Philadelphia's financial agent, holds out this hope, that within two months, two thousand five hundred dollars could be raised on a loan."

Do not yield under the pressure of much work, "adds Francis Patrick:" "He who placed the burden upon you will not fail to sustain you so long as you make a good endeavor. Whatever help I can give you is at your command."

On January 19 of the following year, 1845 good news must have come to Philadephia, for the Bishop writes to his brother of St. Louis: "I am pleased to know that you have gotten a loan of money at a low rate of interest."[4]

The Association for the Propagation of the Faith, which had been one of the mainstays of Bishop Du Bourg and Rosati, seemed to be faltering in its intentions towards St. Louis. "The journey to France has yielded me no profit financially, neither the petitions of my friends" . . . . wrote the Bishop's brother from Paris, "I am afraid they, the Association for the Propagation of the Faith, may give you the same treatment, without considering the debt which has burdened the diocese from the beginning of your administration. You will have to exercise very great care, therefore, so as to keep the burden of debt under control."[5]

All this was good advice; but what could be done to carry it out? Bishop Kenrick realized that he must help himself. His appeal lay to the wealthy families, Irish and French, of the episcopal city, and right nobly some of them responded to the call. The family of the Mullanphys was preeminent in the line of large donations for new churches and institutions, but did not feel inclined to help liquidate the diocesan debt. Mrs. Anne Biddle, a daughter of John Mullanphy, was a liberal contributor to all movements for the advancement of religion in St. Louis diocese, but in all business matters, loans included, she proved to be as slow and circumspect as any banker.[6] Mrs. Anne Hunt, the daughter of

---

3   Kenrick-Frenaye Correspondence, pp. 178 and 179.
4   Kenrick-Frenaye Correspondence, p. 182.
5   Kenrick-Frenaye Correspondence, p. 219.
6   Mrs. Anne Biddle's Letters in Archives of St. Louis Archdiocese.

J. B. C. Lucas, perhaps the greatest benefactress of the diocese, was no less willing to leave the diocesan debt to the care of the Head of the diocese. The Catholic immigrants, German and Irish, were themselves struggling with the hard conditions of life in a new land. Financial panics had shaken the country to its foundations. Money was scarce and could be had only on the best security and at a high rate of interest, sometimes as high as 24%. We have seen what difficulties Bishop Kenrick met in seeking to make a comparatively small loan in Philadelphia. The Catholic immigrants of the city were, for the most part, honest, hard-working and thrifty people. Be their earnings ever so small, a certain portion would be laid aside for future use. But as their little store of dollars accumulated, they felt obliged to look for a place of safe-keeping. Many of the banks had failed, and the others had lost the confidence of the public. It would be a great charity to these people to provide a safe money depository for them, one that would assure them of a fair return in interest. The first priest to realize the twofold advantage inherent in the condition of affairs, that is, the safe-keeping of the Catholic immigrant's small savings and the accumulation of larger amounts of money that could be used for the clamorous needs of the congregations and religious institutions, springing up everywhere, was Father Ambrose Heim. As assistant at the German Church of St. Mary's, he had opportunities in plenty to see what was needed; his easy familar ways and, above all, his kindness and charity won all German hearts to him. He soon found himself the custodian of their accumulations, and he began to feel that the responsibility he had undertaken, was too great and dangerous for a private individual. The Bishop, hearing of this, transferred Father Heim to the Cathedral in 1846, and in the following year made him his Secretary. The hitherto latent business sense of Bishop Kenrick had now found its great opportunity. In Father Heim he recognized a member of that immortal band of those whom the great apostle of the Lord described as "nihil habentes, et omnia possidentes."[7]

The confidence reposed by all classes of Catholics in the Bishop's honesty and ability, was the capital on which the "Bishop's Bank" was established. When the announcement was made that the Bishop of St. Louis was willing to accept any amounts, large or small, on deposit and promised a fair rate of interest, money flowed in from all sides. A small room in the Bishop's house was set apart for the banking enterprise, but in the course of time a separate location became a necessity. Father Heim, as the Bishop's Secretary, was employed in the office. A layman came in a little later. But Peter Richard Kenrick, always

---

[7] Corinthians, II, c. 6, v. 10.

mindful of the fact that not only his personal honor, but also the good
name of the diocese and of the Church, were pledged, would never en-
trust anyone with the management of his Bank, but continued to the end
to give his personal attention to all its business transactions. He was its
actual manager. He supervised all the departments. He spent his days
in the bank's private office. Because of this very individual investigation he was able to almost instinctively judge of the wisdom of financially
aiding a given enterprise. As for instance, during the Great Panic
of 1857, when banks were crashing all over the United States, and
public enterprises and cities were in alarm over the stoppage of many
public works, the "Archbishop's Bank" was not only solid as the Rock
of Gibralter, but was able to show such trust in the City of St. Louis, that
the Archbishop could advance on its Scrip and Treasury Warrants
for payments of its public works, the great sum of $150,000.

Owing to the ever-increasing number of Catholic immigrants in
St. Louis, the business of the so-called Bishop's Bank soon attained
a very large volume. "I am not envious," wrote the Bishop's Brother
from Philadelphia, "I am more amazed, that, fortune smiling on you, I,
by some happy luck, may have a way soon to cancel the money-changer's
account. Counting money will hardly be accounted a loss in the sacred
ministry. This is evident from the reproach which they fling at the
Coadjutor of Philadelphia."[8]

And again in asking for the annual contribution from St. Louis for
the support of several distinguished converts, the Coadjutor of Philadelphia pleasantly adds "It is quite fitting that a prelate who is very
wealthy should lead the rest by example and counsel."[9]

But what use did the Bishop make of the money thus placed in
his hands? He invested largely in real estate, he built large blocks of
stores and dwellings, the rent of which went towards reducing the indebtedness of the diocese.

The improvements made on property of the diocese for instance on
lot 63, cost the sum of $58,900, and the buildings on lots in block 59,
along Second Street, $36,231.62, and on the same block, along Third
Street, $19,084.50, making a total expense of $114,216.12. But these
properties now brought fair returns and when they were sold by the
Archbishop, they brought the net sum of $499,620.80.[10]

The productive improvements on the east side of the Church-block
implied the destruction of the Old Cathedral Residence and the erec-

---

8   Kenrick-Frenaye Correspondence, p. 407.

9   Idem, ibidem, Francis Patrick, writing in a bantering tone, addressed Peter
Richard: "To his brother, now grown wealthy, the Archbishop, of Baltimore,
poor and lowly."

10   Kenrick's Account Book, pp. 73 and 83.

tion of the present building. The total expense on this item was $8606.64. The subscriptions from the parishioners amounted to $2369.50, leaving a deficit of $6237.14, to be paid by the Archbishop. This occurred in 1852. In the following year the sacristy and school house were added to the Cathedral building, the total cost was $7316.55. The subscription paid by the parishioners amounted to $2046.76, leaving another deficit to be liquidated by the Archbishop, amounting to $5269.79. A special bequest of $6000.00 by John Thornton for church and school house, reduced the Archbishop's contribution for these two purposes by about one-half.[11] The Archbishop's Bank furnished loans on easy terms to struggling parishes in city and country and to the religious communities for new buildings and repairs on the old. The city was growing with a rapidity that was witnessed nowhere else. New churches were built year by year, and needed large loans.

It was in 1858 that the great turn in Archbishop Kenrick's fortunes came through the bequest made by John Thornton a wealthy Catholic of St. Louis County, to the Archbishop of St. Louis, for charitable and religious purposes. In the Will, Peter Richard Kenrick, Edward Walsh and John Withnell were named as executors. The sum total received by the Archbishop of St. Louis through the Thornton bequest was $461,-488.41. The first settlement was made in 1858, the third and final settlement, in March 1861. The distribution of this legacy for charitable and religious purposes was carried out by Archbishop Peter Richard Kenrick within the years 1858 to 1862.

In 1862 Archbishop Kenrick drew up a *Synopsis of the Distribution of the Thornton Bequest for Charitable and Religious Purposes,* under four headings:

No. 1·   Charitable: Convent Expenses of Charitable Institutions .................................$ 96,688.24

No. 2.   Charitable: Expenses of Buildings and other permanent improvements in Religious Establishments for Charitable Purposes .............. 127,192.40

No. 3.   Religious: Convent Expenses of Religious Institutions for the promotion of Religion ...... 29,461.68

No. 4.   Religious: Churches, the indebtedness of which has been liquidated, as explained at the end of this Synopsis ............................ 225,470.99

$478,813.31

---

[11] Kenrick's Account Book, p. 48.

Thornton Bequest ....\.....................$461,488.41
From other sources .......................  17,324.90

- $478,813.31

In 1887 the Archbishop drew up a general Statement of his receipts and expenditures in behalf of the diocese from 1842 to date:

The Receipts were.....................................$877,807.32
The Expenditures were..............................  849,509.10

Balance .............................................$28,298.22[12]

In this statement the two following very interesting items occur, in regard to loans or donations made to Churches and Religious Institutions. The question whether the Archbishop's advances were donations or loans was frequently agitated. The *Western Watchman* in its issue of October 16, 1869 has this caustic remark: "The Archbishop has built our churches for us, or if he only loaned the means by which they were built, his numerous creditors construe this obligation to refund very lightly,"

Here are the facts as taken from the Account Books of Archbishop Kenrick:

*Money advanced to various religious and Charitable Institutions,* partly for the support of the Communities, partly for the erection, improvement and repair of Buildings.

St. Anne's Asylum....................................$ 61,844.73
House of the Angel Guardian..........................  22,027.80
La Salle Institute...................................  26,692.37
For the Poor (per Sister Florence of St. Philomena's House)  11,311.15
St. Louis Hospital...................................  83,640.60
St. Vincent's Hospital...............................  80,771.60
House of St. Philomena...............................  32,949.36
Convent of Good Shepherd.............................  66,979.73
St. Bridget's Asylum.................................  21,109.40
Visitation Convent................................... 113,862.90
Miscellaneous Contributions..........................  39,474.64
Original debt on Cathedral...........................  58,000.00
Church of the Annunciation, 2nd loan.................  17,875.00

636,539.37[13]

---

12  Kenrick's Account Book, pp. 34 s. s.
13  Kenrick's Account Book, 34-37.

*Church Debts remitted.*

| | | |
|---|---|---|
| 1858 St. Lawrence O'Toole | ............................. | $ 3,816.70 |
| 1861 Holy Trinity Church | ............................. | 1,934.62 |
| 1866 St. Theresa's Church | ............................. | 14,005.46 |
| 1870 Church of the Assumption | ........................ | 1,742.56 |
| 1870 Church of the Holy Cross | ........................ | 1,032.00 |
| 1870 Church of S. S. Peter and Paul | .................... | 1,946.27 |
| 1870 Church of the Annunciation | ....................... | 34,950.58 |
| 1870 Church of the Holy Trinity | ....................... | 5,576.68 |
| 1870 Church of the Immaculate Conception | .............. | 21,693.90 |
| 1870 Church of St. Michael | ............................ | 4,209.36 |
| 1870 Church of St. Mary (Carondelet) | .................. | 7,864.04 |
| 1870 Church of St. Nicholas | ........................... | 16,264.16 |
| 1870 Church of St. Liborius | ........................... | 965.74 |
| 1870 Church of St. Boniface | ........................... | 11,630.81 |
| 1870 Church of St. Patrick | ............................ | 1,249.72 |
| 1870 Church of the Holy Angels | ........................ | 21,544.49 |
| 1870 Church of St. Lawrence O'Toole | ................... | 16,422.17 |
| 1870 Church of St. Malachy | ............................ | 15,855.05 |
| 1870 Church of St. Mary | ............................... | 5,985.11 |
| 1870 Church of St. Bridget | ............................ | 9,883.55 |
| 1870 Church of St. John | ............................... | 14,394.67 |

212,968.64[14]

The various sums advanced by the Archbishop to the Churches and Religious Institutions of the diocese made a total of $849,508.01 and, together with the value of taxable real estate of the diocese, would seem to cover all the Archbishop's Bank owed to depositors. But the Notes of the Religious Institutions were, in a large measure, only nominal, as at least one-third of their borrowings were understood to be allowances from the John Thornton bequest for Charitable and Religious purposes. Only the loan of the Visitation Convent came in no wise under the provisions of the Thornton Bequest.

As far as the loans to Churches were concerned, the obligation to refund was somewhat stricter, although many of the priests who borrowed the money, seem to have considered the loans as absolute donations; whilst others promptly paid interest and capital.

The churches that shared in the original distribution of the John Thornton Bequest were: St. Mary's, St. Michael's, Holy Trinity, St. John Nepomuk, St. Boniface, St. Mary's, Carondelet, St. Bridget's, The Annunciation, The Assumption, St. Malachi's, St. Patrick's, S. S. Peter and Paul, Immaculate Conception, St. Lawrence O'Toole, St. John.

---

[14] Kenrick's Account Book, p. 71.

Three of these churches had before 1862 paid back their borrowings with interest: namely, St. Mary's, S. S. Peter and Paul, and St. John Nepomuc, and consequently, they were not benefited by the act of remission in that year. Others had increased their borrowings and were, therefore, fully liable for the notes of a later date than 1858; and others again, that were not included in the distribution of the Thornton Bequest, borrowed large amounts from the Bishop's Bank, with full obligation of repayment with interest.

In regard to the beneficiaries of the Thornton Bequest, Archbishop Kenrick made this proviso: "that the sums devised for the building of churches and Religious Institutions have been provisionally distributed, on the following condition: Should the assets of the undersigned (Archbishop) suffice to meet the immense indebtedness he has contracted in building so many churches and religious institutions, then the foregoing distribution is to be considered as permanent, and the churches and institutions named therein to be considered as discharged from all obligations by reason of the advances so made by the undersigned (Archbishop). Should the other assets of the undersigned not suffice for all demands on him or his representative, then the aforesaid churches and institutions to be called on to supply the deficit up to the amount of their respective indebtedness to the undersigned, or up to such proportion of their respective indebtedness as will suffice for the above purpose. He wishes the churches to be first called on, and the whole amount of the deficit to be levied on them, before any of the Religious Institutions be called on, unless these latter should by gift, bequest or otherwise, be able to discharge their indebtedness." This document was written and signed by Peter Richard Kenrick, Archbishop St. Louis, 31st December 1862.[15]

In 1870 it became clear to all that the Archbishop's assets did not cover his indebtedness to the depositors of his bank, and that, consequently, the churches that were indebted to him, were obliged to make up the deficit. On July 16, 1870, Joseph O'Neill, the Manager, stated: "The Pastor of St. Nicholas paid full debt. St. John's, St. Malachy's and Holy Angels' have made similar arrangements. "The incorporated parish of the Holy Trinity cancelled its note of $30,000.00, in full after organizing a bank of their own, on about the same lines, but on a parochial scale. Most of the churches paid back only half of their borrowings. In a public announcement in 1870 Archbishop Kenrick stated that, as he needed cash to pay off his depositors, he would ask the churches for half the debt due him, and promised on that payment to remit the other half. "Most of them, perhaps all, made ready use

---

15　Kenrick's Account Book, p. 39.

of this generous offer. Thus we read in the morning paper of January 5, 1871, under the caption, "Debt of St. John's: The Very Rev. Father Ryan announced last Sunday at Mass that the entire debt of St. John's Church $37,000, had been liquidated, and that in consequence, the door collection would now cease, and the former Mass collection be resumed.

He paid about $30,000 in money and by the Archbishop's recent liberal offer (fifty cents on the dollar, for amounts paid since May) was enabled to clear the entire amount. Equally successful have been the churches of St. Nicholas, St. Malachy and St. Bridget, and St. Louis Catholics have abundant reasons to congratulate themselves on the result. The offer of the Archbishop stimulated earnest action and is another proof of his financial foresight."[16]

Among the institutions that were erected at the expense of the Archbishop's Bank, the Convent of the Visitation on Cass Avenue was at last sold by the Sisters to the Archbishop, and the amount of the old debt taken in part payment on the deal.

The Archbishop felt this daily attendance at the Bank as a heavy burden, which he would gladly have placed on other shoulders, did his conscience allow it. He asked for a coadjutor, as the double burden began to press heavily on him. From Francis Patrick came the brotherly advice: "You ought not to be thinking of a coadjutor. I, who am nearly nine years your senior, have no such thought."[17] And upon further remonstrance, the Bishop of Philadelphia wrote: "The administration of temporalities ought to be kept in control; for this you could choose one of your priests to work with you, as is the Practice of the Vicar-General of the Bishop (Vicar-Apostolic) in London. I know, indeed, that these things are not so easily arranged (as they are counselled); but I am hopeful and trust that things will arrange themselves in your favor."[18]

That the Archbishop of St. Louis was wiser in this than his brother is evidenced by the fact that Bishop Purcell of Cincinnati, who entrusted the care of a similar Bishop's Bank to his own brother, Father Edward was forced into bankruptcy, which entailed untold heart-burnings and miseries upon those who trusted him, not wisely, but too well.[19] No one lost a cent on Archbishop Kenrick's banking enterprise.[20]

---

[16] The debt of St. John's Church in 1862, was $37,049.95; in 1870, it had been reduced to $14,394.67. As the Archbishop offered to remit half, i.e., $7,197.33, Father Ryan was obliged to pay $7,197.33 in order to liquidate the debt.

[17] Bishop James Duggan was given the Archbishop as Coadjutor, May 3, 1857.

[18] Kenrick-Frenaye Correspondence, p. 328.

[19] Cf. Lamott, John H., "History of the Archdiocese of Cincinnati," p. 189-212. Bishop Purcell's Banking enterprise failed with two and one-half million liabilities above all available assets. The properties of the individual parishes

The immediate cause of the Bank's suspension of business was the Vatican Council, which had been called for the year 1870. As the Archbishop would not break with his practice of personal attention to all phases of his business, he felt that the only alternative was to close his banking establishment. He began to pay off all whose money was in his care. In 1867 and 1868 he put on the market a large quantity of valuable real estate, which realized the sum of almost half a million dollars. Advertisements were placed in the papers towards the end, that all accounts not withdrawn would be turned over to another bank just then organized and under charge of Mr. Joseph O'Neill. By 1870 everything was wound up. . . .And the Archbishop had left St. Louis for the Vatican Council. The people of St. Louis gave him $2500.00, to defray travelling expenses to the Council of the Vatican.

As the turbid waters of the Missouri and those of the crystal clear Mississippi, after their junction above St. Louis, flow on side by side, without mingling, yet form the vaster stream that gives life to the city and the country round about, so the priestly and the business life of Peter Richard Kenrick flowed on in close touch, yet uncommingled, "*ad laetificandam civitatem Dei.*" The Archbishop always remained the great prelate, even when seated in the counting-room, for his thoughts and aspirations were always with his diocese. It was not love of money, but love of Holy Church, that urged him on. And so it was not failure that made him close his banking career. From afar he may have heard the warning voices; but there were no rapids in his business career. Of his own will, when his purpose had been accomplished, he paid back all he owed. And the Archbishop's Bank ceased to exist, leaving in its wake a long trail of blessings, the Churches, Schools, Convents, Hospitals and Orphanages, that could not have been built without its ever-ready help.

---

were not held to be involved in the case, except those that had been built with money from John B. and Edward Purcell. The amount paid by these churches to the creditors of the Bank was $140,780.55. The creditors received only 8⅓% of their claims. The creditors appealed to the Pope for redress, and Archbishop Elder, the successor of Archbishop Purcell, did all he could to satisfy them by appeals to the Pope, the hierarchy of the United States and the General Catholic public. Archbishop Purcell's failure occurred in 1878, ten years after Archbishop Kenrick had wound up his banking enterprise.

20 The Archbishop did not try to profit even by the Legal Tender Act of March 3, 1863, which made the paper currency a legal tender for all debts, whether contracted on a gold basis or not. At times gold was at a premium of from fifty to one hundred per cent. The Archbishop paid his creditors in gold, dollar for dollar. The National Archives at Notre Dame University, Indiana, contain a number of letters from Archbishop Kenrick of St. Louis to Archbishop Purcell of Cincinnati, touching these delicate matters. Others treat of the system of pew-renting, seat money and kindred subjects.

## CHAPTER 22

## CATHOLIC CEMETERIES IN ST. LOUIS

The first Catholic Cemetery in St. Louis occupied the northern half of the church-block on Market Street, between the Rue de l'Eglise and the Rue des Granges, that is Second and Third Streets. This cemetery was closed in 1828, after a new burying ground had been opened on the St. Charles Road, a little more than one mile west of the city limits, i. e., Seventh Street, on a four acre tract, acquired by the Wardens of the Cathedral Parish from William Stokes. This cemetery was closed in 1849, and most of the bodies were removed to the newly opened Cemetery on Bates and Sarah Streets, which was called the Rock Spring Cemetery and represented the first burying ground in the city over which the Bishop exercised full control, and from which he derived a regular, though rather variable income, all the years from 1849 to 1867.

The Parish of St. Vincent's founded by the Lazarist Fathers, had its own cemetery on Park and Ohio Avenues. It was opened in 1845 and closed in 1865.

In the cholera period of 1849, from June 22—July 30. "St. Vincent's Cemetery" and the "Catholic Cemeteries, Old and New," are mentioned as burying places for cholera victims.

To give but one example from the daily litany of sorrow:

"Wednesday Morning June 27.

Interments and Cholera—For Monday, June 25.

| | | | | |
|---|---|---|---|---|
| City Cemetery | 20 interments; | Of cholera | | 18 |
| German Protestant | 14 | ,, | ,, ,, | 12 |
| Holy Ghost | 29 | ,, | ,, ,, | 24 |
| Christ Church | 2 | ,, | ,, ,, | 1 |
| · Lutheran | 6 | ,, | ,, ' ,, | 4 |
| Presbyterian | 4 | ,, | ,, ,, | 1 |
| Catholic (Old) | 27 | ,, | ,, ,, | 20 |
| Catholic (New) | 7 | ,, | ,, ,, | 7 |
| St. Vincent | 17 | ,, | ,, ,, | 12 |
| | 126 | | | 99 |

The Baptist, United Hebrew, Methodist and Wesleyan Cemeteries failed to send in their returns."[1]

---

[1] "Missouri Republican," June 22-July 30, 1849.

The year of the cholera epidemic was the last year of one Catholic Cemetery and the opening of another: but both were in use during those dreadful days of June and July 1849.

The "Old Catholic Cemetery" was the one situated on Franklin Avenue somewhere around the present Seventeenth Street. In 1924 during excavations for a building on 2617 Franklin Avenue, many bones and entire skeletons were found which were supposed to have been originally buried in the middle of the Old Catholic Cemetery. If there was another Catholic burying ground on Franklin near Jefferson Avenues, it must have belonged to one of the parishes, as there is no mention of it in Archbishop Kenrick's accounts.

The New Catholic burying ground is the above-mentioned Rock Spring Cemetery, which, in the nineteen years of its existence, brought the Archbishop an annual income, from $3000 to $500 dollars.[2]

The cause of this shrinkage was the opening of the Holy Trinity Cemetery in 1864, on a tract of land adjoining the present O'Fallon Park. Trinity Cemetery was in use from 1864 to 1871. This Archbishop's revenue from this burying ground rose in three years from $1200 to $1900 and then became stationary at a little more than $600.[3]

As Trinity Cemetery was on the north side of the city, the Catholics of South St. Louis, in 1870, received a burying ground of their own, dedicated in honor of S. S. Peter and Paul. The net proceeds derived by the Archbishop from S. S. Peter and Paul's Cemetery, in the first year of its existence, amounted to $2483.66.

S. S. Peter and Paul's Cemetery is still in use, having not only resisted the tide of invasion, but also spread its peaceful slumberers over a very large and valuable territory. It is the property of the diocese, but under the management of one of the Clergy of S. S. Peter and Paul's Parish. One by one, the Old Catholic Cemetery, the Rock Spring Cemetery and Holy Trinity Cemetery have disappeared from view, and the remains of the dead they once enshrined have been transferred either to Calvary or to the vault below St. Bridget's Church.

The expansion of the city convinced Archbishop Kenrick of the necessity of providing for the Catholics of St. Louis a large and beautiful cemetery in a location that would not, for a long period of time, feel the invasion of the City's noise and bustle.

In 1853 the Clay Farm, northwest of the city, was offered to him at a reasonable figure and was bought, and a number of adjoining lots were added to the tract. At first only a part of the land was laid out for Cemetery purposes. The old mansion on the place was for a time the favorite residence of the Archbishop. Later on, it became the

---

2  Archbishop Kenrick's Account Book, m. s.
3  Kenrick, 1. c.

temporary home of the Carmelite Nuns. The Cemetery was called Calvary. It was opened for burials on April 1, 1854. "In 1857 the consecration of the "Priests Lot" and the original four sections marked the first official act of the new coadjutor, Bishop Duggan, former pastor of the old Immaculate Conception Church on Eighth Street in this city, and later Bishop of Chicago."[4]

Thus we have a succession of Catholic Cemeteries, in a direct line from 1770 to the present day.

After the opening of Calvary many reinterments were made from the graveyard on Franklin Avenue and Seventeenth Street, the Rock Springs Cemetery and also from the Holy Trinity Graveyard, to the new and beautiful God's Acre, established by Archbishop Kenrick. "Not long before the outbreak of the Civil War all the dead kept under the Cathedral in the lower church were removed to Calvary; and ten years later, when St. Vincent's Graveyard on Jefferson and Geyer was abandoned, all reinterments were made in the larger place, even those dead unclaimed by relatives being buried in several immense graves in Section Twelve. In this part of the Cemetery is also seen the beautiful and interesting lot of the Vincentian Fathers, where many names recall bright pages of religion in St. Louis."[5]

In March 1867 Archbishop Kenrick, for the purpose of organizing the Calvary Cemetery Association, named the following gentlemen: P. A. Berthold, Joseph O'Neill, John Byrne, Jr., H. L. Patterson, H. J. Spaunhorst, P. J. Hurck, J. E. Yore, Charles Slevin, J. C. Burg, Thomas Ferguson and John Withnell.

These gentlement drafted a Constitution of the Association, which was approved by the Archbishop and obtained a charter. The first officers were:

President, Archbishop Peter Richard Kenrick.

Vice President, Vicar-General Philip P. Brady.

Treasurer, Dr. F. L. Haydel.

Secretary, Thomas J. Gibbons.

Superintendent, Matthew P. Brazill.[6]

To this Calvary Cemetery Association Archbishop conveyed "that certain tract of land known as the Calvary Cemetery situate in the

---

[4] Smith, Mary Constance, "Our Pastors in Calvary." Reminiscence of Michael Dwyer, altar boy at the Old Cathedral in the days of Coadjutor Bishop Duggan, and afterwards sexton for Father Paris. Mr. Dwyer also stated that Sarah Street was cut through the site of Rock Springs Cemetery near Van de Venter and Manchester and that the Old Catholic Cemetery at Franklin and Seventeenth was in charge of Mr. McEnnis, the grandfather of Mrs. James Ring of ·this city.

[5] Smith, M. C. op. cit.

[6] Calvary Cemetery Association, Historical Sketch, Charter and By-Laws and Rules, St. Louis 1888.

County of St. Louis . . . containing in all about two-hundred and eight acres . . . as a place of burial, agreeable to the rules and conditions laid down in the deeds of burial lots hitherto made, on condition that the Association shall and will pay to the Archbishop of St. Louis out of the revenues of the Cemetery the sum of fifty thousand dollars, and that after this sum is paid, the Association shall and will apply the surplus revenues of the Cemetery to the erection and maintenance of the Cathedral Church, which the Archbishop proposes to erect in the northern division of the block 920 in the city of St. Louis. This deed was made on April 1, 1867.[7]

In June of the following year it was deemed best to reorganize the Calvary Cemetery Association as a stock company, and pay the Archbishop for the ground. The organization was effected with the following named gentlemen as incorporators: Joseph O'Neill, John Byrne, Jr., John Withnell, H. L. Turner, Charles Slevin, Thomas Ferguson, J. B. Ghio, H. J. Spaunhorst, P. J Hurck, P. A. Berthold, and James C. Burg. In October 1868 the question as to the disposition of the profits derived from the Cemetery was discussed. None of the stockholders desired to share in any surplus which might remain after the stock had been paid for. At the Archbishop's suggestion it was decided that the surplus should be applied to the support of the Catholic Orphan Asylums of St. Louis: Subscriptions of stock were now asked and a new organization formed under the name Calvary Cemetery Company. The name of Peter Richard Kenrick and D. H. Donovan were added to those of the original incorporators.[8]

It was intended that parishioners of all Catholic parishes interest themselves, and so subscribe to the capital stock: the promise was therefore made that the profits were to be distributed among all the Catholic Orphans. But it was ascertained that the German Catholics had not generally subscribed, except the parishioners of St. Joseph's. Those of S. S. Peter and Paul and Holy Trinity relying for interments on the cemeteries that bore their respective names, and the others being simply indifferent. In consequence St. Joseph's also withdrew its support.[9]

The organization of the Society of stockholders was now perfected under a new Constitution but under the old name, Calvary Cemetery Association.

The main provisions were: that the Archbishop of St. Louis, shall be, ex officio, President of the Association, the other officers to be chosen annually: that out of the profits of the Association there shall be paid on each and every share of stock subscribed, an amount equal to

---

7   Calvary Cemetery Association, pp. 4-6.
8   Ibidem, p. 6.
9   Ibidem, p. 7.

the par value of said stock and interest on the same at the rate of 6% ; that the residue of the profits be applied:

1. to the work of keeping in order, extending, improving and beautifying the Cemetery.

2. to the use of the Board of Managers of the Roman Catholic Male and Female Orphan Asylums.

The last clause excluded the Orphans of the German St. Vincent's Orphan Home from any share in the surplus of the Cemetery, as they were not under the control of the Board of Managers.[10]

The new organization now being in running order, it remained that the rights of the original Calvary Cemetery Association be transferred to its posession. Archbishop Kenrick did this by deed of May 19, 1871, signed by himself as grantor of the deed of April 1, 1867, and by Joseph O'Neill, as President of "the Calvary Cemetery Association, as it originally existed," by which he conveyed to the new Calvary Cemetery Association the parcels of land forming Calvary Cemetery. On May 6, 1871, Archbishop Kenrick issued a Circular announcing this change:

"Whereas in the year 1867, I found it inconvenient to myself and also to interfere with other important duties devolving on me, to conduct and manage satisfactorily, the Calvary Cemetery, and therefore invited several Catholics to associate with me for that purpose: an incorporation was formed for the proper maintenance of that institution. with the ulterior object of applying its proceeds to the support of the orphans under the care of the Manager of the Roman Catholic Male and Female Orphan Asylums of St. Louis. The Association has now so far succeeded as to have reached the point when, if a portion of the stock subscribed to it in its formation be relinquished, there is an almost positive certainty, that the whole of the proceeds of the Cemetery may, within, eighteen months, or at most two years, be appropriated for the original purpose. The additional liberality will secure for the orphans an unusual income of from $15,000 to $20,000 and will thus prove a relief to the Catholic community to that extent.

Impressed with this feeling, I cheerfully relinquish to the Association the amount of stock standing in my name in its books, and venture to express the hope that others of the stockholders will do the same."[11]

A report was made by the Committee, on October 30, 1872 as follows:

That six hundred and ninety-four and two-thirds shares of par-value $34,733.33 had been donated to the Association.

---

[10] Constitution of the C. C. Ass'n. p. 8-11, passim.
[11] L. C. pp. 12 and 13.

That two hundred and twenty-one and one-third shares had been purchased for $11,066.66 cash.

· That two hundred and eleven shares had been cancelled unpaid, leaving twenty-one shares in force and held by twenty-one different persons to keep the Association alive.[12]

This statement declared that the Association as such owned almost all the shares, and consequently could devote almost all its income to the care, extension, and improvement of the two diocesan Orphan Asylums. On July 10th, 1882 the Association's charter was amended under which the Calvary Cemetery Association continues its operations until this day for the benefit of the two diocesan Orphan Homes under the Board of Managers of the Roman Catholic Male and Female Orphan Asylums.

But there is another aspect of the matter: the Calvary Cemetery is one of the monuments of Archbishop Kenrick, one of the show-places of our city "a thing of beauty and a joy forever." A modern Cemetery must be arranged on the so called park and lawn plan, avoiding as much as possible all unnecessary accumulation of stonework, iron fencing and bars, which disfigure so many of the older Cemeteries. This plan takes nature for its model and in the trees, the shrubbery, the flowers and the neatly kept lawn, gives the burying place of our dear departed ones, the moods of peace, and longing hope, and sympathy. Calvary Cemetery was established in a forest, consequently most of the trees in it are of the native forest-varieties. The evergreens, however, were planted, though without design. The roads of our Calvary bear names taken from the history of the Passion, the Via Dolorosa leading to the Great Cross, and the other ways named after those who accompanied the Lord on his sorrowful journey. Four sections are consecrated, the rest is blessed as it is needed for interments. The priests' lot, where so many of the pioneers of the faith sleep around their great leaders, Archbishops Kenrick and Kain, commands a magnificent view of the mighty river of Father Marquette, as it sweeps along through the lands he discovered and blessed, seeking the far-off gulf.[13]

---

12  Calvary Cemetery Association p. 13.
13  Cf. Report of Superintendent Matthew P. Brazill, 1888.

## CHAPTER 23

# CATHOLIC JOURNALISM IN ST. LOUIS BEFORE THE WAR.

"The Catholic Press" has been since time immemorial the object of special solicitude, though not always of generous support, in the Church. Bishop Kenrick united both functions in his person. An editor himself at the time he was chosen to rule the Church of St. Louis, he maintained all through life a keen interest in the printed word, serving the Catholic cause, just as his predecessor Rosati, had .been. In this work Bishop Kenrick enjoyed the cooperation of a number of distinguished persons, priests and laymen, whose names deserve honorable mention in a history of the diocese. The lives of such men, are generally quiet and rather uneventful, but their work exerts a powerful, because wide-spread, influence on the course of events, either for good or evil. Bishop Rosati was the pioneer in this matter as in many others.

The first Catholic paper published in St. Louis, in fact, the first Catholic paper west of the Mississippi River, was "*The Shepherd of the Valley.*" In the Letter-Book of Bishop Rosati there is, under date of May 19th, 1832, the following entry: "Mr. Taylor leaves Hartford; Catholic Press will be published in St. Louis by July 1st, 1832."[1] Joseph and Deodat Taylor were Converts to the Faith, and men of superior character and ability. A paper by the name "*The Catholic Press*" was published by Joseph Taylor, at Hartford, and was to be transferred to St. Louis. But as this project failed, Mr. Joseph Taylor came to St. Louis and established a new paper under the patronage of Bishop Rosati. Father John McMahon on his way to Galena writes to Bishop Rosati on August 27th, 1832: "A Dialogue on the Real Presence, which passed between an intelligent passenger and myself on our way hither, (i. e. Keokuk) may be somewhat entertaining to some of Mr. Taylor's readers. If you think so, I am determined to lend it to you, you will please hand it to him for insertion."[2] Now, what was the name of the Catholic St. Louis paper edited by. Mr. Taylor, if not "*The Shepherd of the Valley?*"

According to Scharf, *History of St. Louis*, "*The Shepherd of the. Valley*" was "established in 1834 or 1835" "as an organ of the Catholic Church."[3]) This is rather vague and uncertain. The "*Shepherd of the Valley*" certainly did exist in 1835, as Father Lefevere in a letter

---

1 Archives of St. Louis Archdiocese.
2 Archives of St. Louis Archdiocese.
3 Scharf, l. c., p. 945.

(163)

to Bishop Rosati speaks of an advertisement he had seen in it in September of that year. By a favorable chance a complete set of *The Shepherd of the Valley* was discovered in the Library of the St. Louis University. It is bound in two volumes. The first number is dated July 7, 1832 and the final number July 2, 1836. The editor and publisher was Francis H. Taylor. The place of publication is given as 3rd Street, Old Hospital Building. For the first year it is written in English and French; but with the opening of the second volume on September 20, 1833, English alone is used. The format is similar to that of the *Western Watchman* of Father Phelan's later days. The motto is "One Lord, one Faith, one Baptism."

With the second volume the format is about the size of modern papers, but has only four pages. It bears the motto "Thou art Peter and upon this rock I will build my Church." Joseph Taylor is still editor and publisher but now "under the auspices of the Catholic Association." The place of publication has been changed to Church Street. The number for September 20, 1833, contains among many other items of historical interest an obituary of John Mullanphy. Regular installments of the Philadelphia Controversy (Hughes Breckinridge) fill the first page of a number of issues for 1833. The third volume is published by Angewin and Crowe under the auspices of the Catholic Association. It begins October 4, 1834 and bears a new headpiece with a picture of St. Peter's Church. Volume III, May 16, 1835, bears only J. G. Crowe's name as publisher, but under the same auspices. Volume IV, beginning November 7, 1835, has no picture in the headpiece, but the same names of paper and publisher. The January 2 Number, 1836, prints a long letter written by Pierce Connelly to his (protestant) bishop in regard to his conversion to the Catholic Church. In the last number July 2, 1836 there is an urgent call to the subscribers to pay up. Very likely the urgent call to duty was not heeded and the paper went to the wall. At least we know of no subsequent number of "*The Shepherd of the Valley.*"

This was in 1836. Three years after, Thomas Mullen is reported by Scharf in his History of St. Louis, "to have started the *Catholic Banner* whose career is shrouded in oblivion." Whether this is fact or fiction we cannot say, as we found no other mention of this paper;

The coming of Bishop Kenrick as coadjutor and successor to Bishop Rosati gave a fresh impetus to Catholic journalism in St. Louis.

The *Catholic Cabinet* made its first appearance in the year 1843. It was originated and in part at least edited by the Rt. Rev. Peter Richard Kenrick, Bishop of St. Louis. We need not say that it was well edited, as Bishop Kenrick was no tyro in journalism, having edited several years previously the *Catholic Herald* in Philadelphia. The *Catholic Cabinet* was a monthly magazine. Besides editorial matter, it contained essays, historical and critical, poetry and religious intelligence.

William J. Mullin was the publisher. The first number bears date May 1843, the last July 1845. The first number was introduced by Bishop Kenrick himself in an article on "The Present State and Prospects of Catholicism throughout the world." The historical trend of the *Catholic Cabinet* is evidenced in the following quotation taken from the article on the Discovery of the Mississippi," vol. I., No. 4: "Nothing is more astonishing than the fact that hitherto so little has been done to snatch from oblivion the few records yet extant that throw light on the early history of the Catholic Church in this portion of the North American Continent. This inattention is less excusable, as we believe, the subject is one that has frequently suggested itself to the minds of many among our clergy, some of whom were eminently qualified to supply the acknowledged desideratum; but whether from necessity of giving undivided attention to the more immediately important duties of missionary life, or from a want of proper encouragement, or from some other undiscoverable cause, certain it is that, with the exception of a few desultory sketches in our Catholic journals, we are as far at the present day from the realization of our hopes, in this regard, as we were twenty years ago."

Among other things the editor states, that "the *Catholic Cabinet* is not only devoted to the exposition, vindication and illustration of Catholic principles, but is also intended to be a chronicle of religious intelligence." This program was carried out with remarkable ability. A number of the historical articles, especially those on Western Catholic history, have retained their importance to the present day. Based on the numerous documents of the Diocesan Archives, they serve as the foundation for a future history of the Church in the Mississippi Valley. The monthly notices under the caption of Religious Intelligence contain an accurate though not full account of the religious development within the years 1843 to 1845. As the *Catholic Cabinet* was the first literary Magazine published west of the Mississippi River, it certainly was the most important one of its time in the United States. The full title was "*Catholic Cabinet and Chronicle of Religious Intelligence.*" Complete sets of the publication are very rare. The title, perhaps, was not well chosen. At least Kenrick's brother, the Bishop of Philadelphia, thought so: "I am surprised," he writes March 20, 1843, "to learn that you intend to give the name Cabinet to the periodical that you have in mind to establish, a title which belonged to a paper in Baltimore, and has now, for good reasons, been given up."[4]

---

[4] Kenrick-Frenaye Correspondence, Philadelphia, 1920, p. 164.

"A Cabinet," said he on another occasion, "is a museum of curiosities."[5] After the appearance of the first number, the editor's brother wrote: "Up to the present time few people have made any request for the periodical of which you are editor each month."[6] "I received yesterday (August 1, 1843) fifty copies of the periodical known as *The Catholic Cabinet.*" I have sent them to Pittsburg. Mr. Fithian also received a hundred copies. For the rest I will counsel you not to send out the periodical where it is to no purpose. Hardly ten persons have bought it here,"[7]) (in Philadelphia). Even in the matter of distributing the various numbers mistakes were made by the publisher. "I fear that Mr. Holcomb mixes things badly: therefore I counsel you to see to things personally, so as not to lose the results of good endeavors."[8]) No wonder that the much-harrassed episcopal editor grew despondent, so that his brother had to use more cheering words: "What you say of the periodical is not encouraging. I have been pleased with the publication, and I think it ought to be carried on to the completion of the first volume at least, if it cannot be continued further. Indeed, what has been so well begun and merited much approval, should not be too hastily discontinued. It is important for religion that the West should have a publication to uphold the Faith."[9]) On December 4, 1843, the Bishop of Philadelphia writes: "I am pleased to know that you decided to continue to publish month by month the periodical, which treats things sacred with honor to the Catholic religion. I am quite sure, if the publication can be continued for two or three years, it will have many patrons throughout the United States."[10]) So the *Catholic Cabinet* continued its course with renewed energy and interest, for another year and two months: then "constrained by circumstances" it closed its career.

The Catholics of those times were few in number and not greatly blessed with earthly goods. Perhaps the *Catholic Cabinet* was of too high a literary character to suit the general public. And the editor himself was then struggling with an immense diocesan debt his predecessor had left him.

A little later, November, 1845, the "*Catholic News-Letter*" began its weekly appearance and continued until April 1, 1848. The editorial work was done under the supervision of Bishop Kenrick by several of his priests, chief among whom was Father, Afterwards Canon O'Hanlon, the celebrated author of "Irish Saints and Shrines" and "Mission Life in Missouri." There is a complete set of the "*Catholic News-*

---

5 O'Shea, "Life of Peter Richard Kenrick," in "Two Kenricks," p. 419.
6 Kenrick-Frenaye Correspondence, p. 168.
7 Kenrick-Frenaye Correspondence, p. 169.
8 Kenrick-Frenaye Correspondence, p. 171.
9 Kenrick-Frenaye Correspondence, p. 176.
10 Kenrick-Frenaye, Correspondence, p. 178.

*Letter''* in the Library of the St. Louis University. The paper is a weekly, published by W. J. Mullin, and "edited by an Association of Gentlemen." The first number is dated Vol. I, Saturday, Nov. 22, 1845, the second, Vol. II, Saturday, Nov. 29, 1845. This mistake is rectified in No. 3, Volume III, of April 1, 1848 contains an eloquent article on Joseph Goerres, the great Catholic German writer and leader, whom the great Napoleon had styled the fourth great power in league against France. The articles contained in the *Catholic News-Letter* were generally well written. Thus the article on the Papacy in vol. I, No. 24; "A Visit to Liberty, Missouri," (July 1847) ; "Merimac," November 1847; "Cape Girardeau," August 1846; "Legends of St. Charles," February 1847, are articles of historical importance.

Shortly before its suspension, the *Catholic News-Letter* published a series of elaborate lectures, given at the Cathedral by Archbishop Kenrick, on the main doctrines of the Church. They were specially intended for non-Catholics, and paved the way for the conversion of a number of prominent citizens of St. Louis.

In reference to this *Catholic News-Letter* the Bishop of Philadelphia wrote his brother: "I am pleased that you have followed out the design of publishing a Catholic periodical."[11]) For a work once undertaken to uphold religion " is not easily to be abandoned."

After a brief career of two years and four months the *Catholic News-Letter* ceased to appear. Shortness of funds, which in a newspaper is the same thing as shortness of breath in the human body, had put an end to its useful existence."

Another failure, if you will; but Bishop Kenrick was too deeply convinced of the necessity of the Catholic Press. For his new venture which began to appear in the late summer of 1850 revived the name of Bishop Rosati's long-dead paper *"The Shepherd of the Valley."* On November 4, 1850 the Bishop of Philadelphia sent his congratulations on the appearance of the new periodical saying: "it has much merit."[12] But he advised his brother not to edit the paper himself, a thing "hardly to be risked after the unfortunate attempts of the past." Dr. Silliman Ives[13] and Jedediah V. Huntington,[14] the editor of the

---

11 Kenrick-Frenaye Correspondenc, p. 266, November 30, 1847.

12 Kenrick-Frenaye Correspondence, p. 314.

13 Levi Silliman Ives was Protestant Episcopal Bishop of North Carolina in 1831-1852. He became a Catholic at Rome in 1852. He did not receive the order of priesthood in the Catholic Church. He wrote "The Trials of a Mind in its Progress to Catholicism." He died October 13, 1867.

14 Jedediah V. Huntington, Graduate in Medicine in 1838, later Episcopalian minister. Received into the Catholic Church in 1849. Editor of the "Metropolitan" in Baltimore, and of the "St. Louis Leader." Author of a volume of Poems, N. Y. 1843. Translated Franchere's "Narration of a Voyage to the Northwest Coast of America, 1811-1814." "Rosemary," a Catholic novel. Huntington died at Pau, France, March 10, 1862.

*"Metropolitan"* in Baltimore, both converts, were not available as editors of the St. Louis paper. On the 15th day of August 1851, Robert A. Bakewell who had been editing a Catholic paper in Pittsburg, came to St. Louis at the solicitation of Archbishop Kenrick, and became editor of the *"Shepherd of the Valley"* and subsequently its publisher. Financial difficulties ensued. Bakewell grew tired of the double burden. On the anniversary of the Declaration of Independence 1854 the Francis Patrick Kenrick, now Archbishop of Baltimore, wrote his brother of St. Louis: "I feel sorry that Robert Bakewell has gone so far as to give up the work. It seems to me proper to do something in the way of helping him on account of the sterling qualities of his work. You may, if you wish, give him fifty dollars in my name."[15] As the *"Encyclopedia of the History of St. Louis"* justly says: "Throughout its career the *Shepherd of the Valley* was a most uncompromising advocate of Catholicism, and in a time when religious antagonisms were peculiarly bitter."[16] But, as Bakewell himself admitted later on, his zeal was not always tempered with prudence. He would write in the *Shepherd* in a way that, whilst harmonizing perfectly with the teachings of Catholic faith, was certain to be taken advantage of by the enemies of the Church.

One of his editorials in regard to religious liberty made a great stir among the Knownothing preachers of its day and long after, and was even made the subject of an enquiry in the U. S. Senate. Embalmed for preservation in such delectable storehouses on anti-Catholic lies as "Gavin's Masterkey of Popery," it is produced at regular intervals by Protestant controversionalists as a decisive proof of Catholic intolerance. What Bakewell wrote is this: "The practical toleration to which we are accustomed in our age and country is not the result of any principle of Protestantism; it is not the consequence of any doctrine; it has been brought about by the force of circumstances; it is owing to the fact that no denomination can pretend to exclusive dominion; it will last only as long as the state of things continues. If the Infidels, the Mormons, the Presbyterians or the Catholics, at any future time, gain a decided superiority, it is at an end. If the Catholics ever gain—which they surely will do, though at a distant date—an immense numerical superiority, religious freedom in this country is at an end. So say our enemies. So we believe; but in which sense do we believe it? In what sense are we the advocates of religious intolerance. In the sense in which the enemies of the Church understand the word? By no means. We simply mean that a Christian people will not consider the ridicule of Christianity, the denial of its fundamental truths, of the immortality of the soul and of the existence of God, the over-

---

15   Kenrick-Frenaye Correspondence, p. 372.
16   Vol. III, p. 1896.

throw of all religion and morality, matters beneath their notice and condemnation; that the foundation will be laid for a legislation which shall restrain the propagation of certain doctrines; that man shall no longer be permitted to attack dogmas with which morality is inseparably connected.''[17]

The *Shepherd of the Valley* though established in 1850 was edited and published by Bakewell from January 1852 to July 1854. Financial difficulties owing to a lack of support from the Catholic public was the cause of its demise. Bakewell in the meantime had studied law and in 1875 became a member of the Court of Appeals, a position which he held with great credit and distinction until 1885.

''A city is fortunate that has good conscientious journalists; they can instruct and mold the dormant public conscience, and oftentimes its course of conduct.''[18] Such men St. Louis Catholic journalism has had among the editors, mostly converts, whom we have so far recounted. The peer of the best we now approach in the person of Jedediah V. Huntington, the founder and editor of the ''*St. Louis Leader*,'' which ran from March 10, 1855 to October 13, 1856 as a weekly, and as a daily until 1858, The ''*Leader*'' was the original ''great religious daily'' of St. Louis, as the Encyclopedia says ''though it flavored its religion largely with Democratic politics,''[19] Dr. Huntington had been conducting a Catholic magazine *The Metropolitan,* in Baltimore. In February 1855 Archbishop Kenrick of Baltimore wrote to his brother, Peter.Richard: ''I hope that you may be able to retain that excellent man Huntington, in your city and that you will favor him with kindly patronage.''[20] In February of the following year he writes: ''Huntington thanks me for the hundred dollars, but says nothing of my subscription.''[21] And on April 16, 1858: '' as that very worthy man Huntington, is returning, I am writing to you.''[22] Huntington was editor in chief; associated with him we find Donald McLeod, William A. Seay, and Edward W. Johnson. ''The Sunday edition, as Hyde tells us, was under the charge of Donald McLeod, who was educated for the priesthood, but had chosen literature in preference to the pulpit. McLeod formed a scandalous alliance with a noted St. Louis beauty, and the affair reaching the public ear, he repented and went into a

---

[17] ''Shepherd of the Valley,'' November 22, 1851, quoted in full in Shea, ''History of the Catholic Church in the United States,'' vol. IV, pp. 606 and 607. For a defense of the letter, cf. O'Shea, ''The Two Kenricks,'' pp. 480-485.

[18] ''Modern View,'' St. Louis.

[19] L. C., vol. III, p. 1634 and 35. Cf. Scharf's ''History of St. Louis,'' vol. I, p. 921.

[20] Kenrick-Frenaye Correspondence, p. 386.

[21] Kenrick-Frenaye Correspondence, p. 410.

[22] Kenrick-Frenaye Correspondence, p. 410.

monastery in Cincinnati. Huntington in 1858 descended from the tripod of the *"Leader"* and was succeeded by his colleague Johnson, with Seay as political editor, who quickly ran the paper into the ground."[23]   We have given this piece of scandal in regard to Donald McLeod from the pen of William Hyde, simply to set it right. There was no "scandalous alliance," though the case was very mysterious. Here is what Bishop Purcell of Cincinnati states in his Memoir of the Rev. Donald Mac-Leod introducing his beautiful book *"History of Roman Catholicism in North America"*: "After his abandonment of the ministry and religious opinions of the Reformation, Mr. MacLeod, for some years, devoted his time to literary pursuits. In St. Louis, where he was connected with the editorial department of a newspaper or magazine, he became attached to an accomplished young lady of the best society; but after having gone even to the Altar for the marriage ceremony, the match was, for some reason, for which neither himself nor the lady was to blame, suddenly broken off. We have the assurance of a highly respectable priest of St. Louis, who was perfectly cognizant of all the proceedings, that the conduct of Mr. MacLeod was all that could have been expected in the premises, from a Christian and a man of honor." Donald MacLeod did not enter a monastery, but Mount St. Mary's Seminary, both as professor and theological student and was raised to the priesthood in October 1860. He died on an errand of priestly duty, being struck by a passing train June 30, 1865."[24]

But to return to the fortunes of the *"St. Louis Leader."* The paper had been established as the organ of the Catholic Church," says Hyde: but it was also a democratic party organ; a combination that certainly did not augur much good. Yet under the circumstances, when the issues were Union or Disunion, every honest man felt bound to take sides. The Democratic party of Missouri wished to preserve the Union with peaceful means: the Republican party attained the preservation of the Union by War. The *Leader* opposed the very man that made the rebellion possible and dangerous, Buchanan, whilst the *Republican* supported him. This must suffice on the matter of mingling religion and politics. It would be well, if it were possible, that religion had more influence on politics without politics controlling religion. We believe Jedediah V. Huntington honestly tried to do so.

There is but one solitary number of the *"St. Louis Leader"* in the Congressional Library, dated December 27, 1856: and one also in the Library of the Missouri Historical Society of May 27, 1857. The latter

---

23   In Missouri Historical Society Publications, 1896, p. 11.

24   "History of Roman Catholicism in North America," by the Rev. Xavier Donald MacLeod, New York. "The Devotion to the Blessed Virgin in this country from its settlement to the present day" is the theme of this beautiful book, the last and ablest offering of the genius of Xavier Donald MacLeod.

number has a leading article on "God versus Law." In the report of the Circuit Court proceedings there is this interesting item: "Circuit Court, Hon. Alexander Hamilton Judge. "Dred Scott, his wife and children emancipated."

"Taylor Blow appeared before His Honor, the Circuit Judge yesterday (May 26, 1857) and emancipated Dred Scott, his wife and Eliza and James, their two children."

In the year 1858 B. Doran Killian, began the publication of the *"Western Banner."* This paper may be classed among the Catholic periodicals having a national bias.

Archbishop Kenrick contributed $3000 to make it a Catholic paper. This came about in the following way. "On leaving St. Louis in 1858 Dr. Huntington left with the Archbishop a note for about $2000, for the purpose of establishing a Catholic paper in the city. Relying on the payment of this note, the Archbishop gave $3000 to establish the *Western Banner.*"[25] But not more than fifty per cent was realized on the note. The *Western Banner* was discontinued about 1860.

This was the Archbishop's last venture in the field of Catholic newspaperdom.

---

[25] Archbishop Kenrick's Account Book, p. 66.

## CHAPTER 24

GERMAN CATHOLIC VENTURES—JOURNALISM

There had been German Catholics in St. Louis since the foundation of the city. The first canonical Pastor P. Bernard de Limpach, a Capuchin was a German, as well as Father Paul de Saint Pierre, the one-time Pastor of Cahokia and Ste. Genevieve. By the time of Bishop Du Bourg's coming the number of German Catholics and Priests had increased considerably, and in 1837 Bishop Rosati wrote: "We have a large number of German Catholics in the diocese. German services are held for them in St. Louis, Dardenne, St. Charles, St. Thomas, Ill., St. Andrews, Ste. Genevieve, Quincy, Ill., Westphalia, Apple Creek and New Madrid. The number of emigrants from Germany is constantly increasing." The high tide of German Catholic immigration came in 1840 and continued to 1850. These Catholic Germans were not of the class of "Latin Farmers" or the Forty-Eighters, men of University training and revolutionary antecedents. They were, however, for the most part, people of sufficient intellectual culture to appreciate an honest outspoken press in their own language. Of the first efforts made in St. Louis to satisfy this natural desire of the Catholic Germans of St. Louis we find the following notice in Schem's Deutsch Amerikanisches Konversations Lexikon[1] article Missouri: The *Katholisches Sonntagsblatt*, (Sunday Paper) of E. Kessel, appearing for the first time on December 1, 1850. in the following year changed its name to "*Herold des Glaubens*," "Herald of the Faith organ of the Catholics," and the "*Tages-Chronik*," The Daily Chronicle, published by Francis Saler[2]), a Catholic daily, edited first by August Boeckling, later on by Adalbert Loehr and Ernst Kargan, was at last merged in the *Anzeiger des Westens*, 1863."

We will have to treat these two Catholic ventures of Francis Saler separately, giving precedence to the "*Herold des Glaubens*," the first Catholic paper of St. Louis destined to weather the storms of the years until the present day.

---

1 Schem's German-American Cyclopedia contains valuable information for the history of German-American life all through its 8 volumes.

2 Francis Saler, a native of Vorarlberg, was architect, builder, publisher and printer and bookseller all in one. He amassed a fortune and then lost it and died a poor man, though always highly respected. Father Holweck has given him a place among the "Friends of the Pastoral-Blatt."

The *"Herold des Glaubens"* appeared for the first time on the first Sunday of January 1850 under the editorship of P. Martin Seisl, S. J., then Pastor of St. Joseph's Church. The publisher was P. Kessel, formerly employed in Saler's printing office. Originally the paper's name was *"Katholisches Sonntagsblatt"* but it was soon changed into *"Herold des Glaubens,* ein Katholisches Sonntagsblatt.'' After a struggle of two years with adverse circumstances, mostly financial, Francis Saler, then at the height of prosperity, came to the rescue. The paper was enlarged. Dr. Thomas Baumstark a distinguished convert, became its editor about 1861 serving in that capacity until the close of the Civil War, when he was succeeded by J. B. Mueller, formerly teacher in Dutzow, Missouri. But the failure of Francis Saler in 1874 threatened to cut short the life of the *"Herold des Glaubens."* Rev. C. Wachter volunteered to conduct the paper until other arrangements could be made. In May 1875 Vicar-General Muehlsiepen, called a meeting of Catholic laymen for the purpose of forming an association which should take over the paper. A committee of five was chosen to arrange matters; 365 dollars were paid for the good will of the paper, and Mr. Cramer appointed editor and general manager. Father Muehlsiepen and Mr. Joseph Gummersbach[3]) were the mainstays of the enterprise. On the 5th day of February 1878 Cramer resigned and was succeeded by William Schwarz, the genial ''Schneider Spitzig.'' Since the autumn of 1878 Mr. Louis Blankemeir was business manager. For a long time the *"Herold des Glaubens"* prospered and grew in influence, but with the gradual extinction of the German language among the native born, a gradual decline set in. On the first day of November 1916 the *"Herold des Glaubens"* found a new home in the Amerika Building and was subsequently combined with the semi-weekly edition of the *Amerika* under the title *"Amerika-Herold des Glaubens."*

The *Herold des Glaubens* always had a wide circulation, not only in St. Louis, but throughout the West and Southwest. Its columns contain a chronicle of the leading events in the history of the Church for the last seventy years. An almost complete set of the publication is preserved in the Office of the *"Amerika."* For many years the Herold Company also published an Almanac, the *"Familienfreund,"* in which a number of the best American writers offered valuable contribution of a literary and historical character.

Franz Salers *"Der Hinkende Bote am Mississippi"* was also a very welcome guest in many a German home.

The *"Herold des Glaubens"* being but a weekly, did not supply the needs of the time. A daily German Catholic paper was felt to be a

---

3 The founder of the firm, B. Herder Co., in St. Louis.

necessity, especially as the "Anzeiger des Westens" and other liberalistic organs of the German Forty-Eighters made frequent attacks upon the Faith and Morals of Catholics.

"In 1851," says the Encyclopedia of the History of St. Louis, "Mr. Franz Saler began publishing the "*Tages-Chronik*," a German two-cent morning newspaper with strong Catholic bias. Among the early editors Mr. Anton Boeckling and Mr. Adalbert Loehr. After twelve years its business interests were transferred to the "*Anzeiger des Westens*," and it ceased to exist. This would place the "*Tages-Chronik's*" date of demise in 1863. By a lucky chance a copy of weekly edition of the Chronik of 1861, the *Wochen-Chronik*, turned up, the only remnant of the paper we know of, and from its columns we get a few interesting items.[4]) The editor August Kruer[5]) seems to have been an able journalist. The place of publication in 1861 was the S. W. Corner of 2nd and Market Streets. The subscription price was $2.00.

In Friedrich Muench's "Der Staat Missouri," I found the following item: "The *St. Louis Chronik* is conservative and opposed to a change in the present system of slavery. The paper is mainly read by Catholics." This very likely means nothing more, than that the "*Tages-Chronik*" was democratic in principle and practice. In the *Wochen Chronik* of June 6, 1861, the leading article is devoted to Stephan A. Douglas, then recently deceased, who is extolled "as the most honored leader, the peerless champion, the most adroit defender, the unconquered hero of the Union cause." The great opponent of Lincoln is reported to have died a Catholic.

William Hyde, one time editor of the now defunct "*Republican*," sometime in 1896 read a paper before the Missouri Historical Society on "Newspapers and Newspaper People of Three Decades," in which he makes the following statements in regard to Franz Saler's Chronicle: The "*Tages-Chronik*," (Daily Chronicle), was located in third story of the *Republican* office. Francis Saler was proprietor. The local editor was an obese and rather inactive man named Meyer, who made a practice, instead of hustling around for news himself, of taking copy off the Republican foreman's hook, translating as much as he wanted of it, and returning the original. I tired of this and set a trap for

---

4  Cf. "Amerika," October 21, 1921.

5  In Kargau's "St. Louis in Frueheren Jahren," 1893, I found a brief notice of A. Kruer. He had edited a newspaper in Madison, Wisconsin, and been librarian of the State Library. After serving on a paper in Chicago he followed Adalbert Loehr in the editorial management of the "Tageschronik," January 1, 1861, but resigned within a year. He was elected Justice of the Peace in South St. Louis (Frenchtown) in 1863 and died in 1865.

the unsuspecting Mr. Meyer. With the aid of Wm. McHenry, there was prepared an elaborate account of the murder in her bed of a white woman by a colored man, who had been living in the same dwelling, and of the suicide of the black fiend. The scene was located—the rear of a house on Pine Street, between Third and Fourth. The narrative, which was quite lengthy, was nothing more nor less than the story of Desdemona, some eminent actor having played Othello the night before at DeBar's old theatre. Meyer took the cork clear under. and, if he had stuck to the text, it would not have been a bad item, but of course, supposing it would appear in the *Republican*, he put in extraneous facts that spoiled the article as a travesty, and only made him laughed at the more."[6]

Now, whether this item be fact or fancy, it gives us a pleasant insight into the old genial newspaperdom before the advent of the linotype and the cylinder press, the days when all things were as yet primitive and more human.

About ten years had passed since the discontinuance of the *Tages-Chronik*. The German Catholics were without a daily paper. Muehlsiepen at the request of Henry J. Spaunhorst and Anthony Roeslein called a meeting of prominent German priests and laymen. The meeting was held in St. Mary's School Building, October 5th 1871. The plan for a new Catholic daily was formed, a directory chosen, with Mr. Spaunhorst as President. But almost a year was consumed with the preparations. The name "*Amerika, a newspaper for Truth and Justice*" was adopted upon motion of Mr. Roeslein. No. 415 Olive Street was the house of the publication. The first number, of four pages in very large format appeared October 17, 1872. Anton Hellmich was the editor. He came from Mud Creek, St. Libory, Illinois, had been a school teacher, possessed a massive figure and a mighty voice, and always wore a Turkish Fez on his Olympian head and dangled a long German students-pipe from his mouth. According to all accounts Mr. Anton Hellmich as editor, was vox et praeterea nihil. The real editor from the start was that noble convert from Lutheranism, Dr. Edward Preuss. Dr. Preuss had been minister of the Gospel and Professor of Theology. After his conversion he turned to journalism. Editor Hellmich resigned January 17, 1878 and the assistant editor, Dr. Preuss,[7] became editor-in-chief. November 27, 1872 the "*Amerika*" office was removed to 106 N. Third Street. To show the policy of the new paper a quotation

---

6 Missouri Historical Society Publications. Vol. I, No. 12, 1896. p. 14 and 15.

7 Dr. Edward Preuss wrote a beautiful work in praise of the Immaculate Conception of the Blessed Virgin Mary. His conversion was mainly brought about by his studies to refute the controversial writings of Cardinal Bellarmin.

from its first editorial will be most appropriate: "We declare hereby, that the "*Amerika*" will not be what is commonly called a religious or a church-paper. Theological disquisitions and fruitless polemics we will always exclude from our columns, on the other hand we will be ever ready and prepared fearessly to meet every attack upon our rights as Catholics and promptly to repel all malicious charges, and that in a way consonant with the motto we have chosen. and the dignity of our cause. What we demand for ourselves, we shall be ready to concede to others, truth and justice. Politically the "*Amerika*" will maintain strict independence of all party-organizations." Among the distinguished men employed by the "*Amerika*" during its early days we would mention Louis Willich, the future editor of *Puck,* who served as local editor.

In 1907 the *Amerika* moved into its own building on Sixth Street. After the death of Dr. Edward Preuss July 11, 1904, the Doctor's son, Arthur who for a few years previous had been assistant editor, became editor for a short time to be succeeded by Mr. F. P. Kenkel who held the position with great credit until May 1920. Once more Mr. Arthur Preuss assumed the management at the urgent request of the directors of the paper.[8]

Dr. Edward Preuss as well as Mr. F. P. Kenkel are converts to the Faith. Arthur Preuss can also be counted among converts. All these have proven themselves as men of strong character, deep convictions, great learning, a clear incisive style of writing and above all, of the most loyal devotion to the Church. Under such leaders the "*Amerika*" prospered, but the War and its consequences almost closed the paper's career just on the eve of its Golden Jubilee. The papers brought notices like the following one clipped from the *St. Louis Star*:

"Die Amerika, founded at the time when German immigration was at its height, served a most useful purpose in familiarizing the newcomers with the ideals, customs and standards of their adopted country. Its passing on October 30 after half a century of good work can be attributed altogether to the stoppage of that same immigration.

In the last two decades the flow from Germany to America fell to a mere trickle. Since 1914 there has been no movement whatever. What with the growth of educational opportunities and the earnest desire of the average German immigrant to become nationalized to his new environment there has of necessity been a narrowing of the circle of German newspaper readers."[9]

---

[8] Mr. Arthur Preuss continued until October 30, 1921, to edit and manage the "Amerika."

[9] "St. Louis Star."

But the end was not yet at hand, though the death-stroke had been given. The main stockholders sold their shares to a consortium of non-catholics. Most of the catholic employes were retained, and the editorial management remained Catholic. It was but a provisional arrangement. After a year's manful struggle, a journalistic adventurer got hold of the helm and cheerfully ran the proud ship upon the breakers. The last of the German Catholic Dailies, the *Amerika*, was no more.

The German-speaking Clergy of St. Louis, since 1866 have enjoyed the distinction of having a monthly theological visitor, the *Pastoral Blatt*. Complete files of this important publication are very scarce, as far as I know there are but four, one with the editor himself, another in the Salesian Library, the third in the New York Public Library, and the fourth in the parish residence of St. Joseph's Church, St. Louis. Father Holweck has written a succinct history of this Pastoral Review as we may call it, on the occasion of its Golden Jubilee[10]) The founder was Archbishop, then only Father Michael Heiss of Milwaukee. Father Muehlsiepen was selected as its first editor; a circle of St. Louis priests pledged the pecuniary support of the venture. The first number appeared in September 1866 from the printing-shop of Franz Saler. The Professors of the Salesianum at Milwaukee were to supply the literary matter. In the prospectus written by Father Heiss, the third point reads: "This paper should serve as a sort of archives for interesting accounts and documents concerning the history of our holy Church in this country."

This promise was fulfilled in the olden as well as in more recent times: and the historical articles now form the priceless value of the *Pastoral Blatt*. From the great number of titles we can select but a few.

Father Nicolas Merz, Pastor of the German Parish in Baltimore; Bishop Lawrence Grassel; Rev. Paul Helbron; Rev. Joseph Pellentz, S. J.; P. James Frombach, S. J.; P. Ferdinand Steinmayer, S. J.; Father Raffeiner; P. Theodor Schneider, S. J., and P. W. Wappler, S. J., Father L. Geissler, P. Anthony Kohlmann, S. J., Rev. Louis de Barth, Rev. Jos. Schueller. All these and many more brief biographies of the early Catholic missionaries in the East, are found in the various numbers of the *Pastoral Blatt*. On January 1, 1873 Father William Faerber, a giant in body, as well as in learning succeeded Father Muehlsiepen as editor. Under his editorship the *Pastoral Blatt* manifested a deeper interest in the ecclesiastico-political questions agitating the world in his time. "Fears and Hopes for the Catholic

---

[10] "Pastoral Blatt," vol. 50, No. 12.

Church and Schools in the United States'' was the title of one of the articles that called down upon the devoted editor of the *Pastoral-Blatt* the wrath of many men high in the councils of the American Church. That the *Pastoral-Blatt* was right and the modernists wrong is now plain to all. A great deal of the contemporary church history is stored up for the future historian in the files of the *Pastoral-Blatt* under Father Faerber's editorship. At his death April 17, 1905, Monsignore, then Father F. G. Holweck succeeded to the editoral chair.

In the year of its Golden Jubilee 1916 the *Pastoral-Blatt* began the publication of a very important series of biographical sketches of German-American pioneers of the Church. Vicar-General Muehlsiepen, the apostle of the German and Polish Catholics of the Archdiocese of St. Louis, Father William Faerber, one of the real authorities on Catechetical methods; Father Innocent Wapelhorst, O. F. M., president of a Great Seminary and then a lowly Franciscan monk, author of the best American book on the Rites of the Church, are treated in the opening chapters. All of these were St. Louis priests, and men of whom our State will be proud forever.

But the Editor, finding that these historical articles supplied a real want, continued his researches and brought to light many an interesting fact of our early days. The papers that have appeared in monthly instalments are devoted to a number of men of note in their day, but whose memory was fast vanishing from view. Bishop Melcher of Green Bay, once Vicar-General of St. Louis; Father Oshwald the quaint mystical writer and founder of the communistic colony of St. Nazianz in Wisconsin, Father Francis Goller of SS. Peter and Paul's, the pastor par excellence, Father Brickwedde, the first missionary to the Germans of Quincy, Illinois, the Abbe Joseph Lutz, pioneer missionary among the Kansas Indians, Father Caspar Ostlangenberg, founder of a number of parishes in Illinois, the rough but loveable Father Ursus Meister, Father Helias, S. J., Father Saulnier, Father Charles De la Croix, and a host of others, of the West and East and South find themselves immortalized in the pages of the *Pastoral-Blatt* from 1917— 1924. Here we also find the best history of the diocese of St. Louis, written by the editor. No library of Catholic Americana can be called complete without a set of the seven last volumes of the *Pastoral-Blatt*.

# THE SECOND SYNOD OF ST. LOUIS

A little less than eleven years had elapsed since the First Synod of the diocese of St. Louis was held in the Cathedral by Bishop Joseph Rosati, when his successor, Peter Richard Kenrick, now Archbishop of St. Louis convoked the Second Synod, to be held in the week of the Fourteenth Sunday after Pentecost.[1] The letter of convocation was dated May 25th, 1850; the Synod was opened on the Feast of St. Louis, August 25th, 1850. The Archbishop in his Pastoral Letter issued after the Synod, wrote, that he had long desired to assemble the Clergy in Synod, but that various impediments had hitherto prevented the accomplishment of his wish, and that even now he would not have felt justified in calling them from their respective stations, but for the necessity that existed for arranging several matters connected with the present state, and future prospects, of Religion in the diocese. There were forty-three priests in attendance, and four absent. Only such priests as had the care of souls were called to attend, the priests teaching that were employed in Colleges and Seminaries were not expected to attend. Only a few of those who had been present at the First Synod, were still among the living; John Elct, S. J. Edmund Saulnier, Augustus Paris, Joseph Renaud, Lewis Tucker, Saint Cyr, Ferdinand Helias, S. J. and Ambrose Heim.

Joseph Melcher was now the only Vicar-General of the Archdiocese: he was appointed Promotor of the Synod; Patrick O'Brien was made Secretary, and Edmund Saulnier, Notary. From Monday to Thursday members of the secular priests made a Retreat at the Seminary under the spiritual presence of the Jesuit Father Peter Speicher; on Friday morning all the Fathers attended the Solemn Requiem for the repose of the soul of Bishop Joseph Rosati and all the deceased priests of the Archdiocese: the second session was held on Friday.

The following Fathers responded to the roll call:

Adm. Rev. Josephus Melcher, V. G.   Rev. D. Patricius O'Brien
Adm. Rev. P. Johannes A. Elct,   Rev. D. Bernardus Donnelly
   S. J.   Rev. D. Thomas Scanlon
Adm. Rev. D. Johannes Lynch,   Rev. B. Johannes Higginbotham
   C. M.   Rev. D. Johannes O'Hanlon
Adm. Rev. D. Antonius O'Regan   Rev. P. Johannes Baptista Miége,
Rev. D. Simon A. Paris   S. J.

---

[1] The substance of this chapter is taken from the Acta et Decreta of the Second Synod of St. Louis, 1850.

Rev. D. Edmundus Saulnier

Rev. D. Josephus Renaud

Rev. D. Petrus Donnelly

Rev. D. Ambrosius J. Heim

Rev. P. Felix Verreydt, S. J.

Rev. P. Ferdinandus Helias, S. J.

Rev. P. Petrus De Smet, S. J.

Rev. P. Judocus Van Asche, S. J.

Rev. D. Ludovicus Tucker

Rev. P. Andreas Ehrensberger, S.J.

Rev. D. Josephus Meister

Rev. D. Antonius Penco, C. M.

Rev. D. Jacobus Rolando, C. M.

Rev. P. Arnoldus Damen, S. J.

Rev. D. Jacobus Murphy

Rev. D. Gulielmus Wheeler

Rev. D. Dionysius Byrne

Rev. D. Franciscus Rutkowski

Rev. D. Georgius Ortlieb

Rev. D. A. Saunier

Rev. D. Jacobus Stehle

Rev. D. Simon Siegrist

Rev. D. Franciscus Weiss

Rev. D. Ludovicus Rosi

Rev. D. Johannes Anselm

Rev. D. Josephus Blaarer

Rev. D. Patricius Ward

Rev. D. Jacobus Fox

Rev. D. Edwardus Hamel

Rev. D. Georgius Tuerck

Rev. D. Josephus Rauch

Rev. D. Remigius Gebhardt

The absent ones were:

Rev. D. J. M. St. Cyr

Rev. D. Johannes Cotter

Rev. P. Antonius Eysvogels, S. J.

Rev. D. Thomas Cusack

After roll-call the following Reverend gentlemen were appointed Synodal Examiners: Joseph Melcher, V. G., John A. Elet, S. J., Anthony O'Regan, Anthony Penco, C. M., Joseph D. Marchi, C. M. and Peter Speicher, S. J. After several decrees of the Council of Trent, and of the Fourth Plenary Council of Baltimore were read. At the afternoon session which was held under the presidency of the Promotor of the Synod, the various decrees which the Archbishop intended to promulgate at the Saturday session, were read and discussed by the clergy, and on Saturday the Archbishop made a long address to the Synod in which he promulgated and explained the decrees, as approved by the Synod. On Sunday morning Father Lewis Tucker sang a solemn Highmass in honor of the Blessed Trinity, and Father John Lynch, C. M., preached an eloquent sermon.

The Archbishop then announced the appointment of the Very Rev. Joseph Melcher as Vicar-General with full powers, even in matrimonial cases; of Edmund Saulnier as Chancellor, and of Ambrose J. Heim as Secretary.

The members of the Arch-episcopal Council were the following: Joseph Melcher, Anthony O'Regan, Simon Paris, and Ambrose J. Heim.

With this the Synod came to an end, and all returned to their posts of duty.

The Reverend Chancellor Edmond Saulnier compiled the following instruction table from the report made just previous by the Synod, in 1850.

## STATISTICS OF THE ARCHDIOCESE OF ST. LOUIS, MISSOURI, 1850

| Place | County | Patron | Pastor | No. of Souls | Bapt. | Mar. | Fun. | Con. |
|---|---|---|---|---|---|---|---|---|
| St. Louis | St. Louis | Cathedral, St. Louis | Rev. Archbishop with 6 Priests | 4450 | 317 | 128 | | 15 |
| St. Louis | St. Louis | St. Mary of Victory | Jos. Melcher | 2500 | 178 | 69 | 38 | 2 |
| St. Louis | St. Louis | St. Francis Xavier | A. Damen, S. J. | 3000 | 278 | 95 | 30 | 60 |
| St. Louis | St. Louis | St. Patrick | Wm. Wheeler | 5000 | 458 | 168 | | |
| St. Louis | St. Louis | St. Joseph's | J. B. Hofbauer, S. J. | 4000 | 301 | 83 | 120 | 2 |
| St. Louis | St. Louis | St. Vincent de Paul | F. X. Dahmen, C. M. | 1500 | 214 | 63 | 259 | 5 |
| St. Louis | St. Louis | St. John Apostle | P. O'Brien | 1065 | 161 | 52 | | 2 |
| St. Louis | St. Louis | Ss. Peter and Paul | S. Siegrist | 2000 | 213 | 77 | 12 | 3 |
| St. Louis | St. Louis | Holy Trinity | J. Anselm | 1700 | 120 | 33 | 13 | 3 |
| St. Louis | St. Louis | St. Michael | J. Higginbotham | 2000 | 8 | 3 | 2 | 1 |
| Apple Creek | Perry | St. Joseph | Fr. Trojan | 413 | 35 | 1 | 15 | |
| Armagh | Franklin | St. Patrick | E. Hamil | 600 | 14 | | | |
| Barrens | Perry | St. Mary | J. Lynch, C. M. | 3500 | 123 | 16 | 72 | 3 |
| Benton | Scott | St. Mary | Jac. Stehle | 609 | 40 | 10 | 23 | 5 |
| Cape Girardeau | Cape Girardeau | St. Vincent's | Rich. Hennessy | 607 | 28 | 4 | 19 | 5 |
| Carondelet | St. Louis | Ss. Mary and Joseph | Geo. Ortlieb | 2000 | 73 | 21 | 27 | 2 |
| Central Tp. | St. Louis | St. Martin | J. Higgins | 120 | 31 | 3 | 1 | 4 |
| Dardennes | St. Charles | St. Peter | N. Neumann | 1480 | 26 | 2 | 8 | 2 |
| Deepwater | Henry | St. Ludger | J. Blaarer | 50 | 4 | 1 | 6 | |
| Florissant | St. Louis | St. Ferdinand | J. Van Assche, S. J. | 1720 | 94 | 18 | 37 | 12 |
| Fredericktown | Madison | St. Michael | L. Tucker | 330 | 40 | 6 | 20 | 4 |
| French Village | St. Francois | St. Ann | A. Saunier | 525 | 51 | 4 | 5 | 2 |
| Hermann | Gasconade | St. George | A. Eysvogels, S. J. (Att. Washington) | 468 | 39 | 2 | 22 | |
| Indian Creek | Monroe | St. Stephen | D. Kennedy | 700 | 32 | | | |
| Jefferson City | Cole | St. Peter | J. U. Meister | 169 | 14 | 2 | 2 | |
| Kansas City | Jackson | St. Francis Reg. | B. Donnelly | 200 | 16 | 1 | 11 | |

STATISTICS OF THE ARCHDIOCESE OF ST. LOUIS, MISSOURI—Continued

| Place | County | Patron | Pastor | No. of Souls | Bapt. | Mar. | Fun. | Con. |
|---|---|---|---|---|---|---|---|---|
| Kirkwood (Gravois) | St. Louis | St. Peter | John Hennessy | 140 | 7 | ... | 2 | ... |
| Liberty | Clay | St. James | J. Murphy | 80 | 12 | 1 | 1 | ... |
| Marshall (Irish Settl.) | Saline | ......... | Thomas Cusack | 400 | ... | ... | ... | ... |
| Mattice Creek | St. Louis | Assumption | Rem. Gebhardt | 700 | 35 | 7 | 19 | ... |
| Millwood | Lincoln | St. Alphonsus | D. Lyne | 400 | 24 | 1 | 4 | 8 |
| Moniteau Creek | Moniteau | Assumption | G. Tuerk | 200 | ... | ... | ... | ... |
| New Madrid | New Madrid | St. John the Baptist | F. Jamison | 300 | 94 | 24 | 3 | 2 |
| North Santa Fe | Clark | St. Patrick | D. Kennedy (Ex. 1850) | 700 | 32 | 4 | 5 | 3 |
| Old Mines | Washington | St. Joachim | J. C. Fitnam | 300 | 29 | 11 | 27 | 1 |
| Portage d. Sioux | St. Charles | St. Francis | L. Verreydt, S. J | 318 | 18 | 4 | 14 | ... |
| Potosi | Washington | St. James | J. Fox | 450 | 20 | ... | 1 | ... |
| Richwoods | Washington | St. Stephen's | L. Rosi | 800 | 30 | 1 | 10 | 5 |
| St. Charles | St. Charles | St. Charles | P. J. Verhaegen, S. J. | 578 | 59 | 9 | 59 | 2 |
| St. Charles | St. Charles | St. Peter's | Jos. Rauch | 700 | 30 | 12 | ... | ... |
| Ste. Genevieve | Ste. Genevieve | Ste. Genevieve | J. M. I. St. Cyr | 900 | 68 | 17 | 52 | 2 |
| St. Joseph | Buchanan | St. Joseph | Ph. Scanlon (Ex. 1850) | 412 | 39 | 3 | 28 | 3 |
| St. Paul's | Ralls | St. Paul | Vacant | 600 | 33 | 11 | 12 | 1 |
| Taos | Cole | St. Francis Xavier | F. Helias, S. J. | 600 | 39 | 6 | 19 | 4 |
| Washington | Franklin | St. Francis Borg. | A. Eysvogels, S. J | 1296 | 65 | 20 | 31 | 1 |
| Weston | Platte | Holy Trinity | F. Rutkowski | 350 | 29 | 3 | 28 | 3 |
| Westphalia | Osage | St. Joseph | Fr. Kalcher, S. J. | 1920 | 87 | 21 | 107 | 1 |
| Zell (German Settlement) | Ste. Genevieve | St. Joseph | F. X. Weiss | 1085 | 47 | 15 | 10. | 1 |
| | | | | 54135 | 3705 | 1032 | 973 | 169 |
| Missions and Stations, say.......... | | | | 4000 | 3705 | | | |
| | | | | 58135 | 3705 | | | |

Parish Churches in City of St. Louis................10
Parish Churches outside City of St. Louis;...........38

Of the forty-three priests mentioned as pastors of souls in the Archdiocese of St. Louis thirty-three were members of the diocesan clergy and only ten of religious Orders. From now on the diocesan priests under the immediate command of the Archbishop were the leaders in the Church's progress in the Archdiocese:

They were the bond which drew together the scattered flock; they were the builders. Many of them were never known outside of parishes where they labored; yet it is to such unheralded men that the progress of the Church in Missouri was mainly due. And from the ranks of such men came, in the nineteenth century also, the majority of the great bishops and archbishops of the West.

The extent of their field of labor may be better judged by the subjoined table of Missions and Stations given in the Report of 1851 as attended from the following places.

Armagh: Johnstown, afterward Pacific.

Barrens: Mattingly's, Reiney's and Manning's, Vysfel Settlement; St. Mary's Landing and Bois Brulé Bottom.

Benton: New Hamburg, Tywappoti Bottom and Nova Yorka.

Cape Girardeau: Jackson.

Carondelet: Jefferson Barracks, visited by V. Rev. O'Regan.

Dardenne: Upper Dardenne, afterward Josephville.

Deepwater: Hog Creek and Windmill (Tipton).

Fredericktown: Iron Mountain, Pilot Knob and New Tennessee.

Indian Creek: Salt River and Brush Creek.

Jefferson City: Fulton and Columbia.

Kansas City: Independence and Lexington, Sibley.

Liberty: Fredericksburg, Far West, Carrolton.

Mattice Creek: Maxville.

Millwood: Louisiana, Pike Co., Portland, Callaway Co., Danville, Montgomery Co.

New Madrid: Point Pleasant.

North Santa Fe: Edina, Knox Co., Mudd Settlement, Scotland Co., Tully, Alexandria.

Old Mines: Valle's Mines, Jefferson Co.

Potosi: At Bryan Pratt's house, Big River, St. Francois Co.

Richwoods: Sandy Creek, Jefferson Co., Gallaher's Mills, Franklin Co., Reed's Settlement, Gasconade Co.

Ste. Genevieve: Bloomsdale (Fourche a Duclos).

St. Joseph's: English Grove.

Washingon: Gildehouse, Port Hudson, Augusta, Dutzow, Peers, Loutre
    Island, afterward Starkenburg, Little Berger.
Weston, Deister's Settlement: Kesler's Settlement, Parkville, Fort
    Leavenworth.
Westphalia: Loose Creek, Richfountain, St. Thomas.
Zell: Riviere Aux Vases and Saline.

The reported number of Catholics in the Archdiocese of St. Louis,
in 1850 was 58,135 it exceeded the number of those that were reported
to the First Synod held by Bishop Rosati eleven years previous, by
twenty thousand souls. Yet, there may have been many more un-
reported Catholics in the diocese in 1839 than there were in 1850. On
the other hand, it must be remembered that Bishop Rosati's Synod
represented the Catholic population, not only of Missouri, but of Illinois,
Arkansas and the Far West, which was no longer the case in 1850
when the archdiocese of St. Louis was confined to the state of Missouri.
The record of the intervening eleven years shows a phenomenal growth
of Catholicity in Missouri, in the city as well as in the country places.

It represents the will and generous initiative of the great prelate
placed by Divine Providence over the vast fruitful field; it represents
no less the readiness of the priests to accept responsibility and finally
the true Christian spirit the hardy immigrant brought along with them
from their Catholic homes beyond the sea. Not that all were good and
faithful; for an admixture of indifference and supine neglect was
noticeable then as it is today. Hence we need not wonder that among
the dioceses of the Synod there are not a few that contain severe
strictures on certain grave abuses:

The Pastoral Letter of September 1, 1850, issued in connection
with the Diocesan Synod, directed the attention of priests and people
to a few of the most important subjects, the reception of the Blessed
Sacrament, Marriage and Christian Education.

"How many are there not who, despising the bounty of their
Savior, in the incomprehensible mystery of His love prepare then only
to eat the Bread of Life, when they are at the end of their pilgrimage;
whereas it was given to sustain them during their progress through
its difficulties and dangers. How often have we not had occasion to
apprehend, in regard to such persons, the fulfillment of the Apostolic
menance: "God is not mocked:" (Gal. VI., 7.) when we have seen such
neglectful Christians, incapable of receiving the Holy Eucharist at
the hour of death! And is there not every reason to fear that, even when
this Divine Gift is received in such circumstances, the graces which it
is capable of communicating, are withheld, by reason of the hard and
impenitent heart of those who receive it, more through the impulse of
fear than from a principle of love?

"Brethren, we entreat you, by the love you bear your own souls, and by the love of Him who gave His life a ransom for those souls, to shake off this fatal lethargy, in which so many of you lie enthralled; to run to those fountains of salvation which our Divine Saviour has opened in His Church; to wash yourselves therein from all defilement of the flesh and of the spirit, by the worthy reception of the Sacrament of Penance; to arise and eat of the supernatural food which not an angel, but the God of angels Himself, points out to you, as the source of strength and perseverance in your journey to the Mountain of God."

As to the Sacrament of Matrimony the Letter says:

"This institution, which has God for its author, has been elevated by our Savior to the dignity of a Sacrament of the New Law. It is declared by the Apostle, St. Paul, to be a great sacrament in Christ and in the Church: (Eph. V. 22.) because it was, from the beginning, a figure of the union of the Son of God and the Church, His Spouse. The Divine Author of our religion has, evidently, designed that this expressive type of his Love for the Church, and of the Church's obedience and fidelity to Him, should be the model for his followers engaged in this state; and accordingly He has not left it unprovided with those graces, by means of which the married couple may be enabled to imitate the sublime example placed before them. (Eph. V. 25). Besides, as this institution, is the foundation of society everything connected with it, is of immense importance, even in reference to the present order of things."

"We scarcely need remind you, brethren, of the doctrine of the Church regarding the indissoluble nature of the marriage tie. That doctrine is implied in the words of Christ: "What God hath joined together, let no man put asunder: (Matth. XIX. 6) as well as in those of the Apostle St. Paul: "The woman hath an husband, whilst her husband liveth, is bound to the law; but if her husband be dead, she is loosed from the law of her husband." (Rom. vii. 2). Nothing, then, but the death of one of the parties can authorize the other to contract a new engagement. Every marriage contracted by either party during the lifetime of the other, is no marriage in the sight of God, no matter before whom such marriage may have been celebrated; and persons living in such state are to be considered as notorious and scandalous sinners, and dealt with accordingly in life and at death."

"We earnestly desire to see the custom of celebrating a marriage in the church, and of receiving the Nuptial Benediction during the Mass for "Bridegroom and Bride," which the Church has prepared for the occasion, preserved where it exists, and as far as circumstances may permit restored, where it has been suffered to fall into disuse. To Christian marriage thus celebrated, the words of Tertullian in the second century of the church, are literally applicable: "How shall I be able to express the happiness of those nuptials which the church joins—which sacrifice confirms—which benediction seals—which the angels announce, and the Father ratifies!" (Lib. II, ad uxorem c. ult.).

The Pastoral now turns to the fruit of Christian marriage, the children entrusted by God to the parents, to be prepared for their glorious destiny by Christian education:

"Whatever be the designs of God on your children, you are bound by every principle to give them a Christian education. Wherever this duty is generally neglected, none but the most afflicting results need be looked for. The necessity of educating youth is everywhere admitted; but, unfortunately, there prevails most serious errors as to the nature of what constitutes education. This does not consist, as many appear to imagine, merely in the cultivation of the intellectual powers, and in the acquisition of that knowledge which constitutes learning. Education necessarily implies the cultivation of the will as well as of the mind, and the acquisition of moral and religious habits; without which the most brilliant talents and the most varied intellectual acquirements become only instruments of evil. The supernatural end for which man has been made, must ever be had in view, in the education by which he is to be enabled to attain it; and every system which is not founded on this principle or seeks, through expediency or apparent necessity, to limit its application; every system in which the principles of the Catholic Church are not deeply imprinted on the youthful mind by the religious practices in which they are embodied; every system in which the Divine gift of faith is exposed, or the tender plant of youthful innocence and piety is liable to be blasted by the contagion of evil example—every system, no matter whatever advantages it may possess, must be regarded by the Catholic as incomplete or positively wrong. We therefore, exhort our venerable brethren of the clergy to encourage the establishment of truly Catholic schools and houses of education in their respective districts; and we rely on the esteem in which the laity hold Christian education, as affording an assurance, that they will cheerfully and liberally cooperate with the Rev. pastors in the establishment and we would hope, the permanent endowment of such schools."

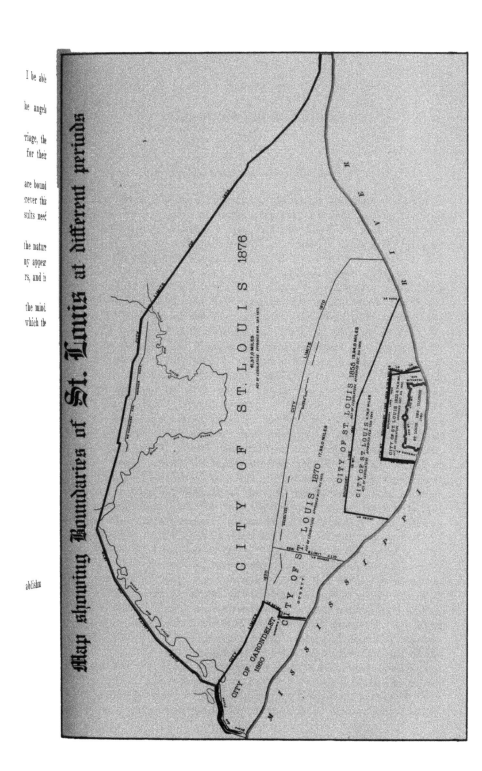

Map showing Boundaries of St. Louis at different periods

CHAPTER 26

## A DECADE OF CHURCH-BUILDING

### I

#### ST. BRIDGET AND ST. MALACHY

The decade of years immediately following the Second Synod of St. Louis was a period of remarkable parish-foundations in the city and country. St. Bridget's was built in 1854, St. John Nepomuc in 1854, St. Lawrence O'Toole in 1855, St. Liborius in 1855, St. Malachy in 1858, the Annunciation in 1859, St. Boniface in Carondelet in 1860 and the Assumption in 1861. These parishes form, as it were, the second line of religious advance in the city, the Cathedral of St. Louis and the church of S. S. Mary and Joseph in Carondelet, with the church of St. Mary of the Victories as a connecting link, forming the base, and the churches S. S. Peter and Paul, St. Vincent de Paul, St. John the Apostle, St. Francis Xavier, St. Joseph, St. Patrick, St. Michael and Holy Trinity in the suburb of Bremen forming the original first line, all radiating from the Cathedral on the river-bank, and pressing against the somewhat irregular concave inner line of the city-limits of 1855 (Grand Avenue). The new foundations do not offer so many distinctive traits or memorable circumstances, as the earlier parishes. Most of them were financed, at least in part, by the Archbishop's Bank. Three nationalities, the Irish, German and Bohemian, were prominently represented in this up-building. Some of them have maintained a high degree of efficiency up to the present day, others have declined from their former splendor: but all have done distinguished work for holy Church: and all of them have had pastors whose names are still in honor and benediction. The Church of St. Bridget on Jefferson Avenue and Carr Street, once one of the most flourishing Churches of the city is now but a shadow of its former self. Yet the title of the mother church of the central part of St. Louis still clings to her. It was in 1853 that Father John Christopher Fitnam was appointed pastor of the wide district around what is now Jefferson Avenue, and commissioned to build a temporary church for the scattered Irish families of the westward movement. On June 5th, 1853, the Rev. Anthony Penco, C.M. blessed and placed the corner-stone of the little building, which was dedicated on the 28th day of the following August. Father Fitnam was a native of Ireland, having been born in Cork on November 12th, 1825. He was raised to the priesthood by Bishop Miége in St. Xavier's Church on April 27th, 1851. His first field of labor was at Old Mines; in 1852 he became pastor of St.

(187)

Patrick's Church in St. Louis, and in May 1853 pastor of St. Bridget's. He left the archdiocese on June 19th, 1856.[1]

Father David F. Lillis, who was appointed to St. Bridget's in June 1856 and, in the course of time, built the present church of St. Bridget, was born in Limerick, on May 11th, 1827. Coming to St. Louis in 1850 he persued his studies at the Seminary in Carondelet and was ordained priest on the 10th of April 1852, by Archbishop Kenrick at the Cathedral. After spending four laborious years in the parish of St. Stephen at Indian Creek, he received this appointment to St. Bridget's Parish. The corner stone of the new church, was laid by Archbishop Kenrick on August 7th, 1859. The dedication took place on December 2nd, of the following year.[2] The first church, is still in use, but only for sodality purposes. Father Lillis had but one assistant all the years of his pastorship, which lasted until the end of 1862. It was Father E. Berry. These two priests were the first ministers of mercy to arrive at Camp Jackson after its capture on May 10th, 1861, and to minister to the wounded.

Father Lillis was one of God's beloved, called away to his reward in his thirty-fifth year. "He was brimful of wit and gentle humor,"[3] like a child, but before God a true man, with a full sense of his responsibility.

"Father Lillis died on Nov. 28th, 1862, and was buried on the feast of St. Andrew, Nov. 30th. The Sunday previous apparently in the best of health, he gave one of the most impressive sermons, and it proved to be his last, in the Convent chapel (St. Louis) on the Gospel of the day—The last Judgment. The following Sunday he was dead."[4]

His successor was the Rev. William Walsh, who remained at St. Bridget's until his death, December 20th, 1898, fully thirty-six years. Monsignor William Walsh was born in the parish of Abington, in the County of Limerick, Ireland, on October 5th, 1829. He came to America in 1851, first going to Chicago and then to St. Louis, he began his theological studies in the Seminary at Carondelet. He was ordained June 10th, 1854, and assigned by Archbishop Kenrick to the pastorate of Jefferson City and its neighboring towns. Here for ten years he

---

1 Chancery Records. The dedication was recorded by Rev. John C. Fitnam, in the baptismal record of 1853, as follows: "In the Year of our Lord 1853, on this 28th day of August, I, the undersigned priest by authority of the Most Rev. Peter Richard Kenrick, Archbishop of St. Louis, dedicated this temple to God under the invocation of St. Bridget, Virgin." The Rev. clergy present were: Rev. Thomas Scanlon, Rev. Bernard Donnelly, Rev. Patrick Feehan, Rev. John Higginbotham and a great concourse of people."

2 Chancery Records.

3 Smith, Mary Constance, "Our Pastors in Calvary, p. 9.

4 Ibidem, p. 9.

labored valiantly, building a church at Jefferson City, another at California, Mo., and a third at one of his mission stations. Bishop Hogan's tribute to his friend during these happy, though laborious days, deserves to be recorded here:

"Rev. William Walsh, the devoted zealous pastor of St. Peter's Church, Jefferson City, ever a loving, faithful friend of the emigrant, took the greatest possible interest in every effort made to lead the good Irish people from the railroad shanties and the back streets and cellars of cities to locate them on lands."[5]

On January 1st, 1863, the Archbishop transferred Father Walsh to St. Bridget's church, St. Louis. The church was heavily in debt to the Archbishop's Bank. After paying a sum of $23,000 Father Walsh built two schools, one for girls and the other for boys. Then he built the parochial residence. Some years later he completed the steeples of St. Bridget's. St. Bridget's school, with its seven hundred pupils, was the joy and pride of Father William Walsh. The boys were in charge of the Christian Brothers, the girls were taught by the Sisters of St. Joseph. Father Walsh was a watchful shepherd of his flock. Frequent visits to the poorer quarters of his parish brought him into immediate contact with those who needed his ministrations most. The dance halls were an abomination to him, and the Saturday evening dances often came in for a sound castigation. He was considered a strict pastor, yet with him mercy always outran justice. Two years before his death Father Walsh was invested with the title of Domestic Prelate to His Holiness. Monsignor Walsh died in 1898, on December 15th, after having been pastor of St. Bridget's for thirty-six years less ten days. During his long administration he had as assistants, Fathers Edward F. Fitzpatrick, James Archer, Edward Fenlon, J. J. Ryan, Jeremiah J. Harty, F. P. Gallagher, E. A. Casey, J. A. Connolly, J. Th. Tuohy, John O'Shea, J. Gavin, C. F. O'Leary, J. Cooney, Thomas J. Walsh, and O. J. McDonald. In 1899 Rev. Edward Fenlon became pastor of St. Bridget's and remained until March 15th, 1907, the day of his death.[6]

The year 1853, that witnessed the erection of St. Bridget's first church, also saw the beginnings of the first church of the Immaculate Conception in St. Louis. On December 11th, of that year the Very Reverend Anthony O'Regan

---

[5] "Our Pastors in Calvary," p. 67.

[6] Ibidem, p. 68. It was under Father Feulon's successor, Patrick Dooley, that the Boys' Highschool was transferred to St. Bridget's. On Father Dooley's premature death Father Arthur J. White succeeded to the pastorate. The cyclone of 1927, which shattered the Little Seminary Building, drove the young aspirants to the priesthood to the hospitable shelter of St. Bridget's School. The parish is now in charge of the Vincentians.

blessed and laid the corner stone for the Church of his friend, Father James Duggan. On September 10th, of the following year Archbishop Kenrick dedicated the modest edifice, which graced the corner of Eighth and Chestnut Streets until June 1874. Father Duggan became Vicar-General in 1856, and on May 3rd, 1857, was consecrated Bishop of Antigone and Coadjutor to the Archbishop of St. Louis; and finally, in 1859, Bishop of Chicago.[7] His assistant, Father John Bannon, had meanwhile undertaken the erection of St. John the Apostle's church. Father Patrick Feehan succeeded to the pastorship of the Immaculate Conception in July 1859, and continued there until 1866. Archbishop Feehan's career is too well known to require a lengthier notice here. Suffice it to say that he was known in particular for his love for the poor, the outcasts, and above all, the wounded soldiers and prisoners of the civil war. A hospital for wounded soldiers was established in his parish and given in charge of the Sisters of Charity. Every moment he could spare from his other grave duties was devoted, by day and far into the night, to these pathetic victims of war.

On July 7th, 1865 Father Feehan was appointed Bishop of Nashville, and on November 1st, he was consecrated by Archbishop Kenrick in the St. Louis Cathedral.[8] After a brief interval, filled by the temporary appointment of Father Charles Ziegler of St. Patrick's, Father Frances M. Kielty succeeded to the pastorate of the Immaculate Conception, to be followed by Father Patrick Cronin in 1869, who in turn succeeded Father Capezuto at the church of the Assumption in 1870.

Father Constantine Smith, who at the time was in Europe as Archbishop Kenrick's theologian at the Vatican Council, had been promised the succession to the Immaculate Conception Parish, but Vicar-General Ryan conferred the pastorate on Father Francis Patrick O'Reilly. Born on January 6th, 1840 in beautiful County Wicklow, and being gifted with poetic feeling, Father O'Reilly liked to refer to his birth-place as "the sweet Vale of Avoca." Coming to St. Louis he attended the St. Louis University, but returned to Ireland to make his theological studies at Carlow, where he was ordained on May 22nd, 1866. After a brief stay at St. Patrick's and then at St. Lawrence O'Tooles, he was made chaplain of the Visitation Convent on Cass Avenue.

Coming to the Immaculate Conception Parish in 1870 Father O'Reilly found himself in rather unpleasant circumstances. The church, standing on the line of the tunnel that was being built to connect the

---

7  Chancery Records.

8  Cf. Kirkfleet, C. J., "The Life of Patrick Augustine Feehan," 1922. First three chapters, passim.

Union Depot with Eads Bridge was badly shaken by the work going on under Eighth Street, so that it became dangerous. In consequence Father O'Reilly was commissioned to build a new church of the name at Jefferson Avenue and Locust Street. As the location was intended then for the new Cathedral, he erected only a frame church.[9] The territory of the old Immaculate Conception Parish was divided among the adjacent parishes, and nothing remained of the first Immaculate Conception but the beautiful name, which however was transferred to the new parish church on Jefferson Avenue and Lucas Place. Father O'Reilly resigned in 1887, and received as his successor the Reverend Gerard D. Power.

Father Gerard D. Power was born at Cork, Ireland, on February 23, 1842. At an early age he joined the Dominican Order of which his uncle, The Very Rev. B. T. Russell, D.D., was the Provincial in Ireland.

Father Power studied in France and at Perugia, finished his studies at the Minerva University in Rome. He was ordained in the Church of St. John Lateran by Cardinal Patrizzi, March 15, 1866. After his ordination he was employed in giving missions in England, and Ireland, and at last, became president of St. Thomas Dominician College at Newbridge, County Kildare. Having obtained permission to leave the Order, "that as secular priest he might assist his father and Mother." Father Power came to St. Louis in 1875, and after several assignments, became pastor of the Immaculate Conception, where he remained until 1901. Father Power was a priest of scholarly attainments and refined manners.[10] He was noted for his polished sermons, and considered himself a man of importance, an opinion that was not shared by all his confreres. One of his neighbors went so far to denounce, from the pulpit and in print, the Sunday-School of the Immaculate Conception Church, and Archbishop Kain when it was reported to him, contented himself with joking about the affair. Archbishop Kain was at the time intent upon gathering in all the funds he could control, for the erection of a new Cathedral. The lot upon which Father Power's Church stood, was one of the assets of the Archdiocese, which he determined to sell for the Cathedral fund. The parish was small and unprogressive. "Since you think so much about the parish," the Archbishop replied to a remonstrance offered, "you ought to purchase Dr. Boyd's Church for $50,000."[11] The little frame Church on Jefferson Avenue was demolished, the lot was sold, and the parish itself divided among the neighboring parishes, and once more, nothing was left of the Church of the Immaculate Conception, save the hallowed

---

[9] Chancery Records and "Our Pastors in Calvary," pp. 121-122.
[10] Chancery Records and "Our Pastors in Calvary," pp. 105-106.
[11] M. S. notices in Archives.

name, which was destined, after a brief interval, to be adopted by
the parish of St. Kevin's, for its fine new church on Lafayette and
Longfellow Avenue.

The church of St. John Nepomucene, the first national church
of the Bohemian Catholics in the United States and, as some assert,
the first Bohemian church ever built outside the Kingdom of Bohemia,
owes its origin to the unremitting zeal of some early members of S.S.
Peter and Paul's Parish. On May 17th, 1854, the erection of a small
frame building was begun on the site of the present St. John's Church
on the corner of Soulard and Rosati Streets, and dedicated by Vicar-
General Duggan on May 13th, 1855. The land was donated to the
Congregation by Father Joseph Renaud, the former Secretary of Archbishop Kenrick. The first pastor of the new parish was Father Henry
Lipowski, a native of Bohemia.[12]

Father Lipowski had a strangely checkered career behind him,
when he was commissioned to take charge of the Bohemian Catholics.
of the City. Born at Stetkovic in the year 1818, the son of the Bohemian
Knight, Wenceslaus Lipowski, he received his classical education at
home under private tutors, and after completing it, was sent to Prague
for his philosophical career. At Gratz in Steiermark he entered the
Society of Jesus, and made his novitiate in Salzburg. But in 1846,
the novice, now in his twenty-eighth year, obtained his release from
the Order, and joined an Austrian regiment as lieutenant. Under
Field Marshal Radetzki, Lipowski took part in the battles of Mentana
and Novara. But at the end of the war the glamour of a soldier's life
was gone: Lieutenant Lipowski laid down his sword, and came to
the land of liberty, America. Here his former ideal of the priesthood
returned to the weary pilgrim: he completed his theological studies
under Father Anthony O'Regan at Carondelet Seminary, and received
ordination on December 17th, 1853.

Father Lipowski, being a fine German scholar, was sent as assistant
to Vicar General Melcher of St. Mary's Church, and at the same time
was entrusted with the editorial management of the German Catholic
Weekly. *The Herold des Glaubens.* Being appointed by the Archbishop to attend to the spiritual wants of the Bohemians, Father Lipowski gathered the children of that race around him at St. Mary's Church,
to prepare them for first Holy Communion. When the little church
on Soulard Street was ready for occupancy, he moved to the parish
residence adjoining it, and began his pastoral work among the people.
It was hard uphill work, and not much to the taste of the scion of
nobility. Collecting funds for the payment of church-debts seemed
too plebeyan an employment. Besides he had the care of the two

---

12 Holweck, F. G., in "Pastoral-Blatt," vol. 52, No. 11.

churches on the Meramec, the Immaculate Conception in Jefferson County and the Assumption in St. Louis County. Everywhere the good Father's soldierly manner estranged the people from him. On July 15th, 1856, he resigned his charge at St. John's Church and returned to his native land. [13]

The Reverend Francis Trojan, native of Jaromer in the diocese of Brünn in Moravia was his successor. Coming to America with Vicar General Melcher's first band of recruits, Francis Trojan was ordained to the priesthood on January 12th, 1851, and was employed for two years at St. Joseph's Church, Apple Creek. In 1853 he was Professor of Music at the College, in Cape Girardeau. In the two following years his name is not mentioned in the Records, but from 1856 to 1864, he was pastor of the Church of St. John Nepomuc in St. Louis. In 1856, he was stationed at Chester, Illinois.[14]

The priest most closely identified with the Bohemian church of St. John, is the saintly Father Joseph Hessoun. He was born in Bohemia, on August 8th, 1830, and ordained to the priesthood for the diocese of St. Louis, on October 1st, 1865. For more than forty years Father Hessoun presided over the destinies of St. John's Church. On May 15th, 1870, the corner stone of the new church was laid, and in November 1872, the building was dedicated. It was a handsome brick-structure of the Gothic order, with a seating capacity of five hundred. The cost of the building was $50,000. Father Hessoun also built two large school houses near the church on Rosati Street. The Sisters de Notre Dame have been in charge of the school since its foundation in 1866. The actual membership of the parish in its most prosperous days numbered five hundred. Realizing the importance of the Catholic press Father Hessoun in 1872, began the publication of a Catholic weekly paper, the "Hlas," in the Bohemian tongue. In 1890, Father Hessoun was honored by the Holy Father with the title of Domestic Prelate to His Holiness, an honor which the distinguished prelate bore in the spirit of humble submission. Six years later the fine church building was almost completely destroyed by the terrible cyclone of May 27th, 1896, but the congregation soon built it up again, though not quite as beautiful as it had been. Having lived to celebrate his Golden Jubilee in 1903, Monsignor Hessoun died on July 4th, 1906. He was succeeded by Father Charles Bleha.[15]

To care for and provide a Catholic education for Bohemian orphans, the Bohemians of St. Louis in 1905, established the Hessoun Bohemian Catholic Orphange at Fenton, Mo., and placed it in charge of the Notre Dame Sisters. It is supported by dues of Bohemian

---

13  Holweck, ibidem, and Chancery Records.
14  Chancery Records.
15  Chancery Records, and personal reminiscences.

Catholic Orphan Aid Societies; collections in Bohemian Catholic churches; entertainments and picnics of Bohemian Catholics and donations of subscribers to the "*Hlas*" Bohemian Catholic Newspaper. It is conducted by the Hessoun Bohemian Catholic Orphanage, who own the property, including buildings.

Through the manifold efforts of this truly apostolic priest, St. John Nepomuc's became, not only a very prosperous parish, but also, the center of the Bohemian Catholics in the United States, so that Father Hessoun may be fitly called "the Apostle of the Bohemians of America."

The church of St. Lawrence O'Toole on Fourteenth and O'Fallon Streets was founded in 1855: the corner stone of the new edifice was blessed by Archbishop Kenrick on April 15th, and the building itself was dedicated on December 16th. A lot on the northwest corner of O'Fallon and Fourteenth was donated for the purpose by Miss Jane Graham, a member of the Mullanphy family. The Rev. James Henry was its founder. Father Henry was born in Carrickallen, County Cavan, Ireland, on January 6th, 1828. He was ordained by Archbishop Kenrick on January 6th, 1853, and his first assignment was to St. Patrick's church, St. Louis.[10]

During the Know-nothing riots Father Henry distinguished himself as the bravest of the brave by gathering the men and boys of his parish around him in defense of the Catholic churches in the vicinity. Father Henry commanded his little army in person, and beat off the blood-thirsty mob. Many participants in the fight were wounded, and "Violet," the leader of the Know-nothing mob, was killed. Ever afterwards Father Henry was known as "the warrior priest."[17] After two years service at St. Patrick's Father Henry was charged with the work of building up a parish of his own, St. Lawrence O'Toole's, which eventually became one of the most populous congregations in the city.

Three years later, in 1858, he built a parochial school on the lot adjoining, which had been donated to him by Mrs. Jane Chambers, another member of the Mullanphy family.

In 1864, deciding to construct a larger church on the southwest corner of O'Fallon and Fourteenth, Father Henry had the first one torn down and the materials used in the new building. But just as this second edifice was ready for the roofing a cyclone destroyed it completely. "Now Father Henry begged from door to door and from the workmen on the streets; and being a polite, priestly man, seldom met with a refusal," says an old friend. Rebuilt and completed, the

10  Chancery Records.
17  "Our Pastors in Calvary," p. 42.

new structure was finally dedicated in the summer of 1865. Later he built a second parochial school on Fourteenth, near Biddle. The Sisters of St. Joseph conducted the school.[18]

During the early years of his pastorate at St. Malachy's Father Henry had for his assistant the Rev. Martin Riordon, who in 1865, accompanied his friend Bishop Feehan to Nashville and, becoming Vicar General of that diocese, fell a victim to the Yellow Fever epidemic, September 17th, 1878. "With all respect to those who have succeeded him," writes Father Quinn in his "Heroes and Heroines of Memphis," "I feel convinced that the soul of the late Martin Riordan is the kindred and most beloved spirit in St. Patrick's parish today."[19] His old pastor believed Father Riordan to be "the greatest priest he had ever known." Father Henry died on November 5th, 1891, in Liverpool, England, while on a visit to his brother, Mr. Michael Henry. His remains were brought to St. Louis and buried from St. Lawrence O'Toole's Church with the utmost pomp. "Father Henry," wrote the *Catholic Standard and Times* of Philadelphia, "was known and beloved not only in his own diocese, but throughout the whole country. Every movement for the spread of religion and the advancement of his fellow countrymen had in him a zealous champion." Father Henry's successor as pastor of St. Malachy's was the late gentle, wise and learned Father, Monsignor Martin S. Brennan, who after eighteen years of faithful work, was at his own request, transferred to the rectorship of S. S. Mary and Joseph in Carondelet.

18 Our Pastors in Cálvary, pp. 42, 43.
19 Father Quinn treats of Father Martin Reardon, pp. 148-155.

## CHAPTER 27

# A DECADE OF CHURCH-BUILDING

## II.

### ST. LIBORIUS AND THE ANNUNCIATION

Whilst the Irish Catholics were spreading southward from St. Patrick's, their German brethren in the faith were filling up the space that lay between the St. Joseph's and the Holy Trinity Churches. The foundation of *St. Liborius* Church was the result. On October 30th, 1855 a lot was bought for the purpose on North Market and Hogan Streets, and the corner-stone of the new church was laid by Vicar-General Melcher, on June 15th, 1856. The building was dedicated to divine service by Father P. J. Patschowski, S. J., the pastor of St. Joseph's Church, on January 25th, 1857, and after its completion, consecrated by Archbishop Kenrick, July 17th, 1859. In 1857 the parochial school under the care of a lay-teacher was organized. The original parishioners were immigrants from Westphalia, Oldenburg, Hanover, with a few families from Southern Germany. They had until then attended divine service either at St. Joseph's or Holy Trinity. Under the leadership of Liborius Muesenfechter they had asked Archbishop Kenrick for permission to build a church and the assignment of a priest to them, and the good Archbishop acquiesced. The pastor he sent them was the Rev. Stephen Schweihoff.[1] This noble priest was born about the year 1815 near Rietberg in the diocese of Paderborn. He was ordained in 1840, and for a time acted as chaplain at the pilgrim-shrine of our Lady at Werne.

In 1855 he joined the first band of recruits won for the diocese by Vicar General Melcher, arriving in St. Louis in October 1855.[2] After a brief stay with Father Melcher at St. Mary's, Father Schweihoff assumed charge of the building operations at St. Liborius parish. At first, mass was said in a room of a rented house; the other room being the pastor's residence and office.

On January 25th, 1857, the first mass was celebrated in the new church.

Times were hard, and the people were poor, yet they had the courage of their convictions and determined to build a school. Mr.

---

1 "Zum Goldenen Jubilaeum der St. Liborius Gemeinde in St. Louis," 1907, pp. 9 and 10.

2 Chancery Records.

Theodore Lemkes was employed as schoolmaster and organist, at the meagre salary of $40.00; but even this mere pittance proved too heavy a burden for the young and struggling parish.

In the course of time Mr. Lemkes became teacher and organist at St. Boniface's Church in Carondelet, where he remained until his death, September 22nd, 1885.

A new school house for the girls of the parish was erected in 1859, and was occupied by the Sisters de Notre Dame; the boys remaining in charge of lay-teachers.[3] But even these improvements did not long meet the needs of the rapidly growing parish. A fine two-story brick building was completed in the late Spring of 1865: By October 1st, of the same year a substantial parish residence was ready to receive Father Schweihoff and his assistant, the newly-ordained Rev. Louis Lay, the future pastor of St. Francis de Sales.

Father Schweihoff lived and died poor. All his possessions were his books and his priestly vestments: his books he willed to the Franciscan Fathers, his vestments to St. Libory's parish. Besides these symbols of learning and piety, Father Schweihoff had nothing to leave to his friends, but the memory of a well-spent life. During his long illness Father Engelbert Hoeyinck was sent to him as his assistant and, on the pastor's death, on the last day of the month of our Lady 1869, he became his successor in the charge of St. Liborius parish.[4]

Father Engelbert Hoeyinck was born on September 18th, 1836, in Balve, in Westphalia, diocese of Paderborn. He made his classical and philosophical studies at Münster, Bonn and Berlin, and took the theological course in the Salesianum near Milwaukee, where he was raised to the priesthood, on January 29th, 1869. Within four months after ordination Father Hoeyinck was thrown upon his own resources by the appointment to the rectorship of St. Liborius.[5] The question of enlarging the church was then uppermost in the minds of his parishioners: but the young pastor wisely delayed, and gradually eliminated the useless project, and promoted the idea of a new and really worthy house of God. Among the assistants of Father Hoeyinck there are a number of distinguished names, Joseph Schmidt, John A. Hoffmann, N. Boden, Henry Schrage, W. J. Rensmann and George A. Reis. Among the lay-teachers of the school after Theodore Lemkes, Joseph Albrecht and Joseph Lubeley were the most noteworthy. The school-sisters, as merging their personality in their holy vocation, remain nameless.

From the time that Father George A. Reis entered upon his duties as assistant to Father Hoeyinck, September 14th, 1882, his personality

---

3 "Zum Goldenen Jubilaeum," pp. 17 and 18.

4 Ibidem, p. 30.

5 Chancery Records.

appears as the driving force in St. Liborius parish. It was through his untiring zeal that Father Hoeyinck was enabled to erect the splendid school building in 1886, the magnificent Gothic church in 1889, and the commodious Rectory in 1890. But wearing away under the gnawing tooth of sickness, Father Hoeyinck, toward the end of June 1895, resigned his position and, returning to his birth place, Balve in Westphalia, died on the 4th day of November 1901.[6]

Father George Reis was now appointed pastor of St. Liborius. Under his administration the beautiful spire of red sandstone was erected. Born on December 9th, 1854, in St. Vincent's Parish, St. Louis, George Reis was sent to Rome for his philosophical and theological studies in October 1876. He was ordained on June 3rd 1882, and returned to his native city, where he was destined to spend the long series of years at St. Liborius Church.[7]

St. Liborius Parish has given to the Church a goodly number of recruits for the ministry and the religious life; among them the well known priests John L. Gadell, Henry Thobe, A.A. Jasper, Joseph Lubeley, Dr. A. A. Gass, O. T. Siesener and others: It is regarded as a model parish: its church choir ranks among the best, its schools are efficient and largely attended, its people are pious and generous and docile, and all, priests, teachers and the laity, have given ample proof of their love for the beauty of the House of God.

Exactly four years elapsed after the founding of St. Liborius Church, until another parish foundation was undertaken in the city of St. Louis, the parish of *St. Malachy.* It was on October 24th, that Archbishop Kenrick laid the corner stone of the new church on Clark Avenue and Ewing St., Rev. John O'Sullivan attended the parish from St. Bridget's Rectory, and on October 30th, 1859 occupied the not quite completed building. The dedication of the church by Archbishop Kenrick occurred on September 2, 1860.[8] ''It is English Gothic in style, and built of brick and stone, with fifty-five feet frontage on Clark Avenue by one hundred and twenty feet in depth. The interior, richly frescoed, is of very imposing appearance, the vaulted roof being supported by a double row of fluted columns.''[9] Father Sullivan had for his assistant the Rev. Patrick Ring. In 1862 the Rev. Myles W. Tobyn became pastor of St. Malachy's in succession to Father O'Sullivan. The immediate cause of Father O'Sullivan's removal from the pastorship of St. Malachy's was his hot and out spoken secessionism, which threatened to bring on a conflict with the military authorities. The Archbishop

6  Zum Goldenen Jubilaeum,'' pp. 34 and 40.
7  Chancery Records.
8  Chancery Records.
9  Scharf, ''History St. Louis,'' p. 1662.

however, recommended him to Bishop Juneker of Alton, who gave the exiled priest the fine parish of the Annunciation in Springfield, Illinois.

Father Myles William Tobyn was born in Dublin, Ireland, on July 17th, 1834. He was sent to a boarding college at Clondalkin, in charge of the Carmelite Monks, from which he entered Maynooth to study for the Dublin diocese. His father's death caused him to ask to be sent to an American diocese. And in 1857, after a visit to France, he arrived in St. Louis as deacon, with letters to Archbishop Kenrick. He spent one year at the old Seminary of Carondelet.[10] Father Tobyn was ordained on June 26th, 1858, and assigned to St. John's Church, assistant to Father John Bannon and, after a short period, to St. Patrick's. His rectorship at St. Malachy's lasted seven years. He built the boys' school, a two-story brick building, fifty by one hundred and twenty-nine feet, with a seating capacity of six hundred. In 1869 he was appointed to the Old Cathedral as pastor, and in 1886 transferred to S. S. Mary's and Joseph's Church in Carondelet, where he died on Good Friday, April 21st, 1905.

Father Tobyn was one of the most popular St. Louis priests of his time. Genial and affable in his relations with others, and the very soul of humor and drollery, he was at heart of a very serious disposition. "To those who knew him only slightly," as Father Phelan said, "he was the wit, the raconteur, the polished conversationalist, to those that knew him well, he was the prayerful, pains-taking priest, and the anxious solicitous pastor of souls." "He was the type of an Irishman, rare even in the Green Isle, and fast passing away, a class of genial, cultivated bright bantering spirits, who are always playful and rippling on the surface, but very thoughtful and religious-minded down in the depths of their souls."[11]

"I remember last summer at the annual priests' retreat," said Father Phelan in the funeral sermon of his friend, "during the time of recreation, Father Tobyn and I were talking together, and he said to me: 'Something tells me that this is my last retreat.' It was his last retreat and he was preparing then for the death he died."[12]

Father Tobyn's successor at St. Malachy's was Father Charles Frederick Ziegler a native American of German parentage, whose rigid integrity, unwearied energy and unremitting zeal, made St. Malachy's

---

10 Smith, Mary Constance, "Our Pastors in Calvary," p. 87.

11 From Father Phelan's Funeral Sermon in "St. Louis Post Dispatch," April 22, 1905, and "Globe-Democrat," April 26, 1905.

12 From the same, quoted in "Our Pastors in Calvary," p. 88.

parish what is was in the heyday of its splendid career, and left behind him the memory of a name worthy of the brightest days of the Church.[13]

Father Charles Ziegler was born at Ste. Genevieve, Mo., on September 3rd, 1832, received his classical education at the Barrens, and his theological training at the Seminary in Carondelet. He was raised to the priesthood by Archbishop Kenrick in the Cathedral of St. Louis on October 2nd, 1854. His first appointment was St. Patrick's Church in St. Louis, where Father Higginbotham was the pastor and Father Henry first assistant.

It was not a new thing that a man of Teuton antecedents should be entrusted with the care of Irish immigrants: for the founder of St. Patrick's Church was a member of that race, the Rev. Joseph Anthony Lutz; yet the appointment of Father Ziegler did arouse the spirit nationalism of some of the priests and laymen against the young German priest, who, however, was master of the French and English tongue, but not of the German. Rev. Francis M. Kielty alluded to this early opposition to Father Ziegler and his easy victory over his critics, at the Jubilee festivities of the Rector of St. Malachy's in 1904:

"It was signified to Archbishop Kenrick that an Irish priest would be more suitable. 'I have appointed him and he will suit,' answered His Grace, and added 'the time is not far off, when the American Church must try and have her own native priesthood and be no longer dependent on Europe.' Father Ziegler was given to understand, that his appointment was thought to be injudicious, though they did not blame him for it. It reached his ears that some were exerting themselves to get the appointment changed, feeling aggrieved that a native American should have been placed where one of themselves should have been placed. To those who complained of the appointment he gave this noble Catholic and Apostolic answer: "I am as much an Irishman as St. Patrick was. I am sent here by the Pope through my Bishop, who is an Irishman. I shall do for the children of St. Patrick, what St. Patrick did for their ancestors: They are Hebrews, so am I. They are Israelites, so am I. They are the seed of Abraham, so am I.' "He went to St. Patrick's cheerfully.' "[14]

Father Ziegler soon found a grand opportunity to prove his Catholic loyalty to the Irish Catholics of the city. In 1866 the cholera once again broke out in St. Louis. St. Patrick's, at that time, was the most populous parish of the diocese, and the cholera raged in its homes

---

13  Holweck, F. G., "Pastoral-Blatt," vol. 59, pp. 179-183.

14  Kielty, Francis M. Address at Father Ziegler's Golden Jubilee, 1904, quoted by Holweck, 1. c., p. 179.

with greatest fury. As Monsignor Brennan put it: "Hundreds upon hundreds perished, young and old succumbed to its fell touch, pallid fear and ruthless panic seized on all; confusion dwelt on every face and dread in every heart."[15]

As Father Wheeler, who had succeeded Father Higginbotham at St. Patrick's, was absent in Europe at the time, the entire work and responsibility devolved upon the young priest, until the Archbishop sent Father Robert Tucker to his assistance. Father Ziegler's self-devoting spirit, and his extraordinary prudence and skill in fighting the dreadful disease moved a number of citizens, Catholic and Protestant, to submit a petition to the Mayor of the stricken city, to have Father Ziegler appointed health commissioner: but religious prejudice in other quarters defeated the proposal.

After fourteen years of wise and faithful service at St. Patrick's, Father Ziegler, in August 1868, received the appointment to the parish of St. Malachy. He was received there with pride and joy, and for forty years prayed and studied and labored for the welfare of the parish God had entrusted to his care. "His heart was ever in his work" as Monsignor Brennan attests, "He knows his flock intimately and they know him and revere him. .. . He has certainly borne the burden of the day and the heats, and still, he has always had a rule of life, an order of the day. He rose at four o'clock each morning, made his meditation and prepared for mass. He had his time for study. His life, though an active one, was also a studious one. . . . One of his strong characteristics was regularity, promptness. He had perfect method in all things. . . he was a model of order. He was faithful and punctual in the confessional. He was ever prompt to answer sick calls, and most devoted to the sick. He has certainly been a great catechist. His catechetical instructions were gems of clearness and practical information. . . The great Archbishop Kenrick, had unbounded confidence in Father Ziegler. He appointed him to the office of Secretary of the Archdiocese, and chose him as his theologian to the Council of Baltimore."[16]

When Father Ziegler took charge of St. Malachy's parish—the church was still in heavy debt and unfinished. He knew he was in for hard work, and set to it. He kept no sexton for the church or janitor for the school; he got up early in the morning and often, on a cold winter's morning, he was seen sweeping the snow off the walk around the church and school house, before time to go into his Confessional.

---

[15] Msgr. Brennan's Jubilee Sermon, quoted by Holweck, l. c., p. 179.
[16] From Msgr. Brennan's Jubilee Sermon, 1. c., pp. 179 and 180.

"With hard work, he in a short while cleared the debt off his church, and then set to work, to complete it. The steeple was finished, the sanctuary enlarged, and beautiful carved wood altars installed, walls frescoed, electric lights, and new stations and pews set in place— and last but not least, the red granite steps in front of the church built, which in his own words 'will outlive every one of us.' Father Ziegler was a man of exquisite taste. He was very musical and possessed one of the finest tenor voices among the clergy. To hear him sing High Mass was a treat that his parishioners will never forget."[17]

In the last years of his life Father Ziegler was for a long time, afflicted with blindness, caused by a cataract, which was afterwards cured by an operation. Not being able to read the epistle and gospel, he recited them from memory and did the same with the announcements. His memory seemed to grow stronger when deprived of sight.[18]

On October 5th, 1903, Father Ziegler celebrated his golden jubilee. For the event St. Malachy's parish rallied friends from all parts of the city, to honor the pastor.

Father Charles Ziegler, irremovable rector of St. Malachy's died on November 24, 1908, at the parochial residence, after a long illness. The obsequies took place on November 27, the sermon being preached by Rev. Father Wm. Dalton of Kansas City, and the last absolution being given by Bishop Bonacum of Lincoln, Nebraska.

Father Martin S. Brennan had been Father Ziegler's faithful assistant from 1873 to April 1884, then until 1893 came Father James Keegan, and then to the end of the pastor's life the young priests, W. E. Randall, A. H. Rohling, T. Moynihan, and Joseph Tammany.

During these prosperous years about six hundred families belonged to the church; the school was under the charge of the Christian Brothers, and had six teachers and four hundred pupils. The parochial school for girls was conducted in St. Philomena's Orphan Asylum and School, opposite the church, attended by four Sisters of Charity, and three hundred scholars.[19]

The Church of the *Annunciation* on Chouteau Avenue and Sixth Street remains in its present ruinous condition a pathetic memorial of its great and good founder and first pastor, the Coadjutor of Archbishop Peter Richard Kenrick, and the distinguished Archbishop of Philadelphia, Patrick John Ryan. Its beautiful facade reminds us of some of the churches of Rome. It is, indeed, a perfect piece of architecture, a cathedral in miniature, bearing aloft the glorious title of our Lady, *"Maria, Gratia Plena."* It was nearly demolished by the

---

17 Holweck, 1. c., p. 181.
18 Holweck, 1, c., p. 180.
19 Chancery Records.

cyclone of 1896; and only partially restored; but worst of all, it has lost almost all its parishioners: the children of the men and women, who hung on the lips of the greatest orator St. Louis ever had, are now gone, scattered over the western part of the city, and seemingly oblivious of the glory that was their Father's pride and joy. Annunciation Parish was organized in 1859, the corner stone was laid by Archbishop Kenrick on November 27th, and the beautiful church was dedicated on December 16th, the following year. The total cost was one hundred thousand dollars. The appearance of the building is massive and imposing.[20] The interior was richly frescoed and adorned with costly paintings, one of which, The Spousals of Joseph and Mary, was presented by Louis XVIII of France to Bishop Du Bourg in 1818. A colonnade of Corinthian pillars supports the arched roof; and the altars, three in number, are of purest Italian marble.''[21]

In the days of its prime, the parish numbered about five hundred families. It had a Free School for boys conducted by the Christian Brothers, and a girls Free School conducted by the Ladies of the Sacred Heart. But a sad change came over the scene: The smoke and grime of the factory drove out the thickly settled population. The Ladies of the Sacred Heart flitted to their grand new Convent in South St. Louis, the Christian Brothers school was closed for lack of children and of means, and the church itself fell into pathetic decay.[22]

---

20 Chancery Records.

21 Scharf, ''History of St. Louis,'' p. 1663.

22 In regard to the lot on which the church was built, Archbishop Kenrick states under date of September 5, 1884, ''Mrs. Gighe died today. The Archbishop paid her from the 1st of November, 1872, to the 1st of September, 1884, the day of her death, $17,875.00, her life annuity being the price paid for the property on which the Church of the Annunciation was built.'' P. R. Kenrick, Archbishop.

## A DECADE OF CHURCH-BUILDING

### III.

#### ST. BONIFACE AND THE ASSUMPTION

The year 1859 brought in its ample folds the gift of a new church to the quaint suburb of St. Louis, Carondelet, resting on the very site of the first settlement of the Kaskaskia Indians on the Mississippi River, and of the long departed glories of the Jesuit Mission of St. Francis Xavier on the Riviere des Peres. It was baptized S. S. Mary and Joseph. It took the place of the church built by Father Edmund Saulnier, in 1841, to supplant the log church he had erected in 1839 on the site of the "modest hut of rough boards," which Father De Andreis had placed there in 1819, by order of Bishop Du Bourg. The lot on which these churches stood or stand was set aside for a church and cemetery as early as 1775. From these facts it will appear that the parish of Carondelet has a long and quietly eventful history, since the days of the early Jesuit foundation. Even the name of the settlement was changed a number of times, being called Cahokia, because just across the river lay the ancient Cahokia; then Prairie de Catalan, then in 1790 Louisburg, and in 1794 Carondelet, in honor of the Governor General of Louisiana, Baron de Carondelet. Its nickname was Vide Poche, Empty Pocket. The name of the first rude chapel erected by the Jesuit Fathers Marest and Pinet, was St. Francis Xavier, the two succeeding church edifices bore the name of "Our Lady of Mount Carmel," and the brick church erected in 1849 north of the old church, was dedicated to *S. S. Mary and Joseph.* The corner stone of the present church building was laid on May 29th, 1859, Vicar-General Patrick J. Ryan performing the ceremony and preaching the sermon. Father Philip Lawrence Hendrickx was the builder of the new church. Shortly after his ordination, December 8th, 1857, he was sent to Carondelet as rector of the parish, in which capacity he served from January 8th, 1858, to the summer of 1861, when he made a trip to Europe. After his return he became pastor of Ste. Genevieve.[1] After an interval of four years, came Father Michael McFaul, who had undermined his health in the extensive mission of Janesville, Wisconsin, where he built St. Patrick's church. Coming to the milder climate

---

1 Chancery Records.

of St. Louis in 1860, Father McFaul first made his home with Bishop Ryan, and in 1866 received the appointment to the parish of S. S. Mary and Joseph. In 1875 ill health compelled him to resign. His death occurred on January 9th, 1910.[2]

Father Thomas G. Daly, his successor at Carondelet, was a native of Ireland, born in 1848. Coming to Canada in early youth, the young aspirant to the priesthood was sent across the boundary to the Seminary of St. Francis near Milwaukee for his ecclesiastical studies.

Bishop Melcher of Green Bay ordained him for the Archdiocese of St. Louis in 1870. Having served his apprenticeship in the sacred ministry at St. Malachy's, and St. Bridget's, Father Daly was appointed to the rectorship of Old Mines and finally, in 1875, to the church of S. S. Mary and Joseph in Carondelet.

His most important work in the old parish was the erection of the new school. There were about two hundred families in the parish. The parochial schools, numbering about three hundred and fifty pupils, were conducted by the Christian Brothers and the Sisters of St. Joseph. Father Daly was a man of literary tastes and contributed to religious magazines. Always delicate, he passed away on February 6th, 1886, in his thirty-eighth year, and was buried by the side of old Father Saint Cyr, in the little Cemetery of the Convent of St. Joseph at Nazareth, St. Louis County.[3]

Father Daly's successor, the Reverend Myles W. Tobyn came to S. S. Mary and Joseph from the Old Cathedral: but prior to that he had done excellent work at St. Malachy's. After his death on Good Friday, April 21st, 1905, in his ripe old age of seventy-one years, the pastor of St. Malachy's, Father Martin S. Brennan, received the appointment to S. S. Mary and Joseph's parish.

At the very time when Father Hendrickx was urging onward the erection of the new S. S. Mary and Joseph Church, the German Catholics of Carondelet were straining every nerve to build their church in honor of St. Boniface. About the middle of the forties and fifties, a large number of the German immigrants had found a home in the ancient sleepy hollow of Carondelet. With their advent a new spirit of life entered the community. The Catholic element among the Germans naturally felt, above all things, the need of a church of their own own language. Archbishop Kenrick was pleased with the project, and the newly ordained Father John B. Gamber was sent to take charge of the German Catholics of Carondelet, at first as Father Hendrickx's assistant, and then as rector of a distinct parish.

---

2 Chancery Records and ''Our Pastors in Calvary,'' p. 111.
3 Chancery Records.

Father Gamber was Rector of the Germans of Carondelet until May 1861, and attained real success. At first, mass was held for the Germans in S. S. Mary and Joseph, every Sunday at 8 o'clock. But early in 1860 the young priest called a parish meeting on which the erection of a new church was determined upon.

The congregation purchased a lot with 100 feet frontage on Michigan Avenue and Schirmer street, upon which the erection of a church was begun at once. The corner stone was laid on the third Sunday in May, 1860, by Vicar-General Joseph Melcher, assisted by Rev. H. Muehlsiepen and Rev. P. J. Ryan. Archbishop Kenrick dedicated the structure on December 26th, 1860, in honor of the Apostle of Germany, St. Boniface.[4]

In the same year the parsonage had been erected, and a parochial school organized with a lay-teacher. The first religious to teach the girls and younger boys were the Sisters de Notre Dame, and after 1880 the Sisters of Christian Charity.[5]

In 1861 Father Gamber demanded and received his exeat from the diocese and returned to his native land, where he became pastor of a parish near the city of Mainz. On June 21st, 1861, Father E. A. Schindel was appointed pastor of St. Boniface parish. Coming to Carondelet with his friend, the pastor of Matteese Creek and Maxville, Father Henry Brockhagen, he found a church and a parsonage, but "all void and empty," The church was not completed, there was no plastering on walls and ceiling, no cross on the steeple, no bell in the tower, no paint on the woodwork; but there was a heavy debt on the parish, with no funds to liquidate it, and no promises reliable enough to satisfy the impatient creditors. Archbishop Kenrick came to the rescue of Father Schindel, as he had done once before in favor of Father Gamber. But the war, that worked much hardship and desolation to others, seems to have brought a blessing to Carondelet, as many of its people found employment at the ironworks, building gun-boats and other military craft.

Conditions having improved, Father Schindel built in 1865 the school on Minnesota Avenue and Schirmer Street, and in 1868 the Sisters' residence. He also built a hospital on Grand Avenue and Lemay Ferry Road, at a cost of more than 40,000 dollars, which a few years later was destroyed by fire, being a total loss. Father Schindel died November 1st, 1895, after thirty-five years' labor in the parish. Rev. Herman Nieters, rector of St. Joseph's Church at Neier, Mo., and former assistant to Father Schindel, was appointed rector of St. Boni-

---

4 "Das Katholische Deutschtum in St. Louis," p. 38.

5 Ibidem, and "Goldenes Jubilaeum der St. Bonifatius Gemeinde zu St. Louis," p. 5-11.

face by Archbishop J. J. Kain. Father Nieters took charge of the parish on December 1st, 1895. Under his pastorate the church was thoroughly repaired and a new school built. The parish school is in charge of the Sisters of Christian Charity. It numbers 450 pupils. St. Boniface celebrated its Golden Jubilee on the first Sunday of May, 1910, in a fitting manner.[6]

During his long pastorate Father Schindel was assisted by a series of distinguished priests, J. G. Nordmeyer, Xavier Juetting, Francis X. Willmes, Hermann Nieters, Clement Moenig, M. Helmbacher, and Peter Kurtenbach. The assistants during Father Nieters pastorate were: Father Kurtenbach, H. Amsinger, William Huelsmann and George Dreher. St. Boniface's parish has given to holy Church five priests, three brothers, and thirty-one Sisters of Christian Charity.

In 1870 the city limits of St. Louis were extended southward to the River des Peres, and Carondelet was incorporated in the great Metropolis of the Mississippi Valley. This expansion of the city included another old foundation within its territory, the Church of St. James at what is still called Cheltenham. The parish was organized in 1861 by Father John O'Sullivan, pastor of St. Malachy's Church from 1859 to 1862. When Father Miles W. Tobyn succeeded to the pastoral charge of St. Malachy's in 1862, the care of the mission church at Cheltenham also devolved upon him, until in 1864 Father Michael Welby was appointed rector of St. James Parish. In the Catholic Directory for 1866 Father Welby is mentioned as being stationed at Cheltenham and at the Cathedral of St. Louis. In 1869 Father Thomas Manning officiated at Cheltenham; he was succeeded in 1870 by Father Henry Kelly.

All these years a parochial school had been in operation at the Church of St. James in Cheltenham, but in 1870 when Father Kelly came, the school was closed; and as there was no rectory, he made the building his residence until he built a house.[7]

Father Henry Kelly died on July 13th, 1878. "He was simple and upright, fearing God," says the inscription on his monument in Calvary Cemetery. Father Thomas Ambrose Butler who in 1878 came to Cheltenham from St. John's Church, then the pro-cathedral of St. Louis, was one of the most remarkable men among the St. Louis priests of his day, though he never attained any distinguished place in the Church. According to the well informed authoress of "*Our Pastors in Calvary.*" "Father Butler was born in Dublin, Ireland May 21st, 1837. He was educated in Maynooth, and ordained in Ireland, March

---

6  "Das Katholische Deutschtum," p. 40.

7  Chancery Records.

17th, 1864. The flame of patriotism lit his poet-soul from early childhood, and as a young priest in his native land he plunged into radical
reforms to help the poor and oppressed around him. His zeal, however, brought him into conflict with the authorities, and, having friends
in Kansas, he came to America. He founded the first cooperative
colony of any importance in the United States. It was composed of
600 men and women from Ireland, and the tract they settled upon was
called Fort Butler. Now it is Butler City. It was his own great and
original idea."[8] Whatever may have been the cause of Father Butler's
leaving his colony in Kansas, his reception in St. Louis, April 1875, was
a hearty one. For three years he served as assistant to Bishop Patrick
Ryan at St. John's, and, on July 1878, was promoted to the rectorship at Cheltenham. From this place of vantage he organized the
parish of St. Cronan, and in 1882 took up his residence there, but
continued to minister to the congregation at Cheltenham until March
1884. It was then that Father Patrick McNamee received charge of
St. James, whilst Father Butler continued his labors at St. Cronan's,
until his death on September 7th, 1897. Father Butler was a poet of true
inspiration though he published but one book of poems: *"The Irish
on the Prairies,"*[9] in 1873. Father McNamee administered the affairs
of St. James Parish until November 21st, 1896. His successor was the
Rev. Edmund A. Casey who remained until 1909. Through the extension of the city limits in 1875 Cheltenham became a part of the city
of St. Louis and, since that date, the Parish of St. James is numbered
among the city churches.

There now remains but one Church to be noticed as founded in
the city before the outbreak of the civil war, the Church of the Assumption; on Sidney and Eighth Street. This parish had been organized in
1861 at Lock's Limekiln by Father Raphael Capezuto, a native of Italy
and member of the Congregation of the Mission, who had been attached
to the Cathedral here, an energetic little man, who is remembered as
a most zealous priest. The ground for the church was donated by John
Doyle, the Philanthropist, and Father Capezuto had the construction
of the church well under way, when he disappeared, the probability
being that he had returned to his Religious Order. Father Bernard
O'Reilly finished the church, which was dedicated on Sunday, November
30th, 1862, with Father P. Feehan the preacher of the occasion.

The parish being at the time the only one for the English-speaking Catholics of South St. Louis, became very prosperous, number-

---

8  "Our Pastors in Calvary," pp. 60 and 61.
9  Chancery Records.

ing over two hundred and fifty families, of Irish, French and Anglo-American descent.

The following year Father Martin O'Riordan succeeded as pastor, remaining with some assistance from Father P. J. Ring during 1864, until he was called to accompany Bishop Feehan to Nashville, Tennessee.

Father O'Riordan is best known as the former assistant priest at St. Patrick's, and as the heroic Vicar-General of Nashville diocese during the Yellow Fever epidemic. His successor at the Assumption was Father Thomas M. Kavanagh, born in County Roscommon, on the 11th of September 1837. In 1866 he was appointed pastor of the Church of the Assumption, St. Louis, a typical young Irish priest, zealous and pious, but light-hearted and full of fun. He was a favorite with all, and his premature and sudden death shocked everyone. He had just finished his retreat and returned for the Sunday services when he became ill, and died on Tuesday, July 21st, 1868, in the little rectory then at the rear of the church. He was in his thirty-second year, and the fourth of his ministry.[10]

Father Kavanagh had as his successor a man who had seen long and exhausting service in the country missions, Potosi and Old Mines, the Rev. James Fox, soon to be promoted to old St. Patrick's, the Irish mother church of the city. Then came the pastorate of Father Edward Shea, from 1870 to 1873, and finally the long and fruitful pastorate of the distinguished Father Constantine Smith, who from the edge of his parish of the Assumption founded the new Church of St. Agnes in 1891, thus making two harvests of corn grow where only one grew before.[11] Father Smith took possession of the parish of St. Agnes in September 1891, and was succeeded at the Assumption by the Rev. Patrick Dooley, who in turn gave way to the Apostolic Missionary Band under the leadership of the saintly William E. Randall.

The parish of the Assumption, after the dismemberment, still contained two hundred and fifty families, who supported a parochial school attended by more than three hundred pupils instructed by five Sisters of St. Joseph.

10 "Our Pastors in Calvary," p. 13.
11 Chancery Records.

## CHAPTER 29

## DURING THE CIVIL WAR AND AFTER

With the election of Abraham Lincoln as President of the United States the die was cast that decided the question of war or peace between North and South. The southern States had formed a confederation for the protection of their interests and claimed the right of secession; whilst the prevalent sentiment in the North was that the Union must be preserved by peaceful means or by war. Soon after President Lincoln's inauguration, the United States Fort Sumter in Charleston Harbor was attacked by the troops of the Confederacy under General Beauregard. This was the first blow of the Civil War. (April 12th, 1861) Yet, "it was in Missouri," as John Fiske says, "that the long series of events was set in motion which terminated in the suppression of the rebellion. From the seizure of Camp Jackson in 1861 down to the appearance of Sherman's army in the rear of Virginia in 1865, there may be traced an unbroken chain of causation."[1] The war might have taken a far different turn, if the powerful state of Missouri had been brought to the Southern side in 1861. That this was possible must be plain to all: The sentiment of the people was about equally divided: the government was in the hands of southern sympathizers. The effort was made by Governor Claiborne Jackson and his advisors and supportors. The attempt to surprise the arsenal in South St. Louis, failed through the watchfulness of Frank P. Blair and Captain Nathanial Lyon. The legislature, however, declared itself opposed to secession. Captain Lyon brought together some 500 men, and Blair raised a few regiments of "Home Guards." Then Governor Jackson obtained a supply of arms and ammunition from the Confederate Government and began recruiting volunteers for the defense of the State. The commander of the district, Daniel Frost, under orders from the state authorities, selected a charming spot just southeast of the intersection of Grand Avenue and Olive Street, known as "Lindell Meadow," ostensibly for a week's encampment of the militia of his military district. It was opened on May 3rd, with seven hundred men, and named Camp Jackson, in honor of the Governor of the state: There was nothing unlawful in this except that the arms and ammunitions for the encampment had been obtained from the Confederate government. The leaders of the Union forces determined to obviate the danger by capturing the camp. Blair marched up from Jefferson Barracks with 1,000 men to join Lyon's forces, and the little army

---

[1] Fiske, John, "The Mississippi Valley in the Civil War," p. 7.

pushed out to Grand Avenue, and by two o'clock May 10, invested Camp Jackson and captured it without firing a shot. On the homeward march, however, there was an unfortunate affray between Lyon's troops and a street mob, in the course of which about thirty lives were lost.[2]

The Capture of Camp Jackson was the opening of the Civil War in Missouri. For the Southern states the conflict was practically a defensive war against a foreign aggressor. As for the Northern States, the Civil War meant a war of conquest, in which their own boundaries were never seriously threatened. But in the case of the border states, and preeminently Missouri, the war meant a contest of brother against brother, neighbor against neighbor, friend against friend, a tearing asunder of all bonds that had united community with community. In consequence of this, personal security and peace were often at the mercy of ruffians acting under assumed authority, or by lawless bands acting from private lust of murder, arson and pillage. When the rights of both claimants to power, were still in the balance, it seemed to be the way of prudence to promote peace by all means possible, and to refrain oneself from violence in word and in act.

Archbishop Kenrick's course throughout all this trying period was courageous, but conservative and prudent, and his guidance, both of clergy and people, firm and unfaltering. On the 12th of January, 1861, the following notice was published over his signature as Archbishop of St. Louis:

"To the Roman Catholics of St. Louis: Beloved brethren, in the present distressed state of the public mind, we feel it our duty to recommend you to avoid all occasions of public excitement, to obey the laws, to respect the rights of all citizens, and to keep away, as much as possible, from all assemblages where the indiscretion of a word or the impetuosity of a momentary passion might endanger public tranquillity. Obey the injunction of the Apostle St. Peter: 'Follow peace with all men, and holiness, without which no man can see God.'[3]

Archbishop Kenrick, no doubt, had decided opinions in regard to the two great questions that were agitated between North and South:

---

2 "Taunts were flung by Southern sympathizers at the St. Louis 'Dutch.' Missiles followed, then shots. The story runs that a Union soldier was killed, a captain wounded. Their comrades began firing on the mob. A number were killed, including two women and a child. The command came to stop firing, but too late to correct the blunder or lessen the terror of a frantic populace. Crowds with banners patrolled the streets. Public meetings were prohibited, windows were barred, and drinking places closed. Disaster had become calamity. That night found St. Louis more unsettled, more fearful of the future, than ever in its life of a century. The next day and the day after saw at river wharf and railroad station the exodus of thousands. Rumor distorted fact and hurriedly overspread the city and state." Shoemaker, F. C., "The Week in Missouri's History," May 10, 1925.

3 I Peter 3, 11.

slavery and secession. But, fair and just, as he always was, he took into consideration the point of view of the southern people, as well as that of the abolitionists. The people of the South had invested many millions of dollars in their slaves. The Constitution approved of the institution as an established fact. Were not all the people of the United States bound in honor to reimburse the masters for their liberated slaves? And was the question as to the rights of the individual states, even to the extent of seceding from the Union, not as yet a mooted one? From our point of vantage, long after the war, we can judge more confidently as to the relative measure of right and wrong in the policies of those days of storm and stress—And yet, even today, ''The conquered Banner'' is still a splendid memory.

Archbishop Kenrick's sympathies, as those of the majority of his people and priests, inclined to the southern cause: yet his position as a Catholic prelate forbade an expression on the matter. He was a slave holder, on a very small scale, but his slaves were perfectly contented with the home he gave them. He sympathized with the sufferings of all men, whether black or white or brown, or yellow: but he did not think immediate emancipation of the negro class the only remedy for these sufferings; The various Provincial and National Councils which he had attended, and of which he was a great part himself, had long ago advocated a gradual emancipation, as beneficial to the slaves and fair to their owners. War he ragarded as one of the three greatest afflictions of mankind, greater even than its two dismal sisters, famine and pestilence: and this war seemed to him not only terrible in its nature, but inexpedient and unjustifiable in its cause. Accordingly he took his own advice: ''to avoid all occasions of public excitement, to obey the laws, to respect the rights of all citizens, and to keep away, as much as possible, from all assemblages where the indiscretion of a word or the impetuosity of a momentary passion might endanger public tranquillity.''

As Archbishop Ryan informs us: ''He kept aloof from politics and abstained for a time from reading the newspapers, because he believed that, in the peculiar circumstances of Missouri as a border State, the interests of religion would be best forwarded by prudent silence: yet an impression became general that the Archbishop shared the views of the distinguished jurist, Charles O'Connor of New York, in regard to the relations of the states to the General Government. This fact coming to the knowledge of Mr. Seward, the Secretary of State, this functionary sought through his friend, Archbishop Hughes, to have the prelate of St. Louis removed by the Roman authorities to another see. It is true, he had done no overt act nor spoken treasonable words: but the simple fact that a man of such profound influence in that city and State should hold such views, was deemed, at that critical period, dangerous to the country. But Mr. Seward's little bell did not tingle in the Vatican, and beyond sending the Secretary's letter to Baltimore, from which place it was sent to St. Louis, nothing more was done by the Archbishop of New York.''[4]

Whilst Archbishop Kenrick, almost single-handed, was striving after peace, there were many who were laboring early and late to draw his people into the conflict. Frank P. Blair who had been elected Colonel of the First Regiment of Missouri Volunteers, and as such continued the work of enlistment with feverish haste, asked for the appointment of Father De Smet as chaplain in the army. As this move seemed to be intended as an inducement to Irish Catholics to join the ranks, Father De Smet being among the most beloved and honored priests in the entire country, the Archbishop refused his consent. It is said that Colonel Blair, whose influence in Washington had already removed both General Harney and General Fremont from the Command of the Department of Missouri, was on the point of taking severe measures against the Archbishop, but soon saw the futility of so doing, and desisted.

When the storm cloud at last broke it arrayed state against state, family against family, brother against brother. The children of the Church also were divided on the great issues involved, and stood arrayed against each other in deadly combat. During its first two years, he abstained entirely from preaching, as every word of his would surely be interpreted as a reflection on the war. When Father John Bannon left his newly frescoed Church of St. John without any formality, of leave-taking, the Archbishop simply appointed Father Ring as his successor. "Father Bannon has gone south," said the bearer of a letter to the Archbishop. "I have heard so," came the quiet answer. "And he has left this letter for Your Grace," added the gentlemen: "Keep it," laconically replied the Archbishop. Father John O'Sullivan, Pastor of St. Malachy's Parish was a hot outspoken secessionist, and accordingly came in conflict with the military authorities. The Archbishop permitted his removal from the parish, but recommended him to Bishop Juncker of Alton, who gave him the parish of the Annunciation Church in Springfield, Illinois. In the Northern cities many a Catholic priest and bishop showed his zeal for the success of the Union arms by flying the Star-Spangled Banner from the church tower. Archbishop Kenrick did not favor this practice. When he was requested by an officious provost marshal to float the American Flag from the Cathedral steeple he refused saying: "No other banner may be placed there, for already there stands one, which alone shall stay, the banner of the Church," pointing to the cross on the Cathedral spire.

---

4 Archbishop Ryan of Philadelphia, in "American Catholic Quarterly Review," vol. XXI, p. 426.

No doubt, he had in mind the glorious words of St. Venantius Fortunatus:

> "Vexilla regis Prodeunt,
> Fulget crucis mysterium."

Whatever we may now think of these acts of Archbishop Kenrick, in opposition to the orders of the Gevernment, we must admit that he simply stood upon his rights as the highest representative of the Catholic Church in a country that had guaranteed the free exercise of religion to every citizeñ, and boasted a complete separation of Church and State. The Church as such does not take orders from the State, is what Archbishop Kenrick held, just as St. Thomas a Becket had held in the long ago: and here he showed, if nothing more, at least the courage of his convictions.

The Church in Missouri, especially in the southern portions suffered greatly from the constant marches and countermarches of the contending armies. Many churches were desecrated by being turned into stables for the horses; others were burnt, and again others were stripped of everything portable, as altars, confessionals, pews, and organs, to be used for the camp fires. Great were the ravages of the war, but great also the opportunities for good it offered to the zealous priests and nuns of the Church. Father Patrick J. Ryan, the pastor of the Church of the Annunciation, was appointed by the Archbishop, chaplain of the Gratiot Street Military Prison, where he ministered so earnestly and gently, that about six hundred of the prisoners asked for Baptism. Countless others were put in communication with friends, or helped back to their homes by Father Ryan. A paid Army Chaplainey was extended to him and to Dr. Schuyler of the Episcopal Church: but Father Ryan refused the honor and salary, while continuing to the end in his wonderful work at this prison.[5] A Hospital for wounded soldiers was established in the parish of the Immaculate Conception, and given in charge of the Sisters of Charity. Father Patrick Feehan, the pastor, spent every moment he could spare from his manifold duties in the work of comforting and counseling these poor victims of grim war. After the great battle of Shiloh, boat loads of wounded men were brought in for three days in succession: a large number of them were Catholics, to whom the sacraments of the Church were a wonderful comfort: others, not of the Faith, but seeing the comfort which the sacraments brought to their dying companions, expressed the wish to die in the same way. The Sisters also made the most wonderful impression upon the wounded soldiers, Catholic and non-Catholic. "I want to belong to the religion to which the Sisters belong," cried one; and when Father Feehan came to his bedside and spoke of the main

---

5. Archbishop Ryan, ibidem.

tenets of the Catholic religion, the dying soldier turned to the attending Sister and asked: "Do you believe that?" And when she answered: "O yes, I surely do believe that;" he assented to every question on the assurance of the Sister that she believed what the Father had proposed. He was baptised, and died in the religion to which the Sisters belonged."[6] It is a pleasant coincidence that Father Ryan, who mainly devoted himself to the southern prisoners of war, eventually became Archbishop of the great northern City of Philadelphia, whilst Father Feehan, whose loving kindness was mainly bestowed upon the wounded soldiers of the North, was promoted to the southern stronghold of Nashville, Tennessee, as its bishop. In the grand work of Christian Charity the Church knows no distinction of friend and enemy: the kingdom of God is the realm of peace and love.

But peace and love are based on justice, the eternal will of God. No virtue can subsist without it, no happiness can be attained, no prosperity assured, if justice be not its very soul. And justice requires, that the rights of God and of His Church be respected by the state, as well as by the individual. When the great conflict was decided at Appomatox, and the soldiers of North and South came home, the politicians became active. In Missouri the so-called radicals held, that all southern-sympathizers must be disfranchised. The means for accomplishing this nefarious purpose lay in the new Constitution, which by force and fraud, had become the fundamental law of the State, on July 4th, 1865.[7] Whilst the Protestant clergy had, as a rule, openly supported the southern cause, the public conduct of the priests and their Archbishop had been perfectly correct. Their high calling as ministers of Christ and dispensers of His mysteries forbade them to take sides in the bloody contest. But religious prejudices were active against the Catholic Church. Fear and jealousy were the motives. The Church was growing too rich and powerful to suit the leaders among the political "saviors of the Country."

But they found in the Archbishop of St. Louis a man whom they could not bend nor break: At no time in his life did Peter Richard Kenrick more strikingly show forth the leonine qualities of his character, than in his opposition to the infamous test-oath required by the so-called Drake Constitution.

The new Constitution of Missouri disqualified from voting and from holding any office of honor, trust or profit in the State, any one

---

6 Kirkfleet C. J. "Patrick Augustine Feehan," pp. 31 and 32.

7 On the Drake Constitution, Cf. Barclay, Thomas S., "The Liberal Republican Movement," in "Missouri Historical Review," vol. XX, No. 1, pp. 55-78, and No. II, p. 297-301. See also: Annual Cyclopedia 1865, New York, p. 591. Bishop Hogan's "On the Missouri in Missouri," and Bishop John McMullen's Life and Writings, Appendix, pp. CXVIII-CXXXIII.

who had ever been in armed hostility to the United States, or had ever given aid or comfort or countenance or support, to persons engaged in such hostility, or had ever by act or word manifested his adherence to the cause of such enemies; or his desire for the triumph over the arms of the United States, or his sympathy with those engaged in rebellion.

This was sufficiently obnoxious; but the injustice went farther: "Nor shall any such person be capable of being an officer, a councilman, director or trustee or other manager of any corporation, public or private, now existing or hereafter established by its authority; or of acting as professor or teacher in any educational institution, or if holding any real or other property in trust for the use of any church, religious society or congregation. In Section VI of the Constitution an oath, called at first the oath of loyalty, but, afterwards known as the Test Oath, was prescribed not only for those who desired to vote or to hold an office of honor, trust, or profit under the authority of the State, but also for all the clergy, Catholic and Protestant, of whatever denomination, before the 2nd day of August 1865.

The test oath read as follows:

"I————, do solemnly swear, that I am well acquainted with the terms of the third section of the second article of the Constitution of the State of Missouri, adopted in the year 1865, and have carefully considered same; that I have never, directly or indirectly, done any of the acts in said section specified; that I have been always truly and loyally on the side of the United States against all enemies thereof, foreign and domestic; that I will bear true faith and allegiance to the United States, and I will support the Constitution and the laws thereof as the supreme law of the land, any law or ordinance of any State to the contrary notwithstanding; that I will, to the best of my ability, protect and defend the Union of the United States, and not allow the same to be broken up and dissolved, or the government thereof to be destroyed or overthrown, under any circumstances if in my power to prevent it; that I will support the Constitution of the State of Missouri; that I make this oath without any mental reservation or evasion, and hold it to be binding on me."

Article III of Section 9 of the Constitution:

"Nor after that time shall any person be competent as a bishop, priest, deacon minister, elder, or other clergyman of any religious persuasion, sect or denomination, to teach, preach or solemnize marriages; unless such persons shall have first taken, subscribed and filed said oath."[8]

---

8 Cf. "Messages and Proclamations," vol. IV, pp. 262-264, and Constitution, 1865.

The Constitution prescribed fine and imprisonment as punishment for holding office or performing the functions mentioned without having taken the oath. A priest was therefore liable to fine and imprisonment in the penitentiary if he ventured to preach, or assist at a marriage, or say mass in public. This provision was clearly in conflict with the Constitution of the United States, as far as it interfered with the freedom of worshipping God. It was, moreover an ex post facto law'' in its operations, that is it attempted to punish people for actions that were not punishable at the time they were committed; and at the same time it would force every one that refused to take the oath, to become a witness against himself. The Archbishop of St. Louis took the high ground that to take the oath, was to acknowledge an authority in the State that does not belong to it, and that human authority was above divine. Accordingly Archbishop Kenrick on July 28th, 1865 addressed the following circular letter to his clergy:

"Reverend Sir: Since under the new Constitution a certain oath is to be exacted of priests, that they may have leave to announce God's word, and officiate at marriages, which oath, they can in no wise take without a sacrifice of ecclesiastical liberty. I have judged it expedient to indicate to you my opinion in the matter, that you may have before your eyes a rule to be followed in a case of such delicacy. I hope that the civil power will abstain from exacting such an oath. But should it happen otherwise, I wish you to inform me of the particular circumstances of your position, that I may be able to give you counsel and assistance." The letter was signed Peter Richard Kenrick, Archbishop of St. Louis. All the priests declined to take the oath, but continued their priestly functions. A number of arrests were made of nonjuring priests, as Father David S. Phelan of Edina, Bernard Hillner of Booneville, John Hogan of Chillicothe, and John A. Cummings of Louisana. Father Hogan[9] showed his contempt for the sponsors of such an outrageous law by going to the Courthouse of Chillicothe, dressed in cassock, surplice, stole and biretta: carrying a large crucifix in his right hand and in his left a Folio Bible. This action of the gentle, ever-helpful priest roused the indignation of the Catholics of Brookfield and Linn County to white heat. At a meeting held in Brookfield they denounced the infamous anti-christian measures of the "Radical Constitution" and defiantly unfurled the flag of religious freedom. The arrested priests were placed under bond. The Archbishop himself was made to suffer for noncompliance in regard to the Test Oath. Mrs. Mary L. Lamarque of Old Mines, Washington County, had made a bequest of $20,000.00 to the Archbishop of St. Louis for the education of priests for his diocese. Louis Bolduc and

---

9 "On the Mission in Missouri," pp. 130-131.

others heirs at law of the deceased benefactress, contested the will under the provisions of the Drake Constitution, disqualifying the nonjuring clergy from holding or receiving property in trust for their church or religious society. The Archbishop on the witness stand testified, that only as Archbishop of St. Louis was he entitled to the legacy and only as Archbishop did he desire to receive it. The Court instructed the jury to give a verdict setting aside the will of Mary L. Lamarque. An appeal from Washington County to the Supreme Court of Missouri, in March term, 1870, affirmed the decision of the trial judge: ''Legacy to Peter Richard Kenrick is void and of no effect, as in violation of section 13, article 1, of the Constitution of the State of Missouri.''[10] Bishop Hogan in his Golden Jubilee Sermon aptly said: ''Under radical rule in Missouri a horse thief . . . was competent to be legatee, but not Peter Richard Kenrick, Archbishop of St. Louis.''

Archbishop Kenrick felt that the Test Oath must be wiped out, if the Church was not to suffer humiliation and continued oppression. His opportunity was at hand. Father John A. Cummings, pastor of Louisiana, Pike County, Mo., was arrested, like many others of his brethren, but unlike them, refused to furnish bail, saying, he would in such a case, rather go to jail, and there await the outcome of his trial. To jail he went, and all appeals to ''the little dapper gentleman,'' as he was described by non-Catholics, to accept the offer of bail, were flatly refused.[11]

Father Cummings was convicted in the Circuit Court of Pike County; he appealed to the Supreme Court of the State, where judgment of the Circuit Court was affirmed. He then took his case to the Supreme Court of the United States, where it was argued in December 1866. The Hon. David Dudley Field, and the Hon. Reverdy Johnson argued the case for Father Cummings. The Missourians George P. Strong and J. B. Henderson were the counsel for the State of Missouri. The case was thus stated by Mr. Justice Field, in rendering the decision: ''This case comes before us on a writ of error to the Supreme Court of Missouri and involves a consideration of the test oath imposed by the Constitution of that State. The plaintiff in error is a priest of the Roman Catholic Church, and was indicted and convicted, in one of the Circuit Courts of that State, of the crime of teaching and preaching, as a priest and minister of that religious denomination, without having first taken the oath, and was sentenced to pay a fine of $500., and to be committed to the jail until the same was paid. On appeal to the Supreme Court of the State, the judgment was affirmed.''[12] The Court then decided that the Missouri Test Oath

---

10  Kenrick versus Cole, et al Missouri Reports, vol. 26, p. 85.
11  Barclay, op. cit., pp. 58-62.
12  Barclay, op. cit., pp. 71 and 72.

was in contravention of the provision of the Constitution, that "no State shall pass any bill of attainder," or "ex post facto law." Now, as the disabilities created by the Constitution of Missouri must be regarded as penalties, they constitute "a bill of attainder," and as they endeavor to inflict punishment for an act which was not punishable when committed, they constitute an "ex post facto law" and are therefore null and void. Archbishop Kenrick's contention that the provisions were a denial of liberty of conscience and religion guaranteed by the Constitution was not touched by the Supreme Court's decision: but the case was won by the Archbishop, and Father Cummings, and all other cases under the test oath law were dismissed. The radicals had suffered a crushing defeat: but the Archbishop's triumph was a costly one. The legal expenses amounted to more than ten thousand dollars, all of which were paid by His Grace himself. In effect, it was a triumph of religious liberty, over bigotry and fanaticism. The Drake Constitution and its infamous test oath had to go into innocuous desuetude and final extinction. Archbishop Kenrick's warning: "Noli irritare leonem" had found its perfect exemplification.

## CHAPTER 30

# FATHER RYAN AND FATHER MUEHLSIEPEN CONTRASTED

It was the Springtide of the year 1867. The horrors of the civil war were over: even the painful consequences of the war, the hatreds engendered and the poverty induced by it, and especially, the Drake Constitution with its Test Oath and other abominations, were things that no longer troubled mankind. Such seasons of peace and calm after years of anguish and anxiety are liable to rouse the "wanderlust" in the hearts of men. Accordingly on May 26th, 1867, the papers spread the news: "that Archbishop Kenrick accompanied by Father Ryan of the Annunciation Church will leave for Cape Girardeau tomorrow (May 27th, 1867) whence, after the ordaining of nine priests, they will proceed to Boston, to sail on the Steamer "*Asia*" for Europe on June 5th, enroute for Rome."[1] On November they brought the news that Archbishop Kenrick was at Brussels in Belgium, on his way to the American College in Louvain, and that he was accompanied by Rev. P. J. Ryan, and that it would probably be some months before their return to St. Louis. The occasion of their visit to Rome was the eighteen hundredth anniversary of the martyrdom of S. S. Peter and Paul. The grand celebration over, Archbishop Kenrick and Father Ryan left the Eternal city in order to visit the great centers of religion and culture in Italy, France, Germany, Belgium and Ireland. In Dublin, his native city, he received an enthusiastic greeting from a multitude of his friends, among them the pastor of his early priestly days, Father O'Dwyer. In Dublin's Cathedral the Archbishop preached a ringing sermon on the sorrows of his native land, leading up to the climax in the sentence: "Ireland differs from other nations in this: whilst they have given martyrs to the Church, Ireland was *the* martyr nation." On June 4th, 1868, the Archbishop and his Secretary, Father Ryan, sailed on "*The City of Antwerp*" and arrived in New York, on June 14th. On June 23rd, they arrived in East St. Louis, and were met there by a delegation of priests and prominent laymen who escorted the Archbishop to his residence, there to be welcomed home by Vicar-General Melcher, the administrator of the Archdiocese during the Archbishop's European trip. A public reception was given to the beloved Prelate on June 28th. The procession was nearly three miles long. On assembling before the Archbishop's house, His Grace received them standing on his doorsteps. Mr. Robert A. Bakewell made the address of welcome.

---

[1] "St. Louis Republican," May 26, 1867.

In the meantime, Vicar-General Melcher had been appointed Bishop of Green Bay. His consecration by Archbishop Kenrick took place at St. Mary's Church on July 12, 1868. On July 4th, the *"Guardian"* had stated: "We learn that Reverend P. J. Ryan, D. D., and Reverend Henry Muehlsiepen have been appointed Vicars-General, and that the Rev. Charles Ziegler succeeds Rev. P. J. Ryan as Secretary."

On the first Sunday in July "Rev. Dr. P. J. Ryan preached his first sermon since his return from Europe . . . . The attendance at the Annunciation Church was larger than it has been on any occasion since his departure. It is needless to add that all were delighted with his discourse." But there were rumors in the air that the pastor of the Annunciation would shortly take charge of St. John's Church. The rumor was but too true. On August 8th, "the Guardian" said, "On Sunday last the Very Rev. P. J. Ryan, V. G., preached for the first time to the new congregation over which he has been appointed to preside. The church was more crowded than we ever remember to have seen it. The sermon lasted about an hour, and so touching was his peroration, that there was not a dry eye in the church."

Vicar-General Ryan being supported in the administration of his populous parish by such able assistants as Fathers Constantine Smith, William Brantner, Edward J. Shea and R. J. Hayes, found ample time to use his extraordinary oratical gifts for the advancement of the Church's interests, and for the good of the poor, the orphans, and the oppressed. Hundreds and hundreds of lectures did he deliver throughout the length and breadth of the country. "Few men in the United States have realized so much money by lecturing as Father Ryan has, and no man has gained thereby as little for himself personally. Not one dollar of the many thousands he had earned has ever been appropriated to his own use." This is the deliberate judgment of a fellow-priest, who knew him well.

This noble disinterestedness was one of the secrets of Father Ryan's great success. But without his gift of oratory it would have been impossible. "His eloquence was fascinating and, at times, irresistible, by force of his earnestness." wrote the editor of the *Guardian* on November 14th, 1868, "His reasoning was lucid, severe, logical: his illustrations fresh and apt, his rhetoric pure, his periods flowing and rounded, and his climaxes grand. His enunciation was clear, and his utterance frequently charged with a fire that made it electric. He spoke without notes, with evident spontaneity, and his sermon was altogether a masterpiece."

Towards the Fall of 1869 Archbishop Kenrick was busy with making preparations for his second journey to Rome. This visit was for the purpose of attending the Vatican Council, which had been convoked by the Soverign Pontiff, Pius IX to meet on the Feast of the Immaculate Conception, December 8th, 1869. Very Reverend Patrick J. Ryan was appointed Administrator of the Archdiocese. The *Western Watchman* printed this brief notice:

"In view of his protracted attendance at the General Council, His Grace, Archbishop Kenrick, has appointed Very Rev. P. J. Ryan to administer the affairs of the diocese during his absence.

We congratulate Father Ryan on his deserved promotion. His long and successful labors in the diocese make the appointment eminently meet and proper. The prayers of a devoted people will follow our worthy Archbishop on his long journey, and their grateful welcome will greet him on his return."

On March 5th, 1870, the "*Western Watchman*" broke forth in the following paean: "Father Ryan is stirring up the chronic lethargy, that for more than a quarter of a century has laid like an incubus on the Catholic body. Never, since St. Louis was established as an Episcopal See, have we witnessed a more powerful putting forth of Catholic strength, as we witness at this time. Move on, the whole column, We have the men, let the leaders take the initiative" This clarion call to arms, though rather unjust in its implications as to the past, was certainly justified in its recognition of the signs of the times. In the person of Father Patrick J. Ryan the Church had put its claims before the world embellished by all the graces of Christian eloquence, and the world seemed to be pleased to listen and to learn. Father Ryan had hundreds and hundreds of converts to his credit. Under the old, quiet, humble, plodding regime converts had been comparatively few. Why not adopt the new method and practice it more generally?

Father Ryan had a companion in authority, the Vicar-General for the German Catholics of the archdiocese, Father Henry Muehlsiepen.[2] Equal to him in his devotion to Holy Church and in his friendship for the Archbishop, he formed a complete contrast to him in his manner of operation.

Father Muehlsiepen was not endowed with the brilliant mind and eloquent tongue of his colleague in the administration of the Archdiocese: yet his success in the upbuildinng of the Church, was equally admirable. Vicar-General Muehlsiepen was born on September 5th, 1834, in the parish of Mintard, archdiocese of Cologne. He was sent to the College of Essen. Hearing of the coming of Vicar-General Melcher in search of recruits for St. Louis, the young student hurried to Paderborn, and asked to be received in the company already assembled

---

2 Monsignor Holweck has immortalized the memory of Vicar-General Muehlsiepen in a beautiful sketch of his life and character in the "Pastoral-Blatt," vol. 51, No. I.

for the long journey. On arriving in St. Louis, Muehlsiepen entered the Seminary at Carondelet for the study of philosophy and theology; and after a two years course under the future bishops, Feehan and Hennessey, was ordained to the priesthood on December 8th, 1857. After five years of priestly labors at St. Mary's Church, Father Muehlsiepen took leave of absence for a year, in order to complete his studies at the Seminary of Treves, in his native Rhineland. Returning to St. Louis in August 1863, with health restored and mind expanded, Father Muehlsiepen took over the practical administration of St. Mary's, leaving his pastor the much needed leisure, to devote all his energies to his pressing duties as Vicar-General and Chancellor of the Archdiocese. St. Mary's was at that time a populous parish, recording three hundred and seventy-five Baptisms in the year 1865.

As "the right hand of the Vicar-General" Father Muehlsiepen won for himself golden opinions among the priests and the laity of the Archdiocese, by his ardent zeal, and kindly sympathy and helpfulness.

Two foundations of that day which exerted a wide influence for good, owe their origin, at least in part, to the far-sighted energy of the youthful priest: the "*St. Louis Pastoral-Blatt*," a monthly journal of scientific and practical theology, and the St. Ludwig's Verein for the purpose of spreading Catholic literature among the people. Father Muehlsiepen was the first editor of the *Pastoral-Blatt* which, by the way, out-lasted the changes of half a century; and of the Society for the Spreading of Catholic books, he was the first and last Secretary, the organization being disbanded when its purpose was sufficiently secured by the foundation in the city, of a branch of the house of B. Herder.

On his appointment to the See of Green Bay, Vicar-General Melcher appointed Father Muehlsiepen pastor of St. Mary's, and Archbishop Kenrick, on his return from Europe, confirmed this appointment, and in addition to this, named him his Vicar-General for the German, Bohemian, and Polish Catholics of the archdiocese. A few weeks after his elevation to this high administrative office Vicar-General Muehlsiepen transferred the pastor of Dutzow, Father F. W. Faerber, to St. Mary's Church, (August 15th, 1868) first as his assistant, then as pastor in his own right, for the office of Vicar-General, in those days of rapid development, seemed to require all his time and energy. Still, he accepted the additional duties of Spiritual Director to the Ursuline Nuns, near whose Convent he found a permanent home.

The main qualities of Father Muehlsiepen's character were meekness and humility, the spirit of self-sacrifice, and childlike trust in God. - ·

Enjoying the full confidence of his Archbishop and entrusted with administrative authority over almost half the archdiocese, a bishop in fact, though not in bishops orders, he was still the most affable of men. His regard for his fellow priests was deep and sincere. Anyone, even a delinquent, might approach him with confidence that he would be heard. Yet, in upholding discipline he was firm and uncompromising. He knew no fear, because he always sought to be just. He thought little of his own comfort, but he was ever solicitous for the welfare of his priests. Heat, or cold, or tiresome travel, the rough hospitality of a backwoods homestead, the improvised altar in some railway shanty, had no terrors for him. He not only performed all the duties of a priest, hearing confessions, visiting the sick and instructing the ignorant, but he visited all portions of the archdiocese, acting as pastor of scattered congregations, which had no pastor of their own. He was always ready to help out his priests when they needed a short vacation, either sending them an available helper, or coming himself to attend the parish. He would tramp miles through the snow and arrive at his post with frost-bitten feet and proceed at once to his priestly duties. As for money, he never knew its value, except as a means to help his priests to continue their ministrations in forlorn situations, and to enable struggling parishes to keep up their schools. He was always intent upon looking up the scattered Catholics everywhere, in order to gather them into congregations. He was no great stickler for style in architecture, yet he loved the beauty of the house of God, whether in the grand city church, or in the humble log chapel among the hills. Practical utility was his main concern. He made Archbishop Hughes' fine saying his own: "the school first, and then the Church." Many a poor country church received its parochial school through Father Muehlsiepen's influence with the Ursuline Nuns, and the Sisters of the Precious Blood. His prudence in dealing with factious people was remarkable, and his manner of settling disputes was unique. He would welcome such delegations very kindly, and when they were ready to start, he would light a cigar and take a few puffs. Then he would call on the leader to state his grievance: which done, he would ask the second and then the third to say what they had to say: After all had been said; and he had formed his judgment, he would rise, and address a few remarks to them on the condition of the weather, or the crops, or their health and then dismiss them with the kindly remark: "I don't wish to detain you any longer. Good by."

Father Muehlsiepen, communicative as he was, could keep a secret as securely as anyone. The few puffs at his cigar were only the outward mark of his watchfulness. The scriptural prudence of the serpent, conjoined with the guilelessness of the dove ever stood guard over his life. One time, to give a sample of many cases, a young priest sought to extract an answer on some burning question of the day, from Father Muehlsiepen. Instead of giving him a cold rebuff, he rose deliberately and closed the door of the room, and returning launched out upon a long discourse on the persecutions the Church sustained in its early days, at the end of which the original question remained unanswered and, of course, was not repeated.

Thus meek and humble, kind and helpful and self-sacrificing was the Apostle of the Germans in Missouri; throughout the thirty-five years of his spiritual rule, always directing, guiding, ruling, not by his power, nor by his authority, but by his heart, by his love. And his priests loved him, and trusted him, and confided to him their troubles and cares, and mishaps and successes, and learnt from his counsel and example, how to bear all in patience and in hope.

It was in the Fall of 1869 the Archbishop Kenrick left St. Louis to attend the Vatican Council.

Far away beyond the sea, in the Eternal City, events were shaping themselves which seemed to forbode a great change. Storm clouds arose, gusty winds raised clouds of dust, "the noise was deafening: but all of a sudden came a great calm, and as in the days of old, the Spirit of God was not in the cloud, nor in the wind, but in the fiery tongues that descended upon Peter and the other apostles. 'Roma locuta, causa finita,' said the Christian world, and the future opened full of the brightest prospects."

In the city of St. Louis the Archbishop had left two representatives of his authority, the one, Vicar-General Ryan, representing by preference the outward tendencies of the Church; and the other, Vicar-General Muehlsiepen, seeking to promote its inward life and progress: Both tendencies were good and wholesome: but the working of the Spirit of God in the hearts of Catholic men and women formed the basis from which the conquest of the world must proceed, if its progress is to be something more than a tinkling cymbal and sounding brass.

Whilst then the wonderful eloquence of Father Patrick J. Ryan has done very much to make the Church esteemed and honored by our non-catholic brethren, the humble, quiet, unselfish, and persevering work of the Vicar-General of the German Catholics of the archdiocese, Father Henry Muehlsiepen, has done far more towards consolidating, strengthening, and perpetuating the Church in Missouri. No doubt, both were remarkable men, and both had the same end in view, the glory of God and the salvation of men. Yet to many a priest and layman of that day Father Muehlsiepen appeared as the more apostolic man of the two.

## Chapter 31

EARLY CHURCHES IN ST. LOUIS AND JEFFERSON COUNTIES

The name Meramec is of Indian derivation and was known from time immemorial as the designation of the beautiful stream that rises in the northern part of the Ozark Mountains and, after a long and meandering course through the counties of Dent, Crawford, Washington, Franklin, St. Louis and Jefferson, joins the mighty Mississippi about twenty miles below the metropolis of Missouri. Father Gravier, S. J. long before the foundation of St. Louis. learnt the name from the lips of his Indian converts, but only as the name of a river. At the time of the Second Synod of St. Louis, 1849, and some time previous, it was also applied to the sparsely inhabited countryside, on both banks of the Meramec River, in the counties of Jefferson, St. Louis and possibly Franklin. In our early church records the name is used in this sense, when priests are reported as attending Meramec. When the population increased more rapidly it crystallized around two points on the lower Meramec, having a distinctive German cast, Mattese Creek with its church of the Assumption, in St. Louis County, on the north side of the river, and Maxville, with the Church of the Immaculate Conception, in Jefferson County, to the south. Farther west, in Franklin County, where the Irish immigrants predominated, there lay Armagh, now Catawissa, and Downpatrick, now Pacific. St. Patrick's church of Armagh stood south of the Meramec, and St. Bridget's of Downpatrick, to the north. Both were log structures built by Father Peter Richard Donnelly. In St. Louis County, some twenty-two miles from the Cathedral, stood the Church of St. Peter of Gravois, now Kirkwood, and northeast of Gravois the town of Manchester, without a church and with but a few scattered Catholics. In 1837 Father Van Quickenborne, found in all Meramec only fourteen Catholics: in Manchester ten "among a great crowd of non-Catholics, many of them well disposed toward the Faith,"[1] and in the hills of Armagh and Downpatrick not one.

At this early date the country along the Meramec, was one vast wilderness. The only roads were the narrow dark openings blazed through the forest. The rivers and streams had to be forded, or crossed in canoes hollowed from the trunks of trees. Here and there, at considerable intervals, crouched rudely constructed log houses in little open fields, the humble homes of the pioneers. But the tide of immigration had touched this lonely region during the early fifties.

---

[1] Van Quickenborne's Report in Archives of St. Louis Archdiocese.

Germans, Irishmen, and men from the Eastern and Southern states and even from England, as the names of some of the towns would indicate, were now in peaceful possession.

The first place here mentioned as a center of Catholic life, Gravois, received its little stone church, through the exertions of Father Charles Van Quickeborne, S.J. as early as 1833, twenty years before the organization of the town of Kirkwood. The Jesuit Father H. G. Aelen in 1839 submitted to Bishop Rosati's Synod in 1839, what he called a "Succinct History of the Church of St. Peter in Gravois Settlement:"

"In 1833 (ni fallor) 80 acres, destined for Church property, were purchased from the Government of the U. S. for $1.25 an acre; and the title was transferred to the Right Rev. Bp. Rosati. Jos Sappington and Owen Collins were chosen trustees. By means of the mutual contributions of the congregation, together with those of several offers made by Protestants, a new stone church was erected, and the corner stone laid by the Rev. P. I. Verhaegen, S.J. in August 1833. (ni fallor) The congregation was successively attended by the Rev. Messrs. Saulnier, Condamine, Lefevere, Borgna, Jamison—this latter gentlemen on his return from the Congregation to St. Louis, had one of his legs broken. Of the spiritual fruit, produced by them, nothing is known to me, but two conversions: the one of Elizabeth Wells, consort of Jos. Sappington, baptized (s.c.) by the Revd. M. Borgna in 1835, the 27th of her age: the other of Ethelinda Maria Palmerly, consort of M. Newton, baptized by the Rev. Mr. Jamison in 1837, the 51st of her age.

"During the year 1838 the congregation was attended by the Rev. Mr. H. G. Aelen, S.J. On the 3rd Sunday after Easter, 15 persons from 14 to 22 years of age, made their first Communion: it being the first time that this was done publicly in this church. On the 5th Sunday after Pentecost the Right Rev. Bp. Rosati made his first visit to the congregation to administer the Sacrament of Confirmation to 21 persons: two of whom were converts: the ages of the confirmed ranged from between 14 and 52.

"Shortly after, was baptized Mr. Renicke, in his 25th year of age, by the attending clergyman. In August of the same year the record-books were purchased and brought in order, as far as circumstances did allow."[2]

In 1839 the Reverend Peter Richard Donnelly was appointed to take charge of St. Peter's Church at Gravois. For three years since his ordination, November 20th, 1836, he had led the hard life of a missionary in the wilds of Arkansas. Pine Bluff was his last station there. But his new place was not much better. Not fully recovered from the effects of the hardships endured in the south, Father Donnelly resigned

---

2  Archives of the St. Louis Archdiocese.

his charge and accepted the position of chaplain at the Hospital of the Sisters of Charity. In 1842 he was commissioned to organize the Irish and French Catholics along the Meramec. He did this with creditable success. Though a rather taciturn man, he won the respect and love of his Irish parishioners. He was one of their own, he could hear their confessions in their native Irish tongue. Canon O'Hanlon speaks at length of ''the Irish settlements on the River Meramec founded by Father P. R. Donnelly. These were Armagh in Franklin County, where he dedicated a log church of St. Patrick, and Downpatrick in Jefferson County where a log church was dedicated to St. Bridget and another to St. Columbkille.''[3]

But Father Donnelly was not to remain at Armagh. In 1845 he was sent, for the second time, to the settlement of St. Peter's at Gravois. Four years more did he carry the burden with health impaired but spirit unbroken. Then in 1849, he returned to the Hospital as Chaplain, and remained there until 1864, when Archbishop Kenrick received him into his household, first at the Cathedral, then at St. John's. "He was" as Mgsr. Brennan relates, "very active and quick always; but very reticent, speaking little to anyone but the Archbishop. Hence he was called "the Archbishop's priest.''[4] Father Peter Richard Donnelly died on Friday, June 30th, 1870, at the Sisters Hospital in Chicago, but was brought back to St. Louis for burial in Calvary Cemetery.

After Father Donnelly's departure from Gravois the settlement was visited for spiritual ministration by the neighboring priests, Fathers Joseph C. Fischer, and John Hennessey. In 1854 the place had attained so great importance, mainly on account of the building of the Pacific Railroad through Franklin County, that it was incorporated under the new name Kirkwood, (i. e.) Church Forest, which probably was intended to immortalize the little stone church of Father Van Quickenborne in the woods of Gravois. Father Eugene O'Hea in 1854 became its pastor for a year, and was relieved by Father James Meller, who was promoted to Jefferson City in 1863, the very year that the parochial school of Kirkwood was inaugurated. His successor was the Rev. Henry Van der Sanden. Born in Utrecht, Holland, in 1831, he came to America to make his theological studies at Carondelet and was ordained on June 3rd, 1860. In 1865 the site of the present church was purchased, and on May 26th, 1867, the corner stone of the new St. Peter's was laid by Vicar-General Melcher. The structure was not completed when it was occupied for divine service, on July 19th, 1868, but was blessed by Bishop Ryan on July 4th, 1875. On January 28th, of the previous year, Father Van der Sanden had been named

---

3  ''Life and Scenery in Missouri,'' p. 147.
4  Father Donnelly was born in Roscommon, Connaught, and spoke Irish.

Chancellor of the Archdiocese, a position he was to hold until death called him away, on the eve of his Golden Jubilee, Wednesday, April 13th, 1910.[5] Father Van der Sanden was a student of history, especially of the Church in the Mississippi Valley. His research work in Rome and in American archives brought signal results. His jealous watchfulness over the literary treasures of Bishop Rosati which his Chancellor, Father Saulnier had transmitted to his care, merit the gratitude of all historians, and especially our own. Searching out, copying, and cataloging historical data was his delight: but he was no writer, and so his long-promised History of the Diocese of St. Louis remained a haunting dream. His burly figure with his red flowing beard and his loud reverberating cough, are unforgettable. His knowledge of languages was wonderful and helped him in his mission at the Hospital of the Alexian Brothers. He spoke French, German, English, Flemish and their various dialects. As one of the Brothers said, "He was a man of gruff manner, but kindly and devoted nevertheless."

After Father Van der Sanden came Rev. Thomas Bonacum, the future Bishop of Lincoln, Nebraska; he was followed by Father James J. Daugherty, and in 1879 by Father Gerard D. Power, who was to become pastor of the Church of The Immaculate Conception in St. Louis in 1887. His successor at Kirkwood was Father Bernard Stemker. The present pastor is the venerable Father Eugene Coyle, who held the pastorate of the Old Cathedral since 1886, but was transferred at his own request, to the parish of Kirkwood in 1910.

The next in the order of time, to Kirkwood, were the twin-churches founded by Father Donnelly: St. Patrick's at Armagh and St. Bridget's at Downpatrick. About four miles south of the present town of Pacific, on the right bank of the Meramec river, in Franklin County, the first St. Patrick's Church was erected under the direction of Father Donnelly in 1842. The site chosen was an elevated spot of level ground, overlooking the river at what is called "Priests Ford." The walls were of hewn logs, the roof of clap boards. In the following year the Church of St. Bridget's was erected by Father Donnelly, a few miles north of the present site of St. Bridget's Church in Pacific, near what is now known as Ridenauers Grove. Many of the Irish Catholics, who had helped at the construction of the Pacific Railroad, invested their savings in landed property around these two churches of Father Donnelly. The Church of St. Columbkille was built by Father Donnelly on a beautiful knoll about one mile west of where the village of Byrnesville is now situated.

During Father Donnelly's stay at the Hospital there was no resident priest at Armagh, but regular services were held for the Con-

---

5   Chancery Records.

gregation by Fathers John O'Hanlon, John O'Regan, James Stehle, Patrick Ward, James Fox, Edward Hamill and Patrick Flemming. There was no parochial residence; the visiting priests were lodged in the home of one or the other parishioner.

In 1852 the Catholic flock of Armagh received a new shepherd in the person of the saintly Father Philip Grace, who spent his entire priestly life from April 10th, 1852 the day of his ordination to October 29th, 1859, the day of his death, in the service of the people of Armagh and Downpatrick.[6]

One of the zealous young pastor's immediate cares was to secure a tract of land nearer to the center of the parish, and to erect on it a larger and finer church, than the old St. Patrick's. Twenty acres of land situated three miles south of the original location were donated by Patrick McBrearty.

Father Grace now asked for subscriptions towards a building fund, and started on a collecting tour along the Pacific Railroad from St. Louis to the other end of the state. All went well and the corner stone was laid in 1857. The building was to be constructed of cut stone; hence the work progressed rather slowly, and when the walls had reached the height of ten feet above ground, Father Grace sickened and died at the early age of thirty-five years.

It was on a sick-call to Armagh during the collecting trip of Father Grace, that the faithful pastor of Richwoods, Washington County, Father McCaffrey was killed by being thrown from his horse into the Meramec River. Father Grace was followed at Armagh by Father Francis P. Gallagher, 1863 to 1864, and soon after by Father Michael Flannery, in 1864.

In the following year, 1865, came the priest whose name is an undying memory to the people of Armagh, Father Edward Berry. He arrived from Carlow, Ireland, in priest's orders, on August 18th, 1856, and was assigned to Indian Creek as Rector, and in 1859 to St. Bridget's in St. Louis as assistant, to Father Lillis, and in 1865 received the appointment to St. Pactrick's of Armagh. In addition to this he was given charge of St. Bridget's at Downpatrick and of St. Columbkill's on Big River, Jefferson County, the three parishes forming a circle twenty miles in diameter.

Five years had elapsed since the death of Father Grace. No progress had been made on the new St. Patrick's Church. The building of the new St. Bridget's Church had likewise been retarded. Since the corner stone was laid in 1857, the brick and other building material had been brought to the grounds, but nothing more was done until 1867. The humble log chapel of St. Columbkille could no longer ac-

---

[6] Chancery Records, and a M.S. Sketch of the Rev. Father Berry by one of his parishioners.

commodate the Congregation. The building of three churches at one time must be undertaken by Father Berry. It was a vast undertaking, seemingly impossible of solution: yet it was also a great opportunity for doing something extraordinary for God and His Church. Father Berry, like the brave and good man that he was, felt glad at the opportunity, and set to work resolutely to raise the means for his three projects.

· Being a man of sound principles in business matters, he enjoyed the confidence of his people and of the business and professional men he had to deal with. Money came in from all sides, if not abundantly, still in sufficient amounts at each time of need. Within a short period St. Patrick's was completed, as Father Grace had planned it; the substantial brick building dedicated to St. Bridget was erected, and a fine brick structure replaced the log chapel of St. Columbkille in the Big River Parish.[7]

The one great trial in Father Berry's life was the destruction of his church and parochial residence by fire on the night of Good Friday 1885. The sun of Easter Saturday shone on a mass of smouldering ruins. The work of half a lifetime had passed away in flame and smoke. But the sympathy of his parishioners and friends infused new courage into the good Father's heart. St. Bridget's as well as St. Columbkill's parishes gave substantial aid towards rebuilding St. Patrick's, and in less than a year the new church and pastoral residence were completed, and on Easter Sunday 1886 holy Mass was celebrated in the new temple of God: The dedication was performed by Vicar-General Phillip Brady. When age and its infirmities began to press heavily upon Father Berry, and he was told by friends to exchange his position for a chaplaincy in the city, the good shepherd of the Armagh hills said: "If the Archbishop will but leave me here, I will be well satisfied." And Archbishop Kain said to Father Berry's solicitous friends: "To take him away from those people whom he loves would break the old man's heart." Father Edward Berry remained at his post of duty until death gently called him away, in the early morning of Wednesday, July 28th, 1901.[8]

The twin-settlements of Mattese Creek and Maxville known of old as Meramec, date back to 1874, when John Hildebrand took up his abode near the salt-springs of the Saline Creek, half way between the present towns of Maxville and Fenton. In 1780 the settlers on the southern bank of the Meramec were driven away by the Indians of the neighborhood. Living conditions at this outpost of civilization were rather primitive. Wheat bread was almost unknown: The women manufactured the clothes of the family from skins of wild animals

---

7 Sketch of Father Edward Berry, M.S.
8 Sketch of Father Edward Berry, M. S.

or from flax and cotton.  The usual currency consisted of shaved deer-skins, at the ratio of three pounds of peltry to one dollar.  This con-tinned all through the first quarter of the nineteenth century.

Catholic life received its first impulse in 1839, when Father Joseph Fischer came to the wilds of the Meramec to gather the Catholic settlers around him for divine service.  The settlers were, for the most part, immigrants from Alsace, Bavaria, Baden, and the Rhineland.  In 1839, April 1st., Father Fischer bought, in his own name, 160 acres of land, and induced the parishioners in 1842 to build a log church.  On July 6th, 1844, Father Fischer transferred the title to this land to Archbishop Kenrick for the use of "the parish of the Immaculate Conception at the Meramec."  The town of Maxville grew up around the church, and the parish received large accessions from southern Germany.  A ferry conveyed the people across the river near the town: the main road led southward to Ste. Genevieve and northward to St. Louis. Mattis Creek, the other half of the Meramec region in St. Louis County, had a similar origin: Father Saulnier made a few occasional visits to the place in 1839: but bought seven acres of land, on which a log church was built and dedicated to Our Lady of the Assumption.  The congregation consisted of seven families.  Father Fischer attended to the spiritual needs of the people for two years, from his home at St. Mary's Church in the city.  In February 1844 Rev. Joseph Melcher became resident pastor.  He built a log parsonage, which, in course of time, served as a school, teachers' residence, stable, and finally was burned.  Father Melcher was succeeded in 1846 by Father Zeller, a priest of some medical knowledge and skill, who in turn was followed by Rev. Simon Sigrist;  He attended Mattis Creek until 1849, when he was called to St. Louis to found the parish of S. S. Peter and Paul.[9] The next two pastors of Mattis Creek Settlement, the Rev. Joseph Blaarer and the Rev. Remigius Gebhard, did not last long under the hard and unpleasant conditions obtaining at the Meramec.  Father Blaarer was a native of St. Gall, Switzerland, a man of diminutive size and sensitive soul, who soon tired of the rude manners of the pioneer farmers on the Meramec and returned to his native land. Father Remigius Bebhard, a Bavarian, from the diocese of Augsburg, born July 1st, 1823.  Laboring with truly apostolic zeal in both parts of Meramec, he raised high hopes for a noble career, but in the midst of his priestly service, he was snatched away by the cholera, June 27th, 1852, in his twenty-ninth year.[10]

The brick church at Mattese was built in 1848, the parsonage in 1871 and the teachers' dwelling in 1874.  A parochial school seems to

---

9  Chancery Records, and "Immaculate Conception Church, Maxville, Mo." Souvenir, 1917, pp. 8 and 9.

10  Cf. Holweck, "Drei Baiern," in "Pastoral-Blatt," vol. 51, No. 12.

have been maintained by the Congregation from the very start, but the Franciscan Sisters took charge of it soon after 1872.

The succession of priests attending to Mattese Creek after Father Gebhard, was: Fathers John Reiss; Matthias Lentner, a native of Tyrol, who remained but a few months; James Meller, of the Archdiocese of Cologne, who attended the Meramec Catholics from Kirkwood, where he was pastor from 1855 to 1860. All these gentlemen had charge of Maxville also, where there was a church, but no shelter for the priest, save the old tumble-down log church of 1842. But there was a Catholic School.

Father Henry Brockhagen was the first resident priest at the Church of the Immaculate Conception at Maxville.[11] His appointment bears date of April 7th, 1859. Father Henry Brockhagen was born at Garbeck, Westphalia, on August 6th, 1833. Coming to America in 1857 he was ordained on St. Joseph's Day, 1859, and two months later appointed to the parish of Maxville. Here he found the fine stone church built by Father Gebhard in 1851. But the structure was unfinished. The walls and ceiling were unplastered; there were no pews, no pulpit, no baptismal font. The altar and communion rail, a gift from St. Louis, had just been installed. The church bell hung from a limb of an ancient oak in front of the Church. The old log church had to serve as parochial residence. There were twenty-five people at the first Sunday service. The number of pupils in the school was fifteen. Father Brockenhagen built a school house in 1860, before that period one room of the pastoral residence served for the purpose. In 1871 he erected the stone school house which is still in use. In 1872, during the so-called Kultur-Kampf in Germany, Father Brockhagen visited his native land, and brought along with him some Franciscan Sisters. This event led to the establishment of the Community of the Franciscan Sisters in St. Louis. From September 1875 to April 1877 a colony of these Sisters taught school for Father Brockhagen in Maxville.[12]

Whilst the young enthusiast was at all times intent upon improving the spiritual and temporal condition of his parish of the Immaculate Conception at Maxville, he never lost sight of his early resolution to make the whole County of Jefferson Catholic. After the departure of Father Meller for Jefferson City, in 1859, the Church of the Assumption of Our Blessed Lady in Mattese Creek was added to his cares. That implied the responsibility for all the county of Jefferson. As Father Schlefers tells us in his well written "Souvenir," Father Brockhagen was untiring in his efforts: "In the beginning we see him go to the church of Mattese Creek every other Sunday, then soon thereafter, every Sunday and also on a weekday. In the same year 1859, the Bo-

---

11 Immaculate Conception Parish, Maxville, pp. 15-17.
12 Ibidem, pp. 18-20.

hemians of Rock Creek begged him to help them to establish a church
and procure for them a pastor. He advised them to build a log church
and occasionally gave them service, till the parish was established. In
1861, May 6th, he blessed the new log church. Around Cedar Hill,
near the present Byrnesville, was a settlement of Catholics of Irish
descent. Mr. Patrick Byrnes asked Father Brockhagen if he would not
give these settlers the consolations of holy religion. This appeal
was, of course, not made in vain; and so we see the zealous pastor
every first Monday in the month on his way to Cedar Hill, 23 miles
distant. He also served the people in Crystal City occasionally. Near
the present Horine lived in those olden days three Catholic slaveholders
with many Catholic slaves. Father Brockhagen often said Mass in
their houses, administered the holy Sacraments and instructed their
children, the colored as well as the white. He often said Mass at
Capt. Horine's farm.''[13]

One wonders how one priest could, in those days of almost im-
passable roads attend to the spiritual needs of the Catholics of half
Jefferson County and of the southern part of St. Louis County. Father
Brockhagen performed this work for about six years. He had two
faithful assistants—his two ponies. An old settler informs us enthusiastically: ''These ponies were like the Ford cars of the present day, no
road too muddy, no hill to steep for them, and always running at high
speed.''

A census taken up by Father Brockhagen in the year 1874 shows
that the parish at Maxville numbered 109 families with 585 souls.''

Father Brockhagen's successors at Maxville were: Father John
Wiegers, 1876-1882: Father James Meller, for the second time, 1882-
1883; Father William J. Angemendt 1883-1886; Father John Schramm,
1888-1892. It was the latter's successor, Father Frederick Schulte, that
built the new brick church at Maxville in 1895, the dedication of which
was conducted by Vicar-General Muehlsiepen on October 13th, of the
same year. Under his administration the Ursuline Nuns were engaged as
teachers. His successor Father Christian Hubert Schlefers, after a
successful administration of the parish for more than fifteen years
died, June 22, 1924.

St. Mary's Church at Bridgeton was built in 1852 by the Jesuit
Father John Gleizal, at that time residing at the Novitiate in Florissant.
As early as 1851, he visited the place and said mass at the home of
Dr. Moore. The first resident priest was Father Dennis Kennedy. The
first rectory was built in 1878 by another Jesuit Father B. Masselis.
There is a long succession of priests represented in the Records of the

---

13   Immaculate Conception Parish, p. 17.

Parish, since 1852, as only a few of them held their residence there or stayed longer than two years.[14] Father Joseph Schroeder was resident pastor from 1878 to 1885. Father Peter Wigger added the sacristy to the Church, which though small and old, has real architectural distinction. Father Joseph Wentker built the school house and the pastoral residence. The present pastor is Father George Koob. Bridgeton is one of our oldest towns, being laid out as such by Robert Owens under the name of Village Robert, or Marais des Liards. In the census taken by De Lassus in 1799 the number of inhabitants is given as 376. The common-field of the town was situated in the Marais des Liards. (Marsh of Poplars.)

St. Joseph's Parish of Clayton St. Louis County is the direct successor of St. Martin's Church on the Bonhomme Road. The corner stone of this, and fifth church built in St. Louis County outside the city limits, was laid on September 4th, 1842, and the completed church was solemnly dedicated by Rev. George A. Carrell, president of St. Louis University and future Bishop of Covington Ky., on April 21st, 1844.[15]

The building was of brick, measured thirty-seven feet square, and was situated on a tract of land of four acres, granted for the purpose by the Congregation. The names of the early priests attending St. Martin's Parish are Fathers P. R. Donnelly, James Murphy, James Higgins, Dennis Kennedy, Patrick Brady, Thomas Cleary, Lawrence Smith and James B. Jackson. When the city of St. Louis extended its territory to the present limits and cast off the incumbrance of St. Louis County, the people of the county looked around for a new county seat. The offer of Ralph Clayton to donate a tract of one hundred acres for the purpose, was accepted: and the erection of the County buildings was begun. The County officers donated to Father Jackson of St. Martin's a lot in the new town for church purposes. Father Watson built upon it a frame church and parsonage. The church he dedicated to St. Joseph, St. Martin's Church on the Bonhomme Road was now forsaken. Father Michael Busch, wrecked the old building and used the brick and lumber for a new parochial residence in Clayton: The present pastor of Clayton, Father Victor Stepka, built the new stone church of St. Joseph in Clayton, and tore down the old parsonage of St. Martin's, in order to give the parish cemetery a better appearance. And now nothing remains of St. Martin's on the Bonhomme road but the wall around the cemetery.

---

14 Chancery Records.
15 "Catholic Cabinet," vol. II, No. 1.

The settlement of Manchester as a town dates back to the early part of the Nineteenth Century, but did not receive its present high sounding name until about 1825. A Catholic Church dedicated to St. Malachy was erected in 1839. For a number of years it was visited by priests from St. Louis Cathedral and St. Peter's Church at Gravois. In 1869 Rev. H. V. Kalmer was appointed Parish Priest.

A parochial school has been maintained by the parish of Manchester since 1851; in the same year the present church building was erected.

St. Anne's church at Normandy dates back to the year 1855 when Mrs. Anne Hunt donated to the Jesuits ten arpens of land on which to build a church. The small temporary· chapel was replaced in 1857 by a large and tasteful stone structure. In 1872 this house of worship was enlarged and renovated, and in 1875 a steeple added to it. In 1868 the brick parsonage was erected. The parochial school has been in operation since 1857. The parish is now in charge of the Passionist Fathers. The school is conducted by the Sisters of Loretto.[16]

Two more church foundations of the Jesuits in St. Louis County must be noticed here: the German Church of The Sacred Heart in Florissant and the Church of the Holy Rosary near the Noviatiate.

It was during good Father Van Assche's administration of the parish of St. Ferdinand, that the number of German Catholic immigrants increased to such an extent that a separate church-organization for their use became a necessity. Father Francis Horstmann was stationed at Florissant as Father Van Assche's assistant. Later on Father Ignatius Panken had the spiritual care of the Germans. In 1866 their number had increased to thirty-five families. Archbishop Kenrick as well as the Superior of the Jesuits now sanctioned the building of a church for them. On June 3rd, 1866 the corner stone of the new edifice was laid by the Archbishop. The title of the Sacred Heart, under which the old Church of St. Ferdinand had been blessed in 1821, was bestowed on the new Church. It is situated on high ground in the center of the town, on property that had, at one time, been chosen as the site·of the Convent of the Sacred Heart. Early in 1867 Father Panken was succeeded as pastor by Father Ignatius Peuckert who carried on the building of the church. On Rosary Sunday of the same year Father De Smet blessed it with great solemnity. A parochial school was opened September 15th, 1866, with two Sisters of the Precious Blood and a lay teacher in charge. The school building proving too small for the needs of the congregation, a new school of imposing proportions was erected in 1889. The present beautiful Church

---

16 Scharf, p. 1914.

of the Sacred Heart was dedicated to divine service on November 23rd, 1893 by Archbishop Kain.[17] The erection of the Sisters' House completed the fine group of buildings, which, as Father Garraghan says, "the German Catholics of Florissant have raised to minister to their spiritual needs."

The succursal Church of the Holy Rosary, for the use of the Creole and Negro Catholics living in the vicinity of the Novitiate, was erected in 1871, though the exertions of Father Charles Coppens. Holy Rosary Church is a chapel of ease, without parochial rights, or obligations; the sixty families who attend its Sunday services belong to St. Ferdinand's Parish or to the Sacred Heart.

17  M. S. Notes.

## Chapter 32

# PROGRESS OF THE CHURCH IN SOUTHEAST MISSOURI

The earliest Catholic house of worship in what is now Scott County, was the log chapel built in 1839 by the Lazarist John Brands in Tywappity Bottom and dedicated to St. Francis de Sales. The second was the church of St. Mary in Benton. As early as 1840 the place was visited by the Lazarists of Cape Girardeau. The deed to the church property was recorded on February 13th, 1843, as Father John Brands, C. M. reports; From 1843 to 1846, the church remained in charge of the Lazarists, but in 1847 Father Cajetan Zapotti, one of Vicar-General Melcher's recruits, was appointed pastor of the Congregation.[1]

Before the end of the year Rev. James Stehle takes his place as resident pastor, but is transferred in 1851 to the newly founded parish of St. Lawrence at New Hamburg, only three miles distant from Benton. A Franciscan Monk, Leo Osredkar, was now placed in charge of Benton and Tywappity Bottom. In 1854 the church was dedicated under the patronage of St. Mary. In this vast field Father Osredkar labored for seven years, departing in early June 1859. His report of 1852 has the following item: "Rosenbach, prope Benton 500 souls." From 1860 to September 1861, the parish is attended by Rev. John M. Boetzkes and from that date on, until the end of 1863 by Rev. George Tuerk, the one-time rector of Herman. The church of St. Mary at Benton was destroyed during the Civil War, and its scattered people were attended from New Hamburg. When the county seat was transferred from Benton to Commerce, the congregation was greatly reduced in numbers so that no priest was assigned to it until 1904 when Father Bernard H. Schlatthoelter became its second founder. The new Church was dedicated under the invocation of St. Dionysius. After three years' service in the newly constituted parish, Father Schlatthoelter was succeeded by Rev. Th. G. Dette, March 20th, 1907.

The parish of St. Lawrence the Martyr, at New Hamburg, Scott County, was organized in 1848, when three acres of land were deeded to Bishop Kenrick for the use of the Catholics in that vicinity. In 1851 Father James Stehle removed to New Hamburg, but in the following year left the parish to become pastor of S. S. Mary and Joseph Church at Carondelet. The care for the little congregation now devolved upon

---

[1] All the data, excepting those that refer to the churches of St. Mary at Cape Girardeau and St. John Baptist at Leopold, Bollinger County, were derived from the Records of the Chancery of St. Louis. Hence no special references are given.

Father Leo of Benton, and his successors, Boetzkes and Tuerk. The massive stone church of St. Lawrence suffered greatly from the ravages of the war. In 1862 it was burnt by the soldiers, only the four walls remained standing, to form the substantial part for the present church. It was in 1867 that Father John Anthony Stroombergen, restored the church and blessed it by order of the Archbishop. Father Stroombergen administered the parish from 1866 to 1868.

His successor, Father Martin Scheerer was a man of might, physically and a powerful preacher of the rough popular kind, but in no wise a man of books.

He ruled his parish with an iron hand for well nigh thirty years, and died on February 16th, 1898, respected and, in a manner loved, by all. His successor was the Rev. Clement J. Moenig.

The first, and until recent times, the only parish in the neighboring County of Bollinger was that of St. John the Apostle, in Leopold. The place was originally known as Dallas, then as Vine Mount, and finally as Leopold, a name modified by the Post Office authorities, from the proposed Leopolis. The origin of this parish was rather peculiar. A number of Dutch and German immigrants had found a temporary home in Cincinnati, Ohio, and there formed a parish under the name of St. Willibrord. Their pastor was the Rev. John Van Luytelaar.

These good people decided to remove to Missouri in a body, and found a colony. They bought government land at a bit, (12½ cents) an acre; each family was to receive 160 acres, the division was to be made by lot. Father Van Luytelaar was accompanied by his brother, the Rev. Thomas Van Luytelaar, who however, withdrew within a year. The pastor drew the lot for the quarter section, on which the parish buildings now stand. After each family had received its proper share of land, the question arose, where shall the church be built? The answer came: Where the pastor has his farm, there the church must be. On August 15th 1856, after mass, work was begun on a church and parochial residence. The logs were prepared and placed in position by the people. The church was named for St. John the Apostle. A town called Vine Mount was laid out. It was but one long wide street. Town lots had 100 feet front, and were sold at $1.00 per front foot. All payments were made either in labor or in land. All parishioners were farmers. Most of the land was poor, gravelly soil; the better land along the creeks being already in the hands of American settlers. Yet by industry, thrift and prudence, these Catholic Hollanders overcame adverse conditions, and built up a substantial community and a flourishing parish.[2]

---

[2] The authorities for this account of the foundation of Vine Mount, now Leopold, are its former pastors, Father John Van Luytelaar, the founder, and Father Francis Bettels, who had gained his information from the ancients of the Parish.

In 1856 Father Van Luytelaar went to Holland to collect funds for a new church, returning to Dallas in May 1857. On May 7th, 1858, he transferred to the Archbishop 120 acres of land for the use of the Church. The war of the rebellion made sad havoc in the parish. Father Van Luytelaar withdrew in 1861, to St. John's in Franklin County. For the next two years the place was occasionally visited by Lazarist Fathers from Cape Girardeau, and by Father Van der Sanden from Kirkwood.

On November 10th, 1866 the Rev. John Bertens came to Vine Mount as rector, and remained until March 1878, when he was promoted to the parish of Dutzow, in Warren County. Under his administration a new house and church were built as every vestige of the former buildings had disappeared. On Father Berten's departure in 1878, the Rev. Francis Bettels, a native of Hildesheim diocese, took up the good work of making Vine Mount one of the leading country parishes of the state. Father Bettels came to St. Louis in his youth and entered the Seminary of St. Francis, Milwaukee for his theological training, was ordained by Archbishop Ryan at St. John's Pro-Cathedral, June 4, 1876. His first appointment was St. Henry's parish at Charleston from where after about two years of hard service he was sent to the Church of Vine Mount in Bolinger County.

During his twenty-eight years at St. John's Church, at what is now called Leopold, Father Bettels accomplished wonderful results with the very scant means at his disposal. The fine stone church in Gothic style, and the commodious residence are the lasting monuments of his own zeal and ability, as well as of the true Catholic spirit which his teaching and pastoral care infused into his congregation. The corner stone of the church was laid by Vicar-General Muehlsiepen on July 4th, 1899. On January 5th, 1906 Father Bettels was promoted to the important charge of St. Bernard's in St. Louis, where a new church had to be built. His successor in Leopold, the Rev. Peter Kurtenbach, arrived June 9th, 1906.

The church of St. Benedict in Doniphan, Ripley County, derives its title from the little log church Father John Hogan built for his Irish colonists in the wilderness of Ripley and Oregon counties, not very far from the Arkansas border. During the civil war and long after, the place lay forsaken, but in 1877 a church was building, and the small scattered congregation was attended from Iron Mountain. From the close of 1879 to 1882 Father P. A. Trumm served the Congregation as rector. Then came a three years vacancy, until the Benedictine Fathers Theodore Schmitt and Pius Reiser took charge of the Catholics living in the almost primeval wilderness on both sides of the railroad town of Doniphan. Now the church, begun in 1877, was completed in 1890, and blessed by Vicar-General Muehlsiepen on June

12th of that year. After the departure of the Benedictines the church was attended from Poplar Bluff until 1905. After the period of dependence came a series of resident pastors, S. J. Zielinski, Stanilaus J. Wisniewski, Peter A. Smyth and James Sheil, John A. Hurcik, and Edward S. Filipiak. At present the parish of Doniphan has attached to it as missions, St. Joseph's at Pulaski, St. Elizabeth's at Oxley, and St. Michael's at Flatwood, all in Ripley County.

The parish of the Sacred Heart in Thayer, Oregon County, with its mission of Brandville and its station in the Irish Wilderness, were detached from the parish of Doniphan.

The Church in Perry County owes its first budding forth to the Trappist Prior Joseph Marie Dunand. But its full vigor of the spring-tide came with the advent of the Lazarist Community. Three distinct Congregations surround the mother-church of St. Mary's of the Barrens, and are administered from that renowned center of religion: St. Vincent's at Brewer, St. James' at Crosstown and St. Joseph's at Highland. But there are seven other parishes within the County: St. Joseph's at Apple Creek, now in charge of secular priests, Our Lady's Nativity at Belgique in Bois Brulé Bottom, St. Maurus at Biehle's, Our Lady of the Rosary at Claryville, Our Lady of the Victories at Sereno, and St. Rose of Lima at Silver Lake. These are nine happy daughters encircling their mother, St. Mary's of the Barrens: But in the very shadow of her home there is one more worthy scion, the German Church of St. Boniface in the city of Perryville.

The German Catholics of Perryville in 1866 began to carry out their long nursed desire to have a church and school of their own nationality. The corner stone of the projected building was laid on November 8th, 1866, and building operations continued until the end of that year. At first the new parish was attended from the Barrens, but in January 1869 the Rev. Henry Groll was appointed its first rector. In 1870 the parochial school was established. In April, however, of that year Father Groll was sent to St. Nicholas Church in St. Louis as assistant to its founder, the Rev. Nicholas Staudinger. Father E. Blume then held the rather difficult position at Perryville for two and one-half years, and was succeeded by Father Sosthenes Kleiser, November 1872 to December 1875. In 1873 the Sisters of the Precious Blood received charge of the parochial school. After an interval of seven years, during which the Fathers Peter Bremerich and Wendelin Stultz administered the affairs of the parish, Father Kleiser returned to his old post of duty, December 2nd, 1882, to remain until his death, which occurred April 15th, 1886. Under Father Conrad Mueller's pastorate the church was blessed, and the Ursuline Nuns replaced the Sisters of the Precious Blood in the management of the parochial school. In October 1891 Father Mueller was promoted to the parish of St. Thomas in Cole County, and Rev. Joseph C. Ernst was appointed in his place at Perryville. Father Ernst remained at St. Boniface until July 1894, when Rev. John Hennes took charge until the appointment of Father H. A. B. Kuennen, who remained there about ten years. The present pastor is the Rev. James Huber.

The earliest church in Cape Girardeau was St Vincent's, built by the Lazarists under Father John Timon. The Congregation was composed almost exclusively of native American converts to the Faith. But the German immigration began to set in in 1834, and, in the course of the following years, brought together a little colony of German Catholics at what is still called Dutchtown. But the malarial fevers prevalent in that marshy region forced these newcomers back to the city of Cape Girardeau. Here they attended the Church of the Vincentians. As they grew more numerous, it was but natural that they should desire to have a church in which the Gospel would be preached to them in their mother-tongue. One of the Lazarist professors at St. Vincent's College, Rev. A. J. Meyer, C. M., a native of St. Louis, born of German parents, encouraged them to carry out their plan. At his invitation the Franciscan missionary Father Rainerius Dickneite, gave a mission to the German Catholics of Cape Girardeau in the parish church of St. Vincent's. New life and hope began to spring up in the hearts of these forlorn children of the Church. Their wish of having a German church now became a strong resolution. The question as to where the building should be located was settled by the purchase of the present site.

The laying of the corner stone was performed by Vicar-General Muehlsiepen on August 2nd, 1868. Father Meyer, who had taken such deep and effective interest in the good work, requested the Vicar-General to appoint a pastor for the new parish as soon as possible, as he himself was about to leave the city. The appointee was the Rev. Julius Heerde, who arrived in Cape Girardeau in August 1868. It was a laborius course of duty that awaited Father Heerde in the new parish: The Church was not completed, and the debts were accumulating: Father Herman Leygraaff and, later on, Father Gells, relieved him temporarily of his distressful labors. In July 1870 the Rev. William Hinssen was appointed his successor, and immediately entered upon the task, of finishing the church and reducing the debt sufficiently to allow further improvements.

On June 1st, 1871 Archbishop Kenrick administered the sacrament of Confirmation in St. Mary's Church. The parochial school owes its orgin to Father Heerde. It was conducted at first in a rented room, then in the church itself, and finally in the parochial residence. During Father Hinssen's absence on a trip to Europe, Father Joseph Pope, a quaint, kindly Tyrolese priest, acted as substitute, and succeeded in paying off a part of the church debt. Father Hinssen, on his return, pursued the even tenor of his ways until April 20th 1874, when he was promoted to the rectorship of St. Agatha's parish in St. Louis. His successor at Cape Girardeau, the Rev. Joseph Henry Schmidt, was chiefly instrumental in bringing the Franciscan Sisters to St. Mary's parish, first as teachers of the parochial school, and eventually for the .erection and management of a Hospital. The Hospital was built and dedicated in honor of St. Francis of Assisi proving a real boon to Cape Girardeau and the surrounding country: so much so that the Sisters in 1914 erected a splendid new Hospital, after the completion of which, the old building was sold to St. Mary's parish for a High-school.

Rev. Sosthenes Kleiser became pastor of St. Mary's Church in January 1876, but with Vicar-General Muehlsiepen's approval, turned over the parish to Father William Sonnenschein, in exchange for the charge of funding a parish at Kelso, Scott County. (November 1878) But the Rev. Sonnenschein's administration coming to an end August 27th, 1879, Father, now Monsignor, Francis Willmes, succeeded as pastor of St. Mary's, from 1879 to 1881 and by virtue of his genial nature and administrative ability harmonized the somewhat discrepant elements of the congregation.

His last words spoken to the people on his departure for his new field of labor in St. Charles were "Be sure to build a new school."

The early realization of this injunction, and of many other projects. of a spiritual or temporal nature, was the work of Father Willmes' successor, the Rev. Everard Pruente, who presided over the destinies of St. Mary's, Cape Girardeau for well nigh fifty years.[3]

The parish of St. Mary's has a mission to attend: the earliest settlement of German Catholics .in Cape Girardeau County, Dutchtown, where a church was erected by Father Edward Kern, the pastor of Jackson.

· When the Sisters of St. Francis requested to be relieved from the charge of conducting the parochial school, the Sisters de Notre Dame accepted it, October 1st, 1903.

The Parish of the Immaculate Conception at. Jackson, Cape Girardeau County, founded by the Vincentian Fathers was originally designated as St. Lawrence. But when the present brick church was completed in 1879, it was dedicated under the invocation of the Immaculate Conception. The first resident priest, Father Henry Schrage, bought a large house for the purpose of a

---

3 "Saint Mary's Church, Cape. Girardeau, Missouri Souvenir of its Golden Jubilee," 1918.

school and Sisters' residence, and brought the Ursuline Sisters from St. Louis to occupy it. Father John L. Gadell succeeded Father Schrage, and he in turn was succeeded by the newly-ordained John Rothensteiner. His successor in 1886 was Father John Long.

Father John Long, built a new school, and Father Edward Kern erécted the present parochial residence. The Congregation was small, and consisted of native Americans and Germans, in about equal parts. The parish received a severe setback by the closing of the parochial school under the administration of Father M. D. Collins.

When the German Catholics around Biehle's Station saw that their brethren in Perryville had succeeded to establish a church of their own language, with a resident pastor, they also decided to make a trial. On May 25th, 1867, they bought five acres of land for church purposes and in 1870 built a chapel on it, in honor of St. Maurus. They then requested Vicar-General Muehlsièpen to give them a resident priest. Rev. Joseph Helwing was appointed in 1871. Rev. John Gockel succeeded him in 1872, but died at Dutzow in August 1873. For three years the place had no pastor, but was regularly attended by Father Joseph Pope from Apple Creek. In November 1876 Rev. Conrad Mueller was assigned to the parish, and continued to reside there until May 12th, 1886. Another vacancy now occurred, which was broken by Father Arnold Acker on January 15th, 1887.  ·

The parish numbered only one hundred and one souls in 1898, when Father J. B. Beth took charge: Father Beth remained at Biehle until 1907. His successors were the Rev. Henry Hassel, and in March 1909 the Rev. J. M. Denner.

St. Augustine's Church in Kelso, Scott County, situated about half way between New Hamburg and Cape Girardeau, owes its origin to both parishes. Father Kleiser of St. Mary's was the chief promoter of the new parish, whilst Father Scheerer of St. Lawrence opposed the dismemberment of his own little spiritual demesne. Yet the needs of the Catholic people, on the outskirts of both St. Mary's and St. Lawrence's carried the day.

The people of Kelso, like the good German Catholics they really were, began with the building of a school. "The church will surely follow" said Father Kleiser to them, and in the Spring of 1878 he called a meeting of the Catholics at Kelso.

Vicar-General Muehlsiepen attended this meeting. It was resolved to build a frame church; a Committee of five was appointed to secure subscriptions and to superintend the work. At the same time a gift of three acres of land was received from one of the parishioners, John Blattel. Within six months the building was ready for services. Father Sosthenes Kleiser was transferred from Cape Girardeau to the new parish. Divine services was held for the first time in the new house of

God in November 1878.  Father Kleiser remained at Kelso until July 1882.  The new pastor, Father Frederick Kleinschnittger, or Klein, as he came to be known, achieved great things during his long pastorate in St. Augustine.  The Congregation increased rapidly: the frame church proved too small for the multitude.  In 1889 the beautiful Gothic church, built of .brick and stone, with its lofty steeple and its three fine altars, was ready for dedication (August 28).  The old church was used for school purposes for twelve years.  In 1902 the imposing school building and Sisters' residence was erected.  Within the twenty-five years of Father Klein's administration the number of families had increased from forty to two hundred.  Father Klein died at Kelso on March 21st, 1910, in his fifty-seventh year, and his remains were laid to rest in the Cemetery of St. Augustine's parish.  Father John Muehlsiepen was appointed his successor.  The school is attended by one hundred and eighty children, in charge of the Sisters of the Most Precious Blood.  In 1912 the parish of Illmo branched off from the Church of St. Augustine.

The first settlers of Texas Bend near the northern boundary of Mississippi County, were German Catholics from the vicinity of Cincinnati, Ohio.  The log church at Texas Bend was the successor of the log chapel built in 1839, by Father Brands at Tywappity Bottom, though not built on the same spot.  Both structures have disappeared; only the grave-yard of the second church of St. ;Francis de Sales in Tywappity remains.

In 1873 Father Henry Willenbrink built the frame church in Charleston and named it St. Henry.  This was the parish church of all Mississippi County.  Father Bettels became its pastor in 1876, but resided and taught school at the Bend.  The present fine brick school building was erected by Father Francis Brand.  The ten years between Fathers Bettels and Brand are filled out by the rectorships of Father J. A. Connolly, Frederick Klein, Frederick Pommer, John A. Gadell, Hugh O'Reilly and Henry Thobe.  Father Henry Hussmann, who became pastor of the parish in 1895, built the beautiful new Church of St. Henry, which was dedicated by Archbishop Glennon on June 4, 1907.

On July 1st, 1909 Father Henry Petri succeeded Father Hussmann as pastor of Charleston, the latter having been appointed to St. Henry's parish in St. Louis as successor to Father John A. Hoffmann.

## CHAPTER 33

# GROWTH OF THE CHURCH IN JACKSON AND LAFAYETTE COUNTIES

It was on the 10th day of September 1880 that the southwestern part of the State of Missouri, bounded by the Missouri River on the north, and by an irregular line along the eastern bounds of the counties of Moniteau, Miller, Camden, Laclede, Wright, Douglas and Ozark, having an extension of 23,539 square miles, was taken from the archdiocese of St. Louis and erected into a separate diocese with Kansas City as its episcopal see. Bishop John J. Hogan of St. Joseph was transferred to the new see, and was at the same time appointed administrator of the diocese of St. Joseph. In Kansas City diocese Bishop Hogan found twenty-four parish churches, attended by twenty-three secular priests and seven Redemptorist Fathers. Besides these parish churches, there were twenty-four missions or stations where regular visits were made by the priests holding pastoral charge.

The parish churches in Kansas City itself were the Immaculate Conception, formerly St. Francis Regis, S.S. Peter and Paul, St. Patrick, The Annunciation, and Our Lady of Perpetual Help. The church of the Immaculate Conception was no longer in charge of the pioneer priest Bernard Donnelly, as he had resigned the charge on April 10th, 1880. Father David J. Doherty had assumed the pastorship.

Father Doherty was of a cheerful disposition and frank open character. He was very popular with all classes. He built the parochial residence which was to serve as the first bishop's palace. The church became the Cathedral of the diocese. But when the corner stone of the new Cathedral was laid on May 11th, 1882, by Bishop John Hogan, Father Doherty was recalled to St. Louis and made pastor of St. Thomas of Aquin Church. On April 25th, 1884 he departed for Europe. Father Van der Sanden in 1888 saw his signature in a hotel register in Freiburg, Baden: ''April 1888 D. Jos. Doherty, M. D. Chicago.''[1] Of Father Donnelly's companions and assistants Father Augustus Saunier, during 1849 and 1850, served the Church of St. Anne's in Little Canada, and after 1851 was stationed at Rochester, New York. Father James Halpin who was at St. Francis Regis from 1868 to 1869, was commissioned to build the church of St. Patrick in Kansas City at which he had no great success. In 1872 he departed to parts unknown. His successor as assistant to Father Donnelly, but not at St. Patrick's, Father James Phelan, was appointed

---

1 Chancery Records.

pastor of Warrensburg and remained there until 1878 when he was transferred to Holden. Of Father Francis Curran, Bernard Donnelly's last assistant, we have but to record that he was ordained at Carlow, May 21, 1877.

The first offshoot from the parish of the Immaculate Conception was SS. Peter and Paul. As detailed in a former chapter Father Francis Ruesse of Deepwater, was of great assistance to Father Donnelly in providing for the German members of his parish. The movement to separate the Germans from the Irish and French and to form them into a distinct parish began in 1866, when property was secured and a basement for a good sized church laid down. The Rev. Henry Grosse was the first pastor of the Germans in Kansas City. In 1871 he was succeeded by Father Francis Andres, who in 1873 received as his successor the indefatigable Father, now Monsignor, Ernest Zechenter.

Both Fathers Grosse and Andres had seen missionary service among the hills of Ste. Genevieve County, before they were sent to Kansas City. Both left the archdiocese before Kansas City was made an episcopal see. But Father Zechenter after his ordination on December 19th, 1868 served as pastor of Glasgow from 1869 to 1873, and as pastor of the Germans in Kansas from 1873 until almost the present day. During these fifty-three years Father Zechenter was regarded as one of the mainstays of religion in the western part of the state.[2]

The third parish in Kansas City in point of time is St. Patrick's. The deed for the first property acquired is dated July 25th, 1868. In the following year a church was reported as building. Father James Halpin was replaced in 1872 by Father Thomas Cooney. But the parish did not manifest any real active life, before the advent in 1873 of Father James A. Dunn as pastor, with Father Cooney as assistant. Father Cooney was born on June 9th, 1846 in County Cavan Ireland and came to St. Louis as a boy. He was ordained at St. Francis, Wisconsin, on June 18th, 1870, by Bishop Melcher. His tastes were scholarly and he shrank from active life. As assistant to Father Dunn he was in his proper element. . . Again and again did he return from brief pastorships to the humble position of assistant : once from Lexington, once from Iron Mountain, once from the Assumption Church in St. Louis, and finally from the rectorship of St. Mark's Church to the chaplainey of St. Joseph's Orphanage, where he died on March 30th, 1914.[3]

Father James A. Dunn was raised to the priesthood on July 4th, 1868, and after his priestly apprenticeship at St. Malachy's from 1869 to 1873 was made pastor of St. Patrick's in Kansas City.

---

[2] Father Zechenter died at St. Mary's Hospital, January 27, 1927.

[3] Chancery Records.

He was a man of bright \mind and restless energy. He chose a better location for the new church, the corner stone of which was laid by Bishop Patrick J. Ryan on July 25th, 1875. Much of the stone of the old basement church was used in the construction of the new building. The people of the parish, mechanics, laborers and owners of teams, gratuitously helped to haul the material to the place, and build up the walls. The stone masonry cost almost nothing, and the brick in the walls cost less than five dollars per thousand. The new church was opened on Christmas morn 1876. The parochial residence also, as well as the school, were the result of Father Dunn's industry. Father James Dunn died in Kansas City on June 19th, 1888.[4]

Of the origin, progress, and final doom of the Church of the Annunciation we have a graphic account from the pen of its venerable founder, Father William J. Dalton:

"A Third division of the original parish of Kansas City was made, May 25th, 1872, when Archbishop Kenrick formed the part of the city known as West Kansas into a new parish. The new parish was named Annunciation. The Rev. William Dalton, assistant at Annunciation Church, St. Louis, was assigned pastor. On Sunday, June 27th, Father Dalton said the first mass for the new congregation.

An empty store on Twelfth Street, between Wyoming and Greene Streets, was tendered by its owner for temporary use. July 3rd, three lots of fifty feet each on the southwest corner of Fourteenth and Wyoming Streets were purchased. This property was then a portion of a corn field, and had just been platted into an addition known as Depot Addition. August 22nd following, 100 feet more were purchased on the southeast corner, facing the first purchase. July 13th, a frame church building, thirty by forty feet, was completed and occupied. This building was enlarged fifty feet in length, and in September was moved across the street to the new property. Here the congregation worshiped until November 12th, 1882, when the new brick church was dedicated. This edifice was sixty-eight by one hundred and thirty feet, and cost $30,000. . . Besides the old and new churches, Annunciation Parish erected a large pastoral residence, a dwelling for the teaching sisters and a spacious school house. The growth of the parish, from about fifty families in 1872 was remarkable. In 1882 there were on the church records over twelve hundred families. As the parish was that district of the city where the railroads, stock-yards and machine-shops were gathered, there were many boarding houses kept and tenanted by Catholics. An inundation from the Missouri River in 1882, and the sweeping purchase of entire streets of property by the Stock-yards Company and the Rock Island Railway

---

[4] Chancery Records.

Company in 1883, 1886 and 1892, forced the parishioners to other parts of the city, and reduced the congregation to a number less than were present at the founding of the parish. In October 1898, the church and pastoral residence were bought by the Rock Island Railway Company. It will be only a very short time until the parish will be abandoned. All the territory in West Kansas except a small portion, is now in the hands of railroads, stock-yards and commercial interests."[5]

Father Dalton's assistants were Rev. A. M. J. Hynes, Rev. John Ryan, and Rev. Dennis Keily. Father Hynes in 1874 became rector of Old Mines, but having a disagreement with Archbishop Kenrick, went to Rome in November 1878. Returning from Europe in May 1879 he received the appointment to Pierce City and, as rector of that Church, became a member of the diocese of Kansas City in 1880. Father John Ryan in 1878 became rector of Adair, and remained as such until July 1888, when he was transferred to St. Bridget's Church in St. Louis as assistant. From May 1892 until July 1898 he served as rector of Moberly and after a visit to Europe, received the appointment to Monroe City. The Rev. Dennis Keily who had been ordained at Carlow for the diocese of St. Louis was sent to Kansas City on November 24th, 1879, and on the erection of the diocese, came to St. Louis early in 1881, but returned to Kansas City in March of the same year.[6]

In regard to the early Redemptorists in Kansas City, Father Dalton says:

"In 1876 the Redemptorist Fathers came from New Orleans, Louisiana and purchased ten acres of ground at Westport. The following year they erected a church edifice and monastery at Thirty-third and Wyandotte Streets, at an outlay of $40,000. They soon opened a preparatory college for students, and in 1885 found it necessary to add to their buildings for educational purposes. In 1890 the preparatory department was removed to Kirkwood, Missouri, and the college was devoted solely to use as the Theological Seminary of the Redemptorist Order. In addition to the college faculty and the parish priests, the monastery is the home of nearly a score of missioners who go out to various Western States. From 1878 until April 1895, the people of the parish attended the Redemptorist Church of Our Lady of Perpetual Help. April 21st, 1895, a parish church under that name was opened for divine worship."[7]

In 1879 just before the erection of the new diocese the Church of Our Lady of Perpetual Help was in the care of Fathers Frederick Faivre, F. Luette, J. Schaggeman, Joseph Firle and Joseph Beil, all of the Redemptorist Order.

---

5 "Encyclopedia of the History of St. Louis," vol. I. p. 554.
6 Chancery Records.
7- Encyclopedia, vol. I, p. 554.

The town of Independence, the first home of Father Donnelly in West Missouri was in 1858 turned over to the ministrations of Father Denis Kennedy, who retained the charge until 1872. Ordained by Archbishop Kenrick on January 12th, 1851, Father Kennedy began his priestly career as pastor of Indian Creek. From 1852 he successively held the rectorship of the churches of Bridgeton, and Bon-Homme; but in 1858 he entered upon the more laborious duties of the pastorate of the Holy Cross at Independence, the flourishing town on the Missouri river. The Congregation of Sibley in Jackson County was also placed under his care.[8]

In 1872 Father Kennedy was transferred to Hannibal, where he died on August 29th, 1884. His successor Father Patrick O'Neil, had in early youth joined the Vincentians, but left the Order before receiving the holy priesthood, on August 7th, 1864. After a short stay at St. Michael's Church, St. Louis, and a longer rectorship at Montgomery City, Father O'Neil was appointed pastor of Hannibal, whence he was sent to Independence, whilst the pastor of Independence came to Hannibal.

In 1876 Father O'Neil's name is no longer found in the Directory. At Independence Father Thomas Fitzgerald holds spiritual sway from 1875 and in 1880 continues the administration of the parish under the Bishop of Kansas City. It was under Father Fitzgerald's pastorship at Independence that the Church exchanged its ancient title of the Holy Cross to that of St. Mary. The Sisters of Charity had before 1880 established their Convent and Academy in the town.[9]

The parish of the Immaculate Conception at Lexington, Lafayette County, which had been founded in 1845, and regularly visited by Father Donnelly, was in 1846 taken in charge by the Rev. D. Kenny resident pastor of Irish Settlement near Marshall in Saline County. When Father Kenny entered the Jesuit Novitiate, Father Donnelly resumed the administration of the small congregation. In 1853 Father James Murphy, the elder, became first resident pastor, whilst Father Thomas Cusack in 1854 visited those parts on the railroad between Jefferson City and Herman, not attended by the priest in these two places. Father Cusack's successor in this temporary Railroad Laborer's Mission was Father John O'Sullivan. Father Daniel Healy succeeded Father Murphy in 1855 and was in 1857 succeeded by the Rev. Eugene O'Hea. Father Edward Hamill followed him in 1860 and remained at his post fully eight years. Born at Tynan in the diocese of Armagh in 1819, he was elevated to the priesthood on June 29th, 1849, by Archbishop Kenrick and at once became pastor of Armagh

---

8 Chancery Records.
9 Chancery Records.

on the Meramec river. In 1854.he succeeded to the rectorship of Wellsburg, formerly called Upper Dardenne, which is the present St. Paul
in St. Charles, County. Here he labored until 1859, when he received
the charge of Lexington.[10]

Ten years later the Irish Settlement near Marshall in Saline County
was entrusted to his care. At the erection of the Kansas City Diocese
in 1880 Father Edward Hamil severed his connection with St. Louis.
His successor at Lexington in 1868 was the future Vicar-General of the
Archdiocese of St. Louis, the Rev. Otto J. S. Hoog, who for two years
had as assistant the Rev. Philip P. Brady, also a future Vicar-General
of St. Louis.

Father Hoog was born at Ettenheim in Baden on April 18th, 1845,
and received ordination to the priesthood in December 1867, at the
hands of Bishop Juneker of Alton. His first appointment was Lexington, which he held from 1868 to 1876. The parish at that time numbered 1,100 souls, had a parochial school, and a missionary circuit, with
Carrolton and Sugar Tree Bottom as principal points. On September
20th, 1874 the Coadjutor Bishop Patrick J. Ryan dedicated the new
church Father Hoog had built in honor of the Immaculate Conception.
In September 1870 Father Hoog accepted the rectorship of the Jefferson City parish, and Father Thomas Cooney took his place at Lexington. In 1878 Rev. John Joseph Lilly was transferred from St. Mary's
in Ste. Genevieve County to Lexington. The church of the Immaculate
Conception at Lexington was the missionary center for the missions
and stations, Brownville, in Saline, Concordia in Cooper, Higginsville,
and Odessa and Wellington, in Lafayette.

---

10   Chancery Records.

## Chapter 34

# GROWTH OF THE CHURCH IN SOUTHWEST MISSOURI

St. Peter's parish at Boonville in Cooper County dates back to the days of the Jesuit Father Verreydt, the place having been visited by him and other Jesuit missionaries since 1831. The organization of the parish, however, was effected in 1847, when Father James Murphy began his ministrations from Jefferson City. Since 1853 the place was visited by Father Joseph Ursus Meister from Bruehl's Settlement, and then placed in his charge, as resident pastor. Father Meister remained until July 1856, when Father Bernard Hillner was appointed in his place. In 1869 Rev. Henry Meurs came to stay until March 1875, then to be succeeded by Father John A. Hoffman.

Of Father Meister's simplicity and zeal we have already spoken. From Apple Creek Archbishop Kenrick sent him to Jefferson City, where his native German might prove useful, and his very bad English might not be too great a hindrance; for the great majority of the parishioners of St. Peter's Church were German immigrants; yet he did not stay long in Jefferson City. In 1853 he left the capital of the state and accepted the charge of Father George Tuerk's missions in Moniteau, Morgan, Pettis, Saline and Cooper Counties, residing at Shakelford in Saline County, where Father Hamil in 1869 had built a church and presbytery of logs and named it St. Peters.[1]

In 1860 Father Meister became rector of Boonville, but after six years of good and acceptable work among the rough pioneers of the western country, he left the archdiocese for Indiana, where Bishop Saint Palais gave him the parish of Celestine. He died at St. Anthony's a few miles from Celestine, by the fall of a tree, in his seventy-fifth year. Father Meister was an honest, square, but rough hewn block of a man; a native of the Canton Solothurn in Switzerland. He came to St. Louis, when already in priest's orders, in Vicar-General Melcher's first caravan of 1847. Father Meister's successor at Booneville, Rev. Bernard Hillner, a native of Westerloh,[2] in the diocese of Paderborn, born July 5th, 1826, was sent to Boonville within two weeks of his ordination, July 14th, 1856 and remained at the place until 1869, when he was transferred to Tipton. Father Hillner was one of the brave men, who at Archbishop Kenrick's order, refused to take the Test Oath

---

1 Chancery Records.

2 Westerloh is known in history as the birthplace of the greatest cavalry-leader in the Thirty-Years War, General Count Spork.

under the Drake Constitution and was accordingly arrested.[3]  In 1877
Father Hillner was transferred to St. Thomas in Cole County and finally
to the peaceful haunts of Osage County as pastor of Koeltztown.  Here
he died on November 13th, 1882.  Father Henry Meurs, came to Boonville in 1869 having since his ordination on May 27th, 1866, filled the
position of Rector of Glasgow in Howard County.  His stay in Boonville covered the period of 1869 to 1875.  Father Meurs died as pastor
of Jefferson City on August 25th, 1876.  In March of the same year
the parish of Boonville received the man of strongest character it ever
had, the Rev. John A. Hoffman.  He was born on February 2nd, 1850,
at Mattis Creek in St. Louis County, and was ordained December 22nd,
1872, at St. Francis, Wisconsin, and was sent to Boonville in March 1875.
The parish at the time numbered seventy-nine families, about one fifth
of whom were English speaking Catholics, the other four-fifths Germans:
The Church was dedicated to S. S. Peter and Paul.  The parochial
school under the care of Ursuline Sisters, was dear to him as the apple
of his eye.  Father Hoffman remained in Kansas City diocese for five
years after its erection, though still a member of the Archdiocese of
St. Louis.  In February 1885, he made use of the privilege, of returning
to his first obedience having been appointed Pastor of the new Church
of St. Henry in St. Louis.[4]  Here he remained until September 15th,
1909 the day of his death.  Father Hoffman was a man of rugged constitution and appearance.  Choleric by temperamant, he bore a little
volcano in his breat, that would break forth at times with irresistible
force.  And yet Father Hoffman was one of the most kind-hearted men,
and the very soul of justice and fairness.  His parishioners and friends
knew him and were devoted to him.  With all his faults of temper, they
could not help but love him for what he really was.[5]

The early vicissitudes of the parish of St. Ludgerus at what was
formerly known as Deepwater, and now as Germantown, in Henry
County, have been treated in a former chapter.  A garrison of one
hundred men had been stationed there during the first two years of the
war, and the new church was used by them as a barracks.  But when
the tide of conflict turned against the Confederacy, the people reoc-
cupied their church and held their devotions in it on Sundays and
Holy days: As they had no priest, they recited the Rosary and sang
their old German hymns.  Twenty-six men of the parish were with the
Union forces, three of them fell in battle.

After the war was over, Father John Gruender came to Deepwater, only a few days after his ordination, on July 19th, 1866.  Full

---

3  ''The Guardian,'' vol. I, No. 34, 1865, contains a sharp protest against
the imprisonment of Father Hillner of Booneville for having preached the Gospel
without having taken the test-oath.

4  Chancery Records.

5  From personal observation.

of zeal and energy he at once started the building of a combination school and parochial residence. He taught school, organized a choir, and laid out a part of the church land in town lots, which he sold for the benefit of the parish.

Germantown seemed to be assured of a bright future: but the railroad being built could not obtain the right of way to the town, and so, placed its station about four miles southeast of Germantown and named it Montrose. But St. Ludger's parish continued to grow and prosper, although the people around Montrose built a church of their own under the title of the Immaculate Conception.[6] Father Gruender's administration of St. Ludger's lasted for four years: In 1870 he was transferred to Vienna in Maries County, then to Koeltztown, then to Taos and finally to Loose Creek, where he died, March 29, 1909, in the forty-third year of his priestly life.

From August 1870 to October 1871 Father William S. Boden was pastor of St. Ludger's. Both Fathers Boden and Gründer came from the diocese of Paderborn at the invitation of Vicar-General Melcher in December 1864 and completed their studies at St. Francis, Wisconsin. From 1871 to 1873, Father Boden served as assistant in St. Liborius and Holy Trinity parishes in St. Louis, he then left the archdiocese. On his return in 1877, he became rector of Pilot Grove in Cooper County, and then in various other country parishes: but left the diocese once more for Schenectady, N. Y. He had a restless wandering disposition. His death occurred in the South.

After an interim of a few months, Father J. Hellwing assumed the rectorship and held it two years. He secured the services of two Sisters of the Precious Blood for his school: but on Father Hellwing's departure, they were recalled to the mother house in O'Fallon. In 1874 Father Francis F. Kueper became pastor of St. Ludger's. He erected the new rectory and converted the old one into a residence for the Sisters, who however failed to come. A beautiful memorial of the living faith and gratitude of these staunch German Catholics, is recorded by the chronicler of the parish:

"In the spring of 1874, the grasshopper plague swept through this part of the country and threatened to destroy all the crops. When the farmers saw this destructive army coming, they rushed to the church and there, before the Blessed Sacrament, made a vow, to keep the first day of May as a day of prayer, if this terrible plague would be averted from them. No sooner was the vow made when the grasshoppers took to their wings, arose like an immense army, darkening the sun as they took their flight. The next day the farmers began replanting their corn, and there never was a better crop of corn raised in this locality

---

6 "The Catholic Register," December 4, 1924.

than in the year of 1874. From that time on the first of May has always been kept sacred, as a day of obligation. All the faithful assist at Mass and received Holy Communion, the Blessed Sacrament is exposed throughout the entire day for public adoration in fulfillment of the vow made by their forefathers.''[7]

Father John Hennes, who was pastor of St. Ludger's from 1875 to 1877, engaged a layman to teach the school. In 1876 Bishop J. Ryan confirmed a class of forty-five. In 1875 the first heating apparatus in the humble form of two large stoves, was introduced into the church.[8]

From 1877 to 1887 Father Ivo Prass, a Capuchin, was in charge. Under his faithful administration the church which had suffered severely during the war-time occupation, was enlarged and remodelled. The corner stone was laid on May 6th, 1880, and the completed church was dedicated on October 27th, 1881, by Bishop John Hogan, the newly appointed ruler of the diocese of Kansas City.[9]

The Church of St. Andrew in Maniteau County was originally situated in the prairie about a mile from the point where the railway station Tipton was afterwards located. In 1851 Father Blaarer reports from Deepwater, that he visited the Catholics at a place called Wind-Mill in Maniteau County. Whether this place was the site of St. Andrew's Church we cannot say. But St. Andrew's is mentioned in 1853 as being visited from Boonville by Fathers Meister and Hillner. The people were from the Rhine Province. They had built an humble log church on a five acre tract donated by three good parishioners, where they assembled every Sunday and Feastday, to hold services as well as they could. Great was their joy when at last they received the ministrations of these priests. From November 1860 to August 1862 Fathers William Walsh and H. Van der Sanden, then stationed at Jefferson City, alternated at saying mass at Tipton, every third Sunday of the month. Then there is a blank in the records until 1865, when the Rev. Henry Vincent Kalmer began his priestly ministrations to the people of Tipton. Father Kalmer, a German by birth, became a member of the Vincentians, but some years after his ordination, obtained his release from the Congregation, and was adopted into the diocese of St. Louis. His first appointment, was St. Andrew's parish at Tipton in 1865. Here he labored with zeal and fervor, until 1869. It was under his administration that the five acres of land in the town of Tipton were bought and a frame church was erected. But the principal members of the parish were too much attached to the old location and their primitive log church, to see the advantage of transferring the school and residence of the pastor to the little rail-road town of

7   ''The Catholic Register,'' December 4, 1924.
8   ''The Catholic Register,'' December 4, 1924.
9   Chancery Records.

Tipton. . . Father Kalmer's natural vivacity of youth broke down under the strain. He obtained his transfer to Manchester in St. Louis County in 1869. After serving various Congregations, Father Kalmer became pastor of St. Augustines Parish in St. Louis: Here he died September 14th, 1884.

His successor at Tipton was the Reverend Bernard Hillner 1869 to 1877. Father Hillner had no sooner laid the foundation for the projected brick church, when he discontinued the work, broken down by hard labor and discouraged by opposition. After a period of eight years in 1877, he was succeeded by the present pastor, Dean Francis F. Kueper. Father Kueper was the third pastor of St. Andrew's and the real founder of the parish as it exists today. When he arrived at the place in 1877, it looked forlorn and desolate. The frame church was too small for the congregation, which, however, was torn asunder by the spirit of faction. The school had been suspended for more than a year; not one of the men had complied with his Easter duty. The pastor's residence was a dark dingy room just under the roof of the frame church. In Autumn 1877 the parochial school was reopened. On St. Andrew's day 1879 a Building Society was organized: House Collections were taken up and the erection of the present Gothic brick church was begun in 1883. The dedication services were held May 24th, 1884, by Bishop Hogan of Kansas City. The later development of the Parish of St. Andrew's at Tipton belongs to the History of Kansas City Diocese.[10]

During its early days after 1865 the priest stationed at Tipton had charge of small missions in Johnson and Pettis Counties, one of which at least has taken its position as a well established parish, St. Mary's of Warrensburg. Otterville and Smithton and Knobnoster are the others. From 1865 to 1867 Warrensburg in Johnson County was regularly attended from Tipton. On July 4th, 1867, Father Gruender laid the corner stone of St. Mary's Church, which was completed by Father Kalmer. The first resident pastor of St. Mary's at Warrensburg was the Rev. Hugh Murray, whose pastorate lasted from 1867 to 1870. His successor the Rev. Michael S. Mackin remained until 1872, then came a Benedictine Monk Rev. Eberhard Gahr, who was succeeded by Rev. James Phelan. In 1879 Warrensburg became vacant and was attended from Holden. Otterville and Smithtown remained with Tipton until the erection of the diocese of Kansas City, whilst Knobnoster after 1872 shared the fortunes of Warrensburg.

The second parish established in Moniteau County, dates from 1859, and bears the title of The Annunciation. California is the name of the town. The deed to the church property was made June 7th, 1859.

---

10  Chancery Records and M. S. Sketch in Archives of Kansas City Diocese.

Its membership was, for the most part, composed of Germans. The church was blessed by Archbishop Kenrick on June 22nd, 1860. At first the place was attended by Fathers Walsh and Van der Sanden from Jefferson City. In 1867 it was in charge of the pastor of Tipton, but in 1871 it received its first resident pastor, the Benedictine Father Eberhard. His successor, Father Frederick Kueper, arrived in 1872, and in 1873 Father Joseph Reisdorff succeeded him, then came Father Wendelin Stultz, in 1876, and finally on July 1877 the newly ordained Father Bernard Stemker, who in 1880 resigned his charge in order to return to his native diocese St. Louis. At the time of the transfer the parish of the Annunciation at California, numbered two hundred and fifty souls. Its last St. Louis pastor, the Reverend Bernard Stemker, was born November 14th, 1851, at Rheda, diocese of Paderborn, ordained September 27th, 1874, and died as pastor of Kirkwood.[11]

The Catholics in Sedalia, Pettis County, made the first move to organize a parish on July 17, 1865, Father H. Murray, pastor of Warrensburg, being the promoter. The church was dedicated to St. Vincent de Paul. In 1869 Father Thomas Swift assumed spiritual charge with Father M. G. Mackin as assistant.

Father Swift came from St. Malachy's Church in St. Louis, whilst Father Mackin had been previously stationed at Shelbina. It was Father Francis Graham, however, that put the parish on the way to progress, by laying the corner stone for a new church. . . Father Graham had been rector of Rolla and Springfield. In 1880 he became a member of Kansas City diocese. At present Sedalia has two strong parishes, with parochial schools, and a Hospital conducted by the Sisters of Charity of the Incarnate Word.[12]

The foundation of the church at Springfield, Green County, dates from 1868. The first church was built in 1870 and dedicated to the Immaculate Conception. The founder and first pastor, Father Francis Graham was ordained to the priesthood on September 23rd, 1864, and immediately received the appointment to the parish of Rolla. In January 1868 he was sent to organize the parish of Springfield. Here he labored with restless energy until his appointment to Sedalia, in 1873. His successor at Springfield, Rev. Theodore Kussmann, was born on January 19th, 1843 at Schallern, diocese of Paderborn, came to America in 1847 and was ordained May 27th, 1866. Under Father Kussmann's efficient management the parish grew in proportion to the rapid growth of the city, 'which now has three beautiful churches, schools, an

---

11 Chancery Records and Archives of Kansas City Diocese.
12 Chancery Records and Catholic Directory.

academy of the Visitation Nuns and a hospital, conducted by the Sisters of Mercy.[13]

As early as 1845 the neighborhood of Marshall in Saline County was visited by Father James Murphy from Boonville. In 1846 came Father Dennis Kenny. An Irish Settlement had sprung up with the customary log church. Father Cusack's missionary trips along the railroad brought him also to this Irish settlement, which soon grew into a town named Shakleford. The church was dedicated to St. John Baptist. During the period from 1862 to 1868 the place was attended from Lexington. But from 1868 to 1880 Father Edward Hamill was rector. The Church was renamed the Immaculate Conception.[14]

When the town of Marshall was founded, the Catholics, under the leadership of Father E. Hamill, and his assistant, Father J. T. D. Murphy, secured the lot on which Bishop Ryan laid the corner stone for the church of St. Peter, May 29th, 1870. In 1872 Father John Thomas David Murphy became its rector, Father Hamill retaining his pastorate of Shakleford. Father Murphy was ordained by Archbishop Kenrick on September 30th, 1869, at St. John's Pro-Cathedral, and after two years service as assistant in Potosi, was sent to Marshall where he remained until 1880 and after.[15]

St. Joseph's Church of Pilot Grove in Cooper County is one of the early foundations of Father Helias, S. J. who in 1842 came from Harrville to visit the scattered Catholics in the wide expanse of prairie east of Clear Creek.

In 1847 Father Murphy of Jefferson City took up his laborious service; from 1865 to 1877, the place was attended from Boonville. Rev. William Boden in 1877 was appointed first resident pastor of Pilot Grove. He labored here until 1879. In December of the same year Rev. Nicholas Joseph Reding was transferred from St. Lawrence church, Punjaub, Ste. Genevieve County, to the church of St. Joseph in Pilot Grove. Becoming a member of Kansas City diocese, Father Reding began the life of a wanderer.[16]

Sarcoxie Prairie is the strange name of a mixed Irish and German settlement in Jasper, now Newton County, that was first visited from Springfield in 1871, and from 1875 to 1878 from Pierce City. The church was dedicated to St. Agnes.

On October 10th, 1878 Father William Joseph Angenendt was installed as rector. Father Augenendt was born on September 25th, 1843, at Keymberg, Archdiocese of Cologne, came to St. Louis in 1867,

---

13   Chancery Records.
14   Chancery Records.
15   Chancery Records.
16   Chancery Records.

and was ordained at St. Francis Seminary, Milwaukee, on June 24th, 1878. After the organization of his parish at Sarcoxie Prairie, Father Angenendt became pastor of Vienna in Maries County. At this time St. Joseph's parish numbered two hundred and seventy souls.

Pierce City in Lawrence County had a small congregation in 1872 when it received monthly visits from Springfield. Rev. Henry Hugh O'Reilly was its first resident priest. On February 1877 Father John Hennes was appointed pastor, and at once began the work of building a new church, which Bishop Patrick J. Ryan blessed on September 24th, 1877, under the invocation of St. John the Baptist. On October 17th, 1879, the Rev. A. M. J. Hynes succeeded Father Hennes as Pastor of Pierce City.[17]

Joplin in Jasper County also received its first spiritual ministrations from Father O'Reilly; in 1877 he was appointed to this place from Pierce City. In 1878, however, Father O'Reilly was transferred to North Missouri, and Father James Mackin took his place at St. Peter's Church in Joplin.

Carthage, in Jasper County, did not become a separate parish before the establishment of Kansas City Diocese, but was visited by priests from Springfield, Pierce City and Sarcoxie Prairie. The same is true of the church of Verona in Lawrence County, where Father Theodore Kussmann on January 3rd, 1878 blessed the new church in honor of St. John Nepomuc. Two outmissions of Springfield were Greenfield in Dade, and Honey Creek in McDonald Counties, both organized in 1872, whilst Syracuse and Bond's Mines, in Morgan County received their first religious services from the priests of Jefferson City. But later on Syracuse was attended from Sedalia, and Bond's Mines from California. The church at Bond's Mines was dedicated to St. Patrick. Neosho and Seneca both situated in Newton County, were missions of Springfield and Pierce City; Cole Camp in Benton, and Spring Fork in Pettis, were stations of Sedalia in 1878 and 1879. Dresden, however, in Pettis was attached to Tipton. The church at Spring Fork was dedicated to St. Francis de Sales. Frankfort, in Saline, being attended from Glasgow, received its first church building in 1867 through the exertions of Father B. Meurs, pastor of the Glasgow, and was attended from that center until 1880. St. Patrick's Church at Holden in Johnson County was organized in 1872 with Father Michael Mackin as its first pastor. Father James Phelan succeeded him in 1878. During the last year prior to the erection of Kansas City diocese Holden was the missionary center for Warrensburg, Knobnoster and other stations in the neighboring counties.[18]

---

17 Chancery Records.
18 Catholic Directory, A.D. 1881.

From the rapid review of the parishes and priests in the vast region which in September 10th, 1880, became, through apostolic decree, the diocese of Kansas City, with the Right Rev. John Hogan, until then Bishop of St. Joseph, as its first bishop, it will appear, that the mother diocese of St. Louis, acted right generously towards her youngest daughter of Kansas City.   In addition to the care for Kansas City diocese, Bishop Hogan was permitted to retain the honor and burden, the diocese of St. Joseph had been to him since March 3rd, 1868; for the Holy See appointed him administrator of that diocese also.  This administratorship continued until the transfer of Bishop Maurice F. Burke from Cheyenne to St. Joseph was effected, June 19, 1893.

The territory of St. Louis was now reduced to about half the State of Missouri, but still contained 168 secular priests, 98 regulars, 262 men in religious orders, 1,033 members of sisterhoods, 216 churches, 51 chapels, 6 monasteries, 91 convents, 110 parochial schools, 1 seminary, 4 colleges, 15 academies, 4 industrial schools, 5 orphanages, 6 hospitals, 4 asylums and a Catholic population 145,872 souls. A truly wonderful growth of the Church within the three decades that had elapsed since the second Diocesan Synod, when the entire state of Missouri contained but forty-eight parish churches and a Catholic population of less than sixty thousand, under the care of ninety-two priests.

## CHAPTER 35

# THE FRANCISCAN PROVINCE OF THE SACRED HEART

Since the days of earliest dawn in the heart of this continent, the Sons of St. Francis of Assisi have been among the foremost light-bearers to the benighted nations. The first marytr to bedew the arid soil of the far western part of the diocese of St. Louis, long before there was a St. Louis diocese, was the Franciscan Fray Juan de Padilla.[1] Among the companions of the intrepid explorer La Salle there were three Franciscans, the saintly Gabriel de la Ribourde, who died a martyr's death on the bank of the Illinois river; the picturesque Father Louis Hennepin, and the brave and resourceful Father Zenobe Mambre. The first parish priest of St. Louis, P. Bernard de Limpach, was a son of St. Francis of the Order of the Capuchins.

But with the end of the Spanish regime in the Mississippi Valley, the curtain fell over the activities of the great missionary Order, in as far as the diocese of St. Louis was concerned. Sulpicians, Lazarists, Jesuits, took their place, and filled it with credit. But the year 1858 marked the return of the Franciscans, though of a different family, to their ancient field of labor.

Bishop Juncker of Alton, accompanied by Father Brickwedde, called on P. Gregory Janknecht, the Provincial of the Franciscans of the Saxon Province of the Holy Cross, and obtained a colony of six: three Fathers and three lay-brothers, for his diocese. On August 24th, 1858, they left their Monastery at Warendorf for Illinois. Teutopolis was assigned to them as their first home in the new world. They all made the journey in their religious habit of St. Francis. They immediately began to give missions in Teutopolis and the surrounding places. In order to facilitate their work in a new country, the use of money and of secular garb was permitted them when traveling. In 1859 new accessions were received from Germany:[2] the Fathers Heribert Hoffmann and Ferdinand Bergmeier, and the subdeacons Bernardine Hermann, Mauritius Klostermann, and Raynerius Dickneite. The Fathers of Teutopolis completed the church and built their residence, and in the course of time, constantly receiving recruits

---

1 Cf. ''American Catholic Quarterly Review,'' vol. XV, No. 59, which places the martyr's place of death in Eastern Kansas. The author of the article is Ad. F. Bandelier.

2 July 31, 1859.

from Germany and from their Novitiate, organized a large number of parishes in Illinois.[3]

The first Superior of the Monastery at Teutopolis, and pastor of its church was D. Damian Henewig, a man of prayer and a great lover of poverty, and consequently one well fitted for the task. The great monastery was erected partly in 1867, and 1889 and completed in 1904. In 1862 the Fathers, at the urgent request of Bishop Juneker organized the diocesan Seminary, known as St. Joseph's College, which in 1898 was changed into a training school for the aspirants to the Order.

The second residence of the Order in America, that at Quincy, Illinois, was founded in 1859. The austere yet most gentle and loveable P. Servatius Altmicks was its founder and first Superior. The church was dedicated to St. Francis Solanus. Like the proverbial mustard seed this Franciscan institution, Monastery, Parish, and College, assumed wonderful proportions, stretching its branches across the river, to Hager's Grove, Bowling Green, Louisiana, Clarkville, Ewing, Palmyra, in the State of Missouri, as well as to several mission stations in Iowa and in Illinois.

Prior to the year 1862 the entire American mission remained under the management of the Provincial Minister of the Province of the Holy Cross in Germany. But in that year it was raised to the rank of a Commissariat of the Province, under P. Matthias Hilterman, as Commissary. Father Hilterman had arrived from Germany with a number of clerics and candidates, among them Nazarius Kommersheid, Anselmus Mueller and Paulinus Weiss. With the number of laborers thus increased, new labors could be undertaken. A new residence was founded and, with it, the state of Missouri was opened to their ministrations.

It was in the southern part of St. Louis that Mr. John Withnell gave the Fathers a large plot of ground for church and residence. P. Servatius Altnicks was sent to erect the buildings and to organize the Parish. He arrived about Christmas 1862. A small frame house served as temporary home and church. The Fathers took possession of the parish on February 5th, 1863. It consisted of one hundred families, one fourth of whom were English-speaking people. The first Monastery building was completed on August 1st, 1863. On April

---

3 All the data of this brief account of a most noble religious Order, are taken from two Franciscan publications: ''Catalogus Provinciae S. S. Cordis Jesu O. F. M., 1922,'' and ''Die Franciskaner Provinz vom Heiligsten Herzen Jesu, 1858-1908.'' It was with a feeling of personal loss that many of the St. Louis priests heard of the removal of the seat of the Franciscan Province of the Sacred Heart from our city to the all-consuming metropolis on the Great Lakes. One of the glories of St. Louis is departed; we can but hope and pray that it may return.

10th, the corner stone of the large stone church was laid. Bishop Hogan of St. Joseph's consecrated it on October 10th, 1869. It was dedicated in honor of St. Anthony of Padua. The parish prospered under the wise and loving care of the Fathers.

A school was built in 1869, and enlarged five years later. In 1901 the Brothers of Mary assumed the management of the boys department.

In 1872 the residence was raised to the rank of a monastery, and P. Ferdinand Borgmeir became its first Guardian. When the grand new church was completed under the direction of P. Bernard Wever in 1909, the old rock church was dedicated to the use of the Third Order of St. Francis.

In 1869 the Minister Provincial, P. Gregory Janknecht, again came to inspect the houses of the American Commissariat and brought with him P. P. Eustace Bruggemann and Francis Albers. P. Maurice Klostermann was now elected Commissary. The Order continued to spread far and wide. Of the new residences and parishes founded at this time we can only mention those of the archdiocese of St. Louis although the far greater number of them and the most important ones are situated elsewhere. In the archdiocese of St. Louis there is the residence and parish of St. George at Herman on the Missouri river with the missionary stations: Chamois, Morrison, Berger and Little Berger.

Chamois and Morrison were in the course of time entrusted to the secular clergy. The residence at Rhineland, now Starkenburg, with the parish church of St. Martin was administered for five years by the Franciscan Fathers, but in 1885 Rhineland itself and the neighboring parishes of Case and Hancock Prairie were relinquished in favor of the diocesan clergy.

The Parish of St. Francis Borgia in Washington, Missouri was transferred by the Jesuits to the Franciscans in 1894. The first Superior of this residence, having charge also of Union and Clover Bottom, was P. Paul Teroerde. Of these three Franciscan residences in the archdiocese of St. Louis a more extended account will be given in the proper place.

The year 1875 was the most memorable one in the history of the Franciscan Order in America. The so-called Kulturkampf in Germany, an unprovoked and altogether senseless attack of the German government upon the Catholic Church, culminated in the expulsion of the religious Orders and Congregations. The gentle sons of St. Francis naturally bethought themselves of the flourishing missions their brethren had but recently established on the free and fruitful soil of America.

To America they decided to go. On July 3rd, 1875, the first contingent of twenty-six priests, thirty-nine religious brothers, nine clerics, twenty-three candidates, and twenty lay-brothers, a total of one hundred and seventeen persons arrived at Teutopolis, and were immediately sent to the various missions already founded or to be founded. Among the new residences were those at Jordan, Minnesota; Chicago, Illinois; Indianapolis, Indiana; and Herman, Missouri.

In the following year another large contingent of Fathers arrived, enabling the Order to establish residences in Vienna, Missouri; Joliet, Illinois; Columbus, Nebraska. In 1878 the residence at Chillicothe, Missouri, was founded, and the care of the Indian Mission among the Chippewas of northern Wisconsin was accepted by the Fathers.

Owing to the rapid and yet substantial growth of the American Mission, it was raised to the rank of an Independent Province under the title of the Sacred Heart. P. Vincentus Halbfas was appointed Provincial, and P. Mauritius Klosterman, Custodian of the Province.

The P. P. Vincent and Mauritius must certainly be numbered among the most noteworthy priests of the Franciscan Order. Father Vincent Halbfas was physically and intellectually a distinguished person. Endowed by nature with keen reasoning powers, a tenacious memory, and fertile imagination, he was eminently fitted for the offices of lector of Theology, and of a preacher of missions. He was a strict ruler, but always kind and courteous and, consequently, respected and beloved by all. P. Mauritius Klosterman was an anima candida, a man without guile, who would do good more by example than by precept. Both together formed an ideal leadership.

St. Louis was chosen as seat of the Provincial. P. Vincent was succeeded in his office as Head of the Province by P. Mauritius Klostermann, July 15th, 1885, and he in turn relinquished the high office to P. Ferdinand Bergmeier, July 25th, 1888.

It was under P. Mauritius that the old Spanish mission of Santa Barbara in California was added to the St. Louis Province, and that three new residences were founded, namely: Watsonville, California; Ashland, Wisconsin and Humphrey, Nebraska. St. Augustine's in Chicago, which within a short time rose to the rank of a Monastery; the Parish of St. Boniface in San Francisco, and the parish of St. Turibius in Lake County, California, were also taken over by the Fathers during P. Vincent's administration.

His immediate successor P. Ferdinand Bergmeier extended the Province still farther by accepting the residence at Kansas City. Father Bergmeier was the first American Provincial to attend a General Chapter of the Order held at Assisi in 1889. His successor was P. Michael Richardat. Within the six years of P. Michael's Guardianship eleven new houses of the Order were erected. Five in California, and one each in Wisconsin, Missouri, Minnesota, Nebraska, Arizona and Michigan. The California Missions were joined together in a Commissariat of the St. Louis Province.

P. Ferdinand had served three years in the Prussian army before his entrance into the Order. He was a leader of eminent efficiency. He died a victim of his charity. A half-crazed servant whom he had taken into the house in Santa Barbara Mission, one morning fired four shots at him, in consequence of which the Father died, but not before he received the last sacraments.

For the next three years 1888-1891 P. Theodore Arentz held the office of Provincial: his succesor for two terms was P. Hugolinus Storff.

From 1905 to 1907 a new Monastery of the Order was erected at Cleveland; to serve as the House of Studies for the young clerics. The populous parish of St. Stanislaus was also taken over from the secular clergy. The residence and parishes of St. Boniface and of St. Francis Assisi in Sioux City, and the parish at Hood River, Oregon, were likewise taken in charge.

Under the Provincial P. Cyprian Bauscheid the Franciscan residence at St. Paul, Minnesota, and St. John's Mission among the Pimas Indians near Phoenix, Arizona, as well as the residence at Cowlitz, Washington, were accepted.

And thus the good work of these humble sons of the Seraphic Father went on until the present day. In 1915 the Province of the Sacred Heart had become too large and diversified: consequently all the monasteries and residences in California, Oregon, Washington and Arizona were constituted a new and independent Province under the patronage of St. Barbara. Its first Provincial was P. Hugolinus Storff.

St. Anthony's Church in St. Louis is a parish church with a very large Congregation: and at the same time it serves the religious community within the Monastery as their place of worship. At first the Superior of the house also held the office of pastor; but since 1887 the offices were divided. The first pastor appointed was P. Innocent Wapelhorst, 1887-1889. The name of Father Wapelhorst is known throughout the entire country and beyond its bounds. He was equally distinguished as priest, teacher, religious and writer of books. His "Compendium Sacrae Liturgiae" is a classic.

The Franciscan Fathers have for many years served as chaplains and confessors in a number of our religious and charitable institutions:

the Academy of the Ladies of the Sacred Heart at Maryville, the Con
vent of the Sisters of St. Joseph, in Carondelet, St. Elizabeth's Institute
the Missouri Pacific R. R. Hospital, St. Anthony's Hospital, the Home
for Aged People, conducted by the Little Sisters of the Poor, the
Deaf and Dumb Asylum, and the Convent of the Sisters of St. Joseph
in St. Louis.   Since 1876 the Fathers attend the city institutions in the
southern part of the city, the Insane Asylum, the Poor House, and the
Female Hospital.   Mass is said there every Sunday, and instructions
are given, the sick are visited, the dying are prepared for a happy
death.

## THE REDEMPTORIST CONVENT AND CHURCH

The Congregation of the Redemptorists founded by St. Alphonsus, came into the archdiocese of St. Louis by way of the Old Cathedral. Whilst gracing with their presence this one-time pride of St. Louis, then in its decay, they turned a longing gaze toward Grand Avenue where a church, larger and more beautiful than their present house of worship, was rising under their auspices.[1] It was to be their own exclusive church, the Church of their Order, dedicated to their holy founder. Parish work and parish rank was not at first contemplated. There were but few people living in the neighborhood. Vast stretches of prairie, small cornfields and potato patches here and there, and "marshy places, thickly overgrown with bright green sedges and reeds." But the church was rising higher and higher, until the roof should close in the space between the walls. Contributions came in from the people of St. Nicholas parish, and from the Cathedral parish; a Building Association was formed. Father Eugene Grimm was appointed to succeed Father Dold as Superior, a loan of twenty thousand dollars was obtained from the "Butchers and Drovers Bank" of St. Louis; and deposits, at a low rate of interest, were accepted from the people.

The purpose was to build a church and convent; but the money raised by all these expedients did not suffice for the church alone. Community life, however, was begun at once in temporary quarters, where "the Fathers and Brothers dwelt and worked and prayed," and we must add, suffered for five years. The Fathers took possession of their "convent" in December 1868, about four years before the dedication of the church. But in spite of hard times and other discouragements, as the opposition of some of the prominent secular priests, the work of raising stone upon stone went on steadily. By the proceeds of Father Mueller's lecture tour the debt was reduced to $9,000., and the building was under roof.

On August 4th, 1872, the "Rock Church," as St. Alphonsus has ever since been known among the people, was dedicated to divine service. It had taken almost five years to build it; and even then, the spire was left unfinished.

Archbishop Ryan, the Coadjutor of St. Louis, performed the dedication ceremonies, and the eloquent Redemptorist, Father Wayrich, delivered a masterly sermon.

---

[1] Leaves from the History of St. Alphonsus Church.

Father Nicholas Jaeckel, C.S.S.R. was the celebrant of the Solemn Highmass. Besides a goodly number of Redemptorist Fathers, there were present: Father Servatius and another Franciscan, two Jesuit priests, one Lazarist, and of the secular clergy, Fathers Fox and Van der Sanden, the Chancellor of the Archdiocese.

A chorus of forty members sang in splendid style Mozart's Twelfth Mass.

Gradually the Convent was enlarged, and made more habitable; the present house, built of brick was begun on June 8th, 1871 and in 1884 the north wing was added to the house.

On July 10th, 1874 the St. Louis house of the Redemptorists was raised to the dignity of a Rectorate, with Rev. W. V. Meredith as its first Rector: The community now numbered fourteen members.

The St. Louis house, however, was destined to play a still more important role, for on December 23rd, 1875, the Community received the news from Rome, that a new Province had been erected in the United States, embracing the immense territory extending from the western border of the State of Ohio to the Pacific Ocean, and from British America to the Gulf of Mexico. St. Louis had been chosen the Mother House of the new province, and the residence of the Provincial. The first Provincial of the new province was Rev. Nicholas Jaeckel, who filled that important post from December 23rd, 1875, to June 27th, 1884, when he was succeeded in office by Rev. Wm. Löwekamp. During the administration of Father Jaeckel many important enterprises for the good of the Order were undertaken and brought to a successful termination.

A Novitiate was begun at St. Louis with Father Smulders as Novice-master, but it was removed before long to Kansas City.

It was now resolved, "for strong and prudent reasons," to change the Rock Church from a mission church to a parochial church. Archbishop Kenrick ratified the decision. The boundaries of the new parish were: North, Easton Avenue; South, Washington Avenue; East, Compton Avenue; West, Taylor Avenue. This assignment was reduced in 1891, when Father Tuohy received permission to build the Church of St. Paul. A third and final change of the limits of the Rock Church Parish was made in 1893 by decree of the Archbishop:

Henceforth the limits of St. Alphonsus' parish will be:

North—Easton Avenue to Sheridan Avenue and Sheridan Avenue to Garrison Avenue.

East—Garrison Avenue from Sheridan Avenue to Lucas Avenue.

South—Lucas Avenue to Compton Avenue, and Washington Avenue from Compton Avenue to Sarah Street.

West—Sarah Street.

All arrangements contrary to this are hereby revoked.

Peter Richard Kenrick,

Archbishop of St. Louis.

With the delimitation of the Parish of St. Alphonsus, the main cause of friction between the Order and the neighboring priests was removed. The parish consisted of English speaking, mostly Irish, people, and consequently the Rock Church, though founded by Germans, is not counted among the national churches and has no exclusive jurisdiction over the German Catholics living within its bounds.

The first and most important work of the parish was the establishment of a parochial school. On September 15th, a meeting was held for the purpose of starting a subscription. Only twenty-three parishioners responded. At the second meeting the sum of $2,500, was raised. On May 25th, 1882, ground was broken for a school building "that would be an ornament, not only to Grand Avenue but to the City of St. Louis," a purpose that was fulfilled within a year. On August 24th, the Sisters of Notre Dame took possession of the new building. On the 27th, the Director of the Notre Dame Motherhouse of Milwaukee dedicated the school: It was opened on September 2nd, 1883, with an attendance of 400 pupils. A Convent Building for the Sisters was erected in 1885.

As St. Alphonsus was most tenderly devoted to the Blessed Mother of God, her faithful Sons throughout the world have always striven to exalt her honor. In consequence the devotion to "Our Lady of Perpetual Help" has ever been most elaborately held at the Rock Church of the Redemptorists. The beautiful marble shrine of Our Lady of Perpetual Help, with a replica of the miraculous picture is a fitting monument to this devotion.

St. Alphonsus Church is, as every St. Louisan knows, built in the English Gothic style, built of stone throughout. The altars are of white Carrara marble. But beautiful as the church appeared, its crowning glory, the spire, with its two flanking steeples was still lacking. Early in 1893 a campaign for funds was started, and on Easter Monday the first stone of the steeple was placed in position. The firm of Schrader and Conradia did the work.

It is a marvel of architectural beauty and exquisite workmanship. The completed church holds a prominent place among the really handsome churches of this country. In fact, it was the first large church built of stone in the City.

Through this monument of Gothic art the Redemptorist Fathers have been instrumental in raising the standard of church-building in our city to a much higher level, and thus helping to make St. Louis a city of beautiful churches.

Whilst the proper activities of the Order, are, by the rule of St. Alphonsus, confined to giving missions and retreats, they have found an extension in this country, through parochial work. The St. Louis Redemptorists have done much good in this line. It is estimated from the Records that from the beginning until 1922 inclusive about one thousand converts have been received, three thousand five hundred infants baptized, eight thousand confirmed, and sixteen hundred couples married. The parish has given to the Church thirty priests and one hundred twenty-five nuns. The parish, like many another St. Louis parish is on the decline, owing to the influx of negroes and Jews within the parish-limits. It now numbers about sixteen hundred souls.

The following priests held office for their respective terms as Superiors of the community and rectors of the parish:

> Rev. Louis Dold, C. SS. R.
> Rev. Eugene Grimm, C. SS. R.
> Rev. Wm. Meredith, C. SS. R.
> Rev. Michael Mueller, C. SS. R.
> Rev. Cyril Dodsworth, C. SS. R.
> Rev. Benedict Neithart, C. SS. R.
> Rev. James McLaughlin, C. SS. R.
> Rev. Thomas P. Brown, C. SS. R.
> Rev. William Löwekamp, C. SS. R.
> Rev. Edward Kennedy, C. SS. R.
> Rev. Jos. Firle, C. SS. R.
> Rev. Jos. Distler, C. SS. R.
> Rev. Charles Kern, C. SS. R.
> Rev. Nicholas Franzen, C. SS. R.
> Rev. John McGinn, C. SS. R.
> Rev. Nicholas Franzen, C. SS. R.
> Rev. Charles Harrison, C. SS. R.
> Rev. Thomas Palmer, C. SS. R.

The St. Louis Province of the Redemptorist Fathers maintains two institutions outside of the city, but within the archdiocese: Mount St. Clements College at Desoto, Missouri, the Novitiate of the St. Louis Province of the Redemptorist, and St. Joseph's College at Windsor Springs, their Preparatory Seminary. The latter property was bought January 25th, 1888 by Very Rev. William Löwekamp.

The grounds on which St. Joseph's College now stands, was formerly the Cleveland estate. The principal building on the property was a two and one-half story, ten room room brick house that had been built about 30 years before the advent of the Redemptorists. This house was used as the convent. The solemn blessing of the new foundation took place July 25th, 1888. Very Rev. Nicholas Jaeckel, C. SS. R. was appointed first Superior.

The construction of the present building was begun May 18th, 1889, and the corner stone was laid August 27th, 1889.

Rectors of St. Joseph's College:

Very Rev. Nicholas Jaeckel, C. SS. R.,...........1888-1890
Very Rev. Joseph Schwarz, C. SS. R.,...........1890-1893
Very Rev. Benedict Neithart, C. SS. R.,.........1893-1895
Very Rev. Patrick Barrett, C. SS. R.,...........1895-1898
Very Rev. Nicholas Franzen, C. SS. R.,.........1898-1904
Very Rev. William Carroll, C. SS. R.,...........1904-1905
Very Rev. Joseph Beil, C. SS. R.,................1905-1907
Very Rev. George Mahoney, C. SS. R.,...........1907-1910
Very Rev. Henry Guenther, C. SS. R.,...........1910-1912
Very Rev. John McGinn, C. SS. R.,..............1912-1915
Very Rev. Eugene Buhler, C. SS. R.,.............1915-1918
Very Rev. Thomas Palmer, C. SS. R.,...........1918-1924
Very Rev. Joseph Fagen, C. SS. R.,..............1924-

The Redemptorist Fathers of the St. Louis Province established Mount St. Clement's College at De Soto, Mo., April 21st, 1897. After using it for a novitiate for three years they converted it into a temporary seminary for the professed students. When they established their permanent seminary at Oconowoc, Wis., in 1911, the Fathers made Mount St. Clement's College the Novitiate of the St. Louis Province. Since then 168 Novices made their religious profession, and 80 students were prepared for ordination. Archbishop John J. Kain held ordinations here in 1901, and Archbishop John J. Glennon, in 1903. The Mission Band, that has been stationed at Mount St. Clement's College from 1902 to 1925, conducted 1,040 spiritual exercises, heard 475,965 confessions, and instructed 442 converts.

# PROGRESS OF ST. LOUIS UNIVERSITY

On December 3rd, 1839, the Jesuit Mission of Missouri was raised to the rank of a Vice-Province: three years later the number of members in the Vice-Province had reached a total of one hundred and thirteen. In 1840 Father Van de Velde succeeded Father Elet as President of the University. He remained in office until 1843, when he was made Vice Provincial of the Society of Jesus in Missouri.

Father Van de Velde was eminently fitted for university work. He was a master of languages, both ancient and modern. The purity and accuracy of his English was as that of one to the manner born. The financial crisis of 1842 necessitated a reduction of the fee for board and tuition, but did not reduce the number of pupils.

When Father James Van de Velde was appointed Vice-Provincial, September, 1843, Rev. George A. Carrell became President of the University. He was a man of scholarly attainments, "peculiarly happy in imparting his own ideas with force and clearness whether in the pulpit or in the class room. Yet as President of the University he was austere even to severity."[1]

Father Carrell eventually, in 1853, became Bishop of Covington, Ky. His successor at the University, the Rev. John R. Druyts, had been employed as professor and disciplinarian for twelve years before his promotion. He was a man of gentle manners and perfect poise. Nothing could ever ruffle his temper or deflect his purpose. He was, accordingly an excellent President.

On June 3rd, 1848, Father Van de Velde retired from the office of Vice-Provincial, and was succeeded by Reverend John A. Elet, one of the original members of the Missouri Colony of Jesuits. This memorable year of revolutions in Europe, brought, among other great blessings, not intended by the revolutionists, a large increase of Jesuit priests and scholastics to the Missouri Vice-Province. About forty of these exiles found a home at the University. Such a large increase of membership enabled Father Elet to take charge of St. Joseph's College at Bardstown, of which Father P. J. Verhaegen was appointed President. Father John Elet, having resigned his office at Vice-Provincial, sickened and died on October 2nd, 1851, and was succeeded by Rev. William S.

---

1 Hill, op. cit., p. 65. Father Fanning in the Memorial Volume, p. 83, calls him a "Christian gentleman and scholar, a self-denying man of God, and a genial companion" and refers also to his "fine personal appearance."

Murphy, who came to the Missouri Vice-Province from the New York and Canada Mission. He was a man of keen observation and judgment of character, thoroughly efficient in the administration of his office. Father Elet was a man of singularly amiable disposition, of deep piety, great learning and marked talent for organization.

On May 19th, 1851, the Church of St. Francis Xavier had been transferred by Father Elet, the Vice-Provincial, to the control of the St. Louis University, with the proviso that the University assume an uncancelled debt of $38,750.00 still resting on the property.

In 1853 Rev. J. B. Druyts, President of the University, decided to begin the erection of a series of commodious and attractive buildings, the first one, forming the east wing of the intended complete structure, was commenced in 1853 and finished in 1855. The public entrance was on Washington Avenue. It contained the chapel and study hall, the second, the Library and Museum and the third, an exhibition hall. The plan, as a whole was never carried out.

During the years from 1851 to 1856 the number of students increased from 218 to 321. At the beginning of the season 1854-55 Father Druyts was succeeded by the Rev. John S. Verdin. Affable and kind, yet firm in maintaining discipline, he made his tenure of office a prosperous one. He retired from the presidency of the University, to succeed Rev. William S. Murphy in the office of Vice-Provincial. The new Vice-Provincial· made it his chief aim to educate thoroughly the scholastics of the Order in those sciences that would fit them for their future duties as professors, missionaries and pastors. He instituted a full course of study for them in the Scholasticate on College Hill, which was placed in charge of Father F. X. Wippern.

In 1857, at the request of Bishop O'Regan of Chicago, Father Arnold Damen was sent to found a residence of the Jesuit Fathers in that city. The corner stone of the Church of The Holy Family was blessed by Bishop O'Regan on August 25th, 1857: the completed church was dedicated by Bishop Duggan in August 1860, Archbishop Kenrick preaching in the English language, Bishop Henni of Milwaukee in German. St. Ignatius College was begun on September 24th, 1867. In the summer of 1861 the eloquent preacher and lecturer Father Cornelius Smarius was sent to aid Father Damen in giving missions. Father Arnold Damen's two hundred and eight missions averaging a duration of two weeks each, brought into the Church the surprisingly large number of twelve thousand converts. The illustrious Father F. X. Weninger also had his home for a while within the hospitable walls of the University. His never failing and never disappointed trust in God's mercy and power cast a sacred spell over his audiences wherever he went. This circumstance and ¡his superabundant energy and earnestness, explain the wonderful effects of his spoken word.[2]

On March 19th, 1859, Rev. Ferdinand Coosemans was installed President of St. Louis University in succession to Father Verdin. The Jesuit Scholasticate was now transferred from College Hill to Boston. Owing to serious illness of the Vice-Provincial, Rev. J. B. Druyts, Father William S. Murphy was recalled from New Orleans to fill the position temporarily. After the Camp Jackson affair, May 10th, 1861, the warlike feeling in St. Louis and the State grew so intense, that the large number of southern boys in the University became very anxious to get home before the military lines were closed. In consequence all classes were suspended, and most of the students left for home.

On July 16th, 1862, Rev. Ferdinand Coosemans was appointed Vice-Provincial of Missouri, and Rev. Thomas O'Neill succeeded him as President of the University. The session 1862-63 began with a sufficiently large number of students, considering the manifold evils of the times. In the spring of 1864 a new building for class-rooms was begun, and by the following autumn it was ready for occupancy. It was four stories high and contained ten large class-rooms, a dormitory on the fourth story and a "Philalethic Hall" in the third story. This building faced eastward on Ninth Street.

The Vice-Province of Missouri was elevated to the rank of a Province December 3rd, 1862. It contained one hundred and ninety-three members within its jurisdiction.

The infamous Drake Constitution of 1865 imposed a heavy burden of taxes on churches, schools, hospitals, orphan asylums and even on the graves of the dead. The tax-gatherer collected from St. Louis University on its buildings, church and grounds for one year, the total of ten thousand dollars:

The sum was later on remitted by order of the legislature.

Property on Grand Avenue, between Lindell and Baker Avenues, was purchased for the University, May 25th, 1867, with a view of removing the institution to that locality of quietness and peace. The price paid for it was more than fifty-two thousand dollars. On July 2nd, 1868 Rev. Francis H. Stuntebeck was installed as President of the University, to succeed Father Thomas O'Neill who had retired.

On July 26th, Father Verhaegen died, having just completed his sixty-eighth year. He was the best educated of Father Quickenborne's little band of scholastics at the Novitiate in Florissant, and as such

---

[2] Father Weninger's writings cannot compare in power and persuasiveness with the spoken word, supported by his surprising mannerisms and the reputation of his strong Christian character.

became the guide of his companions in the study of philosophy and dogmatic theology. His sermons were distinguished by an eloquent simplicity. He was a tall and very handsome man, who walked with a dignified air; his genial countenance was lit up with merry twinkling eyes.

There were three hundred and forty-six students enrolled for the session of 1868-69.

On July 31st, 1871, Rev. Thomas O'Neil succeeded Rev. Ferdinand Coosemans as Provincial. More remarkable for piety and humility, than for brilliancy of mind or depth of learning, Father Coosemans governed with practical good sense, and so his administration of nine years proved a real blessing to the Province. The University, now under the rule of Father Joseph Zealand, showed a remarkable progress over the former session, there being a total of four hundred and two students in attendance. The 6th day of October 1871, was the fiftieth anniversary day of the entrance into the Society of Jesus of the six novices that accompanied Fathers Van Quickenborne and Timmermans from White-marsh, Md. to Florissant in Missouri to found the first residence and novitiate of the Order in the unknown wilderness of the West. Father Timmermans had died long since: Father ¡Van Quickenborne had entered into rest eternal after a life of heroic efforts in the cause of Holy Church. Of the six novices, Fathers Verhaegen, Elet and Smedts had died after most happy and laborious lives: only three were still among the living: Fathers De Smet, Van Assche, and Verreydt.

The first of these three, Peter J. De Smet, the illustrious Indian missionary departed this life at the University on May 23rd, 1873.

Father Hill in his excellent History of the St. Louis University sums up the leading traits of Father De Smets life and character:

"Perhaps no Jesuit since the restoration of the Jesuit order, in 1814, has gained so widespread a celebrity as Father De Smet. As long ago as 1843, a volume of his letters, in which, with his own peculiar power of narrating and describing events and scenes witnessed by him, he gave an account of his first journey to Oregon, and among the Indian tribes of the Rocky Mountains, was read extensively and with avidity in the United States and throughout Europe. On the various trips undertaken in order to advance the welfare of the Indian missions, Father De Smet traveled over one hundred thousand miles; he collected principally in Belgium and Holland, one million of francs in money, and in valuable objects for the altar, which were devoted to the various missions of Kansas and in the Rocky Mountains; during the period of forty years he induced a hundred young men to offer themselves to the Province of Missouri, most of them with the view of going on the Indian missions; and finally, not here to estimate the amount of good done for the Indian race through these different means, he baptized many of these aborigines with his own hands. His name is still in benediction, and his love for the red men is still gratefully remembered among the tribes of the Rocky Mountains, with whom his influence was so great that the United States authorities more than once used his moral power over those savages to pacify them, when irritated into violence by the cupidity and injustice of dishonest agents, or by sharp traders that had swindled or robbed them.''[3] In exemplification, ''he assured us that he had not known a single instance in which war was not occasioned by a breach of faith on the part of the whites. The horrors of the Chivington massacre in which a whole nation of Indians, men, women and children, were mowed down by United States howitzers, after they had stacked arms and assembled to accept the 'peace terms of Chivington,' had sowed the seeds of that terrible crop of vengeance which Captain Jack of the Modocs was wreaking on the Whites in 1873.'' Said the venerable Father, ''Among the white people, if a husband and father has seen his wife and children murdered, he generally seeks revenge; and the poor children of the forest, have this feeling of manhood within them, in common with the rest of mankind. We must not blame the Indians too much for exercising the same spirit of retaliation which their white neighbors have taught them.'' In 1870, ''Father De Smet received from the government at Washington the exclusive right of nominating all Indian agents for Catholic tribes, or Catholic sections of tribes; he exercised this office till a few months before his death, when he was compelled, by ill health, to resign the trust.[4] ''Father De Smet's remains were buried on the little mound, shaded by the tall black-thorn trees, by the catalpa, and the weeping willow, in the garden at St. Stanislaus Novitiate, near Florissant, Missouri, where are now buried all except one of the party who first reached that spot, in June, 1823.''[5]

Good Father Jodocus F. Van Assche was the second member of the trio just mentioned to be called away from the scene of his long and faithful labors. He died at St. Stanislaus Novitiate on June 26th, 1877, in the seventy-eighth year of his age. On the 26th of May he started on horseback to visit the sick, carrying with him the Blessed Sacrament. When two miles from Florissant, out on the Cross Keys Road, he was suddenly attacked with paralysis, falling from his horse. The faithful animal stood still, seemingly waiting for him to rise and remount. He lay helpless on the ground, till a gentleman, happening to pass that way, assisted him upon his horse. He wished to go on to the

3  Hill, ''History of St. Louis University,'' p. 116.
4  Chittenden and Richardson, Father De Smet, pp. 1298, 1334, 1541, 1547.
5  Hill, l. c., p. 116.

P. J. De Smet S. J.

house of the sick person; but after riding a short distance he felt that he could proceed no further, and he turned about and returned to his home at Florissant, which he reached with much difficulty. Dr. Hereford being called, found the attack to be a serious one, that offered little hope of recovery. The patient was removed to the St. Stanislaus Novitiate, where, despite all that medical art and kindness of friends could do for him, he gradually sank until he breathed his last.

A quaint little gentleman, of very benign appearance and somewhat eccentric habits, Father Van Assche realized, in his whole life and conduct, the ideal of a Christian pastor, made perfect beyond all ordinary men, by a charity that was unfeigned, because it knew no exception, it refused no work, and it feared no sacrifice.

Father Felix Verreydt, the Kickapoo Missionary and Companion of Father De Smet in the Potawatomi Mission near Council Bluffs outlived all his companions of the journey from Whitemarch, Maryland to Florissant, Missouri. He died at Cincinnati, Ohio, March 1, 1883 in the eighty-third year of his age, full of merit, and the peace of God.

The founders of the Western Province of the Society of Jesus are long since dead; but the work they accomplished with heroic courage and endurance is still bearing rich fruit, in the University, the Colleges, the parochial schools and the parishes they helped to found. Their honored names can never pass away from the memory of the cultured Catholics of our land.

## CHAPTER 38

## THE CHRISTIAN BROTHERS AND THE PAROCHIAL SCHOOLS

The third religious order of men to take up the work of education in the diocese of St. Louis was that of the "Brothers of the Christian Schools," who on August 18th, 1849, opened a parochial school at the Cathedral of St. Louis. This Institute was founded by John Baptist de la Salle in 1679 at Rheims, where as Canon of the Cathedral he established several free schools and introduced community life among the teachers. The saintly founder received this community into his own house and became their spiritual director and superior. In 1705 he established the novitiate at St. John, which was at a later date, removed to Vangirard, near Paris. The rule of the Institute was approved by Pope Benedict XIII, in 1725. The order was intended to conduct schools. No member was permitted to strive after the dignity of the priesthood, lest the proper purpose of the organization, Christian education, become a secondary matter. The Institute had a rapid and healthy growth throughout the states of Europe and even in Asiatic Turkey and Africa.[1] America received its first regular establishment of the Brothers of the Christian Schools in 1846 when Archbishop Eccleston called them to Baltimore. On August 18th, 1849, Archbishop Peter Richard Kenrick introduced them into his diocese of St. Louis.

Whilst this is a faithful outline of the establishment of the Christian Brothers among us there are several earlier historical incidents connecting the Christian Brothers with our diocese. On the authority of Brother Barbas, one of the five incorporators of the Academy of the Christian Brothers in 1849, it is stated: "In 1718 M. Charron, one of the founders of the Hospital in Canada, came to St. John and asked for four brothers. The "Venerable," being consulted, at first advised that they should be given. All arrangements were made, when, unexpectedly the Holy Founder returned from his prolonged prayer, and begged Brother Barthelemy to withdraw the promise. "But," said the Superior, "we have followed your advice." "If the Brothers go, they will not succeed," replied M. De la Salle. The negotiations were annulled and Charron afterwards admitted that he had intended to send them separately into the villages as teachers. This account Brother Barbas stated, was derived from the Life of the Holy Founder; preserved in the Motherhouse at Paris. To this was appended the following note: "One hundred years

---

[1] Azarias, "Educational Essays."

later (1817) four Brothers were sent to New Orleans (Louisiana) where, contrary to agreement, they were separated, and sent to various missions. Deprived of the graces of community life, they soon tired, and withdrew from the Institute. Thus the previsions of the Ven. De la Salle were confirmed. In 1853, one of these former Brothers asked to make a spiritual retreat in the Christian Brothers College St. Louis, Missouri.[2] St. John Baptist De la Salle died on April 7th, 1719, and was canonized in 1900.

After touching on this early attempt of the Christian Brothers to establish their Institute in this diocese, we will now take up the story of their successful entrance upon the work of education among us. In 1849 three Brothers, Elizaire, Peter and Dorothy came to St. Louis at the invitation of Archbishop Kenrick and, after a brief stay in a house west of the Cathedral, took possession of the Rider Mansion, at the corner of Eighth and Cerre Streets, where they founded their first college. But their first charge in the city was the care of the Cathedral school. The school consisted of two classes, and a third was added in November. Within a few months the number of Brothers was increased to twelve. Additions to the brick building on Cerre Street were made, and in 1852 the College was opened. Brother Patrick was placed in active charge of the Community, and for eight years conducted its affairs with distinguished success. In 1855 the Academy of the Christian Brothers was chartered by the State Legislature, the incorporators being Brothers Patrick, Paulian, Barbas, Dorothy and Lawrence. A branch of the Institute was formed on the North Side, 7th & Cass Avenues, called St. Patrick's Academy. The parochial schools of St. Patrick's, St. Lawrence O'Tooles, St. Bridget's, St. John's and St. Malachy's parishes were for years conducted by the Christian Brothers; but at present there is not one parochial school in the city remaining in charge of the Order.

In 1882 the College was removed from Eighth and Cerre Streets to Cote Brilliante on Kingshighway. The succession of Superiors up to the removal of the College was, Brother Patrick, Brother Ambrose, Brother Edward and Brother James.[3] It was under Brother James' administration in 1871 that the Brothers purchased the Cote Brilliante property, comprising about twenty-one acres, from James H. Lucas. The structure erected upon it was in the shape of a cross, three stories high, with a frontage of three hundred and seventy feet. The building was considered a model of elegance and usefulness at the time. The College prospered at first; but in the early nineties misfortune began to overtake the promising venture. A decree came from

---

[2] From M. S. in Archives of St. Louis Archdiocese.
[3] Catholic Directory, 1850-1875.

Rome, dated January 11th, 1900, forbidding the members of the Order to teach the classical languages in their schools. The reason for this prohibition was the purpose of preserving the Institute for the primary schools. Without Latin and Greek there cannot be a college. The Brothers reluctantly submitted to the decree which shattered their most sanguine hopes. But as their own Superiors in Europe were in favor of the decree as being more in accordance with the spirit of the Institute,[4] nothing was to be done, but to eliminate the classics from the collegiate course. Parochial schools were no longer within reach.

But a fond hope sustained the Brothers that all would be well. The headquarters of the St. Louis Province of the Christian Brothers was established at La Salle Institute, Glencoe, Missouri. This place was formerly the property of the Catholic Orphan Board, and intended as a protectorate for wayward boys. Archbishop Ryan was closely identified with the establishment of the Protectory in 1871 and the following years. The farm of 320 acres with all that pertained to it cost the sum of $27,263.00. Liberal contributions were made by a number of wealthy Catholics, chief among them John Doyle, John Withnell, Joseph O'Neill, J. B. Ghio and Mrs. Winifred Paterson. Vicar-General Muehlsiepen made a strong appeal to the German Catholics of the archdiocese, but with no great practical result. The Protectorate languished and died for want of support; and the assets were taken over by the Brothers of the Christian Schools who made it their Novitiate with the title of the *La Salle Institute*.

The Novitiate had heretofore been situated on Fourth and Market Streets.

In 1926 there were at the La Salle Institute twenty-nine Brothers, thirty-four scholarties, seventeen novices and twenty-five postulants. Father Daniel W. Dowling was their chaplain.

The Christian Brothers College on Cote Brilliante continued to struggle along under a heavy debt and various other burdens, until the fateful day, October 5th, 1916, when all its grandeur, with the exception of the bare walls, was consumed by fire.

Although, for the remainder of that year (1916-1917), classes were held in temporary quarters, conditions, resulting from the World War then raging, made it impossible to secure suitable accommodations for the student body, and it became necessary to suspend activities until adequate facilities could be provided. Accordingly, a new site of ten

---

4 "The Institute of the Brothers of the Christian Schools accepts the direction of any kind of male educational institution; provided the teaching of Latin be excluded; but its principal object is the direction of elementary gratuitous schools." Brother Paul Joseph in Catholic Encyclopedia, vol. VIII, p. 56.

acres was purchased directly west of Forest Park, in one of the most picturesque sections of St. Louis County, on which was erected the present modern fireproof structure.

Although great credit attaches to the Brothers of the Christian Schools in our episcopal city for the substantial work they have done for higher education among us, yet their most meritorious work was accomplished in the parochial schools. When they arrived in St. Louis in 1849, they numbered only three members: In 1870 their number had increased to fifty-seven, with a novitiate that averaged thirty aspirants. Besides their college with an attendance of 350, and their Academy, with an attendance of 250, they attended eight parish schools, St. Vincent's, St. John's, the Annunciation, St. Patrick's, St. Lawrence's, St. Bridget's, St. Michael's, and St. Mary's, Carondelet, with 1,660 pupils, under twenty-one teachers. This was a magnificent start, assuring a permanent establishment of our Catholic School System.

The German parishes of the city, however, did not engage the Christian Brothers in their schools. The absolute need of German at the time forced them to employ lay-teachers or members of the German Sisterhoods, or, as in the case of Father Goller of S. S. Peter and Paul's,[5] leading them to organize a German religious Brotherhood of their own. St. Mary's Parish school was in care of one lay-teacher and a number of Sisters with four hundred pupils. S. S. Peter and Paul's Parochial School, with two secular teachers and twenty Sisters de Notre Dame, had one thousand pupils. St. Joseph's School, conducted by secular teachers and Sisters de Notre Dame, had an attendance of one thousand. St. Liborius Parish, with four hundred pupils was in charge of lay-teachers and Sisters de Notre Dame, Holy Trinity had an equal number of teachers and pupils. The school of the Bohemian Parish of St. John had two hundred pupils under secular teachers and Sisters de Notre Dame.

This makes a total of 3,200 pupils of the German and Bohemian Schools under control of the Sisters de Notre Dame and a few Catholic lay-men as teachers. Two-thirds of the children in parochial schools were of German descent, and one-third of Irish parentage. The Cathedral School with two hundred and seventy pupils was now in charge of secular teachers.

The Sisters of St. Joseph, with about 1,300 girl pupils, and, in a lesser degree, the Sisters of Charity, the ladies of the Sacred Heart, and the Sisters of St. Francis shared with the Sisters de Notre Dame and the Christian Brothers the great honor and burden of establishing the Parochial Schools in our city.

---

5 Concerning Father Goller's ephemeral foundation of a religious Brotherhood, Cf. Holweck, F. G., in "Pastoral-Blatt," vol. 51, No. 7, p. 99.

The Catholic Directory of 1871 adds to these statistics the significant remark: ''Parish schools are also attached to most of the country churches.''

The secret of success or failure, comparatively speaking, of a religious Institute is found in the closer or laxer adhesion to the scope and purpose for which the Rule was designed and approved. The Catholic School system is now firmly established in the diocese of St. Louis, and its wealthier parishes would certainly be well able to open a new field to the Brothers of the Christian Schools. From the smoldering wreckage of their beautiful College the Brothers of the Christian Schools rose with dauntless courage to start all over; they will, no doubt, take up again in our city the most meritorious work appointed for them by their Holy Rule, the education of youth in our parochial Schools.

# EXPANSION OF THE EARLY SISTERHOODS OF ST. LOUIS

The truly wonderful development of the religious Sisterhoods in the diocese of St. Louis is owing, under God's Providence, to these two circumstances: first the deep and strong and self-sacrificing spirit of their pioneer leaders, and second, to the generous financial aid extended to them in their early struggles by Archbishop Kenrick and other wealthy patrons, individuals, and associations.

Wealth also, as well as wisdom and power, is a driving force, and may become no less honorable than they, when employed for the advancement of mankind, and especially, when employed for the advancement of religion. May the old Syriac word Mammon signify *"divitias de iniquitate collectas,"* riches collected from inquity, yet the things summarized under the expression of wealth are creatures of God and may, therefore, become honorable, if properly used. Good Bishop Rosati was dreadfully hampered by the lack of means: and so at the start was Bishop Kenrick. But since the surprising windfall of the Thornton Bequest of almost half a million, in 1858, the Archbishop was able, and perhaps all too willing, to advance large sums at nominal interest or even in form of a donation, to the established Sisterhoods and to new ones, for the purpose of building for them a better and more beautiful home. Other Sisterhoods had noble patrons among the men and women of great wealth in the city; and others were supplied, though more sparingly, by the Missionary Societies of Europe.

The Ladies of the Sacred Heart, the Sisters of Charity, the Sisters of St. Joseph were already firmly established in the diocese at Bishop Kenrick's coming to St. Louis in 1842. The first home of the earliest Sisterhood in the diocese, the Sacred Heart Nuns, was at St. Charles, a small log cabin surrounded by fruit trees and shrubbery. Here they prayed and suffered and waited, until their house in Florissant was completed early in 1819, when the entire Community proceeded under command of the Pastor of St. Ferdinand of Florissant to take possession of it. But they found it even poorer than the house they had left, and the place seemed even less promising for their purpose. The rising town of St. Louis invited the Nuns to establish their Convent and School within its precincts. Mother Duchesne was anxious to go; Mother Barat in Paris was in sympathy with the project. But whence shall the means come? "Mr. John Mullanphy, a magistrate of the town, mentioned by Mother Duchesne as "a man of wealth and merit, and capable of governing a kingdom," offered to make over to the Society of the Sacred Heart, twenty-four acres of land, in the centre of which stood a large building overlooking the Mississippi, on the condition that the nuns would agree to take into the house a specified number of orphans. Mother Barat sanctioned the acceptance of these conditions.

On the twenty-seventh of May, 1826, Mother Duchesne, and one orphan, left Florissant for St. Louis. The orphanage was soon installed, but the opening of the young ladies' academy was delayed until the fall. It was the first Catholic Academy in St. Louis. But the neighborhood of the Convent was gradually relinquished to less desirable occupants, and the buildings became encrusted with the dust and grime and smoke.

"In 1872, the boarding school was transferred to Maryville; in 1893 the "Old City House" was abandoned; the community moved to Maryland Avenue, taking with them the twenty orphans, their talisman of golden charity."

Of course, every St. Louisan knows the great Convent of the Madams of the Sacred Heart at Maryville, near St. Anthony's Church. For fifty-six years the Academy of the Sacred Heart of Maryville has been a living center of true culture and refinement, where "fundamental principles of education have remained firm amidst the vagaries of twentieth-century pedagogy, and whose high ideals embody the Christian philosophy of sacrifice and charity."[1]

The spiritual direction of the community is with the Franciscan Fathers. There are sixty-eight Sisters in the Convent. The academy is attended by about one hundred and sixty pupils.

Maryville was and is a board-school; the second great Institution of the Religious of the Sacred Heart, known as the "Academy of the Sacred Heart and Mullanphy Orphan Asylum," is a day-school, attended by about three hundred pupils, and the specified twenty orphans. There are about forty Sisters in the Community. Both of these Institutions have tasteful and commodious buildings, and are placed amid beautiful surroundings.

St. Charles, that had lost the Sisters of the Sacred Heart in 1819, was to welcome them back to the old log house in 1825. The old convent building is still in use surrounded on three sides by newer and much finer structures.

There are twenty-six Religious in the Community.

The Academy has an attendance of more than a hundred pupils. The blessing of Saint Madelin Barat and her most saintly daughter, Madam Duchesne, still rests, and we trust, shall ever rest upon these Institutions.

---

1 Anna C. Minogue, "The Oldest Academies in Missouri, founded by Mother Du Chesne," in "Western Watchman," October 27, 1918.

The Sisters of Charity had for their patrons the various members of the Mullanphy family and the great Archbishop of St. Louis. "In 1828, under the auspices of Bishop Rosati, and thanks to the enlightened generosity of John Mullanphy, the first hospital west of the Mississippi river, had been opened in a house donated for the purpose and put in charge of a colony of four Sisters of Charity of Emmitsburg, Md.

After some time a building, quite modest at first, but soon to reach more ample proportions, was erected on the corner of Spruce and Fourth Streets. As the "Sisters' Hospital," as it was commonly called, was for many years the only institution devoted to the care of the sick, it was well patronized by all classes of people, one-third of the inmates being habitually charity patients.

The number of Sisters had gradually to be increased, so that in 1847, there were twelve Sisters lending their ministrations to an average of 175 patients."

Mrs. Eliza A. Seton was the American founder of this Sisterhood. Hence the members were often called Mother Seton's Daughters. But in 1850 Father Etienne, Superior of the Daughters of Charity of France, effected the affiliation of the Sisterhood at Emmitsburg with the Daughters of Charity of St. Vincent de Paul. Since that time the designation Mother Seton's Daughters is restricted to the Cincinnati Branch of the Order.[2]

In July 1874 the "Sisters' Hospital" was transferred to the large block on Montgomery and Bacon Streets which it still occupies.

For five years from 1858 to 1862 Archbishop Kenrick contributed about $7,000. annually to help defray the expenses of the St. Louis Hospital. Eighteen Daughters of Charity of St. Vincent de Paul form the Community at the Institution, now designated as the St. Louis Mullanphy Hospital.[3]

The number of patients during the year 1926 was 2,399, outdoor clinic patients, 10,560. Connected with the Hospital is St. Louis (Mullanphy) Training School for Nurses.

The second Institution founded and controlled by the Daughters of Charity of St. Vincent de Paul, St. Vincent's Institution for the Insane, was established in 1858. The old-Sisters' Hospital on Fourth and Spruce Street had a department for the insane. In time it became necessary to provide a separate home for them, which was located on Ninth and Marion Streets.

In 1861 the State Asylum at Fulton was suspended, and the patients returned to their homes. At the request of the County of St. Louis St. Vincent's received ninety patients in addition to the forty

---

2 Catholic Encyclopedia.
3 The cyclone of 1927, did heavy damage to the Mullanphy Hospital.

that were already there.   Only eleven Sisters were in charge and their number could not be increased for lack of housing space.

The Sisters erected a new building, eight miles from the Court-house, which was opened June 25th, 1895.   About one-fourth of the inmates were charity patients.   The Institution was subsidized by Arch-bishop Kenrick from 1858 to 1862 to the amout of $17,885.00 in all.[4]

St. Ann's Widow's Home, Lying-in Hospital and Foundling Asy-lum, also in charge of the Daughters of Charity of St. Vincent de Paul, was organized on May 12, 1853.

The foundation started with four Sisters in the one-time home of Father Cellini on Menard and Marion Streets.   As a Foundling Asylum it was the first institution of its kind in the United States. As John Mullanphy left a bequest for the support of ten widows, the Widow's Home was added to the Foundling Asylum, the combined institutions being placed in a new building erected by the Archbishop on a lot donated by Mrs. Ann Biddle on Tenth and O'Fallon.   This occurred on September 8th, 1858.   The Maternity Hospital formed and still forms a part of St. Anne's, as the Institution is popularly called. In 1904 the corner stone for the new St. Anne's, 5301 Page Boulevard, was laid, and the Sisters took possession. . . The erection of St. Anne's Asylum cost Archbishop Kenrick the sum of $47,166.   His contributions towards the support of the three combined institutions for the five years from 1858-1862 amounted to $10,758.00.[5]

The fourth institution of the Daughters of Charity of St. Vincent de Paul is St. Philomena's Technical School.

In 1834 Bishop Rosati gave to the Sisters of Charity a small house at Third and Walnut Streets, to be used as an asylum for boys and girls.   In 1841, the boys were transferred to St. Joseph's Asylum, in charge of the Sisters of St. Joseph.   Times were hard, suffering great, many poor to be sheltered, and again the little house became insufficient to accomodate even the girls.   Archbishop Kenrick, therefore, in 1845, erected a large building on Fifth and Walnut Streets, where the St. James Hotel now stands, for training the more advanced girls.   Thus was organized St. Philomena's Industrial School, which was incorporated in 1864.   At this period, working-girls, out of employement, also found a home there.   This charity was continued twenty years by generous donations from His Grace: the exact total is $32,389.00.

During the war suffering and destitution were so great, that two sisters had the sole duty of visiting the sick and relieving the distressed. Food and provisions were distributed to the needy.   For this purpose the Archbishop contributed within five years a total of $8,000.

---

4   Encyclopedia of the History of St. Louis, vol. IV, p. 1977.

5   Encyclopedia of the History of St. Louis, vol. IV, p. 1949 s., and answers to Questionnaire.

In 1864 the location began to prove unsuitable to the work. Property was purchased on Clark and Ewing Avenue, and a new home erected, to which the Sisters moved in 1868.[6]

In this parish, a new branch of work was taken up by the institution. St. Malachy's parish was without a building for the girls' parochial school. The Sisters opened four rooms in St. Philomena's, and later on, two more rooms were added.

For over thirty years, St. Malachy's School remained in charge of the Daughters of Charity of St. Vincent de Paul.

In 1895, the parish erected a suitable building for the girls' school, and the Sisters continued to teach, to visit the sick and relieve the poor throughout the parish, until they found it impossible to support the children of the Industrial School.

In September 1910, the faculty took possession of its new building, Union and Cabanne Ave.

To more fully emphasize the nature of the teaching imparted, and to obviate any misconception of the character of the institution, the new home was incorporated under the title of St. Philomena's Technical School.

When the Foundling Asylum conducted by the Daughters of Charity was transferred to its new home on Tenth and O'Fallon Streets, the Sisters established in the vacated house their Home of the Guardian Angel. It was at first intended as a Female Protectory, but it gradually extended its usefulness under the new name, The Guardian Angel Settlement. The Settlement includes Day Nursery, Kindergarten, Sewing School, Lunch Room, Sunday School, Working Girls' Club, Junior Girls' Club, Playgrounds, Free Employment Bureau, Young Ladies' Sodality. The Sisters also visit the poor and sick.

There were fifty children in the house in Mother Rose's time. But since its organization as a Neighborhood Settlement, on February 27th, 1911, the number has grown to one hundred and eighty. The immediate occasion for this change was the large number of children in the neighborhood whose mothers were obliged to work for their support.

.Sequence of Sisters in Charge to date: Sr. Gertrude Stein; Sr. ·Cecilia Craign; Sr. Constantia Mahoney; Sr. Margaret Garvey.

"On a beautiful day, May 27th, 1896" writes the historian of the Sisters, "between five and six o'clock in the evening, just as the workmen were finishing a stairway that led up to the fourth floor, a cyclone struck our city and home: completely wrecked the new addition, tore the roof, broke windows, but not one person was injured.

---

6 "St. Philomena's Technical School," by a Sister of Charity, M. S.

The children, Sisters and workmen all rushed to the chapel at the first sign of danger and remained there until all was over."[7]

Among the minor beneficiaries of Archbishop Kenrick's Charity the *St. Vincent's School* established in 1843 at Tenth and St. Charles Street, deserves special mention. It was for a long time in charge of Sister Olympia of the Daughters of Charity, and was generally designated by her name. It enjoyed great popularity and patronage: but when the business portion of the city had spread beyond their home and school, the Sisters sought another location. An extensive building was erected at the corner of Grand and Lucas Avenues, of which the Sisters took possession on November 1875. The institution was now known as St. Vincent's Seminary. Sister Olympia, the first Superior, died in 1875, and was succeeded by Sister Lucina. In 1911 St. Vincent's Seminary was discontinued, and on August 12th, 1912 the building was leased to the Catholic High-School Association, for the use of the newly established Free High School for Girls, called the Rosati-Kain.

Of the latest Foundation, the Marillac Seminary and Central House and Seminary of the Daughters of Charity of St. Vincent de Paul, St. Louis Province, in Normandy we will have to treat in a later chapter.

The third Sisterhood established in St. Louis before the coming of Bishop Kenrick was the Congregation of the Sisters of St. Joseph. Their first establishments were situated in Carondelet and Cahokia. The Cahokia establishment was destroyed by the flood of 1844: but the foundation at Carondelet grew and flourished, and remains to this day the Motherhouse and Novitiate of the Sisters of St. Joseph of Carondelet.

It was early in 1860 that Mother St. John Facemaz, on the advice of Archbishop Kenrick took up the movement to bring the scattered members of her Sisterhood under a general government similar to that adopted by the Sisters of St. Joseph of Lyons, in France. Her plan suggested three provinces: one of St. Louis, one of Canada and another of the Eastern States: all provinces to be visited under a Superior General with residence at the Motherhouse in Carondelet. The plan was accepted by the majority of the houses: and Mother St. John was elected Superior General for six years.[8] It now remained to secure the approbation of the Holy See for the Congregation in the United States. On the recommendation of Archbishop Kenrick and a number

---

7  M. S. Account of Guardian Angel Settlement.

8  Savage, Sister M. Lucida, ''The Congregation of St. Joseph of Carondelet'' 1923, pp. 116-119.

of bishops the Decree of Approval of the Congregation was granted on September 9th, 1863. The Constitution was approved on July 3rd, 1867.

But previous to these happy events, on January 21st, 1858, a fire broke out in the Convent and destroyed the older parts of the buildings, among them the old log cabin Convent of the Sisters' earliest days: the north wing, however, was saved by the heroic work of the faculty and students of the Theological Seminary of Carondelet. In 1859 Mother St. John made arrangements for the opening of St. Bridget's Orphan Asylum in St. Louis, to which the Orphan girls were removed from St. Vincent's. This new institution, sometimes also called Half-Orphan Asylum was founded by the Archbishop at a cost of $21,109.49. In the following year the Sisters of St. Joseph took charge of St. Bridget's Parochial School, the teachers residing at the Orphan Asylum. In 1872, the Sisters opened a School in St. Lawrence O'Toole's Parish.

Mother St. John's successor as Superior, Mother Agatha Guthrie, was a strong advocate of the parochial schools, and during her first six years of office supplied sisters for twelve parish schools in St. Louis Province alone. The most prosperous were those of St. John's and St. Patrick's Parishes. Other St. Louis Schools provided with teachers by Mother Agatha at this time were: St. Nicholas in 1843, St. Francis Xavier in 1875 and St. Michael's in 1876. It was Rev. Mother Agatha, who in 1877 obtained in Rome the numerous relics now forming the richest treasure of St. Joseph's Convent in Carondelet. These relics were taken from the Catacombs in the first years of the nineteenth century, by order of Pope Pius VII and given to Count Nicholas Savorelli, from whose family Mother Agatha was so fortunate as to obtain the larger portion for her Convent.[9] For a time from 1872-1880 the Novitiate of the Sisters of St. Joseph was at Nazareth, five miles south of Carondelet, in the center of a sixty-acre farm. Here mass was celebrated for the first time on June 22nd, 1872, by Father

---

[9] The solemn translation of Relics at St. Joseph's Convent, took place on Wednesday, the 17th, 1880. The relics are fourteen hundred in number and vary in size from a skull or thigh-bone down to a drop of blood, or a few small hairs. All are beautifully mounted or set, and ornamented. The most complete and elaborately mounted and decorated are the entire bodies of St. Aurelia, a martyred virgin, St. Berenice, a martyr also. There are several other entire bodies encased in wax to give them the human shape. Vases, four in number, hold drops of martyr's blood. The collection is accompanied by several marble tablets taken from the catacombs which were used to mark the resting place of the martyrs. The collection of relics is the largest on this continent. They were removed from the relic room to the chapel in the Convent of Sisters of St. Joseph. The procession was composed of twenty-four priests and eighty sisters, led by a large number of young lady pupils and sisters. Priests bore the relics, then followed the Bishop, last of all. After the relics had been placed in their receptacles, Solemn High Mass was celebrated. Father Vincent O.F.M. officiated, assisted by two Franciscan Fathers." "Western Watchman," November 27, 1880.

J. M. I. Saint Cyr, the chaplain and spiritual guide of the Novices until his death.[10]

In 1880 Mother Agatha brought the novices back to Carondelet, where she erected a new wing to the building in 1883.

The Academy connected with the Convent had grown rapidly, and attained great prominence under the direction of Sister William McDonald 1873-1886.

In 1883 the Sisters of St. Joseph were established in the school of St. Anthony's Parish, and in 1886 in St. Teresa's Parish and that of the Holy Name, all three in St. Louis.

To the Schools already mentioned as being in charge of the Sisters of St. Joseph were added St. Leo's in 1893, the Holy Rosary in 1900, St. Ann's in 1901, All Saint's, and St. Matthew's in 1902.

In 1885 Mother Agatha established a central house, to which the teachers of the various schools of the city removed. The Convent was blessed by Vicar-General Brady, August 24th, 1885, and placed under the patronage of Our Lady of Good Counsel. It was at the Convent of Our Lady of Good Counsel, of the Sisters of St. Joseph of Carondelet, that the first teachers' institute was held in 1894, in which Sisters of the various teaching Orders of St. Louis participated.

St. Teresa's Convent, 5831 Cabanne Ave., is another Home for Sisters teaching in Parochial Schools. Sister M. Alacoque is the Superior.

The other institutions conducted by the Sisters of St. Joseph in the diocese of St. Louis are: St. Joseph's Deaf Mute Institute, 901 N. Garrison Ave., Sister M. Mercedes, Superior.

St. Joseph's Male Orphan Asylum, 4701 S. Grand Ave.

St. Agnes Convent, Sidney St. and McNair Ave.; 14 Sisters of St. Joseph. Mother Rose Mary Superior.

Ste. Genevieve. Convent of St. Francis de Sales—Sisters of St. Joseph. Sister St. Patrick, Superior.

The Congregation of the Sisters of St. Joseph was steadily increasing in numbers, the statistics of 1875 showing a total of four-hundred and fifty-three members. These were located in ten dioceses, and had under their care thirteen thousand two-hundred and twenty children.

Two other Sisterhoods were already established in the diocese of St. Louis, though not in the episcopal city, at the time when Bishop Rosati consecrated his Coadjutor, Peter Richard Kenrick: The Sisters of Loretto, officially styled "The Friends of Mary at the Foot of the Cross;" and the Visitandines or Sisters of the Visitation. Strictly

---

10 It was at Nazareth in the summer of 1878 that the writer paid a visit to Father Saint Cyr. Though blind the saintly old man said mass daily for the Sisters.

speaking, these two Sisterhoods take precedence in the order of time to all others, save the Ladies of the Sacred Heart. For the Convent and School at Kaskaskia was founded by the Visitandines in 1833; and the Convent of the Lorettines at the Barrens dates back to 1823. But, as we are here mainly concerned with the really wonderful growth of the early Catholic Sisterhoods in the city of St. Louis, and in connection with its masterful course of progress, we have taken the dates of the earliest influence exerted by them on the life and culture of the metropolis of the Mississippi Valley.

The Sisters of Loretto, so-called because their Motherhouse was named Loretto by their saintly Founder, arrived at the Barrens, Perry County on May 12th, 1823. The convent they built there was called Bethlehem. Until it should be completed they accepted the hospitality of the widow Clement Hayden, until July 4th, when they took possession of their own dear Bethlehem.[11] From here they sent out colonies of Sisters to Apple Creek in 1831; to St. Michael's Fredericktown, and to New Madrid in 1832; to Ste. Genevieve in 1837. These three earliest foundations from Bethlehem were discontinued, after a short trial: Ste. Genevieve in August 1858. But from Ste. Genevieve Convent the little band of Lorettines went out to Father Schoenmaker's Osage Mission, and from the same center the Convent at Pine Bluff was organized under Mother Agnes Hart, to be transferred, one half to Little Rock, the other to the Post of Arkansas.

In October 1838 the Lazarist Father Brands pastor of St. Vincent's Church, Cape Girardeau, received a community of seven Sisters of Loretto, with six boarders, who had come from their dismantled Convent of Bethlehem at the Barrens for the purpose of founding a new house of their Order in his parish. Father Brands vacated his house for their use. It was in the old mansion once occupied by the Spanish Commandant of the district that they opened their school. In spite of opposition from certain bigots, they gained the good will and confidence of the people. A year later the Sisters were able to erect their own buildings. Yet they were years of privation, those early years at Cape Girardeau. In 1850 a terrible tornado laid St. Vincent's Convent and Academy in ruins. It could not daunt the spirit of these Sisters: the Convent and Academy was rebuilt in short order and St. Vincent Academy continued to prosper with the years.[12]

---

[11] There are two "Lives," in English, of Father Nerinckx, one by Bishop Maes, the other by Father Howlett. Numerous articles have been published in regard to various phases of the Founder and the Foundation of the Lorettine Sisterhood, some of which are mentioned in this bibliography.

[12] Preunte, Rev. E., Cape Girardeau, in the "Church Progress," January 27, 1894.

Still greater things, were in store for the Sisters of Loretto. In 1846 the Ladies of the Sacred Heart had decided, though reluctantly, to suppress the Convent at Florissant. Mother Duchesne felt relieved when told "that the Sisters of Loretto at the Foot of the Cross, had taken up at Florissant the work so dear to her heart."[13]

"The history of Loretto of Florissant during its probationary period, was the history of the Barrens repeated; wrote the historian of the Lorettine Sisterhood in Missouri; "here also the Sisters were blessed with true and loyal friends, in the Jesuits. The community was governed by Mother Elenore Clarke, and never was a Superior more sorely tried by poverty and debt; even the necessaries of life were sometimes lacking: But a friend was at hand in the pastor of Florissant, Father Van Assche, S. J., and through his aid the Sisters were able to purchase the property from the Ladies of the Sacred Heart, and Loretto of Florissant entered upon an era of prosperity which continues to the present. To its classic halls came the daughters of some of the best families of the South and West; they in turn sent their daughters; and now a third generation is growing up under the fostering care and direction of the Sisters."[14] The first school conducted in St. Louis by the Sisters of Loretto was situated on the corner of Tenth and Morgan Streets. It was opened in 1862 under the name of St. Mary Academy. This they subsequently discontinued, taking charge of the parochial school connected with St. Michael's Church and also St. Joseph's School in Edina.

The property at Jefferson Avenue and Pine Streets was donated to the Sisters of Loretto by Mrs. Anne L. Hunt in 1868 for educational purposes. The foundation for an academy and boarding-school for young ladies was laid during the same year, but the projected building was not finished and the property was offered for sale with the consent of Mrs. Hunt.

No acceptable offer being received, the Superior of the Academy at Florissant, Mother Anne Joseph Mattingly, began the erection of a superstructure on the foundation already laid, but on a modified plan. The new building was to serve the purpose of an Academy for day scholars only. It was ready for occupancy September 7th, 1874. The name it bore was Loretto Academy. Its chapel was dedicated to divine worship on December 8th, 1874, under the title of "The Seven Dolors."

The Loretto Academy is well patronized, there being a regular increase of pupils every succeeding term. The total number of scholars registered for the session ending June 21st, 1875, was 50; the total number registered for the session ending June 21st, 1882, was 148; the

---

13 Erskine, Marjorie, "Mother Philippine Du Chesne," p. 363.

14 Minogue, A. C., "Sisters of Loretto," in "Sunday Watchman," October 27, 1918.

number registered for the session of 1882-83 up to January 23rd, 1883, was 156.

A few years ago Loretto Academy moved to its handsome new home on Lafayette Avenue where the Sisters teaching in the parochial schools of the city have their home. The city schools in charge of the Sisters of Loretto before the Third Plenary Council of Baltimore were the following: St. Michael's parochial school, St. Louis, 1869; Sacred Heart parochial school, 1871; Old Cathedral parochial school, 1875; Immaculate Conception parochial school, 1876: After the Council the movement set in with renewed energy: the Visitation parochial school, St. Louis, was opened in 1886; St. Ferdinand parochial school, Florissant, in 1887; St. Charles Borromeo parochial school, St. Charles, in 1893; St. Edward and St. Rose parochial schools, in 1896; St. Cronan parochial school, in 1903; St. Pius parochial school, Immaculate Conception parochial school, Maplewood, in 1906; Our Lady of Mt. Carmel parochial school (Baden), and St. Catherine parochial school, in 1912. The new foundation of the Lorettine Sisterhood in Webster Groves, as belonging to the splendid era of Archbishop Glennon, must be reserved for a later chapter.

The fifth and last religious Sisterhood established in the diocese of St. Louis prior to the advent of Bishop Kenrick was that of the Visitation Nuns. It was in the "year of the great waters" 1844, that St. Louis drew to itself the Sisters of the Visitation founded in 1833 by Bishop Rosati in Kaskaskia, Illinois. The ancient parishes along the east-bank of the Mississippi were then no longer under the care of the Bishop of St. Louis. Chicago had become the see for all Illinois. But Bishop Kenrick had asked for a colony of the Visitandines from Kaskaskia for the episcopal city, and his request was readily granted. On the morning of April 14th, 1844, Mother Agnes Brent with five companions started for St. Louis by steamer and within six hours they arrived at their destination and were housed for eight days with the Sisters of Charity. They rented a house on Sixth Street and fitted it up, as best they could, for a Convent and school. Meanwhile the Mississippi river was playing havoc with the Convent they had just left.[15] The dramatic incidents of the rescue of the Sisters remaining at Kaskaskia from the flood have been related in a former chapter. Suffice it to say that the entire Community of Kaskaskia found itself in St. Louis. As the house on Sixth Street was altogether too small to accomodate them all, the Community under Mother Isabella King took up their abode in the house of Mrs. Anne Biddle. This noble benefactress of the Church, then established the refugees from Kaskaskia in

---

15 Shipman, Paul R., "Establishment of the Visitation Nuns in the West," in "American Catholic Quarterly," January, 1886, p. 36.

her spacious mansion on Broadway, where the Sisters erected a two-story building for the School.

In July 1846, after two years of separation, the two branches of the Visitation Sisterhood were reunited under Mother Agnes Brent as Superior and took possession of the Archbishop's place on Ninth Street, where they made various improvements.[16]

A large lot on Cass Avenue had been bequeathed to the Sisters by Mrs. Anne Biddle, on which they began to build their Convent and Academy. The Archbishop advanced the funds necessary for completing the building, about $120,000.

At last the time for removal came. The Archbishop accepted the improvement made by the Sisters on his property on Ninth Street in lieu of rent due him, and in the Spring of 1858 the Sisters were installed in their beautiful Convent and Academy of the Visitation. In order to encourage them and to help them to keep down their indebtness, the Archbishop, in the six years from 1863 to 1868, paid for the education of poor children the sum of $15,692.65.[17]

The Visitation Convent appears in old prints as a stately building, three stories high, in the midst of woodland scenery. We subjoin the course of studies followed at the Young Ladies' Academy of the Visitation in 1881:

"The Course begins each year on the First Monday in September.

"THE COURSE OF STUDIES of the first class comprises Astronomy, Chemistry, Physics, Physiology, Botany: History, Ancient and Modern, Sacred and Ecclesiastical; Rhetoric, Prose and Poetical Composition, English Literature and Elocution; also, Geometry, Algebra, and the more advanced portions of Arithmetic, Mental and practical, and Book-keeping.

"The studies of the Second Class comprise Classical, Sacred and Physical Geography, Ancient and Modern; Sacred and Ecclesiastical History, Mythology, Grammar, Rhetoric, Botany, Prose and Epistolary Composition, Mental and Practical Arithmetic, Geometry, Book-keeping, Reading and Penmanship.

The studies of the Third Class comprise Ancient and Modern History, Mythology, Modern and Physical Geography, Orthography, Grammar, Familar Science, Prose and Epistolary Composition, Dictation and Reading, Mental and Practical Arithmetic, and Penmanship.

The studies of the Fourth Class comprise Modern Geography, History, Orthography, Grammar, Epistolary Composition, Dictation, Reading, Penmanship, and Mental and Practical Arithmetic.

---

16  Shipman, ibidem, p. 37.
17  Archbishop Kenrick's Account Book.

In the Junior Department the course of studies comprises History, Geography, Orthography, Penmanship, Reading, Epistolary Composition, Dictation, Mental and Practical Arithmetic.

Vocal and Instrumental Music, Drawing, Oil and Water Color Painting, Sewing, Wax, Lace and Hair Work.

Latin and all Modern Languages are taught.''[18]

On August 16th, 1887 the Sisters of the Visitation opened a dayschool farther west, the St. de Chantal Academy, and then acquired, far out on Cabanne Avenue, a beautiful site for the new Convent and Academy of the Visitation, which was finished in the summer of 1892. According to their agreement made with Archbishop Kenrick in 1869, ''that they should give the Archbishop or his legal representative the proceeds of whatever portion of their property they might be empowered to sell,''[19] the Sisters of the Visitation transferred to His Grace the Convent property on Cass Avenue in cancellation of their debt to him.

Within its hallowed walls the Diocesan Seminary was reestablished after a lapse of years, under the guidance and control of the Vincentian Fathers.

---

18  From an advertisement in Mueller, Schematismus, 1882.
19  Archbishop Kenrick's Account Book.

## CHAPTER 40

## ARCHBISHOP KENRICK'S VISIT TO ROME

The close of the year 1866, November 30, marked an epoch in Archbishop Kenrick's life. On that very day, the Feast of St. Andrew, twenty-five years ago, he had received episcopal consecration in Philadelphia at the hands of the sainted Bishop Rosati of St. Louis. Archbishop Kenrick wished to spend this memorial day in quiet contemplation without any public manifestations as are usual on such occasions. But the German Catholics of the city expressed their loyalty by a grand torchlight procession; and the Archbishop accepted the ovation with meek submission and gentle patience.

Twenty-five years of constant labor and self-sacrifice had merited for him a vacation. The Eternal City was his goal. The occasion was the Eighteen Hundredth Anniversary of the Martyrdom of St. Peter, which was to be celebrated in Rome in 1867. A large part of the Catholic episcopacy of the world was expected to attend the festivities.

On May 27, 1867, Archbishop Kenrick, accompanied by Father Patrick J. Ryan,[1] then pastor of the Annunciation Church, left St. Louis for Cape Girardeau whence, after the ordination of nine priests, they proceeded to Boston, and there took the Steamer *Asia* on June 5, en route for Rome. They landed in Ireland, and, after a brief stay, journeyed to Rome, where they were received with high honors. There they attended the celebration that had called them to Rome. In union with the assembled prelates, the Archbishop signed the solemn protest against the spoliation of the Holy See by the Italian revolutionists, and a declaration that the temporal power of the Pope was necessary for the freedom of the Church. Passing through Italy, Germany and France, the Archbishop returned to Dublin, where he spent delightful days of rest amid the familiar scenes of his early life. It was in his native Dublin that he uttered from the pulpit the touching testimonial of his love for his native land: "Ireland differs from other nations in this, that whilst these have given martyrs to the Church, she is the martyr-nation of the world."

On June 16, 1868, the Archbishop and his companion landed in New York and on June 23 arrived in St. Louis. He was met by a delegation of priests and laymen, who escorted him to his residence near St. John's Church. On the following Sunday a public reception

---

[1] Father Patrick J. Ryan in the course of time became Coadjutor to the Archbishop of St. Louis and Archbishop of Philadelphia.

was held in honor of the Archbishop's return. The procession was nearly three miles long. His Grace received the greetings of his episcopal city standing on the doorstep of his house. Mr. R. A. Bakewell delivered the address of welcome; and the Archbishop responded briefly.

During the Archbishop's absence the Vicar-General of the Archdiocese, Father Melcher, had exercised the functions of government, and the Bishop of Alton, Damien Henry Juncker, had administered the sacrament of Holy Orders to four candidates for the ministry, among them the future Vicar-General of the Archdiocese, Father Hoog. On July 12 the Archbishop consecrated Joseph Melcher Bishop of Green Bay, Wisconsin. This solemn function took place at St. Mary's Church.

Fathers Patrick J. Ryan and Henry Muehlsiepen were now appointed Vicar-Generals, and Father Charles Ziegler succeeded to the office of Secretary. Vicar-General Ryan became pastor of St. John's Church in place of Father Ring.

On September 12th, the Archbishop consecrated his old friend John Joseph Hogan Bishop of St. Joseph, Missouri.

The year 1869 brought to the Archbishop the old round of duties; cornerstone-layings, church dedications, ordinations, services and sermons in his pro-cathedral of St. John. In the meantime events of great moment were unfolding themselves in the Church Universal. On July 3, 1868, His Holiness Pope Pius IX had issued the call to the Bishops of the Catholic World for an ecumenical Council, to assemble at the Vatican Basilica on the Feast of the Immaculate Conception, December 8, 1869. A little later a very fatherly invitation went out from the Pope to the separated brethren of the Eastern schismatic churches and to the Protestant Christians throughout the world. It was the first ecumenical Council within three hundred years since the great Council of Trent. Since those early days of Protestant storm and stress, a saddening change had come over Christendom. The spirit of protest against some of the tenets of the Church had at last resulted in the spirit of absolute negation of all revealed truth. Indeed, the Catholic Church, and she alone, had remained firm in the joyful profession of all the sacred truths once delivered to the saints. And now the Church was girding herself to take up the gage of spiritual warfare, and to strike the blow that should lay low the triple head of the dragon, infidelity, heresy and schism.

Archbishop Kenrick was deeply interested in these preparations for the inevitable conflict. In his Pastoral Letter of 1865 he had taken occasion to publish the much maligned "Syllabus of the Principal Errors of our Time," adverting to its importance in the following words:

"The Holy Father has availed Himself of the publication of the Jubilee-Indulgence to condemn certain prevalent errors of our times, as also to promulgate in a collected form, condemnations of the same or similar errors, made by him since he ascended the Pontifical chair. These authoritative declarations we receive with all the reverence and respect which is due to the voice of the Vicar of Christ; recognizing in that voice our only sure and safe guidance amidst the labyrinth of human errors; as also obeying the authority of Him who speaks to us, on this occasion, through the successor of Peter, placed as was Peter to confirm his brethren."[2]

Whilst, however, accepting the guidance of the Pope without reserve and without fear of consequences, Archbishop Kenrick had some misgivings in regard to the question of Papal infallibility which he felt sure, would be proposed to the deliberation of the Council. Of course, he never for a moment, doubted the infallibility of the Church in all matters of Faith and Morals. Nor did he doubt the infallibility of the Pope, when speaking as the Head of the Church in union with her members. It was this very faith that made him extol, even beyond the bounds of truth, that famous saying of St. Vincent of Levins: "Quod semper, quod ubique, quod ab omnibus creditum est, id est Catholica veritas," as if these words could also be applied in a negative way: quod non semper, quod non ubique, quod ab omnibust creditum est, id non est Catholica veritas."[3] The fact is: before the Vatican Council there were two schools of Catholic thought, one commonly designated as ultramontane, the other roughly comprised under the title of Gallican. Like the schismatic Orient, the Gallican believed in synthetic organization. The single churches being grouped together in a larger unit; the ultramontane builded constructively from the center of Unity—from Rome. "Among the native Catholics of England," wrote a keen observer of the times, "and more with the clergy

---

2 The Syllabus, sent to the Bishops of the Catholic Church by Pope Pius IX on December 8, 1864, together with the Encyclical letter, "Quanta Cura," is an authoritative condemnation in eighty propositions, of an equal number of errors of this time, ranging from pantheism to liberalism. The sixteen propositions condemned by the Encyclical *Quanta Cura* certainly fall under the judgment of Papal infallibility. As to the rest, theologians are not agreed, some holding that all those condemnations are made by infallible authority; others maintaining that the negative character of the propositions leave a certain liberty of interpretation as to the dogmatic sense of each. All Catholics must hold, however, that the entire Syllabus, being an emanation from the Supreme pastoral and teaching office of the church, must be accepted by all with the submission of mind and will.

3 "What was believed always, and everywhere, and by all, that is Catholic truth," St. Vincent. "What was not always believed, nor everywhere, nor by all, that is not Catholic truth."

probably than with the laity, there was a considerable survival of what is called Gallicanism, a sort of national pride and tendency in religion, as opposed to the other extreme known as Ultramontanism. Manning described himself as an Ultramontane, and Newman as a Gallican. Of course, there is between these two views no disagreement in faith, though one would sometimes suppose differently from the heated language occasionally indulged in by one or the other towards the opposite party.''[4]

Archbishop Kenrick's view of the Church and its Head inclined to that of the Gallicans. He, as so many another leader of thought and spokesman of the Faith of his day, believed, that it was the office of the Bishop of Rome, as Supreme Pontiff, to decide controversies and condemn errors, and that such decisions and condemnations must be regarded as final and infallible, *if accepted by the Universal Church.* According to this view, the College of the Bishops, whether assembled in Council or dispersed in their sees, in union however with the Roman Pontiff, was the true seat of infallibility; but the Pope, separated from the body of the Bishops, if that were possible, did not enjoy the gift. Practically, there was no difficulty, as the Pope's decrees and decisions in matters of Faith and Morals, had always been accepted by the Church as infallible utterances. For this very reason many considered a formal decision on the matter altogether unnecessary, and in a way hurtful to the Church.

Among the Catholics of England the two great leaders of thought, Manning and Newman, both converts to the Faith, held opposite views, not on Papal infallibility itself, but on the opportuneness of its definition. ''The great Archbishop of Westminster,'' says a contemporary writer, ''was, before and during the Vatican Council, the strongest of the many strong promoters of the definition: whilst the humble son of St. Philip Neri, though ready to receive a clear definition of that doctrine, did not think it opportune at that time. His own treatise on development showed that the entire scroll, of the truth had been held by the Church free from injury from the very beginning, but that it was unfolded by the Church during the ages only just as fast as intellectual progress, and denials or discussions brought each several phase of the truth more and more into intimate relation with the thought or the needs of the time. Like many other Catholics whose faith was absolutely unimpeachable, he dreaded the effects that would follow, as he believed, on the definition of infallibility among the great masses of non-Catholics who did not understand the mean-

---

[4] Thomas F. Galway, ''American Catholic Quarterly Review,'' vol. 31-25. The word ''Gallican'' was used by Manning, not in reproach, but merely to define his own and Newman's position as to Papal Infallibility, which both believed.

ing of papal infallibility as held by Catholics, and would perversely persist in misunderstanding it.'' In 1866 he wrote that he thought ''its definition inexpedient and unlikely. Manning, at this time, was quite sure of the contrary, and was fretted by the attitude of Newman and those in England who thought with Newman. Both were Catholics of sound Faith, but each placed a particular emphasis on that by which he had been drawn to the church.''[5]

Archbishop Kenrick entertained a very high regard for both Manning and Newman, but his preference between the two was Newman. Not that the influence of Newman, in any way, warped his judgment on this or any other matter. Archbishop Kenrick was an independent thinker, and simply held the opinion he had always held since he came to man's estate, as he tells us in his *''Concio Habenda at non Habita:''* ''Almost forty years have passed since I there (in Maynooth College) pursued the study of Theology under the learned John O'Hanlon, then lecturer in Theology, now professor of higher theological science in the same college. The treatise *De Ecclesia* by that man of venerated memory, Delahogue, one of the French emigres in the time of the great French Revolution, contained nothing on the infallibility of the Pope, except a thesis conceived in these words: ''Infallibilitas Summi Pontificis non est de Fide.''

''In 1831, the aforesaid lecturer on Theology, O'Hanlon, of his own accord, gave us the thesis—'The Pope, speaking *ex cathedra is infallible,*' not to convince us of it, but to give us the opportunity of becoming acquainted with this weighty opinion, by the reasons in favor of it, adduced from various quarters. I confess that I was one of those who took the affirmative. But the new and hitherto unheard-of procedure did not meet the approval of all the professors, one of whom, the lecturer on Holy Scripture, who afterwards became President of the College, expressed his displeasure in pretty plain terms, to my classmate, now Bishop of Clonfert, from whom I learned the fact.''[6]

Such reminiscences served the Archbishop as premonitions of the great struggle in which he was to figure far more prominently than he expected or desired. Yet he felt assured that all would be well with the Church. As to himself personally he had but little concern. *Securus judicat orbis terrarum,*[7] was his watchword as it had been that of Newman.

---

5 Galway, ibidem.

6 Cf. Peter Richard Kenrick's Concio Habenda at non Habita, in ''Inside View of the Vatican Council,'' p. 149.

7 It was Wiseman's quotation of St. Augustine's word, ''Securus judicat orbis terrarum,'' which has been interpreted to mean ''Catholic consent is the safe judge of controversy,'' that finally decided Newman's conversion.

But the time had now arrived when he must start for the Eternal City. In view of his protracted attendance at the Council he appointed Vicar-General Ryan as administrator of the Archdiocese with Vicar-General Muehlsiepen in charge of the German and Bohemian parishes. The date of this double appointment was October 8th, 1869. The Archbishop landed in Ireland. In Dublin, in November he was joined by Father Constantine Smith, whom he had chosen as his secretary and theologian. Journeying to Paris, he spent three weeks, visiting the various places of interest in that renowned capital. "One day," writes Father Smith, "the Archbishop had just recounted to me the history of the various treasures of the sacristy of Notre Dame, and as we re-entered the Cathedral, I saw standing looking towards its pulpit an ecclesiastic of imposing figure and striking countenance. Archbishop Manning stood before us. The two prelates saluted and spoke to each other for a few moments. They dined a few evenings after together. Thus chance brought about the meeting of the two prelates who were destined to exercise, each in his way, a most decided influence on the deliberations of the Vatican Council."[8]

Archbishop Connolly of Halifax, and Father Hecker, the founder of the Paulists, joined Archbishop Kenrick on the journey from Paris to the Holy City. On their way they visited the Cathedral of Strassburg and spent a few days in Munich. They then entered Tyrol, crossed the Brenner Pass, and followed the Eisack and the Adige rivers into the Trentino. As they passed the historic town of Trent, they gazed upon the church in which the most renowned Council of the Church's history had been held three hundred years previous. Shortly afterwards, the travelers emerged from the narrow defiles of the valley and entered the plains of Lombardy. They passed through Florence and in the morning of December 1st, arrived in Rome. Apartments in one of the ancient palaces were assigned to the Archbishop and his Secretary.

"One week after our arrival," wrote Father Smith, "on the morning of the Feast of the Immaculate Conception, December 8th, 1869, amid salvos of artillery from the castle of St. Angelo and the pealing of bells and the play of fountains in the great square of St. Peter's, descended the scala regia in rich pontificals, the Bishops of the Catholic world, called to take part in the deliberations of the Vatican Council. Along the Grand Vestibule, at either end of which is an equestrian statue of Constantine and Charlemagne, and on through the great doors of St. Peter's the procession moved. Up an Avenue through St. Peter's, formed by two lines of soldiers of the Antibe Le-

8 The Catholic Standard and Times, Philadelphia, March 21, 1896.

gion, it proceeded till it reached the confessional, or high altar, where it turned to the right and entered the council chamber. At this door I left the side of the Archbishop and was conducted to a seat in one of the loggias. Solemn Pontifical Mass commenced. At the farther end of the chamber sat Pio Nono upon his throne, having his Cardinals seated on each side of him in the form of wings. Immediately before and facing him sat the Patriarchs. Further on to his right, on ascending tiers the archbishops and bishops were arranged according to seniority. I noticed that my Archbishop ranked that day the seventh oldest in the world. When the ceremonies of the Mass were completed, the Pope rose and in a tone of voice of marvelous clearness and almost preternatural power entoned the ''Te Deum.'' The thousand assembled prelates took it up, the joyous wave of sound swelled beyond the enclosure of the Aula and re-echoed back from more than 100,000 human voices, and reverberating through the vast edifice died away in the great dome. The Vatican Council was opened.''[9]

---

[9]    C. F. Smith, ''Catholic Standard and Times.''

## ARCHBISHOP KENRICK'S PART IN THE COUNCIL

The Vatican Council was, even from the historical point of view, one of the greatest events of the Nineteenth Century. The number of prelates from all parts of the globe assembled in Rome, about nine hundred, was far greater than that of any previous Council of the Church. The Pope, as spiritual ruler of the Church Universal, was still the temporal Sovereign of Rome and the surrounding territory called the Patrimony of St. Peter. All the magnificence of pomp and ceremony with which the greatest artistic force of the world was able to produce was thrown around the wonderful gathering. The mystical Orient and the rationalistic Occident were looking on with rapt interest and expectation. The statesmen of Europe, Bismarck, Gladstone, Napoleon III, Prince Hohenlohe, the leaders in historical science, Doellinger, Lord Acton, Maret, Dupanloup and a host of others were calling the world's attention to the prospects of the historic assembly, for good or for evil, according to the position of the observers. The meeting place was the right transept of the mightiest Cathedral of Christendom, specially fitted up for the occasion. The Pope himself presided at the public sessions, whilst the General Congregations were conducted by one of the five Cardinals appointed for the purpose by the Holy Father. The subject matter to be submitted to the Fathers of the Council had been previously prepared by a special commission of learned theologians and canonists from various nations. It was arranged under four heads:

I.   Concerning Faith.
II.  Concerning Discipline.
III. Concerning Regular Orders.
IV.  Concerning Oriental Rites.

The first section, concerning Faith, was subdivided into three schemata:

I.   On Catholic Doctrine.
II.  On the Church, and its Head, and its Relation to Civil Society.
III. On Matrimony.

By order of the Pope four standing committees or deputations of twenty-four members each, were formed, all except the presiding Cardinal, elected by the Council. These deputations were to receive all the objections and emendations the Fathers thought proper to make

(303)

in regard to the various schemata submitted to them in printed form, with the Pope's declaration that they were "nulla nostra approbatione munita," that they were, therefore, subject to discussion. The Holy Father stated at the same time, that the Fathers of the Council were at Liberty to propose any new matter that was of real benefit to the Church.

The order of proceeding as defined by His Holiness was as follows: The Fathers of the Council were to examine each schema, and then submit their criticisms and emendations, to the deputation that had charge of the particular matter. The deputation was then to examine the remarks of the Bishops and decide whether they were pertinent and acceptable or not. One of the delegation then was to refer the matter to the General Congregation, which was almost daily in session; and it was the privilege of each member of the Council to express his opinion on the matter or form of the proposed schema. When completed, the Constitution, as it was then called, was to be submitted to the vote of the assembled Fathers and finally announced to the world by the Holy Father himself.[1]

The first public session of the Council was held on the Feast of the Immaculate Conception, December 8, 1869, for the purpose of organization. In the second public session, which was held on the Feast of the Epiphany, January 6, 1870, the Holy Father first made the solemn Profession of Faith, and then the Fathers of the Council, after hearing the profession of Faith read to them, approached the papal throne, and each took the oath on the Gospels; "Ego, N. N. Episcopus N. N. spondeo, voveo et iuro iuxta formulam praelectam. Sic me Deus adjuvet et haec Sancta Dei Evangelia."

The real work of the Council was done in the General Congregations, the first one of which was held on December 10, 1869, under the presidency of Cardinal de Luca. There were present six hundred and seventy-nine Fathers. Of English speaking Bishops Manning, Spaulding, Leahy and Alemany, of Germans and Austrians Simor, Ledochowski, Senestrey, Gasser and Bishop Martin of Paderborn were members of the standing Committee or Congregation that had charge of Matters on Catholic Faith.

The Schema on Catholic Doctrine was up for discussion. Cardinal Rauscher of Vienna made the first address and was followed by Archbishop Kenrick of St. Louis. The Archbishop spoke briefly and to the point, saying that the schema did not meet his approval, as it was too lengthy, and as its form deviated from that of conciliar decrees. He would advise that a selection of these chapters be made for discussion which seemed most necessary, and that the deputation

---

1 The Acts and Decrees of the Vatican Council fill volume VII of the great Collectio Laceusis.

on matters of Faith then elaborate an exposition of the Faith and submit it to the Council for approval.[2]

The discussions on the Schema concerning Catholic Doctrine as opposed to the principal errors of the times, being finished in the Forty-Sixth Congregation, the Third Public Session of the Council was called for April 24, 1870. About four and one-half months had been consumed in accomplishing such a small part of the matter proposed to the Council. Immediately after the solemn promulgation of the Constitutio Dogmatica De Fide Catholica, a large number of the Fathers were permitted to leave for home. Some had been excused from further attendance on the sessions of the Council two months previous, among them the American Bishops Melcher, Hogan, Lamy, Feehan and O'Gorman. These prelates received leave to return to their dioceses on account of the urgent wants of their new ecclesiastical districts.

On March 6, 1870, Archbishop Kenrick directed a letter from Rome to his faithful friend, Vicar-General Muehlsiepen, in which he gave expression to his feeling of weariness and dissatisfaction:

"Most of us are very tired of Rome, and would willingly leave it. The Council has been now three months in session, and nothing has been done. The body is too big for work, unless divided into sections; and those who had the management of matters were, and are, unwilling to attend to the suggestions made to them by those who had experience in similar assemblies. Should you ever come across an article which appeared in the Moniteur of Paris, about three weeks ago, you will find a detailed and realistic account of what has been the character of our proceedings and the cause of their insuccess.

"The regulations first made have been found insufficient, new ones have been promulgated; with what results remains to be seen. They appear to many, among whom I count myself, to be highly objectionable, and scarcely reconcilable with the liberty a Council should have. Their immediate effect is to suspend our ordinary general congregations, of which we have had three or four every week. In the last twelve days we have had none; and it is said that two or three weeks more may elapse before we be again summoned to meet.

"The Council appears to have been convoked for the special purpose of defining the Papal Infallibility and enacting the propositions of the Syllabus as general laws of the Church. Both objects are deemed by a minority, of which I am one, inexpedient and dangerous, and are sure to meet with serious resistance. The minds of both parties are considerably excited; and there is every reason to fear, that the Council, instead of uniting with the Church those already separ-

---

[2] Archbishop Kenrick had taken the same stand on a similar occasion at the Second Plenary Council of Baltimore.

ated from it, will cause divisions among ourselves most detrimental to Catholic interests. Let us pray that the Providence of God may over-rule the passions of men.''[3]

The next subject to be treated by the Council was the Schema De Ecclesia. This Schema, in its original form, treated (1) of the Church as the Living Body of Christ, (2) of the Pope as the Head of the Church, (3) of the relations existing between the Church and Civil Society. But in accordance with Archbishop Kenrick's sugges-tion, though not in consequence of it, the Presiding Cardinals sub-stituted that part of the matter which seemed most important to them, and to many Fathers of the Council. As early as Christmas day, 1869, the Archbishop of Malines had made use of his privilege to call for the immediate treatment of the Supreme Power in the Church.

The doctrine of Papal Infallibility is clearly announced in the Archbishop's proposal, though the word itself it not used. In the meantime Archbishop Manning was busy getting the signatures of some four hundred Fathers of the Council to a petition for the dog-matic decision on the Infallibility of the Pope. This petition was sent to the Presiding Cardinal on January 28, 1870, to be submitted to His Holiness. The petition had its intended effect. Instead of the original Schema De Ecclesia Christi, the Constitutio Prima De Ecclesia Christi, containing a brief introduction and three chapters on the Primacy of the Supreme Pontiff and a fourth chapter on His Infallibility was submitted.[4]

It seems now that the storm which had been raging around the Council Chamber raised a serious disturbance among the Fathers in Council assembled. There was a comparatively small, but very able and tireless minority, whose members opposed the definition of the Infallibility of the Pope, who, however, were held together, not on a fixed principle of accord, but by an agreement to defeat, if possible, the majority of the so-called infallibilists.

To analyze the constituent parts of this body we shall, with Cardi-nal Gibbons, class them according to ideas:

---

3   Original in Archdiocesan Chancery of St. Louis.

4   Before the opening of the Vatican Council Archbishop Kenrick's stand on Papal Infallibility was substantially that of his brother, the Archbishop of Baltimore: ''That way of speaking is not approved, according to which the Pope is declared to be infallible of himself alone; for scarcely any Catholic theologian is known to have claimed for him as a private teacher the privilege of inerrancy. Neither as Pope is he alone, since to him teaching, the college of bishops gives its adhesion, which, it is plain, has always happened. But no orthodox writer would deny that pontifical definitions accepted by the college of bishops, whether in council or in their sees, either by subscribing decrees, or by offering no objection to them, have full force and infallible authority.'' Theol-ogia Dogmatica, quam concinnavit Franciscus Patricius Kenrick, vol. I, p. 241, 242.

"The first class comprised those, who, believing the doctrine themselves, or at least favoring it speculatively, did not think it capable of definition, not deeming the tradition of the Church clear enough on this point.

"A second class, the most numerous, regarded the definition as possible, but practically fraught with peril to the Church, as impeding conversions, as exasperating to governments. For the sake of peace, and for the good of souls, they would not see it proclaimed as of faith.

"All of these dissident prelates," adds the gentle Cardinal, the last survivor of the Council, "acted with conscientious conviction of the justice of the cause they defended. They were bound in conscience to declare their opinions, and to make them prevail by all lawful influence. If on one side or the other of this most important and vital question, they went beyond the limits of moderation, or used means not dictated by prudence or charity, it is nothing more than might have been expected in so large a number of persons, of such varied character and education."[5]

Our own Archbishop Kenrick was a member of this party, and in particular, one of the first class, as described by the Cardinal, favoring Papal Infallibility speculatively, as a theological opinion, but one not capable of definition."

We, the Church's children of a later day, for whom the clear, concise and comprehensive definition of the Vatican Council has removed all doubt, and most difficulties, may wonder, how a churchman of Archbishop Kenrick's undoubted loyalty, genuine piety and strict orthodoxy could stand up before the assembled Bishops of the world, to oppose the doctrine of the Pope's infallibility; for oppose it he did, though not to the point of absolute denial. Archbishop Kenrick was too strong and outspoken a character to fear the possible effects of a truth, when he was convinced that it was a truth. He cannot, therefore, be called a mere opportunist, as some would have him considered. He held that the doctrine was not as yet sufficiently clear, nor firmly established in the consciousness of the Church to merit a dogmatic definition. In this sense he might have been called an inopportunist. On listening, however, to the arguments of the opposition leaders, a number of whom were really great and good men, and himself revolving in his mind the numerous historical facts that seemed to contradict the opinion of the doctrine's defenders, an honest doubt arose in his mind, whether the Pope could judge securely and infallibly, unless he acted in union with the Universal Church, of which the Bishops were divinely appointed spokesman.[6]

---

5 Life of Cardinal Gibbons, by Allen Sinclair Will, vol. I, p. 126.

6 On the title page of his *Concio* Archbishop Kenrick quoted the words of Sacred Scripture, "O Timothee, depositum custodi, devitans profanas vocum novi-

Of course there never was the least doubt in the Archbishop's mind, that infallibility was present in an ecumenical Council, where the Head and the Members, the Pope and the Bishops, concurred in rendering a decision on Faith or Morals. Nor did he ever doubt, that, if the Pope spoke as Head of the Church, even without the Concurrence of the Bishops, his decision was infallible, if the Bishops of the world accepted it within reasonable time. *"Roma locuta, causa finita."* All this the great Archbishop saw as plainly as any one. But what he does not seem to have seen for a time was that the Pope's decisions must be infallible in themselves or, as the Council expressed it, *"ex sese, non ex consensu Ecclesiae irreformabiles."* Yet such is the fact. For if the Pope could err in official decisions on Faith or Morals, whilst the Bishops of the Church, either in Council assembled, or dispersed throughout the world, faithfully held to the truth, the seamless garment of the Church would be rent asunder, the unity of faith would be lost.

The debate on the Fourth Chapter of the First Constitution on the Church, which treats of the Pope's Infallibility was begun immediately after the third public session. A very large number of the Fathers announced their intention to address the Council on the question. Archbishop Kenrick at first intended to maintain silence, as he "took for granted anything pertinent to the subject would be more fully and forcibly said by others." But as Archbishop Cullen of Dublin, a member of the deputation on matters of Faith, had from the pulpit said some things in which the American Prelate's honor was sorely wounded, he felt obliged to answer his charges, and, as he was not permitted to reply at once, he joined the long series of the Fathers who had asked and received permission to make an address at the proper time. This happened in the Fifty-fifth General Conference, May 20.

Archbishop Kenrick attended the long succession of Congregations or meetings of the Council and listened attentively to the exhaustive and often exhausting streams of eloquence for and against the matter proposed. Cardinal Gibbons, then only Bishop Gibbons, describes him in a few choice words in his *"Retrospect of Fifty Years*: "Archbishop Kenrick of St. Louis was among the most noteworthy prelates from the United States. Archbishop Kenrick spoke

---

tates et oppositiones falsi nominis scientiae, quam quidam promittentes circa fidem exciderunt. I Tim., 6-20, 21 intimating thus that the doctrine of Papal Infallibility did not belong to the depositum fidei. By adding the dictum of Paschasius Radbertus, "Not upon Peter alone, but upon all the apostles and successors of the apostles was the Church of God founded," Lib. VIII, in Matt. 16, he intimated that the entire college of Bishops, with the Pope as the head, was the true seat of infallibility.

Latin with most admirable ease and elegance. I observed him, day after day, reclining in his seat with half-closed eyes, listening attentively to the debates, without taking any notes. And yet so tenacious was his memory that, when his turn came to ascend the rostrum, he reviewed the speeches of his colleagues with remarkable fidelity and precision without the aid of manuscript or memoranda.''[7]

The meetings were held during the hours between 9 and 12 in the morning. The afternoons and evenings were free, for rest, study and social calls. Archbishop Kenrick's secretary, Father Constantine Smith, has left us a fine description of what occupied the minds of the opposition members of the Council.

''Frequent meetings of various shades of opinion as to the opportuneness or the inopportuneness of the definition of the Papal Infallibility were now held outside the Council chamber. Effectually, Rome was divided into two camps. For three months, the greatest intellectual men of the Church were almost equally divided against each other.

Manning, the consummate ecclesiastical statesman, rather than the profound theologian, in virtue of his great eloquence, controlled in a masterful way the forces of the infallibilists. With him were the Bishops of Malines, Ratisbonne and Paderborn. The chief among the French opponents were Dupanloup and Darboy; also Cardinal Mathieu and Bonnechose. The chief Austrian opponents were Cardinals Schwarzenberg and Rauscher and Bishop Strossmayer. Bishop Hefele headed the German opposition. Archbishop Kenrick stood at the head of the opponents belonging to the American episcopate. But there was one man, not attending the Council, not a Cardinal, not a Bishop, who wielded among English-speaking peoples an influence more potent, though silent, against the definition of the dogma of the infallibility than any other, viz., John Henry Newman, afterwards created a Cardinal.

After three months of debate, during which period, the intellectual forces were equally divided, after the intellectual opponents had exhausted every lawful method of debate, every resource that could be devised; after every argument, philosophical, scriptural, social, moral, civil, had been exhausted in trying to defeat or even postpone the definition, on this 13th of July the contest ended, the most memorable that had ever taken place in the annals of ecclesiastical history. It was well. Both sides acknowledged that no more could be done; God alone could decide it. Up to this, for His own wise ends, God permitted the full play of human reason, often swayed by deepest feeling. But now the Divine illumination came.''[8]

---

[7] Cardinal Gibbons, Retrospect of Fifty Years, vol. I, p. 32.

[8] The Catholic Standard and Times, Philadelphia, March 21, 1896.

But before this final act, Archbishop Kenrick took a step that was to bring upon him the harsh judgment of many Catholics and the still more disagreeable plaudits of the secretaries and so-called liberals, without accomplishing the least practical result. One hundred and eleven Fathers had announced their intention to address the Council: Forty-six had spoken by the beginning of July. Sixty-five names were still on the list. Dark war-clouds had arisen on the horizon; if the question of Papal Infallibility were not acted upon within a short time, the whole matter would have to rest in abeyance. The honor of the Church required that the center of unity, the Divine institution of the Papacy, should not receive such a terrible setback. The vast majority of Fathers was in favor of the definition of the infallibility of the Supreme Pontiff. The members of the opposition were using dilatory tactics. In the Eighty-second Congregation held July 4, the Presiding Cardinal suggested that the Fathers who were still booked to speak, should renounce their right. All the orators, excepting two, acquiesced. There were four hundred and sixty-nine Fathers present at this Congregation. Archbishop Kenrick was not present and thereby lost his right to speak. But he was determined to bring his views to the knowledge of the Fathers of the Council. He sent his Secretary, Father Smith, to Naples to supervise the publication of his pamphlet entitled, *"Concio Petri Ricardi Kenrick, Archiepiscopi S. Ludovici in Statibus Foederatis Americae Septentrionalis in Concilio Vaticano Habenda at non Habita, Naples, 1870."*[9] This publication was intended for the Fathers only, but to be circulated outside the Council chamber. It was in substance a belated attempt to refute the strictures, Archbishop Cullen of Dublin and Archbishop Manning of Westminister had made on his objections to the Schema on the Church of Christ.

In his Concio Archbishop Kenrick speaks in the highest terms of admiration of these two distinguished churchmen: "It was with great delight that I listened to the recent speech of the Archbishop of Westminister in this assembly. I was at a loss which most to admire, the eloquence of the man, or his fiery zeal in moving or rather commanding us to enact the new definition. The lucid arrangement of topics, the absolute felicity of diction, the singular grace of elocution and the supreme authority and candor of mind which was resplendent in his speech almost extorted from me the exclamation: *'Talis cum sis, utinam noster esses.'* "

Archbishop Kenrick's Concio is not so much an attack upon the Pope's Infallibility, as rather a defense of the infallibility of the Bishop's united with the Pope. It has become one of the rarest of

---

[9] Cf. Granderath, S. J., Geschichte des Vatikanischen Konzils, vol. III, ch. 10, pp. 288-292.

books: however, it is reprinted in Professor Friederich's *Documenta and Illustrandum Concilium Vaticanum.* The American Tract Society published an English translation, edited by Leonard Woolsey Bacon.

The decisive moment came on July 13. The Eighty-fifth general Congregation, which was attended by six hundred and one Conciliar Fathers, four hundred and fifty-one voted, Placet; eighty-three, Non placet, and sixty-two: Placet Juxta modum. The question had been decided by an overwhelming majority; the minority realized that their cause, so bravely and skillfully defended, was lost: but not convinced of the opposite view, they decided to absent themselves from the final public session on July 18. By order of the Pope, the Secretary read the Constitutio Dogmatica Prima De Ecclesia Christi, and then invited the Fathers to give their vote, either Placet or Non Placet. All but two voted, Placet; and these two immediately after the definition gave in their adhesion.[10]

The Holy Father then rose and confirmed the Constitution with his supreme authority, and addressed a few touching words to the assembled Fathers: "The highest authority of the Roman Pontiff does not oppress but erect, does not destroy but builds up, and frequently confirms in dignity, unites in charity and strengthens and supports the rights of the Bishops. Therefore, those who now judge in a state of commotion, should know that a few years hence, they who once held the contrary judgment will abound in our judgment, and then they will judge *"in spiritu aurae lenis."*[11] How beautifully these prophetic words of Pio Nono were fulfilled in the case of Archbishop Kenrick, we shall see in the following chapter.

---

10 Only two Bishops voted *Non Placet,* one of them was Bishop Fitzgerald of Little Rock. But both Bishops immediately accepted the dogma, Bishop Fitzgerald saying to the Pope: "Now I believe, Most Holy Father."

11 Granderath, vol. III, p. 500.

## Chapter 42

# ARCHBISHOP KENRICK'S SUBMISSION TO THE VATICAN DECREES

After the promulgation of the infallible teaching authority of the Roman Pontiff in the Fourth open session of the Council the participants received permission to absent themselves until November 11, on which day the discussion of the remaining schemata should be taken up. The work of the deputations, however, was to continue throughout the summer months. But it appeared before long that this plan could not be carried out. On July 19 the war between Germany and France broke out, and at the withdrawal of the French garrison from Rome, the troops of Victor Emmanuel took possession of the Eternal City. Under these circumstances the Pope, on October 20, suspended the sessions of the Council.

Archbishop Kenrick had left Rome with the other members of the minority, sad at heart and undecided as to what his future course should be. There were some men of honored name who tried to draw him into open rebellion against what had now been declared a dogma of Faith. But those who knew that Archbishop Kenrick never failed to make his daily meditation, had no fear for him in this regard. Such a man of prayer would not follow in the footsteps of a Doellinger or a Reinkens. Yet the future looked dark and perplexing.

On his homeward journey this spiritual conflict was carried to the proper conclusion. The cause for which he had fought during the Council was, after all, only a part of the truth: the infallibility of the Bishops in union with the Pope. According to the decision of the Council where Pope and Bishops had acted in unison, the full truth was the infallibility of the Pope, not only when speaking by advice or consent of the episcopate, but always when speaking ex cathedra, and defining a doctrine of Faith or Morals for the universal church. Practically the Archbishop had always held this to be true, though not satisfied with the reasons put forward to prove it. But the Council had spoken; and the Catholic world had, to all appearances, accepted the decision as final. Most of the opponents had submitted to the decision. As for the objections he had urged against the doctrine, and which he still considered true, he had to admit they were not conclusive, and hence, as mere difficulties, he should not allow them to raise a single doubt in his mind, now that the Council had spoken. The dogma, no matter by what means it was brought to a passage, was clearly a truth of Divine revelation.

This course of reasoning is but the interpretation of the Archbishop's own words, addressed to Lord Acton: "Sufficient time seems to have elapsed to allow the Catholic world to decide whether or not the decrees of the Council were to be accepted. The greater number of Bishops in minority had signified their assent to them. Among other names published in one of the Brussels papers, I read with surprise that of Mgr. Maret. Although some still held out, they were so few that hesitating to declare my submission would have had the appearance of rejecting the authority of the Church. THIS I NEVER INTENDED TO DO. I could not defend the Council or its action; but I always professed that the acceptance of either by the Church would supply its deficiency. I accordingly made up my mind to submit to what appeared inevitable, unless I were prepared to separate myself, at least in the judgment of most Catholics, from the Church."[1]

The Archbishop arrived in St. Louis on December 31st, 1870, after an absence of more than fourteen months. His return was quiet and unobtrusive, as he had declined a public reception. Yet an ecclesiastical reception was arranged for the following Sunday. It was held at St. John's Church, and all the bells of the Catholic Churches of the city were rung in honor of the occasion. An address was read by the Vicar-General, Very Rev. P. J. Ryan, in St. John's Church, in the presence of many of the secular and regular clergy of the diocese. The Archbishop responded feelingly, saying: "To that portion of the address which refers to my course in the Vatican Council, I have this to say: Up to the very period of that Council I had held as a theological opinion what that Council has decreed to be an article of Christian Faith, and yet I was opposed, most strongly, to the definition. I knew that the misconceptions of its real character would be an obstacle in the way of the diffusion of Catholic truth. At least I thought so. I feared, in certain parts of Europe especially, that such a definition might lead to the danger of schism in the Church; and on more closely examining the question itself, in its intrinsic evidence, I was not convinced of the conclusiveness of the arguments by which it was sustained, or of its compatibility with certain well ascertained facts of ecclesiastical history which rose up strongly before my mind. These were the motives of my opposition. The motive of my submission is simply and singly the authority of the Catholic Church. That submission is a most reasonable obedience, because of the necessity of obeying and following an authority established by God; and having the guaranty of our Divine Savior's perpetual assistance is in

---

[1] The letter of Archbishop Kenrick to Lord Acton was first published in Prof. Schulte's "Der Altkatholizismus" Giessen, 1887. It was republished in the St. Louis daily papers on March 29, 1891.

itself evidence, and cannot be gainsayed by any one who professes to recognize Jesus Christ as his Savior and his God.

"Simply and singly on that authority I yield obedience and full and unreserved submission to the definition concerning the character of which there can be no doubt as emanating from the Council and subsequently accepted by the greater part even of those who were in the minority on that occasion. In yielding this submission, I say to the Church in the words of Peter and of Paul, "To whom, O Holy Mother, shall we go, but to thee? Thou hast the words of eternal life; and we have believed and have known that Thou art the Pillar and the Ground of Truth."[2]

Some theologians found fault with the phrase, "*simply and singly on the authority of the Church I yield obedience and unreserved sub-mission to the definition*," as if the Archbishop meant only an ex-terior act without an interior conviction. This was a rank injustice, as implying that he, for the sake of being left in place, consented to say what he did not believe. As Archbishop Ryan wrote in his brief Memorial on the death of his friend: "Submission to a doctrine means believing it, and without such faith submission were hypocrisy, of which no man ever dared to accuse the departed prelate."[3] The writer then goes on to prove the Archbishop's absolute sincerity by quoting the introductory words of his address on the occasion of his home-coming: "Up to the very period of the assembling of the Coun-cil I had held as a theological opinion what that council had decreed to be an *article of Christian Faith*."[4] But how did the Archbishop surmount the historical difficulties that seemed to stand in the way of his sincerely accepting the truth of the definition. Let us consider his own explanation:

"I reconciled myself intellectually to submission by applying Father Newman's theory of development to the case in point. The pontifical authority, as at present exercised, is so different from what it is supposed to have been in the early Church, that it can only be supposed in substance by allowing a process of doctrinal development. This principle removed Newman's great difficulty, and convinced him that, notwithstanding the difference, he might and should become a Catholic. I thought that it might justify me in remaining one. The positive arguments supplied by tradition for the power as actually exercised are not stronger than those brought forward by the advo-

---

2 Cf. The Two Archbishops Kenrick, by John J. O'Shea, pp. 332 and 333. O'Shea's sketch of Peter Richard Kenrick is a poorly written compilation, but contains a number of important documents.

3 American Catholic Quarterly Review, vol. XXI, p. 427.

4 Ibidem, p. 428.

cates of papal infallibility; nor is it easier to reconcile the Acts of the Fifth Council in reference to Vigilius with the one, than the condemnation of Honorius by the Sixth with the other.''[5] And again: "I submitted most *unreservedly*, not availing myself of any of the ingenious explications of the dogma, set forth by Mr. Maskell, but taking the words of the decree in their strict and literal significance.''[6]

But how shall we reconcile these clear-cut statements with the following words from the same letter: "I gave as the motive of my submission 'Simply and singly' the authority of the Church by which I was well understood to mean that the act was one of pure obedience, and was not grounded on the removal of my motives of opposition to the decree as referred to in my reply, and set forth in my pamphlets.''[7]

In order to understand the full import of this declaration, we must make a distinction. There is a difference between the motives of Catholic Faith, and the motives of credibility of a doctrine. The motive of Faith can be but one, the revelation of God made known to us by the infallible authority of the Church. The motives of credibility are many and manifold, some appealing to one, some to another mind; the motive of faith refers to the revealed truths, the motives of credibility to the fact of revelation; the motive of faith produces absolute certitude, the *motiva credibilitatis* only moral certitude. Now, in Archbishop Kenrick's pamphlets published at the time of the Council, the motives of credibility advanced by his opponents in favor of papal infallibility were attacked as either insufficient or utterly worthless. But the promulgation of the infallible teaching authority of the Pope by the Council furnished an all-sufficient motive of credibility as well as the true and only motive of Christian Faith: "It is revealed doctrine."

In one particular, and that a very important one, the Archbishop candidly admits having made a mistake in his argument. "My statement, to which your Lordship refers, that Papal Infallibility could not become an article of faith even by the definition of the Council

---

[5] Letter to Lord Acton. Concerning Pope Vigilius, who approved the Acts of the Fifth Council, condemning the teachings of Theodore of Mopsuestia, after he had refused to attend the sessions of the Council. Pope Honorius was condemned by the Sixth Council for a letter he was supposed to have written to Sergius on the two operations in Christ, not defining the question, but counselling silence. In both cases the question of Papal Infallibility was supposed to have been denied. But the case of Vigilus militated against the infallibility of the Council, as much as the case of Honorius did against the infallibility of the Pope. The fact is that neither case had anything to do with an ex cathedra pronouncement.

[6] Letter to Lord Acton.

[7] Letter to Lord Acton.

resolves itself into two others; namely that what is not already a doctrine of faith cannot be made so by a conciliar definition, and that papal infallibility, anterior to the definition, was not an article of faith. The first of these propositions is undeniable. The second, it appears, must be given up. My proof of the second was incomplete, as it chiefly referred to countries where the English language is spoken. Even in regard to these countries it does not appear to be satisfactory, as the principles recognized by the ecclesiastical authorities, in such countries, and generally entertained by the faithful in them, appear to establish the contrary. The power of the Pope in doctrinal matters was universally recognized as a rule of faith; nor was this principle materially affected by the tacit assent of the Church, which even Gallican divines, held to be sufficient to give his decision all the weight of conciliar definitions.''[8]

Whether the Archbishop was right in rejecting all and sundry motives of credibility urged by his opponents is not the question here. He may have been mistaken and, in some cases, certainly was mistaken; but the removal of his motive of opposition to the decrees, as set forth in his pamphlets, was not required to enable him to make a sincere and genuine act of faith in the decrees after their approval.

Archbishop Kenrick's letter to Lord Action does sound one discordant note, in saying: ''Notwithstanding my submission, I shall never teach the doctrine of papal infallibility, so as to assure from Scripture or tradition in its support, and shall leave to others to explain its compatibility with the facts of ecclesiastical history, to which I referred in my reply. As long as I may be permitted to remain in my present station, I shall confine myself to administrative functions, which I can do the more easily without attracting observation, as for some years back I have seldom preached.''

''I have steadfastly refused to publish a Pastoral Letter on the Council, although urged thereto by one of my suffragans, by the Archbishop of San Francisco and indirectly, through the suffragan bishop referred to, by Cardinal Barnabo. I have also declined to write to the Pope, although the last named (Barnabo, in sending me some marriage dispensations for which I had asked, invited me to do so. I have also refused to take any part in the demonstrations which have been made generally in the United States in favor of the Temporal Power, and my name is not found among those which, in this city, prepared and sent to Rome an address to the Pope on the occasion of the Italian occupation of his territory.[9] I mention these cir-

---

8 Letter to Lord Acton. Strictly speaking, not an article of faith, but belonging to the deposit of Faith.

9 On June 25, 1871, the twenty-fifth anniversary of the elevation of Pope Pius IX to the chair of St. Peter was celebrated in the city of St. Louis with im-

cumstances to show your Lordship that in what I have done I have not been actuated by any desire to stand well with the Church authorties in Rome.''[10]

These last signs of Archbishop Kenrick's irritation do not refer to the dogma of papal infallibility, but rather to the manner in which it was secured. For he plainly states that he accepted the dogma unreservedly, "simply and singly on the authority of the Church." But how could he preach on the doctrine without touching "on the motiva credibilitatis?'' And these he did not consider to be convincing. For the same reason, a Pastoral on the Council seemed out of question. As for writing to the Pope or protesting against the spoliation of Rome by the Italians, the Archbishop thought he had no particular reason, especially as his doing so, would have been interpreted by many as a measure inspired by fear. He felt that he had done no more than was his right and duty in the matter, and that he had no apology to offer. We can understand the Archbishop's feelings under such trying circumstances. Yet it would have seemed more consonant with the greatness of his mind if he had, like Fenelon, the Archbishop of Cambrai, under similar circumstances, immediately ascended the pulpit to condemn his pamphlets and throw them into the fire; but the intense and almost unbearable strain of his conciliar activities had seriously reduced his vitality and rendered his nerves all too sensitive. Besides there was a special occasion for the regrettable outbreak.

Archbishop Kenrick's letter to Lord Action is dated March 29, 1871. More than two months previous he had written his letter of submission to the Cardinal Prefect of the Propaganda, Barnabo. So all requirements seemed fulfilled to place or rather leave Archbishop Kenrick in good standing with the Head of the Church. Only the *Concio* published in Naples in the heat of combat, seemed to threaten a new storm. The pamphlet had been submitted to the Congregation of the Index, and had been condemned as containing grave errors, but through personal consideration had not appeared among the list of prohibited works. Cardinal De Angelis exhorted Kenrick to anticipate its public condemnation by adhering strictly to the decrees of the Council. Pope Pius himself is reported to have said to the Rector of the American College when he announced to him the Archbishop's submission: "Still he must retract those pamphlets pub-

---

posing ceremonies. There was a parade of Catholic societies four miles in length and a general illumination of the city at night. Bonfires and pyrotechnic displays were also features of the demonstration of loyalty to the Holy Father. The Archbishop was not in the city on that day.

10  Letter to Lord Acton.

lished at Naples.''[11] If the Pope really said this, he certainly made no great effort to obtain this retraction. But the rumors were irritating. The Pamphlets did not get on the Index of Forbidden Books and their author was never again reminded of them. Pope Pius was later on reported to have said: ''Mgr. Kenrick is a great man, but he is as pious as he is great, and he is as orthodox as he is pious and great.''[12] And still later, Pope Leo XIII, according to the account of Cardinal Gibbons, uttered this beautiful and in the main just judgment on Archbishop Kenrick:

''The metropolitan of St. Louis was a noble man and a true Christian Bishop. When he sat in Council as a judge of the Faith, he did according to his conscience, and the moment the decision was taken, although it was against him, submitted with the filial piety of a Catholic Christian.''[13]

---

11   Letter to Lord Acton.
12   Cardinal Gibbons Retrospect of Fifty Years, vol. I, p. 32.
13   A. C. Will, Life of Cardinal Gibbons, vol. I, p. 129.

## CHAPTER 43

## ARCHBISHOP KENRICK'S TWO CHIEF ASSISTANTS

During his long stay in Rome in 1870 Archbishop Kenrick, as a matter of course, visited the Cardinal Prefect of the Propaganda, his immediate Superior, to render an account of the condition and progress of his diocese. Among other things the Archbishop expressed a desire for a coadjutor. He was now in his sixty-fifth year, and had by his manifold labors in the cause of holy Church, certainly merited the *otium cum dignitate*. Father Constantine Smith has left us the following account of this interesting episode: "An intimation was sent to him through the Propaganda for him to assemble the Archbishops of the United States and the Bishops of his province to choose a coadjutor with right of succession. I accompanied him to the American College, where the assemblage took place. After the election, as he entered the carriage, he remarked to me: "They have given me the man of my choice, Father Ryan of St. Louis." I said to him: "Should the votes of the St. Louis priests be taken, their choice would have been the same." "He is a man" said he, "of many gifts, but his quality of heart I prize most."[1] This event took place towards the end of the Council. But the official act of appointment by Propaganda was delayed for about a year. Early in March 1872 the news of Father Ryan's appointment was published in the daily papers of St. Louis. "Archbishop Kenrick has been officially notified by the Holy See of the appointment of Father Ryan. It was made at the Archbishop's instance, with the affirmative votes of all the Bishops of the Province, and Archbishops of the country. The time for the ceremony of consecration has not been fixed on, as the "Bulls" have not arrived, but are now on the way. Due notice will be given of the ceremony. The appointment is made with the right of succession."[2]

On the last day of March 1872 the papers brought the welcome news: "The consecration of Very Rev. Father·Ryan as Bishop of Tricomia in Partibus will take place on Sunday the 14th inst., at St. John's church. Father Ryan will now have new duties and new responsibilities for the display of the estimable qualities which have ever characterized his conduct and won for him the esteem and affection of all who know him."[3]

---

1 Father Constantine Smith in "Globe Democrat," reprinted in "The Catholic Standard and Times," Philadelphia, March 21, 1896.

2 "Western Watchman," March, 1872.

3 "Western Watchman," March 31, 1872.

The consecration of Bishop Patrick Ryan was duly performed by Archbishop Kenrick on Sunday, April 14th, at St. John's Church. Thousands of the young prelate's friends filled and surrounded the procathedral to witness the ceremony. Archbishop Hennessey of Dubuque preached the sermon. The praises of the new bishop were on all lips: His devotion to prayer and study, his labors during the war for the prisoners in Gratiot Street Prison, his many conversions effected among them, his great kindness of heart to all, and his wonderful eloquence. Few churchmen have ever received such genuine and universal praise as the Coadjutor-Bishop to Archbishop Kenrick, and the happiest man of the occasion was the old Archbishop himself.

From that day on Bishop Ryan performed all the episcopal functions, whilst he shared with Father Muehlsiepen, the Vicar-General for the German part of it, the government of the archdiocese. The supreme direction of affairs, however, both in temporal and spiritual matters, was retained by the Archbishop. During the fourteen months of his administratorship of the Archdiocese and the following fourteen months prior to his Episcopal consecration, Father Ryan had ample opportunity for gaining the experience requisite in a bishop. He had visited the most remote parts of the archdiocese, laying corner stones for new churches, blessing them when finished, preaching and lecturing at home and abroad, and getting acquainted with priests and people. In 1870 the Administrator performed six functions of this kind and established five new parishes: the Immaculate Conception at Iron Mountain, St. Gertrude's at Krakow, the Visitation at Vienna, St. Maurus at Biehle, and St. Francis de Sales at Lebanon. At the end of the year 1870 the Archdiocese numbered twenty-four parish churches in the city and ninety outside of the City of St. Louis, and about thirty missions or stations. The number of priests was one hundred and seventy-three secular and regular.

In 1871 the Archbishop ordained three priests for the Archdiocese, the last of whom was the Rev. Francis F. Kueper. Three new parishes were established in the City of St. Louis, the Sacred Heart, St. Agatha's and St. Bonaventure's, an early Italian Church on Sixth and Spruce Streets. In the country five new parishes were established in 1871: St. John's at Rock Creek, St. Joseph's at Canton, the Assumption at O'Fallon, the Annunciation at California and St. Francis Regis at Westport.

On May 19th, 1872, Bishop Patrick John Ryan held his first ordination, Father Peter Bremerich, John Van Krevel, S. J., John Ring, O. S. F., and Clementine Deymann, O. S. F., being the first priests ordained by him. Two more ordinations followed in 1872, on September 8th, and November 10th. Four new churches were blessed during the year, either by Bishop Ryan or Vicar-General Muehlsiepen: the Church of St. Charles at St. Charles was consecrated by the Coadjutor. Six new parishes were established: St. Lawrence at Lawrenceton, St. Patrick's at Holden, St. Columbkille's at Carondelet, Our Lady of Mount Carmel at Baden, the Annunciation at Kansas City, and St. Peter's at Marshall, Saline County.

The corner stone for the new and permanent Church of the Annunciation in Kansas City was laid in September 1872 by Bishop Ryan. Confirmation was administered to more than eighty children in the temporary church. Father William Dalton had made all preparations for the imposing celebration.[4]

On August 10th, the Coadjutor Bishop dedicated the fine rock church on Grand Avenue to the Honor of God and St. Alphonsus. On December 8th, Bishop Ryan laid the cornerstone of the new St. Louis Hospital on Montgomery Street in charge of the Sisters of Charity. The total Catholic population of the St. Louis Archdiocese was estimated at one hundred and seventy thousand, distributed in one hundred and twenty-eight parishes, and thirty-nine stations. As eleven of these parishes were vacant, ordinations were held in 1873, on six distinct occasions, by which five secular priests, and four members of religious orders were added to the clergy of the archdiocese. Bishop Ryan blessed three new churches, and Vicar-General Muehlsiepen laid the corner stone of two others. Three new parishes were established. St. Joseph's at Cottleville, St. John the Baptist in Moberly, Mary the Help of Christians at Lowell.[5]

A confirmation visit of Bishop Ryan to Lexington is fondly described by a correspondent of the *Western Watchman* of June 28th:

"Our Catholic friends have been holding a grand jubilee the last day or two in connection with the visit of Rt. Rev. Bishop Ryan of St. Louis. On Thursday evening St. Joseph's total Abstinence and Benevolent Society in full regalia with their magnificent gold and silken banner floating over them and headed by the Lexington Silver Cornet Band, marched to the river, met the distinguished prelate and escorted his carriage to the church. Here Hon. James O'Gorman, in behalf of the congregation, delivered a feeling and appropriate address of welcome. The Bishop responded briefly, thanking the members of the church and society for their kindness, stating that he had nowhere else in the state ever received such an ovation, and assuring them, that he would remember it with pleasure for many years to come. The ceremonies yesterday were solemn, impressive and sublime. High mass was celebrated at ten o'clock by Rev. Francis Graham of Sedalia: Deacon Rev. J. T. D. Murphy of Marshall; Subdeacon Rev. Francis

---

4  Chancery Records, and Newspaper Reports.
5  Chancery Records.

O'Reilly of Plattsburg, Master of Ceremonies Rev. John Fitzgerald of Edina. The other priests in attendance were Rev. Father Hamill of Irish Settlement, Saline County, Rev. Father Niedekorn, S. J. of Westphalia; Rev. J. Hayes of Carrollton; and Rev. J. Phelan of Warrensburg. The church was densely crowded. Over two hundred persons were confirmed. At the conclusion of the imposing ceremonies Bishop Ryan delivered an eloquent and beautiful sermon. The visitors were warm in their praises of the pastor, Rev. Father Hoog, for his zealous and effective labors in the upbuilding of his congregation. The occasion will be long and fondly remembered by every Catholic who attended, as the grandest religious ceremonial that ever took place in our city.''[6]

Among the other works of religion and charity that held the lively interest of Bishop Ryan at this time, were the building and completion of the Parochial School at St. John's Church, that monument of his pastoral zeal and love for the children of his immediate flock; then the Church of St. Elizabeth for the Colored Catholics of St. Louis; the establishment and development of the Catholic Protectory for wayward boys at Glencoe; and the upbuilding of St. Boniface's Hospital in Carondelet, and of the Hospital-chapel of the Little Sisters of the Poor. In regard to the Catholic Protectory the *Western Watchman* brought the following editorial:

''We have much pleasure in announcing to our readers this week that the Board of the Catholic Protectorate have at last secured the services of a priest to manage and control the affairs of that institution. With the consent of the Archbishop, and at the earnest request of Bishop Ryan, Father O'Reilly of the Immaculate Conception Church, has accepted the position of collector, and we might add, general manager of the new institution. We can but express the earnest wish that his zealous efforts may be crowned with satisfactory results, and that under his direction the Catholic Protectorate may, in a short time, become an accomplished fact. In his letter of appointment Bishop Ryan assures the Catholics in St. Louis, that their donations will be received with gratitude, and will be scrupulously applied to what is truly the most important and most pressing of our charities. Father O'Reilly will enter immediately upon his arduous and responsible duties.''[7]

The Chapel of the Little Sisters of the Poor, situated on Nineteenth and Hebert Streets was dedicated on November 23rd, 1873, by the Coadjutor Bishop of St. Louis. In 1874 Bishop Ryan held four ordinations. Two of the priests ordained on September 22nd, were the well known Fathers Henry Schrage and Bernard Stemker, who had finished their

---

6 ''Western Watchman,'' June 28, 1873.

7 ''Western Watchman,'' November 15, 1873.

theological studies at Paderborn in Westphalia. On April 12th, 1874, the Coadjutor Bishop laid the corner stone of the third church of S. S. Peter and Paul, the present magnificent stone structure. A number of Catholic Societies honored the occasion by their presence. Father Louis Hinnsen of Belleville preached the German panegyric, and the Bishop himself addressed the assembled multitude in his mellifluous English: "And now you see rising around you a church which will be the largest and most splendid church of any denomination in the city. From having no school, you see the spacious schools that are around you, accommodating thirteen hundred children, and they have risen by your generosity and the indefatigable zeal of your pastor."[8]

On May 17th, the Church of Our Lady of Perpetual Help was dedicated by Vicar-General Muehlsiepen. As usual, the Catholic Societies of St. Louis turned out to honor the occasion. On Corpus Christi Day, June 4th, Bishop Ryan laid the corner stone of the new Church of St. Peter at St. Charles, Mo. This church when finished will be one of the largest and handsomest in the State, the cost being over forty thousand dollars. The parishioners, who are all farmers, have given in subscriptions enough already to pay the full amount, many giving from one thousand to fifteen hundred dollars. On July 5th, Bishop Ryan laid the corner stone of St. Joseph's Church, Edina, Mo. On this occasion he preached a grand and impressive sermon . . . In the evening the St. Joseph's and St. Boniface's Societies serenaded the Bishop and Hon. A. J. P. Garesche, who were guests of Father Fitzgerald.

On July 20th, the Coadjutor Bishop blessed the new St. Joseph's Church at Louisiana.

The new Church of the Immaculate Conception at Lexington was dedicated by Bishop Ryan on Sunday September 20th. The *Lexington Caucasian*, said of it:

"Father Hoog is energetically pushing the work on the stately and elegant Catholic Church, which rears its lofty front on 3rd Street, near the Bluffs. When completed it will be the largest and handsomest religious edifice in Western Missouri, an honor to the liberal people who have built it, and an ornament to our city of temples and schools. The wood-work now being done on the inside, is only intended to be temporary. The permanent interior finishing will cost $7000, and the entire cost will not fall far short of $50,000, most of which is already paid."[9]

Father Muehlsiepen's share of dedications was that of St. Anne's Church at French Village. In the city he laid the corner stone of St.

---

8  "Western Watchman," April 15, 1874.
9  "Lexington Caucasian," September 21, 1874.

Augustine's temporary brick church.   Father Henry Van der Sanden was now Chancellor of the Archdiocese.   The new foundations for the year 1874 were : St. Augustine's in St. Louis; St. Mary's at St. Mary's Landing; St. Henry's at Charleston and St. Bernard's in what was then Rock Spring.   The total number of priests was two hundred and ten, of parish churches one hundred and seven and of missions fifty-nine.

On August 4th, the apostle of Central Missouri, Father Helias died in calm old age at his post of duty, the parish of St. Francis Xavier at Taos.   About the middle of September 1874 Bishop Ryan, at the invitation of his dear friend, Bishop Hogan of St. Joseph, made a flying visit to a pair of noble foundations in that diocese, which were organized by Father James Power in the days when the northwestern territory of Missouri was still a part of the archdiocese, Maryville and Conception.

At Maryville, Mo., near St. Joseph, Mo., Bishop Ryan administered confirmation on Monday, September 5th.   The pastor at the time was Father Adelamus of the Order of St. Benedict, who came from Canton Unterwalden, Switzerland, to take charge of this congregation.

He was ably seconded in his efforts by five sisters of the Order of the Perpetual Adoration, who were also from Switzerland, and had charge of the schools.   These good sisters are from the convent of Reichenbach on the banks of Lake Thun, one of the most lovely and picturesque places in Central Switzerland.   From Maryville Bishop Ryan proceeded Monday evening to Conception.   The town of Conception, founded by Father J. Powers in the center of his colony was now the seat of a Benedictine Monastery and had a conventual church of high artistic beauty.

It was almost two years since the Bishop of St. Joseph had applied through the Abbot of St. Meinrad's Indiana, to the Abbot of Engelberg, Switzerland, for a colony of Benedictine Fathers to found a monastery and open missions in the diocese.   Immediately some Fathers came, and then some novices and scholastics and lay-brothers, and the sisters above mentioned, who are all now engaged in their respective duties, bringing down the blessing of God and the people upon him for changing the desert prairie of Missouri to bloom as a garden of roses.   Bishop Hogan, now, for the first time, came to visit this sacred refuge of peace and prayer in the wilderness.   Bishop Ryan accompanied him on the pilgrimage.''[10]

The ordinations of the year 1875 added five priests to the diocesan clergy.   Vicar-General Muehlsiepen blessed five new churches; Bishop Ryan on his part, blessing five and consecrating one, making a total of eleven new churches for the archdiocese.   Three new parishes were

---

10   ''Die Benediktiner in Conception, Mo.'' p. 5 s. s.

established in this year: St. Mary's at Adair, St. Joseph's at Pierce City; Our Lady of Perpetual Help at Weingarten. The archdiocese lost seven priests by death: but the total had grown to two hundred and twenty-nine. The Catholic population now numbered two hundred and fifty thousand. On June 4th, the following year 1876 Bishop Ryan ordained Fathers Peter Lotz, Lawrence Wernert, Henry Hukeskein, Francis Bettels, Patrick W. Tallon and Edward John Hamill, all for the archdiocese of St. Louis. The first four young men had made their theological studies at the Seminary of St. Francis near Milwaukee. Fathers Tallon and Hamill at Cape Girardeau. With them were ordained a large number of Jesuits and Franciscans.

Of church dedications held in 1876 that of St. Kevin's occurred on Sunday, February 13th, of the Church of the Holy Name on Sunday, October 29th, and of St. Theresa's Church on December 22nd. St. Kevin's later on became the third Parish of the Immaculate Conception in St. Louis. Its dedication was performed by Vicar-General Muehlsiepen. The Church of the Holy Name succeeded to the original Church of St. Thomas in Lowel.

Besides St. Kevin's, Father Muehlsiepen blessed St. Bernard's Church, Rock Springs on October 15th, and Our Lady of Help of Christians at Weingarten on October 29th. The chapel of the Catholic Protectory at Glencoe also was blessed by the Coadjutor Bishop. Concerning this special care of the good Bishop the *Western Watchman* of that day has the following description:

"Established four years ago under the care of the Christian Brothers, the Catholic Protectorate has been successful from the start, when it had a dozen boys. When the number increased to thirty, it was found impossible to take any more, the "Old Yeatman Property" having no more accommodations . . A move was then made to erect a large and better building . . . This is 185 feet long and three stories high, having room for 150 boys. Mr. James McGrath drew the plans. The massive walls of limestone, and the roof of slate, the ground plan is divided in play-rooms and a large bath. On the second floor are the school rooms and chapel, and on the third floor the dormitories."[11]

During the year 1876 death claimed four of the diocesan clergy: Fathers James Archer, M. S. Maddock, Henry Meurs and John Dougherty. The passing of Father James Archer, one of the special friends of Bishop Ryan, was truly edifying. He was taken sick in the confessional, ten o'clock Saturday night. It was not until midnight of Tuesday that he was made aware of his critical condition. When about 12 o'clock at night Bishop Ryan bade him prepare for the worst, he

---

[11] "Western Watchman," October 25, 1876.

resigned himself at once to the will of God. His Grace asked him if anything troubled him, when he answered promptly "Nothing." For hours before his death he kept repeating "into thy hands, O Lord, I commend my spirit."[12]

On October 22nd, 1877, the limits of the City of St. Louis being extended so as to take in Carondelet, Cheltenham, Baden, Lowell and Rock Springs the following nine Parish churches were included in the list of city parishes: They are here enumerated according to the date of their erection:

1. Our Lady of Mount Carmel, now called
   St. Mary and St. Joseph.............1827, Thomas G. Daly, Pastor
2. St. Boniface.....................1860, E. A. Schindel, Pastor
3. St. James...........................1860, H. Kelly, Pastor
4. Holy Cross.....................1863, Herman Wigger, Pastor
5. St. Thomas, now Holy Name..........1865, P. J. Gleason, Pastor
6. St. Columbkille.....................1872, M. O'Reilly, Pastor
7. Our Lady of Mount Carmel..........1873, David S. Phelan, Pastor
8. Our Lady of Perpetual Help........1873, August Schilling, Pastor
9. St. Bernard...................1874, Joseph Schaefers, Pastor

This raised the number of city churches to forty, whilst the loss to country was partly made good by the erection of three new parishes. St. Ignatius at Peers, St. Joseph's at Pilot Grove and St. Peter's in Joplin, the exact number of country parishes being one hundred and four.[13]

In the year 1878 Bishop Ryan ordained: Edward J. Dempsey, Jeremiah J. Harty, Joseph A. Connolly, Peter A. Trumm and Francis Jones for the archdiocese, besides ten Franciscans and two Jesuits.

Three new parishes were erected in the course of the year, and the usual number of church dedications were held. On December 8th, Bernard Donnelly was commissioned to bless the Convent and Chapel of the Redemptorist Fathers in Kansas City. The statistics for 1878 give:

      Churches with parochial schools attached............103
      Persons engaged in teaching parochial schools.......267
      Children taught in parochial schools...........15,416[14]

The following year 1879 was not as eventful in church affairs as the preceding ones: Three priests were ordained for the diocese, eight for the Franciscan Order. The Coadjutor Bishop laid the cornerstone for St. Cronin's Church and blessed the church on July 27th. Father

---

12 "Our Pastors in Calvary," p. 25, and "Western Watchman."
13 Chancery Records.
14 Chancery Records.

Muehlsiepen laid the corner stone for St. Francis Church at Portage, and blessed it five months later: He also blessed the Church of St. Stephen at Richwoods and of St. Augustine at Kelso.

On November 16th, the Rev. James Henry laid the corner stone of the combination church, school and parsonage of the Holy Ghost Parish, Father Hukestein preached the sermon.

Of the parish churches dedicated by the Coadjutor Bishop in 1880, Father Weiss' church at Ste. Genevieve is by far the most important: the church at Richfountain is also an imposing stone structure: yet the little Church of St. Paul's at Fenton in St. Louis County probably caused the greatest amount of joy on its day of dedication, November 6th.

"The Church, St. Paul's," chanted one of the proud Catholics of Fenton, "is beautifully situated in that beautiful little town. It stands at the foot of a hill just where the Meramec is spanned by a neat bridge. It is a pretty frame structure, handsomely painted, with a belfry, spire and all complete. But better still, a credit to the pastor and trustees, not a cent of indebtedness hangs over it. The trustees are Messrs. A. Kelsey, Andrew Owens, J. McGuire, and M. Vogelsang. The purchase of a graveyard and the enclosure of the church with a suitable fence are contemplated by the enterpising parishioners.

Within the church on the day of its dedication everything was new, carpet, censer, incense-boat and all little accessories.''[15]

By Papal Bull, dated September 10th, 1880, the territory of the diocese of St. Louis lying south of the Missouri River and west of the eastern boundary of the counties of Moniteau, Miller, Camden, Laclede, Wright, Douglas and Ozark, containing 23,539 square miles, with twenty-four parish churches, twenty-four missions, or stations, and thirty priests, twenty-three of whom were of the secular clergy, seven of the Redemptorist Order. Bishop John Hogan of St. Joseph, was transferred to Kansas City, but retained charge of St. Joseph as administrator. This, the sixth dismemberment of the archdiocese of St. Louis reduced its area to about one half of the state of Missouri. The number of parish churches in the city of St. Louis was forty-three, outside the city ninety-one, missions thirty-nine; stations seventeen. The total number of priests was two hundred and thirty-two.

The Catholic population of the archdiocese made good its losses in the west by corresponding gains in the east, and still numbered about one hundred and forty-five thousand souls.

The year 1880 marked the passage of good Father Tucker of Fredericktown into a blissful eternity, November 30th. On April 24th,

---

15. ''Western Watchman,'' Correspondence from Fenton.

of the following year the Church of the Immaculate Conception at Hannibal was dedicated by the Coadjutor Bishop and on September 7th, the Church of St. Stanislaus at Wardsville by Vicar-General Muehlsiepen; likewise the Church of the Sacred Heart at Festus. The Rev. Dr. John H. May was the first pastor of Festus. Four priests of the archdiocese died within the year 1881, among them the saintly Father Herman Leygraaff.[16]

On April 23rd, of the following year 1882, Bishop Ryan opened with the dedication of the Church of the Visitation in St. Louis, of which Father Edward Fenlon was the first pastor, and on May 21st, the Vicar-General followed with blessing All Saints Church at St. Peter's. Then on September 17th, the Coadjutor Bishop laid the cornerstone of the Holy Rosary Church at Truesdale, and on August 18th, dedicated St. Peter's Church at Jefferson City, whilst the Vicar-General of the Germans blessed St. Peter's Church at Kirkwood, on October 15th, and two days later, laid the corner stone of St. Francis Xavier Church at Taos. On November 12th, the Right Rev. Bishop closed the year's church dedications at the Polish Church of St. Staunlaw, in St. Louis, the pastor of which was the Franciscan Father Leo Brandys.[17]

The dedication of Father Hoog's new church at Jefferson City August 12, 1883 deserves a little more than a passing notice, on account of the distinguished clergymen taking part. High Mass was celebrated by Rev. Father Francis Goller, with Father Schaefer, deacon and Father Stemker as subdeacon. Father Van der Sanden was master of ceremonies. The Right Rev. Bishop was assisted by Father Philip Brady of St. Louis, and Father Edward Fitzgerald of Edina. Father Dickman preached in German and Father Cook in English."[18]

---

16   Chancery Records.

17   Chancery Records and ''Western Watchman.''

18   ''Missouri Volksfreund,'' October 7, 1896.   Golden Jubilee Edition.

CHAPTER 44

A CLUSTER OF SEVEN NEW SISTERHOODS

I

The increase and expansion of religious communities has always been regarded as one of the chief glories of the diocese of St. Louis. Bishop Rosati never missed an opportunity of fostering the religious life in the communities established in his diocese, and of introducing new Congregations and Orders from abroad. Archbishop Kenrick following in his footsteps, more than trebled the number of those already established. Of the beginnings of the Ursuline Nuns, the Sisters of the Good Shepherd and the Sisters of Mercy brief accounts have been given in a former chapter. The Sisterhoods introduced into the archdiocese after the outbreak of the Civil War and before the coming of Archbishop Kain, the School-Sisters de Notre Dame, 1858; the Carmelites, 1863; the Little Sisters of the Poor, 1869; the Sisters of St. Mary, 1872; The Sisters of St. Francis, 1872; the Oblate Sisters of Province, 1880; the Sisters of the Precious Blood, 1882, now claim our attention. Without the generous and self sacrificing cooperation of these and the older religious Congregations and Orders of the archdiocese, our present parochial and diocesan high school system could never have been established.

The *School Sisters de Notre Dame,* a Congregation specially devoted to the education of female youth in parochial schools and orphan asylums had been invited to America by Bishop Michael O'Connor of Pittsburg at the request of the Redemptorist Fathers. The first members of the community came from the Motherhouse in Munich, Bavaria. Baltimore was selected as the location of their Motherhouse in America. The saintly John Neumann, the Superior of the Redemptorists, had helped the Sisters to secure a house near St. James Church, the present Motherhouse of the Eastern Province. This was in October 1847. Before a year had expired, three parochial schools were placed in charge of the new Sisterhood. On October 10th, 1850, Mother Caroline, the youngest of the Sisters, that had founded the Congregation in Baltimore, was named Vicar-General for America, and was sent to establish the Western Province de Notre Dame in the city of Milwaukee. King Louis I. of Bavaria paid the expense of the new foundation. On Christmas day 1850 Bishop Henni sang Highmass in the convent chapel, and on the second day of January, 1851, Mother Caroline opened the first parish school of the Order in the West, at St. Mary's Church, Milwaukee. Mother Caroline was a highly cul-

(329)

tured, amiable, and religious woman. With a zeal and vigilance that never relaxed, she built up the great Motherhouse of the Sisters of Notre Dame in Milwaukee.[1]

To Father Joseph Patchowski, S. J., of St. Joseph's Church, belongs the credit of having brought this excellent Sisterhood to St. Louis, May 1858.

The following year on October 2nd, Father Francis S. Goller of S. S. Peter and Paul's parish obtained three Sisters as teachers for the three hundred pupils of his parochial school. On the same day Father Stephan Schweihoff of St. Liborius Church entrusted his school of seventy pupils to the care of the Sisters de Notre Dame. That was the humble beginning of a mighty work of religion and culture in our city and state. An even, steady growth of the Western Province occasioned a subdivision in 1895. St. Louis was made the seat of the southern part; its motherhouse was named "Sancta Maria in Ripa."

This noble institution was projected in 1884, but had to wait ten years before it could be accomplished. A sixty acre tract named Grand View, fronting on the Mississippi river was purchased in 1894 by Father Peter M. Abbelen. There was a ten room mansion on the place, in which six Sisters under Mother Bonaventure took up their abode. In the chapel of this house Father Goller offered mass for the first time on March 19th, 1895. The new building was begun on June 1st, 1895: the corner stone being laid by Vicar-General Muehlsiepen on October 15th, 1895. The dedication of the Convent chapel was performed on July 7th, 1897 by Archbishop Kain. In the erection of this magnificent institution two distinguished men and one saintly woman, deserve the highest meed of praise. Msgr. Francis Goller of S. S. Peter and Paul's, Msgr. P. M. Abbelen, the Spiritual Director of the Motherhouse at Milwaukee, and Ven. Mother Petra Pfeiffer, the second Superior of the Southern Province. For three years had Mother Petra served as First Assistant to Mother Bonaventure. It was the time when the building of the Motherhouse was in progress. In February 1901 Mother Petra succeeded to the high and most laborious office of Provincial. For the next nine years she labored faithfully and well, to develop all the possibilities, spiritual and temporal, of the new foundation. After the usual interval of three years she was re-elected as Provincial. Her last years were an agonizing martyrdom, which she bore in loving patience and self-oblation. Her death occurred on the Feast of the Immaculate Conception, 1924. Mother Petra was a truly remarkable woman, spiritual to the core, yet endowed with all the natural powers and graces that constitute inspiring leadership. Sancta Maria in Ripa is her monument. In "Sancta Maria in Ripa," just outside the southern

---

[1] Abbelen, P. M., "Mutter Carolina Fries." Fries, Frederick, "Mother Mary Teresa of Jesus, Gerhardinger."

city limits, hard by the waters of the great river, hundreds of teachers receive their normal training; from this haunt of peace and Christian charity they go forth to educate the youth of our City and State and even beyond, to instill knowledge and the love of virtue into the plastic hearts and minds entrusted to their motherly care, here the Sisters meet after the work of the school session is over to recuperate and gain new strength and energy; here too is the reposeful retreat from the manifold cares and distractions of the life they have to lead as teachers, in the world but not of the world. The Sisters of Notre Dame have thirty-three houses in the diocese of St. Louis, whilst in all the provinces of the United States there are 333 houses of the Order with 200,000 children attending the schools taught by the Sisters.

In view of these wonderful results of practical piety and devotion it would seem that the next Order in point of time, brought into the diocese by Archbishop Kenrick, the contemplative *Order of the Carmelite Nuns*, was far beneath the former in value and importance. Yet, the words of Pope Pius IX cannot be gainsaid: "The want of the American Church is religious Orders of prayer, the extension of Contemplative Orders." The spirit of action pervades all classes of our people; and the Orders and Congregations devoted to the works of education and charity are liable to become absorbed in these outward duties and occupations. Reflection and contemplation must restore the balance. The contemplative Orders were intended to be the teachers and bright models of interior prayer. Our own Archbishop Kenrick, thorough man of the active life, yet at the same time, a lover of quiet meditation, is reported to have answered the query: Why introduce an Order that does nothing but pray: with the words: "I have a number of Orders for the works of charity and education, but I want an Order that will pray forever for my priests." Archbishop Kenrick was the true founder of the St. Louis Carmel.[2]

The foundation of the Carmelite Order, to vary a well known saying of "Lord Macaulay: " is lost in the twilight of legend;" yet the beginnings of Carmel in America are as clear as the noonday sun. It was in 1790, the year when the Constitution of the United States was born, that Father Ignatius Matthews, a Jesuit of Maryland, wrote to his sister, the prioress of the Carmelite Convent at Hoogtraeten, in Belgium, these ever memorable words: "Now is your time to found in this country, for peace is declared and religion is free."

The Carmel at Hoogstraeten had among its pupils a number of American children, some of whom had entered the Order, among them Miss Ann Matthews, the Mother Bernardine of Father Matthew's letter, prioress of the Convent. Mother Bernardine and three other Sisters,

---

2 ''Carmel in St. Louis,'' A Souvenir Booklet.

began their voyage to America on April 19th, 1790; and on July 2nd, after suffering many hardships and privations, landed at New York. They established themselves near Port Tobacco, in Charles County, Maryland, in a house given them by Mr. Baker Brooke. It was a poor habitation, on top of a high hill, exposed to the inclemencies of the changeful weather, a solitary place, "suitable," as the Sisters wrote, "to our eremitical Order."

In 1831 they were forced by lack of support to move into the city of Baltimore where Archbishop Whitfield secured a house for them In 1872 they took possession of their new Convent at the corner of Caroline and Biddle Streets, in Baltimore, Md.[3] It was the good fortune of St. Louis to receive the second foundation of American Carmelites. Francis Patrick Kenrick, the Archbishop of Baltimore, a short time before his death, on July 6th, 1863, proposed to the prioress of the Carmelites in Baltimore the desire of his brother Peter Richard of St. Louis to have a community of Carmelites in his diocese. The prioress was favorably impressed with the idea of a new foundation, but the unexpected death of the Archbishop of Baltimore left the matter uncertain. A letter to Archbishop Kenrick of St. Louis, however, brought a cordial invitation to come at once, in consequence of which the prioress with four sisters and their Chaplain started for St. Louis, on September 29th, 1862.

Archbishop Kenrick had offered the Sisters his own country residence, the old Clay Mansion, which stood at the edge of Calvary Cemetery. It was a beautiful spot with its farm and vine-yard, and no public roads leading up to it.

The Archbishop himself conducted the Sisters and their Chaplain to their Carmel in Calvary, and, after saying mass for them the next morning, placed the Blessed Sacrament in the tabernacle, before which the Sisters were to find strength and comfort in many tribulations. For tribulations came in plenty. The management of farms and vine-yards was not to their taste: and yet they must live, and to live they must labor. So they undertook the making of artificial flowers, plain sewing, and other work of this kind for their support; but the returns were meager and precarious. Their trust, however, was in the Lord, and the Lord did not forsake them. Gradually friends came forward and offered help, and after fifteen years, they provided for them a new home within the city. The community had in the meantime increased in number, so that four of the sisters could in 1877 be sent to New Orleans to establish a new monastery of the Order.

For the first eight months Father Edmund Saulnier, Secretary to the Archbishop, was the Sisters' Chaplain. After his death the Arch-

---

3  Boscawen, T. L., "The Story of Carmel" in Souvenir Booklet.

bishop himself acted as their Chaplain for eighteen months, and continued as their confessor for nearly three years.[4]

It was in the year 1878, that the St. Louis Community moved to the new location at the corner of Eighteenth and Victor Streets. The site of the building was donated by Mrs. Patterson. Here then, in happy seclusion, the Carmelite Sisters have been carrying on their apostolate of prayer, almost unnoticed by the world, but shedding, through their generous self-oblation, innumerable blessings upon its denizens, burning day and night as living flames of love before the altar of God a work that they now continue in their new home near Kirkwood.

After the Carmelite Nuns came the *Little Sisters of the Poor,* ever up and doing, like the little Marthas they are, with a most liberal infusion of the contemplative spirit of Mary. As the Catholic Encyclopedia informs us, the Little Sisters of the Poor are an active, unenclosed religious Congregation founded at St. Servan, Brittany, in 1839, through the instrumentality of Abbé Augustine Marie La Pailleur. The Congregation is included in the class of hospitallers. Its constitutions are based on the Rule of St. Augustine. The sisters take simple and perpetual vows of poverty, chastity and obedience, to which they add a fourth, hospitality. They receive into their houses aged men and women who have no other shelter. For the support of their foundation the Sisters are dependent absolutely on charity, having no fixed income or endowment. Most of what they need, they procure by begging. Their constitution was definitely approved by Pius X., on May 7th, 1907. The Motherhouse is at La Tour St. Joseph, France.[5] They have about fifty houses in America, two of them in St. Louis. Owing to the fact that there were many poor in St. Louis, Archbishop Kenrick asked the Little Sisters of the Poor to begin a foundation in his episcopal city. The invitation was gladly accepted. Six Little Sisters arrived in St. Louis on May 1st, 1869, from their Mother house in Brittany, France. The Archbishop heartily welcomed them and led the little band of strangers to the Convent of the Ladies of the Sacred Heart, who not only gave them hospitality but also, with great kindness, furnished them with all things necessary for their chapel. On May 3rd, the Little Sisters took possession of four small houses, which they had rented. But the rooms were "void and empty." "What would they do in an empty house?" they were asked: "It is always in holy poverty that we begin; Divine Providence will provide,"[6] answered the Sisters. Their confidence was not in vain. On the first day some one brought a stove, another a temporary altar, others brought brooms, buckets

---

4  Lord, D. A., "The Carmel in St. Louis," in Souvenir Booklet.

5  Martin, T. T., "A Voice from the West," p. 137. The Catholic Encyclopedia, Article "Poor," Answers to Questionnaire.

6.  Communicated in Questionnaire.

kettles and pans and all the other necessaries for housekeeping. On the second day they received the first old lady. Beds were sent, and even a horse and wagon was furnished. Within two months there were fifty old people in the Home. Their first chaplain was Father J. Lambelin, S.J.

Archbishop Ryan, Coadjutor to Archbishop Kenrick, said one time, the Little Sisters of the Poor were so original in their proceedings, and as an illustration related the following incident: "I knew them when they first came to St. Louis. They had not even straw to lie on, and I, meaning well, sent an old lady who wished to enter the Home, and was willing to give the Sisters the thousand dollars she had accumulated. But the old lady returned to me crying: "They would not admit me on account of my $1,000." The Bishop added, I am certain this work will prosper, for when an edifice is built on poverty, Providence itself cements it together."[7]

"In effect, his words have been fulfilled," the Sisters wrote on July 5th, 1891, "Since that episode, the Home for the old people has been enlarged three times, and the debts are all paid. But seeing the wants of so many poor old people in this large city who claim admission, His Grace the Archbishop, gave his consent two years since to establish a second Home, but we are waiting until our Lord inspires some benevolent benefactor to take the first steps in establishing this second House."

The second Home of the Aged in St. Louis was established on December 3rd, 1900. The beautiful words of praise given our Little Sisters by the "Old Man Eloquent of the Ave-Maria," Father Daniel Hudson, came in like a sweet Amen to what we have tried to say:

"Doubtless one reason why the Little Sisters of the Poor have been so wondrously blessed is that they have strictly adhered to the purpose of their founder. They have never engaged in any work but the one for which the Order was designed, and blessed by the Church. In spite of all recommendations to modify their rule, or solicitations to undertake other good works, they continue to take charge of the aged, homeless poor. When offered an annuity from the estate of a wealthy citizen of Illinois, a non-Catholic, by the way, the Mother-General "declined with thanks," saying: "If we were to accept such gifts instead of begging, we should cease to be the Little Sisters of the Poor, and would become the Little Sisters of the Rich."[8]

The "*Sisters of Mary of the Third Order of St. Francis*," as their official title reads, or "The Sisters of Mary," "die Marienschwestern," as the popular voice has it, came to St. Louis in 1872. The history of their early wanderings, ere they found a secure resting place

---

7 Questionnaire.
8 From Notes and Comment in "Ave Maria."

and home, is a beautiful exemplification of the mysterious ways by which Divine Providence attains the ends proposed by Divine Love.[9]

The Foundress of the Congregation whose main calling is to nurse the sick in hospitals, and the sick poor at their homes, was Catherine Berger, in religion Mother Odilia, a native of Bavaria. Born in the village of Regen, on April 30th, 1823, of wealthy and sincerely religious parents, she was placed with the Ursulines for her education. She soon manifested a strong desire to enter the Convent: her mother, however, refused to let her go. At last she was permitted to enter the Franciscan Community at Pirmasens, Bavaria, where on May 7th, 1857, she received the habit and her name Odilia. Sister Odilia, with a companion Sister, was sent out to solicit alms. In 1866 these journeys brought her and her companion to Paris. Here they were requested to found a convent. On arriving home, they acquainted the Superioress of the request, and received permission to accept the offer. Five Sisters with Mother Odilia founded the Community in Paris October 17th, 1866. The Sisters went out to nurse the sick and kept a home for girls out of employment. All went well until the outbreak of the Franco-Prussian war in 1870. Being of German birth, Mother Odilia with her Sisters was forced to leave France. They went to Elberfeld, where they were given charge of nursing the wounded soldiers in one of the military hospitals.[10] After the closing of the hospital Mother Odilia rented some rooms and undertook to nurse the sick in private families. After the war came the Kultur-Kampf, and the Sisters felt it expedient, if not necessary, to leave their native land, Vicar-General Muehlsiepen of St. Louis advised them to come to St. Louis. Mother Odilia was delighted with the prospects. Accordingly, she and her little band of five sisters with all their poverty sailed from Hamburg on October 8th, and, after a stormy voyage, arrived in St. Louis, November 6th, 1872. Father Muehlsiepen entrusted them to the guidance of Father William Faerber of St. Mary's Church, who in the Providence of God was to remain their Spiritual Director until his death, April 17th, 1905. Hospitality was offered the newcomers at the Ursuline Convent. After three weeks Mother Odilia rented the upper part of a tenement just opposite St. Mary's Church. By the generosity of Father Faerber and the Ursulines, the two rooms were fitted up for occupation, the one serving as parlor and oratory, the other as dining room and community room. The attic was used for a dormitory.[11]

Almost immediately after their arrival in St. Louis, the Sisters were called upon for active service. Smallpox had just begun to rage with great violence in the city; so the Sisters found abundance of work to

---

9   Melies, J. C., ''A History of the Sisters of Mary of St. Louis,'' 1922.

10   Melies, op. cit., p. 12.

11   Ibidem, pp. 14 and 15-17.

do. Their constancy and devotion to this labor of love earned for them the name of ''Smallpox Sisters.'' When in 1873, cholera became prevalent, and there was a return of smallpox, the Sisters were again at the bedside of the afflicted, passing days and even weeks in the infected rooms of the poor; for it was pre-eminently to the poor that the Sisters offered their services.

The fervor of religion and charity in these ministering angels, drew kindred souls into the charmed circle. Not only did the three candidates that had come to St. Louis with Mother Odilia, receive the habit, but others also applied for admission. This, of course, necessitated larger and better accommodations. The Sisters obtained permission to erect a house of their own on the vacant lot south of St. Mary's Church. Building operations were began in the Spring of 1873. Mother Odilia went out on begging expeditions, to secure the necessary means. The Sisters eagerly watched the progress of construction. Early in October the building was completed and furnished. On the Feast of St. Teresa, October 15th, the Convent was blessed by Vicar-General Muehlsiepen, and the fifteen Sisters that now formed the community took possession of the first motherhouse of their Order in the new world.[12]

On the Feast of the Immaculate Conception the first investiture in the new chapel was held by Vicar-General Muehlsiepen, assisted by Father Faerber. The three candidates received the following names: Sister M. Clara, Sister M. Ludovica, and Sister M. Agnes. They had spent the months of probation in the rooms ''across the street,'' they had also taken part in the work of the Sisters among the sick and poor.

In 1874 the smallpox epidemic raged even more fiercely than before, and the Sisters had hard work to answer every call.

In 1875 four more young ladies received the habit, and at the end of the year, the community numbered twenty-three Sisters and seven candidates. At the last solemn reception held in the Convent Chapel on Third Street six young ladies answered the call: ''Come, follow me.''[13]

In 1876 the growing community moved to a new location, a ten acre tract of land on Arsenal Street and Arkansas Avenue, where stood a large brick dwelling and two smaller buildings. The property was the gift of a pious lady, Mrs. Elizabeth Schiller. The main condition, however, was that the Sisters establish and conduct an Orphan Asylum on the place. The Sisters took possession of their new home on July 4th, 1876, and some time later made it the Motherhouse of the Sisters of Mary under the title St. Joseph's Home.

The number of members in the Community increased from year to year. The Franciscan Fathers now received the spiritual charge of the Institution, although the Pastor of St. Mary's remained Spiritual

---

12   Melies, op. cit. p. 19.
13   Ibidem, p. 25.

Director. The old Convent adjoining St. Mary's Church was reserved for the Sisters employed in the care of the sick in the city.

The Ladies of the Sacred Heart on Convent Street assisted the Sisters of Mary in their works of charity by making clothing for poor children. In 1882 the Sisters of Mary found it necessary to relinquish St. Joseph's Home, which was, at a later date, purchased by the Sisters of the Precious Blood.

Serious difficulties were experienced by the Sisters in nursing the sick in their homes, especially among the poor. Lack of the necessaries of life, the difficulty of securing medical aid, and the unfavorable conditions obtaining in these homes, often retarded recovery. A hospital of their own seemed to promise the remedy for these disadvantages. After due consideration, a plot of ground on Fifteenth and Papin Streets was bought. A fine substantial mansion stood upon it. This was the nucleus of what was to become St. Mary's Infirmary. A small but very beautiful chapel was added to the building; and dedicated to the Sorrowful Mother. The first sick person admitted was a charity-patient. Sister M. Clara was the first Superior of St. Mary's Infirmary.[14]

The Charity of these angels of mercy was not confined to the city of St. Louis. As early as 1873 St. Charles on the Missouri river had experienced the blessings of their presence among their sick and dying during the epidemic of the smallpox. The Southland also was to experience them.

When in 1878 an epidemic of yellow-fever broke out in the Southern states, the Sisters of St. Mary offered their services. In August of that year five left for Memphis, and the next month three others also went to Memphis. At the request of Bishop Elder five Sisters went to Canton, Miss., where the plague was also raging. Of the thirteen Sisters who went South, five died of the disease, and the remaining eight, although having contracted it, recovered, and returned to St. Louis in November.

Mother Odilia was almost prostrated at the news of the loss of these five good and heroic Sisters: But her confidence never failed her that all was well with them. Father Faerber wrote her a beautiful letter from Paris, in which he extolled these martyrs of their vocation: "What a privilege it is to die in, and for one's vocation!"[15]

In 1880 the Congregation of the Sisters of Mary was approved by Rome, and on the Feast of St. Francis of Assisi, Vicar-General Muehlsiepen, after the Solemn Highmass sung by Father Faerber, received

14   Melies, op. cit. pp. 41-43.
15   Ibidem, pp. 47-56.

the vows of the Sisters and placed the blessed ring on each one's finger. But the happy event of October 4th, was the prelude for the happy death of Mother Odilia on the Feast of her chosen patron, Blessed Margaret Mary, October 7th, 1880. Sister Seraphina was appointed her successor.

The good work done by the Sisters of Mary in private homes had not escaped the city authorities. In 1883, when there was another epidemic of smallpox in St. Louis, the Health Commissioner, General Stevenson, requested them to undertake the nursing of the smallpox patients at the Quarantine. Reassured by the acquiescence of the religious authorities, the Sisters accepted the offer, and from May, 1883, to May, 1885, nursed at the Quarantine Hospital between 1400 and 1500 patients, a large percentage of whom recovered. The Board of Health did all in its power to alleviate the irksomeness of the task, and, among other things, a room was given them for a Chapel, where the Blessed Sacrament was preserved and Mass was said from time to time.

Two of the Sisters fell victims to the virulent disease. In November 1886 when an epidemic of diptheria broke out in the City, the Board of Health requested the Sisters to receive patients, mostly children, into the Infirmary. The request was complied with. The Missouri Pacific Railroad Hospital was in charge of the Sisters from 1884 to 1889. The Railroad Hospital in Sedalia was also intrusted to their care in 1885. The memory of the good Sisters' charitable work in St. Charles in 1873, was still alive in the hearts of the people, when ten years later they decided to establish a Hospital in their city. Mr. Franz Schulte had left a house with a large plot of ground to Father Willmes for hospital purposes, and Father Willmes now offered it to the Sisters. The offer was accepted, and the Hospital was opened on November 4th, 1885, under the patronage of St. Joseph. Sister M. Elizabeth was its first Superior. In 1890 the erection of the present St. Joseph's Hospital was begun on a large scale, and dedicated by Vicar-General Muehlsiepen in August 1891. An addition was made to the building in 1904, and another in 1924.[16]

The first St. Mary's Infirmary in St. Louis was only a private residence fitted up for hospital purposes: the new building was erected on the same site in 1887. The corner stone was laid by Vicar-General Muehlsiepen, July 11th, 1887, and the building was privately blessed on February 12th, 1889, by Father Faerber. The money for the enterprise was borrowed from kindly disposed persons on the security, as the Sisters put it, "of Divine Providence and St. Joseph." St. Mary's Infirmary enjoys the reputation of doing the largest amount

---

16 Melies, op. cit. pp. 65-66.

of charity work in the city. A bare mention must suffice for St. Mary's Hospital in Chillicothe, Missouri, the so-called German Hospital in Kansas City, and St. Mary's Hospital in Kansas City. Mount St. Rose Sanatorium for consumptives as well as St. Mary's Hospital at Jefferson City, and the subsequent expansion of the Congregation, must be reserved for treatment in a later chapter.

In recounting the glories of Archbishop Kenrick's administration, the rapid growth of the Congregation of the Sisters of Mary from humblest beginnings to its present magnificent proportions, must appear as one of the most marvelous. These Sisters are preeminently devoted to the sick poor, and the blessing that attaches to the care for these helpless children of God, has been theirs in a signal manner.

A CLUSTER OF SEVEN NEW SISTERHOODS

II

"In my Father's house there are many mansions," said our Blessed Savior; in the Church of Christ there are many religious Orders and Congregations in which the will of God is realized in equal approach to perfection, but in diverse manner. Divine Charity is one, but it has many ways and means of manifesting itself. Hence the large number and variety of Institutions of men and women in the Church Catholic; hence also the multiplicity of religious Orders and Congregations established by Archbishop Kenrick in the diocese of St. Louis.

In this chapter the origin and early growth of the three last Sisterhoods to take root in that generous soil, shall be treated; the Sisters of the Most Precious Blood, the Franciscan Sisters of the Province of St. Clara, and the Oblate Sisters of Charity. The period of their respective foundations extended from 1872 to 1882.

The early history of the *Sisters of the Most Precious Blood* reads like a little Aeneid. Living in peace and security in their castled monastery of Gurtweil, in Baden, they are suddenly driven from hold and home. They sail away across the sea to a foreign western shore. They find a temporary home; but ere long they are driven away once more, not so much by unfriendly power, but rather by the secret decrees of Providence. Farther west they find a hearty welcome and a permanent home.[1]

The original founder of the Congregation was Mary de Mattias under direction of Caspar de Buffalo. The time and place was Rome, 1834. But the rule of the Congregation of "the Adorers of the Precious Blood" was in 1857 adapted to the needs of Germany by the Rev. Herman Kessler, pastor of Gurtweil, when he obtained six Sisters from Ottmarshausen in Alsace, for the care of his institution for neglected children. In order to give steady employment and proper means of support to the community he introduced among them the art of embroidery. The Congregation grew rapidly, and the number of orphan children in their care in 1858 rose to sixty. Orders for Church vestments came in from all parts of Germany. In 1865 Father Kessler resigned his charge of the parish of Gurtweil to devote all his time and energy to the Sisters as their Spiritual Director. The cause of education had a strong attraction for the learned Father, and it led him to establish a parochial and high school under the Sisters' management.

---

[1] Zur Erinnerung an das Silberne Jubilaeum der Schwestern vom Kostbaren Blute.

Father Kessler, having accomplished his great life work, was called away by death on October 23rd, 1867.[2]

The government of Baden, at this time, was not friendly to the Catholic Church. In fact, the coming Kultur-Kampf was already casting its threatening shadows before. Its full destructive force broke out in 1871: it came in the wake of the victorious war of 1870. It was, though bloodless, the most oppressive war ever waged by a Protestant government against the Church in Germany. Bishops and priests were imprisoned, and numerous religious institutions were dissolved, and their members sent into exile.[3]

Even before the outbreak of the Franco-Prussian war, the signs of a coming storm were in evidence. The Sisters of Gurtweil realized that ere long the heavy weight of oppression would fall on them. As they were looking around for a safe place of refuge, a letter arrived from Father Blasius Winterhalter, pastor of Belle Prairie, now Piopolis, in Illinois, inviting a colony of the Sisters to take up their work in the Far West, stating, at the same time, that a house was ready to receive them. The invitation was gratefully accepted. On February 2nd, 1870, nine sisters set out on the French steamer, *"The Harmonica,"* for New York, where they arrived on February 16th. They travelled by rail to Cincinnati; then by boat to Shawneetown, Illinois, then by ox teams to their destination, fifty miles to the western border of the state. Great was the joy of the people at seeing the Sisters among them, and the Sisters too were comforted at seeing the kindness of the people amid the rude surroundings. Labor conquers all trouble, and the sense of God's presence sheds a heavenly brightness even on the wilderness.[4] Bishop Juncker of Alton had invited the Sisters to his diocese without assigning them a place for their Motherhouse: His successor, Bishop Baltes, desired that they should establish themselves in the city of Springfield. The Sisters acquiesced, but Belle Prairie was not to be given up. The nine Sisters, however, were not able to bear the double burden; their Superior, therefore, Sister Albertina, journeyed back to Gurtweil, to obtain more Sisters. She returned to America in August 1871, with a colony of twelve other Sisters. Father J. Niehaus, had in 1870 succeeded Father Winterhalter as pastor of Belle Prairie. The Sisters had taken over the schools at Effingham and Edwardsville. The Springfield Motherhouse was in flourishing condition: all seemed to promise a rapid and substantial progress.

But a heavy trial fell upon the hopeful community, the disagreement with the Bishop of the diocese in which they had found

---

2 Op. cit., p. 1-4.
3 Op. cit., p. 6.
4 Op. cit., pp. 7 and 8.

their new home. Bishop Baltes had made it a condition sine qua non, that all the Sisters property must be held as diocesan property, a condition which the Superior, Sister Augusta, refused to accept. The Bishop ordered the Sisters to leave Springfield.[5] The Sisters obeyed and wended their way to Belle Prairie, where they were received with great rejoicings, as it now seemed that the Motherhouse would be established there. In the summer of 1871 all the Sisters spent their vacation at Belle Prairie, but it seemed evident to the more far sighted that Belle Prairie could not receive the Motherhouse. Like Springfield it was in Bishop Baltes' diocese. The Sisters must seek a new home beyond the Mississippi. Mother Auguta wrote to Vicar-General Muehlsiepen, and received a kindly response. The parishes of St. Agatha in the city of St. Louis, and at Herman and St. John's in the diocese, were anxious to obtain the services of the Sisters for their schools. In 1872 another colony of Sisters arrived from Gurtweil. Speedy action was required to provide for all these homeless ones; Vicar-General Muehlsiepen asked the entire community to come to St. Louis and assigned them temporary shelter with the Ursulines, whose Spiritual Director he was: They arrived on December 11th, 1872, twenty-one sisters; and were most hospitably received by Mother Aloysia Winkler, the Mother Superior of the Ursulines.

In the meantime the pastor of St. Agatha's parish, Father Hermann Leygraaff, was working hard to complete his new school and Sisters residence. On February 11th, 1873, they entered the new home, and began to teach in the school. The entire community of the Sisters of the Precious Blood remained at St. Agatha's until the Motherhouse at O'Fallon, St. Charles Co., Mo., was ready for occupancy, July, 1875. In the meantime the news arrived that the Convent at Gurtweil was dissolved by decree of the government. Mother Augusta immediately started for the old home, to bring over to America the remaining members of the Congregation. Forty-nine Sisters entered upon the journey for the West on August 26th, 1873. The French steamer *L'Europe,* brought them safely to New York on September 11th. Vicar-General Muehlsiepen met them on landing and with fatherly care escorted them to St. Louis. The temporary home at St. Agatha's being much too small for the entire community, the Novitiate with Mother Clementina as Mistress of Novices, was transferred to Belle Prairie.[6]

The Catholics of O'Fallon were delighted to have such a large and distinguished Sisterhood in their town, and did all in their power to further the progress of building the Motherhouse.

In the beautiful month of June 1875, the Sisters began to remove their belongings to O'Fallon, when all unexpectedly, the almost in-

---

5   Op. cit., p. 8.
6   Op. cit., p. 9

credible news arrived from Belle Prairie, that the Novitiate under Mother Clementine had accepted the conditions of Bishop Baltes and thus seceded from the main body of the Congregation. The four Sisters at Belle Prairie followed Mother Clementine, but a number of the novices were brought to O'Fallon by their parents. The Motherhouse and Novitiate of Mother Clementine's branch of the Sisters of the Most Precious Blood is now established at Ruma, Illinois.[7] The Motherhouse at O'Fallon prospered in signal manner. Its artistic products in the line of church vestments have became renowned. In 1882 St. Elizabeth's Institute in St. Louis was opened by the Sisters. Today the school numbers three hundred pupils. In 1878 the incorporation of the Commuunity under the laws of the state of Missouri was effected with the legal title of "St. Mary's Institute of O'Fallon, Mo."

The Sisters have schools in the archdiocese of St. Louis, in the dioceses of Springfield, Illinois, Omaha, Lincoln, and St. Joseph. ·

The Normal School at the Motherhouse in O'Fallon, Mo., trains its teachers to meet the growing demands of the day in a most efficient and practical way. The Junior College Department of the Community is accredited with the University of Missouri, Columbia, Mo.

The Community has ever been governed by the Superior General and her Council. The Constitutions and Rules were very soon adapted to the new field of labor and in 1879 obtained the sanction of the ecclesiastical authorities as a Diocesan Community under the late Archbishop Kenrick.

*The Franciscan Sisters of the Province of St. Clara* owe their establishment in St. Louis to the Rev. Ernest Andrew Schindel, the pastor of St. Boniface's Church in Carondelet. After having built the church and school, Father Schindel determined to provide a hospital for the sick poor of his parish and vicinity. His success in this difficult undertaking was remarkable, the actual cost being about $50,000.00. As the building neared completion, Father Schindel sent his friend and neighbor at Mattis Creek, Father Brockhagen, to his native land for Sisters, who would undertake the management of his hospital. Bishop Conrad Martin of Paderborn had referred him to the Motherhouse of the Franciscan Sisters at Salzkotten. This branch of the Franciscan Community was established there in 1863.

On December 3rd, 1873, the first three Sisters, St. Mary Philomena, St. Mary Dorothy and St. Mary Alphonse, entered upon their journey to America in company with Rev. H. Brockhagen, who acted as their guide. They arrived safely in Carondelet, and were heartily welcomed by Father Schindel. As the hospital was not yet finished, the new comers stayed for several months with the good Sisters of St. Joseph.[8]

---

7  Op. cit., p. 4. Cf. Ruma.

8  "Geschichte der Ehrw. Franciskaner Schwestern der Provinz zur Hl. Clara," pp. 5-7.

In the year, 1873, the building was completed and occupied. In the meantime eight more Sisters arrived from the general motherhouse under the protection of Father Schindel, who, with this end in view, had taken a trip to Europe. On the 7th of September, 1873, the new hospital was blessed by the Very Rev. H. Muehlsiepen, Vicar-General. under the name and patronage of St. Boniface. The house was soon filled with patients, but there was on it a debt of $40,000. Thus the Sisters found it necessary to continue their collecting tours which they had begun soon after their arrival.

On August 1st, 1875, eight more Sisters, arrived at the St. Boniface Hospital. The Sisters became known and respected for their arduous and noble works of charity, and requests came in from various places to send Sisters to conduct hospitals, schools and household work in institutions of learning.[9]

The last month of 1875, five Sisters, who were on the way to America, lost their lives on the ill-fated steamer, *Deutschland*. Their burial took place on December 13th, at Stratford, England. Cardinal Manning gave a most sympathetic and impressive sermon, which is still preserved. The small church could not accommodate the crowd, which had gathered to pay their respects to the martyrs of a holy cause. About fifty priests took part in the ceremonies. A modest tombstone marks the place where the mortal remains of the good Sisters are buried.[10]

Within two years of this sad event, the hospital building itself was consumed by fire. On August 6th, 1877, one hour before noon, lightning struck the southeast corner of the roof, and in a few minutes the entire upper story was wrapped in flames. Nothing was saved, except the lives of the inmates and a statue of the Mother of God. The patients were tenderly cared for by the Sisters at Gilleck's Hall. As no priest was present, Mother Cecilia removed the Blessed Sacrament to a place of safety, in the little room above the bakehouse, whence Father Schindel on his arrival, carried it to the parish church. As the amount of insurance money was rather small, and no other resources for rebuilding were at hand, the plan was dropped, and the Sisters departed for St. Louis.[11] But even before this change of location, the Franciscan Sisters had sent out little colonies, either as teachers in parochial schools, at Mattis Creek, or as hospital sisters and school teachers in Cape Girardeau. At the request of Rev. Joseph Schmidt, then Rector of St. Mary Parish at Cape Girardeau, the first branch house was established. In the month of September, 1875, the three Sisters, Philomena, Engelberta and Felicitas arrived in Cape Girardeau. It was difficult work

---

9    Geschichte der Franziskaner Schwestern, p. 8.
10   Op. cit., pp. 13-15.
11   Op. cit., pp. 22-25.

to found this pioneer hospital of Southeast Missouri; yet the Sisters' work and prayers were crowned with singular success. After the opening of the hospital the Sisters at the request of Father Schmidt, also took charge of the parish school. In 1878 a site for a permanent hospital was bought on Sprigg and Williams streets. The building was erected the same year.[12] The present St. Francis Hospital, a magnificent structure, completely fitted up for its purpose, was dedicated November 15th, 1914. The old hospital building was purchased by St. Mary's Parish and turned into a high school in charge of the Sisters de Notre Dame.

Almost at the same time, that the first branch house was planted, the Sisters, upon urgent request of the Rev. Rector Theodore Brünner, accepted the management of the household affairs of the Pio Nono Teachers' College and the Deaf-Mute Institution at St. Francis near Milwaukee, Wis. On September 16th, 1878, a number of the Sisters were sent from the General Motherhouse at Salzkotten to enable the American community to meet the increased demands for service. In the year 1876 the first Mother Provincial was appointed in the person of the Venerable Sister Bernarda. Upon the recommendation of Archbishop P. R. Kenrick, the place of founding the new motherhouse in the City of St. Louis was seriously considered. The execution of this plan was accelerated by the burning of St. Boniface Hospital at Carondelet, on August 6th, 1877. In January of the year 1878 a lot on 14th and O'Fallon streets was bought from Father Henry, Rector of St. Lawrence O'Toole Church, for the sum of $10,000. On February 7th, 1878, the new community was incorporated under the title "Franciscan Sisters."[13]

In the summer of the same year, when the yellow fever raged in the South, five sisters were sent to Memphis to assist in the care of the numerous victims of the terrible plague. In St. Louis the hospital under the name Pius Hospital and the motherhouse were finished in the year 1874 and blessed on October 27. Adjoining the hospital a house for servant girls was built and was soon well patronized. As the number of Sisters increased, and the location became more and more undesirable, the hospital and motherhouse were transferred to the new St. Anthony's Hospital, Grand Avenue and Chippewa Street, which was blessed by Archbishop Kain on April 17th, 1900. The site is ideal, and the hospital provided with the most modern equipments. The beautiful chapel was blessed on April 17th, 1906 by Archbishop Glennon.

Besides the hospital in Cape Girardeau, the other branches are: St. Joseph Hospital on Fourth and Reservoir, Milwaukee, Wis., established in 1879; House of Providence, 1121 Orleans, Chicago, es-

---

12 Op. cit., pp. 10-12.

13 Op. cit., pp. 28-30.

tablished in 1882; St. Mary Hospital, Racine, Wis., established in 1882; St. Clara Orphanage, 3800 W. Twenty-ninth, Denver, Col., established 1890; St. Andrew Hospital, Murphysboro, Ill. established 1897; St. Elizabeth Hospital, Appleton, Wis., established 1899; Sacred Heart Orphanage, Pueblo, Col., established 1902; St. Rose Convent; a home for ladies, remodeled in 1909; St. Francis Hospital, Waterloo, Iowa, established 1909.

The next Order of women introduced into our diocese is that of the *Oblate Sisters of Providence,* a religious community of women of African descent, who have chosen as their special work the care and instruction of negro children.[14]

This congregation of Sisters was established in Baltimore on June 5th, 1829, by the Rev. James Hector Nicholas Joubert de la Muraille. Born in France, at St. Jean d' Angeli, on September 6th, 1777, he was sent in his youth to San Domingo, and became a victim of the insurrection of the blacks in that island, barely escaping with his life. At Baltimore he entered St. Mary's Seminary, and was ordained priest. He joined the Sulpician Society, and determined to do all he could for the regeneration of the race that had so grievously injured him. He taught a Sunday school class of colored children, and, seeing how neglected they were, determined to found a sisterhood of their own people for their education.

Consulting his friends, Father Tessier and Badaade, he was directed to four young women, who were then teaching a private school of their own. In June 1825, the first meeting was held with the purpose of forming a religious community. The approval of Archbishops Marechal and Whitfield having been obtained the four novices, on June 13th, 1829, established community life in a rented house in St. Mary's Court. Father Joubert drew up a Constitution and Rule for them. The Archbishop of Baltimore, on June 5th, 1829, gave his approbation, of the Rule with hearty praise for the Institution. Father Joubert died on November 5th, 1843, but other members of the Sulpician community continued his good work for the new Sisterhood. For a time a threatening cloud rested over them; some of the members were induced to leave the Oblate Sisters of Providence, and join a separate congregation founded by Father Gillet and Poilvache at Monroe, Michigan. Archbishop Eccleston was not favorable to them. But amid all their severe trials the Oblate Sisters placed their trust in Providence. The saintly Father John Neuman, the Provincial of the Redemptorists, had compassion on them and permitted Fathers Tschakert and Smulders to preach a retreat for them: Then Father Thaddeus Anwander, C.S.S.R., became their spiritual director; then the Jesuit Father P. L. Miller was assigned to the work. Fathers Joubert, An-

---

14 ''Blossoms Gathered from the Lower Branches,'' by a Oblate Sister, 1914.

wander and Miller are still held in highest veneration by the Oblate Sisters of Providence.[15]

The St. Louis branch of the Oblate Sisters was established October 16th, 1880, by the Jesuit Father Ignatius Panken, the pastor of St. Elizabeth's Church. The three Sisters began at once to teach school in the basement of the church. Father Pauken secured a neat three-story house on Seventeenth Street to which the Sisters moved and in which they opened school with fifty pupils in attendance. Another teacher now became necessary, for the rapidly increasing number of children.

On January 13th, 1883, the Sisters moved to Morgan Street, near Fourteenth. Kind benefactors came forward to help them in their need. New obligations had to be met. A number of orphan children had already been placed in their care. And applications came in from all sides. Sister Mary Dominica conceived the idea to open as asylum for negro orphan children. Archbishop Kenrick was well-pleased with the project.[16]

The Taylor Mansion on Page Avenue was bought by the Sisters for the purpose. It was a difficult and dangerous venture: but Divine Providence raised up new friends and benefactors. The Archbishop promised them $1,000 out of the Annual Collection for the negro and Indian Missions. On August 2nd, 1888, two Sisters and two postulants from St. Elizabeth's school on Morgan Street, were sent to open the asylum, with nine orphans: soon more orphans came. On May 27th, 1889, the new home was dedicated by Father Panken in honor of St. Frances of Rome, the patron saint of the Order. In 1889, Sister Dominica became Superior at the Orphan Home. Privations, and even real want, were of frequent occurrence: but in their greatest need God was always nearest to them. When the Oblate Sisters bought the Page Avenue property, there were but few houses in the neighborhood: but in a few years the location was improving so fast that they found it impossible to meet the demands that would soon be made on them. Besides the number of orphans had increased to such a degree that the home was again inadequate. In October 1896, they purchased the present site in Normandy. The purchase included eight acres of ground, an orchard, and two brick buildings. The Page Avenue property was sold and, on April 23rd, 1897, the Asylum was moved to Normandy, where the Sisters found new friends and benefactors.[17]

Of the second foundation of the Oblate Sisters in St. Louis, St. Rita's Academy for Colored Girls, only a brief mention can here be made, as it belongs to a later date.[18]

[15] Blossoms, pp. 1-15, passim.
[16] Ibidem, p. 26.
[17] Ibidem, p. 29.
[18] Blossoms, pp. 52 s. s.

## CHAPTER 46

## LATER JOURNALISTIC VENTURES

Times of open persecution are best calculated to rouse oppressed humanity to a clearer sense of its natural rights and duties in the matter of using the weapons of resistance. One of the permanent good results accruing to the Catholics of the archdiocese of St. Louis from the Drake Constitution and its infamous test-oath was their increased interest in the Catholic Press, the mighty weapon for defense and attack, so often praised and blessed, but so seldom adequately supported.

Bishop Rosati's and Archbishop Kenrick's journalistic ventures had failed through the indifference of the people. In times of peace there seemed to be no pressing need of a Catholic Press. The secular papers did all that was necessary in the matter of enlightenment. But when the bitter party spirit engendered by the war for the Union, led men to deny the right of the Church to preach the Gospel, to administer the sacraments and to engage in the work of christian education, except by sanction of the State, then the absolute need of a Catholic paper was deeply felt. The first attempt of supplying this need was not very promising. It was called *The Guardian* and bore the legend: "Arcet, Tuetur,[1] Justice a breastplate, true Judgment a helmet, equity and invincible shield, Wisdom, V. 19. James Clements is named as editor, and John Daly's Printing House as place of publication.

The paper began in 1865. There is in each number a column of Catholic affairs,

No. 2 of vol. 1. has a leader on "Epiphany, Twelfth Day."

No. 34 an article on "The Holy Father" and a sketch of the "House of the Angel Guardian."

There is also a sharp protest against the imprisonment of Father Hillner of Booneville for having preached the Gospel without having taken the test-oath; which among other things required that priests and ministers should declare that they had always been truly and loyally on the side of the United States against all enemies thereof, foreign and domestic. In Vol. II. No. 47, a certain Daniel McAuliffe volunteers for the Papal army, whilst the editor himself declares, that St. Louis is destined to be the Capital of the United States.

---

1 "It repels evil and guards the good" seems to be the sense of the Latin Motto.

Mr. Clements managed the *Guardian* editorially and in a business way until 1868, when he disposed of the material to the Rev. D. S. Phelan, owner of the *Western Watchman.*

The *Edina Watchman*, Weekly, made its first appearance at Edina, Missouri, in 1865 under the editorial and business management of Rev. D. S. Phelan, then pastor of that largely Catholic place. Having refused to subscribe to the test-oath prescribed by the Drake Constitution, he was imprisoned for a time, and, on being released, made vigorous use of the columns of his paper in an endeavor to secure the repeal of this obnoxious legislation. This made the priest-editor still more obnoxious to the radicals, who went so far as to charge him in the courts as a perjurer. Justice, however was not dead, but only sleeping. Judge Burkhard adjudged Father Phelan not guilty and assessed the costs of the trial to the County of Knox.[2] In August, 1868, he was transferred to the church of the Annunciation in St. Louis and brought his paper with him. From that day his management has been uninterrupted until his death.

"*The Western Watchman*," as the paper was now called appeared for the first time on February 6th, 1869. Its initial number brought a lenghty salutatory and an official announcement by Archbishop Kenrick. "The undersigned begs leave to recommend to the support of the Catholic public, the *Western Watchman*, a weekly paper, which is about to be published in this city, the character of those who have undertaken it, affording a reasonable assurance that it will be a useful auxiliary to religion, and be conducted in such a manner as to secure permanent success.

Peter Richard Kenrick,

Archbishop of St. Louis

St. Louis, December 26th, 1868."[3]

The paper was regarded for some time as the official journal of the Archdiocese, but as this claim brought on misunderstandings, the Editor dropped the claim.

The *Western Watchman* is still among the Champions of the Church, though it has lost much of the fighting spirit of former days. The *Western Watchman* really was Father David S. Phelan. They belonged together like Lindbergh and the Spirit of St. Louis. Father Phelan's spirit delighted in controversy. His had the wit, the general knowledge and the copious choice of words, to make him a most dangerous antagonist. "Let him alone," said Archbishop Kenrick to a good priest that came to complain of some rough treatment by the

---

[2] "Western Watchman," August, 1869.
[3] "Western Watchman," February 6, 1869.

*Watchman,* "let him alone: Father Phelan is a dangerous man." As a newspaper man, he was unique, and always interesting even to those who did not share his opinions, nor enjoy his pleasant pastime of excoriating his critics. No doubt, much good was done by this militant exponent of Catholicity, in strengthening the position of Catholics among their fellow citizens. No doubt, also, much harm was occasioned by his violent attacks upon the clergy, high and low, that opposed his views in regard to the school question, and what was called Cahenslyism, and Americanism. In treating of these matters all dignity of speech was forgotten: the rapier of controversy was changed into a flail. Father Phelan took a certain pride in his opposition to what he believed to be mere assumption of power by some of the leaders of the Church. He wrote in 1896:

"From its beginning the *Western Watchman* has been noted for its self-assertion and vigor of expression. It has been condemned by some bishops for its opposition to American interference in the strife between the Pope and the Italian government. Again it has been censured by some bishops for its opposition to episcopal interference in the affairs of patriotic societies. Again, it was condemned for its defense of the lower Clergy against what he held to be the uncanonical arbitrariness of certain bishops.[4] A fourth time it was condemned, and this time by the Archbishop of the city where it was published, for its assertion of the rights of the Catholic press."[5] And we may add a fifth time by the Papal Delegate for disrespectful language concerning him.

For Archbishop Ireland and Cardinal Gibbons the *Western Watchman* always professed the highest admiration. The Fairbault plan of the former prelate seemed to him the practical solution of the question of Catholic education; and when Rome gave its judgment: "tolerari potest," "it can be tolerated," he uttered the jubilant cry: "it is fully approved." Though tainted with the liberalism of the age, Father Phelan's Catholic faith was strong and impulsive. And though lacking in reverence for persons of exalted position, he bowed to authority, even if at times, ungraciously. As to his ability and wealth of illustration there can be no question: neither of his sincere love for Mother Church. Many a battle royal did he fight against the defamers of religion.

He was feared by many; yet loved by more, partly because he was a tower of strength for the present, partly because he had bravely stood his place at a time when it was dangerous to do so.

---

4  Father Phelan's "Canon Law" was rather uncanonical at times.
5  Encyclopedia of the History of St. Louis, vol. III, p. 1896.

· The *Western Watchman* has always been a Democratic, as well as a religious paper. In 1887 it advocated free silver. It opposed the War with Spain, but, since transoceanic territory has been acquired, it urged its retention. It advocated the present public school system for all the people, and a strictly religious parish school system for Catholics. The *Western Watchman* circulated largely throughout the Mississippi Valley in the West, and in the Northwest. There must be many copies of this paper preserved by its readers in memory of great events there chronicled, and, no doubt, our libraries have been laying aside the numbers as they were issued. The *"Watchman"* is a chronicle of the Church's history in the West for more than sixty years.

The year 1872 gave birth to a pair of lesser lights in Catholic journalism: *The Central Magazine,"* edited and published by Mary Nolan, a sixty-eight page monthly, of which the first issue appeared in July, 1872, and the last in 1877. It was not high . class, yet readable. Its most important contents are the Obituaries of priests and Catholic laymen.

"The *La Salle Journal,"* a religious and literary monthly, was begun in January 1872 by George A. Schuette, who afterwards became a member of the Christian Brothers. It continued about two years.

Of the Bohemian Catholic Weekly *"Hlas"* we have no personal knowledge, except that the management gives all assurance of its thoroughly Catholic tendency.

It covered a wide field at the time of its first appearance, there being then no paper of its class nearer than Chicago, on the one side, and Texas, on the other. It dates from 1871 and was published by the Bohemian Literary Society. It is still hale and hearty in its 56th year, and appears twice a week. Father (afterwards Msgr.) Joseph Hessoun was its founder and first editor. For considerably more than half a century has the *Hlas,* that is, the Bohemian Voice, been a bond of love and mutual helpfulness between the Bohemian Catholics throughout the United States. The Bohemian Literary Society also publishes a magazine for women, the *Ceska Uena*, which was started in 1908 and appears twice a month.

It is a strange fact that not a single Catholic book in the French language was ever published in St. Louis, or, for that matter, in the entire state. There was a French newspaper established in the city in 1854. Its editor M. Louis Cortambert, was a gentleman of fine literary attainments. The paper was called *Revue de'L Ouest*. It has long since disappeared from the field of journalism.

In this place we must allude to the tragic failure of B. M. Chambers' attempt to make the fourth *St. Louis Times* a Catholic Daily.[6] This paper was founded in July 1877 by Stilson Hutchins, Dr. H. Mahoney and John Hodnet as a democratic journal, "entirely southern in tone." Hutchins became editor-in-chief. After a most interesting career under various publishers and editors the *St. Louis Times* was in May 1877 bought, at public sale, for fifty thousand dollars, by B. M. Chambers, a staunch Catholic, who wished to make it a Catholic family daily. Mr. Chambers appointed R. H. Sylvester, managing editor, and C. S. Fisher, business manager. The promised support from Catholic circles did not come forward in the manner expected. "Chambers' money kept the paper afloat until November 1878" as Scharf says, when it was consolidated with the *Journal* of Walcot and Hume, under the name *The Times-Journal*. In 1879 Chambers who owned three-fifths of the stock, placed A. S. Mitchell in charge as editor, and advertised the paper for sale. In August 1879 Chambers sold the concern to Dr. James P. Beck, who being disheartened by the continuous opposition, threw the paper back on Chambers' hands. Finally J. H. D. Cundiff bought it, October 1879. After a stormy career of two and a half years B. M. Chambers had sacrificed a fortune in the attempt to conduct a secular daily from the Catholic point of view, such as the *St. Louis Leader* had been; and such as the German *Amerika* was at that very time and long years after.[7]

It may be objected that secular journals do not really come in the purview of the Catholic Press. But they do. Religious and ecclesiastical papers we have in abundance: they do a noble and most necessary work. But the Catholic's point of view on secular matters is not that of the world. The spirit of the age is socialistic, a distinct contradiction to the spirit of the Church.

To judge Catholic matters in the light of eternity—and secular matters in the light of socialistic principles is intellectually and morally wrong. We Catholics, therefore, need a secular daily press, conducted by men who are inbued with the principles of Catholic philosophy, and know how to apply them to the current questions in education, sociology, politics, jurisprudence and medicine. Such a paper, no doubt, Mr. Chambers intended to give us. That he failed, in the attempt is not to his dishonor.

---

6  Complete files of Mr. Chambers' "Times," May 7, 1877, to Nov. 20, 1878, are to be found in the St. Louis Mercantile Library. Also, of the "Times-Journal" to Dec., 1879. A few numbers in Library of State Historical Society, Columbia.

7  As reason must be enlightened by faith to judge aright, so the secular press must be guided by the principles of the Christian Religion, otherwise it becomes a blind leader of the blind, as we see it today.

The *"Church Progress,"* weekly, for many years edited by Mr. Paul Chew, now requires our attention. Like all our Catholic papers it also had a checkered though, in the main, rather prosperous career, to the present day. It seems to have been founded for a special purpose, namely to minister to the wants of the American descendants of both the German and Irish immigrants.

There were in St. Louis since 1840 two strong currents of national life, in the Church, flowing side by side, the Irish and the German. In comparison with these the French and Anglo-Americans seemed negligible quantities. The French Catholics gradually relinquished their language for the American, the Germans alone held fast to a foreign tongue in their new home. Their feeling towards the Fatherland was merely sentimental, in no wise political: whilst the Irishman's affection for "Old Ireland" was both political, religious, and sentimental. Irish·priests were their ideal, whereas the German was contented, if his priest could speak the German language. But Archbishop Kenrick, fair as he was to all, provided German priests for the Germans, Irish for the Irish, and later on Polish for the Poles, and so on.

All these national fragments also desired to have papers in their own language.

The Irish had their *Western Watchman,* the Germans their *Amerika* and *Herold des Glaubens,* and the *Church Progress* was started to meet the wishes of the native born of both races.

The rather complicated origin of the *Church Progress* is clearly stated by a contributor to the Encyclopedia of the History of St. Louis: "The *Church Progress* and *Catholic World,"* weekly, is a consolidation of two Catholic papers, the titles of which appear in its present name. The *"Church Progress"* was published at Marshall, Illinois, from its beginning in 1878 until 1888 when it was consolidated with the *"Catholic World"* (of St. Louis). At the outset the *"Church Progress"* was a Monthly Parish Record, but soon became a weekly, devoted principally to Catholic news and literature. It covered a large field and attained a circulation of 6,000 copies, a phenomenal number to emanate from a country town. The Rev. Father C. Kuhlmann was editor and publisher. The *"Catholic World"* of St. Louis was founded in 1885, being published by the World Publishing Company, in 1887 it was purchased by the St. Louis Catholic Publishing Company, which, in February 1888 bought the *"Church Progress"* and consolidated the two papers. The Rev. C. F. O'Leary was the first editor of the *"Catholic World."*

In the great religious controversy conducted in the Globe Democrat in consequence of Archbishop Ryan's lecture: "What Catholics Do Not Believe," 1882, Father O'Leary, then pastor of St. Brendan's Church, Mexico, Mo., took a distinguished part with what he called

*"Father O'Leary's Letters to The Heretics,"* which displayed considerable erudition and versatility. His editorship of the *"Catholic World"* terminated in August 1886.

Condé B. Pallen a graduate of St. Louis University, succeeded to the editoral management serving until 1896, when he resigned, and the paper was conducted by an executive Committee. This arrangement continued until March 1899, when Mr. Pallen resumed its editoral control. The *"Church Progress* and *Catholic World* is calm and dispassionate in tone, yet never hesitates to advocate a just cause, or to antagonize a wrong one as its editor regards it."[8] This was written in 1889 about forty years ago. The *Church Progress* like all its predecessors and contemporaries, is a store-house of information on historical matters. We would call attention to the three historical series we published in its columns. The "Historical Gleanings from Forgotten Fields," February 1,—March 22nd, 1917; "The Catholic Garner" March 30,—October 1, 1917; and the "First Native Missourians in the College of the Propaganda at Rome." December 10, 1918—February 20, 1919.

Father Tuohy, the erratic free-lance of journalism, was one of the early editors of the *Church Progress*. The only sample of personal journalism St. Louis can boast of is the *"Fortnightly Review"* of Dr. Arthur Preuss, now in its 35th year. It was established April 1st, 1894, at Chicago, as a monthly, but six months later became a weekly. In July, 1895, Dr. Preuss moved the paper to St. Louis. The learned Doctor still wields his trenchant pen in the *Review,* "discussing largely questions of philosophic lines."[9]

It is, of course, Catholic to the core, although it no longer bears the motto: "Christianus, mihi nomen, Catholicus cognomen." The editor, while not exactly persona grata with all higher ecclesiastics, nevertheless has the ear of most of them and the kindly interest and support of many of the best of them.

Among priests the *"Fortnightly"* is a welcome visitor, sometimes exasperating, generally enlightening, and always thought-compelling. Mr. Preuss, though a layman and father of a large family, is one of the ablest theological writers in our country. His translation of Pohle's Dogmatic Theology, and his adaptation of Koch's Moral Theol-

---

8   Encyclopedia of the History of St. Louis, vol. III, p. 1897.

9   Dr. Arthur Preuss is the eldest son of the distinguished convert from Lutheranism, Dr. Edward Preuss.

ogy would amply prove this statement. He is also the best Catholic authority we have on Freemasonry. The *Fortnightly Review* is indispensible to the student of contemporary history, ecclesiastical and cultural. .

Mr. Kenkel resigned his position as Editor-in-chief of the *Amerika* in 1920 with a view of devoting his time and talents to the development of the "Central Bureau" of the German Catholic Societies, and its monthly publication the *Central-Blatt and Social Justice*, two magazines, as it were, in one. This periodical was established in 1909 to bring about a better understanding between the members of the Central Society and to promote the study of sociology. Mr. Kenkel is one of the recognized authorities in matters of social science and its application. At stated intervals the magazine contains four pages of German-American history. Both English and German are used for the editorials. Brief reports on society matters are generally given in German. The editor has a staff of very able writers of sociological questions, as Father Engelen, Professor Bruehl, D. D., of Philadelphia, Professor Muench, D. D., of Milwaukee and Mr. A. Brockland, the assistant manager of the Central Bureau. The *Central-Blatt and Social Justice* represents and defends the Catholic view on great social questions that agitate the minds of men in our day, questions that must be solved, and solved right, if the world is to regain industrial and social peace.

According an honorable mention to the *Negro Child* and to the *Echo from Africa*, and Father Dunne's *"Newsboy,"* we come to the excellent Jesuit Magazine, *The Queen's Work*, edited since 1914 by Father Garesché. It styles itself "A National Magazine of Catholic Activities; primarily, devoted to the spread of devotion to the Blessed Virgin." Its circulation is 75,000. Since 1918 St. Louis has its Catholic Historical Society, founded by Archbishop Glennon; and this organization published a quarterly called *The St. Louis Catholic Historical Review*. "The first editor of the publication was the Rev. Dr. Charles L. Souvay, C. M., who by his learning and energy gave the *Review* a standing among the best of the country. The *Review* published original articles on subjects of the ecclesiastical history of the Mississippi Valley, and documents from the archives of the Society. It completed its fifth volume in 1923 to enter upon a long period of suspended animation.

Last but not least comes the *St. Louis Catholic Herald*, the third Catholic weekly in the English language, to cheer and enlighten the reading public of St. Louis and vicinity. It was established in 1921.

The year 1924 witnessed the demise of the *Daily Amerika,* after a long and faithful course of manifold service to the Archdiocese in general and to the German Catholics of the Northwest.   In 1925 the *Pastoral-Blatt* followed the *Amerika* into the tomb of the unforgotten dead.   They have not lived in vain.   Though often disregarded, their activities have left a mark on some, at least, perhaps, on many minds; and so their good influence may still be active among us, although unknown to fame.   For ideas are immortal, though their outward form and expression be very perishable.

Posterity owes all these priests and laymen, who as journalists wore out their lives in the service of truth and justice, a heavy debt of gratitude.

## Chapter 47

# PROGRESS OF THE CHURCH IN CENTRAL MISSOURI

## I

Father Ferdinand Helias D'Huddeghem, commonly called Father Helias, in 1838, laid the broad foundation for the Church in Central Missouri by erecting the mission of Westphalia into a Jesuit Residence. Not that he could claim priority in all its Catholic establishments, for others had preceded him in the missionary field; but it was Father Helias who built up at least twenty missions, the majority of which developed into strong parishes, in the counties of Cole, Osage, Gasconade, Boon and Callaway. The first religious center established by him, was at Westphalia, in Osage County: but baffled here by the stubborn pride of some of the "Latin farmers,"[1] he retired to St. Louis. During this brief period of rest from missionary labors he rallied from his pessimistic feelings, and in September 1842, returned to the attack, making his headquarters in Haarville, subsequently called Taos, in Cole County, where in 1840 he had built the Church of St. Francis. Here the indefatigable missionary was destined to remain until his death in 1874. Up to the date of Father Helias' departure from Westphalia in 1842 only three churches were in existence in all his missionary district, the Church of St. Joseph at Westphalia, St. Francis Xavier in Cole County, and the Sacred Heart in Richfountain. The fourth to be built was that of St. Ignatius Loyola at Jefferson City. Its construction was begun in 1841 and it was completed before 1843. A fifth church, that of Assumption at Cedron, in Moniteau County, was built before 1843.

April 6th, 1844, the corner stone was laid of the new church of St. Francis Xavier in Haarville. The edifice, 60 by 38 feet, could claim the distinction of being the first Catholic stone church to be built in the interior of Missouri. It was occupied for the first time on May 11th, 1845, Father Helias on this occasion addressing the congregation in English, German and French.

Towards the end of 1844, the Church of St. Thomas the Apostle was built at Indian Bottom, Cole County, near a bend in the Osage River. Finally, on Ascension Day, May 1st, 1845, the Church of the Immaculate Conception at Loose Creek, in Osage County, on the main

---

[1] Latin farmers, was the name applied to that class of German settlers who had attended a gymnasium before coming to the Wild West. They often were dissatisfied with their hard lot and rather critical in regard to their surroundings.

public road between Jefferson City and St. Louis, was opened for divine service. Thus by the middle of 1845, Catholic churches had been .built at Westphalia, Haarville, Richfountain, Jefferson City, Moniteau, Indian Bottom and Loose Creek. These seven churches, attesting the progress Catholicity had made in Central Missouri, were among the results of Father Helias' first seven years of labor in that part· of St. Louis diocese.[2]

Regular monthly services were held by Father Helias on consecutive Sundays at Haarville, Jefferson City, Loose Creek, and Richfountain. The fifth Sunday of the month or a Feastday occurring in the month was assigned to St. Joseph's Church at Westphalia. Besides this monthly round of visits, services were held three or four times a year at the Assumption on Moniteau Creek, at St. Thomas the Apostle, Indian Bottom, Cole County, and at Holy Cross in Pilot Grove, Cooper County. Moreover, visits were paid once or twice a year to Booneville, Columbia, Hibernia, Cote-sans-dessein and other stations.

Father Helias in his letter of January 6th, 1845, contributed to the Berichte der Leopoldinen Stiftung XIX, gives a summary of his ministry in the various parishes and stations of this Mission for the period 1838-1844.

|                        | 1838 | 1839 | 1840 | 1841 | 1842 | 1843 | 1844 |
|------------------------|------|------|------|------|------|------|------|
| Number of souls ...... | 620  | 700  | 950  | 1500 | 2000 | 2000 | 2500 |
| Infant Baptisms ...... | 23   | 36   | 37   | 125  | 150  | 149  | 175  |
| Easter Communions ...  | 423  | 560  | 700  | 1094 | 1090 | 1100 | 1300 |
| First Communions ..    | 9    | 15   | 16   | 20   | 60   | 90   | 100  |
| Conversions .........  | 3    | 4    | 5    | 4    | 4    | 3    | 4    |
| Marriages ...........  | 3    | 3    | 14   | 26   | 23   | 27   | 36   |
| Burials .............. | 12   | 9    | 17   | 24   | 19   | 50   | 155[3] |

As money was very scarce among the early settlers of the country, Father Helias depended for the funds necessary for the erection and furnishing of his seven churches on the generosity of his Flemish relatives and friends, chief among them, his mother, the Countess Helias D'Huddeghem. The generous help of the Leopoldine Association of Vienna in Austria was also laid under contribution for the benefit of the missions. His income from the congregations was never large; his life was a life of poverty and content. He travelled either on horseback, or by steamer up and down the Missouri river. He never had a housekeeper, but kept house himself, preparing his own meals, and occasionally took dinner with one of his parishioners. But a

---

2 Cf. Garraghan, G. J., in "St. Louis Catholic Historical Review," vol. II, p. 171.

3 "Berichte der Leopoldinen Striftung," Heft XIX.

lover of poverty, as Father Helias was, there was nothing too good and beautiful for the house of God.

His friendship with the General of the Jesuits in Rome was the means of obtaining some very fine old paintings for the church at Taos, supposed to be original works of Guido Reni.[4]

Father Helias wrote and spoke French, German, English and his native Flemish; he had a remarkable fluency in writing Latin prose and verse. His interest in Catholic education led him to establish a parochial school at Taos. As a preacher he was not a success; although what he said, being enforced by the holiness of his life, went to the heart of his hearers.

"The year 1844," as Father Garraghan tells us, "was a calamitous one for Father Helias. The Missouri river flood of that year, the greatest in the history of the river, followed by a protracted drought, brought widespread sickness in its wake. There was no house without its patient, and in most houses all the inmates were down with disease at the same time. In one dwelling which he visited, Father Helias found no fewer than twenty persons in the last stages of disease. The one compensating circumstance was that it was a season of divine grace for many of the victims, who found their way back to God's friendship, as the shadows of death crept upon them. Father Helias himself was not to escape the consequence of the great physical strain and constant exposure to infection put upon him by the exercise of his ministry at this critical time. His health broke down and he began to waste away, his skin, as he expressed it in Scriptural phrase, cleaving to his bone. The doctors could do nothing for him and despaired of his recovery. And yet, he passed through the crisis, regained his strength and was able in time to take up again his burden of parochial missionary duties. The next year 1845, he was repeating his experience of the past year, wearing himself out with attendance on the sick and running every risk of infection. A second collapse followed and the Father lay on what seemed from every human outlook his bed of death. The most skillful physicians in the county pronounced him beyond reach of medical aid. For some days he lay in a coma, a cold sweat bathing his forehead, and the extremities of his body stiff with the icy rigors of approaching dissolution. Funeral arrangements began to be made, and the parishes were notified to send their quota of pallbearers. But at the last moment the skill of a worthy widow, Gertrude Evens by name, saved the priest's life. She succeeded in forcing a long reed tube between his firmly clenched teeth, with the result that some needed medicine was successfully

---

4 _ Garraghan, 1. c., pp. 172 and 173.

administered. He rallied, grew steadily stronger and in a short while was again performing his customary round of labors."[5]

Though broken in health and exhausted by the constant strain, Father Helias would not leave his post of duty. It was suggested to him that he return to Belgium, for the declining years of his life, but he refused to consider the offer. "Father Helias declines to return to Belgium, desiring to consummate the sacrifice of his health and life," wrote the Vice-Provincial of the Jesuits of Missouri, "let him then remain where he is."[6]

A partial relief, however, came to Father Helias on December 8th, 1846, in the person of Father James Cotting, who had arrived from Switzerland in 1840, and now became the missionary's assistant. Father Cotting was, in Father Helias' own words, "an exceeding zealous and active young missionary" and an admirable companion, a man of "sympathetic charity" that cheered the good old Father more than words could tell. At Father Cotting's arrival the fever that had greatly troubled Father Helias for months disappeared, and left him in the enjoyment of fresh health and strength.

In addition to this relief, the parishes of Jefferson City and Maniteau were taken over by a secular priest, Father James S. Murphy Sr. Father Murphy was a native of Dublin and, after his ordination to the priesthood, set out for the wilds of Missouri. He arrived in Jefferson City in July 1846, and took up his abode in a blockhouse on Richmond Hill. The church, a small structure of heavy oak planks, stood on High Street. Father Murphy remained in Jefferson City until December 1848, when he was appointed pastor of Lexington. During the Know-nothing movement in 1850 he left the country for Ireland and soon after died in his native city, Dublin.[7]

Of Father Murphy's successor in Jefferson City, Father Joseph Ursus Meister, Monsignor Holweck has given a brief character-sketch in the *Pastoral-Blatt* of St. Louis. Father Meister was born in Switzerland and served the Parish of Etzikon as pastor, when Vicar-General Melcher engaged him for the American missions. He was pastor of Jefferson City from March 1849 to August 1853. Later on he did missionary work in the Counties Moniteau, Morgan, Pettis, Saline and Cooper. Father Joseph Ursus Meister was an original character, simple almost to rudeness, but a zealous priest withall.

The third pastor of Jefferson City, Father Joseph Blaarer, a countryman of Meister and one of his companions on the voyage to America, served the Church of Jefferson City less than a year and had as his successor the Rev. William Walsh, the future pastor of St.

---

5   Garraghan, 1. c., p. 174.
6   April 16, 1846.
7   Chancery Records.

Bridget's Church in St. Louis. Father William Walsh was born October 5th, 1829, in County Limerick, Ireland, and came to St. Louis in 1851. He received Holy orders at the hands of Archbishop Kenrick on June 10th, 1854, and immediately after was appointed to the parish of Jefferson City.

Father Walsh turned the old Church of St. Ignatius into a schoolhouse and replaced it by a new structure of brick which was dedicated under the invocation of St. Peter, under which title the parish of Jefferson City has been known ever since. In the early days of Father Walsh the congregation at Jefferson City numbered forty families; but the pastor and his assistants also attended the Catholics of Hermann and of the various stations along the railroad as far as Sedalia. Columbia and Fulton also were attended from Jefferson City.

Father Henry Van der Sanden, the future Chancellor of the archdiocese, was Father Walsh's assistant from August 29th, 1860 to August 29th, 1862.[8]

On Father William Walsh's appointment to St. Bridget's parish in St. Louis, Father Jacob Meller became pastor of Jefferson City, the fifth in line. Father Meller was born on December 22nd, 1831, in Kerpen, Rhenish Prussia, and coming to St. Louis in 1852, was raised to the priesthood June 29th, 1855. His priestly activities in Jefferson City extended from 1863 to 1875. Of his assistants, Fathers Schrage and Kueper deserve special mention.[9]

The sixth pastor of Jefferson City, Henry Meurs, was already favorably known as the founder of St. Mary's Church at Glasgow. He was a countryman of Father Meller, whom he succeeded in 1875 as pastor of Jefferson City. He is the only priest of all those that labored in the State Capital, to find his last resting place there. His epitaph in the chapel records the facts that he was born September 3rd, 1839, ordained May 10th, 1866, and died August 24th, 1876.[10]

The seventh in line of Jefferson City's pastors, the Very Rev. Otto Joseph Stanislaus Hoog, was born April 18th, 1845 at Ettenheim in Baden, and came to St. Louis with his parents in 1854. In his ninth year the boy Otto lost both parents as victims of the cholera. He was brought to the German St. Vincent's Orphan Asylum; where he remained six years. He made his classical studies at the St. Louis University, entered the Seminary of St. Francis, Milwaukee, in 1861, and completed his theological studies at the Diocesan Seminary at Cape Girardeau. At the request of Archbishop Kenrick the young

---

8  "Missouri Volksfreund," (Jubilee Edition, October 6, 1896), and Chancery Records.

9  "Missouri Volksfreund."

10  "Missouri Volksfreund."

levite was raised to the priesthood by Bishop Juncker of Alton on December 21st, 1867. Father Hoog's first appointment was to the parish of Lexington, where he remained until August 1875, when he received his appointment as successor to Father Meurs.[11]

A man of gentle retiring disposition and endowed with winning manners, Father Hoog in a short time, enjoyed the affectionate regard of his people. He was scrupulously exact in the performance of his priestly and business obligations. Although not gifted with conspicuous ability, and utterly averse to the vulgarity of competition, he won the sincere regard of his Superiors and attained the highest dignities in the archdiocese below the episcopate, as city pastor, Vicar-General and Roman Prelate. Father or rather Monsignor Hoog's, twenty years administration of St. Peter's at Jefferson City, forms the brightest and happiest period of its history. It was during this period that the beautiful church was built, and the magnificent school and parish residence was erected. It was through Father Hoog that the religious life of the parish was brought to its highest level. Father Hoog's Silver Jubilee Celebration, December 21st, 1892, was a revelation of universal regard the pastor held in the hearts of his people, and of his brethren in the priesthood.

Of the long line of assistants to Father Hoog at Jefferson City, we can mention but a few: Father Joseph, Fr. M. Diel, the genuinely pious, though slightly erratic, brother of the Rhineland's poet-priest John B. Diel, S. J.

Father Bernard Stemker, the future pastor of Kirkwood; Father, now Monsignor F. G. Holweck, D. D. Vicar-General, and author of important historical and antiquarian volumes;

Father Sebastian Sennerich, a representative of "that classic eloquence, whose practice and grandeur belong chiefly to the past."

Father John Schramm, the founder of the church at Elston in Cole County;

The Reverend Joseph Selinger, D. D., for many years Professor of Dogmatic Theology at the Seminary of St. Francis, Milwaukee, and eventually Father Hoog's successor as pastor of St. Peter's Church in Jefferson City;

Father Joseph Wentker, one of our best exponents of Catholic Sociology; and finally, Father Simon, J. Orf, D. D., a native of Josephsville, St. Charles County, author of the "Manual of the Forty Hours' Adoration."

After this lengthy disgression which is intended to show how the good seed of Father Helias bore fruit under the care of diocesan

---

[11]  Missouri Volks freund., l. c.

priests, we must now return to the personal efforts of Father Helias and his spiritual brother in arms, Father Cotting.

It was Father Cotting who undertook the reconquest of Westphalia; where a new stone church was in process of erection. The corner stone had been laid on March 19th, 1848, amid the booming of "Mexican cannon, trophies fresh from the siege of Sacramento,"[12] that roused the joy of the people to the highest pitch.

Father Cotting made a good impression on his flock of hard-headed Westphalians who, by the way, were not Westphalians. But the small determined faction that had made life at Westphalia unbearable to Father Helias, now turned their batteries of calumny and abuse on Father Cotting.

"Unfortunately," as Father Garraghan says, "some unguarded statements of the priest, who was quick-tempered and frank of speech, were eagerly seized on by the enemies and turned to his disadvantage. A riotous disturbance which occurred in Westphalia on February 2nd, 1848, was laid to his charge. A lawsuit followed at Jefferson City, in which the Father appeared as defendant. The suit went against him, and only the intervention of Father Helias with some of the public officials saved Father Cotting from the payment of a heavy fine. Father Cotting was thereupon removed by his Superior from Westphalia, to which he bade farewell, January 18th, 1849. His connection with the Missouri Vice-Province ceased at the same time, and he spent the remainder of his days a member of the Maryland Province of his Order.[13]

"Father Cotting's place at Westphalia was filled by Father Andrew Ehrensberger, a Bavarian, one of the exiled German Jesuits who found a home in the Vice-Province of Missouri in 1848. Father Ehrensberger took up his residence at Westphalia on November 17 of that year. From this time forward there were two independent residences in Central Missouri, Westphalia and Taos. Father Ehrensberger gave much of his time and attention to the neighboring Bavarian settlement at Richfountain. Some little skill which he possessed as a painter he turned to good account by decorating the parish church. Father Helias's estimate of Father Ehrensberger's capabilities as a pastor of souls was high. He called him a capital preacher, 'optimus concionator,' and summed up his record as a pastor of Westphalia in the words, 'that redoubtable companion of Christ has so acquitted himself that no one can speak ill of him without untruth.' Father Ehrensberger left Westphalia in 1851 to take up the duties of a professor in St.

---

12 Garraghan, 1. c., p .175.
13 Garraghan, p. 175. "Historia Westphaliae."

Xavier's College, Cincinnati. He was subsequently recalled to Germany where he achieved distinction as a missionary and preacher."[14]

"Father Ehrensberger was succeeded as Superior of the Westphalia Residence by Father Kalcher of the Austrian Province. Father Helias styles him 'an excellent operarius.' Thenceforward the line of Superiors at Westphalia down to the period of the Civil War, includes the names of Father Joseph Brunner, Anthony Eysvogels and John Baptist Goeldlin. Other Fathers attached to the residence as assistants during the same years were James Busschots, Joseph Weber, James Bruehl, John Schulte, William Niederkorn and Henry Van Mierlo."

The steeple of the new stone church of St. Joseph in Westphalia was not finished until some years later than the dedication of the church, a circumstance which seemed to lend point, according to the author of the "Annual Letters," to the Latin inscription over the church door, placed there by the architect;

"Concordia res crescunt, discordia dilabuntur."

Happily the mischief-making tendencies of a part of the congregation during the early period of its history had been corrected, so that Father Goeldlin, Superior of the Westphalia Residence, could write in 1862: "The spirit of the people is in general, good. They have learned that in annoying and contradicting their priests there is neither peace nor the blessing of God."[15]

After 1860 Father J. B. Goeldlin was pastor of Westphalia, with Fathers William Niederkorn and P. M. Grietens as assistants. Other assistants were: Father Peter Paul von Haza-Radlitz, the celebrated missionary, and Frederick Hageman, who at a later date' served as pastor of St. Joseph's Church, St. Louis, and then as Master of Novices in Florissant. Father William Niederkorn[16] entered upon a ten year term as pastor in September 1871. From September 1881 to September 1883 Father Peter Krier held the rectorship with Fathers Ganzer and Valazza as assistants. With them the Jesuit administration of the parish of Westphalia ceased, and Father F. Anton Diepenbrock, a secular priest, was appointed as head of the ancient church, the earliest foundation of good old Father Helias.

---

14 Garraghan, 1. c., p. 176.

15 Goeldlin, "Missio Missouriensis."

16 Father William Niedenkorn is my own spiritual father, he having baptized me in St. Joseph's Church sixty-eight years ago.

## CHAPTER 48

## PROGRESS OF THE CHURCH IN CENTRAL MISSOURI

### II

The bulk of the Catholic population of Osage County is composed of Germans of three distinct racial affiliations: the people of Westphalia being for the most part Westphalians, the people of Loose Creek, Rhinelanders, and the people of Richfountain, Bavarians. The Creole element, the earliest of all, and the Irish and native American, are represented by relatively small quotas. The parishes of a later date, carved out of the territory of these original foundations, may possess a mixture of these elements: but these three original centers maintain a distinct identity as to descent and social characteristics. *Loose Creek*, probably corrupted from the French L'ours, Bear Creek, was the name of a small tributary of the Maries river, and as such, came to designate the circumjacent territory and its natural center, the town that sprang up around the Church of the Immaculate Conception in Osage County.

At the time of its organization as a distinct parish, October 10th, 1848, Loose Creek comprised, the original Loose Creek of Father Helias, as also the older German settlement of Westphalia around Father Meinkman's chapel of St. John's on the Dohmen farm, together with Cadets Creek and French Village. Before this date, mass had been said at Loose Creek in the public school house, and at Cadets Creek and French Village in private residences.[1]

At French Village the ministrations of Father Helias do not seem to have found due appreciation; The zealous Father notes a number of singular visitations of God upon some of the neglectful Creoles of French Village and Cadets Creek.

At last he decided to discontinue his visits to both places, inviting the inhabitants to attend services at Loose Creek.

On September 28th, 1843, six acres of land were bought for Church purposes, at less than a dollar per acre, and soon after the erection of a log house for holding divine services was begun. It was dedicated on May 1st, 1845, and every third Sunday of the month, rain or shine, Father Helias came over from Taos to say mass and administer the sacraments. On October 10th, 1848 the mission of Loose Creek became a parish, and early in 1849 Father T. P. Busschots took up the pastoral duties in the place, though still domiciled at Westphalia. After

---

[1] Garraghan, G. J., "The Mission of Central Missouri," in "St. Louis Historical Review," vol. II, p. 177.

a one-room house had been fitted up for his residence, Father Busschots came to reside in his parish. But even then he took his meals with a neighboring family. The parish of Loose Creek, at this time, was very large, extending from the Missouri river to Linn, and from Baily's Creek and Chamois to the Maries river. The Parish Records were begun September 1st, 1851. In 1852 the first schoolhouse was built and school opened with a lay teacher. During the early fifties the settlement was visited by various diseases, chief among them the cholera. In 1852 Father Busschots recorded fifty-six burials. In 1855 the death rate reached its climax with seventy-eight. After that, health conditions improved and the death rate gradually returned to normal figures. In spite of these severe losses, however, the parish constantly grew in numbers, through a constant flow of immigration, and the number of worshippers outgrew the capacity of the log church. The wealth of the .people, also, had assumed respectable proportions. A new church to be built of brick, now seemed within reach. The decision was made: and all hands went to work. The stone masons and carpenters among the parishioners, and the workmen and farmers, gave a good part of their time, skill and labor free of charge: even the children were employed in carrying brick. When the church was completed there was but a small debt resting upon the property. It was Father Niederkorn, the successor of Father Busschots in 1868 who carried the building operations to a gratifying conclusion. Archbishop Kenrick had laid the corner stone in the Fall of the year 1868: on October 10th, 1870, the building was solemnly dedicated to the honor of God and the Immaculate Virgin. It took seven years more to finish the great work.

The Irish laborers on the Missouri Pacific Railroad whom the Jesuit Fathers had befriended during the cholera epidemic, expressed their gratitude by donating to the church the two side altars of our Blessed Lady and St. Joseph. Father Niederkorn was relieved in 1871 by Father Paul von Haza-Radlitz, to become the rector of Westphalia; but in 1881 he returned to Loose Creek for a second term of two years. In the meantime Father von Haza-Radlitz had introduced the Sisters of the Precious Blood into the school, and built a convent for them. Father P. A. Krier was the last Jesuit pastor of Loose Creek. He built the priest's residence of solid limestone. In September 1885 Father Francis Braun arrived from St. Louis to make arrangements for turning over the parish to the secular priest Father John Gruender.[2]

Father Gruender was born in Dringenberg, Prussia, September 2nd, 1842, came to America in 1864 and was ordained priest July 19th, 1866. He had been pastor successively of Germantown in Henry County, Koeltztown in Maries County and Taos in Cole. He labored with zeal

---

[2] Souvenir of the Diamond Jubilee of the Immaculate Conception Church of Loose Creek.

and success in his new field for twenty-three years, showing special care for the beauty of the House of God. In 1891 the Sisters of the Precious Blood relinquished the school in favor of the Sisters de Notre Dame, who have remained in charge to the present day. Father Gruender suffered a stroke of paralysis on November 10th, 1908, two days after the close of the Forty Hours Adoration but lingered on until death relieved him on March 29th, 1909. Father John B. Bachmeier, his former assistant, and the pastor of Frankenstin was the successor of Father Gruender. The present Pastor is Father Henry S. Kueper.[3]

The Church of Richfountain, some five or six miles south of Westphalia, ranks third in the series of Father Helias' seven churches, having been built before the Father's retirement from Westphalia 1841. The little frame structure was dedicated to the Sacred Heart. The first mass in the place was said on May 11th, 1838 by Father Helias in the home of John Struempf in honor of whom the place was originally called "Struempf Settlement." Father Helias conferred upon it the poetic name it now bears, derived from a beautiful spring of crystal water in the neighborhood. Richfountain was settled by Bavarians. These good people stood high in the regard of their Jesuit pastors who visited them every second Sunday in the month. In 1846 the Rev. John Bax, S.J. was appointed first resident rector of Richfountain.

"In 1849, when the cholera was at its height, the congregation of the Sacred Heart vowed an annual exposition and adoration of the Blessed Sacrament for ten hours. Everyone in the parish escaped unharmed from the scourge. Accordingly, every year on the Sunday within the Octave of the Feast of the Sacred Heart, the people were wont to fulfill their vow with great devotion. Years after, when cholera again broke out in the state, no case was reported from Richfountain an indication, as the author of the "Annual Letters" observes, of how pleasing to the Lord was the pious faith of the congregation. Another instance of the piety of the parishioners of Richfountain was the annual Solemn High Mass for a successful harvest. The Mass stipend was made up by small contributions from the farmers."[4]

In the list of Father Bax's successors we find the honored names of Fathers F. N. Schulak, M. Haering and Martin Seisl. It was Father Aloysius Averbeck that built the new church in 1879 and 1880. The Coadjutor Bishop Ryan blessed it on October 16th, 1880. The old school erected in 1858 bore the motto, engraved in stone: "Spes Patriae"—"The Hope of Our Country."—The Jesuit Father Averbeck enjoys the credit of having added hundreds of acres of the best land to the district of Richfountain. A shallow lake of stagnant water in the vicinity of the village was wont, in summer time, to spread the germs of fever far

---

3   Chancery Records.
4   Garraghan, G. J., l. c., pp. 177 and 178.

and wide, so that almost every one was afflicted with malaria. Father Averbeck succeeded, with the aid of the U. S. Government, to drain the lake, thus eliminating the breeding place of disease and reclaiming a large tract of land for farming purposes.[5] The Sisters de Notre Dame came to take over the school of Richfountain on September 12th, 1883. One year after that date, September 1st, 1884, the Jesuit Father F. J. Valazza turned over the parish to the Rev. Joseph Pope, a native of southern Tyrol. The school contained but one room: Father Pope planned the building of a commodious structure containing three class-rooms and a hall. But as the Sisters were withdrawn in 1891 and did not return until 1894, when Father Pope had completed his new residence, the erection of the new school-building was delayed until 1904. Father John Schramm, having succeeded Father Pope in April 1904, deserves the credit of having built the school. Father Pope returned to his native village, Villanders in Tyrol.[6] The Richfountain school district never had more than one Protestant landowner, and the school directors are always members of the parish. The building is Church property. The textbooks are those prescribed by the state. The salaries of the teachers are paid by the school directors. The school, though not parochial, is practically Catholic. All the buildings of the parish, except the first church, were constructed of local limestone.

The parish at its organization contained about thirty families, almost all from the Kingdom of Bavaria; but has grown, in spite of its having the parish of Freeburg carved out of its territory and membership, and today it numbers one hundred and thirty-five families, Bavarian in substance, with a slight sprinkling of Westphalians, and Rhinelanders. The parish has given the Church six priests and twenty sisters in various Sisterhoods. The Congregation lacks but one mark of American Catholicity, it has no debt.

Passing over the Church of the Assumption which Father Helias built before March 1843 at the present Cedron in Moniteau County, we come to the Church of St. Thomas at what was called Indian Bottom in Cole County, near a bend in the Osage river. The date of its erection is given by Father Helias himself as either 1843 or 1846. Indian Bottom, now known as St. Thomas is eight miles south of Jefferson City. There were but three or four families to be found when Father Helias first visited the place; at the time of the erection of the log church there were seven. The number had increased to twenty-one in 1854, when a frame church was put up by Father Busschots and the log church was turned into a presbytery. Father Eysvogels, who in 1856 succeeded Father Busschots as missionary for St. Thomas, removed

---

5 Questionnaire Answers from Richfountain.
6 Chancery Records.

both church and presbytery to a more accessible location, where a
settlement gradually formed under the name of St. Thomas the Apostle.
In 1860 the parish numbered thirty-five families. The Jesuit Fathers
stationed at Westphalia continued their visits until 1869, when Rev.
Aloysius Meyer was appointed its first resident pastor. Father Meyer,
a native of Bavaria, born October 19th, 1819, and ordained August
3rd, 1860, as a member of the Society of Jesus, remained in the wil-
derness of Indian Bottom until 1875, when the young diocesan priest
Father Francis Kueper was sent to supplant him as pastor of St.
Thomas.[7] In 1877 Father Bernard Hillner relieved him, to be relieved in
turn by Father Joseph Hellwing in January 1878. In January 1879 came
Father Peter Bremerich. During Father Bremerich's incumbency the
Rev. O. J. S. Hoog was sent to lay the corner stone for a new church,
August 22nd, 1883, and on October 22nd, of the following year Vicar-
General Muehlsiepen performed the solemnity of dedication. It was a sub-
stantial structure of brick. Father Bremerich continued his priestly
labors in St. Thomas until September 16th, 1888, when he was pro-
moted to the rectorship of the Parish of St. Bernard in St. Louis, and
Father Joseph C. Ernst became pastor of St. Thomas.

The first Sisterhood in charge of the school was that of the Precious
Blood, who came from Ruma, Illinois, in 1895. They were succeeded by
the "Poor Handmaids" of Fort Wayne. In 1913 the Sisters de Notre
Dame came to St. Thomas. Two priests and eight Sisters are credited
to the parish. The parish of Meta derived most of its people from St.
Thomas.

In regard to the origin of Koeltztown, in Osage County we cannot
do better than quote the words of Father Garraghan, the historian of
the Jesuit foundations in Central Missouri:

"Ten miles south of Westphalia, was a settlement originally known
as St. Boniface, from the name of the parish church, and later as Koeltztown, from the name of the chief property owner of the locality. In
1856 the sale of public lands to the south of Westphalia at attractively
low prices induced many of the parishioners of St. Joseph to move in
that direction. A Protestant lady, Mrs. Koeltz, who had purchased
several thousand acres of land in the locality in question, conceived
the idea that the best means of attracting settlers would be the erection
of a Catholic church. She accordingly offered ten acres of land for
this purpose and, besides, promised to contribute generously to the
building fund. In 1857 Father Goeldlin, then Superior at Westphalia,
was invited to come down to the new settlement to superintend the
construction of the proposed church. However, the Father was under
strict orders from the Vice-Provincial to open no more stations and

---

[7] Chancery Records and Garraghan, 1. c., p. 178.

wished, moreover, first to see the site offered for the church, as an imprudent choice of location had just made it necessary to move the Church of St. Thomas to another place at a considerable outlay of money. But the promoters of the new church at Koelztown were impatient of delay and sent a delegation to Archbishop Kenrick of St. Louis to offer him the church property, which was accepted. Foundations for an elaborate stone edifice which was to eclipse St. Joseph's in Westphalia, were immediately laid and in July 1858, Father Goeldlin, according to others, Vicar-General Joseph Melcher, at Archbishop Kenrick's request, laid the corner stone. However, a young carpenter, who had ventured to play the role of architect of the new church, finding himself incompetent to prosecute his task, made off with a considerable part of the building fund. The original plan was thereupon discontinued, and a modest frame church erected, more in keeping with the humble circumstances of the settlers."[8]

"The difficulty of securing a pastor for the new church had now to be met. The Archbishop of St. Louis had no one to send. The Jesuits were again petitioned to assume charge of the station, but had to decline. However, an arrangement was made between Archbishop Kenrick and Father Coosemans, the Jesuit Vice-Provincial, by which Koeltztown was to be attended from Westphalia until a diocesan priest could be found for the post. Accordingly, beginning with June 1861, the place began to be visited by one of the Westphalia Fathers every second Sunday of the month."[9]

In November 1866 the place was visited by Father E. Holthaus from Jefferson City, and in the following year, Father Holthaus was made resident pastor. In 1868 he was succeeded by Rev. William Klevinghaus who ministered to the spiritual wants of the people, until 1872, when he was relieved of the burden by the Rev. John Gruender. Father Joseph Hellwing who was pastor from 1875 to 1878 laid the corner stone for a new church on June 5th, 1877, but in the following year he was supplanted by Father Bernard Hillner. On November 13th, 1882, Father Hillner died here, having for his successor the Rev. H. Kellersman who was destined to carry on the good work far into the Twentieth Century.[10]

The parish of the Visitation of the Blessed Virgin at Vienna in Maries County owes its origin to a band of sturdy Irish Catholics who were drawn from the cities by a widely advertised sale of public lands. A howling wilderness was soon changed into a smiling land of farmsteads. After the Irish came numerous German families, many of them Catholic. As the settlers were scattered over a wide extent of territory, two sta-

---

8 Garraghan, 1. c., pp. 178-179. Also Questionnaire Answers from St. Thomas.
9 Idem, ibidem. p. 179.
10 Chancery Records.

tions were formed, where divine service was held. The one in the town of Vienna, where the first church in Maries County was erected in 1859; the other at a distance of eight miles from Vienna, which after 1862 was regularly visited from Westphalia.

St. Mary's, as the Church of Vienna was called, was a neat frame structure, and had an attendance of about thirty-five families. The Jesuit Father John Goeldlin, the zealous rector of the Westphalia residence from 1858 to 1871, remarks in the *Annual Letters.* "that when a new station is formed, all things have, so to speak, to be created anew. Not only does lack of money retard the work, but the parishioners, however devoutly they may have lived in the cities, are not easily brought to put up with the inconvenience of bad roads." The parishioners of Vienna," continues the Father, "are chiefly Irish who give promise of becoming not less fervent than the rest of their countrymen, nor less generous, provided Heaven blesses their efforts and brings their good intentions to fruition."[11]

Being a mission of the Jesuit Fathers until 1867, all records were entered on their books: but on April 3rd, 1867, the Baptismal Record was opened by the diocesan priest J. W. Graham. The priests whose names appear on its pages are J. W. Graham, Thomas Moran, John Gruender, Henry Deimel, Joseph Hellwing, Peter Bremerich, Henry Hukestein, W. J. Angemendt, P. A. Trumm, C. Seeberger, Joseph Diel. On June 8th, 1885, the Rev H. A. B. Kuennen began his long and happy pastorate during which the new substantial church was built. Father John Fugel succeeded him on June 15th, 1896. When the school of Vienna was opened is not known. For the last thirty years it has been in charge of the Sisters of the Precious Blood. The present church built of cement-stone was erected in 1907. The parish has a membership of eighty-five families, and has given six of its children to the religious life.[12]

"Toward the close of 1861" as Father Garraghan tells us, "the Jesuit pastors assumed charge of another station, about sixteen miles east of Westphalia, known as St. Isidore's where a group of French settlers had put up a little church. The site had been chosen and the building begun by the settlers on their own initiative and without consulting the Fathers of Westphalia.

Unfortunately the location of the church was a poor one. Moreover, the church was destitute of proper furniture and vestments, whilst the *Annual Letters* note, "It will require great zeal and labor and a considerable measure of divine grace to realize any fruit." About the same time that St. Isidore's was taken in charge, two additional

---

11   Annual Letters, 1863.
12   Chancery Records.

stations, one six and the other about twelve miles south of St. Isidore's were started and attended from Loose Creek.''[13]

These stations were called ''Mary, Help of Christians'' and St. Ignatius. The former was situated near Isabel Station at the Missouri Pacific Railroad and was organized in 1862 by Father Busschots, S.J. the latter was at Baily's Creek, and was attended by ten or twelve families, all Americans. A log church was built here in 1859.

St. George's parish in Linn the county seat of Osage County was organized by the Jesuit Father John Goeldlin in 1867. From an unpublished History of St. George's Church in Linn written by Joseph F. Luecke, we cull the following data: After the close of the Civil war the town of Linn took on new life and vigor. An addition to the village was laid out by two enterprising citizens, who also, though Freemasons, started to move for the erection of a Catholic church. The intention was to draw German Catholic settlers to the new county-seat. These gentlemen then offered Archbishop Kenrick a lot for Church purposes. The offer was accepted and the deed was delivered. Father John Goeldlin of Westphalia drew the plan of the church, the necessary brick were made, and building began. The corner stone was blessed by Father Goeldlin on Pentecost Monday, 1867. His assistants at the ceremony were the Jesuit Fathers Holthaus and Schulak. Sermons were preached in English, French and German. The church was dedicated to St. George, probably to please the two men who had donated the lot on which it was built. The committee appointed to conduct the work and raise the funds consisted of two Catholics and one Lutheran. The building was roofed in before the end of the year, but it was an empty shell, without plastering, ceiling, altar, and everything needed for Catholic worship. Father Goeldlin, who for some time attended the place from his home at Westphalia, retired in favor of Father William Neiderkorn. It was Father Niederkorn, the genial unassuming successor to Father Goeldlin in 1873, that saved the young and struggling mission from utter failure. On St. George's day April 1874, the church and its bell were blessed by Vicar-General Melcher. In 1885 Father Aloysius Averbeck, S.J. became the parish of Linn's first resident pastor, but only for one year. The Jesuit Fathers had been recalled from Westphalia on September 5th, 1882, and Father Averbeck was recalled from Linn in November 1885.

His successor was the diocesan priest Joseph Schroeder, known to all St. Louisans as the builder of the magnificent Church of the Holy Trinity in St. Louis. The Rev. Benjamin Tannrath came to Linn May 1st, 1887, and died there June 13th, 1890.

But it is high time to return to good Father Helias, from whom all these restless activities emanated. We shall find him in his chosen

---

13 Garraghan, 1. c., p. 180.

center, his beloved Taos in Cole County, active as ever, and absorbed in his multifarious engagements.

"At Taos, where Father Helias resided ever since his withdrawal from Westphalia, in 1842, he had the satisfaction of seeing his parish of St. Francis Xavier grow steadily in loyalty to its pastor and regard for ecclesiastical authority. The old attempt at schism on the part of a small but aggressive faction which had provoked warning letters to the congregation from Bishop Rosati and his successor, Bishop Kenrick, were no longer renewed. The material condition of the colonists likewise went on improving. Many of them who had enlisted in the Mexican War shared in the bounty of the Government, which settled a quarter section of land on each of the volunteers when they were discharged from service at the end of the war."[14]

The original members of the parish of Taos were immigrants from the Kingdom of Hanover, and from Belgium. As to the latter we would quote the words of Father Garraghan:

"The arrival in the autumn of 1847 of a party of fifty Belgian emigrants from the neighborhood of Ghent, who came highly recommended by M. Beaulieu, Belgian Minister in Washington, boded well for the future of the parish. They had probably been attracted to Central Missouri by a report published at Brussels by the Baron Van der Straten-Pantholz, Secretary of the Belgian Legation at Washington. The Baron made a trip through Osage and Cole Counties in 1845 to ascertain by personal observation the prospects it held out to Belgian emigrants. Clad in a heavy buffalo robe, for it was the depth of winter, and accompanied by Father Helias who was similarly protected, he visited the various stations of the mission, entering the farm houses and chatting pleasantly with the occupants on the success, or perhaps the lack of it, that had attended their efforts. Much useful information was in this way gleaned for the benefit of such of his countrymen as might care to try their fortune in the New World. The actual arrival in Cole County in 1847 of the party of Belgian emigrants above referred to gladdened the heart of Father Helias:

"I am delighted with the new parishioners; they are good Catholics and always ready to render me a service. Mr. Pierre Dirckx, my nearest neighbor, is a constant visitor at the presbytery and shows me every attention. Together with his partner, Mr. Charles Beckaert, he runs a successful farm of which he is the owner and which yields him a handsome income. Their hired men, Edward Van Voeren, Francois Steippens, Francois Goessens, etc., are mostly Belgians. These young fellows are all equipped with trades, not only useful but highly lucrative in a country like this which has just been thrown open to civilization. For example, Francois Goessens is an excellent maker of wooden

---

14 Garraghan, l. c., p. 180.

shoes. People come from twenty miles around to fit themselves out at his shop. I have, known him to sell as many as five hundred sabots in a single day. It's a smooth business, for wood here costs nothing or almost nothing.''

We may conclude our account of Father Helias and his ministry at Taos by citing the words in which he pictures the condition of the parish in the decade immediately preceding the Civil War: ''While in so many localities both of the Old and New World, corruption, the fruit of wicked doctrines, makes incessant headway, the moral condition of our settlement recalls the beautiful days of the primitive Church. Here one may, without the slightest risk, go away from his house, leaving the doors right open. You need have no fear of theft or trespassing of any kind. Irreligious or licentious publications fail to reach our excellent people. Libertinism is unknown: God's name is not, as elsewhere, the object of profanity. My priestly heart experiences a joy ever new in seeing our churches, crowded on Sundays and Feastdays, with throngs of faithful souls who emulate one another in singing the praises of the Lord.''[15]

Father Ferdinand Helias was born in Ghent, Flanders, on August 3rd, 1796, and came to Westphalia in May 1838. He died August 11th, 1874, in his seventy-eighth year. The cause was a stroke of apoplexy, as he had expected. He was accustomed to ring the Angelus morning, noon and evening. On August 11th, the morning Angelus did not ring: the people coming to Church found him lying in the yard near his residence, dead, his pipe beside him. He had written the memorial of his death in German, English and Flemish: Pray for the soul of Ferdinand Benedict Mary Gislenus Helias, S.J., missionary. Born at Ghent, the 3rd day of August 1796, died in America in full submission to the will of God. (August 11th, 1874) ''Take heed, watch and pray, because you know not when the time shall come.''[16]

With Father Helias' death the Jesuit administration of Taos closed, and Father Gruender became its first pastor from the ranks of the diocesan clergy. With the natural vivacity and energy of youth Father Gruender brought new life into the old parish of St. Francis Xavier. He built the new schoolhouse, made improvements on the parochial residence and erected a large brick church. Father Gruender's successor in 1885 was Father Joseph H. Schmidt.

---

[15] Garraghan, l. c., pp. 180-181.

[16] Scrap of paper in Father Helias' handwriting found among Chancery Records. The date is inserted by another hand.

CHAPTER 49

THE CHURCH IN NORTHEAST MISSOURI

I

A decade had elapsed in 1852 since Father Cusack's entrance upon the missionary field of Northeastern Missouri, and much had been accomplished with sadly inadequate means. The Catholic population was rapidly increasing and spreading out westward. In consequence increased efforts must be made to keep the Faith alive among them. So far, four Catholic centers had been established in this region: St. Paul's in Ralls County commonly called Salt River, with Brush Creek and several other dependencies; St. Patrick's near North Santa Fé, in Clark County, with Edina in Knox, Mudd Settlement, in Scotland with Tulley and Auxandria as outmissions; St. Stephen's at Indian Creek in Monroe County which in 1851 had Salt River and Brush Creek as missions; St. Alphonsus at Milwood in Lincoln County, having the care of Louisiana, Pike County, Portland, Callaway County, and Danville in Montgomery County. Hannibal and Palmyra, the missions of Father O'Hanlon, were vacant at the time.[1]

Of the priests ordained since the close of the Synod Father Dennis Kennedy was appointed to succeed Father Cusack at Indian Creek; and to extend his visits to Salt River, until a resident priest could be sent to that place. But on Father Kennedy's appointment to the church at Bridgeton near St. Louis, Father David Lillis became pastor of Indian Creek. Hannibal now received a resident priest in the person of James Murphy, Jr., as he styled himself in distinction from the elder Father James Murphy, the pastor of Jefferson City, and many other places. Father John Cullinan, a recent accession from the Quebec diocese, was sent to Tully in Lewis County, a town with a fine steamboat landing and nothing else worth speaking of, and he came and saw and left for home. Fathers John O'Sullivan, and Simon Grugan also soon tired of their appointed station, St. Paul's at Salt River, leaving a vacancy from 1858 to 1861.

From 1861, however, Father Francis M. Kielty, held the place, until 1863, and for the next three years Reverend Patrick Cronin. Father David S. Phelan for the next two years, 1865 and 1866, visited Salt River from his parish at Indian Creek, then comes another blank

---

[1] These and almost all the other items in this chapter are derived from the Chancery Records of the Archdiocese of St. Louis. Where other sources were available, they are indicated.

in the Record until the advent of Father Patrick Clark in 1869. Father Eugene Coyle in 1873 prepared the way for Father Dennis Byrne, who had the patience and energy to continue his priestly labors in this lonely place from July 1876 to December 1885. Father Luke Kernan, just four years after his ordination at Carlow, accepted Salt River, and for the next nine years, struggled along as best he could. The succeeding three priests, William Stack, Joseph Sheil and F. J. Ernst bring the record of Salt River down to December 1902.

Father Ernst, however, did not reside at St. Paul's, but at New London, from which prosperous parish he attended Centre, under which new name St. Paul's of Salt River now figures. New London's Church was dedicated in honor of St. Joseph on July 11th, 1875 by Bishop Patrick J. Ryan. So the mother church of Northeast Missouri became subject to one of her younger daughters.

As early as 1836 Indian Creek in Monroe County possessed a log church and a five acre tract of land. Two years later it was visited by Father Lefevere and the Jesuits from St. Charles. Father Thomas Cusack at first came occasionally to Indian Creek; from 1845 to 1850 he was its resident pastor. Father Cusack's immediate successor, Dennis Kennedy, was succeeded in 1852 by Father David Lillis, a newly ordained priest, who remained in charge until 1857, when he became pastor of St. Bridget's Church in St. Louis. His successor, the saintly Father Edward Berry, was called away from Indian Creek within two years of faithful labor to build up the churches of Armagh and Downpatrick. His departure left a vacancy at Indian Creek that lasted two years. Father Thomas Ledwith came to Indian Creek in 1861 from St. Michael's Church in St. Louis, and left the place in 1863 to assume charge of Hannibal. The three pastors of Indian Creek, next in order of time, David S. Phelan (1864 to 1866) John Cummings (1866 to 1871) and Thomas Bonacum (1871 to 1874) are memorable names in our long and eventful history: Father Cummings as the main defendant in the suit to break the tyrannical test oath of the Drake Constitution: Thomas Bonacum, as the fighting Bishop of Lincoln, Nebraska, and David S. Phelan as the militant journalist in the ranks of the St. Louis clergy. Strange to say that their one time home has the reputation of being the most orderly and quietsome community in the world, a veritable ''ancient haunt of peace.''[2]

Father Michael Walsh whose checkered career brought him to Indian Creek in 1873 as assistant to Father Bonacum, within a year carried him to Armagh as assistant and, in 1879, as rector to Bloomsdale in Ste. Genevieve County, and finally, in 1881, to Bonne Terre. In 1874 the Rev. D. J. Dougherty with Father Thomas Conners took

---

2 Indian Creek.

charge of Indian Creek: but on February 4th, 1875 Father Conners died at his post of duty, and his pastor, D. J. Dougherty, within a month followed him into eternity.

Father Edward J. Shea was now appointed pastor with Father Patrick Morrisey as assistant and remained until 1879. On February 7th, 1880, Father Shea's former assistant was promoted to the rectorship at Indian Creek; which he retained for nine years and then became assistant at St. John's Church in St. Louis.

His successor Father J. J. Mahon died at Indian Creek in the fourth year of his rectorship. Father Edward Thomas Gallaher, a former member of the Redemptorist Congregation, came to Indian Creek on February 1st, 1893, was formally adopted as a member of the Archdiocese, and confirmed as rector of the parish in September of the same year. He resigned the charge in 1898 to become pastor of Old Mines. Father Gallaher died as Pastor of Catawissa in March 1906. The remaining St. Louis priests in charge of the parish of St. Stephen's at Indian Creek until its absorption into the diocese of St. Joseph, Cornelius Kane, John Lyons, Stephen S. Brady, and Patrick Cooney, will receive proper notice in later chapters of this work.[3]

The humble log church of earliest days was swept away by a cyclone on March 10th, 1876, and a small but decent brick structure took its place.

The missionary station of Humnwell, in Shelby County which, from its foundation in 1872 until 1879, was attached to Indian Creek, afterwards received ministrations from Macon City, then from Shelbina and finally from Monroe City.

In 1846 the Lazarist Thomas Burke had turned over the parish of St. Patrick's near North Santa Fe in Clark County to the diocesan priest Dennis Byrne, who held it in charge until his transfer to Edina in 1852. The County of Clark is one of the most favored spots in the Mississippi Valley not only for its beautiful scenery of level plains and gracefully rounded hills, its very rich soil, and its memories of the Santa Fe trail of which it was the head, but also claims to be, with what justice, we cannot decide, the actual site of Father Marquette's first landing on the banks of the mighty river he had discovered. In the northeast, the boundary of Clark County is the Des Moines river, on the northern bank of which, about five miles inland, Marquette and Joliet are commonly believed to have found the villages of the friendly Illinois Indians. The historian of Clark County, Missouri, claims the honor for the southern bank of the Des Moines river.

St. Patrick's in Clark County was one of the favorite missions of old Fathers Lefevere and Cusack. On its Baptismal Records we find

---

3 This is the claim made by the historian of Clark and Lewis County.

the names of Fathers James Murphy, Edward Hamill, Joseph Cullinan, probably visiting priests. But in 1854 Father Bernard McMenomee, of whom we shall hear some favorable particulars later on, became the pastor of St. Patrick's, and in 1862 he, on his appointment as rector of Edina, relinquished North Santa Fé and Tully, where he had his residence for a time, to Father James Murphy, the former rector of Hannibal. In Father Patrick Gleason's time, about 1865, there seems to have been a dismemberment of the Congregation in Clark County, one part having a small church near Tully, the other building a new church in honor of St. Patrick at what was for a time designated as St. Marysville, Clark County. It was Father Gleason who gave it that name, in place of North Santa Fé, and it was Father Eugene Coyle, who in 1880 named the Post Office in honor of St. Patrick, because the name St. Marysville was often confused with Maryville in Nodaway County. Father Gleason, however, remained at St. Patrick's until 1870, when he removed to Canton in Lewis County, and in 1873 became pastor of Louisiana. Father Gleason was originally a Lazarist, and seems to have been adopted by the archdiocese without having obtained his release from the Vincentian Order. He was known in the circle of his friends as "devoted, if rather strenuous."

The Rev. William Maddock, who served as pastor of St. Patrick's from 1871 to 1876 was ordained June 6th, 1868, as a member of the Carmelite Order, but was adopted by the archdiocese in August 1870. He died by drowning in the Mississippi river, June 7th, 1876. Father Eugene Coyle succeeded the ex-Monk and remained in charge of St. Patrick's until September 15th, 1884, when Father J. J. Mahon came to take his place. After June 1st, 1889, the parish was attended from Canton, by Father John Cosgrove.

Of the two other places in Clark and Lewis Counties visited by Father Lefevere in 1837, Lagrange was the successor of "Godfrey Le Scur's Trading Post at the Mouth of the Wyaconda river," 1795: Father Francis Kielty on July 7th, 1867, blessed the Church of the Immaculate Conception at Lagrange, which in 1893 was sold by Father Cosgrove for $250.00 because, as he stated, there was no congregation left in the place, and that the church itself was in ruins. But Chancellor Van der Sanden, finding that there was a Congregation of twenty-three families, had the property deeded back to the Archbishop for a consideration of $395.00.[4] Alexandria in Clark County had a church building in 1859 when it was attended from St. Marysville. In 1866 the church is reported as needing repairs, and in 1897, as having been swept away by the Mississippi. Tully in Lewis County with its fine steamboat landing was destroyed in 1851 by a flood, and

---

4 M. S. Account of these transactions in Archives of St. Louis Archdiocese.

from that time on Canton, which had been laid out in 1830, began to grow rapidly. Canton's Church of St. Joseph, whose foundations were laid down in 1866, was at first attended from Marysville and then from Palmyra. Father Patrick J. Gleason became its resident pastor in 1871; Father J. Mackin took up the threads of duty in 1875. Father H. H. O'Reilly succeeded him in 1879, Father John O'Shea in October 1883, Father John Cosgrove in February 1884, and Father P. J. Cooney in August 1894. The Church of Canton was never strong. Lagrange is still a mission of Canton. Both places have never had a parochial school.

St. Joseph's Parish, Edina, dates back to 1837, a period when Knox County was still the southern portion of the border county of Scotland. For in that year Father Hilary Tucker, then pastor of the English-speaking Catholics at Quincy, Illinois, came to the neighborhood of the future city for the purpose of receiving the wife of James A. Reid into the Church. James A. Reid, Richard V. Cook, Patrick Jarvis and Richard Welsh were the Catholic pioneers, and when the town of Edina was laid out in 1839 they were among its first citizens.[5] There was no church edifice, as yet. In the Spring of 1841 came the man who deserves the title of founder of the Church of Edina, a layman and bachelor, Peter Early, in company with John Moore and John Cady. Peter Early was a native of County Tyrone in Ireland, and coming to America at an early age resided for a while in Perry County, Ohio. He was possessed of some means, which enabled him and his companions to enter a large quantity of land in the new country of Northeast Missouri. Peter Early was a man of strong religious faith and determined that the faith of his fathers should take deep root in the soil of his new home. All the landed property of the Church of Edina must be credited to the foresight and determination of Mr. Early. The first mass in the town was said in 1843 by Father Cusack, pastor of Indian Creek, in the log house of James A. Reid.

With the aid of the few Catholics of the neighborhood, Peter Early began in that very year the erection of the first Catholic church in Edina. They hewed the logs in the timberland along the river and dragged them to town with yokes of oxen. Within three days the logs were raised in position, about two-thirds of the men of the County assisting in the work. The church was under roof in the Fall of 1844. As there was no money to buy windows, doors and the nails for fastening the flooring, Peter Early went on a collecting tour to his former home in Ohio and extended it to Kentucky. The church was now completed

---

5 ''Catholicism in Knox County,'' probably written by Bishop Christopher E. Byrne, formerly pastor of Edina and published in the ''Church Progress,'' March 17, 1894.

and fitted up for divine worship: but the people were as yet too poor to support a priest of their own.[6] Father De Marchi, C. M., paid them a visit in 1845, the year when Edina was made the county seat of Knox. In the following year Father Dennis Byrne of St. Patrick's, North Santa Fé, began his regular visits to the place for the purpose of spiritual ministrations. But in 1852 this good priest received the appointment as pastor of Edina and the surrounding missions. When in 1856 Father Byrne took his exeat from the diocese, only to be re-admitted in 1876, the Rev. John Power entered upon the difficult work and put his whole earnest soul into it. He built a brick church, which was dedicated in 1857. But the young priest's health was too delicate for the rough prairie settlement. He died at Edina about the middle of August 1858 and was buried in St. Joseph's Cemetery. The early members of St. Joseph's in Edina, Knox County, were almost exclusively Irish.[7] The families of Reid and Cook were Maryland Catholics. H. Robin, a convert to the Faith, was from Tennessee, John Winterbotham, another convert, and former preacher, was a native of England. During the following year Father Julian Turmel, a young priest from the diocese of Nantes, France, who since January 24th, 1858 held the post of Louisiana, made several visits to Edina, but in 1861 the Pastor of St. Patrick's, North Santa Fé, took Edina in charge as a mission, to become its resident pastor two years later. Father Bernard McMenomy, ordained in St. Louis Cathedral on February 24th, 1854, and immediately appointed to North Santa Fé, is described as a man of pleasing countenance, and of rare oratorical ability. He was popular with all classes and his sermons attracted many non-catholics to the Church.

Meanwhile the number of Catholics had increased year by year. But the outbreak of the Civil War, took away a large number of the young men of the parish, who formed two companies in the twenty-first Missouri Regiment of Infantry. Father McMenomy was a strong Union supporter, and enjoyed the confidence of all classes. When General Price marched through North Missouri in 1864, Father Mc-Menomy saved the life of the Methodist Bishop Hawley, who had made himself obnoxious to secessionists, by coming up from Hannibal to dedicate the Methodist Church, North, at Edina.

The "Drake Constitution," adopted after the war, by the fanatics of Missouri, had fanned anti-catholic sentiment to an unprecedented fury. Father McMenomy, like many others, refused to take the "Test Oath," and was indicted for "Officiating at a marriage." Father McMenony, disgusted with such proceedings left the state for Council Bluffs, Iowa, and never returned.

---

6  "Catholicism in Knox County," l. c.

7  "Edina Pastors" in "Church Progress," March 22, 1894.

Father Martin Walsh was now sent to Edina, in the second year of his priesthood. He did not remain long, only about three months. Like his immediate predecessor, Father McMenomy, he was also indicted for non-observance of the Test Oath law, but he left the state in time to escape arrest. With his friend, the newly consecrated Bishop of Nashville, Patrick Feehan, Father Walsh left the archdiocese for the South where his sympathies lay. He did good work in Memphis, where he built St. Bridget's Church. When the great yellow fever epidemic broke out in Memphis in the summer of 1878, Father Walsh remained faithful to his post, attending the sick night and day, until he himself was stricken down. He was one of the first, if not the first, of the Memphis priests to die of the fever.[8]

Father Patrick J. Gleason, the pastor of the church in Clark County came to Edina late in the Fall of 1865 and returned in the early Spring to the parish from which he had come. Father David Samuel Phelan was now called here from Indian Creek. Father Phelan was born in Nova Scotia, but came to St. Louis in early life. After his ordination on May 30th, 1863, he served as assistant at the Cathedral and in 1864 was sent to Indian Creek, and in May 1866 began his journalistic career in Edina. There was one paper in Knox County, the *Knox County Gazette*, and it was for sale. Father Phelan bought it with borrowed money and changed its name to *Missouri Watchman*. As an outspoken defender of Catholic rights he was indicted, but took a change of venue to Macon County. Father Phelan was young, bright, and full of sparkling fun, and more than a match for the radicals and anti-catholics of North Missouri. He had many friends among the veterans of the war. When the test case of Father Cummings was decided by the Supreme Court, the cases of Father McMenomy and Phelan, and Sisters Dosithes, Patricia and Eleonora were dropped. Father Phelan was appointed pastor of the Church of the Annunciation in St. Louis. The plant of the *Watchman* remained for a time at Edina under the nominal editorship of William Clancy. ''Blue-eyed, light-haired, demure little man,'' is the description given of Father Phelan's successor at Edina, Father John Fitzgerald. Ordained on December 21st, 1867 by Bishop Juncker in St. Vincent's Church St. Louis, having served the Church of the Assumption in St. Louis during Father Kavanaugh's last illness, Father Fitzgerald received his appointment to St. Joseph's Church, Edina in August 1868.

Peter Early was still among the living, having been very active during all these disturbances in building up the parish. In 1860 he had begun to erect out of his own means a priest's residence, but could not then complete it. In 1864 he gave it to the Sisters of Loretto for a

---

8  Quinn, D. A., ''Heroes and Heroines of Memphis,'' pp. 156-159.

Convent, on condition that the parish should build a parochial residence. Father Fitzgerald was cautious and slow to act, especially in the matter of church building. But he made use of a fine opportunity to increase the number of Catholic immigrants. He prevailed on a young man of literary accomplishments, William Clancy, to write laudatory letters about the County of Knox in Northeast Missouri to the Catholic papers in the East, and he got a Lutheran minister to translate these letters into German. Immigration was certainly increased thereby. About one-fourth of the population of Knox County today is Catholic.

In February 1871 the construction of the new St. Joseph's Church was commenced. The brick were burned in 1873. On July 5th, 1874 Coadjutor Bishop Ryan blessed the corner stone, and in 1875 the church, the present magnificent St. Joseph's, was completed and opened for divine services, its dedication taking place on the 10th of October of that year. Bishop Ryan performed the dedication services, and Father James Murphy, then of Sedalia, preached the sermon. The church is an ornament to Edina and is one of the finest church edifices in all northeast Missouri. It is the crowning glory of Father Fitzgerald's life in the sacred ministry. Its dimensions are: length, 137 feet and width, 66 feet, height of steeple, 212 feet.[9]

About 400 families attend the Edina Church. These families are mostly Irish or of Irish descent. There are however many Germans in the congregation whose spiritual wants were attended to by German assistant priests, among them Fathers Bernard Stemker, Frederick Pommer, H. Kuennen, Francis K. Straubinger, Herman Wagener, Henry Thobe, Clement Moenig, H. J. Muckerman and J. J. Rapien. Some miles distant from Edina are the stations of McFarland, where there is a church dedicated to the Blessed Virgin under the title of the Sacred Heart, and Millport with its Church of St. Joachim. Both of these missions date from the early seventies.

St. Joseph's Academy of the Sisters of Loretto at Edina was opened September 1st, 1865, and St. Joseph's College for boys in 1883.

---

9 "Edina Pastors," in "Church Progress," l. c.

## CHAPTER 50

## THE CHURCH IN NORTHEAST MISSOURI

### II

The expansion of the Church in Northeast Missouri naturally followed a westward course, which, however, was reinforced by a northward movement from the Missouri River settlements. As the vast prairie lands adjoining the Counties of Clark, Lewis, Marion, Ralls, Pike, and Lincoln were gradually reclaimed from the state of wild nature, little towns and villages sprung up, forming the center of new Catholic congregations. We have sketched this process in its initial stages; we must now proceed with the subsequent developments. In Marion County there are two early Catholic centers, Palmyra and Hannibal, both of them missionary stations of Father Cusack of Indian Creek and Arrow Rock, since 1845. Palmyra was visited even before this date, by the Jesuit Father Van Lommel from St. Louis, 1831. Services were held in a private house until 1865, when the Congregation, now numbering fifty members, bought a Protestant church, and had it blessed and dedicated to divine worship by Archbishop Kenrick under the invocation of St. Joseph.

In 1867 the Franciscan Fathers of Quincy accepted charge of the place as an outmission. Father Anselm Mueller, then Rector of the College of Quincy, had the Church of St. Joseph remodelled at an expense of $3,000., and established a parochial school. In 1869 Father Theodore Kussman of the diocesan clergy, was made resident pastor of Palmyra. He built the parsonage in 1870. On his appointment to the Church of Springfield, Missouri, the Franciscan Fathers of Quincy, Illinois assumed charge once more. Preeminent among them were the P. P. Paschalis Nolte, who erected the stations of the Way of the Cross in March 1884; and Leonard Neukirchen, a native of Remagen on the Rhine. In 1894 P. Ulric Petri, O. S. F., became pastor of Palmyra, in succession to the six years' term of P. Leonard, who had been called to Rome. P. Ulric was succeeded in 1903 by his Franciscan brother, Marcelline Kollmeyer.[1]

The second parish establishment in Marion County, was that of the Immaculate Conception in Hannibal. From 1845 to 1850 the small congregation, was visited by the pioneer missionaries Cusack, and O'Hanlon: In 1851 the Rev. Patrick Flemming, of the diocese of Lim-

---

[1] Chancery Records and personal communications from Msgr. Holweck and Father Coyle of Kirkwood.

erick, and until then Professor at Carondelet Seminary, organized the parish and became its first resident priest. In 1853 he joined the diocese of Chicago. In 1854 Father James Murphy, Jr., built a church of brick, which was dedicated by the Coadjutor-Bishop James Duggan, on April 24th, 1855, on which occasion the future Coadjutor Patrick Ryan preached the sermon. This church served the Congregation throughout the rectorships of Fathers James Murphy, Bernard O'Reilly, Thomas Ledwith, Patrick Cronin, the future editor of the *Catholic Union and Times,* F. O'Neill, and John Quinlan, who died here in June 1871. In the eighth year of Father Dennis Kennedy's rectorship, October 9th, 1880, the Congregation bought the old Congregationalist Church, and on April 24th, 1881, it was blessed by Coadjutor Bishop Patrick J. Ryan. Father Kennedy died on August 29th, 1884. His successor, the scholarly priest and accomplished musician, Rev. M. J. McLoughlin, continued the pastorship, until December 27th, 1903. The parish now had a membership of 1,500 souls.[2]

The county immediately west of Marion is Shelby, its county seat Shelbina. Here a plot of ground was deeded to the Church on July 26th, 1879. But Father Michael S. Mackin had been rector of the place since his ordination in 1868. As Shelbina was too poor to support a resident pastor, Father Mackin was transferred to Sedalia in the following year, and Shelbina became an outmission of Macon City in the adjoining County of Macon, and in 1876 to 1878 was attended from Indian Creek.

In 1880, however, when Father Mackin was assigned to the Parish of Macon City as assistant, Shelbina also was placed under his charge: Father Mackin died at Macon City in June 1881.

After the death of Father Mackin, Father Thomas J. Moran was appointed rector of Shelbina, on May 10th, 1884, he was succeeded by Father Edmund Casey, who applied the money realized from the sale of the church at Clinton, Monroe County, to the Church of Shelbina. On January 2nd, 1889 came Father D. F. Sullivan. On December 1890 Shelbina was again reduced to the state of an outmission, attended from Monroe City.

The parish of Macon City with its Church of the Immaculate Conception dates from 1867 when Rev. Michael Walsh was appointed its rector.

On May 22nd, 1870, Coadjutor Bishop Ryan laid the corner stone of the church. In the same year Father Patrick McNamee became its pastor and remained until 1874. The new church, a large brick structure, bought from the Presbyterians, was remodelled and fitted up by October 12th, 1875, when Bishop Ryan blessed it, the Rev. P. B. Cahill,

---

2  Chancery Records.

now being rector of the parish. In 1893 the name of the town is abbreviated to "Macon." From December 1898 to January 1902 Rev. Cornelius F. O'Leary held the reins of government in Macon, to relinquish them to Father Daniel Healy. The parish of Macon attended several missions in Macon County, among them, the Sacred Heart Church at Bevier and St. Joseph's at La Plata.[3]

To the north of Macon County lies Adair, which is a branch of Edina. The church at Adair in the County of the same name, is dedicated to St. Mary.

It was Father McNamee, pastor of Macon City from 1870 to 1873, who found ninety families in Clay township and environs. In 1875 Father John Daly was appointed to organize the parish of Adair within the territory from Memphis in Scotland County to the Chariton river, and from Macon to the Iowa line.

In 1877 Father L. Madden was sent to Adair in place of Father Daly: Father John Ryan followed in 1878 and remained fully ten years. His successor Father John O'Shea administered the affairs of the new flourishing parish for more than twenty years. Under his wise and earnest management the parish buildings were removed to a more favorable site in the town of Adair. The present church is described as "by far the prettiest country Church in North Missouri." The second church in Adair County, is at Kirksville. It is dedicated to Mary Immaculate, and was founded by Father John O'Shea from Adair, in 1888. The church was dedicated July 2nd, 1893, but destroyed by a cyclone April 27th, 1899.

Turning to the Counties immediately west of Ralls; the one-time center of Father Lefevere's missions, Monroe and Randolph Counties, we experience the first northward influences from the old Jesuit missions along the north bank of the Mississippi river.

The Church of St. Stephen at Indian Creek in Monroe County is among the earliest centers of the Northeast, and as such has found most honorable mention in the foregoing chapter. There remains the church of the Immaculate Conception in Monroe City, the county seat, established in 1888, when the corner stone for the church was laid (October 14th). It was attended from Shelbina until December 1st, 1890, when Father D. F. Sullivan became its rector. On Father Sullivan's appointment to the irremovable rectorship of Hannibal, January 4th, 1904, Father John Lyons became rector of Monroe City; his successor in 1905 was the Rev. Thomas Mullen.

The earlier stations of Father Cusack in Monroe County, Florida and Clinton, never prospered: Clinton being suppressed, when in 1884 not one Catholic was left within six miles of the church.

---

3 Chancery Records.

The earliest church foundation in Randolph County, St. John the Baptist at Moberly, dates from 1873 when that sturdy missionary Father Francis McKenna and his assistant Father William O'Shea took charge. A church was built and blessed in 1875. Bishop Ryan officiated at the dedication. Father McKenna continued his ministrations until his death April 22nd, 1892. Among the large number of his assistants the names of Fathers Cahill, Tuohy, Moran, O'Donohoe, Straubinger and Tim Dempsey deserve notice. Father McKenna's successor as pastor of St. John's Church at Moberly was the Rev. John Ryan. Father Straubinger is specially noteworthy as being the founder of the first German Church in Northeast Missouri, the Immaculate Conception Church at Moberly. Father Francis A. Straubinger was Father McKenna's assistant from February 19th, 1888 to May 12th, of the same year, and as such was commissioned to organize the German Catholics of Moberly and vicinity into a new parish.

On November 4th, 1888 Vicar-General Muehlsiepen blessed the combination church and school building erected by the parish, under the invocation of the Immaculate Conception. Father Straubinger, joined the Redemptorist Order in June 1891 and was succeeded at Moberly by Father Louis Schlathoelter. Then came Father J. Hennes, who in August 1903 assumed charge of the parish, but died January 26th, 1904. The Rev. Charles H. Schaefer now became pastor for the German Church at Moberly. The parish of St. Joseph in Louisiana, Pike County, first visited by the Jesuit Van Lommel about 1831, remained a dependency of St. Paul's, Salt River, and of Millwood for about thirty-five years. The priests mentioned as visitors to Louisiana are James Murphy, Dennis Byrne, Patrick Brady, D. Lyne, Julian Turmel and Daniel Houlihan. This primitive missionary condition of the place lasted until 1865 when Father John Cummings was appointed its pastor. Father Cummings built a small church on the declivity of a hill facing the Mississippi. In 1866 when Father Cummings was transferred to Indian Creek, Louisiana returned to its old missionary condition, being attended from Hannibal. Then came Father Hugh Murray and, in 1870, Father Keane, who remained until 1873.

The building of the bridge across the Mississippi at Louisiana inspired the Catholic people of the place with fresh hope and energy. Father Patrick J. Gleason began the erection of a new church, the corner stone of which was laid by Bishop Ryan on July 26th, 1874. Building operations progressed rapidly, but funds came in slowly. At the completion of the bridge, most of the workmen left the town for other fields of labor. Father Gleason found himself unable to pay the cost of his church. The property was about to be put up for sale, when Vicar-General Muehlsiepen on his own account raised the sum of $12,000, and paid all claims. Father H. V. Kalmer succeeded Father

Gleason, remaining about a year. The parish was then entrusted to the Franciscan Fathers of Quincy, but in August 1882 the Rev. Doctor John May became its rector. Dr. May opened a parochial school in charge of the Ursuline Nuns: He then started out on a collecting tour for the purpose of reimbursing Vicar-General Muehlsiepen, but soon tired of the unpleasant task. Father F. G. Holweck took charge of the parish on August 26th, 1884, and continued the labor of collecting funds until November 23rd, 1885, and then turned over the place to Father John Joseph Hughes, who was to remain its pastor for the next thirteen years. Of the later pastors of St. Joseph's in Louisiana we can but mention the names of Fathers R. Healy, Patrick Bradly and J. H. Tettemer. The parish is in a fairly prosperous condition, and has a parochial school under the direction of the Sisters de Notre Dame.

Clarksville in Pike County never outgrew the missionary stage of development, being attended from Louisiana, Millwood, Quincy, Illinois, Bowling Green and from 1885 to 1891 from Louisiana. But in the latter year, the Catholics have left the place and, the church being in a very decayed condition, the last vestiges of the mission were removed, and Clarkesville, ceased to figure on the pages of the Catholic Directory.

The Catholic population of Louisiana was almost exclusively Irish, from the west coast of Ireland. They used the Irish language in conversation and in prayer. Every morning before mass began, Father Holweck relates, a few old Irishmen would recite the Rosary in church, each for himself, and all in Irish. Father Gleason's church had pews without kneelers and kneeling space: the people might sit or stand in church, but kneel they could not, unless they took to the aisles.[4]

Millwood in Lincoln County, sometimes designated as Mudd Settlement, emerges into the light of history about 1836 when the ubiquitous Father Lefevere came for his first visit. Father Walters, S. J., held services for a time in the home of Judge Henry T. Mudd, but in 1842 built a log church which cost $300., and which was used until 1856.[5] In 1845 Father James Murphy of Salt River parish visited the place, and in 1849 Father Dennis Byrne of North Santa Fé. The old log church was as yet without a name; but the brick church built by Father Daniel Lyne in 1850 was dedicated by Archbishop Kenrick in honor of St. Alphonsus. The second church was swept away by the cyclone of March 10th, 1876, and was replaced by a frame structure in 1878. At

---

[4] Chancery Records, and reminiscences of Msgr. Holweck; County Histories were also consulted.

[5] ''History of Millwood and St. Alphonsus Parish by Andrew Mudd'' is a well written booklet and reliable in most particulars. An interesting account of Father Walters, S.J., is given on pp. 16 and 17. Father Lefevere, who performed the first marriage ceremony August 9, 1836, was not a Jesuit.

this time the parish numbered one hundred and thirty families, of Irish, French, German and Bohemian nationalities. The succession of Millwood's resident priests is as follows:

Robert Wheeler 1848, Daniel Lyne 1850, Daniel Healy 1859, Edward O'Regan 1862, Thomas Cleary 1865, who died here December 30th, 1895.

A parochial school was established in Millwood by 1849, through the initiative of the people.

Father Lyne, the real founder of the parish of St. Alphonsus at Millwood, enjoyed the reputation of being a highly cultured man and eloquent preacher. He was ordained by Archbishop Kenrick on December 9th, 1849 and returned to Ireland in Easter-tide of 1859. Millwood was the only field of labor Father Lyne ever had in the archdiocese.[6]

Of Father Healy and O'Reagan nothing of importance is related in the chronicles of Millwood. Of Father Cleary, however, we can give interesting accounts, thanks to the investigation of Mr. Mudd:

Rev. Thomas Cleary arrived in Millwood in the fall of 1864, and though he was 52 years of age at the time, he remained pastor of the parish for a longer time than any other priest. During his residence of 31 years here, he christened children, afterward married them, christened their children also, and afterward administered the sacrament of Communion to them. In all he baptized 953 children and performed 197 marriage ceremonies. Though he lived through an age of improvement, he found the parish extremely poor when he took charge of it, and no man was better adapted to handle the situation than he. He possessed an iron constitution, enabling him to withstand many hardships, and his wants were simple and few. He loved the country and avoided the cities. He was extremely zealous in the discharge of his duties towards his people and he had their spiritual welfare at heart up to the last minute of his life. Besides this parish, he also had charge of Troy and the Bohemian settlement.

When the brick church was blown down, Father Cleary once more shared the poverty of the people and, calling them together at an early meeting, suggested the use of the old hall as a temporary place of worship. Accordingly they moved whatever altar fixtures and other church furniture they could to the hall and celebrated mass there in a rather humble manner for about one year . . . In the meantime plans were progressing for the building of a new frame church . . . . .

It was finished in March of the following year at a final cost of $5500, and dedicated by Archbishop Kenrick.

---

[6]  Mudd, Andrew, "History of Millwood," pp. 22-25.

In 1877, Father Cleary in a series of lectures, stressed the value of religious education for children as conducted by the various orders of sisters and urged the building of a convent school. At his instigation a convent building was erected at a cost of $3000 on the lot north of the church, and the Ursuline Sisters established there in 1888. This was the last of Father Cleary's active work in the parish, as he had now reached the age of 76, and his strength had begun to decline. In the fall of 1893, Father P. J. Carroll was removed from Troy to assist Father Cleary through the remainder of his days.[7]

Father Cleary was of the scholarly type of men, careless of dress, and of money, but devoted to his books in English, French, German and Latin.

Walking alone in the fields with his favorite dogs, or mingling in crowds, his venerable appearance was sure to attract the passing stranger. To successive generations of his parish he was the embodiment of all a priest should be. He departed this life on December 30, 1895, fully eighty-three years old.

Father Cleary's successor, Father Philip J. Carroll died on March 15, 1898. After a brief interval came Father Peter F. Quigley, 1899-1914. He enlarged the old frame church and built a modern parochial residence. His death occurred on January 6, 1914.

Father Quigley's assistant and successor, the Rev. W. F. Carr, a native of St. John's Parish, St. Louis, erected the present magnificent church. The temporary frame structure had been consumed by fire, December 28, 1924.[8]

Of St. Simon's Church at Louisville, Lincoln County of which Father Lefevere of St. Paul's, as well as the Jesuit Father Walters of Dardenne make mention, nothing is known after Father Cusack's visit in 1842. The town of Troy, organized in 1875, was for some years attended from Millwood and later on from St. Charles, but became a full fledged parish in 1891 with the title of the Immaculate Conception, and Rev. E. J. Lemkes as its pastor.

The Bohemian Settlement of Mashek in Lincoln County has a church dedicated to St. Mary, and was visited by the Bohemian priests of St. John Nepomuc Church in St. Louis. Since 1901, however, the place is attended from Troy.

Old Monroe in Lincoln County is not one of the old Catholic settlements.

In 1867 the Rev. Gerard Fuerstenberg, O. C. organized the congregation and began building a church which was blessed on March

---

7 Mudd, 1. c., pp. 28-31.
8 Cf. Mudd 1. c., pp. 32 and 36-38.

25th, 1868 under the invocation of the Immaculate Conception. In 1869 Father Fuerstenberg was appointed rector. He continued to build up the parish until July 28th, 1875, when he departed. Father Joseph Gerard Sudeik was the second rector of Old Monroe. He was ordained on June 29th, 1875, and during his priestly life of almost fifty years, remained faithful to his first appointment, Old Monroe. He was a nervous little man, with a slight stutter, but a model priest throughout. During his illness from March 4th to June 15th, 1891. Fathers Aertker and May supplied his place. In 1906 he built the present elegant church, which was blessed by Archbishop Glennon on October 8th of that year.

The parish of St. Clement in the adjoining County of Pike was founded in August 1871, and the church was dedicated two years later. In 1882 on November 18th, it received its first resident priest, Father Charles Brockmeier. In May 1885 Father Brockmeier made a trip to Europe, leaving Father Arnold Acker as substitute. In November of that year, however, Father H. S. Aertker was appointed pastor; He remained pastor of St. Clement's until his death in 1899.

Father Aertker built the present church in 1897-1899, and had it dedicated by Archbishop Kain, May 11th, 1898.

Father Aertker's successors were the Rev. Fathers M. M. Rupprechter 1899-1904, August F. Happe 1905-1908, Henry Minges 1908 to the present day. The parish supports a school of eighty-four pupils, under the Sisters of St. Francis of Oldenburg.[9]

---

9   Chancery Records.

## CHAPTER 51

# WARREN, MONTGOMERY AND AUDRAIN

The county of Warren, cradled with that of St. Charles in the last big bend of the Missouri river, bears quite a different appearance, ecclesiastically, from that of her sister. In 1833 it had but three centers, Warrenton, Pinkney and Marthasville, and not one of them was destined to become the seat of a Catholic church. Marthasville, however, enjoys the distinction of having attracted, through the fame which Duden's celebrated book had conferred upon it, a large number of Catholic immigrants to the hospitable West.[1] Though the "Church of St. Martha at Marthasville" has no foundation in fact, but is only a pious legend, the Church of S. S. Peter and Paul and its successor, the Church of St. Vincent de Paul at Dutzow, must be acknowledged as the first blossoming of religious life in Warren County. As the nucleus of the future parish of Dutzow was within easy reach of Marthasville, that name was often applied to the German settlement that was forming around the church of S. S. Peter and Paul. The place was first visited in 1836 by the early Jesuit Fathers from St. Charles and, after the appointment of Father Busschotts to the parish of Washington just across the river, by the Jesuits settled at that place. Among the missionaries making monthly visits at what was still called Marthasville, we find the names of Busschotts, Eysvogels and Van Mierlo. There were about sixteen families in and around Marthasville.

On July 1st, 1856, Father Christian Wapelhorst attended the place for a little less than a year. In April 1857 the Rev. Bernard Seeling was selected to take charge of the parish. Under his administration, on July 18th, 1858, Vicar General Melcher blessed the church, placing it under the patronage of St. Vincent de Paul. Father Seeling's Report of 1859 is dated: "St. Vincent a Paulo, Duseau:" Still the designation "Marthasville" with the addition "Duseau" remains in use until 1865. The Germanized form of the name Dutzow seems to have prevailed over Duseau and Dujeau in Father William Färber's time, that is between the years 1865 and 1868. He built the parsonage and so became the first resident priest of the place. Father Färber held the pastorship of Dutzow only three years, the first three years after his ordination by Archbishop Kenrick. In July 1868 he became assistant to Father

---

[1] Duden, Gottfried, "Bericht ueber eine Reise nach der Westlichen Staaten Nordamerikas," Eiberfeld, 1829. The book contains a glowing account of the beauty and fertility of Missouri, especially the counties along the north bank of the Missouri River. Duden had his residence in the vicinity of Marthasville.

Muehlseipen at St. Mary's Church, St. Louis, and in August of the same year, pastor of St. Mary's and Spiritual Director of the Sisters of St. Mary. We shall meet him again in various capacities as the course of our History runs on.

Viear-General Muehlsiepen now sent the Rev. John Gockel in place of Father Faerber to the Church of St. Vincent de Paul at Dutzow, Warren County, and in 1872 supplanted him with Father John Heckmann. It was by Father Heckmann's energy and business sense that the new church was erected, which Vicar-General Muehlsiepen dedicated to divine service on September 19th, 1875.

Father Heckmann in 1878 had as his successor the Rev. John Bertens, who presided over the destinies of the parish almost thirty-two years. He died at Dutzow, January 26th, 1900. Father Francis Boehm succeeded him in the rectorship. As early as Father Faerber's time there were two outmissions attached to Dutzow: Holstein, which was afterward named Peers, and Augusta, situated in St. Charles County near the boundary line.[2]

The Church of the Immaculate Conception at Augusta had its origin on August 1st, 1851 when three acres of ground were secured for a site by the Jesuit Fathers of the Washington Residence. The congregation, visited monthly by these Fathers, numbered eighteen German families. From 1857 to 1867 the Jesuits of St. Charles attended the church of Augusta, then still going under the name of Mt. Pleasant. Fathers Van Mierlo, Seisl, Eysvogels, Haering, Bemis, Peuckert and Maes, are the names we recovered from the Records. The visits of these Fathers, at first few and irregular, gradually became more frequent. A messenger on horseback would announce the coming of the priest at the various homesteads: and great was the joy of the people at the good tidings. The first improvised church was but a barn, and the homemade candles were almost black: yet the humble worship of this simple flock was surely acceptable to God. When at last the question of a church building was proposed, some were in favor of placing it half way between Dutzow and Augusta. But Archbishop Kenrick decided that each Congregation should have its own church. So it was ordered and so done. The plot of ground was donated by Herman Aufenorde. The church was built in 1851. It was a small wooden structure; the pews were placed on the bare ground; only the aisles had a floor. Father Van Mierlo was the first priest to say mass in the new house of God on November 2nd or 3rd, 1851. In 1854 Archbishop Kenrick on his Confirmation tour dedicated the building and parish in honor of the Immaculate Conception: Shortly before the outbreak of the Civil War the church was enlarged: a tower was placed on it in

---

2 Souvenir of the Fiftieth Anniversary of St. Vincent de Paul Church, Dutzow, Missouri, 1925. Answers to Questionnaire.

1865. School was held in the church, the children using the seats as writing-desks, whilst kneeling on the ground. Later on, a log house was built for the school. Father Wapelhorst visited the place in 1856, then came Father Seling from Dutzow until 1858. And finally the Jesuits of St. Charles were called upon to renew their care of Dutzow, Holstein and Mt. Pleasant. Father Faerber introduced a novel arrangement: The Catholics of Augusta went to Dutzow for services every Sunday, with the exception of one, when the pastor and people of Dutzow came to the church of Augusta. This arrangement continued until Augusta received its own resident pastor in 1905.[3]

It was Father Francis Boehm, as pastor of Dutzow, that built the new church, a neat frame structure in 1901 and had it dedicated by Archbishop Kain on November 6th, 1901. Father A. A. Jasper was the first resident pastor of the Church of Augusta.

The second mission attended from Dutzow was the Church of St. Ignatius at Holstein (now Peers) in Warren County, where Father P. J. Verhaegen secured a tract of forty acres for the use of the church. The place was at first attended by the Jesuits of the Washington Residence: from 1867, however, until 1877 by the pastors of Dutzow. The first resident priest was Rev. M. Grosholz, who was a carpenter by trade, but later in life was raised to the priesthood. He was succeeded in 1879 by Rev. William Boden, and at the close of 1880 by Rev. William Sonnenschein. Both Reverend Gentlemen were engaged for the Archdiocese by Vicar-General Melcher on his third and final visit to Europe towards the end of 1864.

In 1882 Father Joseph Schmidt was appointed to Holstein, to be supplanted on April 7th, 1883 by the youthful and energetic Rev. John Francis Reuther. At his appointment to the parish of the Creve Coeur, in 1895, the tall sepulchral figure of the first pastor of the parish reappeared upon the scene, to be supplanted on September 14th, 1897 by the Rev. Sebastian Sennerich. Father Sennerich was a man of more than ordinary education, though not of conspicuous ability. He remained at Holstein, now called Peers, until his death.[4]

Prior to 1852 the site of Montgomery City as well as the surrounding country was an unbroken prairie, trackless and unsubdued. Most of the land was still in Government possession. In 1852, however, Benjamin Curd bought the tract on which the city now stands, and laid it out as a town. Settlers came in from beyond the Missouri river, and the irrepressible Jesuit missionary followed in their wake. It was Father John Setters, S.J., that came up from St. Charles in 1857, and built the first church in the frontier town of Montgomery. On April 24th, 1864,

---

[3] Rapien, ''Silver Jubilee of the Parish of the Immaculate Conception, Augusta.''

[4] Chancery Records.

the church authorities secured the present site for the Catholic parish then forming. In the following year the Rev. P. M. O'Neill assumed the duties of a resident parish priest. The church dedicated to the Immaculate Virgin, though humble enough, was then the only Catholic landmark in North Missouri to the West before Independence and Kansas City. Father O'Neill erected a parish residence of equally humble proportions. His real home was among his people along the line of the Wabash Railroad. He built the first church at Mexico, and at Sturgeon. At the end of three years of hard service the pioneer priest was glad to turn over the burden to Father Michael J. McCabe who, after carrying on the good work for five years, resigned his charge into the hands of Father John Daly. Two years later, in 1875, another change occurred in the parochial affairs of Montgomery. It was then that Father J. J. Head began his thirteen years' administration of the parish and of the seven or more missions attached to it. At the time of his coming to Montgomery, Father Head found a Congregation of one hundred and forty families, among them a large percentage of distinguished converts to the Faith: Judges, physicians and military gentlemen. The missions attached to Montgomery were Jonesburg, Martinsburg, Wellsville, Truesdale, Wentzville, New Hartford, Hancock Prairie. Starkenburg was also attached to it for a short time.

A vast amount of labor awaited Father Head; he was to rouse the latent spiritual life in that still formless congregation to united efforts and, with the natural vivacity of youth, he set about its accomplishment. As the passenger train, in those early days, did not run on Sundays, he purchased a three wheel hand car on which he would ride over the tracks from station to station to meet his scattered people. In this manner he was able to say mass in two missions each Sunday, and at night have Vespers, Sermon and Benediction in Montgomery. On Christmas day he attended three missions, and returned to Montgomery for the usual evening services. There were many converts in those days, who in their fervor and joy at having received the light of Faith acted as Father Head's lay-apostolate. Father Head himself, "hale and light-hearted," as he was, found a hearty welcome wherever he went. The church at Truesdale was built by him in 1882, with the generous help of a wealthy convert, Mrs. Ann Gaffney, who willed her residence to Father Head for this purpose. General Bernard Pratte, a former Mayor of St. Louis, a year prior to his death, deeded two hundred and twenty-six acres of land for the erection of a new church at Jonesburg to be dedicated to the Sacred Heart and St. Bernard. The parish of the Immaculate Conception fostered the vocations of three priests, William Moran, George Kuhlman, and George B. Black.

There was a parochial school at Montgomery since 1875 taught by a lay teacher. Since 1882 Father Head obtained some relief through the work of his assistants, Fathers P. A. Trumm, Sebastian Sennerich and Joseph Haar: The corner stone of the second church in Montgomery was laid July 4th, 1885, and the edifice was dedicated on July 4th, of the following year. Vicar-General Brady officiated on both occasions. Unsparing of his strength, as Father Head had been, he was forced, at last, by failing health to seek rest in California. Father P. O'Donohue was appointed as his substitute, and on January 17th, 1888, Father Head took his departure, never to return to Montgomery City as Pastor. For on his return from California he was appointed Bishop Ryan's successor at the Church of the Annunciation in St. Louis. Father Edmund A. Casey was installed as pastor of Montgomery. During his administration Mrs. E. Gray left $3,000 to the parish for a new school. Arrangements were now made to introduce the Dominican Sisters. Father Casep sold the old school building and erected the fine structure still in use. After an incumbency of seven years Father Casey was given the appointment to the pastorate of St. James at Cheltenham, where he, the "big, handsome, intensely human and humorous man," died of heart disease, January 23rd, 1916.

Father John L. Gadell succeeded him in the parish of Montgomery, to be, succeeded in turn, by Rev. Paul Gross. Father Gross published "Historical Sketches of the Church in Montgomery County."[5]

Of the seven churches attended from Montgomery City under Father Head's administration, at least six have attained the dignity of well established parishes: St. Patrick's of Jonesburg, the Resurrection of Wellsville, St. Patrick's of Wentzville, St. Joseph's of Martinsburg, and the central mission itself, the Immaculate Conception of Montgomery. The churches of Truesdale, New Hartford, and Hancock Prairie remained missionary stations unto the present day.

The church of Jonesburg was attended from Montgomery City for seventeen years since its foundation, but in October 1894 received its first resident pastor the Rev. B. H. Schlathoelter, who bent all his energies towards the upbuilding of a strong Catholic organization: but he died a little more than three years after his coming to Jonesburg. Father H. J. Shaw remained less than a year: and Father M. D. Collins filled out the period from January 2nd to December 1903, when Father J. T. Tuohy was appointed in his place.

St. Patrick's Church in Wentzville, St. Charles County, represents a departure from the ordinary run of churches round about it; it is an Irish parish, whilst the others are predominantly German. Father Head of Montgomery City was commissioned by Archbishop Kenrick to provide for the needs of these excellent Catholics, which he did by visiting the place every second Sunday of the month. The church

---

5 Questionnaire Answers by Father Head. Concerning Wentzville, Questionnaire Answers.

was built in 1882. At first there were but fifteen families, the number has now increased to seventy, but the accessions were mostly of German descent. St. Patrick's of Wentzville became a parish in 1905, with the Rev. Peter J. Byrne as its first pastor. The parochial residence was erected in 1909, and the parochial school in 1910, the pastor at the time being Father John Krechter. The Sisters of the Precious Blood from O'Fallon are in charge. As to the origin of St. Joseph's parish of Martinsburg its present pastor writes: ".Towards the middle of the century the place where Martinsburg now stands was the edge of a large prairie. With the completion of the North Missouri railway, in 1857, the town of Martinsburg was laid out. The first Catholics to settle there were Irish railroad laborers. Foremost among these was Denis Scannell, the section boss.''

Father Hogan said Mass in the section house in 1861. After him came the Fathers P. M. O'Neill, M. J. McCabe, Francis McKenna, John Daly, J. J. Head and Cornelius F. O'Leary, all of them stationed at either Montgomery City or Mexico.

The first church, a frame building 20x40 feet, was erected under the direction of Father C. F. O'Leary in the fall of 1876. There were 15 to 20 families here then. After the church had been built, the congregation was in charge of Father O'Leary and his assistant, Rev. Wm. Stack and later of Rev. J. T. Tuohy, assistant to Father McKenna, then at Moberly. In 1881 the parish was attached as a mission to Montgomery, thus passing under the care of Rev. J. J. Head who blessed the church, naming it St. Martin's. His assistants, Rev. Peter A. Trumm and Rev. Sebastian Sennerich, were in charge of the mission. A frame rectory was built in 1884 at the cost of $800. Father Muehlsiepen came from St. Louis occasionally to hear confessions of the German-speaking farmers, of whom the first, Bernard Fennewald, had settled here in 1871.

In the seventies, daring and patient pioneers undertook to cultivate the prairie. Hitherto the prairie had been overgrown with wild grass, and the land was swampy and considered unfit for cultivation. The plowing of the virgin soil and the solicitations of Father Muehlsiepen brought several farmers from Osage County, Mo. A larger church became necessary. The second church of frame construction 40x80 feet with a seating capacity of 350, was built under the direction of Father Joseph Haar and cost a little over $4,000. It was blessed by Archbishop Kenrick, December 5th, 1886, and called St. Joseph's. Father Haar had begun his ministrations at Martinsburg in the capacity of assistant to Father Head, but on January 4th, 1885, he received his appointment as resident pastor of the place.

In September of that year the parochial school was opened with an enrollment of 23 children. After mass a curtain was drawn before the sanctuary and the church converted into a school with Father Haar as teacher. When the second church was completed, the old one became St. Joseph's school. Lay teachers were in charge from 1887 to 1900. In September 1900 the Sisters of the Most Precious Blood of O'Fallon, Mo., were secured as teachers.

Father Joseph Haar, was born at Jefferson City, July 4th, 1859, and after completing his theological studies at St. Meinrads Abbey, was ordained to the priesthood March 7th, 1882. That he was a priest of more than ordinary zeal and capability is witnessed by the fact that his parish, in a few years outstripped its parent and neighboring parishes in spiritual and material progress. His greatest distinction is that his parish in the fifty years of its existence has given eight priests and twelve nuns to Holy Church. Father Haar died December 24th, 1917, at Martinsburg. Of the second pastor, the Rev. Henry J. Freese we will have something to say in a later chapter. The Church of the Resurrection at Wellsville in Montgomery County remains in charge of the pastor of Montgomery City from 1881 until 1907 when it received its first pastor Father P. J. Flannigan. In 1897 the Census reported forty-three families as members of the Church.[6]

The district comprising the parishes of Starkenburg and Rhineland was originally known as "Loutre Island." This name does not designate an island in the Missouri river, but a certain triangular part of the mainland inclosed between the Missouri river and the two branches of the Loutre Creek. It was the original home of the Missouri Indians; the first settlement of whites was made there in 1779. As early as 1847 the Jesuit Father Eysvogels built a rather large log church on land secured by Father Verhaegen at what is now known as Rhineland. Father Eysvogels and his associates in Washington continued to visit the place until 1861, when Father Van der Sanden made a series of weekday calls on the congregation, already numbering one hundred families. From May 1862 to 1867 the care of the people rested upon Father Francis Ruesse, and his successor in the pastorate of Herman. After 1865 the name of the place is given as Rhineland. The title of the church was St. Martin.

Rhineland's first resident priest, the Rev. Joseph Hellwing, was ordained at Cape Girardeau by Archbishop Kenrick on May 24th, 1866, and after one year's service at the Church of the Holy Trinity in St. Louis, was given the task of organizing the Catholics of the lower part of Montgomery County. In 1871, however, he was sent to Biehle in Perry County. He held in quick succession the pastorates of Deepwater, Vienna, Koeltztown, and St. Thomas, and early in 1880 was found to have lost his mind. Father Frederick Volm, an inmate of the

---

6   Freese, Henry J., "Souvenir of Martinsburg," 1926.

Alexian Hospital, "a quite saintly-looking little man with a white beard," as he is described, supplied the place for a brief spell after Father Hellwing's departure, until Father Joseph Schaefer, arrived on the scene in October 1872. Father Schaefer's appointment constituted a turning point in the history of the parish of St. Martin's Rhineland. He was certainly one of the most persuasive talkers, in the pulpit and out of it, the Archdiocese has ever had. Besides he was endowed with singular business tact and shrewdness. He determined at once to erect a new church of stone, and succeeded in bending every other will to his purpose . . . Preparations were begun, a quarry was opened in the Missouri bluffs, and on June 13th, 1873, Vicar-General Muehlsiepen blessed and laid the corner stone of the proposed structure.

Within a year the building was ready for occupancy, and Archbishop Ryan came to dedicate it to God, under the invocation of St. Martin of Tours. When in November 1875 Father Schaefer was transferred to St. Bernard's Rock Springs, he could leave the scene of his three years' labors with the glad consciousness, that the parish, with its fine new church, had no debt whatever. During the year 1876 the parish was vacant, the Franciscan Father John Rings faithfully serving the people from Hermann. The next year Father Bernard Stemker served as pastor, and then asked to be relieved. The Franciscan Father Rings was now assigned by his Superiors to the parish. A convent was built in 1878 by Father Lullus Mues, the Superior of the little Franciscan Community. In 1887 came Father Anselm Puetz, and after him in 1882 P. Arsenius Fahle, who continued for the three following years to exercise the functions of Superior of the Residence and pastor of the parish: The assistant attended the missions Case and Hancock Prairie; P. Marianus Glahn built the beautiful little church at Hancock Prairie.

In 1885 P. Nemesius Rohde was sent to make arrangements for closing the convent, as the parish was to revert once more to the secular clergy. Father Sebastian Sennerich, the new pastor, did not meet with the hearty reception he may have expected; and soon asked for a leave of absence to make a trip to Europe. On his return from abroad he found that the parish of Rhineland was still without a resident priest, and forthwith asked for his reinstatement, which was granted, but he soon grew dissatisfied. On October 12th, 1887, Father George W. Hoehn was appointed rector of St. Martin's, Rhineland, and the missions, where he was to spend the largest part of his priestly life. In 1889 Father Hoehn changed the name of the place to Starkenburg, in memory of the mighty castle that still towers above his ancestral home on the Rhine. Father Hoehn's great work at Starkenburg is the beautiful Pilgrim chapel he built in honor of the Sorrowful Mother. "Our Blessed Lady of the Woods" is the official title of the place of pilgrimage. Thousands upon thousands have come to this shrine of Mother Mary and found peace for their souls. Father Hoehn did not originate the devotion: that was the inspiration of a young student for the priesthood August Mitsch, who found the old statue of the Blessed Virgin, that had in former times graced the altar of the old log church and placed it in the woods under a canopy of fragrant blossoms. This was in the Month of May 1888. Then two other students built a tiny chapel to shelter the statue against rain and snow and wind.

At last Father Hoehn built the present chapel. Whilst, therefore, he was not the originator, he was certainly the loving and efficient promoter of this favorite place of pilgrimage. As for the parish itself, Father Hoehn enlarged the church which the Franciscan Fathers had erected and added the massive tower.[7]

In 1902 Father J. M. Denner was sent to Father Hoehn's assistance, to attend the missions of Case, Hancock Prairie and Rhineland: St. Michael's Church had been built in the little Railroad town of Rhineland about three miles from the old landing. This mission became a parish in 1914, when a new church and school were built there, under the invocation of St. Joseph. Father Francis Holweck was its first resident pastor.

In 1925 the parish of Starkenburg and the pilgrim chapel of the Sorrowful Mother was placed in charge of the Oblate Fathers.

---

[7] Höhn, G. W. "The Silver Pilgrimage Jubilee of Our Blessed Lady of Starkenburg," 1913. Also: Answers to Questionnaire.

## CHAPTER 52

# AUDRAIN, CALLAWAY, BOONE, HOWARD & CHARITON

The westernmost religious centers of Central Missouri north of the Missouri river, Mexico in Audrain County, and Glasgow in Howard County, were of comparatively recent origin, and consequently did not come under the spiritual care of the early Jesuit Fathers, an honor that could be claimed by a number of their missionary stations, as Fulton, Hancock Prairie, Columbia, Fayette, Brunswick and Chariton. The new places proved to have more of the spirit of progress in them than the old. This was partly owing to the prevailing scarcity of priests, and partly to the more central location of the favored few. Most of those missions lay on the outer fringe of civilization. We gain a better idea of the situation when we read that the priest stationed at Montgomery City had charge of the Catholics round about the present seat of the State University, whilst the pastor of Glasgow attended the little flock at Salisbury, and the rector of Mexico ruled the distant church of Fulton.

The Church of the Sacred Heart at Columbia, Boone County, owes its origin to the Jesuit missionary Felix Verreydt, who visited the place in 1831. Whether the pastor of Salt River in Ralls County, the ubiquitous Peter Paul Lefevere, said mass in Columbia in 1835 or at any other time, is doubtful. But that mass was regularly said there in private homes by Jesuit Fathers from Washington and Harrville, is certain. In 1845 Father Lefevere's successor at St. Paul's, Salt River, Father James Murphy, then on his way to Boonville, said mass at the home of John H. Lynch, the only Catholic in the town of Columbia. Two years later he made a second visit to the place from his parish of Boonville. During the period from 1848 to 1867 there is no record, but during the following two years the pastor of Glasgow attended the long-forsaken people. Father Ernst Zechenter, of whom we shall hear greater things when we meet him in Glasgow, was this friend in need. The congregation he found in Columbia and its environs consisted of not more than twenty persons, but they were loyal and generous supporters of the Church.

In 1870 the requirements of the church at Glasgow demanded a change; the outmission of Columbia was placed in charge of the pastor of Montgomery City, and his assistant until the year 1874, when it was assigned to the pastor of Mexico, Father C. F. O'Leary. Two years later Columbia became a mission of Moberly, and on January 17th, 1886 it received its first resident pastor, Father John N. Kern.

In 1876 on June 3rd, Archbishop Ryan said mass in the courthouse for lack of a church building, and on the same day delivered the baccalaureate sermon to the students of the University, his subject being: "Christ as a Model." From that time until the completion of the church, regular services were held in the Courthouse.

The Catholic women of the town, led by a member of the Lynch family, were chiefly instrumental in building the church. Work was begun on August 16th, 1880, and on June 9th, of the following year the first services were held within its walls. Father Cornelius F. O'Leary, the pastor of Mexico, had as assistant the Rev. William F. Stack. On November 27th, 1880, Archbishop P. J. Ryan gave the Rev. Father Stack "permission to collect in the city of (St. Louis) the means of completing the new Catholic church at Columbia, Mo. As there are very few Catholic residents in Columbia, and they have already contributed as much as could be reasonably expected from them, it is hoped that the faithful in St. Louis will aid in the completion of this new church."

It was Father O'Leary that selected the lot on which the church was built.

The edifice was blessed by Vicar-General Muehlsiepen around 1886, under the pastorate of Father Kern, although it had been used for divine services since 1881.

From 1883 to January 17th, 1886, the Church of Columbia was attended by Father Francis McKenna of Moberly.

Father John N. Kern, resided at Columbia for only one year. After his departure the place relapsed to its former condition of a mission, being occasionally visited by Father P. A. Trunn. In 1891, however, Father George A. Watson was given the task to reorganize the parish; · which he did within three years.

Then came the Rev. P. F. O'Reilly, a man of importance and lordly bearing, and four years later, the present Bishop of Galveston, Christopher E. Byrne, a prelate of profound scholarship and calm persuasive eloquence. Father Byrne remained at Columbia two full years: His successor Father Arthur O'Reilly, also two years; then came the saintly martyr of fervor, Father William E. Randall, the son of that noble convert to the Faith, Major B. H. Randall of Fort Ridgely, Minnesota. His successor, the Rev. Dr. John B. Pleuss, remained at this post of duty until 1908, when Father Thomas J. Lloyd took up the reins to hold them for ten long years. It was Father Pleuss that erected the present parsonage, and it was Father Lloyd that opened the parochial school and built the present beautiful stone church. The school is conducted by the Sisters of St. Joseph.[1]

---

[1] "Sketch of the Sacred Heart at Columbia," by Rev. John P. Lynch, M.A.-M.S.

As the parish contains, besides the resident Catholics of Columbia and vicinity, a transient contingent of Catholic students attending the University, Father Lloyd, with the approval of the Church authorities of the three dioceses of the state, prevailed upon the Knights of Columbus to erect a Students' Home in the city of Columbia.

Mexico, the judicial seat of Audrain County, is delightfully situated on the divide that separates the Mississippi and Missouri Rivers. The town was laid out in April 1836 by the Rev. Robert C. Mansfield and James H. Smith. On June 23rd, 1866 a lot was acquired for the purpose of erecting a Catholic church, to be known as St. Stephen's. This church was never blessed. In 1869 the Rev. Francis McKenna was transferred from New Madrid to organize the Catholics in and around Mexico. Father McKenna was a native of County Monaghan, Ireland. After completing his ecclesiastical studies at Cape Girardeau, he was raised to the priesthood by Archbishop Kenrick on May 30th, 1867. The historian of Audrain County describes him as "that sturdy pioneer, able and eloquent, Father McKenna." After his promotion to the Church of St. John at Moberly, Father McKenna continued to minister to the Catholics of Mexico, until 1874, when Father Cornelius O'Leary took charge of the pastorate of Mexico. Father O'Leary came to this country from County Kerry, Ireland at the age of seventeen. He was ordained on May 22nd, 1873, and after a brief apprenticeship at St. Columbkille's Church, Carondelet, received his first pastoral appointment to Mexico, where he was to remain until 1880. Father O'Leary was a man of conspicuous ability, learned in Canon Law, and the history of the Saints, a fine preacher and lecturer, though devoid of the winning graces of the true orator, and somewhat lacking in cool judgment. With characteristic energy he commenced building a new church to be dedicated to St. Brendan, and completed the work within a year. It was blessed by Archbishop Ryan in 1878.

In 1880 Father William Stack was assigned to Mexico as assistant to Father O'Leary, for the mission of Fulton in Callaway County and several missionary stations. At the appointment of Father O'Leary to Downpatrick, near St. Louis, the Rev. E. D. Dempsey became pastor of Mexico with Father Stack and in 1881, with Father John T. J. Tuohy as assistants. The arrangement was continued until 1883 when Father Dempsey, having lost his assistant, struggled on alone until June 2nd, 1899, the day of Father John J. Dillon's appointment to the pastorate of Mexico.[2]

St. Peter's Church at Fulton was a mission of Mexico until the year 1905, but there was an interval of a few years (from 1883 to 1887) during which the place received priestly ministrations from Moberly

---

[2] Chancery Records—History of Audrain County.

and Columbia. The church was built in 1875. Since 1900 it is known under the title of the Immaculate Conception. No parochial school was ever attempted. The congregation is steadily declining. The census of 1897 gave the Catholic population as thirty families with one hundred and forty-three souls: the latest report gives "ten families, and exactly fifty-one souls." Father Joseph Gilfillan was the first pastor of the church holding the office from 1905 to 1912. His residence, however, was at the Hospital in Jefferson City. The succession of pastors since 1912 is: Rev. Joseph Hirner, Rev. C. J. White, Rev. P. J. Canty and Rev. J. A. Murray. Since 1889 Laddonia, Audrain County, constituted one of the missions of Mexico. It had no church. The census of 1897 reports sixteen Catholic and ten mixed families, one hundred and two souls in all. Since its erection into a parish in 1912 a healthy growth is noticeable. In November 1924, Mokane in Callaway County, became a mission of Fulton.

Glasgow in the northwestern part of Howard County, on the Missouri River, was laid out as a town in 1836 and incorporated in 1845. The church lot was acquired in 1847, probably through Father James Murphy of Jefferson City. After this event the pall of oblivion rested over the Congregation of Glasgow, until 1866, when Father Henry Meurs arrived as its first pastor. Father Meurs opened the Register of Baptisms in the new parish on August 12th, 1866.

Father Meurs' days at the new place were days of real apostolic zeal. On his coming here he found neither church nor home. Some of the best buildings of the town had been laid in ruins during the battle of Glasgow, October 15th, 1864, others were plainly showing the ravages of time and neglect. Little wonder then that the courage of the people was not very high. Yet Father Meurs did not despond. Being a man of good education and exemplary character, he soon ingratiated himself with the scattered members of his congregation. He found a temporary home with one of his parishioners. But the congregation must have a place of worship. This also was provided in a private house, where several rooms were transformed into a chapel. Here he said mass for his people. Here also he administered the sacraments, instructed the children and attended to such duties as required by our Holy Faith. From Glasgow as a center, Father Meurs made regular visits to the various outlying missions, Salisbury, Columbia, Brunswick, Roanoke, Cambridge and Frankfort. During the pastorate of Father Meurs the building of the first Church commenced.

Though few in number, the members of the little congregation decided to put up a brick building. Whilst the church was being erected Father Meurs held services on Sundays in the Public School building, which was placed at his disposal for that purpose.

Coincident with the erection of the first church, Father Meurs also commenced the parochial school. Together with Mr. Hines as teacher, he provided for the spiritual and secular training of the children. After a very successful missionary pastorate of about three years, Father Meurs was transferred to Boonville and later on to St. Peter's Church at Jefferson City, Mo., where he died and was buried. Father Meurs found a fitting successor to continue the good work which he had commenced so auspiciously, in the person of the Very Rev. Ernst Zechenter.[3]

Father Ernst Zechenter was born at Breman in the Empire of Austria, on December 9th, 1845, received his college education at Krems on the Danube and came to the United States in 1866 in company with Dr. Joseph Salzman, who was the founder of the great western Seminary of St. Francis at Milwaukee, commonly called the Salesianum. His other companion on the journey was the most widely revered and beloved priest we ever knew, Father Joseph Rainer of the Seminary of St. Francis. On December 19th, 1868, Father Zechenter was ordained to the priesthood at the Salesianum, by Bishop Marty and celebrated his first mass on Christmas morning at St. Mary's Church, in St. Louis. Glasgow was his first field of priestly labor. He completed the church and had it dedicated under the invocation of Virgin Mary by Father James Meller of Jefferson City. As an Austrian of the old school, Father Zechenter retained to the last "a sort of old-world distinction." In manner he was gentle, kind and affable. His sermons showed a beautiful serenity. He served the Church of Glasgow with patient zeal, and four years after his assignment, was sent to Kansas City to take charge of the German Church of S. S. Peter and Paul, where he rounded out his fifty years of pastorship. Father Zechenter died at Kansas City on January 27th, 1927, after a life of almost sixty years in the priesthood, full of untiring benevolence in service and charitable gifts. Monsignor Zechenter's lifelong friend, Monsignor Rainer, preceded him into eternity on January 12, 1927.[4]

The Reverend Michael Busch succeeded Father Zechenter in 1873. After having first made his residence with Mr. Mitchel and then at the home of Mr. Reich, he built a neat brick building north of the church as a permanent rectory.

Reverend H. Willenbrink came to Glasgow in 1876 from Charleston, Mo. While he found a church and a neat residence, he also found a debt resting on church and house. Times were hard, and Father Willenbrink was glad to be able to keep up the interest payments. Under his administration the School Sisters of the Most Precious Blood

---

3 "St. Mary's Church, Glasgow, Mo.," 1916, pp. 40 s. s.
4 Obituary of Father Ernst Zechenter in "Catholic Register," Kansas City.

took charge of the parish school. He remained in Glasgow for two years and was then transferred to St. Bernard's Church, St. Louis, Mo. where he passed to his eternal reward, September 12th, 1888.[5]

Reverend Anton Panek was then given charge of St. Mary's, Glasgow, December 28th, 1878 to February 25th, 1891. He came from St. Charles, Mo., where he had been assistant to Reverend F. H. Willmes of St. Peter's Church. He was Pastor of St. Mary's Church twelve years, and proved a very energetic worker, intent on improving in every way possible the charge that had been entrusted to him. Through him was bought a lot adjoining the parish property for the consideration of $1500.00. After it had been leveled and graded, he built thereon a four room residence for the School Sisters. Shortly before he left Glasgow, he also enlarged the Rectory. In addition to the great work in his own parish, Father Pauk also organized the Missions of Salisbury, Fayette and Frankfort. To the sorrow and regret of many friends whom his genial and gentle disposition had won for him, he was called to St. Louis in 1891 to found and establish the new parish of St. Engelbert.

On February 25th, 1891, Reverend Henry Thobe arrived as successor to Father Pauk. Father Thobe was born in St. Liborius parish, St. Louis, September 12th, 1860. He was ordained by Archbishop Ryan, then Coadjutor of St. Louis, on the 22nd of May 1884.

His several appointments as Assistant Pastor, were at Hannibal, Mo., Holy Trinity Parish, St. Louis, Charleston, Mo., and then as Pastor of Glasgow. His activities in his new parish were many and various. First of all, he had the interior of the church decorated in a most becoming manner. . . To the Sisters Home he built an addition, so that they could occupy the upper rooms as living quarters and use the lower floor as class rooms. . . When the Heriford Residence, across the street on the South, from the church, considered in those days "a gorgeous mansion," was for sale, Father Thobe acquired it and transformed it into a Parochial Residence. . . The former rectorate was then occupied by the Sisters, and the children, "occupied" lawn and home west of the church. . . It must here be mentioned that about this time Richard Graham died and bequeated to the parish his property and estate, the lot north of the Sisters' House, which, however, later on was sold, the proceeds being used for the good of the parish.

On account of impaired health, Father Thobe was transferred from Glasgow to Creve Coeur, Mo., where he remained but a short while, to accept the appointment as Rector of Holy Ghost Parish, St. Louis. On the 30th of May 1909 he celebrated in St. Liborius Church of his boyhood, the 25th Anniversary of his ordination to the Holy Priesthood. . . His health failing again, he went to El Paso, Texas, where

---

[5] Chancery Records.

he expired on March 14th, 1910. . . His ever gentle disposition and manly bearing endeared him to all with whom he came in contact.[6]

With Father Thobe's successor, the Rev. John Waelterman, a new era of development opens for Glasgow Parish: but these eventful years must be treated in a later chapter. A brief record of the early missionary activities radiating from Glasgow remains to be made. The main points of interest are Salisbury in Chariton County and Fayette in Howard. The churches of both places were under the patronage of St. Joseph. The Church of Fayette was blessed by Vicar-General Muehlsiepen on November 5th, 1890, that of Salisbury probably much earlier. Both missions eventually attained the dignity of parishes. Salisbury in 1890 under Father John L. Gadell, Fayette in 1900 under Father Joseph Kroeger. Salisbury was incorporated in the diocese of St. Joseph under its last St. Louis pastor, the Rev. F. J. Ernst. Fayette, however, remained a part of the archdiocese. But New Franklin in Howard County, having supplanted the ancient town of Franklin where Bishop Du Bourg desired the Jesuits to build a house of their Order, now bethought itself of the advantage of having a Catholic church of its own, and started to build in March 1908 under the pastorate of Father C. J. Kane. This church was blessed by Vicar-General Joseph A. Connolly, on October 15th, of the same year. New Franklin thus outran Fayette its competitor for pastoral honors: Fayette became a mission of New Franklin.

We have now completed the account of the various church foundations in Northeast and Central Missouri up to the declining years of Archbishop Kenrick.

The anxious question, no doubt, arises, in the thoughtful mind, why these rich and beautiful counties along the northern border of the Missouri river have so few and widely scattered Catholic Congregations? The answer is this: Catholic immigration to the north Central parts of the state set in long after the best lands had been preempted by the Virginians and New Englanders who were, for the most part Protestants, perhaps not intensely religious, yet holding in some way the ideals of Christian life and the principles of honor and truth. They had come to the West not merely for the pleasure of adventure, like many of the French wood-rangers, but to become freeholders, to build a home and to found commonwealths. When at last the Maryland Catholics, and the Catholics from Ireland and Germany arrived among them, the most kindly, though often crude hospitality was shown them by the backwoodsmen in their primitive homes. "Take what you want," was the invariable answer to any petition for the loan of anything the neighbor had. In many cases their friendly treatment may have led

---

6 ''St. Mary's Church, Glasgow,'' and personal recollections.

to a close fraternization between Catholics and Protestants, and a gradual weakening of the Faith of the newcomer, as visits from their own priests were so few and far between. There was something attractive hidden under the rough exterior of thé backwoodsman, as James Flint truthfully describes him:

"The backwoodsman of the West, as I have seen him, is generally an amiable and virtuous man. His general motive for coming here is to be a freeholder, to have plenty of rich land and to be able to settle his children around him. I fully believe that nine in ten of the emigrants have come here with no other motives. You find in truth that he has vices and barbarisms peculiar to his situation. His manners are rough. He wears, it may be, a long beard. He has a great quantity of bear or deer skins wrought into his household establishment, his furniture and dress. He carries a knife or dirk in his bossom, and when in the woods he has rifle on his back and a pack of dogs at his heels. An Atlantic stranger, transferred directly from one of our cities to his door, would recoil from an encounter with him. But remember that his rifle and dog are his chief means of support and profit. Remember all his first days here were passed in dread of the savages. Remember that he still encounters them; still meets bears and panthers. Enter his door and tell him you are benighted and wish the shelter of his cabin for the night. The welcome is indeed seemingly ungracious: 'I reckon you can stay,' or 'I suppose we must let you stay.' But this apparent ungraciousness is the harbinger of every kindness that he can bestow and every comfort that his cabin can afford. Good coffee, corn bread and butter, venison, pork, wild and tame fowls, are set before you. His wife, timid, silent, reserved, but constantly attentive to your comfort, does not sit at the table with you, but like the wives of the patriarchs, stands and attends on you. You are shown the best bed which the house can offer. When this kind of hospitality has been afforded you as long as you choose to stay, when you depart and speak about your bill, you are most commonly told with some slight mark of resentment, that they do not keep tavern. Even the flaxen-headed urchins will turn away from your money.' "[7]

---

[7] Flint, James, "Letters from America," reprinted by Thwaites in "Early Western Travels."

## CHAPTER 53

# THE PARISHES OF HERMAN AND WASHINGTON

As the northernmost point of Gasconade County, on the southern bank of the Missouri, lies the thriving town of Herman amid its vine-clad hills. It was founded in 1837 by the German Settlement Association of Philadelphia, an offshoot of the "Giessner Auswanderungsgesell-shaft." This later Society, founded in 1833, was, no doubt, the best-organized of all similar German settlement ventures.

Indeed its grand purpose of founding a German state in the American Union which should perpetuate German culture and language and manners under a free and popular government, was not and could not be attained. Even its plan of forming exclusively German settle-ments in the states already organized was doomed to fail. When the colonists arrived in St. Louis, the society was dissolved, some of the members remaining in that city, others proceeding to Illinois, and others up the Missouri river. In 1836 the plan was taken up once more by a number of prominent Germans in Philadelphia, who organized the "German Settlement Association" on about the same basis as that of the defunct Society of Giessen. A tract of 12,000 acres of land in Gasconade, Missouri was purchased by the Association in 1836, the town of Herman was platted, and the surrounding land was laid out in farms. The country being hilly, it has become, under the hands of its German cultivators, a land of vineyards and orchards, and the town of Herman itself, one of the wealthiest and most progressive in Central Missouri.

The original settlers of the Colony of Herman had among them thirty-three Catholics, who in 1840 organized a Catholic congregation with Magnus Will, Diebold & Bernard Niehoff as trustees. The Jesuit Fathers, stationed at Washington some thirty miles down the river, came at stated intervals to minister unto the people. In 1845 they began to erect a church of native stone in honor of St. George and completed it under the management of their first pastor, Father Lawr-ence Kupfer, 1849 to 1851. After Father Kupfer's departure, Father Blaarer filled the position of pastor for a brief space of time. Then Father George Tuerk appeared on the scene. Father Tuerk was one of those restless characters that could never abide long in one place. This trait stood him in good part, and proved a blessing to many, as it resulted in the missions of Little Berger and Morrison in Gasconade County, Berger in Franklin County, Chamois in Osage County, and Rhineland, Montgomery County. All these places, some of which are now flourishing parishes, Father Tuerk visited with untiring zeal.

At Herman he built the parochial residence, which was still in use in 1914. The anti-catholic spirit of many of the inhabitants of the town made trouble for the good and faithful priest, whose abrupt manners and curt sayings were used as occasions for vituperation. After ten years service Father Tuerk retired from Herman and accepted the post as assistant to Father Doebbener in St. Louis.

In 1861 the pastor of St. Ludger's Church in Henry County, Father Francis Ruesse, was transferred to Herman and remained there until 1866. His successor, Rev. William Klevinghaus, at the very beginning of his parochial administration, enlarged the church by an addition. In spite of his good will, however, Father Klevinghaus, found serious opposition from among his own people and consequently sent in his resignation. It was accepted, and on September 12th, 1868, Father William Hinssen was appointed pastor. Father Hinssen was of a literary turn of mind, and certainly well able to hold his own in discussions with the liberalistic leaders of thought in Herman. He was born November 29th, 1841, in the diocese of Muenster, Westphalia, but ordained to the priesthood in America. His chief concern in Herman was the erection of a parochial school. After a partial success in this matter Father Hinssen made way for the Rev. August Schilling, who achieved complete success by building a combination school and convent, and installing the Sisters of the Precious Blood as teachers.[1]

The month of March 1875 constituted a turning point in the history of St. George's parish Herman; for at that particular period the noble sons of St. Francis Assisi took over the parish and surrounding missions. The first Franciscan pastor sent to Herman was the Rev. P. Liborius Schaefermeier, who was superseded, however, before the end of the year, by the Rev. P. Dominic Droessler. The Rev. P. Lullus Meus, came to Herman, March 1877, but within a few months was transferred to Rhineland which, on account of its location north of the river, was more easily and better served by a resident priest.

In January 1878 P. Felix Hosbach, an eminent missionary preacher, was stationed at Herman. He remained pastor of St. George's Church until July 1886 when he returned to his native land to resume his former activities of missionary. His successor P. Ambrose Jansen built the church tower which was afterwards incorporated in the general plan of the new church. In 1899 came P. Cletus Girschewski, then P. Servatius Rasche, and then P. Suitbert Albersmann, all good and distinguished priests, but prevented from doing remarkable things by the shortness of their stay in the parish. Yet a peal of three large bells was placed in the tower during the second pastorate of P. Servatius

---

[1] Rheindorff, R., and Hollweck, F. G., "Die St. Georg's Pfarrei zu Hermann, Mo.," pp. 1-2.

Rasche in 1907. During the brief pastorate of P. Seraphine Lampe the plan of a new church to take form. The old church, begun in 1845 and enlarged in 1866, had been dedicated by Vicar-General Muehlsiepen on October 24th, 1870.

After 1875 the Franciscan lay-brothers covered the walls, which were partly of stone, partly of brick, with a heavy coating of cement, put in a Gothic ceiling, and decorated the interior. The main altar also was the work of the brothers. On January 16th, 1914, P. Romuald Rheindorff entered upon his pastoral duties at Herman, and on July 5th of the following year broke ground for a new church that should be a credit to the parish of St. George. But the actual building operation had to be postponed until the basement of the new school was covered in and fitted up for services. On the Feast of St. Raphael Archangel, April 16th, the holy sacrifice was offered for the last time in the old church and immediately after the work of dismantling the venerable structure was begun. The tower, erected in 1892 was left standing to form a part of the new house of God. On the Feast of the Assumption the corner stone of the new church was blessed and laid and on July 9th, 1916, the beautiful structure built in early Gothic style, was solemnly dedicated by Archbishop Glennon. Under the administration of P. Hildebrand Fuchs the new school was completed, and the old school building was remodeled for the residence of the Franciscan Sisters, who had supplanted the Sisters, of the Precious Blood in 1887.

The present Franciscan Convent was begun in October 1915 and completed in February 1916. In June the following year P. Romuald returned to Herman as pastor taking up his residence in the Convent, with P. Hagedorn as assistant pastor for Morrison and P. Pashalis Forster, holding the same position in regard to Little Berger. Morrison, formerly known as Gasconade Station, had its church blessed on August 29th, 1875, by Vicar-General Muehlsiepen under the invocation of our Blessed Lady of the Immaculate Conception, a title that was afterwards changed to that of the Assumption. In 1897 it numbered 450 souls. It had a Catholic school of its own.[2]

The succursal church of St. Paul at Berger was for a time attended by Father Van der Sanden from Jefferson City, then by the pastors of Herman, Fathers Tuerk, Ruesse, Klevinghaus, Hinssen and Schilling.

The first Franciscan Father to attend the Church of St. Paul, at Berger, Franklin County, was the Rev. P. Dominic Florian, the last one so far, the Rev. P. Ladislans Czech. On July 31st, 1887 Vicar-General H. Muehlsiepen laid the corner stone for the new church, and

---

[2] Rheindorff and Holweck, ibidem.

on July 4th, 1888 blessed the completed structure. It is now known as the church of SS. Peter and Paul.[3]

The parish of St. Joseph at Little Berger, formed out of territory once belonging to Berger, was assigned to P. Paschalis. The members of both congregations were of German nationality.

The parish of Chamois, whose church was erected and blessed by Father Schilling of Herman is under the patronage of the Most Pure Blood of Mary. It is no longer a mission of Herman, but enjoys the ministrations of a resident pastor of the secular clergy.

In speaking of the missions of Herman, Berger and Little Berger, we have crossed the boundary line between Gasconade and Franklin Counties, and must now take up the story of the Jesuit Residence and parish, established at Washington.

In so doing we are strongly reminded of one of the most loveable men we ever met, the manly yet so beautifully childlike Franciscan P. Arseuins Fahle, who spent thirteen years of his life in the outmissions of Herman, and retired to die in Washington, January 16th, 1918.

The parish of St. Francis Borgia at Washington, Franklin County, about thirty-five miles further down, on the Missouri river, dates back to 1833, when a party of twelve Catholic families, men, women and children, from Hanover, intending to make a settlement in the vicinity of Marthasville, was prevailed upon to land on the opposite bank of the river, and there decided to make the hospitable place their new-world home. The beginnings and curious vicissitudes of the predominately Cathoic and German Settlement have been related in a previous chapter. We shall here take up the thread of the story and follow it to its conclusion.

The Jesuit Father Felix Verreydt visited the little colony in 1834; Father Christian Hoecken in the following year. The earliest baptism in Washington is dated October 11th, 1835. In 1837 Father Cornelius Walters was sent from St. Charles to visit these early settlers. There were now fifteen families in the Congregation. A log church was built on ground donated, and was placed under the patronage of St. Francis Borgia. In 1838 the secular priest Henry Meinkman was appointed as the first resident pastor. On November 25th, 1839, the parish was placed in charge of the Jesuits, and Father James G. Busschotts was appointed as Father Meinkman's successor. In the meantime the congregation had received new accessions from beyond the sea, and the church was found inadequate for their needs. Lucinda Owens, widow of the founder of the town, and her son-in-law offered the present site in Washington, on which Father Anthony Eysvogels, Busschot's successor in 1845, built a church of brick. Here trunks of trees served

---

3 Questionnaire-Answers.

as pews. The rectory was not completed till the following year. In the latter part of 1849 Father Henry Van Mierlo, who had been laboring among the Miami Indians, came as assistant, to attend the outmissions on both sides of the Missouri River.

In November 1853 Father Martin Seisl became pastor of Washington, and Father Eysvogels attended the Irish Catholics in the construction camps along the Missouri Pacific Railroad.

Since the days of Father Busschotts school had been conducted in various farm houses by a lay teacher. When the new church was ready for occupancy, the old church south of town was removed, log by log, to a place in town, to serve as a school building. Father Eysvogels taught the school for a time, until a .lay-teacher could be obtained.

The cholera raged in Washington and along the Railroad from 1853 to 1855 and snatched away many of its members in the prime of life.

In the summer of 1854 Father Michael Haering took the place of Father Van Mierlo as visiting priest to the missions.

As Father Seisl had the promise of the School-Sisters of Notre Dame to send him teachers for his school, he built a convent for them and had it solemnly blessed by Father Smarius, S. J., on May 1st, 1860. On the very day of the dedication Mother Superior brought two more Sisters; Sister M. Pia Blunde was appointed Superior. The School became known as St. Mary's Academy.

At the instance of Father Francis X. Weninger, S. J., the first Corpus Christi procession was held May 26th, 1864. The town and surrounding country suffered greatly by military invasion in 1864 by the southern armies of Marmaduke and Cabell: even the Fathers were robbed, but the Sisters at the Academy were not molested.[4]

As some of the missions, especially Krakow, had a large percentage of Polish Catholics, Father Alexander Matauschek, S. J., was placed at Washington as assistant pastor in 1864. The so-called Drake Constitution with its tyrannical "Missouri Test Oath" was, according to the Archbishop's order, set at naught by the pastor of Washington, as by so many other faithful priests in the state.

Father Seisl never had been a southern sympathizer, and therefore, could have conscientiously sworn, that he had never "by act or word, aided the party of the secessionists, nor manifested adherence to the cause of the enemies, or desire for their triumph or show sympathy with them." But as he realized that taking the oath under the circumstances then obtaining, would be "a sacrifice of ecclesiastical liberty," he did not take the oath as required by law; and continued to perform the

---

4 "Washington, Mo., die gediegene, ruehrige, schoene Stadt am Missouri," in "Amerika," April 29, 1923.

functions of his sacred office. He was reported, witnesses were sum-
moued; two lawyers took up his defense and gave bail for his appearance
at the next session of the court. The trial was to be held at Union
on April 5th, 1886. Father Seisl made his appearance and asked for a
change of venue. On October 23rd he was to appear before the Circuit
Court at Herman.

He appeared there and obtained a postponement of his trial. The
purpose of these delays was to await the expected decision of the higher
courts on the constitutionality of the Test Oath. Father Seisl's trial
was never held.

The plan of building a new church having been accepted by the
Congregation on December 26th, 1865, work was commenced in January of the following year. The corner stone was laid by Archbishop
Kenrick on the Feast of the Ascension, May 10th, 1866. The completed
and richly ornamented church was dedicated by the Jesuit Provincial,
Ferdinand Coosemans, on Easter Monday, April 6th, 1868. The three
church bells were blessed July 4th, 1869.

On September 7th, 1871, the Rev. P. Francis Braun came to replace
Father Seisl as pastor of Washington. Extensive improvements in
church and cemetery were made under Father Braun's administration,
which lasted until July 16th, 1876, when Rev. P. Peter Tschieder relieved him of his pastoral duties. A year later came Father Joseph
Frederick Rimmele as assistant to Father Tschieder.

About Easter 1878 the Rev. P. Michael F. Cornely succeeded Father
Tschieder in the administration of the parish; on September 6th, 1880
Father Alexander Mathauschek succeeded Father Cornely, and on
December 8th, 1885 Father Tschieder returned to Washington in the
twofold capacity of Superior of the Convent and pastor of the parish,
whilst Father Mathauschek assumed control of Krakow and Union. On
March 4th, 1886, however, Father Tschieder was recalled, and Father
Mathauschek again became pastor of Washington.

On October 10th, 1882, the fiftieth anniversary of the arrival of the
first Catholic settlers, the Rev. P. William Niederkorn solemnly blessed
the new pastoral residence that had just been completed. In 1884 the
old church was taken down, and the materials were used on the new
school building that was then in course of erection. But in 1890 the
present school a Sisters' convent was built at an expense of $12,000.00.
On January 6th, 1891, Father Mathauschek had the honor of blessing
this, the last of the buildings erected by the Jesuit Fathers in Washington; for on September 1st, 1894 the parishes of Washington, Union
and Krakow, and Clover Bottom were turned over to the Franciscan
Fathers of the Sacred Heart Province.[5]

---

[5] Washington, Mo.

Among the distinguished laymen of the parish of Washington one outstanding figure must be mentioned here, Henry J. Spaunhorst. He was born on January 10, 1828 at Belm in the Kingdom of Hanover. At the age of eight years he came with his parents to America, and after short stays in Louisville and in St. Louis, took up his abode on a farm near Washington. In 1849 young Spaunhorst established himself at St. Louis, and by steady application acquired an education that specially fitted him for leadership. He was elected State Senator and held the office with distinction and success for three terms. He was the only Catholic member of the Constitutional Convention of 1875, which abolished the penal laws and the test oath of 1865. He was honored with the presidency of the German Roman-Catholic Central Society from 1873 to 1891, and then made honorary President for life. All through life Mr. Spaunhorst showed himself as a bold outspoken defender of Catholic interests. His great speech in the Senate held March 2nd, 1870 on the duties and the limitations of the state in regard to education, he stated clearly and emphatically that he was an "humble member of the Catholic Church" and that he believed in its doctrines as firmly as he believed in his own existence. In the same speech the Senator made a strong appeal for justice.[6]

"The safety of republican government and civil and religious liberty rests upon the virtue and intelligence of the people; and I maintain that the mistake of our day is, that we admit the principle of the State being the educator of our children; which must necessarily leave religious instruction out of the schools. Therefore, I say, let the State gather the common school tax and income from the public school fund and be its custodian, and distribute the funds equitably under proper regulations, but leave the choice of the books and teachers to the parents who are the natural guardians of their offspring. Let the State assist and promote education, but not direct the kind to be given."[7]

The parish of St. John the Baptist, formerly known as Rengel and since 1894 as Gildehouse, situated about fifteen miles south of Washington remained under the jurisdiction of the Jesuit Fathers from its organization in 1851 until the arrival of Father John Matthew Boetzkes, a secular priest, as its first resident pastor. In 1824 the place numbered twenty-seven Catholic families, who where attended, once a week, from Washington. In 1858 they had Sunday services once a month. . .Father Boetzkes, who was one of Vicar-General Melcher's recruits, remained but twelve months at St. John's, being sent to Benton in Southeast Missouri. The Rev. August Berger also left the place after one year's service.

---

6  Reavis. "St. Louis the Future Great City of the World," article Spaunhorst.
7  Spaunhorst's Address in "The Acolythe," December 5, 1927.

Early in 1861, however, the parish seemed to be starting on the way of progress under the new pastor, Father John Van Luytelaar.

On July 29th, the corner stone of the new church was blessed and laid by Vicar-General Melcher. Father Luytelaar, however, was intent upon choosing the better part, that is, to enter the novitiate of the Redemptorists: After him came, August 1862, the Rev. J. A. Stroombergen, a good faithful priest, but one that always seemed to enjoy poor health. Father Stroombergen had as his successor in 1865 the Rev. Edward J. Vattmann, but he was to return to St. John's at least three times, thus filling out a pastorate of ten years, in four installments; the final one of four years immediately after Father John S. Nordmeyer's death April 6th, 1894, after a pastorate of twenty-years.

It was from St. John's that the parish of the Immaculate Conception at Union, the county seat of Franklin County, was founded. Father Edward J. Vattmann, pastor of St. John's, a secular priest, was its founder. Father Vattmann came to Missouri with Vicar-General Melcher's third colony from Germany, and was ordained by Archbishop Kenrick on April 1st, 1865. His first and last appointment in the archdiocese was St. John's Parish in Franklin County, 1865 to 1867. Under his direction the church at Union was organized. Christopher Arand, Michael Moutier and Anthony Symanski, bought the old Presbyterian Church for the sum of $200.00. It was dedicated in 1866. There was a congregation of about thirty families, German and Irish. Father Vattman was received into the diocese of Cleveland and later on became chaplain of the United States Army and as such enjoyed the confidence of President McKinley especially during the Spanish-American war. The Jesuit Fathers at Washington were placed in charge of Union after Father Vattmann's departure; the first Jesuit priest to come was Alexander Mathauschek, the last, Father Nicholas Schlechter; their administration lasted about a quarter century: Union with all the other missions or parishes of Washington Residence were ceded to the Franciscan Fathers.

The first church and parochial school at what is now called Neier, a combination structure of logs, was erected about 1850 under the Jesuit missionary P. Anthony Eysvogels; John H. Peveling having donated the church lot. It was named St. Joseph's.

In 1867 a new church, the present brick building, was erected at a cost of $5,000. under the care of Father Alexander Mathauschek, Superior of the Washington Residence of the Jesuit Fathers. In 1873 a parochial residence was built. The priests attending the church of St. Joseph's since Father Eysvogel's day were: Martin Seisl 1853, Michael Haering 1854, Ignatius Penkert 1862, Alexander Mathauschek

1864, Francis Braun 1868, Aloysius Suter 1869, John Aloysius Bauhaus 1869, Joseph Frederick Rimmele 1877, Joseph B. Boeber, 1880 to 1881.[8]

It was early in 1881 that Rev. William F. Boden, a secular priest, was appointed first resident pastor of St. Joseph's Church, Neier, Franklin County. He had been assistant priest at several churches in St. Louis, the pastor of Deepwater, Pilot Grove, Hosten, and just previous to his appointment for Neier, assistant priest at St. Francis de Sales Church in St. Louis. He was one of the less noteworthy priests Vicar-General Melcher brought to America. After his brief stay at Neier, he departed for the East. In 1891 he was living in retirement at Nelsonville, Ohio; but has departed this life since then.

Father Boden's successor at St. Joseph's, the Rev. Sosthenes Kleiser, bore the hardships of the wilderness only two months, and was relieved of his post of duty by Father Michael Grosholz, who lengthened out his own term of office to ten full years. On May 16th, 1892 Father Herman Nieters was appointed pastor. During his pastorship a new parochial school in the present brick building was erected, and blessed by the Very Rev. H. Muehlsiepen, V. G. June 7th, 1893.

Rev. H. Nieters left for his new charge, St. Boniface parish, St. Louis, Nov. 25th, 1895. Rev. G. F. Brand was the next pastor from Nov. 25th, 1895 to July 14th, 1897, when Rev. Geo. Koob took charge July 14th, 1897. During his time a steeple was added to the church, church was frescoed, a pipe organ, new altars and new church windows installed. Rev. George Koob was appointed pastor of Bridgeton, St. Louis County, January 1911 and was succeeded at Neier by the present Rev. C. A. Brockmeier, January 21st, 1911. The parish of Neier gave two priests to the church, and twenty young ladies to the religious life. The congregation numbers one hundred and ten families of German descent.[9]

Krakow in Franklin County, some five miles south of Washington, in 1855 consisted of a chapel and school dedicated to St. Gertrude, with forty-five families living in the neighborhood. In the early days it was known as St. Gertrude's, and was visited from Washington, but only on week days. The people were for the most part, of Polish nationality; but German Catholics were on the increase.

As the broad spaces of woodland were gradually turned into farmsteads, a village sprang up, consisting mainly of Polish people, which was called Krakow. In 1864 Father Alexander Mathauschek, S. J.,

---

8   Questionnaire-Answers.

9   Questionnaire-Answers.

assistant at Washington, was specially designated for the Poles. Father Mathauschek built a new church in the village which was dedicated on November 21st, 1869, and continued his ministrations at Krakow until September 14th, 1880 when he became pastor of Washington.

Father Mathauschek, by his simple, dignified, and beautiful character, won the affection of all. His bearing, especially on horseback, was that of a cavalry officer: and yet in his intercourse with people of town and countryside he was the Father, full of sympathy and disinterested kindness. Father Mathauschek's successor at Krakow was P. Bernard Boewer, and a year later P. Joseph Rimmele. During the next three years the Rev. P. William Neiderkorn had charge of Krakow, and in 1886 Father Mathauschek returned, but only for one year. In 1894 the Franciscan Fathers who had superseded the Jesuits in 1894, turned over the parish to the secular clergy. The Rev. Charles Keller was the first resident pastor. Father George Fugel the second.[10]

About the year 1883 the German Catholics at Krakow began to outnumber the Poles, the latter organized a new mission at Clover Bottom, about five miles west of Krakow. Father Mathauschek was the moving spirit in this venture.

A brick building to be used for school purposes was erected. It was dedicated to St. Anne. The parochial school was the foundation of the parish. About 1900 the Franciscan Father in charge, P. Dominic Czech, obtained the Franciscan Sisters of Lafayette, Indiana for his school. About twenty Polish families belonged to the mission at the start; now thirty German families constitute the parish. The mission has no church but is getting ready to build one.[11]

The mission of the Holy Family at Port Hudson was first visited by Father Eysvogel's, S. J., in 1851. In 1870 its church was blessed. The congregation remained in charge of the Jesuits of Washington until November 4th, 1892, when the secular priest, Father Mathias Thomas Sevcik, became its first rector. In February 1893 Port Hudson returned to its former condition of a Mission and was successively attended from Washington, New Haven and Krakow. In 1896 it had a membership of thirty-one families. The school was attended by twenty children. Father Joseph H. Wippermann was appointed pastor in 1908.

New Haven in Franklin County was originally called Millers Landing. Its church, which was blessed by Archbishop Kenrick on April 6th, 1863, bore the name of St. Mary Magdalene. It was attended by the Jesuits of Washington until 1894 when Father Sevcik took charge. Father Sevcik built the new church, which was blessed October

---

10   Questionnaire-Answers.
11   Questionnaire-Answers.

6th, 1895, under the invocation of Our Lady of the Assumption. Father Francis Goeke became pastor of New Haven in 1905.[12]

The remaining churches of Franklin County, St. Anthony's at Sullivan and the Holy Martyrs of Japan, at Japan, as well as the Holy Trinity at Bem, and the Immaculate Conception at Owensville, the latter two in Gasconade County, were all founded and attended at first from Washington. The congregations at both places were predominantly Bohemian.

In 1887 Sullivan came under the care of the pastor of Rolla, and from 1889 to 1891 under that of St. John's at Rengel. On March 8th, 1891 the new church was blessed by Vicar-General Muehlsiepen. On October 15th of that year Father Henry Hussmann became its first resident rector. The church is dedicated to St. Anthony, the Abbot.

The neighboring mission of the Holy Martyrs of Japan in the southwest corner of the county was organized in 1879, and attended for the next four years by the Jesuit Fathers of Washington. In 1882 it was attended as a mission to St. Joseph's at Neier, in 1885 to Pacific, and from 1887 to 1891 to Neier: But in 1892 Father Hussmann was placed in charge of it. In 1897 the place had a Catholic population of one hundred and twenty-five souls. The churches at both places were frame structures.

The parish of St. Mary's at Mosselle in Franklin County was organized in 1880 by a secular priest, the Rev. John Gerard Nordmeyer, pastor of St. John's at Rengel; but for the next eight years it was attended from Pacific, returning however, in 1889 to its old allegiance. For a few years Mosselle was regularly visited, once a month by Vicar-General Muehlsiepen from St. Louis. In 1892 it was placed in charge of Father Hussmann. The church of Mosselle was built of stone.[13]

Father Nordmeyer was born on December 24th, 1838 in the diocese of Osnabrueck. The Pastor of Pacific at this time was the Rev. John Hennes, a native of the Archdiocese of Cologne, born November 21st, 1849; the Pastor of Neier was the Rev. Herman Nieters, like his neighbor Nordmeyer a native of the diocese of Osnabrueck.

All that remained of the Jesuit Fathers of Washington of their numerous foundations in Franklin County in 1892 were Washington itself with the churches of Krakow, Clover Bottom, and Union. But September 1st, 1894 these parishes also were, with Archbishop John

---

12 New Haven has built a fine church recently. Father Francis H. Schiller is its present efficient pastor. Cf. Souvenir of the Church of the Assumption at New Haven.

13 Sullivan and Mosselle are now fairly prosperous parishes; Mosselle has a school, Sullivan has a mission-station.

Joseph Kain's consent, turned over to the Franciscan Fathers of the Sacred Heart Province. When the people heard of this change, they raised a strong protest and for a time, considered the advisability of carrying their cause to the General of the Society of Jesus in Rome and to the Pope himself, but at last submitted themselves to the inevitable.

On August 31st, 1894 P. Paul Teroerde, O. F. M. and P. Sebastian Cebulla, O. F. M., arrived to take formal possession of the parishes: P. Paul remaining at Washington and P. Sebastian going to Krakow. On the following Tuesday the Provincial Michael Richardt and Brother Oswald Restle came and two days later P. Ubald Otto: the latter to take charge of Krakow and Union, whilst P. Sebastian returned to Washington to serve there as assistant to P. Paul Teroerde.

## CHAPTER 54

## ST. CHARLES COUNTY

The ancient Parish of St. Charles Borromeo in the city of St. Charles, once called the "Little Hills" on the Missouri, was until the coming of the Jesuit Fathers the westernmost Catholic outpost in the state. There is a legendary tradition that in early French days and during the Spanish regime there was at Cote Sans Dessein a regular military, civil and religious establishment which was known under the name of St. Joseph. This may be a poetic reminiscence of the fact that Bourgmond's military expedition up the Missouri river established a fort somewhere on the Northern bank of the Missouri river in the present County of Carroll. But sober history points to St. Charles as the earliest permanent religious establishment on the Missouri river west of St. Louis.

Soon after their arrival in St. Ferdinand de Florissant the Jesuit Fathers were entrusted with the spiritual care of St. Charles and Portage des Sioux. Father Van Quickenborne led an indefatigable search for wandering sheep in the wilderness round about. As the country began to fill up with newcomers, and new towns and villages sprang up here and there and everywhere, the Jesuit Fathers, having increased wonderfully, in numbers, and still maintaining their former zeal and energy, kept pace with ever increasing calls for their ministrations. They not only labored steadfastly to supply their spiritual wants but also encouraged them to build small churches, where they might enjoy the visits of the Lord and His ministers at stated intervals.

It is owing to the wisdom and untiring zeal of these Fathers, that not only the cities but the entire countryside along both sides of the Missouri river as far as the center of the state and farther, is dotted with more or less costly and artistic church buildings bearing aloft the symbol of our redemption. Not all of these temples of God, not even most of them, were actually upraised by Jesuit hands: but most of them, perhaps all of them, sprang up from the good seed that was brought to their fruitful soil, from neighboring Jesuit fields. It was, however, from the northeastern part of the state, the former missionary field of Father Peter Paul Lefevere, that the influence of a similar advance made itself felt in the north-central portion of the Jesuit spiritual domain. Yet even this was of Jesuit origin, as Father Lefevere reports, in most of his missions in Missouri and Illinois, the earlier traces of Fathers Van Quickenborne, Verreydt and Elet. But after Father Lefevere came a numerous band of secular priests, for the most part, of Irish birth and training, advancing westward from the Mississippi with the steady advance of Irish immigration into the prairie lands north of the Missouri.

For this and for other reasons we find here, at the meeting of the ways, a larger commingling of regular and diocesan influences. The ancient city of St. Charles now divided between the two spiritual forces, felt the influx of the Irish element changing the language of the Church of St. Charles from French to English, whilst the secular clergy were installed as rectors of the new parish of St. Peter's for the German Catholics of the city. Father Benedict Richard was the last secular pastor of the Church of St. Charles Borromeo.[1] The old frame church on Jackson Street which had been erected in 1792 with government aid by Blanchette Le Chasseur in place of the earlier log chapel, built by the Capuchin Friar Bernard de Limpach in 1781, was in 1819 reduced to such a ruinous state that, in the words of Father Van Quickenborne, "it much more resembled an old stable than a house of divine worship."[2] Father Van Quickenborne built the third Church of St. Charles, at the time, "the noblest structure in the diocese of St. Louis." A full description of the edifice by Father De Theux was published in the Annals of the Propagation of the Faith. The consecration was performed by Bishop Rosati. Father Van Quickenborne being unable himself, by reason of his manifold occupations as Superior of the Jesuits in the West, to reside in St. Charles, appointed as his successor Father Verhaegen, "a man of destiny in the western church," as Father Conway styles him, "who guided the changing prospects of St. Charles, off and on for well nigh forty years. He was meanwhile, however, founder of the St. Louis University, Vicar-General and Administrator of the diocese of St. Louis, Provincial, General of the Maryland Jesuits, President of St. Joseph's College, Bardstown, Ky., and, finally professor of Moral Theology at the St. Louis University. At intervals, he returned to the home of his young priesthood, and of his earliest spiritual affections: twice before he came to stay: first in 1843, when he remained for a year; secondly in 1851 . . . He then lived here until 1857. In 1858, he returned to stay. He died here in 1868."[3] Father Verhaegen was a many-sided man: "A solid and erudite theologian, an acute but reverent philosopher, an accurate and discriminating historian; and ardent friend of the physical sciences, a constant reader of the polite writers," as Father Conway describes him, a trenchant writer and copious speaker, a gentle friend, a zealous

---

1 Conway, James Joseph, "Historical Sketch of the Church and Parish of St. Charles Borromeo," 1892., p. 9, ss.

2 Conway, 1. c., p. 14.

3 Conway, 1. c., pp. 48-50.

pastor, a holy priest and "the organizer of some of the most efficient forces of the Church in the West and in the East."[4]

The church of St. Charles as the early field of his labors, always held a haunting attraction for him. Father Verhaegen's spirit lived on in the Church of St. Charles Borromeo down to the present day. As Father Conway said: "The seed he had sown of manifold good had taken a lasting root and was fast putting forth one-hundred-fold in church and parish and school . . So that, at the date of his death the little rock church of 1828 had grown too meager and too unworthy of the numbers and piety of the new generation."[5]

It was that rare compound of gentleness and strength, Father John Roes, upon whom the mantle of Verhaegen fell. Father Roes was his coadjutor at the time of his death, in 1868, and understood, better than all others the forecasts and views of the dead pastor. It is little wonder then that Father Roes, immediately after Father Verhaegen was dead, laid the foundation of the fourth church in the parish of St. Charles Borromeo. He had inherited the spirit, learned the secrets and copied the activity of the old master. Its corner stone was laid by Archbishop Kenrick, March 9th, 1869, and the building was pushed forward by Father Roes until the completion about three and a half years afterwards. It was dedicated with great solemnity on the 13th of October, 1872, by Rt. Rev. P. J. Ryan, Coadjutor-Bishop of St. Louis. Bishop Ryan had been consecrated a short time previously. Rev. J. DeBlieck, S. J., preached in English and Rev. P. Tschieder, S. J., preached in German. Many prominent clergymen, both secular and regular, graced the occasion with their presence.[6]

We cannot give more than a bare mention of the long sequence of Jesuit Fathers employed in the Parish of St. Charles, Borromeo up to 1890 as Pastors or assistants: Joseph Goswin Van Zealand, Victor V. D. Putten, Adrian Sweere, Henry Baselmans, Henry Van Mierlo, John Setters, J. R. Rosswinkel, Ignatius Panken, Peter DeMester, William Baldwin Van der Heyden, Francis Kuppens, Florentine Budreaux, George Venneman and the rest, whose memory is in benediction.

On Sunday, October 16th, 1892, the Parish of St. Charles celebrated the Centenary of its foundation. On July 7, 1915, a cyclone struck the Church of St. Charles and completely razed it to the ground. The consternation produced upon the parishioners by the suddenness and violence of the visitation proved to be a blessing in disguise. For the new structure that was immediately begun, far sur-

---

4  Conway, l. c., pp. 50-51.
5  Conway, l. c., p. 51.
6  Conway, l. c., p. 52.

passes the old church in beauty of architecture and is better adapted to the needs of the Congregation.

Although the first church in St. Charles was built by a German priest, P. Bernard de Limpach, pastor of St. Louis and its dependencies, the German Catholics of the town and vicinity did not have a church of their own nationality until seventy years later. The reason for this was that there were no German Catholics in the place before 1830, and only a few before the great waves of German immigration of the forties. In 1848 on the 6th day of May a meeting of the German Catholics was held for the purpose of laying plans for the erection of a church devoted to their own uses.[7]

Archbishop Kenrick readily assented to the request and contributed $100. to the building fund raised among the German Catholics, making a total of $1,806.05. A lot was donated for church purposes, and building operations were begun. Father Simon Sigrist was commissioned to bless the corner stone, September 19th, 1845. The parish was dedicated to the Prince of the Apostles, St. Peter. As the rough structure neared completion the Archbishop was reminded of the promise he had given the committee: "When the church is finished, you will please let me know, so that I may take immediate steps to send you a clergyman." The Archbishop was as good as his word.[8]

On January 1st, 1850, Vicar-General Muehlsiepen installed the first pastor of St. Peter's Church, St. Charles, the Rev. Joseph Rauch. On that very day the first services were held in the new church. But the "completed church" was as yet far from completion. It had an altar, but no pulpit, no pews, no bell, no organ, and worse than all, it was not plastered, and there was no residence for the priest. Father Rauch, a Bavarian by birth and education, was willing to bear all as long as his health permitted, and during the seven years of his stay did much to make life more dignified and pleasant in the new place.[9] But on June 5th, 1857, Father Christian Wapelhorst was sent to continne the good work, as Father Rauch returned to his native land. Father Wapelhorst, one of the most distinguished priests our diocese has been blessed and honored with, was then in the full vigor of early manhood, and took up the threads of duty with singular energy and perseverance. The welfare and progress of the parish in temporal and spiritual things, was his constant care. He established several confraternities, founded the Benevolent Society and introduced the Sisters De Notre Dame in the school. At first school was taught in

---

7 "Andenken an das Goldene Jubilaeum der St. Péter's Gemeinde zu St. Charles," 1900, p. 3.

8 Andenken, p. 4 and 5.

9 Andenken, p. 6.

the lower story of the church building, whilst church services were held on the upper floor. But ere long a new school building was erected. The church, also, had become too small for the rapidly increasing membership. The plan of enlarging the building and transforming it into a more church-like condition by taking out the upper floor and putting in new windows and doors was adopted against the wishes of the more farsighted pastor. But the Almighty gave the whole unpleasant affair a different turn: On March 25th, 1861 a violent storm tore off the roof of the building, and shattered the walls. "Thanks be to God," said Father Wapelhorst, when he heard of what had happened. It meant "not patching, but a new church."

The new structure was erected on the site of the old. On June 30th, the corner stone was blessed and laid by Vicar-General Melcher. The work progressed rapidly. Money was scarce, yet wages were low and building material was cheap.

Dedication services were held on December 18th. The new church was the pride of the people. Though not of a high architectural order, it was very large and substantial for the times. It was consecrated by Archbishop Kenrick on September 4th, 1864. In its remodelled form it is still in use, a monument of the faith and devotion of former days.

After seven years of faithful labor in the parish Father Wapelhorst followed a most honorable call to the Seminary of St. Francis at Milwaukee, Wisconsin, to fill a professor's chair. His distinguished ability as a theologian, and his noble character won for him the proud eminence as Rector of the Salesianum, an institution that was then supreme in efficiency and is second to none today in the United States. But Father Wapelhorst, after a few years, chose the humble position of a Franciscan Monk.[10]

Father Wapelhorst's successor at St. Peter's in 1865 was the Rev. Philip Vogt, who after two years showed signs of collapse under the strain, and put the reins of power in the hands of his assistant, the youthful Theodore Krainhard.

Bells were now ordered, preparations for the erection of a new school and of a priest's residence were pushed; but all too soon the energetic priest was appointed to the neighboring parish of Josephsville. His successor Father E. Holthaus died within six weeks after his appointment of an injury sustained in a ride to Florissant. Father Edward Koch's arrival gave the signal for a steady march of progress. The projected school building and parish residence were built, the church received its bell tower, and a fine organ was installed.

---

10 Andenken, pp. 6-8.

Father Koch died after six years of strenuous labor, only forty-three years old. He was buried in the Cemetery of St. Peter's Church in St. Charles.

Father Joseph Meller came to St. Charles from Jefferson City in 1875, and remained seven years as pastor of St. Peter's Church. He had as assistants Fathers Pauk, Willmes, and Pruente. Under Father Meller's administration the Parish was incorporated. On his retirement in January 1882, the pastor of the St. Mary's Church Cape Girardeau and former assistant to Father Meller, was called to St. Peter's, whilst the assistant at St. Peter's was sent to the church vacated by Father Willmes' promotion. Both have retained their early assignments to the present day with conspicuous success. Of their work we shall have occasion to speak in later chapters of this history.[11]

All Saints Parish of St. Peter's, St. Charles County, was known in early missionary times as St. Peter's of Dardenne or simply Dardenne. This parish originally embraced the northwestern quarter of St. Charles and the southern part of Lincoln Counties; Dardenne was the name of a creek and of a pioneer family, for whom the Creek was named. In the mouth of the people it came to signify the first parish organized in the territory watered by the Dardenne Creek.[12]

The earliest settlers of the place were French Canadians. A few Virginians and Kentuckians came in after the Purchase. These Catholics built a log house for divine service, in 1823. Among the priestly visitors of early days 1823 to 1836, we meet the honored names of the early Jesuits, Timmermans, Verreydt, Van Quickenborne, Verhaegen, Francis Hoecken and Van Assche. The church stood on the east side of the creek, but as the number of settlers increased on the west side, Father Verreidt built the second church on an acre of land given by Paul Troendly, with the condition that it should revert to the heirs, in case it should cease to be used for church purposes. This church was blessed by Father Elet, S. J., in October 16th, 1836. From May 1836 the Jesuit Father Cornelius Walters assumed pastoral duties at St. Peter's Parish at Dardenne.

In 1845 Father Henry Van Mierlo and, for the two following years, Father James Busschotts continued the good work. Such were the humble beginnings of a parish that, in the course of time, was to become the mother of five other flourishing parishes: St. Paul in 1854, Old Monroe in 1867, O'Fallon in 1872, Cottleville in 1880, and then the Parish of the Immaculate Conception at what is now the only bearer of the ancient common designation, Dardenne.

---

11 Andenken, pp. 8 and 9.
12 ''The Centennial of All Saints Parish, St. Peter's, Missouri,'' 1923, p. 4.

From 1830 to 1840 the advance guard of the German immigration from Hildesheim, Hanover, arrived in successive small bands, but in 1840 the high tide of this friendly invasion set in and continued unto 1860, whilst the French Canadians slowly withdrew to other parts of the country.[13]

This circumstance, no doubt, moved the Jesuit authorities to select for the parish two German priests, Father F. Huebner and Father Nicholas Newmann.

As a native of the Fatherland, Father Newmann the last Jesuit to attend Dardenne, found great favor with the old German settlers. It was Father Newmann that wrote in 1850: "Upper Dardenne will be detached from the parish of St. Peter, under the name of St. Joseph's." This arrangement was not completed until May 2nd, 1854, when the Jesuit Provincial, Van de Velde, and his council transferred the forty acre tract of church property at Upper Dardenne to Archbishop Kenrick. The district of Upper Dardenne was composed of two principal settlements, one called Dog Prairie, the other Allen Prairie. The two settlements at first entertained the idea of one church establishment, but in the end each built a church of its own, Dog Prairie selecting St. Paul, and Allen Prairie, St. Joseph as patrons. The first church of Allen Prairie was built of logs, but that of Dog Prairie of stone. As the early settlers of Dog Prairie were Kentucky Catholics, they received for their first resident pastor Rev. Edward Hamill, 1853-1859. The Germans began to arrive in 1838. In 1853 Father Hamill finished the stone church and built a residence for himself. The predominance of the German element in latter sixties brought a German priest, Father Conrad Tintrup, to Dog Prairie, which he immediately rechristened as St. Paul. Father Tintrup became blind in 1892 and retired to Arcadia College where he died. April 10, 1912.[14]

He had been pastor of St. Paul's since 1859 almost a half century. The people of Allen Prairie, however, with their Church of St. Joseph, retained Father Tintrup as resident pastor from 1859 to 1868.

Accordingly Tintrup can be said to have spent almost all his priestly life in Upper Dardenne, from 1859 to 1868 at St. Joseph's, which he christened Josephsville, and from 1868 until 1892 in St. Paul. At times he served both churches, and also Old Monroe in Lincoln County, Wellsburg and several stations on the North Missouri Railroad.

The fine brick church of St. Paul was built by him in 1897.

---

13 The Centennial, p. 6.

14 Registers of St. Paul's Parish, and Chancery Records and papers. The succeeding pastors were Gerard Fick, B. J. Benten, Victor Stepka, P. J. Byrne, and Edward Kern, who built the new rectory in 1928.

Father Theodore Krainhardt came to Josephsville from St. Charles in 1868 and remained until 1899. On October 6th, 1872, Vicar-General Muehlsiepen blessed the new church erected by Father Krainhardt. Father Krainhardt was a German writer of note gifted with an easy natural style, that appealed to the priests and people alike.

But what happened to the mother church of St. Peter's at Dardenne? The Jesuit Newman was supplanted in 1852 by the Rev. Francis Rutkowski, the first secular priest residing at St. Peter's. The location of the old church was found to be rather unfavorable on account of the swamp lands near by. The church itself had become too small for the Congregation. It was decided to build the new church on an elevated spot, where the cemetery had been since 1835, and to dedicate church and parish to All Saints. A proper residence for the pastor was also to be erected. The corner stone for the church was laid on July 4th, 1855.

Within the comparatively short period of a year the edifice was ready for divine service. Father Rutkowski resigned his charge after finishing the building. Father Boetzkes, the pastor of Josephsville and, after nine months, Father Wapelhorst of St. Charles, took charge of the parish. But in May, 1859, Father Charles Kellner came, and soon after, left the place, on account of failing health. Father Wapelhorst once more stepped into the breech: Then Father George Bruner came and left, bringing in Father Wapelhorst for the third time. But brighter days were at hand.[15]

In December 1860 Father Nicholas Staudinger, just ordained to the priesthood, and full of the natural vivacity of youth, entered upon the scene. Father Staudinger was a giant in size and strength, and well able to attend the many calls made upon him. In temporal matters he directed all his energy to the work of beautifying the interior of the house of God. In 1863 the parish under his direction built a brick parsonage. In recognition of his good work Father Staudinger was commissioned in 1866 to build up the Church of St. Nicholas in St. Louis.[16] For the next three years the parish of All Saints, at what was now called St. Peter's instead of Dardenne, was in charge of Father William Sonnenschein. He was succeeded in 1869 by the Rev. Conrad Rotter. A native of Bavaria, born November 25th, 1835, the new pastor had the usual qualities of his countrymen: strong faith, uncompromising conviction, and real kindness of heart under a homely exterior.

Father Rotter was ordained by Bishop George A. Carroll for the diocese of Covington. He did missionary work in Kansas, before he

15 The Centennial, p. 8.
16 The Centennial, p. 9.

came to St. Peter's. Under his supervision the school building was erected, and the Sisters of St. Francis of Oldenburg were installed as teachers of the lower grades, and of the girls of the upper grades, while the boys of the upper grades were taught by a lay teacher.[17]

In 1867 Old Monroe in Lincoln County was detached from the Parish of All Saints, St. Peter's; and O'Fallon followed in 1872. Nevertheless the Congregation had increased to such an extent that a new church appeared as a necessity.

After the usual preparations had been made the work was begun in 1874 and on June 4th, the corner stone was blessed and laid by Archbishop Ryan, the Coadjutor of Archbishop Kenrick. During the years 1874 to 1876 the work was in steady progress: In the latter year the old church was taken down, and divine service was held in the new, which, as usual, was far from being completed.

Father Staudinger, having established St. Nicholas Church on a sound basis, now returned to the church of his early days, relieving Father Rotter, who wished to enter the diocese of Peoria. Father Staudinger, on his return to St. Peter's in 1878, found a debt of $14,500., resting on the property of the church, entailing a heavy interest charge. He set to work resolutely and patiently finished the church during the years 1881 and 1882, and reduced the debt by $9,000. It was a long and strong pull all together that at last brought success. The new Church of All Saints was blessed by Vicar-General Muehlsiepen on May 21st, 1882. It is, even at this late day, one of the really beautiful country churches of the Archdiocese. When Father Staudinger was called to his eternal reward, the debt amounted to 2,500 dollars, and the parish itself enjoyed the reputation of being one of our most flourishing country parishes in the diocese.

Father Staudinger died April 19th, 1894 and was followed by the Rev. Joseph Ernst, who remained pastor for five laborious years, to be succeeded by the genial whole-souled Father John L. Gadell, the future pastor of St. Engelbert's Church in St. Louis. Father Gadell's contribution to the earthly possessions of St. Peter's were the parsonage, Sisters' House and church tower. Father Gadell was one of the ablest preachers of our Archdiocese, frank and fearless almost to a fault, a true man and hater of shams. Father John L. Gadell died at St. Engelbert's rectory, February 15th, 1922. His successor at St. Peter's was the Rev. J. H. Girse.

The parish of O'Fallon, under the patronage of the Mother of God, is a vigorous offshoot from the parishes of St. Peter's and St. Paul's, the former contributing seventeen families, the latter only eight, all of German descent. The organization was effected in the

---

17 The Centennial, p. 10.

Fall of 1869. Great interest in the project was manifested at the first meeting held in the schoolhouse at O'Fallon, but when the pecuniary side of the question was touched it subsided considerably.

But the leaders did not falter and, as they showed the way with generous subscriptions, the followers took courage, and the meeting subscribed the sum of 2,500 dollars. The question as to the material to be used was decided by the offer of a gentleman from St. Louis to donate the necessary brick. Judge A. Krekel donated four acres of land in the village for church purposes.

The next concern of the people was to obtain permission from the authorities to proceed with the work. Father Muehlsiepen was surprised to hear of the project, and as he was unacquainted with the circumstances, neither consented nor refused, but promised to pay the village an early visit. At last, feeling that a successful issue was assured by the piety and good will of these sturdy Germans, he gave his permission, and on Pentecost Monday 1870 laid the corner stone of the Church of the Assumption of the Blessed Virgin in the village of O'Fallon. The good people made the woods round about resound with the expressions of their joy. The work of building went on briskly, so that the structure was covered in by the Fall of the year, and made ready for occupancy in the Spring of 1871. A little schoolhouse of logs was finished about the same time.

The pastor whom the authorities sent to O'Fallon was the Rev. William Sonnenschein. He supervised the completion of the interior of the church, so that Vicar-General Muehlsiepen could come on September 17th, 1871, to dedicate the building to its divine purpose. The church had an altar made by some men of the parish, and borrowed a melodeon from a non-catholic citizen of the town. The various Catholic Societies of St. Louis, St. Charles, St. Peter's, and Josephsville came with bright regalia and flying banners to honor the occasion. Mr. Anthony Roeslein of St. Louis brought along a select choir from the city. It was a great day for little O'Fallon. A house was bought to serve as the priest's residence.[18]

In 1873 the Sisters of the Precious Blood arrived in the town, to establish their Mother house, and the pastor turned over his house to the Community until their own convent should be made ready.

All seemed to prosper, when suddenly and unexpectedly Father Sonnenschein resigned his charge and departed. Father Joseph Pope who was sent to the place did not seem able to control the troubled waters. To allay the excitement and prevent discord the pastor of the Meramec, Father Henry Brockhagen, was appointed pastor of

---

[18] ''Wahrhaftibe Historie von der Parochie Unserer Lieben Frauen in O'Fallon, Mo.,'' in ''Amerika,'' November, 1896.

O'Fallon. His influence for good was not long in making itself manifest. He would tolerate no half measures: either one way or the other,
his will had to go. He was a man of disconcerting frankness of utterance, bluff and independent, and not in the least ingratiating. The
rude tillers of the soil soon found that Father Brockhagen knew more
about farming and cattle raising than they; and that his advice in case
of sickness, though freely given, was worth as much as a doctor's pre-
scription; and above all, that their pastor,'was a man of deep faith and
piety, and that his heart was of gold. All went well with the parish
under such a leader. From his Sanctum in O'Fallon he also ruled
a large circle of Catholic readers through the columns of the *"Haus-
freund,"* a weekly paper of general interest. This crowded life, at
times, especially in the day of decline, met hard rebuffs, bringing him
in conflict with the highest authority of the Church in the country:
but no one that knew him, doubted for a moment his constancy of will
to live and die a Catholic and a priest.

Father Brockhagen built a schoolhouse of brick and, at first,
taught school himself. The Sisters of the Precious Blood accepted
charge of the.school in 1871. The parish at that time contained one
hundred and thirty families, almost exclusively Germans. Father
Brockhagen died in 1910. . . His successor, Father A. Jasper, built
the present fine modern school in 1914 and attained a distinguished
name by his efforts to develop the liturgical spirit among his fellow
priests.

The fourth parish carved out of the territory of the ancient church
of St. Peter of Dardenne, St. Joseph's of Cottleville, was organized
in 1873, by the Benedictine Father Everard Gahr. As early as 1864
the people living at Cottleville were encouraged to form a parish of
their own. A frame structure was erected in 1874, and dedicated to
divine service on August 23rd, by the Franciscan Father Ferdinand
Borgmeier. Father Joseph Reisdorf assumed parochial charge 1876.
There were about thirty-five families in the parish, almost all of German
descent. The parish decreased in numbers when Father Reisdorf
resigned, and Father William Schmidt accepted it as one of his missions.
The later pastors of the church were Fathers Francis Hundhausen,
J. L. Schultz, and H. Strieve. 'The church is a handsome brick
structure.[19]

The ancient name of Dardenne, once the designation of the whole
country side in northern St. Charles County, being discarded by its prog-
eny in favor of the names St. Peter's, St. Paul's, Josephsville, O'Fallon
and Cottleville, remained the exclusive property of a little place that

---

[19] Questionnaire-Answers and Chancery Records.

grew up around the Church of the Immaculate Conception. Vicar-General Muehlsiepen blessed the church on August 29th, 1871. The place was also called Plantersburg. It was attended from 1872 from O'Fallon, then from Cottleville, then again from O'Fallon and finally from Cottleville. But on November 27th, 1880, Father W. A. Schmidt became its rector, though residing at the Convent at O'Fallon. Father Schmidt built the present church, of which Vicar-General Muehlsiepen laid the corner stone on April 22nd, 1896, and performed the dedication services June 1st, 1897.

The Parish of St. Francis Xavier at Portage des Sioux, confined within narrow limits at the junction of the Missouri and Mississippi, had but little of the power of expansion manifested by St. Charles and Dardenne, and cannot, even in its own development, be regarded as one of the eminently progressive parishes of the Archdiocese. Yet, its historic past as the scene of Indian treaty councils, its ancient reputation for piety, and the quiet current of life in the dreamy village during the good old pre-railway, pre-telegraph days, have attractions of their own. Trappist and Lazarist had come and gone.

Father Van Quickenborne, worn out by heroic exertions, died in the little Creole village. His successor De Bruyn soon followed him in death. In June 1839 Father Van Assche entered upon the pastorship, but was recalled in the following year, owing to a notable decline in his health. The Vice-Provincial Father Verhagen then closed the residence, but the Jesuit Fathers stationed at St. Charles continued to attend the place until the appointment of a pastor from the secular clergy in 1875. Father Henry Van Mierlo was the first and the last of these visiting missionaries.

The Parish Registers for the years 1843 to 1875 contain a series of distinguished names, among them James Cotting, John B. Miége, Felix Verreydt, and H. Van Mierlo, who attended the Parish regularly from 1867 to 1878. The first secular priest placed in charge of Portage des Sioux was the Reverend Joseph Schroeder.

Father Schroeder, was born in St. Louis, November 17th, 1849, ordained to the priesthood March 10th, 1875, and appointed to the pastorship of Portage des Sioux early in May of the same year. During his three years' stay Father Schroeder used the old brick church that had been built by Father Verreydt in 1836. But his successor the Reverend Henry Mehring, immediately after his coming, inaugurated a movement for a new church. Father Mehring was a native of Echternach in Luxemburg. Seven years after his ordination he had come to America. After filling a position in Ste. Genevieve County, he received the appointment to Portage de Sioux, June 1878. Vicar-General Muehlsiepen laid the corner stone of the new church of St.

Francis Assisi on April 14th, 1879, and also blessed the completed structure on the following September. On May 1st, 1883, Father William J. Rensman was appointed in Father Mehring's place, but being ill at the time, received a substitute in the person of Father Sebastian Sennerich. On May 21st, however, the pastor came into his parish.[20]

On June 6th, 1884, Father Rensmann started on a trip to Europe and returned October 6th, the interval being filled by the newly ordained author of this History. Father Rensmann continued his pastoral ministrations at Portage des Sioux until his departure for the South.

---

20 Chancery Records, and Answers to Questionnaire.

## THE JESUITS AND THE SPIRITUAL LIFE

Returning now from our long and, perchance, rather wearisome wanderings among the wheat fields and vineyards of God, that were first planted and watered by the devoted Jesuit Fathers along the wide reaches of the Missouri river, we hail once again and with better understanding their earliest home west of the Mississippi, the place of hallowed memories from which they went forth with high hopes and serene confidence, bent on planting the word of God in the heart of the wilderness, and to which they always hoped to return some day, when their work was done, to await the call of God, the St. Stanislaus Seminary and Novitiate of the Society of Jesus at Florissant.

It was the first foundation of the Jesuits in the West, it is the Motherhouse of the Missouri Province, the institution in which hundreds and hundreds of Jesuits were trained by enlightened novice-masters in the spirit and discipline of the Order. Its purpose is not so much to shape and enrich the intellect, but rather to form and inspire the character of the applicant for membership in the Order. The novitiate lasts two years, after which the novice takes the usual three religious vows. He is called a scholastic whilst completing his studies or teaching in one of the schools. After a more or less extended course of studies the scholastic may receive the priesthood, if he be called, and then makes his third year of the novitiate which is called the tertianship.

The St. Stanislaus Novitiate began in 1823 in a miserable log house on the Jesuit farm near Florissant, with Father Van Quickenborne as Novice-Master, and six young men from the Novitiate at Whitemarsh, Md., among them the greatest of all our Indian Missionaries, Father Peter De Smet. In Father Van Quickenborne the two offices of Superior and Novice-master were combined. But as he was often called away from home by his other duties as missionary and pastor and organizer, Father Theodore de Theux supplied his place as Master of Novices from 1827 to 1831; and from February 4th, of that year, he held the office in his own right until the summer of 1837. Father De Theux was one of the most remarkable men in the Order. His interesting antecedents as a scion of nobility and then as the devoted chaplain of Napoleon's military prisoners at Liege, cast a glamor around his personality. He was a man of varied talents, and held high office in the administration of the Province: but above all "He was a man of holiness, regularity and vigorous exactitude, raised far above all human respect, severe to himself, and requiring of those under him the strictest detachment from comfort and emolument in their manner of exercising the apostolic ministry."[1]

He had a tender devotion to the Blessed Virgin. It was he who advised Bishop Purcell of Cincinnati, during the "Know-nothing" agitation of 1844 to petition the Sovereign Pontiff for the privilege of adding the word "Immaculate" to "Conception" in the Preface to the Mass. This petition was granted, long before the promulgation of the dogma of the Immaculate Conception by Pius IX.[2] In 1838 Father De Theux was transferred to Chicago, but returned to St. Louis diocese and in 1845 became pastor of St. Charles, where he died on February 8th, 1846.

His successor as Master of Novices was Father Peter De Vos, who was to hold the office until 1843. Father De Vos' name is not among the select few that grace the pages of the Menology of the Missouri Province. His piety and zeal, however, as well as his spirit of self-sacrifice is made manifest by the fact that he in 1843 joined Father De Smet's noble band of missionaries to the Indians of the Oregon Country. Father De Vos was followed by Rev. J. B. Smedts, who remained in the office till July 23rd, 1849.

Father Smedts was one of the twelve Jesuits that came from Whitemarsh, Maryland, to St. Ferdinand, Missouri, in 1823 under the leadership of Father Van Quickenborne. His name is inscribed on many a page of the history of the diocese, as Pastor of Portage des Sioux, and of St. Charles. His incumbency of these old French parishes was eminently fruitful in results, stirring up the dormant life of the sadly neglected people. On Father De Vos departure for the Flathead mission, Father Smedts was adjudged as eminently fitted for the office of Master of Novices. Father De Smet sums up Father Smedts' character in these words: "His whole life was irreproachable and exemplary. Shunning the world, simple in his manners and patient in suffering, he exhausted his strength in the service of the Lord."[3]

Few men have more faithfully illustrated the Beatitudes in their lives than Father Smedts. He died in St. Louis May 19th, 1855.

Father Smedts was succeeded by Rev. John Lucien Gleizal, who remained till July 3rd, 1857. Father Gleizal says the Menology " was a Frenchman, remarkable for his enlightened spirituality, deep piety and great zeal for religious perfection. His was a spirit which drew all hearts to a love of virtue, notwithstanding the indifferent English style of his instructions . . . . Combined with his persuasiveness of speech and

---

1 "Menology of the Society of Jesus, Province of Missouri," 1926, p. 26.

2 Menology, ibidem. De Smet, P. J., "Western Missions and Missionaries," p. 480.

3 De Smet, P. J., "Western Missions and Missionaries," pp. 492-494.

personal magnetism of virtue, there was manifested in all his private life a degree of mortification, which inspired his novices with a zeal for self-sacrifice and fortitude in the path of high perfection.''[4] There was nothing morose, however, or sombre about his seriousness. This saintly novice-master died in St. Louis on August 6th, 1859, at the age of fifty-one years. After Father Gleizal followed in the office of Novice-Master at St. Stanislaus Novitiate the Rev. Isidor Boudreaux, who filled it till Jan. 17th, 1880, when he was succeeded by Rev. Leopold Bushart. Father Isidor Boudreaux, an American, descended from a French family of Lower Louisiana, together with his distinguished brother Florentine, entered St. Louis University in 1832, and eventually became a member of the Society of Jesus. His lifework was done in Florissant, Mo., where for nigh on twenty-four years, as Superior and Master of Novices, he formed the future professors, pastors and missionaries of the Missouri Province. Father Boudreaux was distinguished for his gentleness of manner, and speech, blending the language of affection with the dignity of his office. As an instance of his lively faith the Menology relates the following incident. ''In 1849, when he, Father Isidor Boudreaux, was director of the Boys' Sodality in St. Louis University, the Asiatic cholera broke out and wrought great havoc in the city. There was imminent danger of the plague seizing on the college. In the emergency, Father Boudreaux induced the students, Protestants included, to make a pious vow, that they would adorn the statue of the Blessed Virgin in the church with a silver crown, if all the inmates of the University were preserved. At the same time, medals of the Immaculate Conception were affixed to the gates and doors and windows which faced on the streets. On the 8th of October following, the crown was solemnly placed on the statue, and a marble slab was inserted in the wall, aside of the Blessed Virgin's Altar, recording in letters of gold that, whereas in the space of a few months, six thousand citizens had perished, yet, through the intercession of Mary, not even one out of two hundred and more boarders had been infected with the plague . . .''[5]

Father Boudreaux died in Chicago on February 11th, 1885. His successor at the Novitiate in 1880 was the Rev. Father Leopold Bushart. Father Bushart was a man of many parts, and filled every office of importance in the Province, and eventually became Procurator of the St. Louis Province in Rome. ''His chief characteristic'' says the Menology, ''was sanctified common sense.'' He was not without imagination and humor. His quick flashing wit was as harmless, as the lightning of a summer night, for he held his naturally quick temper in firm control, and his gentlemanly instincts never forsook him. Incessant

---

[4]  Menology, pp. 73 and 74.
[5]  Menology, pp. 20-22.

labor, ubiquitous exertion, and constant prayer, made up his life. Like St. Paul, he desired "to be dissolved and to be with Christ," but, as he said, "he was ashamed to meet Our Lord with so little to offer Him."[6]

Father Leopold Bushart died in St. Louis in 1909. In Nov. 1881, Rev. Frederick Hageman became master of novices and continued to exert his blessed influence upon the on-coming recruits for the Jesuit army of God, for more than a quarter century 1881-1908. Father Hageman is still among the living, and though, no longer active, yet enjoying the dignified leisure of serene old age. He had made part of his studies at the Seminary of St. Francis near Milwaukee, but had entered the Society of Jesus before his ordination. It can be truly said that Father Hageman left an indelible impress on the Jesuit Community of the West. For whoever came under the fascination of his personal influence was from that moment on a better and nobler man. Those eyes, so keen and yet so kindly won you over, whether you would or not. And then, how skillfully would he adapt what he had to say to the circumstances of the localities and of the persons he was addressing. Really inspiring was his inveterate hopefulness of disposition. It is a pity that such men must grow old and helpless, before the last call.[7] Father Hageman turned over the office of Master of Novices to Father James T. Finn. "In Father Finn," says the Menology, "a frail physique, and an almost feminine refinement of manner belied the strong resolute purpose and strength of soul that abounded within. He sought to instill into his novices a vigorous and virile spirituality, and to school them in absolute fidelity to the Jesuit rule of life." The conventions and courtesies of social intercourse," he said, "should not be neglected or disdained, as they were "natural aids to the promotion of God's work."[8]

Father James T. Finn, having held the office of Novice-Master for seven years, was succeeded by dear old Father John Louis Mathery whom God preserve for many years! And Father Mathery in turn, by Father William Mitchel, and Father Mitchel finally by Father Krenz whose efforts were, no doubt, attended by most blessed results.

What a noble panorama they form, these artists of the spiritual life, with the many hundreds of masterpieces, more or less perfect, in the background; and every one of these masterpieces a living spiritual force for incalculable good. Great are the outward results attained by the Society of Jesus in the West, the Universities they founded and control, the parishes they erected and govern, the publications they issue, the societies and sodalities they promote: but greater still is the spirit

---

6 Historical Sketch of St. Louis University, in "Souvenir of Diamond Jubilee," pp. 101-102. Menology, pp. 82-83.

7 Hageman.

8 Menology, pp. 62 and 63.

of divine love and humble prayer that animates its members and radiates, not only from those who go out to meet the world, to reclaim it for God, but also from those whose lives are hid with God.

It will appear as a matter of course that in a great institution like the St. Louis University there must have lived and labored men of remarkable traits of character, depth and variety of learning, and ever-ready helpfulness extended to the wrecks and waifs of life, who however, for one reason or another, have not been granted the opportunity of distinguishing themselves in the outward upbuilding of the Kingdom of God in the Archdiocese of St. Louis. Some may have been learned professors, others patient and kind confessors, others again missionaries, and others writers of books, and still others who never knew that there was anything good or in the least remarkable in their make-up and who were always humbly grateful to God for any kindness shown them. Many of these men, no doubt, had an element of greatness in them, of which the noisy world knew nothing. Some remained only a short while among us, and we remembered them only when they had attained distinction in some other diocese. Only a few spent the greater part of their life in the diocese: most of them "had their exits and their entrances," and some others among them in turn "played many parts," though not among us.

Of the many distinguished Jesuit Fathers who for some time have made their field of labor among us in such a manner of quiet and unobtrusive life, only a few can find even a passing notice here. The full yield would fill a volume. We can choose but a limited number and those almost at random.

The different classes of men, with three representatives of each, shall here pass in quick review: spiritual writers, pastors of souls, heroic lovers of some particular virtue, zealous missionaries, and self-sacrificing bishops.                                   .

The three spiritual writers we have singled out from among the throng are Father Florentine J. Boudreaux, Rudolph J. Meyer and Peter J. Arnoudt. Father Florentine was one of the nine orphan children of the Boudreaux family of St. Michael, Louisiana, whom Bishop De Neckere had befriended in their great hour of need. Four boys of the family entered St. Louis University, Florentine among them. But the lively lad loved tools more than books and, after the first dull year of enforced study, he betook himself to a farm and then to a tinshop. His brother Isidor, in 1836, became a novice in the Society of Jesus: but Florentine seemed to be content with his position in the world. On the Feast of the Conversion of St. Paul, however, a vivid light came suddenly, and the young man hurriedly called on Father Verhaegen and asked to be received into the Order. Father

Boudreaux lived fifty-three years in the Society. His special study was chemistry, which he taught with delight and excellent results. But above all things he was a man of prayer. He had passed through a long period of dark desolation, which left with him a pathetic earnestness and fervor, even after the cloud had lifted. . From these experiences and the meditations with which he had conquered, he wrote his two beautiful books, "God Our Father" and "Happiness in Heaven." They were published in many editions, and were translated into German, Italian, French, Dutch and Danish. Father Florentine Boudreaux died in Chicago, on January 30th, 1894. He spent thirty-one years at the St. Louis University.[9]

Father Rudolph Meyer, was born in South St. Louis, on November 8th, 1841. He attended St. Louis University from 1853 to 1858, and entered the Novitiate at Florissant on Sunday, July 11th, 1858. At Woodstock he made his theological studies, and was chosen in 1874 to make a public defense of all philosophy and theology, of which he acquitted himself brilliantly. He filled all the grades of authority, from minister and prefect of studies to that of English assistant. Whilst assistant in Rome he wrote the first draft of the "Letter of the English Bishops on Liberal Catholics." Father Meyer was a master of languages, English, German, French and Spanish. His Latinity won him high praise from eminent critics. Yet, all these accomplishments and greatly enlarged responsibilities, which brought him into contact with many distinguished persons, only served to stimulate the religious life he loved so dearly. As a writer of long practice, Father Meyer gave the world, besides a number of other valuable works, the truly admirable book entitled: "First Lessons in the science of the Saints."[10]

Father Rudolph J. Meyer died at St. Louis in 1912.

Father Peter Joseph Arnoudt was a Belgian by birth, but American by choice. Having held a professorship at the University from 1843 to 1849, he served as a missionary at Florissant, and as operarius at the Novitiate. His was a life without stirring incidents of a personal kind. What distinguished him was his great desire for union with the Sacred Heart of Jesus. "Once," as the Menology says, "when suffering from a dangerous malady, he pledged himself to labor with increased zeal for the propagation of this special devotion. In accordance with this promise he wrote his well-known work on "The Imitation of the Sacred Heart of Jesus." The book was written in Latin; but his

---

9  Menology, pp. 15-16.

10  Menology, pp. 104-105. "Diamond Jubilee of St. Louis University," pp. 105-106.

friend and fellow-Jesuit, Father Fastré, translated it into English: Editions in various other languages soon followed.[11]

Father Arnoudt died at Cincinnati in 1865.

Father Joseph Anthony Fastré the translator of Father Arnoudt's classical work "De Imitatione Sacri Cordis," even more properly than Father Arnoudt himself, merits the title of an "Apostle of the Sacred Heart for the English-speaking world," on account of his tireless efforts, in the pulpit, in the class-room, and in his daily intercourse with people of the world, in behalf of this now favorite devotion.

Father Fastré also wrote "The Acts of the Early Martyrs," in five volumes, and was author of a number of plays and poems. His death occurred at Cincinnati, September 22nd, 1878.[12]

The third member of the St. Louis trinity of early promoters of the devotion to the Sacred Heart was Father Henry C. Bronsgest, the builder of "The Church of St. Francis Xavier's, from corner stone to steeple cross,'" and its beloved pastor for twenty-six years. As the Menology says, "Fathers Arnoudt and Fastré with their successors in Cincinnati, Fathers Walsh, Brady and Henry Bronsgeest, are accountable, probably more than any others, for the wonderful spirit of devotion to the Sacred Heart prevalent in the Middle West."

Before his appointment to St. Francis Xaxier's Church in St. Louis Father Bronsgest had been stationed for a few years at the Jesuit College in Cincinnati; where he was entrusted also with the care of the negro community, and for five years served as Pastor of the Church of the Sacred Heart in Chicago.[13]

One more Jesuit pastor of high distinction, to complete the trio, the saintly Father Joseph Weber, who was connected with St. Joseph's Church first as assistant, then as pastor, and finally as assistant for another long period. With the exception of two years spent at Westphalia in Osage County, Father Weber's entire priestly life in Missouri was devoted to the parish of St. Joseph's in St. Louis. Father Weber was born November 21st, 1815, at St. Gall, Switzerland, and received ordination in 1846. The commotions that shook all Europe in 1846, carried many Jesuit Fathers to America, Father Weber among them. After some years of wandering in the East, he came to St. Louis diocese in 1852, and found his true field of labor at St. Joseph's Church in 1854. In 1859 he succeeded Father Joseph Patschowski as pastor of that, the most important German parish of the city at the time. Father Weber was a most gentle and loveable man, of childlike faith, a master in the direction of souls. It is said that he was the confessor

---

11  Menology, p. 69.
12  Menology, p. 12.
13  Menology, pp. 45-47.

of more than half of the priests of the city. He well understood the art of combining the interests of God with the welfare of his people. When in 1866 the cholera broke out a second time, Father Weber proposed to his parishioners that they make a vow to St. Joseph, that they would subscribe for a new high altar in the honor of the Saint, if he would obtain for them and their families deliverance from the danger of infection. The entire Congregation took up the suggestion and subscribed $4,000. for the proposed Memorial in honor of St. Joseph. Not one of the subscribers was attacked by the epidemic.[14]

We now come to a class of Jesuit Fathers whose saintliness of life shone forth in an eminent degree, and, at least in one case, bore the sign manual of a well authenticated miracle. The first of these chosen men was Father Peter Koning, Professor of the natural sciences and architecture, who had also the care of souls among the slaves. When Father Koning in 1862 took seriously ill, many prayers went up to God that the dear good Father be spared, but the Almighty decreed otherwise. Now, when the body of the dead Father was exposed for veneration in the College Church, a young lady, Mary Wilson by name, came with some of her Catholic friends to the church. She was not, at the time, a Catholic, but as she used to tell the story—when she approached and touched the deceased priest, the truth of Catholicity suddenly flooded her mind, like a sunburst among clouds. She was not merely converted to the faith; she soon entered the Society of the Religious of the Sacred Heart. It is well known that St. John Berchmans appeared to her during her novitiate and cured her miraculously. This was one of the miracles accepted at Rome in the cause of St. John Berchmans canonization."[15]

Of Father Daniel McErlane, the next of our Jesuit priests of heroic virtue, we have no report of miracles; but his entire priestly life was one great miracle of love. He had special .charge of the jail and the public hospital for twenty years. "The more helpless called most appealingly for his sympathy," says the Menology, "and he pursued the hard-hearted sinner with an irresistible, patient and prudent love," a "love that seemed to take the form of motherly pity. He veiled all fault, no matter how glaring, and found virtues in the most abandoned souls. He won to the faith practically every condemned criminal of his time. He went to the gallows with each of them, and though the ghastly affair unnerved him, that he did not go to bed for two nights following, he was ready and eager to accompany the next one on his sad road to eternity." He was called the Angel of the Outcast.

---

[14] Questionnaire-Answers from St. Joseph's Church. Also History of St. Joseph's Church in "Das Katholische Deutschtum von St. Louis." p. 74.

[15] Menology, p. 11.

Most interesting were the arts and decoys he used in infinite variety to capture his game as a hunter of souls.

When Father McErlane died in 1910 the whole city turned out to honor him, the papers were full of praise for him.[16]

Nothing illustrates the spirit of the Society of Jesus more beautifully than the high regard in which the Fathers hold the Brothers of the Order as co-workers in their own high vocation. Of the seventy-five names in the Menology of the Missouri Province, two are those of Bishops, fifty of priests, fourteen of Brothers, and eleven of scholastics.

One of these servants of the servants of God was Brother Andrew Mazella, an Italian, who died at St. Mary's, Kansas, in 1867. Having entered the Society at Naples, in 1823, he was destined for his ministry of service unders Fathers Van Quickenborne and Christian Hoecken, at the village of the Kickapoo Indians. Then, transferred to the Potawatomi at Council Bluffs, he accompanied these Indians to their reservation in Kansas, where he spent the rest of his life. "While still at Council Bluffs, Brother Mazella was prostrated with a dangerous malady. Father De Smet and Verreydt were preparing to recite the prayers for the agonizing, when the saintly Brother asked, in a feeble and dying voice, for some drops of St. Ignatius water. He received them, and forthwith exclaimed: "I am cured." So he was, being reserved for twenty-eight years more of self-sacrifice among the Indians." At St. Mary's he was carpenter, shoemaker, tailor, farmer, cook, sacristan, infirmarian, and doctor. And Father De Smet gave him the testimonial: "All that Brother Mazella did was done well."[17]

Of the numerous Missionary Fathers of the Missouri Province, the following three well known men of God shall stand as representatives: Father Francis Xavier Weninger, Father Cornelius **Smarius** and Father Henry Moeller.

Father Weninger was, like so many of his brethren, carried to America on the waves of the revolution of 1848. He was born near Wartburg in Styria, of a well to do family. Through' the kindness of the imperial family he obtained his education at the University of Vienna. At the age of twenty-three he received ordination, but continued his studies for two more years, and won the doctorate of Divinity. As he was "persona grata" with Emporer Francis I and his consort, he might have ascended, step by step, to the highest honors in the Church. But he determined to enter the Society of Jesus. He began his novitiate at Gratz, on this twenty-seventh birthday, 1832. In 1840 he completed preparations for the active life by the so-called Tertianship. He was now sent to Innsbruck as prefect of studies and professor of

---

16 Menology, pp. 51-53.
17 Menology, pp. 50-51.

Sacred Scripture, Hebrew and Ecclesiastical History. It will appear from this brief account, that Father Weninger was a man of deep and varied learning, not the ignorant fanatic he was sometimes represented to be by some who judged him on short acquaintance. But Father Weninger had a higher ideal than that of a merely learned man. He was preeminently a man of action, and whole-hearted determination. The salvation of souls, was the grand object for which all his talents and acquirements were ranged into one serried column of attack and defense. In this sense we must interpret the idiosyncracies and peculiarities of his missionary activities. His whole soul was in his sermon, and the souls of his listeners were always deeply influenced.

Father Weninger's plan of a mission can be called a forerunner of the new Laymen's Retreat Movement that is becoming so popular in our day. He was not content to preach the ordinary mission sermon, but sought to eradicate the special obstacles to a truly Christian life, as they were found in the peculiar conditions of the various classes, the married men, the married women, the young ladies, the young men and finally the children. In the presence of a mixed congregation it was very difficult and certainly not advisable to speak fully and plainly on these delicate matters. He would, therefore, give special instructions for each class or state of life, from which all others were excluded. All classes, however, were expected to attend the sermons of a more general nature: To preserve the fruits of a mission, Father Weninger relied upon the influence of good books, a series of which he himself published and carried along with him on his journeys.[18]

Father Weninger landed in New York on July 25th, 1848, and eight days after his arrival, proceeded on his way to St. Louis to confer with Father James A. Elet, the vice-provincial of the future Missouri Province. While in St. Louis he preached at St. Joseph's Church. In company with Father Elet he then returned to Cincinnati, where he was to spend a season lecturing on Dogmatic Theology and learning English.

"The efforts to master English, however, left much to be desired. In fact, at one time his poor English became a source of worry to the Jesuits stationed at Cincinnati, as he himself relates: "A mission had been arranged for the then Irish Church of St. Xavier, when at the last moment it was found that no one could be depended on in time to give the mission according to schedule. Father Weninger heard that the mission would probably have to be canceled, and offered to give it himself. After serious doubts on the part of the Rector and the Pastor, this offer was finally accepted. Crowds flocked to the church, so that even the aisles were packed, and though there were very few who could fully understand the preacher's broken English, the mission

---

18 Menology, pp. 60-61.

was a great success.[19]  Of course, a man of Father Weninger's uncompromising loyalty to principle made him many enemies: Yet, he met them fearlessly in the open, but also, at times, and for particular reasons, eluded threatening assaults.

"On one evening, during this cholera period," as he relates, "a sick call came about midnight.  The Pastor was himself sick at the time, and the duty of ministering to the dying naturally fell to Father Weninger.  He immediately prepared himself and set out.  At his destination he found an old lady of 70 years in an unconscious state.  Since confession and Holy Viaticum were out of the question, he administered Extreme Unction and gave the general absolution.  But in the meantime a great noise had arisen outside.  An old man rushed in to announce that a crowd of fanatics had gathered with the intention of doing violence to Father Weninger.  "They want to kill you, Father."  "Why?"  "Because you are a priest."  "Then I will know why I die—".  Taking a light into his hands he boldly stepped into the streets, with the Blessed Sacrament still close to his bosom.  The crowd parted, evidently expecting that several guards were to follow.  After Father Weninger had advanced a bit, he suddenly blew out light and swiftly darted into a near-by restaurant, pursued by a furious mob crying "Down with the priest!  Kill the priest!"  From this place he finally made his way home under the protection of the police."[20]

A profound theologian, a vigorous and eloquent preacher, and a great lover of the common people, Father Weninger will go down in history as one of the most remarkable men of his time.  He died at Cincinnati in 1888, at the age of eighty-three years.

Father Cornelius F. Smarius was a native of Brabant, Holland, born in March 1823.  He attended the University at Tilburg, came to America in 1841, and entered the Novitiate at Florissant, and subsequently filled the offices of professor at the University, Vice-President of that Institution, and Rector of the College Church.  But his best work was done by him as a missionary wandering up and down the country.  He was early recognized as a man of extraordinary talents and brilliant promise.  His favorite study was poetry, and he wrote many fine pieces in Latin and in his own native tongue.  On his arrival in America he tried hard and successfully to master the intricacies of English, so that he spoke it fluently, correctly and with only a slight tinge of a foreign accent.  As a missionary, he manifested wonderful powers.  The simplicity and purity of his intentions, the thrilling tones, the tender appeals, the sublime raptures of his eloquence, seized the hearts of the multitude and carried them to nobler heights of life.

---

[19] "Franz Xavier Weninger" In "Central-Blatt," and "Social Justice," June, July, August, 1927.

[20] Ibidem.

Yet, Father Smarius' nature was as simple and guileless as that of a boy. A poet by nature, an orator by study, and a heart of golden love, was Father Cornelius Smarius, S.J. He died at Chicago on March 1st, 1870.[21]

Father Henry Moeller the third and youngest member of our Missionary band, still lives in the memory of many of our priests and members of the laity, for whom and to whom he has ever given a mission. He was an orator of great power, and he had that certainty of aim in spiritual things, which carries conviction and conversion to the mind and heart. But his distinguishing trait was a deep, sincere humility. In fact, "his humility had a tendency toward undue self-depreciation," At times, after a brilliant exposition of Catholic truth, he would return to the house and sit in gloomy silence at the table, whilst lively conversation ran the round of the circle of priests. But suddenly he would pull himself together, as it were, and be the old cheerful, hopeful Father once more. Father Marshall T. Boarman, the Father Boarman of the powerful voice and the sunny care free disposition, was then his companion on the missions. Surely the names of both are written in large golden letters in the Book of Life.[22]

Of the four or five Bishops the Missouri Province gave to the Church, we will mention only the names, as their lives are part of the history of the Universal Church: James Van de Velde, Bishop of Chicago, and subsequently of Natchez; John B. Miége, Bishop of Messina I.P.I. and Vicar-Apostolic of the Indian Territory; George A. Carrell, Bishop of Covington, and Frederick C. Hopkins, Bishop of Athribis, and Vicar-Apostolic of British Honduras; who, however, was only an adopted Son of the Province.

Many more honored names of Jesuits arise in the memory, some whom I have known personally, others of whom I have read or heard something wise, beautiful, interesting and noble. But this chapter must be closed.

---

21 "Western Watchman," March 5, 1870.
22 Menology, pp. 115. Diamond Jubilee, pp. 108-110. Personal Reminiscenses.

ST. LOUIS UNIVERSITY

## Chapter 56

## ST. LOUIS UNIVERSITY IN ITS NEW HOME

The St. Louis University, founded and conducted by the Missouri Province of the Society of Jesus, has been for well nigh a century so closely aligned with the religious life and progress of the city and diocese, that its history and destiny must forever be enshrined in the Catholic heart. Its very presence among us gives distinction to the community: its far-reaching influence, religious cultural and scientific, is a constant call to our eager and talented youth to strive after the higher things of life, and the crucial test of its high merit is found in the ever increasing number of men who have gone forth from its halls to win a distinguished position in one of the higher professions. Founded in poverty, yet animated with the spirit that overcomes the world, this noble institution has forced its way into the front rank of American Universities. Without a thought of earthly recompense its presidents and professors have sought and found the joy of life in doing their very best for God and the youthful souls entrusted to their care. And their spirit of love and self-sacrifice brought results, all the more admirable, because they were attained without much help from the outside world, and at times, in spite of its cold indifference and even direct opposition.

The earlier period of the history of the St. Louis University has already been treated; the later developments hinge on the removal of the institution from Ninth Street and Washington Avenue to the present location, Grand Avenue and Lindell Boulevard. This removal was first broached as a desirable measure in 1836, under the second President, the Rev. J. A. Elct. The idea seems to have received a quietus, when in 1853 the Rev. John B. Druyts, the fifth President, began the erection of the ample and commodious University building fronting on Washington Avenue. Under Father Druyts administration the institution received a set back in as far as the medical faculty requested to have its University dissolved. The reason given was the fear of injury to the medical department, arising from religious prejudices among the people against Catholics and Catholic institutions. The board of trustees did not then consent; but when the Know-Nothing excitement rose and began to spread like wild-fire in 1854 and 1855, the separation was affected by mutual and friendly consent.[1] It was under the presidency of Father Thomas O'Neil (1862-1868) that the plan

---

[1] Fanning, Father W. H., "Historical Sketch of St. Louis University," in "Diamond Jubilee Memorial," p. 55.

of removing the University to a more suitable location assumed definite form. Owing to the Civil War this period was one of severe trial for the College, and demanded the utmost tact and discretion. In the period of reconstruction after the war it became evident that the boarding school would have to be discontinued, and that it would become advisable to transfer the University to the West end of the City. Father O'Neill, accordingly prepared for these eventualities by purchasing ground on Grand Avenue, which was in 1870 to become the city limits. In 1881 under the presidency of Father Joseph E. Keller the University ceased to be a boarding school. There was a gradual increase of day scholars, the total attendance soon attained the general average. Father Keller was a native of Rhenish-Bavaria, but came to America when but a child. Having entered the Society of Jesus in 1844 at Florissant, he was ordained by Archbishop Purcell of Cincinnati, and served the Order in various positions of trust, among them the presidency of the St. Louis University from 1877 to 1881. "Father Keller was a man of varied and brilliant talents," writes Father Fanning. "Besides being a profound theologian he was a master of English, German, French and Spanish. His Latinity won him high praise from eminent critics. His writings were models of elegance and classical finish. He was of a most humble and retiring disposition and yet combined with it a wonderful executive ability and foresight. Education had no greater friend and advocate. To his efforts was due the inauguration of the post-graduate course."[2]

In 1881 Father Rudolph J. Meyer was appointed President of the University. He was a native of St. Louis, and received his earliest training in S. S. Peter and Paul's parochial school. After a five years' course at the University he entered the Novitiate at Florissant, and made his final vows on February 2nd, 1876. In 1881 we find Father Meyer in St. Louis as Rector of the St. Louis University: After his term as president, he was promoted to the office of Provincial, which he held until January 1889. During the time that Father Meyer was president of the University and Provincial of the Missouri Province, the crypt of the present St. Francis Xavier's Church, and the new St. Louis University were built. The corner stone of the church was laid by Archbishop Patrick J. Ryan on June 8th, 1884. The basement or crypt was opened for divine service on All Saints Day the same year. Vicar-General Brady performed the ceremony of dedication. The Rev. Michael Corbett, S.J., was the first pastor of the new parish. Four years more did old St. Francis Xavier Church continue its religious ministrations with Father Henry Moeller as its pastor. In 1886 the erection of the collegiate and academic buildings were begun extending 270 feet in length on Grand Avenue.

---

2 Historical Sketch, pp. 104-105.

On May 24th, the old College premises were sold. On July 24th, 1888 a reunion of Alumni was held with a farewell banquet in the study hall of their Alma Mater. On August 6th, 1888 public services were held for the last time in the "Old College Church." It was on Christmas day 1885 that Father Henry Moeller had become President of the University. The new University was then in process of erection and it devolved upon him to superintend the progress of the construction. After the building was ready for occupancy came the tedious work of removal. With the Archbishop's consent Father Moeller blessed the Chapel and the college on July 31st, 1888. The university was now duly constituted in its new location on Grand Avenue. But Father Moeller's worries were not over as yet. Grand Avenue was far away from the heart of the city. The street car service was even then slow and irregular. Indeed, the poor two-horse or mule power cars were a thing of the past, but the cable or electric power successors were divided into a number of companies, each one charging an extra fare. Many of the poorer students found it too costly to attend the far away University. Yet in spite of these losses, the roll call showed an attendance of four hundred students. Father Moeller guided the University through the first year of its new course and then turned it over to Father Edward Gleeson, in 1889.

This was the year in which the post-graduate School of Philosophy and Science was opened at the University, a stately Hall being erected for its accommodation on Lindell Boulevard.

Father Joseph Grimmelsman, President of the University from 1891 to 1898, was born in Cincinnati on March 17th, 1853. He entered the Novitiate at Florissant on August 9th, 1871. After a most successful course of studies at the College of Woodstock, Maryland, and at the University of Louvain the young priest returned to America to teach Philosophy at Woodstock. As President of St. Louis University he completed the magnificent Gothic Church of St. Francis Xavier. Its dedication and opening for public service on January 16th, 1898, was a notable event.

The church is one of the finest in the entire West. It is built of stone, in the pure English Gothic architecture of the thirteenth century, combining grandeur of proportions, with exquisite beauty of finish. The attractive Hall of the Divinity School on Pine Street was erected in 1899 by Father Grimmelman's successor in the office of President, Rev. James F. K. Hoeffer. On February 14th, 1899, Father Grimmelsman received his appointment as Provincial Superior of the Missouri Province of the Order.

The St. Louis University, at this time, had two faculties: 1) the faculty of Divinity. 2) the faculty of Arts and Sciences, which embraced three distinct departments. The faculty of Law which had been established in 1843 under the guidance of the Hon. Richard Aylet Buckner, was discontinued after a few years. "As a lawyer Mr. Buckner ranked with Henry Clay, Hardin, Underwood, Rowan and others who have shed lustre on the Kentucky Bar."[3]

The death of Mr. Buckner on December 8th, 1847, dispelled the last hope of reviving the Law Department of the St. Louis University.

The faculty of Medicine which was lost to the University in 1855, was restored by the tireless efforts of Father Hoeffer's immediate successor, William Banks Rogers, the eighteenth President of St. Louis University.

Father Fanning in the *Memorial Volume of the Diamond Jubilee* gives a clear and succinct account of this transaction:

"On May 1st, 1901, the Marion Sims College of Medicine was consolidated with the Beaumont Hospital Medical College. This was the result of an effort to unite in one large institution two separate schools for the purpose of strengthening the advantages which each offered. Each one of these had maintained a large faculty with equipment and facilities adequate for the stage of medical education which each represented. The consolidated school thus presented opportunities for medical instruction far in advance of what had before been possible.

Following the tendency in higher medical education, the need for a close university connection was made manifest, and this need was fully supplied when the Marion-Sims-Beaumont College of Medicine become a component part of the St. Louis University. To develop a true universty school of medicine, it is essential that the fundamental departments of medicine be placed upon the same plane as other university branches. This requires that anatomy, chemistry physiology, bacteriology and pharmacology be taught by specialists, who devote their time exclusively to teaching and research. This plan inaugurated by the University during the session of 1903-4 was fully accomplished in 1904, and the instruction of the first two years was placed permanently upon a University basis.

The buildings of the Medical department were located on Compton Hill, the highest point in the city of St. Louis. The College property included an acre and a half of ground, upon the corner of Grand Avenue and Caroline Street, and comprised the Medical Building, the Rebekah Hospital Building, and the Laboratory Building, which was completed, October 1, 1901, and which was devoted exclusively to laboratory instruction in pathology, chemistry, physiology, histology and clinical microscopy.

By the union of the two schools and the association with St. Louis University extraordinary advantages for hospital and clinical instruction were presented to the students. The following hospitals and

---

3 Diamond Jubilee, St. Louis University, p. 137.

clinics came directly under control of the school of members of its faculty: Rebekah Hospital, Alexian Brothers Hospital, St. Mary's Infirmary, St. John's Hospital, Mt. St. Rose Hospital, Josephine Hospital, St. Anne's Lying-In Infirmary, St. Vincent's Asylum, St. Louis Marine Hospital, Obstetric Clinic, Grand Ave., Dispensary, St. John's Clinical Dispensary, and Obstetric Dispensary with the additional facilities afforded by the City Hospital, City Insane Asylum and Poor House.[4]

The course of instructions was to cover four years.''

The Medical Department of the St. Louis University has now been in operation for a quarter century and has by dint. of severest strain achieved a high rank among the medical schools of the land. If it were asked why should a Jesuit Institution of learning devote a large portion of its comparatively slender resources to medical education, it might be answered that medical science, simply because it is a science, belongs to the curriculum of a true University. The earliest university was the medical school of Salerno; The second was the law school of Bologna, and the third, that of Paris, a school of divinity. We need Catholic Doctors of Medicine and Law as much as Doctors of Divinity. ''When Father Rogers in 1903, organized the medical school under the leadership of St. Louis University, there were approximately 300 students in the school. Of this number, scarcely fifteen were Catholics. Today there are 520 students in the institution, and the percentage of Catholics is approximately sixty-five. The last graduating class of one hundred and sixteen men had a percentage of sixty Catholics, and these boys come from practically every state in the union and from many foreign countries. They leave St. Louis imbued with a greater understanding of their faith, by reason of their contact with the men who have taught them during five and more years. They leave St. Louis with a better understanding of the importance of Catholic professional men in the furtherance of the Catholic cause in this country. Not only that, but their own religious faith has been strengthened—their Catholic outlook on life has been retained amidst studies which would under circumstances, have a deteriorating effect upon the spiritual life of the individual, and they leave their Alma Mater, not only more learned and more ambitious men, but better and more Catholic men.''[5]

''Besides the non-Catholic members of the student body have not failed to catch some of this Catholic influence. Their contact with Catholic professors, priests and students tends to dispel bigotry and fanaticism.''[6] After Father Roger's second term in the presidency Rev. John P. Frieden held the office from 1908 to 1911.

---

[4] Diamond Jubilee, pp. 137-139.

[5] From an Address by Father Schwitalla, S. J., in the ''Mariner,'' July 19, 1927.

[6] Ibidem.

Under Father Frieden's efficient management the Dental College and the School of Advanced Science and Law were established in 1908, the Department of Meteorology and Seismology in 1909, the School of Commerce and Finance in 1910. The Rev. A. J. Burrows was President from 1912 to 1913, and the Rev. Bernard J. Otting from 1913 to 1920.

Under Father Otting's administration the University was named chief beneficiary of the many million dollars estate of James Campbell. The fund was to be used for the benefit of the Medical School only; and was not to come into the hands of the University authorities until a more or less extended period had elapsed. Father Otting's successor, the Very Rev. William F. Robinson (1920-1924) set his main efforts on raising an adequate endowment fund for the University. His precarious health prevented him from attaining full success: During a part of his administrative period, his place was supplied by Father Michael J. O'Connor. In 1924, Father Charles H. Cloud was installed as Rector of St. Louis University.

For more than a century this great institution has been among us as a living, acting reality, and it still remains with us full of the wisdom that age confers, but full, also, of the vigor of ever renewed life: a busy life of learning and scholarship, a bulwark of the Church's defense against the false philosophy of the day, the truthful Mother, Alma Mater, of leaders of the people, one of the transcendent glories of the City and Archdiocese of St. Louis.

## CHAPTER 57

## THE CATHOLIC SOCIETIES OF THE ARCHDIOCESE

The Catholic Church is a complete organization in itself, divine in its origin, its faith, its authority and its sacramental system, but human in its membership and administrative personality. She does not need any subsidiary organizations, yet, as like begets like, she has always produced them in various forms and for various purposes, in likeness to her own form and mode of activity, adapted, however, to the varying needs and conditions of successive ages. Our own Archdiocese formed no exception to this rule. We have had and still have a large number of associations, helpful in the work of holy Church and blessed or approved by her supreme authority.

As the chief activities of the Church are concerned with man's relations to God, to his neighbor and to himself, so these church organizations may be divided into Religious, Charitable and Benevolent Societies or Associations.

We will treat of these three classes of Church organizations, as sprung up or were adopted in the diocese of St. Louis.

### 1. RELIGIOUS ASSOCIATIONS

The Sodality of the Blessed Virgin Mary was the earliest, as it is best of all the religious societies established within the territory of Archdiocese. It was founded in 1563 at Rome in the Roman College of the Society of Jesus.

Pope Sixtus V granted permission to erect more than one sodality in the same college. After the suppression of the Jesuits in 1773, the sodalities were kept in existence by zealous priests, probably former members of the Order.

After the reestablishment of the Society of Jesus in 1814 Pope Leo restored the Jesuits' old rights and privileges in regard to the Sodalities. Now, we have no evidence that the Jesuits at Kaskaskia established the Sodality of the Blessed Virgin among their neophites; yet it is probable that they did. But the Jesuit Fathers that established the St. Louis University and St. Francis Xavier's Church, and St. Joseph's Church, in the city, and the numerous parishes along the Missouri River certainly did found the first Sodalities west of the Mississippi River.

It was on the first day of April 1835 that the Senior Sodality was established at the University, under the invocation and title of the Assumption. But in 1859 this title was changed at Rome to that of

(451)

the Immaculate Conception. Father J. B. Druyts, S. J., had requested the change.

The officers of the first year were: Father J. B. Smedts, S. J., Director; Isidore J. Boudreaux, Prefect; Michael Hebert, First Assistant: Sylvester Delouche, Second Assistant; Russell Curtis, Secretary; Gustave H. Kernion, Treasurer. The first year the Sodality numbered thirty members.[1] In 1838 at a mission given by Father John Gleizal, the Sodality was established at Florissant for the pupils of the Sacred Heart Convent. In 1854 Father Patschowski introduced the Sodality for the young ladies in St. Joseph's Parish. In the course of time a number of parishes in country and city requested the establishment of the Sodality for the various classes of their membership.

Another most praiseworthy Society that took deep root in the soil of the diocese is the Confraternity of Christian Mothers. The Third Order of St. Francis, with headquarters at St. Anthony's Church, has done much for the promotion of piety and the practice of charity among its members which were drawn from all the parishes of the city. The Holy Name Society has, of late, been established in a large number of parishes. Its Annual Rally is one of the great diocesan events.

It would be impossible in this chapter to mention all, or even the greater number of pious associations that had a share in building up and strengthening the Church in the one-time territory of St. Louis Archdiocese, and to give due credit to their officers and members. We must pass on to the second class:

## 2.  CHARITABLE SOCIETIES

The first charitable society of St. Louis was organized at the house of Governor McNair in 1824. It was called The Female Charitable Society. Mrs. George F. Strother was its first President with Mrs. McNair as Vice President.

The membership was composed of Catholic and Protestant ladies; the purpose was to afford relief to the poor. On Palm Sunday 1824 the Rev. Francis Niel delivered a fiery sermon at the Cathedral to the members of the society, "producing a happy union of Catholic and Protestant, French and American ladies in the formation of a society, which promises so much to the poor and the needy."

*St. Louis Enquirer* of May 10th, 1824 gave copious extracts from the sermon, which was reprinted in the *United States Miscellany* of June 24th, of the same year.[2]

---

[1] Fanning, Father S.J., "Diamond Jubilee of St. Louis University," pp. 165-170.

[2] "United States Catholic Miscellany," Charleston, S. C., Vol. III. No. 2, and ibidem, pp. 43-46.

The Missouri Hibernian Relief Society was organized three years later (1827), by the enterprising Irish emigrants, who then outnumbered all other Europeans except the French. James C. Lynch was the first President, and William Piggot its first Secretary. The object of the Society was "to relieve those distressed in their native land and assist those who desired to emigrate to our shores."

In 1838 the "Society for the Diffusion of Alms" was formed by a number of Catholic gentlemen with the announcement: "We, the undersigned, do resolve ourselves into a society for the general diffusion of alms, and without heeding anything of the poor save their honest poverty, do pledge our exertions to bestow our units upon them with impartial observance." M. Philip Leduc was President, Christopher Garvey, Vice-President, L. A. Benoist, Treasurer; A. W. Manning, Secretary. Many of the historic Catholic names of early St. Louis occur in the List of Officers of the Society.[3]

The Catholic Orphan Association of St. Louis was founded February 13th, 1841 by a band of Catholic ladies under the leadership of Miss Angela Hughes. But it was not long before the men joined them in their laudable effort for the orphans. The board of Managers in 1849 consisted of John B. Sarpy, Edward Walsh, Bryan Mullanphy, Amadee Valle, Joseph Murphy, John Haverty, Thomas Gray, Thomas Flaherty and Patrick J. Ryder. Under this management the Association was incorporated as the "Roman Catholic Male and Female Orphan Asylum of St. Louis." On September 17th, of that year John B. Sarpy was elected President, John Haverty, Vice-President, Amadee Valle, Treasurer, and Thomas Flaherty, Secretary. The Association had the management of the two Archdiocesan Orphan Asylums and of the Catholic Protectorate at Glencoe.[4]

The St. Vincent de Paul Society, founded at Paris, in May 1833, by Frederic Ozanam was introduced into St. Louis Catholic life in 1845 by Dr. Timothy Papin, aided by Bryan Mullanphy.

The first meeting took place in the house adjoining the Cathedral on Thursday evening, November 20th, 1845; Bryan Mullanphy presided. The election of officers resulted in the following: Dr. M. L. Linton, President, Bryan Mullanphy, First Vice-President, Dennis Galvin, Second Vice-President, James Maguire, Jr., Secretary, and Patrick Ryder, Treasurer. This first Conference of the St. Vincent de Paul Society branched out, as the various Parishes of the city arose, and today is represented by seventy-two Conferences in the city, working under the Metropolitan Central Council and the Particular Council of St. Louis.

---

3   Scharf, "History of St. Louis," p. 1753.
4   Scharf, "History of St. Louis," p. 1759.

There are Conferences of the St. Vincent de Paul Society in St. Charles, Ste. Genevieve and De Soto.

The St. Louis Conference of the Old Cathedral enjoys the distinction of being the very first offshoot of the great Association on American soil.[5]

The German St. Vincent's Orphan Society owes its foundation to the beautiful spirit of charity aroused among the German Catholics of St. Louis by the dreadful ravages of the cholera in 1849. On June 12th, 1850 an appeal was issued by Vicar-General Melcher and a Committee of priests and laymen, calling upon the German Catholics of the city to form a Society for the care of the orphans. The appeal resulted in the organization of the German St. Vincent's Orphan Society, with Frank A. Stuever, President, J. F. Mauntel, Vice-President, Francis Saler, Treasurer, Charles Blattau, First Secretary, and Edward Buse, Second Secretary.

On President Stuever's death, Valentine Reiss succeeded to his office. The Society is still alive and active, having only recently erected a new home of magnificent proportions for the German Catholic Orphans, situated in Normandy. All German Parishes of the City, and some of the county also, have each a Branch of the German St. Vincent Orphan Society.[6]

## 3. BENEVOLENT SOCIETIES

The first Benevolent Society organized in St. Louis was called the "Erin Benevolent Society." On February 9th, 1818, a meeting of Irishmen was held at the house of Jeremiah Connor for the purpose of forming a society for mutual aid in case of sickness and for the support of the families of deceased members. Thomas Brady was elected chairman and Thomas Hanley, Secretary. A Committee of five, Jeremiah Connor, James McGunnegle, John Mullanphy, Alexander Blackwell and Arthur McGinniss, were appointed to frame resolutions. The meeting adjourned to meet Tuesday, February 24th, at the house of Thomas Brady.

The actual organization occurred on October 10th, 1819, at the house and under the presidency of Jeremiah Connor, when the constititution was adopted for the Erin Benevolent Society. On October 21st, 1819, the election of officers was held: Jeremiah Connor, President, Thomas Hardy, Vice-President, Hugh Ranken, Treasurer, Lawrence Ryan, Secretary, Thomas English, James Timon, Robert N. Catherwood, Joseph Charles and Hugh O'Neill, Standing Committee:

---

5   Schulte, Rev. Paul, in "St. Louis Catholic Historical Review," vol. III, 1-13.

6   Remembrance: Diamond Jubilee of the German St. Vincent's Orphan Society, 1925.

John Timon, Robert Ranken and Francis Rockford, Visiting Committee.

On March 17th, 1920, the first observance of St. Patrick's Day was held, by a parade of the Society and a dinner at which a number of toasts and sentiments were given, the first one being: "The Seventeenth of March, the 1326th Anniversary."[7]

The German Catholics followed the example of their Irish brethren by establishing the German Roman-Catholic Benevolent Society. This Society was founded December 13th, 1846. John Amend was elected President: Joseph Kulage, Vice-President; Joseph N. Hendricks, First Secretary, and F. Wellmann, Treasurer. In September 1848 the members turned out in a body to assist at the corner stone laying of the first Church of S.S. Peter and Paul.

On February 24th, 1849, the Society was incorporated, and in June of the same year presented itself with banners and regalia at the dedication of Holy Trinity Church in what was then called Bremen. On March 24th, 1850, John Amend resigned the presidency, and Anton Holle was elected in his place. From the day of its organization until very recent times, there was no corner stone laying or dedication of a Catholic Church in or around St. Louis, at which the so-called "Old Guard" did not take part. On November 19th, 1854, John Amend, having returned from California, was re-elected President of the Society and retained his office till death called him away to his eternal home, November 17th, 1885. "Papa Amend," as he was lovingly called by all that knew him, was a remarkable man, full of strong living faith, charitable to all and eminently fair in all his dealings.

His word was always "as good as gold." John Amend was one of the leaders in the movement to unite all the German Catholic Societies of the United States in a national organization, the so-called Central Verein. This great Association was formed at Baltimore in 1855 and incorporated in the State of Missouri in 1883. The fifth Annual Convention of the Central Verein was held in St. Louis, 28-30 of May, 1860. John Amend presided over the deliberations. The main work of the convention was a clear and comprehensive statement of the Society's aims and purposes in regard to the Church and the world round about. The chief enemy of Catholic life was declared to be found in the numerous Secret Societies of this country.

John Amend held the presidency of the Central Verein from 1860 to 1867 when he declined a re-election. In 1873 another prominent Catholic of St. Louis, Henry J. Spaunhorst was called to the high office and retained it till 1890.

---

[7] Scharf, "History of St. Louis," p. 1758, and O'Leary, Father Cornelius, in "Journal of American-Irish Historical Society," vol. IX, p. 210.

Four more conventions of the Central Verein were held in St. Louis, the latest one in 1917, under the presidency of Joseph Frey of New York, at which the Apostolic Delegate John Bonzano paid a beautiful tribute to the loyalty and patriotism of the German Catholics, which were then suspected and maligned by many: "No institution under the sky assists so much in fostering loyalty to one's country, as the Catholic Church. If I did not believe that you are good, loyal patriotic American Citizens, I would not be here today."[8]

But we must return to our earlier days.

In 1848 the pioneer of all the Catholic Temperance Societies, the "Catholic Total Abstinence and Benevolent Society" was founded. It was organized on August 15th of the above mentioned year by the Rev. John Higginbotham, then pastor of St. Michael's Church. He remained at the head of the Society until 1856 when he resigned his pastorate of St. Patrick's Church, left St. Louis for Halifax, as it is said, to organize a similar society, and then to enter the British service as an army chaplain.

Father Higginbotham was born February 2, 1820, in the diocese of Dublin, entered the Seminary in 1843 and was ordained to the priesthood in the Cathedral of St. Louis on September 21, 1845. His successor in the presidency of the Catholic Total Abstinence and Benevolent Society was the founder and first pastor of St. John's Church, St. Louis, the Rev. James Bannon, who, at the outbreak of the Civil War, entered the Confederate service as army chaplain.

The third president was Father James O'Brien, the fourth, Father James Henry.

Until the Civil War the society enjoyed great prosperity, and had at one time an enrollment of one thousand members. The war caused a serious division, many of the members enlisted either in the northern or southern army. Originally established as a temperance society, pure and simple the Society found it expedient to adopt certain beneficiary features.[9]

The "Catholic Total Abstinence and Benevolent Society" suffered its severest setback by the establishment of a number of similar organizations in the city. The first of these was the *Shamrock Society*. In the summer of 1854 a riot occurred in St. Louis, continuing three days, and among the victims were many Irishmen. To relieve the wants of their distressed countrymen some of the leading Irishmen in September 1854 organized the Shamrock Society. The object was declared to be beneficiary, embracing sick-benefits, and an assessment of one dollar per member, in case of death. The Society drew the bulk of the

---

8  Annual Reports of the Conventions.
9  Scharf, "History of St. Louis," p. 1766.

young Irishmen to its membership, at one time having an enrollment of nearly three hundred. During the Civil War it suffered from political dissensions. The first President was Edward Lester. Though an exclusively St. Louis organization, it maintained correspondence with the Irish Catholic Benevolent Union.[10]

The United Sons of Erin Benevolent Society was the second of these rival organizations. It was formed in 1866. Among its early members and promoters were Rev. James Henry, Francis Noonan, Dr. W. H. Brennan and James Bligh. It had about two hundred members. Its weekly sick-benefit was six dollars; in the event of a member's death, the heirs received one dollar from each surviving member.

The officers in 1882 were: Father Henry, Spritual Adviser; M. Whalen, President, John Costello, Secretary; Richard O'Neill, Treasurer; Dr. W. N. Brennan, Medical Examiner.[11]

Among the German Catholics of the City the German Roman-Catholic Benevolent Society of 1850 had ruled supreme and alone in the city for upwards of eighteen years, drawing its new blood from all the parishes.. But in 1868 the men of S.S. Peter and Paul decided to have a Society of their own, modelled however after the plan of the "Old Society," as it was soon to be known. The name of the Society was St. Paul's Unterstuetzungs-Verein. Frederick Arendes was its first Président. The greater number of the German parishes of the city followed the example of S.S. Peter and Paul: the Holy Trinity, St. Francis de Sales, St. Augustine, St. Joseph, St. Anthony, St. Aloysins, Holy Ghost and many of the German parishes in the .smaller cities and villages, as Carondelet, St. Charles, Herman and others now embraced in the Catholic Union of Missouri.

The Ancient Order of Hibernians, established in New York in 1847, for the relief of the distress of the thousands of Irish immigrants arriving in that part every year, took root in St. Louis in 1870. The first division was soon followed by a second and a third until every district of the city had its division of the Order.

The Order provided sick benefits and death benefit of $1,000. No one but a Catholic Irishman could obtain membership. The Order found some opposition from the Church authorities in some parts of the United States, but in St. Louis enjoyed official sanction and support.[12]

The year 1870 was also marked by the foundation of the "Father Mathew Young Men's Total Abstinence and Benevolent Society." The

---

10 Scharf, "History of St. Louis," pp. 1767-1768.

11 Scharf, "History of St. Louis," pp. 1765.

12 Scharf, "History of St. Louis," pp. 1764-1765. Archbishop Feehan was the Order's great defender at the Council of Baltimore.

object of this association was to inculcate and encourage temperance and provide a fund for the families of 'deceased members.'' All its members were of Irish lineage. Among the charter members we find such honored names as Thomas Fox, Edward Devoy, James Hagerty, John D. Hagerty, James McGraw. The Society was confined to St. Louis, and there was but one Council in the city. In 1873 the Council had thirteen hundred members, but declined to three hundred and fifty in 1883.

The Order of the ''Knights of Father Mathew'' was instituted on Ascension Day.

May 9th, 1872, with Thomas Fox as President, Thomas Phelan Vice-President, John Rohlf, Corresponding Secretary; John McGrath, Financial Secretary, and John B. Hagerty, Treasurer. ''Total Abstinence was the corner stone of the organization. All members were required to appear in uniform on public occasions, and to be thoroughly drilled.'' On July 18, 1881, the Order was incorporated. The members were required to be Catholics and total-abstainers.

The membership now increased to nearly one thousand. Father John O'Neill, S. J., was the Order's first Spiritual Director. His successors up to 1883 were:

Fathers E. A. Noonan and P. F. O'Reilly. The Order then had twelve Councils in St. Louis.[13]

In 1874 the Order of the Catholic Knights of America, sponsored by Bishop Feehan, then of Nashville, and later Archbishop of Chicago, spread like wildfire over the city. Without restriction as to nationality, but still maintaining some sort of parochial affiliation, the ''New Order within thirty years, with generous efforts amid financial reverses, established thirty-four branches with 2,819 members in the city of St. Louis, forty-one branches with 876 members in the other cities and towns of the State of Missouri. The organization of St. Louis Council of the Knights of Columbus in 1899, checked the rapid growth of the Catholic Knights of America, to some extent: but now both organizations, with a number of later foundations, are doing good work for the benefit of their members and the interests of holy Church.[14]

In a general history of a great Archdiocese the numerous societies of a local character had to be passed over in silence, as pertaining strictly to the history of the individual parish. Yet those of a more general nature, as well as those that distinguished themselves by some notable work or enterprise, deserved special mention in this History of the Archdiocese. They formed the militia of the Church, ready at a moment's notice, to come to the assistance of the standing army of priests, and religious, in defense of the Faith, and in the celebration of

---

13  Scharf, p. 1769.
14  Kirkfleet, ''Life of P. A. Feehan,'' pp. 236-238.

the glories of God's Kingdom on earth. Their very existence was a safeguard against the inroads of the secret societies; their public demonstrations on festive occasions, as Papal and Episcopal Jubilees, corner stone layings, and church dedications, their St. Patrick's Day parades, were public professions of Faith that cheered the faithful and commanded respect with those that were not of the fold.

The service rendered by the Catholic Societies as a defense against the encroachments, public and secret, of Masonry and its innumerable affiliations, is accentuated by the position Archbishop Kenrick was forced to take in regard to the Fenian Brotherhood, many of whose adherents were unsuspecting young men gradually drawn into bad company under the banner of patriotism.

This Irish-American revolutionary Society, whose members were commonly styled Fenians, was founded by John O'Mahoney, a distinguished Celtic Scholar who, after the downfall of William Smith O'Brien's rising in 1848, escaped abroad, and in 1852 came to New York. After the Convention at Chicago, in November 1863, the Brotherhood began to wield a powerful influence. The time seemed propitious for a new rising in Ireland. It was hoped that, after the close of the war between North and South, many who had borne arms in that great conflict, would return to their homes in Ireland. The members of Fenian Brotherhood "bound themselves by an oath of allegiance to the Irish Republic now virtually established to "yield implicit obedience to the commands of their superior officers."

As early as 1858 B. Doran Killian, a strong advocate of Fenianism, began the publication of the *Western Banner* in St. Louis, but discontinued it about 1860.

Being a secret, oath-bound Society with revolutionary tendencies, the Fenian Brotherhood, ipso facto, fell under the ban of the Church. The Church could not act otherwise, however deeply she sympathized with the Irish people in their struggle for freedom. For, as the *American Catholic Quarterly Review* wrote, "there cannot be the slightest doubt of the position which the hierarchy and clergy are bound to take up, when questions of the moral law becomes entangled with the political problems of the hour. The Church must uphold the moral law, no matter whom its procedure may offend. When it ceases to do that, it abnegates its proper functions and renounces its divine commission."

Archbishop Kenrick never was a timeserver or a respecter of persons. Here as everywhere else, his course was outspoken and unequivocal: as the following letter shows:

"To the Roman Catholics of St. Louis:

The undersigned has read in the *Republican* of this morning an announcement of a funeral to take place next Sunday from St. Patrick's

Church in this city, of a deceased member of the Fenian Brotherhood, who died at St. Paul, Minn., on the 24th instant. The occasion is evidently made for a display on the part of those in St. Louis who are members of that association, hence the deferred interment, and the pageant which is to accompany the burial. The connection of St. Patrick's Church, where the religious service is announced as to take place, and where, without any authority from the pastor of that church, it would appear, an oration, by a gentleman of this city, is to be delivered, imposes on me the obligation of forbidding, as I have done, the pastor of that church to permit any funeral service or other religious ceremony to take place on that occasion. I have furthermore directed the superintendent of that Calvary Cemetery not to admit any procession of men or women bearing insignia of Fenianism within the gate of the cemetery. I use this occasion to state publicly, what I have uniformly stated in private conversation, that the members of that Fenian Brotherhood, men or women, are not admissible to the sacraments of the church, as long as they are united with that association, which I have always regarded as immoral in its object, the exciting of rebellion in Ireland, and unlawful and unlegal in its means, a quasi military organization in this country while at peace with England, to be made, effective in the event of war with that power.

"Peter Richard Kenrick,
Archbishop of St. Louis"
"St. Louis, August 30, 1865."

## CHAPTER 58

CITY CHURCHES FOUNDED BETWEEN 1865-1885

I.

HOLY NAME—ST. TERESA—HOLY ANGELS—SACRED HEART

Towards the middle of our Civil War there came over the people of St. Louis, a certain feeling of exhaustion and languid expectancy in the matter of church extension, as well as in all civil matters, a lull in their building activities awaiting the return of peace. At the close of the war these activities broke forth with fresh vigor, in city and in country. The half-decade from 1865 to 1870, witnessed the establishment of at least sixteen parishes in the country districts and of six in the city of St. Louis.

The first of these new city parishes was dedicated to the glory of God and the *Holy Name* of Jesus. The territory of the parish of the Holy Name and its German twin sister, the parish of the Perpetual Succor, was formerly the "College Farm" belonging to the St. Louis University, then located on Ninth Street and Washington Avenue. The farm buildings served as a summer resort for the students and scholastics. There were but few houses round about, yet the Jesuit Fathers had erected a small chapel for their students and for the scattered Catholics of the neighborhood. This chapel was dedicated to St. Thomas the Apostle. In 1865 the "College Farm" was laid out as a subdivision to the city, and in consequence the number of worshippers at St. Thomas chapel increased to such an extent, that the formation of a regular parish became a necessity.[1] The Jesuit Fathers now turned over their chapel of St. Thomas to the Archbishop, who then appointed the Rev. Patrick J. Gleason as its first pastor, 1875. Father Gleason immediately set to work to establish the parish on a secure foundation. The chapel was inconveniently situated for the majority of the Congregation: it was therefore resolved to build a new church on a lot farther east, near the intersection of Grand and Florissant Avenues. The name of the parish was changed to "The Holy Name of Jesus." A substantial rectory was built near the church. The parish lacked only a school to make it fairly prosperous. But Father Gleason's administration was cut short through a chain of regrettable circumstances, brought on by some indiscretion on the part of the pastor. He was cited to appear before an ecclesiastical court, appointed by

---

[1]. Cf. Garrahgan, G. J., "St. Louis Catholic Historical Review," vol. V, pp. 122-128.

Archbishop Kenrick.  Father Gleason "trusting too implicitly in his conscious innocence, allowed the vile charge brought against him to go unanswered, when he was officially cited to answer."  He was condemned by the Court, and removed from his parish.  Almost all the priests of the city believed him to be innocent, and signed an appeal for his reinstatement.  This encouraged Father Gleason to appeal his case to Rome.  He was acquitted, and the Archbishop was ordered to restore him to his parish of the Holy Name.  This Archbishop Kenrick refused to do.  Archbishop Ryan on his visit to Rome straightened out the whole matter, by showing that Father Gleason, as a member of a religious Order, from which he had not been released, when he took up his work in the archdiocese, had no legal right to the place.  Archbishop Kenrick was sustained by Rome, and Father Gleason left the Archdiocese.[2]  His successor of the Holy Name, Father Thomas Bonacum, remained in charge from May 1st, 1882, to July 27th, 1887, when he was appointed Bishop of Lincoln, Nebraska.  During his administration as rector of the Holy Name a commodious school building was erected.  The school was placed in charge of the Sisters of St. Joseph.  Father Patrick W. Tallon succeeded Bishop Bonacum in the administration of the parish.  He was very popular with every element of his parish.  The congregation soon attained a total of four hundred families of various nationalities working together harmoniously.  The school numbered four hundred pupils in charge of six Sisters.  After the death of Father Edward Dempsey in 1910, Father Tallon was appointed to succeed him at the church of the Visitation.  Here also Father Tallon labored with eminent success in consolidating the parish.  It was at the Visitation that he received the title of "domestic prelate to His Holiness, the Pope."  Father Tallon's services in the cause of God extended far beyond the limits of his parish.  He was a distinguished orator of the Archbishop Ryan school.  His sermons and lectures were poetic in thought, with a firm hold on the realities of life.  His manner of delivery was less flowing than emphatic.

But to return to the Church of the Holy Name, Father Tallon had as his successor the Rev. Christopher E. Byrne, now Bishop of Galveston, Texas.  Father Byrne enjoys the proud distinction of having erected one of the most beautiful churches in the rich corona of the churches of St. Louis.  The style is a modern Romanesque, rarely seen in the West.  The material used in the construction is of the best.  Hard brick with terra cotta trimmings.  The square bell tower at the rear is a marvel of beauty and grace.  Three years after the completion of the new church Father Byrne was nominated Bishop of Galveston and Father P. P. Crane succeeded him at the Holy Name.  The parish now

---

[2] "Western Watchman," June 7, 1884, "Our First and Last Word on an unpleasant Subject."

numbers one thousand families.[3]  A dismemberment of the parish has has never taken place, but in 1873, the German Catholics living in and around its territory combined to form a parish of their own nationality.  They petitioned Vicar-General Muehlsiepen and began building a church just across from the chapel of St. Thomas.  But the development of this second offshoot of St. Thomas the Apostle must be reserved for a later chapter.

The second City church organized in 1865, is that of *St. Teresa,* on Grand Avenue and North Market Street.  The parish was founded by Father Francis P. Gallagher in 1865.  A few months previous to Father Gallagher's coming, Father James O'Brien, then assistant priest at the Immaculate Conception, who disappeared soon after and reappeared three years later in Cape Girardeau, had issued a circular letter calling upon the Catholics along North Grand Avenue to organize a parish.  The corner stone of the first church was blessed and laid on May 14th, 1865, and the completed edifice was blessed by Archbishop Kenrick on September 23rd, of the following year.  The building was of brick, in the Byzantine style of architecture.  Father Gallagher was a good classical scholar, and loved to intersperse his conversation with scraps from the Latin poets.  Father Phelan had a very high regard for Father Gallagher's scholarship.  Father O'Bannon was one of his most devoted friends.  Father Edward I. Fitzpatrick, one of the most widely read men of his day, was his assistant before he accepted a professor's chair at the Salesianum in Milwaukee.  In 1875 ill health forced the pastor to resign the charge of St. Teresa's and retire to the country.  His successor was the Rev. William H. Brantner.  On August 1st, 1876 St. Teresa's parish was incorporated under the laws of the State of Missouri a "St. Teresa's Roman Catholic Parish Association."  The parochial school was organized in 1870 and conducted by four teachers, it numbered three hundred pupils.  Father Brantner, during his seventeen years administration of the parish, enlarged the church and school building and erected an suitable rectory.  Father Brantner was a native of St. Louis and after the usual course of priestly studies at the Seminary at Cape Girardeau, attended the University of Louvain.  Here he was raised to the priesthood on July 9th, 1868 by Cardinal Joachim Pecci, afterward Pope Leo XIII.  His death occurred on July 29th, 1892.  Father Brantner was but forty years old when, as Father Robert Hayes so beautifully said; "death, like a harper laid his open palm upon his heart to still its vibrations."[4]

On September 1st, 1892, Father Joseph A. Connolly, the pastor of Desoto, received the appointment as successor to Father Brantner.

---

3  "The Church Progress." March 23, 1916.
4  "Our Pastors in Calvary," pp. 45-46.

One of Father Connolly's first labors at St. Teresa's was the enlargement of the school to three times its original size. But the steady growth of the parish demanded a new and entirely adequate church. The corner stone of the present St. Teresa's church was laid on Pentecost Sunday, June 3rd, 1900 by Bishop Montgomery of Los Angeles, who at that time performed the episcopal functions in the archdiocese for the absent Archbishop. Archbishop Kain, however, after his return from Rome, blessed the new church on October 6th, 1901. The school was in charge of the Sisters of Notre Dame. On December 14th, 1903, Father Connolly was made Vicar-General of the Archdiocese, in 1911 Roman Prelate and on Thursday, September 28th, 1922, he was called to his eternal reward.

Father Connolly was a truly loveable man, though hiding his kindly spirit under the appearance of a rigid disciplinarian. He had an extensive knowledge of ecclesiastical science, especially liturgy and Canon Law. In character he was the very soul of honor. As Archbishop Glennon said of the departed; "He never failed; he never forgot, he never broke a promise, he never deceived."[5] Vicar-General Connolly's successor as pastor of St. Teresa's was the Rev. Joseph P. Newman.

The church of the Holy Angels on St. Ange Avenue and Lasalle Street was founded in 1866 on land donated by Mr. John Dillon, one of the parishioners. The Congregation at the time of its organization and long after consisted of a large number of old and distinguished Catholic families, like the Delaneys, Barrys, Papins, Boislinieres, Primms, and Dillons. The neighborhood was one of the finest residence districts of Old St. Louis. The nearest churches were the Annunciation, St. Vincent's, the Immaculate Conception, and the College Church of the Jesuits. Father Michael Welby was the first pastor. The corner stone of the Holy Angels, a neat brick structure of Gothic design, was laid by Archbishop Kenrick on July 9th, 1866, and the church was dedicated to divine service on January 1st, of the following year. Father Welby remained with the parish till February 16th, 1869. He was succeeded by the Rev. Francis M. Kielty. Father Kielty had charge of the parish for thirty-eight years. He was ordained at Cape Girardeau on June 3rd, 1860, by Archbishop Kenrick. His first appointment was the ancient parish of St. Paul in North Missouri. In 1863 he became pastor of the Cathedral in St. Louis, in 1866 he was transferred to the rectorship of the Immaculate Conception, Eighth and Chestnut Street, and finally in 1869 he assumed charge of the Holy Angels Parish. Towards the middle of Father Kielty's priestly life many of his parishioners joined in the exodus to the West End, which was then

---

5 "Our Pastors in Calvary," pp. 161-162.

depopulating the down town parishes. The Congregation in its palmiest days numbered about thirteen hundred souls. Neither Father Welby nor Father Kielty favored the parochial school system, the latter having had many a bout on the question with the tireless champion of the parochial school, Father Francis Goller.

Father Kielty was a writer of note, though he never published anything more extensive than an occasional newspaper article: He dealt with questions of the day in a most interesting and enlightening manner. He had a keen sense of the ridiculous and dearly loved a bit of humor. His great hero was Archbishop Kenrick. During the first twelve years of his pastorate at the Holy Angels Father Kielty had for his assistant the Rev. M. J. McLaughlin, who remained his closest friend for the rest of his years and, when Father McLaughlin died, he also took sick and never rallied. His death occurred on Saturday, September 22nd, 1906, at St. Anthony's Hospital. His Library of three thousand volumes was given by him to the St. Louis University in recognition of the fact that he owed his education to the Jesuits.[6] To many he appeared repellant and censorious. But often, in criticising others, he but used their faults "as modest means to introduce their praise."

On February 8th, 1907, Father Patrick F. O'Reilly, who had been rector of the New Cathedral Chapel, succeeded to the Parish of the Holy Angels, but in September 1908 he resigned the charge and asked for a long leave of absence from the diocese. His resignation was not accepted, but the leave of absence was granted. In the meantime, Father Thomas V. O'Reilly who had served the Church as assistant priest since June 1900, acted as administrator and remained in charge of the parish until his appointment as Pastor of St. Margaret's.

The parish now maintains a parochial school with an enrollment of about two hundred pupils, who are taught by four Sisters of St. Joseph.

The parish of the Sacred Heart was organized in 1871 by the Rev. James J. McCabe. Father McCabe was ordained at Baltimore on July 2nd, 1866, and coming to St. Louis, was assigned to St. Michael's Church as assistant to Father Patrick O'Brien. In March 1871 he was commissioned by the Archbishop to organize a parish west of St. Michael's. Father McCabe built a brick chapel on University and Twentieth Streets, which was dedicated by Vicar-General Patrick Ryan on May 28th, 1871. In 1882 he enlarged the chapel. The parish school was established in 1873 with four Sisters of Loretto in charge. The parish prospered and became one of the most flourishing in the city. The beautiful new church of stone, unique in its architecture, with the

---

6 "Our Pastors in Calvary," pp. 90-91.

colossal marble statue of the Sacred Heart surmounting the dome, is the crowning glory of the long and laborious priestly career of Father James J. McCabe, the founder of the parish. The church, a veritable "Shrine of the Sacred Heart," was completed on June 19th, 1899, the Feast of the Sacred Heart. Father Michael J. McCabe, the pastor's brother, served as his assistant at the Sacred Heart from 1873 until his own appointment in 1896 to the pastorate of the mother church, St. Michael's.

The McCabe brothers came to America in early youth with their parents; the family located in St. Louis. The youthful aspirants for the priesthood, James and Michael, entered St. Vincent's College at Cape Girardeau, and after completing the classical course, proceeded to St. Mary's Seminary at Baltimore. They were ordained on the same day, July 2nd, 1866 by Archbishop Spalding. The future Archbishop Kain, a fellow student of theirs was ordained with them. This circumstance, no doubt, had a far reaching influence on the destinies of St. Louis Archdiocese. Father James McCabe was preparing to celebrate his golden Jubilee on July 2nd, of 1916, but he was called away from the scene of his labors and sacrifices on January 20th.[7] His brother Michael survived him until August 28, 1925.

---

[7] "Our Pastors in Calvary," p. 131.

## CHAPTER 59

CITY CHURCHES FOUNDED BETWEEN 1865-1885

II

ST. NICHOLAS—ST. FRANCIS DE SALES—ST. AGATHA

The German pioneer churches of S. S. Peter and Paul, and St. Joseph, within the brief period from 1865 to 1871, gave rise to three new parishes, that were soon to be numbered among the strongest and most progressive church organizations of the city: St. Nicholas on Nineteenth and Lucas Ave.; St. Francis de Sales on Ohio Ave., and Lynch St.; and St. Agatha on Ninth and Utah Streets. The two latter parishes are still full of life and vigor, whilst St. Nicholas, lying in the heart of the business district, has at last become a missionary church, especially for the colored Catholics of the neighborhood.

St. Nicholas Parish was organized in November 1865. The ground for the church was bought November 8th, of that year. On April 29th of the following year the corner stone of the church was laid by Archbishop Kenrick, who on that occasion preached a sermon in the German language. Until the completion of the edifice, the Congregation worshiped in St. Bridget's Church. The Rev. Nicholas Staudinger was their pastor. On May. 19th, 1867, Archbishop Kenrick dedicated their church in honor of St. Nicholas of Myra. In 1868 the newly ordained Father Henry Groll joined Father Staudinger as assistant and remained with him until 1872.[1] At the start the membership comprised fifty families, but grew rapidly to about three hundred. Yet a hard struggle for existence had to be fought. The building of the church had left a heavy debt of $71,000.00 on the congregation.[2] Prices were high, and money was scarce, and the people, though willing, were mostly poor beginners. Yet a parish school was opened on September 5th, 1865, in the basement of the church, and in 1876 the parish erected a school-house at a cost of $23,000.00. In 1870 the Sisters of St. Joseph were in charge of the school. Father Staudinger resigned the rectorship on February 12th, 1876, and returned to his former charge at St. Peter's in St. Charles County. His successor at St. Nicholas Church, Rev. Casper Doebbener, having returned to St. Louis from the diocese of Vincennes, died October 28th, 1878, and was buried in S. S. Peter and Paul's Cemetery. Meanwhile the church debt had

---

1 Zum Goldenen Priester-Jubilaeum des Hochw. Heinrich Groll.

2 At a meeting of the St. Vincent Conference for the Poor, a number of Catholics of St. Nicholas and St. Joseph's Parishes founded the Biddle Bank, which advanced the loan to the Parish.

increased to dangerous proportions.   It was Father Joseph Schaefers, then pastor of St. Bernard's Church, who was selected to bring order out of chaos.   Father Schaefers, born August 28th, 1848 at Dorren-hagen near Paderborn was then in the prime of manhood, an excellent preacher and shrewd financier.   He had a way of ingratiating him-self with the people; his very presence in St. Nicholas reestablished confidence.   The church debt was reduced in a substantial way from year to year and, at the same time, the church was fitted up with all things necessary and ornamental.   In 1880 the Sisters of Christian Charity of Wilkesbarre, Pa., took over the conduct of the parochial school, lay-teachers remaining in charge of the older boys.

In 1886 Father Schaefers erected the parish residence and also the St. Nicholas Hall.   On the death of Father Joseph Schroeder of the Holy Trinity Parish, Father Schaefers was transferred to the irre-moveable rectorship, but lived only a short time to enjoy his promo-tion.   His successor, the Rev. Herman G. Adrian, a native of Missouri, labored earnestly to stem the downward trend of his parish, which was caused or at least seriously furthered by the constant influx of colored people in the neighborhood.   Father Adrian continued his ministrations to the few German and Irish Catholic families that came to him: and turned over the school building to the colored children in care of the Jesuits assisted by two Sisters of the Blessed Sacrament.

The parish of St. Nicholas gave three priests to the Church, among them the distinguished Redemptorist Father Frank Straubinger.[3]

The first step towards the organization of the Parish of St. Fran-cis de Sales was made April 22nd, 1867, when the representatives of seven German Catholic families assembled at the home of A. Van Mierlo to discuss plans of establishing a church somewhere in the western part of the parish of S. S. Peter and Paul.   Father Francis Goller did not look favorably upon this move: yet a site was selected on Ohio Ave., and Lynch St., a building committee was appointed, and subscription lists were circulated.   These preliminary steps were taken without ecclesiastical authorization.   The contract for building a church which was to cost $12,500.00, was awarded to the well known con-tractor Henry Kotte.   It was high time now to secure ecclesiastical approval.   Vicar-General Melcher was glad to smooth out matters.

On September 1867 the corner stone of the new church was laid by Father Melcher assisted by the Pastor of S. S. Peter and Paul's, the Rev. Francis Salesius Goller, and the Franciscan P. Servatius Altmicks.

---

3   Chancery Records.

of St. Anthony's Church. Eleven Catholic Societies took part in the celebration.[4]

One month after the corner stone laying the youthful Father Louis Lay was appointed pastor of St. Francis de Sales. The first mass in the new church was celebrated on Christmas morning, 1867. The scene was a picture of desolation. The walls of the buildings were bare, and cold. A temporary altar of rough boards was the only ornament in the building: the pews were almost empty, as the bad roads and the severe cold kept the people at home. A number of the parishioners still clung to the mother church. There were to be three masses on Christmas day, but Father Lay felt himself unable to proceed and sent those that came later in the day to St. Anthony's, or S. S. Peter and Paul's for Highmass.

The church was completed in the Spring of 1868. The dedication ceremonies were performed on May 24th, by Vicar-General Melcher, now Bishop Elect of Green Bay. Father Francis Ruesse of S. S. Peter and Paul celebrated the Highmass, and Father Staudinger of St. Nicholas preached the sermon.

The parish of St. Francis de Sales at this time numbered about 800 souls, but every year brought large accessions. The last undertaking of Father Lay in the parish was the erection of a commodious residence for the priest. Father Louis Lay was a convert from Protestantism. After his conversion he began the study of Theology at the Seminary of St. Francis near Milwaukee and received ordination September 17th, 1865. Young and inexperienced as Father Lay was when he took upon himself the government of a difficult parish, he felt himself unable to reconcile the conflicting claims of his people, and accordingly, gave up the struggle and resigned his charge in August 1869.[5] For the next six weeks the Franciscan Father Paulinus Weiss acted as administrator; but on September 17th, the Rev. Peter Wigger arrived from Germany and took up the reins of government in the parish: Father Wigger was a native of staunchly Catholic Westphalia. He was raised to the holy priesthood by Bishop Conrad Martin on August 20th, 1858. His first and only field of priestly labor in America was at St. Francis de Sales. Here he found a parish in the crudest state of formation, encumbered with a debt of $20,000.00, and facing the need of a school building. Father Wigger set to work resolutely, built the school and introduced the Franciscan Sisters of Oldenburg. For the first five years Father Wigger had no assistant. Then came Father Joseph Schroeder and, in June 1876, the Rev.

---

[4] Goldenes Jubilaeum der St. Franz von Sales Gemeinde, 1917, pp. 17, 21 and 25.

[5] Ibidem, p. 29.

Peter Lotz, who was to become the third pastor of St. Francis de Sales. Father Wigger died on March 11th, 1878, and his remains were laid to rest in Calvary Cemetery.[6]

Father Peter Wigger was gifted with fine literary talents, and for six years edited the *Herold des Glaubens*. His home was a favorite center for ecclesiatical students. Father Peter Wigger's brother, Herman, and three nephews of the same honored name were called to serve in the ranks of the clergy of St. Louis. Father Wigger's faithful assistant, Peter Lotz, was now pastor of the parish. His entire energy was directed to the liquidation of the church debt of $30,000.00. In this laborious task he succeeded within a few years, so that he could undertake the enlargement of the church. In 1880 Father Lotz received an assistant in the person of Rev. H. S. Aertker: after Father Aertker's transfer to Rolla his place was taken by an elderly priest, Father William Boden, who in turn was superseded by Father Francis Reuther. Then came Fathers E. A. Diepenbrock and Frederick G. Holweck, Arnold Acker, Frederick Schulte and Francis Brand. On June 10th, 1888 the corner stone of a new school building was laid by Archbishop Kenrick. Father Holweck now became assistant at St. Francis de Sales for the second time, whilst the pastor was absent on a vacation in Europe.

On Father Holweck's appointment as pastor of St. Aloysius Church, Father Albert Mayer continued to serve the church as assistant priest and, on November 1892, Father Lotz received a second assistant, Father Anthony Dempf.

During the next few years the pastor and his assistants labored with untiring zeal in the contruction of a new church building, on the recently acquired triangular site on Iowa Avenue. It was to be the largest and finest church in St. Louis. On his visit to Europe in 1894 Father Lotz had secured a plan in imitation of the famous St. Paul's Church in Berlin. The cost was estimated at $135,000. The laying of the corner stone took place August 11th, 1895. The ceremony was performed by Vicar-General Muehlsiepen. Work had not progressed very far, when the cyclone of May 27th, 1896 razed the old church to the ground. As many of the parishioners had suffered severely by the general catastrophe, it was decided to finish the basement as quickly as possible and to postpone the erection of the superstructure until 1901. In the meantime the detailed plans had arrived, showing that the Church would cost more than half a million. This brought further discouragement, and the work of completing "the largest and finest church in St. Louis" was left to Father Lotz's

---

6  "Goldenes Jubilaeum der St. Franz v. Sales Gemeinde," pp. 29, 33.

successor. Only the basement was completed and fitted up for divine worship.

On the appointment of Father Mayer to Linn in Osage County in 1896, and the sudden death of Father Dempf, June 1899, there was a rapid succession of assistant priests at St. Francis de Sales until 1903, when on May 14th, just after the opening of the Forty Hours' Adoration, Father Lotz succumbed to an attack of angina pectoris. The last of his assistants, Father George Fngel, administered the parish until May 27th, when Father F. G. Holweck was appointed pastor.[7]

Father Holweck's great work was the execution of Father Lotz' magnificent plan in a simplified form. Work was resumed in April 1907 and progressed rapidly, so that the roof could be finished by January 2nd, 1908. The grand structure was dedicated by Bishop Janssen of Belleville, the Archbishop being in Rome. Three Bishops, one Benedictine Abbot, more than a hundred and twenty priests took part in the celebration. The beautiful High Altar and the other church fixtures were donated by the Parish Societies. The artistic wall decorations were Jubilee offerings of the Parish of 1917.

The building of a dwelling for the teaching sisters of the parish school, and the establishment of the school as a free institution were other works of Father Holweck's pastorate. The parish now numbers about 1,200 families. It was mainly through Father Holweck's distinguished personality that the Church of St. Francis de Sales became the representative organization of the German Catholics of St. Louis, a distinction long held by S. S. Peter and Paul. Many prelates of high and highest rank and influence were frequent guests at its hospitable rectory. But its whole hearted, unassuming and ever sympathizing Rector wielded even greater power through his writings and correspondence. Few men have had such a wide circle of friends. With all his varied learning, and his manifold accomplishments, Father Holweck remained simple, plain and approachable. His urbanity and absence of ostentation acted like a charm and made every one feel at home in his presence. Father Holweck accomplished a mass of work in his lifetime that is truly astonishing.[8]

Born at Wiesloch in Baden, Germany, he made his classical studies at Freiburg and Karlsruhr, before coming to America at the age of twenty years. Here he entered the Salesianum in Wisconsin for his theological studies and was ordained there by Bishop Heiss of La Crosse on June 27, 1880.

He came to Missouri in the same year, and his first pastorate was a temporary charge in Jackson, Cape Girardeau County. He served

---

7 Goldenes Jubilaeum, pp. 37, 41.

8 Goldenes Jubilaeum, pp. 41, 45, 49.

for three years as an assistant to the Rev. O. J. S. Hoog, in St. Peter's Church, Jefferson City. In April 1883, he was made an assistant at St. Francis de Sales Church here. In the following year he was transferred to Louisiana, Mo., and in 1885 was sent to Riviere aux Vases, Ste. Genevieve County, where he remained three years, building a school and parochial residence. He returned to St. Francis de Sales' as assistant in 1888, and remained four years. In 1892 he was named as the first pastor of St. Aloysius' church, and remained in that position until May 1903, when he was made pastor of St. Francis de Sales.

Amid all these varied and exhausting missionary labors Father Holweck found solace and support in the pursuit of knowledge, be it in the general history of the Church, or in the field of Latin and Greek Hymnology, or in the boundless expanse of Hagiology, or in the sacred realms of Sacred Liturgy, or in the special department of the Feasts of our Blessed Lady and Her Divine Son, or lastly in the almost untrodden region of our local church history. In all these departments of ecclesiastical science Father Holweck has left us works of real distinction and merit. After thirty-two years of patient research-work he published in 1925 his opus magnum, the "*Biographical Dictionary of the Saints,*" which an English Critic declared to be "the best work of its kind, within the last four hundred years." The Catholic Encyclopaedia contains numerous articles from his facile pen. His Fasti Mariani a treatise in·fluent and correct Latin, on the various Feasts that are or were kept by christian people the world over, appeared in a second and greatly enlarged edition under the title "Calendarium Liturgicum Festorum Dei et Dei Matris," a book that has no equal in all literature. For twenty years Father Holweck was Editor of the St. Louis *Pastoral-Blatt*, and one of the Contributing Editors of the *St. Louis Catholic Historical Review*. For both these publications Father Holweck wrote, in his lucid winning way, a large number of valuable articles, biographical and historical notes, which will be of great service to the coming historians of the Church in our country. In this noble work of preserving the memory of our forebears and local worthies in Church and state, and of rescuing their deeds and sacrifices from the all devouring tooth of time, Father Holweck may have found his highest claim to earthly immortality.

Father Holweck's last few years brought a full meed of high and well deserved honors: the appointment by the Holy Father as a prelate of the Papal household, the election to the doctorate of divinity by the University of Freiburg, and the nomination as Vicar-General of the Archdiocese. No one could bear these honors more gracefully than Monsignor Holweck did for the brief space of years still granted to him. Then came death, gently though unexpectedly, on February 15th, 1927.[9]

Among the diocesan priests successively assigned as assistants to Father Holweck the following deserve special mention: John Wehner, George Fugel, John Peters, George Meyer, Frederick Fuchs, Simon Forster, Francis Mispagel, Engelbert Heimerscheid, Charles Keller, Francis Kehlenbrink, Bernard Kramper, A. J. Sauer, Leo Ebel, Anthony Strauss, Francis A. Baumann and Aloysius A. Ripper.

Twenty generous sons of the Parish have been elevated to the priesthood, and forty-four young ladies have taken the veil in various Sisterhoods.

On the death of Monsignor Holweck Father John Waelterman, the eldest of the many clerical sons of the parish, became its fifth pastor.

St. Francis de Sales parish from its very start had a parochial school. The teachers of the boys were laymen: the girls were in charge of the Sisters of Christian Charity of Oldenburg, who however, were supplanted in the summer of 1873 by the Sisters of the Precious Blood. When Father Lotz became pastor the Sisters of Divine Providence supplanted the Sisters of the Precious Blood. There were then seven hundred children in eleven classes. After the death of Father Lotz these Sisters also retired from the management of the school and now the School-Sisters de Notre Dame began their efficient administration. In the year of Jubilee 1917, the entire school with the exception of the seventh and eighth grades for boys, was taught by the Sisters.

Mr. Michael Bauer, the lay-teacher, was so long and so intimately connected with the progress of St. Francis de Sales parish, that he deserves a special mention in this place.

St. Agatha's Parish was organized in 1871. Rev. J. A. Stroombergen was selected by Archbishop Kenrick to do the work. He found one hundred families in the contemplated territory who signified their willingness to subscribe $5,000.00, towards erecting a church in that vicinity. Father Stroombergen, however, was taken ill, and feeling himself unable to accomplish what was expected of him, resigned the charge. He found a successor in Rev. Henry Leygraaff.[10] A suitable lot having been purchased, the erection of a church was begun. Vicar-General Muehlsiepen laid the corner stone on October 29th, 1871. On July 14th of the following year the new church was dedicated by

---

9 Leaflet of Zentral-Stelle der Zentral Vereins, ''Einem unserer Allerbesten'' and Personal Reminiscenses.

10 St. Agatha's Parish, ''Souvenir of the Golden Jubilee,'' 1921, p. 21. Father Leygraaff published a Book of Travels, in the Holy Land.

Coadjutor Bishop Ryan in honor of St. Agatha. The building was a two-story brick, the lower floor serving for school and Sisters' home, the upper floor for church, which at the time resembled, as Father Leygraaff said, the room of the Last Supper, being bare of everything save the table of the Lord. The congregation was glad to have a church of their own. The school also prospered at once, being opened on September 1872 with one hundred and fifty pupils in care of the Sisters of the Precious Blood.

There was as yet no parochial residence, and Father Leygraaff boarded with a neighboring family. In 1873 the parish built a small house for the pastor, and enlarged it in 1877. Father Leygraaff was a man of saintly life and strong character, but of delicate health, and so not very well fitted for the rough work of pioneering. When, therefore, the honorable call came to him to take a professor's chair in the Seminary of St. Francis at Milwaukee, he felt it was the will of God that he should accept. On May 10th, 1874, there arrived from Cape Girardeau the Rev. William Hinssen,[11] as Father Leygraaff's successor. Young and energetic as well as learned and eloquent, Father Hinssen soon increased the active membership of the parish to more than two-hundred families. He devoted great care and spared no sacrifice in securing the beauty of the house of God. Everything promised a long and happy period of successful labor, to both pastor and people. But it was not to be. On February 25th, 1883, the Reverend William Hinssen left the diocese of St. Louis for that of Covington, Ky. His work at St. Agatha's was taken up by the Rev. Henry Schrage, a native of St. Louis. He was born November 27th, 1851, attended St. Joseph's School and the St. Louis University, and was sent to Muenster in Westphalia for his philosophical and theological training. Returning to America in 1874 he was raised to the priesthood by Coadjutor Bishop Ryan at St. John's church, St. Louis, and immediately sent to Jefferson City as assistant to Father Meller. After filling several other subordinate positions he was appointed pastor of St. Agatha's church on March 2nd, 1883, to remain there unto his death, fully twenty-eight years. During Father Schrage's pastorate the large fine church, the commodious parish residence and the magnificent hall were erected. The corner stone of the present church was laid on April 12th, 1885, by Vicar-General Muehlsiepen, and the dedication ceremonies were performed by Bishop Joseph Rademacher of Nashville, Tenn. In 1892 the Sisters' residence was built at a cost of $12,000.00. In 1899 the church was enlarged by the addition of the transept, sanctuary, and sacristy. Archbishop Kain conducted the dedication ceremonies. Through the special exertions of the Rev. L.

---

11 ''St. Agatha's Parish,'' p. 22.

Kutz, assistant to Father Schrage the fourteen beautiful art glass windows were put in the church. In 1907, the parish debt having been reduced to a minimum, it was decided to build "a new School and Hall." By Thanksgiving day 1908 the building was completed, and Father Schrage's days of labor and worry were over. For years his health had been impaired. All efforts to restore it had failed; towards the end of 1910 his condition became hopeless. In January 1911 he retired to St. Mary's Hospital, whilst Father Henry Geers became administrator.

On October· 1st, the Feast of the Holy Rosary, the faithful pastor was called away to his eternal rest. During his long priestly career Father Schrage hardly knew what rest was. He never spared himself; he was a man of rule and order; yet, though at times he seemed harsh and unsympathetic,·he had a tender heart for the sorrows and anxieties of others.[12]

Father Henry B. Geers, the fifth pastor of St. Agatha's, had been assistant to Father Faerber at old St. Mary's, then pastor at Glasgow, and for twenty-two years, assistant at S. S. Peter and Paul's church, St. Louis. At St. Agatha's he remained until his death April 26th, 1918.[13] Father Otto T. Siesener, a native of St. Louis, succeeded to the pastorate of St. Agatha's in July 1918.[14]

The parish of St. Agatha celebrated its Golden Jubilee in 1921. During all those eventful years the Sisters of the Precious Blood have taught the School of St. Agatha Parish: yet the Parish is proud of the distinction of having had from its very start a succession of lay-teachers for the older boys, among them such men as C. Willenbrink, J. P. Daleiden, A. Sprengnether, A. Schulte, C. Adams and H. F. Stucke. Since 1887 a regular assistant was assigned to St. Agatha's Church. The series began with Father G. H. Schaefer. Then came J. H. Moorbrink, J. H. Muehlsiepen, F. A. Dette, John Girse, L. A. Kutz, Henry Kuper, William Fischer, D. D., W. Gruender. The parish of St. Agatha was right fruitful in vocations to the holy priesthood and the religious life. Twelve priestly sons stand to her credit.

---

[12] "St. Agatha's Parish," p. 22.
[13] St. Agatha's Parish, p. 23.
[14] Ibidem, p. 24.

## Chapter 60

## CITY CHURCHES FOUNDED BETWEEN 1865-1885

### III

OUR LADY OF PERPETUAL HELP—ST. AUGUSTINE—ST. BERNARD—HOLY
GHOST

The parish of *Our Lady of Perpetual Help,* in German *"Maria Hilf,"* founded in 1873, is one of the strongest and most prominent German-American parishes in the city. It is commonly called "College Hill" Parish, from the fact that its territory encompasses most of the former College Hill farm, owned by the St. Louis University. After the Jesuits had established their novitiate there, they built a chapel dedicated to St. Thomas, the Apostle, where the few Catholics of that vicinity were privileged to worship. This chapel stood near the site of the present Church of Our Lady of Perpetual Help. In 1872 the Jesuits subdivided their college farm into lots, which caused a good many Catholics to settle down in the territory, the place now being called Lowell. St. Thomas' Chapel was then turned over by the Jesuits to the Archbishop to be attended by a secular priest. It formed the nucleus of Holy Name Parish. The German Catholics residing in that territory, however, about fifteen or twenty families, petitioned Vicar-General Muehlsiepen for the privilege to organize a new parish. Their petition was granted and an organization meeting called. Sufficient funds were in sight to commence the work at once. A site for a church and school on Twentieth and Linton Streets, was purchased of the Jesuits for $1,600 cash. Rev. A. J. Stroombergen was appointed as first pastor of the new parish. On October 5th, 1873, the corner stone of the new church was laid by Vicar-General Muehlsiepen. A house in the neighborhood was rented at once and a parish school opened therein, which was attended by fifty children. Meanwhile the building of the church progressed rapidly. It was to be a two-story brick building. The upper story was to serve for a church, the lower story for the school.

On May 17th, 1875 the church was completed and blessed by the Coadjutor Bishop Ryan. The parish had now grown to about fifty families. A parsonage was next added to the parish buildings. Owing to continuous ill health the pastor, Rev. A. J. Stroombergen, resigned the pastorate in January 1875. On January 11th, 1875 he received a successor in the person of Rev. A. J. Schilling, formerly rector at Hermann, Mo. Father Schilling served the parish nearly thirty years.

Under his circumspect administration the parish continued to grow and prosper beyond all expectations. On October 22nd, 1877 the town of Lowell was incorporated in the City of St. Louis. The parish now comprised over two hundred and fifty families. The church and school buildings proved more and more inadequate; It was therefore decided to build a new and larger church. The corner stone for the new structure was laid by Vicar-General Muehlsiepen on April 22nd, 1888. The building progressed rapidly, so that its consecration could take place on September 29th, 1889. Bishop Thomas Bonacum of Lincoln, Neb., former rector of the neighboring Holy Name Parish, acted as consecrator, while Bishop John Janssen of Belleville, Ill., celebrated the Pontifical High Mass. Since December 3rd, 1889 a long series of young priests were stationed at Our Lady of Perpetual Help as assistants to Father Schilling: L. F. Schlathoelter, John Waelterman, M. J. Bahr, H. J. Muckermann, William Schulte, and Francis Holweck. Father Schilling died May 6th, 1904, and on September 1st, Archbishop Glennon called one of his Vicars-General, Monsignor Otto Joseph Stanislaus Hoog, from Jefferson City, Mo., to the rectorate of Our Lady of Perpetual Help.

On Monsignor Hoog's appointment to the Parish of S. S. Peter and Paul the Rev. Joseph Wentker was appointed pastor.

The parish numbers over six hundred families. Its schools are conducted by one secular teacher and six Sisters of Notre Dame, and are attended by about six hundred and fifty pupils. Though St. Engelbert's Parish was fashioned out of the territory of Our Lady of Perpetual Help, in 1891, the latter parish has continued to grow and prosper. Five sons of the parish have become priests.[1]

When in 1874 the ecclesiastical authorities determined to establish a German parish in the vicinity of the old Fair Grounds, the Rev. Henry Jaegering, the assistant priest at St. Nicholas, was sent to perfect the organization. In August he purchased ground on Hebert and Lismore Streets for the use of the new parish. On October 7th, Vicar-General Muehlsiepen laid the corner stone of an edifice under the title of St. Augustine, the upper story of which was to be used for church-purposes, the lower, as school and parochial residence. The building was dedicated by Father Muehlsiepen on June 6th, the following year. In September the parish school was opened with an attendance of seventy-five pupils. Father Jaegering continued his priestly ministrations at St. Augustine's for seven years, but in June 1881 the state of his health seemed to require an ocean voyage. The Rev. H. V. Kalmer, was appointed pastor, and Father Jaegering, on his return from Europe,

---

[1] Adapted from "Sunday Watchman," October 27, 1918. "Das Katholische Deutschtum in St. Louis," pp. 102-105.

August 6th, 1882, entered upon his long and faithful service as Chaplain of St. Mary's Sisters on Papin Street and Secretary of the Priests Purgatorial Society. He died on Monday, August 11th, 1919. Father Kalmer, assisted by the Rev. Dr. John May carried on the good work of developing the parish until he died September 14th, 1884. Father Henry Hukestein received the appointment as pastor of St. Augustine's. Father Hukestein, after his ordination by Bishop Ryan on June 4th, 1876, had served as assistant to Father Faerber at St. Mary's Church until January 15th, 1879, when he was appointed rector of the Church of Vienna in Maries County. After a trip to Europe in 1880 Father Hukestein became Rector of Wardsville in Cole County. In his early administration of St. Augustine's the church and school building were enlarged. The rapid development of the parish, however, made the erection of a larger church imperative. The corner stone of the monumental structure was laid by Archbishop John Joseph Kain on the first Sunday in May 1896. The building was dedicated on August 29th, 1897 by Archbishop Kain. St. Augustine's is one of the really beautiful churches of the city built in the thirteenth century Gothic style. In 1904 the Congregation erected a commodious rectory south of the church. The parish numbered about six hundred families.[2]

Father Hukestein for a long time held the office of Spiritual Director of the Franciscan Sisters. In his old age he wished to resign his pastoral charge at St. Augustine's, but the Archbishop would not permit him to do so: yet an administrator, Father John Waelterman. and later on, Father J. A. Dubbert, being appointed, Father Hukestein withdrew to the calm and peace of St. Anthony's Hospital, where he died, soon after the celebration of his Golden Jubilee of the priesthood.

The district, in which St. Bernard's Parish was organized, was originally known as Rock Spring, but as the town was incorporated in St. Louis in 1877, the parish now ranks as the thirty-sixth in the long series of city parishes. The first steps at organizing were taken with the advice and consent of Vicar-General Muehlsiepen, on January 16th, 1875 at a meeting in the home of Mr. Christophel. Under the leadership of Ailrath Wester, Albert Aiple and M. Foerstel, the erection of a German parish was decided on, although there were a number of English speaking Catholics in the neighborhood. Father Muehlsiepen took temporary charge of the congregation. saying mass for them in a private residence. A parochial school was established in February 1874 with a lay teacher in charge. In the meeting of April 4th, 1874, M. Foerstel was empowered to purchase a plot of five acres of land which, with the buildings on it, cost the sum of $19,000. The contract was signed May 7th, 1874. The house was now fitted up for school and church purposes.

---

2 ''Das Katholische Deutschtum in St. Louis,'' pp. 21-23.

On Thursday, July 16th, of the same year Father Henry Kalmer was appointed pastor. As the two most generous contributors, Berman and Winhof, bore the honored name of St. Bernard, the new parish was named for them.

As Father Kalmer was sent to Louisiana, Missouri in 1875, the Rev. Joseph Schaefers was appointed to St. Bernard's, where an efficient financier seemed to be necessary. In order to reduce the very pressing debt of the parish, the southern half of the church land was laid out in lots and sold. The erection of a new church was next in order. On June 11th, 1876 Vicar-General Muehlsiepen blessed and laid the corner stone, and on the 15th of October of the same year dedicated the new structure.

In October 1878 the devoted pastor was transferred to St. Nicholas Parish, where he was destined to remain for the next thirty years. Father Schaefers held the position of pastor of Holy Trinity Parish for only two months and died December 9th, 1907. Father John Heckman, a recent arrival from Paderborn, was appointed to succeed Father Schaefers at St. Bernard's, but died within three months. Early in 1879 came Father H. Willenbrink to assume charge of the pastorate. He introduced the Ursuline Sisters of Louisville in the school. In 1885 the important parish of St. Henry was formed from the territory of St. Bernard's and seven years later, the parish of St. Bernard was dismembered for a second time by the erection of St. Aloysius Church.

In 1888 the parish decided to enlarge the church, but before the addition to the church was roofed in, Father Willenbrink died, September 12th, 1888. The Rev. Peter Bremerich was then called to the parish. In 1890 the roomy school house and parish hall was erected. In 1900 the rectory was built and at the same time it was decided to build a new church. The corner stone was laid by Monsignor Muehlsiepen on July 31st, 1898. By November the basement was made ready for occupancy. It was blessed by the Vicar-General on November 20th. Father Bremerich continued his labors for seven additional years. He was assisted by Fathers Victor Stepka, W. Schulte, H. Hassel and Joseph Wigger. Father Bremerich's death occurred, November 24th, 1905.

Peter Bremerich was a native of Westphalia, and came to America in 1869, in company of five other students for the ministry. He made his studies at the Seminary of St. Vincent's, Cape Girardeau and was raised to the priesthood by Coadjutor Bishop Ryan, May 19th, 1872.

Father Bremerich was succeeded at St. Bernard's by the Rev. Francis Bettels, a native of the diocese of Hildesheim.

Father Bettels began his priestly life in 1876 as pastor of St. Henry's Church, Charleston, Mo., where he held services and taught school for a period of two years: He was then appointed pastor of the lonely parish of St. John in what was successively called Dallas,

Vine Mount, and Leopold in Bollinger County, where he built among other things a beautiful stone church and a commodious rectory. After thirty-one years of patient labor and joyful service, Father Bettels was promoted to the rectorship of St. Bernard's Church in St. Louis. Here he erected the superstructure of the church intended by Father Bremerich, but not as planned by him. Father Bettels was far more solid than brilliant. His was a practical mind, utterly averse to all needless ornament. His preaching was clear, correct and earnest. He was in a high degree, a man of God. He sought no honors or distinctions. To be a good priest was all in all to him. His Golden Jubilee in the priesthood was the crowning glory. He died September 5, 1926.[3]

About the year 1879 the need of a German parish in the northwestern part of the city manifested itself in various ways. A large number of former parishioners of St. Joseph's and St. Nicholas' had established homes on the almost open prairie beyond Grand Avenue. Rev. Michael Busch was charged with the organization of the new parish. A temporary structure, combining church, school and priest's residence, was begun late in 1879. Father Henry laid the corner stone, November 16th, and in May of the following year the building was dedicated by Vicar-General Muehlsiepen in honor of the Holy Ghost.

Father Busch was born in Luxemburg, but came to America in early youth. He made his ecclesiastical studies at the Salesianum, where also he was ordained in 1872. He is described as "a man of sanguine temperament," who from the first had great hopes of building up the parish. To this end he invested in landed property, and went to great work and trouble having improvements made, and inducements offered to Catholic home seekers. The district, at the time was but sparsely settled, and the people were poor. Yet he planned a magnificent church, and started to carry out his plan without duly considering how limited his means really were. Only half of the basement was completed when he found himself unable to meet his building obligations. The people had lost confidence, and the church property, with the exception of the old church and school, were sold under the sheriff's hammer. Father Busch resigned under compulsion, a victim of overconfidence; and Father Augustine Huettler was commissioned to reorganize the parish. And most wonderfully did he succeed in this work. Being a singularly handsome man, a preacher of great ability in French, German and English, a virile thinker in all matters pertaining to theology and philosophy, an ideal priest, strong-bodied, quickwitted, hospitable and courteous, Father Huettler seemed preordained to undertake the most difficult tasks. The hearts of the people were gladdened by his cheerful and affable manner. On the personal re-

3 "Das Deutschtum in St. Louis," pp. 33-35 and Personal Reminiscenses.

sponsibility of Mr. Jacob Mueller and a few of his friends the sum of $10,000. was raised, to repurchase the basement and to fit it up for divine service. School was continued in the old building; the Ursuline Sisters being in charge; and the parish grew in numbers and strength, when he, who had inspired all, suddenly fell a victim of duty, of an illness of three weeks duration, April 27th, 1899.

The people's sadness and consternation was relieved in a measure when the new pastor, the Rev. Henry Thobe, appeared on the scene. He was a native of St. Liborious Parish, St. Louis, and received his early training in the parish school. After completing his theological course of studies at St. Francis Seminary Milwaukee, he was ordained on May 27th, 1884, by Archbishop elect of Philadelphia, Patrick J. Ryan. He was sent to Hannibal to look after the German members of that Parish. He successively administered the parishes of Charleston, Glasgow, Creve Coeur. After eight years of steadily declining health, and feeling himself physically unable to build a church such as the exigencies of the parish seemed to require, he resigned the pastorship to spend his last days in retirement and peace. Father Thobe died March 14th, 1910, far from home and friends, but was brought back to St. Louis for burial. His successor, appointed May 1907 was the former pastor of St. Michael's Church, Fredericktown, Rev. John Rothensteiner. During his administration the parish of the Holy Ghost built the church rectory and school and rounded out the Church property by purchasing the remaining frontage on Taylor Avenue between Garfield and North Market Streets.

Father Huettler had as assistant the Rev. Ferdinand Mumbour, who died July 20, 1923, as Pastor of Walsh, Illinois.

Father Thobe's assistants were the following Fathers: Edmund Salland and John Paffhausen.

Father Rothensteiner had but two assistants in twenty years, Father Francis Mispagel, now Pastor of Fredericktown and Father George Haukap.

The parish has nurtured the vocations of four of its boys, and ten of its girls. The membership of 300 families is scattered over the wide territory between Union and Grand, Lindell Blvd. and Natural Bridge Road.[4]

---

4 ``Amerika,'' November 21, 1909.

## CHAPTER 61

## CHURCHES DEDICATED BY BISHOP RYAN

The quintette of city parishes grouped together in this chapter, St. Columbkille, Mount Carmel, St. Kevin's, afterwards rededicated as The Immaculate Conception, St. Cronan's and the Visitation,[1] owe their origin in a measure to the impulse that went out from the zealous and devoted Coadjutor Bishop Patrick J. Ryan, just as the German Churches grouped together in the preceding chapter are indebted to the foresight and energy of Vicar-General Henry Muehlsiepen for their existence and continued progress. Yet Archbishop Kenrick, though in voluntary retirement, followed this church development on parallel lines with deep interest. In fact, nothing was done in this matter without his knowladge and consent. Hence the chief glory of the church's wonderful progress during the decade of the Archbishop's self-effacement from public view, must still belong to him, however great and meritorious the labors of his two coadjutors in governing the archdiocese may have been.

In 1872 the southern suburb of St. Louis, Carondelet, had spread over so large a territory that another church, in addition to its two existing organizations, seemed called for. It was Father Michael O'Reilly, who had been in charge of Potosi since his ordination in 1866, that was commissioned to carry out the work.

A building containing church and school was erected on Davis Street and Michigan Avenue. The corner stone was laid June 23rd, 1872 and the church was blessed on March 16th, of the following year, the Coadjutor Bishop performing the function on both occasions. The church was named for St. Columbkille. The Vulcan Iron Works were in full blast in those days, giving employment to hundreds of workmen, many of whom were Catholics. Father Michael, being ''a strong character and one who exacted respect,'' succeeded in welding these rough iron molders together into a harmonious organization of Catholics. Teaching the children their Catechism, and even the rudiments of Latin, was his delight. The late Monsignor Connolly and Father Francis Jones were •among his Latin pupils. Father O'Reilly loved his parish of St. Columbkille's and everything connected with it, and bitterly resented the slur one time cast upon his people by Editor

---

[1] The main facts embodied in the sketches of this chapter were derived from Thornton, Adelman and Barnett's ''The Notable Catholic Institutions of St. Louis and Vicinity,'' tested by the Chancery Records. The personal references are partly from ''Our Pastors in Calvary,'' partly from personal recollections.

McCullagh of the *Globe-Democrat.* Hence the sobriquet of "Militant defender of the Church," applied to him by Bishop Ryan. For the time the prospects of building a new church, seemed bright : but before a beginning could be made, the iron works closed down and the parish dwindled down to a small number of people. The brick building blessed in 1873, still served the double purpose of church and school. Father Michael O'Reilly died on February 5th, 1888. His former assistant, Francis J. Jones, succeeded him as pastor of St. Columbkille's. Father Jones remained in charge from February 5th, 1888 to June 11th, 1908, when he was transferred to the parish of St. Thomas of Aquin. Father J. J. Furlong of New Madrid,, the indefatigable missionary of the far Southeast, was appointed pastor of St. Columkille's. The parish numbered about one hundred and fifty families; the school was attended by one hundred and twenty-five pupils, in care of four Dominican Sisters and subsequently of four Sisters of St. Joseph. Father Furlong never complained of anything : he bore all troubles and trials with equanimity, and in this spirit met death, being overcome by the excessive heat of August 1913. His final illness lasted but one day. Father Furlong was succeeded in the pastorate by the venerable pioneer of the Church in North Missouri, the living fountain head of information on our early Catholic struggles and triumphs, Father John J. Head.

The Church of Our Lady of Mount Carmel founded in 1872 took over its beautiful title from the ancient parish of Carondelet, which vacated it in 1859 in favor of S. S. Mary and Joseph. The Coadjutor Bishop of St. Louis blessed the corner stone November 10th, 1872, and dedicated the church on May 4th, 1873. Father David Samuel Phelan, was its founder and remained its pastor for the rest of his life. Originally all the people of the district were affiliated with Holy Cross Parish. Strong in numbers and enthusiastic, as they were, they built a large school house, near the German Church, which after the dismemberment of the parish, was sold to the school board. In later years Father Phelan repurchased the school property for the use of Our Lady of Mount Carmel's parish; the people of the Holy Cross parish having previously established a parochial school of their own. Father Phelan, as owner and editor of the *Western Watchman,* had to depend on his assistants for a good part of the parish work. They were Father William Noonan, John L. Gadell, John J. Dillon, P. Woods, James Sheil, John N. Kern, and William Moran. Up to a few years before Father Phelan's death the Rector of Our Lady of Mount Carmel also acted as Chaplain of Calvary Cemetery. This perquisite has now passed to the Rector of the Church of the Nativity. The Church S. S. George and James at Ferguson was attended from Our Lady of Mount Carmel until 1908, when the parish at Ferguson received a resident pastor in Rev. V. J. McCartney.

For well-nigh forty-two years Father Phelan was identified with the Church of Our Lady of Mount Carmel. He was a ready and forceful speaker. His sermons were orthodox in matter and clear-cut and logical in manner. The preacher however, and still more, the journalist, was not averse to an occasional commotion of the stagnant waters of self-complacency, but his intentions were not evil, and he always bore life's repercussions with equanimity. Father Phelan's Sermons were published by B. Herder in two stout volumes. Father John J. Dillon succeeded to the pastoral charge of Our Lady of Mount Carmel in 1915. The parish now has over three hundred and fifty families.

The parish of the Immaculate Conception with its beautiful Gothic Church on Lafayette Avenue and Longfellow Boulevard, is the third distinct parish of that name in the city of St. Louis. The first, centering around Eighth and Chestnut Streets, was abolished in 1874; the second around Jefferson Avenue and Locust Street, was abolished in 1902; the present flourishing parish of the Immaculate Conception was originally known as St. Kevin's, but received its new title on May 10th, 1908, when Archbishop Glennon blessed the church erected by Father Edward Shea, and when the old church of the parish of St. Kevin's was converted into the parish school.

St. Kevin's parish was the foundation of Father Patrick Lawrence McEvoy who was ordained on October 28th, 1866, for the Order of Carmelites, but was duly incardinated in the Archdiocese of St. Louis in 1872. After a brief stay at the Cathedral he was deputed in November 1875 to organize a new parish in the West End. He erected a temporary church building which was dedicated on January 13th, 1876, by Vicar-General Muehlsiepen in honor of Dublin's patron saint. On August 1st, 1879, Father McEvoy resigned his charge and withdrew from the archdiocese, probably to return to his monastery. The Reverend Edward J. Shea was transferred from Indian Creek, where he had labored for the preceeding four years, to the rectorship of the struggling city parish, with its seventy-five families and its heavy debt. St. Kevin's, however, grew apace and prospered under Father Shea's wise and firm administration. On April 7th, 1889, Vicar-General Philip Brady laid the corner stone for a new church, which the Rev. James J. McCabe dedicated on September 15th, 1889, under the invocation of St. Kevin.

When a new church seemed to be called for by 1904 Father Shea decided to move nearer to the center of the parish. A fine site was purchased about six blocks south of the old establishment. Here the church was erected, a noble Gothic structure of stone, with an abbreviated tower. The new church was dedicated on December 19th, 1908 by Archbishop Glennon in honor of God and the Immaculate Conception of the Blessed Virgin Mary. The former St. Kevin's has been entirely given to the use of the parish school of which the Sisters of Loretto have charge. It is attended by four hundred and fifty pupils.

Father Shea's assistants since 1879 were the Fathers: John O'Shea, John N. Kern, Philip Carroll, P. Morrissey, A. J. O'Reilly, J. F. Foley, W. L. Shea, J. A. Pleuss and D. Courtney.

Father Edward Shea was privileged to keep the Golden Jubilee of his ordination on July 4th, 1918. His death occurred on September 23rd, 1920, after forty-one years of most fruitful service in the parish of the Immaculate Conception.

Of St. Cronan's parish we have already written in connection with Father Ambrose Butler, its founder and first pastor. Father Butler died on September 6th, 1897, and was succeeded by the Rev. Jeremiah T. Foley. His assistant for the last ten years was the distinguished convert to the Faith from the Protestant ministry, the Rev. Russel Ignatius Wilbur.

Two years after the establishment of the Holy Ghost parish in the wide prairie district west of Grand Avenue and between Lindell and Natural Bridge Road, the Irish Catholics were organized into a separate parish bearing the title of the Visitation. Father Edward Fenlon served as its first rector, having entered upon his pastoral duties in 1881. A temporary church was erected and a school and rectory provided for. The Coadjutor Bishop laid the corner stone of the church on November 13th, 1881, and blessed the completed structure on April 23rd, 1882. On July 27th, 1885, Father Fenlon took a trip abroad: during his absence the Rev. Charles Van Tourenhout administered the parish. On September 16th, 1890, Father Fenlon received his first assistant, the Rev. John Lyons. After the death of Monsignor William Walsh in 1899 Father Fenlon was promoted to the pastorate of St. Bridget's Parish, which was then showing the first signs of decline from its former greatness. He never became quite resigned to his change from the Visitation, and died on March 15th, 1907.

Father Edward J. Dempsey, who had been pastor of Mexico, Mo., for the previous eighteen years, was made pastor of the Visitation on June 2nd, 1899. During his twelve years incumbency Father Dempsey built the fine church and rectory on Evans and Taylor Avenues, for which Archbishop Glennon laid the corner stone on April 4th, 1909. The good Father, a priest of genuine simple piety, sickened and died September 28th, 1910.

Under the terms of his will the Church of the Visitation received approximately twelve or thirteen thousand dollars. The school in his day had an enrollment of about three hundred and thirty pupils in charge of seven Sisters of Loretto. Father Dempsey's successor at the Visitation was the Rev. Patrick William Tallon, a native of Wicklow, who came to America in his sixteenth year. After completing his theological studies at Cape Girardeau, young Tallon was ordained by the Coadjutor Bishop Patrick Ryan, June 4th, 1876. The main points of his priestly life are well summed up by one who knew him well:

"Father Tallon's first appointment was assistant to Father Henry, pastor of St. Lawrence O'Toole's Church, at which post he remained eleven years. He was transferred from there to the Holy Name Parish, succeeding Rev. Thomas Bonacum. After 25 years at the Holy Name church, Mgr. Tallon was given charge of the Visitation Church, following the death of Rev. E. J. Dempsey, its builder. During his first five year's administration Mgr. Tallon paid off the entire debt of $50,000. He was one of the consultors of the Archbishop, was a member of the Orphan Board and for a score of years was president of the Kenrick Seminary Board, and one of the directors of the St. Louis Catholic Historical Society."

In recognition of his long and faithful service the Holy Father in April 1916 conferred on Monsignor Tallon the dignity of a Papal Prelate. He was a great friend of Father D. S. Phelan and served as associate editor of the *Western Watchman* for a number of years. His death occurred on Thursday morning, January 15th, 1920, Bishop Gilfillan, of St. Joseph, preached his funeral sermon.

Father Tallon passed the biblical three-score and ten by one year. He was, as the preacher said, a many-sided man, and he filled many parts, and he filled them all creditably."

After his death the Rev. Joseph Collins became pastor of the Visitation Parish. Two of Father Tallon's assistants, the Reverend Fathers J. A. Dockery and P. C. Gavin deserve special mention here as they were greatly instrumental under the pastor's guidance in cancelling the heavy debt contracted in the erection of their fine church.

## CHAPTER 62

## THE COLORED HARVEST IN ST. LOUIS

The thirty-third parish of St. Louis in the order of erection, and yet the first and only parish, so far, for the colored Catholics of the City, is that of St. Elizabeth, founded in 1873. From the city's very foundation, St. Louis had a negro population which increased in proportion to the general growth of the community. And of these colored people a fair proportion must have been Catholics. Why have they made so little outward progress as a distinct racial body within the Church? Why have they but one church of their own, where the City boasts of more than a hundred? It is a sad story, and yet there are gleams of comfort and encouragement in it, which we must point out in connection with the account of St. Elizabeth's.

The Catholic Church, being the loving Mother of all the faithful, makes no distinction between Black and White, just as she made no distinction between Greek and Barbarian in the days of her youth. Every soul is called to the faith, every soul is welcome to her fountains of grace. Side by side the colored servant and the white mistress kneel at the altar to partake of the banquet of the Lord. No priest would ever refuse to minister to a negro Catholic on his sick bed. No bishop, no priest would exclude any negro, man, woman or child from participation in the august sacrifice of the mass. Whence then the complaint that the colored Catholics have not received from their Church all that was due to them.

In order to understand and properly value this reproach, in as far as it applies to the archdiocese of St. Louis, we must take a glance at the extraordinary conditions under which the negroes became members of our civic and religious organizations.

The institution of African slavery was introduced into the vast territory of Louisiana, when "the merchant-prince Anthony Crozat," was granted the exclusive commerce of Louisiana in 1712. "Crozat's charter permitted him to send annually a vessel to Guinea for negroes, whom he might sell in Louisiana, to the exclusion of all others[1]. . . . But few negroes were introduced, and these were bought by private persons as domestic property.

In 1717 Crozat surrendered his charter, and the exclusive commerce of Louisiana was granted to the Company of the West, organized for that purpose. The new Company heeded the demand for more

---

[1] Crozat's Charter, in "Sidney Breese." "Early History of Illinois," p. 284. Cf. Monette, vol. I, p. 227, or "Historical Collections of Louisiana," vol. III, p. 42.

laborers and soon imported five hundred negroes from the coast of Africa. They disembarked at Pensacola, and a part of them were sent to open a plantation nearly opposite the post at New Orleans. A second cargo of five hundred negroes reached the colony in 1720, and landed in Mobile. In the following year Biloxi received a third cargo of the same size. In the spring of 1722, a Guineaman brought two hundred ninety African negroes to Mobile, and another brought three hundred more during the summer. But 1732, the number of negroes in the colony had increased to two thousand.''[2] It was under the rule of the Company of the West that Philip Francois Renault left France in the Spring of 1719, with two hundred miners and laborers, destined for what was then called ''the Illinois.'' On the voyage to Louisiana he purchased at St. Domingo five hundred Guinea negroes to work in the mines of what is now Missouri and Illinois. This was the beginning of negro slavery in the territory of the archdiocese of St. Louis. Many of our Catholic negro families claim descent from these pioneers. Under the early French and Spanish regimes in the Mississippi Valley practically all the slaves were Catholics: yet their religious and moral development was slow and naturally attended with difficulties. The memories of their former wild rites of paganism were not easily uprooted. Then the masters were often averse to the general advancement of their slaves through education: even religious instruction was often discountenanced. ''The impression gained ground that the negro would become discontented and rebellious, and so become less useful as a laborer if his mind were enlightened.''[3]

It is to the credit of the French and Spanish missionaries that they defied such laws or rather prejudices, and insisted on the education and Christian training of the slaves. The so-called ''Code Noir'' or Black Code obliged every slaveholder to have his negroes instructed and baptized. It allowed the slave time for instruction, worship and rest, not only every Sunday, but every festival usually observed by the Roman Catholic Church. It prohibited under severe penalties all masters and managers from corrupting their female slaves. It did not allow the Negro husband, wife, or infant children to be sold separately. It forbade them the use of torture, or immoderate and inhuman punishments.[4] With perfect justice, then, did one of the leaders of the American Negroes, J. M. Smith in his attack on the supine indifference of the Churches in regard to the welfare of his race, declare with emphasis: ''Such are the churches . . . with one exception let it be

---

2  Slavery in Louisiana in the ''Louisiana Historical Quarterly,'' p. 206-207.

3  Rutsch, Joseph, ''Negro Catholics in the United States.'' ''Catholic Historical Review,'' vol. III, p. 36.

4  ''Black Code,'' Art. 2, 4, 5, 6, 8, 11, 38. Gayarre, ''History of Louisiana,'' vol. I, pp. 531-540.

written upon every Protestant brow, for that one is the Roman Catholic Church her doors and her consolations are open alike to black and white, bond and free.''[5]

''Catholic faith and discipline,'' says an authority on the subject, ''are known to have a wholesome effect on the race. Observing men and judges of courts have remarked on the law-abiding spirit existing in Catholic colored communities. . . . And contrary to a prevalent opinion, the negro, when well grounded in the Catholic faith, is tenacious of it.''[6] Under the blighting rule of slavery, the Catholic Church was the negro's main defender, teacher, and consoler. No doubt, through her benign influence many a slave lived a happy and contented life: yet it would be a misconception of the true state of his feelings to say that the negro was better off and more satisfied in slavery than after his enfranchisement. His consciousness of the injustice of slavery and the corresponding desire for freedom are forced upon the mind of the student of recent publications on the matter, ''as is also the fact that from beginning to end, these emotions are rooted in an undoubtedly sincere and a deeply religious nature.''[7]

The emancipation of the slaves in 1862 brought a new great opportunity to the Church, and the Church realized it at once. The Fathers of the Second Plenary Council of Baltimore, held from the 7th to the 21st day of October 1866, issued a Pastoral Letter to the Clergy and Laity of their charge, in which the following passage is to the point:

''We must all feel, Beloved Brethren, that in some manner a new and most extensive field of charity and devotedness has been opened to us by the emancipation of the immense slave population of the South. We could have wished that, in accordance with the action of the Catholic Church in past ages in regard to the serfs of Europe, a more gradual system of emancipation could have been adopted, so that they might have been, in some measure, prepared to make a better use of their freedom, than they are likely to do now. Still, the evils which must necessarily attend upon the sudden liberation of so large a multitude with their peculiar dispositions and habits, only make the appeal to our Christian charity and zeal, presented by their forlorn condition, the more forcible and imperative.

We urge upon the Clergy and people of our charge the most generous co-operation with the plans which may be adopted by the Bishops of the Dioceses in which they are, to extend to them that Christian

---

5 ''The Mind of the Negro as Reflected in Letters Written During the Crisis 1800-1860,'' edited by Carter G. Woodson. Washington: The Association for the Study of Negro Life and History.

6 Woodson, ''The Education of the Negro Prior to 1861.''

7 Ibidem.

education and moral restraint which they so much stand in need of. Our only regret in regard to this matter is that our means and opportunity of spreading over them the protecting and salutary influences of our Holy Religion, are so restricted."[8]

Among the decrees of the Council in this matter the following are to be noted: "Wherever it seems advisable to erect seperate churches for the Negro Catholics, it may be done; but wherever it is judged more proper and profitable for the Negroes, that they attend the same church with the whites, the Ordinary must see to it that all cause for accusations against the Church be removed. Hence all must have free access to Christ, all that desire the holy sacraments, must be made welcome to receive them, and a place must be provided for all where they can assist at the tremendous sacrifice of the mass on Sundays and other days of obligation. But the obligation imposed upon the clergy and the people would be only partially fulfilled, if they only received the willing, but refused to seek the unwilling and erring. Missions should therefore be held in the larger communities of negroes, to which non-Catholics as well as Catholics were to be invited. The Superiors of Religious houses are requested to come to the assistance of the Bishops; the secular priests, willing to devote their lives to the cause of christianizing the negro, are praised for their charity. Priests of foreign countries are also invited to participate in the great work. Orphan Asylums for colored children should be founded."[9]

The Third Plenary Council of Baltimore held in 1884, extended this legislation by the appointment of a commission whose object should be to aid the missions among the Indians and Negroes of the United States and by appointing an annual Collection for these missions to be taken up in every diocese.

In the archdiocese of St. Louis the colored people of the city and its vicinity were placed in charge of the Society of Jesus with headquarters at the St. Louis University; whilst in the country parishes and missions they were treated as members of the Congregation. In many churches a certain number of pews were assigned for their use, whilst the main part of the church was reserved for the other parishioners. As early as 1858, the Jesuit Father William Koning, being appointed to labor specially among the negroes fitted out the upper gallery of old St. Xavier's Church as a chapel for his wards. Father Ignatius May carried on this work in 1861, and Father Henry Baselmans in 1862, the year of Father Koning's death. Then came Fathers Philip Colleton and James M. Hayes, each for one year, and in 1866, Father Michael Callaghan was given the post. Father Van der Heyden, his successor, had charge of it for two years, when he departed.

---

8   Pastoral-Letter of the Second Plenary Council of Baltimore, 1866.
9   Concilium Baltimorense Secundum, 1866, passim.

A new era was now to begin in the pastoral work for the colored folks of St. Louis. In 1872, Father Ignatius Panken, S. J., was called from Leavenworth to take charge of the colored Catholics of St. Louis.

In Christmas week of that year a Fair was held for the benefit of the Congregation of Colored Catholics in a hall that previously served as a Baptist, and then as a Presbyterian Church, but now bore the name of Vinegar Hill Hall. Father Panken attended the entertainment, when the idea occurred to him that the Hall would make a serviceable church for his people. The hall was bought for $5,000, and quickly fitted out with all things required for a true house of God.

On May 18th, 1873, there was a grand parade of more than 10,000 people, at the conclusion of which the Coadjutor Bishop dedicated the church to the glory of God under the invocation of St. Elizabeth. It stood on Fourteenth and Gay Streets. For twenty-two years, from 1872 until 1894, Father Panken continued, with one short interruption, to guard and guide the fold of the Lord's sheep at St. Elizabeth's. In 1890 he was sent to assist Father Ponziglione at St. Stephen's Indian Mission. During his absence Father Martial T. Boarman was in charge.[10]

"The most important event in Father Panken's career," the historian of St. Elizabeth's parish tells us, "was the coming of the Oblate Colored Sisters of Providence on October 12th, 1880, to assume direction of his school. Hitherto the school had been conducted in the basement of the church: but three weeks after the arrival of Sister Mary Louis Noel and her three companions, it was removed to a building that had been purchased for $2,700, a few weeks before. This new school added to its former day school a boarding school and finally an orphanage, which latter presently fissured off and became the most conspicuous work of the Oblate Sisters, the Orphan Asylum for colored children at Normandy. In 1883 and 1884, the expansion of the Sisters' school on 16th Street cost $11,500. Again, in 1890, Father Boarman bought a lot for $2,000 and Father Panken put up an $11,000 structure for the use of the Sodalities and school rooms.[11]

The Rev. Ignatius Panken was born at Duizel, Holland, November 28th, 1832. He offered himself to Father De Smet for the Indian Missions, and entered the novitiate at Florissant, January 9th, 1857, was stationed at Florissant and St. Charles, established the Sacred Heart Parish at Florissant in 1865, accompanied Father De Smet to Dakota, in 1870. From 1872 to 1894, he was pastor of St. Elizabeth's. In 1890, when Father Martial T. Boarman supplied his place, Father Panken was absent from St. Elizabeth's, attending the Arrapahoe and Shoshone

---

10   Questionnaire-Answers, and Chancery Records.

11   "Blossoms Gathered from the Lower Branches," by an Oblate Sister, pp. 25-34.

Indians in Wyoming. In 1894 he retired to Florissant where he acted as Spiritual Father until his death, March 20th, 1906.

Few priests in St. Louis were better known and loved than St. Elizabeth's first pastor. He endeared himself to Catholics and Protestants alike, and it was no small tribute to his merits that he directed for years the conscience of the learned and venerable Archbishop Kenrick.[12]

"After Father Panken, came Father Meuffels and in 1895, Father Michael F. Speich, the last-named, continuing the work for sixteen years. The long pastorate of Father Speich left its impression on the parish; he found it in a nascent state, and when called in 1911, to take charge of a Jesuit community in Florissant, Mo., left it well organized, free from debt, with a number of promising sodalities, societies, clubs, etc.''

In recent years the surroundings of St. Elizabeth's changed so much from previous conditions that it was deemed advisable to seek another and more central point for church activities. This was the task of Father McGuire, the successor of Father Speich in 1912.

After much deliberation the property at 2731 Pine Street, known as the Old Walsh Mansion was selected as the site of the new St. Elizabeth's Chapel and parish home. This stately old dwelling, while occupied by a St. Louis Club, had been enlarged by a double hall, and the whole plant afforded ample room for a chapel, school, club-rooms, and other appurtenances of a Community Center. The removal from the old to the new site was a red-letter day in the history of St. Elizabeth's. The leading Catholic Societies of the city turned out in parade, and after the dedication of the chapel, Archbishop Glennon and Mayor Kiel addressed an immense audience on the plans of the new St. Elizabeth's and the good it was to effect among the colored people of St. Louis. In 1914 Father McGuire secured for his school Mother Drexel's Sisters of the Blessed Sacrament, an Order devoted exclusively to work among colored people and Indians.

Their advent was to mark the beginning of a home for working girls and a hospital, two institutions bulking large in the plan of settlement work formed by the church. War clouds for a time darkened the pastor's prospects. The dull condition of the market prevented him from selling to advantage the old church property on Fourteenth Street, and his white brethren, who helped the colored cause in the past, and on whom he relied for present assistance, were too hard pressed to respond.'' Yet Father McGuire's courage did not fail or falter.

To quote his own words: "The divine mission of St. Elizabeth's is more than to minister to those who have the true faith; it is to mark

---

[12] Father Pauken was Archbishop Kenrick's Confessor for a number of years prior to the Prelate's death.

as her own the entire colored population of this great city. In this church the negro will find light and leading; her beautiful ceremonial will impress and instruct him, her grand system of sacraments will strengthen him to run his course like a giant, her priests and nuns will counsel him and devote their best energy to all his needs.''[13]

In 1918 Father Joseph Lynam came from Cincinnati to relieve Father McGuire. Father Lynam was a native of St. Louis, where he had a large circle of friends and acquaintances. He had spent many years as. a missionary among the natives of British Honduras, and his wide knowledge and experience eminently fitted him for the arduous work, in which he was engaged for seven years.[14]

Father Joseph Milet, S. J., succeeded to the pastoral charge of St. Elizabeth's in 1825. The present pastor is the Rev. William N. Markoe, S. J. There are from 2,000 to 3,000 Catholic negroes in St. Louis today, scattered over the greater part of the city. St. Elizabeth's Church is far too small for that number of worshippers. Besides, a part of the multitude is too far away from the church. Consequently very many colored Catholics attend the parish churches in their neighborhood, where they are heartily. welcome, but are generally assigned pews or seats separate from the main part of the Congregation. This, at times, arouses indignation on the part of the colored Catholics, who pretend to see in it a sign that they are not welcome.

In the fall of 1923, four catechism centers were successively established: at St. Joseph's (Biddle and 11th Sts.), Convent of the Helpers of the Holy Souls (Washington Ave.), St. Nicholas' (Lucas and 19th Sts.), and St. Patrick's (Biddle and 6th Sts.) St. Joseph's center was subsequently discontinued. At St. Nicholas' center a school was opened in 1924 which has over 400 colored children at present. At St. Patrick's a special Sunday Mass is said for colored Catholics. Confirmation is administered regularly at St. Nicholas and St. Patrick's.

In St. Louis County the Jesuit Father Arnold J. Garvey of St. Stanislaus Seminary has charge of two Catholic Congregations of colored folk, one at Anglum consisting mainly of descendants of former slaves of the Seminary, and the other at South Kinloch.

---

13 From an Account of St. Elizabeth's Church by Father Maguire, S.J., in ''Sunday Watchman,'' October 27, 1918.

14 Chancery Records.

## CHAPTER 63

## ARCHBISHOP KENRICK AND HIS SECOND COADJUTOR

Ever since the Archbishop's return from the Vatican Council most of his manifold duties devolved upon two most efficient and faithful men, the Coadjutor Bishop Ryan and the German Vicar-General Muehlsiepen. And excellently well did they fulfill the trust reposed in them. Running in parallel lines of duty, their plans never came in conflict, their labors ever tended to mutual support. This was owing in part to the fact that their initiative was always controlled and supported by the real ruler of the great archdiocese, Peter Richard Kenrick. He, with the deep wisdom gained by long years of labor and prayer, and with the dominant power of will that sought only the glory of God in the advancement of the Church, held his hand to the pulse of his people, and when no longer in immediate contact with them, inspired, guided and controlled the ideas and actions of those whom he sent out as the leaders of his priests and their congregations.

It was not a life of absolute retirement that the Archbishop led during the twelve years of Bishop Ryan's coadjutorship. The visitation of the parishes, the dedication of churches, the administration of the sacrament of Confirmation, the ordination of candidates for the ministry of the altar, no longer filled the days of the Archbishop with their diverse calls. Yet doing these works through others, he shared in their merit and consolation and, at the same time, trained his coadjutor in the practical virtues of Episcopal life. Bishop Ryan himself has borne testimony to this fact:

"It is only just for me to say that whatever qualities I may possess, whatever wisdom of government I may have shown, are due to the direct influence, the wisdom of the head and purity of heart of the man to whom I am coadjutor. My sacerdotal and episcopal education of mind and heart has been obtained under that man of general learning and consummate priestly character, one of the greatest men among the great, under him, to whom I know no superior in the Church of God today."[1]

The mutual relations that existed between the two great men, the Archbishop and his Coadjutor, were of the most harmonious kind. It was a true friendship that bound them together. "A friendship most beautiful in the annals of the American Church, a friendship that recalls the twin lives of Paul and Timothy, and of Basil and Gregory. Archbishop Kenrick always regarded Bishop Ryan as a child of his

---

[1] Farewell Address of Archbishop Ryan in "Western Watchman," August 23, 1884.

heart, and his predilection for him was as pure as it was honorable to both. As he said on one occasion, it was not his mind that attracted him, nor yet his manner; it was his big heart that won him. Archbishop Ryan fairly worshipped his father and friend. On a certain public occasion he declared that he was the greatest man he knew in the Church of God. As an indication of the lofty character of their communings he said on one occasion that never, in all his long intercourse with Archbishop Kenrick, had he ventured one familiar word."[2] Father Walsh was right in saying: "No two men were ever better fitted to carry on a common work. Such was their mutual respect and mutual confidence that a serious misunderstanding or disagreement was well nigh an impossibility. The one commanded as was his right, the other obeyed as was his duty."[3]

Of course, these friendly relations being unknown to the world at large, there were many rumors afloat as to the ecclesiastical status of the Archbishop. Some attributed his silence and retirement to a certain taciturnity of pride, others to a broken spirit, and others again to a direct command from Rome. Some time in March 1882, the *Spectator* a weekly paper of St. Louis of a literary and social trend, had begun the publication of a series of biographical notices of the prominent men of St. Louis and, among them, gave a very eulogistic summary of the life and labors of Bishop Ryan; and incidentally disposed of the archbishop by the bold assertion that he had been retired from all ecclesiastical functions. Catholics felt hurt at this slur upon a man who was held in such high regard at Rome and throughout the Catholic world as Archbishop Kenrick. Under date of March 25th, 1882, the Coadjutor, "fortiter in re," though "suaviter in modo," demolished the blundering impertinence of Editor Reavis: "Editor of the Spectator: Will you permit me to correct a mistake which occurs in the very friendly notice of me published in your last issue? Were the matter purely personal to me, I should not trouble you; but as its interest is of a general character, and as possibly other people may labor under the same impression as the writer of the article, I desire that the correction may be full and emphatic. The writer says, 'owing to the fact that Archbishop Kenrick has been practically relieved from all active duties since he took so strong a position in the Ecumenical Council against the dogma of infallibility, Bishop Ryan has been the real Archbishop,' etc. This is *not* the fact. The Archbishop possesses all the powers and faculties he ever enjoyed, and I am simply his Coadjutor. If I perform most of the episcopal work, it is solely because the Archbishop so desires it; and surely, after fifty years of great

---

2  "Western Watchman," June 14, 1884.
3  Walsh, William, "The Life of Peter Richard Kenrick," p. 36.

labor and great self-sacrifice in the ministry, he should rest a little in the evening of his day.

"Whilst the Catholic Church demands entire acceptance of a dogma once defined, she allows great liberty of thought and expression previons to such definition. Among the strongest opponents of the advisibility of defining Papal infallibility were the present Cardinal Primate of Hungary and Cardinal Newman; yet both have been created Cardinals since the definition—the former by Pious IX, and the latter by Leo XIII. Like our Archbishop, both submitted to the definition when once promulgated. A new argument was furnished to them— namely the decision of a tribunal which their reason had already accepted as the authorized and unerring interpreter of God's words to man."[4]

On March 7th, 1883, Bishop Ryan ordained Francis Anthony Diepenbrock, Joseph Leo Haar and Jeremiah F. Foley, and one Jesuit, to the holy priesthood. On May 12th, however Bishop Machebeuf held ordinations at the pro-cathedral of St. John. The corner stone layings and church dedications, with the exception of the Church of St. Thomas Aquinas, in St. Louis, St. Peter's in Jefferson City, and St. Patrick's at Wentzville, fell to the lot of several prominent priests: Fathers David S. Phelan, Henry Brockhagen, O. J. S. Hoog, J. J. Head, Peter Wigger and Henry Van der Sanden. Vicar-General Muehlsiepen was absent, at the time, on a visit to Europe. He returned to his post of duty on the eve of the Feast of the Immaculate Conception. In its issue of August 1883, the *Western Watchman* made the following announcement, which proved to be founded on fact: "In a few weeks coadjutor Bishop Ryan will set out for the Eternal city to take part in the most important deliberative assembly that was ever engaged exclusively with the affairs of the American Church. It is quite evident from the notes received by the Archbishop that this Roman conference will be called upon to formulate a general code of laws for the government of the Church in the United States. All previous attempts at such legislation have proved abortive, the acts of our Plenary Councils of Baltimore being little more than easy lessons in Church Latin. These Bishops will act as a regular committee on laws and will report their work to a Plenary Council to be held soon after their return. They will have the assistance of the best canonists of Rome in preparing their draft of an organic law for the American Church, and the general discussion that will be evoked by the confronting of ancient use with the experience and knowledge of the American prelates, will result in a clear presentation of the actual situation of affairs in this country,

---

4 "The Spectator" was a weekly paper founded and edited by John R. Reavis, devoted to art, society, the drama, literature, and matters of general social interest, 1880-1883.

and enable Rome to take a active part in our legislation which she never took before. Rome is slow to commit herself to any policy; but once committed, she is immovable. All we have to say is: May God direct the work to the happiest results for His Own Glory and the advancement of our young, but glorious Church.''[5]

Bishop Ryan sailed for Europe on Saturday, September 29th. He was accompanied by the Rev. P. J. O'Reilly, as Secretary. In Rome he attended the meetings of the American bishops as Archbishop Kenrick's representative. The Roman authorities, favorably impressed by the sterling qualities of his mind and heart and his stately bearing, conferred upon him, in recognition of his worth, the title of Archbishop of Salamis. It is reported that, on this occasion also, his appointment as Archbishop Wood's successor at Philadelphia was decreed by the Propaganda. The Prefect of the Propaganda, Cardinal Simeone, had proposed his name. Archbishop Ryan, it seems, knew nothing about the influences at work, and probably would not have been well pleased at the efforts made to separate him from his dearest friend on earth, Archbishop Kenrick. He returned home with his new title of Archbishop of Salamis and entered once more upon the work laid out for him as Coadjutor to the Archbishop of St. Louis. On May 22nd, 1884, he, at the pro-cathedral of St. John raised a number of young clerics to the holy priesthood, among them Henry Thobe, John Rothensteiner, five Jesuits and seven Franciscans. It was the last ordination held in St. Louis by Bishop Patrick J. Ryan, for on June 8th, of the same year, he was transferred to the Archdiocese of Philadelphia as the sixth incumbent of that noble See.[6]

When the news of Archbishop Ryan's promotion to the metropolitan See of Philadelphia reached St. Louis, as it quickly did, there came a feeling of mingled sorrow and pride over all the people. At first it seemed impossible that he should have his home anywhere but in St. Louis. Father Phelan well expressed these conflicting feelings:

''The clergy and people of the diocese, and indeed the people of the West, regardless of creed, will be sorry to part with Archbishop Ryan, for they have come to regard him as a very prominent item in that sum total of advantages, upon which they base their religious worth and social consequence. . . . The departing prelate has been identified with all that is pure and noble and grand in this city for thirty-two years. He grew into manhood here and developed into greatness under our very eyes. He is a rare exotic, but he had grown so magnificently under these western heavens, that we would fain claim him a product of our soil. He leaves millions of people who have come to reverence his worth; he is torn from a body of priests who honored, loved and

---

5  ''Western Watchman,'' August 11, 1883.

6  Chancery Records.

cleaved to him. Although never clothed with powers of administration among us, we have come to regard him as a parent, and his departure is to us like the announcement to a family that their widowed mother is to wed again.

"Archbishop Ryan is a man of powerful influence, far-reaching, yet sweetest withal. His activity is wide and deep, yet pervaded with the perfume of gentleness, that makes its positiveness persuasive and its vigor most refreshing. His opinions are most pronounced, his conceptions of duty fixed and uncompromising; yet he knows how to curb the impetuosity that would lead to collisions and to soften the asperities that would produce only friction and discouragement. He is a man with whom it is impossible to fall out more than once and not that once long. As there is no see in the world he would not adorn, so there is no clergy his presence would not bless.

"The transfer of Archbishop Ryan is a very great but justly deserved promotion. He is now only titular Archbishop; in Philadelphia he will be metropolitan of the grandest city on the continent. New York may be our greatest financially; Chicago may be our most enterprising and promising, but Philadelphia will be the paragon city of our American civilization. Matthew Arnold delared it "The city of America," and his judgment was nothing at fault."[7]

And again: "Archbishop Kenrick will be the heaviest loser by the transfer of Archbishop Ryan; but he is so detached from the things of this world that he will regard this as a challenge to approach nearer to his Divine model, Him, 'who emptied Himself, becoming obedient even unto death.' Some surmises have been indulged in as to the character of the Pope's mandate and its effect in controlling Archbishop Ryan's action under the trying circumstance of the call. These speculations are vain: Archbishop Ryan will go where he is sent. Personal preferences, personal friendships, all give way before the call of God, and the will of His Vicegerent."[8]

At the farewell banquet given by the Priests of the Archdiocese in honor of Archbishop Ryan, the great and gentle prelate pronounced these touching words in praise of Archbishop Kenrick:

"He was my leader, and I followed, but now I am left alone at the helm. I shall not now be able to say, as many of you remember I have often said: "I will speak to the Archbishop." There is no chance of that now. Sometimes, no doubt, you have thought that this was a most convenient mode of getting out of a difficulty, but I felt my dependence upon the Archbishop, and it was not the mere trick of a diplomat. It was due to a feeling that there was a much stronger man— a man of whom I have naturally looked up to from the age of twenty-

---

[7] "Western Watchman," June 14, 1884.
[8] "Western Watchman," June 14, 1884.

one, when I came here a priest—a man strong in his wisdom and experience to whom I could appeal.''[9]

Archbishop Ryan arrived in Philadelphia on August 19th. His
reception by clergy and people was truly magnificent, the installation
services at the Cathedral were held on August 30th, the impression
made by the Archbishop was decidedly favorable. All was well with
Archbishop Ryan.

But what were the feelings of the lonely Archbishop in St. Louis,
bereft of his coadjutor? Archbishop Kenrick was not accustomed to
indulge his feelings: he was a man of quick action:

On Friday, September 1st, Archbishop Kenrick officially notified
Rev. Philip P. Brady, rector of the Church of the Annunciation, that
he had appointed him Vicar-General of the diocese. It was assumed
by many that this appointment was but a preliminary to the higher
dignity of coadjutor, with the right of succession, especially as Father
Brady had been twice recommended by the bishops of the Province
for episcopal honors.[10]

The new Vicar-General was not a man of exceptional talents or
scholarship; but he had been a most laborious and successful priest.

Father Muehlsiepen, the Vicar-General for the Germans and Bohemians and Poles, was expected home to take up again his work in the
diocese. And now the aged Archbishop rose to the height of the occasion: he was done with coadjutors, he would do his own work. And he
was as good as his word. He came forth from his retirement of more
than twelve years and resumed the work of a bishop, apparently with
the same vigor with which in 1842, he had begun his episcopal career.

"He," as Father Walsh assures us, "visited every part of the
diocese, confirmed great numbers of children, and did all the work implied in an Episcopal visitation. Since his resumption of the active
duties incumbent upon the head of the diocese, he has confirmed at
least six thousand children every year.''[11] His confirmation tours begin
early in Spring and continue all summer. On his travels he is usually
accompanied by his Vicar-General Father Brady. The Archbishop bears
the fatigues and worries of travel over rough roads or no roads at all,
with remarkable patience and endurance. Every year he holds one
or two ordinations. In the seven years between Archbishop Ryan's
departure and his own Golden Jubilee he has ordained fifty-five priests,
and consecrated as Bishops two of his priests. In the summer of 1886,
he made the journey to Baltimore to invest Cardinal Gibbons with
the insignia of a Prince of the Roman Church. But along with this
and more than this, he has continued the headwork of the Archdiocese,

---

9  "Western Watchman," August 23, 1884.
10  "Western Watchman," September, 1884.
11  Walsh, "Life of Peter Richard Kenrick," p. 39.

the "sollicitudo omnium ecclesiarum," of a true shepherd of the flock of Christ. In November 1884, he made the long and tiresome journey to attend the Third Plenary Council of Baltimore, and sang the Pontifical Highmass at the opening of the Council, whilst his former Coadjutor preached the opening sermon on "The Church in Her Councils." He took part in the deliberations of the Council, and in forming that noble code of laws and regulations which under the name of "Decrees of Third Council of Baltimore" remains to this day in binding force in all matters not abrogated by the Codex Juris. The Archbishop was accompanied by Fathers Francis Goller and Thomas Bonacum in the capacity of theologians. Archbishop James Gibbons, as Apostolic Delegate, presided over the sessions of the Council. Fourteen archbishops, sixty-one bishops, six abbots and one General of a Religious Congregation were in attendance. The Council was formally opened on November 9th, and continued for four weeks, closing on Sunday, December 7th, 1884.[12] Archbishop Kenrick with his almost four score years, began another period of seven years of tireless episcopal activity. Some of the priests still among us remember with honest pride the day or the days when they had him as guest in their humble home in the city or in town or village, administering the sacrament of Confirmation to the lambs of their flock and speaking in a low melodious voice to the people that crowded around to hear him, speaking distinctly and intelligibly on some exalted theme. His frail form somewhat bent, but his eyes under the shaggy eyebrows luminous with a subdued glow, and every word, every gesture announcing though unconsciously, the splendid daring and gentle patience of a truly great man and servant of God.[13]

Whilst the venerable Octogenarian Peter Richard was busily engaged, not only in what may be called the head-work of the diocese, but also in the exhausting labors of visiting the parishes, administering confirmation to thousands, and ordaining priests, the Holy See removed two of his most zealous and faithful priests from the ranks and elevated them to the full power and dignity of the episcopacy.

On November 30th, 1887, Archbishop Kenrick consecrated the Rt. Rev. Thomas Bonacum, Bishop of Lincoln, Nebraska, and on the same day of the following year, the Rt. Rev. John Joseph Hennessy, Bishop of Wichita, Kansas, received, as the last one of a long line of Bishops, the imposition of his consecrating hands. Both events took place in St. John's Pro-Cathedral. It may be well to insert here the full list of Bishops that are, through Kenrick, linked with the apostolic succession:

---

12  Acta et Decreta Concilii Plenarii Baltimorensis Tertii, 1886, passim.
13  Personal Recollections.

1849, February 11, James Van de Velde, S.J. Bishop of Chicago; 1850, November 10, John McGill, Bishop of Richmond; 1851, March 25, John B. Miege, S.J., Bishop of Messenia; 1854, July 25, Anthony O'Regan, Bishop of Chicago; 1857, May 3, Clement Smyth, Coadjutor of Dubuque; 1857, May 3, James Duggan Coadjutor of St. Louis; 1859, May 8, James Whelan, Coadjutor of Nashville; 1859, July 24, Thomas Grace, Bishop of St. Paul; 1859, May 8, James O'Gorman, Bishop of Raphanea; 1865, November 1, Patrick A. Feehan, Bishop of Nashville; 1866, September 30, John Hennessy, Bishop of Dubuque; 1868, July 12, Joseph Melcher, Bishop of Green Bay; 1868, September 12, John Joseph Hogan, Bishop of St. Joseph; 1872, April 14, Patrick J. Ryan, Coadjutor of St. Louis.

Then the last of the series Thomas Bonacum of Lincoln and John Joseph Hennessy of Wichita making thirteen in all. The number of priests ordained by him exceeds three hundred, whilst those ordained by Bishop Ryan as Coadjutor numbered eighty-nine, and by other Bishops, at the Archbishop's request, twenty-six.

On August 5th, 1888 Mass was said for the last time in St. Francis Xavier's Church, Ninth and Lucas, the last church built in St. Louis before Peter Richard's coming as Coadjutor. The building was then turned over to the purchaser to be demolished. On July 31st, the chapel and college of the St. Louis University on Grand and Lindell Avenues were blessed by Father Henry Moeller, S.J.

The westward urge of the churches and institutions had begun. The old order was changing, a new era was soon to open.

CHAPTER 64

## ST. LOUIS PARISHES FORMED IN ARCHBISHOP KENRICK'S LAST YEARS

The last ten years of Archbishop Kenrick's actual regime, 1882 to 1892, saw ten new parishes established within the city of St. Louis, some with churches that are numbered even today among our architectural monuments, like St. Francis Xavier's, and St. Agnes; others that had to be content for a shorter or longer space of time, with more humble temples of God, but at last attained their ideals in church construction, as St. Henry, St. Rose of Lima, St. Engelbert, the Holy Rosary and St. Aloysius. Some of these parishes are now among the strongest and most prosperous church organizations in the diocese, and might appear to require the same minute and extensive treatment as those that have gone before. Yet, we must remember that we are now arrived among the living, of whom we cannot speak so freely as of the dead, for fear of either offending their finer sensibilities with excessive praise, or hurting their feelings with unfair criticism. Moreover, these later parishes, when placed in proper correlation to what has gone before and what has so far resulted from them, do not possess the same importance, in a historical sense, as pioneer parishes like the Old Cathedral, St. Mary's, St. Joseph's, St. Patrick's, St. Vincent de Paul's, or S.S. Peter and Paul. The earlier churches were conquests from the wilderness, the later ones but extensions and divisions of these conquests. And the impulse that formed the latter was but the necessary result of the life and vigor going out from the pioneers. The glamor that clings to the pioneer is lacking both in their priests and people. It is the Spring's shy return, more than the full splendor of the summer sun, that is regarded as the most interesting season of the year; so the beginnings of the Church in St. Louis, amid poverty, hardships and constant struggle, demand of the historian a larger share of interest, than the living present. In order to get the true perspective of events we must look at them from a certain distance of years: as to the events of the present or the recent past we can only give the bare facts.

The parish of *St. Thomas of Aquin* in South St. Louis was carved out of the territory of the parish of the Franciscan Fathers, which was originally organized as a mixed German-English congregation and remained so for twenty years. In 1882 the members of St. Anthony's parish, that were not of German descent, separated from the main body of the congregation and obtained permission to organize

(502)

a new parish within the territory bounded by Utah Street, the Mississippi River, Delor Avenue and the City Limits. On October 8th, Rev. John J. Hennessy laid the corner stone, and on April 29th, 1883, the Coadjutor Bishop blessed the Church. Rev. David J. Doherty served as pastor of St. Thomas of Aquin from 1883 to April 28th, 1884.

His successor was the venerable Father Martin S. Brennan, then in his manly prime. A parish residence and a school were added under his administration.

On Father Brennan's transfer to St. Lawrence O'Toole's, on December 28th, 1891, the Rev. Dr. John H. May was appointed to the rectorship of St. Thomas of Aquin's, and held the position until his death on January 15th, 1908. Dr. May enlarged the church, and Archbishop Kain blessed it on October 1st, 1893.

After a brief administratorship Rev. Francis J. Jones was made pastor, May 27th, 1908. Father Jones remained faithful to his parish until his death on July 7, 1926. The school with an attendance of 200 pupils is taught by seven religious of the Sacred Heart.[1]

The beginnings of the parish of *St. Rose of Lima* date back to the early seventies when the pastor of St. Anne's Church of Normandy, Father Adrian Van Hulst, S. J., built a rude wooden chapel on what is now Hamilton and Minerva Avenues, for the use of the few scattered Catholics living west of Grand Avenue.

Small as the chapel was, it also served as a school, in which two Sisters of Mercy from Normandy taught the children of the neighborhood. Two other Jesuit Fathers interested themselves in the early parishioners of St. Rose's: Father F. X. Kuppin and Joseph Real. In 1883 Father Gerard D. Power, then chaplain of the Loretto Convent in St. Louis, began to attend the mission on Sundays and Holy days of obligation. He did not, however, reside at the place. On June 25th, 1884, almost immediately after his ordination, Father James J. McGlynn was appointed as the first pastor of St. Rose of Lima's parish. He found only thirty-five families in his district; but others were coming, and he soon realized the necessity of building a new church. But it was decided that it would be to the interest of the parish to erect a building at a location further east. The new St. Rose's Church and School were erected on Goodfellow and Etzel Avenues. On October 26th, Vicar-General Brady laid the corner stone of the church, and on June 21st, of the following year the structure was ready for occupancy, after being blessed by Father Brady. Its seating capacity was for five hundred people. In 1893 the new school was built

---

[1] Chancery Records and Thornton Adelman Barnet, ''The Notable Catholic Institutions of St. Louis,'' p. 83.

and placed in care of the Lorettine Sisters. Although large and important Congregations like St. Mark's, St. Edward's, St. Barbara's, All Saint's, St. Roch's, The Nativity Church, and St. Catherine were, in the course of years, formed out of St. Rose of Lima's parish, the mother church continued to increase and multiply spiritually. Thirty priests and forty Sisters were born within the limits of its former territory. A new and much larger school was built in 1900, accommodating seven hundred pupils, and the crowning glory of the parish, the beautiful stone church, was commenced in 1909. The corner stone was laid on June 27th, of that year, the day making the twenty-fifth anniversary of Father McGlynn's ordination, whose entire priestly life was spent in the service of St. Rose of Lima's parish. On Sunday, September 18th, 1910, this the third church of the parish, was dedicated by Archbishop Glennon.[2]

Of *St. Francis Xavier's Church* adjoining St. Louis University, we took occasion to speak in connection with the later history of that grand institution. Suffice it to say in this place that the parish, in Father H. J. Bronsgeests days, numbered about one thousand families, and that the parish school numbered two hundred and fifty pupils, who were in charge of the Sisters of Charity of the Blessed Virgin from Dubuque, Iowa.

*St. Henry's Church* on California Avenue and Rutger Street is numbered as the forty-eighth church in the city. It was erected by and for German Catholics.

On January 16th, 1885, Father John A. Hoffmann, who had been recalled from the temporary administration of the church at Boonville, in Kansas City diocese, was commissioned by the ecclesiastical authorities to organize a new German parish in the territory bounded by Grand and Geyer Avenues, and Eighteenth and Clark Streets. At a meeting held in a public hall, the organization was formed, and on March 13th, the tract of land now in use for the church and school were bought. The corner stone for the new church and school was laid on June 28th, and the building dedicated in honor of St. Henry, on on Sunday, September 13th, by Vicar-General Henry Muehlsiepen. In 1890 a parsonage was built, facing on Rutger Street. The parish school numbered about 200 children, in charge of Sisters of St. Francis.

The parish prospered under the able leadership of its energetic and zealous pastor, so that in 1896 the building of a new church had been decided on.

But the cyclone of May 27th of that year laid St. Henry's church and school in ruins. A temporary church was hastily erected out of

---

2 Cooke, Anna Dolores, St. Rose's Church, 1910.

boards, to serve as a place of worship, until the old church and school could be rebuilt. It was dedicated by Archbishop Kain on November 26th. The erection of the contemplated new church had to be temporarily abandoned, but was again taken up in the spring of 1909. .

The corner stone of the structure was laid by Archbishop Glennon in May 1909. As the entire sum necessary for building operations was on hand, the church was completed early in May 1910.

The precarious condition of Father Hoffmann's health caused him to ask for an administrator of the parish with the right of succession, and he obtained the person of his choice, his former assistant, the Rev. Henry Hussmann, rector of St. Henry's church, Charleston, Mo. Father Hoffmann did not live to see the completion of his life's monument. He died on September 15th, 1909.

Father Hussmann having become pastor of St. Henry's, carried out all the plans and ideas of the founder. The dedication service were held on June 12th, 1910, Archbishop Glennon officiating. The parish also celebrated the 25th anniversary of its organization in connection with the dedication of its new church.[3]

Of the assistants to Father Hoffmann at St. Henry's from 1890 until 1909 we may subjoin the honored names of the Fathers Henry Hussmann, George Koob, A. J. Von Brunn, Joseph F. Lubeley and Henry C. Petri, all of them still among the living and active members of the diocesan clergy.

The parish of *St. Leo* on Twenty Third and Mullanphy Streets was organized in 1888. At that time the mother church, St. Bridget's, was perhaps the most populous of the city. Father Jeremiah Harty, the future Archbishop of Manilla, and subsequently of Omaha, but then only a young assistant to Father William Walsh of St. Bridget's, was entrusted with the organization of a new parish in the territory, which was to be taken from the northern part of the mother church. A suitable site was purchased, and a temporary church structure was dedicated by Vicar-General Brady. On May 31st, 1889, Father Harty received an assistant in the person of Father James J. O'Brien. The Bishop of Wichita, J. J. Hennessy, came on September 1st, of the same year, to bless and lay the corner stone of the new church of St. Leo, which was completed in the following year and dedicated by Archbishop Kain. A school building and parsonage were also erected by Father Harty.

In 1904 Father Harty was elected to the archiepiscopal See of Manilla, Philippine Islands. He was succeeded as pastor of St. Leo's by the Rev. James T. Coffey, formerly rector of St. John's. The parish continued to prosper, and became one of the largest in the city. Its

---

3  ''Das Katholische Deutschtum von St. Louis,'' pp. 65-68.

parochial school in charge of the Sisters of St. Joseph, showed an enrollment of eight hundred and fifty children. This is certainly an
unmistakable index of the condition of the parish at that time. The
present number of pupils is about six hundred and eighty. Father
James T. Coffey remained in charge of the parish to the present day.
The clergy of St. Leo's have charge of the chapel of St. Louis in
the Home for the Aged of the Little Sisters of the Poor.[4]

*St. Engelbert's* parish in Northeast St. Louis was from the start
one of the most promising church organizations in St. Louis, and
now, after a long period of rest, is making good its early promise. It
is a parish of German Catholics, and was organized in 1891 in the
region occupied by truck gardeners and dairymen.

Father Anthony Pauck was its founder and first pastor. A tract
of six acres was bought for the parish. The first meeting of the new
congregation took place on March 30th, 1891, in the home of the leading parishioner Engelbert Schaefer. The plans for the proposed Church
of St. Engelbert, including school and Sisters residence were accepted.
In 1891 the foundation was laid and the church was opened for divine
worship, Vicar-General Muehlsiepen performing both functions of
corner stone laying and dedication, the latter on November 22nd, 1891.
The rectory was built on Marcus Avenue adjoining the site of the
present imposing Church of St. Engelbert. The immediate vicinity
of the church began to build up rapidly after proper grades and a
system of sewerage were established.[5]

Rev. Father Pauck came to St. Engelbert's parish from Glasgow,
Mo., where he had labored as pastor for sixteen years. He died April
14th, 1908.

"Father Anthony Pauck was of a genial disposition," wrote the
Rev. Dr. Selinger, "He had the rare gift of interesting young men in
the choice of their future vocation. A number of priests owe to him
the first awakening of their call to the ministry of Christ. He made
personal sacrifices of his money and time. He started them in Latin by
instructions and assisted them financially to continue their studies.
After their ordination he continued as their Father by advice and warning. Always busy with parish work he still found leisure to help
educate boys for the priesthood. He had winning ways with the
people. In St. Charles, where he was assistant, he is still remembered
for his charities. In Glasgow where he was pastor, the fruits of his
ministration still endure."[6]

Father Pauck's successor at St. Engelbert's, Rev. Frederick H.
Schulte died February 27th, 1916. After him came the Rev. August

---

4  Thornton, 1. c., 195 s. s.

5  "Das Katholische Deutschtum," pp. 53-56.

6  Selinger, Dr. Jos., in "Our Pastors in Calvary," p. 101.

Happe who resigned his charge, October 6th, 1918, whereupon that genial priest and devout client of Mary was Father John L. Gadell appointed rector. Father Gadell's death occurred within three years of his appointment, February 15th, 1922. His successor, the Rev. August Von Brunn, at once took measures to erect the long-discussed Church of St. Engelbert which is now the pride and joy of the people.

The Church of the *Holy Rosary* was organized in July 1891 and governed by Father Daniel J. Lavery from that time on to the present day. The first church, a modest brick structure, was blessed by Vicar-General Brady, on December 20th, of the same year. The school was established about the same time and placed in charge of five Sisters of St. Joseph. In 1909 it showed an enrollment of two hundred and thirty children. The parish has had a steady growth and has not even now reached its climax. A new and quaintly beautiful church was accordingly provided for its use. Its dedication by Archbishop Glennon took place in 1923. The Rev. Dr. Lavery holds the position of Defensor Matrimonii in the Matrimonial Court of the archdiocese.[7]

*St. Agnes parish* was the result of a misunderstanding. Prior to 1890 the Rev. Constantine P. Smith was pastor of the ancient church of the Assumption. As the neighborhood of the church had been gradually turned into the great brewery center of St. Louis, and for that matter, of the United States, the quiet, studious pastor determined to supersede the Assumption church with a new one in a new location, farther west and to give it the name of St. Agnes. The corner stone was laid on September 28th, 1890 by Vicar-General Brady. The church was dedicated December 6th, of the following year by Bishop Edward Fitzgerald of Little Rock, Arkansas. The dedicatory sermon was preached by Archbishop Ryan of Philadelphia. After the completion of St. Agnes church, Archbishop Kenrick declined to abolish the old church of the Assumption, and appointed the Rev. Thomas Cooney to take charge of the eastern part of the dismembered parish. Father Cooney had as successors at the Assumption the Rev. Fathers Patrick Dooley, and William Randall. The latter made the place the center of the diocesan Missionary Band. It is still a live parish with a school of three hundred children under six Sisters of St. Joseph and one lay-teacher. The present pastor is the Rev. William L. Shea.

The parish of St. Agnes remained in charge of Father Constantine Smith until the autumn of 1897, when ill health forced him to lay down the burden. He sought to regain health in travel, but died in New Orleans on January 5th, 1898.

---

7  Thornton, p. 201, and Chancery Records.

Father Constantine Smith was born June 2nd, 1838, in County Cavan, Ireland, and came to America when he was only twelve years old. He made his theological course at Cape Girardeau and, after his ordination at the hands of Archbishop Kenrick, was appointed assistant priest at St. John's Pro-Cathedral. Here his love for sacred learning found a congenial home in Archbishop Kenrick's excellent library. Here he became one of the most scholarly priests in the West, and here he contracted the staunch friendship with his great archbishop, that was a comfort for both in the days of supreme trial: "those stormy days when minds were severely tried," as Father Phelan remarked, "and our great Metropolitan's intellect received the terrible wrench from which it never recovered."

Father John J. Tannrath, who had acted as administrator of the parish since December 27th, 1897, was now appointed as its pastor. Father Tannrath built the present fine school of St. Agnes, which was opened in September 1905, with four hundred and fifty pupils in charge of nine Sisters of St. Joseph. On Monsignor Tannrath's appointment to the pastorship of the Old Cathedral, Father John S. Long succeeded him at St. Agnes.[8]

*St. Aloysius parish*, in the southwestern part of the city, was organized by Vicar-General Muehlsiepen in January 1892.

On May 27th, 1892, Rev. F. G. Holweck, assistant at St. Francis de Sales, parish, received the appointment as the first Rector of St. Aloysius parish. But because no one could be found at the time to replace him at St. Francis de Sales, Vicar-General Muehlsiepen acted as administrator at St. Aloysius. The building of the temporary church was begun on August 16th.

Rev. F. G. Holweck assumed charge of the parish on Sunday, September 4th. On the next day the parochial school was opened. Twenty-four pupils answered the roll call, most of whom formerly attended St. Bernard's school. A census of the parish was taken soon after, which showed sixty families; mostly of the laboring class. Ten acres of land had been purchased on Reber Place, and laid out in three blocks, the middle one being reserved for church purposes, the other two being divided up into lots for sale to Catholic Germans. The youthful pastor was accordingly compelled to take up the duties of the real estate business in addition to his pastoral and other obligations. These lots soon found ready sale, and the parish grew rapidly until it contained about one hundred and thirty families. As the old frame church could no longer accommodate the congregation, a new

8 "Western Watchman," February 8, 1898.

substantial building was determined on in 1898, of which the corner stone was laid on May 7th, by Vicar-General Muehlsiepen. A spacious basement was built, and covered in for temporary use: "In 1900 the parish numbered 200 families, including an Italian colony. The school numbered 200 pupils, and was in charge of the Sisters of Notre Dame. After the demise of Father Peter Lotz of St. Francis de Sales church. May 14th, 1903, Father Holweck was appointed as his successor, and the Rev. Francis G. Brand, as rector of St. Aloysius.[9]

Father Brand, at the time of his coming to lead and govern the parish for almost a quarter century, had a distinguished record of varied and successful missionary labor. He was born at Taos, the favorite mission of the saintly Jesuit Father Helias, from whose hands he received his first holy Communion. After his ordination by Archbishop Kenrick on May 30th, 1885, the young priest was assigned to St. Francis de Sales church as assistant. In 1888 he was sent to Charleston, where he built the fine school and, in addition to St. Henry's Church of Charleston, attended the scattered missions of New Madrid, Caruthersville and Cooter, Belmont, East Prairie, Bird's Point, Texas Bend and Sikeston. From Charleston he also organized the Church of Oran and built its first church. In Sikeston he bought a Protestant church and arranged it for the use of the Catholic Congregation. This vast mission field Father Brand was requested to leave in order to organize a new parish in Shrewsbury, a suburb of St. Louis. Here also he had established church and school, when Archbishop Kain sent him to the northeast corner of the State for the same purpose. With his usual energy Father Brand set out for the long neglected field of labor. Kahoka in Clark County was his place of residence: here he built a church and rectory, and from here he attended the missions of Wayland, Chambersburg and Mudd Settlement, and said mass in private houses at Downing, Memphis, Hitt, Avela, Acasto, Athens, St. Francesville, Alexandria, Wyaconda and others. Some of these names sound sweetly reminiscent to the readers of Father Lefevere's letters of the early thirties of the nineteenth Century.

And now after fifteen years of hard, rugged journeys through the swamps of the Southeast and the hill country and prairie lands of the Northeast, Father Brand was to complete the work that was hardly begun among a poor and listless following. There was but a basement church and a heavy debt. Yet the obstacles and pitfalls of the situation did not seem insurmountable. He paid off the old debt, he

---

9 Holweck, F. G., in ''Das Katholische Deutschtum in St. Louis,'' pp. 10-14.

built a new church and a house for the sisters, and a house for the priest and lastly a house of God that is a real credit to the parish and a source of pride to the diocese. In November 1924 ground was broken for the new edifice, and the corner stone was laid by the Archbishop under the most auspicious circumstances on Sunday, May 2, 1925.[10]

The dedication of the really noble structure by Archbishop Glennon took place, April 25, 1926.

---

[10] Rev. J. W. Souvenir Album of Rev. H. F. M. Brand's 25th Anniversary, 1910, pp. 19-28.

## CHAPTER 65

## THE ALEXIAN BROTHERS

"The fruit which we have gained forever, is that which thou, O God, hast accepted," may be appropriately said of the unknown founders of the Alexian Brotherhood, who banded themselves together at Mechlin in Brabant during the terrible ravages of the pest in the fifteenth century. They were laymen, having taken no vows nor adopted any rule of life, except the Christian rule of Charity to succor their brethren stricken with the plague. This sentiment also guided them in selecting their heavenly patron, that perfect model of most generous contempt of the world, St. Alexius. The son of a Roman Senator in the Fifth Century, born in a palace on the Aventine Hill, Alexius might have risen to high position in the Empire. In obedience to his Father's will he married a lady of beauty and wealth and of a gentle, religious disposition, but as he had learnt that "riches given, remain our own," and fearing that the fascination of temporal honors and pleasures might gradually undermine the best intentions, he left his bride immediately after the marriage ceremony, using the Christian liberty of separation before consummation, and led the life of a lonely pilgrim, unknown to all the world, and died under the stairs of his father's home as an unknown beggar.

Contempt for the world was one side of St. Alexius' character; deep helpful love for the poor, sick and wounded, and outcasts of society was the other. Visiting the hospitals was his dearest occupation. The choice of such a patron saint would indicate, that the Alexian Brotherhood had appointed as the life work of its members, the care of the poor sick, and afflicted in body or in mind. And this is exactly the case: In all countries the members have been known and revered for their devotion to the sick in cities, and to the wounded on the battlefields. According to a statement made by one of their members: "The Alexian Brothers are a Community of Lay Brothers, who have their Motherhouse in the ancient City of Aix la Chapelle, Germany, and their Novitiate and Nurses' Training school at the Alexian Brothers Hospital, Chicago, Illinois, where the Novices receive a training which entitles them to the privilege of making their State examination for Registered Nurses, either in the State of Missouri or Illinois, the school having been registered with the State board of education and registration."

The first settlement of the Brotherhood in America was made in Chicago in 1866 by Brother Bonaventure Thelen, with the hearty approbation of Bishop Duggan.

(511)

The Alexian Brothers' Hospital of St. Louis was founded in September, 1869, by Brothers Paulus Tollig and Alexius Bernard, who had been sent from Chicago by their Provincial, Brother Bonaventure Thelen.

In St. Louis they were encouraged from the start by Archbishop Kenrick and the two Vicars-General, Father Patrick J. Ryan and Father Henry Muehlsiepen, the latter entertaining them at his residence until they found a location.

On September 21st, 1869, they purchased the old Simons Mansion surrounded by five acres of land and commanding a good view of the river. The price was $25,000, and they had only one thousand to pay down, but the owner, James Lucas, donated the sum of a thousand, and almost everywhere the Brothers went to collect they were received kindly and their request answered with generosity. Begging from door to door for some time, they were at last able to equip their new home and prepare a chapel. On December 7th, the Hospital was dedicated by Vicar-General Muehlsiepen, and in April they were ready to receive patients. The first one who applied for medical treatment was a priest, Father Stroombergen, a circumstance the Brothers considered auspicious.

The opening of the Hospital, therefore, dates from April 12th, 1870. The Hospital having become inadequate to meet the many applications for admittance, the corner stone for a new and more spacious building was laid on Pentecost Monday 1873, by the Coadjutor-Bishop Patrick J. Ryan, and on the 4th of July 1874, the new hospital was consecrated by the same prelate.

On May 2nd, 1889, a contract was awarded for another wing to the hospital, doubling its capacity, which was opened and dedicated in October 1890, by Very Rev. Van der Sanden, Chancellor of the Archdiocese, who was resident chaplain for the Brothers during twenty-three years.

In 1924 a Nurses' Home was erected, and in 1925 a new Dispensary Building in place of an old Residence adjoining the Hospital, which had been in use as a Dispensary for some years.

The Alexian Brothers Hospital, has a capacity of 250 beds, for male patients only, and is located on the Corner of South Broadway and Osage Streets, on a plot of five acres, surrounded by gardens and parks overlooking the Mississippi River. The hospital is divided into two General Departments. The first department is the hospital for the care of surgical, medical, eye, ear, nose and throat, and genito-urinary ailments. The second department separated from the foregoing, consists of two divisions: one for enebriates, and the other for the milder nervous ailments. The Hospital is managed, and the patients are nursed by the Alexian Brothers.

The cyclone of 1896 unroofed part of the Alexian Brothers Hospital and damaged several of the walls. Attending to the consequent repairs, the Brothers took the opportunity of adding another story to the building.

The present equipment is splendid, particularly the laboratory, but there is a growing ambition of the Brothers to have the best of every scientific device known to alleviate the sufferings and cure the diseases of their patients. The Alexian Brothers Hospital consists at present of three units, namely: The hospital for surgical and medical cases, the sanatorium for nervous and mental cases, and the dispensary where all deserving patients, both male and female, are given treatment and medicine without cost.

The staff of the hospital consists of twenty physicians and surgeons of first rank, and the patients of other recognized members of the medical profession are welcomed at all times. In addition there are eight resident physicians and internes. In fact, the work of the Alexian Brothers is distinguished by a spirit of broad Christian charity.

The Free Dispensary is a blessing to the poor of South St. Louis, of whom over three thousand are treated in the course of one year, in its different departments, making on the average from 12 to 14,000 visits, as many have to call several times before a cure is effected. No poor sick man, no matter what may be his color, creed or nationality, is refused admission to the Hospital, as long as there is a vacent bed in the house. The Brothers are twenty-two in number. The life they lead is indeed most self-sacrificing, and it is a life hidden with God. Many a story, bright, cheering and hopeful, could those silent walls relate, of men that came here or were brought here, to find relief from bodily pain and anguish of mind, and who found all that, and much more, the peace of a good conscience restored. And how many other stories sad, tragic, heartrending, of those who came to say a last fond farewell to those they loved more than all on earth, and whom they would never again meet in life. But the weather-beaten walls remain silent, and the Brothers keep no record, save that of name, and date of birth and death. Charity hides the rest. One of the saddest things in life is to witness day by day, not only the countless ills that afflict mankind, but also the trembling sorrow and struggling hope of those that are doomed to overpowering bereavement. The Alexian Brotherhood has chosen this very saddening life as its course of Christian activity, and for this reason alone, if for no other, it deserves the highest respect from all.

## CHAPTER 66

## THE PASSIONIST RETREAT AND PREPARATORY SEMINARY

The last of the religious Orders of Men received into the Archdiocese by Archbishop Kenrick was the Congregation of the Passionist Fathers, in 1884. "The Passionists are neither monks, nor friars nor canons regular:" yet they have the charm of monasticism about them. Their homes are called Retreats, their superiors simply Rectors. To the simple vows of poverty, chastity and obedience, they add the fourth to promote love and devotion to the Passion of Our Lord. Hence their popular name, Passionists.

The chief work of the Fathers is the giving of missions to the people and retreats to the clergy and Religious Communities. They do not, as a rule, take charge of parishes, but act as a reserve corps in the Church and are ever ready to come to the aid of the diocesan clergy.

These items about the Passionists in general are taken from the beautiful book "The Passionists" by Rev. Felix Ward, one of the early American members of the Order.

The founder of the Congregation of the Passion, Paul Danei, now canonized as St. Paul of the Cross, a singularly gifted, stately and handsome youth, came of a noble but impoverished family of Northern Italy. It was the scoffing age of Voltaire, in which he lived: but his faith and his virtues shone all the brighter for the darkness and misery that lay all around him.

In 1714 he joined the Venetian army against the Turkish invaders. In the midst of the turmoil of war came the call of God, that he should found a new Order of Religious. His efforts met with success. Pope Benedict XIII approved the Congregation. Paul and his brother John were ordained to the priesthood by the Pope himself. In 1740 the saintly founder revised the rules of his Congregation, and on May 15th, of the following year Pope Benedict XIV gave his formal approval, by rescript, and in 1801, the martyr-pope Pius VII confirmed it solemnly by the Bull *Gravissimas inter causas*. Pope Clement XIV assigned to the Passionists the Church of S.S. John and Paul with the house attached to it for a Retreat. S. S. John and Paul has been the headquarters of the Passionists ever since. St. Paul of the Cross died on October 13th, 1775, at the age of eighty-one years and nine months, "Read the Passion of Our Lord for me" were his last words on earth. On September 22nd, 1784, Pius VI declared the servant of God, *Venerable,* in October 1852, Pius IX declared him Blessed, and on June 29, 1867, he canonized St. Paul of the Cross. At the death of the Founder there were two Provinces, twelve Retreats and two hundred and eighty professed Passionists. Emperor Napoleon dissolved the Congregation; but at the return of Pious VII to Rome it was restored. Pope Pius IX who, as Count Mastai-Feretti had desired to join the Passionists, became their great protector and friend. The quick expansion of the Order was one of the marvels of the age. England, once "Our Lady's Dowry," received them with gladness. Father Dominic, the Passionist, was chosen by Divine Providence to receive England's most distinguished convert the future Cardinal John Henry Newman into the Church.

America, too, gave a hearty welcome to the loving, genial sons of St. Paul of the Cross. Bishop Michael O'Connor of Pittsburg, when at Rome in 1843, visited the shrine of St. Paul, and then went straightway to the Second Founder, Father Anthony of St. James, to ask for a colony of Passionists for his far-away diocese. The choice for the mission fell on Father Anthony Callandri, Albinus Magno, Stanislaus Parezyki, and Brother Lawrence Di Giacomo. During their stay at Philadelphia they received gracious attention from the saintly Bishop Neuman. Bishop O'Connor offered them the choice of two sites for their Retreat, one at Lawrenceville on the Allegheny River, the other on a hilltop high above the town of Birmingham. The solitary, hilltop covered by the forest primeval was chosen by Father Anthony. Here the Fathers built their Retreat and began their work of preparation for their mission. Father Anthony was regarded by all as a saint. Under his wise and benign administration the good work made progress in every way. Wonderful conversions were made; from all sides came the requests for missions and retreats: also from St. Louis. Archbishop Kenrick, one of the most intimate friends of the Bishop of Pittsburg, had as early as 1865, invited the Passionists to locate in his archdiocese, offering them a very desirable place in the suburbs of the rapidly growing city. This generous offer the Fathers were forced to decline, owing to the scarcity of members in the promising, but as yet very small American Province.

In the fall and winter of 1883-4, whilst the Passionists were engaged in giving missions in St. Louis, the subject of accepting a foundation in the archdiocese was frequently spoken of by some of the leading priests of the city, as Fathers Harty, Tobyn and Hennessey. Both clergy and people seemed very anxious to have the Fathers in their midst.

In 1884, during a mission in St. John's Church, Father Charles Lang, Rector of Sacred Heart Retreat, Louisville, Ky., approached Archbishop Ryan on the subject of the new foundation. The Archbishop was pleased with the idea and assured the Father, that it met his entire approval. He added that he would mention the matter to Archbishop Kenrick. Everything being satisfactorily arranged, the Fathers purchased a plot of ground on Page Avenue, known as the Foster Place. It was beautifully located and convenient to the city.

There was a handsome residence on the grounds, a great barn, a house for the servants, and a conservatory for flowers.

The little community took possession of Foster Place on November 1st, 1884. Mass was offered for the first time in the chapel of the Retreat on November 10th. One of the Fathers, Gaudentius, was appointed chaplain to the Christian Brothers whose College was nearby. Father Charles as Rector, and Father, Gaudentius, Peter Hanley, Xavier Sutton and Brother John, formed the first Passionist Community in St. Louis. But as the westward movement in the city continued and threatened to disturb the solitude of the Retreat, the Fathers resolved to secure a more suitable place. This they found in Normandy, just outside the city limits. A fine tract of twenty acres was purchased, and the property on Page Avenue was sold. Father Charles, who had in the meantime been occupied in giving missions, among them one very fruitful one in the little parish of Jackson in Southeast Missouri, returned to Hoboken; and Father Felix Ward was made Superior. On January 1st, 1889, the Fathers took charge of the quaintly beautiful Church of St. Anne in Normandy. This church had hitherto been in charge of the Jesuit Fathers who now, with the permission of the Archbishop and the Hunt heirs, courteously and graciously transferred their rights to the Passionists. The people of Normandy were grieved at losing their Jesuit Fathers, but their grief was relieved in a measure, when their departing pastor, Father De Mestre, spoke to them in such a touching manner about those that were to succeed him, as the friends of the Society of Jesus, the sons of St. Paul of the Cross.

On September 24th, 1889, ground was broken for the new Retreat and on November 28th, the corner stone was laid. The ceremony was performed by Rt. Rev. J. J. Hennessey, Bishop of Wichita, the former pastor of St. John's. Father Phelan made an appropriate address. There were present on the occasion, besides Bishop Hennessey, Bishop Glorieux, of Boise, Idaho, Vicars-General Brady and Muehlsiepen, about fifty priests, regular and secular, and a large number of the laity. The contract for the building was given to Mr. William J. Baker. The formal opening of the Retreat of Our Lady of Good Counsel took place on Sunday, June 7th, 1891. Vicar-General Brady was commissioned by the Archbishop to perform the ceremony. Father Peter Hanley was now made Rector of the Retreat. The annual spiritual exercises of the St. Louis Clergy were held at the Passionist Home in October 1891.

Originally this Institution was a Retreat of Monastic Observance where the austere Rule of Life followed by the Passionists was rigorously observed, and where professed students of the Order prepared themselves for ordination. In 1920, however, the Preparatory Seminary was transferred from Cincinnati to Normandy. And now boys seeking admission into the Order are educated here in the preparatory department of ecclesiastical studies, and receive likewise the first training in the life of a Passionist. At present there are in the Community, thirteen Priests; four Brothers; and forty-five Students. The Very Rev. Anselm Secor, C.P., is the first Rector of the Seminary.

Since 1923 a wing has been added to the original building enabling the Fathers to receive more than double the present number of vocations. A beautiful chapel has likewise been built wherein both community and public services are held.

Of the various religious institutions in Normandy attended by the Passionist Fathers, the first mention is due to the "School of the Immaculate Heart" under the management of the Sisters of the Congregation of Our Lady of Charity of the Good Shepherd. This foundation was an offshoot from the Provincial Monastery of the Religious of the Good Shepherd in St. Louis. In September, 1882, the erection of the buildings was begun on a large tract of land donated to the Sisters by Madame R. C. Hunt. On August 26th, 1883, the Institution was formally opened under the title "The Industrial School of the Immaculate Heart of Mary."

On December 16th, 1891, the Institution was incorporated under the new title: "The Catholic Protectorate and Industrial School of St. Louis," which Protectorate was to operate and maintain either in the City or County of St. Louis, or in both, Protectorates for girls and children of the female sex, where such might be shielded from vice, instructed in the branches of common school education and works of industry suited to their age, sex, and condition, under the management of the Religious of the Congregation of Our Lady of Charity of the Good Shepherd.

On the 6th day of October, A. D. 1899, the Corporation name of the Protectorate was changed to that of "School of the Immaculate Heart," Normandy, Mo.

The second institution attended by the Passionists of Normandy is the Orphan Asylum for Colored Children founded in 1897, by the Oblate Sisters of Providence. Since the erection of the German St. Vincent's Orphan Asylum of Normandy the Passionist Fathers have charge of the Community of twenty-eight Sisters of Christian Charity.

The succession of Rectors of the Passionist Retreat embraces the honored names of Fathers Sebastian, Robert, Casimir, Denis and Alfred.

The faculty of the Seminary is made up of priests in the Community. Besides these professors, there reside at the Seminary, the Pastor of St. Ann's Church in Normandy, the chaplains of the local institutions, and missionaries engaged in Apostolic work.[1]

---

[1] Authorities used: Rev. Felix Ward, "The Passionists," Chapter 48, pp. 369-378, and Personal Communications from the Normandy Retreat. There is a very readable article on the Passionists in "Western Watchman," September 4, 1892.

## Chapter 67

# STE. GENEVIEVE COUNTY

The three parishes of Bloomsdale, Lawrenceton and French Village, forming the ragged outline of an isosceles triangle, with its base in Ste. Genevieve County, and its apex in the neighboring County of St. Francois, have at various times been administered as one parochial entity.[1] Bloomsdale was the oldest and most important of the three, being known as early as 1839 under the name La Fourche a Duclos, a name that was dropped in 1874 in favor of the more poetical one of Bloomsdale. The corner stone of the first church in honor of St. Philomena was placed and blessed on June 30th, 1851, by the pastor, the Rev. August Saunier, who had recently been transferred from Westport on the Kansas river to Ste. Genevieve County. In 1858 Father John Anselm was placed in charge of both Bloomsdale and French Village or Little Canada, as it was then called. He had been pastor of Holy Trinity parish for six years previous to his coming to Ste. Genevieve County. Both places remained in his care until 1867, when Father Theodore Kussmann was appointed to St. Anne's of French Village with Bloomsdale as a Mission. This arrangement was continued under Father E. Blume, the successor to Father Kussmann.

On June 4th, 1871 the Lazarist Father, F. M. Donaghoe, laid the corner stone for a new church at French Village, and the following year Father John Daly was appointed rector. Bloomsdale was still an outmission, but not of French Village. A new church had been built at a place called Punjaub, and afterwards Lawrenceton; Vicar-General Muehlsiepen had dedicated it in 1872 in honor of St. Lawrence. The Rev. Peter Moellenbeck was its first pastor. But on November 29th, 1874 the Vicar-General dedicated the new church at French Village. Father Moellenbeck, and after his departure, Father Henry Mehring, pastors of Lawrenceton made regular visits to French Village until 1877. In 1878 both places were occasionally visited from Iron Mountain.

The appointment of Fathers George A. Watson for French Village in 1878, and to Father Michael Walsh for Bloomsdale in 1879, and of Fathers Reding and Grosholz for Lawrenceton served the association of these three churches for a time. Father Watson was succeeded by Father Thomas Moran, and Father Walsh by the Rev. P. A. McNamee

---

1 All the facts of the first half of this chapter are derived from the Chancery Records and from Personal Reminiscences.

(518)

and the Rev. Doctor John H. May, whilst the Rev. M. Grosholz per-servered at his post at Lawrenceton until 1882.

In August 1882, however, the three parishes were once more united under the pastorship of Father Augustine Huettler. Father Huettler took up his residence at Bloomsdale, but visited his two missions of Lawrenceton and French Village in rotation every Sunday morning for the purpose of saying mass and performing the other functions of his pastoral office. After a year of such strenuous missionary labor Father Huettler was appointed assistant to Father Weiss of Ste. Gen-evieve, September 29th, 1883.

On January 11th of the following year the Rev. Peter A. Trumm succeeded Father Huettler at Bloomsdale and continued the visits to Lawrenceton and French Village until September 28th, 1887, when the Rev. Charles L. Van Tourenhout, was put in charge of Lawrenceton with French Village as a mission. French Village remained in this condition of dependence on Lawrenceton under the long succession of pastors, A. H. Schaefer, J. H. Muehlsiepen, H. Minges, Christian H. Schlefers, Henry Fabry, Henry Hassel, and Aloysius J. Reh.

At Bloomsdale the Rev. P. A. Trumm was succeeded in February 20th, 1899 by Father Louis Schathoelter. The succession of Blooms-dale's resident priests since Father S. Kurtenbach's brief pastorate, which ended in January 1895, is as follows: Fathers Michael Helm-bacher; Michael Bush, under whose administration the church of St. Philomena was visited with an interdict; then Rev. John H. Krechter and Rev. Joseph Preuss. In 1898 Bloomsdale parish numbered 673 souls.

The German settlement at New Offenburg, afterwards renamed Zell, was organized as a mission in 1845, when the Lazarist Gandolfo laid the corner stone of its church in honor of St. Joseph. This church, built of stone, was completed and dedicated in 1847. Father Francis X. Weiss served as its pastor from July 1848 to August 1862. The Records show that German Catholics came to Zell from very great distances to receive the sacraments, or to have Baptism administered to their little ones. In 1862 seventy-nine children were baptized by Father Weiss. On his appointment to Riviere aux Vases, which had until 1863 been an outmission of Ste. Genevieve under the title of S. S. Philip and James, the Rev. Theodore Stein was appointed its rector. Under this distinguished priest's administration Vicar-General Muehl-siepen laid the corner stone for the addition to the church. Father Stein was specially noted for his ability in imparting catechetical in-struction. As a preacher also he showed more than ordinary ability and above all, he was a most zealous priest, faithful and true in all things, although the vile tongue of slander took advantage of an act of imprudence to make his stay in the parish unbearable to his sensitive spirit. He retired to his native diocese of Rottenburg in Bavaria. His successor at Zell was the well known Father Henry Pigge, until then, assistant priest to Father Faerber at St. Mary's church, St. Louis. Father Pigge, big, burly man that he was, had a most gentle disposition, and always followed the even tenor of his ways until death called him to his eternal rest. At times he had the care of the neighboring church of Weingarten in addition to his own. The principal fruit of his early labors in Zell was the parochial school. The parish built a combination school and convent for the Sisters of the Precious Blood who arrived from O'Fallon, Mo., in September 1888. Since 1895, however, the school was in charge of the Sisters of the Precious Blood of Ruma, Illinois. In the course of thirty-four years seventeen young ladies of the Parish have entered the Convent.

In the building line the parochial residence falls to the credit of Father Pigge, as well as the tower of the church. The faithful priest died in Easter week, April 21st, 1912. The Highmass on Easter day was his last public function.

After a brief interval, during which Father Adelbert Thum administered the parish until the new pastor, Father Fr. Heimerscheid entered upon his charge. Father Weiss remained at Riviere aux Vases from 1863 to 1865, to become pastor of the mother church of Ste. Genevieve County. The church of Riviere aux Vases, after an interval of three years during which it was attended from New Offenburg, received a pastor of its own once more in 1869. It was the Rev. H. V. Kalmer. After Father Kalmer's two years' administration came the Rev. F. Andres, and a year later in 1871 the Rev. T. Wachter who carried the burden for the better part of four years. Then Father John Wiegers succeeded Father Wachter, and in 1876, Father Joseph Pope, Father Wiegers, and in 1878, Father Joseph Schmidt, Father Pope, and on November 23rd, 1885 Father Frederick G. Holweck, Father Schmidt. From October 22nd, 1886 to February 23rd, 1887 Father John Rothensteiner acted as substitute of Father Holweck during his absence on his first trip to Europe. Father Frederick H. Schulte received the reins of government out of Father Holweck's willing hands on July 1st, 1888, and transmitted them to Father Herman Wagener in October 1892. Father A. H. Schaefer, who came to Bloomsdale on March 1st, 1894, accepted the upbuilding of the parish of S. S. Philip and James as his life work. For the Church of Bloomsdale alone he lived and at Bloomsdale he died. In the meantime Father Francis Weiss had erected his new church of Ste. Genevieve, partly on the foundation of the stone structure of Father Francis X. Dahmen's day, and had it dedicated on September 29th, 1880. Up to this time he had done all the work single-handed. But feeling that old age was creeping up, he concluded to ask for an assistant, and his choice fell on his Fellow-Alsatian, the young and energetic Father Augustin Henry Julian Huettler. Born November 19th, 1857 at Colmar, a former imperial city but then under French rule, the young Augustine, full of energy and romantic dreams, attended the schools of his native city and of Strassburg, and came to America in May 1881. After passing a year at the Salesianum near Milwaukee making his final preparation for the ministry, he was ordained for the archdiocese of St. Louis by the Venerable Archbishop of Milwaukee, Michael Heiss, on June 25th, 1882. A little more than a year after his ordination Father Huettler was appointed assistant to Father Weiss of Ste. Genevieve.

Gifted with a keen incisive intellect and always ready for an argument on any possible subject: endowed likewise with distinguished oratorical ability, using with almost equal power and fluency the three languages of Ste. Genevieve County, French, German and English, and above all, imbued with the simple Catholic faith of his people, the young priest easily won the respect and affection of all. His practical interest in local politics may, at times, have estranged some of his people from him. But, as he never showed resentment, his own faults were quickly forgotten. He may have expected that Father Weiss would, in the course of time, resign the honor and burden of the pastorship in his favor. Certain it is, that Father Weiss did intend to do so about 1887, but was prevailed upon by his friends to change his purpose, or perhaps, rescind his act. Father Huettler on June 22nd, 1887 asked for his own transfer to the vacant parish of Maria Weingarten; the seventh in the order of filiation from the mother church of Ste. Genevieve. The Church of Our Lady, Help of Christians at what was originally called "Maria Weingarten," Mary's Vineyard, was founded in 1872, though the church building, a fine spacious structure of stone, was not completed until 1874. The parish numbered eighty families, all of German descent. At first they received occasional visits from some Franciscan Fathers. At last they received a resident priest, Father Sebastian Sennerich, who on December 16th, preached his first sermon. Father Sennerich, was a native of Baden, born February 11th, 1845, and ordained in Freiburg, May 20th, 1875, for the archdiocese of St. Louis. Weingarten was his first appointment. After laboring faithfully for eight years in consolidating the new congregation, he entered Cape Girardeau College for the purpose of learning English. But his perseverance did not correspond with his spirit of enterprize. On May 4th, 1883, he took the place of Father

Rensman at Portage, during that Reverend gentleman's sickness. The forsaken parish of Maria Weingarten, however, after some brief attempts by several priests like Fathers Diel, Schaeffer and Trumm was assigned to Father Huettler, September 28th, 1887. About six years later Father Huettler obtained leave of absence for a journey home, but returning in September 1893, he took up the duties once more as pastor of Weingarten. Father Huettler succeeded in establishing a school at Weingarten, taught by lay teachers. The parish residence was enlarged, a pipe organ was installed in the church, and stained glass windows were bought. The church choir was reorganized, the devotion of the Forty Hours was introduced, and a lively interest was cultivated in parish and county affairs. On June 15th, 1896 Father Huettler was promoted to the Church of the Holy Ghost in St. Louis.

Father Huettler's successor at Weingarten was the Rev. John Henry Muehlsiepen, who spent there more than sixteen years of quiet priestly labor and rare success.

After Father Huettler's departure from Ste. Genevieve and the very time of his appointment to Weingarten, Father Weiss received as his assistants the Rev. J. A. Schultz, and in June 1888 the Rev. F. X. Gnielinski. On January 5th, 1889, however, came the priest who was to rival Father Huettler in the affectionate regard of his people and eventually to succeed good old Father Weiss in the pastorate of Ste. Genevieve, Father Charles Lewis Van Tourenhout a native of S. S. Peter and Paul's Parish, St. Louis. His appointment as assistant to Father Weiss was dated January 5th, 1889. Father Weiss, in his simple, dignified, and beautiful old age, placed a good part of the administrative work of the parish in Father Van Tourenhout's able hands. It was mainly through the latter's energy that, in 1895 the new school house was erected, thereby giving the entire convent as a residence for the Sisters, and the rock building as the exclusive residence for the priests.

The preliminary arrangements for the venture, however, were made by the pastor in 1890, as the following letter from St. Joseph's Convent South St. Louis, dated July 5th, 1890 would show:
"Reverend and dear Father Weiss:

We ought to have written you more promptly in reference to the subject treated of between us while at Ste. Genevieve: but the matter had to be brought before the Council of the Community which necessarily occasioned some delay.

"I am now authorized to say, that the Community is willing to give you as much ground for your school building and school-yards as may be needed, for the sole consideration of being released from the obligation put upon us by the donation of Mr. and Mrs. Valle. We would then, of course, expect a salary for each teacher, as this would be the only means of support to the Community and to keep up the necessary repairs of the place.

"We went to see His Grace, the Archbishop, to obtain his sanc. tion for this transaction, but found he had just left the city. We have, however, not the slightest doubt but he will consent to our project.

"Rev. Mother Agatha, Mother St. John, and your humble cor. respondent, beg to present their best respects and good wishes for the happy success of your proposed honorable undertaking and earnestly commend themselves and Community to your holy prayers."[2]

The obligation imposed upon the Sisters of St. Joseph by the dona. tion of Felix Valle, amounting to $7,500., were the free services "of three able teachers for the parochial school of Ste. Genevieve, one for the boys under twelve years, and two for the girls. The considera. tion offered Father Weiss for their release from these obligations, was "as much ground for your school-building and school-yards as may be needed." Now, as the new Parochial School adjoins the Sisters Con. vent and stands on ground that formerly belonged to them, this offer must have been accepted. Father Van Tourenhout's next great con. cern was the Golden Jubilee of his Pastor. The day for the Jubilee services was set for Wednesday, April 27th, 1898. It was to be the grandest spectacle Ste. Genevieve had ever witnessed, being the first Golden Jubilee ever celebrated publicly by a priest of the Arch. diocese. The town was crowded with visitors from far and near. Every house was decorated, and joy reigned supreme. Wednesday morning Solemn High Mass was celebrated by the Venerable Pastor in the presence of His Grace, Archbishop Kain, of St. Louis, Rev. Fathers Schaefer of River aux Vases and Wagner of St. Mary's were deacon and subdeacon respectively. Sermons were delivered in French by Rev. A. J. Huettler, in English by Rev. Charles Ziegler, and in German by Rev. F. Goller, all of St. Louis. At one o'clock P. M., the banquet was served at the School Hall to the clergy; and at eight o'clock in the evening the festivities ended with a grand torchlight procession, about five blocks in length, the largest thing of the kind ever witnessed in Ste. Genevieve.[3]

---

2  Archives of the Church of Ste. Genevieve.

3  "Fair Play," of Ste. Genevieve, April 30, 1898. "Ste. Genevieve Herald." "St. Louis Republic," April 26.

The Jubilee was over, and the recipient of such honors was almost ready to resign in favor of his efficient assistant. On August 19th, 1900 the Board of Trustees made this step possible by voting an annuity of $600. to the pastor emeritus, assuring him of the continued love, reverence, and devotion of the parish, and expressing the hope that the balance of his life might be spent among them with that tranquillity, contentment and happiness, which his long and faithful services so richly merited.

Father Van Tourenhout was now pastor of Ste. Genevieve. One year after the change, Father Weiss sickened and died; March 3rd, 1901. His earthly remains were laid to rest in the Valle Spring Cemetery at Ste. Genevieve. His name and his fame remain among the proudest possessions of the people of Ste. Genevieve County.

## Chapter 68

LATER DEVELOPMENTS IN JEFFERSON AND ST. FRANCOIS
COUNTIES

When in the early fifties the construction of the St. Louis-Iron
Mountain Railroad was proceeding its feverish way a number of new
towns sprang up, and old ones were resurrected along the road or
within easy reach of it, the chief among them being De Soto in Jefferson County.   Herculaneum, the ancient shipping place for the lead
mines in the vicinity, and the proud possessor of the first shot tower
ever operated in the Mississippi Valley, had long ago lost its trade to
Selma and Rush-Tower farther down the Mississippi River, and its
early political distinction of being the county seat of Jefferson County,
to Hillsboro, the former Monticello.   Hillsboro itself remained in
dreamy seclusion, as also did Maxville on the Meramec.

De Soto's first building was erected in 1885 and the town of
De Soto was incorporated in 1857.   The population in 1861 did not
exceed two hundred souls.   But when the Railroad Company placed its
machine shops in the valley of the Joachim Creek, the town began to
prosper, especially since 1883.   The residence part of De Soto is on
the heights overlooking the busy scene in the Valley.   As most of the
laborers on the Railroad were Irish Catholics, Father James Fox of
Old Mines, Father Lewis Tucker of Fredericktown, and others visited
their camps to bring them spiritual succor and consolation.   When
De Soto became an established town its Catholic Congregation was
placed in charge of Father Theodore Kussman of French Village in
the neighboring County of St. Francois.   But in 1870 De Soto was
established as a parish under the patronage of St. Rose of Lima with
Father Patrick T. Ring in charge.   Father Ring had been rector of
St. John's Church in St. Louis from 1861 to 1868 but could not hold
his position in that important and laborious charge, as his nervous
system was wrecked by an awful experience at sea when the ship on
which he travelled was burnt, and he and his companions of the
voyage were saved in the last extremity.   Father Ring's death occurred
at the Mullanphy Hospital on February 7, 1887, where he had served
as chaplain since 1881.

On September 21st, 1881 the parish of St. Rose was intrusted
to the energetic but somewhat erratic Father Cornelius Francis O'Leary.
Father O'Leary left his native County Kerry in Ireland for the mission
in America at the age of seventeen.   He made his studies at St. Vincent's
Seminary, Cape Girardeau and was ordained on May 22nd, 1873.   After

having proved his capacity for church building by erecting the Church of St. Brendan in Mexico and several others, he was appointed to the struggling parish of De Soto to repeat, or even to excel, his former efforts. Father O'Leary accomplished what was expected of him.

The beautiful Gothic structure of stone that crowns the height above the southern part of the city of De Soto, is his work and monument. But the expense incurred was a heavy burden, and as the parish was unable to meet the full obligation, Father O'Leary made use of the lecture platform to help along the good cause. He had accumulated a vast store of desultory knowledge, which he used with care and elegance in defending the doctrines and practices of the Church, as well as the cause of Ireland's liberation. It is regretable that the peculiarities of his temperament, his lack of prudence, his gift, if gift it be, of quick caustic retort, and above all, his habit of universal criticism should have accompanied him all through life, and made him many enemies and detractors. "No sphere not state was immune from his censorship," said one who knew and loved him well. Yet, there was no malice or envy in his make-up. He loved truth, and would never minimize it. He saw many things that he thought needed correction and, as he never shirked a duty, he was often in contention, and rarely yielded his position. The fact is, he felt himself out of sympathy with the tendencies of the age, and he struggled valiantly, but in vain, to set things aright. During the railroad strike of 1886 his imprudence in speech brought the threat of an early removal of the machine shops from De Soto. This led to his transfer to Webster Groves in October 1886. On March 16th, 1887, he left the diocese, and his name no longer appeared in the Directory: On January 3rd, of the following he is readmitted and begins his six years' service as assistant or perhaps as guest at several St. Louis Churches. On February 5th, 1896, Father O'Leary was made pastor of Bonneterre, but on July 12th, of the following year he asked for his exeat to go to Ireland. In January 1898, however, he returned and on June 1st, 1902, was commissioned by Archbishop Glennon to found the parish of Notre Dame de Lourdes in Wellston. Here he built a frame church and a brick school house and laid plans for a permanent church. But on May 30th, 1917, when a tornado wrecked the railroad station at Mineral Point, Missouri, where he, with a number of other priests, were awaiting the train from St. Louis, Father O'Leary was seriously injured, and after lingering for more than a month, died on July 17th, 1917.[1]

Father O'Leary had the future Vicar-General of the archdiocese, Father Joseph Aloyosius Connolly, for his successor at De Soto, on November 3rd, 1886. Father Connolly was the very soul of order and

---

[1] Father Patrick Dooley's Funeral Sermon and Chancery Records.

promptitude. The thorough organization of the parish of St. Rose of Lima at De Soto was his work. He established the school with the Ursuline Nuns in charge. And he paid the debt still resting on the Congregation. In consequence he was promoted to the more important charge of St. Teresa's in St. Louis, and the Rev. William Noonan became his successor, at De Soto, September 1st, 1892. Toward the end of Father Noonan's rectorship at De Soto, the parish had become so strong financially that Archbishop Kain considered it worthy of being governed by a permanent rector: Father Noonan accordingly became what is usually called an "irremovable rector." When he died in 1910, the place had to be filled by Concursus. Father Peter Joseph Byrne, whom Archbishop Kain had brought along from Ireland in 1893, and whom he had made his Secretary, was the successful candidate. Father Byrne took charge of his irremoveable rectorship in 1910. His death occurred unexpectedly on Thursday, November 13th, 1919, in New York City, where he had arrived two days before from a visit to Ireland.

The recent pastors of St. Rose of Lima Parish in De Soto were the Revs. Joseph P. Newman and Edward A. Rogers.

A short distance south of De Soto the railroad makes a detour from the airline into Washington County along the old mining towns, of which we have already written, and on bending eastward again, strikes the town of Delassus, which is the point of departure for the city of Farmington in St. Francois County, although that city now has also a station of the Frisco line.

The Church of Farmington, at present so strong and prosperous, had a rather checkered career since 1869, when three lots on the outskirts of the town were acquired by the few Catholics residing in the vicinity. As a mission it was attended from 1873 to 1875 from French Village; from 1875 to 1879 from Iron Mountain; from 1880 to 1883 from St. Joe Mines and from 1883 to 1889 again from Iron Mountain. In 1890 the parish received Father H. J. Shaw as its first rector. The church, a small frame structure, was dedicated to St. Joseph.

The series of pastors since 1892 was as follows: Rev. John N. Kern to July 1893; Rev. Arthur F. O'Reilly to August 1897; Rev. J. J. Toomey till April 21st, 1906. Father James Toomey was a native of County Limerick, Ireland, and received his education at Carlow and Paris. He became a Christian Brother, taught in Ireland and in Montreal, Canada, and there studied for the priesthood. As Pastor of Farmington he at once opened a school in the sacristy of his church.

In September 1903 he built the new school house and introduced the Dominican Sisters as teachers. When these Sisters retired from the place, Father Toomey taught school himself for two years. He died at Farmington on April 21st, 1906.

Father Bernard Stolte continued the excellent work of Father Toomey until October 1907. It was Father Joseph A. Collins, that built, the present beautiful Romanesque church with campanile in rear, adjoining the sanctuary. He also introduced the Ursuline Sisters for his school.

The present pastor is the Rev. F. H. Skaer.

Bismark, a little railroad town at the juncture of the main line and the Belmont Branch of the Iron Mountain Railroad, has a small Catholic Congregation, which worships in an humble nameless frame church. The place never had a resident priest, but was attended from 1879 to 1893 from Iron Mountain and, after the latter date until 1908, from Farmington.

The mission of Doe Run organized from Farmington in 1889 and dedicated to St. Francis Xavier is still a dependency of that parish.

The State Hospital No. 4 for the Insane and the St. Francois County Poor Farm are in charge of the Pastor of Farmington, who says mass occasionally at both places. Libertyville, and Knob Lick have a few scattered Catholics.

The parish of Bonneterre, St. Francois County was organized in 1872. It was dedicated to St. Joseph. From its foundation to 1879 it was a dependency of Old Mines. It became a parish on November 24th, 1879, the Rev. E. J. Dempsey being appointed its first rector. From September 14th, 1881, till October 1888, Rev. Michael Walsh served as pastor, and was succeeded on January 20th, 1889 by Rev. P. O'Donohoe. In May 1892 Rev. H. J. Shaw arrived and remained until February 1896.

From February 1896 to July 1897 Father C. F. O'Leary was pastor of St. Joseph's. Then Rev. C. M. Canning, a recent arrival from Ireland, held the reins until October 3rd, 1905, when Father M. T. Sevcik began his very efficient administration. The present pastor is the Rev. S. W. Brinkman; Father John Simon Moser is his assistant. The parish of St. Joseph, Bonneterre, has a parochial school with 181 pupils, taught by four Ursuline Sisters. The priests also attend the mission of Leadwood, founded 1906, which was formerly attended from Owensville.

The true mother of churches in St. Francois County is neither Farmington nor Bonneterre, but the little Church of St. Anne at French Village.

Little Canada or French Village, received its first resident priest in the person of the Rev. John Anselm. He had been pastor of Holy Trinity Church in St. Louis for six years previous. Both St. Anne's Church in Little Canada and St. Philomena's Church at Bloomsdale remained in his care until 1867, when Father Theodore Kussmann was appointed to St. Anne's of French Village, with Bloomsdale as a mission. This arrangement was continued under Father Blume, the successor of Rev. Kussmann. On June 4th, 1871 the Lazarist Father T. M. Donaghoe laid the corner stone for a new church at French Village. In the following year, Father John Daly was appointed rector of French Village, whilst Bloomsdale remained an outmission, no longer of French Village, however, but of the new parish called Punjaub or Lawrenceton, where the church had been blessed by Vicar-General Muehlsiepen in 1872. Father Peter Moellenbeck was its first pastor.

French Village was now a full fledged Parish, with Father John Daly, as its rector for the next two years. The church was not completed until November 9th, 1874, when Vicar-General Muehlsiepen blessed it with the usual ceremonies. In 1878 the place was attended from Iron Mountain. In 1878 the Rev. George A. Watson was appointed to the rectorship. Father Watson is still remembered by the older people as a man of kindly disposition and good humor, whose whimsical delight in teasing everybody he met, friend or casual acquaintance or even stranger, made many go out of their way to escape his sallies. His faith was strong and simple and childlike. He was a saintly priest and confessor. In 1880 he was succeeded by the Rev. Thomas Moran.

After June 20th, 1881, Bonneterre, Bloomsdale and Lawrenceton were successively in charge of this "ancient haunt of peace," and in charge of Lawrenceton it still remains. In 1847 it had only forty-five Catholic and twelve mixed families, fifty-seven in all.

Valle's Mines was visited for church services by the Lazarist Fathers from Old Mines. The place had no church building: mass was said in private houses where the neighbors were gathered. From 1843 to 1845 Father Wiseman, a learned writer of books, came to Valle's Mine a few times a year from his parish at Richwoods. After 1850 the place no longer finds mention in the Church Records. The Congregation was absorbed by the Parish of Desloge which was organ-ized as a mission in 1900 and received a resident pastor in 1903 in the person of Father James Sheil. Father Sheil, an Irishman by birth, was well liked by the people, although he was very frank and outspoken, in the pulpit as well as in private conversation.

The Church of Desloge was dedicated to the Blessed Virgin under the glorious title of the Immaculate Conception. In February 1904 Father Joseph Casey had succeeded to the pastorate. Since 1905 there is at Desloge a small Congregation of Catholics of the Greek Ruthenian rite, which at first was attended by the Rev. Czaplinski. They are not properly of the diocese of St. Louis, but have a Bishop of their own, who is in communion with Rome.

The town of Herculaneum was founded in 1808, and the first Post Office in Jefferson County was established within its limits in 1843. In that year the Rev. pastor of Gravois, that is, Kirkwood, Father Peter Fischer, visited the Catholics of the place, until the opening of the Twentieth Century, when Father M. T. Sevcik organized a Congregation in April 1916, and then turned it over to the Rev. L. W. Brinkmann as pastor. War-time requirements brought new life to Herculaneum. A combination church and hall was dedicated under the title of the Assumption of the Blessed Virgin Mary, by Archbishop Glennon on December 8th, 1916. The school opened in Fall 1917 with two lay-teachers in charge. The parish numbered about one hundred and ten families, mostly of French descent, of whom only forty-five remain. The entire town, with the exception of the Church grounds, is owned by the St. Joseph Lead Co. Father Joseph McGinly is the present rector.

The mission Church of the Assumption at Hillsboro had its corner stone laid by Vicar-General Patrick J. Ryan, on May 16, 1869, and the completed structure blessed by the same dignitary on July 2nd, 1871. It was attended from De Soto until 1888. After that date the church was closed and sold.

The 21st day of May 1877, witnessed the blessing of the new St. Joseph Church at Kimmswick by Vicar-General Henry Muehlsiepen: The Congregation seems to have been organized by the Franciscan Fathers, who were in charge of it until 1889, when it passed over to the care of the pastor of Festus, the Rev. Francis Boehm. Father Ruesse from S.S. Peter and Paul in St. Louis visited the place once a month in 1892 and 1893. Then priestly visits were made from Maxville until on October 3rd, 1905, Father Edmund F. Salland received the appointment as first pastor of St. Joseph's Church in Kimmswick. Father Salland in 1927 built a new church and was, even before its dedication, transferred to the neighboring church of Maxville.

The last of the churches of Jefferson County to find a place in this chapter is that of the Sacred Heart at Festus. The church was built in 1881 on a lot purchased on February 22nd of the same year. Rev. Dr. May was its first rector. Father John L. Gadell succeeded Dr. May on October 4th, 1884 and remained until April 1885, when Rev. Francis Boehm was sent to assume charge.

Father Boehm had the Rev. Victor Stepka as successor. In April 1904 Father Adolph Holtschneider entered upon his long and eventful course of pastoral labor and building operations of which the fine new Church of the Sacred Heart is the most notable result. Festus is now one of the really flourishing parishes, possessing all things that pertain to a parish. The school is taught by six Ursuline Nuns and two lay-teachers. It has an attendance of 430 pupils.[2]

---

[2] Chancery Records.

There remain a few parishes of this period situated in St. Louis County, which may find a place in this connection, as they did not originate by filiation from any city parish but rather from one or the other older establishments in the County. Some had corporate existence before the advent of Archbishop Kain, yet as all of them enjoyed their greatest prosperity under his regime they will be fitly treated here:

The oldest of these parishes is St. Monica, Creve Coeur.

Prior to the year 1872 the few Catholic families that lived in the district known as Creve Coeur attended Holy Mass at St. Joseph Church, Manchester, Missouri.

Very Rev. H. Muehlsiepen, then Vicar-General of the St. Louis Archdiocese, soon took a lively interest in their spiritual welfare, occasionally said Mass for them in various farm houses, and finally induced the Franciscan Fathers of the St. Louis Province to look after their spiritual wants.

Rev. Chrysostom Beineke, O.F.M., was appointed pastor, organized the parish and built a church on a plot of ground that had been donated by the Emerson family. An altar was improvised in the so-called Lake House on the Olive Street Road, and Father Chrysostom celebrated Holy Mass for his little flock twice a month.

On the 4th of October 1872, the new church, a brick structure, was dedicated by Very Rev. H. Muehlsiepen, V.G., and placed under the patronage of St. Monica.

Subsequently St. Monica's parish, which at that time numbered about sixty families, was attended from the Franciscan Monastery, St. Louis.

Rev. Joseph Diel was the first resident pastor. After a stay of five months he was succeeded by Rev. Aertker, who built the priest's house (now Sisters' residence) and labored there until the year 1885.

In 1885 Rev. Charles Brockmeier took charge. He soon happily succeeded in implanting new life in the parish, built the present handsome church, commodious priest's residence, and converted the old church into a school. On the fifth day of May, 1888, the corner stone of the new church was laid by Very Rev. H. Muehlsiepen, V.G., in the presence of twenty-two priests and about 3000 lay-people. In 1894 Father Brockmeier left for a climate more congenial to his health and became pastor of St. Francis of Assisi Church, New Orleans, La.

From 1894 to 1922 the following Rev. Fathers have labored during their respective terms, for the spiritual and material welfare of St. Monica's parish: Rev. J. S. Strombergen, 1895, about four months; Rev. M. Grosholz 1895, about eight months; Rev. J. F. Reuther, 1895-

1898; Rev. H. Thobe, 1898, about six months; Rev. H. Minges, 1899-1908; Rev. A. J. Happe, 1908-1916. The present incumbent, Rev. J. F. Hoeschen has been in charge since July, 1916.

In 1918 the old school was wrecked and replaced by a modern, up-to-date building at a cost of approximately $20,000. The school is in charge of the Ursuline sisters and attended by eighty-one pupils.

The parish of St. John and St. James, at Ferguson, in St. Louis County was organized in October 1881 by Father David S. Phelan. The first church in the place was dedicated by Archbishop Ryan. A new church of granite is now building: the basement was dedicated December 8th, 1918. The new school built of granite was opened November 1925. It is in charge of the Sisters of St. Joseph. At the time of its organization, the parish numbered ten families: it now has two hundred: Father Phelan attended the place for twenty-five years. He was succeeded by Father Vincent McCartney. Since May 11th, 1911, the Rev. J. J. Godfrey has pastoral charge.

The parish of Our Holy Redeemer in Webster Groves dates from October 1886. Father Cornelius O'Leary was its founder and first pastor. In March 1887 the Rev. P. J. Kane was appointed in his place. The first church, built by Father Kane, was blessed by Vicar-General Brady, June 19th, 1887. The second house of worship, an all-rock structure, was built during the period 1895 to 1897. It was dedicated by Archbishop Kain, May 2nd, 1897.

At first the parish numbered only one hundred and forty souls, Irish and German.

But in 1896 the Germans formed a parish of their own and named it St. Michael's, Shrewsburg. Three other parishes were formed, at least in part, out of the territory of Our Holy Redeemer's: the Immaculate Conception, Maplewood, St. Mary Magdalen's, Brentwood; and Mary Queen of Peace, Glendale. Father P. J. Dooley succeeded to the pastorate October 15th, 1925.

The School is in charge of four Dominican Sisters, and numbers one hundred and seventy pupils.

## CHAPTER 69

## THE CHURCH IN THE INTERIOR OF SOUTHEAST MISSOURI

It is a noteworthy fact that the final advance of the Church into the heart of southern Missouri followed three concentric movements, from New Madrid in the East, from Doniphan in Father Hogan's ''Irish Wilderness,'' in the West, and from Iron Mountain and Arcadia in the North. None of these points of vantage possessed strong Catholic organizations; but their spiritual leaders had the spirit of faith and the zeal for souls, that would not bow to adverse circumstances.

At the erection of the diocese of Kansas City, the western boundary of the Archdiocese of St. Louis was drawn along the western limits of the counties of Cole, Maries, Pulaski, Texas and Howell. Of these counties Cole and Maries belonged to the Jesuit sphere of influence, and have therefore been treated separately. Pulaski and Texas, as well as the adjoining counties of Dent, and Shannon and Carter, are still abiding in the darkness, or possibly in the twilight, as regards the Faith. But a great amount of evangelization and organization has been accomplished in regions that were utterly unknown to Archbishop Kenrick in the early years of his administration.[1]

It is true that the material results attained by these missionaries, the property acquired, and the buildings erected, were not, as a rule, of magnificent proportions. The early churches were, for the most part, rude log or frame structures costing but a few hundred dollars. But these humble beginnings were due, not to the lack of generosity, but rather to the lack of means in the early settlers. And in spite of its poverty, the little church was the house of God to the faithful round about, it offered them every spiritual union, elevation and comfort that the grandest Cathedral could afford; it was their visible bond of union with the Church universal. It would have been seriously and sincerely missed, if it had been destroyed by the rude elements or the ruder hand of man, as it sometimes happened: and even when, through age and decay, it was found inadequate for their needs, it retained its place among their treasured memories.

In opening the view of this widespread panorama it seems to be eminently proper to start with the record of the slow but steady advance of the Church in the great swamp region of Southeastern Missouri, New Madrid, Pemiscot, Dunklin and Butler Counties. The rich alluvial soil has always attracted settlers, wherever the land rose

---

[1] All data given in this chapter are derived from the Chancery Records of the Archdiocese, and the Questionnaire-Reports from the various pastors.

above the waters of the spring tide. But the usual penalties of low-land regions, malarial fever and the plague of mosquitoes, prevented a more rapid growth of population. The extensive system of drainage has, however, wrought a wonderful change and promises to make the former swamp lands the garden spot of Missouri.

But the beginnings of the Church in this favored land of corn and cotton date back to the Spanish regime under which the town of New Madrid and its parish of St. Isidore were founded. In a previous chapter an account of the earlier vicissitudes of New Madrid and its dependencies has been given. We now turn to their later affairs.

Father Heim's departure from New Madrid in 1842, was a real calamity, in as far as three long years had to pass, ere another priest was sent there, the well-remembered Father Lewis Tucker, grandson of Joseph Tucker, the earliest Catholic settler of Perry County, Mo. Having been raised to the priesthood in the Cathedral of St. Louis by Bishop Rosati, September 21st, 1835, Father Tucker received his first appointment to St. Michael's, now Fredericktown, and then to Potosi. At New Madrid he remained from February 18th, 1845 to October 15th, of the same year, a period of eight months. The young priest's health began to fail, and he was appointed pastor of his first mission, St. Michael's, where he remained until his death, November 30th, 1880.

After an interval of two years, during which the Lazarist Father Louis Scaphi served as pastor of the place, the Rev. Aloysius Rosi was appointed to New Madrid and remained for one year, 1848-1849. Father Rosi has become a legendary personage in Ste. Genevieve County, probably owing to his having lost his life by drowning, on the occasion of a sick call. He is buried in the Church of Bloomsdale. Father Rosi found no immediate successor at New Madrid. For the period of a year the pastor of Benton, Scott County, paid occasional visits to the place. But from 1850-1851, Father John Hennessey, the future Arch-bishop of Dubuque, filled the position, to be succeeded in 1851, by the Rev. F. B. Jamison, 1851-1853. In November 1853, Rev. Jamison was suspended. Again there is an interval of half a year, to be broken by Father Simon Grugau in 1854. Then comes the brief pastorship of Rev. James Murphy, and another sad vacancy from 1856-1857. The years 1857 and 1858, are marked by the pastoral efforts of Father Julian Turmel, and then, from 1859 to 1867, New Madrid is dependent for spiritual ministrations on the occasional visits of missionary priests.

These years are marked by the great Civil War, that was especially harrassing and destructive on the border between North and South. Some of the important battles of the Civil War were fought in the vicinity of New Madrid. The old Church of St. John was consumed by fire within this period. A good part of the records were lost with the church or even at an earlier date. Father Francis McKenna, born August 15th, 1832, ordained May 30th, 1867, became pastor of New Madrid almost on the day of his ordination in 1867. He remained in charge until 1869. His administration is noteworthy through the fact that it saw a new church arise under the new title of The Immaculate Conception. The Church Records of New Madrid state that the edifice was dedicated on the 9th day of May, 1869, by the Reverend John F. McGerry, C.M., at the request of the pastor Father McKenna. The attendants of the solemnities were Fathers A. Nerrina, C.M., and Francis O'Brien. In 1869, Father McKenna was appointed to the parish of Mexico, and in 1873, to that of Moberly, where he died in 1892.

From 1870-1872, New Madrid had as its pastor Rev. Philip Patrick Brady, who in the course of time became Vicar-General to Archbishop Kenrick, and died as Pastor of St. John's Pro-Cathedral, in St. Louis, March 6th, 1893.

Father Edward Smith was pastor of New Madrid from 1872 to 1874, and after a few years interval during which the parish was attended from Charleston, and the church building itself had to be dragged away from the river bank to save it from the waters of the Mississippi (1875). New Madrid received its most zealous and successful pastor since the days of Father Ambrose Heim, in the person of Joseph Aloysius Connolly, our late lamented Vicar-General. Ordained June 18th, 1878, Father Connolly became pastor of New Madrid in the very year of his ordination and remained at his post of duty until May 1st, 1882. We found a characteristic letter of the youthful Pastor among the treasures of our Archives and, as a beautiful monument to the zeal and staying qualities of our dead Monsignor, we will reprint its main items. It is dated January 9th, 1881. After stating that he visited Caruthersville, and Center, in Pemiscot County, and Osceola in the State of Arkansas, he writes:

"Last Monday I opened a parochial school, which may be termed a 'Catholic free school.' The children receive their instruction free. The parents paying only for seats and desks. None but Catholic children received. Would I receive all applicants and demand a monthly fee, I would have more children under me than I could well find room for. In the course of time I expect we will be able to build a small school house, when all children will be received and charged for, but all under the regular Catholic school discipline. After long deliberation I concluded to adopt the present plan, believing it would, in a year or so, be productive of much good, and a Catholic school a fixity in New Madrid, so long as a priest will be left here, which I trust will be always. At present I will offer no objection if I be the one. To attempt a regular parochial school at present would be a failure, but this·being carried on as I have commenced will lead only to permanent results. All the Catholic children in town, but five, have been attending—the latter's excuse being distance,—though some living five times the distance were in attendance.

"As it would be rather long to wait till I should get to St. Louis to confer about the records of this church, I think it better to write you all that is attainable. The old church was destroyed during the war, and part of the records lost then, or before. There are but three old books, and the fragments of a fourth; this is the marriage register. The oldest record is that of baptisms, commencing "Die 24 Martii, 1821," "Franciscus Cellini, P.C.M." From April 1821 to "le 7 Septembre, 1832, P. Paillasson," there is no record. Father Paillasson's records extend to June 18th, '36, after which I find the following names J. Bouillier, C.M., J. M. Odin, C.M., J. M. Simonin, C.M., B. Rolando, C.M., Hippolitus Gandolfo, C.M., to December 1837, when Father A. J. Heim assumed charge. He remained here until—at least the last register entry is "twelfth of May, 1844." After him I find, from "third of November 1844" to "first of November 1845," "L. Tucker, P.P." Then follow several Lazarists.

I have been able to find only a few fragments of the marriage register, 1821, a few 1835, '40 '46, etc. All thus far, except Father Tucker's, were transcribed by Father Scafi, C.M., "to 15 of November 1847," so that many records must have been lost, or very few marriages performed, as the first is in 1821, the next being second on same page, is in 1834. I have collected the fragments, sewn them together, and put them in a book, several marriages have been recorded on the same page as baptisms i.e. a baptism or two, then a marriage or so, and thus for several pages. Our present register will contain all baptisms and marriages for the next fifty years unless there be a great change in this part of the world."

Father Connolly's hopes in regard to a permanent parochial school in New Madrid were realized: and the parish has had a resident priest ever since except for a period of two years, 1884-1886, and again from 1888-1889, when it was attended from Charleston. The succession of pastors was as follows:

Patrick McNamee, 1882-1884.

Hugh O'Reilly, October 15, 1884 to November 15, 1885. From that date on, Father O'Reilly resided in Charleston, and from there attended New Madrid until 1886.

Philip Joseph Carroll, June 16, 1886, to September 28, 1887.

Edward Smith, February 15, 1888, to April 13, 1888.

Thomas Edward Gallaher, for one month in 1889. Taking sick with fever he asked to return to Old Mines where he remained until 1893.

James Joseph Furlong, became pastor of New Madrid October 7, 1889, and remained until June 11th, 1908, almost nineteen years, during which time he built a number of churches in the little mission stations of New Madrid and adjoining Counties; at Caruthersville, Portageville, East Prairie and Malden. In the city of New Madrid Father Furlong established the Parochial School under the management of the Benedictine Sisters. At present, the Sisters of Loretto are in charge. In October, 1905, Father Furlong received an assistant in the person of Rev. C. J. Kane. Father Furlong died as Pastor of St. Mary and Joseph Church in Carondelet, October 15, 1913. He was a most humble, kind and considerate man, and shrewd withal in business matters, but towards the end, rather negligent of his personal appearance.

The inward growth and outward development of New Madrid and its dependencies since the departure of Father Furlong is too recent for historical treatment. We would but mention the names of his successors, the Fathers M. J. Taylor, D. W. Clark, and D. J. Ryan. The first of the three, Father M. J. Taylor, built the present church edifice in the city of New Madrid in 1911.

But it must be remembered that at least three of the former missionary stations attended by Father Furlong, Caruthersville, Portageville and Malden, are now well-appointed parishes, with resident pastors, and all the appurtenances of modern religious centers. The seed. of God's word could not be destroyed by the fury of the elements, nor by the malice of the wicked, or the shortcomings of the good.

The parish of Caruthersville is the development of former dependency of New Madrid at Little Prairie in Pemiscot County. As early as the days of Father Gibault religious services were held here. Before the great earthquake of 1811 to 1812, Little Prairie contained two hundred families, mostly French and Catholic. But after the earthquake the whole country was depopulated; Many of the former inhabitants never returned to their lands: As Flint says: "The aspect of Little Prairie was one of decay, desolation and desertion." In 1815, Congress passed an Act by which landholders in New Madrid district were permitted to exchange their present holdings in the ravaged district for public lands. The exact location of the ancient village of Little Prairie was found by Nuttall below Point Pleasant, but there was only a single house remaining.

In 1840, Rev. Ambrose Heim reports that he has made all arrangements for a new chapel at Point Pleasant six miles from New Madrid on the Mississippi. There was a chapel there in 1847, when the Lazarist Fathers Scaphi and Rossi visited the place. By 1890, the church had disappeared, its twelve souls having been added to the membership of New Madrid parish: since March 24th, 1905, it figures as a mission of Portageville. In Father Heim's day, the church at Portageville in Pemiscot County, was known as St. Philips. It was no longer in existence in 1890; but regular services were held at the place by priests from New Madrid. Father James Furlong built the church and named it St. Eustace. On March 24th, 1905, Portageville received its first resident pastor in the person of Joseph J. McMahon. Father McMahon removed the church-building to a better location in the town, enlarging and remodelling it so as to render it a practically new structure. He then built a commodious parochial residence. His successor and namesake Father Joseph A. McMahon built the school and placed it in charge of the Sisters of Mercy. When the church burnt to the ground it was replaced by the present pastor Father Willima F. Galvin with one of the finest church-buildings outside the city of St. Louis.

The Church of St. Patrick at Malden in Dunklin County was erected in 1894, by Father Furlong pastor of New Madrid. Its dedication took place on July 15th, 1895. At the time of its organization the parish contained only fourteen families, all native Americans. There was a gradual increase to forty families. The missions attached to the parish are Dexter, and Bloomfield in Stoddard, and Kenneth in Dunklin Counties. The succession of pastors after Father Furlong includes Father F. Peters, V. Tesselaar, O.S.M. and B. Ponce de Leon, O.S.M. Gayoso in Pemiscot County was attended from 1889 to 1898, from New Madrid. It never had a church building, and is supposed to have been swept away by the Mississippi. Dexter also received its first spiritual ministrations in 1889, but from Doniphan in the Irish Wilderness: From 1892 to 1908, it was supplied from Poplar Bluff, then from Sikeston and finally from Malden. The mission of Dexter once bore the name of St. Anthony; but is now under the patronage of the Sacred Heart; the Church of Kenneth bears the name of St. Anne. East Prairie in Mississippi County also is visited by the pastor of Malden: Its church is named for St. Joseph. At Malden, the mother church of these missions, there is a new church in course of construction which is to be named St. Anne's.

"Good old Father Tucker," of St. Michael's Fredericktown, was the first priest to make regular missionary excursions to the little stations in Iron, Wayne, Butler and Dunklin Counties. Among his few extant letters there are two that refer to his visit to Bloomfield in Dunklin. All through St. Francois and Iron Counties his name it still a household word among the older people. For it was Father Tucker that attended the little congregations at Iron Mountain and Pilot Knob from 1851 to 1869. In 1870, Iron Mountain in St. Francois County was established as a parish under the Rev. John Joseph Hennessy the future Bishop of Wichita. On

March 6th, of that year Vicar-General Patrick J. Ryan laid the corner stone of the Church of the Immaculate Conception. Pilot Knob in Iron County, where a church had been erected in 1867, and dedicated to Our Lady Help of Christians, was now placed in charge of Father Hennessy. But his sphere of influence extended much farther. To the north there were the congregations of Bismark and Farmington and Graniteville, to the South Des Arc, Piedmont and Popular Bluff. Des Arc and Piedmont were first mentioned in the records of 1873, Poplar Bluff two years later. During the early part of his pastorate in Iron Mountain Father Hennessy had in rapid succession the following assistants: James Phelan, J. J. Ryan, and J. J. Head. But in 1876, the Rev. Lawrence C.·Wernert came to stay, first as assistant to Father Hennessy, and then as Chaplain of Arcadia Convent and Academy and finally as pastor of Arcadia.

Father Hennessy was a priest of graceful bearing and courteous manners with a fair admixture of business tact and shrewdness. It was through his prudent management that Arcadia Convent, the gem of Arcadia Valley, was established. From 1875 until his promotion to the pastorate of St. John's Church in St. Louis in 1880, he made regular visits to Poplar Bluff in Butler County, and other stations by the way.

When the Ursuline Convent at Arcadia received its first contingent of Nuns, a chapel, and a chaplain became necessary. The chapel was dedicated to St. Joseph and served the people of Arcadia as their place of worship. Father Herman Leygraaff, in view of his deep piety and profound scholarship, was appointed chaplain of Convent and Academy. But as the good Father's health was seriously impaired by faithful service in the missions and in the Seminary, the young and energetic Father Lawrence C. Wernert was sent in his place in 1879.

Besides giving classes in the Academy and attending to his parish of Arcadia, he had charge of the mission of Pilot Knob, whilst Father Thomas Cooney, the successor of Father Hennessy as pastor of Iron Mountain, made regular visits to Granitville, Bismark and Farmington. The more distant missions, Des Arc and Gatewood in Ripley County, Piedmont in Wayne, and Poplar Bluff in Butler, had been placed in care of the pastor of Doniphan, Father P. A. Trumm, as being more conveniently located for his ministrations.

But when in 1883, Father Trumm retired from Doniphan, Des Arc, Piedmont and Poplar Bluff came under the jurisdiction of Father Wernert, pastor of Arcadia. Father Cooney filled the pastoral charge of Iron Mountain until November 1885, when the unfortunate Father Hugh H. ·O'Reilly succeeded him. In 1892 and 1893, Iron Mountain was attended from Farmington and then owing to the closing of the Mines the parish was abolished, the church closed, and the Post Office disestablished. Iron Mountain had become a deserted village, and its few remaining Catholic people were placed in care of the pastor of Arcadia. After 1885, the Church of Doniphan roused itself from its temporary lethargy. Granite Bend in Wayne County, Peace Valley in Howell, Dexter in Stoddard were organized, and Popular Bluff itself was attended by its clergy until 1892. After that period Poplar Bluff, having received a pastor of its own in October 1891, took the lead in the ecclesiastical affairs of the southern counties of Missouri.

The man who wrought this change was the Irish Cistercian, Daniel A. Donovan, a former Seminary professor and author of a valuable work on Moral Theology, and a zealous energetic priest withall.

His first concern was the erection of the stations of the Way of the Cross in the Church of the Sacred Heart at Poplar Bluff. Besides his own parish, Father Donovan received the charge of the former missions of Doniphan, and bent all his efforts to rouse the scattered Catholics of his immense territory to greater, more generous efforts, but the cheerless outlook at last discouraged him, and in 1895, he returned to his Convent in Ireland. In October of the same year, Father Daniel W. Clarke succeeded him in the parish. In February 1897, came Father C. J. Kane, in 1899, Father L. N. Larche, and on December 3rd, 1901, the Rev. Maurice O'Flaherty.

Father Francis Joseph Adrian, on his arrival in 1919, succeeded in infusing new vigor into his people. The school conducted by the Ursulines was fairly prosperous, the parish was growing steadily. The missions, however, were a heavy burden. There were seven of them: Dudley in Stoddard, Fisk, Harriell and Neelyville in Butler, Hiram, Piedmont and Williamsville in Wayne. After a brave and restless struggle of five years the youthful missionary's devotion to an exalted purpose ended in death. His parish and missions are now in charge of the Rev. R. L. Foristal, whilst the parish of long and friendly rivalry, St. Benedict's of Doniphan, for some years in charge of Father John A. Hurcick, is now placed in care of Father Edward S. Filipiak.

The veteran leader of this advance, the revered and beloved Father Lawrence C. Wernert of Arcadia is still pastor of Arcadia and surrounding missions, as well as chaplain of the Convent. In full possession of his mental strength and bodily health, this pioneer priest of Southeast Missouri recently celebrated the fiftieth anniversary of his ordination to the priesthood.

## CHAPTER 70

# FROM THE MISSOURI TO THE CREST OF THE OZARKS

There remain a few parishes in Maries and Cole Counties that grew up in the eighties of the last Century in consequence of the religious impetus given to these localities by the early Jesuit missionaries, although they were actually organized by secular priests: Viessmann, planted in 1874, but since 1903 designated as Brinktown, Maries County: and Wardsville and Elston in Cole.[1]

The Church at Viessmann, built some time after 1874 on a four acres tract of land, bore the title of the *Holy Trinity*. It was at first attended from Vienna. In 1880, however, the Rev. Benjamin V. Tannrath seems to have been appointed rector of the place, as the Catholic Directory for 1881 prints the item. Yet the fact is, that this appointment was rescinded on account of the vacancy occurring at that time in Fredericktown, through the death of Father Lewis Tucker, which Father Tannrath was appointed to fill.

Accordingly Viesmann continued to be served by the pastor of Vienna for three more years. In 1891 the Rev. Louis Schlathoelter appears to have attended the congregations until Otcober 15th, when Father Gerard Herman Brand took charge as rector. A parochial school was opened about 1894, the school-building like the Church and parish residence, was of frame. A lay-teacher had charge.

There were at this time about forty-four families in the parish, two-thirds of German extraction, the rest Irish. In 1903 the names of both the place and the church were changed to Brinktown, and The Guardian Angel. In November 1895, Thomas A. Dette relieved Father Brand of his burden. During Father Dette's rule of more than thirteen years no important developments were noticeable: the membership increased to fifty-four families. On Father Dette's appointment to the parish of Benton in Scott County, Father B. A. Schlathoelter came to Brinktown. Father Patrick Lyons supplied the place for a short while. Then came the Rev. Francis Schiller, and finally the Rev. Charles F. Schilling, the present incumbent. Father Gerard Herman Brand died on November 5th, 1907, as rector of Gildehouse.

The Church of *St. Stanislaus*, at *Wardsville*, Cole County, has a somewhat more diversified history than the parish of Brinktown. Father Henry Anthony Hukestein was its founder. Originally a schoolmaster, he was encouraged to study for the priesthood and attained

---

[1] Authorities: Chancery Records and Answers to Questionnaire.

his purpose in 1876, June 4th, when he was ordained by the Coadjutor Bishop of St. Louis in the pro-cathedral of St. John. After filling the position of assistant at St. Mary's Church, St. Louis and that of pastor in Vienna, Maries County, for about four years, Father Hukestein was sent to Cole County to form a new parish some ten miles distant from Jefferson City. In November 1880 a parcel of land had been secured for the new parish. Father Hukestein arrived at his destination on November 9th of the same year and immediately began preparations for the erection of a church.

He found about seventy-five families in his district, all German. On September 7th, 1881, Vicar-General Muehlsiepen laid the corner stone for the church which was to be of brick. On October 10th, 1883, the church was blessed by Father Hermann Wigger, under the patronage of St. Stanislaus: Father Hukestein continued his kindly yet energetic rule of the parish until July 18th, 1884, when the opportunity offered itself of building the grand Church of St. Augustine in St. Louis. His successor at Wardsville, the Rev. Joseph Charles Ernst, had come to America from Cologne in the heyday of the Bismarkian persecution of the Church. He had received holy orders from the Martyr-Bishop Paulus Melchers in 1872. When the noble prelate was dragged to prison for religion's sake, the young priest also, like a number of others, got in conflict with the civil authorities and, in consequence, fled the country. His family name was Ritzenhoff, Ernst Joseph, were his baptismal names, which he used in America to hide his identity. He returned to the Rhineland in July 1899. He functioned as pastor of Wardsville until 1888, became successively pastor of St. Thomas, Perryville, St. Peter's, and Assistant to Father Hukestein at St. Augustine's, St. Louis.

The next pastor of Wardsville was the Rev. J. F. M. Diel, who held a watchful eye upon his flock until June 1895. It was the next pastor, Father Bernard John Benten, that built the school and introduced the Ursuline Sisters as teachers. On Father Benten's promotion to the Church of St. Paul in St. Charles County, the Rev. J. H. Krechter assumed pastoral charge; in 1908 came the Rev. Paul Gross, a former religious of the Congregation of the Holy Ghost, whom Father Francis W. Gerhold succeeded in 1913. Father Gerhold built a fine church which was dedicated on June 28th, 1925. The parish is in flourishing condition, although its membership was considerably reduced by the establishment of two new parishes within its former territory: St. Anthony of Padua at Folk and St. Margaret, at Osage Bend.

The first dismemberment took place in 1905 when the parish of St. Anthony at Folk was founded with Father John Hoeschen as pastor, and twenty-five families, all of German descent. The church was dedicated on June 11th, 1905, the parochial residence was erected in 1906. The school was opened in 1914 with a Catholic lay teacher. It is supported by the County: Since its organization, the parish increased to fifty-five families and still continues to grow.    Since 1916 the Rev. Joseph A. Richarz has occupied the pastorate.

The second dismemberment was occasioned by the establishment of St. Margaret's Church at *Osage Bend* under the leadership of Father Peter Joseph Wigger.  The dedication of this new house of God took place on July 22nd, 1908.  The original membership of the parish, twenty-two German families, has grown, in the course of near twenty years, to thirty.  Each of these two daughters of Wardsville has given one son to the priesthood of the Church.

Father Wigger's successors were Henry Kuper, 1913 to 1917; Rev. J. M. Denner, the present pastor the Rev. Herman Wagener. Wardsville itself the mother church, has ten members of religious orders to her credit, but no priestly son so far.

The Church of St. Martin at *Elston*, Cole County, was officially founded by Father John Schramm in June 1885.

On August 26th of that year Vicar-General Muehlsiepen blessed the church, which was built by the people under Father Schramm's directions.  But the origin of the parish dates back to 1860.  There was a place called Stringtown, some distance from Jefferson City, which Father Van der Sanden, then stationed at the State Capital as assistant priest to the pastor of St. Peter's Church, was accustomed to visit once every six weeks.  Fifteen German families had their homes around Stringtown, but the place had no church, and although Father Van der Sanden on March 19th, 1862 blessed and laid the corner stone for a proposed church in honor of St. Joseph, the building never materialized.  Yet the priests of Jefferson City came to say mass at Stringtown in private homes until 1885.  The last good missionary to do so was the Rev. John Schramm.  In 1885 the mission was discontinued and, to supply its place, a parish was organized at Elston, with Russelville as a mission.  The church was dedicated in honor of St. Martin by Vicar-General Muehlsiepen on August 26th, 1885.

Of course the people of Stringtown became members of the new parish of Elston; The total membership at its foundation was thirty-five families, German and Irish.  The school was opened about 1888, in charge of a secular teacher, until the advent of the School-Sisters of St. Francis in 1912.

Elston is a railroad town about ten miles from Jefferson City, with coal and lead mines in the vicinity.

In 1890 the population was two hundred and fifty souls.  In November 1898, during the pastorate of Rev. Charles Keller, the church with all its furnishings was burned to the ground.  Nothing daunted, however, priest and people, had a new church under way in a little while, and saw it completed in June 1899.

Vicar-General Muehlsiepen conducted the solemnities of dedication on October 18th. The succession of pastors at Elston after Father Schramm's departure on September 28th, 1887, was Rev. Sebastian Senneerich to 1894; Rev. Joseph Wentker to 1896; Rev. Charles Keller to 1900; Rev. Henry Fabry to 1901; Rev. C. H. Schlefers to 1908; Rev. J. B. Pleuss, D.D., and Rev. John Wehner, the present pastor.

The parish is rapidly decreasing in numbers owing to the young peoples' drifting to Jefferson City to find employment in the shoe factories. The establishment of the former mission of Russelville into a distinct parish was also a loss to Elston.

St. Michael's Church of *Russelville,* Cole County dates from April 13th, 1887, when Father Schramm, the pastor of Elston, laid the corner stone for its church. In the meantime the place was attended from Elston, even after the dedication of the church by Vicar-General Muehlsiepen, on October 22nd, 1890. In 1897 the school was established with a lay-teacher in charge. By September 26th, 1906, the mission had developed into a parish with Rev. Joseph Wehner as its first pastor. After him came Fathers Richarz and Reh. The outlook is not very flattering at present, but gives no reason for desponding.

As the latest flourishing branches of the mighty spiritual tree planted by Father Helias and his associates in the soil of Osage and Cole Counties, the remaining parishes of Freeburg, Meta, Bonnot's Mill, Osage Bend, Chamois and Argyle may find a place here, although they really belong to a later period.

The town of *Freeburg,* the center of the parish of the Holy Family, was founded in 1902, when the Rock Island Railroad built its line along the southern part of Osage County. The pioneers of this enterprising community were German Catholics. In 1903, December 29th, the Rev. Gerard Fick, was made rector of Freeburg. A native of Richfountain, Osage County, Father Fick had the necessary knowledge of local conditions, and so was well fitted to organize and build up the parish. The people in glad anticipation of soon getting a pastor, had begun the erection of a temporary church building, but the young pastor supervised its completion. His pastoral residence was a little cubby-hole in the sacristy. In 1905 the church was enlarged, and the erection of the school and Sisters' residence soon followed. Then the parishioners insisted that their pastor must have a proper dwelling. Father Fick's great ambition was to erect a dwelling for the Lord which should by its beauty and majesty overshadow everything around it. His expressed wish found a hearty response.

On July 28th, 1920, Msgr. J. J. Tannrath, laid the corner stone of the proposed church. The dedication of the imposing structure took place on August 8th, 1921, Archbishop Glennon officiating. The parochial school was taught by four School-Sisters' De Notre Dame. In 1904 it was made a public school, but continued its teaching faculty. At the beginning there were about forty-six families in the parish, at present there are one hundred and twenty. Four girls of the parish have become Sisters.

The parish of *Meta*, Osage County, is dedicated to St. Cecelia. In 1904 the people of the place obtained the Archbishop's permission to begin building a church, and then sat down to await developments. In October of that year the Rev. Herman Wagener announced himself as their rector. On November 5th, 1904 the Rev. Father wrote the chancellor of the Archdiocese: "We are using a rented house for church and school." In the Spring of 1906, however, a beginning was made with building operations. Vicar-General Hoog blessed and laid the corner stone for the Church of St. Cecilia. The parish has a school taught by a lay-teacher, and at times by the pastor himself.

One of the most beautiful locations for a temple of the Most High is that of *Bonnot's Mill* in Osage County. Halfway up the hillside stands the church of St. Louis, with miles and miles of diversified country before it, and the silvery windings of the Missouri connecting scene with scene. The Rev. Charles Even, a native of the County, built it in 1905. Church, rectory and school are frame structures. The corner stone of the church was laid by Father Rupprechter, then pastor of Linn. The parish school was established in 1916. The parish numbered about fifty families, French and German, the latter being the more numerous and constructive force. The outlook until 1918 was promising, but through the prevalence of automobile traffic, the commercial and social importance of Bonnot's Mill has gradually faded away, and in consequence the independent growth of the Church is now in danger. Father Even, the founder of the parish, died there on April 17th, 1923, in his sixty-third year. The successive pastors were Fathers John Schramm, John Lakebrink, and C. Schmidt.

Chamois with its Church of the Most Pure Heart of Mary was attended from Herman, but in 1910 the Franciscan Fathers turned over the parish to the secular clergy. Father Joseph George Hoelting was its first resident priest. Father Joseph H. Winkelmann succeeded him. The mission of St. Ignatius at Baily's Creek is attached to Chamois.

The school is now in charge of the Sisters' de Notre Dame.

The Church of St. Aloysius at *Argyle* was founded in 1910 by the Rev. Joseph J. Rapien; it was for the last ten years administered by the Rev. Joseph M. Clooney.  There remains but one more church to find mention here, that of the Immaculate Conception in Jefferson City carved out of the ancient parish of St. Peter.  The Rev. Dr. John B. Pleuss was its founder and first pastor.  The school is táught by four Sisters of Charity of the Incarnate Word.  Since the days of Msgr. Hoog, Jefferson City has a Catholic Hospital in care of the Sisters of St. Mary.

South and southeast of Cole and Osage Counties which contain the earliest missionary centers of the central portion of the State, there are nine counties that were rather slow at receiving the light in its meridian brightness; the Counties of Maries, Phelps, Crawford, Pulaski, Dent, Texas, Shannon, Howell and Oregon.  Far inland as they were and remote from what were then the highways of commerce and immigration, the great rivers, they naturally developed at a slower pace.  But as the counties of Cole and Osage grew in Catholic population and formed new parishes in the seventies and eighties, so the counties to the southwest also took their part in the conquest of the wilderness for Christ the Lord.

The link between north and south is the Church of St. Patrick in *Rolla,* Phelps County.  It was organized as a mission in 1862 by Rev. Francis P. Gallagher, and became a parish in 1864.  Father Gallagher having been recalled to St. Louis in 1865 to build the first St. Teresa's church after Father James O'Brien's premature death, had as his own successor in Rolla the Rev. Francis Graham, who received the appointment immediately after his ordination by Archbishop Kenrick, September 23rd, 1865.

On Father Graham's transfer to Springfield, January 1868, the Rev. Thomas Moran took over the charge of Rolla, until 1875.  Father Edward Smith, one of the assistants at the Cathedral, was then appointed to the pastorate and remained there until 1879.  The Rev. Thomas Bonacum, the future Bishop of Lincoln, served as pastor of Rolla for the next two years.  Then followed the long pastorate of the Rev. Patrick O'Loughlin, lasting almost four decades.

The missions organized and attended from Rolla, were very numerous, spreading out over the counties of Phelps, Crawford, Dent, Texas and Pulaski:

The mission of the Immaculate Conception at *St. James,* Phelps County, was organized in 1871.  On the 16th day of July of that year Vicar-General Patrick J. Ryan blessed the church.  The mission remained a dependency of Rolla until 1906, when it was attached to Knob

View. Salem in Dent County received priestly ministrations from Rolla since 1880. It had a frame church in 1898 which was attended from Rolla until 1908. Now it is a mission of Cuba, Crawford County. The third mission of Rolla was Leasburg in Crawford County, which had a frame church dedicated to the Sacred Heart. It was organized by Father O'Loughlin. It is now an outmission of Cuba.

Holy Cross Church of *Cuba* itself is an offshoot of the church of Rolla. It was organized as a mission in 1883. Previous to that date mass was said occasionally by Father Gallagher who was stationed at Rolla from 1862 to 1865. When the Frisco Railroad was building, a large number of workmen and their families settled in and near the town. The first church in Cuba was erected by Father Bonacum. This edifice was blown to pieces by the cyclone of 1877. The present church was erected by Father O'Loughlin in 1879, and enlarged by him in 1898. At the time of its foundation Holy Cross Parish at Cuba numbered twenty-families, all Irish, with the exception of two who were German. It has grown rapidly in late years, so that on October 26th, 1914, it could be raised to the dignity of a parish, with Rev. Curtis J. Hornsby as its first pastor. With the old missions of Salem and Leasburg, the new missions of St. Francis at Burbon, Crawford County, and the former Jesuit mission of the Japanese Martyrs at Japan in Franklin County, were attached to the church of Cuba, but the latter has recently been formed into a separate parish under Father Lakebrink. St. Michael's Church at Cabool, in Texas County was attended from Rolla since 1888, and Haley's Settlement since 1889. But on September 15th, 1896 the care of Cabool was assigned to White church in Howell County, and subsequently, to Thayer and finally restored to White Church.

Four other missionary stations were mentioned in 1907 as pertaining to Rolla:

Newburg in Phelps, Pina Station in Texas, Richland and Dixon in Pulaski Counties.

*Knobview* and Phelps County is a parish composed chiefly of Italians. In 1900 a group of forty Italian families settled in the district by invitation from the Frisco Railroad. They petitioned Archbishop Glennon for a priest and were gladdened in April 1906 to receive the Rev. Ottavio Leone as their pastor. They were living in extreme poverty, but they were willing to make any sacrifice to have a church and priest of their own. The first church was dedicated in 1908 under the title of St. Anthony, but in 1918 church and parish residence were destroyed by fire.

The new brick church was dedicated in May 1919: the parish residence was built in 1920. There were about two-hundred souls in the parish at its foundation, all Italians: but there are many fallen-away Catholics in the district. It speaks well for the community, that four of its young ladies consecrated themselves to the religious life.

Father Leone was born in Italy in 1867, became a member of the Passionist Order, but received his exeat from the Order in 1904 and joined the ranks of the secular Clergy. He was succeeded in 1923 by the Rev. C. B. Faris.

## CHAPTER 71

# DECLINE OF THE EARLIEST CHURCHES OF THE CITY

During these more than fifty years of Church extension from the original and only parish church Peter Richard Kenrick found in the city of St. Louis on his arrival from Philadelphia, until in 1893, their number amounted to fifty-five, only three fell by the way: the first Church of the Immaculate Conception on 8th and Chestnut Street St. Bonaventure on 6th and Spruce, and St. Francis Xavier's on 9th and Lucas. Catholic sentiment is strongly opposed to forsake a place that was once chosen as the visible habitation of God among men. At first there was no need, except in the three cases enumerated, of abolishing any of the constantly increasing number; each parish, new or old, had a sufficiency of support, and was not as yet accustomed to demand more than the things really necessary. The sources of income were not uniform. The German parishes adhered to the practice of pew-renting, whilst in the English-speaking parishes the custom of paying 10c for a seat was in vogue.[1] Subscriptions for special purposes were taken up in all the churches. The Easter collection for the parish clergy was in full force as a law, but not everywhere in practice. As early as 1869, the *Western Watchman* speaks of it as a time-honored institution. So all churches bore, neither the burden of poverty nor of great wealth, but the sweet yoke of humble content.

Under these circumstances it is remarkable, how within the three years of Bishop Kenrick's Coadjutorship, St. Louis was enriched with five splendid Churches so well planned and built, that even today, after the wear and tear of more than eighty years, they with the exception of the first St. Francis Xavier's, remain with us as worthy monuments of the old days and ornaments of the present: St. Mary's of the Victories, St. Patrick's, St. Joseph's, St. Vincent de Paul's. But what is still more remarkable is, that this cluster of old churches, together with the Old Cathedral, still serve the holy purposes for which the faith and love of their founders destined them. St. Francis Xavier's Church, perhaps the most beautiful of the five, was demolished when

---

[1] Archbishop Kenrick's Order in regard to the temporalities of the churches is dated October 1, 1868, and signed, "By Order the Archbishop, Charles Ziegler, Secretary." The following two clauses are to the point: "It is expected that everyone of the faithful, on entering the church, contribute at least 5 cents. It is not intended to keep anyone that does not contribute from entering the church but it is expected that only a few of the poorest will decline to fulfill this duty of piety and justice. At the High Masses, all the pews not rented shall be locked and opened only for those who have a ticket from the ushers for ten cents."

the St. Louis University was moved to Grand Avenue, and it is still a matter of regret that is was not left at its old hallowed place.

It would, of course, be wrong to apply the term of ''prosperous'' to any of these five ancient parishes and churches. In fact, some of them can hardly claim to have a resident congregation, but only more or less regular attendants. Though enjoying all parochial rights and well-defined parish bounds, they have become practically missionary churches. St. Vincent's is, and St. Patrick's may be still a full fledged parish: but St. Mary's, St. Joseph's and the Old Cathedral draw their chief support from the scattered children and children's children of those who helped to build and beautify them.

What a wonderful attraction the *Old Cathedral* on Walnut Street near the river has upon the people of the city. How they crowd its pews and aisles on the Solemn Feasts of the Church, or at the Sunday Highmass and at the midday service in Lent. And how many hundreds visit this Church of their Fathers day by day, to offer a prayer of petition or thanksgiving at one or the other of its beautiful shrines. And how restful the care fretted heart finds the quiet air of peace that broods within those massive walls and mighty pillars. Now and then its sombre majesty brightened up with the presence of the great prelates of the land; as at the Golden Jubilee of Archbishop Kenrick: at other times it spoke even more eloquently through the contrast, of the vanity of all terrestrial things, as at the funeral services for the same Archbishop Kenrick, and for his successor Archbishop Kain. But even independently of these haunting memories, the old Church has attractions of a real and most sacred nature: its numerous relics, and its singular indulgences. We use the word singular advisedly: for there seems to be no case of such peculiar indulgences being granted to any church in Christendom save the Cathedral church of St. Louis built by Bishop Joseph Rosati, namely the indulgences of the Seven Churches of Rome. It was an ancient tradition current in St. Louis that Bishop Rosati, during an audience with Pope Gregory XVI, his former classmate, told of his cathedral built in the wilderness on the western bank of the Mississippi, and asked the Holy Father to endow it with special favors. When asked what he wanted, Bishop Rosati said: ''I wish for my cathedral the indulgences attached to the seven Basilicas of Rome.'' We are told that the Holy Father protested that those indulgences were never granted to other churches. ''That is exactly why I want them.'' replied Bishop Rosati. That he was successful in his audacious request is seen by the list of indulgences granted by the decree of the same Pope, dated April 3, 1841. It reads as follows:

Holy Father: Joseph Rosati, Bishop of St. Louis, humbly prostrate at the feet of your Holiness, asks that your Holiness deign to grant in perpetuity, the usual conditions being observed.

1. A Plenary Indulgence daily to the faithful visiting the Cathedral Church of St. Louis.

2. The Indulgences of the Seven Churches of Rome to those visiting the four altars of the said Cathedral Church.

3. The Indulgences of the Stations of Rome to those visiting the said Cathedral Church on the days of such Stations.

4. A Plenary Indulgence on the anniversary of the dedication of the same Church and during the Octave of such dedication, and on the Octave day.

5. A Plenary Indulgence on the Feast of St. Louis, the Patron of the Cathedral Church, and throughout the Octave."

This is the petition of Bishop Rosati, as far as it refers to his Cathedral; what now follows is the Pope's act of granting the petition in perpetuity:

"In audience with His Holiness held on the third of April, 1841, our Most Holy Lord, Gregory XVI, by divine Providence Pope, on the statement of the undersigned Secretary of the Sacred Congregation of the Propagation of the Faith, having duly considered the matter of the petition, graciously grants in perpetuity all the Indulgences asked for in the petitioning brief. All things to the contrary notwithstanding.

Given at Rome, from the Offices of the said Sacred Congregation, on the day and year as above. Entirely free from any renumeration under any head.

I. Arch. Spolet."

This signature stands for the full name and title of Cardinal Ignatius Cadolini, Archbishop of Spoleto, who was Secretary of the Sacred Congregation de Propaganda Fide from 1838 to 1843. By the second clause, therefore, of this document the singular privilege was granted those who should visit the four altars of the Old Cathedral Church, that they might gain the many rich indulgences attached to the Seven Basilica-Churches of Rome, Viz: To St. Peter's, on the Vatican; St. Paul and St. Sebastian outside the walls: St. John Lateran; The Holy Cross in Jerusalem; St. Lawrence, outside the walls, and St. Mary Major. An unique privilege, indeed, when we consider that yearly, thousands of Pilgrims from all parts of the world make their visits to the Holy City and to the above mentioned churches to be enriched with the Indulgences attached thereto.

But the Old Cathedral for many years has had only three altars, the fourth having been removed when St. Mary's Chapel in the basement of the Cathedral was closed. Was this indulgence then lost with the loss of the fourth altar? This question was settled by Pope Pius IX July 9th, 1848, when the following petition of Archbishop Kenrick was acted upon favorably:

"Most Holy Father:—Peter Richard Kenrick, Archbishop of St. Louis, most humbly submits to your Holiness, that among the privileges granted by Gregory XVI, of happy memory, to his predecessor, is that daily Plenary Indulgence gained by those who visit the Seven Basilicas, which was granted to those who visit the four altars of the Cathedral of St. Louis. But as there are only three altars in the Cathedral, the fourth being in the basement Chapel, and as your petitioner for grave reasons intends to close the latter, and there would seem to be little likelihood in the present condition of affairs, of another Altar being erected in the Church, your petitioner humbly asks that the above mentioned indulgence be accorded to those who visit the three altars of the Church, or more, should more in the course of time be erected. In an audience with His Holiness on the ninth of July, 1848, our Most Holy Lord, Pius IX, by divine Providence Pope, on the statement of the undersigned Pro-Secretary of the Congregation of the Propagation of the Faith, having duly considered the matter of the petition, graciously assents in all things accordingly as they are asked, all things to the contrary notwithstanding. Given at Rome, from the Offices of the said Sacred Congregation on the day and year as above.

Free from any remuneration under any head.

Alexander Barnabo,
Pro-Secretary.''

Cardinal Alexander Barnabo was Secretary of the Sacred Congregation De Propaganda Fide from 1848 to 1865, in which latter year he became Prefect of the Propaganda in succession to Cardinal Fransoni.[2]

A matter of such vast spiritual import and of such unique occurrence surely will merit for the Old Cathedral perennial youth and vigor, no matter whether the fluctuation of population may tell for it or against it. The Old Cathedral will and must remain the great religious shrine of the city. But under faithful shepherds, as the small scattered congregation has had for a number of years, and with the aid of the parochial school which it supports, even its pastoral functions will be required more and more.

The Church of *St. Mary of the Victories*, the earliest church the German Catholics, had, as we have seen, a long line of distinguished pastors: Father John Peter Fischer, a native of Lorraine, served in that capacity, during the first three years of its existence, but accepted the post of assistant on the arrival of Vicar-General Melcher and served as such until June 1856, when he returned to his

---

2 The official documents are preserved in the Archives of the Old Cathedral. The concession of 1841, is printed in ''Synodus Sti. Ludovici, III,'' 1896, pp. 159-160. Cf. ''Catholic Herald,'' vol. V, No. 6.

native land. Father Melcher remained pastor of St. Mary's until his elevation to the see of Green Bay, March 3, 1868. During the twenty-one years of his management of the parish, Vicar-General Melcher was faithfully assisted by the future Vicar-General of the diocese, Father Henry Muehlsiepen. In this period the church was completed according to the original cruciform plan, and a massive campanile, was erected on the north side of the church. The completed edifice was solemnly consecrated by Archbishop Kenrick on May 13th, 1860. Probably in no church of the city at this time the Highmass was more solemnly held than at old St. Mary's. After Bishop Melcher's departure, Father Muehlsiepen became pastor of the parish and Vicar-General for the German, Bohemian and Polish Catholics of the archdiocese. The new Vicar-General now recalled the pastor of Dutzow, Father Frederick William Faerber, to St. Mary's and entrusted to him the care of the parish, and soon afterward appointed him pastor. In order to give his friend and successor perfect freedom of action, the Vicar-General changed his own place of residence to the Ursuline Convent, of which he was Spiritual Director. At the time of Father Faerber's early pastorship the parish of St. Mary of the Victories had already passed the meridian of its numerical strength and importance. To the southwest stood the Church of St. Vincent, whose parish was organized on German-English lines. Directly west the parishes of St. Nicholas and St. Henry had been formed out of its former territory. But its greatest and irreparable loss resulted from the gradual deterioration of that part of the city that lies along the river between the Courthouse and the so-called Frenchtown due south of St. Mary's Church. Factories, and wholesale business houses took the place of the residences of many of the city's best families.[3]

Within the period from 1859 to 1868 the number of annual Baptisms had decreased from 400 to 220. But the parish still ranged among the best. The succession of Father Faerber's assistants includes such honored names as Henry Jaegering, Henry Pigge, Henry Hukestein, John L. Gadell, William Rensmann, Henry Geers, A. Happe, John J. Tannrath and Aloysius Gorthoeffner.

But the decline went on and at last seemed to threaten extinction. Father Faerber in 1891 resorted to a rather peculiar measure to infuse new life into the old organism. He bought a plot of ground on Morisson Avenue, one block west of Twelfth Street, to which he proposed to transfer St. Mary's church. The new location was within the limits of St. Vincent's parish: but as it was not intended to win over the English speaking people of the district, and as it was hoped that the German Catholics attending St. Vincent's would be gladly transferred

---

3 "Amerika," October 26, 1919. (Father Holweck's article).

to a purely German parish within their reach, Vicar-General Muehl-siepen obtained the Archbishop's consent to the new venture.

The plans for church and school were ready, contributions were being collected, and building operations were about to begin, when there came a thunder-clap that stopped the proceeding.

The Vincentian Fathers, who had charge of St. Vincent's parish, through their Visitor had entered a protest with Archbishop Kenrick, stating that their parish had been a mixed French-English-German or-ganization from its very inception, and that it would be an injustice to draw away from them the wealthy Germans of the parish, and that it was against all law to build a new parish church within the limits of another parish enjoying equal rights   The Vincentians were right in their contention and the Archbishop decided against Father Faerber's project.   Father Faerber's appeal to Rome was rejected.   The loss sustained by St. Mary's parish fell, at least, in part, to the lot of Vicar-General Muehlsiepen.   St. Mary's Church had to remain in the old location amid the factories and slums.[4]

Towards the end of 1901 Father Faerber took up his abode with the Community of the Sisters of St. Mary, which he had been chiefly instrumental in founding.   Always busy with his literary work, he left the administration of his parish to his assistant, Father Aloysius Garthoeffner, who at Father Faerber's demise, April 17th, 1905, became pastor.   Father Garthoeffer paid the debts resting on the parish, re-stored the crumbling buildings and, with a large legacy from the Heit-kump family, placed church and school on a sound financial basis. The school, in Father Garthoeffner's day had become a rather cosmo-politan institution, eight nationalities being represented.   For the last sixty-five years the Notre Dame Sisters have had charge of it.   When Father Garthoeffner became Director of Schools and chaplain of the Ursulines, the parochial duties devolved upon his assistant, the Rev. Herman E. Amsinger, whilst the pastor exercised the financial manage-ment.   At the death of Father Garthoeffner April 27th, 1917, Father Amsinger was appointed Administrator of the parish, and has held the position ever since.

St. Mary's Church enjoys the distinction of having given the Arch-diocese its first Superintendent of Schools.

On the death of Father James Archer, April 5th, 1876, Father James McCaffrey succeeded to the pastorship of *St. Patrick's parish.* He had for assistants a number of prominent priests of the diocese, as Father William O'Shea, E. J. Hamill, R. J. Hayes, J. J. Ryan, D. Healy, J. T. Foley, Eugene Coyle, C. F. O'Leary, O. J. McDonald and J. J. Toomey.

---

4  ''Amerika,'' October 26, 1919.

ST. VINCENT'S CHURCH AND SCHOOL

On his appointment to the new Cathedral Chapel, October 15th, 1896, Father J. T. Tuohy became pastor of St. Patrick's. During these twenty years a complete transformation had taken place in its human make-up: Originally all Irish, the parishioners were now of almost all nations of Europe, except the Irish.

The church was shorn of its towers by the cyclone of 1896. But the school endured. St. Patrick's Day was always one of the most splendidly celebrated days in St. Louis. Under the pastorship of Father Dempsey from July 11th, 1898 to the present day old St. Patrick's has more than all the splendor of its early days in the institutions founded by Father Tim. Year by year on the feast of Erin's great Saint a vast assembly of clergy and laity gather within its walls to do honor to God in His saint, and in His faithful and great-hearted servant, the pastor of St. Patrick's.[5]

The Church of *St. Vincent de Paul* of which the corner stone was laid on March 17th, 1844, and which was solemnly consecrated by Bishop Kenrick on November 5th of the following year, has remained in charge of the Vincentian Fathers since its foundation. The church building, too, remained the same, only that the beautiful facade and the tower were added after the consecration. The congregation was and is composed of three nationalities or their descendants: the French, Irish and German. Services have accordingly been held in English and German, the French not being required since the earliest days. The list of subscribers to the Church building fund is equally creditable to the two leading nationalities. Most of them were recent arrivals from beyond the sea. Poor in worldly goods they were, but rich in faith and the love of God, and glad and proud of the beauty of His house. They were sturdy men of the artisan and laboring classes, not highly educated but endowed with a larger share of good common sense. And above all, they held on to their magnificent inheritance, the ingrained Catholic culture they had brought along from the home of their childhood.

They also clung to their inherited language. It was this twofold bond of love, one supernatural, the other natural, that moved their hearts to give generously from their little store of wealth or from the meagre results of their daily toil. From its inception St. Vincent's parish enjoyed the signal blessing of a parochial school. In 1851 Father John Gerard Uhland, a man of small stature, but of a great loving heart, came to St. Vincent's as Director of Schools, and Rector for the German part of the Congregation. He was, certainly one of the most popular, and best-beloved priests our City ever had. He remained at St. Vincent's until his happy death which occurred on February 17th,

---

5  Chancery Records.

1885. He was a true father to all classes. Old and young, rich and poor, cultured and rude, native or foreigner, all were dear to his paternal heart.

As the parish increased in numbers a new school building was erected for the Christian Brothers, the teachers of the boys. But the Sisters of Charity also, having a constantly increasing number of girl pupils to provide for, needed a new building. Mrs. Soulard donated a piece of property on Eighth and Marion Streets, on which the school was erected. It was opened in the Spring of 1853. At that time nine hundred pupils of both sexes were educated at the Schools of the Parish: Now the attendance had dwindled to about one-third of that number:[6]

It is, of course, to be presumed, that St. Vincent's Parish, in its blessed course of almost ninety years, must have had many priests of distinction, many whose names are still in benediction. The series of pastors alone is rich enough in distinguished men to prove this assumption, men who have acquired extraordinary reputation, as preachers and public speakers, of men who have greatly stimulated the religious life of the parish, or have attained to greatly enlarged responsibilities either in the Order, or in the episcopacy. The peculiar atmosphere of religious thought pervading the community house certainly had a share in these results. There is first of all the founder of the parish in 1838, Father John Timon, then Superior of the Missions, and Vicar-General of the diocese, and subsequently Bishop of Buffalo. Father Timon was a man who saw clearly, reasoned incisively and acted without timidity or temerity. The first pastor of St. Vincent's, the one-time Napoleonic calvaryman, Father Francis Xavier Dahmen, light-hearted as a true son of the Rhineland, in all humility relinquished to the abler administrator and business manager, Father Blasius Raho, the honor and merit of building the church and having it consecrated. Father Raho, being full of the missionary spirit of the Vincentian Order, was especially noted for his extraordinary meekness and patience, all of which he had so beautifully exemplified in his foundation of. the La Salle Mission. In 1847, he was sent to St. Vincent's Seminary at New Orleans, and was succeeded as Pastor of St. Vincent's parish, by Father Francis Burlando. As St. Vincent's parish had a very strong German membership, there was always a German Vice Pastor appointed to take care of them. The first one to fill this important office was Father John Gerard Uhland. Father Uhland was for thirty-four years the only firm and fixed point in the constant change of pastors at St. Vincent's.

---

6 Diamond Jubilee of St. Vincent de Paul Church, 1919. "Church Progress," November 20, 1919.

Father Burlando had filled the office of Missionary Professor and Superior of the Seminary at St. Louis before he received the appointment as Pastor of St. Vincent's.

In 1850, he made a visit to the Orient, and was subsequently appointed Spiritual Director of the Daughters of Charity, at whose House in Emmitsburg he died on February 16th, 1873, fifty-eight years of age. In 1850, Father Dahmen was reappointed pastor and held the office until September 27th, 1852. In that year his Superior sent him to the Motherhouse in Paris. Here he died on March 27th, 1866. Father Dahmen was not a grave man of learning, but alert in mind and direct in rugged speech, yet a very loveable character withall.

Of Father Anthony Penco, who filled the rectorship of St. Vincent's Parish from 1852 to 1855, a sufficient account can be found in the chapter treating St. Vincent's Seminary at Cape Girardeau. He returned to his native Italy. Father Penco's successor at St. Vincent's, Father James Rolando, was pastor of the Parish from 1855 to 1858, and Superior of the Mission from 1872, to 1874. He died at Germantown, November 26th, 1883.

The next Vincentian to administer the pastoral cares of St. Vincent's, was the bright, witty, and humorous Irishman, Father John O'Reilly. He was both talented and energetic, a hater of all shams and insincerities and ever ready champion of the oppressed, in manner ardent, but always maintaining a fine priestly bearing. Father John O'Reilly came to St. Louis from the La Salle Mission and held the rectorship of St. Vincent's from 1858 to 1860. He died March 4, 1862.

"During the period of the Civil War the Rev. Stephen Ryan held the office of Visitor of the Province: but the pastor of St. Vincent's parish was the Rev. Thomas Burk. Those years of danger and distress, no doubt weighed heavily upon the hearts of these two noble priests; yet beyond the horizon that bounded their fears and sorrows, they saw in spirit the light of a brighter day which was sure to break, and they devoted all the energies of their powers to keep the organizations over which God had set them, from disruption and ruin. Father Stephen V. Ryan, on becoming Visitor, took up his abode at St. Vincent's Rectory, St. Louis; but when the Motherhouse and Novitiate of the Community of the Lazarists, was removed to Germantown, he made it his residence, until he was elected to the See of Buffalo as successor to Bishop John Timon.

Father Thomas Burk's monument in Calvary bears the inscription: "Friend of the Poor," but his most beautiful and enduring monument is the little army of souls he has led into the ways of justice and righteousness during the twenty-two years of his pastorate at St. Vincent's. Father Tom Burk as he was lovingly called by his priest-friends and intimates, died October 31st, 1877. During his incumbency of St. Vincent's Father Burk had a number of good and faithful assistants chief among them were Fathers Edmund Hennessey, Hermann John Koop, Thomas Smith, A. Krabbler and Peter O'Neill: The most interesting personage of all these men of distinction was the "Metaphysician" Father Hermann John Koop. Father Shaw, who knew him well at La Salle Mission, describes him as a man of diminutive size, but possessed of a mighty spirit, that found delight in soaring to the highest heights of philosophical truth, who pursued the even tenor of his way, at ease with the world and its ways and without any desire for applause or even recognition. Father Koop was the most intimate friend the great convert Orestes A. Brownson had in his later days. Father Koop died in St. Louis, July 6th, 1880. Another one of Father Burk's assistants, the Rev. Edmund M. Hennessey, who filled the position from November 1877 to 1879, when Father Denis Leyden was put in his place, until Father James McGill was recalled from California to take charge of St. Vincent's. Father McGill resigned his charge into the hands of Father Michael Richardson in 1884. It was under his administration that good old Father Uhland died and received as his successor to the pastorship of the German part of the parish the well-known Father Pius G. Krentz. Father Krentz had served as assistant since 1880, and now continued to serve as Vice-pastor until 1891, when Father Henry Augustine Asmuth came to take his place. Father Krentz closed the line of his earthly days in La Salle, Illinois, on January 26th, 1897. The later pastors of St. Vincent's parish were: Father David William Kenrick (1892-1903) one of the most scholarly priests of the city, who also held the office of Procurator of the Western Province of the Order. Father Kenrick died on January 31st, 1903, at El Paso, Texas, the victim of an accident. He was returning from Los Angeles and, when nearing his destination, walked out on the platform and fell off the train. His body was brought to St. Louis for burial,

His successor at St. Vincent's was Father Francis V. Nugent, the noble minded man, great orator, missionary, and Seminary president. Father Nugent held the position of pastor of St. Vincent's from 1903 to 1912. During his pastorate the important post of Director of Missions of the Western Province of Vincentian Fathers was entrusted to him. Early in 1912, he went to New Orleans to accept the pastorate of St. Stephen's Church where he stayed until 1917, when he returned to St. Louis. He served as Chaplain at Marillac Seminary from this time until his death on June 1st, 1918.

The pastoral succession since that day was: Father J. E. A. Linn, Father Martin Gabriel Hanley, and the present pastor. Father S. P. Hueber.

On November 19th, 1919, the parish of St. Vincent kept with great solemnity the Diamond Jubilee of its foundation. Three Archbishops, Patrick J. Ryan of Philadelphia, John Joseph Kain of St. Louis, and John Ireland of St. Paul; one Bishop, Stephen V. Ryan of Buffalo, and a large number of minor prelates and priests were in attendance. Archbishop Kain celebrated the Jubilee Highmass, and Archbishop Ryan paid a glowing tribute to the clergy and people of St. Vincent's parish.[7]

*St. Joseph's*, the fourth parish erected under Peter Richard Kenrick's coadjutorship, has also a bright galaxy of pastors to show, whose names and characteristic marks deserve to be inscribed on the pages of our history. It was the Jesuit trefoil, Father James Cotting, a native of Switzerland, Father James Busshotts, a native of Flanders, and the Austrian Father Nicholas Hofbauer, to whom the care of the German Catholics worshiping at St. Aloysius Chapel were entrusted. When in 1843, Mrs. Ann Biddle donated the lot on Eleventh and Biddle Streets for the purpose of a church for the Germans, Father Cotting started a collection for the building fund, which amounted to more than thirteen hundred dollars. The corner stone was laid on April 21st, of the following year. It was Father Nicholas Hofbauer that carried the undertaking to a successful issue. During Father Hofbauer's first year he was greatly assisted in the work of collecting funds by Father Joseph Patschowski. The total cost of the church was $10,776. And the parish had no school as yet and no residence for the priests. The church was dedicated on August 2nd, 1846 by the Jesuit Provincial. In 1847, Father Patschowski was transferred to Cincinnati, and Father Martin Seisl, a native of Tyrol, was sent to take his place. A school building for the boys was now erected, as well as a rectory. The Sisters of Charity had opened a school for girls some years previous.

In 1849, the parish of St. Joseph received two severe checks: the first by the erection of the parish of the Holy Trinity within its former boundaries, and secondly by the small pox and cholera epidemics which visited many of its families. Father Seisl obtained from the Provincial, Father Elet, the plot of ground upon which the German St. Vincent Orphan Society erected the German Orphan Home. In 1851, Father Patschowski replaced Father Hofbauer as pastor of St. Joseph's and in 1854, when the Sisters of Charity asked to be relieved of the schoolwork in the parish, Father Patschowski invited the Sisters de Notre Dame, and at once made preparations for a larger school building to be ready against the coming of this new Sisterhood. But the zealous

---

[7] Diamond Jubilee in ''Church Progress,'' November 20, 1919. Bishop Stephen V. Ryan is author of a volume against the validity of Anglican Orders, and Protestant Misstatements of Catholic Faith.

Father's death occurred on January 10th, 1859. Father Patschowski was a man of extraordinary ability and zeal. Archbishop Kenrick, in his funeral sermon said of him: ''I have never known a more worthy, zealous and selfsacrificing priest, than Father Patschowski.'' Father William Niederkern now became pastor of St. Joseph's with Father Joseph Weber as assistant. But in 1861, Father Weber was made pastor with Fathers F. Wieppern, and Peter Tschieder as assistants, and governed the parish until 1870. This was the period of its highest prosperity and splendor. The church could no longer hold the crowds of people that frequented the various masses. The lot adjoining the church to the north was leased from the Biddle Estate for the period of three hundred years, a building fund of $27,000 was subscribed within a few days, and in the Fall of 1865, the Archbishop laid the corner stone for the addition to the church. The practically new church measured one hundred and eighty-five feet in length and eighty-five feet in width. The priests residence, which was built at the same time, contained twelve rooms. St. Joseph's Parish was dismembered at this time by the erection of St. Liborius, and lost territory also to the new St. Nicholas Parish: But its schools still numbered eleven hundred children. In 1870, Father Tschieder replaced Father Weber as pastor, but the latter remained at St. Joseph's in the capacity of assistant. Father Hagemann followed Father Tschieder in the pastorate (July 20, 1876) and in 1881, Father Lambert Etten succeeded Father Hagemann. The work of completing the church by the addition of the majestic facade with the two mighty towers was begun in 1881. On November 23rd, 1881, a solemn Highmass of thanksgiving was celebrated in the completed structure. Father Weninger preached the sermon. On April 15th, 1894, St. Joseph's celebrated its Golden Jubilee as a parish. Bishop Burke of St. Joseph Diocese was celebrant of the Solemn Highmass, with Vicar-General Muehlsiepen, and Fathers Goller, Faerber, Hoog and Schilling assisting. A large gathering of priests honored the occasion with their presence. The parish had been under severe losses of parishioners for some time previous, but still numbered six hundred and fifty-three children in the school. In the following year, Father Lambert Etten after a pastorate of seventeen years was transferred to Florissant and Father Francis X. Valazza took his place at St. Joseph's: Father Valazza had as assistants the Rev. Fathers Francis Braun, Charles Bill, Schlechter and some Polish missionaries. Father Valazza remained pastor of St. Joseph's from 1895-1904, when Father Etten returned from Florissant. He died in the Spring of 1907. He was in every way an able pastor of souls; zealous, vigilant, practical, and attentive to the spiritual and material well-being of the parish. After Father Etten's death came Father Peter Krier who had as assistants the Fathers Charles Bill, Francis Moorfeld and Stephen

Hoehn. Father Krier, a native of Luxemburg, was born March 9th, 1845. He died in December 1909. Shortly before his death Father Valazza had returned to his pioneer place, and subsequently became pastor of St. Joseph's for a second term. From 1918 to 1920, Father Anthony Hartman held the position. Father Ferdinand A. Moeller a brother of the late Archbishop of Cincinnati, came to St. Joseph's in 1920. Father Henry Grotegeers is its present pastor with Fathers Francis Moorfeld and Theodore Hegeman as assistants. The parish has now lost almost all its parishioners, and the attendance at the school has dwindled to about one hundred and fifty children of various national antecedents. Yet the spirit of St. Joseph's parish is still alive and active through the religious influence of many of its former parishioners now scattered throughout the western city parishes.[8]

There is one mighty institution of national importance that in a large measure owes its existence to the parish of St. Joseph. The German Roman Catholic Central Society. "The German Roman-Catholic Benevolent Society" founded and built up under the leadership of such men as John Amend, Henry Spaunhorst, Frederick Arendes formed the center around which the Benevolent Societies of the various German churches of the city grew up, and together with similar organizations in other States of the Union, expanded into the great national association, mentioned above. John Amend was for many years the President of the national body as well as of the "Old Society" as the original Society was called unto the present day.

---

8 "Diamantenes Jubilaeum der St. Joseph's Gemeinde," St. Louis, in "Amerika."

## Chapter 72

## AMERICANISM VERSUS CAHENSLYISM

During the tempestuous years just previous to the Third Plenary Council of Baltimore until the coming of Archbishop Kain when a strong and agressive party in the Church raised the battle cry of "Americanism against Cahenslyism," St. Louis was regarded by many as the ecclesiastical storm center of the country, and three of its prominent priests as the fomentors of most of the trouble. Others again regarded these same men as the fearless defenders of what was just and right and proper against unjust agression. They were characterized by one of our noblest ecclesiastics as "the pious Father Muehlsiepen, the learned Father Faerber, and the astute Father Goller," a combination that would, indeed, seem dangerous in a bad cause, and irresistible in a good one. The storm clouds have long since rolled away, although angry mutterings are still heard at times in posthumous diaries and memoirs, like echoes of a fray that seemed forgotten. Americanism, as a religious issue, is as dead as Marley, and Cahenslyism never was any more real than Marley's ghost.[1] The parochial school is firmly established everywhere, and the use of the German language in school and in the pulpit is either obsolete or obsolescent. The Church has not suffered seriously by the conflict of opinions. What was sane in the demands of the one side and of the other remains intact for the good of both.

"The learned Father Faerber," pastor of St. Mary's Church and second editor of the *Pastoral Blatt,* was a man of tall stature and huge girth, but also of genuine childlike piety and vast extent of learning. His style of writing was clear, concise and direct. His only concern in life was, besides the salvation of souls, the preservation of the German language, German customs and German thoroughness in the children of the German immigrants. Not that he wished to Germanize the Church in this country. Such a crude idea never entered his mind. So much was admitted even by opponents, as the following quotation from a critique of Father Faeber's articles would show:

"The author repudiates any idea of establishing in America a New Germany or of prepetuating any national discord among Catholics, but contends that the transition from their mother language to the language of the country, must develop itself gradually in a 'natural manner.' This we believe to be the wisest course in the German

---

[1] Cf. Dickens, "A Christmas Carol."

congregations, especially as the author states that the children must be taught English in the school.''[2]  But Father Faerber honestly believed that the preservation of these German characteristics was, if not necessary, at least highly conducive to the preservation of the Faith of the German immigrants and their children.  A transition he knew, must come some day; but to hurry on the development of a German into a hundred percent American was tyrannical, imprudent and worse than useless.  Not force, not intimidation, not superior airs should be employed against freemen in a free country, and least of all, by the Church that knows neither Greek nor Jew, but loves all with equal affection.  In this matter Father Faerber was easily roused to outbursts of fiery indignation, at times, perhaps, beyond the line of Christian prudence and charity: but no one can refuse him the tribute of respect for the honesty of his faith and purpose.[3]

Father Muehlsiepen, a man of singularly amiable disposition and slow steady energy, shared Father Faerber's convictions, but did not give them such forceful expression.  Yet every one knew that he stood in firm league with the editor of the *Pastoral-Blatt*.  In fact, his position as Vicar-General for the German, Bohemian and Polish Catholics of the Archdiocese, seemed to justify his predilection for the languages, customs and traditions of the foreign-born Catholics, whilst it laid some restraint upon his course of action in the matter.  ''The astute Father Goller'' was just as firm and determined in this regard as Father Faerber himself; he spoke in season and out of season on the rights of every man to use his mother tongue, whenever and wherever he pleased, and to transmit to his posterity the noble inheritance of his race.

But he did not use the *Pastoral-Blatt* for his not very frequent and not very lengthy communications on the subject.  His favorite organ was the *Amerika*, a German Daily of high reputation for accuracy, respectability and literary excellence, the editor of which, the noble convert from Lutheranism, Dr. Edward Preuss, was his welcome guest at dinner every Sunday throughout the year.  Of course, there were other participants in the fray, but these three seemed to be the leaders, and must bear the weight of the praise and blame.

The movement, however, was not intended to disturb the peace, but rather to lay the foundations of a true and lasting peace.  That German

---

2  Zwierlein, F. J., ''Life and Letters of Bishop McQuaid,'' vol. III, p. 44.

3  Father William Faerber has immortalized his name by the composition of two books of perennial value, the ''Catechism for the Catholic Parochial Schools of the United States'' and the ''Commentary on the Catechism.''  When the history of catechetical literature in the United States comes to be written, Father Faerber's name will surely be placed among the immortals, as one who succeeded splendidly, when so many others have failed dismally.

and other national churches should be regarded as mere "chapels of ease," seemed to many an unbearable humiliation, and to seek redress through the highest Church authority, when every other means had failed, seemed but a praiseworthy act of Christian manhood.

"Of course, the Germans have one grievous cause of complaint," wrote Bishop McQuaid "in the way they are treated in St. Louis. It is not fair to make their churches succursal to the English churches."[4] To be ostracised, in a manner, for being of German blood, seemed to call for a protest. And the protest came in the form of two articles in the *Pastoral Blatt,* November 1883 and April 1884, which were translated into English and published in pamphlet form under the title "The Future of Foreign-Born Catholics," and "Fears and Hopes for the Catholic Church and School in the United States, 1884." The first article was written by Father Faerber, the second by Father Innocent Wapelhorst, O.F.M. Father Wapelhorst had been recalled from his post as Professor in the Salesianum in 1873 to become Chancellor of the Archdiocese but in 1874 had returned to the Salesianum as Rector. In 1879 he became a member of the Order of St. Francis, under the name of P. Innocent. He was then in the 47th year of his age. Father Wapelhorst's tastes were scholarly, his love for virtue intense. The celebrated work "Compendium Saerae Liturgiae" gives ample testimony both to the piety and the exactitude of this worthy Franciscan.

From the character and the avowed purpose of these men it would appear, that their fight against the tendencies that were summed up under the vague term "Americanism" was an honest defense of religious principles and personal rights, the permanence of the parochial school system and the use of any language in the church that might be instrumental in preserving and propagating the Faith.

That they were right in their defense of the parochial school system is evinced by the final decision of the Holy See;[5] that there were certain liberalistic or rather naturalistic tendencies among the men whom the friends of the *Pastoral-Blatt* attacked, is proved by the Encyclical on Modernism;[6] and that the latter were not altogether wrong in their defense of a modified and gradually waning Germanism remains to be proved, that they were disloyal to their adopted country, as the Americanist party was wont to intimate, if not to charge

---

4 McQuaid to Gilmour, apud. Zwierlein, op. cit., vol. III, p. 41.

5 The injunction of the Roman authorities in regard to parochial schools was recently renewed in the Letter of the Papal Delegate to all the Ordinaries of the United States, by order of the S. Congregation for Seminaries and Universities, January 24, 1928. Cf. "Ecclesiastical Review," July, 1928.

6 The Encyclical on "Modernism" was preceded by a Papal document on "Americanism."

publicly, was utterly devoid of proof and simply foolish as an assumption.[7] For the German government, Prussian and Lutheran as it was, had never shown anything but aversion and contempt for the German Catholics in foreign parts, after its persecuting methods had driven them from hearth and home. Their feelings towards the Fatherland were sentimental and religious, not in any way political. Their love for German speech and German manners and customs was simply the natural love for themselves. And surely, there was no reason that they should love their American or Irish neighbors more than themselves.

The great mass of German Catholics were recent immigrants, and as such necessarily strangers to the natives. But as an Irish lecturer, Henry Giles, tells us, "strangeness, at first a feeling, may become, at last a habit." "It is natural" he continues, "that for a long while, they (the immigrants), should feel as in a strange land; and how can they more easily relieve this feeling than by holding communion with those who share their native memories and with whom they can interchange native sympathies."[8]

This is true of the Irish as well as of the German immigrant. Yet to the Irish, America was a distant, but not a foreign land, because his language was spoken all around him, whilst the German had to learn it with painful effort, and mostly with rather poor success. Every man has a right to his native tongue, and for anyone to despise it, would prove him a man without the sense of honor. No one was more severe on such turncoats, than the Irish Statesman John Philpot Curran. To a pretentious witness who feigned ignorance of Irish, and spoke English badly he said: "I see, Sir, you are more ashamed of knowing your own language than of not knowing any other."[9]

---

7 It was the Rev. Dr. McGlynn of Henry George fame that first made out the charge of "Constructive treason" against the German-American Catholics, for desiring the appointment of German speaking Bishops. Dr. McGlynn perhaps never knew that Cardinal Fransoni, as Prefect of the Propaganda, had on July 3, 1847, decreed this very measure, which was condemned as treason by the Americanists, namely that priests proposed as Bishops of Dioceses where a larger proportion of German Catholics resided, should be able to speak German. But here is this decree, as addressed to the Sixth Provincial Council of Baltimore, by Cardinal Fransoni:

"Inter qualitates vero in Episcopis requirendas, locum certe tenet scientia linguae, qua untuntur Fideles quibus iidem praeesse debent. Itaque, cum ingens sit numerous eorum qui ex Germania quotannis migrant ut in Foederatis Provinciis sedem sibi domiciliumque constituant, dabitis operam in posterum ut. S. Congregationi Presbyteros quos reperiri licebit linguae Germanicae peritia praeditos, pro iis duoecesibus eligendos curetis, in quibus populus ex Germania profectus reperiatur." Printed in "Acta et Decreta Concilii, VI," Baltimorensis. Collectio Lacensis, vol. III, p. 106.

8 Giles, H., "Lectures and Essays," p. 160.

9 Giles, ibidem, p. 109.

The German American priests sympathized with their people, and consequently loved to speak to them in the language of their native land; but they neglected no effort to bring them into harmony with the institutions of their new home. There was no disloyalty in their minds and hearts; they who had since 1848 resisted the encroachments of Protestant and infidel princes on the rights of the Church in Germany, and who had, in many cases, fled from their home country to find in America the liberty to serve God in the old Catholic way, surely could not desire anything like Prussianism in their new homes.

The troubles and trials of the Catholic Germans in this country were considerably enhanced by the fact that after the revolution of 1848 a large number of so-called liberal Germans sought refuge on our hospitable shores. They were for the most part young men who had received their education in the colleges and universities of Germany; some of them able men, who quickly made themselves a name in social, political and military life, but whose narrow ideas of civil and religious liberty led them to regard Roman Catholics as their deadly enemies and often to treat them as consummate fools. Boasting of the military record in "the war for liberty against the tyrants of Germany," they put themselves forward and were, to a large extent, accepted as the leaders and representatives of the German-American citizens of the country. Men like Carl Schurz, Daenzer, Preetorius, Boernstein, were indeed, no ordinary persons, though their minds were warped by a false philosophy of life. The mass of their followers, however, was of far less conspicuous ability, yet endowed with an inordinate vanity and a volubility of language, that was only surpassed by the meagreness of their ideas. These German radicals formed a well-organized body, and sought to dominate their Catholic countrymen. Their weapons against the recalcitrants were the usual ones of ridicule and slander. While boasting of their love of liberty, in thinking and writing, they covered with the poisonous darts of vituperation those who claimed the same right and professed the same love, but used it in a more decent manner.[10]

As the language these men employed by profession, was German, the Catholics of other nationalities, were not much affected by these diatribes; but the German Catholics felt them deeply, especially as only a few of their number were sufficiently educated to defend themselves against these unfair tactics. It certainly redounds to their credit, that they did not lose the courage of their convictions and that their Amer-

---

[10] It is almost incredible how coarse and even blasphemous such high class journals like the "St. Louis Puck" could write whenever anything Catholic was the theme, as for an instance, the account of the miraculous healing of a sick child in the Hospital of the Sisters of Charity, in 1871, "Puck," vol. I, No. 31.

icanization was more rapidly and thoroughly accomplished than that of the liberal and evangelical elements of the German race.

Standing alone in a new world of strange surroundings, viewed with suspicion by many of their own religion, and attacked, cajoled, and maligned by the prominent members of their own nationality, the German Catholic immigrants and their children had a hard battle of the spiritual kind to wage; and they fought it boldly and valiantly. It was therefore, a measure of Christian prudence, if not of necessity, to keep the children of the Faith away from these deleterious influences, and to band them together in strong Catholic organizations, where they might hold communion with those who shared their native memories and with whom they could interchange native sympathies.

That the Press as well as the Pulpit was employed for this purpose was but natural and perfectly right, both being powerful organs of the Catholic apostolate: These staunch old German priests deserve, instead of reproach, the highest praise, for having preserved the great mass of German Catholic immigrants from the fate of being swallowed up by the antichristian lodges and the German Free Thinker-Societies.[11]

This tender care for the German immigrant also lay at the root of what was derisively called "Cahenslyism." There was and still is an organization in Germany, called the St. Raphael's Society for the protection of German emigrants on their way to their new homes in America. It has its American headquarters at the Leo-House in New York, which, by the way, was founded mainly through the efforts of our St. Louis "Cahenslyites." It seeks to direct Catholic immigrants to such places as will offer them, not only the opportunity of making a livelihood, but also of practicing their religion.

In the early nineties, the distinguished President of the St. Raphael's Society, Peter Paul Cahensly,[12] who at the same time happened to be a member of the Centre Party in the German Reichstag, came to this country to study the workings of his Society and the condition of immigrants in general, irrespective of nationality and religion. The hue and cry was raised against him, as a political emissary of the German Emperor, and a dangerous plotter against the unity of the Church in America. Of course, nothing of the kind was intended or attempted. Mr. Cahensly's visit and his later activities had only the charitable object, to safeguard the emigrants from Germany and to ameliorate their spiritual condition in the New World. Archbishop

---

[11] Kenkel, Die Stellung der Deutschen Radikalen in Amerika zur Kirche und ihren Stammesgenossen, "Zentral-Blatt," December, 1920.

[12] The name is pronounced with the accent on the first syllable: Cáhensly, hence the designation Cahenslyites was a double violation of an honored name; one through malice and the other through ignorance.

Katzer[13] of Milwaukee, at the great German Catholic Convention in Buffalo, in September 1891, indignantly repelled the false aspersion of disloyalty, and distinctly stated on his honor as an Archbishop, that there was no trace of a disloyal or schismatic movement among the German Catholics of the United States. That ought to be proof sufficient, and yet Marley's ghost will not down. Just as in our early days, some Knownothings of the East objected to the charitable activities of the Leopoldine Association of Austria in supplying men and money for the struggling dioceses of the United States,[14] so in this case, some Know-alls of a later date held up to obloquy, under the name of Cahenslyism, the charitable activities of the St. Raphael's Society for the temporal and spiritual welfare of the Catholic immigrants. It seems preposterous that even churchmen of distinction should have taken the part of the enemies of a large portion of the Church's faithful children. Only a short while since, Bruce M. Mohler, Director of the Bureau of Immigration of the National Catholic Welfare Conference, after a three months study of the immigration situation in Europe, complains, "that the Catholics in some European countries have been somewhat slow to grasp the importance of the immigration question, as it pertains to America, and are not completely organized." He then adds ruefully: "This situation is a serious handicap to the Catholic immigration agency in this country," and he finally holds out the hope that "Catholics throughout Europe, have awakened to the needs of the immigration situation. They have begun to take an earnest interest and promise to put themselves in a position to co-operate effectively with the now highly efficient N.C.W.C. Catholic immigration organization on the receiving end in this country."[15] This is exactly what the St. Raphael's Society of the German Catholics has been doing for many years past, and what Mr. Cahensly proposed to further and expand in this country.

It was a total misconception of facts that made the so-called Americanists apply an opprobrious term to a thoroughly Catholic and, in a manner, patriotic movement. The pious Father Muehlsiepen, the learned Father Faerber and the astute Father Goller, therefore, deserve, not only admiration for their gallant fight for equal rights of all races in the Church, but also, the gratitude of all Catholics for their victorious defense of our Parochial Schools. Peace be to their ashes.

---

13   Archbishop Katzer was an Austrian and certainly had no use for Prussian protestantism and imperialism.

14   Protest against Leopold I of Austria in the New York "Observer" of 1834.

15   National Catholic Welfare Conference News Service, August 22, 1924.

# THE YEAR OF THE GOLDEN JUBILEE

In the year of Our Lord 1891 the city of St. Louis was destined to witness the most magnificent, as it was the most spontaneous, outburst of love and regard for a Catholic prelate, ever recorded in the Annals of the American Church.

The occasion was the fiftieth anniversary of the consecration of Peter Richard Kenrick as a Bishop, at the hands of the first Bishop of St. Louis, Joseph Rosati, in St. Mary's Church, Philadelphia. It was the first Golden Jubilee celebrated by a member of the American hierarchy, and the entire hierarchy was determined to honor their oldest and most distinguished member, Archbishop Peter Richard Kenrick.

Some nine years previous when the fiftieth anniversary of his ordination to the simple priesthood was approaching, and clergy and people of St. Louis were preparing to celebrate it, the archbishop forbade the ceremony, preferring to spend the day alone with God in his own thoughts. But at the urgent request of his Coadjutor Bishop Ryan, His Grace smiling significantly said: "It can be done should that time ever come." The clergy and people of the Archdiocese very properly held their archbishop to his promise.[1]

Early in the year preparations for the celebration were begun. As the archbishop's house was too small and unimposing for the occasion, a Committee of laymen raised funds for a new residence on a lot on Lindell Boulevard.

The lot was secured on March 1st, 1891, building operations proceeded rapidly, the house was furnished by a number of prominent ladies. On April 26th, both Vicars-General, Muehlsiepen and Brady, sent out notices to the clergy to assemble at St. John's Hall and to form an organization for the purpose of making arrangements for the Jubilee. Invitations were extended to all the members of the American episcopate and to prominent clergymen throughout the United States, and, of course to all the priests of the diocese.

All roads led to the "Rome of America," as St. Louis was popularly called since the celebration of the Golden Jubilee of Pope Pius IX. From all parts of the land there came distinguished ecclesiastics. The archbishops and bishops alone numbered about sixty; the priests of high or lower rank, at least five hundred.

---

[1] All the papers of the Jubilee Week were filled with glowing descriptions of the event, and published the more important addresses.

The Golden Jubilee festivities began on Sunday morning, with Pontifical High Mass, at St. John's Pro-Cathedral, celebrated by the Archbishop of Philadelphia. In other churches of the city thousands of fervent Catholics received Holy Communion for their beloved good shepherd, whilst the Jubilarian himself said mass privately in his chapel. In many of the churches eloquent discourses were preached by visiting prelates in praise of the great archbishop of St. Louis. The weather was clear and cold, the sun shone down on the streets from an unclouded sky.

All morning, almost from the hour of sunrise, the streets enclosing the Old Cathedral had been swarming with people who were anxious to get at least a glimpse of the evermemorable scene to be enacted there. A constant stream of prelates and priests came pouring into the courtyard between Cathedral and parish residence. At 10:10 o'clock the bells pealed forth the opening of the Jubilee. The procession, with the golden cross at its head came out of the courtyard into the full view of the spectators in the street. First came five hundred priests walking two abreast, with bowed heads; then the Superiors of Religious Orders, four Monsignors, two Mitred Abbots, forty Bishops and fourteen Archbishops, all these prelates in full canonicals. Then before the eyes of the vast multitude appeared the gracious figure of Peter Richard Kenrick, the central figure of the jubilee. Walking slowly, with bowed head beneath the canopy, humble and calm of face and bearing on the occasion of the greatest honor ever paid to an American prelate, the Archbishop came like the vision of a medieval saint before the reverent gaze of the people. His face, gentle and peaceful, showed no sign of any other emotion than that of quiet thankfulness, and his blue eyes, dimmed by the flight of more than four-score years, were bright, but tranquil in their brightness. Vicar-General Muehlsiepen and Father William Walsh were Deacons of Honor to the Archbishop.

Immediately behind the Jubilarian, and crowning the order of formation of the procession, as the highest representative of His Holiness, Pope Leo XIII, came His Eminence James Cardinal Gibbons, Archbishop of Baltimore, in the princely purple of His great office. With slow and measured step, he walked beneath the canopy held above his form. His pale and thoughtful countenance was the cynosure for thousands of wondering eyes. His attendants were Vicar-General Philip Brady, as Archpriest, and the Rev. Fathers D. W. Kenrick, C. M., and Joseph Hessoun as Deacons of Honor to the Celebrant.

As the last of the picturesque figures had disappeared within the sacred precincts of the Cathedral, the bells became silent: the solemn Pontifical Mass celebrated by Cardinal Gibbons, had begun. Archbishop Ryan preached the Jubilee Sermon. As an introduction to his masterly oratorical effort, he read the letter that had been addressed by the first Bishop of St. Louis, Joseph Rosati to his clergy and people on the occasion of the consecration of his Coadjutor, the present Archbishop of St. Louis, on that morning fifty years ago:

"Dearly Beloved Brethren:—The Very Rev. Peter Richard Kenrick, Vicar-General of the Diocese of Philadelphia, whose apostolical zeal has been so conspicuous in this city, and to whose merits all the Prelates of the American Church give honorable testimony, has been elected Bishop of Drasa and our Coadjutor. An express command of the Sovereign Pontiff having precluded every way of shrinking from the dignity to which he has been called, he .has submitted to the will of Heaven. We, assisted by his venerable brother, the Coadjutor and Administrator of the Diocese of Philadelphia, and by the Rt. Rev. Bishop Lefevre, coadjutor to the Bishop of Detroit, had the happiness of consecrating him in the church of St. Mary in Philadelphia, on the day consecrated to the memory of the Apostle St. Andrew, and had the satisfaction of receiving general congratulations .on the precious acquisition to us and to our diocese of so worthy a prelate.

Our heart overflows with joy at this happy event which, we consider, is the greatest blessing which Divine Providence had ever been pleased to bestow upon our diocese and upon you, dearly beloved brethren. He will continue to be your Father for a long succession of years."

The preacher then dilated on the Jubilarian's great qualities, his unaffected piety, his dauntless courage, his administrative wisdom, his love of study and contemplation combined with his supreme devotion to duty, his utter unselfishness, his high standard of sacerdotal virtue, and his universal sympathy for mankind.[2]

After the sermon the High Mass continued. The mass over, the procession of the Church dignitaries passed out as it had entered the Cathedral. The Cardinal, the Archbishop, and all the participating clergy then repaired to the Lindell Hotel for the banquet. Nearly six hundred guests were feasted and entertained there for four hours. The banqueting continued from 3 to 5 when the toastmaster announced that the addresses would proceed. Vicar-General Brady opened "the feast of wit and flow of soul" with an address to His Grace Peter Richard Kenrick. The Archbishop rose and in a few beautiful words expressed his gratitude to his priests and his hope to be able to devote the remainder of his life to the realization of the solid interests of religion and morality.

After the long and hearty applause had subsided the toastmaster announced "The address of welcome to the Cardinal, the visiting Prelates and Clergy," by the Rev. Francis Goller. Father Goller was long

---

2 Reprinted in full, "The Two Kenricks," pp. 345-357.

recognized as the intellectual leader of the German-American priests of
the Archdiocese of St. Louis and far beyond, one of the great promoters
and defenders of the parochial schools, absolutely loyal to his archbishop
and perfectly frank with him in all matters.    The Archbishop had
a sincere regard and liking for Father Goller.    It must be
remembered that the jubilee year was also the year of the
hightide of "Americanism."    Father Goller saw his opportunity
of setting his compatriots right in the matter by holding up the object
of his and the noble assembly's veneration, Archbishop Kenrick, as a true
shepherd of his entire flock, who knew his German Catholic people and
his German priests, and who entertained no suspiscion in regard to their
ecclesiastical or civic loyalty.    After a few happy words of welcome
Father Goller said:

"There is no act of his eventful, efficacious life in which the
genius of Peter Richard Kenrick shines more luminously then in the
generous, wise and just treatment he accorded to the brethren of the
faith who arrived in his diocese during the fifty years of his episcopate.
From every country of Europe, but preeminently from Ireland, Germany, France and Italy, mighty armies of peaceful men and women
have landed on our shores.    They came at America's generous invitation
to seek new homes in a land where all men are free and equal before the
law.    They felt that life, liberty, and the pursuit of happiness were
among the inalienable rights of man, and they began to love the country
that guaranteed them the free exercise of their rights. ' They proved
themselves worthy of being ranked among the most loyal and active
defenders of the Union.    If you rejoice in the fact that America is
great and glorious and free today, that the United States forms the
most prosperous, the most enlightened, the most powerful empire of
the world, then you owe heartfelt thanks and praise to the adopted sons
and daughters of America.    Do not call them foreigners, for they are
true Americans.    Learn to abstract the essentials from the accidental,
the primal duties of citizenship from the customs and manners of private life.    They are loyal Americans, for they love liberty and independence above all earthly goods, above the gaudy pomps of royalty, above
imperial splendor.    They have demonstrated on many fields of battle
how they love their country—America.

"They may still retain a fond regard for the land of their birth:
they may still treasure in their hearts the sweet memories of childhood;
for only the renegade can forget the mother that bore him—but far
dearer to them than the memories of childhood is the strong and
beautiful bride, Columbia, who taught them to walk erect on God's
earth in the proud consciousness of manhood.

"And the very love they bear their bride, Columbia, renders them
anxious to remove every blemish from her countenance and every speck

from her bright raiment, and makes them rise in solemn protest when self-seeking men endeavor to shield their evil deeds with her sacred name.

"In this free land they claim the right of fair criticism and of shaping public opinion according to their honest convictions. With all its faults we love the Union, yet, in the words of one of the brightest and most patriotic sons of America.

> "As honor would, nor lightly to dethrone
> Judgment, the stamp of manhood, or forego
> The son's right to a mother, dearer grown
> With growing knowledge.

"We have a country, but we are not as yet a nation in the full sense of the term: we are, as it were, "the rudis indigestaque moles" of a nation in the state of formation. All Europe, not England alone, is our mother, and we disdain to become a mere second edition of John Bull. A grander destiny awaits us. From the "disjecta membra" of many tribes and peoples we are gradually forming a new national type: we are absorbing the noble traits of various foreign nationalities. A hundred, perhaps more, years must roll on ere the typical American will be produced, embodying in himself the common sense and business capacity of the Anglo-Saxon, the patient research of the German, the keen wit of the Celt, the brilliant dash of the children of France, the childlike piety of Catholic Italy: but when he does make his appearance, all the world will recognize in him the ideal man.

"Archbishop Kenrick discovered in Catholic immigration, not a danger to the Republic, but a priceless acquisition. Mindful of the word of Sacred Scripture: 'Do you, therefore, love strangers, because you also were strangers in the land of Egypt,' our noble prelate welcomed all the children of the Church, unconcerned about their disparity in language and manner. For he based his hopes of a bright future upon the unifying bond of faith. . .

" 'In necassariis unitas, in dubiis libertas, in omnibus caritas.' This is the noble principle from which he never deviated in his intercourse with his priests and with his people. He was firm in exacting what was just, yet ever ready to grant freedom of action in all matters not defined by Divine or human law.

"Such is the man you are assembled to honor. He undertook many noble works for the honor of God. Divine Providence blessed his labors and crowned him with glory and honor. And honored forevermore shall be the name of Peter Richard Kenrick." [3]

---

3  Cf. "The Two Kenricks," pp. 364-367.

At the conclusion of Father Goller's adress there were loud and prolonged calls for Archbishop Ireland of St. Paul, and again at the end of the Cardinal's eloquent words in praise of the Holy Father, Leo XIII. The Archbishop of St. Paul rose in his place and made a brief response, winding up with the statement: "We recognize in civil matters no other power than the authorities at Washington, and in religious matters no other power than the Pontiff of the Vatican." Father Goller's remarks may have been regarded by many as uttered *magis importune quam opportune* yet the point he made, that the proper care and solicitude for the Catholic immigrant from beyond the sea, served as the main factor in the winning of the West for the Church of God, was was adverted to and favorably stressed by all the distinguished speakers of the evening, Archbishop Corrigan of New York, Archbishop Janssens of New Orleans, and Archbishop Hennessey of Dubuque. At the end of the banquet all the guests hurried away to prepare for the festivities of the night, the grand torchlight procession in honor of the Jubilarian and his guests.

It was a magnificent parade, a revelation of the strength of the Church in St. Louis, as well as a token of the affectionate regard the Catholics of St. Louis entertain for their venerable Archbishop. At least twenty thousand stalwart men and active youths, with banners afloat, and bands playing, bore their flaming torches on a parade that took two hours to pass a given point on the line of march. It was a glorious sight, that endless stream of men, eight abreast, under the mellowed glitter and glare of their twenty thousand torches. About 9 o'clock the head of the parade with Governor Francis and Mayor Noonan in the lead, reached the Archbishop's residence, His Grace stood at the window, with Archbishop Ryan at his side, until the last of the marchers were past. The last great torchlight procession in St. Louis had become a part of its history.

Tuesday morning witnessed the most touching of all the Jubilee greetings, the children's tribute to their Father and Friend. It took place in the grand Music Hall of the Exposition Building. The Hall was almost filled with children from the various parochial schools and diocese institutions; all the other seats were occupied by priests and sisters. About one hundred visiting prelates sat on the stage. The Archbishop occupied the center of the stage. The scene before him was one of marvelous beauty. The little girls from the German schools were all dressed in white, with golden wreaths on their heads, the others were dressed in sombre colors and wearing red hats. Every child bore an American flag. There they sat, the hope of the Church, under a waving mass of red, white and blue, the Irish and English, the German, the Polish, the Bohemian, the Italian children. Delegation after - delegation from the parochial schools approached His Grace, offered their happy greeting in their mother tongue, and stepped back for others. Round after round of applause swept over the house, as a delegation of the Colored Orphans stepped forward and presented their address to the Archbishop. Then came the orphans of St. Joseph's and of St. Mary's Home: then six children from St. Vincent German Orphan Home. The most touching part of the ceremony was the address of the deafmutes, spelled out in pantomine and immediately translated into English. "Hail Columbia, Happy Land" was then sung by the assembled multitude of children. with an enthusiam and precision that filled the Archbishop's heart with delight. "It is simply overwhelming," said the good old man, from the fullness of his great paternal heart. He could say no more: Archbishop Ryan spoke for him: "Overwhelming it is, the confession of all the varied nationalities mingled in this glorious country, united by the love of Jesus Christ, united in patriotism to the adopted country, the flag and the inspiration of these flags waving upon them, the flag bearers, singing, "Hail Columbia." . . . My heart is touched as it never was before. I cannot give expression to the thoughts that flash from the intellect, and the emotions that stir the soul to its deepest depths, and fill every fiber of my heart, as I look upon you, dear lambs, of the flock, now in the morning of your life, now with the flowers of promise blooming around you, now beginning life, coming to him who is approaching its end, and with your young hearts full of tenderness towards him, paying your aged Father the tribute of your veneration and love, in every tongue."[4]

One more demonstration was on the program of the Jubilee: the Public tribute to the representative of the Church in St. Louis and in the State of Missouri, by the representatives of the State and of the City, Governor David R. Francis was the main speaker of the occasion. The Governor's remarks were thoughtful, warm in tone and all in good taste. He closed with the remarkable ·words:

"Many thoughtless persons habituate themselves to the belief that, because there is no open union, there is total disseverance between the two mightest forces, the spiritual and the secular governances. It is a complete delusion. The strength of the one is derived from the stability of the other.

---

4 "The Two Kenricks," pp. 383-387.

We feel not the weight of the air, nor perceive it, as we respire it, yet we may not exist without it, and its weight would crush us, were we otherwise built, though it seems imponderable as it is. So works the unwritten and invisible harmony between Church and State in every civilized community.''

Thus ended the unique event, that stirred the heart of the entire country and awaked fresh interest in the Church everywhere, Archbishop Kenrick's Golden Jubilee.

## ARCHBISHOP KENRICK'S LAST YEARS

The crowning event of Archbishop Kenrick's life was over. The guests had departed, the noise and bustle was stilled. The old frame of his body felt tired but not exhausted. The four-score and five years seemed to rest lightly on his silvery crown of hair. A part of the energy of his youth seemed to have been roused in him by the memories evoked during the golden days of his Jubilee. It was, indeed, the sunset glow of a noble and blessed life, yet it had one effect, that was not transient: The diocesan Seminary was its enduring monument.

For a number of years St. Louis had a Seminary Board, but no Seminary. Funds were raised by annual collections for the education of candidates for the priesthood. Ordinations were held every year in the pro-cathedral of St. John the Apostle. From the time of Archbishop Ryan's departure for Philadelphia until the Jubilee, fully seven years, Archbishop Kenrick had ordained sixty priests, about one-fourth of that number for the diocese, the others for the various religious orders. Besides these, there were fourteen others that were ordained for St. Louis in Rome or·Baltimore or elsewhere, where they had been sent for their ecclesiastical studies. The majority of our students, however, attended the Seminary of St. Francis near Milwaukee. A number of our older diocesan clergy look back with pleasure and gratitude to the happy years they spent in that noble institution of learning by the shore of Lake Michigan.

Viear-General Muehlsiepen was President of the Seminary Board, and being of German antecedents, naturally favored the Seminary conducted on German lines of simplicity of life and thoroughness of training. But as it was the natural desire of many, to have a Seminary of their own, Archbishop Kenrick, seeing the opportunity offered to him of reestablishing the only institution still lacking in his otherwise so richly endowed archdiocese, quickly took action in the matter.

The Sisters of the Visitation, whom he and Bishop Timon in 1844, had rescued from the waters that engulfed their first home in the West, at Kaskaskia, and brought to St. Louis, had established a great Convent and School on Cass Avenue and Nineteenth Street. The Archbishop's Bank had furnished them a large building loan, the better part of which still remained uncancelled. In the course of time a change of location seemed desirable to the Sisters. With the assistance of friends, they

(577)

found a fine site in Cabanne Place, and having begun to build, were anxious to dispose of the old property. The Archbishop met their wishes most graciously, and thus the old Visitation Convent became his property for any purpose he might put it to.

What will he do with it? Was the question asked by many. "It shall serve for a Seminary, at least for a beginning."

The Archbishop's first choice for a teaching staff was reported to be the order of the Sulpicians: But Father Magnien declined the honor, because the men for the purpose were not available. The Vincentian Fathers were then approached. As they accepted the charge, the title to the property was transferred to them, on condition, that they conduct a first class Seminary. The buildings were remodeled and repaired. On the part of the Vincentians the Very Rev. Aloysius J. Meyer, C.M., one of their most distinguished educators, together with a full staff of professors took charge. The new institute was named the Kenrick Seminary in honor of its founder.

Classes opened on December 4th, 1892. Father Meyer retained the presidency until December 8, 1894. His successors were Father P. V. Byrne, F. V. Nugent, William Musson, M. S. Ryan, and Charles L. Souvay, all Lazarists, of course.

In the first ten years of its existence "one hundred and fifty-four students, representing twenty-five dioceses, have been ordained priests from Kenrick Seminary. But, as its founder anticipated, the time came when the location should no longer be suitable and the buildings should have become inadequate. The Kenrick Seminary was transferred to an ideal location, in the silvan solitude of the County, on what was called the Drummond Estate, now Glennon Park.

The Archbishop had never in all his life been seriously ill. As a man of extraordinary energy, combined with a singular regularity of life and of frugal habits, he had reached a hale and hearty old age, still able to do the work assigned to him, and very willing to do it. His old and trusted Vicar-General, Father Muehlsiepen, still enjoyed his gracious confidence, although a passing cloud in the matter of Father Faerber's unwarranted attempt to erect a new St. Mary's Church beyond the territory assigned to him, disturbed the confidential relations between the two good friends for a time. Vicar-General Brady, a much younger man, was very devoted and attentive to his venerable chief, confirming himself more and more in his good graces.

But sorrow came to the lonely house. The Archbishop's niece, Miss Elizabeth Eustace, who had kept house for him for a number of years, died after a brief illness; and then death called away his cousin, Jane Eustace, and finally Father Andrew Eustace, the pastor of St.

Michael's Church departed this life: The desire for a coadjutor, who would relieve him of his burden and carry it onward to greater and more blessed results, again and again rose in the heart of the austere recluse, as he took his lonely, though not lonesome walk, or sat in his study, or received a friendly call. The matter had been urged upon him repeatedly by men of high and low station. He had at first received these suggestions unkindly, then with some slight favor, and at last, with acquiescence. It now became apparent that Father Philip Brady was his choice for the office of his coadjutor, with the right of succession. The majority of the priests were not favorably disposed towards the Archbishop's probable choice.

On November 17th, 1892, the Archbishops of the United States were to hold their annual meeting in New York. Matters of great import were to be discussed and possibly settled. The storm that had been raging for some time in regard to the so-called school question was to be allayed. The Archbishop sent his Vicar-General, Brady, to attend the meeting as his representative. Father Brady was admitted to the sessions. It was at this meeting that Archbishop Satolli announced himself as the Apostolic Delegate to the United States. Although the deliberations of such an assembly are hedged in by the law of secrecy, a number of things that happened have become known. One of these was that Archbishop Kenrick's representative submitted a letter of His Grace requesting that the Archbishops immediately petition the Holy See to give him a Coadjutor in the person of the Very Rev. Philip Brady, V.G., of St. Louis. This was the old way of proceeding in the matter of episcopal appointments: But the Third Plenary Council of Baltimore had made new regulations, placing the choice of three candidates in the hands of the Diocesan Consultors and Irremoverable Rectors, which three names were to be forwarded to Rome and to the other bishops of the Province. The Bishops might reject one or all of the names submitted, but would have to give their reason for their action. Now the Archbishop of St. Louis had not appointed any Consultors or Irremover-able Rectors: and consequently the proper way of proceeding in the case seemed blocked, whilst the old way was no longer acceptable. It was, therefore, suggested to the priests of St. Louis to take action and submit a terna to the Archbishops for transmission to Rome. What was done at this meeting is briefly expressed by the following letter, dated St. Loins, Mo., November 17, 1892, which was sent to all the pastors and rectors of the Archdiocese:

"The Priests of the city have considered this an opportune time to express their wishes as regards the Coadjutor for the Most Rev. Archbishop, as he is no longer, on account of advanced age, able to attend to the visitation of the Diocese.

Upon conclusion of the oldest Priests of the city, the names mentioned in the petition were in the majority, and hence, were placed there.

The enclosed document has already been sent to his Eminence, Cardinal Gibbons. The time being so limited that we could not consult with all the Pastors of the Diocese, we therefore take this means of informing you what we have done, and ask you to express by letter your wishes in the premises.

The Reverend Clergy, regardless of nationality, gave us an enthusiastic reception. Every Secular Church in the city was visited; only four of the Rectors refusing to sign.

We remain your Brethren in the Priesthood,

C. Ziegler.
Jas. McCaffrey.
Jas. T. McCabe.
J. T. Foley.

Address:

Rev. C. Ziegler
St. Malachy's Church,
No. 2904 Clark Ave.,
St. Louis, Mo.''

The Letter to Cardinal Gibbons read as follows:

St. Louis, Mo., November 14th, 1892.

''To His Eminence, Cardinal Gibbons:

Your Eminence—We, the undersigned Rectors of St. Louis, respectfully request that a Coadjutor to His Grace, Archbishop Kenrick, cum jure successionis, be appointed at once, and that he be selected from the following list: Right Rev. J. J. Kain, of Wheeling; Right Rev. J. L. Spalding, of Peoria; Right Rev. Edw. Fitzgerald, of Little Rock.

Signers.

C. Ziegler, Pastor St. Malachy's Church.
F. M. Keilty, Rector of Holy Angels' Church.
James McCaffrey, Pastor of St. Patrick's Church.
Jas. J. McCabe, Rector of the Church of the Sacred Heart.
M. J. McLaughlin, Immaculate Conception, Hannibal.
C. P. Smith, St. Agnes Church.
F. Goller, Rector S.S. Peter and Paul, substituting Bishop
    Zardetti for Bishop Fitzgerald.
Eugene Coyle, Rector of the Cathedral.
Wm. Walsh Rector of St. Bridget's Church.
G. D. Power, Rector of Immaculate Conception Church.
E. J. Shea, Rector of St. Kevin's Church.
J. A. Hoffmann, Rector of St. Henry's Church.

Myles W. Tobyn, Rector of SS. Mary and Joseph's.
John H. May, Rector of Thomas Church.
Thos. Cooney, Rector of the Church of the Assumption.
E. Berry, Franklin County, Mo.
E. A. Schindel, Rector St. Boniface Church.
H. Schrage, Rector St. Agatha.
J. Hessoun, St. John of Nepomuc.
J. J. Head, Church of the Annunciation.
Wm. Faerber, St. Mary's Church.
T. A. Butler, St. Cronan's Church.
Edw. Fenlon, Church of the Visitation.
Daniel J. Lavery, Holy Rosary Church.
P. W. Tallon, Church of the Holy Name.
Jas. McGlynn, St. Rose of Lima.
M. Busch, Church of Holy Ghost.
D. S. Phelan, Church of Mount Carmel.
H. Hukestein, St. Augustine Church.
A. J. Schilling, Our Lady of Perpetual Succor.
A. Pauck, St. Engelbert's Church.
H. Wigger, Holy Cross Church.
Jos. Schroeder, Holy Trinity Church.
P. Gross, St. Stephen's, Richwoods.
Jas. Bourke, Administrator St. Michael's Church.
F. H. Gnielinski, St. Casimir's Church.
Engelbert Hoeynk, St. Liborius Church.
Urban Stanowski, St. Stanislaus Church.
Andreas Eustace, Rector St. Michael's Church.
Thos. Cleary, Lincoln County, Mo.
P. J. McNamee, St. James Church.
P. Bremerich, St. Bernard's Church.
Patrick Bernard Cahill, Pastor, Macon City.
Joseph Schaefers, Rector of St. Nicholas' Church."[1]

Two of the rectors refusing to sign the petition were the Reverend Fathers Harty of St. Leo's, afterward Archbishop of Manilla, and Joseph A. Connolly of St. Teresa's, the future Vicar-General of Archbishop Glennon. That the action taken by the priests of St. Louis met popular favor, is evidenced by the numerous expressions of joy and gratitude extended by the *Western Watchman* to the unanimity of the assembly and, especially, to the modest reserve shown by the German rectors in refraining from submitting a list of candidates of their own. Indeed Father Goller had submitted the name of Bishop Zardetti for that of Bishop Fitzgerald. But he stood alone in this,

---

1 Copy of Circular in Archives of the St. Louis Archdiocese.

and the name of Zardetti seems to have been finally dropped in favor of that of Bishop Marty. There was some talk about Archbishop Hennessey of Dubuque, but no action was taken. Although the *Western Watchman* stated in its issue of November 20th, 1892, that "the action of the priests cannot be interpreted as opposition to any priest in the diocese," the failure to put the Archbishop's favorite on the list shows conclusively that there was reason for such an interpretation. Two articles in the *Western Watchman*, December 4th, 1892, announced with glowing eloquence the satisfaction every one seemed to feel that the question of the Coadjutorship had brought on a veritable "Treuga Dei," a Truce of God, between the two contending wings of the St. Louis Clergy. Father Brady bore up bravely under his disappointment; for the Archbishop's confidence in him never wavered. But the knowledge that his brethren in the ministry had not only ignored him in their petition for a Coadjutor, but had actually arraigned him before the tribunal at Rome, as one unworthy of the high dignity, at last broke his spirit. He died at St. John's Parochial Residence on March 5th, 1893. Archbishop Ryan of Philadelphia preached his funeral sermon.

Father Philip P. Brady was born in Ireland, on April 4th, 1847, but came to America when two years old. He was educated for the priesthood in St. Vincent's Seminary at Cape Girardeau. Father Brady served first as assistant priest in Lexington, then as pastor in New Madrid. In 1874, he was appointed pastor of the Annunciation Church in St. Louis. Here he maintained two parish free schools, one for the boys in charge of the Christian Brothers, and one for the girls, in which the Religious of the Sacred Heart gave their services. In 1884, when Archbishop Ryan was appointed to the see of Philadelphia, Father Brady was made Vicar-General of the English speaking priests of the Archdiocese of St. Louis. And a few years later. when Bishop J. J. Hennessy was consecrated for the diocese of Wichita he was chosen to succeed him as pastor of St. John's Church. He was not a man of profound scholarship or of oratorical power. His health had been impaired by the privations and exposures of missionary life in the swamps of southeast Missouri. The qualities of his character fitted him better for a subordinate postion than for the high and arduous duties of an archbishop. At least, that was the opinion of his fellow priests, who must have known him well.

The news of Father Brady's sudden and unexpected death, following so closely in the wake of a mutual disappointment, fell upon the Archbishop's spirit with the sense of a personal loss. Now, indeed, he was alone. Archbishop Ryan lingered in St. Louis for a month to comfort his bereaved father and friend. The Archbishop had been ailing during the winter of 1892 to 1893: in fact his sickness was more serious than people knew. It had affected his mind in such a way, that he was rendered incapable of administering the affairs of the Archdiocese. The Holy See now took action on the priest's petition for a Coadjutor, and appointed the Rt. Rev. John Joseph Kain, the Bishop of Wheeling, West Virginia, to the position, constituting him titular Archbishop of Oxyrinchia and Coadjutor of Most Reverend Peter Richard Kenrick, Archbishop of St. Louis. Archbishop Kain arrived in St. Louis on August 3st, 1893, accompanied by an escort of twenty-two priests from the Archdiocese who had gone to Wheeling to welcome him to his new home in the West.

On December 14th, 1893, the Archbishop Coadjutor was appointed Administrator of the Archdiocese.

The sad story of Peter Richard Kenrick's last days as Archbishop of St. Louis, the one time "fountain of jurisdiction in the whole Northwest," is given in the Reminiscences of Father John T. Tuohy, a writer and editor of the day: the following is its substance:

"Unlike Archbishop Ryan and the Very Rev. Vicar-General Brady, who both lived in their own houses and simply paid weekly visits to the Archbishop for the business of the Diocese, the new Coadjutor went directly to the Archbishop's residence and took up quarters. The Seminary at the time had prepared the Archbishop's rooms and evidently expected to have the honor of housing him. But it was advised differently. Archbishop Kenrick evidently had not taken kindly to or did not recognize the fact that he had a claimant in his house. However this be, during the absence of the new Coadjutor at the Catholic Congress in Chicago, Archbishop Kenrick, probably acting on the advice of an overzealous visitor or two, appointed a Vicar General in place of Father Brady, for the Diocese.

This caused no little suprise, and might have led to complications, were it not for the good sense and judgment of the appointee, who later formally resigned the honor. The venerable Archbishop would keep the reins. He would settle his various finances, close the several annuities which he had been administering for years. Some expressed anxiety as to diocesan property and diocesan funds." Though there was little occasion for this uneasiness, the Archbishop-Administrator, having the full responsibility, naturally became urgent to take matters in charge. By civil process Archbishop Kenrick was divested of the administration of the temporalities of the Archdiocese, and the Coadjutor was invested with it. These proceedings proved most unpopular and brought much criticism on the Administrator. Nevertheless he was obliged to proceed still further. On May 21st, 1895, the Holy See created John Joseph Kain, Archbishop of St. Louis and the Most Reverend Peter Richard Kenrick titular Archbishop of Marcianopolis. Archbishop Kain was now free to act. But he had no home. Taking his breakfast and attending official calls at the Archiepiscopal residence, he was soon gone for the day. Various pastors of the city in turn had him as guest.''[2]

His first years in St. Louis were a sore trial to him. There was the constant warning over the entrance to his house: ''Noli irritare leonem.''[3]

---

[2] Historical Sketch of the Archdiocese of St. Louis, by Rev. J. T. Tuohy, L.L.D.

[3] Archbishop Kenrick's coat-of-arms bore the inscription, ''Noli irritare leonem,'' ''Do not irritate the lion.'' It was placed on the front-door arch of the Archbishop's residence.

PART THREE

———

THE ARCHDIOCESE OF ST. LOUIS

BOOK II

*Archbishop John Joseph Kain*

John J. Kain
Abp. St Louis

PART III

BOOK II

CHAPTER 1

ARCHBISHOP KAIN'S ANTECEDENTS IN THE EAST AND
BEGINNINGS IN THE WEST

The new Coadjutor to Archbishop Kenrick, John Joseph Kain, was born May 31, 1841, at Martinsburg, Virginia, now West Virginia, in the very year his predecessor had come to St. Louis. At the age of sixteen, he was sent to the Sulpician College of St. Charles, Ellicot City, Maryland, to make his collegiate studies. On the completion of the course in 1862, he passed on to. the Seminary of St. Mary's, at Baltimore. At College the future Archbishop of Dubuque, John J. Keane, was a classmate of his. At Baltimore he had for fellow-students the brothers James J. and Michael McCabe who, later on, as pastors of two prominent St. Louis churches, were instrumental in placing John Joseph Kain's name on the priests' list for the St. Louis Coadjutorship. Throughout his collegiate, philosophical and theological studies the young John Joseph evinced rare talent and a capacity for hard work. In the judgment of their Sulpician professors "John J. Kain was the more solid, John J. Keane the more brilliant" student, a judgment that was·borne out by the event. John Joseph Kain was ordained a priest by Archbishop Martin J. Spalding, in Baltimore Cathedral, July 2, 1866.

Being a member of the diocese of Richmond, which then embraced all Virginia and the eastern counties of West Virginia, the young and energetic priest was appointed by Bishop John McGill to the pastorship of Harper's Ferry. The parish covered eight counties in West Virginia and parts of four in the Old Dominion. The territory was for the most part rugged and pathless and desolate. Having hardly emerged out of the primeval wilderness, it experienced all the horrors of civil war. Churches lay in ruins, as that of Winchester and of Broken Spring, the homes of the farmers and miners were destroyed or impoverished. Harper's Ferry was full of memorials of John Brown and the subsequent struggle between the North and South. Father Kain's home town, Martinsburg, also lay within his parish.

(587)

A young man of magnificent physique and remarkable power of endurance, the pastor of Harper's Ferry drew new courage from the difficulties and hardships in prospect. Nothing could daunt him, nothing could cast him down. Even the constant exuberant praise he heard everywhere of his predecessor in office, then the Bishop of Wheeling, did not discourage the humble beginner. On the contrary, as the little church on the rock of Harper's Ferry had been the stepping-stone of Father Whelan to episcopal honors, so it was to be Father Kain's, to the see of Wheeling, and finally, his own successor's in the pastorate, Father Van de Viver, to the see of Richmond, just vacated by Bishop James Gibbons. But this is running ahead of time. Father Kain, as pastor of Harper's Ferry and the surrounding counties, gained for himself an enviable reputation among high and low, throughout Virginia and West Virginia and Maryland. His intensive activity seemed to be his characteristic mark. He always prepared his sermons. They contained no lofty flights of eloquence, but were always plain and direct and full of the Christian spirit. And their influence was heightened by the force of his personal example. Wherever and whenever he could get a knot of people together in a court-house or under the forest trees, or in some hospitable home in the mountains, it was his delight to expound the teachings of the Gospel. And the people loved to hear him speak in his earnest kindly way. They were poor, indeed, in earthly goods, but rich in Faith.

Father Kain's financial ability and business tact, an ability almost indispensible in a priest, was made manifest by the churches he built in his missions, and for which he paid. When he was ordained in 1866, many thought that he was a victim of consumption; but as he himself said on the occasion of his Silver Jubilee in the priesthood, he no doubt, owed it to the exercise forced upon him in the nine years of his pastorate at Harper's Ferry, that his voice was stronger, and his health better than when he was ordained a priest.

After nine years of such faithful, yet ever humble service in the rugged vineyard of the Lord, Father Kain's hour of exaltation came. The saintly Bishop Richard Vincent Whelan died on July 7, 1874; the last words were: "My work is done." By Apostolic letters bearing date of February 12, 1875, Rev. John Joseph Kain, Pastor of Harper's Ferry, was appointed his successor as Bishop of Wheeling.

Rt. Rev. John J. Kain's consecration took place in the Wheeling Cathedral, May 23, 1875. Archbishop Bayley of Baltimore, assisted by Bishop James Gibbons of Richmond, Virginia, and Thomas A. Becker of Wilmington, Delaware, were the consecrating prelates. The Bishops that honored the occasion by their gracious presence were Rosecrans of Columbus, Ohio, Domenec of Pittsburg, Pa.; Shanahan of Harrisburg, Pa.; and O'Hara of Scranton, Pa.

About twenty-four diocesan priests and eminent clergymen of other dioceses were in attendance. Bishop James Gibbons of Richmond preached the consecration sermon: "A new captain comes forward today to lead you on to fresh battles and unless I am very much deceived, he will never say: 'Go' but will always say: 'Come let us go together.'— "The diocese of Richmond" concluded the preacher, "in losing Father Kain, had lost a valuable member, and the clergy an affectionate brother, but Richmond's loss was Wheeling's gain . . . May this day be the harbinger of a bright and glorious future for the diocese of Wheeling."

The diocese of Wheeling was erected out of the western part of the territory of the diocese of Richmond, on July 23, 1850, and the Bishop of Richmond, Richard V. Whelan was transferred to the new See. It embraced the State of West Virginia except eight counties which remained with Richmond; but in lieu of these, Wheeling received jurisdiction over eighteen counties of the Old Dominion. The diocese covered 29,172 sq. miles. The Catholic membership was estimated at one-twentieth of the total population and was scattered over a very large and difficult area. Consequently, there were but few parishes strong enough financially to support a resident priest. The only religious Order of men represented in the diocese, was that of the Capuchins. The Sisters of St. Joseph had their Motherhouse and Novitiate, and also a Hospital in Wheeling; the Sisters of the Visitation conducted an Academy for girls at their Convent, and the Sisters of Divine Providence were in charge of the Orphan Asylum. The number of priests in the diocese to cover the twenty-nine thousand square miles was about thirty-five, although Bishop Kain had labored very hard to increase their number. The Bishop himself lived the life of a missionary. In 1876 Bishop Kain applied to Rome for a redistribution of the dioceses of Wheeling and Richmond, so that Wheeling should receive the eight West Virginia counties in exchange for that part of the diocese that lay in Old Virginia. Cardinal Franchi, Prefect of the Propaganda, sent a copy of Bishop Kain's letter to the Bishop of Richmond, James Gibbons, afterwards Cardinal Archbishop of Baltimore, who objected to the proposed move. Whereupon Propaganda declined to authorize any change.[1]

At the Third Plenary Council of Baltimore, Bishop Kain was one of the leading spirits, being a member of the Deputation of Bishops on the Catechism. He took prominent part in the discussions on the procedure in clerical trials, on "the wicked custom of demanding an entrance fee from all those who go to hear Mass," on the "custom of having dances for the promotion of pious works," on the spiritual care of poor immigrants, and other kindred topics.[2] Bishop McQuaid

---

1 Will, Allen Sinclair, "Life of Cardinal Gibbons," vol. I, p. 151.
2 Concilia Plenarii Baltimorensis III. Acta et Decreta, passim.

of Rochester regarded Bishop Kain as a supporter of the high aspirations of Baltimore as against New York. Baltimore wants to set up as the American Vatican, with its curia under the management of the Sulpicians," he wrote to Bishop Gilmour; and then, criticizing the Commission on the Indian and Negro Missions, he added: "All are Sulpicians, Gibbons, Kain, Curtis. Here in the North we do not propose to be tied to the chariot-wheel of Baltimore."[3]

The Silver Jubilee of Bishop John J. Kain's ordination to the priesthood was kept on July 2, 1891. The church services were held in St. Joseph's Cathedral of Wheeling. The preacher on the occasion, Monsignor Sullivan, adverted in particular to the outstanding virtues of the Rt. Rev. Jubilarian; as manifested among them during his sixteen years as bishop: namely, "his zeal, piety, efficiency and learning," and in conclusion expressed the hallowed wish: "Ad multos Anuos."[4] Bishop Kain's remaining years in Wheeling were not destined by Heaven to be many. Only two years after this event Bishop John Joseph Kain was constituted Archbishop of Oxorynchia and Coadjutor to the Most Rev. Peter Richard Kenrick, Archbishop of St. Louis. That meant a long farewell to his mountain-home of liberty; a life of severe strain and heavier disappointment than Harper's Ferry or Wheeling had ever imposed upon him.

The people of St. Louis did not realize the serious particulars of Archbishop Kenrick's condition. He still had a partial use of his mind; but the duties and responsibilities of his office were so numerous and so grave, that the Coadjutor must feel himself bound to assume them entirely, as the Archbishop would in no wise share them with him. Accordingly, Most Rev. John Joseph Kain on December 14, 1893 was appointed Administrator of the Archdiocese.

The Archbishop-Elect still remained under some restrictions: Ordinations of eight St. Louis Priests were held by neighboring bishops or in Foreign Seminaries. A number of corner stones were laid and churches blessed but not by the Administrator. On September 20, 1893, however, Archbishop Kain began to perform such ceremonies, but after May 21, 1895, when the Holy See created him Archbishop of St. Louis, the ordinations were generally performed by him in person.

Archbishop Kenrick's old and trusted Vicar-General Henry Muehlsiepen, was continued in office, though no longer enjoying the full powers of the Vicar-General of the German and Polish priests and parishes. In 1895 fifteen priests were ordained for the diocese and two others were re-

---

3 Zwierlein, Frederick J., "Life and Letters of Bishop McQuaid," vol. I, p. 152.

4 To the Rt. Rev. John T. Sullivan's Memorial Booklet, at the Sacerdotal Silver Jubilee of Rt. Rev. John J. Kain, July 2, 1891, we owe a number of biographical data.

ceived from abroad. On April 28, Archbishop Kain laid the corner stone of St. Casimir's church in St. Louis and on September 1, blessed it with the usual solemnity, whilst the Vicar-General blessed the Bohemian church of St. Wenceslaus July 21. In the meantime Father Muehlsiepen laid the cornerstones of the new churches of the Immaculate Conception at Maxville, of St. Francis de Sales in St. Louis and of the Assumption church at New Haven. On October 13 the church of the Immaculate Conception was blessed by the Vicar-General. The following five city parishes were erected in 1893. St. Matthew's, St. Louis, by Rev. Joseph T. Shields; St. Mark's, St. Louis, by Rev. John Dillon; St. Edward's, St. Louis, by Rev. L. J. Wynne; St. Barbara, German, St. Louis, by Rev. John Schramm; Holy Innocents, St. Louis, by Rev. John White. Only one Parish was formed this year in a country district: St. Aloysius, Baring, Knox Co. by Rev. James J. O'Reilly.

In 1894 the following churches received their first resident pastor: Our Lady of Good Counsel, St. Louis, Rev. P. O. Donohue; Guardian Angel, Oran, Scott Co., Rev. George Koob; St. Patrick's, Jonesburg, Andrian Co., Rev. B. H. Schlathoelter; The Assumption, formerly St. Magdalen parish at New Haven, Franklin Co., Rev. M. T. Sevcik.

In 1895 the following six parishes were established: St. Wenceslaus, St. Louis, Rev. H. Peocar; St. Theodore, Flint Hill, Rev. G. W. Kurtenbach; St. Michael's, Shrewsbury, Rev. F. Brand; St. Joseph's, White Church, Rev. John Waeltermann.

At the close of the year 1895 the diocese contained 2 Archbishops, 214 diocesan priests, 127 priests of Religious Orders: Parish churches in the city 60; chapels with daily mass 27: Parish churches outside the city 114; missions with churches 94; stations 35.

On March 4, 1896 died the Most Reverend Peter Richard Kenrick, titular Archbishop of Marcianopolis, having been Archbishop of St. Louis from July 20, 1847 until May 21, 1895.

## CHAPTER 2

ARCHBISHOP KENRICK'S DEATH AND OBSEQUIES

Archbishop Kenrick's death, though long expected, at last came to find his attendants unprepared; his last moments were spent alone with God. A Brother from the Alexian Hospital had been with the venerable patient for the last few months, but had been dismissed by the Archbishop as no longer needed. Father Panken, S.J. of St. Elizabeth's, the Archbishop's confessor, and Father Bronsgeest of the College church, the pastor of the district in which the Archbishop's House was situated, had regularly brought him Holy Communion ever since he had ceased to say Mass; but neither good Father was aware of any serious change in his condition. The Archbishop's faithful servant Tom was most assiduous in his attentions, but had no inkling that the end was so near. Archbishop Kain had left the house in the morning after a brief call in the sick room, and took dinner at the Planters' Hotel with Father Tuohy. The morning wore on without any apparent change, save this that the Archbishop declined dinner. At about one in the afternoon, the servant asked: "would His Grace have the bedroom made warmer, and the answer came faintly: "Yes." It was the last word of the Archbishop heard on earth. When Tom returned to the bedside the Angel of Death had departed with the great soul of Peter Richard Kenrick. Archbishop Kain returned to the house shortly after death had set in. The solemn obsequies of the great and good Archbishop were held in the Old Cathedral on Walnut Street. Here the last earthly remains of the man who had built up the church in the Mississippi Valley and ruled it for more than half a century, lay in state, to receive the homage of reverence and love for the last time. Cardinal Gibbons presided at the solemn Requiem. In the Sanctuary knelt Archbishops Ryan of Philadelphia, Feehan of Chicago, Ireland of St. Paul, Elder of Cincinnati, Katzer of Milwaukee and Kain of St. Louis; as well as Bishops Hennessy, Scannell, McCloskey, Foley, Heslin, Rademacher, Ryan of Alton, Janssen and Cotter. The sanctuary and the front pews were filled with Priests of the diocese and a vast number from outside: fully thirty thousand were gathered in and around the Cathedral; people of all classes and religious denominations and walks of life.

Archbishop Ryan, the almost lifelong friend of the dead prelate, preached the funeral oration. In his own masterly way the preacher passed in review the characteristic traits of Archbishop Kenrick's personality: his indomitable missionary spirit, his tireless devotion to duty, his captivating eloquence and his fearless adherence to what he believed

(592)

to be true and right. The emotion which the preacher exhibited was deep and genuine and found a full response in the hearts of the assembled multitude, to whom the departed had been a father and friend, guide and model.

After the requiem, the prayers of the last absolution were pronounced by Cardinal Gibbons, and then the funeral cortege started for Calvary Cemetery, where the casket was gently lowered into the grave, there to await the resurrection day. As Archbishop Ryan so beautifully and touchingly expressed it in his grand funeral sermon: "We saw him, a stately lily in the garden of the Church, and we saw the lily droop, till the powerless stem could no longer keep elevated the golden chalice; and when the lily drooped, the stem and lily fell; and we felt that the flower hath fallen."

As the years of Archbishop Kenrick's manifold labors and successful endeavors in the cause of Christ and then the few lengthening years of weariness and sorrow slowly recede from the view of the rising generation, the greatness and beauty of his character as reflected from the bright mirror of contemporary opinion and regard, are beginning to grow clearer and brighter in the minds of those that were young in his days of decline.

In outward appearance, during the later years, Archbishop Kenrick was of medium size and harmonious build; only the broad forehead with its eagle eyes under shaggy gray eyebrows immediately fastened upon the mind on first meeting him as something out of the regular order. His clothing was old-fashioned, though by no means slovenly. His walk was slow and pensive. Like a true gentleman of the old school, he always, when out walking, wore the regulation silk hat. On his daily walk along Pine Street he commanded respect and attention even among strangers, by his poise and gentlemanly bearing. His punctuality in coming and going is still remembered by many who lived in the vicinity of St. John's church. His speech was slow but distinct, "With the faintest suggestion of the charming brogue of Ireland." In manner he was not austere but temperate. His personal peculiarities were intimately bound up with his highest qualities, his love of study and meditation. He possessed a considerable amount of dry humor. He loved solitude, but not from any sullen contempt of his fellowman; his was not the "taciturnity of pride," as Walter Savage Landor expresses it, but the yearning love of a great heart for the infinite Silence of God's Presence. The ruling phase of his character was an abiding faith in God, a childlike trust in His Providence. He had a high regard for the episcopal office, in himself as well in his fellowbishops. As one who, by Divine ordinance represented Christ, to his flock, he accepted the reverence and love shown to him; but outside of that he cared not for anything the world might offer him. He stood for justice like an impregnable tower, against the preachers of hate and iniquity, against the vaunting politicians of test-oath days, against his own brethren at the Council. Though mistaken in the latter case, and perhaps on some others, he never spoke or acted against the voice of his conscience; He was loyal to Holy Church, always and everywhere, although, in the fervor of debate, he said some things that had better been left unsaid. But he said them boldly, because he believed they had an important bearing on the destinies of the Church; and when he found that he was mistaken, he gave, in the words of Archbishop Ryan, ''The strongest proof of his loyalty,'' by accepting something simply because it was the teaching of the Church. ''He was loyal to the Pope as the head of the Church. As to his practical infallibility in teaching on matters of faith and morals, he had never entertained a doubt—But he did not believe the promulgation of the doctrine opportune at the time, and consequently urged a number of historical facts that seemed to call for a longer clarifying process, before the matter should be finally adjudicated. This was an error of judgment and was afterwards recognized by him as such. He had made his opposition ''salvo meo ordine,'' ''without prejudice to my order,'' as a Bishop, ''whom the Holy Ghost had appointed to rule the Church of God:'' he humbly submitted when the Holy See showed him the full truth by the decree of the Church Universal. His episcopal dignity still remained the symbol of his honor and power.

Among the most lovable traits of the Archbishop's character is his absolute contempt ''for all the world of fat prosperity.'' He knew the value of money in the Church's battle of life. But his treatment of money stood in gracious relief from some of our modern methods of money-getting. The vulgarity of competition had no part in him. He was one of those

> ''brave hearts that never did aspire
> Wholly to things of earth.''

And in the sequence he had lost all thought of earthly recompense.

He was ever the friend of the oppressed, the weak and the needy, although he made no great to-do about his charities. He sometimes passed a gentle censure on a priest as a means to introduce his praise. He was the embodiment of Sidney's gentleman: ''high erected thoughts seated in a heart of courtesy.'' Thus Archbishop Kenrick lived, blending the interior Christian life with the exterior duty of a Catholic Bishop. He was a distinguished orator; his preaching was direct and paternal; and as Archbishop Ryan said, ''he preached with a power, a logic and an unction, that convinced the intellect and touched the heart.'' ''He knew his duties well and fulfilled them; he knew his rights and always maintained them.'' On the American Church he left the indelible impress of his individuality, that of a really great man. This perfect consistency of character, simple, dignified and beautiful, was Archbishop Kenrick's most valued gift to his beloved archdiocese of St. Louis and to the people of the entire territory of his early days.

And what a vast and unpromising diocese it was when Peter Richard Kenrick entered upon its administration, comprising the present states of Arkansas and Missouri, the western moiety of Illinois and everything west of Arkansas, Missouri and Iowa. The territory of Iowa had already been detached from the diocese in Bishop Rosati's time, as the temporary care of Chicago also ceased before Bishop Kenrick's advent on the field. Besides the archdioceses of Chicago and Dubuque with their seven suffragan sees: Belleville, Peoria, Rockford, Springfield, Davenport, Des Moines and Sioux City, the territory of which was dismembered from the original diocese of St. Louis under Bishop Rosati, the early diocese of Bishop Kenrick has in the course of fifty years lost by filiation and dismemberment the territory of the present sees of Little Rock in Arkansas: St. Joseph and Kansas City in Missouri, the archdiocese of St. Paul with Duluth, St. Cloud, Winona in Minnesota; Wichita, Leavenworth and Concordia in Kansas; Lincoln and Omaha in Nebraska; Denver in Colorado; Fargo in North Dakota; Sioux Falls in South Dakota; Helena in Montana; Cheyenne in Wyoming; Salt Lake City in Utah; Boise in Idaho; and Tucson in Arizona. What a marvelous development within the short period of fifty years; and what a glorious prospect for the future of the Church in what was once a single struggling diocese. Great credit is due to many devoted men and women who have given of their best to the upbuilding of the Church in the West, but as Archbishop Hennessy of Dubuque expressed it in glowing terms, ''Of all the great men that will have labored to build her: of all the bright names that will have shed the lustre of their learning and their virtues around her, the brightest far and the most cherished will be that of Peter Richard Kenrick. He it was who ruled all that territory, and only he, since it became the abode of white men; he it was who with sound judgment divided it up into dioceses and provinces, selected the rectors of the assembly and recommended their rulers, gathered or brought them together in council, enacted wise and timely laws for their guidance, engraved on them, to some extent, the impress of his own character, gave them constantly the edifying example of his own bright and beautiful life to allure and encourage them along the narrow, rough road before them.

''Fifty years ago, when the venerable Archbishop of St. Louis was consecrated, there was but one Archbishop in the entire United States, with but fifteen other Bishops. There were 500 priests, with 518 churches and chapels. There were thirty-three Catholic schools, containing some 5,200 pupils, and a Catholic population estimated at 1,300,000. Now the ratio of our increase is this: for every priest then ministering at the altar there are now sixteen others, for every church and chapel there are eighteen, and most of these churches are more beautiful and far more enduring. The Catholic population has multiplied seven times over, and for every pupil then attending a Catholic school, there are now 120, and our schools themselves have multiplied at the ratio of a hundred for a single one.'"[1]

---

1 From Archbishop Hennessey's Address at the Golden Jubilee Banquet.

# WAITING FOR THE PALLIUM

The First great religious event in St. Louis after the historic scene of Archbishop Kenrick's funeral was the official visit of Cardinal Satolli, the Apostolic Delegate, to Archbishop Kain's episcopal city, in the second week of April 1896. The Cardinal arrived in the city on Wednesday, April 8. On Thursday morning His Eminence held a Solemn High Mass. Father David S. Phelan preached the sermon in his usual sparkling style on the text: "Thou art Peter." In his peroration he said: "Francis Satolli has overcome all opposition and won all hearts in this great American Republic. He came to us ·as a Roman of the Romans, he leaves us as an American of the Americans. He comes today to honor us with his visit and at the same time to bid us farewell. He has done great service to the Church of America. He came as an alien and uninvited, among us, he leaves us as a friend whose departure makes us sad. He will take the comfort along with him to Rome that he has gained the esteem of all and that he made more close and strong the bands that unite our hearts with Rome."

After Highmass the clergy repaired to the Kenrick Seminary to attend the banquet in honor of Cardinal Satolli. The function of toastmaster fell to Father Myles Tobin. Archbishop Kain addressed a hearty welcome to His Eminence, in which he alluded to Cardinal Satolli's high regard for American institutions. The next speaker, Father Francis Goller, made a beautiful talk in classical Latin on the great Encyclicals of Leo XIII; Father Tallon's topic was the Apostolic Delegation; Father McLaughlin's, the Church in America; and Father James Coffey's, the Archdiocese of St. Louis. All the speakers seemed to hold the rapt attention of His Eminence; His response was given in Latin. It was an informal talk expressing the gratitude of his heart for the grand welcome extended to him, and the high admiration, he entertained for St. Louis and its Catholic people. The number of guests taking part in the demonstration in honor of the Pope's Representative was one hundred and eighty-four. A Latin ode in the Alcaic measure composed by Father Holweck was recited at the banquet in honor of Cardinal Satolli,

"Quem mittit almus rex senio gravis,
Qui iam labantis pondera sacculi
   Pronasque regnorum ruinas
   Consilioque humerisque sistit."[1]

---

[1] Almost prophetic words of the down-fall of civilization and the ruin of kingdoms we have witnessed in the World War.

A tour of the city was the next thing on the program. Brief visits were made by the Cardinal to a number of Religious Institutions, the Asylum for the Deaf Mutes, St. Vincent's Orphan Asylum, St. Ann's Home and St. Joseph's Church. These visits were resumed on Friday morning to the House of the Good Shepherd, the Carmelite Nuns and the Ursuline Convent. A great surprise awaited His Eminence at S.S. Peter and Paul's. As the Papal Delegate entered the Sanctuary of the beautiful Church, there was before him a broad and deep expanse of upturned faces, children's faces, fourteen hundred of them, all pupils of the School of S.S. Peter and Paul. After the last tones of the German hymn of praise had died away, the pastor, Father Francis Goller, delivered the following address, again in the majestic language of Rome:

"Your Eminence: Entering our Church of S.S. Peter and Paul you meet more than twelve hundred children who are acquiring the rudiments of Christian Doctrine in our parochial school and receive from the care and zeal of our good Sisters instructions in good morals, as well as in the sciences and arts, so that they may become good citizens of the state and worthy members of the kingdom of God. For in this, our country, where the Catholics are living dispersed among so many unbelievers and heretics, it is almost impossible, certainly very difficult, that Catholic truth should remain the rule of life, unless it be instilled into the minds of the young from their earliest years. Therefore, I do not hesitate to affirm that, in the shadow of every church that is really flourishing and bringing forth fruit for everlasting life, you will find a parochial school; where, however, you find no parochial school, the church will appear neglected and, I fear, will soon fall to ruin.

And if you should find at times such a parish, showing some life and progress, it is because it is drawing its vigor and vital spirit from other parishes, that are blessed with parochial schools, whilst its own offspring is gradually dying out. This temple has been built by the parents of these children, 'and it is filled three times on every Sunday and Feast, from the altar to the portals, by the multitude of the faithful. But I am fully convinced, that, if the parochial school should be suspended, after thirty years only a few pious women and their infants would be present at the solemnities of the Church."[2]

In response His Eminence congratulated the priests and people on the magnificence and solidity of their church edifice and for their zeal in caring for the lambs of the flock. He had now learned to regard his stay in America as a psalm of praise, of which his visit to St. Louis was the Gloria Patri et Filio et Spiritui Sancto, and his present visit to the church of S.S. Peter and Paul as the final Alleluia."

---

2 "Church Progress," April, 1896.

There were many more visits paid by Cardinal Satolli on that day, but the grandest and most touching of all was his visit to Archbishop Kenrick's grave. It was the Cardinal's own request. He desired to kneel at the grave of the grand old Metropolitan who for more than fifty years had held sway over the Archdiocese of St. Louis. And then when church bells were ringing and worshipers hurrying along the streets of the great city there in the golden glow of the warm Sunday morning, surrounded by the voiceless dead and the dumb tombstones, that bore the legend of their birth and death, there on the fresh grass of early Spring, knelt the Pope's Representative, a Cardinal of the Roman Church, to pay homage to the lifeless dust of Peter Richard Kenrick, and chanted over his tomb the prayers of Holy Church. After the prayer Cardinal Satolli remained on his knees in silent meditation for several minutes; then he arose and walked in silence to the carriage in waiting. He departed for Washington, Monday morning.

On May 10, 1896, the Archdiocese was to be honored and gladdened by the investiture of its new Archbishop with the Sacred Pallium. The Pallium, a circular band made of white wool, worn over the shoulders and having two pendants of the same material is the symbol of archiepiscopal power. It is blessed by the Pope and sent by him to an Archbishop-elect at his petition and it typifies his participation in the Pope's supreme pastoral power in the Province assigned to him. The solemn function of conferring the Pallium was held in the Old Cathedral. Cardinal Gibbons, assisted by twenty-five Archbishops and Bishops, with the clergy of the Diocese and numbers of visiting priests and minor prelates filled the Sanctuary. Cardinal Gibbons celebrated Pontifical High Mass; but before doing so he received the profession of Faith and the oath of Office from Archbishop Kain and then placed the Pallium over his shoulders. All this was done in the strictly rubrical way; but now came a novelty that surprised everybody save the Archbishop. A delegation of laymen, headed by the Hon. R. Graham Frost, entered the Sanctuary and offered an address of welcome to their new Archbishop. The reply of Archbishop Kain was an expression of gratitude and affection. At the close of the Pontifical Highmass, Bishop John J. Kean, then Rector of the Catholic University of Washington, D. C., delivered a forceful discourse on the words of Our Lord: "Feed my Lambs, feed my sheep," closing with a warm eulogy on the virtues of the new Archbishop. A splendid banquet at the Kenrick Seminary closed the festivities.

Being now invested with the full jurisdiction of his exalted office the new Archbishop of St. Louis laid plans for a large amount of constructive work, spiritual and material. To gain an adequate knowledge of the diocese, of the number and quality of the clergy, of the resources of the parishes and religious institutions, had already been the object of his attention. He had learnt from the reports handed in at the Chancery that there were two hundred and twenty-seven diocesan priests and one hundred and twenty-seven Fathers belonging to various religious communities, under his pastoral care. Also, that the number of churches with resident priest was one hundred and sixty-five and of mission-churches sixty-nine, making a total of two hundred and thirty-four church buildings in the diocese. Besides these places of worship there were fifty-four chapels connected with religious houses in which holy mass was said daily or at short intervals. There also were twenty-six stations where mass was said occasionally in private houses. The diocesan Seminary harbored seventy-two ecclesiastical students. In addition to this, five Religious Orders each conducted a Seminary of its own, with a total of two hundred and sixty-five students. The number of colleges and Academies for boys and young men was three, with a total attendance of seven hundred and eighty-five. Of Academies and other institutions of learning for girls and young ladies there were nineteen with 1500 pupils. Of the one hundred and sixty-five parishes one hundred and thirty-five had parochial schools, which were attended by 23,527 pupils. The five orphan asylums of the city took care of the spiritual and bodily needs of 800 orphan children. The house of the Good Shepherd offered a Christlike welcome to 250 wayward and unfortunate women. In the two Deaf-Mute Asylums seventy-five afflicted children were educated in religion and the arts of life. The three industrial schools numbered 150 pupils. The grand total of all the children being educated in these Catholic schools was 26,817. The Charitable Institutions of the diocese were known far and wide for their truly charitable work. The Hospitals and Infirmaries, thirteen in number, ministered to 6000 patients a year. The Catholic population of the diocese was computed at 200,000. This was the spiritual inheritance of which Archbishop Kain now had full jurisdiction. Strong and vigorous as the vineyard appeared to him, he felt it his duty to retrench some of its wilder shoots and bring out its latent possibilities. Archbishop Kenrick's mild and almost impersonal government exercised either by himself or through his coadjutor and Vicar-General, was liable to form a clergy imbued with a highly developed spirit of initiative and self-reliance. A vast field of labor lay before them and the laborers were few. It was the Bishop's office to say where the next efforts at subduing the wilderness should be undertaken; the order was given and the chosen ones proceeded on their way, practically without staff or scrip, determined on doing their best. There was no holding back, no complaining, no murmuring. A priest's life was one of sacrifice. Why then should any one be exempt?

It was through this spirit of unselfishness in the clergy, that the people were slowly won over to make corresponding sacrifices. In a short while a nucleus was formed which in most cases developed into a parish of life and strength. Of course, not all, perhaps not many were of altogether heroic mold; yet the spirit here described was predominant among the clergy that grew up under Archbishop Kenrick's regime. They felt that their leader placed implicit confidence in their sense of duty and, for the most part, they repaid this trust with their very best efforts.

Yet, this very spirit of initiative, though held in proper subjection by the sincere and deep respect all entertained for the person of the great Archbishop, was liable to assume a certain feeling of independence, when the old and venerated Archbishop was supplanted by the new and somewhat choleric prelate from the East. It did not amount to more than a poorly concealed suspicion, that a strict surveillance of all diocesan activities was now to be introduced. It is to be regretted that the Archbishop, who really wanted to be a Father and Friend to his priests, should, through a wrong interpretation of this spirit, have been brought into open collision with some of his best and some of his ablest priests. It must be still in the memory of many, how on April 15, 1894, the Archbishop ordered that a circular denouncing the *Western Watchman* as "a paper utterly unfit to be brought into a Catholic home," should be read from every pulpit in the diocese, and how on April 28 every pulpit resounded with the Archbishop's recall of the circular, "inasmuch as the Rev. David S. Phelan, Editor and Proprietor of the *Western Watchman*, had fully complied with our injunctions and has, in a manner creditable to himself as a priest and the responsible manager of a Catholic newspaper, published the Apology and Retraction, which we felt it our duty to require."

A clash more regretable occurred at a meeting of the priests, held in Kenrick Seminary on February 7, 1896. Cardinal Satolli was expected to come and bring the Pallium to St. Louis. The Archbishop desired that the occasion should be made a memorable one. In his address he requested the assembly to give His Eminence a banquet. Father Ziegler arose and demanded to know whether His Grace really desired his priests to offend against the spirit of Lent, by attending a banquet. The Archbishop, thrown off his guard by the unexpected attack from one of the most honored and honorable priests of the diocese, dropped a few slighting remarks on the dead Archbishop, when Father Ziegler exclaimed: "I hope the pallium celebration will be a great success, but the reception to the Cardinal a great fiasco." The proposition to honor Cardinal Satolli with a banquet in Kenrick Seminary was then put to a vote: thirty-seven priests voted with Father Ziegler, forty-three with the Archbishop. Father Ziegler then gave his parting shot: "If Cardinal Satolli comes now, we should not hold a banquet, but a black fast." The old lion was dead, but the spirit of the lion was still alive "Noli irritare leonem."[3]

3  Holweck, F. G., Article of Father Ziegler in "Pastoral-Blatt," December, 1925.

## CHAPTER 4

## THE THIRD SYNOD OF ST. LOUIS

The first Diocesan Synod of St. Louis was held on April 1839 by Bishop Joseph Rosati; the second in August 1850 by Archbishop Peter Richard Kenrick, and the third in 1898 by Archbishop John Joseph Kain.

A Diocesan Synod as distinguished from a National Synod, is an assembly of the priests of the diocese under their bishop, whose purpose it is to treat of matters that relate to the pastoral charge or the care of souls. "Only the priests having the cura animarum and those constituted in any dignity, are bound to attend. The Bishop is the sole lawgiver in these assemblies; the other members have but a consultative voice."

The Third Diocesan Synod of St. Louis was convoked by Archbishop Kain for Monday, September 8th, 1896, but the work of preparation was begun almost a year prior to that date, namely in the early part of November 1895. Seventeen priests of the diocese, both regular and secular, were selected by the Archbishop as a General Commission. Three members of this commission were appointed as a Special Commission for the purpose of preparing a working scheme of all things to be treated in the Synod. These Reverend gentlemen were Father William Faerber, Father Edward Fitzpatrick, and the Rev. Doctor John May. The Special Committee divided the General Commission into six subcommittees of three or two members each, and assigned to them the following topics:

I. On the Care of Souls.
II. On the Education of Youth.
III. On Divine Worship.
IV. On the Administration of the Sacraments.
V. On Holy Matrimony.
VI. On the Temporalities of the Church.

Each committee discussed its assigned topic, and sent in its report to the Special Commission of Three who were to digest the entire matter into proper form and have it printed for the members of the Synod. The Archbishop then sent out the call for the Synod to all the clergy, requesting them to send in any observations they might think proper and useful as well as their choice of three priests for the office of diocesan Consultors.

The Synod opened on September 8th, with a Pontifical Mass by the Archbishop. Father William Faerber was announced as Promoter;

Vicar-General Muehlsiepen, Father William Walsh and Father D. G. Kenrick, C.M. as Judges of Complaints and excuses; Fathers J. J. McCabe and F. G. Holweck, as Procurators of the Clergy and the Rev. Doctor John May as Secretary. The roll call showed the presence of 219 members, thirty-five were absent for sufficient cause.

The Archbishop then proposed the names of eleven priests who were to form the Board of Diocesan Examiners: they were elected by acclamation. The names of the six consultors were then announced and immediately afterwards the names of fifteen Irremovable Rectors, thus making a total of twenty-one members of the electoral college of the Archdiocese as prescribed by the Third Plenary Council of Baltimore for the purpose of presenting candidates for episcopal honors to the Holy See.[1]

Then the usual episcopal courts were constituted; Very Rev. Henry Muehlsiepen was confirmed in his office of Vicar-General, and Rev. Henry Van der Sanden as Chancellor of the Archdiocese. Father F. G. Holweck received the appointment as Censor Librorum.

In the afternoon session the Decrees of the Third Plenary Council of Baltimore were promulgated. The Statutes also of the former Synods and the Decrees of the Provincial Councils of St. Louis were again confirmed and their observance enjoined on the clergy.[2]

The Decrees of the Synod were admitted by all to be wise and salutary. Many of them are but literal transcripts of the legislation of the former Synods, or of the Third Plenary Council of Baltimore. This is especially noticeable in the treatment of the question of education. Every pastor of souls is required to establish a parochial school near his church within two years, and the parents are required under severest penalties to have their children educated in these Catholic schools; recalcitrants being threatened with refusal of absolution in the tribunal of penance. As to exceptional cases the Archbishop is the judge: in country parishes the rector must decide. The schools should be supported by all the parishioners, whether they have children of

---

1 It was remarked with some surprise that the two priests having the highest number of votes for the office of consultor, Fathers Walsh and Goller, should not be appointed, for the reason that they were named irremovable rectors. This reason for superseding the clergy's choice did not meet with general approval, although no formal protest was made, as everybody recognized the Archbishop's right to choose whomsoever he desired. Yet, in as far as the clergy's expression had been asked and was so very decided, and as the office of consultor meant far more to them than the title of irremovable rector, it was felt that their choice should have been accepted. Dr. John May, the Secretary of the Synod, explained the Archbishop's position in this matter in a communication to the "Ecclesiastical Review" of Philadelphia, but the Editor chose to disagree with him, and there the matter rested.

2 Synodus Diocesana Sti. Ludovici Tertia, 1896.

school age or not. The pastors are required to visit their schools at least twice a week. A School-commission is established for the purpose of unifying the educational methods of the schools, introducing a uniform series of text-books and thus establishing the Parochial School-System of the Archdiocese of St. Louis, where there were only individual schools before. The children were to be taken to confession four times a year and admitted to First Holy Communion between the ages of ten and fourteen. The first-communicants were to be well instructed by the pastor in person and were to be urged to make a solemn promise of abstaining from intoxicating drink until their twentieth year.

"The fifth chapter of the Synodical decrees contains our formal and explicit declaration that the German, Polish and Bohemian parishes enjoy all the rights and privileges of English-speaking parishes. But the members of any parish established on the lines of any foreign nationality may, provided they understand English sufficiently well, attach themselves to the English-speaking parish in which they live. In this case the pastor of the English-speaking church must notify the former pastor of these persons of the fact that they have chosen to become members of his church. Once, however, they have made this choice, they will not be permitted to rescind it."[3] This is the Archbishop's own summing up of the Synod's legislation on the vexed question of ecclesiastical status of the German, Bohemian and Polish parishes in the city of St. Louis. Archbishop Kenrick had, in his early days, declared them to be mere succursal churches for the use of their respective nationality; but their pastors were to enjoy full pastoral rights in regard to their own people. They were accordingly neither full-fledged pastors nor unfledged assistants, whilst their churches in many cases, surpassed the others in numbers and progressive spirit. This caused much irritation and friction among the clergy, and aroused a spirit of emulation among the people which almost amounted to jealousy. This anomolous condition of affairs was one of the complaints brought to the notice of Rome in November 1886. In consequence of the agitation that set in, the Archbishops of the United States, assembled in Philadelphia, submitted to the Propaganda, the following three basic principles:

1) That there should exist among all the parishes of the United States, without distinction of nationality, a perfect equality, and that each should be independent of the other.

2) That it was not necessary that any privilege should be accorded any nationality in the administration of dioceses and parishes.

---

3 Pastoral Letter of the Most Rev. John Joseph Kain, D. D., Archbishop of St. Louis, 1896.

3) That it was the plain duty of every Bishop to do his utmost, that all the faithful, of all languages, who might be in his diocese, be taken care of with the same charity.''

As Rome approved these principles of the Archbishops, Archbishop Kain could not but declare that the parishes of any other than the English language, the German, Bohemian, Polish, should be on an equal footing with those using the English language and fully independent from them, and that no distinction exists between them in regard to parochial rights and privileges.'' This decree was perfectly satisfactory to all whom it concerned, although some critical busybodies raised objections.

The Synod enjoined the annual celebration of the Forty Hours Adoration on every pastor, and recommended the erection of the Sodality of the Blessed Virgin, the Association of the Holy Family and the Conference of St. Vincent de Paul for the Poor in all Parishes. A warning against all secret societies is issued, Saturday night balls and excursions at night are condemned. Newspaper attacks by Catholic writers, lay or cleric, on ecclesiastical persons, especially on Bishops in regard to the government and administration of their diocese, are declared to be scandalous acts worthy of the severest censure.

Among the statutes of a positive nature are those requiring an annual report on the spiritual and temporal activities of each parish, fixing the Cathedraticum at 5% of the ordinary income of the churches, and approving the Easter offering to the Clergy of the parishes. The Diocesan Records are then touched upon; two new buildings for the Orphans; the adequate support of the Seminary and the erection of a new Cathedral are announced.

The Synod closed with bright prospects of renewed life and vigor for the diocese. Some of the decrees were superseded by later legislation of a general nature; others secured a permanent place in the living practice of priests and people. Some hopes never attained fulfillment, or were fulfilled in a manner never dreamt of at the time: and some others took root in stony soil and died of the drought that supervened.

# VARIOUS ACTIVITIES OF ARCHBISHOP KAIN

"For years the clergy and laity of St. Louis have recognized the necessity of a new Cathedral Church," said Archbishop Kain in his Pastoral letter of October 28, 1896, "but the rapid expansion of our city renders it difficult to select a suitable location. Perhaps it is well that final selection was delayed. But the time had surely come for securing the location. This we have done, and we believe the site selected has given general satisfaction."[1] It was the block bounded by Lindell Boulevard, Maryland Avenue, where the massive majestic Cathedral of Archbishop Glennon now lifts up its Cupola crowned with a cross of gold. The parish of the future Cathedral was made up of territory dismembered from St. Francis Xavier's. The organization of the parish was placed in the hands of the Rev. James McCaffrey, who was transferred from St. Patrick's after a pastorate of thirty-five years. The Archbishop had erected a commodious chapel and rectory on the corner of Newstead and Maryland Avenues. The Cathedral Chapel, however, was but an earnest of the great Cathedral he was planning. Of this grand church, which never took form, a glowing description was given in the St. Louis Republic of June 9, 1901, from which a few particulars may be of interest. It was to be after the style of the Roman Basilica, with transept and clerestory. The towers will be disengaged from the main building and will be one hundred feet high. The entire exterior will be either of white marble or gray granite. The interior will be on a scale more elegant even than that of the exterior. The Baptistery will be to the right of the vestibule, the Bishops chapel to the left. From the vestibule which is the main entrance to the church proper, each side aisle is separated from the nave by groups of pilasters of great girth, from which spring the arches supporting the clerestory, 75 feet high, and the great octagonal dome 200 feet above the floor. The pilasters and cornices of the main story are florid angular Ionic, those of the clerestory and dome are of the Corinthian order. "A special feature of the interior," concludes the elegant description "will be the lighting effects produced by concealed electric lights emphasizing the cornices, arches, niches and other architectural effects of the interior of the building and dome, when required for grand ceremonial. The building represents, in fact, the matured thought of His Grace, the Archbishop, who has with his architects,

---

[1] Pastoral Letter of Archbishop Kain, pp. 20-21.

(607)

Barnett, Haynes and Barnett, for the last two years studiously collaborated on the problem, which, as represented, embodied the ideas gathered both here and abroad, and when finished the structure will be one that not alone the Catholic community, but the entire city, can point to with pride, as, in comparison with others, as to cost and design, it will be second to none in this country.''[2]

On May 27, 1896, St. Louis was struck by a tornado, which occasioned an appalling loss of life and property, laying waste an area of about two miles wide and three miles in length. A heavy downpour of rain increased the horror of the situation. The devastated district lay in darkness. When the morning broke, the full force of the disaster was realized. About forty thousand persons required assistance. More than three hundred buildings were entirely destroyed; about five thousand were injured more or less. The money-value of the losses was over ten millions. The loss on schools and churches alone amounted to half a million dollars. A number of the finest Catholic churches of the city either lay in ruins or stood unroofed and dilapidated. The Archbishop felt the awful visitation deeply, and did what he could to inspire confidence among priests and people. The prospects for an early realization of his Cathedral plans vanished with the cyclone. In fact the haunting dream of the good Archbishop was never to be realized; Yet as Archbishop Glennon said in his sermon in the Cathedral chapel on the first Sunday of February 1905: ''The strength and depth of his devotion to this, his accepted life-work, is amply proved by his making the proposed Cathedral the beneficiary, not only of his life's sacrifice, but of any property of a personal nature he was possessed of at the time of his death.''[3]

It was the desire of studying some of the great Cathedrals of Europe, no less than the necessity of seeking relief from the sorrows and cares and fatigues incident to the episcopal office, that determined Archbishop Kain to make an extended trip abroad. Besides, an ad limina visit was a duty he could not and would not shirk. Father Muehlsiepen, now raised to the dignity of a Roman Prelate, was appointed Administrator of the Archdiocese during the Archbishop's absence from home.

On July 31, 1897, Archbishop Kain, accompanied by Fathers James McCabe and O'Connor embarked for Europe and, after visiting some of the chief cities of Ireland and Scotland, arrived in London on the eve of September 1st. From here they journeyed by slow stages to Antwerp, thence up the Rhine to Cologne and westward again to Paris, Lourdes and the South, Carcassonne, Marseilles and Cannes. On October 1st, the party arrived in Genoa and proceeded by way

---

2   Souvay, Dr. Charles L., ''The Cathedrals of St. Louis,'' pp. 29-30.

3   Ibidem, p. 30.

of Pisa and Florence to the Eternal City. From there they made a pilgrimage to the Holy House at Loretto. Bologna, Venice and the Swiss Lakes were next on their itinerary, and on November 3, they were back again in Rome where they spent three weeks in pleasant sightseeing and official visits. The Archbishop had a delightful audience with the Cardinal Prefect of the Propaganda, and on November 8th the Holy Father Leo XIII received him in private audience. On November 22, the party of three started for Naples, whence they sailed for Gibraltar and the open sea, homeward bound. On the whole journey the thought of the unfortunate Tuohy case was uppermost in the Archbishop's mind; in almost every one of his numerous letters, brief as they were, the name of Father Tuohy was sure to occur.. The Archbishop had for good reasons, removed the pastor of St. Patrick's Church from his pastorate, but Father Tuohy refused to vacate. Vicar-General Muehlsiepen, whom the Archbishop had left in charge of the diocese, was instructed to appoint Father Hayes to the parish, as soon as Father Tuohy should have submitted. "I hope the latter will give no trouble. I hope that his case has been finally disposed of," wrote the Archbishop. On September 15, he wrote from Paris: "By the way, this is the day set for final disposition of the Tuohy case. I again express the hope that he will give no further trouble." On October 3, the case was set for final settlement within a week. "Father Muehlsiepen seemed to be inclined to give the Reverend gentleman all the time he asked for, and Father Tuohy was not at all backward in asking for it" "I have had no later news of Father Tuohy than that received from you," answered the Archbishop, "I shall be pleased if that matter has been finally disposed of before my return." "Not having received any word of the Tuohy case," wrote his Grace on November 3, "I conclude it has not been finally settled. I am of course, fully aware that he will hold on as long as he can, and will submit only when he has exhausted all possible resources. And Father Muehlsiepen acts wisely in taking no steps that will not be fully sustained. I should be glad however, if the matter were disposed of before my return."[4]

The Archbishop was in mid-ocean on the Feast of the Immaculate Conception praying that all might be well at home. The Tuohy case, however dragged on its weary length for months and months. At last on March 17, 1898, the *Globe Democrat* announced in bold type that "the Tuohy case may become an affair of national, nay, of international importance." Although Father Tuohy conscientiously refrained from exercising his priestly office, he fought tooth and nail, to hold possession of the pastoral residence; at last he was obliged to yield, but, as the Archbishop had predicted, only when he had "exhausted all possible

---

4 Archives of 'St. Louis Archdiocese, Letters of Archbishop Kain.

resources.'' There can be no doubt, that the Tuohy case contributed largely to the Archbishop's rapid decline, so noticeable since 1896.

After his return from abroad Archbishop Kain took up the reins of government with his usual firm grip; yet his appearance betokened the fact that his health and vigor were slowly failing. His friends, especially the members of his household noticed this, and urged him to take better care of himself and to put himself under Doctor's orders Rest and change of scene were enjoined, and the Archbishop reluctantly submitted to the decree.

A part of the Summer of 1899, was spent by the Archbishop at Atlantic City, where he met Cardinal Gibbons and a number of friends. The weather was cool and the water cold; yet the place seemed restful after the turmoil of St. Louis. A brief visit was made to Harper's Ferry and Martinsburg, his ''old field of operation.'' The Tuohy ease still followed him: ''Tuohy has written to me protesting against my collecting the amount of judgment from the Security Company. I did not answer his letter, but wrote to Judge Dillon to insist on the Company being held to its obligation.''

The Archbishop's health was good, although he reports an attack of vertigo which lasted all day. On August 21, he was home once more and ready for episcopal functions.

Among the diocesan needs proposed to the charity of the Catholics of St. Louis by the Pastoral Letter of 1896, the two diocesan orphanages of St. Joseph and St. Mary met with a specially generous response. St. Mary's Orphanage for girls on Tenth and Biddle Streets had been erected fifty years before through the munificence of Mrs. Anne Biddle, daughter of John Mullanphy. The Sisters of Charity had charge of the new home since January 22, 1845. The institution remained here until 1890, when the girls were transferred to the Orphan Home on Fifteenth and Clark, just vacated by the orphan boys, who had been brought to their new home on Grand Avenue. Here St. Mary's Orphan Home remained till 1900, when, through the liberal donation of $85,000 by a gentleman whose name was never divulged, the new magnificent Orphanage for Girls was erected on Emerson and Harney Avenues.

The building on Fifteenth and Clark Avenues which was occupied successively by the boys and the girls, had to be enlarged several times. Through the munificence, however, of Mrs. Eliza Patterson, the boys' Orphanage could in 1890, be located on a large lot on Grand Avenue and Itaska Street. The bequest of Mrs. Patterson to the Orphan Board amounted to $100,000. The Sisters of St. Joseph have charge of this asylum. These two diocesan orphanages, sheltering some four hundred children, are supported by an annual tax on the English-speaking parishes of the diocese. The net revenue of Calvary Cemetery also goes to the support of the two diocesan Orphan Homes.

On April 28, 1900, Archbishop Kain set out from New York on his second voyage to Europe. On May 28th he arrived in Rome. The companions of his journey were Fathers Phelan and Tracy. The Archbishop and his companions made their four visits a day for ten days to the four great Basilicas of Rome, without availing themselves of any dispensation. The Archbishop was very anxious to hear about affairs in St. Louis, where Monsignor Muehlsiepen administered affairs and Bishop Montgomery performed episcopal functions for him. But his interest was also devoted to matters of general Church policy.

"I had my audience with the Holy Father on last Wednesday, May 30th. In the throne-room awaiting their turn were some twenty Bishops. When I had seen the Holy Father in the company with the Archbishop of Alexandria, the Bishops of Zanzibar, Tonquin, Gilbraltar, one or two from Australia and the Bishops Eis and Forest, I requested a talk with him alone, which he granted. Among other matters discussed, was the Dubuque vacancy. When I informed him that Archbishop Keane was the first choice of the Bishops of the Province, and that all the Archbishops of the country had indorsed that choice, he assured me (this must be for a time confidential) that he would confirm him. So I now consider his appointment at an early date as a forgone conclusion. Even Cardinal Satolli will support his appointment."

That there were other candidates, real or imaginary, for episcopal honors, appears from a passage of the Archbishop's letter of August 21, from Lisdoonvarna, Ireland: "I see, by the way, that they are stealing a march on me. Someone sent Father Tracy a clipping from P.D. announcing that Father Harty was to be Auxiliary-Bishop of St. Louis. This was news to me, but queer things are sometimes done at Rome. On Sunday September 16, Archbishop Kain and his party set sail from Queenstown for New York. At the opening of October he arrived in St. Louis. Father Muehlsiepen had mapped out a full month of episcopal visitations for that month. The Archbishop only "hoped that the weather would be favorable."

In the following year 1902, on the 9th day of April, Archbishop Kain convoked his clergy once more for a diocesan synod, the Fourth Synod of St. Louis. The date of meeting was the ninth day of September, the place was the Kenrick Seminary on Cass Avenue. The Preparatory Commission consisted of the Fathers William Faerber, John H. May, D.D., and Francis Gilfillan, S.T.L. Two hundred and nine priests responded to the roll call. The various diocesan officials were then nominated by the Archbishop. The Decrees of the various plenary Councils of Baltimore and all the Statutes of the Third Diocesan Synod were again promulgated as binding, with a few slight modifications. The statute of the Third Synod forbidding the celebration of mixed marriages in private houses, which had been publicly criticized as too severe, was dropped. The former legislation in regard to the Parochial Schools is sustained in all its vigor, even to the refusal of absolution in the Sacrament of Penance to recalcitrant parents. The annual examinations of the Junior Clergy for the period of five years as a means of testing their fitness for pastoral charges was confirmed by Synodal statute, having been in practice since 1896.

The Synod closed with a Solemn Te Deum.

## CHAPTER 6

## NEW PARISHES IN THE RURAL DISTRICTS

The first four years of Archbishop Kain's administration, as Coadjutor, then as administrator, and lastly as Archbishop in his own right, were filled with many wasting cares and labors: He felt them keenly, but could not be turned aside from his appointed task of extending and consolidating his part of the Kingdom of God on earth. After his arrival in St. Louis from Wheeling, on August 3rd, 1892, in company of a large delegation of priests from St. Louis, he immediately took up the reins of government. He found two faithful official helpers, the venerable Vicar-General Muehlsiepen and the bluff hearty Chancellor Henry Van der Sanden. The latter was sent to bless the new church of the *Nativity* at Belgique, Perry County, on September 12th, 1893, as he had blessed the first church in the place in 1895. Belique is a colony of staunch Belgian and Dutch Catholics in what was formerly called Bois Brulé Bottom.

Father D. L. De Ceunyuck was the founder of the parish and its pastor from 1884 to 1907, when he resigned his charge. His successor was the Rev. J. M. Denner. In 1899 the parish numbered 314 souls. On March 30th, 1909, Father Charles Einig succeeded Father Denner as pastor of Belgique. The present pastor in succession to the Rev. Charles E. Schmalle, is Father John S. Kelley.

The first new parish established in the diocese by Archbishop Kain was that of *St. Aloysius* at Baring Knox County, with Father James J. O'Reilly as pastor.

The Archbishop blessed the new church on November 12th, 1893. Father O'Reilly was ordained at St. John's Church, on May 30th, 1885, by Archbishop Kenrick, and served as assistant at Hannibal from November 1885 until his appointment to Baring, where he remained to the end of his life, a highly respected, and really loveable, though naturally somewhat quick-tempered priest.

The parish of the *Guardian* Angel at Oran, Mississippi County was organized August 19th, 1893. The pastor of Charleston, Father Francis Brand, built the church, which was dedicated by Vicar-General Muehlsiepen on May 30th, 1894.

In the interval of church-building Father Brand came up from Charleston to hold services in a warehouse. The parish consisted of forty families all German Alsatians. On July 12th, 1894, Father George Koob was appointed pastor of the thriving parish. On his promotion to the Church at Neier, Franklin County, June 1897, Father

Michael G. Helmbacher took charge of the destinies of Oran parish. Father Helmbacher was born in St. Louis, and ordained by Bishop Janssen in Belleville Cathedral, on January 29th, 1893.

For two years he served as assistant at St. Boniface Church, Carondelet; then he received the appointment as pastor of Bloomsdale, and finally as pastor of the Guardian Angel Church at Oran, which position he still holds after a lapse of thirty years. Father Helmbacher has effected a complete transformation of the parish. From forty families the enrollment increased to one hundred and seventy-five, almost exclusively of German descent. In 1907 Father Helmbacher built his rectory at a cost of $7,500.00, and then the beautiful brick-church, during 1916 and 1917, at a cost of $44,000.00 and lastly the Sisters' Residence. The new church was dedicated August 8th, 1917. The Parish owns thirty-eight acres of land. The original church, a frame structure was remodeled and now serves as the school, which is attended by one hundred and fifty children. From 1893 to 1898 the school was taught by lay-brothers.

· For the next two years, the Benedictine Sisters from Jonesboro, Ark., were in charge: Then came the Sisters of the Most Precious Blood of Ruma, Ill., who have continued this blessed work, with a brief intermission, until the present day.

Jonesburg, in Montgomery County, was attended as a mission from Montgomery City, from 1877 to October 1894, when it became a parish under the Rev. B. H. Schlathoelter as its first pastor. The church was dedicated to *St. Patrick*.

On January 25th, 1898, Father Schlatthoelter was succeeded by the Rev. H. J. Shaw, whose labors were cut short by death, on December 20th, of the same year. The Rev. Michael D. Collins, Father Shaw's successor, remained at his post until December 1903, when Father Tuohy was appointed in his place. Father Tuohy, one of the early students at the Catholic University of Washington, was a learned, forceful, but somewhat erratic and self-willed gentleman. He came to Jonesburg from his exile in the East after the death of Archbishop Kain.[1]

The Parish of New Haven, Franklin County was established in 1894; but its Catholic settlement dates back to the days of the Jesuit missionaries. The first church was blessed by Archbishop Kenrick on April 6th, 1873. The first secular priest in charge of the mission was Father Francis Reuther, who in 1893 occasionally came from "Across the river," that is, from Holstein. The church at New Haven was originally called *St. Magdalen's*. But the people generally attended mass at Washington. In August 1894 Father Mathias Thomas Sevcik

---

[1]  Chancery Records and Questionnaire-Answers.

who, since his adoption into the diocese, November 4th, 1892, had been rector of Port Hudson, until his transfer to St. John Nepomuc's Church in St. Louis, was brought back to Franklin County, with headquarters at New Haven. Father Sevcik tore down the old dilapidated chapel, and having bought a new location for the future church buildings, and erected a parish residence thereon, began in 1895 to erect a new church out of the material of the old, but on the new location. Father Muehlsiepen laid the corner stone on October 6th, 1895. This brick church was intended to serve as a school, when the parish should be able to erect a worthy temple of God. The name of the church was changed from *St. Magdalen*, to the *Assumption* of the Blessed Virgin. In these building operations Father Sevcik served not only as architect, superintendent and financial manager, but as bricklayer, carpenter and hod carrier. Most of the money needed was obtained by Father Sevcik from St. Louis friends. In October 1905, the Rev. Francis Goeke succeeded Father Sevcik as pastor of New Haven. Not of very strong constitution, Father Goeke devoted all his energies to the spiritual advancement of his people. He remained at his post for fifteen years, being succeeded on September 8th, 1920, by Father Francis Schiller, the efficient assistant of Msgr. Tannrath at the Old Cathedral. Archbishop Glennon had given the young and energetic priest the mandate to build a new fine church at New Haven; and Father Schiller started at once to plan and to find material for earring out the wish of His Grace. During Father Goeke's pastorship many had clamored for a new church: but when Father Schiller said: "I am sent here to build a church," the clamors changed into murmurs of dissent. The pastor brought together a number of parishioners to clean up the place, now overgrown with weeds and covered with rubbish. So he became acquainted with his parishioners. When they saw that at the end of the year there was a balance of almost $1,000, they regained courage and confidence. By the end of March 1921, all began talking about "the new Church." In April a parish meeting selected trustees and a building committee.

On May 1st, the Parish decided to build a church that would cost at least $25,000. The amount was to be raised by freewill offerings. At this meeting more than $18,000 were subscribed.

The corner stone was laid by Monsignor Tannrath on May 8th, 1922, Father Van Tourenhout of Ste. Genevieve preached the sermon. In somewhat less than two years the church was completed, the bells were installed in the massive tower, and everything was ready for the dedication, which was to take place on Labor-day, September 1st, 1924. The church is a handsome stone structure in the Romanesque style, fronted by a mighty tower 117 feet high. Archbishop Glennon performed the solemn rite of dedication; On the 15th of April of the following year, Monsignor Tannrath consecrated the altar.[2]

*St. Joseph's* parish of White Church, Howell, County had a rather peculiar origin.

When Father Joseph Schaefers was pastor of Rhineland about 1872 a number of German families of the parish and its vicinity determined to seek new homes farther West. They started in covered wagons in a southwesterly direction: but in the course of their journey some of their animals died, and sickness broke out among the women and children. They simply broke down, as the people themselves confessed, and determined to stay where they found themselves. The town of Peace Valley was near by and its little white church of the Methodist gave its name to the place they had chosen for their Settlement. Government land was plentiful and cheap, and though the soil was not rich, it would repay their work. They set to work to put up a frame church in which every piece of lumber was hand-sawed by the parishioners. At first Father Donovan came over from Poplar Bluff to hold services for them: but as the journey overland was very tiresome, he advised them to ask the Archbishop for a priest of their own. Father Holtschneider, then assistant at St. Nicholas Church, St. Louis, at Vicar-General Muehlsiepen's request, went to their wilderness-home, but only for one or two Sundays: living conditions were, indeed, primitive. The kindhearted Vicar-General then undertook to visit the forsaken people at least once a year to enable them to fulfill their Easter duty.

It was in 1895 that Father John Waelterman organized the parish. In the night following the day of his arrival a violent storm poured in a little flood upon the sleeper's bed, which stood in a cabin next to the church. He found, after a diligent search, that his parish of White Church including West Plains, Pomona, Mountain View, and Cottbus, all in Howell County, consisted of sixty-five families, or about 350 souls. Father Waelterman remained at White Church until June 1897. He enlarged the church and built a parish house. An episcopal visitation of the parish by Archbishop Kain accompanied by his ever faithful Father Muehlsiepen in 1896, greatly encouraged priest and people of White Church and its dependencies, Cabool, Willow Springs, West Plains, and Thayer, in every one of which the Archbishop delivered a sermon or lecture.

Small though the parish was, it never lost its identity. The succession of pastors after Father Waelterman was: Rev. Victor Stepka, 1897—June 1900; Rev. F. K. Reker to 1902; Rev. Conrad Brockmeier to June 1905; Rev. J. A. Richarz to June 1906: Rev. Joseph Wipperman

---

[2] Souvenir of the Church of the Assumption, New Haven.

to August 1908; Rev. Daniel O'Brien, Daniel Courtney, Sidney Paul Stocking, and the present pastor Rev. E. P. Ryan.

Of all these Reverend gentlemen, Father Stepka specially distinguished himself by building a school. White Church was a missionary center from the start.

In 1824 the Missions were: Cabool, Willow Springs, West Plains, the Stations: Houston, Texas County; Hutlin Valley, Howell County; Mountain View, Howell County; Raymondville, Texas County. Willow Springs, as a mission, passed from Rolla to White Church.

Whilst White Church lies fondly nestled in the hill country of the southern slopes of the Ozarks, the Parish of Thayer basks in the plain, stretching southward into Arkansas. Thayer lies on the Kansas City, St. Louis and Memphis Railroad which crosses Howell County diagonally into the border land of Oregon. Thayer is the last station on the Missouri side.

In 1900 it had a population of about 2,000 souls, very few of whom were Catholics. Yet it was visited since 1890 by priests from Doniphan, who said mass in a private house. On May 29th, 1893, the Congregation, then in care of the priests of Poplar Bluff, bought a lot in the town for church purposes.

In 1897 the membership had increased to thirty-seven souls. From 1895 to 1897 the congregation of Thayer was attended by Father Waelterman, and from the latter date on until 1902 by Father Francis Reker, both stationed at White Church.

When Father Waelterman first saw Thayer, he found only four walls of a frame church, roughly weather-boarded, and perfectly innocent of plaster. Until the roof was put on the structure, he said mass at a private house. His congregation consisted of twenty families, most of them residing in the town.

Father Waelterman visited the place once a month. Mammoth Springs in Arkansas was also within the jurisdiction of the pastor of White Church.

This arrangement was continued under the rectorship of Father Victor Stepka from June 1897 to June 1900. Father Francis X. Reker then succeeded Father Stepka at both White Church and Thayer, but in 1902, he transferred his residence to Thayer, whilst Father Conrad Brockmeier assumed pastoral charge of White Church and the Howell County missions.

In 1904 came Father Joseph G. Hoelting, and in 1905 Father Frederick Peters.

In October 1906 the Rev. P. J. Carney took over the reins of government from the hands of Father Peters, to relinquish them in November 1907 into the hands of the Rev. Clement Fehlig. Father T.

J. Aylward is the present pastor of Thayer.  He has charge of the mission of Brandsville and the Stations of Couch, and Irish Wilderness; the scene of Bishop Hogan's early efforts at colonizing.[3]

It would appear from this brief account of religious conditions in the Ozark Mountain Country, that there is no special receptivity for Catholic truth among its people, partly because the great streams of Irish and German immigration barely touched its fringes, and partly because the early prejudices imbibed by the natives from the preaching of their many circuit-riding parsons have crystallized their minds and hearts into incontestable convictions.

Yet the work of these priests was not in vain.  Whilst no memorable outward results have been attained, a few thousand souls of good will have enjoyed the happiness of their ministrations and have lived a better, nobler life, and died a more blessed death through the constancy and fidelity of these shepherds in the wilderness of South Central Missouri.

From the far-away Ozarks we must now return to the regions north of the Missouri river, to Flint Hill in St. Charles County and its church of *St. Theodore*.  As early as July 10th, 1883 the Reverend Henry Brockhagen was commissioned by Father Muehlsiepen to lay the corner stone of the new church which was in charge of Father Theodore Krainhardt.  The church was finished within a month and five days.  Father Brockhagen blessed the humble wooden structure on August 15th, 1883.  For the next twelve years the place is attended by priests from Allen Prairie or Josephsville.  In September 1895, Father G. W. Kurtenbach was appointed pastor of St. George's Church, but dying on January 19th, 1898, the Rev. August J. Von Brunn took his place.  Father Von Brunn built a new church, the corner stone of which was laid on May 6th, 1900.  The church was blessed by Vicar-General Muehlsiepen on September 16th, of the same year.[4]

On July 31st, 1897, Archbishop Kain started on his ad limina trip, and incidentally visited Ireland, England, Scotland, Belgium, France, Germany and Italy.  In that year the archdiocese was served by 377 priests, 233 of the secular and 144 of the regular clergy.  The parochial schools numbered 138 with 24,454 pupils, and the religious institutions had an enrollment of 5,033.

The Archbishop's decline in health was becoming more noticeable in 1897; yet his strong will sustained and urged him on to inaugurate another series of parishes in the county districts.  It must have been noticed that in the treatment of the parishes founded under the regime of Archbishop Kain, the chronological order, pure and simple, is used.

---

3 Chancery Records and Questionnaire-Answers.
4 Chancery Records and Questionnaire.

The parishes are no longer grouped together in regard to their local position, as they were in the account of the steady progress of the Church under Archbishop Kenrick on a long concentric movement into ever new territory. By the time of Archbishop Kain's arrival the wilderness was practically conquered, and all that remained for him and his successor was to fill up the intervening spaces and thus to consolidate the conquest.

In 1898 Archbishop Kain requested Father Francis Brand, who had just then established the suburban parish of St. Michael's Shrewsbury, to undertake the arduous task of a missionary in the far northeastern counties of the diocese.

Father Brand accepted the honorable commission, and started for his new field.

After learning the condition of affairs and the prospects of success, he selected Kahoka in Clark County as his headquarters. Here he built a neat frame church and a parochial residence. Archbishop Kain blessed the church on September 19th, 1898. But the good shepherd was always on the road. Travelling on horseback at times, and at times in buggy, and again on the rough seat of a farmer-wagon, he visited the neighboring places. For the more remote stations he used the cab of a freight train, and frequently an engine or a hand car. So he made his way to bring the consolations of religion to his scattered flock in town and country side. His missions were Wayland, Chambersburg, Mudd Settlement: his stations for occasional mass in private homes were Memphis, Hitt, Avela, Neva, Acesto, Athens, St. Francisville, Alexandria, Wyaconda, Neeper and Medill. For five long and wearisome years Father Brand labored with distinguished success in this far-away missionary field: In June 1903 he was appointed to the pastorship of St. Aloysius Church in St. Louis. Father H. Muckerman became his successor at Kahoka. Father Joseph Westhus received the charge of St. Michael's Church, Kahoka in 1907.[5]

Ozora in Ste. Genevieve County was formerly known as New Bremen. Father Martin A. Bahr, a native of Ste. Genevieve, was constituted its first pastor, October 29th, 1898. On August 22, 1899, Monsignor Muehlsiepen blessed the church, Father Bahr had built. In January 1903, Father John Peters took charge of the parish, but in September of the same year Father George L. Fugel succeeded him.

In 1907 the Rev. Charles Keller was appointed to the rectorship of *St. Martin's*. The present pastor Father Bernard Kramper built a very handsome church of native stone, which was dedicated by Msgr. Holweck.

---

5  J. W., Souvenir of Father Brand's Silver Jubilee.

The church of Carruthersville, whose early history is so intimately connected with that of New Madrid, received its first resident priest in 1900 in the person of Father William Schulte. On the 22nd, of July, 1894 Vicar-General Muehlsiepen had blessed the new church of the Sacred Heart, built by Father Furlong. Father Schulte built the parsonage and enlarged the church. Father Francis Mispagel in 1918 bought a fine residence in the town and had it removed to the church grounds to serve as school and Sisters' residence.

The Church of the Sacred Heart at New Franklin in Howard County was attended in 1897 by Father B. H. Schlathoelter from Jonesburg; in 1898, and 1899 by Father A. Holtschneider from Starkenburg and Fayette, and from 1899 to 1902 by Father Joseph Kroeger from Fayette. In 1902 Father Kroeger took up his residence in the place, but on November 28th, 1907 accepted the appointment to Gildehaus in Franklin County. Father Kroeger's successor at New Franklin was the Rev. C. J. Kane.[6]

The Church of *St. Joseph* at New London, Ralls County, dates back to the days of Father Lefevere, but received a resident priest as late as 1901. Rev. Frederick J. Ernst was its first rector. The new church built by Father Ernst was blessed by Archbishop Kain in 1901. The parish did not thrive and eventually returned to its former condition as a mission of the church of Center in Ralls County, which was transferred to the diocese of St. Joseph in 1911.

The little congregation of eighteen families living at what is now called Augusta in St. Charles County, was an early mission of the Jesuit Fathers of Washington and St. Charles. This continued until 1866 when it was attended from Dutzow.

In 1901 Archbishop Kain blessed the new Church of the *Immaculate Conception* at the place, and in September 1905, the Rev. Anthony A. Jasper became its first resident priest. The first decade of Father Jasper's life was spent by turns, as assistant of Father Willmes in St. Charles and as an invalid in Europe. But the care of the parish of Augusta restored him to health and energy. Father Anthony Straus is now in charge of the parish. The school is conducted by the Sisters of St. Francis, Oldenburg.

The parish of the *Immaculate Conception* at Desloges in St. Francois County, a former mission of Bonne Terre, received the Rev. James Sheil as rector in 1903. Its first church had been dedicated on December 8th, 1901. In February 1909, the Rev. Joseph Casey succeeded Father Sheil.

Desloges was the last country parish established by Archbishop Kain: there remains but the suburban parish of *Notre Dame de*

---

6 Chancery Records.

*Lourdes,* the last foundation of Father Cornelius O'Leary, of whose tragic death we have written in connection with the account of his great monument, the church of St. Rose at De Soto. But this foundation, as well as a few others, was really inspired by the Coadjutor Bishop John Joseph Glennon. Archbishop Kain, for about a year previous to his death, was prevented by serious illness to meet the duties of his office.

The slowly dying prelate asked Rome for an auxiliary, naming Father Connolly as his choice, but his petition was not granted. Bishop Hennessey of Wichita, and Bishop Montgomery, the Coadjutor of San Francisco, were called in for ordinations. The old faithful Vicar-General Monsignor Muehlsiepen, too, had now become stricken with what proved to be his final illness. Again the helpless Archbishop petitioned Rome for an auxiliary, naming Father Harty, the pastor of St. Leo's Church. Propaganda replied by sending a decree which enjoined that in case of Auxiliaries to Archbishops, nominations must follow the provisions laid down by the Third Council of Baltimore. There the matter rested for a while, whilst the Archbishop's condition grew worse.

## Chapter 7

# THE CITY CHURCHES ORGANIZED UNDER ARCHBISHOP KAIN'S RULE

During the ten years intervening between Archbishop Kain's, entering upon his episcopal duties in the Archdiocese of St. Louis and his death in St. Agnes Sanitarium near Baltimore, nineteen parishes were erected in the city of St. Louis: ten for English-speaking people, three for the Italians, two for Germans, one for English and German people, and one each for Bohemian, Slovak and Syro-Maronite Congregations. The very noticeable decline in the erection of German parishes is owing to two distinct causes: 1) the decline of German immigration during the heyday of German imperial power, and 2) to rapid Americanization of the German Catholics of the second and often of the first generation after the arrival of the immigrants. As a consequence, new parishes using the German language though, at times, desirable, seemed no longer of compelling necessity. The six new parishes erected in this period for immigrants from other foreign parts were certainly needed, and will be needed for a long time to come.

In this chapter, the history of the English and German foundations will be briefly narrated; the data concerning the Italian, Syrian, Slovak, Bohemian and also of the Polish Parishes of St. Louis will require separate treatment.

*St. Matthew's* church is situated on Kennerly Avenue and Sarah Street, in the center of the parish, which is now one of the leading church organizations of the city, in numbers as well as in financial resources. Its humble origin dates back to 1893, when Father Joseph Shields built a temporary church on the site of his present parish buildings. The territory assigned to St. Matthew's extended from Vandeventer to Goode Street and from Easton Avenue to Natural Bridge Road. It was but sparsely populated at the time. The Catholics numbered about one hundred families, Irish and American. There were a number of German Catholics within reach of St. Matthew's Church, but they belonged to the church of the Holy Ghost which Father Michael Busch had founded at what was then called Elleardsville. The first Church of St. Matthew was dedicated in July, 1893. The blessing of God rested upon the parish. It grew steadily until it numbered twelve hundred families, or almost six thousand souls. The school which was established in 1902 and placed in charge of fourteen resident Sisters of St. Joseph, numbered seven hundred pupils; and of consecrated persons that call St. Matthew's their native parish, there are eighteen priests and seventeen nuns. The good spirit that animates this parish is further evidenced by the grand new Gothic church, of which the corner stone was laid by Vicar-General Connolly on August 12, 1906, whilst the completed structure was dedicated on September 22, 1907, by His Grace the Archbishop.[1]

After St. Matthew's came *St. Mark's* Parish, but the difference in age is as small as that of Jacob and Esau. Both churches were started on their way in 1893. In April of that year Father John J. Dillon was commissioned to obtain a suitable site for a church in the northwestern part of the city. A large plot of ground was secured on Page and Academy Avenues, in the vicinity of the Christian Brothers' College. A temporary church was soon erected. On May 14th, the Rev. Chancellor of the Archdiocese, Henry Van der Sanden, blessed it. On April 29, 1895, Father Dillon resigned his charge and accepted the rectorship of Byrnesville. Father James Joseph Flanagan, his successor, died within less than three weeks after his appointment. Then·Father Thomas Cooney became administrator and, in 1896, rector of St. Mark's with Father Peter J. O'Rourke as assistant from 1897 to June 2, 1899. It was then that the latter superseded Father Cooney at St. Mark's, Father Cooney accepting the chaplaincy of the Boys' Orphan Home. As the westward trend of the city had by this time filled up most of the vacant spaces in the territory of St. Mark's, the church naturally possessed its full share of the increase in population. The erection of a fine commodious church, a worthy monument to its piety and zeal was resolved on. The corner stone of the new St. Mark's was laid on July 9, 1901. The dedication service by Archbishop Glennon took place in November 1902. The building is a handsome structure of Gothic design and built of Bedford limestone. The parish then erected a magnificent school building with all modern requirements, which was opened in September 1909. Father Peter O'Rourke is still in charge of the pastorate of St. Mark's.[2]

The third church of St. Louis built in 1893, is that of *St. Edward's* on Clara and Maffit Avenues. Its founder was the Rev. Edward J. Wynne. He had been successively placed at Byrnesville, Silver Lake, St. Mary's Landing, and received charge of St. Edward's parish in St. Louis in May, 1893. The congregation numbered two hundred and fifty families, the parish school had an equal number of children. The basement of the future church was used for school purposes.

The Parish of the *Holy Innocents* is the fourth St. Louis parish organized in 1893. It is situated in the southwestern part of the city.

---

1 Chancery Records and Answers to Questionnaire.
2 Chancery Records.

The Rev. John White was its founder; the date of its foundation is uncertain: only the year is known. The congregation still worships in the poor frame structure of the long ago. But in 1922, the Rev. Timothy O'Sullivan established a parochial school, with Sisters of the Precious Blood as teachers. Since 1922, the parish seems to have taken a new start on life. The Rev. Leo A. McAtee is the pastor.

The church of *St. Barbara*, the Virgin Martyr, was in some ways, the successor to the little Church of St. Rose of Lima built on a hill in the wildwood of St. Louis County, by the Jesuit Fathers residing at Normandy, and used by Father James McGlynn in the early years of St. Rose's parish. While living here, Father McGlynn had built a fine roomy parsonage. When the new church had been completed on Etzel and Goodfellow Avenue and the transfer had taken place on June 21, 1891, the little Church of St. Rose stood deserted until two years later. But a most happy change came over the scene when, on May 12, 1893, the Church authorities delegated Rev. John Schramm to gather the scattered German Catholics of the district and organize a new parish. This was the first time that Father Schramm saw the old church and learned its history. A better opportunity had seldom been offered to any priest, and so Father Schramm, with the sanction of Vicar-General Muehlsiepen, bought this property for the small sum of $8000. The deed carries the date of June 10, 1893. On Sunday June 4, 1893, the first services were held. Vicar-General Muehlsiepen delivered the first German sermon in what is now St. Barbara's church The parish grew in bounds and as early as 1900 numbered 150 families.

Correctly appreciating the necessity of a Catholic education for Catholic children, the founder and pioneers of the parish lost no time in planning the establishment of a school, with such success, that less than three months after the first services had been held in their modest little church, classes were opened in a small frame building which stood to the rear of the church. During its first year the school was conducted by a lay-teacher, after which it passed into the care of the Sisters of Notre Dame, who are in charge today.

Father Schramm, the founder and first pastor of St. Barbara's, after ten years of faithful service, asked to be relieved of the ever-increasing burden of the parish. The Archbishop, complying with the request, assigned him to the pastorate of the Church of the Sacred Heart at Richfountain, Osage County, and appointed the Rev. E. J. Lemkes of Manchester to take his place. This was in the early spring of 1904.[3]

The pastor, prior to his appointment to his present charge, had served three years as assistant priest of St. Peter's Church at St.

---

[3]  Chancery Records, and "Sunday Watchman," October 27, 1918.

Charles, Mo., and thirteen years as pastor of St. Joseph's at Manchester, Mo. He is a native of St. Louis and hails from St. Boniface Parish in Carondelet.

The great St. Louis World's Fair was held in that year. This event was destined to exert a great influence on the development of St. Barbara's, particularly as to its numerical increase. Immediately after the Fair, and largely brought about by the same, the entire "west end" experienced an almost phenomenal boom. A new and populous section of the city began to spring up. Among the many who came out to establish new homes away from the grime and smoke of the down-town districts, there were many Catholics, and St. Barbara's got its liberal quota of these. So much so that within one year the church and school facilities became quite inadequate to accommodate the new-comers. As consequence, the need of a new church became apparent and so, obeying necessity's law, preliminary measures towards such an undertaking were at once entered upon. In due time, plans were drawn and the work put under way, with the result, that as early as May 1906, the corner stone was laid and on July 4, 1907, the solemn blessing of the church took place, Archbishop Glennon officiating on both occasions. In 1908 one wing of the new school was built and in 1912, the building was completed. The Sisters' convent was erected in 1916, and in 1917, the Hall was added to the cluster of buildings, belonging to the parish, a large auditorium, spacious assembly rooms, billiard rooms, hand-ball courts and bowling alleys, all serving the cultural and social activities of the members of the congregation.

The Parish of *Our Lady of Good Counsel* with its church almost adjoining the stately Church of the Holy Trinity, was founded in 1894, by the Rev. Patrick O'Donahoe. Its territory was dismembered from St. Michael's parish. The corner stone for the church was laid on June 3, by the Vincentian Father A. Mayer; the dedication of the building took place on November 4; the officiating clergyman being the Rev. J. McCaffery. There were seven hundred families in the membership of the parish, all of Irish or Anglo-American descent. The parish having but two blocks in width, and the territory east of Broadway being encroached upon by lumber yards were the main obstacles to a healthy growth. Father O'Donahoe died on April 6, 1901, and the Rev. Joseph A. Tracy was appointed to take charge. After a pastorate of eight years at Our Lady of Good Counsel Father Tracy was transferred to Byrnesville. The Rev. Joseph R. Watson now holds the position as pastor. There is no school in the parish.[4]

*St. Michael's Parish* of Shrewsbury Park, though not situated within the city limits of St. Louis, is officially numbered among the city

---

[4] Questionnaire-Answers.

churches. It owes its origin in great part to the energy of the Rev. Francis Brand. A large plot of ground with a fine stone house, the old Murdock mansion, was acquired by purchase, and a frame structure was erected to serve as a provisional church. School was opened at once with the Ursuline Sisters as teachers. When Father Brand was sent to Cahokia, October 1898, the Rev. J. A. Strombergen became rector, but resigned the charge in September 1900. The Rev. Charles E. Einig then began his eight and one half years' pastoral ministrations at the place, to be superseded in February 1909, by the present pastor, Father Joseph Preuss. The school is now taught by the Sisters of Notre Dame. In the spring of 1910, an addition was made to the church, doubling its seating capacity.

*The New Cathedral Chapel* which comes next in the order of time, but being mainly the creation of Archbishop Kain, found its place in the account of the life and labors of that distinguished prelate. Its line of pastors was: Rev. James McCaffrey, Rev. P. F. O'Reilly, Rev. Francis Gilfillan. The chapel was in use until the completion of the great Cathedral, in 1914, when it was demolished. On July 8, 1922, the last pastor of the Cathedral Chapel, Father Gilfillan, was appointed Coadjutor Bishop of the diocese of St. Joseph. Monsignor John J. Tannrath succeeded Bishop Gilfillan as pastor of the Cathedral parish. The congregation numbered at the start about one thousand families, all native American; the annual increase is large and steady. The Archbishop's sermons always draw large crowds. The Schools of the parish from 1916 to 1921, were in charge of the Madames of the Sacred Heart, after that date the Sisters of St. Joseph entered upon the promising field.

The antecedents of *St. Anne's* parish on Whittier and Page Boulevard appear rather complicated, as various cross-currents of ecclesiastical activity had influenced them. It will be remembered that the Redemptorist Church of St. Alphonsus was not intended at first as a parochial church, and consequently had no parish limits assigned to it. In September 1881, however, the authorities changed its status, and assigned to it a territory bounded on the North by Easton Avenue, South by Washington Avenue; East by Compton Avenue and West by Taylor Avenue. But in 1891, it was deemed advisable to erect a new parish in the western part of the city, and the plan, having been laid before Archbishop Kenrick, was approved by him. Now the greater part of this new parish was to be taken from the western end of St. Alphonsus parish, thus withdrawing from it all the territory between Taylor Avenue and Sarah Street. Father John Thomas Joseph Tuohy fresh from his two years' course at the Catholic University, Washington, D.C., was the moving spirit in this undertaking. He built a small frame chapel on Finney and Grand Avenues only a few blocks distant from St. Alphonsus. On January 10, 1892, Vicar-General Brady blessed this primitive structure in honor of St. Paul the Apostle. Father Tuohy had won, and held his position until 1896, when Archbishop Kain appointed him to the pastorate of St. Patrick's venerable church. On October 2, of that year the pastorship of St. Paul's parish devolved upon Father O. J. McDonald, who after a few months consideration found the location unsuitable, and on July 13, 1897, established the church at Page Boulevard and Whittier Street. The name of the parish was changed to St. Anne, and the Church of St. Paul the Apostle was demolished. The corner stone for St. Anne's Church was laid by Archbishop Kain on February 22, 1897. The basement completed and fitted up for divine service, was blessed by Vicar-General Muehlsiepen on September 12, 1897. Here the congregation consisting of three hundred and twenty-five families of Irish descent, worshiped and prospered under the pious care of Father McDonald. Within less than thirteen years, however, the church was completed and the congregation exchanged its gloomy catacomb for the bright sunlit marble sanctuary above. The dedication services were held on May 13, 1910. St. Anne's Parish supported a fine parochial free school, taught by the Sisters of St. Joseph. The enrollment was two hundred and seventy children, but parish and school are declining of late, owing to the overwhelming influx of negroes into its territory. Two months after Father McDonald's death in March 1911, Father Thomas Walsh succeeded to the rectorship of St. Anne's; Father James E. Douglass was appointed pastor, October 28, 1925.[5]

The *Holy Family Parish* may look to the year 1898, as the year of its birth. It was to Vicar-General Muehlsiepen that the need of a parish in the Tower Grove Park district made its first appeal. It was he who brought this knowledge to the attention of the late Archbishop Kain, who immediately mapped out the territory of the new parish, and requested the Rev. J. F. Reuther, then pastor of St. Monica's parish in Creve Coeur, to begin the work of organization. After a thorough canvas of the district, it was found that one hundred and seventy-three answered to the name Catholic; but even this small number was further decreased by the fact that many of them had fallen away from the practice of their Holy Faith, and no argument could induce them to return.

An old house on Wyoming Street was rented and two rooms on the first floor were furnished as a chapel. An altar, the gift of Rev. E. Lemkes, was erected, and by the generosity of some other benefactors, all things necessary for the celebration of the Holy Sacrifice were provided. On November 10, 1898, the first Holy Mass was offered up to

---

[5] Chancery Records. Cf. Leaves from the History of St. Alphonsus Church, pp. 34-35.

God in the new parish. Then even the two small rooms which served as a chapel proved amply sufficient for the number of people who came to worship on that first Sunday.

Next in importance to the organization of the parish, was the opening of the parish school. What joy for the pastor and flock was the announcement that on January 12, 1899, the parish school would commence its important work in the same rooms that served as a chapel. The school Sisters de Notre Dame were engaged to teach, but by reason of the scarcity of room, they returned to their Mother House each night after their day's work was finished.

In the Autumn of 1898, the Trustees purchased a plot of ground on the north side of Humphrey Street, 350 by 125 feet. The Spring of 1899, saw the parish actively engaged in building operations. Undeterred by the inclement weather of April and May of the year 1899, the building made rapid strides towards completion. In the presence of a large number of parishioners and societies of the city and a host of priests, Vicar-General Muehlsiepen laid the corner stone of the new church on the Feast of St. Joachim, August 20, 1899. On November 12, 1899, just one year after the organization of the parish, the new church was blessed for the service of God, by the Very Rev. H. Van der Sanden, Chancellor of the diocese.

In the year 1900, the Sisters of the Congregation of the Most Precious Blood assumed charge of the parish school. Under their able and zealous care the school grew apace with the parish. The Sacrament of Confirmation was administered for the first time by Archbishop John Joseph Kain on April 8, 1901.

The completion of the church and the erection of a Sisters' home was commenced in 1906, and, by winter of that year, both buildings were under roof. The new buildings being equipped, the blessing of the new church took place on 9th day of August, 1907. The new Vicar-General O. J. S. Hoog performed the solemn function.

At this time the necessity of providing more school rooms arose; consequently in the year 1912, a new building containing four school rooms and a parish auditorium was provided.

The parish of the Holy Family grew and prospered. A large number of old parishioners of SS. Peter and Paul's established their homes in this attractive part of the city. On November 22, 1927, the corner stone for a new substantial church edifice was laid and on June 19, 1927, the massive imposing structure of granite was dedicated by Archbishop Glennon. On Father Reuther's death, August 2, 1927, Father W. H. Huelsmann succeeded to the pastorship.[6]

The year that saw the organization of the Holy Family Parish also witnessed the humble beginnings of *St. Margaret's*, on Flad and

---

6 Questionnaire-Answers.

Vandeventer Avenues. When the need of an English-speaking parish north of Tower Grove Park became obvious Archbishop Kain, late in 1899, charged Father James J. O'Brien, then assistant priest at St. Leo's Church, with the work of its establishment. The outlook seemed very promising, when in the early months of 1900, Father O'Brien made a thorough canvass of the district assigned to him. A vacant store building on the southeast corner of Russell and Vandeventer Avenues was rented; the store-room was then arranged for church services, and the upper story served for the pastoral residence. Here the congregation worshipped for several years, until the members felt able to erect a permanent establishment. A fine site was purchased on Flad and Vandeventer Avenues and the corner stone for the present Church of St. Margaret was laid on April 3, 1906, by Vicar-General Hoog. On Thanksgiving day 1907, the massive building was dedicated by Archbishop Glennon. The erection of a parochial school was postponed until 1911, when it was organized with nine Sisters of St. Joseph in charge. In 1922, Father James O'Brien was called away by death from the parish he had founded. Rev. Thomas V. O'Reilly, succeeded Father O'Brien in the Fall of 1922, and under his energetic administration the parish continues to be one of the most prosperous in the city.[7]

It was Father O'Brien's childhood friend, the Rev. John S. Long that in 1902, founded the parish of *All Saints* on the western boundary of the city, and built for its temporary home the great frame, two and one-half story combination church, school, parish residence and community center on Sixty-Third Street and Maple Avenue, which has now made way for the elegant church erected by Father McMahon. The school is conducted by six Sisters of St. Joseph.

The last of the churches of Archbishop Kain's administration enumerated among the city churches, though not strictly in the city, is that of Notre Dame de Lourdes at Wellston. There is nothing French about the parish save two or three old families and the form of its name. Father Cornelius F. O'Leary founded it after his return from Ireland. Wellston was part of St. Rose's parish. The first church was built in 1903. It was wrecked in 1924, to make room for the edifice, the foundation of which was laid down by 1925. The parochial school was established in 1909, in a frame building, which was superseded by a fine large brick school. The educational management of the school is in the hands of the Sisters of St. Joseph. The series of Pastors of Notre Dame de Lourdes contains but three names: Father Cornelius F. O'Leary (1902-1917), Father William Nugent (1917-1919) and Father Stephen J. Brady (1919-1925). In 1928 the Rev. Wilbur Russell became Pastor of Wellston Parish.

---

7 "Sunday Watchman," August 23, 1925.

## CHAPTER 8

## ARCHBISHOP KAIN'S LAST DAYS.

The Third Plenary Council of Baltimore, 1884 in its "Titulus II. De Personis Ecclesiastics" decreed that in designating a Coadjutor-bishop cum jure successionis the following procedure must be observed: The consultors and irremovable rectors of the diocese must be assembled to select three names to be submitted to the bishops of the Province, who discuss the names thus proposed or others proposed by themselves and then submit three names to the Holy See. In case the Coadjutor is intended for an archdiocese, the Archbishop himself presides at the meeting of the diocesan consultors and rectors. The bishop in this case may suggest the names of those whom he prefers for the office. A latter decree of the Holy See prescribed the same course for the election of an auxiliary.

Archbishop Kain convoked his consultors and rectors for this purpose and presided over the deliberations. Vicar-General Muehlsiepen, though an invalid, was present at the meeting which took place at the Archbishop's residence on January 6th, 1903. The names selected by the assembled representatives of the diocese were 1. Bishop John Joseph Glennon of Kansas City; 2. Bishop Dunne of Dallas, and 3. Bishop Messmer of Green Bay. The Bishops of the Province and the Archbishops of the United States passed on the nominations. By April 27th, 1903 the Right Reverend John Joseph Glennon, Bishop of Pinara and Coadjutor of Kansas City, was appointed by Rome Coadjutor to the Archbishop of St. Louis with the right of succession.

Unheralded and alone the newly appointed Coadjutor Bishop, John J. Glennon, arrived in St. Louis and reported for duty at the episcopal residence. He was well known to Archbishop Kain. At his invitation he had preached the sermon at the Eucharistic Congress held in St. Louis in November 1901, and since that day he had been called in repeatedly to assist the stricken prelate.

He had been informed by letter of his appointment, but the official documents arrived only a few days before Archbishop Kain's departure for St. Agnes Sanitarium, Baltimore. The Coadjutor was now appointed administrator, and the Archbishop left for the East on May 9th, 1903. For a time, good news of the distinguished patient's couvalescence came from Baltimore: but the disease was making steady progress. His Chaplain, Father P. J. Byrne, said mass every morning in the Archbishop's room, until on October 13th, 1903, death came to call him away: He was in his 62nd year, and survived his predecessor by seven years and eight months.

There was a movement among the dead Archbishop's eastern friends to hold the burial services in Wheeling: but Cardinal Gibbons is reported to have insisted on the absolute propriety of bringing the remains to St. Louis.

The old historic Cathedral in which Archbishop Kain had been invested with the sacred pallium, was also to witness the last sad rites of holy Church over his remains. Cardinal Gibbons was celebrant of the Pontifical Requiem Mass. Four Archbishops and fifteen Bishops were in the sanctuary. The absolutions were given by Archbishops Elder of Cincinnati, Keane of Dubuque, Harty of Omaha, and Glennon of St. Louis.

Archbishop Keane, the earliest friend of the dead prelate paid the last tribute of love and respect to his brother Metropolitan. The remains were laid to rest in Calvary Cemetery. ''After Life's fitful fever he sleepeth well.''

Archbishop John Joseph Kain, though not one of the great leaders of his time, nevertheless had many elements of distinction. He was a man of executive ability, endowed with a strong sense of order and a high regard for his office. He had no use for misdirected energy either in the Church at large or in his own diocese. His nature was a rugged, honest, zealous and hard working one. He was respected by priests and people, ''not because he did everything in the best way, nor because he made no mistakes, but rather because he was strong and earnest and had clearly defined views and firmly fixed principles which he tried to carry out and live up to.''

Bishop McQuaid, the great fighting Bishop of the East, wrote of him to Archbishop Corrigan in 1894: ''Archbishop Kain has a great deal of backbone.'' His administration extended through most trying times: he was dragged into the miserable quarrels between the ultra-progressive and conservative factions in the American Church, but he refused to become a partisan of the one as well as of the other. His stand on the school question, and the language question, and the question of nationalism was correct and dignified. He was a man of solid practical learning, with no inclination for literary effort, but gifted with an easy flow of language. His sermons were always clear-cut, direct and concise, breathing the freshness of a meditative mind. Every sentence, every clause embodied a thought the preacher had weighed: Personally he combined an irascible temper with true kindliness of heart. His earnest will was to be just to all. No doubt, some of his stormy outbreaks were mainly due to the condition of his health. He was straightforward in all his dealings: diplomacy was not one of the elements of his spiritual make up.   He was not exactly a loveable character: his appearance and manner of speech seemed to preclude familiarity: yet he craved warm loyalty and whole-souled regard.   The multitude of priests and laymen who came in contact with him, still treasure his memory, the memory of a high minded prelate, a faithful and kindly priest, a strong, fearless and sincere man. As to his high office in the Church of St. Louis he formed the golden link uniting the olden days of missionary effort and labor with the glorious promise of a new era of unprecedented spiritual progress and outward expansion.   Archbishop Kain spent ten years of his life as the head of the Archdiocese of St. Louis.   But the first three years were passed under the shadow of a mighty name, and the last two under the enveloping wings of pain and sorrow and anguish of spirit.   His best work was done and his greatest successes were achieved within the remaining period of five years.   His labors and successes were, for the most part, preparatory for the greater things to come.

PART THREE

———

# The Archdiocese of St. Louis

## BOOK III

*Archbishop John Joseph Glennon*

Archbishop of Saint Louis.

## CHAPTER 1

## ARCHBISHOP GLENNON OF ST. LOUIS

In writing of the new era inaugurated by Archbishop John Joseph Glennon, the historian labors under two serious difficulties: the main actors of the period are still among the living, and the events are too recent to arrange themselves in proper perspective. The first fact imposes upon him a certain reticence in distributing praise or blame, and can be overcome only by letting the facts speak for themselves. The other solves itself, at least in a good measure, by the concomitant fact that the vast increase of events and personalities emphasizes the absolute necessity of following only the main lines of development and treating as concisely as possible of individual efforts and attainments.

Archbishop Glennon was born in the village of Kinnegad, County Westmeath, Ireland, in the vicinity of Clonard, where St. Finian in the sixth century had founded an abbey, from which he took his title as Bishop of Clonard. Out of St. Finian's school came several of the principal saints and doctors of Ireland, as Kiaran the Younger, Columbkille, Columba, and the two Brendans.

The young John Joseph grew up amid the traditions of Ireland's sacred glories, and at an early age, conceived a strong desire for the holy priesthood. After completing his primary course of studies at the school of his native village, he was sent to the Diocesan College of St. Finian at Mullingar, and having completed his classical course, entered All Hallow's College, near Dublin. In this missionary Seminary the young theological student was assigned to the Diocese of Kansas City, and being under the canonical age for holy Orders, continued his studies under Bishop John Hogan. He was ordained by Bishop Hogan in the Cathedral of Kansas City on December 20th, 1884.

Father Glennon's first appointment was as assistant to Father Dunne of St. Patrick's Church, Kansas City. In 1887 Bishop Hogan gave Father Glennon leave of absence for a tour of travel and study in Europe. After a period of study at the University of Bonn on the Rhine and a tour through France and Italy, Father Glennon was

(635)

appointed assistant at the Cathedral of the Immaculate Conception, Kansas City, where a little later he became pastor in succession to Dean Curran. Then came another promotion, that of the Vicar-Generalship, and on June 9th, 1896 the appointment to the Coadjutorship of Kansas City with the title of Bishop of Pinara, an ancient see, now extinct, near the famous city of Troy. The consecration took place in the Cathedral of Kansas City, June 29th, 1896: Archbishop Kain of St. Louis was the consecrating prelate.

Bishop Hogan, then a worn old man, having spent forty-four years in the priesthood, twenty-eight of them in the episcopate, was glad to put the burden and responsibility of his arduous office upon the shoulders of the young, strong and energetic coadjutor, but like many another old man, could not altogether refrain himself from interfering now and then in matters of importance. Bishop Glennon's seven years of Coadjutorship at Kansas City, requiring meekness, patience, prudence and tact, were a good school and novitiate for the future Archbishop of St. Louis; for "they rule best, who have learnt to obey."

All the accounts of Archbishop Glennon's early movements and public functions in St. Louis are full of honest admiration for his outward appearance, and distinguished personality. His tall dignified figure, his graceful movements and gestures, his voice, sweet, yet resonant, his soft and rich complexion, his ever-ready wit, his smile that seldom vanishes. The magic of his tones and the witchery of his manner, his majestic bearing at public functions, and his affability among the people, all of these points and many more were recorded in the papers and books of travel of those early days. "Those who do not know him," said one of his admirers, "are never in danger of mistaking his rank, and those who do know him are never reminded of it." And again: "Amid all the vast cares that are laid upon his shoulders, he bears without abuse, the grand old name of gentleman."

But Archbishop Glennon was more than a gentleman; he was a great churchman fitted by nature and grace to govern a grand archdiocese and to minister by word and deed to the spiritual needs of the lowly as well as the highest.

In September 1903 the Golden Jubilee of Archbishop Patrick J. Ryan, Archbishop of Philadelphia, brought a vast concourse of people from all parts of the Country to the City of Brotherly Love. Bishop Glennon and Archbishop Harty assisted the Jubilarian in receiving the guests. At the banquet that followed the church solemnities Bishop Glennon paid a beautiful tribute to Archbishop Ryan and his former chief in St. Louis, Archbishop Peter Richard Kenrick. It was a magnificent response to the toast "The Archdiocese of St. Louis," and once more turned the eyes of the East to the "Rome of the West." "By the rolling waters of the Mississippi the Lion of the West lies sleeping, and if the waters could speak as they flow, their every wavelet would echo the greatness of his name. For there is not a stream tributary to that mighty river that does not reflect the golden cross of St. Louis.'' Since that memorable day Archbishop Glennon was recognized by the hierarchy of the United States as the worthy heir to the oratorical laurels of Archbishop Patrick J. Ryan, and on almost every grand occasion, East, West, North and South, the Archbishop of St. Louis was chosen to preach the sermon.

But the Archbishop did not confine himself to preaching before distinguished audiences and on great national occasions. In his monthly sermon at the Cathedral chapel, and on his confirmation tours in city and country-side he showed himself as the pastor-orator: entertaining, keen, kind, pleasant, one who never tires, never overawes, never overwhelms his audience, but wins each hearer by apt illustrations and argument clothed in words that reach the mind through the heart. But "suaviter in modo, fortiter in re" was the Archbishop's rule. There was no minimizing in regard to Catholic faith and morals. There was no popularity seeking in his dealings with non-catholics.

When at the time of the World's Fair Congresses, the Protestant Ministers' Alliance made an effort to hold a little Congress of Religions and asked the Archbishop of St. Louis to give his adhesion, they received the unequivocal answer: "A Catholic bishop cannot join in any non-catholic religious service anywhere."

In October 1903 the Archbishop participated in the Diamond Jubilee Solemnities held in honor of the foundation of the St. Louis University. The theme of his sermon was the wonderful work accomplished by the University in the religious, scientific and social advancement of St. Louis and the entire Mississippi Valley, but incidentally touched upon the obstructive work of Socialism. The Archbishop met the socialist counter-attack in a forceful letter addressed to the Clergy of the archdiocese.

The first official act of the new Archbishop was to complete the organization of the diocese: The venerable Vicar-General of his two predecessors, Msgr. Henry Muehlsiepen, had died shortly before his own coming into the archdiocese.

Archbishop Glennon now designated Father Joseph A. Connolly of St. Teresa's Parish, and Father Otto J. S. Hoog of St. Peter's Church. Jefferson City, as his Vicars-General and confirmed Father Henry Van der Sanden in his office of Chancellor of the Archdiocese. According to the requirements of Canon Law he sent the formal petition for the pallium to Rome and, at the same time, requested that, in the interval, he be permitted to exercise all the functions of an archbishop. The request was graciously granted, and the pallium was promised to arrive in due time.

The year of our Lord 1904 was the year of the St. Louis World's Fair, held in honor of the purchase of Louisiana from France. It was bound to be reminiscent of many things and events essentially Catholic. The formal opening took place on April 30th, and its close was fixed for December 1st. As many notables from all parts of the globe, men distinguished in statesmanship, war, and the arts of peace, leaders in science and culture, above all, men of high ecclesiastical rank, were drawn to St. Louis, it was felt as a real godsend that a man of such varied talents and accomplishments, of such poise and self-possession, and of such imposing presence, presided over the destinies of the Church in the City of the World's Fair. This natural pride in having a man at the head of Church affairs was greatly augmented by the frequent words of praise uttered by distinguished visitors. One quotation must suffice, that of the author of "In the Land of the Strenuous Life," the Abbe Felix Klein, of the Catholic University of Paris:

"The bluff good-nature of the Bishop of Rochester, the charming cleverness of Archbishop Ireland, the shining candor of Archbishop Kain, are not the predominating qualities of Archbishop Glennon. He is very simple, but distinction is his dominant trait. Very young, very tall, very handsome, very eloquent, he begins by so astonishing you, evidently without any intention on his own part, with his external gifts, that you are inclined to regard these as excessively developed. Gradually, however, his qualities of mind and heart make themselves appreciated, and you yield to their charm. During my stay I perceived that he produces the same effect on everybody; and in what I learned of him later, I became convinced that the Church in America considers him one of its future glories."

The visit of Cardinal Satolli to the Fair was made the occasion of a great Catholic demonstration. Archbishop Glennon, Judge O'Neill Ryan, Frederick W. Lehman, Cardinal Satolli, and Msgr. Dennis O'Connell, were the speakers at the Reception in honor of the representative of the Pope.

It was Archbishop Glennon's gracious but compelling personality that obtained for the Catholic Church the recognition it deserved, not only from the authorities, but also from countless visitors. "All who have visited St. Louis during the many ceremonies of the Exposition," wrote the New York Sun, "have been struck by the character displayed by Archbishop Glennon, whose handsome boyish face gives no inkling of the qualities of aggressive leadership he has of late so often manifested. He is the coming man." And yet he was only forty-two years of age, twenty of which he had spent in the priestly state. His immediate jurisdiction at the end of the year extended over seventy-one parishes in the City and 126 in the Country towns and villages of Eastern Missouri, with a diocesan clergy numbering two hundred and seventy-four. The priests belonging to Religious Orders within his diocese numbered two hundred and nine, making a total of four hundred and eighty-three, only sixty-two less than could be found in all the United States, when Archbishop Kenrick began his wonderful career in St. Louis, three score years before.

## CHAPTER 2

## PLANNING THE NEW CATHEDRAL

The first public utterance of Archbishop Glennon in regard to the erection of a Cathedral that should be worthy of St. Louis "the Mother-See of the West," was made in a powerful sermon in the Cathedral chapel on the first Sunday of February, 1905. Starting from the inspired words of Solomon: "Now the Lord hath given me rest round about, and there is no adversary, nor evil occurrence. Wherefore, I propose to build a temple to the name of the Lord my God,"[1] the speaker represented his purpose as the fulfillment of the desires and prayers and frustrated efforts of the past to give to St. Louis "a Cathedral commensurate with its importance as an Archdiocese and its greatness as a city, the symbol of unity, and the center of religion." Archbishop Kenrick, he said, had purchased the site and formed a society for the purpose of procuring the necessary funds: but the needs of the parishes and the cause of charity, and financial depression brought delay upon delay, until the illustrious Archbishop sank to rest without having attained his fervent desire. Archbishop Kain, accepting the trust of his predecessor's unfulfilled desire, strove with might and main to realize it: he purchased the present site, had sketches prepared of a Cathedral in the Roman Basilica style and formulated plans for the payment of it: when he, all too soon, was called away from his labors. Having thus prepared the way the Archbishop unfolded his own magnificent plan: "From the first day I came amongst you I found pressing on me with ever increasing urgency this great work, the fulfillment of which is so evidently the will of God. Indeed, we would be recreant to the duties of our holy office, faithless to the traditions of the Diocese and to the memories of the dead, forgetful of your spiritual interests, were we to delay any longer in the performance of this manifest duty. We must not do so, and with God's help we hope to see the work soon commenced; and should we not live to see its completion, we can at least feel, in joining the group in Calvary, that their hopes were ours also; their ideas we endeavored to cherish and their sacrifices we struggled to imitate, and that it was God's will that we should leave to others the task we fain had believed was our own."

"In this matter I feel I am only echoing your wishes, and that you are as anxious as I am to begin the great work.

"We have a right to think, to hope and to expect that a great and noble building will be erected commensurate at once with your

[1] III Kings, 5, 3.

civic pride, your Catholic faith and your generous giving. To say that your Cathedral should cost a' million of dollars is certainly not an extravagant idea: and if your spirit and generosity make it possible, it will soon become a great reality. Great things have been done here in the past—noble works and princely gifts for faith and charity. Many of the generous ones are now at rest. They were your fathers and your friends; if they could speak today, they would say to you, their children, to build in God's name this Cathedral. They would say to you by the faith they loved and the city they loved: Don't let the flag of faith be lowered; don't let the fleur-de-lis of St. Louis be stained!'' Lifted up in the olden days, the twin symbol of civic pride and religious life, they should still be carried forward, and onward to victory. If St. Louis of old spent his life and his fortune in an attempt to rescue the tomb of the Savior from the hand of the pagan, is there not even a higher reason for us to spend our lives and fortunes that His (the Savior's) home might be made glorious?

"That tomb which St. Louis would rescue was an empty tomb; in the Christian tabernacle we look with eyes of faith, not to an empty tomb, but to an omnipotent Presence, and kneeling down adore. Should not the place of our adoration be in some way worthy of that august Presence?

"Can you afford to gather gems you may not wear, and collect tapestries you have to hide, and walk on floors of tesselated colors, or beneath ceilings rich with artists' colors, and make your homes rich with all these things, while you leave the home of the Savior in solitary desolation? There was no room for Him in the inns at Bethlehem; will we seek to follow Bethlehem in its selfishness, forgetting that all good gifts come from Him whom we would now reject as an intruder?

"You have churches—many of them—in the city and the Diocese: but they are orphaned till the mother church, the Cathedral church is, built. It stands to them and the Diocese what the parish church is for the parish. The circle is not complete; the crown is not reached. The work of God is unfinished as long as we remain without the crowning edifice, which will be a parish church for you, a cathedral for the Diocese. The battle cry of the crusaders—of St. Louis the King—the cry that led them on to victory or consoled them in defeat was: 'God wills it!' 'God wills it!' So in the name of the Crucified One we take up this new crusade. Shall we build for Christ this temple? Yes, for surely 'God wills it'.''[2]

No doubt, these words were received at first with mingled feelings of joy and serious misgivings: joy, because a new Cathedral was desired by all: misgivings, because the amount of a million dollars seemed be-

---

2  Cf. ''The Cathedrals of St. Louis,'' Dr. Souvay, pp. 30-31.

yond reach. In 1905, money was not as plentiful and cheap as it became during the war. But the Archbishop seemed confident and spoke with an assurance that was plainly inspired by a full knowledge of the circumstances, favorable and unfavorable.

The eloquent appeal was read with deep interest, and eventually obtained universal approval. The realization of the long delayed dream was fast approaching.

And now, on the 14th day of Our Lady's Month, the response of the clergy and laity to the Archbishop's appeal was to come. The occasion was the ceremony of conferring the sacred Pallium on the new Archbishop. Cardinal James Gibbons, the highest dignitary of the Church in America, was to officiate at the solemnity.

On the morning of May 14th, the third Sunday after Easter, 1905, the Old Cathedral on Walnut Street witnessed a scene of unprecedented beauty and splendor. The noble altar banked with flowers, and the sanctuary flooded with light, formed a majestic background, for the Archbishop, resplendent with glory, surrounded by priests clad in gold vestments, the venerable Cardinal at his right, and his brothers in the Episcopacy before him. It was as if the old pile, the joy and pride of Bishop Rosati, stood transfigured with youthful rapture, to bid farewell and godspeed to its ever memorable founder's third successor, on his way to a new, far greater and nobler Cathedral. The Archbishop of St. Paul, John Ireland, voiced the sentiment in his scholarly address, the conclusion of which must be given here:

"Archbishop Glennon, as I love the church of America, I love the church of St. Louis: I wish her to do her full part in the battles of the future: hence my joy in seeing the pallium of Rome descending upon your shoulders. It befits you. As years go by, may it befit you more and more. You are rich in talent: you are rich in good will and energy: you are fashioned to conquer: and youth is yours. Youth burns with the fire of enthusiasm, so important in him who is called to do great things: it allows far-reaching vision and wide and thoughtful planning. I envy your youth on the threshold of the Twentieth Century, when such wondrous opportunities are unfolded, when the trumpet blast summons to such portentous battles. Forward to your God-given work. Clergy and laity trust you and pledge to you unreserved and unwavering loyalty. Forward, in the might of your soul, in the might of Divine Grace. Great things must you do for St. Louis and for America. You will build a cathedral for St. Louis. Already your hand is in the work. Yes, build it. The honor of St. Louis demands a cathedral: the complement and the crown of its many other religious glories. It demands a cathedral worthy of its own past and of its future—towering high to the skies, as towers the historic eminence of

St. Louis: rich and rare in its beauty in sanctuary and aisle, as is rich and rare the faith, the piety of the church of St. Louis. Build your cathedral. Take up the memories of the old cathedral! the cathedral of Rosati and Kenrick: the cathedral of the pioneer Catholics of St. Louis, perfuming with them the new Cathedral. Build your cathedral, but remember that when your career is over, the Cathedral must draw its highest and sweetest honor from this, that it is a monument of the glorious deeds done by you in the spiritual work of your episcopate— deeds done for God and for souls, for church and for country.''[3] .

Archbishop Glennon with his youthful fire of enthusiasm, his far reaching vision and wide thoughtful planning did not require such an urgent appeal: yet it was welcome as an inspiration to his people. At the close of the ceremonies in Church, a banquet was given by the clergy to the Archbishop and the Cardinal and visiting dignitaries, at which the sum of $60,000.00 in cash, the personal gift of the priests of the diocese, was presented to his Grace for the Cathedral. The amount eventually reached $71,200. The same evening, in the course of a reception tendered to the Archbishop and his guests, public announcement was made by the Hon. R. C. Kerens that thirty-two lay members of the Church of St. Louis had subscribed for the Cathedral a sum aggregating $260,000, four of these donors contributing $25,000 each. This spontaneous act, on the part of the laity was a great surprise and still greater encouragement to the Archbishop. Adding together the sum of $250,000. that had been accumulated by his predecessors, and was now in his hands, and the liberal contributions from the clergy and the laity, the Archbishop could announce an initial fund of $600,000. To raise the remaining amount of $400,000, to make up the required million, seemed but a matter of time: the erection of the great Cathedral was now assured.

But there were many other matters of importance that required attention and study: the choice of an architect and the selection of a plan.

"As it stands today," says Dr. Souvay in his historical Sketch, "The Cathedral of St. Louis is the result of a building process that has been carried on since the summer of 1905, when designs were drawn up by various architects of America, France and Germany, according to the plan of Archbishop Glennon, for a competition contest. The mot d'ordre was: We want a million dollar structure that shall not be classic, Gothic or Renaissance."[4] Three styles of Church-buildings were excluded: the classic, the Gothic and Renaissance, perhaps

---

- [3]  Archbishop Ireland's Sermon, "Globe-Democrat," May 15, 1905.
  [4]  "The Cathedrals of St. Louis," p. 34.

for no other reason than that the cities of America, and St. Louis in an eminent degree, already contained a large number of beautiful reproductions of European Churches in one or the other of these accepted forms of architecture. A number of famous architects of St. Louis, Boston, New York, Paris, Vienna and Cologne were invited to submit sketches. It was to be the largest church in the United States, with a seating capacity of 4,500, it must be magnificent in outward appearance, and the cost of the rough structure was not to exceed $1,300,000. At the same time a building Committee consisting of prominent Catholics of the city was appointed to study the sketches and to select and pass on their respective merits. On the first of August the Archbishop sailed from New York to Ireland to visit his venerable father. Then he started out to study the most famous Cathedrals of England, France and Germany, especially Paris, London and Cologne. During his absence the affairs of the Diocese were administered by the two Vicars-General, J. A. Connolly, and Otto J. S. Hoog. The Archbishop arrived in Queenstown on August 5th. At Thurles he met Archbishop Ryan of Philadelphia. He sailed from Queenstown on September 9th, and reached home on Tuesday September 18th, unheralded and unattended. As to his Cathedral project, he said, that the building was to be a combination of Romanesque, Byzantine and Renaissance, and that the end of October had been fixed as the time when the plans for the structure must be in the hands of the Committee. On the very day of his arrival in St. Louis the Archbishop announced that Fathers Crane and Randall had been appointed diocesan missionaries and would depart in October for Washington to enter the Paulist College for a special course of instruction.''

The Fifth Diocesan Synod of St. Louis was opened at Kenrick Seminary on October 3rd, 1905, with Pontifical Mass. Within less than three hours the business of the Synod was transacted, the consultors and other boards of the diocese were named, and the Decrees of the Fourth Synod were promulgated anew, with a few unimportant changes in regard to church-music, theological conferences, and the transition from one parish to another. Father Van der Sanden was retained as Chancellor and Fathers Hoffman, Tallon, May, Holweck, Coffey and Tannrath formed the Archbishop's Board of Consultors. Father Francis Goller's elevation to the dignity of a Roman Prelate was announced.

The Archbishop spoke in a general way about the new Cathedral, but divulged none of his plans regarding the building. He thanked the priests for their liberal offering, but urged them to impress on their parishioners the necessity of assisting, even in a small way, the large undertaking.

The special committee appointed to make a selection from among the designs submitted, after a long session held on February 12, 1906, and enlivened by several spirited arguments, finally rendered its verdict in favor of the designs presented by Messrs. Barnett, Haynes and Barnett, of St. Louis. The architects at once set about to draw their detailed plans. In announcing, on September 2nd, 1906, that the work on the building would commence as soon as the architects were ready, the Archbishop remarked: ''We hope to have a very large and beautiful structure. Its seating capacity is estimated at between 4,000 and 5,000, and its cost will be at least $1,000,000. We do not expect to go into debt. It is a bad thing to have a mortgage between you and the Almighty.''[5]

Thus the project of the Cathedral building rested for a year; whilst the building fund was increasing from day to day, and the architects were laying down the details of their magnificent plan.

---

5  ''The Cathedrals of St. Louis,'' p. 34.

## CHAPTER 3

## THE LAYING OF THE CORNER STONE

Wherever there are many minds employed on a great undertak-, ing, there will arise a number of doubts and misgivings to threaten its success or at least to delay its progress. After the plans of the Cathedral had been completed, questions that seemed to have been definitely settled, arose once more: Is the chosen site in every way satisfactory? Should the Cathedral not be placed further West? And can the ground really support the tremendous mass of stone and mortar that is to be raised upon it? A special committee was appointed to canvass the various sections of the West End for a better location: Their report was in favor of the site chosen by Archbishop Kain. To satisfy every lingering doubt, the soil was tested down to rock bottom and found to be fully satisfactory.

Ground was broken for the structure on May 1st, 1907, by the Archbishop, attended by Archbishop Harty of Manilla, Father Francis Gilfillan, the new pastor of the Cathedral chapel, and Father Tannrath of St. Agnes Church, as well as George D. Barnett, the architect, and Jerome F. P. Casey, contractor. No speeches were made. The foundation was expected to be completed within six months. Bids for the contract for the main structure were to be opened on July 15th, 1907. The parochial residence which stood on the site of the proposed Cathedral was put on rollers and removed to the northwest corner of the block, within sixty days. Work on the foundations was progressing rapidly; and the time seemed near for awarding the contract. But now another delay occurred. The circumstances that led up to it are succinctly stated by Dr. Souvay in his sketch: "Early in April was the date scheduled for the awarding of the contract. But then much discussion arose as to the kind of stone to be used in the construction; some of the members of the Cathedral Board suggested granite, others, Bedford stone, others still, granite and Bedford stone combined. The committee of five appointed to decide definitely upon the material, reported on Thursday evening April 9th, 1908, in favor of granite, whereupon granite was unanimously decided upon by the Board. All the bids submitted took Bedford stone into consideration; the verdict of the Board, therefore, involved the resubmission of the bids, as granite in the ornamentation alone raised the. cost of the structure $300,000 more. The granite to be used was understood to be the gray or white sort quarried in Vermont and New Hamsphire

(646)

On May 10th, the contract for the superstructure, amounting to \$1,-000,000, was let to the firm of J. E. Robinson and Son, of New York.''[1]

On June 26th, 1908 the Sixth Diocesan Synod was held at the Kenrick Seminary: the Archbishop presided; the Rev. Dr. Joseph Selinger as Promotor Synodi and the Rev. J. J. Tannrath as Secretary. After mass was said by Vicar-General Connolly, about four hundred priests responded to the roll call. The Papal Encyclical ''Pascendi Gregis'' regarding Marriage was enthusiastically accepted. The recent Papal Decree ''Ne Temere'' regarding Marriage was explained in all its bearings, and the rules and regulations of the Diocese in regard to this matter were altered in conformity with the Decree. The Law of the Baltimore Council, regulating the sale and use of intoxicants at Church festivities was enjoined upon all the clergy, in order that Church discipline and decorum might be evident in all the gatherings of our people. The various church boards were reappointed, as no changes seemed necessary. In regard to the Cathedral, His Grace asked and exhorted the clergy to raise a fund of \$500,000 among the laity of the diocese. No parishes at present were to be assessed; but the members of the many parishes throughout the Diocese were expected to contribute according to their means for the up-building and perfecting of this great undertaking.

At the request of the Synodal Board His Grace, promised to issue a special Pastoral Letter, ''De Aedificanda Cathedrali.'' The Special Committee appointed to assist the Archbishop in the collection of the fund of half a million from the members of the various parishes of the diocese was composed of Fathers P. W. Tallon, H. Hukestein, Patrick Dooley, E. J. Lemkes, Timothy Dempsey, P. J. O'Rourke, William Randall, J. J. Tannrath and Francis Brand, with a representative from each one of the four great missionary Orders of the diocese, the Jesuits, Redemptorists, Vincentians and Passionists.

The Pastoral Letter was issued August 25th, 1908, and read in all the Churches of the diocese on the following Sunday: The main points of the document are contained in the following extracts:

''It does not appear unreasonable nor unfair to invite the numerous and devoted people of this diocese to now enter into this great work and bring the project to a satisfactory conclusion. If a few have been able to do so much, then many should certainly be able to do the rest. It is our ambition to have every family of the Diocese represented in this work.

''This Cathedral is to be the Mother Church of the Diocese, not for the wealthy few, nor even for the generous subscribers, but for

---

1 ''The Cathedrals of St. Louis,'' p. 35.

all the people of the Diocese, and this is an added reason why all the people of the Diocese should have their hand in its upbuilding and be among the subscribers. As with the subscriptions received heretofore, so it shall be with all subscriptions to be received in the future, namely, that only one-fifth of the amount subscribed would be asked for this year and so until it is all paid.

"Our appeal is now made to the generous and devoted people of the Archdiocese of St. Louis. We ask for five hundred thousand ($500,000) dollars, which, with the eight hundred thousand already subscribed, will complete and fully equip your new Cathedral."[2]

At the same time the announcement was made that the ceremony of laying the corner stone of the New Cathedral would take place Sunday, October 18th, and would be preceded by a Catholic parade, to add to the impressiveness of the scene, and to show by its number and decorum that the faith of St. Louis is still alive and has a work to do.

All the parishes of the city, seventy-seven in number, as well as those of the neighboring towns, immediately began organizing their contingents on military lines. Only men were to participate in the parade. Under the Grand Marshal Amedeé V. Reyburn three divisions were formed under Joseph P. Hartnett, Thomas A. Dooley and Casper Wolf, as division commanders. Each division had two brigades. Great enthusiasm was manifested everywhere: The estimates as to the numbers that would take part in the demonstration ranged from twenty to thirty thousand. At last the great day dawned, Sunday, October 19th. It was a beautiful, bright and balmy day. The column started from Beaumont and Pine Streets, with every side street to Grand Avenue filled, both north and south, with reserve platoons of marchers, waiting for their turn to fall in line. Down Pine Street to Theresa Avenue moved the glittering hosts, over Theresa Avenue to Lindell Boulevard and west on Lindell Boulevard to Kingshighway, and thence to the Cathedral site. Thousands of floating Church banners and flags of our Country, martial music from forty bands, and the steady tread of forty thousand marching men, twelve abreast, between two deep, solid ranks of cheering men and women, formed the grandest religious demonstration ever given west of New York. Every nationality of the Caucasian race and a few others were represented in this wonderful manifestation of Catholic faith.

Standing bareheaded, clothed in his official regalia, tall and distinguished among his brother Archbishops and Bishops, Archbishop Glennon watched the procession on its stately way. Beside him stood

---

[2] The Pastoral Letter appeared in the "Sunday Watchman," September 6, 1908.

the Apostolic Delegate, Archbishop Diomede Falconio, who had come
to bless the corner stone. All around them stood the Archbishops:
John M. Farley of New York, John Ireland of St. Paul, James Blenk
of New Orleans, Kelly of Sidney, Australia, Patrick Quigly of Chicago,
and Bishops J. D. O'Connell, Rector of the Catholic University at
Washington. Edmund M. Dunne of Peoria; Theophile Meerschaert of
Oklahoma; Nicholas A. Gallagher of Galveston; John B. Morris of
Little Rock; Richard Scannell of Omaha; Maurice F. Burke of St.
Joseph; John F. Cunningham of Concordia; James J. Hartley of
Columbus; Camillus Maes of Covington; John P. Carroll of Helena;
Thomas Lillis of Leavenworth; Patrick A. Ludden of Syracuse, and
John H. Hennessey of Wichita. Before the end of the parade the
Papal Delegate and Archbishop Glennon quickly left the reviewing
stand: then His Excellency, attended by the two Vicars-General of the
diocese blessed and laid the corner stone on the southeast corner of the
spacious Cathedral foundations. Monsignor Francis Goller served as
assistant Priest, Fathers John A. Hoffmann and Patrick Tallon as
Deacon and Subdeacon, Fathers Tannrath, M. S. Ryan and J. Spencer
as Masters of Ceremonies. In the meantime the Archbishop returned
to the grand stand and, at the close of the parade, delivered an address
full of gratitude and reverence for the ever memorable past, and of
joyous hope for the future, concluding with a variation on the majestic
words graven on the corner stone: "To Christ, the Victor, we raise
this temple; to the worship of the One True God; in the faith of
St. Louis and St. Peter, to the perpetuation of the faith of our
Fathers."

During the Archbishop's impassioned address darkness gradually
settled down upon the vast multitude gathered in a compact mass
around the foundations.

Only the great derrick, that had lifted the corner stone in place,
stood out in bold relief against the darkened sky, with its mighty arm
extended over the spectral scene, when suddenly, a flaming cross burst
forth and hovered high in air over the site where all the pomp and
ceremony of the Church had attended the laying of the corner stone.
And underneath its full brightness stood the Archbishop, speaking to
his people, with an eloquence born of the occasion; speaking of the
faith and courage of his predecessors: it was all so strange, so overwhelming in its significance: The electric lights that had been lit to
illumine the scene, had become the flaming symbol of the Catholic
faith of St. Louis.[3]

---

3 The papers of the day relate that hundreds of people from a distance saw
the flaming cross and hurried westward to see what it meant.

As the Archbishop ceased speaking the Apostolic Delegate chanted the papal blessing bestowed in a cablegram from the Holy Father Pius X. So ended the greatest day the Catholic Church, in St. Louis had śeen, a day that was not to be equalled until the consecration of the Cathedral eighteen years later. .

Two weeks after this event the Archbishop was on his way to the Eternal City, to make his report to the Holy Father. In his absence the affairs of the diocese were administered by the two Vicars-General, J. A. Connolly and O. J. S. Hoog.

When he arrived in the center of the Christian world a great change had taken place in the American Church. On November 3, 1908 the rule of the Sacred Congregation of the Propaganda over the ecclesiastical hierarchy of the Church in the United States terminated, and its missionary status was changed into that of canonical dioceses and parishes, all of equal rank with the older church organizations of Europe, dealing directly with the Pope. In this sense, also, the Archbishop, at the corner stone laying stood at the threshold of a new era.

## CHAPTER 4

## CATHOLIC SOCIAL WORK

Five years had now elapsed since Bishop Glennon became Metropolitan of St. Louis. During this time he busied himself with a multitude of important matters of a charitable nature which must now be recorded. Whilst perhaps the building of the great Cathedral was uppermost in his mind, yet his interest in various branches of social work, held even a prior claim on his affections. Since his consecration as a Bishop of the Church of God, the claims of God's favorite children, the poor, the forsaken, the persecuted, and even the straying and wayward, have constantly engaged his attention as expressed in sermons, in lectures and in organized activities. As Archbishop of St. Louis, however, he found greater opportunities of realizing his ideas and plans for the betterment of social conditions among his people.

First and foremost, there is the institution sponsored by Archbishop Glennon as having the purpose of counteracting the evils of a homeless and roving life, the Home that now bears the name "Father Dempsey's Hotel," instead of the original title "The Exile's Rest." It was on July 11th, 1898 that Father Timothy Dempsey was appointed pastor of St. Patrick's Church. The district in which St. Patrick's church is situated has greatly deteriorated since its foundation in 1844: in fact it might be designed by the malodorous title of "Slums." The good pastor had ample opportunity to study the baneful effects of the dingy saloon and the cheap lodging house on the thousands of men of a roving disposition, who flocked to the city throughout the year. Father Dempsey conceived the idea of a home for the weary wanderers and the men with scant means in their pockets, where, for the price of a dime, a clean comfortable bed, hot or cold bath, stationery and access to the reading-room might be secured. Wholesome food was also to be provided. The conviction of the necessity of such an institution grew stronger from year to year, and at last took outward form. The beginning was made on December 6th of the preceding year, when the old Shield School was bought and work was begun in remodeling the building for hotel purposes. Sunday, May 5th, of that year "Father Demsey's Hotel" as Archbishop Glennon baptized it on its birthday, was opened amid a large assembly of distinguished visitors, among them the Archbishop, the Mayor and the Postmaster of St. Louis. Mayor Wells praised and thanked Father Dempsey for having done an act in the interest of the Commonwealth by making worthy citizens out of the despondent and reckless. Father Demsey's Hotel at the time of its opening had sixty-eight rooms with two hundred and seven beds.

In 1908, not less than 7,953 guests were entertained. The average number throughout the years of its existence was 10,000. The name "Exile Rest" is now applied to Father Demsey's lot in Calvary Cemetery, where the earthly remains of his proteges are to find their last resting place. It contains the graves of more than one hundred and ninety workingmen who might otherwise have been consigned to Potter's Field. In addition to his Hotel for Workingmen "Father Tim," as everybody calls him, has established a similar "Hotel for Working Girls, where they can live in comfort on small pay, secure from the temptations of the Street, the "St. Patrick's Day Nursery and Emergency Home," a "Home for Convalescents." "All these institutions have been enlarged as the needs increased, maintained and have filled fields of the highest usefulness in giving comfort and aid to those who suffer from poverty or misfortune. Father Tim himself is a St. Louis Institution.

"Both employers and employed sought his potent aid in settling their conflicts and bringing peace.

He settled forty-six labor disputes and strikes to the satisfaction of both sides.

The second Institution is Father Dunne's Newsboys' Home and Protectorate, opened on February 6, 1906. Realizing the sad condition of poor boys who are obliged to earn their living as newsboys, or bootblacks, in fact, of all homeless boys who are too old to find shelter in an orphan asylum, Archbishop Glennon decided to establish a home for such children. The proper man for founding and conducting such an institution he found in Father Peter J. Dunne, the assistant at St. Rose's Church. At the quarterly meeting of the St. Vincent de Paul Society, a subscription fund of about $1,200 was raised by individual members as to the nucleus of the great work. The Archbishop headed the list with $100. This was early in 1906.

On February 6th, of that year Father Dunne took possession of a rented house at 1013 Selby Place. Three boys were installed in the Home on the day of the opening. The house was as bare almost as the pavements or doorsteps on which the boys had been accustomed to sleep: but soon Father Dunne found generous friends: not so much among the wealthy, but among the poor. An unexpected difficulty arose: the neighbors did not want to have such an institution among them, and began to agitate against it. Every mischief perpetrated there, was charged to Father Dunne's Boys. Selby Place was no longer an enjoyable place for Father Dunne; but he could not move before he had found a new home. The idea of a Newsboy's Home seemed to have gotten on everybody's nerves. At last the good Father secured a house located at 2737 Locust Street where he removed with his thirty-five boys, May 4th, 1906. All this work had been done by Father Dunne in addition to his priestly duties as assistant at St. Rose's and afterwards at St. Patrick's Church. But now he was freed by the Archbishop from all other duties save that of Head and Factotum of the Newsboy's Home. To feed and clothe his boys, to provide the younger ones with opportunities to attend school, and the older ones with positions in the city, and to supervise the affairs of those selling papers. The duty of attending the Juvenile Court also devolved upon him. Then he established a printing plant in the Home, and issued a monthly publication devoted to the interests of the Home.

Rents were high and present quarters were insufficient for the constantly growing family of boys. Father Dunne wished to buy one of the old mansions that had been forsaken by their former owners. But one of the patrons of the home urged him to build a new home that would serve all his purposes. A plot of ground on the corner of Washington and Garrison Avenue was offered him at the price of $30,000. The amount seemed beyond reach: yet Father Dunne, one of that class of persons whom the Scriptures describe as "having nothing, yet possessing all things," boldly approached thirty of the wealthy business men of the city for a contribution of $1,000 by each and everyone; and he succeeded in a short space to raise the $30,000 and to buy the coveted property. There was an old mansion on the place into which Father Dunne now transferred his establishment on November 10th, 1907. A beautiful chapel was erected in connection with the building and in June 1912 an addition was erected, to serve the growing needs of the Home. In the course of time Father Dunne received many large donations from wealthy citizens, among them one donation of $16,000, from "An Unknown Friend."

As Archbishop Glennon said at the dedication of the Newsboy's Home on Sunday November 10th, 1907, "The work Father Dunne is doing is far more heroic than rescuing women and children from a burning house or the river."

Who Father Dunne is everybody knows, in St. Louis and in the State, and we may add in every town and hamlet of our country. A few words about the early life of such a man will not seem out of place here. In fact, they will furnish encouragement to young men struggling under adverse circumstances, and keep them from complaining, that they never got a chance. Peter Joseph Dunne was born of poor but honest and pious parentage in Chicago, June 29th, 1870. When Chicago was devastated by the great fire of 1873, the Dunne family removed to a farm near Council Grove, Kansas. Here the young Peter Joseph spent eight years of happy childhood, broken, however, in his ninth year by the death of his mother. Early in 1882 his father sold the farm and sought employment in Kansas City. The brothers and sisters of the youthful Peter Joseph were placed in Orphan Homes, but he himself worked his way through life in a printing shop. His Father died on Good Friday 1882. The small sum of money the Father had received for his farm, was lost through a faithless administrator. With the desire in his heart to become a priest, but not knowing how to attain his ideal, he worked in a dairy, then in a blacksmith shop, then as a teamster. His first use of his savings was for the purchase of a scholarship in night school. But mental application was so very difficult that he became discouraged and turned to the business of a dairyman, and finally to that of a horse trader.

Failing in this dangerous trade, Peter Joseph turned his face to St. Louis: He worked with pick and shovel on the city water works, then he became a teamster once more, then he worked for the Mississippi Valley Glass Company, and then invested his savings in a team of mules. When the panic of 1893 reached St. Louis, and almost all public works were stopped, he sold his team and found employment as night watchman at the St. Louis University. It was now, in his twenty-fourth year, that the desire for the priesthood took possession of Peter Joseph's heart with renewed vigor. And he found a friend who made it possible for him to attain his almost hopeless purpose. It was Archbishop Kain who adopted him for the diocese and sent him to Kenrick Seminary. On June 13th, 1903 Archbishop Glennon ordained Peter Joseph Dunne, who had thus passed through the furnace of affliction, to undertake and accomplish a work that is heroic in its nature and stands among the chief glories of the Archdiocese, Father Dunne's Newsboys' Home and Protectory.

Both Fathers Dempsey and Dunne have been honored by the Holy Father with the dignity of Roman Prelates.

Whilst these noble works of social welfare, though inspired and encouraged by the Archbishop, were really the creations of the two distinguished priests whose name they bear, the remaining work of sociological importance to be treated in this chapter, owes its origin to Archbishop Glennon and was carried out almost single-handed by His Grace. It is the Colonization Realty Company organized in 1905.

The purpose of the Archbishop in engaging in the Colonization movement was to attract Catholic colonists from the overcrowded cities of the East and European emigrants, who are for the most part agriculturists, to the fertile fields of Missouri. Coming from Italy, Russia, Poland, and the eastern crownlands of what was Austria, as most of those later immigrants do, they are of the Catholics Faith, but, remaining in the large eastern centers, or being carried into localities where there are no Catholic churches, they often lose all religion. The movement inaugurated by Archbishop Glennon is intended for the benefit of the aliens who need help for building their homes. It is to save them from the squalor and poverty of the large cities and to place them in rural districts where they will be given a good start in the way of home building. "The movement," says the Archbishop, "will aid in building up strong country parishes, where not only the religion, but the language and the national tastes of immigrants will be protected." In July the Archbishop purchased more than twelve thousand acres of land in Dunklin County for the purpose of colonization. Within a short time after this purchase, thirty Catholic families arrived and began the making of homesteads. In October, 1905, Father Frederick Peters was sent to the colony as its rector and general adviser. A sawmill was established to saw the timbers into lumber for the frame houses of the pioneers. Thus a little town grew up which was named Glennonville in honor of its founder. The church is dedicated to St. Teresa. The parish supports a school with eighty pupils. A lay-teacher is in charge. There are two other colonies that owe their existence to the efforts of Archbishop Glennon's Colonization Realty Company, that of Knobview, in Phelps County, where Father Octavio Leone built a small church in honor of St. Anthony and which was dedicated by Archbishop Glennon in 1906. The other colony is that of Wilhelmina in Dunklin County, organized by the Rev. Vincent Tesselaar, O.S.M.

Starting his priestly life as a Professor of Philosophy and the Higher Mathematics, Father Tesselaar was sent to the forest-wilds of Southeast Missouri to recuperate his health, and to transform the wilderness into a Catholic settlement under the auspices of Archbishop Glennon and his Colonization Realty Company. There are about fifty families of Dutch extraction settled at Wilhelmina, and there is room for fifty more. The present chapel of the place was dedicated May 12th, 1910, in honor of the Sacred Heart. In 1920, the pastor introduced the Ursuline Sisters of Mount St. Joseph in the School. About seventy children are in attendance. The parish built a good substantial house for the pastor and another for the Sisters. Two young men of the place have become priests, and two young ladies have joined the Ursuline Nuns, certainly a very good showing for a colonial town.

At the annual meeting of the Archbishops of the United States, at Washington, D. C., on April 27th, 1911, the question of immigration and colonization as advocated by the Archbishop of St. Louis, was discussed, and it was resolved that a special meeting of that body should be held at St. Louis, May 2nd and 3rd, in conjunction with the representatives of the Catholic Colonization Societies of the United States. A national organization was formed, with headquarters at Chicago. The aim of the Society is to protect Catholics of modest means who desire to purchase farmlands.

Of the minor Catholic organizations for social service purposes established under Archbishop Glennon's regime, we can but mention the following:

*Association for the Care of Convalescent Girls and Women,* Mrs. William L. Igoe, President.

*Catholic Instruction League,* Miss Inez Specking, President, with twenty-seven Catechism Centers and two hundred and fifty-three teachers.

*Catholic Outing Home,* Mrs. J. L. Hornsby, President.

*Catholic Women's Association* with employment department, lunch room and hospital Committee.

*St. Louis Catholic Women's League of Missouri* for patriotic, charitable and civic work.

*Guardian Angel Settlement* conducted by Sisters of Charity.

*St. Joseph Social Center* for the purpose of assisting Catholic families not otherwise cared for in religious, economic and physical needs·

*The Queens Daughters* to promote the performance of the spiritual and corporal works of mercy.

*St. Elizabeth's Settlement of the Central Verein* to do constructive social work, to conduct a Day Nursery, Kindergarten, lunch room for school children, and to carry on family visitation. In charge of Notre Dame Sisters and one lay worker, who also renders spiritual and material aid to the Catholic patients in the maternity Ward of the City Hospital. Conducted by the Central Bureau of the Central Verein, 3835 Westminister Place, supported by the Central Verein, co-operating societies and their members.

*Sisters of Mercy Home for Girls.* Corporate name, "St. Joseph's Convent of Mercy." For accommodation of working women, who desire a suitable and safe boarding place; without distinction of class, nationality or creed. The Home is self-supporting. In charge of, and conducted by, the Sisters of Mercy.

All these organizations, and many others of earlier date, were banded together in 1911, under the title of the "Catholic Charities and Kindred Activities of the City of St. Louis."

## CHAPTER 5

VARIOUS ACTIVITIES OF THE CATHEDRAL BUILDER

After a nine weeks trip abroad, during which Archbishop Glennon visited Rome for the Sacerdotal Jubilee of Pope Pius X, the return voyage was made on the steamship Compania. On his arrival in New York the keen student of human nature expressed his judgment of the character of the Supreme Pontiff: "The Holy Father is not only a good man, but an able man also. If he is not so great, perhaps, as some of his predecessors, he is strong, able and good. He is not a politician in the sense of participating in the affairs of the world powers. He is less interested in what is going on in things extra, than things intra (muros ecclessiae).

The Archbishop arrived in St. Louis on January 12th, and immediately took up his usual round of episcopal functions of preaching, confirming, laying of corner stones and church dedications. August 2nd, found him in Mobile, Alabama, making an impressive address on the Catholic University at the great convention of the Knights of Columbus: On August 14th, he preached the sermon at the dedication of St. Mary's Cathedral in Salt Lake City, the peroration of which in praise of noble christian womanhood was pronounced ''one of the most perfect things ever uttered by human lips.''

But a number of important home duties awaited the Archbishop in September. The dedication of the Church of the Visitation in Vienna, of which Father John Eugel was the pastor, and the opening of the Kenrick Seminary, September 22nd, each demanded his presence, and an address. Then preparations had to be made for the Celebration of the Centennial of the City of St. Louis, which was set for the first week of October, a civic affair, to which the Church was to give the proper religious setting. The solemn opening of the celebration took place in the city's first Church, the Old Cathedral, Sunday, October 3rd. Bishop John J. Hennessy of Wichita, a native of the parish, was the celebrant of the mass, Archbishop Glennon spoke in glowing words of the early history of the Church of St. Louis. The heads of the city administration attended the ceremonies. In the afternoon the pupils of the Catholic Schools, 20,000 in number, assembled on Art Hill, Forest Park, to do honor to the Crusader King, the Patron Saint of the City and diocese, whose bronze statue crowns the hill. On the afternoon of the fifth day of the Centennial Celebration, October 7th, thousands of St. Louis Catholics made a pilgrimage to the old Church and Cemetery of Cahokia, the oldest in the Mississippi Valley. It

(657)

was among the silent monuments of the earliest pioneers of the Church of the West, that the inspiration was given by the Archbishop of St. Louis, for the foundation of a Catholic Historical Society ''which will do for Catholic monuments, what the Missouri and Illinois Historical Societies are doing in the civic order.'' On the Sunday after Thanks-giving-day the new Church of the Holy Ghost Parish was dedicated by the Archbishop. On December 13th, he spoke at the dedication of St. Mark's new school on ''The Reason Why the Catholic Church stands for Education.''

December 20th, 1909, was the twenty-fifth anniversary day of Archbishop Glennon's elevation to the priesthood. The priests of the diocese had been making preparations for some time previous for a grand Jubilee celebration: but His Grace forbade any public demonstra-tion, in view of the fact that the Catholics of St. Louis had so gener-ously responded on two recent great occasions, those of the Centennial Week, and the laying of the Cathedral corner stone. All he asked for was a bouquet of masses and prayers. But the movement of honoring the beloved prelate, only gained in strength. Archbishop Ryan. of Philadelphia came to join the priests and people of St. Louis, felici-tating the Jubilarian. The festivities were held at the Kenrick Semi-nary. The Archbishop celebrated Mass at 6 o'clock; at which five candidates for the priesthood were ordained. In his address to the young levites he adverted to the happy day twenty-five years ago, when he himself had been ordained by Bishop Hogan. The celebration in honor of the Jubilarian was held in one of the large study-halls of the Seminary. Seated between Archbishop Ryan and Bishop Hen-nessey he listened to the addresses, poems and songs given by the stu-dents, and afterwards took part in a banquet at the Seminary. Presi-dent Taft offered his congratulations and best wishes in a familiar letter, and the Holy Father sent his fatherly blessing. A brilliant public reception at the Archbishop's House closed the festivities.

On January 9th, 1910, the Papal Delegate D. Falconio and His Grace of St. Louis dedicated the spacious and richly decorated Church of St. Anthony, built by the Franciscan Brother Anselm Wolff. On the 28th, of the same year the Archbishop attended the first Land-Congress ever held in Missouri. The meeting place was Springfield, in the heart of the Ozarks. The distinguished prelate dwelt at length on the advantages of country life, picturing the vision of village joined to village, like the pearls of a necklace; and of the hillsides peopled by the various races of Europe, crowding one another in the large cities, and yet fit to become lovers of their homes and their liberties, and new sources of wealth for the Commonwealth.

On April 9th, Archbishop Glennon dedicated the new church of St. Anne, and gave great praise to its pastor the Rev. O. J. McDonald.

Montreal in Canada, said to be the most thoroughly Catholic City in America, had the distinction of being selected for the first general Eucharistic Congress held in America. It was the twentieth one in the long series of these Congresses; Its three centuries of Catholic life promised a grander demonstration than any so far witnessed in the proudest cities of the Old World. The Holy Father's special representative at the Congress was Cardinal Vincenzo Vanutelli, "old in years but young in spirit and energy." It speaks well for the St. Louis Archbishop's reputation for masterly eloquence that he was chosen to deliver the sermon on September 10th, 1910, at St. Patrick's Church, Montreal, the center of the largest English Congregation in Canada. Cardinal Vanutelli gladly accepted the invitation to visit the city of St. Louis. He arrived on September 24th, and was honored on the 27th, by a magnificent parade of the Catholic children of the city about 25,000 strong. The Cardinal was delighted with the spectacle and clapped his hands, saying: "It is glorious."

From St. Louis Cardinal Vanutelli traveled by slow stages to New York, where the Cathedral of St. Patrick was to be consecrated on Sunday, October 5th. Two other Cardinals, James Gibbons, of Baltimore, and Michael Logue, Archbishop of Armagh and Primate of All Ireland, were also to honor the occasion by their presence. Archbishop Glennon of St. Louis was selected to preach the consecration sermon. "It was described as a masterpiece in thought and expression. A few weeks later the Archbishop, on his confirmation tour in Central Missouri, paid a visit to the Missouri Penitentiary, and in kind hopeful words addressed the convicts there as "My dear Brothers."

Two civic events in which the Archbishop took a leading part may be mentioned here: the unveiling of the Monument to General James Shields at Carrolton on November 12th, and the opening of the McKinley Bridge at St. Louis: In the first event the Archbishop made the address; in the second, he blessed the structure with the usual ceremonial of the Church.

Whilst all these various activities were in progress, the walls of the Cathedral were growing higher and higher in long gray layers of granite; the facade with its great rose window and two mighty campanile towers flanking the facade were nearing completion, and the concrete roof of the dome was being cast. In February 1911 the hope was expressed, that the exterior work would be completed within four months, and that the structure would be ready for use within a year. Four years had now elapsed since work on the foundation was begun; One more year of patient waiting, and then the consecration. But "he gains who loses a vain hope," as the proverb has it. The consecration of the Cathedral was much farther off, awaiting a grander opportunity that would have offered itself in the early months of

1912. It will be October 18th, 1914, before the first mass will be said or sung within the walls of the Cathedral, and thirteen years more must pass before the solemn consecration is held, but then with a splendor and solemnity and the perfection of order and decorum that was to make that day the climax of a long succession of glorious days.

Yet the work on the Cathedral went on steadily all these years. As the plan showed, there were four lateral chapels, each one to be a marvel of decoration in marble and mosaic; they were to be in honor of the Blessed Sacrament, Our Blessed Lady, All Saints, and the Holy Souls: the cost was fixed at $100,000 each.

The Chapel of the Blessed Sacrament was donated by the Hon. R. C. Kerens, onetime Ambassador at Vienna. The Chapel of All Saints was donated by Mrs. Anna Hamilton Baily. The Lady Chapel was the gift of John and Patrick Sheehan, and the Altar in All Souls Chapel was secured by a bequest from Miss Anna S. Meagher. The magnificent High-Altar was presented by Mrs. Katherine Mangan McBride.

On June 19th, 1911, a pro-synodal meeting of the diocese was held; about three hundred priests were in attendance. The Archbishop presided and made various announcements in regard to Church discipline, and the general progress of the Church. The various commissions and boards were continued for another triennium. His Grace insisted that the Decree in regard to early and frequent communion must be fulfilled to the letter. As to the new Cathedral's progress His Grace could give full assurance: the funds necessary for the time were coming in satisfactorily. During the summer, rumors were spread by ill-affected persons that the Cathedral walls were cracking in many places, owing to faulty construction. It was but natural that there should be some uneven settling of the massive structure, but there was not the slightest danger of any serious crack in the walls. In June 1912, Archbishop Glennon gave out the contract for the decoration of All Souls and Our Blessed Lady's Chapels at a cost of $280,000. At that time he said he hoped to have this work completed within a year, and would then quietly open the Cathedral, the day of consecration being set at a later date "The Cathedral, so far is out of debt," he added.

But a grand plan had for some time filled his mind; the erection of a great Seminary. On June 23rd, 1912, at the close of the retreat the announcement was made by His Grace that a site for a new Seminary had been acquired, and that ground would be broken for the construction of the new edifice sometime in the Fall. The building would require an outlay of at least half a million dollars. The site selected was the Old Drummond Farm, a short distance Southwest of Maplewood.

### St. Louis Cathedral

THE CORNERSTONE of this magnificent and imposing structure was laid on Sunday, October 18th, 1908, by the Most Reverend Apostolic Delegate, Diomede Falconio, D. D., Titular Archbishop of Larissa. On that occasion seventy-nine city parishes participated in the grand parade, making the largest demonstration ever seen in the city.

Yet the Archbishop's thoughts were constantly recalled to the Cathedral. On September 15th and 16th, Cardinal Gibbons stopped over in St. Louis on his way to Wichita, Kansas, where he was to consecrate the new cathedral, whilst Archbishop Glennon was to preach the consecration sermon. During his stay with Archbishop Glennon the Cardinal spent a good part of his time inspecting the vast granite pile that represented the Catholic spirit of St. Louis. Thus year succeeded year after the corner stone laying, on October 18th, 1908, years crowded with diverse activities of far-reaching importance, whilst the walls of the Cathedral, and the mighty dome were rising higher and higher. At last, on October 18th, 1914, the Cathedral was blessed and opened for divine service. A picturesque writer of the day described the magnificent scene that presented itself, inside and outside the great building.

"Everything conspired to make the opening ideal. A beautiful early autumn day with glorious sunbeams playing on the Byzantine dome; a magnificent crowd of worshippers and spectators representing every creed, race and social strata; a happy Archbishop in the middle of a colorful company of ecclesiastics and seminarians; a gorgeous ritual from the stately procession of blessing around the walls of the Cathedral to the pulse-quickening recessional, while the great throng burst into a hymn of praise following the Cathedral-filling Te Deum; a Bishop pontificating in the presence of his fellow Bishops; a choir of 300 male voices trained for devotional singing, and a sermon interpreting the architectural splendor which filled the souls of that multitude, drinking in the half-finished glories of the Cathedral and its chapels—these are some of the things that blended in a single religious event, the magnitude of which must have surpassed even the brilliant mind of its own creator."[1]

The Right Rev. John J. Hennessy, Bishop of Wichita, was the celebrant of the Pontifical Mass. For assistant priest he had the Rt. Rev. J. A. Connolly, V. G.: Revs. John J. Tannrath and James T. Coffey, were the deacons of honor, and Revs. Francis J. Jones and E. J. Lemkes deacon and subdeacon of the Mass. Dr. M. S. Brennan, official master of ceremonies, was assisted by Rev. J. P. Spencer. On the archiepiscopal throne sat the Most Rev. John J. Glennon between his two chaplains, Very Rev. Dr. M. S. Ryan, C.M., president of Kenrick Seminary, and Rev. P. W. Tallon, Rector of the Visitation Church. On the opposite side of the temporary altar was the bepurpled choir of bishops: Thomas F. Lillis of Kansas City, John Ward of Leavenworth, J. F. Cunningham of Concordia, Richard Scannell of Omaha and Thomas Garrigan of Sioux City, and besides them Msgr. O. J. S. Hoog, V. G. Thirty or more priests were present in the Sanctuary.

---

1 Gruenstein, "St. Louis Republic," October 19, 1914.

The sermon on the occasion was preached by the Archbishop. Just before the sermon proper, His Grace once more gave out the figures showing the receipts and expenditure to date. The cash receipts, including payments due, were $1,729,648; whereas the expenditures amounted to $1,302,000. "We opened without debt," said the Archbishop, "and we have funds on hand for every contract thus far signed." The prelate then read out the long list of names—hundreds of them—of contributors and subscribers to the edifice. "To-day," he added, "we see the Cathedral finished as a building, though much still is left to be done in its decoration and equipment. It is because of this unfinished decoration and equipment that we have deferred for another year the solemn consecration of this building to the services of religion and the worship of the Almighty."

The Cathedral as a building was finished, a triumph of architecture in the Byzantine style, one of the most noteworthy church buildings in the world. Its chief characteristics are expressed in the words: massive, splendid, original. In its dignified simplicity of the exterior, and the majestic dome that crowns the massive walls, it resembles the Church of Hagia Sophia at Constantinople, from which ancient monument of Christian art the architect derived his inspiration for the salient feature of the design. It is the largest Church in all America, measuring 380 feet in length, with an extreme width of 212 feet and a height of 220 feet from the floor to the top of the dome. The interior was still in the rough, lacking the Byzantine warmth and variety of color, and the countless columns of resplendent marble; and the architraves and balustrades and arches were still awaiting their covering of rich mosaic. The loveliest feature of the present Cathedral, the Altar of exquisite white marble, overarched by the baldachino of silver filigree, supported by great pillars of delicately tinted onyx, was not as yet in place. But massive strength, sublime distances were there, and that in a truly original manner. In this regard the structure of that day might be compared to the barrenness of the desert under the star-bright dome of heaven. But, as the Archbishop said in his comparison of the Byzantine with the Gothic style, the Cathedral "will not be completed until it has set on its wall the luster of every jewel, the bright plumage of every bird, the glow and glory of every metal, the iridescent gleam of every glass."

It took seven years to erect the shell of the vast building with its many recesses and angles. The completion of the interior went forward, somewhat intermittently until 1927. Pillar and pylon and wide spaces of wall were covered with marble: arch after arch, and ceiling and dome were covered with gleaming mosaic, and the four chapels were transformed into veritable jewels of Christian art.

"On July 2nd, 1912, the contracts for All Saints and the Lady Chapels had been awarded to the Tiffany Company of New York. The plans and drawings for these chapels were the work of the Italian architect, Cav. Aristide Leonori, under whose supervision the cartoons were designed and the marbles and mosaics assembled. These two chapels were entirely completed in the summer of 1915, and the first Mass in All Saints' Chapel was celebrated by Archbishop Glennon on October 10th, 1915; it was a Mass offered for the eternal repose of the soul of the donor, Anna Hamilton Bailey."

On August 25th, 1915, Feast of St. Louis, the new chancel organ was blessed by the Archbishop after the solemn Mass in honor of the Patron Saint of the city. By a sad coincidence, that very same week the organ accompanied the chanting of the Mass for the obsequies of John B. Garneau, who, with other members of his family, had donated the instrument."

"Arrangements for the erection of the high altar, the gift of Mr. William Cullen McBride, were entered into with the Gorham Company of New York on November 17th, 1913, according to the plans and specifications submitted by Mr. George D. Barnett, one of the architects of the Cathedral. By All Souls' Day, November 2nd, 1916, the altar was ready for use, and on that day the first High Mass was celebrated at the new altar. It was a solemn Pontifical Mass sung by His Grace, the Archbishop of St. Louis, for the deceased benefactors of the Cathedral."

"The Blessed Sacrament Chapel was ready for use in March 1916, and was employed in Divine Service for the first time on Holy Thursday, April 5th, 1917, the Repository being erected therein. As was already mentioned, it was a gift of the late Hon. R. C. Kerens in Memory of his deceased wife. The work, designed by Mr. George D. Barnett, was executed under his supervision by the Gorham Company."

"The Chapel of the Holy Souls was completed in 1926, by the Emil Frei Company of St. Louis."[2]

On the occasion of his episcopal Jubilee, June 29th, 1921, Archbishop Glennon said: "This Cathedral is not yet finished. Five years hence, a century will have completed its circle since St. Louis, dismembered from New Orleans, was made a separate diocese. Is it not fitting that the celebration of this most auspicious event should mark the completion of the great work, and take place in the Cathedral dedicated to Almighty God with the solemn rites of Consecration?"

---

2 Souvay, Dr. C. L., "The Cathedrals of St. Louis," p. 40.

## Chapter 6

# THE NEW KENRICK SEMINARY

When in 1904 the lure of our World's Fair drew the Abbe Felix Klein of the University of Paris to the "Land of the Strenuous Life," he found many things to praise in Catholic St. Louis, and only one thing to criticise, the Kenrick Seminary. Not, indeed, the Seminary proper, the professors or the student body, but the old ramshackle buildings on Cass Avenue that housed them since 1893: "I confided to Archbishop Glennon, on leaving the Grand Seminary, the painful impression which had been made on me, by the sight of the buildings, the narrow halls, the court devoid of grass, and the generally wretched condition of the place where the clergy of this great diocese are trained; while all the other establishments rejoice in the light, in the open air, in a healthy prosperity. The Archbishop was all the more ready to listen to the expression of these regrets, because he himself feels them, and is resolved to remove their cause. He explained to me that this convent, an old one of the Visitandines, had been adapted as well as could be to the needs of the Grand Seminary, but that this state of things is not to last. Now, that he has full authority, I am sure that one of the first uses he will make of it will be to remove his future priests from a lodging which is at best only suitable for our poor dioceses of Europe."[1]

Archbishop Glennon had, at that time, just entered upon his brilliant career in St. Louis. The great Cathedral was to be his first building venture.

But the need of a new home for the Seminary was in constant evidence, although the limited, though rich resources of the archdiocese, were all necessarily turned into the one great channel of Cathedral building. The purchase of the Drummond Farm, a tract of 373 acres in St. Louis County, now styled Glennon Park, marked the beginning of the new Kenrick Seminary. On St. Anselm's day, April 21st, 1913, the Archbishop turned the first sod for the building, followed by the President of Kenrick Seminary, Dr. Ryan, Vicar-General Connolly, the Members of the Seminary Board, and the Architects, Comes, Imbs and Preuss. The plans call for a building in the English Gothic style, designed to accommodate about 175 students and twelve professors.

On Thanksgiving day the corner stone of the new Seminary was blessed and laid in position by His Grace. The weather was cloudy and

---

[1] Klein, Abbé Felix, op. cit., p. 203.

KENRICK SEMINARY

threatening: nevertheless a large concourse of its clergy and laity witnessed the ceremony.

The Archbishop in his address gave a statement of the financial status of the undertaking. The $50,000. given by the clergy and the $50,000. given by himself and the $100,000. expected to be raised by the Christmas Collection, $200,000. in all, would be supplemented by a bond-issue of $400,000, more than half of which was already sold.

In his Christmas letter the Archbishop dwelt on the importance of this new undertaking: "The Seminary is the heart of the Diocese. It is from it and through it that men are equipped to gò out to the people as the "Ministers of Christ" and the "Dispensers of the Mysteries of God."

"We had a Seminary in Missouri before we had the Diocese of St. Louis. . . We inherit all its glorious memories, all its blessed traditions; among which, not the least are the saintly and learned men, who taught there, and the great and brilliant students, who passed from its portals to the evangelization of the West. . ."[2]

The old building on Cass Avenue has ceased to be a fitting place for a seminary. . . it became imperative to call our young men from there, to lead them out to the quiet retreat as Christ and his disciples to the lonely places, that then He might speak to their hearts."

"The change from the old·to the new means a heavy expense: but we are confident that the devoted priests and people of the Diocese · will make the transaction easy and the financial burden not too heavy."

"We are glad to announce" wrote the Archbishop in conclusion, "that some donations have been made to the new Seminary, and take special pleasure in announcing the donation of the Collegiate Chapel and the High Altar. The donor of it desires to remain unknown, but does expect a Mass in return from each of the young priests who go forth from within its sacred precincts."[3]

The last time ordinations were held at the old Seminary was on Sunday, June 5th, 1915. The ordinandi were seven in number, of German, Irish and Slavonic origin.

At the beginning of September 1915 the grand building was ready for occupancy.

On September 12th, the doors of the Seminary were thrown open to the general public. All were invited to inspect every nook and corner of the vast structure. At least 25,000 persons, priests and laymen, came, saw and admired the massive walls and the noble proportion of the exterior of the building, as well as its picturesque

---

[2] Archbishop's Address, "St. Louis Republic," November 30, 1913.
[3] Idem, ibidem.

setting amid the fine old trees of the Park. The four-story building is in the form of the letter "H" with the chapel in the center. The outside dimensions are estimated at 310 by 275 feet. The main entrance lobby, facing the campus and lake, is reached by a broad flight of steps, under a carved stone porch over which appears in Gothic letters:

"Venite-Filii-Audite-Me     ·
Timorem-Domini-Docebo-Vos."

The Old Kenrick Seminary was no more: On September 14th, 1915, the students from the old Seminary, and a large accession of newcomers from elsewhere, a total of 160 matriculated at the new Kenrick Seminary. Studies were begun at once, but the formal opening was reserved for the Feast of Our Lady of the Miraculous Medal, November 27th. The Archbishop made a short but pithy address to the students in which he dwelt on oratory, public reading, and singing, closing with the words: "The low mass, short sermon and big collection-order is passing away, and the Church's liturgy is gradually coming into its own. Deem yourselves privileged in being permitted to sing the canticles of the Lord; in being allowed to perform on earth the functions that the angels and saints rejoice to perform in heaven."[4]

The dedication of the New Kenrick Seminary set for Thursday, April 27, the thirteenth anniversary of Archbishop Glennon's transfer to the See of St. Louis, proved to be an event of grand proportions as well as of the deepest significance. The Holy Father sent a beautiful autograph letter of congratulation and hearty approval. The Apostolic Delegate, His Excellency John Bonzano, came from Washington to officiate at the services of dedication: four Archbishops, fifteen Bishops, six Papal Prelates and three hundred and fifty priests, participated in the festivity.

After the blessing of the exterior walls, the procession of Seminarians, followed by Archbishop. Glennon and attendants, moved into the chapel chanting the Litany of All Saints. The Archbishop then dedicated the Collegiate Chapel to its sacred purpose. After the dedication the visiting priests and prelates were ushered into the chapel. Last of all came Archbishop Bonzano, the Celebrant of the Dedication Mass. After the Gospel Archbishop Edward J. Hanna, of San Francisco, whose oratorical fame, had preceded him, delivered a masterly sermon, in which the Seminary was shown to be the institution that alone can send forth men fashioned after the divine Model, Jesus Christ, to the conquest of the world. "As teachers they must have

---

4   Kenrick Seminary Prospectus, 1916.

the wisdom of Christ, as offerers of sacrifice they must be holy, as rulers they must be kind, dignified and strong.''[5]

At the conclusion of the Pontifical Mass the distinguished assembly of prelates and priests were entertained at dinner by the Seminary faculty: of the many well known names we will subjoin only those of the Archbishops and Bishops.

His Excellency, Most Rev. John Bonzano, Apostolic Delegate.

Most Rev. Henry Moeller, Archbishop of Cincinnati.

Most Rev. James John Keane, Archbishop of Dubuque.

Most Rev. Edward J. Hanna, Archbishop of San Francisco.

Right Rev. Maurice F. Burke, Bishop of St. Joseph, Mo.

Right Rev. John Joseph Hennessy, Bishop of Wichita, Kan.

Right Rev. Theophile Meerschaert, Bishop of Oklahoma, Okla.

Right Rev. Edward P. Allen, Bishop of Mobile, Ala.

Right Rev. John Francis Cunningham, Bishop of Concordia, Kan.

Right Rev. Thomas F. Lillis, Bishop of Kansas City, Mo.

Right Rev. John B. Morris, Bishop of Little Rock, Ark.

Right Rev. Edmund P. Dunne, Bishop of Peoria, Ill.

Right Rev. John Ward, Bishop of Leavenworth, Kan.

Right Rev. Henry J. Tihen, Bishop of Lincoln, Neb.

Right Rev. Austin Dowling, Bishop of Des Moines, Iowa.

Right Rev. Henry Althoff, Bishop of Belleville, Ill.

Right Rev. Thomas Joseph Shahan, Rector of the Catholic University.

Right Rev. Joseph S. Glass, C. M., Bishop of Salt Lake, Utah.

Right Rev. Ferdinand Brossart, Bishop of Covington.

On the day following the dedication of the Seminary, a Solemn High Mass was sung for the benefactors whose cheerful contributions had really made ''the transition from the old to the new, easy, and the financial burden not too heavy.''

The Lazarist Father U. P. Barr was celebrant, the Apostolic Delegate presided on the Episcopal throne, and Archbishop Glennon made an address in simple heartfelt words.

Friday afternoon and the whole of Saturday were spent by Archbishop Bonzano in visiting a large number of the Catholic Institutions of the city. He was escorted on these visits by Archbishop Glennon, Bishop Shahan, and Fathers M. S. Ryan, P. W. Tallon, and J. J. Tannrath. The Institutions visited on Friday were; the Convent of the Good Shepherd, St. Anthony's Hospital, the Franciscan Monastery, the Sacred Heart Convent at Maryville, St. Joseph's Orphanage for boys, the Convent of the Sisters of St. Joseph in Carondelet, the Alexian Brother's Hospital, S. S. Peter and Paul's Church and Schools,

---

5 Hanna, Archbishop Edward J., in Papers of the Day.

Lorretto Academy, St. Elizabeth's Institute, the Guardian Angel Settlement and St. Mary's Infirmary. Then His Excellency expressed the wish to see the Old Cathedral, thus winding up his manifold experiences with the sight of the oldest Catholic monument of St. Louis.

On Saturday visits were made to St. Louis University, Rosati-Kain High-School, the Home of the Little Sisters of the Poor, the Little Seminary, New Cathedral, St. John's Hospital, Sacred Heart Academy, the Christian Brothers College, Calvary Cemetery, St. Mary's Orphanage, Father Dunne's Newsboys' Home, Father Dempsey's Hotel for Workingmen. Saturday the Apostolic Delegate was entertained at lunch by Father Tallon of the Visitation Parish. On this festive occasion the announcement was made by the Apostolic Delegate that the Holy Father had raised Fathers Tallon and Tannrath to the dignity of Roman Prelates.

On Sunday morning Solemn High Mass was celebrated in the Cathedral by Archbishop Bonzano, whilst the sermon was preached by the Archbishop.

Sunday afternoon at 2:30 the Conference of Catholic Charities was held at the Odeon. It was the fitting climax to Archbishop Bonzano's visit.

Exhibitions, including songs, dances, recitations and drills, were made by the following charitable Institutions: St. Anne's Foundling Asylum, St. Patrick's Day Nursery, St. Joseph's Male Orphan Asylum, St. Frances Colored Orphan Asylum, St. Mary's Female Orphan Asylum, the Deaf-Mute Institution, the Guardian Angel Settlement, and the German St. Vincent Orphan Home. Both the Archbishop and his guest were deeply moved by the efforts of this little army of children, every one of which owed its happy childhood, its continued innocence, its health and, perhaps, its very life to the divine charity actuating these Institutions. The Apostolic Delegate, whose "winsomeness of deep religious faith and piety" won him the heart of St. Louis, was delighted with the city, its Archbishop its clergy and its religious and its people.

"I have been told before coming here," said he, "that St. Louis is a Catholic City: Now I see with my eyes, I have touched with my hands, the proof of the Catholicity of St. Louis. By working this miracle of charity, you have already in your hand the pledge of your salvation. You certainly have great and noble hearts, for only great and noble hearts understand and do such things."

Thus closed the four days' festivities of the dedication of Archbishop Glennon's second crown of glory, the new Kenrick Seminary in Glennon Park.

NEW WILLIAM CULLEN McBRIDE CATHOLIC BOYS' HIGH SCHOOL

## CHAPTER 7

# THE SCHOOLS OF THE ST. LOUIS ARCHDIOCESE

The parochial school-system of St. Louis as such, dates back to the Third Diocesan Synod of 1896, when the decrees of the Third Council of Baltimore regarding the erection and support of parochial schools were promulgated by Archbishop Kain. The Synod made reference to a school-commission, which, however, was not appointed until the Fourth Synod in 1902. It consisted of Fathers Edward Fenlon, Henry Hukestein and Urban Stanowski, representing the three dominant races in the diocese.

Up to this period hundreds of parochial schools had flourished in the city and in the country missions, most of them taught by members of religious orders. But, as they owed the origin and continued life to private effort and enterprize, they were also conducted according to the best judgment of the individual pastors. Wherever they existed, they were considered a necessary adjunct to the Church, rounding out, as it were the parochial ministrations; but where they did not exist, they were frequently designated as necessary evils, or unnecessary impositions on the people. As there was no law or, at least, no law enforced, the status of the parochial school was doubtful, and its future precarious. It is true, the earlier Plenary Councils of Baltimore recognized the great importance of having Catholic Schools in connection with every parish church, yet did not consider it opportune to legislate on the matter, but confined itself to recommend and urge the erection of Catholic schools wherever it was found possible. After the Third Council of Baltimore there could no longer be any doubt as to the standing of the Parochial Schools.

But the work of bringing them into a system, by coordinating the courses of studies, and placing all matters relating to school books, examinations, and diplomas in the hand of a School-Commission, was the work of Archbishop Kain. Theoretically, this seemed to supply a long felt want; but practically it did not work so well. A Superintendent of Schools, was wanted to supervise the work of the teachers. After the Annual Retreat at Kenrick Seminary in June 1910, Archbishop Glennon announced the appointment of Father Aloysius V. Gorthoeffner, pastor of St. Mary's church, as Superintendent of the Catholic Schools of the diocese. There were then about seventy Catholic schools in the city with an enrollment of more than 22,000 children. Father Garthoeffner thus relieved Father Connolly, Vicar-General and President of the School Board, from the many obligations of connection with the latter office. Father Garthoeffner received an efficient assistant in the person of Father Amsinger, at St. Mary's, so that he found ample time to prepare himself for the arduous work of reorganizing the Parochial School system, and raising it to a higher level of usefulness.

At the Sixth Synod of St. Louis held after the Retreat of 1910, Archbishop Glennon made the first move for the establishment of Diocesan High Schools, by appointing a Committee of three for the purpose of investigating the need of such schools, and to make arrangements with the priests of the diocese to establish such schools. On August 18th, 1911, the plan had so far prospered, the School-Superintendent Garthoeffner could announce at the closing session of the Catholic Parochial Teachers' Institute, that three diocesan High Schools would be started early in September; one for boys in the school-building of S. S. Peter and Paul, where even then a parochial high school was in operation, and two for girls, the first in St. Teresa's School taught by the Sisters of St. Joseph and the second in St. Francis de Sales school taught by the Sisters de Notre Dame. The boys were to be taught by the Brothers of Mary. The high school for boys was named for Archbishop Kenrick: the others were to be named for Bishop Rosati and Archbishop Kain. A four-years course, either classical or commercial, was to begin at once. The Archbishop fully approved Father Garthoeffner's plan: ''As we are all agreed in regard to the value and necessity of Catholic education, it becomes a logical duty to perfect the system that bears that name: to strengthen link by link the entire system from the kindergarten to the university.''

On November 14th, 1911, the Catholic High School Association of the Archdiocese of St. Louis was incorporated, with the Archbishop as President. Its purpose was to provide means for the support of the new High Schools. In August 1912, the old St. Vincent's Seminary on Grand and Lucas Avenues was leased for an indefinite term of years to the Catholic High-School Association.

The building was a massive structure, that had been used for many years by the Sisters of Charity for a convent and academy. The Association took possession at once and fitted it up for the high school girls of the Rosati-Kain Schools. Father Garthoeffner supervised the work. In 1913 the Kenrick High School was transferred to a new location on Leffingwell Avenue and Locust Street.

Father Garthoeffner was an excellent educator, but a less competent financier. In February 1914, he as treasurer of the Association and paymaster of the institution sent out circulars asking diocesan support for the diocesan high schools. The enrollment at the Rosati-Kain was one hundred and seventy-six girls, and at the Kenrick sixty-five boys. The Brothers of Mary were in charge, of the boys;

the Sisters of St. Joseph and the School sisters de Notre Dame furnished the teachers for the girls. The total income of the Association in 1915 was a little more than $10,000, of which sum the Sisters of St. Joseph had contributed $1,000., besides accepting no salary: the Sisters de Notre Dame also did their work without an earthly recompense, yet the enrollment had increased to 137 boys and 243 girls. The first class of the classical course graduated in June 1915 with six boys and seventeen girls.

The graduates of the Commercial Course were nine boys and thirty girls. Two of the girl graduates joined the Sisters of St. Joseph, one, the Sister of Notre Dame. Two other graduates entered the Harris Teacher's College, All the boy graduates were placed in good positions. The teaching staff consisted of five Brothers of Mary, five Sisters of St. Joseph and four Sisters de Notre Dame. The Girl's School had been fully accredited to the State University, at Columbia.

In the following year the enrollment in the Kenrick School was one hundred and fifty boys and in the Rosati-Kain School, two hundred and fifty girls. The teaching staff had increased to seventeen. The outlook for the Catholic High-Schools was truly encouraging: but at the very time when matters were taking a favorable turn, death came to take away the "founder, promoter and director of the two splendidly inaugurated Catholic High Schools," as the Archbishop in his eulogy, designated Father Aloysius V. Garthoeffner. The saintly priest died on Friday, April 25th, 1917, at the Ursuline Convent, where he had filled the position of chaplain. After a solemn Requiem on Saturday, the remains of Father Garthoeffner were brought to St. Mary's Church where another Requiem was celebrated on Monday morning by Father Amsinger. On Monday afternoon the remains were conveyed to the New Cathedral, where a guard of honor of the Fourth Degree Knights of Columbus kept watch all through the night and until the hour of the funeral on Tuesday. The Solemn Requiem was sung by a boyhood friend of the deceased, Father Louis Kutz. The Archbishop, in a brief but touching sermon, gave expression to his admiration for the priestly virtues of the deceased and to his own deep sense of obligation to him for the whole-hearted and disinterested work he had done for the diocese of St. Louis. In his address to the graduates of the High-Schools and the Parochial Schools in June 1917, the Archbishop asked a prayer from all present for Father Garthoeffner, "whose life was given to the upbuilding of our Catholic Schools: whose soul, heart and strength were dedicated to the sole object that the Catholic High Schools, which he created, might live."

Father Garthoeffner was a native of St. Louis, having been born in St. Nicholas parish in 1874. He made his classical studies in the

Salesinaum near Milwaukee, and completed his philosophical and theological course at the Kenrick Seminary of his native city, where also he was raised to the priesthood by Archbishop Kain, June 12th, 1896. His first and only appointment for parish work was to Old St. Mary's Church.

Father Garthoeffner's successor in the office of Superintendent of the Catholic High Schools was the Rev. Patrick Dooley, a native of County Tipperary, who came to America to enter St. Mary's Seminary, Baltimore. He was ordained on December 17th, 1892, by Cardinal Satolli. He successively held the position as Assistant, Administrator and Rector of the Church of the Assumption in St. Louis. In January 1904 he became Rector of St. John's Church, and in June 1907 Rector of St. Bridget's. The ancient parish of St. Bridget's had been steadily declining, and the parochial school was reduced in numbers to such an extent that the Boy's High School could find a temporary home within the walls of its capacious building.

Father Patrick Dooley was well fitted to superintend High School Work. "His pamphlet on the subject of High School education attracted the attention of the best educators in this part of the country. He was a man of broad culture, an excellent preacher and an able writer."

At the annual meeting of the Catholic High School Association March 13th, 1918, a substantial increase in the attendance as well as in the finances was reported. The buildings in which the Schools were housed, were not the property of the High School Association: besides, they were old and no longer adapted to the increased demands of modern education. In any case, the Girls' High School Building had been sold and must be vacated.

In a Circular Letter to the Clergy and Laity of the Archdiocese, issued on May 16th, 1919, Archbishop Glennon, assuming that the Catholic people of the city would not allow their High School to fail for lack of funds, requested them to subscribe at least $150,000.00 for the purpose of purchasing a site, and of erecting and equipping a suitable building for the Rosati-Kain High School. Owing, perhaps, to post-war conditions the response was not as prompt and generous, as may have been expected. Yet, the corner lot on Lindell Boulevard and Newstead Avenue was purchased. The residence and garage on the premises were fitted up for the temporary quarters of the Rosati-Kain School.

The erection of a new building was reserved for the following year. School was opened on September 2nd, 1919; but Father Dooley, who had labored so earnestly for the institution was not present. He had died at St. John's Hospital on Friday 8th, of that year, having

just rounded out a half century of life. Though recently appointed to the pastorate of Holy Name Parish. He was buried from St. Bridget's Church with which he had been so long identified. Rt. Rev. Christopher Byrne, Bishop of Galveston, preached the funeral oration. Father Dooley's successor as Superintendent of the Catholic High School was Father Paul Ritchie; Father James P. Murray had been previously appointed Superintendent of Parish Schools.

At the Sixteenth Convention of the Catholic Educational Association which was in session in the City of St. Louis from June 23rd to June 27th, 1919, many of the country's educators of high and even highest standing, were in attendance. Bishop Shahein, Rector of the Catholic University, presided at the general sessions. Archbishop Glennon's sermon at the opening Pontifical High Mass was an impassioned appeal to the American people for a just treatment of our Catholic Schools.

The Twenty-Fifth Anniversary of Archbishop Glennon's consecration occurred on Wednesday, June 29th, 1921. The Jubilarian was averse to any public celebration. But the clergy and people of St. Louis would not let the day slip by without at least a modest but hearty and generous tribute to the high character of their Archbishop as the leader in their religious educational and civic affairs. The Jubilee was celebrated with three large gatherings, at morning, noon and night. It was a diocesan celebration. No one outside the diocese was invited: about three hundred priests attended the luncheon in the Cathedral Hall. Messages of congratulation came from President Harding, Governor Hyde and Mayor Kiel. A cablegram from Rome, sent in the name of Pope Benedict XV by Cardinal Gasparri, acquainted the Archbishop of his being honored by the Holy Father with a new ecclesiastical dignity: "Assistant to the Papal Throne."

Msgr. John J. Tannrath, Chancellor of the Archdiocese, made the presentation speech of the Jubilee Fund Committee: "We, hereby, as a small expression of our deep appreciation offer You a Jubilee gift in the shape of $250,000. It affords us great pleasure to announce to You that Mrs. William Cullen McBride and her daughters, likewise contribute $250,000. for the erection of a school for boys.

Visibly moved, yet with smiling countenance, the Archbishop expressed his gratitude: "For this gift, so generous and so quickly assembled, my thanks and appreciation are due. I know how difficult it must be in these days to collect money for any purpose whatsoever. Wartime and war drives and other drives, one after another, have come as the waves of the sea. My gratitude is not limited to myself personally, but in the name of our schools I thank those who helped so generously."

The erection of a high school building for the girls of the Rosati-Kain School was now assured. A suitable site for the Boy's High School was secured, and the contracts for both structures were given out. The schools had now been in operation for a decade; the Kenrick High School had an enrollment of 359 boys, the Rosati-Kain 517 girls. The graduates of both schools numbered 107.

The Rosati-Kain Building was completed in 1923: but the erection of the William Cullen McBride Memorial Building had to be delayed on account of the exorbitant price of building materials. But by the end of 1924 the beautiful building on Kingshighway was ready for occupancy, and on January 6th, 1925 the five hundred students of the Kenrick High School were transferred to the McBride High School. The new building was dedicated by the Archbishop on Sunday afternoon, April 26th. The enrollment at the time was 517 boys with a teaching staff of seventeen members of the Society of the Brothers of Mary.

The structure was erected according to the plans of Henry P. Hess, architect.

Early in June of this year Archbishop Glennon led a pilgrimage to Rome and was received by Pope Pius XI in private audience. He was back again in New York on August 24th.

## CHAPTER 8

## THE LAST DISMEMBERMENT OF THE DIOCESE

Since the days of Archbishop Kain the small Diocese of St. Joseph in the northwestern corner of the State openly sponsored a movement to have the northeastern corner also placed under its jurisdiction, so that all the territory of Missouri between the Missouri and the Mississippi river should be under the rule of the Bishop of St. Joseph. The Archbishop of St. Louis was not averse to this movement, yet could hardly be expected to promote the proposed dismemberment of his own diocese. In the early years of Archbishop Glennon the matter seemed to be relegated to the realm of fancy: but fancy was in time to become fact, at least in part. But until Rome should make its decision, the Northeastern part of the Archdiocese required the same care as any other portion.

At Kirksville, Adair County, the Rev. Dr. A. B. Gass had built a beautiful little frame church for his small flock; Archbishop Glennon dedicated it on October 8th, 1905, and preached the sermon. Father Tannrath sang the Highmass with Fathers Gadell and Walsh as assistants. The Chronicle of this day of gladness relates, that a man, not as yet of the fold, was heard to say: "The Archbishop satisfied me fully. I do not need to read any further."

From Adair the Archbishop journeyed to Edina, the county seat of Knox, where Father Christopher Byrne had prepared a grand reception for him. When the Archbishop and his companions, Fathers Tannrath, Reiss and Long, alighted from the coach, they were greeted by the strains of welcoming music. Fully five hundred people had assembled to do honor to their distinguished guests. A cavalcade of one hundred and forty men on horseback, and the same number of men marching on foot escorted his Grace to the Parochial Residence, from the veranda of which he expressed his joy and thanks to the enthusiastic crowd. At 7:30 in the evening the Archbishop entered the Church of St. Joseph to administer Confirmation to a class of eighty. In the presence of more than a thousand persons, the mayor of the town stepped up to the communion rail and made an address of welcome. The Archbishop replied in his usual gracious way, and then held his audience spellbound for an hour with the praises of the Blessed Mother of God. On the morning of October 9th, His Grace took the train for Baring, the home of Father James J. O'Reilly, pastor of St. Aloysius church of that place. In the course of his sermon on "The home and the Church," the Archbishop admonished

(675)

the Congregation "To be loyal to their pastor, Rev. James J. O'Reilly, as their pastor was loyal to them: Within the last year, Father O'Reilly had three times refused an appointment to a much larger parish in a much larger city than Baring."

Forty-five persons were confirmed that evening. Once more in the mellow month of October, but two years later, Archbishop Glennon paid a visit to St. Joseph's parish, Edina, this time, to dedicate the handsome school building, Father Byrne had just completed. The Archbishop arrived from Ewing on a special train supplied from Edina. At Ewing, Lewis County, where the Franciscan Father Alphonse Fritz of Quincy was acting pastor, a class of confirmandi had received the sacrament in the morning. About 3 P. M. the procession of children with their teachers, Sisters of Loretto, then a large number of altar boys, followed by the priests, and the Archbishop started on its way. The new St. Joseph's Parochial School was pronounced by many to be "not only the finest building of its kind in Knox County, but also of the state."

In the evening the Archbishop delivered "a most eloquent, forceful and practical sermon on St. Joseph, the just and prudent man," applying the definition of justice to the commercial, civil, social and home life of the day. On the next morning His Grace left Edina by conveyance for Williamstown, a journey of thirty miles to the northern wilds of Lewis County.

Thursday and Friday, July the 1st and 2nd, were great days for the Catholics of Moberly, Randolph County, Missouri: for in the afternoon of Thursday the Archbishop of St. Louis administered the sacrament of Confirmation in the Church of the Immaculate Conception and at 9 o'clock in the morning of Friday in the Church of St. John the Baptist. The pastor of the former church, Father Charles Schaefer, entertained the Archbishop at dinner on Thursday. A public reception was given the Archbishop at Father Carney's residence, at which the Mayor of Moberly tendered a hearty welcome to the honored guest of the city. The Archbishop responded in one of the happiest and most appropriate addresses ever heard in Moberly. "His references to the building of a new church were received with hearty applause."

From Moberly His Grace journeyed to Salisbury, Chariton County, where Father F. J. Ernst presided over a fine large parish, dedicated to St. Joseph. The school was taught by seven Sisters of the Precious Blood and had an enrollment of 144 pupils. From Salisbury the Archbishop proceeded to Glasgow and thence by rail to St. Louis.

It was in the month of October 1909 that Archbishop Glennon made his last confirmation tour through Northeast Missouri, visiting the Churches of Hannibal, St. Paul's on Salt River, Indian Creek, Monroe

City, Palmyra, Shelbina and Macon. At Hannibal he confirmed 160
persons. The Parish had made notable progress under the administration, of the highly cultured and eloquent Father McLaughlin
which extended from 1884 to 1903. On Father McLaughlin's demise,
December 27, the Rev. Daniel F. Sullivan became Permanent Rector.
Ten Sisters of St. Joseph formed the teaching staff of the School. The
old church was still in use as a chapel.

On the following day, October 19th, the Archbishop was at St.
Paul's Church, Salt River, the old missionary center of Father Lefevere.
Here he administered confirmation to 55 persons. St. Paul's in Ralls
County is the same place as the earlier ''Salt River'' and the later
''Center.'' Its long roster of pastors since 1863 contains the names of
Fathers Patrick Cronin, David S. Phelan, P. Clark, Eugene Coyle, D.
Byrne, Luke Kernan, William Stack, James Sheil and F. J. Ernst,
under whom it became a mission of New London.

On October 20th, Indian Creek was the scene of a memorable
Catholic demonstration. The village of Indian Creek housed a population of half a thousand, all, with one exception, of the Catholic faith.
The parish of St. Stephen includes an additional number of Catholics
living on their farms round about their church. The village was
never incorporated, and never felt the need of an officer of any kind.
Only one deed of violence has been recorded in its long history, and that
occasioned by the Civil War excitement. No one has ever been sent
to the poorhouse. ''As peaceful as Indian Creek'' has become a by-
word in Monroe County. It is seven miles from the railroad, the
country round about displays a scene of pastoral beauty, and the
village itself is a veritable haunt of the true joy of life, of which the
Catholic religion forms the main cause and ingredient.

Into this little paradise came Archbishop Glennon on Wednesday,
October 20th, to confirm 80 of its parishioners, descendants of the Catholic immigrants from Kentucky, and Tennessee and Ireland, the Spald-
ings and Mudds and Hayses and Parsons and Smiths and Carricos.
Father Patrick J. Cooney, who had in February 1904, succeeded Father
John Lyons in the pastorate, did all he could to make the occasion a
memorable one. On Thursday October 21st, the Archbishop administered Confirmation in Monroe City to 60 persons. Father John Ryan was
pastor of the Church of the Holy Rosary.

The school was in charge of the Sisters of St. Dominic. Two former
stations of Fathers Lefevere and Cusack, Brusch Creek and Hunnewell
were now attached to Monroe City as missions.

Palmyra with its church of St. Joseph, was the Archbishop's goal
in the afternoon of October 21st. The Franciscan Fathers from beyond the river, held charge of the struggling Congregation since 1873.

The Rev. P. Ernst Kaufhold, O. F. M. was rector. Franciscan Sisters conducted the parochial school. The confirmations on this occasion numbered 27.

From Palmyra the journey went to Shelbina where Father Herman G. Adrian had come into possession of the pastorate in May 1902, after eleven orphaned years of the Parish, and had turned it over in 1906 to Rev. Martin J. Collins. Father Collins had prepared 56 persons for Confirmation. There were two missions attached to Shelbina at that time, Clarence and Lakenan, both in Shelby County. On Sunday, October 23rd, the Archbishop arrived at Macon, to administer confirmation in the Church of the Immaculate Conception which he had blessed on January 12th of the foregoing year. Father Richard J. Healy, the builder of the church, had since then received promotion to Edina, and Father Francis Tracy had succeeded to the rectorship of Macon. The missions of Macon were Bevier and Healy's Settlement. The number of confirmations in 1909 totaled 55. In the following week Archbishop Glennon visited the churches of Wellston, Montgomery City, Jonesburg, Wentzville, Valley Park and Manchester. Of the remaining parishes in Northeast Missouri, Canton in Lewis County, Kahoka and St. Patrick, both in Clark, which were not visited by His Grace on these occassions, a few words must be said:

Canton, with its Church of St. Joseph, in charge of the one time assistant at the Cathedral, Father Denis Patrick Mulcahy, and its school conducted by the Ursuline Sisters, had made noteworthy progress since 1895 under the successive administrations of Fathers P. J. Cooney, M. M. Rupprechter, A. Holtschneider and John Girse. Father Mulcahy's missions were: Lagrange, Monticello, Williamstown and Lewistown.

At Kahoka with its missions of Chambersburg, Mudd Settlement, Wayland, and its stations of Alexandria, Bitt Nation, Hill, in Scotland County and Wyaconda, the Rev. Austin Fleming had succeeded Father Geisert.

St. Patrick, Clark County, formerly called North Santa Fé, was one of the earliest and most important churches of Northeast Missouri, dating from 1842 as a parish with church and resident priest. In 1866 the name was changed to Maryville. Father Keilty on June 30th, 1867 dedicated the new church in honor of Ireland's great patron saint. In 1876 the Rev. Eugene Coyle became pastor and remained as such until September 15th, 1884, when the Rev. J. J. Mahon assumed charge. The later pastors were: Father P. J. O'Rourke, Patrick Cooney, Stephen Brady, and P. J. Carney, who was succeeded in 1909 by the Rev. Edward A. Bolger. The school was conducted by the Sisters of Divine Providence.

On April 20th, 1909 Father Thomas F. Mullen was transferred from Monroe City to St. Malachy's Church, St. Louis.

On January 10th, 1911, the transfer of Father Christopher E. Byrne from Edina to the Holy Name parish St. Louis was announced, Father P. W. Tallon going to the Church of the Visitation. Father Byrne was born in Byrnesville, Missouri, a town named for his family, who were among the early settlers of the Meramec district. On the same day news came from Rome announcing the cutting off from the Archdiocese of St. Louis, and adding to the diocese of St. Joseph, a large portion of territory in the Northeastern corner of the State. The priests in that part of the archdiocese were notified by the Chancellor of the Archdiocese, Father J. J. Tannrath, that, if they wished to express their attitude on the proposed division, they must do so at once. It was within the individual discretion of the priests affected by the change to give up their parishes and remain with the Archdiocese of St. Louis, or retain their pastorate and be subject to the Diocese of St. Joseph.

The counties included in this transfer were those between the Chariton and the Mississippi rivers, exclusive of the river counties: Audrain and Pike and Lincoln. In the first report from Rome, the counties of Audrain and Pike were also mentioned as part of the transferred territory. The Moberly Conference protested in a body against the dismemberment of their parishes from St. Louis: other Conferences in North Missouri were reported to have taken similar action. These protests were forwarded to Rome by Bishop Burke of St. Joseph.

The final decision came within six months. The Letters Apostolic by which the dismemberment was decreed were dated June 16th, 1911. Since that day the diocese of St. Joseph covers all the territory between the Missouri on the west and the Mississippi on the east; and from the Iowa border southward to the Missouri, and the northern border of the Counties of Howard, Boone, Audrain and Pike.

For the Diocese of St. Joseph this transfer meant a substantial gain, an increase of about 35 per cent, as the statistics before and after the 16th day of June 1911 will show:

| *Before June 16th:* | | *After June 16th:* | |
|---|---|---|---|
| Priests, secular | 30 | Priests, secular | 53 |
| Priests, regular | 33 | Priests, regular | 38 |
| Churches with priests | 28 | Churches with priests | 46 |
| Missions | 31 | Missions | 48 |
| Catholic Population | 22,703 | Catholic Population | 35,000 |
| Square miles | 12,848 | Square Miles | 18,206 |

With these additions the Diocese of St. Joseph took its place among the more prosperous of the lesser Dioceses of the United States.

As far as the St. Louis Archdiocese was concerned the change did not materially affect its resources, as only some twenty-five out of three hundred parishes and more notable missions were detached from its jurisdiction. The principal towns included in the transfer were Hannibal, Edina, Moberly, Mexico, and Kirksville.

On November 8th, 1922 the Right Rev. Francis Gilfillan pastor of the Cathedral of St. Louis, received consecration at the hands of his Archbishop as Bishop of Spigas and Coadjutor to the Bishop of St. Joseph.     On the death of Bishop Maurice F. Burke, March 17th, 1923, Bishop Gilfillan succeeded to the See.

The diocese of St. Louis quickly recovered from the check, the last of a long series of dismemberments, that reduced its territory from the magnificent expanse of Illinois, Wisconsin, Minnesota, Iowa, Arkansas, Missouri, and the farthest reaches of the western prairies, as it was in the days of its founder, the first Bishop Joseph Rosati.

## CHAPTER 9

## CATHOLICS FROM ITALY AND THE NEAR EAST

The three Italian churches in the city of St. Louis, St. Charles Borromeo, Our Lady of the Help of Christians, and St. Ambrose, had a rather late origin, all dating from the first three years of the Twentieth Century and all owing their origin and continued prosperity to a priest who is still among the living, the Rev. Father Caesar Spigardi. There were several reasons for this belated appearance of this ancient Catholic people on the scene of our ecclesiastical life. For a long time the Italians could not be prevailed upon to forsake their beautiful country for any other country in the world. Neither penury and oppression at home, nor the siren song of liberty and wealth from abroad, could move them. Under his vine and fig tree the true Italian felt content. Of course, sporadic cases of flight beyond the sea occurred, sometimes on account of crime committed, sometimes on account of vengeance feared. The better classes of people which really form the bulk of the Italian nation, were either too proud or too home-loving or too ignorant of the world to sail away to foreign parts. Accordingly there were but few Italians in Missouri before 1860. A slight advance in numbers is shown in 1870, and an appreciable increase appears by 1880. The Census of 1900, shows a total population of 4,345 Italian immigrants in Missouri, the share of the city of St. Louis being 2,227. To this number should be added the number of children born in America. It is plain, that there was no crying need of a distinctive Italian Church in St. Louis before 1900: besides, if this proof did not seem sufficiently convincing, the sad fate of the earliest Italian Church in the City, St. Bonaventure, would confirm it.

It was mainly through the efforts of Vicar-General Muehlsiepen that, as early as 1871, a church for the Italian Catholics was built on Sixth and Spruce Streets. The parish was placed in charge of the Order of Black Franciscans, so-called from the black habit they wear. They came from Italy. The first pastor was the Rev. J. B. Salvatelli, his assistant, Father Marzetti. On April 21st, 1872, the Coadjutor Bishop Ryan dedicated the new building to the glory of God under the invocation of the great Franciscan Doctor of the Church, St. Bonaventure: Father Salvatelli remained as pastor until 1877; his assistants were successively: Fathers Nazareno Gruziani, F. Schmelzer and Leopold Moczygemba, all members of the Order of Friars Minor Conventuals or Black Franciscans. It was soon found that the location of the church was not favorable, the parish never

(681)

realized the expectations placed in it by good Father Muehlsiepen and his friends. In 1877, Father Salvatelli left St. Bonaventure's and withdrew to St. Mary's Church for a year and then returned to Italy, where he was subsequently elected Provincial of his Order. His successor at St. Bonaventure's was a secular priest, Father Nazareno Orfei, who received faculties from the Italians, but was not adopted into the diocese. Father Orfei, carried on the arduous work until January 30th, 1883, when St. Bonaventure's Church was closed and sold. Father Orfei was sent to Old Mines as Rector, where he labored in the ministry for two years, and then became Chaplain of Calvary Cemetery, in St. Louis. From 1886 till 1900 he served at various churches as assistant and, in 1900, became pastor of Byrnesville, where he died May 29th, 1906. In the meantime Father John S. Long, and the late Monsignor Holweck and the Jesuit Fathers of St. Joseph's Church devoted themselves in a large measure to the care of the Italian Catholics in St. Louis. Father Long had made his theological studies in Rome, and therefore had a good acquaintance with the Italian language and the Italian mentality. From January 1889, to November 1900, he was assistant priest, first at St. Augustine's, then at St. John's and lastly at St. Patrick's. In every one of these parishes there was a considerable number of Italians. In the German parish of St. Aloysius the nucleus of the present strong Italian parish of St. Ambrose was formed by the self-sacrificing care of its founder and first pastor, Father Holweck. The Jesuit Father's zeal for souls of whatever race, needs no further comment.

Father Caesar Spigardi, the organizer and apostle of the Italian Catholics of St. Louis, was born on August 31st, 1859.

In 1899, he arrived in St. Louis and on February 9th, of the following year accepted charge of all the Italians in the city, about ten thousand in number. He rented the old Presbyterian church on Nineteenth and Morgan Streets. Archbishop Kain blessed it on February 11th, under the Invocation of *Our Lady, Help of Christians.*

In 1902, this church was abandoned, and a Protestant church, situated on Tenth and Wash Streets having been bought for a part of the Congregation it was blessed under the same title of Our Lady Help of Christians. It was occupied on the eve of the Feast of the Immaculate Conception 1902. The church was established as a chapel of ease dependent on the parish church of St. Charles Borromeo on Locust and Twenty-ninth. St. Charles Borromeo was originally a Protestant church, like the two preceeding ones, and was bought and fitted up for Catholic worship in 1902. Here was the parochial residence from which Father Spigardi and his assistants attended the Church of Our Lady, Help of Christians, and from 1903 on, the Church of St. Ambrose also.

This church of the Italians in the southwestern part of St. Louis, was blessed by Archbishop Glennon on August 3rd, 1903. It was attended from St. Charles Borromeo's until 1907, when it became an independent parish of St. Ambrose under Father Luciano Carotti.

The priests that have assisted Father Spigardi in his twenty-seven years of hard and successful labor building up these churches are: Father Joseph Marturano, 1903 to 1904; Leonardo Russo, 1903 to 1905; Petrus Bulfamante, 1904-1906; Lucian Carrotti, 1905 to 1907: Leo Manzetti 1906 to 1909, Nicholas Albanese, 1907 to 1909.

St. Ambrose School built by Father Carotti was attended by over three hundred and fifty pupils taught by eight Sisters of Loretto and one lay teacher. In 1923 Rev. Julius Giovannini was appointed pastor, and plans were laid at once for the erection of a church thoroughly worthy of the spirit of the parish. The corner stone was blessed and laid on May 30th, 1925, and the ceremonies of dedication were performed by Archbishop Glennon. The parish numbers 6,500 souls and is still increasing. The people of St. Ambrose are for the most part from the neighborhood of Milan, whilst those of the downtown parishes are largely Sicilans and Neapolitans. St. Charles Borromeo was noted for its noisy, but otherwise orderly, open-air processions in honor of the Virgin Mary, Mother of God; the people of St. Ambrose are equally devout but rather more Americanized.

Two other Italian priests laboring for a time in St. Louis diocese may be mentioned here: Rev. Ottavio Leoni and Rev. P. Celauro. Both came to Missouri in 1906, but neither was received into the diocese. Rev. Celauro attended the Italian Catholics at Keota, Macon County, from 1906 to 1907, and then departed for parts unknown. The Rev. Ottavio Leoni filled the position of Rector of St. Anthony's Church at Knobview, Phelps County, and missionary to St. James for about twenty years after his appointment in July 1st, 1906. The church at Knobview was dedicated on December 9th, 1906.

The latest of national parishes organized in St. Louis was that of *Our Lady of Cavadonga* for the Spanish and Mexican Catholics. The Rev. Jose Picojovar, a Mexican refugee, was its founder. Archbishop Glennon dedicated the humble structure on Sunday, September 1915. Its life was short as the congregation soon dispersed.

It may seem a far cry from the Italians to the Syro-Maronites in St. Louis; yet in the Catholic Church in every nation and people and tribe is represented, the juxta-position in one and the same city causes no comment and therefore need not surprise any one. Both nations have received the Catholic faith in the heroic days of the Church, and have held it tenaciously unto the present day.

The Maronites are a small nation and have their homes on the mountain range of the Libanus and Antilibanus, so often mentioned in the Sacred Scriptures. Their language is the Arabic, their Liturgy is the Syriac. They are governed by a Patriarch, who resides at Antioch in Syria. In order to be recognized by his people the Patriarch must be confirmed in his office by the Pope.

The first Maronite church was organized by the Rev. George Emanuel, a member of the Order of St. Anthony the Hermit in October 1898. The Congregation, numbering about fifty families, met for divine service in a stone building on Broadway and Poplar Street, which was named *St. Anthony the Abbot*. The school was taught by two lay-teachers; it had an enrollment of forty-five pupils. When in 1901 Father Emanuel left the diocese, the Rev. Mataco Noemi was assigned to his place. He also was a member of the Order of St. Anthony. Father Noemi was relieved of his charge in January 1906 by the secular priest Rev. Anthony Slieman. This third pastor of the Maronites bought a piece of property on Hickory Street and St. Ange Avenue on which the church and school of the parish were built. In 1920 the Rev. Francis Chaman was pastor, in 1926 the Rev. Joakin Stephan.

As the Maronite Catholics of St. Louis had increased considerably since 1898, they felt the necessity of another parish organization, which was affected on July 15th, 1913 under the title of St. Raymond. Their church situated in the nine hundred block of La Salle Street, was dedicated in 1913. There were seventy-five families in its membership, and the number is still increasing. The founder and first pastor is the Rev. Joseph Karam. The parish has established a school of its own with two lay-teachers and fifty-two pupils.

## CHAPTER 10

## THE CHURCHES OF THE SLAVIC RACES IN ST. LOUIS

In the early years of Peter Richard Kenrick's regime the great mass of Catholic immigrants belonged exclusively to the Irish or the German race. But in the first half of the fifties another race began to make itself felt in the diocese, the Slavic. They were mostly of that North-Slavic stock, that is commonly designated as Bohemians, although their proper name is Czechs. These new immigrants clustered around a point in South St. Louis that is still marked by the Church of St. John Nepomuc.

About thirty years later came the second friendly invasion by a Catholic division of the Slavic race, also of North-Slavic stock, the Poles. Large numbers of this valiant and devoted people, had for some time prior to the close of the seventh decade of the nineteenth century, settled down in the district south of Cass Avenue, which on account of its predominantly Irish population, was popularly known as Kerry Patch. They attended the Catholic churches in the neighborhood; but feeling the lack of instructions in their own language, and realizing that they were strong enough in numbers and in wealth, they decided to build a church of their own. The organization of the parish was perfected at a meeting at St. Joseph's Church in 1879. The congregation met for divine services in the basement of St. Patrick's school, until the completion of their own church, November 12th, 1882, which was consecrated to God in honor of *St. Stanislaus*. Bishop Ryan officiated. The congregation numbered one hundred and forty families, besides a large contingent of unmarried persons. The Franciscan Fathers, who fortunately had some priests of Polish nationality among their members, came to the aid of the young struggling parish. Their choice for the position of pastor of St. Stanislaus was Father Sebastian Cebulla, O.S.F., who had organized it and built the church. Shortly before its consecration he was superceded by Father Leo Brandys, also a Franciscan, who remained until 1886. The first St. Stanislaus Church was the usual combination structure of church and school. In 1886 Father Urban Stanowskï, a member of the Franciscan Order like his predecessors, was sent to take parochial charge of St. Stanislaus. On December 15th, 1887 Father Urban received the Rev. Francis Gnielinski as assistant. Father Stanowski's success was due in a large measure to his prudent effort in assisting his flock to obtain their own homes. He organized building and loan societies, and in a few years, the church was surrounded with substantial dwellings owned by Catholic Poles.

(685)

This encouragement led to the erection of the present spacious Church at a cost of $150,000. On September 13th, 1891 Vicar-General Muehlsiepen laid the corner stone, and on September 18th, of the following year dedicated the church to divine service.

Father Urban, being a Franciscan Friar needed a special dispensation to live outside of the cloister. In November 1887 he had received dispensation for three years, and in January 1891 it was extended for two more years. But on March 8th, 1892 the Archbishop of St. Louis granted him an indult to remain extra claustra for the rest of his life, and received him as a member of the secular clergy. During all this time and many years after, Father Stanowski faithfully served the Congregation of St. Stanislaus, assisted by the following members of the diocesan clergy, Francis Gnielinski (1887-1888) Victor Stepka (1896-1897) Charles Ruskowski (1897-1898) Simon Joseph Zielinski (1902-1905) Julian Moczydlowski (1903-1905) Stanislaus Wisniewski, 1905, Simon Naurocki, 1905.

St. Stanislaus became the mother-church of the Poles of St. Louis, for through its efforts three other Polish churches, in the course of time, were organized in the city: St. Casimir (1889), St. Hedwig (1904), and our Lady of Czestochowa (1907). St. Stanislaus has a parish school with an enrollment of about 400 pupils. The school is in charge of five Sisters of the Third Order of St. Francis.

Father Urban Stanowski died as Pastor of St. Stanislaus on January 23rd, 1927, in his seventy-seventh year. The first dismemberment of St. Stanislaus Parish, which until then embraced all the Catholic Poles in the city, occurred in 1889, when *St. Casimir's parish* was organized under the rectorship of Father Gnielinski. Father Gnielinski was ordained in Eichstaedt, Bavaria, for the diocese of St. Louis, on July 3rd, 1887, and was appointed assistant to Father Urban, and on June 4th, 1888 was transferred to Ste. Genevieve. On October 6th, 1889, he was constituted rector of St. Casimir's church, which, originally a Protestant meeting house, was blessed on that very day by Vicar-General Brady. St. Casimir's church, was and is situated on Eighth and Mound Streets. It had a parochial school from the beginning, at first taught by a layman. The parish flourished and soon outgrew its early habiliments: a new church was built, for which Archbishop Kain laid the corner stone on April 28th, and performed the dedication service on the following September 1st.

Father Theophile Pudlowski and Simon Zielinski served as assistants to Father Francis Gnielinski during the latter half of his incumbency. In November 1905 the pastor of St. Casimir's left his parish and the diocese, and the Jesuit Father Alexander Matauschek was sent to take charge until the coming of Father Pudlowski as pastor, December 17th, 1905.

Father Pudlowski is an alumnus of the Kenrick Seminary and was raised to the priesthood on June 11th, 1898 by Archbishop Glennon. From 1903 to 1905, he was rector of the Slovak parish of the Holy Trinity. Under Father Pudlowski's able management the parish enrollment increased and multiplied. In 1920 the school was in charge of eleven Polish Sisters of St. Joseph with 760 pupils in attendance.

Father Theophile Thomas Pudlowski was born in Oschen, German Poland, September 26th, 1874, was ordained by Archbishop Kain on June 11th, 1898, and died on April 7th, 1922, after an illness of only two days. He was succeeded in the pastorate of St. Casimiri's by Father Francis A. Pudlowski under whose pastorate the church remained to the present day. The Parish has given two of its young men to the clergy of St. Louis.

The third church of the Polish people in St. Louis was established in 1904, by a native of the City, Father Victor Stepka, in the southeastern part of St. Louis, Compton Avenue and Hiawatha Street. A combination church, school and parsonage structure was built and dedicated to *St. Hedwig*, by Archbishop Glennon, March 26th, 1905. The Parish at its very start numbered one hundred and fifty families, all of Polish descent. The school showed an enrollment of one hundred and fifty-four pupils, taught by four Sisters de Notre Dame. In 1906, Father Stepka was supplanted by the Rev. Simon Joseph Zielinski. Father Zielinski entered Kenrick Seminary from the archdiocese of Guesen-Posen and was ordained on June 14, 1902 by Archbishop Kain. He served as assistant priest at St. Stanislaus and St. Casimir's, then as rector in Owensville and Doniphan, to become pastor of St. Hedwig's on February 1st, 1906. He enlarged the Church in 1907. His death occurred October 24, 1926.

Late in April 1907, the Polish Catholics who had now spread over the greater part of the city, obtained permission from the ecclesiastical authorities to form another parish, under the title of *Our Lady of Czestochowa* the most celebrated miraculous Madonna of all Poland. The parish was organized with the assistance of the Franciscan Fathers, and the church was blessed by Archbishop Glennon on November 17th, 1907. In January the following year, the Reverend Leonard Czopnik was appointed its pastor. A new rectory was built in 1913. The school was opened in 1917, with Polish Franciscan Sisters in charge, and shortly afterward, November 6th, 1917, Father Czopnik died. Father Simon J. Wisniewski succeeded Father Czopnik. It was now, July 15th, 1918, that the new church building was bought from the Lutherans and dedicated by Archbishop Glennon. The parish is of healthy growth and numbers one hundred and fifty families. The school is in charge of the Polish Sisters of St. Joseph.

As related in a former chapter, St. John Nepomuc was the first religious center of the Bohemian Catholics in St. Louis. It was also the mother of the second Bohemian church in the city, as well as the foster-mother of others in the country districts. Through the efforts of Father Hessoun the Parish of *St. Wenceslaus* was organized and supplied with the necessary buildings. The Davenport priest, Rev. John Pekar, was appointed as temporary pastor on May 1895. The church and school building was blessed on June 21st, of the same year. From March 3rd, 1896, to March 1897, the Rev. B. H. Taitlik, a Premonstratensian monk, served in the same capacity; but from that time on until March 1900, Father Charles August Bleha was pastor of St. Wenceslaus Parish, as a distinct entity. Father Bleha was a native of the diocese of Koeniggraetz in Bohemia, made his studies in Louvain and was there ordained for the diocese of New Orleans. Having been adopted by the diocese of St. Louis, Father Bleha in 1895, became assistant at St. John Nepomuc and in March 1897, received the appointment to St. Wenceslaus Church. When Father Hessoun, on March 15th, 1900, was disabled by a stroke of paralysis, Father Bleha was appointed administrator of St. John's and, at the death of the venerable pastor in 1906, became his successor. Father John Nekula, who had served as assistant at St. John's since July 14th, 1895, succeeded to the pastorate of St. Wenceslaus where he remained until his death in June 1922. Father William Hamill was then appointed administrator and subsequently pastor of St. Wenceslaus Parish. Father Charles Bleha, pastor of St. John's died May 8th, 1926, and was succeeded by Father Wenceslaus Linek, one of the priestly sons of St. John of Nepomuc parish, as Father John Nekula was of St. Wenceslaus. Of the numerous assistants Father Hessoun had in his long and laborious apostolate among the Bohemian Catholics the following deserves special notice: Joseph Roszevac (1871-1881) afterwards pastor of the Bohemian Settlement at Rock Creek.

The other outmission attended from St. John's was Hawk Point near Troy in Lincoln County, and the missionaries were Fathers Joseph S. Koudelka (1882-1883) the future Bishop of Cleveland, and second Bishop of Superior, and Peter Houst, an Ex-Franciscan (1833-1895). In 1890, Father Houst published, "A History of the Bohemian Catholic Parishes in the United States." The book brought financial difficulties upon the author, so that eventually he was forced to leave St. John's to the great sorrow of Father Hessoun. Mathias Sevcik (1903-1904) and Charles Bleha, (1895-1900) followed Houst as assistants. In 1900, Father Bleha became administrator, with Rev. Leopold Steffl as assistant, until Father Hessoun's death on July 4th, 1906, when Father Bleha succeeded to the pastorship with Rev. Wenceslaus Stephan as assistant. Two other Bohemian priests devoted some time to their Catholic countrymen in Rock Creek, Rev. John Tichy from September 1898 to November 1899, and Joseph Methodius Hynek from November 1899 to November 1900. Both left the diocese after one year's trial or perhaps trials.

Akin to the Bohemians as the Slovaks are in their racial characteristics and political affiliations, they also were next to the Bohemians in the order of time, as far as St. Louis is concerned. "In the northern part of Central Europe, where the Carpathians slope toward the Hungarian plain, is the country called by its children, "Slovensco" or "Slovakland," says Stephen J. Palikar in his short study: *"The Slovak's in Chicago."* It is an historic race of solid character and exceeding industry, but worthy of the name that has been given to its members: "the very step-children of fortune." It was christianized about 1863, by the Apostles *Cyril and Methodius.* There are about three million Slovaks in Czecho-Slovakia, for the most part excellent Catholics. Slovak emigration to America began in 1873, the largest number in any one year of Slovak immigrants, 52,368, arrived in 1905. Missouri has not received a large proportion of these valuable accessions to our national wealth and strength. They have but one church of their own in St. Louis, the Church of the Holy Trinity of Park Avenue and Twelfth Street. The edifice one time served as a Baptist Church, but was thoroughly renovated and blessed by Archbishop Kain. A parish school was built and blessed in 1910, with Franciscan Sisters in charge. The parish numbered seventy families.

The Rev. Milo Duchon was given faculties for one year, but he left the diocese by August before the expiration of his time of probation, in August 1899. The Rev. Francis Horak was then appointed to take his place, but he also left the diocese on February 4th, 1902, when Father Duchon returned to his post. Father Theophile Pudlowski, a Pole, was then appointed Pastor of the Slovaks and succeeded right well, but was recalled on December 7th, 1905, to fill the vacancy caused at St. Casimir's by the sudden departure of Father Gnielinski. On April 20th, 1906, came the Rev. Francis Horak, who maintained his authority until 1909. His successor was the Rev. Ladislans Neuwirth. After him came Father Wenceslaus Linek, an American of Bohemian descent, as administrator, who remained until he was appointed to his native parish of St. John of Nepomuc.

The only Catholic church in St. Louis of any South-Slavic people is that of the Croatians on Thirteenth Street and Chouteau Avenue. These good people were organized into a parish in 1904, by Rev. Oscar Suster. They purchased the Jewish Synagogue at the place mentioned above and fitted it up as a very neat Catholic church, under the protection of St. Joseph. The parish numbered seventy-five families. Father Suster came from the diocese of Zagreb in Croatia, and was ordained there on July 29th, 1900. He arrived in the diocese of St. Louis in February 1904, and left it for good in 1909. His successor at the Croatian church Father Joseph Kompare was more persevering. .He established a school, with three Sisters of the Precious Blood as teachers. When the Ursuline Sisters had completed the erection of their new Convent at Oakland. St. Louis County, and in consequence offered their property on State Street and Russell Avenue for sale, Father Kompare bought it for his Croatian Congregation. This establishment comprised an entire city-block of large dimensions. The Convent was remodelled to serve the Congregation as a community center with church, school, parochial residence, Society meeting rooms, entertainment hall and gymnasiums. As the chapel of the Sisters, was not large enough for the congregation, an addition was begun at once, in the space where the chapel had been between the two wings of the great Convent building.

The solemn dedication of this new Catholic Croatian church by Archbishop Glennon on April 26th, 1928, was a memorable event for the local Catholic Croatians. The two other previous eventful dates are the corner stone laying and then the grand opening of the Croatian Catholic Community Center. The group of buildings of this parish are truly a monument of this people's faith and zeal. Rev. Ambrose Misetic, O.F.M., is in charge, enjoying the whole hearted cooperation, and liberal support of his faithful parishioners. Numerous clergymen from out of town attended the celebration, among them the Rev. Msgr. Martin D. Krmpotic, of Kansas City, Kansas; Very Rev. Clement Veren, O.F.M., Franciscan Commissary of South Bethlehem, Pa., who preached; and Rev. Bono Andacich and Rev. Bojanich.

Proceeding the solemn dedicatory ceremonies a parade was formed at 8:30 and started from 12th and Russell, moving north to Soulard Street, at which point various Bohemian, Slovak and Ukrainian Societies and the Laclede and Lafayette Council, Knights of Columbus, joined in the ranks, and then this monster parade wended its way to the new church on 12th and Russell Avenue.

There is one noteworthy charitable institution in the diocese that is the product of the united efforts of the four parishes just mentioned, St. John of Nepomuc, St. Wenceslaus, Holy Trinity of the Slovaks, and the Croatian St. Joseph, an institution intended in its foundation as a memorial of their venerable leader and friend, Monsignor Joseph Hessoun: The Hessoun Bohemian Catholic Orphan Home at Fenton, Mo. It was established in 1913.

Father Charles Bleha, pastor of St. John Nepomuc Church was the prime mover in the project; but the Bohemians of St. Louis and, we may say of the United States, grew enthusiastic about it. The erection of this Hessoun Bohemian Catholic Orphanage was approved by the Most Rev. Archbishop. A piece of land was bought near Fenton, Mo.; then collections were taken up among the Catholic Bohemians in St. Louis, many donations being obtained through the appeal of the newspapers. "Hlas" and "Ceska Zena," reaching homes in all America. In the meantime Father Bleha brought over from Bohemia the Sisters *de Notra Domina,* who at once took charge of the institution. That the Orphanage really filled a want is evident from the fact, that in the years 1918 and 1919, when the influenza epidemic proved fatal to many heads of families, as many as fifty-seven orphan children were cared for by the Sisters. At the present time the Hessoun Bohemian Catholic Orphanage is caring for 30 children. When the *De Notra Domina* Sisters decided to take charge of schools and institutions in the States of Iowa and Nebraska, the Sisters of the Holy Cross were brought from Moravia, which Sisters, up to the present date, are taking care of these little orphan children.

The Orphanage is supported by the following parishes: St. John's Nepomuc, St. Wenceslaus, Holy Trinity (Slovak) and the Croatian parish of St. Joseph. The spiritual director of the institution is the present pastor of St. John's, the Rev. Wenceslaus Linek. The two last great divisions of the Slavic race to establish Catholic parishes in St. Louis were the Ruthenians or Little Russians and the Lithuanians. Before the World War the former great people was divided between the Empires of Russia and Austro-Hungary: those living in Austria-Hungary being Catholics in union with the Holy See, but having the privilege of using the modified Greek rite that is known as the Greek-Ruthenian; Those living in Russia were for the most part Greek orthodox. To say a Ruthenian, therefore, means a Little Russian of the Catholic Faith, but of the Greek rite. Now in 1905, there were about one hundred Greek-Ruthenian Catholic families in the city of St. Louis and vicinity; who came together to organize a parish of their nationality. For a few years they worshipped in the chapel of St. John of Nepomuc's church, on Eleventh and Soulard Streets. In 1908, however, the congregation bought the old Episcopal church of St. John, at Dolman and Hickory Streets. Now the name first chosen, St. Andrew, was changed to St. Mary's Assumption. The people are from Austro-Galicia. The services are conducted in the Ruthenian language. Desloge, in St. Francois County, also has a Ruthenian church, which is attended once a month by the pastor of the St. Louis church. The organizer and first pastor of St. Andrew's parish of Ruthenians was the Rev. Joseph E. Czaplinski. On September 21st, 1905, Father Czaplinski stated in a letter to Chancellor Van der Sanden, that "we do not own our own church, but we rent a chapel at St. John." On November of the same year the Rev. P. Dobrotwor appears as his successor. After the church was bought came the Rev. Dymytry

Chomiac who remained during the years 1909 and 1910.  The issues of the Catholic Directories for 1920-1926, give his name among the clergy of Scranton, Pa., whilst Fathers Czaplinski and Dobrotwor continued their ministration to their Catholic countrymen, the one in New Jersey, the other in Michigan.

On May the 28th, 1913, the Holy See established the Ruthenian Greek Catholic Diocese, with the Rt. Rev. Stephen Soter Ortinski as its first Bishop.  All the Ruthenian parishes in the United States were placed under his jurisdiction.  His Cathedral of the Immaculate Conception of the Blessed Virgin Mary is in Philadelphia.  When Bishop Ortinski died March 24th, 1916, the Rt. Rev. Constantine Bohacheffski was appointed in his place.  The parish of the Assumption of the Blessed Virgin Mary in St. Louis and the mission at Desloge were accordingly withdrawn from the jurisdiction of the Archbishop of St. Louis and placed in the hands of the Ruthenian Greek Bishop of the United States.  The Ruthenian priests residing at the Church of the Assumption were the Rev. Vladisner Kopytchak, Basil Merenkow and Miko Romanink.

The Catholic Lithuanians under the leadership of Father Michael Vitkus recently purchased a disused Protestant church on Armstrong and Park Avenues, and remodelled it into a Catholic house of worship. So far they have not established a school, but that, will no doubt, soon make an irresistible appeal to this deeply religious people.

## CHAPTER 11

# THE GREAT WESTWARD MOVEMENT

The westward expansion of the City of St. Louis after the World's Fair was rapidly followed, and at times, even anticipated, by the erection of new Catholic churches and schools. It was not, strictly speaking, new territory in which these parishes were founded: but the Catholic families living scattered in a wide circle on their farms and truck gardens around one or the other early churches, now sold their land, directly or indirectly, to the newcomers and formed with them, in as far as they were Catholics, the nucleus of the new parishes springing up year by year. There are twenty-one of these latest city churches, enclosing in a wide irregular semicircle the City of St. Louis. *The Immaculate Conception* parish at Maplewood was the pioneer in the movement. In 1904, on March 1st, Rev. Daniel W. Clark was appointed Rector of the parish. First services were held in a vacant store building. On November 26th, 1905 Archbishop Glennon blessed the church, a combination building for all church purposes: The school opened in September 1906 with one hundred and fifty pupils, taught by three Sisters of Loretto. There were seventy-five families, Irish and German, but almost all American-born. Father Clark in 1914 exchanged his parish for that of Father M. J. Taylor, New Madrid. His tragic death, July 27th, 1916, is still remembered. His successor at Maplewood Father M. J. Taylor, held the parish until May 25th, 1921. The present pastor J. P. Ryan was appointed January 30th, 1922. Two other parishes, St. Luke's of Richmond Heights, and Epiphany at Gratiot, were established in the original territory of the Immaculate Conception of Maplewood. In 1826 the new church and rectory at Maplewood were built at a cost of $175,000., on a new location that is regarded as one of the beauty spots of St. Louis County.

Early in the following year 1905, the church of the *Nativity of Our Lord*, was founded by the Rev. John C. Granville, who had just then received his honorable discharge from the army. According to the Records he was appointed on January 3rd of that year to found a parish in the northwest portion of the city. Services were held at first, in St. Mary's Orphan Asylum. The first parish building was a combination church and school, which was dedicated October 22nd, 1905. The school was placed in care of the Sisters of St. Joseph. The membership of the new parish was cosmopolitan, and had a rapid growth. The original territory was dismembered into four parishes: St. Adalberts (a Polish parish) Corpus Christi, and St. Philip Neri, being the three daughters of the Nativity. Father Granville died October 26th, 1911. Father Joseph Cruse succeeded him at the Nativity parish on November 11th, 1911. Six Sisters of St. Joseph conduct the parochial school.

The parish of *St. Andrew* was organized on December 24th, 1904 by the Rev. Albert Mayer in the territory between the River Des Peres and Jefferson Barracks, east and west of Broadway. The population was predominantly German, with an admixture of eight or nine other nationalities. The first mass was celebrated in February 1905 in a little chapel on the Mt. St. Rose Hospital Grounds.

A large plot of ground was bought, and the corner stone of the new church, school and Sisters dwelling was laid July 4th, 1905. In the summer of 1905 a rectory was built. The church was dedicated by His Grace on December 19, 1905.

In 1906 the parish purchased a house adjoining the school which was remodeled into a home for the School Sisters of Notre Dame.

In 1907 a new school was built. It is a brick building, 97 feet long and 61 feet wide, with a large basement and a fine hall.

The first census taken up in 1905 enumerated two hundred families. The Congregation increased rather slowly for the first five years; then came a total stand-still which lasted about ten years, and finally an extraordinary growth set in, so that the parish now numbers four hundred and fifty families.

*St. Pius* church on Grand and Utah Avenue is one of the most artistic church buildings in St. Louis. Its pure white facade of Carthage stone with the sculptured entrance and pediment, and the graceful campanile, is a model of the Romanesque style of architecture of the sixteenth century period. The parish of St. Pius was founded on October 3rd, 1905 by Father John Lyons.

Ground was broken for this beautiful new church on July 27th, 1916. The corner stone was laid November 15th, 1916. The dedication took place October 28th, 1917. Archbishop Glennon officiated and Bishop Althoff of Belleville was celebrant of the Solemn Highmass.

The parish school and the rectory, both of which have a stone facade corresponding with the material used in the church building form worthy accompaniments of the beautiful church.

The parish of *St. Cecelia* was organized in October 1906 by the Rev. Bernard J. Benten, until then pastor of St. Paul's, Mo. The membership numbered only three hundred and fifty souls, mainly of German and Irish extraction. But it grew rapidly until it attained the grand total of four hundred and fifty families. The corner stone laying of the combination building for school and church took place May 19th,

1907, and the dedication January 1st, 1908. The erection of the new church was begun in January 1926, and its dedication by Archbishop Glennon followed on Sunday, February 27th, 1927.

St. Cecelia's new church is a structure of beauty and harmony in the Romanesque style of architecture.

The school is in charge of the Sisters of St. Joseph of Carondelet.

The parish of the *Blessed Sacrament* was organized on June 27th, 1907, by the Rev Patrick H. Bradley in territory.taken from the Visitation and the Holy Rosary parishes. The new church was completed and dedicated by Archbishop Glennon on Sunday, March 21st, 1915. At the conclusion of the Mass the Archbishop presided at the Peace-Service prescribed by Pope Benedict for that day in every Catholic church of the Universe.

The church was described by His Grace, as "large, ornate, costly and substantial." The marble main altar, which is of a really novel design, was placed in the church soon after the dedication services. The reredos is formed by the group of the twelve apostles, and the figure of our Blessed Lord is the tabernacle.

The parish of *Our Lady of Sorrows* bears a name reminiscent of its origin and surroundings. It was organized among the cemeteries of South St. Louis, and its first services were held in the Chapel of S. S. Peter and Paul's Cemetery. Father S. A. Stolte was its founder, October 20th, 1907. The parish had a school built by a real estate agent in 1908. But in 1911 Father Stolte erected the usual combination building to serve as church, school and hall. It was dedicated by Archbishop Glennon October 20th, 1911. The parish numbered seventy families, dispersed over a wide area. In the course of time it relinquished a large part of its territory to three new foundations: St. John the Baptist, St. George and St. Mary Magdalen. The parish of Our Lady of Sorrows has already given two priests and five nuns to Holy church.

The church of *All Souls,* Overland Park owes its origin to the exertions of Father John S. Long, pastor of All Saints parish. Father Long began the canvassing of the Overland district of his parish described as No Man's Land two days before Christmas 1907, and on Palm Sunday called a meeting for the purpose of establishing a new parish. April 12th, of the following year a meeting was held, at which a subscription of $700 was raised. Canvassing and collecting was continued during the Spring and Summer months. A frame building accommodating two hundred worshipers was erected and blessed by Father Long on November 29th, 1908, under the invocation of All Souls. Father Long continued his ministrations from All Saints, saying mass at All Souls every Sunday, until January 1910 when the Archbishop appointed the Rev. William L. Shea as the first resident pastor.

Father Shea was born in St. Louis January 1st, 1870, and was raised to holy priesthood on January 8th, 1895. Since October 1897, he had been assistant priest at St. Kevin's church. His successor at All Souls is the Rev. Albert B. Gass, in the capacity of Administrator. Dr. Gaas, also, is a native of St. Louis. As pastor of Kirksville in North Missouri from 1903 to 1910 he built the beautiful church of Mary Immaculate.

The parish of *St. Catherine of Sienna* came into being in August 1909. Mass was said in a tent erected on the grounds, until the church, a frame building of moderate size, was completed and blessed, April 24th, 1910. Father John Nugent became its pastor in November 1909.

The parochial school was established in 1913, in charge of the Sisters of Loretto. The membership of the parish is composed of Irish and German Catholics and grew from two hundred to six hundred souls. St. Catherine's is a flourishing parish.

*St. Paul the Apostle* is the name of a parish of originally seventy families, organized by Father J. H. Tettemer on March 11th, 1909. Its parochial school is taught by Sisters of Loretto.

The parish of the *Epiphany* was founded in 1911 by Father J. F. English, who on his arrival from Ireland in 1905 was appointed Assistant at St. Agnes church and subsequently pastor of the church of the Epiphany. The Sisters of St. Dominic have charge of the school.

*St. Roch's* parish was established in September 1911 in territory cut off from St. Rose's and All Saints.

The pastor of the latter parish was chiefly instrumental in effecting its organization. A meeting called by him was attended by the Archbishop on the Feast of St. Anthony, June 13, 1911.

Among the eight gentlemen who responded were Mr. Walter Scott Clinton, Mr. Robert Tam Brownrigg, Mr. Ed. J. Scott, Mr. Thos. J. Scott and Mr. Frank Casey, Thomas Guggerty, James Costello. His Grace approved the purchase at $55.00 per front foot. This purchase was consummated promptly. It proved to be a very fortunate transaction. Within the short space of one week, a representative of a Real Estate Company, came and tried to buy the same plot of ground, offering $65.00 per front foot, for an apartment house. Father Long had prepared a complete list of the seventy-five Catholic families, living in the territory of the proposed new parish, and had it ready for the Rev. Geo. P. Kuhlman, first pastor, who began building in the summer of 1911.

At first services were held in a store on Kingsbury Boulevard. The corner stone of the church was laid September 18th, 1921 and the completed structure was dedicated by Archbishop Glennon November

22nd, 1922. School was opened in the same year, in charge of the Sisters of St. Joseph. The parish had a remarkable growth, from eighteen to eight hundred families. Father Kuhlman did not live to see the crowning glory of his parish, the church he had planned. On his death August 22nd, 1922, the Rev. John Patrick Spencer succeeded to the rectorship. The new church of St. Roch's was dedicated on November 22nd, 1922, by Archbishop Glennon, assisted by the Bishops of St. Joseph and of Galveston. The structure is built in the Tudor Gothic style with a majestic tower. St. Roch's is one of the very few churches of the city dedicated to a sainted layman.

*St. Rita's* parish, Vinita Park, is another foundation of the former pastor of All Saints, the Rev. John S. Long.

Having had to attend numerous sick calls in Vinita Park for two or three years, Father Long of All Saints Parish, was invited by certain of the community in Vinita Park, to start a new Parish, as it was a growing section of the suburbs. Accordingly the McDonagh family, offered to donate one acre for a Catholic church site on Page just west of Spring Avenue.

The zealous Father made a canvass of the territory and reported to the Archbishop on January 6th, 1913. There was some hesitation as to the site, but he continued his visits among the people and held some meetings. On September 17th, 1913, he received instructions from Archbishop Glennon to "go ahead and build." In the summer of 1914, the first church, a neat frame structure with a seating capacity of about two hundred, was erected on the above named site. On October 1st, 1914, altar and pews were installed and a vestment case soon followed. A meeting was held October 18th, and it was resolved to call the new parish St. Rita's. On October 25th, 1914, the church was dedicated by the Archbishop.

The High Mass of Dedication was sung by Rev. Father Ludgerus, O.F.M., the choir services being rendered by the Knights of Columbus Choral Club. The sermon was preached by Rev. P. P. Crane. Present at the Mass were Rt. Rev. Msgr. O. J. S. Hoog, V. G., Very Rev. Dr. M. S. Ryan, C. M., Rev. C. F. O'Leary and Rev. John Nugent, Rev. E. J. Lemkes, Rev. F. X. Willmes of St. Charles and Rev. Francis, O. F. M.

Father Long gave Mass at St. Rita's every Sunday and Holy Day, coming over from All Saints. On April 24th, 1915, His Grace said to him: "I shall appoint a pastor to St. Rita's as soon as I can." The founder's last Mass at the place was on Sunday, June 27th, 1915, as a resident pastor was assigned in the person of Rev. Daniel J. Buckley.

There were about twenty families in the new parish; they were of Irish and German nationality. The Rev. Daniel F. Buckley was in charge as administrator from June 1915 to January 1st, 1919. As Father Buckley was not a priest of the diocese, he was released from duty on the return of the army chaplains at the end of 1918, and Father William Nugent received the appointment to St. Rita's.

The frame church of Father Long's time was dedicated by Archbishop Glennon in the Fall of 1914.

*St. Luke's* parish, Richmond Heights, founded by Father Joseph McMahon in 1914, for years strove towards the erection of a church befitting the parish in such a rapidly growing section of the city. The Gothic style of architecture was chosen. The corner stone was laid on Sunday, May 6th, 1928. When finished the new St. Luke's will be a worthy rival of St. Matthew's and St. Mark's. The parish is blessed with a parochial school of which the Sisters of St. Joseph are the teachers.

*St. John the Baptist* parish is a daughter of Our Lady of Sorrows: Father John Peters was its godfather. The first Mass was celebrated in a vacant store on February 1914. The temporary brick church was dedicated July 7th, of the same year. The new church was built in 1924 and dedicated in the following year. The parochial school was opened in September 1914. The first week's attendance was 234 pupils. The Sisters of the Precious Blood form the faculty. The pastor of the parish, Father John Peters, is the managing editor of the *Pfarrbote*, a Parish Messenger distributed monthly in a number of our City parishes.

*Corpus Christi* is the name of a parish in the northwest part of the city, formerly called Jennings. Its founder, the Rev. John F. Adrian, made the first proof of his ability in building the really beautiful Chapel of the Ursuline Nuns at Arcadia and there acquired those administrative habits that now promise a substantial development of his rather difficult parish composed, as it is, of German, Irish, Polish, Bohemian and Italian elements. The date of organization was November 7th, 1915. On Thanksgiving day 1917 Archbishop Glennon dedicated the new church and school of the parish, and took occasion to praise the new building as most suitable for its double purpose.

The parish of *Our Lady of Lourdes,* University City, was organized on May 6th 1916, by the Rev. Francis J. O'Connor. There were but few Catholics in the neighborhood, for whom the pastor erected, at his own expense, a small stucco chapel. The school opened September 1917, with five pupils: but when the Sisters of St. Joseph took charge in 1919, the increase in attendance was marked. Now there are one hundred and sixty families in the parish; church, parsonage and school are built of stone: the new church was built in 1917-1918. It is of Norman Gothic architecture, and cost $70,000. Its erection was made possible by the personal donation of a generous benefactor. School and rectory are in keeping, architecturally with the church.

The parish of *St. George* was formed in October 1915 within the southern portion of the parish of Our Lady of Sorrows. Father John Waeltermann was the leader of the exodus. The membership of about three hundred families was composed of Hungarians, Croatians, Lithuanians, Germans, Anglo-Americans, Bohemians, Poles, Belgians and Italians, a truly cosmopolitan aggregation. Yet, there was unity of spirit in the diversity of tongues, as is evident from the magnificent work they accomplished in short time. Father Waeltermann, however, seems to have exceeded the measure of his strength, and resigned his charge in June 1916. Father Joseph Siebert was appointed administrator, an office he holds to the present day. Father Siebert had been a member of the Diocesan Missionary Band. Endowed now with pastoral duties, he set to work to build one of the most imposing churches in the city.

The corner stone was laid in June 1927 and the dedication by Archbishop Glennon took place on April 15th, 1928. The church is designed in the style of architecture known as Lombard. It has a seating capacity of seven hundred and fifty. The Very Rev. Charles L. Van Tourenhout preached one of his most eloquent sermons at the dedication. Father Siebert is a native of Ste. Genevieve. Seven Sisters of the Precious Blood have charge of the school.

The parish of *Our Lady of the Presentation*, St. John's Station, on the road to St. Charles, was organized in October 1916, by Father John Tracy, an old and dear friend of Archbishop Kain. Its territory was dismembered from All Saints.

The preparations, were made by Father John S. Long who, on June 27th, 1915, brought the Archbishop to a meeting at the home of Mr. McManus in the settlement in St. Louis County, known as St. John's Station. Mr. McManus had heard of the neighboring new parishes of All Souls and St. Rita, in Overland Park and Vinita Park, respectively, and conceived the desire of having a Parish also in St. John's Heights. "We had been invited to call on him." He offered a site, 75 ft. by 140 ft. for a Catholic church. The most Rev. Archbishop was evidently pleased, and thanking them, said: "This will be a memorable day." The plot of ground donated by Mr. and Mrs. McManus was later raffled off by Rev. John A. Tracy, the first pastor, for a handsome sum with which he purchased a more suitable location. He began work at once. worked hard, and soon had a substantial brick church erected, which he named the Church of the Presentation. The Rev. John A. Tracy was, appointed by the Most Rev. Archbishop, at Father Long's request.

The corner stone of the church was laid November 21st, 1916, but on March 1st, 1918, Father Tracy died. The church was completed by

Father E. T. Finan, and dedicated July 7th, 1918. The congregation is composed of about one hundred souls, for the most part German-Americans. There are now almost two hundred families in the parish. The school is conducted by the Sisters of St. Joseph.

The church of *St. Mary Magdalen*, Southampton, St. Louis County, was was built up since September 1919, in the southern part of Our Lady of Sorrows parish by Father John J. Thomson, a native of St. Louis. In 1920 he purchased a large residence in the district and fitted it up for school purposes. In 1925 he erected a modern school, for two hundred pupils in care of the Sisters of St. Joseph. The membership of the parish was "decidedly German." The increase is marked, the condition of the parish flourishing.

The parish of *St. Philip Neri*, near the northern Cemetery region of the City, was organized on June 26th, 1919, by Father Thomas Kennedy, immediately after his return from overseas, where he had served as Chaplain, with the rank of Captain.

On November 7th, 1920, the corner stone of the combination church and school building was laid by the Archbishop of St. Louis.

It was completed and ready for school September 1921. The parochial school was opened on September, 1921, the Sisters of St. Joseph having charge.

The parish of *St. Catherine of Alexandria* organized by Father Joseph Westhues north of the city and of Holly Hills, Westmoor, completes the roster of the city churches formed in St. Louis and its environs, mostly by dismemberment of the older parishes, during Archbishop Glennon's administration of the diocese. There were at the end of 1925, one hundred and two parish churches in the city, a fact that evidences a steady and rapid growth of the Catholic population of St. Louis under the fostering care of the Archbishop and through the zeal and energy of the younger clergy that grew up under its inspiration.

# THE RURAL CHURCHES FOUNDED SINCE 1903

Archbishop Glennon, from the start, manifested a deep conviction that rural life was far preferable to life in the city, in as far as contentment of mind, peace and solid prosperity and, above all, the soul's salvation, were concerned; and at the same time, that the future of the Church in the cities depended, in a large measure, on the constant renewal of its religious life, through the sturdy elements communicated to its population by the numerous parishes in the surrounding rural districts. It was therefore, to be expected that he would use special care to strengthen the older country parishes, and to organize as many new ones as he could.

The Church of the *Sacred Heart at Valley Park*, was the firstfruit of this plan: It was organized November 14th, 1903, and the Rev. Henry S. Kister became its first pastor. Through the opening of the St. Louis Plate Glass Company, the Catholic population of Valley Park district had received many accessions who found it inconvenient to attend the mother church at Manchester. Hence the new parish was organized. Thirty-one families of German, Irish and Bohemian nationality or extraction comprised the parish in December 1903.

The School was established in 1904. The Sisters arrived October 7th, and on October 11th, school was opened with forty-six children in attendance.

The first Mass was said in a chapel erected on the Timmermann grounds November 29th, 1903.

The first Mass in the school and church building was said October 23rd, 1904, after its dedication by Vicar-General Hoog. In 1906 this building was destroyed by fire. Father Kister immediately set to work to erect the present fine Gothic church, of which the corner stone was laid by Archbishop Glennon. It was dedicated by Vicar-General Hoog on July 4th, 1908.

The succession of pastors at Valley Park was:

Rev. H. S. Kister, November 1903—January 1911
Rev. William Schulte, January 1911—January 1913
Rev. M. O'Flaherty, January 1913—June 1916

The parish suffered a severe setback in August 1915, when a devastating flood, due to incessant rains, closed down the glass works, the chief industry of the community. People were forced to look elsewhere for work and, since St. Louis offered no opportunities, an exodus to other cities where the glass industry flourished, took place. The flood was followed by a destructive fire, so that the summer of 1917, found the morale of the community at a low ebb, and with the community the parish was also in the throes of despondency.

An effort to revive the glass industry in 1917, resulted in failure, and with the legal closing of the bank in January 1918, the complete financial rout was effected. This was followed by the entrance of the United States into the World War which deprived the parish of its man power, so that in 1920, less than thirty supporting families shouldered the burden of up-keep.

With the ever increasing lure of the Meramec river to the summer vacationist, the community has taken on new life, in which the parish has its adequate share. With the advent of smaller industries to replace those of by-gone days the parish today numbers sixty supporting families with a school enrollment of ninety children.

Father F. X. Recker is its pastor since June 1916.

The other churches founded in 1903, are the *Holy Family of Freeburg,* Osage County, the *Sacred Heart, Thayer,* Oregon County, the *Immaculate Conception, Desloge,* St. Francois County, and *Our Lady of the Rosary, Claryville,* Perry County.

The year 1904, witnessed the foundation of the parishes of the *Immaculate Conception, Owensville,* Gasconade County and *St. Cecelia's, Meta,* Osage County.

Claryville has the mission of St. Teresa, at Lithium attached to it; Owensville, the Missions Belle, Maries County, St. Alexander's and the Stations Bland, Gasconade County; Gerald, Franklin County.

Rev. John J. Martin is pastor. There is a school with two Polish Franciscan Sisters, and forty-two pupils.

The pastor of Claryville is the Rev. George J. Hildner: Father Herman Wagner after founding the parish of Meta established and, for a long time, taught its school. The year 1905, was the banner year of church foundations in the country districts of the diocese. There were eleven: the first one mentioned, Lithium, returned to its former missionary condition: but the remaining ten not only remained alive, but grew strong and fairly prosperous. Bonnots Mill and Folk, Morelle and Augusta, all being in Central Missouri, have all fallen in ranks, when their older neighbors passed in review. But the remaining five now claim recognition.

The *Church of St. Francis at Glennon,* Bollinger County, was founded by Father J. M. Huber, who also attended the church at Advance. He built a church in the forest primeval, but gradually the swamp lands were reclaimed by sturdy settlers from Leopold and Cape Girardeau Counties.

*Portageville* in New Madrid County possesses a church dedicated in honor of *St. Enstachius.* It is a promising parish. Its school numbers 109 pupils, taught by four Sisters of Mercy. *St. Patrick's* parish at *Wentzville,* St. Charles County is in charge of Father Martin Joseph Clarke. Its parish school is taught by a lay teacher. Of the parish of *St. Francis Xavier* at *Sikeston* we learn that it was a Mission of Charleston under Fathers Francis Brand and Henry Hussman, and that it was raised to the dignity of a parish in 1905. Its first pastor was the Rev. Conrad A. Brockmeier. Its buildings, church, school and convent, are frame structures and rather old. The Sisters of Mercy conduct the school. The succession of Pastors since Father Brockmeier are: Fathers Schultz, Moran, George M. O'Ryan, and T. R. Woods. With Advance we close the Record of 1905.

The church of *St. Joseph, Advance,* Stoddard County, owes its first Catholic ministries to Father Everard Pruente who visited the place as early as 1885, and said mass for the people in the hardware store of the Schoenhoff's, who had come from Father Pruente's parish in Cape Girardeau. Then came Father Edward Kern from Jackson and lastly Father Jacob Huber; who built the first church, which however was destroyed by a cyclone, April 29th, 1909.

Father Bonkamp seems to have been made pastor of Advance in 1907 or 1908, but he resided at Glennon, where Rev. J. Huber had started a mission. Rev. Bonkamp built the present church, which was blessed privately, January 9th, 1909, and was solemnly dedicated by Archbishop Glennon, May 19th, 1910.

Father Andrew Toebben succeeded the Rev. Bonkamp as pastor of Glennon and Advance in August 1914. He at first resided at Glennon but, having built the present rectory at Advance, he took up his residence there January 1918. Father Toebben also tried to start a school here; material was bought, a building for the Sisters was bought, but the school was never built owing to the fact that Sisters could not be obtained to take charge.

Father Toebben left the place in November, right after All Souls day, and the Rev. W. Fischer took charge on November 15th of that year.

The rural parishes founded in 1906, four in number, Fenton, Russellville, Knob View and Keota, have already been mentioned; and all retained their standing except one, Keota, which is an Italian Colony, without priest.

In 1907, the parish of *St. Ambrose, Chaffee,* Scott County leads the way. The City of Chaffee owes its existence to the St. Louis-Memphis branch of the great Frisco Railway system.

When the Mississippi was bridged at Thebes, Illinois, and not at Cape Girardeau, the Railroad moved its Division from Cape Girardeau to a more favorable point, and forced its employees to remove with it. Thus a few houses sprung up; a bank was established and the town

of Chaffee found itself full grown almost overnight. Among the first
settlers of the place were some Catholics. As early as the year 1907,
they applied to Archbishop Glennon for a resident pastor. But at the
time, not having a priest available for the place, the Archbishop asked
the Vincentian Fathers of Cape Girardeau to look after the new settlement. On the Feast of the Holy Family, 1907, the first mass in Chaffee
was celebrated by Rev. Frank Freeley, C.M., in Bird's Hall on Yoakum
Avenue.

In June 1907, the attention of the Archbishop being again called
to the number of Catholics in the new town of Chaffee, Rev. Anthony
H. Rohling, was appointed first resident pastor.

A church building was commenced on November 3rd, 1907, and
on January 1st, 1908, the first mass was celebrated in it to the honor
of St. Ambrose, its Patron. In June, 1916, the Archbishop promoted
Rev. Father Rohling to the pastorate of St. Mary's Church, Manchester,
St. Louis County, and in his place appointed the Rev. M. J. Clooney.

The parochial school was established on September 1918, with the
Sisters of Mercy in charge. Father Clooney's successors were Fathers
M. J. O'Leary and John J. Lonergan. The parish now numbers eighty
families, and has one hundred and sixty pupils in its school under a
teaching staff of seven Sisters. Of the other four parishes of 1907,
Osage Bend has already been mentioned with the other Osage Parishes;
*Fulton,* however, in the Kingdom of Callaway, *Glennonville* in Dunklin
County, and *Wellsville,* in Montgomery, await our friendly greeting.
The Church of *Fulton* bears the name of *St. Peter.* The place was
visited by priests since 1831. Its resident priest is the Rev. J. A.
Murray. Of *Glennonville* everybody interested in immigration and
colonization must know, that it is the center of Archbishop Glennon's
famous colony, of which Father Frederick F. Peters is manager, and
pastor. The Church is dedicated to *St. Teresa,* the Spanish Carmelite.
Of *Wellsville* we know but little: only this that its church is named
in honor of the Resurrection of Christ. Father Daniel Hurley was pastor
in 1924, and held this position. Father Hurley's school is taught by
two Franciscan Sisters.

All the rural parishes founded in 1909 and 1910, Chamois, Argyle,
Wilhelmina, and Malden made their bow to us in former chapters: of
Maddenville nothing seems to be known since its foundation as a
parish in 1912; of *Laddonia,* however, in Audrain County we know
that its Church of St. John's is the center of two or three missions.
The pastor, and probably the founder, was the Rev. George Nolte, who
was succeeded since 1924, by the Rev. Anthony F. Schuermann.

*St. Mary Magdalen's* Church of Brentwood is in charge of the Rev.
J. Clement Fehlig.

*Mary Queen of Peace* at *Glendale* was founded in the last week of September 1921, by the Rev. Michael D. Collins. Its territory was carved out of the parishes of Webster Groves, Kirkwood and Brentwood. church and school are temporary frame buildings. No school has so far been established.

*Coffman* in Ste. Genevieve, the ancient New Tennessee Settlement, has a church dedicated to *St. Catherine of Alexandria.* The pastor is Father John F. Walsh. The parish has a mission named Minnith.

Hawk Point, Lincoln County is in charge of the Rev. Wenceslaus Svehla: Mashek is the name of the Mission attached to it. The church is named St. Mary. The people are of Bohemian extraction.

They settled around Mashek about seventy years ago. Mass was at first said in a private house. A log chapel was then built and forty years since, it was supplanted by a frame church, which is still in use. The visiting priests came from St. Charles and Millwood and Troy. From 1907 to 1919, Mashek was a mission of St. John Nepomuc's Church in St. Louis. It never had a resident priest. The parish of Hawk Point was established in June 1919, and on August 15th, of that year Father Wenceslaus Svehla became pastor of both places. Hawk Point is without a church building, whilst the mission of Mashek has. Hawk Point is a railroad town on the Burlington System.

The parish of *St. Joseph* at *Illmo-Fornfelt* was organized in August, 1911, by Father John Muehlsiepen. Divine services were held monthly in Jacob's hall until a suitable building could be provided. In June the following year the corner stone was laid for the new church building. The cost of erection was $1500. It was dedicated on the 27th day of November by Archbishop Glennon of St. Louis. Father Muehlsiepen for a time looked after the spiritual welfare of the parish. The Vincentian Fathers of Cape Girardeau said holy mass during the two months preceeding the appointment of a resident pastor.

Rev. A. B. Lager, D.D., was appointed as the first resident pastor in July 1913. The first three years Dr. Lager lived in a farm house. The parishioners made strenous efforts to provide a residence befitting the position of their pastor. In the spring of 1917, the present parsonage was erected. Father Lager labored faithfully for the spiritual and material welfare of the parish from 1913 to July 1922, when he was succeeded by the Rev. Bernard S. Groner.

The parishioners of Illmo have long realized the need of a parochial school, but the income was not sufficient to warrant the undertaking. But on Sunday, March 1st, 1926, the corner stone for a brick school building was laid by Dean Everard Pruente. In September of the same year the Sisters de Notre Dame took charge of the School.

*Ozora* is the youngest parish of old Ste. Genevieve County; but it has one of the finest churches in a far wider circle. It is dedicated to the *Sacred Heart*. Father Bernard Kramper is the pastor and builder. *Sereno* is the youngest parish in Perry County. *Our Lady of the Victory* is the name of its church. The Rev. William V. Roche is the pastor of Sereno. *St. Joseph's* Church in *Tiff*, Washington County, is in charge of the Rev. John Cook. Its school is conducted by a lay teacher.

*St. Anthony's* Parish at *Centaur*, St. Louis County, was organized on October 18th, 1908, by the Rev. Charles Keller, who said the first mass at the place on that day. Since Father McCartney's arrival the Mission of Chesterfield seems to have outstripped Centaur, as it was there the new church of the parish was built.

The Parish of the *Holy Ghost, Kinloch Park* is one of the latest foundations in the Archdiocese. The Rev. James J. Downes is its pastor. He resides at Villa St. Joseph in Ferguson.

On December 12th, 1924, the last of the churches founded in the immediate neighborhood of the city of St. Louis, the *Immaculate Conception of West Alton*. St. Charles County, began its parochial existence. The territory formed part of the ancient parish of Portage des Sioux. But as it is all bottom land, and at times partly under water, the Catholics living just opposite to Alton on somewhat higher ground asked for the establishment of a separate parish. The first parish building was a combination church and school. It was dedicated May 17th, 1925. The rectory was completed in September of the same year. The congregation consists of forty families, German and Irish. The founder of West Alton parish and its pastor is the Rev. August Fechtel.

CHAPTER 13

CIVIC AND SOCIAL ENDEAVORS

The whole world is God's creation and the object of His providence, Whilst the Church, as its noblest part, requires the supreme attention of all, the state also and the realms of science and art, and all human endeavor, lay claim to a fair share of man's interest and care. A churchman's proper sphere is religion: yet the needs of society, the schemes of politics and statesmanship, the progress of civilization, discovery and invention are not thereby excluded from his solicitude. "Nihil humaniame alienum puto," remains a proper maxime for the spiritual leader as well as for any other leader of men. For the right solution of many civic questions, and the proper adjustment of worldly affairs, have a strong bearing on man's true destiny as an heir of God's Kingdom.

The Federal Census taken up every decade and published to the world is a case in point. The relative strength of Catholicity in this country has been a matter of controversy since the founding of the nation. Our Catholic Directories were considered unreliable as exaggerating the number of Catholics: the Federal Census was condemned for falling short of what was considered a fair estimate. No doubt, both were untrustworthy in many particulars and, consequently, of no scientific value. In order to get the correct data on this interesting and important matter, the Census Bureau in Washington in the Spring of 1907, appointed Archbishop Glennon of St. Louis, a Special Commissioner of the Government to supervise the compilation of an accurate census of the Catholic population of the United States. This appointment was made in accordance with the suggestion made to the Government by the Archbishops of the country. Archbishop Glennon accepted the appointment, and, at once, informed all the bishops of the course of action to be taken. Father J. J. Tannrath was appointed Chief Assistant to the Archbishop. The work accomplished by the Special Commission was embodied in the Federal Census Report, and for the first time gave an approximately correct account of the number of Catholics in the United States.

The local history of the Church also found a strong advocate in Archbishop Glennon. It had been well said that, "we cannot understand anything human unless we know how it grew." The Catholic Church in the Mississippi Valley is a historical fact of outstanding greatness and splendor. All who have eyes to see, can see it. But it remains an impenetrable mystery to the mind unless we know its origin and the

(707)

stages of its development. It was the Centennial Year of the foundation of St. Louis 1909. On October 7th thousands of St. Louis Catholics crossed the river to visit the earliest pilgrim-shrine in the Mississippi Valley in the quaint village of Cahokia. Archbishop Glennon was there, with Bishops Jaussen of Belleville and Hennessey of Wichita. The quaint weatherworn church, and the ancient cemetery with its crumbling tombstones, spoke to the visitors of the humble beginnings and severe trials of the Church they loved and honored. ''We stand here'' said the Archbishop, ''at the well-spring, the fountain-head, whence comes our city's prosperity and wealth. We stand at the fountain-head, and lo, above the fountain is the sign of the cross.'' ''I hope,'' he continued'' that in this meeting there shall be found the inspiration to establish a Catholic Historical Society, which will do for Catholic monuments, what the Missouri and Illinois Historical Societies, are doing in the civic order.''

This opportune suggestion was carried out by the Archbishop himself, on February 7th, 1917, at the close of the Junior Clergy Examinations. His Grace proposed the organization of a Society, whose object it should be to preserve the records and monuments of the Church in the territory subject to St. Louis in the early days. The proposal was accepted and the organization completed by May 1917. The Society published a quarterly Review for five years, under the editorship of the Rev. Charles L. Souvay, C. M., D. D.

On January 22nd, 1916, the Catholic Library, collected by Professor Wright, and devised by will to the Archdiocese, was incorporated in the St. Louis Public Library, to be conducted as a new Branch in the Headquarters of the Catholic Women's Association. It is now housed in the St. Louis University.

In March 1915, the American Headquarters of the Sodality of St. Peter Claver, devoted to the evangelization of Africa, was established in St. Louis. The Sodality publishes a tiny Magazine, called *The Negro Child*.

On January 18th, 1920, Archbishop Glennon dedicated the Catholic Students' Home at Columbus, designed as a community center for Catholic students attending the Missouri State University. Solemn Pontifical Mass was celebrated by Bishop Byrne at Sacred Heart Church : the Archbishop in his sermon emphasized the purpose and scope of a University as being to ''teach all truth:'' ''Though the introduction of a department of Sacred Science is impossible (under present conditions), yet its absence (from the University course) is a misfortune.

For from the totality of knowledge which the complete University is supposed to present, truths most fundamental and far reaching have to be omitted. The horizon of the University is circumscribed. God, heaven, and the human soul have no place there. . . It is to the task of adjusting and supplementing the work of the University that your Students' Hall, must dedicate itself.''

The building was erected through contributions made by the Knights of Columbus and Catholics generally.

On April 25th, 1920, a Pastoral Letter of the Archbishop announced the creation of a Diocesan Interinsurance Exchange, of which churches and all diocesan properties, including religious institutions may be insured. Rev. P. J. Dooley was appointed to take charge of the Exchange. Its capital was $125,000. The maximum amount accepted on any one risk was fixed at $50,000. The Exchange is different from the so-called Mutual Insurance Companies, in the sense that the premiums must be paid in full in cash and that there will be no further liability on the part of the insured: The Exchange has sustained some severe losses through the two destructive hurricanes[1] that visited the city of St. Louis in 1927: but was able to meet all obligations and remain fairly prosperous.

In regard to women's rights and political duties the Archbishop on May 20th, 1920, expressed his views in clearest terms: ''It remains to be determined how far the extension of woman's power in the field of politics makes for her greater dignity or more helpful influence. Time alone can decide. . . Since however, woman suffrage is now an accomplished fact, our Catholic women should realize that, whatever be its intrinsic merit, their duty is to participate in and exercise according to their own high ethical standards, the franchise that is theirs, not forgetting, however, their other high duties and rights, on which, after all, their lasting dignity and greatest influence must necessarily depend. . . Yours is to stand for the principles of the right; yours is the duty to have in mind the sanctity of the home, the protection of the weak, the care of the sick, the establishment of justice, the punishment of crime. In this way you may hope that your influence may be for good all along the line.''

The Students' Mission Crusade founded in 1919, held its first celebration in St. Louis on February 22nd, 1922. A large number of schools were represented.

The Sisters of the Blessed Sacrament, with Mother Catherine Drexel at their head, brought a family of four Winnebago Indians. About twenty religious Orders had interesting exhibits from their missionary fields, among them the Sisters of St. Joseph, the Loretto Sisters, the Little Helpers of the Holy Souls, the Fathers of the Holy Ghost, the Fathers of the Divine Word, the St. Peter Claver Mission Society, the Church Extension Society, the Apostolic Mission House and others.

---

1 May 8 and September 29, 1927.

The Mission Pageant and Exhibit was held at the First Regiment Armory. The religious services were held at the Cathedral. The Archbishop assisted at the solemn High Mass celebrated by Msgr. Beckman, Rector of the Cincinnati Seminary, and preached the missionary sermon.

In 1925 the St. Louis Mission Society was organized by Archbishop Glennon for the purpose of providing spiritual and material support for the home and foreign missions of the Church. It was also intended to serve as a sort of clearing house for all offerings given to the missions. Father Joseph P. Donovan, C. M., was its first President. The grand total received for distribution by the Society for 1926-1927 was $25,699.43: the grand total of mission charity of the Archdiocese was $117,232.45.

The first National Catholic Rural Life Conference was held in St. Louis on November 8-10, 1923. The Archbishop was greatly interested in the Conference and, in a hearty letter of invitation to the priests and people of his jurisdiction, expressed the hope that its deliberations would "result in constructive efforts for the improvement of the social and economic conditions of the farmers, who constitute so important a group in Society and the State."

## CHAPTER 14

## PATRIOTISM AND CHRISTIAN BROTHERHOOD

In brief address to the soldiers at Jefferson Barracks in November 1916, Archbishop Glennon stated his position on war and peace: "I hope our beloved country always will be free from the disasters of war; but if war should ever come, I hope, that not only will every soldier, but every civilian will stand by the flag and the country."

At that time we were still at peace with all the world, and were thankful for the favor. It was, therefore, eminently proper, that on the death of the venerable monarch of the ancient Catholic Empire of Austria, Francis Joseph, a Solemn Requiem should be celebrated for the repose of his soul. December 2nd, 1916, was the day for this memorial service. The Archbishop was celebrant, assisted by Fathers Lubeley and Eggemann. At the close of the ceremonies the Archbishop announced the fact the Requiem had been offered up for the late Emperor Francis Joseph of Austria; this announcement was repeated in German by Father Holweck, in Hungarian by Father Eggemann; by Father Nekula in Bohemian, by Father Linek in Slovak, by Father Kompare in Croatian and by Father Dzenazera in Ruthenian.

On January 27th, 1917, the Archbishop, at the request of the Holy Father, issued a touching appeal in behalf of the starving children of Belgium. Strong, sinister influences had for some time been at work among our people to draw the country into the vortex of the European conflict. In 1917, the United States took the first step for entering the war: diplomatic relations with Germany were broken off on February 4th. The Archbishop stated, that this measure did not necessarily mean war: the matter was in the hands of the President, who, no doubt, had facts in his possession of which the general public knew nothing. On Good Friday the President sent his war message to Congress: war with Germany was thereupon declared. "This is no week for any nation to proclaim war, the Archbishop had said on Palm Sunday, "Christ lifted up on the cross should be the center of our attention, allegiance, and devotion. . . We should not crucify Him anew in the blood of our brothers." Yet, the step taken by the Government was final: and it was now the duty of every American to support the President, loyally and openly, as the representative of lawful authority, leaving the responsibility to him and his advisers. Archbishop Glennon's name was joined to the names of seven other Archbishops of the country in the remarkable document of Catholic loyalty and patriotism sent to the President on April 19th, 1917.

(711)

On the first Sunday in May of the fateful year 1917, the Archbishop declared:

"It is not necessary for victory that we should abuse our enemies. The enthusiasm of patriotism that is inseparable from abuse is not well based. We should look to our conservation and our devotion to duty, praying that under Divine leadership there may come, not only peace, but good will as well, and brotherhood may be established."

The welfare of the American soldiers of the Catholic faith was the first object of the Archbishop's fatherly solicitude. These two hundred thousand young men must be supplied with chaplains; sacred vestments, vessels, and all the paraphernalia for Divine worship must be gathered; articles of devotion in great quantities must be ready for quick distribution; suitable meeting places and opportunities for healthful recreation should be always at hand.

This patriotic work was at once taken up by the Catholic people under the auspices of the Knights of Columbus and carried to a successful issue.

At the military High Mass which was held at Camp Maxwell on July 16th, the Archbishop praised the American soldiers as Sir Galahads, whose strength was as the strength of ten because he was pure of heart." When Pope Benedict's Peace Proposal was submitted to the United States and the Allies, Archbishop Glennon declared that, whilst it "was a great moral issue, it must be looked upon by American Catholics as a political move, which had no binding influence on them any more than on non-catholics. Yet, "it is a move for civilization's sake," said the prelate in conclusion. The Delegate Apostolic, Msgr. John Bonzano, who had just arrived in St. Louis to attend the Sixty-Second Annual Convention of the Central Verein, said in his address: "I feel, that the members of this organization would not be transgressing their rights as citizens, if they were to formulate a petition urging the Government to consider the Pope's pleas for universal peace."

But the war continued to drag along its devastating coils over sea and land. The excitement among a large class of our people grew to fever heat. Under cover of these hysterical manifestations the old Know-nothing hatred of everything German demanded measures that were plainly foolish and unjust.

There were about twenty Catholic parishes in the city that had been founded and kept up by congregations of German antecedents: but the use of the German tongue in Church, had been long ago restricted to a minimum by the pastors themselves, and generally discontinued in the schools. The language question in the German parishes of St. Louis was solving itself in the natural way of gradual reduction and extinction. Force was not necessary, not even advisable. But the war phrensy put it into the heads of some patriots, that the small remnants of Germanism must be eliminated. The request came before the Archbishop, and his answer was clear-cut and strong: "As I understand it, we are not making war on languages, but on false principles. In most of the so-called German Churches English is used to a greater extent than German. The announcements are made in both languages, and as a rule, only one of the Sunday sermons is in German.

"The question of eliminating the German language is being considered, and will, no doubt, be taken up in due time. I have the unquestionable right to suppress disloyalty or heresy in whatever language it is voiced, but no complaint of disloyalty or heresy in any St. Louis Church has come to me."

That pronouncement settled the matter for the Archdiocese of St. Louis. The process of gradual elimination went on as before.

In June, 1918, at the Solemn Military High Mass held on the grounds of the Orphanage of the Sisters of St. Joseph, in the presence of more than thirty thousand persons, the Archbishop took occasion to emphasize this point: "We are not fighting for Anglo-Saxon supremacy: we are fighting for the supremacy of justice and right, rather than the supremacy of race. Neither is this a war of languages. Language is but the vehicle of thought; and is cursed or blessed by the thinker, whose servant it is. Sentiments of disloyalty may find their place in any language, and equally so, sentiments of loyalty and fidelity."

From the start Archbishop Glennon was active in promoting every honorable measure that would secure for the Government the fullest measure "of men to fight, arms to fight with, ships to carry them, and food to sustain them."

The various liberty loan drives, the drive for the Red Cross, and for the Knights of Columbus war fund always found him as a ready spokesman and supporter.

At last came the armistice, the harbinger of peace. On Sunday, November 17th, 1918, a solemn Thanksgiving Service was held in the Cathedral, by the Rector, Father Gilfillan. The Archbishop's sermon on the occasion served to declare that we should rejoice in the victory, "not because our nation is victorious, nor even because our soldiers, our arms, are victorious, but because the principles for which we struggled are asserted in the victory of our arms."

The Archbishop's faith in President Wilson's honesty of purpose was rudely shaken by the cold reception of his appeal for justice to all nations, great or small, and especially "the oldest, most oppressed and most deserving of them all, the Irish nation." Then, came the exclusion of the Pope, the true Prince of Peace, from the Peace Conference at Versailles. And finally, the Treaty of Versailles embodying the Covenant of the League with all the "acts of conquest, every acre of ground stolen, every land looted and taken over by the looter," that we might through its Article X "give our approval and benediction to all the successful crimes of history, but also guarantee protection to the criminals," found the Archbishop's strongest opposition.

Peace was now assured, but it was not a Christian peace of justice tempered with mercy.

Distinguished foreigners, prominent in Church and State, leaders in culture and in war, now came flocking to the hospitable shores of America, to offer us their thanks for our great services, and incidentally to appeal for continued liberality to their impoverished nations. Archbishop Glennon extended a kindly, courteous welcome to them all, and helped to secure a friendly hearing for them. King Albert of Belgium came, and Cardinal Mercier of Malines. At a banquet tendered to the King by the city of St. Louis the Archbishop expressed the beautiful sentiment: "It is meet and just that we should now unite in beseeching the King of Kings and the Master of Nations, to bless us and to bring back to all peoples the reign of justice, prosperity and peace." Cardinal Mercier declared: "Belgium is still in sore straits financially. . .While here I shall discuss with Your Archbishop a plan of forming a Belgian Relief Commission, such as they have in New York, Baltimore and Washington."

On October 25th, 1919, the Cardinal held solemn Pontifical Requiem in commemoration of all the men of the Archdiocese who had made the supreme sacrifice in the World War.

Belgium needed help and received it from the people of St. Louis as well as from the other great cities of the country. But there was another country that found itself in far greater need than Belgium itself, Austria, Catholic Austria, or rather the pitiful remnant of what was once the great ancient empire of Austria, now reduced to actual starvation. "The Holy Father," said the Archbishop, "has asked the children of America to aid the starving children of Austria. . . Even the enemy countries, England, France, and Italy are hurrying to the rescue of these peoples; but so widespread is the misery that their help is insufficient, and especially is this true of Austria, where the shadow of death is over all the land. There are seventy thousand or more children in the diocese; and it is not too much to ask them to forward sixty or seventy thousand dollars." Again and again the Archbishop reverted to the subject of the starving children of Central Europe, especially of Austria, insisting that generous help must be given and given at once.

There are no reports or statistics at hand; but there can be no doubt that the Archdiocese of St. Louis contributed more than ten times its quota to alleviate the misery of the famishing people of Central Europe.

This beginning of the greatest work of charity any nation ever undertook, the rescue and relief of the suffering millions of war-torn Europe, was made in 1920. It was followed by a number of even grander efforts, partly under Catholic, partly under Civil management. The whole movement represented many millions of dollars, and in all of them the people of the St. Louis diocese took a leading part. It was the one bright radiance that illuminated the later days of Pope Benedict XV. The great heart that went out to all the peoples, was stilled in death on January 22nd, 1922. Pontifical Requiem for the repose of the soul of the dead Pontiff was celebrated at the Cathedral on Monday, January 30th. He had twice in 1915 and in 1917 set forth the basis whereon a just and honorable peace should have been concluded. His peace plans were rejected by the pride and fury of the belligerents. The world gained nothing by delaying the end of the conflict, but lost untold treasures in the destruction of the lives of millions of Europe's and America's noblest and best.

On February 7th, Cardinal Achille Ratti was chosen by the Conclave as Supreme Pontiff and assumed the name of Pius XI. The first Encyclical of the successor of Benedict XV gave Archbishop Glennon the occasion to point out the chief cause of war: the heresy of nationalism: ''Patriotism is a virtue; love of country is next to love of God; but nationalism is not dealing with the land we love in itself, for itself and its preservation, but it has to do with its relation toward others. Nationalism means that your nation must triumph over others, not alone by moral power, but by whatever means, diplomacy or arms, may be used in conquering. Nationalism calls for a super-nation.''

The last of the really distinguished public men to visit our city on a mission of comity, was the German Cardinal Michael von Faulhaber, Archbishop of Munich. He arrived in the city on May 8th, 1923, and received a magnificent reception. Like Cardinal Mercier, Cardinal Faulhaber, too, came to us to make propaganda for his country and his people: but he did it in such a consummate way that no one could feel it as irksome. Throughout the trying ordeal he maintained the dignity of a prince of the Church. ''The German people have the will to work,'' he said, ''They do not wish to live by charity, and they know that they cannot expect to eat the bread of other nations; that they must live by labor. I hope that international conditions will be established, which will provide work and subsistence for the people of all countries.'' The Cardinal, who had served as chief chaplain of the Bavarian forces, dwelt upon the friendly feelings entertained by the Bavarian soldiers for our American boys: "Our soldiers esteemed them highly, and I never heard any expression of bitterness regarding Americans. Our men often spoke of the clean soldierly appearances of the American troops, and I have known of our men feasting on hardtack which came over, in some way, from the American lines. Later, when the American soldiers were on the Rhine, all our people felt cordially toward them, and the people of the Rhineland sincerely regretted their departure."

Archbishop Glennon spoke in terms of admiration of the Cardinal's lovable personality as making the best kind of propaganda for his people and his country. Thus the prayer of the Archbishop made on the occasion of our entrance into the world war, was fulfilled: "that under divine leadership there may come, not only peace, but good will as well, and brotherhood may be established."

## CHAPTER 15

## ARCHBISHOP GLENNON AS AN ORATOR

Cardinal Hayes in his address before the Catholic Club of St. Louis on May 7th, 1925 paid the following tribute to Archbishop Glennon: "You have in your midst an eloquent voice that has been lifted up throughout the country. Our own beautiful Cathedral of St. Patrick's, in New York, has echoed his eloquence. And wherever it is announced that Archbishop Glennon is to preach, there are no empty pews. You think he is yours, but in reality he belongs to the entire Catholic Church of America."

This expression of admiration uttered by the Cardinal of New York, is a just, though inadequate, embodiment of a fact of which the Catholics of the United States in general seem to have a more vivid consciousness than the general Catholic public of Archbishop Glennon's own episcopal city. Not that they fail to recognize him as a clear, lucid and attractive speaker: but the fact is, that only the few have so far realized that our Archbishop has been recognized by his brother-bishops in the American hierarchy as the one outstanding pulpit orator since the death of Archbishop Patrick J. Ryan of Philadelphia. The cogent proof for what is here stated is the fact that for the last twenty-five years there was no ecclesiastical event of national importance, at which the Archbishop of St. Louis was not called upon to deliver the sermon appropriate to the occasion. From Montreal and New York, in the North to New Orleans and San Antonio in the sunny South, from Baltimore and Richmond in the East to Salt Lake City and Helena, Montana, in the Far West, in the great cities of the land, Washington, Philadelphia, Cincinnati, Chicago, Milwaukee, Detroit, Kansas City, Denver and quaint old Bardstown, the golden tones of his voice were heard, and their message, whether of joy or sorrow, of triumph or reproach, of clear quiet exposition or exultant fervor, was received with faith and joy into the hearts of thousands and thousands of hearers. There is a distinction which no other Churchman of our time enjoys, and it well merits a page in our history. In a certain sense Archbishop Glennon does "belong to the entire Catholic Church of America."

It would indeed, seem highly appropriate that the long series of Archbishop Glennon's acknowledged masterpieces of oratorical art should have begun at the Golden Jubilee Celebration of Archbishop Patrick J. Ryan of Philadelphia. The mantle of the departing prelate was to grace the shoulders of the rising leader of men. It was a grand opportunity: Archbishop Ryan, who fifty years before had come to St. Louis as a stranger, but had in a brief space "won all the West to the magic sway of his eloquence and amiable personality," was now celebrating the Golden Sacerdotal Jubilee; and the Coadjutor Archbishop of St. Louis had come to awaken the dearest memories of his heart with gentle touch but irresistible power. Archbishop Glennon's address was conceded to be the most eloquent of all, after that of Archbishop Ryan. This was in 1903. The next Church event of national interest and importance was the Centenary Celebration of the Baltimore Cathedral, April 29th and 30th, 1906. It was a deeply impressive celebration, not only through the assemblage of the American hierarchy, to mark an epoch in the life of the Church, but also through the memorable utterances of two high dignitaries of the Church on the great question agitating the nation, socialism and the undue aggregation of wealth. These two sermons, together with Archbishop John J. Keane's sermon in favor of Catholic schools, were extolled at the time, as "superb orations that gave a new impetus to American Catholic eloquences." The orators were styled "the three graces of American Catholic eloquence, Archbishop Ryan, the preacher of faith, Archbishop Glennon the preacher of hope, and Archbishop Keane, the preacher of love."

"I feel" said Archbishop Glennon "that there is spiritual electricity in the atmosphere of today; that there is a force in the very assembly, the most representative held in America in twenty years; that their is before me the synthesis of unusual promise and power."

On November 29th, 1906, the new Cathedral of Richmond, Virginia was dedicated by Cardinal Gibbons, assisted by many prelates and priests from all parts of the country. Archbishop Glennon and Archbishop Keane were chosen as the preachers of the joyful occasion: Archbishop Glennon's theme was "the Catholic Church established by God." "Eloquent and scholarly" were the epithets applied to the St. Louis Prelate's treatment of the subject.

The august ceremony of conferring the pallium on Archbishop Blenk of New Orleans was held on April 24th, 1907, in the ancient historic Church of St. Louis. Cardinal Gibbons, two Archbishops, and seventeen Bishops graced the occasion by their presence. Archbishop Glennon preached a sermon on the history and signification of the Pallium. It was pronounced one of the finest sermons ever heard in that historic edifice where the greatest orators of the Catholic Church have been heard."

After New Orleans came Kansas City, the former home of the Archbishop, with a pressing invitation: His Grace responded with one of the grandest pieces of forensic eloquence "On the Last Rose of Summer of Irish History": The occasion was the Feast of Ireland's

Patron Saint. Such a good judge of oratory as Father Phelan praised
the lecture as fully equal to the best that has been handed down to
us by a long line of Irish orators, all of whom have, at some time of
their life, tried their powers of thought and expression on this exacting
theme.'' In illustration he quotes a passage in which the Archbishop
speaks of the spirituality of the Irish race; the mystic light that has
·touched to transcendent beauty the better part of English poetry:

"That mystic light, it comes from the wild sea that washes the Irish
coasts; from the heather that covers its hills; from the moaning winds
that crowd its woods; from the woods themselves with their silent life
and mystic gloom; from the open meadows and the summer night;
from the banshee's cry, and the fairy's companionship; from out of
the scenery and association and life that become a part of the Irish
character, there comes that strange yearning, that great desire, that
unwillingness to be part of the common-place, that restlessness, energy
and fire which as a dissolvent set here in American life makes crass
materialism impossible and sets across the face of our land a rainbow
of light and hope, which in color, form and setting takes from the
earth its fascination and tells us of the better things and the brighter
land. So in the struggles of the past, the Irish exile has been with you
to fight for Liberty, civil and religious; and in these later days to
stand with those who struggle for law and order and constitutional
liberty, and then and not the least, to light these lives of ours with
the glow of their own color and the brightness of their own heart's
energy.''

The Archbishop was now in constant demand, whenever there was
a great celebration in any part of the country. He had to decline
invitations to Philadelphia and other places. It was the time when bids
for his own Cathedral were opened. New York was· to be the scene
of the Archbishop's next triumph. The Archdiocese of New York
was commemorating the Centenary of its foundation. 'Cardinal Gibbons
of Baltimore and Cardinal Logue, Primate of All Ireland, Msgr. Falconio, the Papal Delegate, ten Archbishops, forty Bishops and eight
hundred Priests were assembled in the historic Cathedral of St. Patrick.
Archbishop Glennon was accorded the distinguished honor of preaching
the sermon before this exalted audience. Needless to say, the Archbishop rose to the occasion with a magnificent discourse on the Divinity
of Christ. The sermon was based on the Encyclical of Pope Pius X,
on Modernism. "Of Archbishop Glennon's many happy efforts it
was beyond question the most filicitous,'' wrote one Catholic Editor,
and "The priests and people of New York are proud of the magnificent
display of Catholicity that was made during the celebration; but summing up the net results, they say, the two features that will remain

indelibly impressed on their memory will be the march of the Catholic millionaires in the street procession, and Archbishop Glennon's sermon.

His Grace, and with him the entire diocese, was busy for months, preceding the 18th of October, 1908, with the preparations for the corner stone laying of the new Cathedral of St. Louis. This in itself was a great national event, and right worthily did our Archbishop commemorate its deeper meaning, in a glowing tribute to the spirit of piety and self-sacrifice of his predecessors. The dedication on August 15th, 1909, of the beautiful Cathedral of St. Mary Magdalene in Salt Lake City marked the culminating point in the marvelous growth of the Catholic Church in Utah. It was the most impressive and solemn ceremony ever witnessed in the western half of the continent. Cardinal Gibbons was there among the princes of the western Church, and his magnetic influence was felt like a blessing; "But the climax came with the soul inspiring eloquence of Archbishop Glennon. He led his hearers like little children, and one felt that he, too, had the heart of a child. . . . As the gifted orator delivered his tribute to the two Mary's, contrasting the meanings of their lives, the great assemblage wept . . . Archbishop Glennon's peroration was one of the most perfect things ever uttered by human lips."

In November 1909, Kansas City was favored by the Archbishop once more. The lecture he delivered was entitled "The Lights of Home." It is a masterly delineation of the Christian home, with its constituent elements and "the lights that shine there, the lights of love, sacrifice and obedience.'"

The 20th day of December 1909, marked the twenty-fifth anniversary of Archbishop Glennon's ordination. As His Grace had forbidden any public demonstration in his honor, a suitable recognition of his standing and accomplishments both in St. Louis, and in the American hierarchy was planned by the priests of the diocese. President Taft sent an autograph letter of congratulation. Pope Pius X sent the apostolic benediction. Archbishop Ryan came in person to offer his best greetings.

Two great ecclesiastical events in the Northeast; the Eucharistic Congress held in Montreal, Canada, September 1910, and the Consecration of St. Patrick's Cathedral at New York in October of the same year brought forth two additional "gems of purest ray serene" in the rich domain of Archbishop Glennon's oratorical masterpieces. Cardinal Vincenzo Vauntelli, old in years, but young in spirit and energy, was the special envoy of the Pope to the Eucharistic Congress. Bishops and priests from all parts of the world were in attendance. It was the greatest convocation of churchmen that ever met on this side of the Atlantic. Three Cardinals, eighty Archbishops, and a vast multitude of Bishops, prelates, and priests, distinguished for sacred science, philosophical depth, administrative ability and effective leadership, crowded around the center of Catholic unity, the Blessed Eucharist. Archbishop Glennon preached a powerful sermon at St. Patrick's church on the Triumph of the Eucharistic King. Cardinal Vanutelli accompanied Archbishop Glennon to St. Louis, and was accorded a general reception by the Catholics of the city. Both dignitaries then wended their way eastward to New York to participate in the Consecration of its great St. Patrick's Cathedral. Archbishop Glennon delivered the consecration sermon. It is a masterpiece of pulpit eloquence, generously instructive and full of timely thoughts couched in beautiful expression. The first part is devoted to the memory of the high-minded generous men who presided over the destinies of the mighty archdiocese of our country: the preacher then drives home a few salutary thoughts:

"Democracy, when right, is divine, but when it goes wrong, it is revolution. The popular will must have leaders, and their leadership must partake the responsibility of an apostle and the unselfishness of a saint. To face the tide of the times the solid principles of justice must be preached: the straight lines of equity must be proclaimed: the changeless teachings of a changeless creed of a changeless God must be told and retold: winged words spoken by lips that are touched by fire must speak for man's social regeneration and his eternal redemption."

The following year, 1911, was saddened for many throughout the land by the death of the good Archbishop of Philadelphia, Patrick J. Ryan.

As a matter of course Archbishop Glennon was invited to preach the funeral sermon. It was a beautiful tribute to the life and achievements of the dead prelate, the eulogy of a friend who felt a deep sorrow and the touch of a personal bereavement.

"Archbishop Ryan, like unto all that are truly great, was an humble man. He sought no preferments: he expected no honors, and consequently he was never disappointed. When the call of Philadelphia came to him in 1883, he was surprised and saddened. He would not come if his own sympathies and sentiments were considered, but the call was from the Vicar of Christ. It was a command, and all commands of the Holy Church were sacred to him. But when he came he brought all the strength and goodness and consecration of his great soul. And if he sometimes cast lingering glances backward to his beloved St. Louis, it was only the natural promptings of his heart, for nearly all the friends he knew were there, and Archbishop Ryan never forgot a friend."

Once more did the city of Baltimore require the presence of Archbishop Glennon. The occasion was the Golden Jubilee of its Cardinal-Archbishop, James Gibbons, October 15th, 1911. Surrounded by the largest number of prelates of the Church that ever came together in the United States, Cardinal James Gibbons celebrated the Golden Jubilee as a priest and the Silver Jubilee as a member of the Sacred College of Cardinals. The venerable Cathedral was crowded and thousands waited outside to view the procession. Archbishop Glennon's sermon paid a loving tribute to the Jubilarian, "the gentlest of gentlemen, and. the most loved public man in America today." comparing his qualities with the devotion for his country of Richelieu, the unstained citizenship of Newman, and the democracy of Manning.

Two Cathedral dedications, one in Wichita, Kansas, and the other in Denver, Colorado, were attended by the Archbishop in the late Fall of 1911.

Cardinal Gibbons and the Archbishop traveled together to Wichita. The subject of the Metropolitan's sermon was: "How we would make America Catholic."

At the Denver celebration, Cardinal Farley of New York took the place of the Cardinal of Baltimore; but the preacher of the occasion was the same Metropolitan of the St. Louis Archdiocese. The theme of his sermon was: "The Sanctity of the Church Yesterday, Today and Forever."

The two years from 1911 to 1913 were busy years of the Cathedral builder of St. Louis. For his great monument was gradually nearing completion and a second mighty effort, the erection of a grand Seminary, was in contemplation. Besides the requirements of his episcopal office consumed much time and energy. Yet His Grace was ready for the call to Belleville when the saintly Bishop Janssen died in July 1913, and at the funeral he spoke touching words of sympathy and love in memory of the beautiful quiet unostentatious life of the departed high priest of the diocese of Belleville.

On May 18th, 1914, the Archbishop of St. Louis announced his proposed visit to Rome. On the 14th day of June, he started for Ireland, and on June 29th, he preached at the consecration of . the Plunket Memorial church in Drogheda, in the very heart of Ulster. Archbishop Oliver Plunket, Archbishop of Arenagh and Primate of all Ireland in the last half of the Seventeenth century, was condemned to death by English Tyranny, hanged and drawn and quartered, July 11th, 1681. "The words of burning eloquence," wrote the *Drogheda Independent* of July 4th, 1914, "in which the Archbishop of St. Louis told us of the sorrows and sufferings and Martyrdoms undergone by our coreligionists

for the faith of which we are all proud. . . will long remain a memory
with those who heard them.''

Archbishop Glennon had a private audience with Pope Pius X:
On his homeward voyage, he remained unaware of the gentle Holy
Father's death: But on August 30th, he gave the Papal benediction to
all the people of the diocese. The ceremony occurred in the Old
Cathedral. ''There is a quality now attached to this privilege which has
in it a great deal of pathos. Since conceding the privilege Pius X has
died. Let us hope that the blessing comes from him above.''

And so occasion after occasion approaches and meets a gracious
response: the Diamond Jubilee of St. Mary-of-the-Woods; the Consecration of Bishop Brossart of Covington; the Centennial of the Bardstown Cathedral designated as ''the historic Shrine of the West,'' the
Centennial of our own dear Old Cathedral, and the Seventy-Fifth
Anniversary of Chicago as a Catholic diocese, all, occasions, well calculated to open the hidden springs of true heart-stirring eloquence.
There are so many others that demand with more than equal right,
a brief mention here: and before all others, the death of Cardinal
Gibbons in 1921 and death of Pope Benedict XV in 1922. The eulogy
on the dead Cardinal of Baltimore emphasized his outstanding great
qualities, as a leader of the army of God, a wise legislator, an educator
of far-reaching vision and a great patriot, all embodied in the ''kindly
gentle old man whose coming was a joy, whose presence was a benediction.''

The eulogy on Pope Benedict, being delivered in the St. Louis
Cathedral, does not, strictly speaking, pertain to this series which is
intended to show that Archbishop Glennon belongs, in a manner, to the
entire country: yet its object of universal sorrow, and its brief, deeply
felt and most touching accents, merit for it a place among the acknowledged masterpieces of the Archbishop: ''Benedict was not neutral, but
as between the warring nations, he was impartial. Undoubtedly protected by the Spirit of God and the charity of Christ, he never faltered
and never yielded. Unswayed he stood above passion, greed and
prejudices of men and nations, and he stood alone. . .''

The Diamond Jubilee of the diocese of Galveston, occurred on March
14th, 1922. The sermon on the occasion was preached by Archbishop
Glennon. It was a song of praise and thanksgiving raised to God for
the strong men of faith who carried the cross from East to West, and
from West to East over the wide savannahs of Texas; the Franciscan
Padres and the Lazarist missionaries.

After the Diamond Jubilee in the South came the consecration of
the Cathedrals of Omaha in the North: then the death of Bishop
Burke of St. Joseph, and then the death of Bishop James Ryan of Alton,

and finally the dedication of the Seminary of New Orleans, all within
the period of two years.   In 1924 followed the consecration of the
Cathedral of Helena, Montana, and the Funeral of Archbishop Moeller
of Cincinnati, in 1925.

There are many more sermons and addresses of Archbishop Glennon, preached on more or less memorable occasions, at home and abroad,
and preserved only in the files of forgotten newspapers, sermons and
addresses which, if gathered would form a conspectus of the high points
of Catholic American History during the Quarter, Century just elapsed.
They show the aptness of the New York Cardinals saying: ''You think
he is yours; but he belongs to the entire Church of America.''

It is a memorable fact that, since his elevation to the Metropolitan
see of St. Louis, he was called upon to give expression to the joy or
sorrow, the triumph and gratitude, the hope and courage and supreme
confidence of the Church of God in America on almost all the great
occasions of the last twenty-five years.

Like all true Irishmen, Archbishop Glennon is a poet at heart,
although he shuns the fetters of verse and rhyme.   His prose is rhythmic
like the sea in its varing moods.   His vision of life is that of a mystic,
a dreamer, if you will, whose dreams are bound to come true, because
they are not mere imaginings, but real visions, with force of character
behind them.   He sees the hand of God in the order and beauty of nature
and the vicissitudes of life, and he has the mysterious power of making
his hearers catch a passing glimpse, here and there, of the unseen world
around them.

## CHAPTER 16

## VARIOUS ECCLESIASTICAL PROMOTIONS

During Archbishop Kenrick's regime St. Louis was known as the Mother of Bishops. And justly so. For from 1849 to 1888 the Archbishop of St. Louis consecrated sixteen Bishops, ten of them having been chosen from the secular clergy of the Diocese and six from various religious Orders, Jesuits, Dominicans and Trappists. Since 1888 that particular glory had departed from the St. Louis, although (in 1903, a member of the St. Louis clergy, Father Jeremiah J. Harty, was chosen by the Holy See as Archbishop of Manila, but received his consecration at Rome,) and on June 29th, 1896, the Archbishop of St. Louis, John J. Kain, was called upon to consecrate a priest of Kansas City, Father John J. Glennon, who was ultimately to succeed him in St. Louis.

But in 1918 a change came over the scene. On November 10th, Archbishop Glennon for the first time had the honor of consecrating a Bishop: It was the former pastor of the Church of the Holy Name in St. Louis, Christopher E. Byrne, a native Missourian, whom the Holy See had appointed Bishop of Galveston. Owing to the influenza, prevailing at the time, church gatherings were prohibited. Hence only a small congregation of friends attended the consecration services, but the clergy were well represented. Bishops Thomas F. Lillis, of Kansas City, and John B. Morris of Little Rock acted as co-consecrators with the Archbishop. Father Patrick Dooley was the preacher of the day. The other Bishops, honoring the memorable event with their presence, were: John J. Hennessy of Wichita, John Ward of Leavenworth, E. P. Allen of Mobile, Thophile Merschaert, of Oklahoma City, Cornelius Van de Ven of Alexandria, La.; Joseph S. Glass, C.M., Salt Lake City; J. H. Tihen of Denver; and J. S. Gunn of Natchez. Besides these prelates there were a number of Monsignori and other distinguished priests from Texas, Illinois, Kansas and Missouri. Bishop Byrne was born at Byrnesville, Missouri, on April 21st, 1867. He made his classical studies at St. Mary's College, Kansas, and his philosophical and theological course at St. Mary's Seminary, Baltimore. He was ordained by Archbishop Kenrick on September 23rd, 1891, and assigned as assistant to St. Bridget's Church, St. Louis. Serving in that capacity until June 16th, 1897, he was made pastor of Sacred Heart Church, Columbia, and on December 6th, 1899 became Permanent Rector of St. Joseph's Church, Edina. On January 27th, 1911, Father Byrne resigned the charge of Edina, and received the appointment to the Holy Name Church in St. Louis.

Here he made large improvements on the school, and increased the attendance threefold. He built the beautiful new church, the first one in the Romanesque style, in the city. He held a number of important diocesan offices and was for six years the Manager of the *"Church Progress."* The Diocese of Galveston, was founded by the St. Louis Lazarists, John Timon and John M. Odin. But long before their coming, ever since Coronado's expedition, the Sons of St. Francis of Assisi, Father Massenet and his noble companions and successors, had labored among the Indian tribes of the country until their Missions were suppressed by the Spanish Government in 1824.

On May 2nd, 1840, Father Odin left the Seminary of St. Mary's in Perry County, Missouri, in company of Father Dutreluingne, on his mission to Texas. Father John Timon, the Superior of the Lazarists had been appointed Prefect Apostolic, but had in turn appointed Father John M. Odin, Vice Prefect-Apostolic. In 1847, the State of Texas was erected into a Diocese, with the See of Galveston, and John M. Odin became its first Bishop. On his appointment to the Archdiocese of New Orleans, Bishop Claude Marie Dubuis succeeded to the See, October 21st, 1862. Bishop Nicholas Aloysius Gallagher was the third Bishop of Galveston. Bishop Christopher E. Byrne is the fourth, a worthy successor to the great and good men that preceded him.

Archbishop Glennon's second consecration of a Bishop took place on November 8th, 1922, in the Cathedral, of which the new Bishop, Francis Gilfillan had been Rector, since its foundation. Bishop Gilfillan had the appointment as Coadjutor to Bishop Maurice F. Burke of St. Joseph, and was soon to follow that learned and pious Prelate as the Ordinary of the See. The Archbishop, as consecrating Prelate, was assisted by Bishops Christopher E. Byrne of Galveston and Thomas F. Lillis of Kansas City. Twelve other Bishops, a number of Monsignori, a large delegation of priests from St. Joseph and more than three hundred visiting and local clergy took part in the sublime ceremonies.

The Bishops were: Jeremiah J. Harty of Omaha; Thomas J. Shahan of the Catholic University at Washington; Joseph Chartrand of Indianapolis; Edmond Heelan of Sioux City, Iowa; John Ward of Leavenworth; Francis J. Tief of Concordia; Kansas; Henry Althoff of Belleville; J. H. Tihen of Denver; Schwertner of Wichita; P. J. Keane of Sacramento, Cal.; Bishop Maurice F. Burke's infirmities prevented his attendance. The Rector of Kenrick Seminary, Dr. Ryan, in the touching peroration of his sermon said: "To us, beloved Bishop, as to yourself, the future is a sealed book; but, judging from your well-known piety and learning, we confidently pray and expect, that the future will reveal the glory of the past not only undimmed but enhanced in splendor."

On Saturday, March 17th, 1923, Bishop Maurice F. Burke departed this life; and Bishop Francis Gilfillan was Bishop of St. Joseph. Archbishop Glennon preached the funeral sermon describing the departed prelate, in the threefold character of the priest, the gentleman and the scholar.''

The year 1923 marked the well merited elevation of four distinguished priests of the Archdiocese to the dignity of Domestic Prelates of the Pope's Household.

Monsignor Frederick G. Holweck, Pastor of St. Francis de Sales Church, was invested with the proper insignia on Sunday, May 6th; Monsignor Timothy Dempsey, Pastor of Old St. Patrick's, on Ascension Thursday, May 10th, in the morning, Monsignor F. X. Willmes, Pastor of St. Peter's church, St. Charles, on the evening of the same day; and Monsignor Martin S. Brennan, Pastor of S.S. Mary and Joseph's, Carondelet, on Sunday, May 27th.

The Archbishop officiated at all these ceremonies, and was delighted with the many marks of approval his four-fold choice of men to be honored above others, met on all sides.

The Centenary Celebration of the coming of the Jesuits to St. Louis, June 21st, 1923, was an event of greatest import and magnificence. There were present in the sanctuary of St. Francis Xavier's church six visiting Bishops, five Provincials of the Society of Jesus, Presidents of eleven Jesuit Colleges of the Missouri Province, members of the St. Louis University faculty and a number of priests of the city and diocese. The Bishops in attendance were: Patrick A. McGovern of Cheyenne; Edmond Heelan of Sioux City; Anthony J. Schuler of El Paso; Francis Gilfillan of St. Joseph, and Patrick Richard Heffron.

Bishop Lillis of Kansas City sang the Solemn High Mass, and Archbishop Glennon delivered the sermon, which was a masterly presentation of the grand and far-reaching works effected within a century by the Missouri Province in education, in the Indian missions, in the defense of the Church against heresy and infidelity, in the ever watchful care for the immigrant in the one time wilderness of the West.

Scarcely ten months had passed when the the Church of St. Francis Xavier once again saw a large gathering of Bishops and high dignitaries in its sanctuary. The occasion was the consecration of Bishop Joseph A. Murphy of British Honduras. Bishop Murphy was a member of the Society of Jesus. He had been stationed at St. Louis University since 1919. Archbishop Glennon was the consecrating Prelate, with Bishops Joseph Chartrand of Indianapolis and Anthony J. Schuler of El Paso. Others of Episcopal rank present in the sanctuary were: Bishops Thomas A. Lillis of Kansas City; Francis Gilfillan of St. Joseph;

Henry Althoff of Belleville; James A. Griffin of Springfield, Ill.; Bishop
F. J. Tief of Concordia; Alphonse Smith of Nashville and E. D. Howard
of Davenport.

Father M. J. O'Connor, S. J., of the St. Louis University at the
close of his sermon paid a glowing tribute to his almost life-long friend
Bishop Murphy:

"Weighty indeed, is the obligation that comes to Father Murphy
this morning; difficult, indeed, the fulfilling of the charge that enters
into his life. And yet, as with glistening eyes we view this splendid
ceremony, to see him take on the character of a bishop, there is no
misgiving in our hearts. For Father Murphy in his priestly years had
proved good and true and loyal; and Bishop Murphy will bear the
burden that is put upon him, grandly." In the month of April 1924,
the Archbishop secured the so-called Walsh Mansion on Lindell Boulevard and Taylor Avenue, and made it the Archiepiscopal Residence,
devoting his old residence, 3810 Lindell Boulevard, to chancery and
other diocesan purposes. The new residence is an imposing structure,
situated only one block from the Cathedral.

Here in May 1925, he received the visit of Cardinal Hayes, Archbishop of New York and a number of other dignitaries of the clergy
and laity. On June 7th, however, he announced his impending departure for Rome. On June 30th, the Archbishop was received in private
audience by the Pope. On August 26th, he was back again at his post
of duty. In an interview given to the *Post-Dispatch* the Archbishop
spoke of his impressions gained in Ireland, France and Italy. Of Pope
Pius XI he said: "He is most affable and cultured. His career before
his elevation brought him into contact with books and people: hence
his knowledge of literature and language. At the audience to the
laity from St. Louis, as the Holy Father had understood that some were
of German extraction, he spoke to them in German. While he under-
stands English well, he does not speak it fluently."

It was the year of the Jubilee 1925: Pilgrimages in great numbers
were made to the Eternal City to gain the indulgence. But for the
great mass of Catholics a journey to Rome was simply impossible.
Hence the Holy Father extended the Jubilee celebration for another
year, with the favor that all visits could be performed in their home-
cities, towns and villages. On February 19th, 1926 the Archbishop
issued his Jubilee Letter.

In St. Louis the churches to be visited were the Old Cathedral,
St. John's Basilica, St. Francis Xavier's church and the Cathedral.
Since the death of Monsignor Hoog on April 1925, the Archbishop had

VICAR-GENERAL MSGR. F. G. **HOLWECK**, D.D.

no Vicar-General. But on January 6th, 1926 His Grace appointed Msgr. Frederick G. Holweck and Father Patrick P. Crane to this, the highest office in the diocese, save that of the Archbishop himself.

Vicar-General Crane is a comparatively young man; but has a wide experience gained as a member of the Diocesan Mission Band, and in general pastoral work.

Monsignor Frederick George Holweck was a many-sided man, distinguished as a pastor and leader of men, as well as a man of science, gifted with a restless spirit of enquiry and research, an authority on liturgy and Canon Law, an historian of note, a critical student of Hagiology, Latin and Greek Hymnology, and the Feasts of Our Lord and His Blessed Mother. In recognition of his extensive and solid learning, as displayed in the "Biographical Dictionary of Saints," and the "Calendarium of the Feasts of Our Lord and His Blessed Mother," (in Latin) the University of Freiburg conferred upon Msgr. Holweck the honorary Doctorate of Theology. During his almost fifty years of priestly life, Father Holweck, as he preferred to be called until the last, was a staunch supporter of the Catholic Press, not only by subscriptions but also by practical cooperation. He contributed more or less regularly to the *Herold des Glaubens,* the *Amerika,* the *Pastoral-Blatt* (of which he was the last Editor) the *Fortnightly Review,* and the *St. Louis Catholic Historical Review.* The *Illinois Catholic Historical Review,* and the *Catholic Historical Review* of Washington, D. C. He also wrote contributions for the *Catholic Encyclopedia* and *Herder's Konversationslexikon.*

The Biographical Dictionary of the Saints is admittedly the best and most complete reference work of its kind in the English language.

The *Calendarium* is simply unique, as there is nothing like it in any language.

Monsignor Holweck, V. G., died February 15th, 1925 at the age of seventy, full of honors, full of merits. "What makes the greatness of this Prelate more apparent," wrote the *Western Watchman* on the occasion of his death, "is that he was ever humble, always condescending. One could seek his advice and find him easily accessible. And one could come away satisfied, knowing that the advice he offered, and the solutions he gave, had for backgrounds long years of profound research, and a record of unblemished virtue." As a man he possessed the saving sense of humor, in an eminent degree: he was full of "quips and cranks," and he had an inimitable way of telling a funny story, but he never used illegitimate means to provoke a laugh, or to convey a sting.

He had the hearty cheerfulness of manner that made every one feel at home in his presence. Its immediate expression was the sympathy for the poor, the suffering, the despised and down-trodden everywhere. Of all the priests in the diocese, there was none that could compare with Monsignor Holweck in the extent of his charities extended to the impoverished and famine-stricken bishops, priests, nuns, and helpless women and children and their husbands and fathers, of Germany and Austria. Many a good and worthy soul would have sunk beneath the heavy load of misery, if Monsignor Holweck had not turned the ever flowing resources of his parishioners and friends, far and near, into the broad stream of Christian charity that, like the gulf stream, warmed and cheered and vivified.

## CHAPTER 17

# THE BROTHERS OF MARY AND THE RESURRECTIONISTS

The latest religious Orders of Men to find a home in St. Louis were the Marianists, commonly called the Brothers of Mary, and the Resurrectionist Fathers. Two others: the Servites (O.S.M.) and the Oblate Fathers of Mary Immaculate (O.M.T.) are employed in missionary and pastoral work, but have not erected an institution of their respective Orders in the diocese.

The Society of Mary, as the Marianists are officially styled, "is composed of priests and brothers, who all make the same vows, observe the same rule, and pursue the same works of zeal under the standard of Mary Immaculate."

A novelty in monastic life is introduced in so far as that "priests and brothers enjoy the same privileges in the Society of Mary. They have the same representation in the administration of the Society, and can hold the same positions, except such as are reserved to the priests by cannon law. They live together, take their meals together, and spend their recreations together."

As in all other religious associations in the Church, the object of the Society is twofold; namely, the personal sanctification of its members, and the salvation of souls. The latter is accomplished principally through the Christian education of youth, with which the Society combines the works of the sacred ministry: preaching, retreats and missions, wherever Divine Providence and the Holy See call the apostolic laborers of the institution."[1]

The founder of the Society of Mary, William Joseph Chaminade, was born in Perigueux, a small city sixty miles northeast of Bordeaux, France, on the eighth of April, 1761.

William Joseph and his brother Louis received their early training for the ministry in the College of Wussidan, near their home town, where their elder brother John, a member of the Society of Jesus, was professor. They attended the University of Bordeaux for philosophy and the Seminary of St. Sulpice in Paris for their course in theology. Both were raised to the holy priesthood in 1784 and returned to the College of Mussidan as professors, and in the following year three Chaminade Brothers assumed control of the College. Everything might have gone well, in a worldly sense, with William Joseph Chami-

---

1 From "A Nineteenth Century Apostle of Mary," passim, and Prospectus of the Society of Mary, p. 23.

nade: for his talents and devotion to duty were bound to attain early recognition.

But the terrors of the Revolution forced the College to close its door, and drove the youthful priest to Bordeaux, where he bought the Villa St. Lawrence, and hid himself from the persecutors. This life of alarms lasted until 1797: but in October of that year divine Providence led him to Saragossa in Spain. It was, on the feast of Our Lady of the Pillar, when he arrived. Here he received the inspiration to found the Society of Mary for men, and the Daughters of Mary for women.

The seed-grain from which the Society of Mary developed was a Sodality. On May 1st, 1817, Father Chaminade addressed Father Lelanne, one of the .most brilliant, energetic and influential sodalists: "Let us form a religious institute, having the three vows of religion, but having no particular name, no distinctive costume, and as much as possible, not even a corporate life."

Father Lalanne gladly accepted the call, and both priests spoke privately to a number of other Sodalists. Seven young men, Father Lalanne included, declared formally and publicly to their director that they placed themselves entirely at his disposal, that they chose him as their religious superior.

They were from various walks of life. Two were preparing for Holy Orders, one was a college professor, two were business men, two were coopers by trade. Thus from the very beginnings, the Society of Mary embodied in itself both priests and lay members. The latter are popularly spoken of as the Brothers, though in the Society this term includes the clerical as well as the lay members."[2]

Father Chaminade pledged his most cherished enterprise, the Society of Mary, to the work of educating youth.

After the first novitiate of the Society was established in the Villa St. Lawrence at Bordeaux, calls for religious came from all parts of France, and even from foreign countries. Before the death of the Founder, in 1850, the Society of Mary numbered four provinces, sixty establishments and nearly five hundred members in France, Switzerland and America.

It was in 1849, one year before the death of the venerated founder, that the Society was introduced into the United States by one of his most cherished and faithful disciples, the Rev. Leo Meyer. It grew and spread quickly and without obstacle, and today there are two flourishing provinces of the Society of Mary in the United States. One has headquarters at Mt. St. John, Dayton, Ohio, and is known as the Cincinnati Province. The other has its central house at Mary-

---

2  ''A Nineteenth Century Apostle of Mary,'' pp. 20-21.

hurst Normal, Kirkwood, Missouri, and is called the St. Louis Province. But how did the foundation of the St. Louis Province of the Brothers of Mary come about? In 1897 the Rev. Francis S. Goller, pastor of S. S. Peter and Paul's parish in St. Louis called at the Novitiate of the Society in Dayton, Ohio, for the purpose of securing brothers for his school. The request was granted. In September the school opened with three Brothers as a Grade and Commercial High School. The High School drew pupils from every part of the city and constantly extended its usefulness. In 1913 the new pastor of S. S. Peter and Paul, Father Hoog placed the higher grades of what was heretofore a parochial institution in charge of the diocesan High School Board under the new designation: The Kenrick High School. The Brothers of Mary were continued in office, and when in 1913, the school was removed to a new and more central location on Locust Street, they furnished the teaching staff. The Commercial High School being gone, S. S. Peter and Paul's School was reduced to its former condition of a grade school, with the Brothers of Mary in charge.

In 1916 the Kenrick High was removed from Locust to Stoddard Street, near St. Bridget's Church and finally, in 1924, to that monument of classic refinement the new High School building, erected on Kingshighway through the munificence of Mrs. William Cullen McBride. As it was intended for a memorial to her departed husband, the name of Kenrick now lapsed in favor of McBride. The present faculty of the McBride High School numbers twenty-two members, who all belong to the Society of Mary.

In 1828 the Archdiocese erected a tasteful and commodious residence for the Brothers. The only other School taken over by the Brothers of Mary was that of St. Anthony of Padua.[3]

But this enterprise was only the opening wedge. In 1908 the Brothers of Mary formed the Province of St. Louis. They established their Postulate and Novitiate at the Villa St. Joseph in Ferguson, St. Louis County. The Postulate is intended to receive and train boys whose age ranges between 13 and 16 years, who earnestly desire to become members of the Society. The Novitiate continues this training under the direction of a priest who is called the Novice-Master. The novices are occupied principally in studies of a religious nature. The novitiate lasts one year: then if the novices persevere, they are admitted to the profession of vows. The first vows are usually made for one year: and never more than three years. After the novitiate comes the scholasticate which extends over a period of several years. The scholastics wear the costume of the Brothers: and they are regarded as members of the Society. Most of them are employed in

---

[3] Answers to Questionnaire.

teaching: those that have a vocation to the priesthood, make the usual course of studies as pursued in other Seminaries.[4]

The home of the postulants and novices of the Society remained at Villa St. Joseph in Ferguson until 1909, when the Chaminade College Building at Clayton was erected. But only the Postulate was transferred to its classic halls, whilst the Novitiate remained at Ferguson. The rapid and substantial growth of Chaminade College obliged the Superiors of the Society to look for a suitable property on which to build the Mother-house of the St. Louis Province. The Brownhurst homestead, situated on the Big Bend and Denny Roads, just outside of Kirkwood was bought in 1918, and the Novitiate of the Order was transferred there. A large building was erected on the grounds. The new property was named Maryhurst. The inauguration of this building as the residence of the Provincial and Inspector and as Postulate and Scholasticate took place on August 15th, 1922. Chaminade College, which had been the Mother-house of the St. Louis Province until 1917, was superseded by Maryhurst; but it continued its remarkable march of progress as an institution of learning. On its opening day in September 1910 it had only seventeen students and fourteen years later two hundred and twelve. The succession of Presidents at the College were: Rev. August Frische, Rev. Andrew Huder, Rev. Louis A. Tragesser, Brother Francis A. Meyer, Rev. Joseph E. Ei, and Rev. Albert H. Rabe.

A Gymnasium costing $90,000., was added to the College buildings in 1921 and a dwelling for the Sisters in 1923. The grounds embrace one hundred acres of rolling prairie and woodland giving exceptional facilities for College purposes.

"The Brothers of Mary are convinced, that the welfare of our country is bound up intimately with the work of the Catholic Church, and that the interests of the Church are best fostered by the thorough Christian education of the youth of our land. But whilst they insist that the eternal welfare of the pupils must be sought above all things, they employ the best means and methods that can assure full success to them in the various careers of social and commercial life."[5]

A similar purpose is manifested by the only Institution of the Resurrectionist Fathers in the Archdiocese, the St. John Cantius House of Studies. The Congregation of the Resurrection was founded in Rome, in 1842 by two Polish priests, Peter Semenenco and Jerome Kaysiewicz. Its members follow a modified form of the rule of St. Benedict. Pope Leo XIII approved the Congregation in 1902. The Mother-house is in Rome.

---

[4] Prospectus of the Society of Mary, pp. 34 and 37.
[5] Dooley, Rev. P., Sermon.

. St. John Cantius' House of Studies, in charge of the Congregation of the Resurrection, was established in the year 1918.

At this Institution the aspirants to the priesthood in the Congregation of the Resurrection make their course of three years philosophical and four years theological studies after having completed a year of Novitiate either at Chicago, Ill., or at Kitchener, Ontario, Canada.

All students attend St. Louis University.

The policy of the Congregation of the Resurrection in regard to the preparation of its Scholastics for the priesthood is to give them the advantages of an education in the Natural Sciences as taught in one of our foremost Catholic Universities in America, St. Louis University, as well as a theological education with the many incidental advantages that are proper to it when obtained in Rome. For this reason the Scholastics of the American and Canadian Provinces of the Congregation of the Resurrection, as a rule, make the three years philosophy, including the natural sciences, at St. Louis University, after which they are sent to the Roman House of Studies, Rome, Italy, for four years of theology where they attend the Pontifical Gregoriana University.

In this manner they are well equipped when priests to take up the work of the Congregation of the Resurrection which is chiefly to conduct colleges in which Catholic young men are prepared for University or Seminary courses and, above all, to be of first rate assistance to the respective bishops in whose dioceses they may be located, by the care of souls in parishes entrusted to their charge.

Owing to the increased number of Scholastics since the establishment of St. John Cantius' House of Studies at St. Louis, a handsome addition providing twenty-four additional rooms, was built in the year 1925.

At this House of Studies there are twenty-four Clerics; three lay Brothers; and three priests.

Very Rev. Robert S. Dehler is Superior and Rector; Rev. Alex Reitzel, C. R., Assistant Rector; Rev. Joseph Ziemba, C. R., Missionary.[6]

---

6 Information furnished by House of Studies.

CHAPTER 18

LATEST DEVELOPMENTS OF THE SISTERHOODS

One of the most beautiful indications of the strength and vigor of Catholic life in the Archdiocese of St. Louis is to be found in the constant growth and expansion of the religious Orders and Congregations of women among us. The life of a religious, to be attractive or even bearable, must be supernatural. The fact, therefore, that so many young ladies of high talent and brightest prospects, year by year, consecrate themselves to the service of God in the cloister, or in the classroom, or in the hospital, or in the orphan asylum, and in the course of years experience no regrets, no hankerings after the pleasures of the world, no disappointments in meeting ingratitude for their consecrated service, this fact alone surely proves that the love of supernatural things is still deep and strong among our Catholic people. It is a pleasure to record the fact that all our Sisterhoods have not only held their own, since Archbishop Kenrick's time, but have made wonderful progress in numbers and in efficiency of service. The blessing of God has been with them; and the good will and the admiration of the Catholic laity as well.

Taking then, the outward manifestation for the symbol and vesture of the living spirit within these sisterhoods, we would place here a page of statistics derived from the Catholic Directory for 1927; in regard to their increase in membership and enlargement of their means of service in the cause of religion, morals and culture.

1. *The Ladies of the Sacred Heart*

"Maryville College and Academy of the Sacred Heart, Meramec St. and Nebraska Ave. Sisters 58; Pupils 136. Lay Teachers 7. Day pupils are not received.

Academy of the Sacred Heart and Mullanphy Orphan Asylum, 334 Taylor Ave. Sisters 44; Lay Teachers 4, Pupils 303, Orphans 20.

Academy of the Sacred Heart, 2nd and Decatur St., St. Charles, Mo. Religious 35, Pupils 105.

2. *The Daughters of Charity of St. Vincent de Paul*

St. Louis Mullanphy Hospital, 3225 Montgomery St., 18 Daughters of Charity of St. Vincent de Paul. Patients during the year, 2718; outdoor clinic patients 14,544. Connected with the Hospital is St. Louis Mullanphy Training School for Nurses. Pupils 55.

(736)

St. Vincent's Sanitarium for Nervous and Mental Disorders. Sisters 35. Patients treated during the year, 523. Inmates in Sanitarium, 362.

St. Philomena's Technical School, 5300 Cabanne Ave., 9 Daughters of Charity of St. Vincent de Paul. 8 Lay Teachers. Girls 70.

St. Mary's Female Orphan Asylum, 5341 Emerson Ave., 10 Daughters of Charity·of St. Vincent de Paul. Orphans 150.

St. Ann's Widows' Home, lying-in Hospital and Foundling Asylum, 5301 Page Ave. Sisters 15. Orphans 148. Patients treated during the year 975. Connected with the Home is St. Ann's Maternity Hospital Training School for Nurses. Pupils 6.

Guardian Angel Settlement, 1029 Marion St. 8 Daughters of Charity of St. Vincent de Paul. Postulants 7. 180 Day Nursery children enrolled. The Settlement includes Day Nursery; Kindergarten, Sewing school, Lunch room, Sunday school, Working Girls'˙ Club, Junior Girls' Club, Playgrounds, Free Employment Bureau, Young Ladies Sodality. The Sisters also visit the poor and sick.

St. Patrick's Day Nursery and Father Dempsey's Settlement, 1209. N. 6th St. 9 Daughters of Charity of St. Vincent de Paul. 1 Lay Teacher. Children 72, average daily.

Normandy. Marillac Seminary—Motherhouse and Seminary of the Daughters of Charity of St. Vincent de Paul. St. Louis Province. Sisters 35. Novices 26.

### 3. *The Sisters of St. Joseph*

St. Joseph's Academy, 6400 Minnesota Ave.—Motherhouse and Novitiate of the Sisters of St. Joseph of Carondelet. Sisters 38. Novices 58. Postulants 23. Pupils in Academy 210.

Fontbonne College, Wydown and Big Bend Rds., 31 Sisters of St. Joseph of Carondelet. 12 Lay Teachers. Pupils 231.

Convent of Our Lady of Good Counsel. 1849 Cass Ave. Sisters 110.

St. Joseph Male Orphan Asylum, 4701 Grand Ave. Sisters 16. Orphans 185.

St. Agnes Convent, 2049 Sidney St. 15 Sisters.

St. Joseph Deaf Mute institute, 901 N. Garrison Ave. Sisters 10. Lay Teachers 5. Pupils 80.

Nazareth, Retreat of the Sisters of St. Joseph of Carondelet. Sisters 38.

Vallé High School and Convent of St. Francis de Sales, Ste. Genevieve, Mo. Sisters 14. Lay Teachers 1. Pupils 70.

#### 4. *The Sisters of Loretto*

Loretto Academy, 3407 Lafayette Ave. 56 Sisters of Loretto at the Foot of the Cross. Pupils. 215. 3 Lay Teachers.

Webster College, Webster Groves, Lockwood and Plymouth Aves. Sisters 36. Lay Teachers 6. Pupils 170. The Reverend Professors of Kenrick Seminary have charge of the Departments of Philosophy, Sacred Scripture, History, Sociology, and Religion.

#### 5. *The Sisters of the Good Shepherd*

Good Shepherd Convent, 3801 Gravois Ave. Provincial house of the Sisters of Our Lady of Charity of the Good Shepherd. Professed Sisters 61. Novices 14. Postulants 2. Magdalen's 73. Girls in Reformatory 293.

School of the Immaculate Heart, 7626 Natural Bridge Rd., St. Louis, Mo. Conducted by the Sisters of Our Lady of the Good Shepherd. In Community 13. Lady Boarders 3. Dependents 10. Pupils 39.

#### 6. *The Visitation Nuns*

Convent and Academy of the Visitation, 5448 Cabanne Place. Sisters 70. Novices 10. Postulants 2. Lay Teachers 4. Pupils 275.

#### 7. *The Ursuline Nuns*

Oakland, Ursuline Convent and Academy.

Arcadia College and Ursuline Academy, Arcadia, Mo. Conducted by the Ursuline Nuns, St. Louis. Sisters 43. Pupils 75.

#### 8. *The Carmelite Nuns*

Carmelite Monastery, Victor and 18th Sts. Discalced Carmelites. Professed Sisters 12. Novices 7. Postulants 2. Extern Sisters 2. The Carmelites are now installed in their new Monastery near Clayton.

#### 9. *The Sisters of Mercy*

Sisters of Mercy Home for Girls, Locust and 23rd Sts. Boarding Home for Business Girls and Women. Professed Sisters 12. Accommodations for 125. Sick visited in their homes. City Jail visited by Sisters.

St. John's Hospital, Euclid and Parkview Aves. 50 Sisters of Mercy. Patients admitted during the year 5,602. A Free Clinical Dispensary is attached to the Hospital. Sisters visit the sick in their homes. In connection with the Hospital the Sisters have opened a Training School for nurses. Nurses 90.

St. Joseph's Convent of Mercy—Motherhouse and Novitiate of Sisters of Mercy. Professed Sisters 20. Novices 6. Postulants 22. Orphan Girls 73. St. Catherine's school for Girls.

### 10. *School Sisters of Notre Dame*

Sancta Maria in Ripa, Ripa Ave. S. St. Louis—Motherhouse and Novitiate and Junior College of the School Sisters of Notre Dame for the Southwestern Province.

Sisters 101. Novices 63. Postulants 58. Pupils in Preparatory Course 47.

### 11. *The Little Sisters of the Poor*

Home for the Aged, 2209 Hebert St.—Little Sisters of the Poor. Sisters 17. Old Persons 227.

Home for the Aged, 3400 S. Grand Ave.—Little Sisters of the Poor. Sisters 19. Old Persons 250.

### 12. *The Sisters of Mary*

St. Mary's Infirmary, 1536 Papin St.—Motherhouse of the Sisters of St. Mary of the Third Order of St. Francis. Patients during year, 2,069. Patients treated in Dispensary, 3301. St. Mary's Training School for Nurses. Professed Sisters 82.

St. Mary's Hospital and Novitiate of Sisters of St. Mary of the Third Order of St. Francis. Clayton Rd. and Bellevue Ave. Professed Sisters 56. Novices 41. Postulants 19. Patients treated during the year, 3,868.

St. Mary's Home, Partridge Ave. between Page Blvd. and Olive Rd.—6 Sisters of St. Mary of the Third Order Regular of St. Francis.

Mount St. Rose Sanitarium, 9101 S. Broadway. 42 Sisters. Patients during the year, 409.

St. Joseph's Hospital, 3rd and S. Clay Sts., St. Charles, Mo. 15 Sisters. Patients 425.

St. Mary's Hospital, Bolivar and Elm Sts., Jefferson City, Mo. 20 Sisters. Patients 860.

### 13. *The Franciscan Sisters*

St. Anthony's Hospital, Grand and Chippewa St.—Provincial Motherhouse and Novitiate of the Franciscan Sisters, Daughters of the Sacred Hearts of Jesus and Mary. Patients during the year, 1,716. Sisters 87. Novices 39. Postulants 12.

St. Anthony's Training School for Nurses, conducted for members of the Community exclusively. Pupils 20.

St. Francis Hospital, Good Hope and Pacific Sts., Cape Girardeau, Mo. 20 Sisters. Patients 1,175.

### 14. *The Oblate Sisters*

St. Francis Orphan Asylum, conducted by the Oblate Sisters of Providence. Girls admitted between the years of 2 and 12 only. 13 Sisters. Orphans 92. Inmates in Asylum, 105.

St. Rita's Convent, 4650 S. Broadway. Oblate Sisters of Providence 7 Sisters. Pupils 48.

### 15. *The Sisters of the Precious Blood*

St. Mary's Institute, O'Fallon, Mo.—Mother-house and Novitiate of the Sisters of the Most Precious Blood. Sisters 259. Novices 31.

St. Elizabeth's Academy, 3401 Arsenal St.—Academy for Young Ladies. 34 Sisters of the Most Precious Blood. Lay Teachers 3. Pupils 350.

### 16. *Helpers of the Holy Souls*

Convent of the Helpers of the Holy Souls, 4012 Washington Blvd. Sisters 18.

### 17. *The Polish Franciscan Sisters*

Convent of our Lady of Perpetual Help, 3419 Gasconade St.— Motherhouse and Novitiate of the Polish Franciscan School Sisters. Professed Sisters 152. Novices 22. Postulants 7. Aspirants 4.

Villa St. Joseph, Ferguson, Mo.—Novitiate of Polish Franciscan Sisters. Sisters 6. Novices 22. Postulants 7. Aspirants 4.

### 18. *The Carmelite Sisters of the D. H. of Jesus*

St. Joseph's Home of Our Lady of Mount Carmel—Conducted by the Carmelite Sisters of the Divine Heart of Jesus. Inmates 15. Patients in Home 21. Sisters 6.

### 19. *Sisters of Christian Charity*

St. Vincent's German Orphan Home, Natural Bridge and Florissant Rd.—28 Sisters of Christian Charity. Orphans 250.

### 20. *Sisters of Charity of the Incarnate Word*

Incarnate Word Convent. Our Lady's Mount-Provincial House and Novitiate of the St. Louis Province of the Sisters of Charity of the Incarnate Word of San Antonio. 9 Sisters. 7 Novices. 5 Postulants.

### 21. *Sisters of the Holy Cross*

Fenton, Hessoun Bohemian Catholic Orphan Home—6 Sisters of the Holy Cross. Orphans 23. Pupils 19. 1 Lay Teacher.

### 22. *Sister Servants of the Holy Ghost of Perpetual Adoration*

American Motherhouse of the Congregation of the Sister Servants. 12 Sisters.

This Sisterhood now has two houses in the city, the old home of the Carmelite Nuns in South St. Louis having been occupied by them.

In addition to these Institutions of Charity and Education, the various Sisterhoods have in charge almost all the parochial schools in the diocese. Without their generous and self-sacrificing cooperation the entire system of Catholic primary education would fall. It is, therefore, a matter of solemn duty to recognize this most momentous service of our Sisterhoods to the cause of Holy Church.

| | Sisterhood | Schools in City | Schools in County | Teachers |
|---|---|---|---|---|
| 1. | Sisters of St. Joseph | 31 | 3 | 224 |
| 2. | School Sisters of Notre Dame | 18 | 18 | 219 |
| 3. | Sisters of the Precious Blood | 6 | 20 | 108 |
| 4. | Sisters of Loretto | 13 | 5 | 105 |
| 5. | The Ursuline Nuns | 1 | 18 | 59 |
| 6. | The Sisters of Charity of Incarnate Word | 5 | 3 | 58 |
| 7. | The Sisters of St. Francis | 5 | 8 | 51 |
| 8. | The Dominican Sisters | 4 | 2 | 41 |
| 9. | The Sisters of Mercy | 0 | 3 | 13 |
| 10. | The Daughters of Charity | 1 | | 9 |
| 11. | Polish Franciscans | 3 | | 9 |
| 12. | Sisters of St. Francis | 3 | | 7 |
| 13. | Sisters of the Blessed Sacrament | 2 | | 6 |
| 14. | Apostolic Zelatrices | 1 | | 6 |
| 15. | Sisters of the Sacred Heart | 1 | | 7 |
| 16. | Sisters of Charity of the B. V. M. | 1 | | 7 |
| | | 95 | 80 | 929 |

The Sisters of St. Joseph, and the School Sisters of Notre Dame furnish the teaching staff of the Rosati-Kain High School for Girls. Each order is represented by twenty-four of its members.

Doing such valiant work in the archdiocese, it seems quite natural that these Sisterhoods should also express their spirit in the outward forms of their institutions. The buildings are, indeed, of secondary importance: yet their beauty of architecture and their orderly arrangement suiting their purpose, and the comfort they offer, represent real elements of success. As long as the true spirit of charity is cultivated within, there is no reason to condemn the outward magnificence and splendor.

A representative number of these more recent monuments of Faith and Charity are here singled out from the large number of new buildings erected by the various Sisterhoods in St. Louis and its immediate vicinity for educational and charitable institutions.

The Convent and Academy of the Visitation in Cabanne Place was erected by the Visitandine Sisters in 1892. It is a fine building, beautiful and substantial, well adapted to its purpose of educating the future leaders of women's religious and social movements.

Sancta Maria in Ripa, the Mother-house of the Southern Province of the School Sisters de Notre Dame is certainly the most beautifully situated of all the Convent buildings of St. Louis. "St. Mary on the bank of the Great River," such is the title of the Institution, and with extended hands, she appears to hold sway and diffuse her sheltering benediction broadcast over the grand old "Father of the Waters" as it flows majestically, ever and ever onward, past the extensive, charming grounds, vineyards and orchards, encompassing the institution,— and over the surrounding picturesque country.

The grand building was dedicated by Archbishop Kain on July 7, 1897.

The Southern Province had at its foundation nineteen houses in Missouri, and twenty-three in other states; the number now exceeds eighty-six. The Sisters de Notre Dame have always adhered to the principle announced by the sainted Mother Caroline. "That the parochial school and the orphanage were the special vocation of the School Sisters; that they would be untrue to their providential calling should they deviate from this principle."

St. Ann's Asylum and Orphan Home on Page and Union Boulevard, St. Vincent's Sanitarium, for Nervous and Mental Disorders and Marillac Seminary, the Mother-house of the Daughters of Charity of St. Vincent de Paul, St. Louis Province, are the three up-to-date buildings of the Sisters of Charity. A fourth one was in contemplation, the new St. Louis Mullanphy Hospital, intended to supplant the old Mullanphy on Montgomery St. In fact, excavations for the purpose were made, but for some unknown reasons, building operations were discontinued. The cyclone of 1927 did serious damage to the St. Louis Mullanphy Hospital, but no loss of life occurred.

The St. Vincent's Sanitarium was occupied by the Sisters of Charity and their afflicted charges in 1896. Hardly had they left the old place on Ninth and Marion Streets when the cyclone of May 27, 1896 razed the buildings completely to the ground.

The Franciscan Sisters of the province of St. Claire started to build their new St. Anthony's Hospital in 1899, after having occupied a temporary building on the site since 1894. The corner stone was laid by Vicar-General Muehlsiepen on Sunday, April 23, 1899 and the completed great building was dedicated by Archbishop Kain on April 17, 1900. This building was now designated as the Mother-house of the Province. Soon after the opening all the patients in the old Hospital were removed to St. Anthony's. The Training School for Nurses was organized October 15, 1901.

Mount St. Rose for the care of consumptives owes its origin to the discovery by Dr. Robert Koch of the tubercle bacilli as the immediate cause of consumption. It was the first institution of its kind in the Middle West. The Institution is in a beautiful park, near the River des Peres. The building presents a magnificent appearance with its towering steeples and verandas.

The second monumental structure raised by the Sisters of Mary for the comfort and healing of suffering mankind is the new St. Mary's Hospital built in 1922. It is a modern up-to-date institution and makes a fine appearance. This building and the four remaining ones, show the marks of the period in which they were erected, as certain vastness of design and classic simplicity and grace of treatment. The cost of St. Mary's Hospital is one million dollars.

St. John's Hospital of the Sisters of Mercy is the latest achievement of this noble Sisterhood in the building way. Archbishop Glennon in laying the corner stone, said: "In the fifty-six years the Sisters of Mercy have been engaged in the work of love in St. Louis, I don't believe there have been fifty-six words printed about their good deeds. In this modern age, it seems, one must talk about one's self to be noticed . . I hope that this new venture of the Sisters will meet with the appreciation it deserves."

Fontbonne College, the great educational institution of the Sisters of St. Joseph is situated on a twenty acre tract, on Wydown Boulevard and Big Bend Road, and consists of seven distinct buildings, The main building is named Ryan Hall, and like all the others is built of Missouri granite, in Gothic architectural style. Through its main corridor the chapel is entered. There is also a music and arts building, a science building, an auditorium, a gymnasium and a service building.

The buildings were dedicated by Archbishop Glennon October 16, 1926, after having been in use for a full college term. The Archbishop's sermon stresses the importance of women's work in modern life.

The Ursuline Nuns, who since 1849 have maintained an Academy in their Mother-house on Twelfth and State Streets have erected a new Mother-house in Oakland, St. Louis County. Their old home in the city is now the Community Center of the Catholic Slovaks of St. Louis.

Only recently the Carmelite Sisters, who have occupied their convent at 18th and Victor Streets for over fifty years, have left it for their new Monastery at Clayton and Price Roads, the Monastery for Carmel of St. Joseph. The convent building is three stories in height, and beautifully situated on elevated, largely wooded ground, perfectly suited to a contemplative Order like the Carmelites.

The latest accessions to the Diocesan Sisterhoods, were the Polish Franciscans, the Helpers of the Holy Souls, the Sisters of the Holy Cross, the Sisters of Charity of the Incarnate Word, the Sisters of the Blessed Sacrament in charge of St. Elizabeth's Settlement, established for colored people in connection with their new church in the Old Walsh Mansion at 2731 Pine Street, the Carmelite Sisters of the Divine Heart of Jesus, and lastly the Sister Servants of the Holy Ghost of Perpetual Adoration, complete the list of our Sisterhoods.

All these organizations of consecrated women fulfill a mission among us. *Ora et labora* is their watchword; their love for Christ the Lord is their chosen duty and sweetest comfort.

## CHAPTER 19

## PROGRESS OF CHURCH ARCHITECTURE IN ST. LOUIS

### I

Christian art has been justly called the eldest daughter of the Church. Like Holy Mother Church, Christian art must, therefore be one and holy and universal. Whether it expresses itself in architecture, painting or sculpture, in poetry, oratory or music, the spirit of the Christian religion must inform, inspire and guide it.

"The true work of art," says Michael Angelo, "is but a shadow of Divine Perfection," or as Richard Chenevix Trench varies the idea, "eternal beauty is the form of art." Christian art follows in the train of Holy Church, as a loving and observant daughter. Indeed, the Church can live and thrive in the Catacombs, in the primitive log house, in the poor frame structures of our earlier days, as well as in the grand Cathedrals, or the Gothic or Romanesque parish churches of the present day. But the love for God quite naturally produces the love for the beauty of the house of God. Whether consciously or unconsciously, the trend to beauty will be present in the church builder, even if he be the most matter-of-fact person; for "a building, fitted accurately to assure its end," says Emerson "turns out to be beautiful, though beauty has not been intended." Those early churches of hewn logs amid the wilderness scenery, of which our fathers so lovingly spoke to their children, surely had an element of beauty in their rude outlines, for they enclosed the throne of the Living God. Not for their own satisfaction or comfort do Catholic people build their churches, but primarily for the honor and glory of the Almighty, for Whom nothing that they can offer, seems too great and rare and costly. Hence the measure of their love is the measure of their giving, and their only limitation in the more or less limited amount of their means.

It is through this spirit that St. Louis has become a city of beautiful churches, and that the rural parishes of the diocese have followed its lead.

But there is also a sort of honest civic pride at the very root of church architecture. When the Israelites lived in tents, the House of God among them, was also a tent, though a more splendid one. When they attained fixed habitations in city and village, their temple became one of the architectural glories of the world.

"Art, especially architecture, gives a history to the state of society," says a noted traveler, and he is right.

During the early missionary period of our diocese, of hard struggle for subsistence, the artistic side of church architecture could find but little attention. Logs from the surrounding forest, rough boards or, at best, rock from a neighboring ledge were the materials. No trained architect was needed to fashion these rude materials into an humble but serviceable temple of the Most High.

Not that the missionaries and people lacked the love for the beauty of the house of God, far from it! They offered the best they had, and God accepted their offering.

Bishop Rosati's great work in church building, the venerable Cathedral on Walnut Street gave the first impulse to the spirit of artistic development in St. Louis. In its severe simplicity and massive forms, this earliest basilica in the Mississippi Valley remains one of the glories of our city, as it was the model and inspiration for church builders far and wide. All through Bishop Rosati's episcopate, St. Louis had but one church, as it formed but one parish. But with the advent of Bishop Kenrick, a rapid development set in.

The great religious Orders of men, the Lazarists, Jesuits and Redemptorists, were fortunate in having among their membership some Father or Brother endowed with a fair measure of taste and skill in architecture: hence the really artistic early churches of the diocese after Rosati's Cathedral, St. Vincent de Paul, the church of the Lazarists in St. Louis, and the interior loveliness of their Church of St. Mary's at the Barrens; then the perennial beauty of the Jesuit Churches of St. Francis Xavier and St. Joseph in St. Louis, and the second Church of St. Charles in the city of that name; and finally the grandeur of the Church of St. Alphonsus of the Redemptorists, began in 1867, and completed in 1872, all bear the imprint, the spirit of art. True it is, that the venerable Churches of St. Michael, St. Lawrence O'Toole and St. Malachy, all in the Gothic style of architecture, are creditable achievements for that early date and that the ancient Churches of St. Patrick and St. Mary of Victories and St. Bridget try to represent the architectural traditions of the Old Cathedral, each one a more or less beautiful center of attraction for the neighborhood, yet they lack the distinction of high artistic conception.

The early seventies of the Nineteenth Century marked the supremacy of the Gothic style in our city, in the two great monuments in stone: St. Alphonsus, with its rich facade, and the great church of S.S. Peter and Paul. Their lead was immediately followed by other more or less distinguished specimens of the Gothic style: St. Agatha's, 1872, Our Lady of Perpetual Help, 1873, St. Augustine's, 1875, St. Liborius, 1889, though the latter's chief beauty, the open work stone tower, is of a later date; then Holy Trinity, which the recent cyclone deprived of the only excrescence that marred its grandeur, the clumsy dome, leaving it

SAINT FRANCIS XAVIER'S (COLLEGE) CHURCH OF SAINT LOUIS

as it now stands forth in its true and splendid perfection; and still later, the new Church of St. Francis Xavier, completed and opened for use in 1898.

St. Francis Xavier is in the English Gothic style, not as plain as the early English, nor yet as elaborate as the decorated. Moreover, it has borrowed not a few features from the French Gothic, such as its polygonal spire, its fine columns, its rose window, and the treatment of the facade, richly diversified and well proportioned. The tower, however, seems to be out of proportion with the side elevation and its long sweep of clerestory windows. The interior is, graceful, well proportioned and tastefully diversified; the sanctuary which pushes itself halfway into the transept, looks up to a delicate and graceful stellar-vault. The altars are of marble, the sculpture on the four side altars, done by the sculptor Libbel, are admirable.

These, together with the older Gothic churches already mentioned, and the two Romanesque churches, the Annunciation, a replica in miniature of St. John Lateran in Rome, and the Church of the Sacred Heart, with its two low hexagon towers flanking the entrance, the grand central cupola bearing up the statue of the Sacred Heart, these formed the artistic inheritance of the diocese from the administration of Archbishops Kenrick and Kane.

With Archbishop Glennon, the representative of triumphant Catholicity, came a new outburst of Christian art in the city and diocese of St. Louis; not only in the rapid increase of new churches, but also in the beautiful diversity of architectural forms, and the splendid accessories of veined marble and brilliant mosaic, stained glass windows and the treasures of marble statues, original paintings and church furniture of costly material and artistic workmanship. The great Cathedral, rearing its majestic walls of grey granite higher and higher, and at last receiving the crown of its outward perfection in the mighty dome; and then, as the years passed away in hurried flight, the constant growth of its inward splendor, of mosaic and marble and columns of precious stone, became the harbinger of a new era, and its constant inspiration.

All the worthy styles of Christian architecture are now represented with marvelous specimens among the hundred and more Catholic churches of the city of the Crusader Saint: and though the builders have drawn upon the great models of the Old World, they have not failed to develop characteristic features of their own, "to please the eye and save the soul besides."

It may be a matter of surprise to many that, in the first six years of Archbishop Glennon's episcopate, no less than eight churches were built in the old familiar Gothic style. Yet, besides the really pronounced advantages of that form of architecture, there was a special reason why it was used: some of these churches were planned, and others were actually begun before 1903.

*St. Barbara's* led the way under the leadership of Father Emile Lemkes. His church, especially in its graceful tower, reminds one of Frankfurt's stately cathedral of St. Bartholomew, in which the erections and coronations of the Roman Emperors of the German Nation were held. Of course, a comparison of the two structures would be out of place; yet St. Barbara's, with its recent addition of the choir, is a really fine sample of the Gothic. Pipers was the architect.

The year 1907 witnessed the completion of *St. Matthew's church,* a large Gothic building in grey brick and stone, of moderate height, the vaulted ceiling of the transept representing a great star. The altar and communion rail, as well as the statues are of Carrara marble. The windows have stained glass, and the walls bear some really fine paintings by a St. Louis artist, Matthew Hastings. Father Joseph T. Shields built this church. Conradi was the architect.

"One of the finest Gothic structures in the West," is the designation Thornton applies to Father E. J. Shea's church of the *Immaculate Conception.* It is a clerestory building of English Gothic style with magnificent rose windows in the facade and at both ends of the transept. The tower is truncated. The church was dedicated on December 19th, 1908. It cost was $200,000.00. "Beautiful in its conception, beautiful in its execution, bearing in every line the beauty of Catholic architecture," was the final judgment of Archbishop Glennon.

The year 1909, witnessed the completion of four notable churches, all Gothic in style, distinct in execution. The church of the *Holy Ghost,* the basement of which dated from the time of Father Busch, but which was built up according to new plans by Weisbecker and Hillebrand, and dedicated in 1909, is a Gothic church of simple yet harmonious outlines and of respectable height. It is cruciform, with the sanctuary gracefully rounded. The church possesses two very fine statues in wood-carving by the noted Tyrolese artist, Valentin Gallmetzer. The stained glass windows of the sanctuary and transept are of exquisite, deep toned coloring.

The church of the *Holy Cross* in what is still called Baden, is similar in many structural points to the preceding building. One of its characteristic marks is the high elevation of the sanctuary, with its long flight of marble steps leading down from the Altar to the communion rail, that is on a level with the floor of the nave. The beautiful stained glass windows add lustre to the beauty of simple architectural forms. The church was built by Father Peter Wigger.

*St. Francis de Sales,* is the crown of the later Gothic churches, vying with St. Alphonsus, S.S. Peter and Paul, St. Francis Xavier and the Holy Trinity for the palm of glorious Christian architecture. The first impression is that of massive strength, then the harmony of all parts, and their subordination to the central idea, opens upon the mind. One of the chief elements of effect is its height, of sixty-five feet from the floor line to the groined ceiling. The magnificent altar, the richly carved pulpit, the highly artistic stained glass windows and, above all, the chapel of Our Lady of Perpetual Succor, with its sparkling mosaic covered walls and ceiling, make St. Francis de Sales one of the sights of the city. Its steeple is said to be the highest one in St. Louis. All in all, the church is one of the most majestic church buildings in the entire country. The cost of the structure exceeded $300,000.00.

The church of the *Visitation* is the Tudor Gothic style, of brick and cut stone construction, with two towers, ornamented with gargoyles, carved in Bedford stone, completes, as Archbishop Glennon said on the day of its dedication, "corona of beautiful temples rising in St. Louis, for the steadfast purpose of honoring Christ the Lord." The church cost $100,000.00. Its builder was Father Dempsey.

In 1910 began the seven years period of Romanesque architecture in St. Louis, with the Franciscan church of St. Anthony of Padua, one of the most spacious, beautiful and majestic churches in the city. Its builder was Father Bernard Wever, O.F.M., the architect was Brother Anselm Wolff, of the same Order.

The exterior of the new St. Anthony's has, indeed, a simple, but most commanding appearance. The proportions of the grand Romanesque structure are extreme outside length, 226 ft., inside length, 205 ft., the inside width, 68½ ft. At the transept, 90 ft. The height of the nave is 62 ft. and that of the side aisles, 30 ft. The width of nave and transept is 38 ft.

The foundation and basement wall are built of Carthage stone. The walls of the superstructure of grey vitrified brick laid up with red cement mortar, with trimmings of Bedford stone. The columns and roof are of steel construction. The roof is covered with dark slate, which beautifully contrasts with the light grey color of the walls. The gorgeous facade, whose gable reaches a height of 86 ft., is flanked by two mighty towers each 175 feet high. Wide granite steps lead up to the three double doors of the front. The carved arches above the doors are supported by a double stone colonnade.

Entering the church proper one is filled with awe at the grand spectacle before him. The imposing high altar in onyx and gold, with its huge canopy, captures the eye at once and thence draws it up to the immense painting of the Adoration of the Lamb, which covers the entire upper apsis of the sanctuary.

The side walls of the sanctuary are ornamented with paintings representing the four great Latin Doctors of the Church, and four of the most celebrated saints of the Franciscan Order, St. Bernardin, St. John Capistran, St. Peter Baptist, and St. Leonard.

On the right hand of the altar there is an oratory for the Friars. From the sanctuary, all along the walls throughout the whole church runs a series of paintings which present historical events from the life of Christ and His Saints, especially of St. Francis and St. Anthony of Padua.

Four large paintings ornament the transept: Jesus and Mary as King and Queen of Heaven, St. Anthony favored by an apparition of the Divine Infant and St. Anthony the Helper of the poor and afflicted. Besides these representations there are to be found in different parts of the church twenty-four single figures and eight groups of figures, representing well-known and beloved saints.

But these numerous pictures are excelled by the grand representations, which in glowing colors ornament all windows of the sanctuary, in the clerestory in the transept and along both side aisles.

The transept has two immense windows, 18 x 35 ft., which call forth general admiration, the Birth of Christ. and the Ascension of Christ into Heaven.

The frescoing of the church is a masterpiece, and harmoniously agrees with the fourteen huge columns finished in dark Sienna Scagliola marble, which carry the mighty groined arches above. The two inside the communion railing in honor of the Sacred Heart of Jesus and the Immaculate Heart of Mary, the two in the transept in honor of St. Joseph and St. Anthony. Besides these, there is an altar in the baptistery in honor of the Mater Dolorosa.

The altars, communion railing, pulpit, all in pure Roman style, are profusely ornamented with gold, marble and onyx, whilst the pews and confessional retain the natural color of oak wood. The stations of the cross are set in pairs along the side walls. They are of exquisite beauty and will induce many a pious worshiper to lovingly gaze upon our Savior in his last bitter agony.

The same year, 1910, witnessed the completion of two other Romanesque churches of real distinction: Father McGlynn's church of St. Rose of Lima, and Father Hussmann's church of St. Henry.

*St. Rose* is built in the subdivision of the Romanesque called the Tuscan or Florentine type of architecture, developed in blue Bedford stone throughout the exterior, with a lofty spire in one corner of the front and suppressed tower on the other. The facade is embellished with highly ornamental entrances, gables and cornices. The sanctuary is enclosed by a chancel railing of simple but elegant workmanship. The cost was $100,000.00. The church was dedicated August 13, 1910.

A less pretentious building, though in its simplicity of treatment, of really striking architectural beauty, is the church of *St. Henry,* planned and begun by Father John A. Hoffman and completed by his successor, Father Henry Hussmann. It follows the Romanesque style of the so-called Hall-church (Hallen-kirche) form. Two rows of stout pillars run along the side walls, at a distance of about four feet from the walls. The main roof rests upon these pillars; the space between pillars and wall is covered in by separate roofing. The large rose window of the facade is supported by eight graceful columns. The main tower is a square, running into an octagon. Among the treasures of the church we would mention the exquisitely carved High Altar of hardwood and very fine statue of the Mother of God and St. Joseph, the carpenter of Nazareth.

The style of St. Bernard's church must be classed as Gothic, although it lacks some of its main characteristics. The facade is bare of all ornament; The windows have no stained glass, and there is no tower. The church cost about $68,000.00. It was dedicated on Thanksgiving day, 1912.

Of *St. Anne's* we have said what was to be said in the history of the foundation of the parish. Of the church of the *Blessed Sacrament* likewise. The latter is a return to the Gothic, but with modern alterations.

The world war was raging since 1914, and threatening to draw our country into its vortex. There came a pause in church building, that lasted till 1916, when another spring tide of St. Louis church architecture opened with the dedication of Father Christopher Byrne's Romanesque church of the *Holy Name,* an event almost simultaneous with the first Pontifical Mass celebrated by Archbishop Glennon, at the marvelously beautiful High Altar of his new Cathedral. But the importance of this new period of architectural development merits a new chapter.

## CHAPTER 20

# PROGRESS OF CHURCH ARCHITECTURE IN ST. LOUIS

## II

It was Bishop Christopher Byrne of Galveston, the former pastor of *St. Joseph's* in Edina and of the *Holy Name* in St. Louis, that was privileged to extoll in our grand cathedral the wonderful achievements of Archbishop Glennon's Quarter Century as Head of the Archdiocese of St. Louis. On this occasion the eloquent Prelate said:

"In your city community there were 67 churches in 1903, today 103 golden crosses point the way to the feet of Christ and God. In the country there were 113 parishes in 1903, and today they number 155. A very noble thing is the splendid architecture of so many of these new churches. The great pleasure of seeing abroad the beautiful churches built in the Ages of Faith is being brought to your own door. Painting and sculpture and mosaic, the best in glass and bronze and wood make beautiful these temples."

The Church of the *Holy Name* is an exemplification of these words. It is in the Romanesque style, of substantial construction and lasting material. The decorations are in terra cotta. The facade is dignified by a clustered stone colonnade supporting the cornice and an arched balustrade. Above it the great rose window its delicate tracery pierces the center of the facade. A crucifixion group of terra cotta crowns the pediment. A striking feature of the church is its campanile, one hundred and twenty-five feet in height, with its graceful colonnaded belfry.

The church of *Our Lady of Lourdes,* on Forsythe Avenue, near Clayton Road, is in the style of the round arched Anglo-Norman plus certain developments into the earliest English lancet Gothic. The square bell-tower resembles the Saxon Towers of early England, such as may be seen at Iffly near Oxford. Of the interior, probably the most notable feature is the fine hammer-beam wooden roof, of true and massive construction, somewhat similar in character and design to the splendid one of the church of St. Stephen, at Norwich, England. (15th Century). Another fine feature is the admirable Norman wheel window of the north front, filled with exquisite geometrical glass, similar in type to some of the early glass in Canterbury Cathedral. Indeed, the central medallion of this window is taken from a head in one of the Chartres windows, and portrays Our Lady as Regina Coeli. The High Altar with the screen back of it is of Caenstone, and in design of the English Decorated Period of Gothic. It is correct and refined in detail. The

(752)

architects Study, Farrar and McMahon have given us a fine example of a typical English Parish church of Rural England as was built and slowly added to and developed during several centuries, and several successive architectural styles and periods. Native rubble stone was used for the exterior walls, with all doors, windows and tracery of Bedford cut stone. The total cost was $80,000.00. Father Francis O'Connor is the builder of the church which was dedicated in 1919.

Similar to the church of the *Holy Name* is the church of St. Pius. Its massive facade is typical of the Romanesque style, its gleaming white stone walls contrast harmoniously with the roof of red Spanish tile. The interior of the church deserves special mention. The customary barrel vault spans the nave, from which the side aisles are separated by arched colonnades. The clerestory is pierced by art-glass windows, which shed a flood of mellow light into the nave. The apse is semicircular in form surmounted by a dome. The facade is ornamented with two works of sculpture; the lower representing the scene of the crucifixion, the upper that of the Battle of Lepanto, having as its central figure, Pope Pius V. The approximate cost was $200,000.00.

Father Kuhlmann's Church of *St. Roch's,* marks a return to the Gothic style, it was executed by the architects of St. Pius and the Holy Name, Messrs. Lee and Rush. Being Tudor Gothic, St. Roch's is rich in ornamentation, really beyond the limit of good taste. The church is rather high for its length. Profusion of detail and florid elaboration of tracery are the characteristics of facade and tower. The church represents an expenditure of $225,000.00. It was dedicated November 26th, 1922, by Archbishop Glennon.

Gothic in style but of the early English or Irish, the Church of the *Holy Rosary,* built by Dr. Daniel Lavery in 1923, makes a pleasing impression with its solid square battlemented tower carrying with it a flavor of antique times of storm and stress. The church is of stone; Its erection cost $245,000.00.

The church of *St. Ambrose* built by the Rev. Julius Giovanini for the Italian Catholics of Southwest St. Louis, bears the imprint of the Lombard Romanesque style and is reminiscent of the antique churches of the *San Ambrogio* and *Santa Maria della Grazie* in Milan. The exterior of the structure, with the campanile in the back is of brick and terra cotta. The interior with its high barrel vaulted ceiling consists of three naves, separated by arches, resting on six columns. There is a profusion of statues upon the altars and in niches all around the walls. The church was blessed on June 27th, 1926.

The Bohemian Catholics of St. Louis also placed a noble monument of their faith and generosity in the corona of beautiful churches by erecting their fine Gothic structure in honor of their national Saint,

King Winceslaus. All the appointments are of the best material obtainable and of excellent workmanship. The cost was $125,000.00.

The second Parish of the *Immaculate Conception* in St. Louis, existing simultaneously not merely successively, was founded in what was originally Maplewood, and is accordingly called the Immaculate Conception of Maplewood. The new church is designed and constructed in the Romanesque style of matt brick with Bedford stone trimmings. It is without the usual colonnaded portico, and the campanile, too, is wanting, it was constructed by Mr. Henry Hess, architect, for the Rev. J. P. Ryan, the pastor. The archbishops dedicated the building, October 10th, 1926.

The new church of *St. Aloysius*, which was dedicated on the 25th of April, 1926, follows the Romanesque style, though in a modified form. "The prevailing idea in its erection was convenience to the worshipers, moderate cost, durability and the production of something different from what had been accomplished in church architecture in this city." This purpose was certainly attained: *St. Aloysius* is unique among the notable churches of the city. The total cost of building and furnishing was $145,000.00. Father Francis Brand who in his long pastoral course built so many churches, may regard the new St. Aloysius as his monument.

The new church of the *Holy Family* was planned and executed by the same architects who built St. Aloysius, Ludwig and Dreisoerner, and bears a marked resemblance to the former building. It is a massive structure of variegated granite from the quarries near Fredericktown, Missouri. The brick arch that spans the sanctuary is the widest known. Father John F. Reuther, who began the work, died before its completion. The church was dedicated in June 1927.

The church of *Our Lady of Sorrows* is another fine reproduction of the Italian basilica, with narthex, clerestory and campanile. The narthex or colonnaded portico on the front, and the placing of the campanile on the side of the church just in front of the transept, though common enough in the style of the church, is an innovation in Catholic church design in St. Louis. The exterior of the church is clothed in buff brick with red terra cotta trimmings, closely following Italian precedent. The main structural features of the imposing interior is the richly coffered flat ceiling. The church at present has not its full complement of interior furnishings. It is contemplated to provide in the very near future a baldachin altar of marble with mosaic dome over the altar and mosaic stations. When completed Our Lady of Sorrows promises to present a very rich and colorful example of Romanesque architecture. The cost of the building up to date is $250,000.00. It was designed by Adolph F. Stauder. Father

Bernard Stolte is the pastor. The dedication took place on February 12th, 1927.

*St. Cecilia's* church is a beautiful Romanesque structure, of matt brick with stone trimmings.   Its facade is flanked by two majestic towers, somewhat resembling in design and execution, the neighboring Church of St. Anthony.   Its interior, being Romanesque and, therefore, depending more on the accessories of beauty than its structural forms, is profusely and splendidly adorned, befitting the majesty of the King, whose home it is.   The entire sanctuary is made brilliant with costly mosaics.   The dome of the apse has a representation of St. Cecilia, Patroness of the church, with a kneeling angel on either side.   The lower portion of the apse is carried out in a tapestry design forming a most interesting background to the high altar.   On the south wall, on a background of gold, there is a representation of the Sacrifice of Abraham, and on the opposite wall a representation of the Sacrifice of Melchisedech.   The ceiling above is carried out in blue with gold stars suggestive of the heavens.   The side chapels continue the scheme of the sanctuary proper with the ceiling in blue with gold stars and walls in gold forming a beautiful background to the side altars and the shrines.   The mosaics are the work of the Emil Frei Studio in Munich, Bavaria.   The beautiful stained glass windows were designed by Mr. Emil Frei also and executed in his Munich studio.   The large transept windows are of the pictorial type.   The two transept windows and the front rose window forms a triangle and suggest the theme of the Most Holy Trinity.   Another outstanding feature of the new church are its altars, five in number, all of Italian marble, produced by the Kaletta Co.   The main altar is of the Ciborium type, Romanesque in design with a touch of modern architecture in places.   The altar proper is constructed of white Italian marble.   Columns supporting the exposition dome in the reredos and on mensa front are of red Verona marble.   The back of the exposition niche is inlaid with Venetian mosaic.   The dome above is surmounted by the Dove representing the Holy Spirit.   DaVinci's Last Supper, carved in Italian marble, rests in the mensa front with relief carvings of grapes and wheat in the side panels.   A Crucifixion Group carved in Italian marble rises up behind the exposition and gives the altar proper its complete finish.   Above this altar rises majestically the Caldachino, resting on four large columns of Breccia violet marble.

St. Cecilia's is one of the sights of the city.   Father Bernard J. Renten, the pastor and his distinguished architect, Mr. Henry P. Hess, deserves great credit.   The church was dedicated on February 26th, 1927. The approximate cost of the building was $300,000.00.

*St. Engelbert's* Church is a fair sample of what the same artist can accomplish in the Gothic form of architecture.   The structure is designed in the later English or Tudor Gothic, with truncated tower and large rose window in the facade. The walls are of matt brick and Bedford stone trimmings. The altar is of marble and has two large mosaic panels flanking the tabernacle, representing the sacrifices of Abraham and of Melchisedech. A fine representation of the crucifixion surmounts the altar. The building and furnishing of the building approximate $200,000.00. Father A. J. Von Brunn is pastor of St. Engelbert's.

The year 1928, saw the completion and dedication to divine service of the grand structure of *St. James the Greater*, built in the Gothic style of the eleventh century, a period when the building of churches was promoted by piety and the spirit of reverence, and the artists and artisans worked with earnest devotion to make beautiful, each by his special skill, the sanctuary of the Lord.

In St. Jame's Church the artisan has exhibited his skill in wood-carvings, wrought iron, leaded glass, cut stone, plastering, painting and floor-laying. The Organ gallery, organ screen, confession boxes, reredos and canopy over the altar are hand-carved and touched with pigments of various colors to emphasize the detail in the carvings and make more effective the natural hues of the chestnut, which is used in all the interior woodwork. The lanterns, gates of the baptistery and net work of altar railings are of wrought iron. The main and side altars are built of Mankato stone. The magnificence of the decorations are most pronounced in the many beautiful windows and tapestries. The scheme of decoration leaves the sanctuary an illuminated harmony of brilliant colors .and the body of the church, except where windows are set like gems, a place of restful sombre hue.

The cost of the church was $225,000.00. O'Meara and Hills were the architects.

Father James O'Connor is the pastor. Dedication services were held by Archbishop Glennon, October 7th, 1928.

One of the finest, perhaps the finest of the recent church buildings in St. Louis, is that of *St. George*. In the erection of this monumental structure the architects O'Meara and Hills scored a special triumph in securing for their basilica and its graceful tower an architectural vista that is unique. From whatever side you approach St. George's parish church, there seems to be a campanile in the middle of the road ahead—a perfect vista, reminiscent of those slender, peaceful looking bell-towers in Italy, dominating the horizon. And as you draw nigh the warm color of the brickwork, terra cotta, tile, marble and stone, the vague horizontal striping in the brickwork, all making for harmony and a friendly atmosphere, "deepen the impression of a little piece of Italy in the spirit of the Middle Ages nestling in its new but congenial setting." "In the detail, St. George himself may be found, slaying the evil dragon at the left hand end of the modeled frieze just above the main door-way.'' There is, strictly speaking, no facade to the building, it is entered by two powerfully developed side entrances. The interior of the church is in harmony with the exterior. The baldachino is of chestnut wood with an insert of a large tapestry of Christ the King. The altars and communion railing are of Colfax stone, the altar brasses of solid bronze, the ceiling and trimmings throughout are of chestnut wood. The windows have stained glass antique, the lighting fixtures are of bronze, the sanctuary lamp of bronze. The cost, including appointments, was $175,000.00. The dedication took place on April 15th, 1928. Father Joseph Siebert and his parish may be justly proud of what they have added to the artistic treasures of St. Louis.

We will close our rapid and rather superfical review of the more recent churches of St. Louis, having an artistic value and interest with the new Church of *St. Luke,* in Richmond Heights, which is now under construction and will be finished in the Spring of 1929. It will cost approximately $250,000.00. The church is designed by Study, Farrar and Rothenheber in the early English Gothic style, blended with certain marked characteristics of the late Norman style, as it appeared in France and England. Its chief characteristics are, its fidelity to the best traditions of the Medieval buildings, where honesty of construction is present. The church is built of solid masonry, the exterior walls being faced with Bedford stone, laid in continuous courses, varying in length and height. The trusses and roof construction are built of heavy timbers, so that the structural members of the roof become the decoration for the ceiling. In other words, throughout the entire church, the actual structural members form all the decorative motifs and details. There is absolutely no false work used in any portion of the church. The tracery for the windows is of stone. The front facade is now almost completed and speaks for itself, to be a noble example of Gothic architecture. The great wheel window in the western facade is a glorious piece of design. The tower, which is now mounting, will be one of the finest and richest in detail in the city. The Archbishop blessed and laid the corner stone on Sunday, May 6th, 1928. Father Joseph A. McMahon is the pastor and builder of the church.

The city of St. Louis is proud of its corona of beautiful churches in the various forms of Christian architecture and no less of the finer appreciation of what is beautiful, manifested therein by the priests and the people that built them. The builders have not labored in vain. The beautiful temples they have prepared for God whom St. Augustine calls ''Beauty, ever ancient, ever new,'' will have a long course of silent but irresistible influence over almost innumerable souls, raising them from the contemplation of the vain and sordid things of life, to visions of the glorious things in store for them in the Home of Our Father. The builders—and by this term I mean all those who contributed by genius of planning, honesty of workmanship, and generosity in furnishing the means, the builders themselves will pass away at the call of God; but their work shall outlast the centuries, to elevate, and inspire, to comfort and delight their children and children's children, for many generations to come.

The writer of this sketch of our beautiful city churches would be happy to append a similar account of the really fine rural churches of the diocese, as those of Freeburg, Farmington, Fredericktown, Charleston, Clayton, Columbia, Festus, Leopold, Martinsburg, Millwood, New Haven, Oran, Ozora, Portageville, Valley Park; and the Chapels of the Seminary, and of the Ursuline Convent in Arcadia, as well as the Pilgrim Shrine at Starkenburg, and a number of others. The readers of this History will kindly take the wish for the deed: as we cannot possibly travel from place to place to gather the necessary impressions. A separate, thorough-going history of church architecture in the diocese of St. Louis would fill a real want. Our two chapters are but an humble plea for something exhaustive on the difficult subject.

*Altar - The New Cathedral - St. Louis*

# THE CONSECRATION OF THE CATHEDRAL

Many a scene of grandeur in the successive manifestations of its Catholic Faith has the city of St. Louis, been privileged to witness since the time of its erection into a diocese of the Church Universal, each succeeding event surpassing in splendor and majesty those that went before: but the climax was reached in the last week of June of the year 1926. It then appeared as if all the splendor and joy and fragrance and pathos, Catholic St. Louis has ever known and taken to heart, were gathered up into one grand sunburst of spiritual exaltation of universal peace and good will.

The Centennial of the diocese of St. Louis was to be marked by the consecration of the grand Cathedral, the crowning glory of one hundred years of spiritual life and corresponding outward progress and expansion. The festivities were to extend over two days, Tuesday and Wednesday, June 29th and 30th. A great gathering of noted churchmen from far and near was expected for the occasion. Rome, the center of the Christian world was deeply interested in the coming event: all Christendom was alive to its magnificent promise. Cardinal Bonzano, the Papal Delegate, with Cardinals and Archbishops and other Prelates from all corners of the world were to take part in the solemn functions.

It was certainly proper and right that the Cathedral Church of the "Rome of the West," that had sent the "many holy men and women who, in apostolic zeal from this center, blazed the way of faith into all this western land," should be consecrated by a papal Legate. But the solemn grandeur of the Cathedral itself merited a consecration that should rival in brilliancy and solemnity any that have taken place outside of the Eternal City." Four Cardinals, fifty-nine Bishops and Archbishops assisted in the ceremonies, which far outranked anything that St. Louis has known. All the wealth and richness of Catholic liturgy was summoned for the occasion, and carried out with becoming dignity and fervor.

The festivities opened with the arrival of the Papal Legate Cardinal Bonzano, at Union and Lindell Boulevards, on Monday evening, June 28th.. The Legate was accompanied by Cardinal O'Donnell, the Archbishop of Armagh and Primate of all Ireland, and a number of Roman Prelates. At least fifty thousand St. Louisans fervently greeted the official representative of the Pope, and thousands of them followed the procession of the Cardinals and their host, the Archbishop

(759)

of St. Louis, to the Cathedral and thence to the Archbishop's Residence. Here they were joined by Cardinal Patrick Hayes of New York and Cardinal Michael von Faulhaber of Munich, Bavaria.

The actual consecration of the Cathedral was performed on Tuesday morning between seven and ten o'clock, by Archbishop Glennon and four of his suffragan bishops: Thomas F. Lillis of Kansas City, Mo., Francis J. Tief of Concordia, Kansas; A. J. Schwertner of Wichita, Kansas, and Francis J. Gilfillan of St. Joseph, Mo. The consecration of the altars of the four chapels was conducted simultaneously by these four bishops; whilst the Archbishop performed the solemn consecration of the main altar and the building itself.

Shortly after ten o'clock the doors were opened to admit all who could possibly find a seat or standing space within. Long before the Papal Legate and the other dignitaries entered in procession, every seat was occupied, and the immense galleries surrounding the auditorium presented a sea of faces. At last came the procession of hundreds of seminarians, members of the Religious Orders of priests and brothers, perhaps more than a thousand secular priests of the archdiocese and from other dioceses; hundreds of monsignori, mitred abbots and bishops streamed into the sanctuary or were given pews in the body of the church. The Archbishops followed, last of whom was Archbishop Glennon, who blessed the kneeling multitude.

Next in order walked Cardinals Faulhaber, Hayes and O'Donnell. The German Cardinal-Archbishop of Munich, Michael Faulhaber, a man of earnest, almost severe countenance and majestic bearing; the American Cardinal-Archbishop of New York, Patrick Hayes, small of stature, but showing in his serene, open countenance, the marks of the determined leader and happy organizer he is; and the lovable Cardinal-Archbishop of Armagh, Primate of all Ireland, Patrick O'Donnell, the most popular figure of all the high visitors, expressing even now in his kindly sympathetic features the irrepressible glint of something pleasant or witty he would like to utter. Cardinal Bonzano followed, imparting as he passed down the aisle his blessing. A man of quiet dignity and graceful movement, the very ideal of an Italian churchman, the Cardinal Legate takes his seat upon the throne. It was 11:30 o'clock when Msgr. Tannrath, pastor of the Cathedral and chancellor of the archdiocese, mounted the pulpit and read, first in Latin and then in English, the Apostolic Brief of Pope Pius XI, authorizing Cardinal Bonzano to preside in St. Louis as his representative at the consecration and the celebration ceremonies of the hundreth anniversary of the establishment of the diocese.

"To Our Beloved Son, John Bonzano of the title of St. Susanna, Cardinal Priest of the Holy Roman Church, Pius XI, POPE.

Our Beloved Son: Greeting and Apostolic Blessing.

Knowing of the auspicious twofold celebration to take place shortly in the diocese of St. Louis, on the coming feast of the Prince of the Apostles—the solemn consecration of the Cathedral church, and the commemoration of the centenary of the erection of the diocese itself—in response to the petition of the Most Reverend John Joseph Glennon, the zealous and illustrious Archbishop of the diocese, WE appoint you, Our Legate to the Eucharistic Congress at Chicago, to preside over these solemn ceremonies.

Inasmuch as whatever furthers the increase of faith and piety is most dear to Our Heart, WE gladly accede to the wishes of the Pastor of that Cathedral church, and his beloved people; We grant this all the more willingly since we know that the Province of Chicago at one time formed a part of the diocese of St. Louis, and that your predecessor in the Apostolic Delegation at Washington laid the corner stone of this new temple.

Wherefore, by these presents, We commission you, Our Beloved Son, in Our Name and by Our Authority, to assist at these sacred ceremonies, and to rightly consecrate this magnificent new Cathedral church.

Furthermore, We trust that this twofold celebration may inspire the faithful with a greater love toward this Apostolic See, and that they may advance daily in the practice and furtherance of religion, which alone can bring peace and prosperity to a country.

Meanwhile, as a harbinger of the divine gifts and a testimonial of Our Paternal interest, to you, Our Beloved Son, to the Archbishop of St. Louis, to his clergy and his people We impart the Apostolic Blessing.

Pius XI Pope.

Given at St. Peter's, Rome, this twentieth day of May, in the year of Our Lord 1926, and the fifth of our pontificate.''

After a brief address to the Papal Legate by Archbishop Glennon and a cordial response by His Eminence, the solemn Pontifical Mass was sung by Cardinal Bonzano, with all the pontifical ceremony prescribed for such occasions. Cardinal Hayes of New York gave a beautiful sermon. He spoke forcefully and earnestly in smooth flowing periods, on the subject that was uppermost in all minds and hearts, the grandeur of the new Cathedral: ''The stones of this edifice, the metal which holds it together, the precious marbles and gorgeous mosaics which adorn it—yesterday purely material and of potter's clay—today, through consecration are living, eloquent, burning tongues of adoration, praise, petition and reparation to the greater glory of God and for man's everlasting benediction.''

It was indeed a scene of marvelous power and beauty; the wide aisles of the Cathedral thronged with a vast multitude of interesting spectators, a veritable sea of upturned faces, suffused with devotion, joy and gratitude; the mellow sunlight streaming down upon them from the great central dome. And in the sanctuary, amid the golden glow of the light reflected from the marbles and mosaics of the altar and baldachino and arch above, the four princes of the Universal Church, amid the shepherds of the people from a thousand places far and near. It was grand, it was overpowering: and the only expression the Catholic heart could utter was the immortal saying of Holy Scripture, "Truly this is the House of God and the Gate of Heaven."

The Mass continued in all its pomp and splendor. Finally the "Ite Missa Est" is sung, and the Papal Benediction pronounced. It was half-past one, before the Mass was over and the crowd left church. The worshipers passed through a vestibule hung with Papal colors of yellow and white, wreathed with emblems and floral adornments.

The day was declining and the shades of the beautiful summer night were falling fast, when another great gathering of people found itself massed in a wide circle around the Cathedral. The sacramental procession over the "sacred way," "the via sacra," as Lindell Boulevard from the Cathedral to the Archbishop's Residence was renamed for the occasion, clings to the memory as the most beautiful and entrancing event of the entire celebration. The procession formed at the Archbishop's house at half-past seven in the evening. Cheer after cheer went up from the immense concourse of people, at least 40 deep on both sides of the line, as the Papal Legate and the Cardinals passed by on their way to the Cathedral. When all the clergy had entered, the usual Benediction with the Blessed Sacrament was given by Cardinal O'Donnell. As the procession emerged from the portal and slowly wended its solemn way up to the wide boulevard, a scene of surpassing splendor opened before them. The sacred way, about eight blocks in length, lay flooded in light from the thousands and thousands of electric globes hiding from view the very stars in the blue dome of heaven. It was a pathway of light and glory, enclosed on all sides by the darkness of night. Along the route of the Sacred Way were lined more than 6000 children from the parish schools of the city and county. Behind this guard of honor stood protecting cordons of Catholic men— 4000 of them from the various Catholic societies of the city.

Against this solid bulwark pressed a living sea of more than one hundred thousand spectators crowding sidewalks and lawns and balconies and every perch of vantage. There was no cheering, no disturbance of any kind, as the great procession of priests and friars and prelates, bishops and archbishops passed along chanting the Litany of all the Saints. As the Blessed Sacrament was carried by, a slight ripple seemed to run along the mighty crowd on both sides of the way, and then came a deep hush: thousands and thousands were kneeling in rapt adoration, saluting the awful presence of their Lord and God.

Benediction with the Blessed Sacrament was given by Cardinal O'Donnell on the lawn at the Archbishop's Home. Then the procession was set in motion once more for the grounds of the Sacred Heart Convent. Here it reached its height of beauty because of the exquisite array of the setting. Against the dark walls had been set a temporary altar on the steps of the convent building. At the bottom were the red kneeling benches. At least five thousand persons were massed in the convent grounds. Up the steps to the lighted altar went Cardinal O'Donnell, the celebrant, and his attendants reached the convent for the last Benediction of the evening.

It was then 9 o'clock, an hour and a half after the procession had started, and an hour after the first Benediction at the Cathedral had been given. The hush that has fallen over the bowed worshipers is broken, as the chimes ring and announce the movement of the Blessed Sacrament in solemn Benediction. The priests and choristers intone "Holy God, we praise Thy Name," and the solemn rites are over. The crowd lingers for a moment to catch a last glimpse of the prelates and then melts away into the adjacent streets.

The next day, June 30th, was set apart for the special Centenary Convention of the St. Louis Archdiocese. The Solemn Pontifical Mass was to be celebrated by the Cardinal Archbishop of Paris, as representative of France. But as His Eminence failed to arrive from Chicago, Archbishop Hanna of San Francisco, took the place of Cardinal Dubois. Archbishop Dowling of St. Paul delivered the Jubilee sermon, a panegyric charged with memories of the heroic men and women who fought the good fight and prepared the way for the Church in the Mississippi Valley.

The Centennial banquet in the Hotel Chase in the evening served as the afterglow of the ever-memorable celebration. It was attended by the Cardinal-Legate and a large number of archbishops, bishops and priests and by the leaders of St. Louis society, Catholic and non-catholic. The speakers, representing both the hierarchy and laity were men of national reputation.

All in all, the ceremonies commemorating the consecration of the St. Louis Cathedral and the Centennial of the Diocese of St. Louis formed a truly historic event emphasizing, as the leading Daily of St. Louis took occasion to state."

"The magnitude and splendor which the Roman Catholic Church has achieved in the Western world." "Its greatness may be symbolized in the glory of its architecture and the robed and mitred majesty of its prelates; but its greatness resides in the fervor of its people, in their worshipful fidelity to its covenants, in their unswerving trust in its authority and guidance. In a time when other sects complain of faltering allegiance and fading prestige, the Roman Catholic Church, so far as an impartial noncommunicant can observe, maintains the full flower and vigor of its dynastic genius.''

The celebration, so deeply significant and so splendidly carried out, was a great triumph of Archbishop Glennon. But we need not praise him; the Holy Father, Pius XI, has done that in a manner worthy to be immortalized, in his letter of congratulation, of September 23rd, 1928:

''Venerable Brother,
Health and the Apostolic Blessing.''

A happy day indeed will dawn for you on the 13th of the coming month of October, the day which will round out twenty-five years of your administration of the extensive Archdiocese of St. Louis. As, on this joyful occasion, all your Diocesans, we understand, wish to tender to you a public testimony of their love and veneration, we deem it fit that you should not fail to receive likewise our congratulations: for this is but the just reward of the deeds which you have accomplished for the sake of the Church of God—and these deeds are many and excellent. We can only summarize; but must say that you are deserving of especial praise, not only for your eloquent preaching of the word of God, and your constant conscientious discharge of your pastoral duties; but also because you have never left anything undone which might contribute to the welfare of the Church confided to you. Indeed there stand remarkable monuments of your activity and zeal: your Cathedral, a most splendid édifice, at the dedication of which, only a short time ago, our own Legate presided; and for the training of the young aspirants to the Priesthood, the Major Seminary erected by your exertions, and, besides, the new building in contemplation, for the construction of which a large amount of money has already been contributed by your good people. Nor should this short enumeration of your deeds pass over in silence the numerous parishes which you have established in order to supply the spiritual needs of the constantly increasing Catholic population.

''For this cause, to You, who are so strenuous in the discharge of your pastoral office, we bear a most particular affection; and with pleasure do we share in your joy and join our own good wishes to the good wishes of your Diocesans. Especially we beg of God in your behalf that He may help You in your holy undertakings, and that He may be pleased to keep you many, yes, very many years to the love of all your people.''

## CHAPTER 22

## EPILOGUE

Here now we rest at the end of our long journey through two and one-half centuries of a forward movement of the Church, unprecedented in the annals of the world. From small, almost insignificant beginnings in the primeval forests and prairies of the Continent of North America, the Church opened a steady advance, slowly, laboriously, but ever hopefully struggling onward, until the true center was found in the city of the Crusader Saint on the banks of the mightiest river of the world.

The diocese of St. Louis once established, the religious advance proceeded irresistably until, after one hundred years, we behold almost every city and town and village and country-side of the western world crowned with dome or tower or spire, which the living faith of millions of Catholic people have erected to the honor and glory of the Living God. It is a miracle of God's power and wisdom and mercy, doing such great things through mortal man.

But the outward splendor and magnificence of our almost innumerable churches, and schools and institutions of religion and culture and charity, is but the symbol of the Living Temple of God, not built by the hands of man or produced by human wisdom but by the love and Wisdom of God. · The Catholic people of the West are as loyal and sincere believers in the Church's sublime teaching, as strong and undaunted defenders of her rights, as high-minded and generous supporters of her manifold undertakings for the honor of God and the welfare of mankind, as may be found anywhere in the wide world.

· Composed of elements from every nation of Europe, Asia, Africa and the Islands of the Sea, they are a unified body, all clinging to the center of Unity, the See of Peter and, though differing in many things one from the other, yet all united in one common impulse to win the world for Christ the Lord of All.

Not that all are saints; far from it, not that all are pleasant people such as the world loves to acclaim; no: but they all know and believe that they have a call to a higher life, than the worldling; and that the grace of God is not wanting to their every effort. To have brought order out of the seeming chaos of many nations with conflicting aspirations and deep-seated prejudices and varied customs and habits of thought, is the greatest glory of the Western Church.

And now, from the point of vantage we have gained, let us look back upon the recorded past, to single out the secret of success. The first was singleness of purpose, the glory of God. *Ad Majorem Dei Gloriam* was, from the beginning, the watchword of the Jesuit Mission-aries, treading the Indian trail or voyaging in the frail canoe or confined to the lonely station amid an alien people who did not care, or if they did, cared only to hate. Not for any earthly consideration did the distinguished men of God, a Gibault, a Bernard de Limpach, a Paul de Saint Pierre, a Gabriel Richard, a Levadoux and Flaget and the rest of their saintly company, live and labor and die, far removed from the comforts of Home.

*Ad Majorem Dei Gloriam* was also the supreme motive of the lowliest of that band.

It almost seemed a hopeless struggle; yet, they would not, they could not lose hope under the banner of Christ, who liveth in the glory of the Father.

And when at last their prayers and labors began to bring victory after victory under such leaders as Du Bourg, Rosati, De Andreis, Van Quickenborne, Elet, De Smet and John Timon, Peter Richard Kenrick and the multitude of their devoted followers, penetrating into the regions of darkness, north, west, east and south, carrying the glad tidings of the gospel to the scattered fragments of many nations, it was again "Ad Majorem Dei Gloriam."

True it is, they too had their failings to trouble them, and their earthly concerns that threatened to turn them aside from the clear path of duty; human they were, but uppermost in their mind and deepest down in their heart was the desire, the will, to do something "Ad Majorem Dei Gloriam."

That was the first secret of their success, singleness of purpose, and that of the noblest kind.

And their second secret, lying at the very root of all that was good and excellent in them, was their strong, living, undaunted faith. No difficulty proposed could disturb them, even if they themselves were unable to solve it. They were convinced with absolute certainty that the doctrines of their religion came from the mouth of God, and needed no defence, but only a lucid statement to be accepted by every man who was of good will. Controversy was not to their liking, and still less the fault of minimizing the import of God's word. Most of these pioneers were not learned in book-lore, nor gifted with the power of human eloquence and, generally, far from being worldly-wise. But they had and cherished the divine gift of an unconquerable faith; and this it was that supported them in the spiritual combat and led them on to renewed efforts in the cause of God.

Their outward labors, successes may seem insignificant and never to be compared to those of a later day. And yet these very men laid the foundations on which the greatness of our day must be acknowledged to rest. Beautiful and spacious churches, grand institutions of learning and charity, political influence, power to compel wealth, all these may be signs and indications of true religion, but they are not religion itself. It is the faith of a people that makes it great, not its greatness that makes it truly faithful.

Strong, living, undaunted faith of its priests and people led them to the glorious heights we now enjoy.

And the third great secret of our early missionaries, although it may not appear as a secret, was their constant desire and effort to make converts, to lead back the separated brethren to the Church, the common home of all. It is the noblest charity to win a soul for Christ, the Good Shepherd. And the pioneer missionaries knew that nothing would give greater pleasure and satisfaction to their Superior or their Bishop, than the announcement of the conversions they had made.

To sum up what has been said: Singleness of purpose, strong, lively and undaunted faith, and the spirit of charity towards erring, forlorn souls, formed the triune secret of success in the past and, as every society must continue in the same state in which it was founded or miserably perish, it would follow that every success that does not, mediately or immediately, spring from these principles, is no true advance, but rather a dangerous reverse.

Some of the signs of the times are ominous: others may only seem so: yet eternal vigilance is said to be the price of liberty: so the continued freedom and healthy progress depend upon the spiritual height and intensity with which the clergy and the people regard and treat all the various concerns of life.

# BIBLIOGRAPHY

It cannot be my purpose here to give in detail all the sources that contributed to the substance of this History. Where only a few facts of minor importance were gleaned the bare mention in the text or the notes must suffice. This refers particularly to the class of unpublished sources, which are so numerous that even the briefest bibliographical notice of them would occupy many pages. Of the published sources a more extended notice is given, as they can be more easily consulted by the student. Of the secondary works, whether relating to the life of the Church itself or to its historical background, a sufficient number of books, pamphlets, and articles will be found. As a Bibliography is intended not only to facilitate the verification of the facts narrated, but also to give the reader some pointers as to further research work, the list of these books is perhaps larger than would seem necessary.

## UNPUBLISHED SOURCES

1. Archdiocesan Report, Memoranda Missionum ante Fundationem Urbis Sti. Ludovici, Archives of St. Louis Archdiocese.

2. Archives of St. Louis Archdiocese, containing a Mass of Petitions, Instructions and Letters of Bishop Du Bourg, Bishop Rosati, Fathers De Andreis, Cellini, Lutz, Lefevere, Roux, Dahmen, Saint Cyr, Timon, the Jesuit Missionaries, Vicar-General Melcher, Bishop Kenrick, and many others, which illustrate the period of our Church history from 1818-1845.

3. Archives of the Missouri Province of the Society of Jesus, St. Louis University.

4. Archives of Baltimore Cathedral, preserving a number of letters from priests of the transition period as Fathers Rivet, De Saint Pierre, Janin, Maxwell, Valiniere, Gibault and numerous others.

5. The Library of Congress, Washington, with its wealth of transcripts from French and Spanish documents found in the Archives of Paris and Sevilla, and other cities.

6. Archiepiscopal Archives of Quebec.

7. Indian Office Letter Books in Department of Indian Affairs, Washington. Correspondence of Bishop Du Bourg and Fathers Van Quickenborne and Verhaegen with Commissioner of Indian Affairs.

8. Taschereau, E. A., Mission du Seminaire de Quebec, chez les Tamarois du Illinois sur les Bords du Mississippi. M. S., dated 1849, in Laval University, Quebec.

9. Kenrick Seminary Archives, Collections of the Letters of Bishops Du Bourg, and Rosati, Fathers Timon, De Andreis and others, in typewritten copies made by the Very Rev. Dr. Charles L. Souvay, C.M., D.D.

10. Archives of the Missouri Historical Society.

11. Archives of the Eastern Province of the Society of Jesus, Baltimore.

12. Archives of the Propaganda, Rome.

13. Archives of Monte Citorio, Rome.

14. Chancery of St. Louis Archdiocese, Registers of Clergy and of Parishes, Account Books, Official Correspondence with Rome, Official Announcements,

(769)

Pastoral Letters. For a list of these documents cf. St. Louis Catholic
Historical Review, vol. I, pp. 24-39 and pp. 276-285.

15. Parish Archives of the Old Cathedral, Ste. Genevieve, Old Mines, Post of
Arkansas, Old St. Michael's, and various city churches.

## PUBLISHED SOURCES

### JESUIT RELATIONS AND ALLIED DOCUMENTS

Travels and Explorations of the French Jesuit Missionaries among the Indians
of Canada and the Northern and North-Western States of the United States 1610-
1791; with numerous Historical, Geographical, Ethnological, and Bibliograhpical
Notes, and an Analytical Index, under the editorial direction of Reuben Gold
Thwaites, LL.D., 73 vols., 8vo., averaging 300 pages. Cleveland, 1896-1901.

An exact verbatim et literatim reprint of the very rare French, Latin, and
Italian Originals, both MS. and Printed, accompanied page for page by a Complete
English Translation. Illustrated with numerous facsimiles, portraits, maps, etc.
The volumes specially important for our purpose were:

# ILLINOIS HISTORICAL COLLECTIONS

Virginia Series and British Series.

## C. W. ALVORD, CAHOKIA RECORDS

## C. W. ALVORD, KASKASKIA RECORDS (1778-1790)

## JAMES A. JAMES—GEORGE ROGERS CLARK PAPERS (1771-1781)

Lettres de Mgr. Rosati, c. XVIII, pp. 542, 545, 553, 574.
Lettres de M. Odin, c. XVIII, pp. 533, 537.
Lettre du P. Van Quickenborne, c. XVIII, p. 512.
Lettre de M. Anduzi, c. XVIII, p. 501.
Lettre de M. J. B. Blanc, c. XVIII, p. 509.
Lettre de M. Bouillier, c. XVIII, p. 515.
Lettre de M. Du Chesne, c. XVIII, p. 571.
Lettre de M. Lutz, missionaire chez les Kansas, c. XVIII, p. 556.
Lettre de M. Ar . . . Um . . . , c. XVIII, p. 525.
Vol. IV, Cahier XIX—XXIV.
Mission du Missouri, c. XXIII, p. 571.
Lettres de Mgr. Rosati, c. XXIII, pp. 593, 595.
Lettres du P. Van Quickenborne, c. XXIII, pp. 572, 590.
Mission du Missouri, c. XXIV, p. 656.
Lettre de Mgr. Rosati, c. XXIV, p. 663.
Lettres de M. Antoine Blanc, c. XXIV, pp. 657, 667, 670.
Lettre de M. Paillasson, c. XXIV, p. 661.
Vol. V, Cahier XXV—XXX.
Mission du Missouri, c. XXIX, p. 563.
Lettres de Mgr. Rosati, c. XXIX, pp. 566, 568, 597.
Lettres du P. De Theux, c. XXIX, pp. 570, 573.
Lettre de M. Bouillier, c. XXIX, p. 59.
Lettre de M. Rondot, c. XXIX, p. 575.
Lettre de M. Paillasson, c. XXIX, p. 587.
Vol. VI, Cahier XXXI—XXXV.
Notice historique sur M. Richard, c. XXXII, p. 147.
Vol. VII, Cahier XXXVI—XLI.
Lettres de Mgr. Rosati, c. XXXVI, pp. 101, 103, 108, 112, 117, 122, 126.
Lettre du P. De Theux, c. XXXVI, p. 105.
Lettre de M. Leclerc, c. XXXVI, p. 115.
Notice sur Mgr. Du Bourg, c. XXXVI, p. 99.
Vol. VIII, Cahier XLII—XLVIII.
Mission du Missouri—
Lettres de Mgr. Rosati, c. XLIV, pp. 262, 273, 276.
Lettres du P. De Theux, c. XLIV, pp. 278, 285.
Vol. IX, Cahier XL—LIII.
Mission du Missouri, c. XLVIII, p. 88.
Relation du voyage chez les tribes Indiennes par le P. Van Quickenborne, c. XLVIII,
   p. 88.
Vol. X, Cahier LIV—LX.
Mission du Missouri, c. LV, p. 129.
Lettre du P. Van Quickenborne, c. LIV, p. 129.
Vol. XI, Cahier LXI.
Notice sur les Pottomatomies, p. 379.
Lettres de M. Petit, pp. 382, 400.
Lettre du P. Verhaegen, p. 469.
Lettres du P. De Smet, pp. 479, 499.

Under the title, ''Letters Concerning some Missions of the Mississippi Valley, A. D. 1818-1827,'' Neina dos Santos translated and published in the Records of the American Catholic Historical Society of Philadelphia (Vol. XIV, No. 2), copious extracts of letters from Bishop Du Bourg, Bishop Flaget, Fathers Michaud, Portier, Odin, Rosati, Anthony and Jean B. Blanc. Other translations have appeared from time to time in the "Illinois Catholic Historical Review."

## THE ANNALS OF THE LEOPOLDINE ASSOCIATION OF THE EMPIRE OF AUSTRIA (1831-1852)

Most important for our purpose were the following Reports:

Report XIX (1846)—
14. Rev. B. Raho, C.M., to Leop. Assoc., St. Louis, September 17, 1845 ____ 51-54
20. Rev. F. Helias, S.J., to Leop. Assoc., Jefferson City, Mo., Jan. 6, 1845 __ 66-76
Report XX (1847)—
9. Rev. J. Patschowsky, S.J., to his Superior, Florissant, Mo., March 17, 1846 _____ 37-43
Report XXI (1848-1849)—
11. Rev. J. Van de Velde, S.J., to Leop. Assoc., St. Louis, Nov. 29, 1846 ____ 35-43
12. Rev. J. N. Hofbauer, S.J., to his Superior, St. Louis, April 8, 1846 ____ 43-51
Report XXIV (1852)—
1. Most Rev. P. R. Kenrick to Leop. Assoc., St. Louis, Oct. 16, 1850 _____ 1-6


### HISTORICAL REVIEWS AND MAGAZINES—ABBREVIATIONS

ACQR   *American Catholic Quarterly Review*, Philadelphia, Pa.

AD   *Acta et Dieta*, published by the Catholic Historical Society of St. Paul, St. Paul, Minn.

Am   *America*, published weekly by the America Press, New York City.

AMK   *Amerika*, Daily and Weekly, St. Louis, Mo.

CHR   *The Catholic Historical Review*, published quarterly by the Catholic University of America, Washington, D. C.

CISHL   *Collections of Illinois State Historical Library.*

CP   *The Church Progress*, St. Louis.

ER   *Ecclesiastical Review*, Philadelphia.

FR   *The Fortnightly Review*, St. Louis, Mo.

GD   *Globe-Democrat.*

HG   *Herold des Glaubens.*

HAHR   *The Hispanic American Historical Review*, published quarterly, Baltimore, Md.

HRS   *Historical Records and Studies*, published by the United States Catholic Historical Society, New York.

ICHR   *Illinois Catholic Historical Review*, published quarterly by the Illinois Catholic Historical Society, Chicago, Ill.

JISHS   *Journal of the Illinois State Historical Society*, published quarterly by the Illinois State Historical Society, Springfield, Ill.

LHQ   *Louisiana Historical Quarterly*, published by the Louisiana Historical Society, New Orleans, La.

MHM   *Michigan History Magazine*, published quarterly by the Michigan Historical Commission, Lansing, Mich.

MHSC   *Missouri Historical Society Collections.*

MinnHB   *Minnesota History Bulletin*, published quarterly by the Minnesota Historical Society, St. Paul, Minn.

MoHR   *The Missouri Historical Review*, published quarterly by the State Historical Society of Missouri, Columbia, Mo.

MVHR   *The Mississippi Valley Historical Review*, published quarterly by the Mississippi Valley Historical Association, Lincoln, Neb.

PastBl   *Pastoral-Blatt*, St. Louis, Mo.

PD   *Post Dispatch.*

RACHS   *Records of the American Catholic Historical Society of Philadelphia*, published quarterly by the Society, Philadelphia, Pa.

SLHR   *St. Louis Catholic Historical Review.*

SLR   *St. Louis Republic.*

TISHS   *Transactions of the Illinois State Historical Society,* published by
         the Illinois State Historical Society, Springfield, Ill.
WF    *Wahrheits Freund,* Cincinnati, O.
WMH   *The Wisconsin Magazine of History,* published quarterly by the State
         Historical Society of Wisconsin, Menasha, Wis.
WW    *The Western Watchman,* St. Louis, Mo.

## PUBLISHED SOURCES—Continued

Acta et Decreta, Concilii Plenarii Baltimorensis Secundi, A. D. 1866.   Baltimore,
     1868.   Concilii Plenarii Baltimorensis Tertii, A. D. 1884, Baltimore 1886.
Allouez.   Journey of Father Allouez to Lake Superior, in ''Early Narratives of the
     Northwest,'' by Louise Phelps Kellogg, N. Y., Scribner, 1917.
Allouez.   Father Allouez's Wisconsin Journey, Ibid.
Alvord, C. W. Sources of Catholic History in Illinois, I. C. H. R., vol. I p. 73.
Archives of St. Louis, Right Reverend James Oliver Van de Velde, D.D., I. C. H.
     R., vol. IX, p. 56.
Ashe, Thomas.   Travels in America, 1806, for the purpose of exploring the Rivers
     Allegheny and Monongahela, Ohio and Mississippi, and to ascertain the
     produce and condition of their banks and vicinity.
Association of the Propagation of the Faith, The.   Metropolitan Magazine, vol. II,
     p. 9, 1855.
Austin's Journal.   American Historical Review, vol. VIII, p. 518.
Bacon, Leonard Woolsey, (Editor).   An Inside View of the Vatican Council.   New
     York, no date.
Barbe-Marbois.   Histoire de la Louisiana.   Paris, 1829.
Beckwith, H. W.   Collections of the Illinois State Historical Library, vol. I con-
     taining, Voyages of Father Marquette, Hennepin's Narrative, LaSalle's
     Voyage, Memoir of H. De Touty.
Benedict XV.   An Appeal to the Catholics of America.   FR, vol. XXVI, No. 19,
     ·  October 1, 1919, p. 289.
Bradbury, John.   Travels in America, 1809-1811; including upper Louisiana, Ohio,
     Kentucky, Indiana and Tennessee with Illinois and western territories.
     Philadelphia, 1819.
Browne, Rev. Patrick W., Translator and Annotator.   Dilhet, Etat de l'Eglise
     Catholique ou Diocèse des Etats Unis dans l'Amérique Septentrionale.
Cabeza de Vaca, Wanderings of.   Edited by Frederick W. Hodge, of the Bureau of
     American Ethnology.   In the Spanish Explorers in the Southern United
     States, 1528-1543.
Calendar of Documents Mississippi Valley.   Publication, Louisiana Hist. S., vol. IV,
     1908, pp. 7, 13, 38, 41, 43, 100.
Carayon, A.   Bannissement de Jesuites de la Louisiana.   Paris, 1865.
Carver, Jonathan.   Travels through interior parts of North America; account of
     Great Lakes, etc.; description of birds, beasts, insects, and fishes; history of
     genius, manners and customs of the Indians.   Philadelphia, 1796.
Carondelet, Baron.   Letter of Instructions of Baron Carondelet to Lieut. Col. Don
     Carlos Howard, Nov. 26, 1796.   MoHSC., vol. III, 1, pp. 71-91.
Castañeda, Pedro de.   Expedition of Coronado.   Edited by Frederick W. Hodge.
———   Pedro de.   Expedition of Coronado.   Edited by Frederick W. Hodge.
———   In the Spanish Explorers in the Southern United States, 1528-1543.
Catholic Church, 1783-1789, The.   (Document) CHR, vol. XV.
Catlin, Geo.   The Manners, Customs and Conditions of the North American Indians,
     written during eight years' travel amongst the wildest tribes of Indians in
     North America. 1832-1839.

Charlevoix, Father. Letters to Duchess of Lesdiguieres; voyage to Canada and travels through that vast country and Louisiana to Gulf of Mexico. London, 1763.

—— Pièrre Francois Xavier de, (S.J.) A voyage to North America undertaken by command of the present King of France, containing the Geographical Description and Natural History of Canada and Louisiana with the Customs, Manners, Trade and Religion of the Inhabitants; a Description of the Lakes and Rivers with their Navigation and manner of passing the Great Cataracts, 2 vols. (Dublin, 1766.)

—— P. F. X. de. History and General Description of New France. Translated and extensively annotated by John G. Shea; with numerous finely engraved portraits, many proofs on India paper, folding maps, etc. 6 vols., New York, 1866.

Chittenden, Hiram Martin and Alfred Talbot Richardson. Life, Letters and Travels of Father Pierre Jean De Smet, S.J., 1801-1873. 4 vols. New York, 1905.

Chouteau, Auguste, Col. Journal of the Founding of St. Louis. Original and Translation. MoHSC., vol. III, 4, pp. 335-366.

—— J. Gilman. The J. Gilman Chouteau Papers. MoHSC., vol. III, 1, pp. 93-94.

Colby, Charles W. The Jesuit Relations. American Historical Review, 1901, pp. 36-55. The Fortnightly Review, April 1918.

Collectio Lacensis. Acta et Decreta Sacrorum Conciliorum Recentiorum. 8 vol., Friburgi 1875-1890.

Collot, Victor. A Journey in North Amercia, containing a survey of the countries watered by the Mississippi, Ohio, Missouri (etc.) and a projected line of frontiers. Firenze, 1924.

Concilia Baltimorensia, habita ab anno 1829, usque ab annum 1849-52-55-58.

Congress, Library of. Handbook of Manuscripts in the Library of Congress. Government Printing Office. FR, vol. XXVI, No. 9, May 1, 1919, p. 144.

Coronado through Kansas, 1540, then known as Quivira. A story of the Kansas, Osage, and Pawnee Indians. Plates. (Seneca, Kas. 1908.)

Correspondence Relating to New Orleans and St. Louis. RACHS, vol. XIX, pp. 185 and 305.

D'Artaguiette. D'Artaguiette's Journal of a tour up the Mississippi to the Illinois Country, 1722-1723; in ''Travels in the American Colonies,'' by N. D. Mereness. 693 pp., N. Y., 1916.

Darby, John F. Personal Recollections. St. Louis, 1880.

Douglass, J. C., Enroll. Agent. Journal of a Migrating Party of Potawatomi Indians, 1838. Indiana Magazine of History, vol. XXI, pp. 315-336.

Duden, Gottfried. Berichte über eine Reise nach den Westlichen Staaten Nordamerika's. Elberfeld, 1829.

—— Gottfried. G. Duden's Report, 1824-1827; by William G. Bek. MoHR., vol. XIII, 3, April 1919, pp. 251-281.

—— And his Critics; by Jessie J. Kile. TISHS., vol. XXI, pp. 63-70.

Fencl, Leonard J. (S.J.) The Death of Father Marquette.

Flaget, Benedict, Bishop. Report of the Diocese of Bardstown to Pius VII. April 10, 1815. CHR, vol. I, p. 305.

Flagg. The Far West. 1838.

—— Flat Boat. Description according to travelers in the beginning of the 19th century; in Pioneer Letters of Gershom Flagg. TISHS XV., p. 152, and 40.

Flint, Timothy. Recollections of last ten years, in Valley of Mississippi from Pittsburgh and the Missouri to Gulf of Mexico and from Florida to the Spanish frontier. Boston, 1826.

Franchere, Gabriel. Narrative of a Voyage to the Northwest Coast of America in 1811—14 or the First American Settlement on the Pacific. Plates. N. Y. 1854.

French, B. F.  Historical Collections of Louisiana; translations of rare valuable documents, relating to natural, civil, and political history, historical and biographical notes, and an introduction; folding map.  8vo., 309 pp., newly bound in half morocco.  Philadelphia, 1850.

—— Part II containing: Translation of a recently discovered manuscript journal of expedition of Hernando de Soto in Florida, by L. Hernandez de Biedma; English province of Carolina, etc., by Coxe; discovery of new countries and nations in North America in 1673 by Père Marquette and Sieur Joliet, etc.

—— Part III contains: Laharpe's Historical Journal, Historical Journal of Father Charlevoix, The Black Code.

Freri, Msgr.  Centenary of the Society for the Propagation of the Faith.  CHR, New S., vol. II, p. 137.

Garraghan, Rev. Gilbert J. (S.J.)  Some Newly Discovered Missouri Maps.  MHSC, vol. V, p. 256.

Gentleman of Elvas, The.  Relacam verdadera dos traballos y governador do Hernando de Soto....passaron.

Griffin, M. T. J.  The American Catholic Historical Researches, Philadelphia, 1887-1912.

Hamilton, Raphael N. (S.J.)  The Journey of the Bishop of Walla Walla.  ICHR, vol. IX, p. 208.

Hennepin, Father Louis.  A New Discovery of a Vast Country in America.  Reuben Gold Thwaites, Editor.  2 vols.  Chicago, 1903.

—— Louis.  The Franciscan.  Minnesota Historical Collections, vol. I, p. 302-313.

Herbermann, Charles G.  Very Rev. Pierre Gibault, V.G.  HRS, vol. VI, Part II. .

Hogan, J. J., Bishop of Kansas City.  On the Mission in Missouri.  Kansas City, 1892.

Holweck, Rev. F. G.  Father Beauprez' Letters.  StLCHR, vol. V, p. 40.

—— Contribution to the "Inglesi Affair."  StLCHR, vol. V, p. 14. ·

—— The Historical Archives of St. Louis.  StLCHR, vol. I, p. 24.

Houck, Louis.  The Spanish Regime in Missouri.  Two vols.  Chicago, 1909.

Howe, Henry.  Historical Collections of The Great West.  Cincinnati, 1855.

Hughes, Thomas Aloysius, (S.J.)  History of the Society of Jesus in North America, Colonial and Federal, 2 vols.  Text 2 vols.  Documents 2 vols.  New York, 1907-1917.

Inama, Father.  Letter, December 27, 1842, in Katholische Blätter aus Tirol, 1843.

Irving, Theo.  Conquest of Florida, by Hernando de Soto; folding map.  New York, 1851.

James, J. A.  George Rogers Clark Papers, 1771-1781.  CISHL, vol. VIII.

—— George Rogers Clark Papers, 1781-1784.  CISHL, vol. XIX.

Jogues.  Journey of Raymbault and Jogues to the Sault, by Father Lalemant, in "Early Narratives of the Northwest," by Louise Phelps Kellogg.  N. Y., Scribner, 1917.

Joliet.  The Mississippi Voyage of Joliet and Marquette, in "Early Narratives of the Northwest," by Louise Phelps Kellogg.  N. Y., Scribner, 1917.

Journal.  Missouri Constitutional Convention of 1875.  Columbia, 1920.

Joutel's Journal of La Salle's Last Voyage, 1648-87; with frontispiece of Gudebrod's statue of La Salle and map of the original French edition, Paris, 1713, in facsimile.  Albany, 1906.

Kain, M. Rev. John J.  Synodus Diocesana Sti. Ludovici Tertia 1896.  Sti. Ludovici 1897.

Kansas Historical Collections, *i. e.* Transactions of the Kansas State Historical Society.  Topeka, Kansas.

Kappler, Charles J. (ed.) Indian Affairs, Laws and Treaties, 2 vols. Washington, 1904.

Kellogg, L. P. Early Narratives of the Northwest, 1634-1699; maps and facsimile. 8vo., pp. 396, cloth. New York, 1917. Nicolet, Radisson, Allouez, Joliet and Marquette, La Salle, etc.

Kelly, Rev. John. The Mission to Liberia. HRS, vol. XIV, pp. 120-153.

Kenrick, The—Frenaye Correspondence. Letters chiefly of F. P. Kenrick and Mark Anthony Frenaye, Selected from the Catholic Archives of Philadelphia; Translated, arranged and annotated as Sources and Helps to the Study of Local Catholic History, 1830-1862. By F. E. T., Turcher, Philadelphia, 1920.

Kip, W. I. Early Jesuit Missions in North America, compiled from letters of French Jesuits, with annotations and the scarce folded map. 12mo., pp. 339, cloth. Albany, 1873.

Koerner, Gustave. Memoirs of, 1809-1896, life sketches written at the suggestion of his children, edited by McCormack; portrait. 2 vols., Chicago, 1918.

Leo XIII on Americanism. Latin and English. January 22, 1899.

Lettres Edifiantes et Curieuses, écrites des Missions Etrangères. With numerous maps. 26 vols., Paris, 1780-1783.

Letters from Archives of Baltimore, vol. XX, pp. 49, 193, 250, 431.

Letters Selected from the Cathedral Archives, Philadelphia, containing a number of Bishop Peter Richard Kenrick Letters. RACHS, vol. XXX, No. 4.

Lewis and Clark. History of the Expedition, 1804-5-6. 2 vols. Chicago, 1902.

Lionel St. George Lindsay. Correspondence between the Abbé Gibault and Bishop Briand. RACHS, vol. II, pp. 406-430.

Louisiana, An Echo of the Old Order of Church and State in. (Father Hilaire de Geneveaux, Prothonotary). RACHS, vol. XXV, No. 4.

Marquette's Last Voyage, 1674-1675, in L. P. Kellogg's, Early Narratives of the Northwest, pp. 259-278.

Mason, Edward G. Illinois in the Eighteenth Century, containing: Chicago, 1881; Kaskaskia and The Parish Records of Old Fort Chartres.

Mazzuchelli, Rev. S. Memoirs, Historical and Edifying, of a Missionary Apostolic of the Order of Saint Dominic, Among Various Indian Tribes and Among the Catholics and Protestants in the United States of America. With an Introduction by the Most Reverend John Ireland, D.D., Archbishop of St. Paul. Saint Clara College, Sinsinawa, Wisconsin, 1915.

—— Memoirs, transl. by Sister Mary Benedicta Kennedy, O.S.D., Chicago. (Rev. ICHR, vol. I, 1, July 1918, pp. 124-125.)

McCann, Mary Agnes, Sister. Bishop Purcell's Journal, 1833-1836. CHR, vol. V, p. 239.

Narratives of the Northwest, pp. 281-320.

Memoir of La Salle's Discoveries, by De Tonty, 1678-1690, in L. P. Kellogg's, Early

Mississippi Voyage of Joliet and Marquette, The. 1673, in L. P. Kellogg's, Early Narratives of the Northwest, pp. 221-257.

Nicolet, John. History of Discovery of Northwest in 1634, with sketch of his life, by C. W. Butterfield. Cincinnati, 1881.

Nutall's Travels into Arkansas Territory, 1819. EWT, vol. XIII.

O'Daniel, Rev. V. F. Some Letters of Fathers Badin and Nerinckx to Bishop Carroll. CHR, vol. VI, p. 66.

O'Hanlon, Canon. Life and Scenery in Missouri. Dublin, 1890.

Ohio Archaeological and Historical Society Publications. Vols. 1 to 10, inclusive. Columbus, 1900.

Pageant of 1671 in Early Narratives of the Northwest, The. pp. 211-218.

Papers Relating to the Church in America. RACHS, vol. VII, pp. 283-388, 434-492; vol. VIII, 195-240, 294-329, 450-512; vol. IX, 1-35.

Paré and Quaife. The St. Joseph Baptismal Register. MVHR, vol. XIII, pp. 201-239.

Pastoral Letter of the Second Plenary Council, 1866.

Payne, Rev. Raymond. Annals of the Leopoldine Association. CHR, vol. I, pp. 52-64 and 175-191.

Peñalver J. Cardenas. Statutes of the Diocese of Louisiana and the Florida. 1795. English and Spanish. 1887.

Pittman, Captain Philip. European Settlements on the Mississippi, 1770. Cleveland, 1906.

Proces-Verbal of Saint Lusson, June 14, 1671. Proces-Verbal of La Salle, April 9, 1682. In Wisconsin Historical Collection, vol. XI.

Propagation of the Faith, Annals of the—; Documents relating to the early Illinois Churches; by Cecilia Mary Young. ICHR, vol. I, 2, October, 1918, pp. 214-224.

Rothensteiner, Rev. John. Bishop England's Correspondence With Bishop Rosati. ICHR, vol. IX, pp. 260, 363; vol. X, p. 59.

———— (Editor) Letters of Bishop B. J. Fenwick of Boston to Bishop Rosati of St. Louis. ICHR, vol. X, p. 145.

———— Kaskaskia—Fr. Benedict Roux. ICHR, vol. I, p. 198.

———— (Editor) Correspondence of Archbishop Whitfield with Bishop Rosati. StLCHR, vol. V, p. 237.

———— The Northeastern Part of the Diocese of St. Louis under Bishop Rosati. ICHR, vols. II, III, IV.

Schoolcraft, H R.. Travels in the Central Portions of the Mississippi Valley; comprising observations on its Mineral Geography, Internal Resources, and Aboriginal Population Maps and illustrations. New York, 1825.

———— Exploring Expedition to Sources of Mississippi River, 1820; resumed and completed, by discovery of its origin in Itasca Lake, in 1832; with appendixes comprising original report of the copper mines of Lake Superior and geology of lake Basins, and summit of Mississippi; with all official reports and scientific papers of both expeditions, woodcut. Philadelphia, 1855.

———— Indian Tribes of the U. S. Historical and Statistical Information respecting the History, Condition and Prospects. Collected and prepared under the direction of the Bureau of Indian Affairs. Illustrated by S. Eastman, many plates in color. 6 vols., Philadelphia, 1851-57.

Seton, Rev. Robert. (Editor) Memoir Letters and Journal of Elizabeth Seton. 2 vols. New York, 1869.

Shabert, Rev. Joseph A. The Ludwig Missions Verein. CHR, New Series, vol. II, p. 23.

Shea, J. G. Discovery and Exploration of Mississippi Valley; narratives of Marquette, Allouez, Membre, Hennepin, and Anastase Douay; with facsimile of the newly discovered map of Marquette's letter and steel portrait of La Salle. Albany, 1903.

———— Early Voyages Up and Down Mississippi. Albany, 1861. The author has collected, translated and annotated various relations concerning voyages of Cavelier, De Montigny de Saint-Cosme, Le Sueur, Gravier and Guignas.

Shepard, Elihu H. The Autobiography. St. Louis, 1869.

———— The Early History of St. Louis and Missouri. Saint Louis, 1870.

Smet, De, Rev. Peter John (S.J.) Letters and Sketches with a Narrative of a Year's Residence among the Indian Tribes of the Rocky Mountains. Philadelphia, M. Fithian, 1843.

Smet, De, Rev. Peter John (S.J.) Oregon Missions and Travels over the Rocky Mountains in 1845-1846. New York, Edward Dunnigan, 1847.

———— Western Missions and Missionaries: A Series of Letters. New York, 1863. James B. Kirker.

———— New Indian Sketches. New York, 1863. D. and J. Sadlier & Co.

———— The Indian Missions in the United States of America under the care of the Missouri Province of the Society of Jesus. Philadelphia, 1841. King and David.

———— Précis Historiques, in Lettres Du R. P. Pierre De Smet. Bruxelles, 1853-1858.

———— Letters, translated by John A. Cahalan. RACHS, vols. IV and V.

Soto, de, Hernando, Expedition of, by the Gentleman of Elvas. Edited by Theodore H. Lewis, of St. Paul, in The Spanish Explorers in the Southern United States, 1528-1543.

Souvay, Rev. Charles L. (C.M.) (Editor) Correspondence of Bishop Du Bourg with Propaganda. StLCHR, vols. I, II, III.

———— Diary of Rosati, 1822-1826. StLCHR, vols. III and IV.

Stoddard, Major Amos. Sketches of Louisiana. Philadelphia, 1812.

Thompson, Joseph J. Illinois' First Citizen, Pierre Gibault. ICHR.

Trail Makers, The. The Journey of Alvar Nunez Cabeza de Vaca, and his companions from Florida to the Pacific, 1528-1536. Translated by Fanny Bandelier. Edited with an introduction by Ad. F. Bandelier.

———— Narratives of the Career of Hernando de Soto in the Conquest of Florida, 1539-1542, as told by a gentleman of Elvas, by Luys Hernandez de Biedma and by Rodrigo Ranjel. Edited with an Introduction by Prof. Edward Gaylord Bourne, of Yale University. In two volumes.

———— The Journey of Coronado, 1540-42. From the City of Mexico to the Buffalo Plains of Kansas and Nebraska. Translated and Edited, with an Introduction by George Parker Winship.

———— History of the Expedition Under the Command of Captains Lewis and Clark to the Sources of the Missouri. Across the Rocky Mountains Down the Columbia River to the Pacific in 1804-6. With an account of the Louisiana Purchase, by Prof. John Bach MacMaster, and an Introduction identifying the route. In three volumes.

———— A Journal of Voyages and Travels in the Interior of North America. By Daniel Williams Harmon, a partner in the Northwest Company, (beginning in 1800).

Trudeau's John B., Journal. American Hist. Review, vol. XIX, Original French, pp. 299-333. The same in English translated by Mrs. H. T. Beauregard. Missouri Hist. Coll., vol. IV, pp. 11-48.

Ulloa Instructions to Rui, 1767. MHSC, vol. III, p. 145.

United States Catholic Historical Magazine, The. New York, 1888-1892.

Vanished Bishopric in Ohio, A. Document. CHR, vol. II, p. 195.

Verwyst, P. Chrys. (O.S.F.) Missionary Labors of Father Marquette, Menard and Allouez in the Lake Superior Region.

Voyage of St. Cosme, The. 1678-1682, in L. P. Kellogg's Early Narratives of the Northwest, pp. 335-359.

Wyeth, Nathl. J. Correspondence and Journals, 1831-6. A Record of two Expeditions for the Occupation of the Oregon Country, with Maps, Introd. and Index. Edited, from the original MS by F. G. Young. Eugene, Oregon, 1899.

# GENERAL WORKS

Abbelen, P. M. Relatio de Quaestione Germanica in Statibus Foederatis, 1886.
—————— Mutter Maria Karolina Friess. St. Louis, 1892.
Abell, Annie Heloise. Indian Reservations in Kansas and the Extinguishment of their Title. Kansas Historical Collections, 8: 77.
Acadians, Were the, "Rebels?" ACQR, vol. XII, p. 32.
Agatha, St., Parish, St. Louis. St Louis, 1921. St. Agatha Gemeinde, 1890.
Albers, B. Francis (O.F.M.) St. Antonius Gemeinde, St. Louis, Mo., 1894.
Alerding, H. History of the Catholic Church in the Diocese of Vincennes. Indianapolis, 1883.
Alexian Brothers Hospital, St. Louis, Mo., Golden Jubilee, 1919.
Alphonsus, St., Church, Leaves from the History of.
Alvord, C. W. The Mississippi Valley in British Politics. CHR, vol. IV, p. 100.
—————— Clarence Walworth. The Illinois, Country, 1673-1818. Springfield, Ill., 1920. Centennial History of Illinois, vol. I.
—————— C. W. The Old Kaskaskia Records. Chicago, 1856.
—————— The Daniel Boone Myth. Journal ISHS, vol. XIX, 1 and 2.
Andreas. History of Chicago. 2 vols. Chicago.
Arnold, Matthew. Civilization in the United States. The Nineteenth Century. No. 134, April 1888.
Assumption, Church of the, New Haven, Mo., n. d.
Atkinson, E. The Winter of Deep Snow, 1831. TISHS.
Atwater, Caleb. History of Ohio. Cincinnati, 1838.
—————— Description of Antiquities discovered in the Western Country, 1833.
—————— Remarks Made on a Tour to Prairie du Chien, and Tour to Washington City, 1829.
Augusta, Immaculate Conception Parish, Mo., 1926.
Babb, Miss Margaret E. The Mansion House of Cahokia and its Builder, Nicholas Jarrot. TISHS, 1924, p. 78.
Babbitt, Charles H. Early Days in Council Bluffs. Washington, D. C., Press of Byron S. Adams, 1916. (Rev. CHR, III, pp. 349-350).
Baltimore. History of the Third Plenary Council of Baltimore. Baltimore, 1885.
Bandelier, Ad. F. Fray Juan de Padilla, the First Catholic Missionary and Martyr in Eastern Kansas. 1542. ACQR, vol. XV, p. 59, 1890.
—————— Contributions to the History of the Southwestern Portion of the U. S. Archaeological Institute of America, Cambridge, 1890.
Barclay, Thomas S. The Liberal Republican Movement in Missouri. MoHR, vol. XX ss.
Barns, Chancy R. (ed.) Commonwealth of Missouri. St. Louis, 1877.
Baunard, Abbé. Life of Mother Duchesne, translated from French by Lady Fullerton. Roehampton, England, 1879.
Baunard-Fullerton. Life of Ven. Madeleine Barat. New York, 1893.
Baunard, Abbé. Histoire de Madame Duchesne. Paris, 1878.
Bek, William G. The German Settlement Society of Philadelphia and its Colony, Hermann, Missouri. Philadelphia, 1907.
Belote. The Scioto Speculation and the Fourth Settlement at Gallipolis. Cincinnati, 1907.
Benediktiner in Conception, Mo., und ihre Missionstatigkeit. Conception, 1885.
Beuckmann, F. History of the Diocese of Belleville. Belleville, 1914.
—————— History of the Diocese of Belleville, St. John's Orphanage Edition. Belleville, 1919.
—————— Civil and Ecclesiastical Jurisdiction in Illinois. ICHR, vol. I, p. 64.

Beuckmann, F.   The Commons of Kaskaskia, Cahokia and Prairie Du Rocher. ICHR, vol. I, p. 405.

Bilger, Karl F.   Geschichte der Gemeinde in Celestine.   Evansville, Ind.

Billon, Frederick L.   Annals of St. Louis in its early days under the French and Spanish dominations.   St. Louis, 1886.

——— Annals of St. Louis in its Territorial Days.   St. Louis, 1888.

Bishpam, C. W.   Fray Antonio Sedella. LHQ, vol. II, No. 1.

Bjork, David K.   (Editor) Documents relating to Don Alexandro O'Reilly. LHQ.

Blanchard, Rufus.   The Discovery and Conquest of the Northwest.   Chicago, 1880.

Bodley, Temple.   George Rogers Clark.   MVHR, vol. XI, No. 2.

Bohemians, The—in America. FR, vol. XXVII, No. 10, May 15, 1920, p. 151.

Bolton and Marshall.   The Colonisation of North America.   New York, 1924.

Bolton, Herbert E.   Spanish Exploration in the Southwest.   New York, 1925.

——— The Location of La Salle's Colony on the Gulf of Mexico.   Reprint from the MVHR, September, 1915.

——— Athanase de Mezières and the Louisiana-Texas Border, 1766-1780.   Two vols.   Cleveland, 1914.

Bonifatiusgemeinde, St. Louis, Mo., Goldenes Jubilaeum.   1910.

Bossu, N.   Travels through that part of• North America formerly called Louisiana.   Translated by J. R. Forster.   London, 1771.

Bourne, E. S.   The Romance of Western History. MVHR, 1906, vol. I, p. 1.

Brand, H. F. M.   25th Anniversary of his Ordination.   St. Louis, 1810.

Breese, Sidney.   The Early History of Illinois.   Chicago, 1884.

Briggs, John Ely.   Louis Joliet. ICHR, vol. VI, p. 28.

Broadhead.   The Louisiana Purchase.   MHSC, 1897.

Bromwell, William J.   History of Immigration.   New York, 1856.

Brower, J. V.   The Missouri River.   St. Paul, 1897.

Brown, Edward.   Alexander McNair, First Governor of Missouri. StLCHR, vol. I, p. 231.

Brown, Stuart.   Old Kaskaskia Days and Ways. ICHR, vol. II, pp. 61, 413.

Bruener, Rev. Theodore.   Katholische Kirchengeschichte Quincy's.   1887.

Buck, Solon Justus.   Illinois in 1818.   Springfield, 1917.

——— Illinois in 1818.   Springfield, 1917.   CHR, vol. IV, p. 112.

Buckingham, T.—Smith.   Colleccion de varios Documentos para la Historia de la Florida y tierras adyacentes.   Madrid, 1857.

Burnham, J. H.   The Destruction of Kaskaskia by the Mississippi River. TISHS, 1914, p. 95.

Burns, Rev. James A. (C.S.G.)   Growth and Development of the Catholic School System in the United States.

Bushnell, D. I. The Cahokia and Surrounding Mound Groups.   Cambridge, Mass., 1904.

Butler, T. Ambrose.   Irish on the Prairies and Other Poems.

Butler, Mann.   History of Kentucky.

Butsch, Rev. Jos.   Negro Catholics in the U. S.   CHR, vol. III, p. 33.

Byrne, P. J.   Centennial of the Catholic Settlement of Ruma, Ill.   Belleville, 1918.

——— Catholic Settlement at Ruma, Ill.   1818-1918.

"Cahenslyism," The truth about.   FR, vol. XXV, No. 22, November 15, 1918, pp. 341-342.

Cailly, Louis De.   Memoirs of Bishop Loras, First Bishop of Dubuque, Iowa.   New York, 1897.

Calvary Cemetery Association, Historical Sketch, Charter, By-Laws and Rules.   St. Louis, 1888.

Campbell, Rev. T. J. (S.J.)   Pioneer Priests of North America.   Vol. I, Among the Iroquois; vol. II, Among the Hurons; vol. III, Among the Algonquins.   The American Press, New York, 1911-1914.

Campbell, Rev. T. J. (S. J.) Pioneer Laymen of North America. 1914.
—— The Jesuits, 1534-1921. New York, 1921.
—— Robert A. Gazetteer of Missouri. St. Louis, 1874.
Cape Girardeau Co., Mo. Recollections of some of the early settlers in Cape Girardeau County. Jackson, Mo., Cash-Book, 1917, March 8.
Cape Girardeau, St. Mary's Church. 1918.
Capek, Thomas. The Cechs (Bohemians) in America. Boston, 1920.
Caraccioli, M. The Life of Pope Clement XIV. Ganganelli, London, 1776. Appendix: The Brief of the Abolition of the Jesuits in Latin.
Carmel of St. Louis.
Carr, Lucien. Missouri: a bone of contention. Boston, 1888. American Commonwealth Series.
Cassilly, Rev. Francis (S.J.) The Old Jesuit Mission in Council Bluffs.
Catalogus Patrum et Fratrum Provinciae SS. Cordis Jesu O. F. M., S. P. N. Francisci. A. D. 1922.
Catholic Cabinet. Vol. I, II and III. St. Louis, 1843 s.
"Centralblatt and Social Justice," The historical numbers of. St. Louis, Mo.
Catholic Charities and Social Activities of the City of St. Louis. St. Louis, 1812.
Chamberlain, Rev. Cecil H. (S.J.) Colonel Francis Vigo and George Rogers Clark. ICHR, vol. X, p. 139.
Charles, St., Mo., St. Peter's Gemeinde, Jan. 1, 1900. St. Louis, 1900.
Chicago in 1867. Atlantic Monthly, March, 1867.
Chittenden, Hiram M. History of Early Steamboat Navigation on Missouri River; life and adventures of Joseph LaBarge, pioneer navigator and Indian trader, for fifty years identified with the commerce of Missouri Valley; map, portraits and plates. 2 vols. New York, 1903.
—— American Fur Trade of the Far West; history of the pioneer trading posts and early fur companies of the Missouri Valley and the Rocky Mountains, and of the overland commerce with Santa Fe. New York, 1902.
Clark, Col. George Rogers. Sketch of his Campaign in the Illinois, 1778-79, introduction by Hon. Henry Pirtle, containing Major Bowman's Journal of taking of Post St. Vincents. Cincinnati, 1907.
Clark, D. E. Early Forts on the Upper Mississippi. MVHQ.
Clark, Charles A. Indians of Iowa. Annals of Iowa, vol. VI, 2.
Clarke, Richard A. Lives of the deceased Bishops of the United States. 3 vols. New York, 1872-1888.
Clayton, Mo. Some History of St. Joseph's Church, Clayton, upon its 75th anniversary. Watchman Advocate, Clayton, Mo., August 3, 1917.
Colley, Rev. R. (S.J.) Life of Ven. Madeleine Sophie Barat, 1779-1865.
Collier, John. America, Treatment of Her Indians. Current History Magazine.
Conard, Howard L. (ed.) Encyclopedia of the History of Missouri. 6 vols. St. Louis, 1901.
Converts, Their Influence and Work in this Country. ACQR, vol. VIII, p. 509.
Conway, Rev. J. J. (S.J.) The Beginnings of Ecclesiastical Jurisdiction in the Archdiocese of St. Louis, 1764-4776. MHS, vol. I, No. 14.
—— Historical Sketch of the Church and Parish of St. Charles Borromeo. St. Charles, Mo., 1892.
Cook, Anna D. History of St. Rose's Church. St. Louis, 1910.
Corrigan, Gertrude. Two Hundredth Anniversary of Fort Chartres. ICHR.
Corrigan, Rev. Joseph M. Father De Smet—Mighty Sower. 1801-1873. RACHS, vol. 27, No. 2 and 3.
Corrigan, Bishop Owen B. Chronology of the American Hierarchy. CHR, vol. I, pp. 367-389; vol. II, pp. 127-145, 283-301; vol. III, pp. 22-32, 151-164.

Corwin, Edward S. The Dred Scott Decision. AHR, vol. XVII, 5.

Côte-sans-Dessein. The Battle of Côte-sans-Dessein. Some Historical Facts concerning a certain Indian Fight in Callaway Co. about the years 1819 to 1822. Hamilton, Mo., Telegraph, 1917, April 6.

Cotterill, R. S. The National Railroad Convention in St. Louis, 1849. MoHR, vol. XII, No. 4.

Culemans, Rev. J. B. Catholic Explorers and Pioneers of Illinois. CHR, vol. IV, p. 141.

———— Father De La Valiniere. ICHR, vol. I, p. 339.

———— Missionary Adventures Among the Peorias. ICHR, vol. V, p. 27.

Currier, Charles W. The Church of Cuba. CHR, vol. I, p. 128 s.

Curtis, G. P. The American Catholic Who Is Who. St. Louis, 1911.

Daurignac-Clements. History of the Society of Jesus, from its Foundation to the Present Time. . From the French, of Daurignac. By J. Clements. With an Appendix, from 1862 to 1877, 2 vols. in one.

Deiler, J. H. Die Europaeische Einwanderung nach den Ver. Staaten. New Orleans, 1897.

———— Zur Geschichte der Deutschen am Unteren Mississippi. New Orleans, 1901.

———— The Settlement of the German Coast of Louisiana. Philadelphia, 1909.

Dennis, A. P. Lord Baltimore's Struggle with the Jesuits, 1634-1649. AHAR, 1900.

Desmond, H. J. A Century of Irish Immigration. ACQR, 1900, p. 518.

Deuther, Charles G. The Life and Times of Rt. Rev. John Timon, D.D. Washington, D. C., 1870.

Deutschtum der Katholiken von St. Louis in seinen zwanzig Gemeinded, Das. Amerika, St. Louis, 1896.

Diary of the Trappist Joseph Marie Dunand. RACHS, vol. 26 and 27.

Directories; The Catholic Almanac and, a full set (1822-1919), is in the Chancery Office. The Historical Library possesses the Directories of 1864, 1868, 1870, 1871, 1886-1893, 1894, 1907, 1909, and 1912.

Directory to the Church Service for the Year of Our Lord 1822, The Laity's. CHR, vol. VI, p. 343.

Donnelly. Rev. Father Donnelly, the pioneer Priest of the Missouri Valley. Kansas City Times, 1917, June 29.

Douglas, Jas. Old France in the New World; Quebec in the 17th Century. Cleveland, 1906.

———— New England and New France. New York, 1913.

———— Walter B. The Sieurs de Saint Ange. TISHS.

———— Lisa, Manuel. MoHSC, vol. III, 3, pp. 233-274 and vol. III, 4, pp. 367-406.

Drake Constitution and the Test Oath in Missouri, The. The Annual Cyclopedia for 1865, Art. Missouri, p. 586.

Drake, Samuel G. The Indians of North America. Boston, 1848.

Du Bourg, Bishop William Louis. Memorial Sketch. 1918.

Du Bourg, J. H. Life of the Cardinal de Cheverus, Archbishop of Bordeaux, Philadelphia, 1839.

Duchesne; Ven. Rose Philippine, A Grain of Wheat. St. Louis, 1918.

Dunand, J. American History in French Archives.

Dunn, John E. Memorial of Rev. Laurence Smyth. Fort Smith, 1900.

Early Franciscan Missions in the Country. ACQR, vol. VIII, p. 121.

Edwards, Ninian. History of Illinois, 1778-1833. Springfield, 1870.

Edwards, R. The Great West and her Commercial Metropolis, and a Complete History of St. Louis, 1861.

———— The St. Louis Press, 1860.

Elliott, Richard R. The Sulpicians at the Cradle of the American Hierarchy. ACQR.

Elliott, Richard Smith. Notes taken in Sixty Years. St. Louis, 1883.

Emigration, A True Picture of, 1831. London.

Emmons, Ben L. The Founding of St. Charles. MHR, vol. XVIII, No. 4.

England, Bishop. United States Catholic Miscellany. From July to Dec. 1824. From Jan. to June 1825.

English, W. H. Northwest of the River Ohio, 1778-1783. Life of Gen. Geo. Rogers Clark. Indianapolis, 1897.

Enzlberger, J. N. Schematismus der Kath. Geistlichkeit in den Ver. Staaten. Milwaukee, 1892.

Epstein, Rev. Francis J. Illinois and the Leopoldine Association. ICHR, vol. I, p. 225.

———— Bishop Quarter's Letters. ICHR, vol. I, p. 372.

———— The Leopoldine Association. ICHR, vol. III, p. 88. .

Erskine, Marjory. Mother Philippine Duchesne. New York, 1926.

Esaray, Logan. A history of Indiana from its exploration to 1850. Indianapolis, L. K. Stewart Co., 1915 (Rev. CHR, vol. I, pp. 340-342). .

———— The true story of Father Pierre Gibault. Indiana Catholic and Record. Indianapolis, January 14, 1916.

Fairchild, Henry Pratt. Immigration. New York, 1913.

Fanning, William F. W. Historical Sketch of St. Louis University, 1908.

Faust, Albert B. The German Element in the United States, with Special Reference to its political, moral, social and educational influence. Boston, 1809.

Fellner, P. Felix (O.S.B.) P. Helbron's Baptismal Register at Sportsman's Hall. RACHS, vol. 27 p. 371.

Fencl, Rev. Leonard J. (S.J.) The Death of Father James Marquette. ICHR, vol. XI, p. 147.

Ferris, Jacob. The States and Territories of the Great West. With map. New York and Auburn, 1856.

Finkelnburg, Gustavus A. Under three Flags, or the Story of St. Louis briefly told. MoHSC, vol. III, 3, pp. 201-232.

Finley, John. The French in the Heart of America. New York, 1915.

Fish, Hamilton. Sickness and Mortality on Board Emigrant Ships. Senate Document, Washington, 1854.

Fiske, John. Overthrow of French Power in America. Harpers, June 1852.

Flick, L. French Refugee Trappists in the United States. RACHS, vol. I, p. 87.

Flint, James. Letters from America. Thwaites', Early Western Travels.

Florissant, Mo., St. Stanislaus Seminary. The Story of a Hundred Years.

Foik, Rev. Paul J. Among the Indian Chiefs at the Great Miami. ICHR, vol. VIII, p. 215.

Foik, Rev. Paul J. (C.S.C., Ph.D.) Homeseekers in the Wilderness. ICHR, vol. IX, p. 327.

Ford, Thomas. A History of Illinois, from its commencement as a state in 1818 to 1847. Chicago, 1854.

Fort St. Charles. The Spanish Forts at the mouth of the Missouri River. MoHSC, vol. III, 3, pp. 269-274.

Fortier, Edward Joseph. Points in Illinois History. A Symposium. ICHR, vol. V, p. 143.

———— The Establishment of the Tamaroi Mission. TISHS, No. XIII, p. 233.

Fowke, Gerard. Aboriginal Inhabitants of Missouri. MHSC, vol. IV, p. 82.

———— Prehistoric Objects, Classified and Described. MHSC.

Franz, Alexander. Die Kolonisation des Mississippitales. Leipzig, 1906.

Franziskaner Provinz vom Hl. Herzen Jesu, 1858-1908. St. Louis, 1908.

Franziskanerschwestern von der Provinz zur hl. Klara in Nord Amerika. St. Louis, 1915.

Freedom of Worship in the United States. ACQR, vol. X, p. 293.

Future of Foreign-Born Catholics, The. St. Louis, Mo. B. Herder, 1884.

Gagnon, Ernest. Louis Joliet. Montreal, 1913.

Galbally, Edward. Father Mazzuchelli (Review). RACHS, p. 270.

Garesché, M. Louisa. Biography of Father James Joseph Conway, S.J.

Garis, Roy L. America's Immigration Policy. North American Review, vol. 220, p. 63.

Garraghan, Rev. Gilbert J. (S.J.) The Emergence of the Missouri Valley Into History. ICHR, vol. IX, p. 306.

———— Selected Letters from the Roux Correspondence. CHR, vol. IV, p. 84.

———— The First Settlement on the Site of St. Louis. ICHR, vol. IX, p. 342.

———— New Lights on Old Cahokia. ICHR, vol. XI, p. 99.

———— Early Catholicity in Chicago. ICHR, vol. I, pp. 8, 147.

———— The Beginnings of the Holy Family Parish, Chicago. ICHR, vol. I, p. 436.

———— St. Regis Seminary. First Catholic Indian School, 1823-1831. CHR, vol. IV, p. 452.

———— The Missouri Centenary. ICHR, vol. IV, p. 300.

———— Father De Smet—History Maker. ICHR, vol. VI, p. 168.

———— The Trappists of Monk's Mound. RACHS, vol. XXXVI, p. 70. Also ICHR, vol. VIII, p. 106.

———— Catholic Church in Chicago, 1673-1871. Chicago, 1921.

———— Catholic Beginnings in Kansas City, Missouri. Chicago, 1923.

———— St. Ferdinand de Florissant; the story of an ancient Parish. Chicago, 1923.

———— New Lights on Old Cahokia. ICHR, vol. XI, No. 2.

———— Some Early Chapters in the History of St. Louis University. StLCHR, vol. V, p. 99.

———— The Kickapoo Mission. StLCHR, vol. IV, p. 25.

———— The Beginnings of St. Louis University. StLCHR, vol. I, p. 85.

———— Bishop Bruté and the Mission of Chicago. StLCHR, vol. I, p. 201.

———— The Mission of Central Missouri. StLCHR, vol. II, p. 157.

———— Some High Lights In Missouri's History. StLCHR, vol. III, p. 232.

———— The Potawatomi Mission of Council Bluffs. StLCHR, vol. III, p. 155.

Gassler, Rev. F. L. Père Antoine, Supreme Officer of the Holy Inquisition of Cartagena, in Louisiana. CHR, New Series, vol. II, p. 59.

Gayarre, Chas. Louisiana and its history as a French Colony; with folding plan of New Orleans in 1770. New York, 1852.

———— History of Louisiana. Four volumes: The French Domination, vols. I and II. New York, 1854. The Spanish Domination, 1854. The American Domination. 1866.

Genevieve, Ste. Valle Chimes, 1925.

Gibault and Vincennes, Fathers. American Historical Review, vol. XIV, p. 544.

Giles, Henry. Lectures and Essays. New York, 1869.

Glasgow, Mo.; St. Mary's Church, 1916.

Glennon, Most Rev. J. J. The Dawn of Missouri's History. StLCHR, vol. III, p. 227.

———— The Coming of the Jesuit Fathers to St. Louis. StLCHR, vol. V, p. 93.

Goebel. Laenger als ein Menschenleben in Missouri.

Goeltz, Chr. History of St. Philip's Parish. East St. Louis, 1917.

Goodwin, Cardinal L. The Trans-Mississippi West and its Settlement. New York, 1922.

———— Early Exploration and Settlement of Missouri and Arkansas. MoHR, vol. XIV, 3—4, April—July, 1920, pp. 385-424.

Gormly, Rev. J. W. Father Dunn's Newsboys' Home. St. Louis.

Granderath, Rev. Theodor (S.J.) Geschichte des Vantikanischen Konzils. Freiburg, 1906. 3 volumes.

Gray, John Gilmore. The Winning of the Illinois Country. Journal of American History.

Gregg, Josiah. The Commerce of the Prairies. New York, 1845.

Griffin, M. I. J. The Angelo Inglese Affair, in Life of Bishop Conwell, Ch. 17 and 18. RACHS, vol. XXVI, 3; vol. XXVII, 1.

Groll, Hochw. Heinrich. 1916.

Gross, Rev. Paul. Historical Sketch of the Church in Montgomery County, Mo.

Grover, Frank R. Father Pierre Francois Pinet, S.J., and his Mission of the Guardian Angel, Chicago, 1696-1699. Chicago, 1907.

Guilday, Rev. Peter. The Sacred Congregation de Propaganda Fidei. CHR, vol. VI, p. 478.

———— The Restoration of the Society of Jesus in the United States—(1806-1815). RACHS, vol. 32, 3.

———— The Life and Times of John Carroll, Archbishop of Baltimore (1735-1815). New York, 1922.

Hagedorn, Eugene (O.F.M.) The Expulsion of the Franciscans From Prussia and Their Coming to the United States in the Summer of 1875. ICHR, vol. VIII, p. 66.

Hamilton, Peter J. Colonial Mobile. Boston and New York, 1897.

Harding, S. B. Missouri Party Struggles in the Civil War. A. H. A. Historical Doc. 548.

Hart, Gerald E. The Fall of New France, 1755-1760. Montreal, 1888.

Hasbrouck, Louisa S. La Salle. New York, 1916.

Hearn, Lafcadio. Creole Sketches. Boston, 1924.

Hebard, Grace Raymond. The Bozeman Trail. 2 vols. Cleveland, O.

Helpers of the Holy Souls, The. St. Louis, 1898.

Herbermann, Very Rev. Charles G. The Sulpicians in the United States. New York, 1916.

———— Pierre Gibault, V. G. HRS, vol. VI, P. II.

Herculaneum, Mo., in 1818. MVHR, vol. VI, 2, September 1919, p. 176.

Herron, Sister Mary Eulalia. The Work of the Sisters of Mercy in the Archdiocese of St. Louis, Missouri (1856-1921). ACQR, vol. 34, No. 3.

Hildreth, S. P. Pioneer History of the Ohio Valley and the Northwest Territory. Cincinnati, 1848.

Hill, Walter H. (S.J.) Historical Sketch of the St. Louis University. St. Louis, 1879.

History of Cole, Moniteau, Benton, Miller, Maries and Osage Counties. Chicago, 1883.

History of Southeast Missouri.

History of Paris, The. Vol. III, containing a notice of the Church of St. Denis. London, 1825.

Hitchcock, Ripley. The Louisiana Purchase. Boston, 1903.

Hodge, Frederick Webb (ed.) Handbook of American Indians. 2 vols. Washington, 1912. Bureau of American Ethnology.

Holman, F. V. McLoughlin (Dr. John, the Father of Oregon). Cleveland, 1907.

Holweck, Rev. F. G. Origin of the Creoles of German Descent (Cote des Allemands, La.) StLCHR, vol. II, p. 114.

────── The Arkansas Mission Under Rosati. StLCHR, vol. I, p. 243.

────── The Language Question in the Old Cathedral of St. Louis. StLCHR, vol. II, p. 5.

────── Beginning of the Church in Little Rock. CHR, vol. VI, p. 156.

────── Rev. John Francis Regis Loisel. StLCHR, vol. I, p. 103.

────── Public Places of Worship in St. Louis, Before Palm Sunday 1843. StLCHR, vol. IV, p. 5.

────── Father Edmond Saulnier. StLCHA, vol. IV, p. 189.

────── Ostlangenburg, Rev. Gaspar Henry. ICHR, vol. III, p. 43.

────── Abbé Joseph Anthony Lutz. StLCHR, vol. V, p. 183.

────── Abbé Joseph Anton Lutz. PastBl, 1918-1919.

────── Abbé Charles de La Croix. PastBl, 1919.

────── Ein Blatt aus Alter Zeit. Cellini und Potini.

────── Kirchengeschichte von St. Louis (Souvenir der 62. General Versammlung des R. K. Centralvereins). St. Louis, 1917.

────── Nach Fünfzig Jahren. St. Louis, 1916.

────── Der Freundeskreis des Pastoralblattes. St. Louis, 1917.

────── History of St. Francis de Sales Parish. St. Louis, Mo., 1917.

────── St. Franz von Sales Gemeinde, 1917.

Hosmer, James K. The History of the Louisiana Purchase. New York, 1902.

Houck, Rev. Geo. F. Church in Northern Ohio and in Diocese of Cleveland, from 1817 to September, 1887. New York, 1887.

Houck, Louis. A History of Missouri. Three volumes, Chicago, 1908.

Howard, James Q. History of the Louisiana Purchase. Chicago, 1902.

Howe, Henry. Historical Collections of the Great West. Cincinnati, 1902.

Howlett, Rev. W. J. Life of Rev. Chas. Nerinckx. Techny, Ill., 1915.

────── Review of Father O'Daniel's Early Secular Missionaries of Kentucky. No date.

────── Rev. Wm. J. Historical Tribute to St. Thomas' Seminary, Bardstown, Ky. St. Louis, 1906.

Hulbert, Archer Butler. Red-Men's Roads. The Indian Thoroughfares of the Central West. Maps and illustrations. Columbus, 1900.

────── The Cumberland Road. Cleveland, 1904.

────── Ohio River. New York, 1906.

────── Centennial of Western Steam Boat Navigation. MVHA, 1911.

Hundt, Ferd. Die Deutschen Katholiken in Amerika. Chicago, Sept. 6, 1887.

Hunt, Gaylord. Life in America One Hundred Years Ago.

Hyde and Conard (Ed.) Encyclopedia of the History of St. Louis. A compendium of Hist. and Biog. for Ready Reference. 4 vols. New York, 1899.

Hyde, William. Newspapers and Newspaper People. MHS, 1896.

Hynes, Rev. Robert. The Old Church at Cahokia. ICHR, vol. I, p. 459.

Indian Treaties, and Laws and Regulations relating to Indian Affairs. North American Review, No. 24, 1927.

Irving, Theodore. The Conquest of Florida by Hernando De Soto. New York, 1851.

Ivory, Bertha May. Fifty Years a Bishop. St. Louis, 1891.

Jacker, Rev. Edward. La Salle and the Jesuits. ACQR, vol. III, p. 404.

Jackson's, Pres. Andrew, Message "On Indian Affairs." March 4, 1829-1830.

James, James A. Detroit the Key to the West during the American Revolution. TISHS, 1900, p. 154.

────── The Significance of The Attack on St. Louis, 1780. MVSR, 1908-1909.

────── The value of the Memoirs of George Rogers Clark as an Historical Document. Proceed. of the MVHA, vol. IX, 1915-1916.

Jenkins, Rev. T. J. Protestant Isms and Catholicity in the United States. ACQR, vol. VII, p. 71.

Jeron, Rev. Otto (O.M. Cap.) The Capuchins. RACHS, vol. V, p. 274.

Johnson, Dr. Peter L. Organization of the Catholic Church in the United States. The Salesianum, vol. XV.

Johnson, Rossiter. History of the French War. New York, 1882.

Johnson, William Henry. French Pathfinders in North America. Boston, 1905.

Joseph's Parish, St. Apple Creek, Mo., 1928.

Journal of American-Irish Historical Society, vol. IX, 1910.

Judson, Rev. Paul J. (O.S.A.) Father Gabriel Richard. RACHS, vol. XXXVII, 3 and 4.

Kain, John Jos. (D.D.) Pastoral Letter 1896. English and German.

Kansas State Historical Society, Transactions of the. Vols. VII and IX.

Kempker, Rev. John F. History of the Catholic Church in Iowa.

——— Very Rev. J. A. M. Felamourgues. An Iowa Pioneer, (Rev. Mazzuchelli). Annals of Iowa, 1904.

——— Catholicity in South Eastern Iowa. RACHS, vol. II, p. 128.

Kennerly, W. C. Early Days in St. Louis. MHSC, vol. III, p. 407.

Kenny, Rev. Laurence (S. J.) Missouri's Earliest Settlement and its Name. StLCHR, vol. I, p. 151.

——— The Gallipolis Colony (1790). ICHR, vol. IV, p. 415.

——— First Ladies, Some of Illinois. ICHR, vol. III, p. 117.

——— The Mullanphys of St. Louis. HRS, vol. XIV, May 1920, p. 70-110.

——— The Jesuits in the Mississippi Valley. MVHR, vol. X, p. 1.

Kenrick, Francis Patrick. The Primacy of the Apostolic See Vindicated. 7th revised and enlarged edition.

——— P. R., Erzbischof von St. Louis, in seinem Leben und Wirken. St. Louis, 1891.

Kenrick Seminary. Webster Groves, 1916.

Keuenhof, R. V. William. Catholic Church Annals of Kansas City, 1800-1859. CHR, vol. III, p. 326.

Kirkfleet, Rev. C. J. Life of Patrick Augustine Feehan, Chicago, 1922.

Klein, Fel. The Land of the Strenuous Life. Chicago, 1905.

Kostbaren Blut Schwestern in O'Fallon, Mo. O'Fallon, 1898.

Kreuzgemeinde, Hl., in St. Louis. 1914.

Lamott, Rev. John H. (S.T.D.) History of the Archdiocese of Cincinnati, 1821-1921. Cincinnati and New York, 1921.

Latrobe, Chas. J. Rambler in North America, 1832-1833; folding map. 2 vols. London, 1800.

Laveille, E. (S.J.) The Life of Father De Smet, S.J. Translation by Marian Lindsay. New York.

Law, Judge. The Colonial History of Vincennes. Vincennes, 1858.

Lebrocquy, Auguste (S. J.) Vie du R. P. Helias D'Huddeghem de la Compagnie de Jesus. Gand, 1878.

Leftwich, Rev. W. M. Martyrdom in Missouri. 2 vols. St. Louis, 1870.

Liberius, Pope, The Alleged Fall of. ACQR, vol. VIII, p. 529.

Liboriusgemeinde, St., St. Louis, Mo. Goldenes Jubilaeum, 13 Oct., 1907.

Lomasney, Rev. Patrick (S.J.) Marquette's Burial Site Located. ICHR, vol. IX, p. 348.

Loose Creek, Mo., Church of the Immaculate Conception.

Lord, Daniel A. (S.J.) Our Nuns. Their Varied and Vital Service for God and Country.

Lord, Trenor, Barrows. The Italian in America. New York, 1906.

Loretto, The Sisters of. Eccl. R., vol. XIX, pp. 259-272, 354-361.

Louis, St., When, was not a part of the United States. Some History of St. Louis under the Spanish and French. St. Louis Republic, 1917, May 13.

Louis History, St., Some early. St. Louis Post-Dispatch, 1917, May 6.

Louis, St., Land Owners in 1805. MHSC, vol. III, p. 183.

Luytelaar, Rev. J. Van (C.S.S.R.) Religious Unity. St. Louis, 1885.

M., G. E. Ven. Philippine Duchesne. New York, 1914.

MacMullen, John. History of Canada from its first discovery to present time. Brockville, 1855.

Maes, Bishop C. P. Rev. John Francis Rivet of Vincennes. ER, July and August 1906.

—— Life of Rev. Charles Nerinckx: with a chapter on the early missions of Kentucky; copious notes on the progress of Catholicity in the United States of America from 1800 to 1825; an account of the establishment of the Society of Jesus in Missouri; and an historical sketch of the Sisterhood of Loretto in Kentucky, Missouri, New Mexico, etc. (Cincinnati, 1880).

—— Bishop Camillus. Hennepin, Louis, O.F.M., Flemish Franciscan Missionaries in North America. CHR, vol. I, pp. 14-16.

—— Path of Hennepin, by Randolph Edgar. Bellman, January 1917.

Mallet, Major Edmund. Origin of the Flathead Mission. RACHS, vol. II, p. 174.

Marshall, Wm. I. History vs. The Whitman Saved Oregon Story. Three essays showing the true history of the acquisition of the Oregon territory. Chicago, 1904.

—— Marcus Whitman. AHR, 1900, p. 219.

—— Thomas Maitland (Ph.D.) A History of the Western Boundary of the Louisiana Purchase, 1819-1841). Berkeley, Cal., University of California Press, 1914.

—— A History of the Western Boundary of the Louisiana Purchase. 1904.

Martin, Francis X. History of Louisiana. 2 vols. New Orleans, 1827-29.

Martin, I. T. A Voice from the West. 1908.

Martinsburg, Mo., Freese, Rev. H., 1926.

Mary, St., Sisters of. St. Louis, 1922.

Mason, Augustine L. Romance and Tragedy of Pioneer Life. Cincinnati, 1884.

Mason, Edw. G. Chapters from Illinois History. Chicago, 1901.

Maxville, Mo., Immaculate Conception Church. 1917.

—— Immaculate Conception Church, Diamond Jubilee, 1917.

McCann, Sr. Mary Agnes. The History of Mother Seton's Daughters.

McCarthy, Rev. Charles F. Historical Development of Episcopal Nominations of the Catholic Church in the United States. RACHS, vol. XXXIX, p. 297.

McElroy, Robert M. The Winning of the Far West. New York, 1914.

McGoorty, J. P. The Early Irish in Illinois. TISHS, 1927, pp. 54-64.

McGovern, James. History of the Catholic Church in Chicago. Chicago, 1891.

McGovern, Rev. J. (O.P.) The Gallipolis Colony. RACHS, vol. 37, No. 1.

—— The Life and Writings of John McMullen, Bishop of Davenport. Chicago 1888.

McMaster, John Bach. A History of the People of the United States from the Revolution to the Civil War. 7 vols. New York.

Menology of the Society of Jesus, Province of Missouri. 1926.

Messmer, Archbishop S. G. The Rev. Hercules Brassac. CHR, vol. III, p. 392.

—— Brassac's Correspondence with the American Bishops. CHR, vol. III, p. 448.

Metzger, Rev. Charles H. (S.J.)  Meurin, Sebastian Louis, S.J.  ICHR, vol. III, pp. 241 and 371; vol. IV, p. 43.

Milburn, W. H.  The Pioneers, Preachers and People of the Mississippi Valley. N. Y., 1860.

Military Bounty Lands between the Mississippi and Illinois Rivers.  Western Monthly Magazine.  Reprinted: The Family Magazine, Cincinnati, 1837.

Minogue, Anna Loretto.  Annals of the Century.  New York, 1912.

Mississippi River, The, History of the Discovery of.  Collections of the Minnesota Historical Society, vol. VIII, pp. 303-418.

Missouri.  North American Review, April 1839, No. 11.

Mitchell's Reference and Distance Map.  Philadelphia, 1835.

Mitchell, Augustus.  Illinois in 1837.  Philadelphia, 1837.

Monette, Dr. J. W.  History of the discovery and settlement of the Mississippi, by Spain, France, and Great Britain, and the subsequent occupation, settlement, and extension of Civil Government by the U. S. to 1846.  Folding colored maps. 2 vols. New York, 1846.

Monroe City, Mo.  Some History of Indian Creek and St. Stephen's Church.  Monroe City, Mo., News, 1917, July 31.

Moore, Chas.  Northwest under Three Flags, 1635-17-96; maps, portraits and numerous other illustrations.  New York, 1900.

Moses, B.  Establishment of Spanish Rule in America.  New York, 1898.

——— J., and Kirkland.  History of Chicago; illustrated with numerous portraits and plates. 2 vols. Chicago, 1895.

——— John.  Illinois Historical and Statistical.  Chicago, 1889.

——— Expedition of G. R. Clark.  Magazine of Western History.

Mudd, Andrew.  History of Millwood and St. Alphonsus Parish.  1927.

Mueller.  Schematismus der deutschen und deutsch-sprechenden Priester in den Ver. Staaten Nord-Amerika's.  St. Louis, B. Herder, 1882.

Muench, Julius T.  Friedrich Muench.  MHSC, vol. III, p. 132.

Mullanphy, John.  How John Mullanphy, St. Louis philanthropist, helped to win the battle of New Orleans.  St. Louis Globe Democrat, 1917, August 12.

Munro, W. B.  The Office of Intendant in New France.  AHR, vol. XII, No. 2.

Murphey, H. K.  The Northern Rail Roads, 1860-1865.

Murray, John O'Kane.  Catholic Heroes and Heroines of America.  New York, 1882. Marquette p. 511; La Salle p. 535; Mother Seton p. 659; Father De Smet p. 835.

Nasatir, A. P.  Jacques D'Eglise on the Upper Missouri, 1791-1795.  MVHR, vol. XIV, p. 47.

Nativism in the Forties and Fifties.  MVHR, vol. IX, No. 3.

Navigator, The.  Directions for navigating the Ohio and Mississippi Rivers.  Pittsburg, 1824.  12th Edition.

Nerinckx, Rev. Charles.  FR, vol. XVIII, pp. 527-530.

Newlin, Sava.  Indian Treaties and National Honor.

Niel, Abbé F.  La Voie Du Salut.  Paris, 1845.

Nolan, Francis.  The Liquor Problem and the Jesuit Missions in New France.  AD., III, 1, July, 1911.

Oblate Sisters of Providence, The.  St. Louis, 1905.

O'Brien, Rev. John J.  Gabriel Richard, Educator, Statesman and Priest.  RACHS, vol. V, p. 77.

Och, Dr. Joseph.  Der Deutschamerikanische Farmer.

O'Daniel, Rev. V. F.  A Long Misunderstood Episode in American History.  CHR, vol. VI, p. 15.

O'Dwyer, George F. Irish Colonization in Illinois. ICHR, vol. III, p. 73.

Oertel. The Reasons of J. J. M. Oertel, late a Lutheran minister for becoming a Catholic. New York, 1840.

O'Gorman, Thomas. A History of the Roman Catholic Church in the United States. New York, 1895.

O'Hara, Rev. Edwin V. Catholic Pioneers in the Oregon Country. CHR, vol. III, p. 187.

———— Catholic Pioneers in the Oregon Country. C. H. R.

O'Malley, Rev. M. J. (C.M.) The Centenary of the Foundation of the St. Louis Diocesan Seminary. StLCHR, vol. I, p. 40.

Orphan Society, the German St. Vincent's, Diamond Jubilee of. 1850-1925.

O'Shea, John. The Two Kenricks. Philadelphia, 1904.

O'Sullivan, D. A. The Treaty of Paris, 1763, and the Catholics in American Colonies.' ACQR, vol. XIII, p. 240.

Padilla. Fray Juan de Padilla, the Protomartyr of the American Missions. FR, vol. XXVI, No. 9, May 1, 1919, p. 142.

Palickar, Stephen J. The Slovaks of Chicago. ICHR, vol. IV, p. 180.

Palladino. Indian and White in the Northwest. Lancaster, Pa.

Papin, Edward V. The Village under the Hill. MHSC, vol. V, p. 18.

Parish, All Saints', St. Peter, Mo., 1923.

Parish, SS. Peter and Paul's. Diamond Jubilee.

Parker, S. Exploring Tour Beyond Rocky Mountains, 1835-1837; folding map of Oregon territory. Ithaca, 1842.

Parkman, Francis. The Pioneers of France in the New World.

———— The Jesuits in North America.

———— La Salle and the Discovery of the Great West.

———— The Old Regime in Canada.

———— Count Frontenac and New France under Louis XIV.

———— A Half Century of Conflict.

———— Montcalm and Wolfe.

———— The Conspiracy of Pontiac.

———— The Oregon Trail: Sketches of Prairie and Rocky Mountain Life. Boston, 1882.

Parrish, Randall. Historic Illinois. Chicago, 1906.

Patten Helen. Old Mission La Pointe du Saint Esprit. ICHR, vol. IV, p. 319.

Payne, Raymond. Annals of the Leopoldine Association. CHR, vol. I, p. 51 and 175.

Pease, Theodore Calvin. The Frontier States. 1918.

Peck, J. M. Historical Sketch of the Early American Settlements in Illinois, 1780-1800. The Family Magazine, Cincinnati, 1840, p. 54.

———— New Guide for Emigrants in the West.

Pekari, Rev. Matthew Anthony (O.M. Cap.) The German Catholics in the United States of America. RACHS, vol. 36, No. 4.

Perrin Du Lac. Voyages dans deux Louisianes et chez les Nations Sauvages, etc. Lyon, 1805.

Perkins-Peck. Annals of the West. St. Louis, 1850.

Pettibone, Levi. With Schoolcraft in Southwest Missouri in 1818. MHSC, vol. 11, No. 1.

Peyton, Pauline L. Pierre Gibault, Priest and Patriot, RACHS, vol. XII, pp. 452-498.

Pfeiffer, Mother M. Petra C. De N. D., 1924.

Phillips, George S. Bishop Duggan and the Chicago Diocese. ICHR, vol. II, p. 365.

Pioneer, The. The Family Magazine, Cincinnati, 1840, p. 147.

Plumer, John, Jr. Iowa Territory. Examiner and Western Monthly Review. Reprint: The Family Magazine, 1840, p. 153.

Ponziglione, Rev. Paul M. (S.J.) Osage Indian Manners and Customs. StLCHR, vol. IV, p. 130.

——— Osage Mission during the Civil War. StLCHR, vol. IV, p. 219.

——— An Adventure of Lucille St. Pierre among the Osage Indians. StLCHR, vol. IV, p. 51.

Precious Blood, Most, The Foundation and Progress of Sisters of the. 1925.

Preuss, E. Zum Lobe des Unbefleckten Empfangniss. Freiburg, 1879.

Primm, Judge Wilson. History of St. Louis. MoHSC, vol. IV, 2, pp. 160-193.

——— New Year's Day in Olden Times in St. Louis. MoHSC, vol. II, No. 1.

——— Biographical Sketch of Judge Wilson Primm. MoHSC, vol. IV, 2, pp. 127-159.

Pruente, Rev. E. The Beginnings of Catholicity in Cape Girardeau, Mo. StLCHR, vol. III, p. 50.

Quaife, M. M. Chicago and the Old Northwest, 1673-1835; maps, portraits and plates. Chicago, 1913.

——— Points in Illinois History—A Symposium, Mooted Questions. ICHR, vol. V, p. 16.

Quebec and Western Policy. Canadian Historical Review, March 1, 1925.

Quinn, Rev. D. A. Heroes and Heroines of Memphis, 1887.

R., H. L. The Suppression of the Jesuits by Pope Clement XIV. ACQR, vol. XIII, p. 696.

Reavis, R. U. St. Louis, the Future Great City. 1870.

Reker, Rev. F. X. Sacred Heart Church, Valley Park. 1928.

Reuss, Francis X. Biographical Cyclopaedia of the Catholic Hierarchy of the United States, 1784-1896. Milwaukee.

Revaux, Abbé. Life of Rev. M. St. John Fontbonne. New York, 1887.

Rezek, Rev. A. J. The Leopoldine Society; A.D., III, 2, July, 1914.

Ricciardelli, Raffaeli. Vita De Servo Di Dio Felice De Andreis. Roma, 1923.

Riegel, Robert E. The Story of the Western Railroads. New York, 1926.

Rochemonteix, P. C. de (S.J.) Les Jesuites et la Nouvelle-France an XVIe siècle. 3 vols. Paris, 1895-1896.

Rosalita, Sister Mary. Education in Detroit Prior to 1850. Michigan Historical Commission.

Rosati. Life of Felix De Andreis. St. Louis, 1900.

——— Catechisme imprimé par l'ordre de Msgr. Jos. Rosati, Evêque de St. Louis. Lyon, 1841. (This Catechism was the property of Térèse Aubuchon).

Rothensteiner, Rev. J. The Flat-Head and Nez Perce Delegation to St. Louis. StLCHR, vol. II, p. 183.

——— Paul de Saint Pierre, the First German-American Priest of the West. CHR, vol. V, p. 195.

——— Rev. Paul de Saint Pierre, O. Carm. Disc. Der erste Deutsch-amerikanische Priester des Westens. Reprint from Pastorall-Blatt, St. Louis, 1918.

——— Historical Antecedents of the Diocese of St. Louis. ICHR, vol. IV, p. 243.

——— Chicago to St. Louis in the Early Days. ICHR, vol. IX, p. 21.

——— Archbishop Kenrick and the Vatican Council. ICHR, vol. XI, p. 3.

——— Interesting Facts Concerning Chicago's First Four Bishops. ICHR, vol. IX, p. 151.

——— The Sulpicians in Illinois. ICHR, vol. VIII, p. 233.

——— The Old St. Louis Calvary. StLCHR, vol. III, p. 39.

——— Early Missionary Efforts Among the Indians in the Diocese of St. Louis. StLCHR, vol. II, p. 57.

Rothensteiner, Rev. J.  Father Charles Nerinckx and His Relations to the Diocese of St. Louis.  StLCHR, vol. I, p. 157.
——— Catholic Historical Society of St. Louis.  StLCHR, vol. I, p. 8.
——— The First Years of Bishop Kenrick's Administration of the St. Louis Diocese.  StLCHR, vol. V, p. 205.
——— Historical Sketch of Catholic New Madrid.  StLCHR, vol. IV, p. 206.
——— Father James Maxwell of Ste. Genevieve.  StLCHR, vol. IV, p. 142.
——— Archbishop Eccleston and the Visitandines of Kaskaskia.  ICHR, vol. I, p. 500.
——— The Trappist Monks in the Mississippi Valley.  St. Louis Church Progress, 1917, June 14 and 21.
——— Historical gleanings from the early History of the Catholic Church in Missouri.  St. Louis Church Progress, 1917, February 1, 8, 15, 22, March 1, 8, 15, 22.
——— The arrival of Bishop Du Bourg in St. Louis, 1818.  The country and its people.  St. Louis Church Progress, 1917, July 26.
——— The Old Cathedral and the St. Louis College, 1818-1823.  St. Louis Church Progress, 1917, August 2 and 9.
——— The Missouri Priest one hundred years ago.  Address of Rev. J. Rothensteiner at the observance of Missouri's Centennial Celebration at Columbia, Mo., January 8, 1918.  St. Louis, 1918.
——— P. Bernard von Limpach und die Anfänge der Kirche in St. Louis, Reprint from Pastorall-Blatt, St. Louis, 1918.
——— The Catholic Church and Civil Liberty.  St. Louis, 1915.
——— Chronicles of an Old Missouri Parish.  St. Louis, 1917.
——— Religious conditions in St. Louis in 1827 as described by Bishop Rosati.  St. Louis Church Progress, 1917, August 30.
Rozier, Firmin A.  History of the Early Settlement of the Mississippi Valley.  St. Louis, 1890.
Ryan, Rev. Edwin A.  Ecclesiastical Jurisdiction in the Spanish Colonies.  CHR, vol. V, p. 3.
Ryan, P. J.  Most Rev. Peter Richard Kenrick, D.D.  ACQR, vol. XXI, p. 82.
Ryan, Most Rev. Patrick John (D.D.,LL.D.)  Fifty years a priest.  ACQR, vol. XXVIII, p. 625.
Ryan, Stephen V.  Claims of a Protestant Episcopal Bishop Disproved.  Buffalo, 1880.
St. George's Parish, Hermann, Mo.
Salaries of Curates and other Ecclesiastical Ministers of the Colony of Louisiana (1786—1787).  MVHR. VI, 1. December 1919, p. 390.
Salzbacher, Dr. Joseph.  Meine Reise nach Nord-Amerika im J. 1842.  Wien, 1845.
Sampson, Francis A.  The New Madrid and other Earthquakes in Missouri.  Reprint from MVHR.
——— Some Descriptions of Missouri in the early days, from the writings of European Travelers.  Columbia, Mo., Times, 1917, June 1.
Sauer, Carl O.  The Geography of the Ozark Highland of Missouri.  Chicago, 1920.
Savage, Sister M. Lucida.  The Congregation of St. Joseph of Carondelet.  St. Louis, 1923.
Schaaf, Ida M.  Henri Pratte, Missouri's First Native Born Priest.  StLCHR, vol. V, p. 129.
Schaefer, Joseph.  The British Attitude toward the Oregon Question, 1815-1846.  AHR, vol. XVI, pp. 273-299.
Scharf, J. Th.  History of St. Louis City and County.  Philadelphia, 1883.
Schmidt, Joseph H.  Recollections of the first Catholic Missions in Central Missouri.  MHR, vol. V, pp. 83-93, 1910-1911.

Schoolcraft, Henry R.  A View of the Lead Mines of Missouri.  New York, 1819.

———— Personal Narrative of Scenes and Adventures in the Ozark Mountains of Missouri and Arkansas.  Philadelphia.

Schools, The Plot against the Parochial.  FR, vol. XXV, No. 23, December 1, 1918, p. 358.

———— Danger to Our.  Ibid., No. 18, September 15, 1918, pp. 281-282; vol. XXVI, No. 8, April 15, 1919, pp. 122-123.

———— Our, and the State.  Ibid., No. 12, June 15, 1919, p. 186.

———— Need of a concerted Policy in regard to the— Question.  Ibid., No. 16, August 15, 1919, p. 247.

———— Language Question in.  A Protest by the Bishop of Burlington.  Ibid., No. 13, July 1, 1919, p. 194.

———— Foreign Languages in American.  Ibid., No. 21, November 1, 1919, p. 327.

———— Non-Catholic Children in Catholic.  Ibid., No. 13, July 1, 1919, p. 194; No. 15, August 1, 1919, p. 233.

Schrage, H.  St. Agatha Gemeinde, St. Louis, Mo., 1899.

Schubert, J.  Kirchendeutsche und Vereindeutsche.

Schulte, Rev. Paul.  The Old Cathedral Conference of the St. Vincent de Paul Society.  StLCHR, vol. III, p. 5.

Schultz, Rev. J. L.  St. Francis Xavier's Church, Sikeston, Mo.

Schuyler, H. C.  The Apostle of the Abuakis.  CHR, vol. I, p. 164.

Sedella, Fray Antonio de, an Appreciation.  LHQ.

Shaughnessy, Rev. Gerald.  Has the Immigrant Kept the Faith.  New York, 1925.

———— Catholic Population Statistics.  Salesianum, Milwaukee.

Shea, John Gilmary.  The Catholic Church in Colonial Days, 1521-1763.  New York, 1886.

———— Life and Times of the Most Rev. John Carroll, 1763-1815.  New York, 1888.

———— History of the Catholic Church in the U. S.  Two vols.  New York, 1892.

———— Defenders of the Faith.  New York, 1891.

———— and H. De Courcy.  History of the Catholic Church in the United States.  New York, 1879.

———— History of the Catholic Missions among the Indian Tribes of the U. S.  New York.

———— The Early Franciscan Mission in this Country.  ACQR, vol. VIII, p. 121.

———— Converts—Their Influence and Work in this Country.  ACQR, vol. VIII, p. 509.

———— What Right Has the Federal Government to Mismanage the Indians.  ACQR, vol. VI, p. 520.

———— The Catholic Church in American History.  ACQR, vol. I, p. 148.

———— The Canadian Element in the United States.  ACQR, vol. IV, No. 16.

Shepherd, William R.  The Spanish Archives and their Importance for the History of the U. S.  AHA, Report, 1903.

Sheridan, Frank.  Influence of the Irish People in the Formation of the United States.  ICHR, vol. IX, p. 377.

Shine, Michael.  The Lost Province of Quivira.  CHR, vol. II, p. 3.

Shipman, Paul R.  Establishment of the Visitation Nuns in the West.  ACQR, January 1886.

Shoemaker, Floyd C.  Missouri's Century of Statehood.  M. Manual, 1921.

———— Missouri Centennial Commission and Celebration.

———— Six Periods of Missouri History.  MHR, vol. IX, No. 4.

Smith, W. R.  Brief History of Louisiana Territory.  St. Louis, 1904.

Smith, Mary Constance.  A Sheaf of Golden Years, 1856-1906.  St. Louis, 1906.

Smith, Mary Constance. Our Pastors in Calvary. St. Louis, 1924.

Snyder, John F. Capt. J. B. Saucier at Fort Chartres, 1751-1763. JISHS.

Sommervogel, Carlos. Bibliotheque de la Compagnie le Jesus. Premiere partie; bibliographie par les Peres Augustin et Aloys de Backer. Seconde partie; histoire par le Pere Auguste Carayon. Bruxelles et Paris; Province (jesuite) de Belgique, 1890-98. 8 vols. F.

Soniat, Charles T. The Title to the Jesuit Plantation. LHS, vol. V, 1911.

Souvay, Rev. Charles L. (C.M.) The Lazarists in Illinois. ICHR, vol. I, p. 303.

——— Around the St. Louis Cathedral with Bishop Du Bourg, 1818-1820. StLCHR, vol. V, p. 149.

——— Episcopal Visitation of the Diocese of New Orleans, 1827-1828. StLCHR, vol. I, p. 215.

——— Du Bourg and the Biblical Society, New Orleans, 1813. StLCHR, vol. II, p. 18.

——— Questions Anent Mother Seton's Conversion. CHR, vol. V, p. 223.

——— Bishop Rosati and the See of New Orleans. CHR, vol. III, p. 3.

——— Rosati's Elevation to the See of St. Louis, 1827. CHR, vol. III, p. 165.

——— A Centennial of the Church in St. Louis. CHR, vol. IV, p. 52.

——— The Cathedrals of St. Louis.

Spalding, Martin J. Sketches of the Life, Times and Character of Benedict Joseph Flaget, First Bishop of Louisville. Louisville, Ky., 1852.

——— Sketches of Early Catholic Missions of Kentucky. Louisville, 1844.

——— Rev. H. S. (S.J.) Who Discovered the Mississippi? ICHR, vol. VI, p. 40.

——— The Life of James Marquette, S.J., ICHR, vol. IX, pp. 3, 109, 223.

Spanish Forts at the Mouth of the Missouri River, The. MoHSC, vol. IV.

Sparks, Jared. Life of Robert Cavelier De La Salle. American Biography New Series vol. I.

——— Life of Father Marquette, American Biography, vol. X.

——— English Settlement in Illinois, The. Reprints of three rare tracts on the Illinois Country. (Birkbeck, Letter from the Illinois (1819) Flower Letters from Lexington and the Illinois (1819) Flower, Letters from the Illinois, 1820-21.) Fldg. map., London, 1907.

Spears, John R. and A. H. Clark. A History of the Mississippi Valley, from its Discovery to the End of Foreign Dominion. New York, 1903.

Spencer, Thomas E. The Story of Old St. Louis. St. Louis 1914.

Spill, William A. University of Michigan, Beginnings vol. I. Father Gabriel Richard's part in its formation. Michigan History Magazine vol. XII, No. 4.

Starkenburg Shrine, Silver Jubilee, 1913.

Steck, Francis Borgia, O.F.M. The Discovery of the Mississippi River. ICHR, vol. VI, p. 50.

——— The Joliet and Marquette Expedition, 1673. Quincy, 1928.

Steckel, Alfred. The German Roman Catholic Central Society. RACHS, vol. VI, p. 252.

Stephenson, George M. A History of American Immigration 1820-1924. Boston, 1926.

Stevens, W. B. Missouri's Centennial. Columbia, Mo., 1917.

——— St. Louis, the Fourth City, 1764-1909. St. Louis, 1909.

——— Laclede, the Founder of St. Louis.

——— Missourians One Hundred Years Ago. Columbia, 1917.

——— One Hundred Years of the St. Louis Republic. St. Louis, 1908.

Steward, J. F. Destruction of the Fox Indians, 1730. Chicago, 1902.

Stuart, Benjamin F. Removal of the Menomene Band of Potawatomi Indians 1838. Indiana Magazine of History, vol. XVIII, pp. 256-261.

Sullivan, J. T. Sacerdotal Jubilee of Rt. Rev. J. J. Kain, second Bishop of Wheeling. Wheeling, 1891.

——— The Catholic Church in Wisconsin. Milwaukee, 1895-1898.

Swanton, John R. De Soto's Line of March, MVHR.

Switzler, Col. W. F. History of Missouri (1841-1877).

Taylor and Crooks, Sketch book of St. Louis, 1858.

Thébaud, S.J., Rev. Aug. J. Freedom of Worship in the United States. ACQR, vol. X, p. 293.

Theux, Le Pere Theodore de. De la Compagnie de Jesus et la Mission Belge du Missouri. Roulers, 1913.

Thomas, W. S. History of St. Louis County, Mo., two vols. St. Louis, 1911.

Thompson, Albert. In and About Kaskaskia. Magazine of Western History, vol. VI, p. 37.

Thompson, Joseph J. Penalties of Patriotism. An Appreciation of the Life Patriotism and Services of Francis Vigo, Pierre Gibault, George Rogers Clark and Arthur St. Clair, "the Founders of the Nortwest." JISHS, vol. IX, 4, January, 1917, pp. 433-445.

———— Illinois—The Cradle of Christianity. ICHR, vol. IX, pp. 193, 291. Vol. X, pp. 3, 123, 379.

———— Father Marquette's Second Journey to Illinois. Persons and Places Associated with History of Father Marquette. Account of the Second Voyage of Father Marquette, Rev. Claude J. Dablon, ICHR, vol. VII, pp. 144, 203, 291.

———— The Cahokia Mission Property. ICHR, vol, V, p. 195, vol. VI, p. 99.

———— Along the Historic Illinois. ICHR, vol. V, pp. 3 and 99.

———— The Illinois part of the Diocese of Vincennes. ICHR, vol. IV, pp. 255, 381.

———— The First Catholics In and About Chicago. ICHR, vol. III, p. 227.

———— The First Chicago Church Records. ICHR, vol. IV, p. 6.

———— Irish in Early Illinois,—Irish in Chicago. ICHR, vol. II, 223, 286, 458, 146.

———— The Illinois Missions. ICHR, vol. I, p. 38.

———— Illinois' First Citizen—Pierre Gibault. ICHR, vols. I-VI, VII, VIII.

———— Along the Historic Illinois. ICHR, vol. V, pp. 3, 99.

Thwaites, Reuben Gold. William Clark, Soldier, Explorer, Statesman. MoHSC, vol. II, 7, p. 1.

———— R. G. French Regime in Wisconsin, 1727-1748, (Wis. Hist. Coll., vol. 17.) Mad, 1906.

———— On the Storied Ohio. Chicago, 1903.

———— Daniel Boone. New York, 1902.

———— Father Marquette. New York, 1902.

———— At the Meeting of the Trails. MVHR, vol. VI.

Tolerari Potest. Buffalo, 1893.

———— Oeniponte, 1893.

Tornado, Pictoral Story of St. Louis Tornado. St. Louis, 1890.

Trails in the Black Hawk Country, Early. JISHS, vol. XVII, No. 4.

Treaty of Paris, and Catholics in American Colonies, The. ACQR, vol. X, pp. 240-255.

Treaty between the French Republic and the United States concerning the Cession of Louisiana, signed at Paris, the 30th of April 1803. LHQ. II, 2. April 1919, p. 139-163.

Trexler, Harrison A. Slavery in Missouri, 1804-1865. The John Hopkins Press, Baltimore, 1914. (Rev. MoHSC, IV, 3, pp. 373-374.)

Troesch, Helen. The First Convent in Illinois. ICHR, vol. I p. 352

Tuohy, Rev. J. T. Religious Institutions in the Archdiocese of St. Louis.

Turner, Fred J. Colonization of the West. AHR, vol. XI, p. 303.

Turner, Frederick (Editor.) George Rogers Clark and the Kaskaskia Campaign. AHR, vol. VIII, p. 491.

Ulloa (Ant. De) Noticias Americanas: Entretenimientos Fisico-Historicos Sobre la America Meridional, y la Septentrional Oriental: Comparacion General de ·los Territorios, Climas y Produccionesen las tres especies Vegetal, Animal y Mineral; con una Relacion Particular de los Indios de aquellos paises, sus Costumbres y usos, etc., Madrid en la Imprenta Real, 1792. Contains accounts of New Orleans an dthe Mississippi, and Lousiana and its Indian inhabitants.

Ursuline Convent and Academy, St. Louis, Mo. St. Louis, 1899.

Vallette, Marc F. Jacques Cartier, ACQR, Jan. 1919, p. 40.

—— Some Early Explorers and Missionaries in the Territory now known as the United States. ACQR, January, 1916.

Verwyst, Chrysostom. Historic Sites on Chequamegan Bay. Wisconsin Historical Collections, No. 13, pp. 426-440.

Villiers, Marc de. La Disconverte du Missouri it l'Histoire du Foot Or'leans, 1673-1728. Paris, 1925.

Vincent de Paul, St. Society, Manual. St. Louis, 1861.

—— Church, Dutzow, Mo. 1925.

—— Eighty-Third Annual Report of the Metropolitan Central Council. St. Louis, 1928.

Vinzenz, Waisenverein, St. St. Louis, Mo., Goldenes Jubilaeum, June 13, 1900.

Violette, E. M. Spanish Land Claims in Missouri. Washington University Studies, vol. VIII, No. 2.

Violette, Eugene Morrow. History of Missouri, New York, 1918.

—— Early Settlements in Missouri. MHR, vol. I, No. 1.

Vogel, Mrs. E. M. The Ursuline Nuns in America. RACHS, vol. I, p. 214.

Waibl, Eug. Die Katholischen Missionen im Nordöstlichen Arkansas.

Walker, C. B. The Mississippi Valley and Prehistory Events. Burlington, Iowa, 1879.

Wallace, Joseph. The History of Illinios and Louisiana under French Rule. Cincinnati, 1899.

Walsh, Wm. Life of the Most Rev. Peter Richard Kenrick. St. Louis, 1891.

Ward, Felix, C. P. The Passionists, Sketches, Historical and Personal.

Webb, Ben J. The Centenary of Catholicity in Kentucky. Louisville, 1884.

Weber, W. A. The Rise of the National Catholic Churches in the U. S. CHR, vol. I, p. 422.

Weld, Laenas G. Decisive Episodes in Western History. State Historical Society of Iowa, 1914.

—— Joliet and Marquette in Iowa. Iowa City, 1903.

White, Charles T. Life of Mrs. Elizabeth Seton. Baltimore, 1879.

Wilkins, W. H. Immigration Troubles of the U. S. The Nineteenth Century, October, 1891.

Will, Allen Sinclair. Life of Cardinal Gibbons, 2 vols. New York, 1922.

Winsor, Justin. Cartier to Frontenac. New York, 1894.

—— The Westward Movement. New York, 1897.

—— The Mississippi Basin. New York, 1897.

—— Narrative and Critical History of America, 8 vols. Boston and New York.

Wislizenus, F. A. Journey to Rocky Mountains, 1839; translated from the German, with life by his son. St. Louis, 1912.

Woodstock Letters. A Record of Current events and Historical Notes connected with the colleges and Missions of· the Society of Jesus. (Woodstock, Md., 1872 ff.)

Young, Cecilia Mary. Annals of the Propagation of the Faith. ICHR, vol. I, p. 214.

Zwierlein, Frederick J. Life and Letters of Bishop McQuaid, 3 vols. Rochester, . 1925-1927.

# INDEX

The Arabic number refers to the page in either volume: the Roman II refers to volume II. When the Arabic numbers precede and follow the Roman II, the former refers to vol. I, the latter to vol. II.

(801)

Lightning Source UK Ltd.
Milton Keynes UK
UKHW020605261118
332889UK00009B/949/P